Statistical Techniques in
BUSINESS & ECONOMICS

The McGraw-Hill/Irwin Series in Operations and Decision Sciences

Statistical Techniques in
BUSINESS & ECONOMICS

NINETEENTH EDITION

DOUGLAS A. LIND
Coastal Carolina University and The University of Toledo

WILLIAM G. MARCHAL
The University of Toledo

SAMUEL A. WATHEN
Coastal Carolina University

STATISTICAL TECHNIQUES IN BUSINESS & ECONOMICS, NINETEENTH EDITION

Published by McGraw Hill LLC, 1325 Avenue of the Americas, New York, NY 10019. Copyright ©2024 by McGraw Hill LLC. All rights reserved. Printed in the United States of America. Previous editions ©2021, 2018, and 2015. No part of this publication may be reproduced or distributed in any form or by any means, or stored in a database or retrieval system, without the prior written consent of McGraw Hill LLC, including, but not limited to, in any network or other electronic storage or transmission, or broadcast for distance learning.

Some ancillaries, including electronic and print components, may not be available to customers outside the United States.

This book is printed on acid-free paper.

1 2 3 4 5 6 7 8 9 LWI 28 27 26 25 24 23

ISBN 978-1-265-32246-5 (bound edition)
MHID 1-265-32246-5 (bound edition)
ISBN 978-1-265-77553-7 (loose-leaf edition)
MHID 1-265-77553-2 (loose-leaf edition)

Portfolio Manager: *Eric Weber*
Product Developer: *Ryan McAndrews*
Marketing Manager: *Harper Christopher*
Content Project Managers: *Jenilynn McAtee; Bruce Gin*
Manufacturing Project Manager: *Laura Fuller*
Content Licensing Specialist: *Sarah Flynn*
Cover Image: *Shutterstock / Double Brain*
Compositor: *Straive*

All credits appearing on page or at the end of the book are considered to be an extension of the copyright page.

Library of Congress Cataloging-in-Publication Data

Names: Lind, Douglas A., author. | Marchal, William G., author. | Wathen, Samuel Adam, author.
Title: Statistical techniques in business & economics / Douglas A. Lind, Coastal Carolina University and The University of Toledo, William G. Marchal, The University of Toledo, Samuel A. Wathen, Coastal Carolina University.
Other titles: Statistical techniques in business and economics
Description: Nineteenth edition. | New York, NY : McGraw Hill, [2024] | Series: The McGraw-Hill/Irwin series in operations and decision sciences | Includes index.
Identifiers: LCCN 2022033304 | ISBN 9781265322465 (hardcover ; alk. paper)
Subjects: LCSH: Economics—Statistical methods. | Commercial statistics.
Classification: LCC HA29 .M268 2024 | DDC 519.5—dc23/eng/20220713
LC record available at https://lccn.loc.gov/2022033304

The Internet addresses listed in the text were accurate at the time of publication. The inclusion of a website does not indicate an endorsement by the authors or McGraw Hill LLC, and McGraw Hill LLC does not guarantee the accuracy of the information presented at these sites.

mheducation.com/highered

DEDICATION

To Jane, my wife and best friend, and our sons, their wives, and our grandchildren: Mike and Sue (Steve and Courtney), Steve and Kathryn (Kennedy, Jake, and Brady), and Mark and Sarah (Jared, Drew, and Nate).

Douglas A. Lind

To Abigail Marchal Nicholson and Andrea.

William G. Marchal

To my wonderful family: Barb, Hannah, and Isaac.

Samuel A. Wathen

Over the years, we received many compliments on this text and understand that it's a favorite among students. We accept that as the highest compliment and continue to work very hard to maintain that status.

The objective of *Statistical Techniques in Business and Economics* is to provide students majoring in management, marketing, finance, accounting, economics, and other fields of business administration with an introductory survey of descriptive and inferential statistics. We use many examples and exercises to illustrate the application of statistics to current business-related questions and problems. To use our text, a previous course in statistics is not necessary, and the mathematical requirement is first-year algebra.

In this text, we show beginning students every step needed to be successful in a basic statistics course. This step-by-step approach enhances performance, accelerates preparedness, and significantly improves motivation. Understanding the concepts, seeing and doing plenty of examples and exercises, and comprehending the application of statistical methods in business and economics are the focus of this book.

The first edition of this text was published in 1967. At that time, locating and accessing relevant business data was difficult. That has changed! Today retail stores collect data from our online searches and purchases and then use the data to selectively target market products and services to each of us. Financial institutions collect data related to our transactions to determine credit scores and target market various financial products. Medical devices automatically monitor our heart rate, blood pressure, and temperature from remote locations. A large amount of business information is recorded and reported almost instantly. CNN, *USA Today,* and MSNBC, for example, all have websites that track stock prices in real time.

Today, the practice of data analytics is widely applied to "big data." The practice of data analytics requires skills and knowledge in several areas. Computer skills are needed to process large volumes of information. Analytical skills are needed to evaluate, summarize, organize, and analyze the information. Critical thinking skills are needed to interpret and communicate the results of processing the information.

Our text supports the development of basic data analytical skills. At the end of each chapter is the section Data Analytics. As you work through the text, this section provides the instructor and student with opportunities to apply statistical knowledge and statistical software to explore several business environments. Interpretation of the analytical results is an integral part of these exercises. In addition, many of the text's exercises ask students to apply statistical techniques using small data sets. Over 350 data sets can be easily accessed in Connect with statistical software.

A variety of statistical software is available to complement our text. Microsoft Excel includes an add-in with many statistical analyses. MegaStat is an add-in available for Microsoft Excel. Minitab and JMP are stand-alone statistical software packages available to download for either PC or MAC computers. In our text, Microsoft Excel, Minitab, and MegaStat are used to illustrate statistical software analyses. The text now includes references or links to Excel tutorials in Connect. These provide users with clear demonstrations using statistical software to create graphical and descriptive statistics and statistical analyses to test hypotheses. We use screen captures within the chapters, so the student becomes familiar with the nature of the software output.

Because of the availability of computers and software, it is no longer necessary to dwell on calculations. We have replaced many of the calculation examples with interpretative ones, to assist the student in understanding and interpreting the statistical results. In addition, we place more emphasis on the conceptual nature of the statistical topics. While making these changes, we still continue to present, as best we can, the key concepts, along with supporting interesting and relevant examples.

WHAT'S NEW IN THE NINETEENTH EDITION?

The Nineteenth Edition benefits from reviewers' thoughtful comments and suggestions. The detailed changes are in the following section on Enhancements to the Nineteenth Edition. In general, we made several changes to the flow and organization of the text. For example, the sampling distribution of the proportion is added to Chapter 8 (Sampling, Sampling Methods, and the Central Limit Theorem), and the one- and two-sample tests of hypothesis for proportions are now included in Chapters 10 (One-Sample Tests of Hypothesis) and 11 (Two-Sample Tests of Hypothesis). The F-distribution now precedes the two-sample tests of hypothesis in Chapter 11. Several chapter introductions are revised to help explain the significance of the chapter's content.

This edition also brings a renewed recognition of diversity, equity, and inclusion to the text, exercises, and examples. As you read the text, you will find an increased diversity of persons and businesses from varied geographic, ethnic, and cultural groups. We hope these changes help promote awareness, consideration, and implementation of diversity, equity, and inclusion in our societies.

Chapter Learning Objectives

Each chapter begins with a set of learning objectives designed to provide focus for the chapter and motivate student learning. These objectives, located in the margins next to the topic, indicate what the student should be able to do after completing each section in the chapter.

▲ MERRILL LYNCH recently completed a study of online investment portfolios for a sample of clients. For the 70 participants in the study, organize these data into a frequency distribution. (See Exercise 43 and LO2-3.)

LEARNING OBJECTIVES

When you have completed this chapter, you will be able to:

LO2-1   Summarize qualitative variables with frequency and relative frequency tables.

LO2-2   Display a frequency table using a bar or pie chart.

LO2-3   Summarize quantitative variables with frequency and relative frequency distributions.

LO2-4   Display a frequency distribution using a histogram or frequency polygon.

Chapter Opening Exercise

A representative exercise opens the chapter and shows how the chapter content can be applied to a real-world situation.

Introduction to the Topic

Each chapter starts with a review of the important concepts of the previous chapter and provides a link to the material in the current chapter. This step-by-step approach increases comprehension by providing continuity across the concepts.

Introduction

The United States automobile retailing industry is highly competitive. It is dominated by megadealerships that own and operate 50 or more franchises, employ over 10,000 people, and generate several billion dollars in annual sales. Many of the top dealerships are publicly owned with shares traded on the New York Stock Exchange or NASDAQ. In 2020, the largest megadealership was Carmax (ticker symbol KMX), followed by Penske Auto Group (PAG), AutoNation (AN), and Lithia Motors Inc. (LAD).

These large corporations use statistics and analytics to summarize and analyze data and information to support their decisions. As an example, we will look at the Applewood Auto Group. It owns four dealerships and sells a wide range of vehicles. These include the popular Korean brands Kia and Hyundai, BMW and Volvo sedans and luxury SUVs, and a full line of Ford and Chevrolet cars and trucks.

Harper Davis is a member of the senior management team at Applewood Auto Group, which has its corporate offices adjacent to Kane Motors. Harper is responsible for tracking and analyzing vehicle sales and the profitability of those sales. To track sales, Harper records

Justin Sullivan/Getty Images

Example/Solution

After important concepts are introduced, a solved example is given. This example provides a how-to illustration and shows a relevant business application that helps students answer the question, "How can I apply this concept?"

▶ EXAMPLE

Morgan Stanley is an investment company with offices located throughout the United States. Listed here are the commissions earned last month by a sample of 15 brokers at the Morgan Stanley office in Oakland, California.

$2,038	$1,758	$1,721	$1,637	$2,097	$2,047	$2,205	$1,787	$2,287
1,940	2,311	2,054	2,406	1,471	1,460			

Locate the median, the first quartile, and the third quartile for the commissions earned.

Self-Reviews

Self-Reviews are interspersed throughout each chapter and follow Example/Solution sections. They help students monitor their progress and provide immediate reinforcement for that particular technique. Answers are in Appendix D.

SELF-REVIEW 4-2

The Quality Control department of Plainsville Peanut Company is responsible for checking the weight of the 8-ounce jar of peanut butter. The weights of a sample of nine jars produced last hour are:

7.69	7.72	7.80	7.86	7.90	7.94	7.97	8.06	8.09

(a)   What is the median weight?
(b)   Determine the weights corresponding to the first and third quartiles.

Statistics in Action

Statistics in Action articles are scattered throughout the text, usually about two per chapter. They provide unique, interesting applications and historical insights in the field of statistics.

STATISTICS IN ACTION

Government statistics show there are about 1.7 automobile-caused fatalities for every 100,000,000 vehicle-miles. If you drive 1 mile to the store to buy your lottery ticket and then return home, you have driven 2 miles. Thus, the probability that you will join this statistical group on your next 2-mile round trip is

Definitions

Definitions of new terms or terms unique to the study of statistics are set apart from the text and highlighted for easy reference and review. They also appear in the Glossary at the end of the book.

JOINT PROBABILITY A probability that measures the likelihood two or more events will happen concurrently.

Formulas

Formulas that are used for the first time are boxed and numbered for reference. In addition, a list of all formulas is included in the back of the text.

SPECIAL RULE OF MULTIPLICATION $P(A \text{ and } B) = P(A)P(B)$ **(5–8)**

Exercises

Exercises are included after sections within the chapter and at the end of the chapter. Section exercises cover the material studied in the section. Many exercises have data files available to import into statistical software. They are indicated with the FILE icon. Answers to the odd-numbered exercises are in Appendix C.

EXERCISES

13. What would you report as the modal value for a set of observations if there were a total of:
    a. 10 observations and no two values were the same?
    b. 6 observations and they were all equal to 21?
    c. 6 observations and the values were 1, 2, 3, 3, 4, and 4?

For Exercises 14–16, determine the (a) mean, (b) median, and (c) mode.

14. The following is the number of oil changes for the last 7 days at the Jiffy Lube located at the corner of Elm Street and Pennsylvania Avenue.

Computer Output

The text includes many software examples, using Excel, MegaStat®, and Minitab. The software results are illustrated in the chapters. Instructions for the software examples are referenced in online tutorials in Connect.

	A	B	Location	Vehicle-Type	Previous		Profit	
1	Age	Profit	Location	Vehicle-Type	Previous			
2	21	$1,387	Tionesta	Sedan	0			
3	23	$1,754	Sheffield	SUV	1		Mean	1843.17
4	24	$1,817	Sheffield	Hybrid	1		Standard Error	47.97
5	25	$1,040	Sheffield	Compact	0		Median	1882.50
6	26	$1,273	Kane	Sedan	1		Mode	1761.00
7	27	$1,529	Sheffield	Sedan	1		Standard Dev	643.63
8	27	$3,082	Kane	Truck	0		Sample Varian	414256.60
9	28	$1,951	Kane	SUV	1		Kurtosis	-0.22
10	28	$2,692	Tionesta	Compact	0		Skewness	-0.24
11	29	$1,206	Sheffield	Sedan	0		Range	2998.00
12	29	$1,342	Kane	Sedan	2		Minimum	294.00
13	30	$443	Kane	Sedan	3		Maximum	3292.00
14	30	$754	Olean	Sedan	2		Sum	331770.00
15	30	$1,621	Sheffield	Truck	1		Count	180.00

Source: Microsoft Excel

BY CHAPTER

Chapter Summary

Each chapter contains a brief summary of the chapter material, including vocabulary, definitions, and critical formulas.

Pronunciation Key

This section lists the mathematical symbol, its meaning, and how to pronounce it. We believe this will help the student retain the meaning of the symbol and generally enhance course communications.

Chapter Exercises

Generally, the end-of-chapter exercises are the most challenging and integrate the chapter concepts. The answers and worked-out solutions for all odd-numbered exercises are in Appendix C. Many exercises are noted with a data file icon in the margin. For these exercises, there are data files in Excel format located on the text's website, www. mhhe.com/Lind19e. These files help students use statistical software to solve the exercises.

Data Analytics

The goal of the Data Analytics sections is to develop analytical skills. The exercises present a real-world context with supporting data. The data sets are printed in Appendix A and available to download from the text's website www. mhhe.com/Lind19e. Statistical software is required to analyze the data and respond to the exercises. Each data set is used to explore questions and discover findings that relate to a real-world context. For each business context, a story is uncovered as students progress from Chapters 1 to 17.

CHAPTER SUMMARY

I. A random variable is a numerical value determined by the outcome of an experiment.

II. A probability distribution is a listing of all possible outcomes of an experiment and the probability associated with each outcome.

  A. A discrete probability distribution can assume only certain values. The main features as follows:

    1. The sum of the probabilities is 1.00.

    2. The probability of a particular outcome is between 0.00 and 1.00.

    3. The outcomes are mutually exclusive.

  B. A continuous distribution can assume an infinite number of values within a specific range.

III. The mean and variance of a discrete probability distribution are computed as follows:

  A. The mean is:

$$\mu = \Sigma[xP(x)] \tag{6-1}$$

  B. The variance is:

PRONUNCIATION KEY

SYMBOL	MEANING	PRONUNCIATION
$P(A)$	Probability of A	P of A
$P(\sim A)$	Probability of not A	P of not A
$P(A \text{ and } B)$	Probability of A and B	P of A and B
$P(A \text{ or } B)$	Probability of A or B	P of A or B
$P(A|B)$	Probability of A given B has happened	P of A given B
$_nP_r$	Permutation of n items selected r at a time	Pnr
$_nC_r$	Combination of n items selected r at a time	Cnr

CHAPTER EXERCISES

31. According to the local union president, the mean gross income of plumbers in the Salt Lake City area follows the normal probability distribution with a mean of $45,000 and a population standard deviation of $3,000. A recent investigative reporter for KYAK TV found, for a sample of 120 plumbers, the mean gross income was $45,500. At the .10 significance level, is it reasonable to conclude that the mean income is not equal to $45,000? Determine the p-value.

32. **FILE** Rutter Nursery Company packages its pine bark mulch in 50-pound bags. From a long history, management knows that the distribution of bag weights is normally distributed with a population standard deviation of 3 pounds per bag. At the end of each day, Jeff Rutter, the production manager, weighs 10 bags and computes the mean weight of the sample. Following are the weights of 10 bags from today's production.

45.6	47.7	47.6	46.3	46.2	47.4	49.2	55.8	47.5	48.5

  a. Can Mr. Rutter conclude that the mean weight of the bags is less than 50 pounds? Use the .01 significance level.

  b. In a brief report, tell why Mr. Rutter can use the z-distribution as the test statistic.

  c. Compute the p-value.

DATA ANALYTICS

(The data for these exercises are available at the text website: www.mhhe.com/lind19e.)

60. Refer to the North Valley Real Estate data, which report information on homes sold during the last year.

  a. The mean selling price (in $ thousands) of the homes was computed earlier to be $357.0, with a standard deviation of $160.7. Use the normal distribution to estimate the percentage of homes selling for more than $500,000. Compare this to the actual results. Is price normally distributed? Try another test. If price is normally distributed, how many homes should have a price greater than the mean? Compare this to the actual number of homes. Construct a frequency distribution of price. What do you observe?

  b. The mean days on the market is 30 with a standard deviation of 10 days. Use the normal distribution to estimate the number of homes on the market more than

---

Software Tutorials

References to tutorials demonstrating how to use Excel to compute various statistics and perform statistical analyses are included throughout the text. See an example of the icon to the right.

Tutorial #3 in Connect

Tutorial #3 in Connect

Answers to Self-Review

The worked-out solutions to the Self-Reviews are provided in Appendix D.

16–5	Ranks			
	Englewood	West Side	Great Northern	Sylvania
	17	5	19	7
	20	1	9.5	11
	16	3	21	15
	13	5	22	9.5
	5	2	14	8
	18			12

BY SECTION

Section Reviews

After selected groups of chapters (1–4, 5–7, 8 and 9, 10–12, 13 and 14, 15 and 16, and 17 and 18), a Section Review is included. Much like a review before an exam, these include a brief **overview** of the chapters and **problems for review.**

Cases

The review also includes continuing cases and several small cases that let students make decisions using tools and techniques from a variety of chapters.

Practice Test

The Practice Test is intended to give students an idea of content that might appear on a test and how the test might be structured. The Practice Test includes both objective questions and problems covering the material studied in the section.

A REVIEW OF CHAPTERS 1–4

This section is a review of the major concepts and terms introduced in Chapters 1–4. Chapter 1 began by describing the meaning and purpose of statistics. Next we described the different types of variables and the four levels of measurement. Chapter 2 was concerned with describing a set of observations by organizing it into a frequency distribution and then portraying the frequency distribution as a histogram or a frequency polygon. Chapter 3 began by describing measures of location, such as the mean, weighted mean, median, geometric mean, and mode. This chapter also included measures of dispersion, or spread. Discussed in this section were the range, variance, and standard deviation. Chapter 4 included several graphing techniques such as dot plots, box plots, and scatter diagrams. We also discussed the coefficient of skewness, which reports the lack of symmetry in a set of data, and the correlation coefficient.

CASES

A. Century National Bank

The following case will appear in subsequent review sections. Assume that you work in the Planning Department of the Century National Bank and report to Ms. Lamberg. You will need to do some data analysis and prepare a short written report. Remember, Mr. Selig is the president of the bank, so you will want to ensure that your report is complete and accurate. A copy of the data appears in Appendix A.5.

Century National Bank has offices in several cities in the Midwest and the southeastern part of the United States. Mr. Dan Selig, president and CEO, would like to know the characteristics of his checking account customers. What is the balance of a typical customer?

How many other bank services do the checking account customers use? Do the customers use the ATM service and, if so, how often? What about debit cards? Who uses them, and how often are they used?

other bank services (a savings account, a certificate of deposit, etc.) the customer uses; (3) whether the customer has a debit card (this is a bank service in which charges are made directly to the customer's account); and (4) whether or not interest is paid on the checking account. The sample includes customers from the branches in Cincinnati, Ohio; Atlanta, Georgia; Louisville, Kentucky; and Erie, Pennsylvania.

1. Develop a graph or table that portrays the checking balances. What is the balance of a typical customer? Do many customers have more than $2,000 in their accounts? Does it appear that there is a difference in the distribution of the accounts among the four branches? Around what value do the account balances tend to cluster?
2. Determine the mean and median of the checking account balances. Compare the mean and the median balances for the four branches. Is there a

PRACTICE TEST

There is a practice test at the end of each review section. The tests are in two parts. The first part contains several objective questions, usually in a fill-in-the-blank format. The second part is problems. In most cases, it should take 30 to 45 minutes to complete the test. The problems require a calculator. Check the answers in the Answer Section in the back of the book.

Part 1—Objective

1. The science of collecting, organizing, presenting, analyzing, and interpreting data to assist in making effective decisions is called _____
2. Methods of organizing, summarizing, and presenting data in an informative way are called _____
3. The entire set of individuals or objects of interest or the measurements obtained from all individuals or objects of interest are called the _____
4. List the two types of variables.

1. _____
2. _____
3. _____
4. _____

Students
Get Learning that Fits You

Effective tools for efficient studying

Connect is designed to help you be more productive with simple, flexible, intuitive tools that maximize your study time and meet your individual learning needs. Get learning that works for you with Connect.

Study anytime, anywhere

Download the free ReadAnywhere® app and access your online eBook, SmartBook® 2.0, or Adaptive Learning Assignments when it's convenient, even if you're offline. And since the app automatically syncs with your Connect account, all of your work is available every time you open it. Find out more at **mheducation.com/readanywhere**

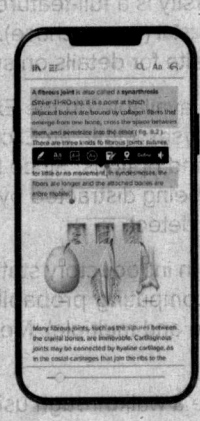

iPhone: Getty Images

"I really liked this app—it made it easy to study when you don't have your textbook in front of you."

- Jordan Cunningham,
Eastern Washington University

Everything you need in one place

Your Connect course has everything you need—whether reading your digital eBook or completing assignments for class, Connect makes it easy to get your work done.

Learning for everyone

McGraw Hill works directly with Accessibility Services Departments and faculty to meet the learning needs of all students. Please contact your Accessibility Services Office and ask them to email accessibility@mheducation.com, or visit **mheducation.com/about/accessibility** for more information.

INSTRUCTOR LIBRARY

The *Connect®* Instructor Library is your repository for additional resources to improve student engagement in and out of class. You can select and use any asset that enhances your lecture, including:

- **Solutions Manual** The Solutions Manual, carefully revised by the authors, contains solutions to all basic, intermediate, and difficult exercises found throughout the chapters.
- **Test Bank** The Test Bank, revised by Wendy Bailey of Troy University, contains hundreds of true/false, multiple choice, and short-answer/discussions, updated based on the revisions of the authors. The level of difficulty varies, as indicated by the easy, medium, and difficult labels.
- **PowerPoint Presentations** Prepared by Stephanie Campbell of Mineral Area College, the presentations contain exhibits, tables, key points, and summaries in a visually stimulating collection of slides.
- **Excel Templates** There are templates for various end-of-chapter problems that have been set as Excel spreadsheets—all denoted by an icon. Students can easily download, save the files, and use the data to solve end-of-chapter problems.

MEGASTAT® FOR MICROSOFT EXCEL®

MegaStat® by J. B. Orris of Butler University is a full-featured Excel statistical analysis add-in that is available on the MegaStat website at **www.mhhe.com/megastat** (for purchase). MegaStat works with recent versions of Microsoft Excel® (Windows and Mac OS X). See the website for details on supported versions.

Once installed, MegaStat will always be available on the Excel add-ins ribbon with no expiration date or data limitations. MegaStat performs statistical analyses within an Excel workbook. When a MegaStat menu item is selected, a dialog box pops up for data selection and options. Since MegaStat is an easy-to-use extension of Excel, students can focus on learning statistics without being distracted by the software. Ease-of-use features include Auto Expand for quick data selection and Auto Label detect.

MegaStat does most calculations found in introductory statistics textbooks, such as computing descriptive statistics, creating frequency distributions, and computing probabilities as well as hypothesis testing, ANOVA, chi-square analysis, and regression analysis (simple and multiple). MegaStat output is carefully formatted and appended to an output worksheet.

Video tutorials are included that provide a walkthrough using MegaStat for typical business statistics topics. A context-sensitive help system is built into MegaStat and a User's Guide is included in PDF format.

MINITAB®/SPSS®/JMP®

Minitab®, Minitab© Express, SPSS®, and JMP® Student Edition are software products that are available to help students solve the exercises with data files. Each software product can be packaged with any McGraw Hill business statistics text.

Minitab, Inc.

This edition of *Statistical Techniques in Business and Economics* is the product of many people: students, colleagues, reviewers, and the staff at McGraw Hill Education. We thank them all. We wish to express our sincere gratitude to the reviewers:

Mark Dahkle
University of Nebraska–Kearny

Mark Haney
Robert Morris University

Miren Ivankovic
Anderson University

Jakeun Koo
Texas Southern University

Subrata Kundu
George Washington University

John Lewis
Midlands Technical College

Keith Lowe
Jacksonville State University

Ed Pappanastos
Troy University

Germain N. Pichop
Oklahoma City Community College

Ildiko Roth
North Idaho College

Jim Shi
New Jersey Institute of Technology

Michael Sinkey
University of West Georgia

Stanley Taylor
California State University–Sacramento

Angela Waits
Gadsden State Community College

Anne Williams
Gateway Community College

Jay Zagorsky
Boston University

Zhiwei Zhu
University of Louisiana–Lafayette

Their suggestions and thorough reviews of the previous edition and the manuscript of this edition make this a better text.

Special thanks go to a number of people. Shelly Moore, College of Western Idaho, and John Arcaro, Lakeland Community College, accuracy checked the Connect exercises. Ed Pappanastos, Troy University, built new data sets and revised Smartbook. Rene Ordonez, Southern Oregon University, built the *Connect* guided examples. Wendy Bailey, Troy University, prepared the test bank. Stephanie Campbell, Mineral Area College, prepared the PowerPoint decks. Vickie Fry, Westmoreland County Community College, provided countless hours of digital accuracy checking and support.

We also wish to thank the staff at McGraw Hill. This includes Eric Weber, Portfolio Manager; Portfolio Manager; Harper Christopher, Executive Marketing Manager; Ryan McAndrews, Product Developer; Jenilynn McAtee, Content Project Manager; Bruce Gin, Assessment Project Manager; Katie Ward, Freelance Product Developer; and Matt Diamond, Senior Designer; and others we do not know personally, but who have made valuable contributions. Also, thanks to Vickie Fry for keeping Connect current.

Based on reviewer comments, we made many important changes to the text.

CHAPTER 1 What is Statistics?

- Updated examples, illustrations, and exercises.
- Revised exercises 11, 13, 17, and 19.

CHAPTER 2 Describing Data: Frequency Tables, Frequency Distributions, and Graphic Presentation

- Improved comparisons and illustrations of raw versus grouped data.
- The mode is introduced to help describe frequency distributions.
- Revised exercises 44, 47, and 48.

CHAPTER 3 Describing Data: Numerical Measures

- New and revised exercises applying the geometric mean.
- Expanded presentations of Chebyshev's theorem and the Empirical Rule.
- The section "Compute the mean and standard deviation of grouped data" is removed from the text.
- Revised exercises: 18, 62, 66, 73, and 74.

CHAPTER 4 Describing Data: Displaying and Exploring Data

- A revised introduction relates the chapter topics to data visualization.
- A "Statistics in Action" section about Florence Nightingale and historical reference to data visualization is reintroduced to the text.
- Additional details of computing boxplot whiskers when there are outliers versus no outliers.
- Additional discussion and integration of the interquartile range.
- Revised exercises: 3, 4, 5, 6, 7, 8, 12, 13, 14, 15, 24, 28, 30, and 31.

CHAPTER 5 A Survey of Probability Concepts

- New chapter opening features a lottery example to introduce probability.
- A revised introduction transitions the reader from descriptive statistics using frequency distributions to the concept of probability.
- The sections on counting, permutations, and combinations now follow the classical probability section.
- Each approach to probability (classical, empirical, and subjective) has its own learning objective.
- Revised exercises: 3, 7, 9, 10, 58, and 60.

CHAPTER 6 Discrete Probability Distributions

- A revised introduction discusses the application of probability distributions to decision support models and data science.
- Revised exercises 65 and 66.

CHAPTER 7 Continuous Probability Distributions

- Revised and expanded uniform distribution section provides more context for its application.
- Standardization of the examples showing how to apply the standard normal probability distribution.
- Moved the empirical distribution section to follow the application of the standard normal table.

CHAPTER 8 Sampling, Sampling Methods, and the Central Limit Theorem

- New section describing and applying the sampling distribution of the sample proportion with associated exercises.
- Revised exercises: 4, 24, and 35.

CHAPTER 9 Estimation and Confidence Intervals

- Revised introduction describing the transition from sampling distributions to the application of sampling distributions to estimate population parameters.
- New exercises 11 and 12.
- Revised exercises: 4, 24, and 35.

CHAPTER 10 One-Sample Tests of Hypothesis

- Revised introduction describes the transition from interval estimation to hypothesis testing.
- Hypothesis testing of a population proportion is now included in this chapter.
- Revised and expanded description and application of Type I and Type II errors.
- New examples contrasting the interpretation of hypothesis tests resulting in "failing to reject the null hypothesis," versus "rejecting the null hypothesis."
- Revised exercises: 1, 2, 3, 4, 5, 6, 7, and 8.

CHAPTER 11 Two-Sample Tests of Hypothesis

- A section on the *F*-distribution and testing the equality of two variances is now in this chapter.
- Many chapter exercises include equality of population variance hypothesis tests in advance of testing the equality of two population means.
- Two-sample tests of proportions is now in this chapter.
- Revised exercises: 13, 14, 15, 16, 17, 18, 19, 20, 21, 22, 39, 40, 41, 42, 43, 44 45, 46, 47, 48, 49, and 60.

CHAPTER 12 Analysis of Variance

- The section on the F-distribution is moved to Chapter 11.

CHAPTER 13 Correlation and Linear Regression

- New "Statistics in Action" feature.
- Revised exercises: 17, 36, 41, and 43.

CHAPTER 14 Multiple Regression Analysis

- Revised introduction relating the importance and application of multiple regression and modeling to the broader context of data science.
- Revised exercises: 5, 6, 7, 8, 9, 10, 11, 12, 14, 18, 19, 22, 23, 24, 26, 28, and 31.

CHAPTER 15 Nonparametric Methods: Nominal Level Hypothesis Tests

- Moved the single population proportion hypothesis test to Chapter 10.
- Moved two-sample population proportion hypothesis test to Chapter 11.
- Revised exercises: 18, 19, 25, 27, 29, 30, and 35.

CHAPTER 16 Nonparametric Methods: Analysis of Ordinal Data

- Revised Example/Solution illustrating the hypothesis test of a median.
- Revised exercises: 11,12, 21, and 24.

CHAPTER 17 Index Numbers

- Examples and exercises are updated with recent data.

CHAPTER 18 Forecasting with Time Series Analysis

- Added a second measure of forecasting error, the mean absolute percent error.
- Examples and exercises are updated with recent data.

CHAPTER 19: Statistical Process Control and Quality Management

- Updated list of Baldrige Award winners.

CHAPTER 20: An Introduction to Decision Theory

- Updated exercises.

APPENDIX A: Updated 2021 Major League Baseball data.

APPENDIX B: The F-distribution table values are presented to two significant digits. All Chapter 12 exercises can be solved with the tables.

APPENDIX C AND D: All solutions updated based on revised or updated exercises and/or data.

CHAPTER 12 Analysis of Variance

- The section on the Poisson distribution is moved to Chapter 11.

CHAPTER 13 Correlation and Linear Regression

- New 'Statistics in Action' feature.
- Revised exercises 17, 39, 41, and 43.

CHAPTER 14 Multiple Regression Analysis

- Revised introduction relating the importance and application of multiple regression and modeling to the broader context of data science
- Revised exercises 5, 6, 7, 8, 9, 10, 11, 12, 14, 16, 19, 22, 23, 24, 26, 28, and 31.

CHAPTER 15 Nonparametric Methods: Nominal level Hypothesis Tests

- Moved the single population proportion hypothesis test to Chapter 10
- Moved two sample population proportion hypothesis test to Chapter 11
- Revised exercises 18, 19, 26, 27, 29, 30, and 35

CHAPTER 16 Nonparametric Methods: Analysis of Ordinal Data

- Revised Example/Solution illustrating the hypothesis test of a median.
- Revised exercises 11, 12, 21, and 21.

CHAPTER 17 Index Numbers

- Examples and exercises are updated with recent data

CHAPTER 18 Forecasting with Time Series Analysis

- Added a second measure of forecasting error, the mean absolute percent error.
- Examples and exercises are updated with recent data

CHAPTER 19 Statistical Process Control and Quality Management

- Updated list of Baldrige Award winners.

CHAPTER 20 An introduction to Decision Theory

- Updated exercises

APPENDIX A: Updated 2021 Major League Baseball data.

APPENDIX B: The F-distribution table values are presented to two significant digits. All Chapter 12 exercises can be solved with the tables.

APPENDIX C AND D: All solutions updated based on revised or updated exercises and/or data.

BRIEF CONTENTS

CONTENTS

8 Sampling, Sampling Methods, and the Central Limit Theorem 249

9 Estimation and Confidence Intervals 286

10 One-Sample Tests of Hypothesis 325

11 Two-Sample Tests of Hypothesis 364

12 Analysis of Variance 413

13 Correlation and Linear Regression 459

What Is Statistics?

rawf8/Shutterstock

▲ **THE FITBIT BLAZE** Smart Fitness Watch has been ranked as the number one best-selling wearable technology device. This wearable technology tracks heart rate and many activities such as running, biking, and cross training. It also monitors sleep patterns. The data can be synced with a phone app that summarizes and displays the user's information. Is the ranking based on a population or a sample? A retailer also reports over 14,000 ratings for the device. Are the ratings based on a population or a sample? (See Exercise 11 and LO1-3.)

LEARNING OBJECTIVES

When you have completed this chapter, you will be able to:

LO1-1 Explain why knowledge of statistics is important.

LO1-2 Define statistics and provide an example of how statistics is applied.

LO1-3 Differentiate between descriptive and inferential statistics.

LO1-4 Classify variables as qualitative or quantitative, and discrete or continuous.

LO1-5 Distinguish among nominal, ordinal, interval, and ratio levels of measurement.

LO1-6 List the values associated with the practice of statistics.

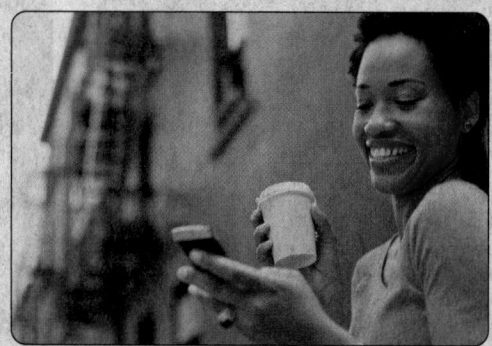

Barry Djomede/Alamy Stock Photo

Introduction

Suppose you work for a large company and your supervisor asks you to decide if a new version of a smartphone should be produced and sold. You start by thinking about the product's innovations and new features. Then, you stop and realize the consequences of the decision. The product will need to make a profit, so the pricing and the costs of production and distribution are all very important. The decision to introduce the product is based on many alternatives. So how will you know? Where do you start?

Without experience in the industry, beginning to develop an intelligence that will make you an expert is essential. You select three other people to work with and meet with them. The conversation focuses on what you need to know and what information and data you need. In your meeting, many questions are asked. How many competitors are already in the market? How are smartphones priced? What design features do competitors' products have? What features does the market require? What do customers want in a smartphone? What do customers like about the existing products? The answers will be based on business intelligence consisting of data and information collected through customer surveys, engineering analysis, and market research. In the end, your presentation to support your decision regarding the introduction of a new smartphone is based on the statistics that you use to summarize and organize your data, the statistics that you use to compare the new product to existing products, and the statistics to estimate future sales, costs, and revenues. The statistics will be the focus of the conversation that you will have with your supervisor about this very important decision.

As a decision maker, you will need to acquire and analyze data to support your decisions. The purpose of this text is to develop your knowledge of basic statistical techniques and methods and how to apply them to develop the business and personal intelligence that will help you make decisions.

LO1-1
Explain why knowledge of statistics is important.

Source: Domo, Inc.
https://www.domo.com/learn/infographic/data-never-sleeps-9

Why Study Statistics?

If you look through your university catalog, you will find that statistics is required for many college programs. As you investigate a future career in accounting, economics, human resources, finance, business analytics, or other business area, you will also discover that statistics is required as part of these college programs. So why is statistics a requirement in so many disciplines?

A major driver of the requirement for statistics knowledge is the technologies available for capturing data. Examples include the technology that Google uses to track how Internet users access websites. As people use Google to search the Internet, Google records every search and then uses these data to sort and prioritize the results for future Internet searches. One recent estimate indicates that Google processes 20,000 terabytes of information per day. Big-box retailers such as Target, Walmart, Kroger, and others scan every purchase and use the data to manage the distribution of products, to make decisions about marketing and sales, and to track daily and even hourly sales. Police departments collect and use data to provide city residents with maps that communicate information about crimes committed and their location. Every organization is collecting and using data to develop knowledge and intelligence that will help people make informed decisions and track the implementation of their decisions. The graphic to the left shows the amount of data generated every minute (www.domo.com).

A good working knowledge of statistics is useful for summarizing and organizing data to provide information that is useful and supportive of decision making. Statistics is used to make valid comparisons and to predict the outcomes of decisions.

In summary, there are at least three reasons for studying statistics: (1) Data are collected everywhere and require statistical knowledge to make the information useful, (2) statistical techniques are used to make professional and personal decisions, and (3) no matter what your career, you will need a knowledge of statistics to understand the world and to be conversant in your career. An understanding of statistics and statistical methods will help you make more effective personal and professional decisions.

What Is Meant by Statistics?

This question can be rephrased in two, subtly different ways: What are statistics, and what is statistics? To answer the first question, a statistic is a number used to communicate a piece of information. Examples of **statistics** are:

- The rate of inflation in the United States economy was 5.4% in July 2020.
- Your grade point average is 3.5.
- The price of a 2022 Tesla Model S sedan is $99,990.

Each of these statistics is a numerical fact and communicates a very limited piece of information that is not very useful by itself. However, if we recognize that each of these statistics is part of a larger discussion, then the question "what **is** statistics" is applicable. Statistics is the set of knowledge and skills used to organize, summarize, and analyze data. The results of statistical analysis will start interesting conversations in the search for knowledge and intelligence that will help us make decisions. For example:

- The inflation rate for the 2020 calendar year was 5.4%. By applying statistics we could compare this year's inflation rate to the past observations of inflation. Is it higher, lower, or about the same? By graphing the reported monthly inflation rates, we can determine the trend in inflation. We can also use the inflation rate to predict future prices and other effects of inflation on the economy.
- Your grade point average (GPA) is 3.5. By collecting data and applying statistics, you can determine the required GPA to be admitted to the Master of Business Administration program at the University of Chicago, Harvard University, or the University of Michigan. You can determine the likelihood that you would be admitted to a particular program. You may be interested in interviewing for a management position with Procter & Gamble. What GPA does Procter & Gamble require for college graduates with a bachelor's degree? Is there a range of acceptable GPAs?
- You are budgeting for a new car. You would like to own an electric car with a small carbon footprint. The price, according to Kelley Blue Book, for a 2022 Tesla Model S Sedan is $99,990. By collecting additional data and applying statistics, you can analyze the alternatives. For example, another choice is a hybrid car that runs on both gas and electricity. A 2022 Prius Limited can be purchased for about $32,920. In 2021, Ford introduced the battery-powered Mustang Mach-e priced at $43,895. What are the differences in the cars' specifications? What additional information can be collected and summarized so that you can make a good purchase decision?

Another example of using statistics to provide information as the basis for making decisions involves the sales and market share of major snack foods in the United States. To create the information, data are collected on the sales volume, measured in pounds, for each of the major snack foods in the United States market. The data also include the pounds of each product line sold by Frito-Lay, a subsidiary of Pepsico. Based on this information, we can calculate the market share of Frito-Lay's brands for each product line. Statistics is used to summarize and present this information as a bar chart, presented in Chart 1–1. The chart shows the total pounds of each product line sold in the United States. Clearly, potato and tortilla chips dominate the market. In addition, the chart shows, both graphically and numerically, Frito-Lay's market share

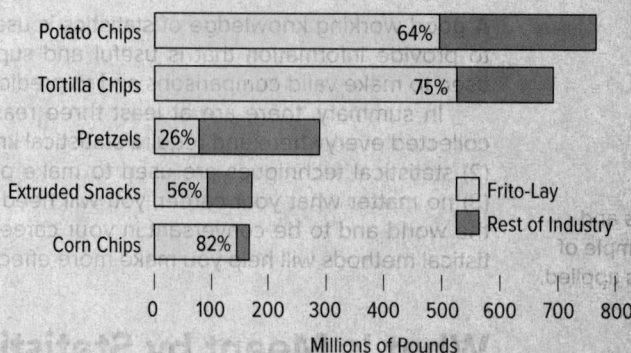

CHART 1–1 Frito-Lay Volume and Share of Major Snack Chip Categories in U.S. Supermarkets

for each product line. Except for pretzels, Frito-Lay products account for more than half of snack food pounds sold in the United States. The information shows that Frito-Lay is the market leader in the U.S. snack food industry.

These examples show that statistics is more than the presentation of numerical information. Statistics is about collecting and processing information to create a conversation, to stimulate additional questions, and to provide a basis for making decisions. Specifically, we define **statistics** as:

> **STATISTICS** The science of collecting, organizing, presenting, analyzing, and interpreting data to assist in making more effective decisions.

In this book, you will learn the basic techniques and applications of statistics that you can use to support your decisions, both personal and professional. To start, we will differentiate between descriptive and inferential statistics.

LO1-3
Differentiate between descriptive and inferential statistics.

Types of Statistics

When we use statistics to generate information for decision making from data, we use either descriptive statistics or inferential statistics. Their application depends on the questions asked and the type of data available.

Descriptive Statistics

Masses of unorganized data—such as the census of population, the weekly earnings of thousands of computer programmers, and the individual responses of 2,000 registered voters regarding their choice for president of the United States—are of little value as is. However, descriptive statistics can be used to organize data into a meaningful form. We define **descriptive statistics** as:

> **DESCRIPTIVE STATISTICS** Methods of organizing, summarizing, and presenting data in an informative way.

The following are examples that apply descriptive statistics to summarize a large amount of data and provide information that is easy to understand.

- There are a total of 46,837 miles of interstate highways in the United States. The interstate system represents only 1% of the nation's total roads but carries more than 20% of the traffic. The longest is I-90, which stretches from Boston to Seattle, a distance of 3,099 miles. The shortest is I-878 in New York City, which is

0.70 miles in length. Alaska does not have any interstate highways, Texas has the most interstate miles at 3,232, and New York has the most interstate routes with 28.
• In 2021, Americans spent an average of $164.76 on Valentine's Day—related gifts, a decrease of 16.07% compared to 2020. The highest average amount spent, $264, was for people between 35 and 44 years of age. More than 25% of Americans buy Valentine's Day gifts for their pets (**https://balancingeverything. com/valentines-day-sales-statistics/**).

Statistical methods and techniques to generate descriptive statistics are presented in Chapters 2 and 4. These include organizing and summarizing data with frequency distributions and presenting frequency distributions with charts and graphs. In addition, statistical measures to summarize the characteristics of a distribution are discussed in Chapter 3.

Inferential Statistics

Sometimes we must make decisions based on a limited set of data. For example, we would like to know the operating characteristics, such as fuel efficiency measured by miles per gallon (MPG), of sport utility vehicles (SUVs) currently in use. If we spent a lot of time, money, and effort, all the owners of SUVs could be surveyed. In this case, our goal would be to survey the **population** of SUV owners.

> **POPULATION** The entire set of individuals or objects of interest or the measurements obtained from all individuals or objects of interest.

However, based on inferential statistics, we can survey a limited number of SUV owners and collect a **sample** from the population.

> **SAMPLE** A portion, or part, of the population of interest.

Samples often are used to obtain reliable estimates of population parameters. (Sampling is discussed in Chapter 8.) In the process, we make trade-offs between the time, money, and effort to collect the data and the error of estimating a population parameter. The process of sampling SUVs is illustrated in the following graphic. In this example, we would like to know the mean or average SUV fuel efficiency. To estimate the mean of the population, six SUVs are sampled and the mean of their MPG is calculated.

Population
All items

Sample
Items selected
from the population

So, the sample of six SUVs represents evidence from the population that we use to reach an inference, or conclusion, about the average MPG for all SUVs. The process of sampling from a population with the objective of estimating properties of a population is called **inferential statistics.**

> **INFERENTIAL STATISTICS** The methods used to estimate a property of a population on the basis of a sample.

Inferential statistics is widely applied to learn something about a population in business, agriculture, politics, and government, as shown in the following examples:

- Television networks constantly monitor the popularity of their programs by hiring Nielsen and other organizations to sample the preferences of TV viewers. During the 2020–2021 season, *The Late Show with Stephen Colbert* was the most-watched late-night show. *Jimmy Kimmet LIve!* ranked second, followed by *The Tonight Show Starring Jimmy Fallon* (**https://deadline.com/2021/06/late-night-ratings-late-show-wins-season-fifth-consecutive-year-1234772290**). These program ratings are used to make decisions about advertising rates and whether to continue or cancel a program.
- In 2021, a vaccination for COVID-19 was freely available. Its benefit is to prevent serious health or fatal outcomes from a COVID infection. Many people did not get vaccinated. To determine why people did not choose to vaccinate, random samples of people were selected and surveyed regarding their opinions. Based on these surveys, public health officials can focus their communication and distribution strategies to increase the number of vaccinated people.

A feature of our text is self-review problems. There are a number of them interspersed throughout each chapter. The first self-review follows. Each self-review tests your comprehension of preceding material. The answer and method of solution are given in Appendix D. You can find the answer to the following self-review in 1–1 in Appendix D. We recommend that you solve each one and then check your answer.

SELF-REVIEW 1–1

The answers are in Appendix D.

The Atlanta-based advertising firm Brandon and Associates asked a sample of 1,960 consumers to try a newly developed chicken dinner by Boston Market. Of the 1,960 sampled, 1,176 said they would purchase the dinner if it is marketed.
(a) Is this an example of descriptive statistics or inferential statistics? Explain.
(b) What could Brandon and Associates report to Boston Market regarding acceptance of the chicken dinner in the population?

LO1-4
Classify variables as qualitative or quantitative, and discrete or continuous.

Types of Variables

There are two basic types of variables: qualitative and quantitative (see Chart 1–2). When an object or individual is observed and recorded as a nonnumeric characteristic, it is a qualitative variable or an attribute. Examples of qualitative variables are, beverage preference, brand of vehicle owned, state of birth, and eye color. When a variable is qualitative, we usually count the number of observations for each category and determine what percent are in each category. For example, if we observe the variable eye color, what percent of the population has blue eyes and what percent has brown eyes? If the variable is type of vehicle, what percent of the total number of cars sold last month were SUVs? Qualitative variables are often summarized in charts and bar graphs (see Chapter 2).

```
                          ┌─────────────────────┐
                          │  Types of Variables │
                          └─────────────────────┘
                    ┌──────────────┴──────────────┐
            ┌───────────────┐            ┌───────────────┐
            │  Qualitative  │            │  Quantitative │
            └───────────────┘            └───────────────┘
                                    ┌──────────┴──────────┐
                            ┌───────────────┐     ┌───────────────┐
                            │   Discrete    │     │   Continuous  │
                            └───────────────┘     └───────────────┘

    • Brand of PC              • Children in a family     • Amount of income
    • Marital status           • Strokes on a golf hole     tax paid
    • Hair color               • TV sets owned            • Weight of a student
                                                          • Yearly rainfall in
                                                            Tampa, FL
```

CHART 1–2 Summary of the Types of Variables

When a variable can be reported numerically, it is called a quantitative variable. Examples of quantitative variables are the balance in your checking account, the number of gigabytes of data used on your cell phone plan last month, the life of a car battery (such as 42 months), and the number of people employed by a company.

Quantitative variables are either discrete or continuous. Discrete variables can assume only certain values, and there are "gaps" between the values. Examples of discrete variables are the number of bedrooms in a house (1, 2, 3, 4, etc.), the number of cars (326, 421, etc.) arriving at Exit 25 on I-4 in Florida near Walt Disney World in an hour, and the number of students in each section of a statistics course (25 in section A, 42 in section B, and 18 in section C). We count, for example, the number of cars arriving at Exit 25 on I-4, and we count the number of statistics students in each section. Notice that a home can have 3 or 4 bedrooms, but it cannot have 3.56 bedrooms. Thus, there is a "gap" between possible values. Typically, discrete variables are counted.

Observations of a continuous variable can assume any value within a specific range. Examples of continuous variables are the air pressure in a tire and the weight of a shipment of tomatoes. Other examples are the ounces of raisins in a box of raisin bran cereal and the duration of flights from Orlando to San Diego. Grade point average is a continuous variable. We could report the GPA of a particular student as 3.2576952. The usual practice is to round to 3 places—3.258. Typically, continuous variables result from measuring.

LO1-5
Distinguish among nominal, ordinal, interval, and ratio levels of measurement.

Ron Buskirk/Alamy Stock Photo

Levels of Measurement

Data can be classified according to levels of measurement. The level of measurement determines how data should be summarized and presented. It will also indicate the type of statistical analysis that can be performed. Here are two examples of the relationship between measurement and how we apply statistics. There are six colors of candies in a bag of M&Ms. Suppose we assign brown a value of 1, yellow 2, blue 3, orange 4, green 5, and red 6. What kind of variable is the color of an M&M? It is a qualitative variable. Suppose someone summarizes M&M color by adding the assigned color values, divides the sum by the number of M&Ms, and reports that the mean color is 3.56. How do we interpret this statistic? You are correct in concluding that it has no meaning as a measure of M&M color. As a qualitative variable, we can only report the count and percentage of each color in a bag of M&Ms. As a second example, in a high school track meet there are eight competitors in the 400-meter run. We report the order of finish and that the mean finish is 4.5. What does the mean finish tell us? Nothing! In both of these instances, we have not used the appropriate statistics for the level of measurement.

There are four levels of measurement: nominal, ordinal, interval, and ratio. The lowest, or the most primitive, measurement is the nominal level. The highest is the ratio level of measurement.

Nominal-Level Data

For the **nominal level of measurement,** observations of a qualitative variable are measured and recorded as labels or names. The labels or names can only be classified and counted. There is no particular order to the labels.

> **NOMINAL LEVEL OF MEASUREMENT** Data recorded at the nominal level of measurement is represented as labels or names. They have no order. They can only be classified and counted.

A classification of M&M candies based on their color is an example of the nominal level of measurement. We simply classify the candies by color. There is no natural order. That is, we could report the brown candies first, the orange first, or any of the other colors first. For the data measured at the nominal level, we are limited to counting the number in each category of the variable. Often, we convert these counts to percentages. For example, a random sample of 100 bags of M&M candies reports the following percentages for each color:

Color	Percent in a bag
Blue	24%
Green	20%
Orange	16%
Yellow	14%
Red	13%
Brown	13%

To process the data for a variable measured at the nominal level, we often numerically code the labels or names. For example, if we are interested in measuring the home state for students at East Carolina University, we would assign a student's home state of Alabama a code of 1, Alaska a code of 2, Arizona a 3, and so on. Using this procedure with an alphabetical listing of states, Wisconsin is coded 49 and Wyoming 50. Realize that the number assigned to each state is still a label or name. The reason we assign numerical codes is to facilitate counting the number of students from each state with statistical software. Note that assigning numbers to the states does not give us license to manipulate the codes as numerical information. Specifically, in this example, 1 + 2 = 3 corresponds to Alabama + Alaska = Arizona. Clearly, the nominal level of measurement does not permit any mathematical operation that has any valid interpretation.

Ordinal-Level Data

The next higher level of measurement is the **ordinal level.** For this level of measurement a qualitative variable or attribute is either ranked or rated on a relative scale.

> **ORDINAL LEVEL OF MEASUREMENT** Data recorded at the ordinal level of measurement is based on a relative ranking or rating of items based on a defined attribute or qualitative variable. Variables based on this level of measurement are only ranked or counted.

Best Business Climate

1. Virginia
2. North Carolina
3. Texas
4. Tennessee
5. Alabama
6. Utah
7. Georgia
8. Florida
9. Arizona
10. West Virginia

For example, many businesses make decisions about where to locate their facilities; in other words, where is the best place for their business? Business Facilities (Search "Rankings" at **https://businessfacilities.com/**) publishes a list of the top 10 states for the "best business climate." There are no rankings shown. They are based on the evaluation of many different factors, including the cost of labor, business tax climate, quality of life, transportation infrastructure, educated workforce, and economic growth potential.

This is an example of an ordinal scale because the states are ranked in order of best to worst business climate. That is, we know the relative order of the states based on the attribute. For example, in 2021 Virginia was rated as having the best business climate and North Carolina was second. Alabama was fifth, and that was better than Georgia but not as good as Tennessee. Based on this ordinal ranking, we cannot say that Virginia's business climate is five times better than Alabama's business climate because the magnitude of the difference between the states is not known. To put it another way, we do not know if the magnitude of the difference between Virginia and North Carolina is the same as between North Carolina and Texas.

Another example of the ordinal level measure is based on a scale that measures an attribute. This type of scale is used when students rate instructors on a variety of attributes. One attribute may be: "Overall, how do you rate the quality of instruction in this class?" A student's response is recorded on a relative scale of inferior, poor, good, excellent, and superior. An important characteristic of using a relative measurement scale is that we cannot distinguish the magnitude of the differences between the responses. We do not know if the difference between "Superior" and "Good" is the same as the difference between "Poor" and "Inferior."

Table 1–1 lists the frequencies of 60 student ratings of instructional quality for Professor Peyton Brunner in an Introduction to Finance course. The data are summarized based on the order of the scale used to rate the instructor. That is, they are summarized by the number of students who indicated a rating of superior (6), good (26), and so on. We also can convert the frequencies to percentages. About 43.3% (26/60) of the students rated the instructor as good.

TABLE 1–1 Rating of a Finance Professor

Rating	Frequency	Percentage
Superior	6	10.0%
Good	26	43.3%
Average	16	26.7%
Poor	9	15.0%
Inferior	3	5.0%

Interval-Level Data

The **interval level of measurement** is the next highest level. It includes all the characteristics of the ordinal level, but, in addition, the difference or interval between values is meaningful.

> **INTERVAL LEVEL OF MEASUREMENT** For data recorded at the interval level of measurement, the interval or the distance between values is meaningful. The interval level of measurement is based on a scale with a known unit of measurement.

The Fahrenheit temperature scale is an example of the interval level of measurement. Suppose the high temperatures on three consecutive winter days in Boston are 28, 31, and 20 degrees Fahrenheit. These temperatures can be easily ranked, but we can also determine the interval or distance between temperatures. This is possible because 1 degree Fahrenheit represents a constant unit of measurement. That is, the distance between 10 and 15 degrees Fahrenheit is 5 degrees, and is the same as the 5-degree distance between 50 and 55 degrees Fahrenheit. It is also important to note that 0 is just a point on the scale. It does not represent the absence of the condition. The measurement of 0 degrees Fahrenheit does not represent the absence of heat or cold. But by our own measurement scale, it is cold! A major limitation of a variable measured at the interval level is that we cannot make statements similar to "20 degrees Fahrenheit is twice as warm as 10 degrees Fahrenheit."

Another example of the interval scale of measurement is dress size. Listed here are the bust, waist, and hip measurements for each dress size.

Size	Bust (in)	Waist (in)	Hips (in)
8	32	24	35
10	34	26	37
12	36	28	39
14	38	30	41
16	40	32	43
18	42	34	45
20	44	36	47
22	46	38	49
24	48	40	51
26	50	42	53
28	52	44	55

Why is the variable "size" measured on an interval scale? The first clue is dress size has no natural zero. The measures associated with a size 0 dress are not zero; they are 24-inch bust, 16-inch waist, and 27-inch hips. Second, the intervals between sizes are consistent. Observe that as the size changes by two units (say from size 10 to size 12 or from size 24 to size 26), each of the measurements increases by 2 inches. Third, the ratios between dress sizes are not consistent. For example, a size 28 dress is not twice the size of a size 14 dress. See that the waist measurement for a size 28 dress is 44 inches and the waist size for a size 14 dress is 30 inches. Clearly, the ratio between the waist size of 44 inches is only 1.5 times larger than a waist size of 30 inches. The same observations can be made for bust and hip measurements.

In short, a variable is measured with an interval scale when no absolute zero exists, the intervals between values are consistent over the range of the scale, and ratios, such as "twice as large" or "half as large" are not consistent over the range of the scale.

Ratio-Level Data

Almost all quantitative variables are recorded on the **ratio level of measurement.** The ratio level is the "highest" level of measurement. It has all the characteristics of the interval level, but, in addition, the 0 point and the ratio between two numbers are both meaningful.

> **RATIO LEVEL OF MEASUREMENT** Data recorded at the ratio level of measurement are based on a scale with a known unit of measurement and a meaningful interpretation of zero on the scale.

Examples of the ratio scale of measurement include wages, units of production, weight, changes in stock prices, distance between branch offices, and height. Money is also a good illustration. If you have zero dollars, then you have no money, and a wage

TABLE 1–2 Sampled University Annual Tuition and Fees for International or Out-of-State Students

University	$US
University of North Carolina, Chapel Hill, U.S.	$37,000*
University of Edinburgh, Scotland	26,000*
National University of Singapore, Singapore	15,000*
University of Sydney, Australia	15,000*
University of Johannesburg, South Africa	2,500
University of Haifa, Israel	9,500

*Rounded to the nearest thousand

CHART 1–3 Summary and Examples of the Characteristics for Levels of Measurement

of $50 per hour is two times the wage of $25 per hour. Weight also is measured at the ratio level of measurement. If a scale is correctly calibrated, then it will read 0 when nothing is on the scale. Further, something that weighs 1 pound is half as heavy as something that weighs 2 pounds.

Table 1–2 illustrates the ratio scale of measurement for the variable, university tuition and fees for international, or out-of-state, students attending one of the listed universities. As a ratio scale, we can validly say that attending the University of Edinburgh is about 70% ($26,000/$37,000) of the cost to attend the University of North Carolina, Chapel Hill. Attending the University of Sydney is about 41% of the cost to attend the University of North Carolina, Chapel Hill. Based on this limited information, international universities may be more affordable than U.S. universities. More information would be required to make a fair comparison.

Chart 1–3 summarizes the major characteristics of the various levels of measurement. The level of measurement will determine the type of statistical methods that can be used to analyze a variable. Statistical methods to analyze variables measured on a nominal level are discussed in Chapter 15; methods for ordinal-level variables are discussed in Chapter 16. Statistical methods to analyze variables measured on an interval or ratio level are presented in Chapters 9 through 14.

SELF-REVIEW 1–2

(a) The mean age of people who listen to talk radio is 42.1 years. What level of measurement is used to assess the variable age?

(b) In a survey of luxury-car owners, 8% of the U.S. population own luxury cars. In California and Georgia, 14% of people own luxury cars. Two variables are included in this information. What are they, and how are they measured?

EXERCISES

The answers to the odd-numbered exercises are in Appendix D.

1. What is the level of measurement for each of the following variables?
   a. Student IQ ratings
   b. Distance students travel to class
   c. The jersey numbers of a sorority soccer team
   d. A student's state of birth
   e. A student's academic class—that is, freshman, sophomore, junior, or senior
   f. Number of hours students study per week

2. *Slate* is a daily magazine on the Web. Its business activities can be described by a number of variables. What is the level of measurement for each of the following variables?
   a. The number of hits on their website on Saturday between 8:00 a.m. and 9:00 a.m.
   b. The departments, such as food and drink, politics, foreign policy, sports, etc.
   c. The number of weekly hits on the USAA Insurance ad
   d. The number of years each employee has been employed with Slate

3. On the Web, go to your favorite news source and find examples of each type of variable. Write a brief memo that lists the variables and describes them in terms of qualitative or quantitative, discrete or continuous, and the measurement level.

4. For each of the following, determine whether the group is a sample or a population.
   a. The participants in a study of a new cholesterol drug
   b. The drivers who received a speeding ticket in Kansas City last month
   c. People on welfare in Cook County (Chicago), Illinois
   d. The 30 stocks that make up the Dow Jones Industrial Average

Ethics and Statistics

LO1-6
List the values associated with the practice of statistics.

On September 20, 2018, Cornell University's provost issued the following statement:

> Consistent with the university's Academic Misconduct policy, a faculty committee conducted a thorough investigation into Professor Wansink's research. The committee found that Professor Wansink committed academic misconduct in his research and scholarship, including misreporting of research data, problematic statistical techniques, failure to properly document and preserve research results, and inappropriate authorship. As provided in Cornell policy, these findings were thoroughly reviewed by and upheld by Cornell's dean of the faculty.

> **(http://statements.cornell.edu/2018/20180920-statement-provost-michael-kotlikoff.cfm)**

Professor Wansink resigned from his position at Cornell. Note the series of findings that describe the nature of unethical statistical practices. Clearly, the unethical conduct of research has serious consequences for the researcher and the consumers of the false research outcomes.

Another instance of unethical behavior began in 2003 when Elizabeth Holmes founded the privately held company, Theranos. The company claimed that it created an innovative technology that could run 200 different blood tests with a single drop of blood. To collect blood samples, Ms. Holmes was able to develop business relationships with large chain stores such as Safeway and Walgreens. The company distributed false and misleading data and information regarding the capabilities of the blood testing technology and misreported projected revenues to investors. In 2014, the company projected revenues of $100 million; the Securities and Exchange Commission (SEC) found the actual revenues to be about $100,000. Investors lost about $700 million. In addition, many customers, patients, and doctors relied on the test results to help them make important health care decisions. Many false and unreliable test results were delivered to these people. The SEC charged the founder with fraud for misrepresenting the capabilities of the revolutionary technology and defrauding investors (**https://knowledge.wharton.upenn.edu/article/lessons-from-theranos/**).

In April 2018, the American Statistical Association (ASA) approved "Ethical Guidelines for Statistical Practice" (**https://www.amstat.org/ASA/Your-Career/Ethical-Guidelines-for-Statistical-Practice.aspx**). The ASA advises us to practice statistics with integrity and honesty and urges us to "do the right thing" when collecting, organizing, summarizing, analyzing, and interpreting data and information. The real contribution of statistics to society is a moral one. Financial analysts need to provide information that truly reflects a company's performance so as not to mislead individual investors. Information regarding product defects that may be harmful to people must be analyzed and reported with integrity and honesty. The guidelines further indicate that when we practice statistics, we need to maintain an independent and principled point-of-view when analyzing and reporting findings and results.

As you progress through this text, we will highlight ethical issues in the collection, analysis, presentation, and interpretation of statistical information. We also hope that as you learn about using statistics, you will become a more informed consumer of information. For example, you will question a report if the data do not fairly represent the population, if the report does not include all relevant statistics, or if the presentation of the report does not include the limitations of the statistical analyses and possible sources of error.

Basic Business Analytics

A knowledge of statistics is necessary to support the increasing need for companies and organizations to apply business analytics. Business analytics is used to process and analyze data and information to support a story or narrative of a company's business, such as "What makes us profitable?" or "How will our customers respond to a change in marketing?" In addition to statistics, an ability to use computer software to summarize, organize, analyze, and present the findings of statistical analysis is essential. In this text, we will be using very elementary applications of business analytics using common and available computer software. Throughout our text, we will use Microsoft Excel and, occasionally, Minitab. Universities and colleges usually offer access to Microsoft Excel. Your computer already may be packaged with Microsoft Excel. If not, the Microsoft Office package with Excel often is sold at a reduced academic price through your university or college. In this text, we use Excel for the majority of the applications. We also use an Excel "Add-in" called MegaStat. If your instructor requires this package, it is available at **www.mhhe.com/megastat**. This add-in gives Excel the capability to produce additional statistical reports. Occasionally, we use Minitab to illustrate an application. See **www.minitab.com** for further information. Minitab also offers discounted academic pricing.

The following example shows the application of Excel to perform a statistical summary. It refers to sales information from the Applewood Auto Group, a multilocation

	A	B	C	D	E	F	G	H
1	Age	Profit	Location	Vehicle-Type	Previous		Profit	
2	51	$2,236	Tionesta	sedan	2			
3	40	$1,144	Tionesta	Truck	0		Mean	1,843.17
4	48	$1,295	Sheffield	sedan	1		Standard Error	47.97
5	39	$996	Kane	Compact	2		Median	1,882.50
6	31	$2,415	Kane	SUV	0		Mode	1,761.00
7	50	$842	Kane	sedan	0		Standard Deviation	643.63
8	48	$2,070	Kane	sedan	1		Sample Variance	414,256.60
9	47	$3,292	Olean	SUV	2		Kurtosis	-0.22
10	40	$1,961	Sheffield	SUV	1		Skewness	-0.24
11	46	$1,818	Kane	sedan	0		Range	2998
12	38	$1,766	Sheffield	sedan	0		Minimum	294
13	72	$1,821	Tionesta	sedan	1		Maximum	3292
14	40	$352	Sheffield	Compact	0		Sum	331770
15	62	$1,538	Olean	Truck	1		Count	180

Source: Microsoft Excel

car sales and service company. The Applewood information has sales information for 180 vehicle sales. Each sale is described by several variables: the age of the buyer, whether the buyer is a repeat customer, the location of the dealership for the sale, the type of vehicle sold, and the profit for the sale. This listing of individual observations and the measurements for each variable is called raw data. We use statistics and statistical software to summarize the raw data. For example, the following shows Excel's summary of statistics for the variable profit. The summary of profit shows the mean profit per vehicle was $1,843.17, the median profit was slightly more at $1,882.50, and profit ranged from $294 to $3,292.

Throughout the text, we will encourage the use of computer software to summarize, describe, and present information and data. To demonstrate the application of statistical analysis in Excel, Connect includes tutorials referenced with the icon shown here. In addition, Connect also includes data files for many exercises that can be opened directly with statistical software and spreadsheets.

Tutorial #20
in Connect

CHAPTER SUMMARY

I. Statistics is the science of collecting, organizing, presenting, analyzing, and interpreting data to assist in making more effective decisions.
II. There are two types of statistics.
    A. Descriptive statistics are procedures used to organize and summarize data.
    B. Inferential statistics involve taking a sample from a population and making estimates about a population based on the sample results.
        1. A population is an entire set of individuals or objects of interest or the measurements obtained from all individuals or objects of interest.
        2. A sample is a part of the population.
III. There are two types of variables.
    A. A qualitative variable is nonnumeric.
        1. Usually we are interested in the number or percent of the observations in each category.
        2. Qualitative data usually are summarized in graphs and bar charts.
    B. There are two types of quantitative variables, and they usually are reported numerically.
        1. Discrete variables can assume only certain values, and there are usually gaps between values.
        2. A continuous variable can assume any value within a specified range.
IV. There are four levels of measurement.
    A. With the nominal level, the data are sorted into categories with no particular order to the categories.
    B. The ordinal level of measurement presumes that one classification is ranked higher than another.
    C. The interval level of measurement has the ranking characteristic of the ordinal level of measurement plus the characteristic that the distance between values is a constant size.
    D. The ratio level of measurement has all the characteristics of the interval level, plus there is a 0 point and the ratio of two values is meaningful.

CHAPTER EXERCISES

5. Explain the difference between qualitative and quantitative variables. Give an example of qualitative and quantitative variables.
6. Explain the difference between a sample and a population.

7. Explain the difference between a discrete and a continuous variable. Give an example of each not included in the text.

8. For the following situations, would you collect information using a sample or a population? Why?

   a. Statistics 201 is a course taught at a university. Professor Rauch has taught nearly 1,500 students in the course over the past 5 years. You would like to know the average grade for the course.

   b. As part of a research project, you need to report the average profit as a percentage of revenue for the #1-ranked corporation in the *Fortune* 500 for each of the last 10 years.

   c. You are looking forward to graduation and your first job as a salesperson for one of five large pharmaceutical corporations. Planning for your interviews, you will need to know about each company's mission, profitability, products, and markets.

   d. You are shopping for a portable generator to provide electricity when you lose power. To buy the best generator, you need to estimate how much electricity your home consumes on a typical day.

9. Exits along interstate highways were formerly numbered successively from the western or southern border of a state. However, the Department of Transportation changed most of them to agree with the numbers on the mile markers along the highway.

   a. What is the level of measurement for the variable, exit number?

   b. What is the level of measurement for the variable, milepost numbe?

   c. Discuss the advantages of the newer system.

10. A poll solicits a large number of college undergraduates for information on the following variables: the name of their cell phone provider (AT&T, Verizon, and so on), the numbers of minutes used last month (200, 400, for example), and their satisfaction with the service (Terrible, Adequate, Excellent, and so forth). What is the level of measurement for each of these three variables?

11. The Fitbit Blaze Smart Fitness Watch has been ranked as the number one best-selling wearable technology device. This wearable technology tracks heart rate, and many activities such as running, biking, and cross training. It also monitors sleep patterns. The data can be synced with a phone app that summarizes and displays the user's information.

    a. As the number one best-selling wearable, would this ranking be more likely based on a population or a sample? Why?

    b. An online retailer reports over 14,000 ratings from people who bought this wearable device. Sixty-four percent of the ratings are five stars. Would these ratings be more likely based on a population or a sample? Why?

12. Using the concepts of sample and population, describe how a presidential election is unlike an "exit" poll of the electorate.

13. Place these variables in the following classification tables. For each table, summarize your observations and evaluate if the results are generally true. For example, salary is reported as a continuous quantitative variable. It is also a continuous ratio-scaled variable.

    a. Salary
    b. Country
    c. Sales volume of treadmills
    d. Energy-drink preference
    e. Temperature
    f. SAT scores
    g. Student rank in class
    h. Rating of a finance professor
    i. Number of home video devices

	Discrete Variable	Continuous Variable
Qualitative		
Quantitative		a. Salary

	Discrete	Continuous
Nominal		
Ordinal		
Interval		
Ratio		a. Salary

14. Using data from such publications as the *Statistical Abstract of the United States, Forbes,* or any news source, give examples of variables measured with nominal, ordinal, interval, and ratio scales.

15. The Struthers Wells Corporation employs more than 10,000 white-collar workers in its sales offices and manufacturing facilities in the United States, Europe, and Asia. A sample of 300 U.S. workers revealed 120 would accept a transfer to a location outside the United States. On the basis of these findings, write a brief memo to Jamie Gonzales, Vice President of Human Services, regarding all white-collar workers in the firm and their willingness to relocate.

16. AVX Home Entertainment Inc. recently began a "no-hassles" return policy. A sample of 500 customers who recently returned items showed 400 thought the policy was fair, 32 thought it took too long to complete the transaction, and the rest had no opinion. On the basis of this information, make an inference about customer reaction to the new policy.

17. **FILE** *Goodcarbadcar* is an online portal (**www.goodcarbadcar.net**) that reports automotive industry data. The table shows the number of cars sold in the United States in 2019 and 2020. The top 34 brands are listed. Sales data are often reported in this way to compare current sales to last year's sales.

Brand	2019 Sales	2020 Sales
Acura	157,385	136,982
Alfa Romeo	18,294	18,585
Audi	224,111	186,625
BMW	324,825	280,297
Buick	206,926	162,749
Cadillac	156,250	129,495
Chevrolet	1,942,039	1,730,033
Chrysler	126,972	110,285
Dodge	422,888	267,326
Fiat	9,204	4,304
Ford	2,284,425	1,929,195

Brand	2019 Sales	2020 Sales
Genesis	21,237	16,384
GMC	564,950	515,313
Honda	1,450,985	1,199,805
Hyundai	688,771	619,925
Infiniti	117,708	79,503
Jaguar	31,005	21,786
Jeep	923,292	795,306
Kia	614,613	586,005
Land Rover	94,736	80,033
Lexus	298,112	275,042
Lincoln	112,107	105,405
Mazda	278,550	279,076
Mercedes-Benz	352,129	324,708
Mini	36,165	28,047
Mitsubishi	121,049	87,386
Nissan	1,227,973	837,762
Porsche	61,568	57,286
Ram	703,023	624,637
Subaru	700,117	611,938
Tesla	195,125	292,902
Toyota	2,085,206	1,837,898
Volkswagen	363,322	355,684
Volvo	108,227	110,130

a. Using computer software, compare 2019 sales to 2020 sales for each brand by computing the difference. Make a list of the brands that increased sales in 2020 compared to 2019; make a list of brands that decreased sales.

b. Using computer software, compare 2019 sales to 2020 sales for each brand by computing the percentage change in sales. Make a list of the brands in order of increasing percentage changes. Which brands are in the top five in percentage change? Which brands are in the bottom five in percentage change?

c. Using computer software, first sort the data using the 2020 year-to-date sales. Then, design a bar graph to illustrate the 2019 and 2020 year-to-date sales for the top 10 brands. Also, design a bar graph to illustrate the percentage change for the top 10 brands. Compare these two graphs in a brief written report.

18. The following chart depicts the average amounts spent by consumers on holiday gifts.

Source: Microsoft Excel

Write a brief report summarizing the amounts spent during the holidays. Be sure to include the total amount spent and the percent spent by each group.

19. The following chart depicts the earnings in billions of dollars for ExxonMobil for the period 2008 until 2021. Write a brief report discussing the earnings at ExxonMobil during the period. Was one year higher than the others? Did the earnings increase, decrease, or stay the same over the period?

Year	Earnings ($ billions)
2008	45.2
2009	19.3
2010	30.5
2011	41.1
2012	44.9
2013	32.6
2014	32.5
2015	16.2
2016	7.8
2017	19.7
2018	20.8
2019	14.3
2020	-22.4

ExxonMobile Annual Earnings

Source: Microsoft Excel

DATA ANALYTICS

20. **FILE** Refer to the North Valley Real Estate data, which report information on homes sold in the area last year. Consider the following variables: selling price, number of bedrooms, township, and mortgage type.
    a. Which of the variables are qualitative and which are quantitative?
    b. How is each variable measured? Determine the level of measurement for each of the variables.

21. **FILE** Refer to the Baseball 2021 data, which report information on the 30 Major League Baseball teams for the 2021 season. Consider the following variables: number of wins, payroll, season attendance, whether the team is in the American or National League, and the number of home runs hit.
    a. Which of these variables are quantitative and which are qualitative?
    b. Determine the level of measurement for each of the variables.

22. **FILE** Refer to the Lincolnville School District bus data, which report information on the school district's bus fleet.
    a. Which of the variables are qualitative and which are quantitative?
    b. Determine the level of measurement for each variable.

Describing Data:

FREQUENCY TABLES, FREQUENCY DISTRIBUTIONS, AND GRAPHIC PRESENTATION

2

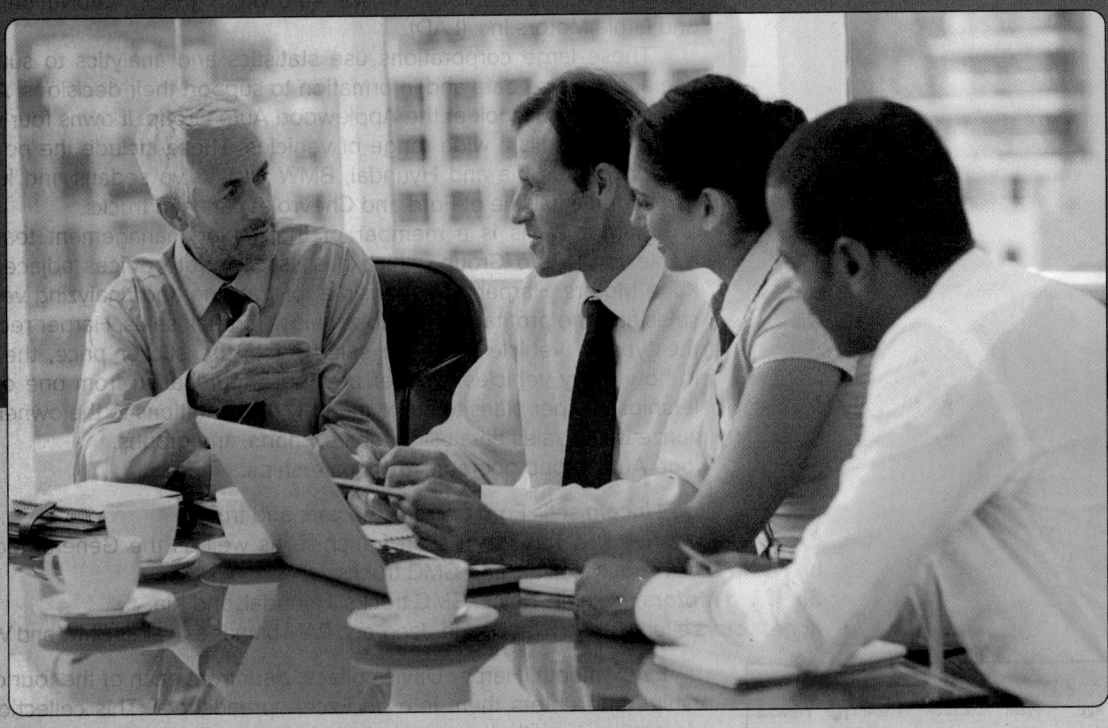

ESB Professional/Shutterstock

▲ **MERRILL LYNCH** recently completed a study of online investment portfolios for a sample of clients. For the 70 participants in the study, organize these data into a frequency distribution. (See Exercise 43 and LO2-3.)

LEARNING OBJECTIVES

When you have completed this chapter, you will be able to:

LO2-1 Summarize qualitative variables with frequency and relative frequency tables.

LO2-2 Display a frequency table using a bar or pie chart.

LO2-3 Summarize quantitative variables with frequency and relative frequency distributions.

LO2-4 Display a frequency distribution using a histogram or frequency polygon.

19

Introduction

The United States automobile retailing industry is highly competitive. It is dominated by megadealerships that own and operate 50 or more franchises, employ over 10,000 people, and generate several billion dollars in annual sales. Many of the top dealerships are publicly owned with shares traded on the New York Stock Exchange or NASDAQ. In 2020, the largest megadealership was Carmax (ticker symbol KMX), followed by Penske Auto Group (PAG), AutoNation (AN), and Lithia Motors Inc. (LAD).

These large corporations use statistics and analytics to summarize and analyze data and information to support their decisions. As an example, we will look at the Applewood Auto Group. It owns four dealerships and sells a wide range of vehicles. These include the popular Korean brands Kia and Hyundai, BMW and Volvo sedans and luxury SUVs, and a full line of Ford and Chevrolet cars and trucks.

Harper Davis is a member of the senior management team at Applewood Auto Group, which has its corporate offices adjacent to Kane Motors. Harper is responsible for tracking and analyzing vehicle sales and the profitability of those sales. To track sales, Harper records the type of vehicle sold, the sales price, the sticker price, the age of the buyer, and how many vehicles a buyer previously purchased from one of the Applewood dealerships. Harper plans to make monthly presentations to the ownership group that summarize these sales data using tables, charts, and graphs.

The Applewood Auto Group operates four dealerships:

- **Tionesta Ford Lincoln** sells Ford and Lincoln cars and trucks.
- **Olean Automotive Inc.** has the Nissan franchise as well as the General Motors brands of Chevrolet, Cadillac, and GMC trucks.
- **Sheffield Motors Inc.** sells Buick, GMC trucks, Hyundai, and Kia.
- **Kane Motors** offers the Chrysler, Dodge, Jeep, and RAM brands as well as BMW and Volvo.

Justin Sullivan/Getty Images

	A	B	C	D	E
1	Age	Profit	Location	Vehicle-Type	Previous
2	51	2236	Tionesta	Sedan	2
3	40	1144	Tionesta	Truck	0
4	48	1295	Sheffield	Sedan	1
5	39	996	Kane	Compact	2
6	31	2415	Kane	SUV	0
7	50	842	Kane	Sedan	0
8	48	2070	Kane	Sedan	1
9	47	3292	Olean	SUV	2
10	40	1961	Sheffield	SUV	1
11	46	1818	Kane	Sedan	0
12	38	1766	Sheffield	Sedan	0
13	72	1821	Tionesta	Sedan	1
14	40	352	Sheffield	Compact	0
15	62	1538	Olean	Truck	1

Source: Microsoft Excel

Every month, Harper Davis collects data from each of the four dealerships and enters them into an Excel spreadsheet. This collection of information is called the raw data. Last month the Applewood Auto Group sold 180 vehicles at the four dealerships. A copy of the first few observations appears to the left. The variables collected include:

- **Age**—the age of the buyer at the time of the purchase
- **Profit**—the amount earned by the dealership on the sale of each vehicle
- **Location**—the dealership where the vehicle was purchased
- **Vehicle type**—SUV, sedan, compact, hybrid, or truck
- **Previous**—the number of vehicles previously purchased at any of the four Applewood dealerships by the consumer

The entire data set is available in Connect and in Appendix A.4 at the end of the text.

LO2-1
Summarize qualitative variables with frequency and relative frequency tables.

Constructing Frequency Tables

Recall from Chapter 1 that techniques used to describe a set of data are called descriptive statistics. Descriptive statistics organize and summarize raw data to show the general pattern of the data, to identify where values tend to concentrate, and to expose extreme or unusual data values. The first technique we discuss is a **frequency table.**

> **FREQUENCY TABLE** A grouping of qualitative data into mutually exclusive and collectively exhaustive classes showing the number of observations in each class.

In Chapter 1, we distinguished between qualitative and quantitative variables. To review, a qualitative variable is nonnumeric—that is, it can only be classified into distinct categories. Examples of qualitative data include political affiliation (Republican, Democrat, Independent, or other), state of birth (Alabama, . . . , Wyoming), and method of payment for a purchase at Barnes & Noble (cash, digital wallet, debit, or credit). On the other hand, quantitative variables are numerical in nature. Examples of quantitative data relating to college students include the price of their textbooks, their age, and the number of credit hours they are registered for this semester.

In the Applewood Auto Group data set, there are five variables for each vehicle sale: age of the buyer, amount of profit, dealership that made the sale, type of vehicle sold, and number of previous purchases by the buyer. The dealership and the type of vehicle are *qualitative* variables. The amount of profit, the age of the buyer, and the number of previous purchases are *quantitative* variables.

Suppose Harper Davis wants to summarize the raw data by grouping last month's sales by location. The first step is to sort the vehicles sold last month according to their location and then tally, or count, the number sold at each of the four locations: Tionesta, Olean, Sheffield, or Kane. The four locations are used to develop a frequency table with four mutually exclusive (distinctive) classes. Mutually exclusive means that a particular vehicle can be assigned to only one class. In addition, the frequency table must be collectively exhaustive. That is, every vehicle sold last month is accounted for in the table. If every vehicle is included in the frequency table, the table will be collectively exhaustive and the total number of vehicles will be 180. How do we obtain these counts? Excel provides a tool called a Pivot Table that will quickly and accurately establish the four classes and do the counting. The Excel results follow in Table 2–1. The table shows a total of 180 vehicles; of the 180 vehicles, 52 were sold at Kane Motors.

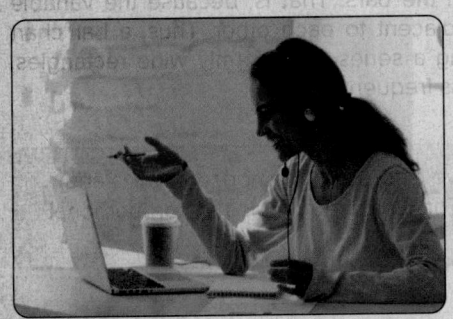
fizkes/Shutterstock

TABLE 2–1 Frequency Table for Vehicles Sold Last Month at Applewood Auto Group by Location

Location	Number of Cars
Kane	52
Olean	40
Sheffield	45
Tionesta	43
Total	180

Relative Class Frequencies

You can convert class frequencies to relative class frequencies to show the fraction of the total number of observations in each class. A relative frequency captures the relationship between a class frequency and the total number of observations. In the vehicle sales example, we may want to know the percentage of total cars sold at each of the four locations. To convert a frequency table to a relative frequency table, each of the class frequencies is divided by the total number of observations. Again, this is easily accomplished using Excel. The fraction of vehicles sold last month at the Kane location is 0.289, found by 52 divided by 180. We can interpret the relative frequency as a percentage. For example 28.9% of total sales occurred at the Kane location. The relative frequency for each location is shown in Table 2–2.

TABLE 2–2 Relative Frequency Table of Vehicles Sold by Location Last Month at Applewood Auto Group

Location	Number of Cars	Relative Frequency	Found by
Kane	52	.289	52/180
Olean	40	.222	40/180
Sheffield	45	.250	45/180
Tionesta	43	.239	43/180
Total	180	1.000	

LO2-2

Display a frequency table using a bar or pie chart.

Graphic Presentation of Qualitative Data

The most common graphic form to present a qualitative variable is a **bar chart.** In most cases, the horizontal axis shows the variable of interest. The vertical axis shows the frequency or fraction of each of the possible outcomes. A distinguishing feature of a bar chart is the distance or gaps between the bars. That is, because the variable of interest is qualitative, the bars are not adjacent to each other. Thus, a bar chart graphically describes a frequency table using a series of uniformly wide rectangles, where the height of each rectangle is the class frequency.

> **BAR CHART** A graph that shows qualitative classes on the horizontal axis and the class frequencies on the vertical axis. The class frequencies are proportional to the heights of the bars.

We use the Applewood Auto Group data as an example (Chart 2–1). The variables of interest are the location where the vehicle was sold and the number of vehicles sold at each location. We label the horizontal axis with the four locations and scale the vertical axis with the number sold. The variable location is of nominal scale, so the order of the locations on the horizontal axis does not matter. In Chart 2–1, the locations are listed alphabetically. The locations also could be in order of decreasing or increasing frequencies.

The height of the bars, or rectangles, corresponds to the number of vehicles sold at each location. There were 52 vehicles sold last month at the Kane location, so the height of the Kane bar is 52; the height of the bar for the Olean location is 40. See the link to a tutorial showing how to create a vertical bar chart in Excel. This graphic clearly shows that the Kane location had the most sales, followed by the Sheffield, Tionesta,

Tutorial #3
in Connect

CHART 2–1 Number of Vehicles Sold by Location

and Olean locations. In this example, the Kane location would be the **mode** of the distribution; it is the location with the highest frequency of cars sold.

> **MODE** The class of a distribution with the highest frequency.

Another useful type of chart for depicting qualitative information is a **pie chart.**

> **PIE CHART** A chart that shows the proportion or percentage that each class represents of the total number of frequencies.

We explain the details of constructing a pie chart using the information in Table 2–3, which shows the frequency and percent of cars sold by the Applewood Auto Group for each vehicle type.

TABLE 2–3 Vehicle Sales by Type at Applewood Auto Group

Vehicle Type	Number Sold	Percent Sold
SUV	72	40
Sedan	54	30
Compact	27	15
Truck	18	10
Hybrid	9	5
Total	180	100

The first step to develop a pie chart is to mark the percentages 0, 5, 10, 15, and so on evenly around the circumference of a circle (Chart 2–2). To plot the 40% of total sales represented by SUVs, draw a line from the center of the circle to 0 and another line from the center of the circle to 40%. The area in this "slice" represents the number of SUVs sold as a percentage of the total sales. Next, add the sedan's percentage of total sales, 30%, to the SUV's percentage of total sales, 40%. The result is 70%. Draw a line from the center of the circle to 70%, so the area between 40 and 70 shows the sales of sedans as a percentage of total sales. Continuing, add the 15% of total sales for compact vehicles, which gives us a total of 85%. Draw a line from the center of the circle to 85, so the "slice" between 70% and 85% represents the number of compact vehicles sold as a percentage of the total sales. The remaining 10% for truck sales and 5% for hybrid sales are added to the chart using the same method. See the link in the margin to a tutorial showing how to create a pie chart in Excel.

Tutorial #4
in Connect

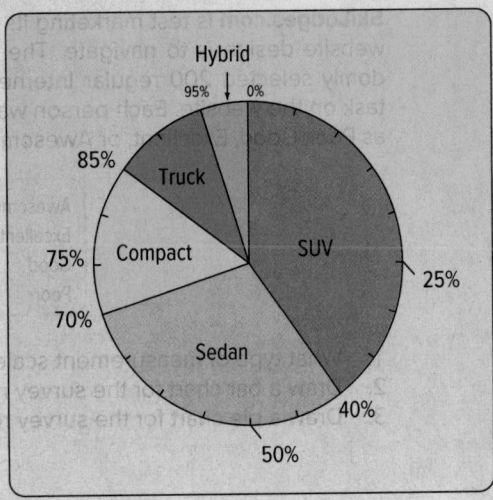

CHART 2–2 Pie Chart of Vehicles by Type

Because each slice of the pie represents the relative frequency of each vehicle type as a percentage of the total sales, we can easily compare them:

- The largest percentage of sales is SUVs; this class is the mode of the distribution of sales by car type.
- SUVs and sedans together account for 70% of vehicle sales.
- Hybrids account for 5% of vehicle sales.

Tutorial #7 in Connect

We can use Excel software to quickly count the number of cars for each vehicle type and create the frequency table, bar chart, and pie chart shown in the following summary. The Excel tool is called a Pivot Table. The instructions to produce these descriptive statistics and charts are provided in the Excel tutorials. See the link in the margin. The Applewood data set is available in Connect.

Source: Microsoft Excel

Pie and bar charts both serve to illustrate frequency and relative frequency tables. When is a pie chart preferred to a bar chart? In most cases, pie charts are used to show and compare the relative frequencies or percentages of observations for each value or class of a qualitative variable. Bar charts are preferred when the goal is to compare the number or frequency of observations for each value or class of a qualitative variable. The following Example/Solution shows another application of bar and pie charts.

▶ EXAMPLE

SkiLodges.com is test marketing its new website and is interested in how easy its website design is to navigate. The Analytics Department at **SkiLodges.com** randomly selected 200 regular Internet users and asked them to perform a search task on the website. Each person was asked to rate the relative ease of navigation as Poor, Good, Excellent, or Awesome. The results are shown in the following table:

Awesome	102
Excellent	58
Good	30
Poor	10

1. What type of measurement scale is used for ease of navigation?
2. Draw a bar chart for the survey results.
3. Draw a pie chart for the survey results.

SOLUTION

The data are measured on an ordinal scale. That is, the scale is ranked in relative ease of navigation when moving from Awesome to Poor. The interval between each rating is unknown so it is impossible, for example, to conclude that a rating of Good is twice the value of a Poor rating.

We can use a bar chart to graph the data. The vertical scale shows the frequency, and the horizontal scale shows the values of the ease-of-navigation variable.

The bar chart of the frequency table clearly shows that the Awesome response was the mode, or the class with the highest frequency. The other classes had lower frequencies.

A pie chart can be used to show the relative frequencies among the four classes. To find the relative frequencies, each class frequency is divided by the total frequency as follows:

Rating	Frequency	Relative Frequency
Awesome	102	102/200 = .51 or 51%
Excellent	58	58/200 = .29 or 29%
Good	30	30/200 = .15 or 15%
Poor	10	10/200 = .05 or 5%
Total	200	

To create the pie chart, 51% of the responses is Awesome. So, partition the pie so that slightly more than half, 51%, of the pie represents Awesome. The next rating is Excellent, with 29% of the responses. Adding 51% to 29%, these two classes will be 80% of the pie, or slightly more than ¾ of the pie. The next class is Good, with 15%. So, the first three classes will account for 95% of the pie. Estimate and insert this partition. The remaining partition is the Poor rating, with 5%.

The pie chart clearly shows that about half of the responses were Awesome, with a combined 80% either Awesome or Excellent. Note that the pie chart also clearly shows that the Awesome response is the most frequent or mode of the distribution.

SELF-REVIEW 2–1

The answers are in Appendix D.

DeCenzo Specialty Food and Beverage Company has been serving a cola drink with an additional flavoring, Cola-Plus, that is very popular among its customers. The company is interested in customer preferences for Cola-Plus versus Coca-Cola, Pepsi, and a lemon-lime beverage. They ask 100 randomly sampled customers to take a taste test and select the beverage they prefer most. The results are shown in the following table:

Beverage	Number
Cola-Plus	40
Coca-Cola	25
Pepsi	20
Lemon-Lime	15
Total	100

(a) Are the data qualitative or quantitative? Why?
(b) What is the table called? What does it show?
(c) Develop a bar chart to depict the information.
(d) Develop a pie chart using the relative frequencies.

EXERCISES

The answers to the odd-numbered exercises are in Appendix C.

1. A pie chart shows the relative market share of cola products. The "slice" for Pepsi has a central angle of 90 degrees. What is its market share?
2. In a marketing study, 100 consumers were asked to select their favorite type of mattress: foam, latex, hybrid, or inner spring. To summarize the consumer responses with a frequency table, how many classes would the frequency table have?
3. A total of 1,000 residents in Minnesota were asked which season they preferred. Of those surveyed 100 liked winter best, 300 liked spring, 400 liked summer, and

200 liked fall. Develop a frequency table and a relative frequency table to summarize this information.

4. Two thousand frequent business travelers were asked which midwestern city they prefer: Indianapolis, Saint Louis, Chicago, or Milwaukee. Of those surveyed, 100 liked Indianapolis best, 450 liked Saint Louis, 1,300 liked Chicago, and the remainder preferred Milwaukee. Develop a frequency table and a relative frequency table to summarize this information.

5. Wellstone Inc. produces and markets replacement covers for cell phones in five different colors: bright white, metallic black, magnetic lime, tangerine orange, and fusion red. To estimate the demand for each color, the company set up a kiosk for several hours in the Mall of America and asked randomly selected people which cover color was their favorite. The results follow:

Bright white	130
Metallic black	104
Magnetic lime	325
Tangerine orange	455
Fusion red	286

a. What is the table called?
b. Draw a bar chart for the table.
c. Draw a pie chart to represent the relative frequencies.
d. If Wellstone Inc. plans to produce 1 million cell phone covers, how many of each color should it produce?

6. A small business consultant is investigating the performance of several companies. The fourth-quarter sales for last year (in thousands of dollars) for the selected companies were:

Company	Fourth-Quarter Sales ($ thousands)
Hoden Building Products	$ 1,645.2
J & R Printing Inc.	4,757.0
Long Bay Concrete Construction	8,913.0
Mancell Electric and Plumbing	627.1
Maxwell Heating and Air Conditioning	24,612.0
Mizelle Roofing & Sheet Metals	191.9

The consultant wants to include a chart in his report comparing the sales of the six companies. Use a bar chart to compare the fourth-quarter sales of these corporations and write a brief report summarizing the bar chart.

Constructing Frequency Distributions

LO2-3
Summarize quantitative variables with frequency and relative frequency distributions.

In Chapter 1 and earlier in this chapter, we distinguished between qualitative and quantitative data. In the previous section, using the Applewood Automotive Group raw data, we summarized two qualitative variables: the location of the sale and the type of vehicle sold. We created frequency and relative frequency tables and depicted the grouped data in bar and pie charts.

The Applewood Auto Group data also includes several quantitative variables: the age of the buyer, the profit earned on the sale of the vehicle, and the number of previous purchases. Suppose Harper Davis wants to summarize last month's sales by profit earned for each vehicle. We can describe profit using a **frequency distribution.**

> **FREQUENCY DISTRIBUTION** A grouping of quantitative data into mutually exclusive and collectively exhaustive classes showing the number of observations in each class.

How do we develop a frequency distribution? The following example shows the steps to construct a frequency distribution. Remember, our goal is to construct tables, charts, and graphs that will quickly summarize the data by showing the shape of the data's distribution.

▶ **EXAMPLE**

Harper Davis of the Applewood Auto Group wants to summarize the quantitative variable profit with a frequency distribution and display the distribution with charts and graphs. With this information, Harper can easily answer the following questions: What is the typical profit on each sale? What is the largest or maximum profit on any sale? What is the smallest or minimum profit on any sale? Around what value do the profits tend to cluster?

SOLUTION

To begin, we need the profits for each of the 180 vehicle sales listed in Table 2–4. This information is called raw or ungrouped data because it is simply a listing of the individual, observed profits. It is possible to search the list and find the smallest or minimum profit ($294) and the largest or maximum profit ($3,292), but that is about all. It is difficult to determine a typical profit or to visualize where the profits tend to cluster. The raw data are more easily interpreted if we group or summarize the data with a frequency distribution. The steps to create this frequency distribution are as follows.

TABLE 2–4 Profit on Vehicles Sold Last Month by the Applewood Auto Group

						Maximum		
$1,387	$2,148	$2,201	$ 963	$ 820	$2,230	$3,043	$2,584	$2,370
1,754	2,207	996	1,298	1,266	2,341	1,059	2,666	2,637
1,817	2,252	2,813	1,410	1,741	3,292	1,674	2,991	1,426
1,040	1,428	323	1,553	1,772	1,108	1,807	934	2,944
1,273	1,889	352	1,648	1,932	1,295	2,056	2,063	2,147
1,529	1,166	482	2,071	2,350	1,344	2,236	2,083	1,973
3,082	1,320	1,144	2,116	2,422	1,906	2,928	2,856	2,502
1,951	2,265	1,485	1,500	2,446	1,952	1,269	2,989	783
2,692	1,323	1,509	1,549	369	2,070	1,717	910	1,538
1,206	1,760	1,638	2,348	978	2,454	1,797	1,536	2,339
1,342	1,919	1,961	2,498	1,238	1,606	1,955	1,957	2,700
443	2,357	2,127	294	1,818	1,680	2,199	2,240	2,222
754	2,866	2,430	1,115	1,824	1,827	2,482	2,695	2,597
1,621	732	1,704	1,124	1,907	1,915	2,701	1,325	2,742
870	1,464	1,876	1,532	1,938	2,084	3,210	2,250	1,837
1,174	1,626	2,010	1,688	1,940	2,639	377	2,279	2,842
1,412	1,762	2,165	1,822	2,197	842	1,220	2,626	2,434
1,809	1,915	2,231	1,897	2,646	1,963	1,401	1,501	1,640
2,415	2,119	2,389	2,445	1,461	2,059	2,175	1,752	1,821
1,546	1,766	335	2,886	1,731	2,338	1,118	2,058	2,487

Minimum

Step 1: **Decide on the number of classes.** A useful recipe to determine the number of classes (k) is the "2 to the k rule." This guide suggests you select the smallest number (k) for the number of classes such that 2^k (in words, 2 raised to the power of k) is greater than the number of observations (n). In the Applewood Auto Group example, there were 180 vehicles sold. So $n = 180$. If we try $k = 7$, which means we would use 7 classes, $2^7 = 128$, which is less than 180. Hence, 7 is too few classes. If we let $k = 8$, then $2^8 = 256$, which is greater than 180. So the recommended number of classes is 8.

Step 2: **Determine the class interval.** Generally, the **class interval** is the same for all classes. The classes all taken together must cover at least the distance from the minimum value in the data up to the maximum value. Expressing these words in a formula:

$$i \geq \frac{\text{Maximum value} - \text{Minimum value}}{k}$$

where i is the class interval, and k is the number of classes.

For the Applewood Auto Group, the minimum value is $294 and the maximum value is $3,292. If we need 8 classes, the interval should be:

$$i \geq \frac{\text{Maximum value} - \text{Minimum value}}{k} = \frac{\$3,292 - \$294}{8} = \$374.75$$

In practice, this interval size is usually rounded up to some convenient number, such as a multiple of 10 or 100. The value of $400 is a reasonable choice.

Step 3: **Set the individual class limits.** State clear class limits so you can put each observation into only one category. This means you must avoid overlapping or unclear class limits. For example, classes such as "$1,300–$1,400" and "$1,400–$1,500" should not be used because it is not clear whether the value $1,400 is in the first or second class. In this text, we will generally use the format $1,300 **up to** $1,400 and $1,400 **up to** $1,500 and so on. With this format, it is clear that $1,399 goes into the first class and $1,400 in the second.

Because we always round the class interval up to get a convenient class size, we cover a larger than necessary range. For example, using 8 classes with an interval of $400 in the Applewood Auto Group example results in a range of 8($400) = $3,200. The actual range is $2,998, found by ($3,292 − $294). Comparing that value to $3,200, we have an excess of $202. Because we need to cover only the range (Maximum − Minimum), it is natural to put approximately equal amounts of the excess in each of the two tails. Of course, we also should select convenient class limits. A guideline is to make the lower limit of the first class a multiple of the class interval. Sometimes this is not possible, but the lower limit should at least be rounded. So here are the classes we could use for these data.

Classes
$ 200 up to $ 600
600 up to 1,000
1,000 up to 1,400
1,400 up to 1,800
1,800 up to 2,200
2,200 up to 2,600
2,600 up to 3,000
3,000 up to 3,400

Step 4: **Tally the vehicle profit into the classes and determine the number of observations in each class.** To begin, the profit from the sale of the first vehicle in Table 2–4 is $1,387. It is tallied in the $1,000 up to $1,400 class. The second profit in the first row of Table 2–4 is $2,148. It is tallied in the $1,800 up to $2,200 class. The other profits are tallied in a similar manner. When all the profits are tallied, the table would appear as:

Profit	Frequency
$ 200 up to $ 600	⅄Ⅼ Ⅰ
600 up to 1,000	⅄Ⅼ ⅄Ⅼ Ⅰ
1,000 up to 1,400	⅄Ⅼ ⅄Ⅼ ⅄Ⅼ ⅄Ⅼ Ⅲ
1,400 up to 1,800	⅄Ⅼ ⅄Ⅼ ⅄Ⅼ ⅄Ⅼ ⅄Ⅼ ⅄Ⅼ ⅄Ⅼ Ⅲ
1,800 up to 2,200	⅄Ⅼ ⅄Ⅼ ⅄Ⅼ ⅄Ⅼ ⅄Ⅼ ⅄Ⅼ ⅄Ⅼ ⅄Ⅼ ⅄Ⅼ
2,200 up to 2,600	⅄Ⅼ ⅄Ⅼ ⅄Ⅼ ⅄Ⅼ ⅄Ⅼ ⅄Ⅼ Ⅱ
2,600 up to 3,000	⅄Ⅼ ⅄Ⅼ ⅄Ⅼ Ⅲ
3,000 up to 3,400	Ⅲ|

The number of observations in each class is called the **class frequency.** In the $200 up to $600 class there are 8 observations, and in the $600 up to $1,000 class there are 11 observations. Therefore, the class frequency in the first class is 8 and the class frequency in the second class is 11. There are a total of 180 observations in the entire set of data. So the sum of all the frequencies should be equal to 180. The results of the frequency distribution are in Table 2–5.

TABLE 2–5 Frequency Distribution of Profit for Vehicles Sold Last Month at Applewood Auto Group

Profit	Frequency
$ 200 up to $ 600	8
600 up to 1,000	11
1,000 up to 1,400	23
1,400 up to 1,800	38
1,800 up to 2,200	45
2,200 up to 2,600	32
2,600 up to 3,000	19
3,000 up to 3,400	4
Total	180

Now that we grouped or organized, and summarized the raw data into a frequency distribution (see Table 2–5), we can describe the profits of the vehicles for the Applewood Auto Group. Observe the following:

1. The profits from vehicle sales range between $200 and $3,400.
2. The vehicle profits are classified using a class interval of $400. The class interval is determined by subtracting consecutive lower or upper class limits. For example, the lower limit of the first class is $200, and the lower limit of the second class is $600. The difference is the class interval of $400.
3. The profits are concentrated between $1,000 and $3,000. The profit on 157 vehicles, or 87%, was within this range.
4. For each class, we can determine the typical profit or **class midpoint.** It is halfway between the lower or upper limits of two consecutive classes. It is computed by adding the lower or upper limits of consecutive classes and dividing by 2. Referring to Table 2–5, the lower class limit of the first class is $200, and the next class limit is $600. The class midpoint is $400, found by ($600 + $200)/2. The midpoint best represents, or is typical of, the profits of the vehicles in that class. Applewood sold 8 vehicles with a typical profit of $400.

5. The largest concentration, or highest frequency, of vehicles sold is in the $1,800 up to $2,200 class. This class is the mode of the distribution. There are 45 vehicles in this class. The class midpoint is $2,000. So we say that the typical profit in the class with the highest frequency is $2,000.

By using a frequency distribution, Harper Davis can make a clear presentation and summary of last month's profits.

We admit that arranging the information on profits into a frequency distribution does result in the loss of some detailed information. That is, by organizing the data into a frequency distribution, we cannot pinpoint the exact profit on any vehicle, such as $1,387, $2,148, or $2,201. Further, we cannot tell that the actual minimum profit for any vehicle sold is $294 or that the maximum profit was $3,292. However, the lower limit of the first class and the upper limit of the last class convey essentially the same meaning. Even if the exact profit of $292 is not presented in the table, Harper will most likely make the same judgment knowing the smallest profit is about $200. The advantages of summarizing the 180 profits into a more understandable and organized form more than offset knowing the exact profit values.

When we summarize raw data with frequency distributions, equal class intervals are preferred. However, in certain situations unequal class intervals may be necessary to avoid a large number of classes with very small frequencies. Such is the case in Table 2–6. The U.S. Internal Revenue Service uses unequal-sized class intervals for adjusted gross income on individual tax returns to summarize the number of individual tax returns. If we use our method to find equal class intervals, the 2^k rule results in 25 classes, and a class interval of $400,000, assuming $0 and $10,000,000 as the minimum and maximum values for adjusted gross income. Using equal class intervals, the first 13 classes in Table 2–6 would be combined into one class of about 99.9% of all tax returns and 24 classes for the 0.1% of the returns with an adjusted gross income above $400,000. Using equal class intervals does not provide a good understanding of the raw data. In this case, good judgment in the use of unequal class intervals, as demonstrated in Table 2–6, is required to show the distribution of the number of tax returns filed, especially for incomes under $500,000.

STATISTICS IN ACTION

In 1788, James Madison, John Jay, and Alexander Hamilton anonymously published a series of essays entitled *The Federalist Papers*. These papers were an attempt to convince the people of New York that they should ratify the Constitution. In the course of history, the authorship of most of these papers became known, but 12 remained contested. Through the use of statistical analysis, and particularly studying the frequency distributions of various words, we can now conclude that James Madison is the likely author of the 12 papers. In fact, the statistical evidence that Madison is the author is overwhelming.

TABLE 2–6 Adjusted Gross Income for Individuals Filing Income Tax Returns

Adjusted Gross Income			Number of Returns (in thousands)
No adjusted gross income			178.2
$	1 up to $	5,000	1,204.6
	5,000 up to	10,000	2,595.5
	10,000 up to	15,000	3,142.0
	15,000 up to	20,000	3,191.7
	20,000 up to	25,000	2,501.4
	25,000 up to	30,000	1,901.6
	30,000 up to	40,000	2,502.3
	40,000 up to	50,000	1,426.8
	50,000 up to	75,000	1,476.3
	75,000 up to	100,000	338.8
	100,000 up to	200,000	223.3
	200,000 up to	500,000	55.2
	500,000 up to	1,000,000	12.0
	1,000,000 up to	2,000,000	5.1
	2,000,000 up to	10,000,000	3.4
	10,000,000 or more		0.6

32   CHAPTER 2

SELF-REVIEW 2-2

In the first quarter of last year, the 11 members of the sales staff at Master Chemical Company earned the following commissions:

$1,650 $1,475 $1,510 $1,670 $1,595 $1,760 $1,540 $1,495 $1,590 $1,625 $1,510

(a) What are the values such as $1,650 and $1,475 called?
(b) Using $1,400 up to $1,500 as the first class, $1,500 up to $1,600 as the second class, and so forth, organize the quarterly commissions into a frequency distribution.
(c) What are the numbers in the right column of your frequency distribution called?
(d) Describe the distribution of quarterly commissions, based on the frequency distribution. What is the largest concentration of commissions earned? What is the smallest, and the largest? What is the typical amount earned?

Relative Frequency Distribution

It may be desirable, as we did earlier with qualitative data, to convert class frequencies to relative class frequencies to show the proportion of the total number of observations in each class. In our vehicle profits, we may want to know what percentage of the vehicle profits are in the $1,000 up to $1,400 class. To convert a frequency distribution to a *relative* frequency distribution, each of the class frequencies is divided by the total number of observations. From the distribution of vehicle profits, Table 2–5, the relative frequency for the $1,000 up to $1,400 class is 0.128, found by dividing 23 by 180. That is, profit on 12.8% of the vehicles sold is between $1,000 and $1,400. The relative frequencies for the remaining classes are shown in Table 2–7.

TABLE 2–7 Relative Frequency Distribution of Profit for Vehicles Sold Last Month at Applewood Auto Group

Profit	Frequency	Relative Frequency	Found by
$ 200 up to $ 600	8	.044	8/180
600 up to 1,000	11	.061	11/180
1,000 up to 1,400	23	.128	23/180
1,400 up to 1,800	38	.211	38/180
1,800 up to 2,200	45	.250	45/180
2,200 up to 2,600	32	.178	32/180
2,600 up to 3,000	19	.106	19/180
3,000 up to 3,400	4	.022	4/180
Total	180	1.000	

Tutorial #8 in Connect

	A	B	C
	APPLEWOOD AUTO GROUP		
1	Profit Class	Frequency	Relative Frequency
2	200-600	8	4.44%
3	600-1000	11	6.11%
4	1000-1400	23	12.78%
5	1400-1800	38	21.11%
6	1800-2200	45	25.00%
7	2200-2600	32	17.78%
8	2600-3000	19	10.56%
9	3000-3400	4	2.22%
10	Grand Total	180	100.00%

Source: Microsoft Excel

There are many software packages that perform statistical calculations. Throughout this text, we will show the output from Microsoft Excel, MegaStat (a Microsoft Excel add-in), and Minitab (a statistical software package). Because Excel is most readily available, it is used most frequently.

Within the earlier Graphic Presentation of Qualitative Data section, we used the Pivot Table tool in Excel to create a frequency table. See the accompanying Excel tutorial that shows how to use a pivot table to create the frequency and relative frequency distributions. The Applewood data set is available in Connect.

SELF-REVIEW 2-3

Barry Bonds of the San Francisco Giants established the single-season Major League Baseball home run record by hitting 73 home runs during the 2001 season. Listed in the following table is the sorted distance of each of the 73 home runs.

320	320	347	350	360	360	360	361	365	370
370	375	375	375	375	380	380	380	380	380
380	390	390	391	394	396	400	400	400	400
405	410	410	410	410	410	410	410	410	410
410	410	411	415	415	416	417	417	420	420
420	420	420	420	420	420	429	430	430	430
430	430	435	435	436	440	440	440	440	440
450	480	488							

(a) For these data, show that seven classes would be used to create a frequency distribution using the 2^k rule.
(b) Show that a class interval of 30 would summarize the data in seven classes.
(c) Construct frequency and relative frequency distributions for the data with seven classes and a class interval of 30. Start the first class with a lower limit of 300.
(d) How many home runs traveled a distance of 360 up to 390 feet?
(e) What percentage of the home runs traveled a distance of 360 up to 390 feet?
(f) What percentage of the home runs traveled a distance of 390 feet or more?

EXERCISES

7. A set of data consists of 38 observations. How many classes would you recommend for the frequency distribution?
8. A set of data consists of 45 observations between $0 and $29. What size would you recommend for the class interval?
9. A set of data consists of 230 observations between $235 and $567. What class interval would you recommend?
10. A set of data contains 53 observations. The minimum value is 42 and the maximum value is 129. The data are to be organized into a frequency distribution.
    a. How many classes would you suggest?
    b. What would you suggest as the lower limit of the first class?

11. **FILE** Wachesaw Manufacturing Inc. produced the following number of units in the last 16 days.

27	27	27	28	27	25	25	28
26	28	26	28	31	30	26	26

The information is to be organized into a frequency distribution.
a. How many classes would you recommend?
b. What class interval would you suggest?
c. What lower limit would you recommend for the first class?
d. Organize the information into a frequency distribution and determine the relative frequency distribution.
e. Comment on the shape of the distribution. Which class represents the mode of the distribution?

12. **FILE** The Quick Change Oil Company has a number of outlets in the metropolitan Seattle area. The daily number of oil changes at the Oak Street outlet in the past 20 days is:

65	98	55	62	79	59	51	90	72	56
70	62	66	80	94	79	63	73	71	85

The data are to be organized into a frequency distribution.
a. How many classes would you recommend?
b. What class interval would you suggest?
c. What lower limit would you recommend for the first class?
d. Organize the number of oil changes into a frequency distribution.
e. Comment on the shape of the frequency distribution. Also determine the relative frequency distribution.

13. **FILE** The manager of the BiLo Supermarket in Mt. Pleasant, Rhode Island, gathered the following information on the number of times a customer visits the store during a month. The responses of 51 customers were:

5	3	3	1	4	4	5	6	4	2	6	6	6	7	1
1	14	1	2	4	4	4	5	6	3	5	3	4	5	6
8	4	7	6	5	9	11	3	12	4	7	6	5	15	1
1	10	8	9	2	12

a. Starting with 0 as the lower limit of the first class and using a class interval of 3, organize the data into a frequency distribution.
b. Describe the distribution. Where do the data tend to cluster?
c. Convert the distribution to a relative frequency distribution.

14. **FILE** The food services division of Cedar River Amusement Park Inc. is studying the amount of money spent per day on food and drink by families who visit the amusement park. A sample of 40 families who visited the park yesterday revealed they spent the following amounts:

$77	$18	$63	$84	$38	$54	$50	$59	$54	$56	$36	$26	$50	$34	$44
41	58	58	53	51	62	43	52	53	63	62	62	65	61	52
60	60	45	66	83	71	63	58	61	71

a. Organize the data into a frequency distribution, using seven classes and 15 as the lower limit of the first class. What class interval did you select?
b. Where do the data tend to cluster?
c. Describe the distribution.
d. Determine the relative frequency distribution.

Graphic Presentation of a Distribution

LO2-4
Display a frequency distribution using a histogram or frequency polygon.

Sales managers, stock analysts, hospital administrators, and other busy executives often need a quick picture of the distributions of sales, stock prices, or hospital costs. These distributions often can be depicted by the use of charts and graphs. Three charts that will help portray a frequency distribution graphically are the histogram, the frequency polygon, and the cumulative frequency polygon.

Histogram

A **histogram** for a frequency distribution based on quantitative data is similar to the bar chart showing the distribution of qualitative data. The classes are marked on the horizontal axis and the class frequencies on the vertical axis. The class frequencies are represented by the heights of the bars. However, there is one important difference based on the nature of the data. Quantitative data are usually measured using scales that are continuous, not discrete. Therefore, the horizontal axis represents all possible values, and the bars are drawn adjacent to each other to show the continuous nature of the data.

> **HISTOGRAM** A graph in which the classes are marked on the horizontal axis and the class frequencies on the vertical axis. The class frequencies are represented by the heights of the bars, and the bars are drawn adjacent to each other.

▶ ## EXAMPLE

Following is the frequency distribution of the profits on vehicle sales last month at the Applewood Auto Group.

Profit	Frequency
$ 200 up to $ 600	8
600 up to 1,000	11
1,000 up to 1,400	23
1,400 up to 1,800	38
1,800 up to 2,200	45
2,200 up to 2,600	32
2,600 up to 3,000	19
3,000 up to 3,400	4
Total	180

Construct a histogram. What observations can you reach based on the information presented in the histogram?

SOLUTION

The class frequencies are scaled along the vertical axis (Y-axis) and either the class limits or the class midpoints along the horizontal axis (X-axis). To illustrate the construction of the histogram, the first three classes are shown in Chart 2–3.

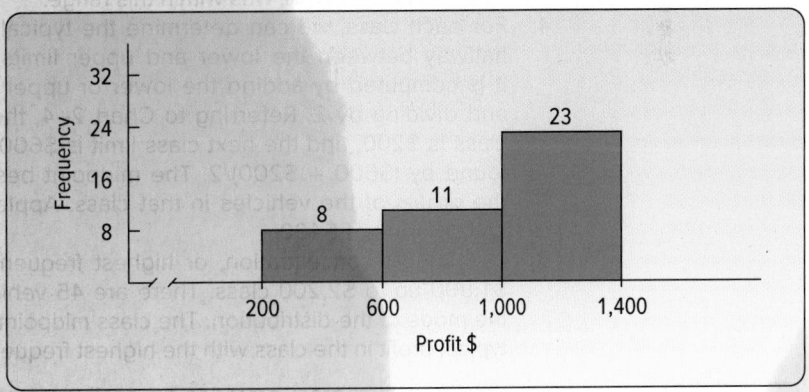

CHART 2–3 Construction of a Histogram

From Chart 2–3 we note the profit on eight vehicles was $200 up to $600. Therefore, the height of the column for that class is 8. There are 11 vehicle sales where the profit was $600 up to $1,000. So, logically, the height of that column is 11. The height of the bar represents the number of observations in the class.

This procedure is continued for all classes. The complete histogram is shown in Chart 2–4. Note that there is no space between the bars. This is a feature of the histogram. Why is this so? Because the variable profit, plotted on the X-axis, is a continuous variable. In a bar chart, the scale of measurement is usually nominal and the vertical bars are separated. This is an important distinction between the histogram and the bar chart.

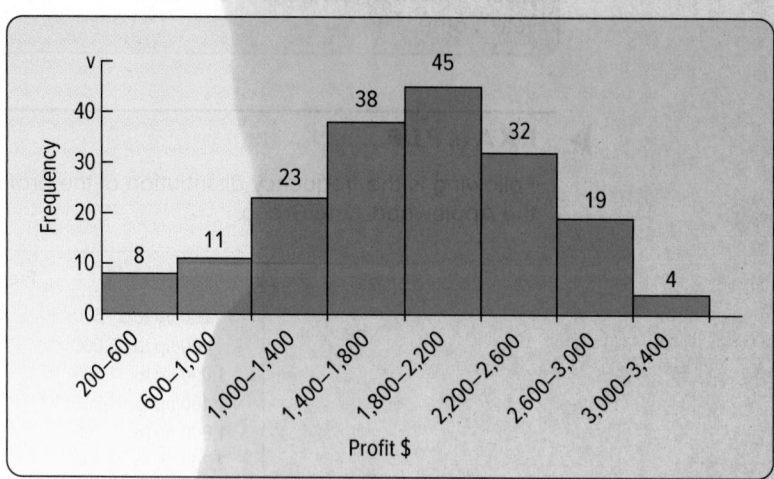

CHART 2–4 Histogram of the Profit on 180 Vehicles Sold at the Applewood Auto Group

We can make the following statements using Chart 2–4. They are the same as the observations based on Table 2–5.

1. The profits from vehicle sales range between $200 and $3,400.
2. The vehicle profits are classified using a class interval of $400. The class interval is determined by subtracting consecutive lower or upper class limits. For example, the lower limit of the first class is $200, and the lower limit of the second class is $600. The difference is the class interval or $400.
3. The profits are concentrated between $1,000 and $3,000. The profit on 157 vehicles, or 87%, was within this range.
4. For each class, we can determine the typical profit or class midpoint. It is halfway between the lower and upper limits of two consecutive classes. It is computed by adding the lower or upper limits of consecutive classes and dividing by 2. Referring to Chart 2–4, the lower class limit of the first class is $200, and the next class limit is $600. The class midpoint is $400, found by ($600 + $200)/2. The midpoint best represents, or is typical of, the profits of the vehicles in that class. Applewood sold 8 vehicles with a typical profit of $400.
5. The largest concentration, or highest frequency of vehicles sold, is in the $1,800 up to $2,200 class. There are 45 vehicles in this class. This class is the mode of the distribution. The class midpoint is $2,000. So we say that the typical profit in the class with the highest frequency is $2,000.

Thus, the histogram provides an easily interpreted visual representation of a frequency distribution. We also should point out that we would have made the same observations and the shape of the histogram would have been the same had we used a relative frequency distribution instead of the actual frequencies. That is, if we use the relative frequencies of Table 2–7, the result is a histogram of the same shape as Chart 2–4. The only difference is that the vertical axis would have been reported in percentage of vehicles instead of the number of vehicles. See the accompanying Excel tutorial that shows how to use a pivot table to create the frequency distribution and histogram. The Applewood data set is available in Connect.

Tutorial #8
in Connect

Frequency Polygon

A **frequency polygon** also shows the shape of a distribution and is similar to a histogram. It consists of line segments connecting the points formed by the intersections of the class midpoints and the class frequencies. The construction of a frequency polygon is illustrated in Chart 2–5. We use the profits from the cars sold last month at the Applewood Auto Group. The midpoint of each class is scaled on the X-axis and the class frequencies on the Y-axis. Recall that the class midpoint is the value at the center of a class and represents the typical values in that class. The class frequency is the number of observations in a particular class. The profit earned on the vehicles sold last month by the Applewood Auto Group is repeated here.

Profit	Midpoint	Frequency
$ 200 up to $ 600	$ 400	8
600 up to 1,000	800	11
1,000 up to 1,400	1,200	23
1,400 up to 1,800	1,600	38
1,800 up to 2,200	2,000	45
2,200 up to 2,600	2,400	32
2,600 up to 3,000	2,800	19
3,000 up to 3,400	3,200	4
Total		180

CHART 2–5 Frequency Polygon of Profit on 180 Vehicles Sold at Applewood Auto Group

As noted previously, the $200 up to $600 class is represented by the midpoint $400. To construct a frequency polygon, move horizontally on the graph to the midpoint, $400, and then vertically to 8, the class frequency, and place a dot. The x and the y values of this point are called the *coordinates*. The coordinates of the next point are x = 800 and y = 11. The process is continued for all classes. Then the points are connected in order. That is, the point representing the lowest class is joined to the one representing the second class and so on. Note in Chart 2–5 that, to complete the frequency polygon, midpoints of $0 and $3,600 are added to the X-axis to "anchor" the polygon at zero frequencies. These two values, $0 and $3,600, were derived by subtracting the class interval of $400 from the lowest midpoint ($400) and by adding $400 to the highest midpoint ($3,200) in the frequency distribution.

Both the histogram and the frequency polygon allow us to get a quick picture of the main characteristics of the data (highs, lows, points of concentration, etc.). Although the two representations are similar in purpose, the histogram has the advantage of depicting each class as a rectangle, with the height of the rectangular bar representing

CHART 2–6 Distribution of Profit at Applewood Auto Group and Fowler Motors

the number in each class. The frequency polygon, in turn, has an advantage over the histogram. It allows us to compare directly two or more frequency distributions. Suppose Harper Davis wants to compare the profit per vehicle sold at Applewood Auto Group with a similar auto group, Fowler Auto in Grayling, Michigan. To do this, two frequency polygons are constructed, one on top of the other, as in Chart 2–6. Two things are clear from the chart:

- The typical vehicle profit is larger at Fowler Motors—about $2,000 for Applewood and about $2,400 for Fowler.
- There is less variation or dispersion in the profits at Fowler Motors than at Applewood. The lower limit of the first class for Applewood is $0 and the upper limit is $3,600. For Fowler Motors, the lower limit is $800 and the upper limit is the same: $3,600.

The total number of cars sold at the two dealerships is about the same, so a direct comparison of the frequency polygons is possible. If the difference in the total number of cars sold is large, then converting the frequencies to relative frequencies and then plotting the two distributions would allow a clearer comparison.

SELF-REVIEW 2-4

The annual imports of a selected group of electronic suppliers are shown in the following frequency distribution.

Imports ($ millions)	Number of Suppliers
$ 2 up to $ 5	6
5 up to 8	13
8 up to 11	20
11 up to 14	10
14 up to 17	1

(a) Portray the imports as a histogram.
(b) Portray the imports as a relative frequency polygon.
(c) Summarize the important facets of the distribution (such as classes with the highest and lowest frequencies).

EXERCISES

15. Sun Ray Candles has several retail stores in the coastal areas of North and South Carolina. Many of their customers ask the store to ship their purchases. The following chart shows the number of packages shipped per day for the last 100 days. For example, the first class shows that there were 5 days when the number of packages shipped was 0 up to 5.

  a. What is this chart called?
  b. What is the total number of packages shipped?
  c. What is the class interval?
  d. What is the number of packages shipped in the 10 up to 15 class?
  e. What is the relative frequency of packages shipped in the 10 up to 15 class?
  f. What is the midpoint of the 10 up to 15 class?
  g. On how many days were there 25 or more packages shipped?

16. The following chart shows the number of patients admitted daily to Memorial Hospital through the emergency room.

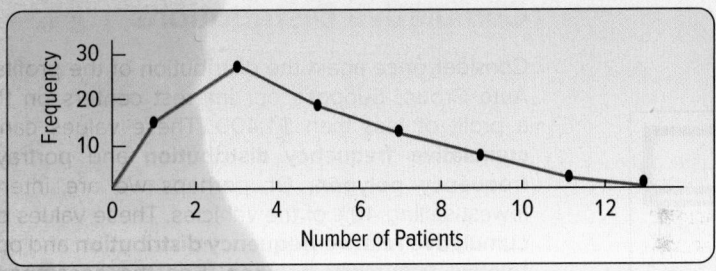

  a. What is the midpoint of the 2 up to 4 class?
  b. On how many days were 2 up to 4 patients admitted?
  c. What is the class interval?
  d. What is this chart called?

17. The following frequency distribution reports the number of frequent flier miles, reported in thousands, for employees of Brumley Statistical Consulting Inc. during the most recent quarter.

Frequent Flier Miles (000)	Number of Employees
0 up to 3	5
3 up to 6	12
6 up to 9	23
9 up to 12	8
12 up to 15	2
Total	50

  a. How many employees were studied?
  b. What is the midpoint of the first class?

c. Construct a histogram.
d. A frequency polygon is to be drawn. What are the coordinates of the plot for the first class?
e. Construct a frequency polygon.
f. Interpret the frequent flier miles accumulated using the two charts.

18. A large Internet retailer is studying the lead time (elapsed time between when an order is placed and when it is filled) for a sample of recent orders. The lead times are reported in days.
a. How many orders were studied?
b. What is the midpoint of the first class?

Lead Time (days)	Frequency
0 up to 5	6
5 up to 10	7
10 up to 15	12
15 up to 20	8
20 up to 25	7
Total	40

c. What are the coordinates of the first class for a frequency polygon?
d. Draw a histogram.
e. Draw a frequency polygon.
f. Interpret the lead times using the two charts.

Cumulative Distributions

Tutorial #13
in Connect

Consider once again the distribution of the profits on vehicles sold by the Applewood Auto Group. Suppose our interest centers on the number of vehicles that sold for a profit of less than $1,400. These values can be approximated by developing a **cumulative frequency distribution** and portraying it graphically in a **cumulative frequency polygon.** Or, perhaps we are interested in the profit earned on the lowest-selling 40% of the vehicles. These values can be approximated by developing a **cumulative relative frequency distribution** and portraying it graphically in a **cumulative relative frequency polygon.** See the accompanying Excel tutorial that shows how to use a pivot table to create the cumulative distribution and the cumulative relative frequency polygon. The Applewood data set is available in Connect.

▶ **EXAMPLE**

The frequency distribution of the profits earned at Applewood Auto Group is repeated from Table 2–5.

Profit	Frequency
$ 200 up to $ 600	8
600 up to 1,000	11
1,000 up to 1,400	23
1,400 up to 1,800	38
1,800 up to 2,200	45
2,200 up to 2,600	32
2,600 up to 3,000	19
3,000 up to 3,400	4
Total	180

Construct a cumulative frequency polygon to answer the following question: Sixty of the vehicles earned a profit of less than what amount? Construct a cumulative relative frequency polygon to answer this question: Seventy-five percent of the vehicles sold earned a profit of less than what amount?

SOLUTION

As the names imply, a cumulative frequency distribution and a cumulative frequency polygon require *cumulative frequencies*. To construct a cumulative frequency distribution, refer to the preceding table and note that there were eight vehicles in which the profit earned was less than $600. Those 8 vehicles, plus the 11 in the next higher class, for a total of 19, earned a profit of less than $1,000. The cumulative frequency for the next higher class is 42, found by 8 + 11 + 23. This process is continued for all the classes. All the vehicles earned a profit of less than $3,400 (Table 2–8).

TABLE 2–8 Cumulative Frequency Distribution for Profit on Vehicles Sold Last Month at Applewood Auto Group

Profit	Cumulative Frequency	Found by
Less than $ 600	8	8
Less than 1,000	19	8 + 11
Less than 1,400	42	8 + 11 + 23
Less than 1,800	80	8 + 11 + 23 + 38
Less than 2,200	125	8 + 11 + 23 + 38 + 45
Less than 2,600	157	8 + 11 + 23 + 38 + 45 + 32
Less than 3,000	176	8 + 11 + 23 + 38 + 45 + 32 + 19
Less than 3,400	180	8 + 11 + 23 + 38 + 45 + 32 + 19 + 4

To construct a cumulative relative frequency distribution, we divide the cumulative frequencies by the total number of observations, 180. As shown in Table 2–9, the cumulative relative frequency of the fourth class is 80/180 = 44%. This means that 44% of the vehicles sold for less than $1,800.

TABLE 2–9 Cumulative Relative Frequency Distribution for Profit on Vehicles Sold Last Month at Applewood Auto Group

Profit	Cumulative Frequency	Cumulative Relative Frequency
Less than $ 600	8	8/180 = 0.044 = 4.4%
Less than 1,000	19	19/180 = 0.106 = 10.6%
Less than 1,400	42	42/180 = 0.233 = 23.3%
Less than 1,800	80	80/180 = 0.444 = 44.4%
Less than 2,200	125	125/180 = 0.694 = 69.4%
Less than 2,600	157	157/180 = 0.872 = 87.2%
Less than 3,000	176	176/180 = 0.978 = 97.8%
Less than 3,400	180	180/180 = 1.000 = 100%

To plot a cumulative frequency distribution, scale the upper limit of each class along the X-axis and scale the number of vehicles from 0 to 180 along the Y-axis. To provide additional information, you can label the vertical axis on the right in terms of cumulative relative frequencies. In the Applewood Auto Group, the vertical axis on the left is labeled from 0 to 180 and on the right from 0 to 100%. Note, as an example, that 50% on the right axis should be opposite 90 vehicles on the left axis and 100% on the right axis should be opposite 180 on the left axis.

To begin, the first plot is at $x = 200$ and $y = 0$. None of the vehicles sold for a profit of less than $200. The profit on 8 vehicles was less than $600, so the next plot is at $x = 600$ and $y = 8$. Continuing, the next plot is $x = 1,000$ and $y = 19$. There were 19 vehicles that sold for a profit of less than $1,000. The rest of the points are plotted and then the dots connected to form Chart 2–7.

We should point out that the shape of the distribution is the same if we use cumulative relative frequencies instead of the cumulative frequencies. The only difference is that the vertical axis is scaled in percentages. In the following charts, a percentage scale is added to the right side of the graphs to help answer questions about cumulative relative frequencies.

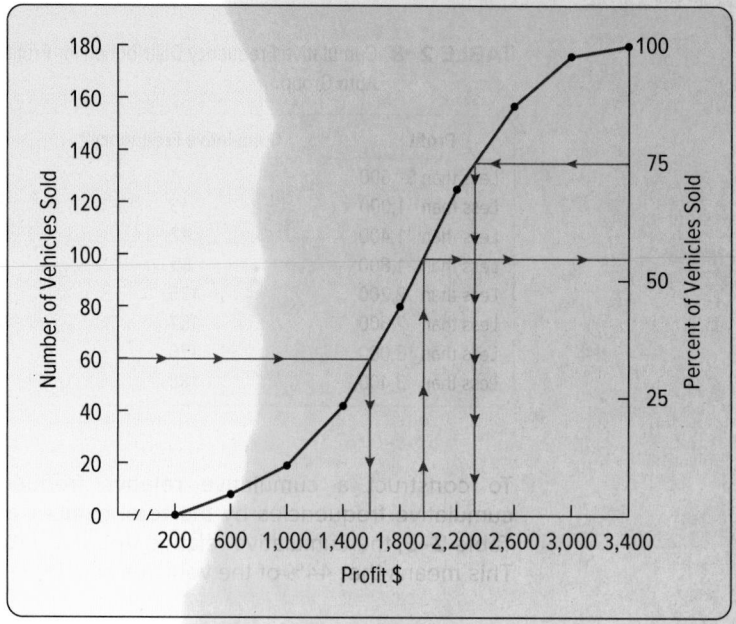

CHART 2–7 Cumulative Frequency Polygon for Profit on Vehicles Sold Last Month at Applewood Auto Group

Using Chart 2–7 to find the amount of profit on 75% of the cars sold, draw a horizontal line from the 75% mark on the right-hand vertical axis over to the polygon, then drop down to the X-axis and read the amount of profit. The value on the X-axis is about $2,300, so we estimate that 75% of the vehicles sold earned a profit of $2,300 or less for the Applewood group.

To find the highest profit earned on 60 of the 180 vehicles, we use Chart 2–7 to locate the value of 60 on the left-hand vertical axis. Next, we draw a horizontal line from the value of 60 to the polygon and then drop down to the X-axis and read the profit. It is about $1,600, so we estimate that 60 of the vehicles sold for a profit of less than $1,600. We can also make estimates of the percentage of vehicles that sold for less than a particular amount. To explain, suppose we want to estimate the percentage of vehicles that sold for a profit of less than $2,000. We begin by locating the value of $2,000 on the X-axis, move vertically to the polygon, and then horizontally to the vertical axis on the right. The value is about 56%, so we conclude 56% of the vehicles sold for a profit of less than $2,000.

SELF-REVIEW 2-5

Jackie's Tire and Auto Repair has 15 employees. Their hourly wages are summarized in the following table.

Hourly Wages	Number of Employees
$ 8 up to $10	3
10 up to 12	7
12 up to 14	4
14 up to 16	1

(a) What is the table called?
(b) Develop a cumulative frequency distribution and portray the distribution in a cumulative frequency polygon.
(c) On the basis of the cumulative frequency polygon, how many employees earn less than $11 per hour?

EXERCISES

19. The following cumulative frequency and the cumulative relative frequency polygon for the distribution of hourly wages of a sample of certified welders in the Atlanta, Georgia, area is shown in the graph.

a. How many welders were studied?
b. What is the class interval?
c. About how many welders earn less than $10.00 per hour?
d. About 75% of the welders make less than what amount?
e. Ten of the welders studied made less than what amount?
f. What percent of the welders make less than $20.00 per hour?

20. The cumulative frequency and the cumulative relative frequency polygon for a distribution of selling prices ($000) of houses sold in the Billings, Montana, area is shown in the graph.

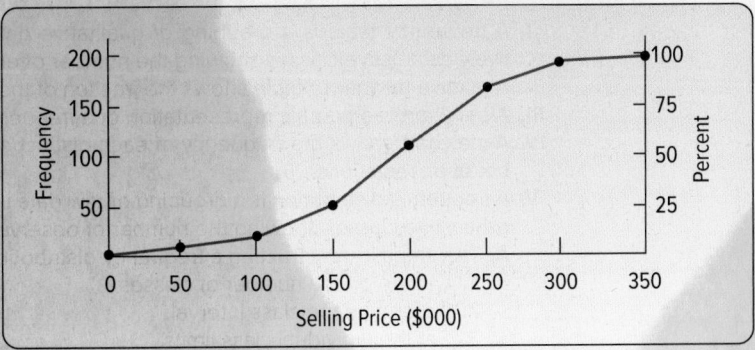

a. How many homes were studied?
b. What is the class interval?
c. One hundred homes sold for less than what amount?
d. About 75% of the homes sold for less than what amount?
e. Estimate the number of homes in the $150,000 up to $200,000 class.
f. About how many homes sold for less than $225,000?

21. The frequency distribution representing the number of frequent flier miles accumulated by employees at Brumley Statistical Consulting Inc. are repeated from Exercise 17.

Frequent Flier Miles (000)	Frequency
0 up to 3	5
3 up to 6	12
6 up to 9	23
9 up to 12	8
12 up to 15	2
Total	50

a. How many employees accumulated less than 3,000 miles?
b. Convert the frequency distribution to a cumulative frequency distribution.
c. Portray the cumulative distribution in the form of a cumulative frequency polygon.
d. Based on the cumulative relative frequencies, about 75% of the employees accumulated how many miles or less?

22. The frequency distribution of order lead time of the retailer from Exercise 18 is repeated here.

Lead Time (days)	Frequency
0 up to 5	6
5 up to 10	7
10 up to 15	12
15 up to 20	8
20 up to 25	7
Total	40

a. How many orders were filled in less than 10 days? In less than 15 days?
b. Convert the frequency distribution to cumulative frequency and cumulative relative frequency distributions.
c. Develop a cumulative frequency polygon.
d. About 60% of the orders were filled in less than how many days?

CHAPTER SUMMARY

I. A frequency table is a grouping of qualitative data into mutually exclusive and collectively exhaustive classes showing the number of observations in each class.
II. A relative frequency table shows the fraction of the number of frequencies in each class.
III. A bar chart is a graphic representation of a frequency table.
IV. A pie chart shows the frequency of each distinct class as a proportion of the total number of observations.
V. A frequency distribution is a grouping of raw data into mutually exclusive and collectively exhaustive classes showing the number of observations in each class.
   A. The steps in constructing a frequency distribution are:
      1. Decide on the number of classes.
      2. Determine the class interval.
      3. Set the individual class limits.
      4. Tally the raw data into classes and determine the frequency in each class.

B. The class frequency is the number of observations in each class.

C. The class interval is the difference between the limits of two consecutive classes.

D. The class midpoint is halfway between the limits of consecutive classes.

VI. A relative frequency distribution shows the percent of observations in each class.

VII. There are several methods for graphically portraying a frequency distribution.

A. A histogram portrays the frequencies in the form of a rectangle or bar for each class. The height of the rectangles is proportional to the class frequencies.

B. A frequency polygon consists of line segments connecting the points formed by the intersection of the class midpoint and the class frequency.

C. A graph of a cumulative frequency distribution shows the number of observations less than a given value.

D. A graph of a cumulative relative frequency distribution shows the percent of observations less than a given value.

CHAPTER EXERCISES

23. Describe the similarities and differences of qualitative and quantitative variables. Be sure to include the following:

a. What level of measurement is required for each variable type?

b. Can both types be used to describe both samples and populations?

24. Describe the similarities and differences between a frequency table and a frequency distribution. Be sure to include which requires qualitative data and which requires quantitative data.

25. Alex Damonte will be building a new resort in Myrtle Beach, South Carolina. Alex must decide how to design the resort based on the type of activities that the resort will offer to its customers. A recent poll of 300 potential customers showed the following results about customers' preferences for planned resort activities:

Like planned activities	63
Do not like planned activities	135
Not sure	78
No answer	24

a. What is the table called?

b. Draw a bar chart to portray the survey results.

c. Draw a pie chart for the survey results.

d. If you are preparing to present the results to Alex Damonte as part of a report, which graph would you prefer to show? Why?

26. **FILE** Speedy Swift is a package delivery service that serves the greater Atlanta, Georgia, metropolitan area. To maintain customer loyalty, one of Speedy Swift's performance objectives is on-time delivery. To monitor its performance, each delivery is measured on the following scale: early (package delivered before the promised time), on-time (package delivered within 15 minutes of the promised time), late (package delivered more than 15 minutes past the promised time), or lost (package never delivered). Speedy Swift's objective is to deliver 99% of all packages either early or on-time. Speedy collected the following data for last month's performance:

On-time	On-time	Early	Late	On-time	On-time	On-time	On-time	Late	On-time
Early	On-time	On-time	Early	On-time	On-time	On-time	On-time	On-time	On-time
Early	On-time	Early	On-time	On-time	On-time	Early	On-time	On-time	On-time
Early	On-time	On-time	Late	Early	Early	On-time	On-time	On-time	Early
On-time	Late	Late	On-time	On-time	On-time	On-time	On-time	On-time	On-time
On-time	Late	Early	On-time	Early	On-time	Lost	On-time	On-time	On-time
Early	Early	On-time	On-time	Late	Early	Lost	On-time	On-time	On-time
On-time	On-time	Early	On-time	Early	On-time	Early	On-time	Late	On-time
On-time	Early	On-time	On-time	On-time	Late	On-time	Early	On-time	On-time
On-time	On-time	On-time	On-time	On-time	Early	Early	On-time	On-time	On-time

a. What kind of variable is delivery performance? What scale is used to measure delivery performance?
b. Construct a frequency table for delivery performance for last month.
c. Construct a relative frequency table for delivery performance last month.
d. Construct a bar chart of the frequency table for delivery performance for last month.
e. Construct a pie chart of on-time delivery performance for last month.
f. Write a memo reporting the results of the analyses. Include your tables and graphs with written descriptions of what they show. Conclude with a general statement of last month's delivery performance as it relates to Speedy Swift's performance objectives.

27. A data set consists of 83 observations. How many classes would you recommend for a frequency distribution?

28. A data set consists of 145 observations that range from 56 to 490. What size class interval would you recommend?

29. **FILE** The following is the number of minutes to commute from home to work for a group of 25 automobile executives.

| 28 | 25 | 48 | 37 | 41 | 19 | 32 | 26 | 16 | 23 | 23 | 29 | 36 |
| 31 | 26 | 21 | 32 | 25 | 31 | 43 | 35 | 42 | 38 | 33 | 28 | |

a. How many classes would you recommend?
b. What class interval would you suggest?
c. What would you recommend as the lower limit of the first class?
d. Organize the data into a frequency distribution.
e. Based on the frequency distribution, describe the distribution of minutes to commute.

30. **FILE** The following data give the weekly amounts spent on groceries for a sample of 45 households.

$271	$363	$159	$ 76	$227	$337	$295	$319	$250
279	205	279	266	199	177	162	232	303
192	181	321	309	246	278	50	41	335
116	100	151	240	474	297	170	188	320
429	294	570	342	279	235	434	123	325

a. How many classes would you recommend?
b. What class interval would you suggest?
c. What would you recommend as the lower limit of the first class?
d. Organize the data into a frequency distribution.

31. **FILE** A social scientist is studying the attendance of college students at on-campus movies. A sample of 45 students showed they attended the following number of movies last semester.

4	6	8	7	9	6	3	7	7	6	7	1	4	7	7
4	6	4	10	2	4	6	3	4	6	8	4	3	3	6
8	8	4	6	4	6	5	5	9	6	8	8	6	5	10

Organize the information into a frequency distribution.
a. How many classes would you suggest?
b. What is the most suitable class interval?
c. What is the lower limit of the initial class?
d. Create the frequency distribution.
e. Describe the shape of the distribution.

32. **FILE** Aki Zhang owns and manages an investment portfolio of 36 stocks. Listed here is the holding time (recorded to the nearest whole year) between purchase and sale for the collection of 36 stocks.

8	8	6	11	11	9	8	5	11	4	8	5	14	7	12	8	6	11	9	7
9	15	8	8	12	5	9	8	5	9	10	11	3	9	8	6				

  a. How many classes would you propose?
  b. What class interval would you suggest?
  c. What quantity would you use for the lower limit of the initial class?
  d. Using your responses to parts (a), (b), and (c), create a frequency distribution.
  e. Describe the distribution of the time Aki holds a stock. Remember to comment on the mode.

33. **FILE** Many companies rely on sales representatives to prospect for potential customers. To connect and speak with a potential customer, representatives often make multiple telephone calls. A sales group at **Indeed.com** recorded the number of attempts to call a potential customer before speaking with the customer.

4	19	29
7	23	32
9	27	32
10	28	36
10	29	51

  a. Create a frequency distribution to summarize the variable.
  b. Describe the distribution of the variable.

34. **FILE** The monthly issues of the *Journal of Finance* are available on the Internet. The following table shows the number of times an issue was downloaded over the last 33 months. Suppose that you wish to summarize the number of downloads with a frequency distribution.

312	2,753	2,595	6,057	7,624	6,624	6,362	6,575	7,760	7,085	7,272
5,967	5,256	6,160	6,238	6,709	7,193	5,631	6,490	6,682	7,829	7,091
6,871	6,230	7,253	5,507	5,676	6,974	6,915	4,999	5,689	6,143	7,086

  a. How many classes would you propose?
  b. What class interval would you suggest?
  c. What quantity would you use for the lower limit of the initial class?
  d. Using your responses to parts (a), (b), and (c), create a frequency distribution.
  e. Describe the shape of the frequency distribution.

35. The following histogram shows the scores on the first exam for a statistics class.

  a. How many students took the exam?
  b. What is the class interval?
  c. What is the class midpoint for the first class?
  d. How many students earned a score of less than 70?

36. The following chart summarizes the selling price of homes sold last month in the Sarasota, Florida, area.

a. What is the chart called?
b. How many homes were sold during the last month?
c. What is the class interval?
d. About 75% of the houses sold for less than what amount?
e. One hundred seventy-five of the homes sold for less than what amount?

37. **FILE** A chain of sport shops catering to beginning skiers, headquartered in Aspen, Colorado, plans to conduct a study of how much a beginning skier spends on the initial purchase of equipment and supplies. Based on these figures, it wants to explore the possibility of offering combinations, such as a pair of boots and a pair of skis, to induce customers to buy more. A sample of 44 cash register receipts revealed these initial purchases:

$140	$ 82	$265	$168	$ 90	$114	$172	$230	$142
86	125	235	212	171	149	156	162	118
139	149	132	105	162	126	216	195	127
161	135	172	220	229	129	87	128	126
175	127	149	126	121	118	172	126	

a. Arrive at a suggested class interval.
b. Organize the data into a frequency distribution using a lower limit of $80.
c. Interpret your findings.

38. **FILE** The numbers of outstanding shares for 24 publicly traded companies are listed in the following table.

Company	Number of Outstanding Shares (millions)	Company	Number of Outstanding Shares (millions)
Southwest Airlines	573.02	Costco	438.19
FirstEnergy	486.02	Home Depot	1,140.00
Harley Davidson	164.95	DTE Energy	181.77
Entergy	180.06	Procter & Gamble	2,490.00
Chevron	1,920.00	Eastman Kodak	42.67
Pacific Gas and Electric	264.38	American Electric Power	493.11
DuPont	524.28	ITT Corp	87.56
Nike	1,270.00	Ameren	244.04
Eversource	316.89	ExxonMobil	4,230.00
Facebook	2,410.00	Boeing	567.88
Alphabet Inc. (Google)	349.62	Consumers Energy	84.10
Apple	4,830.00	Starbucks	1,350.00

a. Using the number of outstanding shares, summarize the companies with a frequency distribution.
b. Display the frequency distribution with a frequency polygon.

c. Create a cumulative frequency distribution of the outstanding shares.
d. Display the cumulative frequency distribution with a cumulative frequency polygon.
e. Based on the cumulative relative frequency distribution, 75% of the companies have less than "what number" of outstanding shares?
f. Write a brief analysis of this group of companies based on your statistical summaries of "number of outstanding shares."

39. A recent survey showed that the typical American car owner spends $2,950 per year on operating expenses. Following is a breakdown of the various expenditure items.

Expenditure Item	Amount
Fuel	$ 603
Interest on car loan	279
Repairs	930
Insurance and license	646
Depreciation	492
Total	$2,950

a. Draw an appropriate chart to summarize the data.
b. Why did you select this type of chart?
c. Summarize your findings.

40. **FILE** Midland National Bank selected a sample of 40 student checking accounts. Following are their end-of-the-month balances.

$404	$ 74	$234	$149	$279	$215	$123	$ 55	$ 43	$321
87	234	68	489	57	185	141	758	72	863
703	125	350	440	37	252	27	521	302	127
968	712	503	489	327	608	358	425	303	203

a. Tally the data into frequency and cumulative frequency distributions using $100 as a class interval and $0 as the starting point.
b. Draw a cumulative frequency polygon.
c. The bank considers any student with an ending balance of $400 or more a "preferred customer." Estimate the percentage of preferred customers.
d. The bank is also considering a service charge to the lowest 10% of the ending balances. What would you recommend as the cutoff point between those who have to pay a service charge and those who do not?

41. Residents of the state of South Carolina earned a total of $69.5 billion in adjusted gross income. Seventy-three percent of the total was in wages and salaries; 11% in dividends, interest, and capital gains; 8% in IRAs and taxable pensions; 3% in business income pensions; 2% in Social Security; and the remaining 3% from other sources. Develop a pie chart depicting the breakdown of adjusted gross income. Write a paragraph summarizing the information.

42. **FILE** A recent study of home technologies reported the number of hours of personal computer usage per day for a sample of 60 persons. Excluded from the study were people who worked out of their home and used the computer as a part of their work.

9.3	5.3	6.3	8.8	6.5	0.6	5.2	6.6	9.3	4.3
6.3	2.1	2.7	0.4	3.7	3.3	1.1	2.7	6.7	6.5
4.3	9.7	7.7	5.2	1.7	8.5	4.2	5.5	5.1	5.6
5.4	4.8	2.1	10.1	1.3	5.6	2.4	2.4	4.7	1.7
2.0	6.7	1.1	6.7	2.2	2.6	9.8	6.4	4.9	5.2
4.5	9.3	7.9	4.6	4.3	4.5	9.2	8.5	6.0	8.1

a. Organize the data into a frequency distribution. How many classes would you suggest? What value would you suggest for a class interval?
b. Draw a histogram. Describe your results.

43. **FILE** Merrill Lynch recently completed a study regarding the size of online investment portfolios (stocks, bonds, mutual funds, and certificates of deposit) for a sample of clients in the 40 up to 50 years old age group. Listed here is the value of all the investments in thousands of dollars for the 70 participants in the study.

$669.9	$ 7.5	$ 77.2	$ 7.5	$125.7	$516.9	$ 219.9	$645.2
301.9	235.4	716.4	145.3	26.6	187.2	315.5	89.2
136.4	616.9	440.6	408.2	34.4	296.1	185.4	526.3
380.7	3.3	363.2	51.9	52.2	107.5	82.9	63.0
228.6	308.7	126.7	430.3	82.0	227.0	321.1	403.4
39.5	124.3	118.1	23.9	352.8	156.7	276.3	23.5
31.3	301.2	35.7	154.9	174.3	100.6	236.7	171.9
221.1	43.4	212.3	243.3	315.4	5.9	1,002.2	171.7
295.7	437.0	87.8	302.1	268.1	899.5		

a. Organize the data into a frequency distribution. How many classes would you suggest? What value would you suggest for a class interval?
b. Draw a histogram of the frequency distribution using class midpoints.
c. Financial experts suggest that this age group of people have at least five times their salary saved. As a benchmark, assume an investment portfolio of $500,000 would support retirement in 10–15 years. In writing, summarize your results.

44. **FILE** According to *PMQ Pizza Magazine* (**https://www.pizzatoday.com/pizzeria-rankings/2019-top-100-pizza-companies/**), an estimate of pizza sales in the United States for the top 100 pizza companies was $45.6 billion in 2019. Following are the top five companies with the number of franchise units and total gross sales in $ millions.

Name	Units	Sales ($ millions)
Domino's	15,914	13,545
Pizza Hut	18,431	12,212
Little Caesars Pizza	5,465	4,770
Papa John's International	5,345	3,500
Papa Murphy's International	1,404	808

To complete this exercise, please access the data set with the top 100 pizza companies.
a. Using the data set, compute the sales per unit.
b. Construct a frequency distribution of companies based on total sales.
c. Construct a frequency distribution of companies based on per unit sales.
d. Write a report comparing the distributions of total sales and per unit sales.

45. Refer to the following chart:

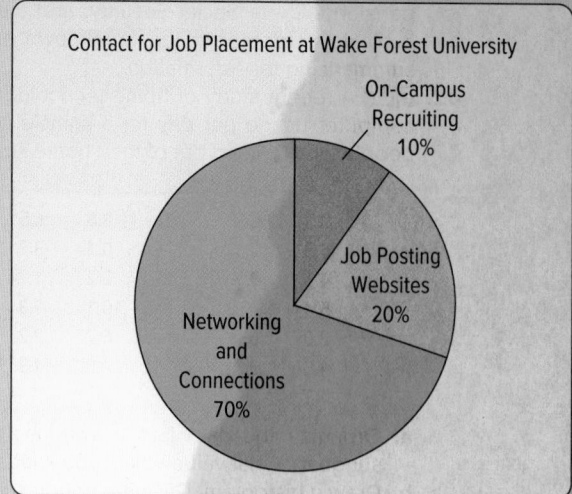

  a. What is the name given to this type of chart?
  b. Suppose that 1,000 graduates will start a new job shortly after graduation. Estimate the number of graduates whose first contact for employment occurred through networking and other connections.
  c. Would it be reasonable to conclude that about 90% of job placements were made through networking, connections, and job posting websites? Cite evidence.

46. The following chart depicts the annual revenues, by type of tax, for the state of Georgia.

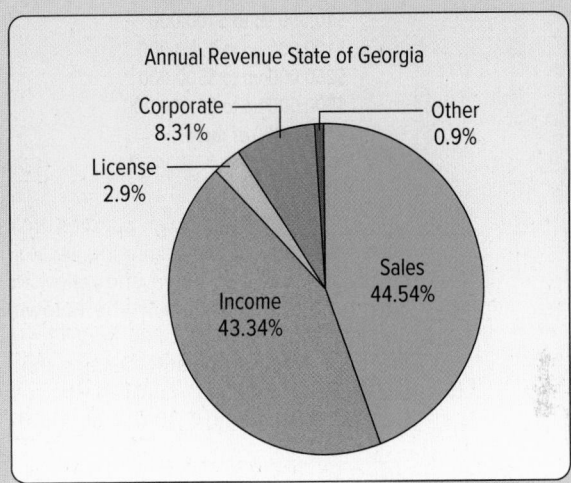

  a. What percentage of the state revenue is accounted for by sales tax and individual income tax?
  b. Which category will generate more revenue: corporate taxes or license fees?
  c. The total annual revenue for the state of Georgia is $6.3 billion. Estimate the amount of revenue in billions of dollars for sales taxes and for individual taxes.

47. In 2020, the United States exported a total of $256.2 billion worth of products to Canada (**https://www.trade.gov/knowledge-product/canada-market-overview**). The top five categories relative to dollar value, in billions of dollars, were:

Product Category	Dollar Value ($ billion)
Machinery	$39
Vehicles	38
Electrical machinery	22
Mineral fuels	16
Plastics	13

  a. Summarize the table with a bar chart using a software package.
  b. What is the percentage of each of the top five products exported to Canada relative to the total exports of products to Canada?
  c. What is the percentage of all other products exported to Canada relative to the total exports of products to Canada?
  d. Create a pie chart of all U.S. product exports to Canada. Which class is the mode of the distribution?

48. In the United States, agriculture is big business. For the period 2020–2021, agriculture accounted for nearly 20% of gross domestic product. Farming is the main driver of the industry. In 2020, there were 2.019 million farms in the United States, comprising a land area of 896,600 thousand acres. The average farm size was 444 acres. Each farm generates sales dollars for its owner.

a. Using the following table based on 2020 data, create a histogram for relative frequency of farms in each sales class.

b. Create a pie chart of percent of total farm land in each class.

c. Write a summary of the results that describes the percent of total farms in each sales class and the percent of total farm acreage in each sales class. Be specific.

Farm Sales Dollars	Percent of Total Farms	Percent of Total Farm Acreage
$1,000 up to $10,000	51.1	9.4
$10,000 up to $100,000	30.4	20.8
$100,000 up to $250,000	6.7	14.7
$250,000 up to $500,000	4.4	14.3
$500,000 up to $1,000,000	3.5	15.4
$1,000,000 or more	3.9	25.4

49. One of the most popular candies in the United States is M&M's produced by the Mars Company. In the beginning M&M's were all brown. Now they are produced in red, green, blue, orange, brown, and yellow. Recently, the purchase of a 14-ounce bag of M&M's Plain had 444 candies with the following breakdown by color: 130 brown, 98 yellow, 96 red, 35 orange, 52 blue, and 33 green. Develop a chart depicting this information and write a paragraph summarizing the results.

50. **FILE** The number of families who used the Minneapolis YWCA day care service was recorded during a 30-day period. The results are as follows:

31	49	19	62	24	45	23	51	55	60
40	35	54	26	57	37	43	65	18	41
50	56	4	54	39	52	35	51	63	42

a. Construct a cumulative frequency distribution.

b. Sketch a graph of the cumulative frequency polygon.

c. How many days saw fewer than 30 families utilize the day care center?

d. Based on cumulative relative frequencies, how busy were the highest 80% of the days?

DATA ANALYTICS

51. **FILE** Refer to the North Valley Real Estate data, which report information on homes sold during the last year. For the variable *price,* select an appropriate class interval and organize the selling prices into a frequency distribution. Write a brief report summarizing your findings. Be sure to answer the following questions in your report.

a. Around what values of price do the data tend to cluster?

b. Based on the frequency distribution, what is the typical selling price in the first class? What is the typical selling price in the last class?

c. Draw a cumulative relative frequency distribution. Using this distribution, 50% of the homes sold for what price or less? Estimate the lower price of the top 10% of homes sold. About what percent of the homes sold for less than $300,000?

d. Refer to the variable *Bedrooms.* Draw a bar chart showing the number of homes sold with two, three, four, or more bedrooms. Write a description of the distribution.

52. **FILE** Refer to the Baseball 2021 data that report information on the 30 Major League Baseball teams for the 2021 season. Create a frequency distribution for the *Team Salary* variable and answer the following questions.

   a. What is the typical salary for a team? What is the range of the salaries?

   b. Comment on the shape of the distribution. Does it appear that any of the teams have a salary that is out of line with the others?

   c. Draw a cumulative relative frequency distribution of team salary. Using this distribution, 40% of the teams have a salary of less than what amount? About how many teams have a total salary of more than $205 million?

53. **FILE** Refer to the Lincolnville School District bus data. Select the variable referring to the number of *miles traveled since the last maintenance,* and then organize these data into a frequency distribution.

   a. What is a typical amount of miles traveled? What is the range?

   b. Comment on the shape of the distribution. Are there any outliers in terms of miles driven?

   c. Draw a cumulative relative frequency distribution. Forty percent of the buses were driven fewer than how many miles? How many buses were driven less than 10,500 miles?

   d. Refer to the variables regarding the bus *manufacturer* and the bus *capacity.* Draw a pie chart of each variable and write a description of your results.

3

Describing Data:

NUMERICAL MEASURES

Cheryl Ann Quigley/Shutterstock

▲ **THE KENTUCKY DERBY** is held the first Saturday in May at Churchill Downs in Louisville, Kentucky. The race track is one and one-quarter miles. The table in Exercise 74 shows the winners since 1990, their margin of victory, the winning time, and the payoff on a $2 bet. Determine the mean and median for the variables winning time and payoff on a $2 bet. (See Exercise 74 and **LO3-1**.)

LEARNING OBJECTIVES

When you have completed this chapter, you will be able to:

LO3-1 Compute and interpret the mean, the median, and the mode.

LO3-2 Compute a weighted mean.

LO3-3 Compute and interpret the geometric mean.

LO3-4 Compute and interpret the range, variance, and standard deviation.

LO3-5 Explain and apply Chebyshev's theorem and the Empirical Rule.

Introduction

Chapter 2 began our study of descriptive statistics. To summarize raw data into a meaningful form, we organized qualitative data into a frequency table and portrayed the results in a bar chart. In a similar fashion, we organized quantitative data into a frequency distribution and portrayed the results in a histogram. We also looked at other graphical techniques such as pie charts to portray qualitative data and frequency polygons to portray quantitative data.

This chapter is concerned with two numerical ways of describing quantitative variables, namely, **measures of location** and **measures of dispersion.** Measures of location are often referred to as averages. The purpose of a measure of location is to pinpoint the center of a distribution of data. An average is a measure of location that shows the central value of the data. Averages appear daily on TV, on various websites, in the newspaper, and in other journals. Here are some examples:

- The average U.S. home changes ownership every 8.17 years.
- The U.S. Postal Service processed and delivered a daily average of 429.9 million mail pieces.
- The average American home has more video devices than people. There are about 10 video devices and 2.53 people in a typical home.
- In 2020, the average cost of a wedding ceremony and reception was $19,000. In 2019, the average was $28,000. The decrease is attributed to the COVID pandemic that caused many wedding planners to reduce the size of the ceremonies.
- The average price of a theater ticket on Broadway is $189.

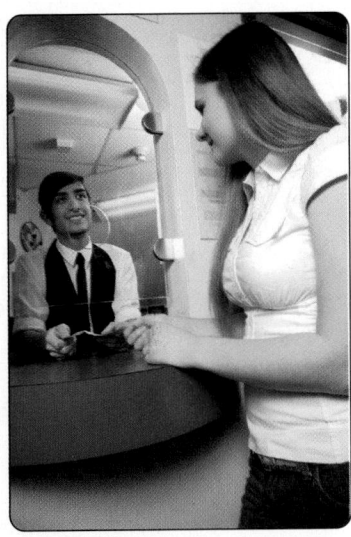
Steve Debenport/iStock/Getty Images

If we consider only measures of location in a set of data, or if we compare several sets of data using central values, we may draw an erroneous conclusion. In addition to measures of location, we should consider the **dispersion**—often called the *variation* or the *spread*—in the data. As an illustration, suppose the average annual income of executives for Internet-related companies is $80,000, and the average income for executives in pharmaceutical firms is also $80,000. If we looked only at the average incomes, we might conclude that executives in both industries receive the same annual income. However, if we review the data and analyze the dispersion of income in each industry, the distributions of annual income are much different. The salaries for the executives in the Internet firms range from $70,000 to $90,000, but salaries for the marketing executives in pharmaceuticals range from $40,000 to $120,000. Thus, we conclude that although the average salaries are the same for the two industries, there is much more spread or dispersion in salaries for the pharmaceutical executives. To describe the dispersion, we will consider the range, the variance, and the standard deviation.

Measures of Location

We begin by discussing measures of location. There is not just one measure of location; in fact, there are many. We will consider five: the arithmetic mean, the median, the mode, the weighted mean, and the geometric mean. The arithmetic mean is the most widely used and widely reported measure of location. We study the mean as both a population parameter and a sample statistic.

LO3-1
Compute and interpret the mean, the median, and the mode.

The Population Mean

Many studies involve all the individuals in a population. For example, there are 12 sales associates employed at the Reynolds Road Carpet Outlet. The mean amount of commission they earned last month was $1,345. This is a population value because we considered the commission of *all* the sales associates. Other examples of a population mean would be:

- The mean closing price for Johnson & Johnson stock for the last 5 days is $164.38.
- The mean number of overtime hours worked last week by the six welders employed by Butts Welding Inc. is 6.45 hours.
- Caryn Tirsch began a website last month devoted to organic gardening. The mean daily number of hits on Caryn's site for the 31 days in July was 84.36.

For raw data—that is, data that have not been grouped in a frequency distribution—the population mean is the sum of all the values in the population divided by the number of values in the population. To find the population mean, we use the following formula.

$$\text{Population mean} = \frac{\text{Sum of all the values in the population}}{\text{Number of values in the population}}$$

Instead of writing out in words the full directions for computing the population mean (or any other measure), it is more convenient to use the shorthand symbols of mathematics. The mean of the population using mathematical symbols is:

POPULATION MEAN	$\mu = \dfrac{\Sigma x}{N}$	(3–1)

where:

μ represents the population mean. It is the Greek lowercase letter "mu."
N is the number of values in the population.
x represents any particular value.
Σ is the Greek capital letter "sigma" and indicates the operation of adding.
Σx is the sum of the x values in the population.

Any measurable characteristic of a population is called a **parameter.** The mean of a population is an example of a parameter.

PARAMETER   A characteristic of a population.

▶ **EXAMPLE**

There are 46 exits on I-75 through the state of Kentucky. Listed here are the distances between exits (in miles).

11	4	10	4	9	3	8	10	3	14	1	6
4	3	5	2	2	5	4	2	3	2	5	5
1	1	2	7	8	10	2	3	7	5	4	3
2	1	1	2	1	1	2	1	2	1		

Why is this information a population? What is the mean number of miles between exits?

SOLUTION

This is a population because we are considering all the exits on I-75 in Kentucky. We add the distances between each of the 46 exits. The total distance is 192 miles. To find the arithmetic mean, we divide this total by 46. So the arithmetic mean is 4.17 miles, found by 192/46. From formula (3–1):

$$\mu = \frac{\Sigma x}{N} = \frac{11 + 4 + 10 + \cdots + 1}{46} = \frac{192}{46} = 4.17$$

How do we interpret the value of 4.17? It is the typical number of miles between exits. Because we considered all the exits on I-75 in Kentucky, this value is a population parameter.

TY Lim/Shutterstock

The Sample Mean

As explained in Chapter 1, we often select a sample from the population to estimate a specific characteristic of the population. Smucker's quality assurance department needs to be assured that the amount of orange marmalade in the jar labeled as containing 12 ounces actually contains that amount. It would be very expensive and time consuming to check the weight of each jar. Therefore, a sample of 20 jars is selected, the mean of the sample is determined, and that value is used to estimate the amount in each jar.

For raw data—that is, the data are not grouped as in a frequency distribution—*the mean is the sum of all the sampled values divided by the total number of sampled values.* To find the mean for a sample:

$$\text{Sample mean} = \frac{\text{Sum of all the values in the sample}}{\text{Number of values in the sample}}$$

The mean of a sample and the mean of a population are computed in the same way, but the shorthand notation used is different. The formula for the mean of a *sample* is:

SAMPLE MEAN	$\bar{x} = \dfrac{\Sigma x}{n}$	(3–2)

where:

- $\bar{x}$ represents the sample mean. It is read "x bar."
- n is the number of values in the sample.
- x represents any particular value.
- Σ is the Greek capital letter "sigma" and indicates the operation of adding.
- Σx is the sum of the x values in the sample.

The mean of a sample, or any other measure based on sample data, is called a **statistic.** If the mean weight of a sample of 10 jars of Smucker's orange marmalade is 11.5 ounces, this is an example of a statistic.

STATISTIC A characteristic of a sample.

▶ **EXAMPLE**

Verizon is studying the number of hours per day that people use their mobile phones. A random sample of 12 customers showed the following daily usage in hours.

4.1	3.7	4.3	4.2	5.5	5.1
4.2	5.1	4.2	4.6	5.2	3.8

What is the arithmetic mean number of hours per day used last month?

SOLUTION

Using formula (3–2), the sample mean is:

$$\text{Sample mean} = \frac{\text{Sum of all values in the sample}}{\text{Number of values in the sample}}$$

$$\bar{x} = \frac{\Sigma x}{n} = \frac{4.1 + 3.7 + \cdots + 3.8}{12} = \frac{54.0}{12} = 4.5$$

The arithmetic mean number of hours per day that people use their mobile phones is 4.5 hours.

Properties of the Arithmetic Mean

The arithmetic mean is a widely used measure of location. It has several important properties:

1. **To compute a mean, the data must be measured at the interval or ratio level.** Recall from Chapter 1 that ratio-level data include such data as ages, incomes, and weights.
2. **All the values are included in computing the mean.**
3. **The mean is unique.** That is, there is only one mean in a set of data. Later in the chapter, we will discover a measure of location that may have more than one value.
4. **The sum of the deviations of each value from the mean is zero.** Expressed symbolically:

$$\Sigma(x - \bar{x}) = 0$$

As an example, the mean of 3, 8, and 4 is 5. Then:

$$\Sigma(x - \bar{x}) = (3 - 5) + (8 - 5) + (4 - 5)$$
$$= -2 + 3 - 1$$
$$= 0$$

Thus, we can consider the mean as a balance point for a set of data. To illustrate, see Chart 3–1. It shows a balance beam with the numbers 1, 2, 3, . . . , 9 evenly spaced on it. Suppose three bars of equal weight were placed on the board at numbers 1, 3, and 8. To balance the beam, we compute the mean of the three values; it is 4. If we balance the beam at 4, we will find that the board is balanced perfectly! The sum of the deviations below the mean (−4) exactly offsets the deviation above the mean (+4). The sum of the deviations is zero.

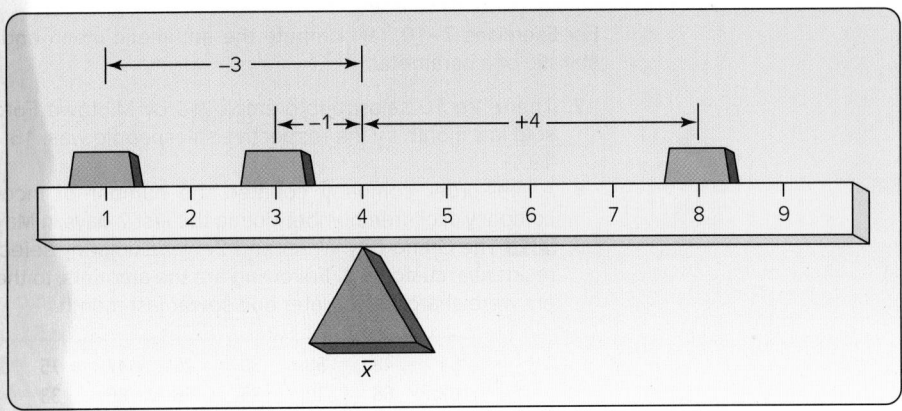

CHART 3–1 Mean as a Balance Point

The mean does have a weakness. Recall that the mean uses the value of every item in a sample, or population, in its computation. If one or two of these values are either extremely large or extremely small compared to the majority of data, the mean might not be an appropriate average to represent the data. For example, suppose the annual incomes of a sample of financial planners at Merrill Lynch are $62,900, $61,600, $62,500, $60,800, and $1,200,000. The mean income is $289,560. Obviously, it is not representative of this group because all but one financial planner has an income in the $60,000 to $63,000 range. One income ($1.2 million) is unduly affecting the mean.

SELF-REVIEW 3–1

The answers are in Appendix D.

1. The annual incomes of a sample of middle-management employees at Westinghouse are $62,900, $69,100, $58,300, and $76,800.
   (a) What is the formula for the sample mean? Using the formula for the sample mean, explain how to compute the sample mean.
   (b) Find the sample mean.
   (c) Is the mean you computed in (b) a statistic or a parameter? Why?
   (d) What is your best estimate of the population mean?
2. The six students in Computer Science 411 are a population. Their final course grades are 92, 96, 61, 86, 79, and 84.
   (a) Give the formula for the population mean. Using the formula for the population mean, explain how to compute the sample mean.
   (b) Compute the mean course grade.
   (c) Is the mean you computed in part (b) a statistic or a parameter? Why?

EXERCISES

The answers to the odd-numbered exercises are in Appendix C.

1. Compute the mean of the following population values: 6, 3, 5, 7, 6.
2. Compute the mean of the following population values: 14, 10, 14, 6, 14, 8.
3. a. Compute the mean of the following sample values: 5, 9, 4, 10.
   b. Show that $\Sigma(x - \bar{x}) = 0$.
4. a. Compute the mean of the following sample values: 1.3, 7.0, 3.6, 4.1, 5.0.
   b. Show that $\Sigma(x - \bar{x}) = 0$.
5. Compute the mean of the following sample values: 16.25, 12.91, 14.58.
6. Suppose you go to the grocery store and spend $61.85 for the purchase of 14 items. What is the mean price per item?

For Exercises 7–10, (a) compute the arithmetic mean and (b) indicate whether it is a statistic or a parameter.

7. There are 10 salespeople employed by Midtown Ford. The number of new cars sold last month by the respective salespeople was: 15, 23, 4, 19, 18, 10, 10, 8, 28, 19.

8. A mail-order company counted the number of incoming calls per day to the company's toll-free number during the first 7 days in May: 14, 24, 19, 31, 36, 26, 17.

9. **FILE** The Grand City Water and Sewer Company selected a random sample of 20 residential customers. Following are the amounts, to the nearest dollar, the customers were charged for water and sewer last month.

54	48	58	50	25	47	75	46	60	70
67	68	39	35	56	66	33	62	65	67

10. **FILE** A Human Resources manager at Metal Technologies studied the overtime hours of welders. A sample of 15 welders showed the following number of overtime hours worked last month.

13	13	12	15	7	15	5	12
6	7	12	10	9	13	12	

11. AAA Heating and Air Conditioning completed 30 jobs last month with a mean revenue of $5,430 per job. The president wants to know the total revenue for the month. Based on the limited information, can you compute the total revenue? What is it?

12. A large pharmaceutical company hires business administration graduates to sell its products. The company is growing rapidly and dedicates only 1 day of sales training for new salespeople. The company's goal for new salespeople is $10,000 per month. The goal is based on the current mean sales for the entire company, which is $10,000 per month. After reviewing the retention rates of new employees, the company finds that only one in 10 new employees stays longer than 3 months. Comment on using the current mean sales per month as a sales goal for new employees. Why do new employees leave the company?

The Median

We have stressed that, for data containing one or two very large or very small values, the arithmetic mean may not fairly represent the central location of the data. The center for such data is better described by a measure of location called the **median.**

> **MEDIAN** The midpoint of the values after they have been ordered from the minimum to the maximum values.

To illustrate the need for a measure of location other than the arithmetic mean, suppose you are seeking to buy a condominium in Palm Aire. Your real estate agent says that the typical price of the units currently available is $110,000. Would you still want to look? If you had budgeted your maximum purchase price at $75,000, you might think they are out of your price range. However, checking the prices of the individual units might change your mind. They are $60,000, $65,000, $70,000, and $80,000, and a superdeluxe penthouse costs $275,000. The arithmetic mean price is $110,000, as the real estate agent reported, but one price ($275,000) is pulling the arithmetic mean upward, causing it to be an unrepresentative average. It does seem that a price around $70,000 is a more typical or representative average, and it is. In cases such as this, the median provides a more valid measure of location.

The median price of the units available is $70,000. To determine this, we order the prices from the minimum value ($60,000) to the maximum value ($275,000) and select the middle value ($70,000). For the median, the data must be at least an ordinal level of measurement.

Prices Ordered from Minimum to Maximum		Prices Ordered from Maximum to Minimum
$ 60,000		$275,000
65,000		80,000
70,000	← Median →	70,000
80,000		65,000
275,000		60,000

Note that there is the same number of prices below the median of $70,000 as above it. The median is, therefore, unaffected by extremely low or high prices. Had the highest price been $90,000, or $300,000, or even $1 million, the median price would still be $70,000. Likewise, had the lowest price been $20,000 or $50,000, the median price would still be $70,000.

In the previous illustration, there are an *odd* number of observations (five). How is the median determined for an *even* number of observations? As before, the observations are ordered. Then by convention to obtain a unique value we calculate the mean of the two middle observations. So for an even number of observations, the median may not be one of the given values.

▶ **EXAMPLE**

Facebook is a popular social networking website. Users can add friends and send them messages, and update their personal profiles to notify friends about themselves and their activities. A sample of 10 adults revealed they spent the following number of hours last week using Facebook.

| 3 | 5 | 7 | 5 | 9 | 1 | 3 | 9 | 17 | 10 |

Find the median number of hours.

SOLUTION

Note that the number of adults sampled is even (10). The first step, as before, is to order the hours using Facebook from the minimum value to the maximum value. Then identify the two middle values. The arithmetic mean of the two middle observations gives us the median hours. Arranging the values from minimum to maximum:

| 1 | 3 | 3 | 5 | 5 | 7 | 9 | 9 | 10 | 17 |

The median is found by averaging the two middle values. The middle values are 5 hours and 7 hours, and the mean of these two values is 6. We conclude that the typical adult Facebook user spends 6 hours per week at the website. Notice that the median is not one of the values. Also, half of the times are below the median and half are above it.

The major properties of the median are as follows:

1. **It is not affected by extremely large or small values.** Therefore, the median is a valuable measure of location when such values do occur.
2. **It can be computed for ordinal-level data or higher.** Recall from Chapter 1 that ordinal-level data can be ranked from low to high.

The Mode

As demonstrated in Chapter 2, the **mode** is useful in summarizing qualitative, nominal data. As an example, a company developed five new bath oils. A marketing survey was designed to determine consumer bath oil preferences. The raw data are summarized by grouping the data into a frequency table. Chart 3–2 presents these frequencies. The largest number of respondents favored Lamoure, as evidenced by the highest bar. Thus, Lamoure is the mode.

> **MODE** The value of the observation that appears most frequently.

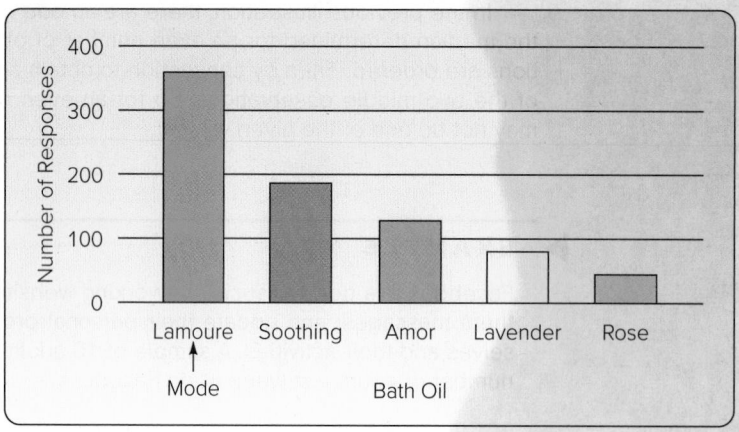

CHART 3–2 Number of Respondents Favoring Various Bath Oils

The mode can also be applied to find the central location of quantitative, raw data. For quantitative, raw data, the mode is the value that occurs most frequently. In the following sorted data of 10 observations,

10 10 10 10 10 11 11 13 14 14

the value 10 occurs five times. So, it is the mode of the data set.

An advantage of the mode is that extremely high or low values do not affect its value. The mode does have disadvantages, however, that cause it to be used less frequently than the mean or median. For many sets of data, there is no mode because no value appears more than once. For example, there is no mode for this set of sorted price data because every value occurs once:

$18 $19 $20 $21 $23

Conversely, for some data sets there is more than one mode. Suppose the ages of the individuals in an investment club are:

22 26 27 27 31 35 35

Both the ages 27 and 35 are modes. Thus, this grouping of ages is referred to as *bimodal* (having two modes). One would question the use of two modes to represent the location of this set of age data.

▶ **EXAMPLE**

FILE Recall the data regarding the distance in miles between exits on I-75 in Kentucky. The information is repeated here.

11	4	10	4	9	3	8	10	3	14	1	6
4	3	5	2	2	5	4	2	3	2	5	5
1	1	2	7	8	10	2	3	7	5	4	3
2	1	1	2	1	1	2	1	2	1		

Determine the values for the median and mode.

SOLUTION

The first step is to organize the distances into a frequency table. This will help us determine the distance that occurs most frequently. Notice that we decided to use classes based on each value of distance between exits. This choice results in a clear summary and presentation of the variable, distance between exits.

Distance between Exits (Miles)	Frequency
1	9
2	10
3	6
4	5
5	5
6	1
7	2
8	2
9	1
10	3
11	1
14	1
Total	**46**

Which of the three measures of location (mode, mean, or median) best represents the central location of these data? Is the mode the best measure of location to represent the Kentucky data? Perhaps. The mode represents a frequency. When compared to all other possible values, the mode infers that while driving I-75 in Kentucky, you have the highest likelihood of finding two exits that are 2 miles apart. While the mode provides interesting information, it does not, as in this example, always provide a good measure of a distribution's central location.

Is the mean the best measure of location to represent these data? On page 57, we calculated the mean distance between exits to be 4.17 miles. Recall Chart 3–1 and the balance beam. When determining the location of a distribution, we would like a "middle value." For "distance between exits," there are many cases with short distances and a few cases with long distances between exits. The mean or balance point of the distribution would be influenced by the longer distances making the mean too large. For this data, the mean is not a good measure of location.

What about the median? Recall that the median relies only on the sorted ranking of the raw data. In the sorted list, the median is the distance associated with the middle value. The median distance is 3 miles. That is, half of the distances between exits are 3 miles or less; half are 3 miles or more. With this data, the median of 3 miles between exits is probably the best measure of location for the distance between exits.

SELF-REVIEW 3–2

1. A sample of single person households in Towson, Texas, receiving Social Security payments revealed these monthly benefits: $852, $598, $580, $1,374, $960, $878, and $1,130.
   (a) What is the median monthly benefit?
   (b) How many observations are below the median? Above it?
2. The number of work stoppages in the United States over the last 10 years are 22, 20, 21, 15, 5, 11, 19, 19, 15, and 11.
   (a) What is the median number of stoppages?
   (b) How many observations are below the median? Above it?
   (c) What is the modal number of work stoppages?

Software Solution

We can use a statistical software package to find many measures of location.

Tutorial #20
in Connect

▶ **EXAMPLE**

Table 2–4 on page 28 showed the profit on the sales of 180 vehicles at Applewood Auto Group. Determine the mean and the median selling price.

SOLUTION

The mean, median, and modal amounts of profit are reported in the following output (highlighted in the screen shot). See the Excel Tutorial to learn how to create the following statistical summary. There are 180 vehicles in the study, so using a calculator would be tedious and prone to error.

	A	B	C	D	E	F	G	H
1	Age	Profit	Location	Vehicle-Type	Previous		*Profit*	
2	21	$1,387	Tionesta	Sedan	0			
3	23	$1,754	Sheffield	SUV	1		Mean	1843.17
4	24	$1,817	Sheffield	Hybrid	1		Standard Erro	47.97
5	25	$1,040	Sheffield	Compact	0		Median	1882.50
6	26	$1,273	Kane	Sedan	1		Mode	1761.00
7	27	$1,529	Sheffield	Sedan	1		Standard Dev	643.63
8	27	$3,082	Kane	Truck	0		Sample Varia	414256.60
9	28	$1,951	Kane	SUV	1		Kurtosis	-0.22
10	28	$2,692	Tionesta	Compact	0		Skewness	-0.24
11	29	$1,206	Sheffield	Sedan	0		Range	2998.00
12	29	$1,342	Kane	Sedan	2		Minimum	294.00
13	30	$443	Kane	Sedan	3		Maximum	3292.00
14	30	$754	Olean	Sedan	2		Sum	331770.00
15	30	$1,621	Sheffield	Truck	1		Count	180.00

Source: Microsoft Excel

The mean profit is $1,843.17 and the median is $1,882.50. These two values are less than $40 apart, so either value is a reasonable measure of central location for profit. The mode is $1761.00; of the 180 observations, $1761.00 occurred only twice. The mode is not a good measure of central location. We can also see from the Excel output that there were 180 vehicles sold and the sum total of profit was $331,770.00. We will describe the meaning of standard error, standard deviation, and other measures reported on the output later in this chapter and in later chapters.

EXERCISES

13. What would you report as the modal value for a set of observations if there were a total of:
    a. 10 observations and no two values were the same?
    b. 6 observations and they were all equal to 21?
    c. 6 observations and the values were 1, 2, 3, 3, 4, and 4?

For Exercises 14–16, determine the (a) mean, (b) median, and (c) mode.

14. The following is the number of oil changes for the last 7 days at the Jiffy Lube located at the corner of Elm Street and Pennsylvania Avenue.

| 41 | 15 | 39 | 54 | 31 | 15 | 33 |

15. The following is the percent change in net income from last year to this year for a sample of 12 construction companies in Denver.

| 5 | 1 | −10 | −6 | 5 | 12 | 7 | 8 | 6 | 5 | −1 | 11 |

16. The following are the ages of the 10 people in the Java Coffee Shop at the Southwyck Shopping Mall at 10 a.m.

| 21 | 41 | 20 | 23 | 24 | 33 | 37 | 42 | 23 | 29 |

17. **FILE** Several indicators of long-term economic growth in the United States and their annual percent change are listed here.

Economic Indicator	Percent Change	Economic Indicator	Percent Change
Inflation	4.5%	Real GNP	2.9%
Exports	4.7	Investment (residential)	3.6
Imports	2.3	Investment (nonresidential)	2.1
Real disposable income	2.9	Productivity (total)	1.4
Consumption	2.7	Productivity (manufacturing)	5.2

    a. What is the median percent change?
    b. What is the modal percent change?

18. **FILE** Sally Reynolds sells real estate along the coastal area of Northern California. Following are her total annual commissions between 2012 and 2022. Find the mean, median, and mode of the commissions she earned for the 11 years.

Year	Amount (thousands)
2012	292.16
2013	233.80
2014	206.97
2015	202.67
2016	164.69
2017	206.53
2018	237.51
2019	225.57
2020	255.33
2021	248.14
2022	269.11

19. **FILE** The accounting firm of Rowatti and Koppel specializes in income tax returns for self-employed professionals, such as physicians, dentists, architects, and lawyers. The firm employs 11 accountants who prepare the returns. For last year, the number of returns prepared by each accountant was:

| 58 | 75 | 31 | 58 | 46 | 65 | 60 | 71 | 45 | 58 | 80 |

Find the mean, median, and mode for the number of returns prepared by each accountant. If you could report only one, which measure of location would you recommend reporting?

20. **FILE** The demand for the video games provided by Mid-Tech Video Games Inc. has exploded in the last several years. Hence, the owner needs to hire several new technical people to keep up with the demand. Mid-Tech gives each applicant a special test that Dr. Ohana, the designer of the test, believes is closely related to the ability to create video games. For the general population, the mean on this test is 100. Following are the scores on this test for the applicants.

| 95 | 105 | 120 | 81 | 90 | 115 | 99 | 100 | 130 | 10 |

The president is interested in the overall quality of the job applicants based on this test. Compute the mean and the median scores for the 10 applicants. What would you report to the president? Does it seem that the applicants are better than the general population?

The Relative Positions of the Mean, Median, and Mode

Which of the three measures of location, mean, median, or mode, would be reported as the location of a set of data? The answer depends on the shape of the distribution.

A distribution, as shown in Chart 3–3, is symmetrical in shape. It is symmetrical because the shape of the curve is the same on either side of the distribution's center. A symmetrical distribution is special because all three measures of location are at the center of the distribution. In this case, the mean is usually reported as the distribution's location.

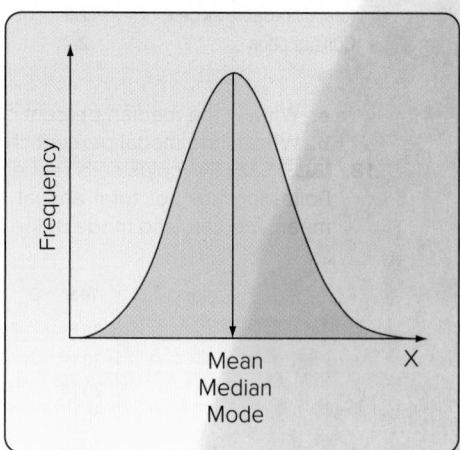

CHART 3–3 A Symmetric Distribution

As an example, Donahue's donut shop counted the number of customers per day for the last 73 days. The frequency distribution of the data can be described as fairly symmetrical. That is, the mode is in the center of the distribution and class frequencies decrease as they diverge from the mode. The mean number of customers is 36.1;

the median and mode are both 36. The three measures of location should be approximately equal for symmetrical distributions. The mean of 36.1 customers per day would be reported as the measure of location for this symmetrical distribution.

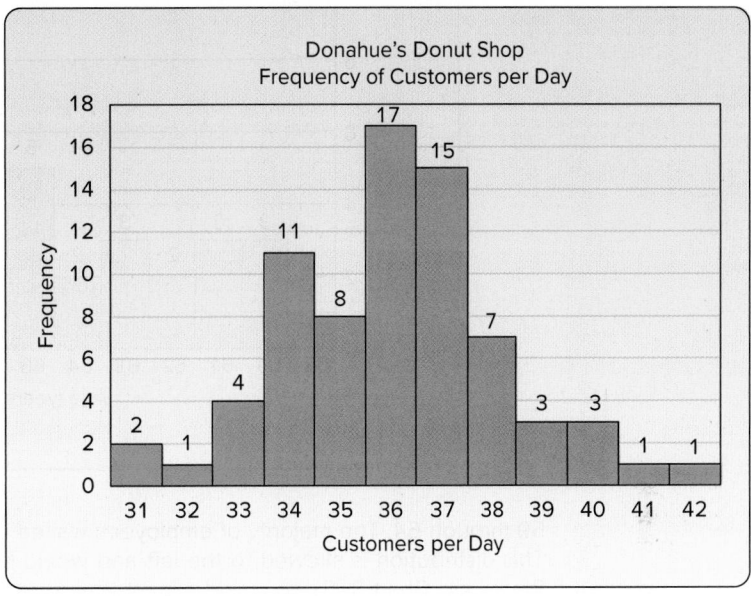

The distributions, as shown in Charts 3–4 and 3–5, are not symmetrical in shape. The shapes are described as skewed. Chart 3–4 has a long tail to the right and is positively skewed; Chart 3–5 has a long tail to the left and is negatively skewed. For these shapes, the measures of location of each distribution are different. Because the calculation of the mean sums all the values, including the relatively infrequent, extreme values, the value is pulled toward the direction of the distribution's skew. Review Chart 3–1 to see the effect of extreme values on the mean.

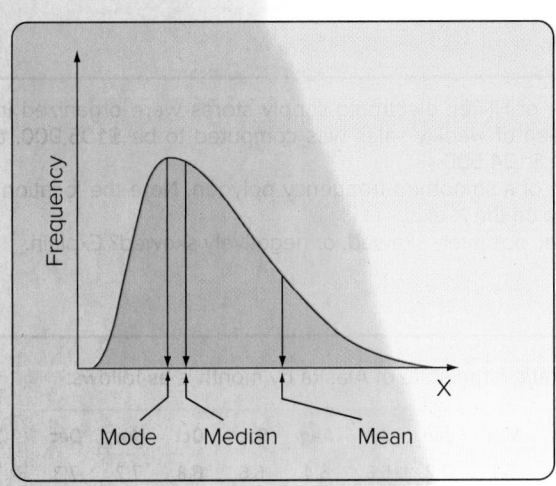

CHART 3–4 A Positively Skewed Distribution

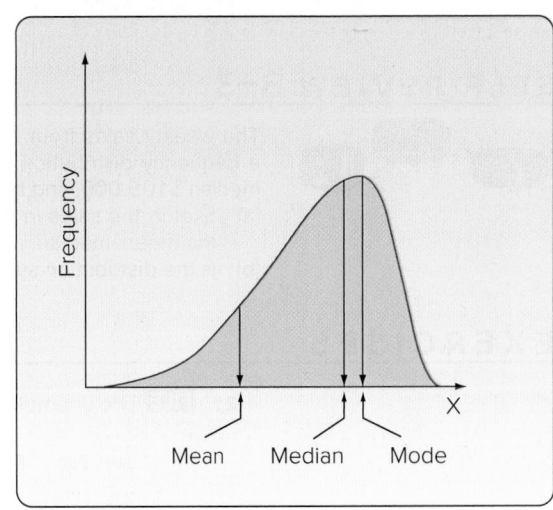

CHART 3–5 A Negatively Skewed Distribution

G. G. Green Manufacturing reviewed the employment records of the most recent 45 retirees and recorded their ages when they retired. The frequency distribution shows one employee retired at 58 years of age followed by two to three employees for ages

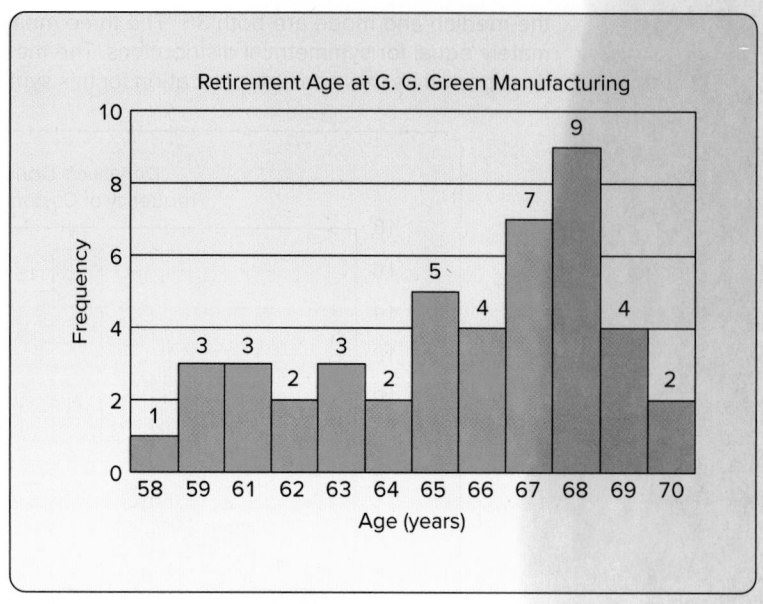

59 through 64. The majority of employees waited until the age of 65 or older to retire. This distribution is skewed to the left and would be described as negatively skewed. Reviewing Chart 3–5, we would expect the values of the mean, median, and mode to be different. From the frequency distribution, the mode is 68 years of age. Knowing that the distribution summarizes 45 employees, the value of the median would be the age of the 23rd employee in a sorted list of employees. Using the frequency distribution, we know that the 23rd employee would be in the age class of 66, so the median is 66. The median also indicates that 50% of employees retired between 58 and 66 years of age, and 50% retired between years 66 and 70. The computed mean is 65.4 years of age. The numerical order of the mean, median, and mode (65.4 < 66 < 68) matches the negatively skewed shape of the distribution. Reporting all measures of location provides complete information about the distribution of retirement age.

SELF-REVIEW 3–3

The weekly sales from a sample of Hi-Tec electronic supply stores were organized into a frequency distribution. The mean of weekly sales was computed to be $105,900, the median $105,000, and the mode $104,500.
(a) Sketch the sales in the form of a smoothed frequency polygon. Note the location of the mean, median, and mode on the X-axis.
(b) Is the distribution symmetrical, positively skewed, or negatively skewed? Explain.

EXERCISES

21. **FILE** The unemployment rate in the state of Alaska by month is as follows:

Jan	Feb	Mar	Apr	May	Jun	Jul	Aug	Sep	Oct	Nov	Dec
7.8	7.9	7.7	7.3	7.1	7.2	6.6	6.4	6.6	6.8	7.2	7.3

a. What is the arithmetic mean of the Alaska unemployment rates?
b. Find the median and the mode for the unemployment rates.
c. Compute the arithmetic mean and median for just the winter (Dec–Mar) months. Is it much different?

22. FILE Big Orange Trucking is designing an information system for use in "in-cab" communications. It must summarize data from eight sites throughout a region to describe typical conditions. Compute an appropriate measure of central location for the variables wind direction, temperature, and pavement.

City	Wind Direction	Temperature	Pavement
Anniston, AL	West	89	Dry
Atlanta, GA	Northwest	86	Wet
Augusta, GA	Southwest	92	Wet
Birmingham, AL	South	91	Dry
Jackson, MS	Southwest	92	Dry
Meridian, MS	South	92	Trace
Monroe, LA	Southwest	93	Wet
Tuscaloosa, AL	Southwest	93	Trace

LO3-2

Compute a weighted mean.

The Weighted Mean

The weighted mean is a convenient way to compute the arithmetic mean when there are several observations of the same value. To explain, suppose the nearby Wendy's Restaurant sold medium, large, and biggie-sized soft drinks for $1.84, $2.07, and $2.40, respectively. Of the last 10 drinks sold, 3 were medium, 4 were large, and 3 were biggie-sized. To find the mean price of the last 10 drinks sold, we could use formula (3–2).

$$\bar{x} = \frac{(\$1.84 + \$1.84 + \$1.84) + (\$2.07 + \$2.07 + \$2.07 + \$2.07) + (\$2.40 + \$2.40 + \$2.40)}{10}$$

$$\bar{x} = \frac{\$21.00}{10} = \$2.10$$

The mean selling price of the last 10 drinks is $2.10.

An easier way to find the mean selling price is to determine the weighted mean. That is, we multiply each observation by the number of times it occurs. We will refer to the weighted mean as $\bar{x}_w$. This is read "x bar sub w."

$$\bar{x}_w = \frac{3(\$1.84) + 4(\$2.07) + 3(\$2.40)}{10} = \frac{\$21.00}{10} = \$2.10$$

In this case, the weights are frequency counts for each value. However, any measure of importance could be used as a weight. In general, the weighted mean of a set of numbers designated $x_1, x_2, x_3, \ldots, x_n$ with the corresponding weights $w_1, w_2, w_3, \ldots, w_n$ is computed by:

WEIGHTED MEAN	$\bar{x}_w = \dfrac{w_1x_1 + w_2x_2 + w_3x_3 + \cdots + w_nx_n}{w_1 + w_2 + w_3 + \cdots + w_n}$	**(3–3)**

This may be shortened to:

$$\bar{x}_w = \frac{\Sigma(wx)}{\Sigma w}$$

Note that the denominator of a weighted mean is always the sum of the weights.

EXAMPLE

The Carter Construction Company pays its hourly employees $16.50, $19.00, or $25.00 per hour. There are 26 hourly employees; 14 employees are paid at the $16.50 rate, 10 at the $19.00 rate, and 2 at the $25.00 rate. What is the mean hourly rate paid to the 26 employees?

SOLUTION

To find the mean hourly rate, we multiply each of the hourly rates by the number of employees earning that rate. From formula (3–3), the mean hourly rate is:

$$\bar{x}_w = \frac{14(\$16.50) + 10(\$19.00) + 2(\$25.00)}{14 + 10 + 2} = \frac{\$471.00}{26} = \$18.1154$$

The weighted mean hourly wage is rounded to $18.12.

SELF-REVIEW 3–4

Springers sold 95 Antonelli men's suits for the regular price of $400. For the spring sale, the suits were reduced to $200 and 126 were sold. At the final clearance, the price was reduced to $100 and the remaining 79 suits were sold.
(a)   What was the weighted mean price of an Antonelli suit?
(b)   Springers paid $200 a suit for the 300 suits. Comment on the store's profit per suit if a salesperson receives a $25 commission for each one sold.

EXERCISES

23. In June, an investor purchased 300 shares of Oracle (an information technology company) stock at $65 per share. In August, she purchased an additional 400 shares at $90 per share. In November, she purchased an additional 400 shares at $80. What is the weighted mean price per share?

24. The Bookstall Inc. is a specialty bookstore concentrating on used books sold via the Internet. Paperbacks are $1.00 each, and hardcover books are $3.50. Of the 50 books sold last Tuesday morning, 40 were paperback and the rest were hardcover. What was the weighted mean price of a book?

25. The Loris Healthcare System employs 200 persons on the nursing staff. Fifty are nurse's aides, 50 are practical nurses, and 100 are registered nurses. Nurse's aides receive $12 an hour, practical nurses $20 an hour, and registered nurses $29 an hour. What is the weighted mean hourly wage?

26. Bouchard and Associates specialize in corporate law. They charge $100 an hour for researching a case, $75 an hour for consultations, and $200 an hour for writing a brief. Last week one of the associates spent 10 hours consulting with a client, 10 hours researching the case, and 20 hours writing the brief. What was the weighted mean hourly charge for the associate's legal services?

LO3-3

Compute and interpret the geometric mean.

The Geometric Mean

The geometric mean is useful in finding average rates of change over time. The rates can be expressed as percentages, ratios, or indexes. A percentage change is expressed as (1.0 + %change). If $1,000 has a positive 7% change, then $1,000 increases to $1,000(1.0 + 0.07) = $1,070. If $1,000 has a negative 4% change, then $1,000 decreases to $1,000(1.0 − 0.04) = $960.

The geometric mean has wide application in business and economics because we are often interested in finding the percentage change over time in sales, salaries, or economic figures, such as the gross domestic product. The geometric mean of a set of n positive numbers is computed as the nth root of the product of n values. The formula for the geometric mean is written:

GEOMETRIC MEAN	$GM = \sqrt[n]{(x_1)(x_2) \cdots (x_n)}$	(3–4)

The geometric mean will always be less than or equal to (never more than) the arithmetic mean. Also, all the data values must be positive.

To show how the geometric and arithmetic means differ, suppose that your monthly salary was $3,000. Then 3 months later you received a 5% increase, then 3 months later you received a 15% increase. The result of each raise follows:

Raise 1: $3,000(1 + 0.05) = $3,1500.00, which is $150 more than $3,000

Followed by:

Raise 2: $3,150(1 + 0.15) = $3,622.50, which is $472.50 more than $3,150

Overall, your monthly salary increased $622.50.

To calculate the average percent increase over time, you might average 5% and 15% and say that your average percent increase was 10%. Then, your two adjusted salaries would be

Raise 1: $3,000(1 + 0.10) = $3,300.00

Followed by:

Raise 2: $3,300(1 + 0.10) = $3,630.00

Using an arithmetic mean increase of 10%, the total increase is $630; this is not correct. This average does not account for the sequential timing of the raises. In this case, the geometric mean must be used to compute the average percent increase:

$$GM = \sqrt[2]{(1.05)(1.15)} = 1.09886$$

The average percent increase in salary is (1.09886 – 1.0) = 0.09886 or 9.886%.

So, using the geometric mean of 9.886% we can correctly calculate the salary after the second raise as:

Raise 1: $3,000.00(1.09886) = $3,296.58

Raise 2: $3,296.59(1.09886) = $3,622.50

The following example shows the geometric mean of several annual percent changes.

▶ **EXAMPLE**

The return on investment (ROI) earned by Atkins Construction Company for four successive years was 30%, 20%, −40%, and 200%. What is the average annual percentage return on investment?

SOLUTION

First, each ROI percentage should be converted to values representing increases or decreases. A positive 30% ROI is a 1.30 increase; a positive 20% ROI is a 1.20

increase; a negative 40% ROI is a 0.60 decrease; a positive 200% ROI is a 3.00 increase.

The geometric mean assumes the total return each period is reinvested and becomes the base for the next period. Then the geometric mean rate of return is 29.4%, found by:

$$GM = \sqrt[4]{(1.30)(1.20)(0.60)(3.00)} = \sqrt[4]{2.808} = 1.294$$

The geometric mean is the fourth root of 2.808. So, the average annual percent change in ROI is (1.294 − 1.000) or 29.4%. Notice also that if you compute the arithmetic mean ROI [(30% + 20% − 40% + 200%)/4 = 52.5%], you would have a much larger number, which would overstate the true rate of return! The tutorial referenced in the margin shows how to compute the geometric mean from a series of percentages.

Tutorial #16
in Connect

A second application of the geometric mean is based on the beginning and ending values over a specified time period. For example, if you earned $45,000 in 2010 and $100,000 in 2022, what is your average annual percentage rate of increase? The rate of increase is determined by the following formula. In this case, n is the number of years over the period, 2010 and 2022, and is equal to 12.

RATE OF INCREASE OVER TIME $GM = \sqrt[n]{\dfrac{\text{Value at end of period}}{\text{Value at start of period}}} - 1$ **(3–5)**

Applying the geometric mean, the value at the start of the period is $45,000; the value at the end of the period is $100,000; n is 12.

$$GM = \sqrt[12]{\frac{\$100,000}{\$45,000}} - 1 = \sqrt[12]{2.222} - 1 = 1.0688 - 1 = 6.88\%$$

The average annual percentage increase is 6.88%.

▶ **EXAMPLE**

According to the United Nations, Africa is the fastest growing continent. The fastest growing African city is Gwagwalada, Nigeria. In 2011, its population was 189,000; in 2021 its population increased to 443,000. What is the average annual percent growth rate over this time?

SOLUTION

The beginning value is 189,000 people in 2011; the ending value is 443,000 people in 2021. There are 10 years between 2011 and 2021, so $n = 10$. Then the geometric mean formula (3–5) is applied:

$$GM = \sqrt[10]{\frac{443,000}{189,000}} - 1 = \sqrt[10]{2.344} - 1 = 1.0889 - 1 = 8.90\%$$

The annual rate of Gwagwalada's population growth between 2011 and 2021 is 8.90%.

SELF-REVIEW 3-5

1. The percent increases in sales for the last 4 years at Combs Cosmetics were 4.91, 5.75, 8.12, and 21.60.
   (a) Find the geometric mean annual percent increase.
   (b) Find the arithmetic mean annual percent increase.
   (c) Is the arithmetic mean equal to or greater than the geometric mean?
2. Production of Cablos trucks increased from 23,000 units in 2012 to 120,520 in 2022. Find the geometric mean annual percent increase.

EXERCISES

27. Compute the geometric mean of the following monthly percent increases: 8, 12, 14, 26, and 5.
28. Compute the geometric mean of the following weekly percent increases: 2, 8, 6, 4, 10, 6, 8, and 4.
29. Listed here is the percent increase in sales for the MG Corporation over the last 5 years. Determine the geometric mean percent increase in sales over the period.

9.4	13.8	11.7	11.9	14.7

30. You have funds invested in a mutual fund of S&P 500 stocks. Over the last 5 years, the annual percent returns of the S&P 500 are 19.42%, − 6.24%, 28.88%, 16.26%, and 14.49%. What is the average annual percent return on the S&P 500 stocks over the last 5 years?
31. You currently have $10,000 invested. If your goal is to increase this investment to $1,000,000 in 30 years, what annual percent growth rate would be needed?
32. In 2014, 125,821,000 taxpayers in the United States filed their individual tax returns electronically. By the year 2019, the number increased to 151,812,000. What is the geometric mean annual increase for the period?
33. The Consumer Price Index is reported monthly by the U.S. Bureau of Labor Statistics. It reports the change in prices for a market basket of goods from one period to another. The index for 2010 was 213.967. By 2020, it increased to 260.474. What was the geometric mean annual increase for the period?
34. JetBlue Airways is an American low-cost airline headquartered in New York City. Its main base is John F. Kennedy International Airport. JetBlue's revenue in 2015 was $6.416 billion. In 2020, the COVID pandemic caused revenue to decrease to $2.957 billion. What was the geometric mean annual revenue change for the period?
35. In 2010, there were 232.2 million cell phone subscribers in the United States. By 2020, the number of subscribers increased to 276.7 million.
   a. What is the geometric mean annual percent increase for the period?
   b. Using the annual percent increase, forecast the number of cell phone users in 2022.
36. The table shows the average annual tuition and fees for public and private colleges in 2011–2012 and 2021–2022. For the period between 2011–2012 and 2021–2022, what is the annual rate of change in the cost to attend each type of college? Compare the rates.

Type of College	2011–2012	2021–2022
Public (four-year)	$ 8,244	$10,338
Private (four-year)	$28,500	$38,185

LO3-4
Compute and interpret
the range, variance, and
standard deviation.

STATISTICS IN ACTION

The U.S. Postal Service has tried to become more "user friendly" in the last several years. A recent survey showed that customers were interested in more *consistency* in the time it takes to make a delivery. Under the old conditions, a local letter might take only 1 day to deliver, or it might take several. "Just tell me how many days ahead I need to mail the birthday card to Mom so it gets there on her birthday, not early, not late," was a common complaint. The level of consistency is measured by the standard deviation of the delivery times.

Why Study Dispersion?

A measure of location, such as the mean, median, or mode, only describes the center of the data. It is valuable from that standpoint, but it does not tell us anything about the spread of the data. For example, if your nature guide told you that the river ahead averaged 3 feet in depth, would you want to wade across on foot without additional information? Probably not. You would want to know something about the variation in the depth. Is the maximum depth of the river 3.25 feet and the minimum 2.75 feet? If that is the case, you would probably agree to cross. What if you learned the river depth ranged from 0.50 foot to 5.5 feet? Your decision probably would be not to cross. Before making a decision about crossing the river, you want information on both the typical depth and the dispersion in the depth of the river.

A reason to study dispersion is to compare the spread in two or more distributions. Suppose, for example, that the new Vision Quest LCD computer monitor is assembled in Baton Rouge and also in Tucson. The arithmetic mean hourly output in both the Baton Rouge plant and the Tucson plant is 50. Based on the two means, you might conclude that the distributions of the hourly outputs are identical. Production records for 9 hours at the two plants, however, reveal that this conclusion is not correct (Chart 3–6). Baton Rouge production varies from 48 to 52 assemblies per hour. Production at the Tucson plant is more erratic, ranging from 40 to 60 per hour. Therefore, the hourly output for Baton Rouge is clustered near the mean of 50; the hourly output for Tucson is more dispersed.

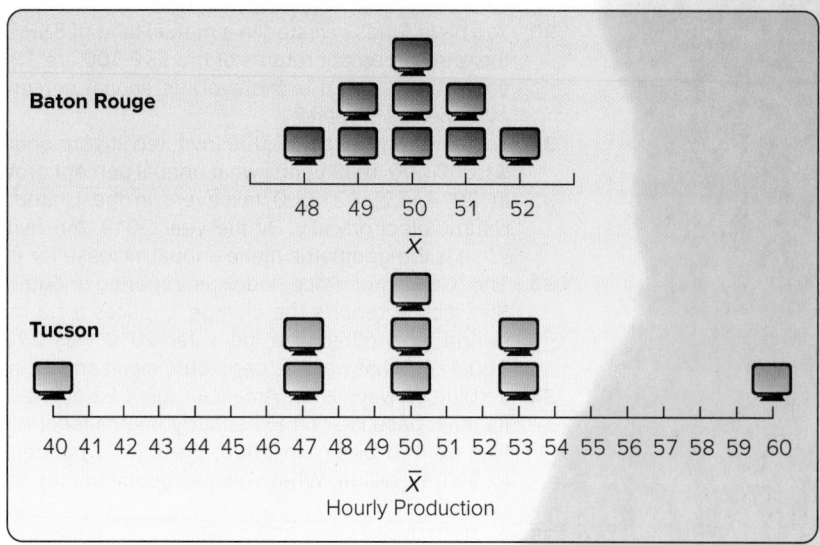

CHART 3–6 Hourly Production of Computer Monitors at the Baton Rouge and Tucson Plants

We will consider several measures of dispersion. The range is based on the maximum and minimum values in the data set; that is, only two values are considered. The variance and the standard deviation use all the values in a data set and are based on deviations from the arithmetic mean.

Range

The simplest measure of dispersion is the **range.** It is the difference between the maximum and minimum values in a data set. Note that sometimes the range is interpreted as an interval. For example, the age of high school students ranges between 12 and 20 years. In statistics, the range of ages would be 8 and calculated as follows:

| **RANGE** | Range = Maximum value − Minimum Value | **(3–6)** |

The range is widely used in production management and control applications because it is very easy to calculate and understand.

▶ **EXAMPLE**

Refer to Chart 3–6. Find the range in the number of computer monitors produced per hour for the Baton Rouge and the Tucson plants. Interpret the two ranges.

SOLUTION

The range of the hourly production of computer monitors at the Baton Rouge plant is 4, found by the difference between the maximum hourly production of 52 and the minimum of 48. The range in the hourly production for the Tucson plant is 20 computer monitors, found by 60 − 40. We therefore conclude that there is less dispersion in the hourly production in the Baton Rouge plant than in the Tucson plant because the range of 4 computer monitors is less than a range of 20 computer monitors.

Variance

A limitation of the range is that it is based on only two values, the maximum and the minimum; it does not take into consideration all of the values. The **variance** does. It measures the mean amount by which the values in a population, or sample, vary from their mean. In terms of a definition:

> **VARIANCE** The arithmetic mean of the squared deviations from the mean.

The following example illustrates how the variance is used to measure dispersion.

▶ **EXAMPLE**

The chart here shows the number of cappuccinos sold at the Starbucks in the Orange County airport and the Ontario, California, airport between 4 and 5 p.m. for a sample of 5 days last month.

California Airports	
Orange County	**Ontario**
20	20
40	45
50	50
60	55
80	80

Source: Microsoft Excel

Sorbis/Shutterstock

Determine the mean, median, range, and variance for each location. Comment on the similarities and differences in these measures.

SOLUTION

The mean, median, and range for each of the airport locations are reported as part of an Excel spreadsheet.

◢	A	B	C
1		California Airports	
2		Orange County	Ontario
3		20	20
4		40	45
5		50	50
6		60	55
7		80	80
8			
9	Mean	50	50
10	Median	50	50
11	Range	60	60

Source: Microsoft Excel

Notice that all three of the measures are exactly the same. Does this indicate that there is no difference in the two sets of data? We get a clearer picture if we calculate the variance. First, for Orange County:

F	G	H
Calculation of Variance for Orange County		
Number Sold	Each Value - Mean	Squared Deviation
20	20 - 50 = -30	900
40	40 - 50 = -10	100
50	50 - 50 = 0	0
60	60 - 50 = 10	100
80	80 - 50 = 30	900
	Total	2000

Source: Microsoft Excel

$$\text{Variance} = \frac{\Sigma(x - \mu)^2}{N} = \frac{(-30^2) + (-10^2) + 0^2 + 10^2 + 30^2}{5} = \frac{2,000}{5} = 400$$

The variance is 400. That is, the average squared deviation from the mean is 400.

The following shows the detail of determining the variance for the number of cappuccinos sold at the Ontario Airport.

Calculation of Variance for Ontario		
Number Sold	Each Value - Mean	Squared Deviation
20	20 - 50 = -30	900
45	45 - 50 = -5	25
50	50 - 50 = 0	0
55	55 - 50 = 5	25
80	80 - 50 = 30	900
	Total	1850

Source: Microsoft Excel

$$\text{Variance} = \frac{\Sigma(x - \mu)^2}{N} = \frac{(-30^2) + (-5^2) + 0^2 + 5^2 + 30^2}{5} = \frac{1,850}{5} = 370$$

So the mean, median, and range of the cappuccinos sold are the same at the two airports, but the variances are different. The variance at Orange County is 400, but it is 370 at Ontario.

Let's interpret and compare the results of our measures for the two Starbucks airport locations. The mean and median of the two locations are exactly the same, 50 cappuccinos sold. These measures of location suggest the two distributions are the same. The range for both locations is also the same, 60. However, recall that the range provides limited information about the dispersion because it is based on only two values, the minimum and maximum.

The variances are not the same for the two Starbucks stores. The variance is based on the differences between each observation and the arithmetic mean. It shows the closeness or clustering of the data relative to the mean or center of the distribution. Compare the variance for Orange County of 400 to the variance for Ontario of 370. Based on the variance, we conclude that the dispersion for the sales distribution of the Ontario Starbucks is more concentrated—that is, nearer the mean of 50—than for the Orange County location.

The variance has an important advantage over the range. It uses all the values in the computation. Recall that the range uses only the highest and the lowest values.

SELF-REVIEW 3–6

The weights of containers being shipped to Ireland are (in thousands of pounds):

| 95 | 103 | 105 | 110 | 104 | 105 | 112 | 90 |

(a) What is the range of the weights?
(b) Compute the arithmetic mean weight.
(c) Compute the variance of the weights.

EXERCISES

For Exercises 37–42, calculate the (a) range, (b) arithmetic mean, (c) variance, and (d) interpret the statistics.

37. **FILE** During last weekend's sale, there were five customer service representatives on duty at the Electronic Super Store. The numbers of HDTVs these representatives sold were 5, 8, 4, 10, and 3.

38. **FILE** The Department of Statistics at Western State University offers eight sections of basic statistics. Following are the numbers of students enrolled in these sections: 34, 46, 52, 29, 41, 38, 36, and 28.

39. **FILE** Dave's Automatic Door installs automatic garage door openers. The following list indicates the number of minutes needed to install 10 door openers: 28, 32, 24, 46, 44, 40, 54, 38, 32, and 42.

40. **FILE** All eight companies in the aerospace industry were surveyed as to their return on investment last year. The results are: 10.6%, 12.6%, 14.8%, 18.2%, 12.0%, 14.8%, 12.2%, and 15.6%.

41. **FILE** Ten young adults living in California rated the taste of a newly developed sushi pizza topped with tuna, rice, and kelp on a scale of 1 to 50, with 1 indicating they did not like the taste and 50 that they did. The ratings were:

| 34 | 39 | 40 | 46 | 33 | 31 | 34 | 14 | 15 | 45 |

In a parallel study, 10 young adults in Iowa rated the taste of the same pizza. The ratings were:

| 28 | 25 | 35 | 16 | 25 | 29 | 24 | 26 | 17 | 20 |

As a market researcher, compare the potential for sushi pizza in the two markets.

42. **FILE** The personnel files of all eight employees at the Pawnee location of Acme Carpet Cleaners Inc. revealed that during the last 6-month period they lost the following number of days due to illness:

| 2 | 0 | 6 | 3 | 10 | 4 | 1 | 2 |

> All eight employees during the same period at the Chickpee location of Acme Carpets revealed they lost the following number of days due to illness:
>
> | 2 | 0 | 1 | 0 | 5 | 0 | 1 | 0 |
> |---|---|---|---|---|---|---|---|
>
> As the director of human resources, compare the two locations. What would you recommend?

Population Variance

In the previous example, we developed the concept of variance as a measure of dispersion. Similar to the mean, we can calculate the variance of a population or the variance of a sample. The formula to compute the population variance is:

POPULATION VARIANCE	$\sigma^2 = \dfrac{\Sigma(x - \mu)^2}{N}$	**(3–7)**

where:

σ^2 is the population variance (σ is the lowercase Greek letter sigma). It is read as "sigma squared."
x is the value of a particular observation in the population.
μ is the arithmetic mean of the population.
N is the number of observations in the population.

The process for computing the variance is implied by the formula.

1. Begin by finding the mean.
2. Find the difference between each observation and the mean, and square that difference.
3. Sum all the squared differences.
4. Divide the sum of the squared differences by the number of items in the population.

So the population variance is the mean of the squared difference between each value and the mean. For populations whose values are near the mean, the variance will be small. For populations whose values are dispersed from the mean, the population variance will be large.

The variance overcomes the weakness of the range by using all the values in the population, whereas the range uses only the maximum and minimum values. We overcome the issue where $\Sigma(x - \mu) = 0$ by squaring the differences. Squaring the differences will always result in nonnegative values. The following is another example that illustrates the calculation and interpretation of the variance.

▶ **EXAMPLE**

The number of traffic citations issued last year by month in Beaufort County, South Carolina, is reported as:

						Citations by Month					
January	February	March	April	May	June	July	August	September	October	November	December
19	17	22	18	28	34	45	39	38	44	34	10

Determine the population variance.

SOLUTION

Because we are studying all the citations for a year, the data comprise a population. To determine the population variance, we use formula (3–7). This table details the calculations.

Month	Citations (x)	$x - \mu$	$(x - \mu)^2$
January	19	−10	100
February	17	−12	144
March	22	−7	49
April	18	−11	121
May	28	−1	1
June	34	5	25
July	45	16	256
August	39	10	100
September	38	9	81
October	44	15	225
November	34	5	25
December	10	−19	361
Total	348	0	1,488

1. We begin by determining the arithmetic mean of the population. The total number of citations issued for the year is 348, so the mean number issued per month is 29.

$$\mu = \frac{\Sigma x}{N} = \frac{19 + 17 + \cdots + 10}{12} = \frac{348}{12} = 29$$

2. Next we find the difference between each observation and the mean. This is shown in the third column of the table. The sum of the differences between the mean and the number of citations each month is 0. This outcome illustrates the principle that for any interval or ratio variable, the deviations or differences of the individual values from the mean always sum to zero.

3. The next step is to square the difference for each month. That is shown in the fourth column of the table. All the squared differences will be positive. Note that squaring a negative value, or multiplying a negative value by itself, always results in a positive value.

4. The squared differences are totaled. The total of the fourth column is 1,488. That is the term $\Sigma(x - \mu)^2$.

5. Finally, we divide the squared differences by N, the number of observations in the population.

$$\sigma^2 = \frac{\Sigma(x - \sigma)^2}{N} = \frac{1,488}{12} = 124$$

So, the population variance for the number of citations is 124.

Like the range, the variance can be used to compare the dispersion in two or more sets of observations. For example, the variance for the number of citations issued in Beaufort County was just computed to be 124. If the variance in the number of citations issued in Marlboro County, South Carolina, is 342.9, we conclude that (1) there is less dispersion in the distribution of the number of citations issued in Beaufort County than in Marlboro County (because 124 is less than 342.9), and (2) the number of citations in Beaufort County is more closely clustered around the mean of 29 than for the number of citations issued in Marlboro County. Thus the mean number of citations issued in Beaufort County is a more representative measure of location than the mean number of citations in Marlboro County.

Population Standard Deviation

When we compute the variance, it is important to understand the unit of measure and what happens when the differences in the numerator are squared. That is, in the previous example, the number of monthly citations is the variable. When we calculate the variance, the unit of measure for the variance is citations squared. Using "squared citations" as a unit of measure is difficult to interpret.

There is a way out of this difficulty. By taking the square root of the population variance, we can transform it to the same unit of measurement used for the original data. The square root of 124 citations squared is 11.14 citations. The units are now simply citations. The square root of the population variance is the **population standard deviation.**

POPULATION STANDARD DEVIATION	$\sigma = \sqrt{\dfrac{\Sigma(x - \mu)^2}{N}}$	**(3–8)**

SELF-REVIEW 3-7

The Philadelphia office of PricewaterhouseCoopers hired five accounting trainees this year. Their monthly starting salaries were $3,536; $3,173; $3,448; $3,121; and $3,622.
(a) Compute the population mean.
(b) Compute the population variance.
(c) Compute the population standard deviation.
(d) The Pittsburgh office hired six trainees. Their mean monthly salary was $3,550, and the standard deviation was $250. Compare the two groups.

EXERCISES

43. Consider these five values a population: 8, 3, 7, 3, and 4.
   a. Determine the mean of the population.
   b. Determine the variance.

44. Consider these six values a population: 13, 3, 8, 10, 8, and 6.
   a. Determine the mean of the population.
   b. Determine the variance.

45. The annual report of Dennis Industries cited these primary earnings per common share for the past 5 years: $2.68, $1.03, $2.26, $4.30, and $3.58. If we assume these are population values, what is:
   a. the arithmetic mean primary earnings per share of common stock?
   b. the variance?

46. Referring to Exercise 45, the annual report of Dennis Industries also gave these gross profits ($1,000) for the same 5-year period: 13.2, 5.0, 10.2, 17.5, and 12.9.
   a. What is the arithmetic mean gross profit?
   b. What is the variance?

47. Plywood Inc. reported these gross profits ($1,000) for the past 5 years: 4.3, 4.9, 7.2, 6.7, and 11.6. Consider these as population values.
   a. Compute the range, the arithmetic mean, the variance, and the standard deviation.
   b. Compare the gross profits ($1,000) for Plywood Inc. with that for Dennis Industries cited in Exercise 46.

48. The annual incomes of the five vice presidents of TMV Industries are $125,000; $128,000; $122,000; $133,000; and $140,000. Consider this a population.
   a. What is the range?
   b. What is the arithmetic mean income?
   c. What is the population variance? The standard deviation?
   d. The annual incomes of officers of another firm similar to TMV Industries were also studied. The mean was $129,000 and the standard deviation $8,612. Compare the means and dispersions in the two firms.

Sample Variance and Standard Deviation

The formula for the population mean is $\mu = \Sigma x/N$. We just changed the symbols for the sample mean; that is, $\bar{x} = \Sigma x/n$. Unfortunately, the conversion from the population variance to the sample variance is not as direct. It requires a change in the denominator. Instead of substituting n (number in the sample) for N (number in the population), the denominator is $n - 1$. Thus the formula for the **sample variance** is:

SAMPLE VARIANCE	$s^2 = \dfrac{\Sigma(x - \bar{x})^2}{n - 1}$	(3–9)

where:

s^2 is the sample variance.
x is the value of each observation in the sample.
$\bar{x}$ is the mean of the sample.
n is the number of observations in the sample.

Why is this change made in the denominator? Although the use of n is logical since $\bar{x}$ is used to estimate μ, it tends to underestimate the population variance, σ^2. The use of $(n - 1)$ in the denominator provides the appropriate correction for this tendency. Because the primary use of sample statistics like s^2 is to estimate population parameters like σ^2, $(n - 1)$ is used instead of n in defining the sample variance. We also will use this convention when computing the sample standard deviation.

▶ **EXAMPLE**

The hourly wages for a sample of part-time employees at Pickett's Hardware Store are $12, $20, $16, $18, and $19. What is the sample variance?

SOLUTION

The sample variance is computed by using formula (3–9). First, we compute the sample mean. Then we complete the following table by computing the squared deviations from the sample mean. Last, sum the squared deviations and divide by $(n - 1)$.

$$\bar{x} = \frac{\Sigma x}{n} = \frac{\$85}{5} = \$17$$

Hourly Wage (x)	$x - \bar{x}$	$(x - \bar{x})^2$
$12	−$5	25
20	3	9
16	−1	1
18	1	1
19	2	4
$85	0	40

$$s^2 = \frac{\Sigma(x - \bar{x})^2}{n - 1} = \frac{40}{5 - 1}$$

$$= 10 \text{ in dollars squared}$$

The sample standard deviation is used as an estimator of the population standard deviation. As noted previously, the population standard deviation is the square root of the population variance. Likewise, the *sample standard deviation is the square root of the sample variance.* The sample standard deviation is determined by:

> **SAMPLE STANDARD DEVIATION** $s = \sqrt{\dfrac{\Sigma(x - \bar{x})^2}{n - 1}}$ **(3–10)**

▶ **EXAMPLE**

The sample variance in the previous example involving hourly wages was computed to be 10. What is the sample standard deviation?

SOLUTION

The sample standard deviation is computed using formula (3–10).

$$s = \sqrt{\frac{\Sigma(x - \bar{x})^2}{n - 1}} = \sqrt{\frac{40}{5 - 1}} = \sqrt{10}$$

$$= 3.16 \text{ dollars}$$

Note again that by taking the square root of the variance, the units of the standard deviation is in the same units, dollars, as the original data.

Software Solution

On page 64, we used Excel to determine the mean, median, and mode of profit for the Applewood Auto Group data. You also will note that it lists the sample variance and sample standard deviation. Excel, like most other statistical software, assumes the data are from a sample. See the Tutorial to learn how to use Excel to compute the list of descriptive statistics.

Tutorial #20
in Connect

	A	B	C	D	E	F	G	H
1	Age	Profit	Location	Vehicle-Type	Previous		*Profit*	
2	21	$1,387	Tionesta	Sedan	0			
3	23	$1,754	Sheffield	SUV	1		Mean	1843.17
4	24	$1,817	Sheffield	Hybrid	1		Standard Error	47.97
5	25	$1,040	Sheffield	Compact	0		Median	1882.50
6	26	$1,273	Kane	Sedan	1		Mode	1761.00
7	27	$1,529	Sheffield	Sedan	1		Standard Deviation	643.63
8	27	$3,082	Kane	Truck	0		Sample Variance	414256.60
9	28	$1,951	Kane	SUV	1		Kurtosis	-0.22
10	28	$2,692	Tionesta	Compact	0		Skewness	-0.24
11	29	$1,206	Sheffield	Sedan	0		Range	2998.00
12	29	$1,342	Kane	Sedan	2		Minimum	294.00
13	30	$443	Kane	Sedan	3		Maximum	3292.00
14	30	$754	Olean	Sedan	2		Sum	331770.00
15	30	$1,621	Sheffield	Truck	1		Count	180.00

Source: Microsoft Excel

SELF-REVIEW 3–8

The years of service for a sample of seven employees at a State Farm Insurance claims office in Cleveland, Ohio, are 4, 2, 5, 4, 5, 2, and 6. What is the sample variance? Compute the sample standard deviation.

EXERCISES

For Exercises 49–54, do the following:
   a. Compute the sample variance.
   b. Determine the sample standard deviation.

49. Consider these values a sample: 7, 2, 6, 2, and 3.
50. The following five values are a sample: 15, 7, 12, 8, and 8.
51. **FILE** Dave's Automatic Door, referred to in Exercise 39, installs automatic garage door openers. Based on a sample, following are the times, in minutes, required to install 10 door openers: 28, 32, 24, 46, 44, 40, 54, 38, 32, and 42.
52. **FILE** The sample of eight companies in the aerospace industry, referred to in Exercise 40, was surveyed as to their return on investment last year. The results are 10.6, 12.6, 14.8, 18.2, 12.0, 14.8, 12.2, and 15.6.
53. **FILE** The Houston, Texas, Motel Owner Association conducted a survey regarding weekday motel rates in the area. Listed are the room rates for business-class guests for a sample of 10 motels.

| $101 | $97 | $103 | $110 | $78 | $87 | $101 | $80 | $106 | $88 |

54. **FILE** A consumer watchdog organization is concerned about credit card debt. A survey of 10 young adults with credit card debt of more than $2,000 showed they paid an average of just over $100 per month against their balances. Listed are the amounts each young adult paid last month.

| $110 | $126 | $103 | $93 | $99 | $113 | $87 | $101 | $109 | $100 |

LO3-5

Explain and apply Chebyshev's theorem and the Empirical Rule.

Interpretation and Uses of the Standard Deviation

The standard deviation is commonly used as a measure to compare the spread in two or more sets of observations. For example, the standard deviation of the biweekly amounts invested in the Dupree Paint Company profit-sharing plan is computed to be $7.51. Suppose these employees are located in Georgia. If the standard deviation for a group of employees in Texas is $10.47, and the means are about the same, it indicates that the amounts invested by the Georgia employees are not dispersed as much as those in Texas (because $7.51 < $10.47). Since the amounts invested by the Georgia employees are clustered more closely about the mean, the mean for the Georgia employees is a more reliable measure than the mean for the Texas group.

Chebyshev's Theorem

We have stressed that data values with a small standard deviation are located relatively close to the mean. Conversely, data values with a large standard deviation are widely scattered about the mean. The Russian mathematician P. L. Chebyshev (1821–1894) developed **Chebyshev's theorem** that better defines the dispersion of data around the mean. It computes the minimum proportion of data set values that lie within a specified number of standard deviations of the mean. The theorem applies regardless of the distribution's shape. Chebyshev's theorem states:

> **CHEBYSHEV'S THEOREM** For any set of observations (sample or population), the proportion of the values that lie within k standard deviations of the mean is at least $1 - 1/k^2$, where k is any value greater than 1.

For example, a data set has 100 observations; the mean and standard deviation for the data set are 10 and 1. We are interested in the proportion of the 100 observations that are within 2 standard deviations of the mean. The dispersion of values would be computed as 2 standard deviations less than the mean [10 −2(1)] and 2 standard deviations greater than the mean [10 + 2(1)]; the range is between 8 and 12. According to Chebyshev's theorem with $k = 2$ standard deviations, the proportion of the data set's values that lie between 8 and 12 is at least [1 − 1/(2)²], or 75%. Remember that 75% is a minimum proportion. The actual proportion could be more.

If we are interested in the proportion of data within 3 standard deviations of the mean, then $k = 3$ standard deviations. In this case, the proportion is [1 −1/(3)²] or 88.9%. For a data set with 500 observations, a minimum of 88.9%, or about 445 observations, are within plus or minus 3 standard deviations of the mean.

▶ **EXAMPLE**

Dupree Paint Company employees contribute a mean of $51.54 to the company's profit-sharing plan every 2 weeks. The standard deviation of biweekly contributions is $7.51. According to Chebyshev's theorem, at least what proportion of employees contribute between 3.5 standard deviations and minus 3.5 standard deviations of the mean, that is, between $25.26 and $77.83?

SOLUTION

In this case, $k = 3.5$ standard deviations, the computed proportion is:

$$1 - \frac{1}{k^2} = 1 - \frac{1}{3.5^2} = 1 - \frac{1}{12.25} = 0.92$$

If there are 100 employees, then at least 92 employees contributed between $25.26 and $77.83. There may be more than 92 employees in this group.

The Empirical Rule

Chebyshev's theorem applies to any set of values; that is, the distribution of values can have any shape. However, if the data have a symmetrical, bell-shaped distribution such as the one in Chart 3–7, we can be more precise in explaining the dispersion about the mean. These relationships involving the standard deviation and the mean are described by the **Empirical Rule**, sometimes called the **Normal Rule.**

> **EMPIRICAL RULE** For a symmetrical, bell-shaped frequency distribution, approximately 68% of the observations will lie within plus and minus 1 standard deviation of the mean, about 95% of the observations will lie within plus and minus 2 standard deviations of the mean, and practically all (99.7%) will lie within plus and minus 3 standard deviations of the mean.

These relationships are portrayed graphically in Chart 3–7 for a bell-shaped distribution with a mean of 100 and a standard deviation of 10.

Applying the Empirical Rule to the bell-shaped distribution in Chart 3–7, about 68% of the observations are within 1 standard deviation of the mean, that is 100 −1(10) and 100 + 1(10), or between 90 and 110. Approximately, 95% of the observations are within 2 standard deviations of the mean, that is 100 −2(10) and 100 + 2(10), or between 80 and 120. Nearly 99.7% of the observations are within 3 standard deviations of the mean, that is 100 −3(10) and 100 + 3(10), or between 70 and 130.

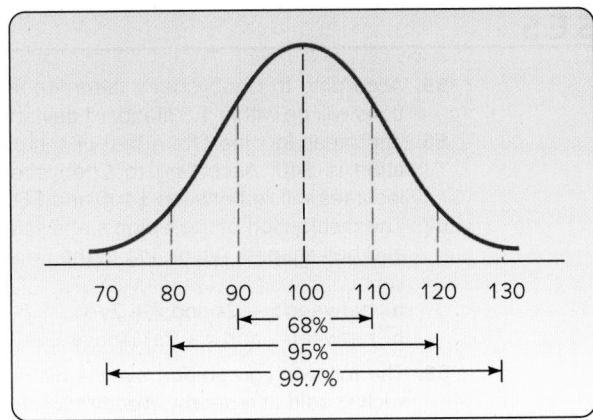

CHART 3–7 A Symmetrical, Bell-Shaped Curve Showing the Relationships between the Standard Deviation and the Percentage of Observations

The Empirical Rule can also be used to estimate a bell-shaped distribution's standard deviation. The rule states that nearly all observations (99.7%) are within 3 standard deviations of the mean. If we only know the range of the data, then we can estimate the standard deviation as the range divided by 6 (within 3 standard deviations of the mean). For example, if we know the range of a data set is 210 and assume that the data have a bell-shaped distribution, then the distribution's standard deviation is estimated as 210/6, or 35.

▶ **EXAMPLE**

The monthly apartment rental rates near Crawford State University approximate a symmetrical, bell-shaped distribution. The sample mean is $500; the standard deviation is $20. Using the Empirical Rule, answer these questions:

1. About 68% of the monthly rentals are between what two amounts?
2. About 95% of the monthly rentals are between what two amounts?
3. Almost all of the monthly rentals are between what two amounts?

SOLUTION

1. About 68% are between $480 and $520, found by $\bar{x} \pm 1s = \$500 \pm 1(\$20)$.
2. About 95% are between $460 and $540, found by $\bar{x} \pm 2s = \$500 \pm 2(\$20)$.
3. Almost all (99.7%) are between $440 and $560, found by $\bar{x} \pm 3s = \$500 \pm 3(\$20)$.

SELF-REVIEW 3–9

The Pitney Pipe Company is one of several domestic manufacturers of PVC pipe. The quality control department sampled 600 10-foot lengths. At a point 1 foot from the end of the pipe, they measured the outside diameter. The mean was 14.0 inches and the standard deviation 0.1 inch.

(a) If we do not know the shape of the distribution of outside pipe diameters, at least what percent of the observations will be between 13.85 inches and 14.15 inches?

(b) If we assume that the distribution of diameters is symmetrical and bell shaped, about 95% of the observations will be between what two values?

EXERCISES

55. According to Chebyshev's theorem, at least what percent of any set of observations will be within 1.8 standard deviations of the mean?

56. The mean income of a group of sample observations is $500; the standard deviation is $40. According to Chebyshev's theorem, at least what percent of the incomes will lie between $400 and $600?

57. The distribution of the weights of a sample of 1,400 cargo containers is symmetric and bell shaped. According to the Empirical Rule, what percent of the weights will lie:
   a. between $\bar{x} - 2s$ and $\bar{x} + 2s$?
   b. between $\bar{x}$ and $\bar{x} + 2s$? Above $\bar{x} + 2s$?

58. The following graph portrays the distribution of the number of spicy chicken sandwiches sold at a nearby Wendy's for the last 141 days. The mean number of sandwiches sold per day is 91.9 and the standard deviation is 4.67.

Sales

If we use the Empirical Rule, sales will be between what two values on 68% of the days? Sales will be between what two values on 95% of the days?

Ethics and Reporting Results

In Chapter 1, we discussed the ethical and unbiased reporting of statistical results. While you are learning how to organize, summarize, and interpret data using statistics, it also is important to understand statistics so that you can be an intelligent consumer of information.

In this chapter, we learned how to compute descriptive statistics. Specifically, we showed how to compute and interpret measures of location for a data set: the mean, median, and mode. We also discussed the advantages and disadvantages for each statistic. For example, if a real estate developer tells a client that the average home in a particular subdivision sold for $150,000, we assume that $150,000 is a representative selling price for all the homes. But suppose that the client also asks what the median sales price is, and the median is $60,000. Why was the developer only reporting the mean price? This information is extremely important to a person's decision making when buying a home. Knowing the advantages and disadvantages of the mean, median, and mode is important as we report statistics and as we use statistical information to make decisions.

We also learned how to compute measures of dispersion: range, variance, and standard deviation. Each of these statistics also has advantages and disadvantages. Remember that the range provides information about the overall spread of a distribution. However, it does not provide any information about how the data are clustered or concentrated around the mean of the distribution. As we learn more about statistics, we need to remember that when we use statistics we must maintain an independent and principled point of view. Any statistical report requires objective and honest communication of the results.

CHAPTER SUMMARY

I. A measure of location is a value used to describe the central tendency of a set of data.

   A. The arithmetic mean is the most widely reported measure of location.

      1. It is calculated by adding the values of the observations and dividing by the total number of observations.

         a. The formula for the population mean of ungrouped or raw data is

$$\mu = \frac{\Sigma x}{N} \tag{3-1}$$

         b. The formula for the sample mean is

$$\bar{x} = \frac{\Sigma x}{n} \tag{3-2}$$

      2. The major characteristics of the arithmetic mean are as follows:

         a. At least the interval scale of measurement is required.

         b. All the data values are used in the calculation.

         c. A set of data has only one mean. That is, it is unique.

         d. The sum of the deviations between each observation and the mean is always 0.

   B. The median is the value in the middle of a set of ordered data.

      1. To find the median, sort the observations from minimum to maximum and identify the middle value.

      2. The major characteristics of the median are as follows:

         a. At least the ordinal scale of measurement is required.

         b. It is not influenced by extreme values.

         c. Fifty percent of the observations are larger than the median.

         d. It is unique to a set of data.

   C. The mode is the value that occurs most often in a set of data.

      1. The mode can be found for nominal-level data.

      2. A set of data can have more than one mode.

   D. The weighted mean is found by multiplying each observation by its corresponding weight.

      1. The formula for determining the weighted mean is

$$\bar{x}_w = \frac{w_1 x_1 + w_2 x_2 + w_3 x_3 + \cdots + w_n x_n}{w_1 + w_2 + w_3 + \cdots + w_n} \tag{3-3}$$

   E. The geometric mean is the nth root of the product of n positive values.

      1. The formula for the geometric mean is

$$GM = \sqrt[n]{(x_1)(x_2)(x_3) \cdots (x_n)} \tag{3-4}$$

      2. The geometric mean is also used to find the rate of change from one period to another.

$$GM = \sqrt[n]{\frac{\text{Value at end of period}}{\text{Value at beginning of period}}} - 1 \tag{3-5}$$

      3. The geometric mean is always equal to or less than the arithmetic mean.

II. The dispersion is the variation or spread in a set of data.

   A. The range is the difference between the maximum and minimum values in a set of data.

      1. The formula for the range is

$$\text{Range} = \text{Maximum value} - \text{Minimum value} \tag{3-6}$$

      2. The major characteristics of the range are as follows:

         a. Only two values are used in its calculation.

         b. It is influenced by extreme values.

         c. It is easy to compute and to understand.

   B. The variance is the mean of the squared deviations from the arithmetic mean.

1. The formula for the population variance is

$$\sigma^2 = \frac{\Sigma(x - \mu)^2}{N}$$

(3–7)

2. The formula for the sample variance is

$$s^2 = \frac{\Sigma(x - \bar{x})^2}{n - 1}$$

(3–9)

3. The major characteristics of the variance are as follows:
   a. All observations are used in the calculation.
   b. The units are somewhat difficult to work with; they are the original units squared.

C. The standard deviation is the square root of the variance.
   1. The major characteristics of the standard deviation are as follows:
      a. It is in the same units as the original data.
      b. It is the square root of the average squared distance from the mean.
      c. It cannot be negative.
      d. It is the most widely reported measure of dispersion.
   2. The formula for the sample standard deviation is

$$s = \sqrt{\frac{\Sigma(x - \bar{x})^2}{n - 1}}$$

(3–10)

III. We use the standard deviation to describe a frequency distribution by applying Chebyshev's theorem or the Empirical Rule.
   A. Chebyshev's theorem states that regardless of the shape of the distribution, at least $1 - 1/k^2$ of the observations will be within k standard deviations of the mean, where k is greater than 1.
   B. The Empirical Rule states that for a bell-shaped distribution about 68% of the values will be within 1 standard deviation of the mean, 95% within 2 standard deviations, and virtually all within 3 standard deviations.

PRONUNCIATION KEY

SYMBOL	MEANING	PRONUNCIATION
μ	Population mean	*mu*
Σ	Operation of adding	*sigma*
Σx	Adding a group of values	*sigma x*
$\bar{x}$	Sample mean	*x bar*
$\bar{x}_w$	Weighted mean	*x bar sub w*
GM	Geometric mean	*G M*
σ^2	Population variance	*sigma squared*
σ	Population standard deviation	*sigma*

CHAPTER EXERCISES

59. The accounting firm of Crawford and Associates has five senior partners. Yesterday the senior partners saw six, four, three, seven, and five clients, respectively.
   a. Compute the mean and median number of clients seen by the partners.
   b. Is the mean a sample mean or a population mean?
   c. Verify that $\Sigma(x - \mu) = 0$.

60. Owens Orchards sells apples in a large bag by weight. A sample of seven bags contained the following numbers of apples: 23, 19, 26, 17, 21, 24, 22.
   a. Compute the mean and median number of apples in a bag.
   b. Verify that $\Sigma(x - \bar{x}) = 0$.

61. **FILE** A sample of households that subscribe to United Bell Phone Company for landline phone service revealed the following number of robocalls received per household last week. Determine the mean and the median number of robocalls received.

52	43	30	38	30	42	12	46	39	37
34	46	32	18	41	5				

62. **FILE** The Citizens Banking Company is studying the number of times the ATM located in a Loblaws Supermarket at the foot of Market Street is used per day. Following are the number of times the machine was used each day over the last 30 days. Determine the mean number of times the machine was used per day.

83	64	84	76	84	54	75	59	70	61
63	80	84	73	68	52	65	90	52	77
95	36	78	61	59	84	95	47	87	60

63. **FILE** A recent study of the laundry habits of Americans included the time in minutes of the wash cycle. A sample of 40 observations follows. Determine the mean and the median of a typical wash cycle.

35	37	28	37	33	38	37	32	28	29
39	33	32	37	33	35	36	44	36	34
40	38	46	39	37	39	34	39	31	33
37	35	39	38	37	32	43	31	31	35

64. **FILE** Trudy Green works for the True-Green Lawn Company. Her job is to solicit lawn-care business via the telephone. Listed here is the number of appointments she made in each of the last 25 hours of calling.

9	5	2	6	5	6	4	4	7	2	3	6	3
4	4	7	8	4	4	5	5	4	8	3	3	

    a. Construct a frequency table for the number of appointments made per hour. Use the number of appointments as the class.
    b. Find the mode.
    c. Find the median.
    d. Compute the mean.
    e. Interpret the mode.
    f. Interpret the median.
    g. Interpret the mean. Then use the mean to estimate the average number of appointments made in a 7-hour workday.

65. The Split-A-Rail Fence Company sells three types of fence to homeowners in suburban Seattle, Washington. Grade A costs $5.00 per running foot to install, Grade B costs $6.50 per running foot, and Grade C, the premium quality, costs $8.00 per running foot. Yesterday, Split-A-Rail installed 270 feet of Grade A, 300 feet of Grade B, and 100 feet of Grade C. What was the mean cost per foot of fence installed?

66. Chris Proust is a sophomore in the College of Business at Scandia Tech. Last semester Chris took courses in statistics and accounting, 3 hours each, and earned an A in both. Chris earned a B in a 5-hour history course and a B in a 2-hour history of jazz course. In addition, Chris took a 1-hour course in the rules of basketball to get a referee's license and officiate high school basketball games. Chris got an A in this course. In computing a grade point average, assume each A gets 4 points, each B gets 3 points, each C gets 2 points, and each D gets 1 point. Calculate the GPA for the semester. What measure of central location did you calculate? What method did you use?

67. The table shows the percent of the labor force that is unemployed and the size of the labor force for three counties in northwest Ohio. Jon Elsas is the Regional Director of Economic Development. He must present a report to several companies that are considering locating in northwest Ohio. What would be an appropriate unemployment rate to show for the entire region?

County	Percent Unemployed	Size of Workforce
Wood	4.5	15,300
Ottawa	3.0	10,400
Lucas	10.2	150,600

68. **FILE** The American Diabetes Association recommends a blood glucose reading of less than 130 for those with Type 2 diabetes. Blood glucose measures the amount of sugar in the blood. Following are the readings for February for a person recently diagnosed with Type 2 diabetes.

112	122	116	103	112	96	115	98	106	111
106	124	116	127	116	108	112	112	121	115
124	116	107	118	123	109	109	106		

   a. What is the arithmetic mean glucose reading?
   b. What is the median glucose reading?
   c. What is the modal glucose reading?

69. The first Super Bowl was played in 1967. The cost for a 30-second commercial was $42,000. The cost of a 30-second commercial for Super Bowl 55, which was played on February 7, 2021, in Tampa Bay, Florida, was $5.6 million. What was the geometric mean rate of increase for the 54 years between 1967 and 2021?

70. A recent article suggested that, if you earn $25,000 a year today and the inflation rate continues at 3% per year, you'll need to make $33,598 in 10 years to have the same buying power. You would need to make $44,771 if the inflation rate jumped to 6%. Confirm that these statements are accurate by finding the geometric mean rate of increase.

71. The ages of a sample of Canadian tourists flying from Toronto to Hong Kong were 32, 21, 60, 47, 54, 17, 72, 55, 33, and 41.
   a. Compute the range.
   b. Compute the standard deviation.

72. The weights (in pounds) of a sample of five boxes being sent by UPS are 12, 6, 7, 3, and 10.
   a. Compute the range.
   b. Compute the standard deviation.

73. **FILE** The undergraduate enrollments for the 13 public universities in the state of Ohio for the fall of 2020 are listed here.

University	Enrollment
University of Akron	13,651
Bowling Green State University	14,998
Central State University	4,021
University of Cincinnati	28,657
Cleveland State University	11,245
Kent State University	21,621
Miami University	16,522
Ohio State University	46,984
Ohio University	18,913
Shawnee State University	3,304
University of Toledo	14,406
Wright State University	8,332
Youngstown State University	10,468

a. Is this a sample or a population?
b. What is the mean enrollment?
c. What is the median enrollment?
d. Is there a mode for this distribution?
e. Would you select the mean or the median as most representative? Why?
f. What is the range of the enrollments?
g. Compute the standard deviation.

74. **FILE** The Kentucky Derby is held the first Saturday in May at Churchill Downs in Louisville, Kentucky. The race track is one and one-quarter miles. The following table shows the winners since 2000, their margin of victory, the winning time, and the payoff on a $2 bet.

Year	Winner	Winning Margin (lengths)	Winning Time (minutes)	Payoff on a $2 Bet
2000	Fusaichi Pegasus	1.50	2.02000	2.30
2001	Monarchos	4.75	1.99950	10.50
2002	War Emblem	4.00	2.01883	20.50
2003	Funny Cide	1.75	2.01983	12.80
2004	Smarty Jones	2.75	2.06767	4.10
2005	Giacomo	0.50	2.04583	50.30
2006	Barbaro	6.50	2.02267	6.10
2007	Street Sense	2.25	2.03617	4.90
2008	Big Brown	4.75	2.03033	6.80
2009	Mine That Bird	6.75	2.04433	103.20
2010	Super Saver	2.50	2.07417	18.00
2011	Animal Kingdom	2.75	2.03400	43.80
2012	I'll Have Another	1.50	2.03050	32.60
2013	Orb	2.50	2.04817	12.80
2014	California Chrome	1.75	2.06100	7.00
2015	American Pharoah	1.00	2.05033	7.80
2016	Nyquist	1.25	2.01517	6.60
2017	Always Dreaming	3.75	2.03983	11.40
2018	Justify	2.50	2.04333	7.80
2019	Country House	1.75	2.0561	132.4
2020	Authentic	1.25	2.00366	18.8
2021	Medina Spirit	0.5	2.017	26.2

a. Determine the mean and median for the variables Winning Time and Payoff on a $2 bet.
b. Determine the range and standard deviation of the variables Winning Time and Payoff on a $2 bet.
c. Refer to the variable Winning Margin. What is the level of measurement? What measure of location would be most appropriate?

75. **FILE** The Apollo space program lasted from 1967 until 1972 and included 13 missions. The missions lasted from as little as 7 hours to as long as 301 hours. The duration of each flight is as follows:

9	195	241	301	216	260	7	244	192	147
10	295	142							

a. Explain why the flight times are a population.
b. Find the mean and median of the flight times.
c. Find the range and the standard deviation of the flight times.

76. **FILE** Creek Ratz is a very popular restaurant located along the coast of northern Florida. They serve a variety of steak and seafood dinners. During the summer beach season, they do not take reservations or accept "call ahead" seating. Management of

the restaurant is concerned with the time a patron must wait before being seated for dinner. Listed here is the wait time, in minutes, for the 25 tables seated last Saturday night.

28	39	23	67	37	28	56	40	28	50
51	45	44	65	61	27	24	61	34	44
64	25	24	27	29					

a. Explain why the times are a population.
b. Find the mean and median of the times.
c. Find the range and the standard deviation of the times.

77. **FILE** A sample of 25 undergraduates reported the following dollar amounts of entertainment expenses last year.

684	710	688	711	722	698	723	743	738	722	696	721	685
763	681	731	736	771	693	701	737	717	752	710	697	

a. Find the mean, median, and mode of this information.
b. What are the range and standard deviation?
c. Use the Empirical Rule to establish an interval that includes about 95% of the observations.

DATA ANALYTICS

78. **FILE** Refer to the North Valley Real Estate data and prepare a report on the sales prices of the homes. Be sure to answer the following questions in your report.
    a. Around what values of price do the data tend to cluster? What is the mean sales price? What is the median sales price? Is one measure more representative of the typical sales prices than the others?
    b. What is the range of sales prices? What is the standard deviation? About 95% of the sales prices are between what two values? Is the standard deviation a useful statistic for describing the dispersion of sales price?
    c. Repeat parts (a) and (b) using FICO score.

79. **FILE** Refer to the Baseball 2021 data, which report information on the 30 Major League Baseball teams for the 2021 season. Refer to the team salary variable.
    a. Prepare a report on the team salaries. Be sure to answer the following questions in your report.
        1. Around what values do the data tend to cluster? Specifically what is the mean team salary? What is the median team salary? Is one measure more representative of the typical team salary than the others?
        2. What is the range of the team salaries? What is the standard deviation? About 95% of the salaries are between what two values?
    b. In 2000 the average player salary was $1.99 million. In 2021, the average player salary is $4.17 million. What was the rate of change over the period?

80. **FILE** Refer to the Lincolnville School District bus data. Prepare a report on the maintenance cost for last month. Be sure to answer the following questions in your report.
    a. Around what values do the data tend to cluster? Specifically what was the mean maintenance cost last month? What is the median cost? Is one measure more representative of the typical cost than the others?
    b. What is the range of maintenance costs? What is the standard deviation? About 95% of the maintenance costs are between what two values?

Describing Data:

DISPLAYING AND EXPLORING DATA

4

Shutterstock/Kwangmoozaa

▲ **MCGIVERN JEWELERS** recently posted an advertisement on a social media site reporting the shape, size, price, and cut grade for 33 of its diamonds in stock. Develop a box plot of the variable price and comment on the result. (See Exercise 29 and LO4-3.)

LEARNING OBJECTIVES

When you have completed this chapter, you will be able to:

LO4-1   Construct and interpret a dot plot.

LO4-2   Identify and compute measures of position.

LO4-3   Construct and analyze a box plot.

LO4-4   Compute and interpret the coefficient of skewness.

LO4-5   Create and interpret a scatter diagram.

LO4-6   Compute and interpret the correlation coefficient.

LO4-7   Develop and explain a contingency table.

Introduction

The charts and graphs in Chapters 2 and 4 are an introduction to the creative process of data visualization. Data visualization is the depiction of data and information in a graph, chart, or other visual images. The images can graphically show trends, clusters, and patterns that may exist in large amounts of data. The products of data visualization can provide meaningful ways to present and interpret large amounts of data. The graphic on page 2 in Chapter 1 depicts the vast amount of data and information created and consumed every minute. Data visualizations can summarize a lot of information as shown in another example of global water supply and demand **(https://visme.co/blog/wp-content/uploads/2021/08/consumption-of-water.png)**.

Chapter 2 began our study of descriptive statistics. To transform raw or ungrouped data into a meaningful form, we organize the data into a frequency distribution. We present the frequency distribution in graphic form as a histogram or a frequency polygon. This allows us to visualize where the data tend to cluster, the largest and the smallest values, and the general shape of the data.

In Chapter 3, we first computed several measures of location, such as the mean, median, and mode. These measures of location allow us to report a typical value in the set of observations. We also computed several measures of dispersion, such as the range, variance, and standard deviation. These measures of dispersion allow us to describe the variation or the spread in a set of observations.

We continue our study of descriptive statistics in this chapter. We study (1) dot plots, (2) percentiles, and (3) box plots. These charts and statistics give us additional insight into where the values are concentrated as well as the general shape of the data. Then we consider bivariate data. In bivariate data, we observe two variables for each individual or observation. Examples include the number of hours a student studied and the points earned on an examination; if a sampled product meets quality specifications and the shift on which it is manufactured; or the amount of electricity used in a month by a homeowner and the mean daily high temperature in the region for the month. These charts and graphs provide useful insights as we use business analytics to enhance our understanding of data.

Dot Plots

Recall for the Applewood Auto Group data, we summarized the profit earned on the 180 vehicles sold with a frequency distribution using eight classes. When we organized the data into the eight classes, we lost the exact value of the observations. A **dot plot,** on the other hand, groups the data as little as possible, and we do not lose the identity of an individual observation. To develop a dot plot, we display a dot for each observation along a horizontal number line indicating the possible values of the data. If there are identical observations or the observations are too close to be shown individually, the dots are "piled" on top of each other. This allows us to see the shape of the distribution, the value about which the data tend to cluster, and the largest and smallest observations. Dot plots are most useful for smaller data sets, whereas histograms tend to be most useful for large data sets. An example will show how to construct and interpret dot plots.

> **DOT PLOT** A dot plot summarizes the distribution of one variable by stacking dots at points on a number line that shows the values of the variable. A dot plot shows all values.

▶ **EXAMPLE**

The service departments at Tionesta Ford Lincoln and Sheffield Motors Inc., two of the four Applewood Auto Group dealerships, were both open 24 days last month.

Listed here is the number of vehicles serviced last month at the two dealerships. Construct dot plots and report summary statistics to compare the two dealerships.

Tionesta Ford Lincoln

Monday	Tuesday	Wednesday	Thursday	Friday	Saturday
23	33	27	28	39	26
30	32	28	33	35	32
29	25	36	31	32	27
35	32	35	37	36	30

Sheffield Motors Inc.

Monday	Tuesday	Wednesday	Thursday	Friday	Saturday
31	35	44	36	34	37
30	37	43	31	40	31
32	44	36	34	43	36
26	38	37	30	42	33

SOLUTION

The Minitab system provides a dot plot and outputs the mean, median, maximum, and minimum values, and the standard deviation for the number of cars serviced at each dealership over the last 24 working days.

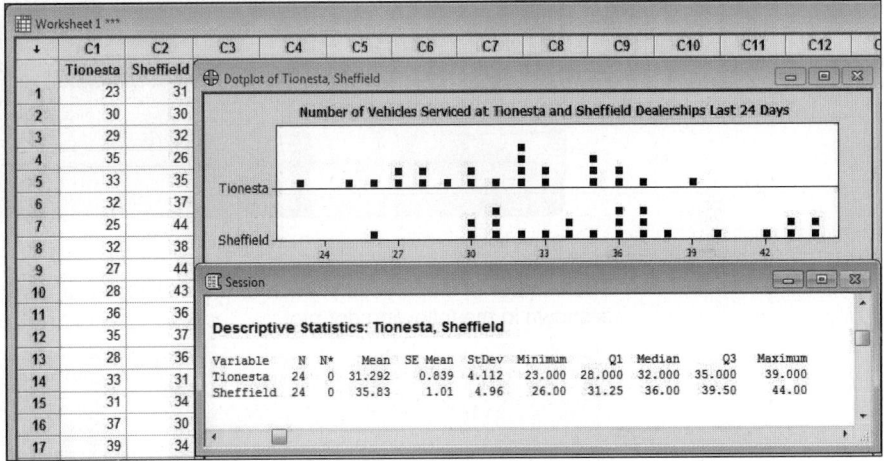

Source: Minitab

The dot plots, shown in the center of the output, graphically illustrate the distributions for each dealership. The plots show the difference in the location and dispersion of the observations. By looking at the dot plots, we can see that the number of vehicles serviced at the Sheffield dealership is more widely dispersed and has a larger mean than at the Tionesta dealership. Several other features of the number of vehicles serviced are:

- Tionesta serviced the fewest cars in any day, 23.
- Sheffield serviced 26 cars during their slowest day, which is 4 cars less than the next lowest day.
- Tionesta serviced exactly 32 cars on four different days.
- The numbers of cars serviced cluster around 36 for Sheffield and 32 for Tionesta.

From the descriptive statistics, we see Sheffield serviced a mean of 35.83 vehicles per day. Tionesta serviced a mean of 31.292 vehicles per day during the same period. So Sheffield typically services 4.54 more vehicles per day. There is also more dispersion, or variation, in the daily number of vehicles serviced at Sheffield than at Tionesta. How do we know this? The standard deviation is larger at Sheffield (4.96 vehicles per day) than at Tionesta (4.112 cars per day).

SELF-REVIEW 4–1

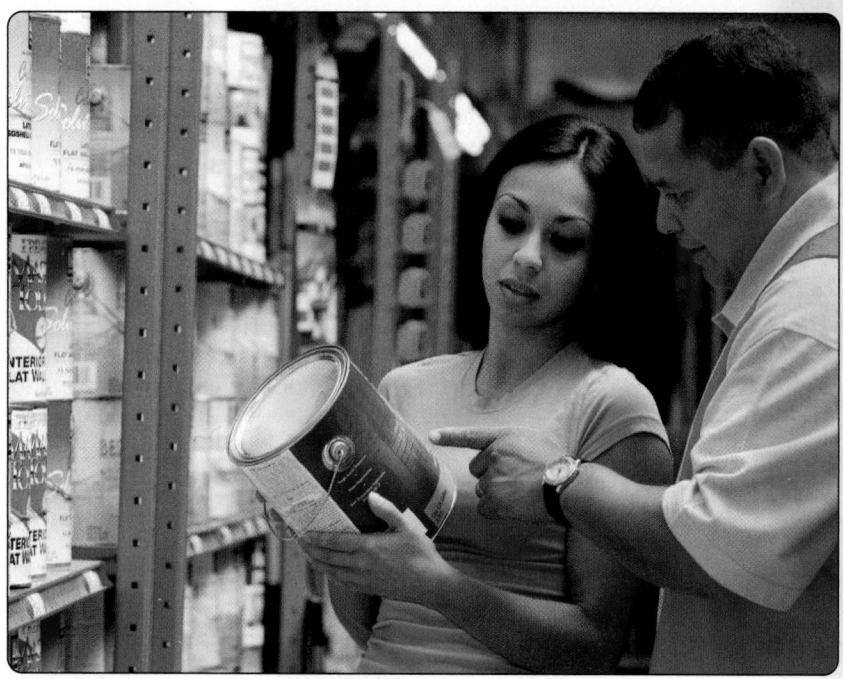

Steve Hix/Corbis/Somos Images/Getty Images

The number of employees at each of the 142 Home Depot stores in the Southeast region is shown in the following dot plot.

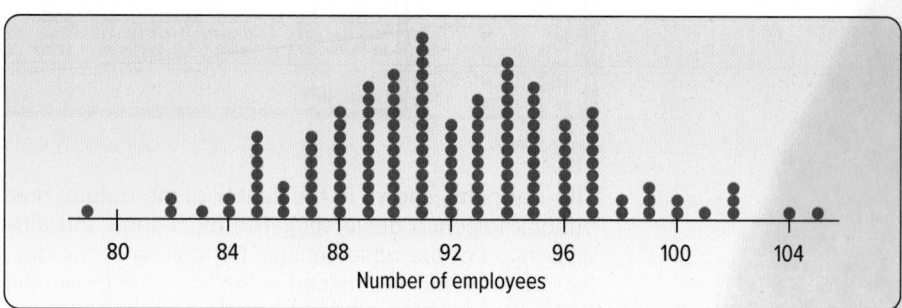

(a) What are the minimum, maximum, and range of number of employees?
(b) How would you describe the shape of the distribution: bell shaped, negatively skewed, or positively skewed?
(c) Visually, estimate the central location of the distribution.
(d) Find the mode of the distribution. Why is this value the mode?
(e) Find the median of the distribution. Why is this value the median?
(f) Using the weighted mean, calculate the mean. Hint: Use the frequencies as the weights.
(g) How do the values of the mode, median, and mean compare?

EXERCISES

1. Describe the differences between a histogram and a dot plot. When might a dot plot be better than a histogram?
2. When are dot plots most useful?
3. The following chart presents a visual summary of a study's data.

   a. What is this chart called?
   b. How many observations are in the study?
   c. What are the minimum, maximum, and range of the data?
   d. How would you describe the shape of the distribution: bell shaped, negatively skewed, or positively skewed?
   e. Visually, estimate the central location of the distribution.
   f. Find the mode of the distribution. Why is this value the mode?
   g. Find the median of the distribution. Why is this value the median?
   h. Using the weighted mean, calculate the mean. Hint: Use the frequencies as the weights.
   i. How do the values of the mode, median, and mean compare?
4. The following chart reports the number of cell phones sold at a big-box retail store for the last 26 days.

   a. What are the minimum, maximum, and range of number of cell phones sold?
   b. How would you describe the shape of the distribution: bell shaped, negatively skewed, or positively skewed?
   c. Visually, estimate the central location of the distribution.
   d. Find the mode of the distribution. Why is this value the mode?
   e. Find the median of the distribution. Why is this value the median?
   f. Using the weighted mean, calculate the mean. Hint: Use the frequencies as the weights.
   g. How do the values of the mode, median, and mean compare?

LO4-2

Identify and compute measures of position.

Measures of Position

The standard deviation is the most widely used measure of dispersion. However, there are other ways of describing the variation or spread in a set of data. One method is to determine the *location* of values that divide a set of observations into equal parts. These measures include **quartiles, deciles,** and **percentiles.**

Quartiles divide a set of observations into four equal parts. To explain further, think of any set of values arranged from the minimum to the maximum. In Chapter 3, we called the middle value of a set of data arranged from the minimum to the maximum the median. That is, 50% of the observations are larger than the median and 50% are smaller. The median is a measure of location because it pinpoints the center of the data. In a similar fashion, **quartiles** divide a set of observations into four equal parts. The first quartile, usually labeled Q_1, is the value below which 25% of the observations occur, and the third quartile, usually labeled Q_3, is the value below which 75% of the observations occur.

Similarly, **deciles** divide a set of observations into 10 equal parts and **percentiles** into 100 equal parts. So if you found that your GPA was in the 8th decile at your university, you could conclude that 80% of the students had a GPA lower than yours and 20% had a higher GPA. If your GPA was in the 92nd percentile, then 92% of students had a GPA less than your GPA and only 8% of students had a GPA greater than your GPA. Percentile scores are frequently used to report results on such national standardized tests as the SAT, ACT, GMAT (used to judge entry into many master of business administration programs), and LSAT (used to judge entry into law school).

> **QUARTILES** Values of an ordered (minimum to maximum) data set that divide the data into four intervals.
> **DECILES** Values of an ordered (minimum to maximum) data set that divide the data into 10 equal parts.
> **PERCENTILES** Values of an ordered (minimum to maximum) data set that divide the data into 100 intervals.

To formalize the computational procedure, let L_p refer to the location of a desired percentile. So if we want to find the 92nd percentile we would use L_{92}, and if we wanted the median, the 50th percentile, then L_{50}. For a number of observations, n, the location of the Pth percentile, can be found using the formula:

LOCATION OF A PERCENTILE	$L_p = (n + 1)\dfrac{P}{100}$	**(4–1)**

An example will help to explain further.

▶ EXAMPLE

Morgan Stanley is an investment company with offices located throughout the United States. Listed here are the commissions earned last month by a sample of 15 brokers at the Morgan Stanley office in Oakland, California.

$2,038	$1,758	$1,721	$1,637	$2,097	$2,047	$2,205	$1,787	$2,287
1,940	2,311	2,054	2,406	1,471	1,460			

Locate the median, the first quartile, and the third quartile for the commissions earned.

SOLUTION

The first step is to sort the data from the smallest commission to the largest.

$1,460	$1,471	$1,637	$1,721	$1,758	$1,787	$1,940	$2,038	$2,047
2,054	2,097	2,205	2,287	2,311	2,406			

Yuji Kotani/Digital Vision/Getty Images

The median value is the observation in the center and is the same as the 50th percentile, so P equals 50. The median or L_{50} is located at $(n + 1)(50/100)$, where n is the number of observations. In this case, that is position number 8, found by $(15 + 1)(50/100)$. The eighth-largest commission is \$2,038. So we conclude this is the median and that half the brokers earned commissions more than \$2,038 and half earned less than \$2,038. The result using formula (4–1) to find the median is the same as the method presented in Chapter 3.

Recall the definition of a quartile. Quartiles divide a set of observations into four equal parts. Hence 25% of the observations will be less than the first quartile and 75% of the observations will be less than the third quartile. To locate the first quartile, we use formula (4–1), where $n = 15$ and $P = 25$:

$$L_{25} = (n + 1)\frac{P}{100} = (15 + 1)\frac{25}{100} = 4$$

And to locate the third quartile, $n = 15$ and $P = 75$:

$$L_{75} = (n + 1)\frac{P}{100} = (15 + 1)\frac{75}{100} = 12$$

Therefore, the first and third quartile values are located at positions 4 and 12, respectively. The fourth value in the ordered array is \$1,721 and the twelfth is \$2,205. These are the first and third quartiles.

In the previous example, the location formula yielded a whole number. That is, we wanted to find the first quartile and there were 15 observations, so the location formula indicated we should find the fourth ordered value. What if there were 20 observations in the sample, that is $n = 20$, and we wanted to locate the first quartile? From the location formula (4–1):

$$L_{25} = (n + 1)\frac{P}{100} = (20 + 1)\frac{25}{100} = 5.25$$

We would locate the fifth value in the ordered array and then move .25 of the distance between the fifth and sixth values and report that as the first quartile. Like the median, the quartile does not need to be one of the actual values in the data set.

To explain further, suppose a data set contained the six values 91, 75, 61, 101, 43, and 104. We want to locate the first quartile. We order the values from the minimum to the maximum: 43, 61, 75, 91, 101, and 104. The first quartile is located at:

$$L_{25} = (n + 1)\frac{P}{100} = (6 + 1)\frac{25}{100} = 1.75$$

The position formula tells us that the first quartile is located between the first and the second values and it is .75 of the distance between the first and the second values. The first value is 43 and the second is 61. So the distance between these two values is 18. To locate the first quartile, we need to move .75 of the distance between the first and second values, so .75(18) = 13.5. To complete the procedure, we add 13.5 to the first value, 43, and report that the first quartile is 56.5.

We can extend the idea to include both deciles and percentiles. To locate the 23rd percentile in a sample of 80 observations, we would look for the 18.63 position.

$$L_{23} = (n + 1)\frac{P}{100} = (80 + 1)\frac{23}{100} = 18.63$$

To find the value corresponding to the 23rd percentile, we would locate the 18th value and the 19th value and determine the distance between the two values. Next, we would multiply this difference by 0.63 and add the result to the smaller value. The result would be the 23rd percentile.

Statistical software is very helpful when describing and summarizing data. Excel, Google Sheets, Minitab, and MegaStat, a statistical analysis Excel add-in, all provide summary statistics that include quartiles. For example, the Minitab summary of the Morgan Stanley commission data, shown here, includes the first and third quartiles and other statistics. Based on the reported quartiles, 25% of the commissions earned were less than $1,721 and 75% were less than $2,205. These are the same values we calculated using formula (4–1). This is also referred to as the **Exclusive Method** for determining quartiles.

Sheet1 ***			Session
↓	**C1**		**Descriptive Statistics: Commissions**
	Commissions		
1	1460		Variable N N* Mean SE Mean StDev Minimum Q1 Median Q3 Maximum
2	1471		Commissions 15 0 1947.9 77.1 298.8 1460.0 1721.0 2038.0 2205.0 2406.0
3	1637		
4	1721		

Source: Minitab

Morgan Stanley Commisisons			
$2,038			
1,758	Method	Exclusive	Inclusive
1,721	First Quartile	1,721.0	1,739.5
1,637	Median	2,038.0	2,038.0
2,097	Third Quartile	2,205.0	2,151.0
2,047			
2,205			
1,787			
2,287			
1,940			
2,311			
2,054			
2,406			
1,471			
1,460			

Source: Minitab

There are ways other than the Exclusive Method to locate quartile values. Another method called the **Inclusive Method** uses the formula $0.25n + 0.75$ to locate the position of the first quartile and $0.75n + 0.25$ to locate the position of the third quartile. In the Morgan Stanley data, this method would place the first quartile at position 4.5 (.25 × 15 + .75) and the third quartile at position 11.5 (.75 × 15 + .25). The first quartile would be interpolated as one-half the difference between the fourth- and the fifth-ranked values. Based on this method, the first quartile is $1,739.5, found by ($1,721 + 0.5 [$1,758 – $1,721]). The third quartile, at position 11.5, would be $2,151, or one-half the distance between the eleventh- and the twelfth-ranked values, found by ($2,097 + 0.5 [$2,205 – $2,097]).

Excel, as shown in the Morgan Stanley and Applewood examples, can compute quartiles using either of the two methods. **Please note the text uses the Exclusive Method [formula (4–1)] to calculate quartiles.** Please also see the Excel tutorial referenced in the left margin for instructions for computing quartiles and percentiles.

Tutorial #26
in Connect

Applewood				
Age	Profit	Method	Exclusive	Inclusive
21	$1,387	First Quartile	1415.5	1422.5
23	1,754	Median	1882.5	1882.5
24	1,817	Third Quartile	2275.5	2268.5
25	1,040			
26	1,273			
27	1,529			
27	3,082			
28	1,951			
28	2,692			
29	1,206			
29	1,342			

Source: Minitab

Is the difference between the two methods important? No. Usually it is just a nuisance. In general, both methods calculate values that will support the statement that approximately 25% of the values are less than the value of the first quartile, and approximately 75% of the data values are less than the value of the third quartile. When the sample is large, the difference in the results from the two methods is small. For example, in the Applewood Auto Group data there are 180 vehicles. Both methods of computing quartiles are shown on the previous page. Based on the variable profit, 45 of the 180 values (25%) are less than both values of the first quartile, and 135 of the 180 values (75%) are less than both values of the third quartile.

When using Excel, be careful to understand the method used to calculate quartiles. The Excel function, **Quartile.exc,** will result in the same answer as the Exclusive Method (formula 4–1). The Excel function, **Quartile.inc,** computes quartiles using the Inclusive Method.

SELF-REVIEW 4–2

The Quality Control department of Plainsville Peanut Company is responsible for checking the weight of the 8-ounce jar of peanut butter. The weights of a sample of nine jars produced last hour are:

| 7.69 | 7.72 | 7.80 | 7.86 | 7.90 | 7.94 | 7.97 | 8.06 | 8.09 |

(a) What is the median weight?
(b) Determine the weights corresponding to the first and third quartiles.

EXERCISES

5. **FILE** Determine and interpret the median and the first and third quartiles in the following data.

| 46 | 47 | 49 | 49 | 51 | 53 | 54 | 54 | 55 | 55 | 59 |

6. **FILE** Determine and interpret the median and the first and third quartiles in the following data.

| 5.24 | 6.02 | 6.67 | 7.30 | 7.59 | 7.99 | 8.03 | 8.35 | 8.81 | 9.45 |
| 9.61 | 10.37 | 10.39 | 11.86 | 12.22 | 12.71 | 13.07 | 13.59 | 13.89 | 15.42 |

7. **FILE** The Thomas Supply Company Inc. is a distributor of gas-powered generators. As with any business, the length of time customers take to pay their invoices is important. Listed here, arranged from smallest to largest, is the time, in days, for a sample of the Thomas Supply Company Inc. invoices.

| 13 | 13 | 13 | 20 | 26 | 27 | 31 | 34 | 34 | 34 | 35 | 35 | 36 | 37 | 38 |
| 41 | 41 | 41 | 45 | 47 | 47 | 47 | 50 | 51 | 53 | 54 | 56 | 62 | 67 | 82 |

  a. Determine and interpret the first and third quartiles.
  b. Determine and interpret the second decile and the eighth decile.
  c. Determine and interpret the 67th percentile.

8. **FILE** Blair Jokinen is a sales manager for Pearson, one of the top publishing companies in the world. Blair manages 40 sales representatives who visit college professors in Europe. On Saturday mornings, each representative sends Blair a report that includes the number of professors visited during the previous week. Listed here, ordered from smallest to largest, is the number of visits last week.

| 22 | 22 | 23 | 23 | 23 | 23 | 23 | 24 | 24 | 24 | 24 | 24 | 24 | 24 | 24 | 25 | 25 | 25 | 25 | 25 |
| 25 | 25 | 25 | 25 | 25 | 25 | 25 | 25 | 26 | 26 | 26 | 26 | 26 | 26 | 27 | 27 | 27 | 27 | 28 | 28 |

a. Create a visual presentation of the data with a dot plot.
b. What are the minimum, maximum, and range of number of sales calls?
c. How would you describe the shape of the distribution: bell shaped, negatively skewed, or positively skewed?
d. Visually, estimate the central location of the distribution.
e. Find the mode of the distribution. Why is this value the mode?
f. Find the median of the distribution. Why is this value the median?
g. What is the first quartile of sales? What does it mean?
h. What is the third quartile of sales? What does it mean?
i. What is the ninth decile?
j. What is the 33rd percentile?

LO4-3

Construct and analyze a box plot.

Box Plots

A **box plot** is a graphical display using a five-number summary of a distribution. The five numbers or statistics are the minimum, first quartile (Q_1), median, third quartile (Q_3), and maximum values.

> **BOX PLOT** A graphic display that shows the general shape of a variable's distribution. It is based on five descriptive statistics: the maximum and minimum values, the first and third quartiles, and the median.

The following example/solution shows how to use the five statistics to create a box plot that graphically illustrates the location and dispersion of a distribution.

EXAMPLE

Alex's Pizza offers pizza delivery within 15 miles of the pizzeria. Alex, the owner, wants information on the time it takes for delivery. How long does a typical delivery take? Within what range of times will most deliveries be completed? For a sample of 20 deliveries, Alex determined the following information:

$$\text{Minimum value} = 13 \text{ minutes}$$
$$Q_1 = 15 \text{ minutes}$$
$$\text{Median} = 18 \text{ minutes}$$
$$Q_3 = 22 \text{ minutes}$$
$$\text{Maximum value} = 30 \text{ minutes}$$

Develop a box plot for the delivery times. What conclusions can you make about the delivery times?

SOLUTION

The first step in drawing a box plot is to create an appropriate scale along the horizontal axis. Next, we draw a box that starts at Q_1 (15 minutes) and ends at Q_3 (22 minutes). Inside the box we place a vertical line to represent the median (18 minutes). Finally, we extend horizontal lines from the box out to the minimum value (13 minutes) and the maximum value (30 minutes). These horizontal lines outside of the box are sometimes called "whiskers" because they look a bit like a cat's whiskers.

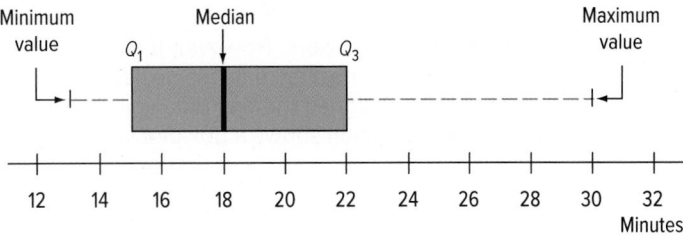

The box plot allows us to visualize several things about the distribution of delivery times. First, the minimum and maximum values are 12 and 30 minutes. Using the median, the location of the distribution is 18 minutes. So, 50% of deliveries take between 13 and 18 minutes; 50% of deliveries take between 18 and 30 minutes. In addition, the first quartile indicates that 25% of delivery times are between 12 and 15 minutes while the third quartile indicates that 25% of the delivery times are between 22 and 30 minutes.

In addition, a boxplot shows the **interquartile range.** The interquartile range is the distance between the first and third quartiles. Furthermore, given the interpretations of the first and third quartiles, 50% of the observations are in the interquartile range. In the previous example/solution, 50% of delivery times are between 15 and 22 minutes.

> **INTERQUARTILE RANGE** The range of values between the first and third quartiles; 50% of a distribution's values are located within this range.

The box plot also reveals that the distribution of delivery times is positively skewed. In Chapter 3, we defined skewness as the lack of symmetry in a set of data. How do we know this distribution is positively skewed? In this case, there are actually two pieces of information that suggest this. First, the dashed line to the right of the box from 22 minutes (Q_3) to the maximum time of 30 minutes is longer than the dashed line from the left of 15 minutes (Q_1) to the minimum value of 13 minutes. To put it another way, the 25% of the data larger than the third quartile are more spread out than the 25% less than the first quartile. A second indication of positive skewness is that the median is not in the center of the box. The distance from the first quartile to the median is smaller than the distance from the median to the third quartile. We know that the number of delivery times between 15 and 18 minutes is the same as the number of delivery times between 18 and 22 minutes.

Sometimes, there are observations that are inconsistent with the data. That is, the observations are far from the location of a distribution; relative to the distribution, the values are either very small or very large. These observations are called **outliers.** In terms of a box plot, an outlier is either greater than the upper boundary or less than the lower boundary as defined by the following:

$$\text{Upper outlier boundary} = Q_3 + 1.5(Q_3 - Q_1)$$
$$\text{Lower outlier boundary} = Q_1 - 1.5(Q_3 - Q_1)$$

> **OUTLIER** A data point that is unusually far from the others. An accepted rule is to classify an observation as an outlier if it is 1.5 times the interquartile range above the third quartile or below the first quartile.

If there are no outliers, the minimum and maximum values should be used as the ends of the whiskers. However, if the data include outliers, the upper whisker should be assigned the first data value less than the upper boundary; the lower whisker should be assigned the first data value greater than the lower boundary. The following Example/Solution shows a box plot with outliers.

▶ **EXAMPLE**

Refer to the Applewood Auto Group data. Develop a box plot for the variable age of the buyer. What can we conclude about the distribution of the age of the buyer?

SOLUTION

Tutorial #27 in Connect

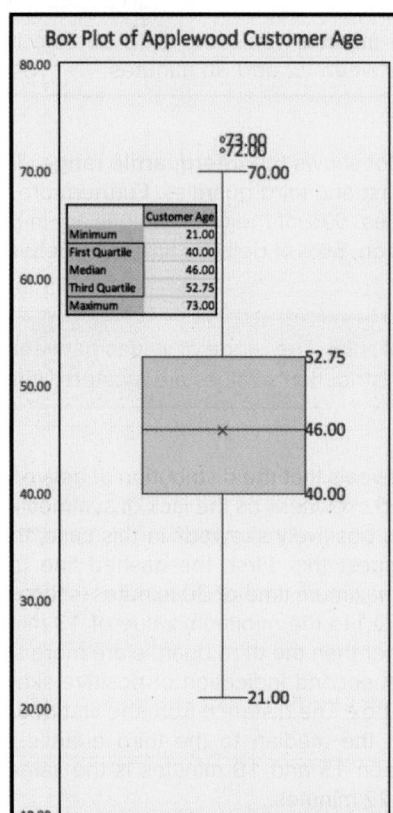

Excel was used to develop the adjoining chart and summary statistics. See the Excel tutorial referenced here.

The median age of the purchaser is 46 years, 25% of the purchasers are less than 40 years of age, and 25% are more than 52.75 years of age. Based on the summary information and the box plot, we conclude:

- The interquartile range shows that 50% of the purchasers are between the ages of 40 and 52.75 years.
- The distribution of ages is fairly symmetric. There are two reasons for this conclusion. The length of the whisker above 52.75 years (Q_3) is about the same length as the whisker below 40 years (Q_1). Also, the area in the box between 40 years and the median of 46 years is about the same as the area between the median and 52.75.

There are two points above the upper outlier boundary of 70 years. What do they indicate? These points represent purchasers who are much older than others in the sample. They are outliers with ages of 72 and 73.

The whiskers are determined as follows:

Upper outlier boundary $= Q_3 + 1.5(Q_3 - Q_1) = 52.75 + 1.5(52.75 - 40) = 71.875$

Reviewing the sorted raw data, 70 is the first value less than 71.875. So, the upper whisker is labeled 70 years of age.

Lower outlier boundary $= Q_1 - 1.5(Q_3 - Q_1) = 40 - 1.5(52.75 - 40) = 20.875$

Reviewing the sorted raw data, 21 is the minimum value. So, the lower whisker is labeled 21.

By reviewing the raw data, there are actually three purchasers older than 70 years of age; none are less than 21 years of age. Sometimes in box plots and other types of graphs, a single point may represent more than one observation.

SELF-REVIEW 4–3

The following box plot shows the assets in millions of dollars for credit unions in Seattle, Washington.

(a) What are the minimum and maximum values?
(b) What is the median?
(c) What are the first and third quartiles?
(d) Interpret the interquartile range, and the first and third quartiles.
(e) Is the distribution symmetrical? Why?
(f) Compute the upper outlier boundary. Based on the upper boundary, are there any outliers?

EXERCISES

9. The box plot shows the amount spent for books and supplies per year by students at four-year public colleges.

   a. Estimate the median amount spent.
   b. Estimate the first and third quartiles for the amount spent.
   c. Estimate the interquartile range for the amount spent.
   d. Beyond what point is a value considered an outlier?
   e. Identify any outliers and estimate their values.
   f. Is the distribution symmetrical or positively or negatively skewed?

10. The box plot shows the undergraduate in-state tuition per credit hour at four-year public colleges.

   a. Estimate the median.
   b. Estimate the first and third quartiles.
   c. Determine the interquartile range.
   d. Beyond what point is a value considered an outlier?
   e. Identify any outliers and estimate their values.
   f. Is the distribution symmetrical or positively or negatively skewed?

11. In a study of the gasoline mileage of model year 2022 automobiles, the mean miles per gallon was 27.5 and the median was 26.8. The smallest value in the study was 12.70 miles per gallon, and the largest was 50.20. The first and third quartiles were 17.95 and 35.45 miles per gallon, respectively. Develop a box plot and comment on the distribution. Is it a symmetric distribution?

12. **FILE** A sample of 28 time-shares in the Orlando, Florida, area revealed the following daily charges for a one-bedroom suite. For convenience, the data are ordered from smallest to largest.

$116	$121	$157	$192	$207	$209	$209
229	232	236	236	239	243	246
260	264	276	281	283	289	296
307	309	312	317	324	341	353

a. List the minimum, first quartile, median, third quartile, and maximum values.
b. Construct a box plot to represent the data.
c. Comment on the shape of the distribution.

Skewness

LO4-4

Compute and interpret the coefficient of skewness.

In Chapter 3, we described measures of central location for a distribution of data by reporting the mean, median, and mode. We also described measures that show the amount of spread or variation in a distribution, such as the range and the standard deviation.

Another characteristic of a distribution is the shape. We briefly described this in the previous chapter. There are four shapes commonly observed: symmetric, positively skewed, negatively skewed, and bimodal. In a **symmetric** distribution the mean and median are equal and the data values are evenly spread around these values. The shape of the distribution below the mean and median is a mirror image of the distribution above the mean and median. A distribution of values is **skewed to the right** or **positively skewed** if there is a single peak, but the values extend much farther to the right of the peak than to the left of the peak. In this case, the mean is larger than the median. In a **negatively skewed** distribution there is a single peak, but the observations extend farther to the left, in the negative direction, than to the right. In a negatively skewed distribution, the mean is smaller than the median. Positively skewed distributions are more common. Salaries often follow this pattern. Think of the salaries of those employed in a small company of about 100 people. The president and a few top executives would have very large salaries relative to the other workers and hence the distribution of salaries would exhibit positive skewness. A **bimodal distribution** will have two or more peaks. This is often the case when the values are from two or more populations. This information is summarized in Chart 4–1.

STATISTICS IN ACTION

The late Stephen Jay Gould (1941–2002) was a professor of zoology and professor of geology at Harvard University. In 1982, he was diagnosed with cancer and had an expected survival time of 8 months. However, never one to be discouraged, his research showed that the distribution of survival time is dramatically skewed to the right and showed that not only do 50% of similar cancer patients survive more than 8 months, but that the survival time could be years rather than months! In fact, Dr. Gould lived another 20 years. Based on his experience, he wrote a widely published essay titled "The Median Isn't the Message."

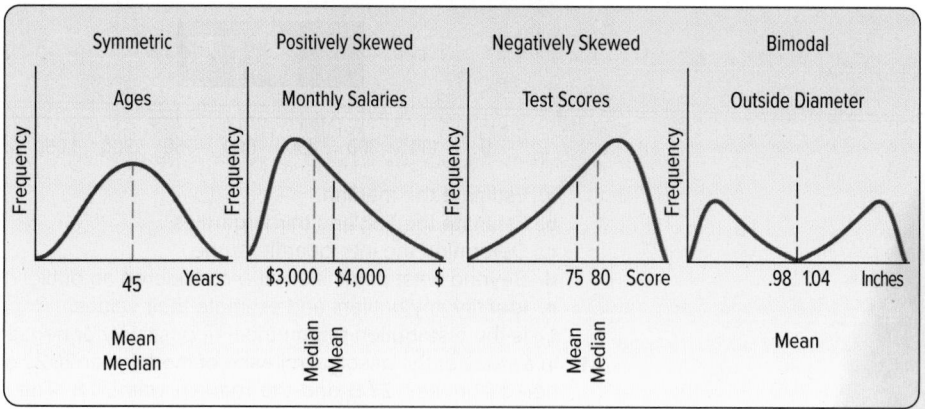

CHART 4–1 Shapes of Frequency Polygons

There are several formulas in the statistical literature used to calculate skewness. The simplest, developed by Professor Karl Pearson (1857–1936), is based on the difference between the mean and the median.

> **PEARSON'S COEFFICIENT OF SKEWNESS**
> $$sk = \frac{3(\bar{x} - \text{Median})}{s}$$ **(4–2)**

Using this relationship, the coefficient of skewness can range from −3 up to 3. A value near −3, such as −2.57, indicates considerable negative skewness. A value such as 1.63 indicates moderate positive skewness. A value equal to 0 occurs when the mean and median are equal, indicating there is no skewness.

In this text, we present output from Minitab and Excel. Both of these software packages compute a value for the coefficient of skewness based on the cubed deviations from the mean. The formula is:

> **SOFTWARE COEFFICIENT OF SKEWNESS**
> $$sk = \frac{n}{(n-1)(n-2)}\left[\Sigma\left(\frac{x-\bar{x}}{s}\right)^3\right]$$ **(4–3)**

Formula (4–3) offers an insight into skewness. The right-hand side of the formula is the difference between each value and the mean, divided by the standard deviation. That is the portion $(x - \bar{x})/s$ of the formula. This idea is called **standardizing.** We will discuss the idea of standardizing a value in more detail in Chapter 7 when we describe the normal probability distribution. At this point, observe that the result is to report the difference between each value and the mean in units of the standard deviation. If this difference is positive, the particular value is larger than the mean; if the value is negative, the standardized quantity is smaller than the mean. When we cube these values, we retain the information on the direction of the difference. Recall that in the formula for the standard deviation [see formula (3–10)], we squared the difference between each value and the mean, so that the result was all nonnegative values.

If the set of data values under consideration is symmetric, when we cube the standardized values and sum over all the values, the result will be near zero. If there are several large values, clearly separate from the others, the sum of the cubed differences will be a large positive value. If there are several small values clearly separate from the others, the sum of the cubed differences will be negative.

An example will illustrate the idea of skewness.

▶ **EXAMPLE**

Following are the earnings per share for a sample of 15 software companies for the year 2022. The earnings per share are arranged from smallest to largest.

$0.09	$0.13	$0.41	$0.51	$ 1.12	$ 1.20	$ 1.49	$3.18
3.50	6.36	7.83	8.92	10.13	12.99	16.40	

Compute the mean, median, and standard deviation. Find the coefficient of skewness using Pearson's estimate and the software methods. What is your conclusion regarding the shape of the distribution?

SOLUTION

These are sample data, so we use formula (3–2) to determine the mean.

$$\bar{x} = \frac{\Sigma x}{n} = \frac{\$74.26}{15} = \$4.95$$

The median is the middle value in a set of data, arranged from smallest to largest. In this case, there is an odd number of observations, so the middle value is the median. It is $3.18.

We use formula (3–10) to determine the sample standard deviation.

$$s = \sqrt{\frac{\Sigma(x - \bar{x})^2}{n - 1}} = \sqrt{\frac{(\$0.09 - \$4.95)^2 + \cdots + (\$16.40 - \$4.95)^2}{15 - 1}} = \$5.22$$

Pearson's coefficient of skewness is 1.017, found by:

$$sk = \frac{3(\bar{x} - \text{Median})}{s} = \frac{3(\$4.95 - \$3.18)}{\$5.22} = 1.017$$

This indicates there is moderate positive skewness in the earnings per share data.

We obtain a similar, but not exactly the same, value from the software method. The details of the calculations are shown in Table 4–1. To begin, we find the difference between each earnings per share value and the mean and divide this result by the standard deviation. We have referred to this as standardizing. Next, we cube, that is, raise to the third power, the result of the first step. Finally, we sum the cubed values. The details for the first company, that is, the company with an earnings per share of $0.09, are:

$$\left(\frac{x - \bar{x}}{s}\right)^3 = \left(\frac{0.09 - 4.95}{5.22}\right)^3 = (-0.9310)^3 = -0.8070$$

TABLE 4–1 Calculation of the Coefficient of Skewness

Earnings per Share	$\dfrac{(x - \bar{x})}{s}$	$\left(\dfrac{x - \bar{x}}{s}\right)^3$
0.09	−0.9310	−0.8070
0.13	−0.9234	−0.7873
0.41	−0.8697	−0.6579
0.51	−0.8506	−0.6154
1.12	−0.7337	−0.3950
1.20	−0.7184	−0.3708
1.49	−0.6628	−0.2912
3.18	−0.3391	−0.0390
3.50	−0.2778	−0.0214
6.36	0.2701	0.0197
7.83	0.5517	0.1679
8.92	0.7605	0.4399
10.13	0.9923	0.9772
12.99	1.5402	3.6539
16.40	2.1935	10.5537
		11.8274

When we sum the 15 cubed values, the result is 11.8274. That is, the term $\Sigma[(x - \bar{x})/S]^3 = 11.8274$. To find the coefficient of skewness, we use formula (4–3), with $n = 15$.

$$sk = \frac{n}{(n - 1)(n - 2)}\Sigma\left(\frac{x - \bar{x}}{s}\right)^3 = \frac{15}{(15 - 1)(15 - 2)}(11.8274) = 0.975$$

We conclude that the earnings per share values are somewhat positively skewed. The following Minitab summary reports the descriptive measures, such as the mean, median, and standard deviation of the earnings per share data. Also included are the coefficient of skewness and a histogram with a bell-shaped curve superimposed. Note that Excel also can compute the list of descriptive statistics that includes skewness. See Excel tutorial to the left.

Tutorial #20
in Connect

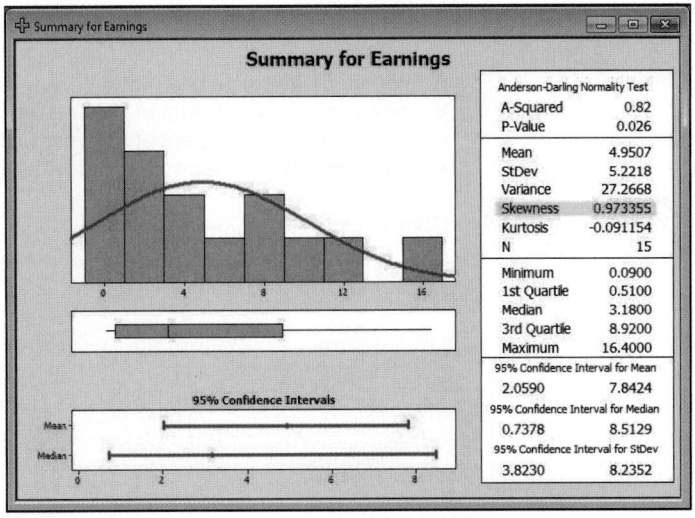

Source: Minitab

SELF-REVIEW 4–4

A sample of five data entry clerks employed in the Horry County Tax Office revised the following number of tax records last hour: 73, 98, 60, 92, and 84.
(a) Find the mean, median, and the standard deviation.
(b) Compute the coefficient of skewness using Pearson's method.
(c) Calculate the coefficient of skewness using the software method.
(d) What is your conclusion regarding the skewness of the data?

EXERCISES

13. **FILE** The following values are the starting salaries, in $000, for a sample of five accounting graduates who accepted positions in public accounting last year.

36.0	26.0	33.0	28.0	31.0

    a. Determine the mean, median, and the standard deviation.
    b. Determine the coefficient of skewness using Pearson's method.
    c. Determine the coefficient of skewness using the software method.

14. **FILE** Listed are the salaries, in $000, for a sample of 15 chief financial officers in the electronics industry.

$516.0	$548.0	$566.0	$534.0	$586.0	$529.0
546.0	523.0	538.0	523.0	551.0	552.0
486.0	558.0	574.0			

    a. Determine the minimum, first quartile, median, third quartile, and maximum values.
    b. Plot the data using a box plot.
    c. Determine the coefficient of skewness using Pearson's method.
    d. Determine the coefficient of skewness using the software method.
    e. Comment on the shape of the distribution using your answers to parts (b), (c), and (d).

15. **FILE** Listed are the commissions earned ($000) last year by the 15 sales representatives at Furniture Patch Inc.

$ 3.9	$ 5.7	$ 7.3	$10.6	$13.0	$13.6	$15.1	$15.8	$17.1
17.4	17.6	22.3	38.6	43.2	87.7			

a. Determine the minimum, first quartile, median, third quartile, and maximum values.
b. Plot the data using a box plot.
c. Determine the coefficient of skewness using Pearson's method.
d. Determine the coefficient of skewness using the software method.
e. Comment on the shape of the distribution using your answers to parts (b), (c), and (d).

16. **FILE** In 2021, 188 women played the Ladies Professional Golf Association (LPGA) tour. A random sample of 30 players is selected and their winnings recorded. The sample is listed here.

Jin Young Ko	$1,656,415	Stephanie Meadow	$140,897
Minjee Lee	$1,363,781	Muni He	$128,032
Lexi Thompson	$1,032,787	Ana Belac	$116,832
Hyo Joo Kim	$ 827,654	Andrea Lee	$107,165
Pajaree Anannarukarn	$ 663,169	Alena Sharp	$ 90,166
Ally Ewing	$ 605,336	Mo Martin	$ 50,945
Matilda Castren	$ 596,365	Kelly Tan	$ 48,910
Elizabeth Szokol	$ 510,203	Brianna Do	$ 30,153
Gaby Lopez	$ 468,574	Maria Fernanda Torres	$ 28,305
Eun-Hee Ji	$ 392,616	Jillian Hollis	$ 23,971
Sarah Schmelzel	$ 250,553	Ruixin Liu	$ 23,594
Haeji Kang	$ 210,653	Peiyun Chien	$ 17,279
Gerina Piller	$ 199,594	Vicky Hurst	$ 13,388
Celine Herbin	$ 176,811	Haru Nomura	$ 3,373
Mi Jung Hur	$ 146,811	Katelyn Dambaugh	$ 2,362

a. Determine the minimum, first quartile, median, third quartile, and maximum values.
b. Plot the data using a box plot.
c. Determine the coefficient of skewness using Pearson's method.
d. Determine the coefficient of skewness using the software method.
e. Comment on the shape of the distribution using your answers to parts (b), (c), and (d).

LO4-5
Create and interpret a scatter diagram.

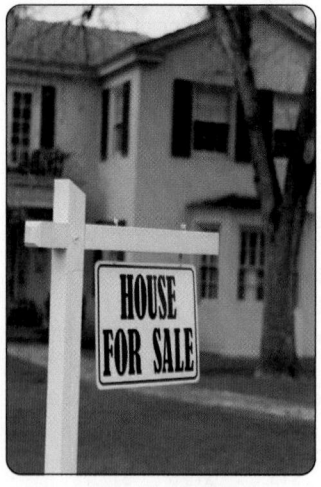
Steve Mason/Photodisc/Getty Images

Describing the Relationship between Two Variables

In Chapter 2 and the first section of this chapter, we presented graphical techniques to summarize the distribution of a single variable. We used a histogram in Chapter 2 to summarize the profit on vehicles sold by the Applewood Auto Group. Earlier in this chapter, we used dot plots to visualize a set of data. Because we are studying a single variable, we refer to this as **univariate** data.

There are situations where we wish to study and visually portray the relationship between two variables. When we study the relationship between two variables, we refer to the data as **bivariate.** Data analysts frequently wish to understand the relationship between two variables. Here are some examples:

- Tybo and Associates is a law firm that advertises extensively on local TV. The partners are considering increasing their advertising budget. Before doing so, they would like to know the relationship between the amount spent per month on advertising and the total amount of billings for that month. To put it another way, will increasing the amount spent on advertising result in an increase in billings?

- Coastal Realty is studying the selling prices of homes. What variables seem to be related to the selling price of homes? For example, do larger homes sell for more than smaller ones? Probably. So Coastal might study the relationship between the area in square feet and the selling price.
- Dr. Naveen Chatterjee is an expert in human development studying the relationship between the height of fathers and the height of their sons. That is, do tall fathers tend to have tall children? Would you expect LeBron James, the 6′8″, 250-pound professional basketball player, to have relatively tall sons?

One graphical technique we use to show the relationship between variables is called a **scatter diagram.**

> **SCATTER DIAGRAM** Graphical technique used to show the relationship between two variables measured with interval or ratio scales.

To draw a scatter diagram, we need two variables. We scale one variable along the horizontal axis (X-axis) of a graph and the other variable along the vertical axis (Y-axis). Usually one variable depends to some degree on the other. In the third example just presented, the height of the son *depends* on the height of the father. So we scale the height of the father on the X-axis and that of the son on the Y-axis. *Caution:* You should always be careful of the scale. By changing the scale of either the vertical or the horizontal axis, you can affect the apparent visual strength of the relationship.

LO4-6
Compute and interpret the correlation coefficient.

Correlation Coefficient

In addition to a scatter graph, a statistic called the **correlation coefficient** can be calculated to measure the direction and strength of the relationship between two variables. At this point, we will provide a brief introduction to the statistic and its interpretation. The correlation coefficient is computed as:

> **CORRELATION COEFFICIENT** $r = \dfrac{\Sigma(x - \bar{x})(y - \bar{y})}{(n - 1)s_x s_y}$ **(4–4)**

The formula is fairly complex, but, given a set of data, Excel and other statistical software easily compute the correlation coefficient. The sample correlation coefficient, specified by r, ranges from −1.0 to +1.0. Based on the value of the correlation coefficient, it can complement the interpretation of scatter diagrams. For example, if r = −1.0 the relationship between the two variables is perfectly negative; if r = +1.0 the relationship is perfectly positive. These two cases are illustrated as follows:

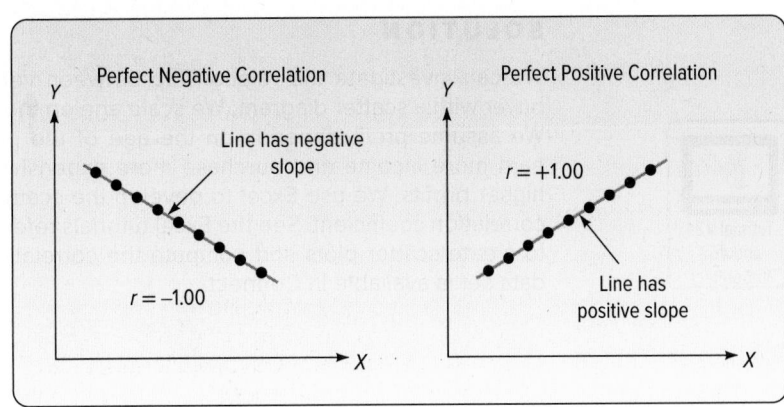

The correlation coefficient can be any value between −1.0 and +1.0. The closer the coefficient is to −1.0 or +1.0, the stronger the relationship. If *r* is close to 0.0, there is no relationship between the variables. Following are three scatter diagrams (Chart 4–2). The one on the left shows a rather strong positive relationship with a correlation coefficient of 0.99 between the age in years of a bus and its maintenance cost. Note that as the age of the bus increases, the yearly maintenance cost also increases. The example in the center shows the scatter plot of a baseball team's season total home runs versus the team's season batting average. The correlation is −0.08. The scatter plot shows no obvious relationship, and this observation is supported by a correlation coefficient that is very close to 0.0. The example on the right shows a rather strong indirect relationship, with a correlation coefficient of −0.80, between the price of a house and the days the house has been on the market. The relationship is that price decreases as the days on the market increases.

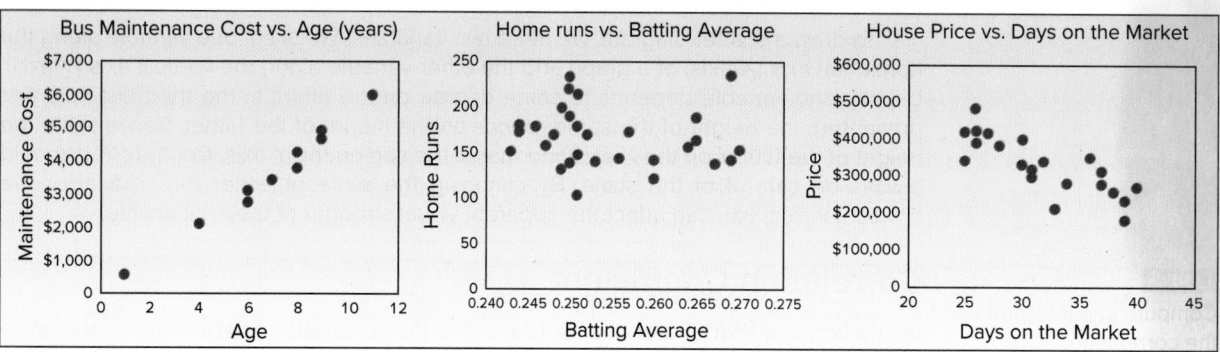

CHART 4–2 Three Examples of Scatter Diagrams

▶ **EXAMPLE**

In the introduction to Chapter 2, we presented data from the Applewood Auto Group. We gathered information concerning several variables, including the profit earned from the sale of 180 vehicles sold last month. In addition to the amount of profit on each sale, one of the other variables is the age of the purchaser. Is there a relationship between the profit earned on a vehicle sale and the age of the purchaser? Would it be reasonable to conclude that more profit is made on vehicles purchased by older buyers?

SOLUTION

Tutorial #24
and #62
in Connect

We can investigate the relationship between vehicle profit and the age of the buyer with a scatter diagram. We scale age on the *X*-axis and profit on the *Y*-axis. We assume profit depends on the age of the purchaser. As people age, they earn more income and purchase more expensive cars, which in turn produces higher profits. We use Excel to develop the scatter diagram and to compute the correlation coefficient. See the Excel tutorials referenced to the left that show how to create scatter plots and compute the correlation coefficient. The Applewood data set is available in Connect.

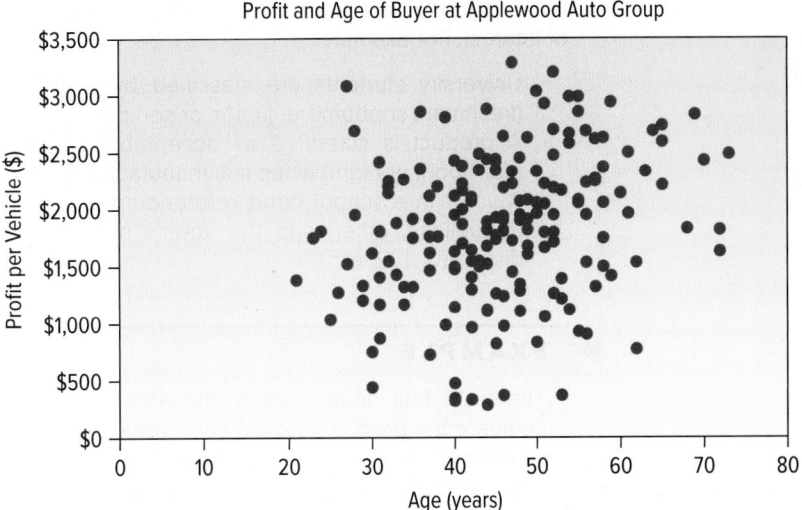

The scatter diagram shows a rather weak relationship between vehicle profit and the age of the buyer. The correlation coefficient of 0.26 supports this observation. In Chapter 13, we will study the relationship between variables more extensively, even calculating several numerical measures to express the relationship between variables.

In the preceding example, there is a weak positive, or direct, relationship between the variables. There are, however, many instances where there is a relationship between the variables, but that relationship is inverse or negative. For example:

- The value of a vehicle and the number of miles driven. As the number of miles increases, the value of the vehicle decreases.
- The premium for auto insurance and the age of the driver. Auto rates tend to be the highest for younger drivers and lower for older drivers.
- Businesses strive to increase product or service quality. Higher quality is often related to fewer defects, fewer customer complaints, or decreased rework.

LO4-7

Develop and explain a contingency table.

Contingency Tables

A scatter diagram requires that both of the variables be at least interval scale. In the Applewood Auto Group example, both age and vehicle profit are ratio-scale variables. Height is also ratio scale as used in the discussion of the relationship between the height of fathers and the height of their sons. What if we wish to study the relationship between two variables when one or both are nominal or ordinal scale? In this case, we tally the results in a **contingency table.**

> **CONTINGENCY TABLE** A table used to classify sample observations according to two identifiable characteristics.

A contingency table is a cross-tabulation that simultaneously summarizes two variables of interest. For example:

- University students are classified by residency (in or out of state) and class (freshman, sophomore, junior, or senior).
- A product is classified as acceptable or unacceptable and by the shift (day, afternoon, or night) when it is manufactured.
- A voter in a school bond referendum is classified by party affiliation (Democrat, Republican, other) and the voter's number of children attending school in the district (0, 1, 2, etc.).

▶ **EXAMPLE**

There are four dealerships in the Applewood Auto Group. Suppose we want to compare the profit earned on each vehicle sold by the particular dealership. To put it another way, is there a relationship between the amount of profit earned and the dealership?

SOLUTION

In a contingency table, both variables only need to be nominal or ordinal. In this example, the variable dealership is a nominal variable and the variable profit is a ratio variable. To convert profit to an ordinal variable, we classify the variable profit into two categories, those cases where the profit earned is more than the median and those cases where it is less. On page 61, we calculated the median profit for all sales last month at Applewood Auto Group to be $1,882.50.

Contingency Table Showing the Relationship between Profit and Dealership					
Above/Below Median Profit	**Kane**	**Olean**	**Sheffield**	**Tionesta**	**Total**
Above	25	20	19	26	90
Below	27	20	26	17	90
Total	52	40	45	43	180

By organizing the information into a contingency table, we can compare the profit at the four dealerships. We observe the following:

- From the Total column on the right, 90 of the 180 cars sold had a profit above the median and half below. From the definition of the median, this is expected.
- For the Kane dealership, 25 of the 52, or 48%, of the cars sold were sold for a profit more than the median.
- The percentage of profits above the median for the other dealerships are 50% for Olean, 42% for Sheffield, and 60% for Tionesta.

We will return to the study of contingency tables in Chapter 5 during the study of probability and in Chapter 15 during the study of nonparametric methods of analysis.

SELF-REVIEW 4–5

The rock group Blue String Beans is touring the United States. The following chart shows the relationship between concert seating capacity and revenue in $100,000s for a sample of concerts.

Seating Capacity	Amount ($100,000s)
5,700	2.0
5,700	3.0
5,950	2.9
6,000	4.3
6,050	3.8
6,200	3.6
6,500	6.0
6,550	6.1
6,600	3.9
6,650	4.1
6,700	6.0
6,800	6.2
7,000	6.8
7,350	7.3
7,300	7.4

(a) Create a scatter plot.
(b) Compute the correlation coefficient for the relationship.
(c) Estimate the revenue for the concert with the largest seating capacity.
(d) How would you characterize the relationship between revenue and seating capacity? Is it strong or weak, direct or inverse?

EXERCISES

17. **FILE** Create a scatter diagram and compute a correlation coefficient. How would you describe the relationship between the values?

x-Value	y-Value	x-Value	y-Value
10	6	11	6
8	2	10	5
9	6	7	2
11	5	7	3
13	7	11	7

18. Silver Springs Moving and Storage Inc. is studying the relationship between the number of rooms in a move and the number of labor hours required for the move. As part of the analysis, create a scatter plot and compute a correlation coefficient. Comment on the relationship.

Rooms	Labor Hours	Rooms	Labor Hours
1.0	3	2.5	17
1.0	15	3.0	18
1.5	8	3.0	35
1.5	16	3.5	28
2.0	17	4.0	19
2.0	15	4.5	33
2.5	16	5.0	40
2.5	24		

19. The Director of Planning for Devine Dining Inc. wishes to study the relationship between the time of day a customer dined and whether the guest orders dessert. To investigate the relationship, the manager collected the following information from a sample of 200 recent customers.

Dessert Ordered	Time of Day		Total
	Lunch	Dinner	
Yes	32	85	117
No	68	15	83
Total	100	100	200

a. What is the level of measurement of the two variables?
b. What is this table called?
c. Do the data suggest that customers are more likely to order dessert? Explain why.
d. Do the data suggest that customers at lunch time are more likely to order dessert? Explain why.
e. Do the data suggest that customers at dinner time are more likely to order dessert? Explain why.

20. Ski Resorts of Vermont Inc. is considering a merger with Gulf Shores Beach Resorts Inc. of Alabama. The board of directors surveyed 50 stockholders concerning their position on the merger. The results are reported here.

Number of Shares Held	Opinion			Total
	Favor	Oppose	Undecided	
Under 200	8	6	2	16
200 up to 1,000	6	8	1	15
Over 1,000	6	12	1	19
Total	20	26	4	50

a. What level of measurement is used in this table?
b. What is this table called?
c. What group seems most strongly opposed to the merger?

CHAPTER SUMMARY

I. A dot plot shows the range of values on the horizontal axis and the number of observations for each value on the vertical axis.
   A. Dot plots report the details of each observation.
   B. They are useful for comparing two or more data sets.
II. Measures of location also describe the distribution of observations or data.
   A. Quartiles divide a set of observations into four equal parts.
      1. Twenty-five percent of the observations are less than the first quartile, 50% are less than the second quartile, and 75% are less than the third quartile.
      2. The interquartile range is the difference between the third quartile and the first quartile. Fifty percent of observations occur within the interquartile range.
   B. Deciles divide a set of observations into 10 equal parts and percentiles into 100 equal parts.
III. A box plot is a graphic display of a set of data.
   A. A box is drawn enclosing the regions between the first quartile and the third quartile.
      1. A line is drawn inside the box at the median value.
      2. Dotted line segments are drawn from the third quartile to the largest value to show the highest 25% of the values and from the first quartile to the smallest value to show the lowest 25% of the values.
   B. A box plot is based on five statistics: the maximum and minimum values, the first and third quartiles, and the median.

IV. The coefficient of skewness is a measure of the symmetry of a distribution.
    A. There are two formulas for the coefficient of skewness.
        1. The formula developed by Pearson is:

$$sk = \frac{3(\bar{x} - \text{Median})}{s} \tag{4–2}$$

        2. The coefficient of skewness computed by statistical software is:

$$sk = \frac{n}{(n-1)(n-2)}\left[\Sigma\left(\frac{x-\bar{x}}{s}\right)^3\right] \tag{4–3}$$

V. A scatter diagram is a graphic tool to portray the relationship between two variables.
    A. Both variables are measured with interval or ratio scales.
    B. If the scatter of points moves from the lower left to the upper right, the variables under consideration are directly or positively related.
    C. If the scatter of points moves from the upper left to the lower right, the variables are inversely or negatively related.
    D. The correlation coefficient measures the strength of the linear association between two variables.
        1. Both variables must be at least the interval scale of measurement.
        2. The correlation coefficient can range from −1.00 to 1.00.
        3. If the correlation between the two variables is 0, there is no association between them.
        4. A value of 1.00 indicates perfect positive correlation, and a value of −1.00 indicates perfect negative correlation.
        5. A positive sign means there is a direct relationship between the variables, and a negative sign means there is an indirect relationship.
VI. A contingency table is used to classify nominal-scale observations according to two characteristics.

PRONUNCIATION KEY

SYMBOL	MEANING	PRONUNCIATION
L_p	Location of percentile	L sub p
Q_1	First quartile	Q sub 1
Q_3	Third quartile	Q sub 3

CHAPTER EXERCISES

21. Southeast Florida University surveyed a sample of students about the number of social activities in which they participated last week. The following chart was prepared from the sample data.

    a. What is the name given to this chart?
    b. How many students were in the study?
    c. How many students reported attending no social activities?
22. Doctor's Care is a walk-in clinic, with locations in Georgetown, Moncks Corner, and Aynor, where patients receive treatment for minor injuries, colds, and flu, as well as

physical examinations. The following chart reports the number of patients treated in each of the three locations last month.

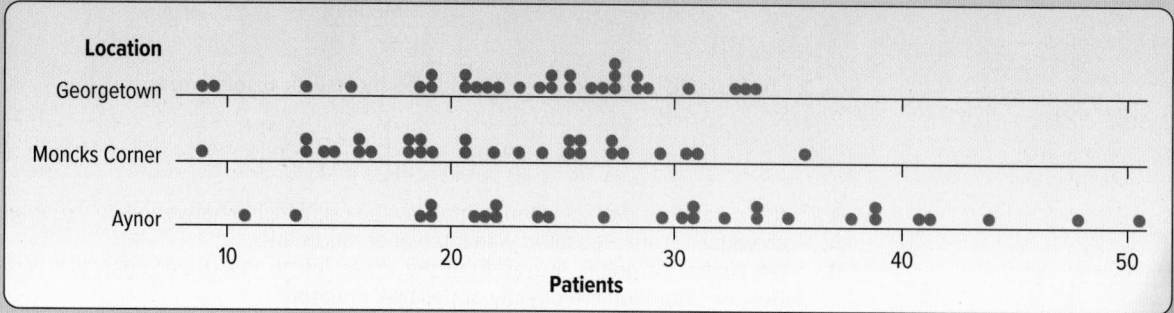

Using the charts, compare the three locations based on the number of patients served per day.

23. **FILE** In recent years, homeowners in Spain refinanced their home mortgages due to low interest rates. Santana Sosa is a mortgage officer at Open Bank, S.A. Following are the amounts refinanced for 20 loans Santana processed last week. The data are reported in thousands of euros and arranged from smallest to largest.

59.2	59.5	61.6	65.5	66.6	72.9	74.8	77.3	79.2
83.7	85.6	85.8	86.6	87.0	87.1	90.2	93.3	98.6
100.2	100.7							

a. Find the median, first quartile, and third quartile.
b. Find the 26th and 83rd percentiles.
c. Draw a box plot of the data.

24. **FILE** Listed are the 30 companies that make up the Dow Jones Industrial Average (DJIA) and their percent dividend yields (October 2021). Make a box plot of the percent dividend yields for these companies. Write a brief report describing the information represented by the box plot.

Company	Dividend Yield (%)	Company	Dividend Yield (%)
3M	3.29	Intel	2.92
American Express	0.92	Johnson & Johnson	2.66
Amgen	3.59	JPMorgan Chase	2.42
Apple	0.62	McDonalds	2.32
Boeing	0.00	Merck	3.40
Caterpillar	2.29	Microsoft	0.80
Chevron	4.84	NIKE B	0.76
Cisco Systems	2.79	Procter & Gamble	2.63
Coca-Cola	3.14	Salesforce.Com	0.00
Disney	1.04	Travelers	2.20
Dow	4.79	UnitedHealth Group	1.38
Goldman Sachs	2.03	Verizon Communications	4.86
Home Depot	1.93	Visa A	0.61
Honeywell International	1.80	Walgreens Boots Alliance	3.92
IBM	5.16	WalMart	1.50

25. **FILE** The corporate headquarters of *Bank.com*, an online banking company, is located in downtown Philadelphia. The director of human resources is making a study of the time it takes employees to get to work. The city is planning to offer incentives to each downtown employer if they will encourage their employees to use public transportation. The following is a listing of the time to get to work this morning according to whether the employee used public transportation or drove a car.

Public Transportation									
23	25	25	30	31	31	32	33	35	36
37	42								

Private									
32	32	33	34	37	37	38	38	38	39
40	44								

   a. Find the median and the first and third quartiles for the time it took employees using public transportation. Develop a box plot for the information.
   b. Find the median and the first and third quartiles for the time it took employees who drove their own vehicle. Develop a box plot for the information.
   c. Compare the times of the two groups.

26. The following box plot shows the number of daily newspapers published in each state and the District of Columbia. Write a brief report summarizing the number published. Be sure to include information on the values of the first and third quartiles, the median, and whether there is any skewness. If there are any outliers, estimate their value.

Number of Newspapers

27. The Gogel Company is an industrial supplier of fasteners, tools, and springs. The amounts of its invoices vary widely, from less than $20.00 to more than $400.00. During the month of January, the company sent out 80 invoices. Here is a box plot of these invoices. Write a brief report summarizing the invoice amounts. Be sure to include information on the values of the first and third quartiles, the median, and whether there is any skewness. If there are any outliers, approximate the value of these invoices.

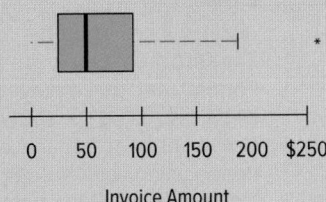

Invoice Amount

28. **FILE** For each U.S. state and the District of Columbia, the following table lists the total employees and number of total employees represented by unions.

State	Number Represented by Unions	Total Employees	State	Number Represented by Unions	Total Employees
Alabama	164,000	1,896,000	Montana	54,000	419,000
Alaska	55,000	280,000	Nebraska	94,000	890,000
Arizona	207,000	2,909,000	Nevada	186,000	1,208,000
Arkansas	69,000	1,158,000	New Hampshire	70,000	629,000
California	2,655,000	15,069,000	New Jersey	660,000	3,719,000
Colorado	202,000	2,470,000	New Mexico	64,000	743,000
Connecticut	282,000	1,533,000	New York	1,784,000	7,552,000
Delaware	44,000	424,000	North Carolina	161,000	4,128,000
District of Columbia	33,000	343,000	North Dakota	25,000	338,000
Florida	644,000	8,155,000	Ohio	686,000	4,815,000
Georgia	271,000	4,173,000	Oklahoma	114,000	1,501,000
Hawaii	130,000	508,000	Oregon	293,000	1,694,000
Idaho	47,000	732,000	Pennsylvania	775,000	5,307,000
Illinois	788,000	5,178,000	Rhode Island	87,000	455,000
Indiana	270,000	2,838,000	South Carolina	77,000	2,036,000
Iowa	128,000	1,401,000	South Dakota	21,000	385,000
Kansas	144,000	1,282,000	Tennessee	137,000	2,678,000
Kentucky	160,000	1,694,000	Texas	642,000	11,607,000
Louisiana	113,000	1,682,000	Utah	75,000	1,403,000
Maine	93,000	559,000	Vermont	36,000	265,000
Maryland	380,000	2,690,000	Virginia	201,000	3,703,000
Massachusetts	383,000	2,982,000	Washington	596,000	3,201,000
Michigan	661,000	3,974,000	West Virginia	75,000	666,000
Minnesota	427,000	2,515,000	Wisconsin	264,000	2,592,000
Mississippi	86,000	1,034,000	Wyoming	22,000	240,000
Missouri	254,000	2,525,000			

Use statistical software to answer the following questions.

a. For Number Represented by Unions, determine the minimum, first quartile, median, third quartile, and maximum values.

b. For Number Represented by Unions, determine if any observations are outliers. If so, report the lower and upper outlier boundaries.

c. For Number Represented by Unions, plot the data using a box plot.

d. For Number Represented by Unions, determine the coefficient of skewness using the software method.

e. Comment on the shape of the Number Represented by Unions distribution using your answers to parts (a), (b), (c), and (d).

f. Compute and add a variable, Percent of Employees Represented by Unions.

g. For Percent of Employees Represented by Unions, determine the minimum, first quartile, median, third quartile, and maximum values.

h. For Percent of Employees Represented by Unions, determine if any observations are outliers. If so, report the lower and upper outlier boundaries.

i. For Percent of Employees Represented by Unions, plot the data using a box plot.

j. For Percent of Employees Represented by Unions, determine the coefficient of skewness using the software method.

k. Comment on the shape of the Percent of Employees Represented by Unions distribution using your answers to parts (g), (h), (i), and (j).

l. Does Number Represented by Unions or Percent of Employees Represented by Unions better reflect union representation?

29. **FILE** McGivern Jewelers is located in the Levis Square Mall just south of Toledo, Ohio. Recently it posted an advertisement on a social media site reporting the shape, size, price, and cut grade for 33 of its diamonds currently in stock. The information is reported as follows:

Shape	Size (carats)	Price	Cut Grade
Princess	5.03	$44,312	Ideal cut
Round	2.35	20,413	Premium cut
Round	2.03	13,080	Ideal cut
Round	1.56	13,925	Ideal cut
Round	1.21	7,382	Ultra ideal cut
Round	1.21	5,154	Average cut
Round	1.19	5,339	Premium cut
Emerald	1.16	5,161	Ideal cut
Round	1.08	8,775	Ultra ideal cut
Round	1.02	4,282	Premium cut
Round	1.02	6,943	Ideal cut
Marquise	1.01	7,038	Good cut
Princess	1.00	4,868	Premium cut
Round	0.91	5,106	Premium cut
Round	0.90	3,921	Good cut
Round	0.90	3,733	Premium cut
Round	0.84	2,621	Premium cut
Round	0.77	2,828	Ultra ideal cut
Oval	0.76	3,808	Premium cut
Princess	0.71	2,327	Premium cut
Marquise	0.71	2,732	Good cut
Round	0.70	1,915	Premium cut
Round	0.66	1,885	Premium cut
Round	0.62	1,397	Good cut
Round	0.52	2,555	Premium cut
Princess	0.51	1,337	Ideal cut
Round	0.51	1,558	Premium cut
Round	0.45	1,191	Premium cut
Princess	0.44	1,319	Average cut
Marquise	0.44	1,319	Premium cut
Round	0.40	1,133	Premium cut
Round	0.35	1,354	Good cut
Round	0.32	896	Premium cut

a. Develop a box plot of the variable price and comment on the result. Are there any outliers? What is the median price? What are the values of the first and the third quartiles?

b. Develop a box plot of the variable size and comment on the result. Are there any outliers? What is the median price? What are the values of the first and the third quartiles?

c. Develop a scatter diagram between the variables Price and Size. Be sure to put Price on the vertical axis and Size on the horizontal axis. Does there seem to be an association between the two variables? Is the association direct or indirect? Does any point seem to be different from the others?

d. Develop a contingency table for the variables Shape and Cut Grade. What is the most common cut grade? What is the most common shape? What is the most common combination of cut grade and shape?

30. FILE Listed is the amount of commissions earned last month for the eight members of the sales staff at Best Electronics. Calculate the coefficient of skewness using both methods. What do the skewness statistics indicate about the distribution? Hint: Use of a spreadsheet will expedite the calculations.

980.9	1,036.5	1,099.5	1,153.9	1,409.0	1,456.4	1,718.4	1,721.2

31. **FILE** Listed is the number of car thefts in a sample of seven large cities over the last week. Calculate the coefficient of skewness using both methods. What do the skewness statistics indicate about the distribution? Hint: Use of a spreadsheet will expedite the calculations.

3	12	13	7	8	3	8

32. The manager of Information Services at Wilkin Investigations, a private investigation firm, is studying the relationship between the age (in months) of a combination printer, copier, and fax machine and its monthly maintenance cost. Create a scatter graph and compute the correlation coefficient. Describe the results of your analysis.

Months	Monthly Cost
33	88
35	97
35	111
36	90
37	79
37	93
38	105
39	109
43	98
43	107
44	100
41	123
41	126
47	121
48	109

33. **FILE** An auto insurance company reported the following information regarding the age of a driver and the number of accidents reported last year. Develop a scatter diagram for the data and write a brief summary.

Age	Accidents	Age	Accidents
16	4	23	0
24	2	27	1
18	5	32	1
17	4	22	3

34. Wendy's offers eight different condiments (mustard, ketchup, onion, mayonnaise, pickle, lettuce, tomato, and relish) on hamburgers. A store manager collected the following information on the number of condiments ordered and the age group of the customer. What can you conclude regarding the information? Who tends to order the most or least number of condiments?

	Age			
Number of Condiments	Under 18	18 up to 40	40 up to 60	60 or Older
0	12	18	24	52
1	21	76	50	30
2	39	52	40	12
3 or more	71	87	47	28

35. Here is a table showing the number of employed and unemployed workers 20 years or older by gender in the United States.

Gender	Number of Workers (000)	
	Employed	**Unemployed**
Men	70,415	4,209
Women	61,402	3,314

    a. How many workers were studied?
    b. What percent of the workers were unemployed?
    c. Compare the percent unemployed for the men and the women.

DATA ANALYTICS

(The data for these exercises are available in Connect.)

36. **FILE** Refer to the North Valley real estate data recorded on homes sold during the last year. Prepare a report on the selling prices of the homes based on the answers to the following questions.
    a. Compute the minimum, maximum, median, and the first and the third quartiles of price. Create a box plot. Comment on the distribution of home prices.
    b. Develop a scatter diagram with price on the vertical axis and the size of the home on the horizontal. Is there a relationship between these variables? Is the relationship direct or indirect?
    c. For homes without a pool, develop a scatter diagram with price on the vertical axis and the size of the home on the horizontal. Do the same for homes with a pool. How do the relationships between price and size for homes without a pool and homes with a pool compare?

37. **FILE** Refer to the Baseball 2021 data that report information on the 30 Major League Baseball teams for the 2021 season.
    a. In the data set, the year opened is the first year of operation for that stadium. For each team, use this variable to create a new variable, stadium age, by subtracting the value of the variable year opened from the current year. Develop a box plot with the new variable, stadium age. Are there any outliers? If so, which of the stadiums are outliers?
    b. Using the variable salary create a box plot. Are there any outliers? Compute the quartiles using formula (4–1). Write a brief summary of your analysis.
    c. Draw a scatter diagram with the variable wins on the vertical axis and salary on the horizontal axis. Compute the correlation coefficient between wins and salary. What are your conclusions?
    d. Using the variable wins draw a dot plot. What can you conclude from this plot?

38. **FILE** Refer to the Lincolnville School District bus data.
    a. Referring to the maintenance cost variable, develop a box plot. What are the minimum, first quartile, median, third quartile, and maximum values? Are there any outliers?
    b. Using the median maintenance cost, develop a contingency table with bus manufacturer as one variable and whether the maintenance cost was above or below the median as the other variable. What are your conclusions?

A REVIEW OF CHAPTERS 1–4

This section is a review of the major concepts and terms introduced in Chapters 1–4. Chapter 1 began by describing the meaning and purpose of statistics. Next we described the different types of variables and the four levels of measurement. Chapter 2 was concerned with describing a set of observations by organizing it into a frequency distribution and then portraying the frequency distribution as a histogram or a frequency polygon. Chapter 3 began by describing measures of location, such as the mean, weighted mean, median, geometric mean, and mode. This chapter also included measures of dispersion, or spread. Discussed in this section were the range, variance, and standard deviation. Chapter 4 included several graphing techniques such as dot plots, box plots, and scatter diagrams. We also discussed the coefficient of skewness, which reports the lack of symmetry in a set of data, and the correlation coefficient.

Throughout this section we stressed the importance of statistical software, such as Excel. Many computer outputs in these chapters demonstrated how quickly and effectively a large data set can be organized into a frequency distribution, several of the measures of location or measures of variation calculated, and the information presented in graphical form.

PROBLEMS

1. **FILE** The duration in minutes of a sample of 50 power outages last year in the state of South Carolina is as follows:

124	14	150	289	52	156	203	82	27	248
39	52	103	58	136	249	110	298	251	157
186	107	142	185	75	202	119	219	156	78
116	152	206	117	52	299	58	153	219	148
145	187	165	147	158	146	185	186	149	140

Use a statistical software package such as Excel or Minitab to help answer the following questions.
   a. Determine the mean, median, and standard deviation.
   b. Determine the first and third quartiles.
   c. Develop a box plot. Are there any outliers? Do the amounts follow a symmetric distribution or are they skewed? Justify your answer.
   d. Organize the distribution of funds into a frequency distribution.
   e. Write a brief summary of the results in parts (a) to (d).

2. **FILE** Listed are the 46 U.S. presidents and their age as they began their terms in office.

Number	Name	Age	Number	Name	Age
1	Washington	57	24	Cleveland	55
2	J. Adams	61	25	McKinley	54
3	Jefferson	57	26	T. Roosevelt	42
4	Madison	57	27	Taft	51
5	Monroe	58	28	Wilson	56
6	J. Q. Adams	57	29	Harding	55
7	Jackson	61	30	Coolidge	51
8	Van Buren	54	31	Hoover	54
9	W. H. Harrison	68	32	F. D. Roosevelt	51
10	Tyler	51	33	Truman	60
11	Polk	49	34	Eisenhower	62
12	Taylor	64	35	Kennedy	43
13	Fillmore	50	36	L. B. Johnson	55
14	Pierce	48	37	Nixon	56
15	Buchanan	65	38	Ford	61
16	Lincoln	52	39	Carter	52
17	A. Johnson	56	40	Reagan	69
18	Grant	46	41	G. H. W. Bush	64
19	Hayes	54	42	Clinton	46
20	Garfield	49	43	G. W. Bush	54
21	Arthur	50	44	Obama	47
22	Cleveland	47	45	Trump	70
23	B. Harrison	55	46	Biden	78

Use a statistical software package such as Excel or Minitab to help answer the following questions.

a. Determine the minimum, first quartile, median, third quartile, and maximum values of age.

b. Determine and interpret the interquartile range.

c. Develop a box plot. Are there any outliers? Do the amounts follow a symmetric distribution or are they skewed? Justify your answer.

d. Organize the distribution of ages into a frequency distribution.

e. Write a brief summary of the results in parts (a) to (d).

3. **FILE** Listed are the 2019 U.S. Census Bureau estimates of median annual family income for the 50 states, the District of Columbia, and Puerto Rico (**https://www.census.gov/programs-surveys/acs/data.html**).

State	Median family income (dollars)	State	Median family income (dollars)
Alabama	$ 66,171	Montana	$ 73,014
Alaska	91,971	Nebraska	80,062
Arizona	74,468	Nevada	76,124
Arkansas	62,387	New Hampshire	97,112
California	91,377	New Jersey	105,705
Colorado	95,164	New Mexico	61,826
Connecticut	101,272	New York	89,475
Delaware	87,148	North Carolina	72,049
District of Columbia	130,291	North Dakota	87,055
Florida	71,348	Ohio	74,911
Georgia	74,833	Oklahoma	68,358
Hawaii	96,462	Oregon	82,540
Idaho	72,365	Pennsylvania	81,075
Illinois	87,771	Puerto Rico	25,388
Indiana	73,876	Rhode Island	89,373
Iowa	78,152	South Carolina	70,537
Kansas	79,006	South Dakota	76,826
Kentucky	66,183	Tennessee	69,993
Louisiana	65,105	Texas	76,727
Maine	76,316	Utah	86,152
Maryland	105,679	Vermont	83,458
Massachusetts	108,348	Virginia	93,497
Michigan	75,703	Washington	94,709
Minnesota	93,584	West Virginia	60,920
Mississippi	58,503	Wisconsin	81,829
Missouri	73,457	Wyoming	79,946

Use a statistical software package such as Excel or Minitab to help answer the following questions.

a. Determine the minimum or lower outlier boundary, first quartile, median, third quartile, and maximum or upper outlier boundary values of median family income.

b. Determine and interpret the interquartile range.

c. Develop a box plot. Are there any outliers? Do the amounts follow a symmetric distribution or are they skewed? Justify your answer.

d. Organize the distribution of funds into a frequency distribution.

e. Write a brief summary of the results in parts (a) to (d).

4. A sample of 12 homes sold last week in St. Paul, Minnesota, revealed the following information. Draw a scatter diagram. Can we conclude that, as the size of the home (reported in thousands of square feet) increases, the selling price (reported in $ thousands) also increases?

Home Size (thousands of square feet)	Selling Price ($ thousands)	Home Size (thousands of square feet)	Selling Price ($ thousands)
1.4	100	1.3	110
1.3	110	0.8	85
1.2	105	1.2	105
1.1	120	0.9	75
1.4	80	1.1	70
1.0	105	1.1	95

5. Refer to the following diagram.

    a. What is the graph called?
    b. Estimate the median, and first and third quartile values.
    c. Is the distribution positively skewed? Tell how you know.
    d. Are there any outliers? If yes, estimate these values.
    e. Can you determine the number of observations in the study?

CASES

A. Century National Bank

The following case will appear in subsequent review sections. Assume that you work in the Planning Department of the Century National Bank and report to Ms. Lamberg. You will need to do some data analysis and prepare a short written report. Remember, Mr. Selig is the president of the bank, so you will want to ensure that your report is complete and accurate. A copy of the data appears in Appendix A.5.

Century National Bank has offices in several cities in the Midwest and the southeastern part of the United States. Mr. Dan Selig, president and CEO, would like to know the characteristics of his checking account customers. What is the balance of a typical customer?

How many other bank services do the checking account customers use? Do the customers use the ATM service and, if so, how often? What about debit cards? Who uses them, and how often are they used?

To better understand the customers, Mr. Selig asked Ms. Wendy Lamberg, director of planning, to select a sample of customers and prepare a report. To begin, she has appointed a team from her staff. You are the head of the team and responsible for preparing the report. You select a random sample of 60 customers. In addition to the balance in each account at the end of last month, you determine (1) the number of ATM (automatic teller machine) transactions in the last month; (2) the number of

other bank services (a savings account, a certificate of deposit, etc.) the customer uses; (3) whether the customer has a debit card (this is a bank service in which charges are made directly to the customer's account); and (4) whether or not interest is paid on the checking account. The sample includes customers from the branches in Cincinnati, Ohio; Atlanta, Georgia; Louisville, Kentucky; and Erie, Pennsylvania.

1. Develop a graph or table that portrays the checking balances. What is the balance of a typical customer? Do many customers have more than $2,000 in their accounts? Does it appear that there is a difference in the distribution of the accounts among the four branches? Around what value do the account balances tend to cluster?

2. Determine the mean and median of the checking account balances. Compare the mean and the median balances for the four branches. Is there a difference among the branches? Be sure to explain the difference between the mean and the median in your report.

3. Determine the range and the standard deviation of the checking account balances. What do the first and third quartiles show? Determine the coefficient of skewness and indicate what it shows. Because Mr. Selig does not deal with statistics daily, include

a brief description and interpretation of the standard deviation and other measures.

B. Wildcat Plumbing Supply Inc.: Do We Have Gender Differences?

Wildcat Plumbing Supply has served the plumbing needs of Southwest Arizona for more than 40 years. The company was founded by Mr. Terrence St. Julian and is run today by his son Cory. The company has grown from a handful of employees to more than 500 today. Cory is concerned about several positions within the company where he has men and women doing essentially the same job but at different pay. To investigate, he collected the information below. Suppose you are a student intern in the Accounting Department and have been given the task to write a report summarizing the situation.

Yearly Salary ($000)	Women	Men
Less than 30	2	0
30 up to 40	3	1
40 up to 50	17	4
50 up to 60	17	24
60 up to 70	8	21
70 up to 80	3	7
80 or more	0	3

To kick off the project, Mr. Cory St. Julian held a meeting with his staff and you were invited. At this meeting, it was suggested that you calculate several measures of location, create charts or draw graphs such as a cumulative frequency distribution, and determine the quartiles for both men and women. Develop the charts and write the report summarizing the yearly salaries of employees at Wildcat Plumbing Supply. Does it appear that there are pay differences based on gender?

C. Kimble Products: Is There a Difference In the Commissions?

At the January national sales meeting, the CEO of Kimble Products was questioned extensively regarding the company policy for paying commissions to its sales representatives. The company sells sporting goods to two major markets. There are 40 sales representatives who call directly on large-volume customers, such as the athletic departments at major colleges and universities and professional sports franchises.

Commissions Earned by Sales Representatives Calling on Athletic Departments ($)

354	87	1,676	1,187	69	3,202	680	39	1,683	1,106
883	3,140	299	2,197	175	159	1,105	434	615	149
1,168	278	579	7	357	252	1,602	2,321	4	392
416	427	1,738	526	13	1,604	249	557	635	527

There are 30 sales representatives who represent the company to retail stores located in shopping malls and large discounters such as Kmart and Target.

Commissions Earned by Sales Representatives Calling on Large Retailers ($)

1,116	681	1,294	12	754	1,206	1,448	870	944	1,255
1,213	1,291	719	934	1,313	1,083	899	850	886	1,556
886	1,315	1,858	1,262	1,338	1,066	807	1,244	758	918

Upon his return to corporate headquarters, the CEO asked the sales manager for a report comparing the commissions earned last year by the two parts of the sales team. The information is reported below. Write a brief report. Would you conclude that there is a difference? Be sure to include information in the report on both the central tendency and dispersion of the two groups.

PRACTICE TEST

There is a practice test at the end of each review section. The tests are in two parts. The first part contains several objective questions, usually in a fill-in-the-blank format. The second part is problems. In most cases, it should take 30 to 45 minutes to complete the test. The problems require a calculator. Check the answers in the Answer Section in the back of the book.

Part 1—Objective

1. The science of collecting, organizing, presenting, analyzing, and interpreting data to assist in making effective decisions is called _____.

2. Methods of organizing, summarizing, and presenting data in an informative way are called _____.

3. The entire set of individuals or objects of interest or the measurements obtained from all individuals or objects of interest are called the _____.

4. List the two types of variables.

5. The number of bedrooms in a house is an example of a _____. (discrete variable, continuous variable, qualitative variable—pick one)

1. _____

2. _____

3. _____

4. _____

5. _____

6. The jersey numbers of Major League Baseball players are an example of what level of measurement?   6. _____
7. The classification of students by eye color is an example of what level of measurement?   7. _____
8. The sum of the differences between each value and the mean is always equal to what value?   8. _____
9. A set of data contained 70 observations. How many classes would the 2^k method suggest to construct a frequency distribution?   9. _____
10. What percent of the values in a data set are always larger than the median?   10. _____
11. The square of the standard deviation is the _____.   11. _____
12. The standard deviation assumes a negative value when _____. (all the values are negative, at least half the values are negative, or never—pick one)   12. _____
13. Which of the following is least affected by an outlier? (mean, median, or range—pick one)   13. _____

Part 2—Problems

1. The Russell 2000 index of stock prices increased by the following amounts over the last 3 years.

| 18%   4%   2% |

What is the geometric mean increase for the 3 years?   _____

2. The information refers to recent selling prices ($000) of homes sold in Warren, Pennsylvania.

Selling Price ($000)	Frequency
120.0 up to 150.0	4
150.0 up to 180.0	18
180.0 up to 210.0	30
210.0 up to 240.0	20
240.0 up to 270.0	17
270.0 up to 300.0	10
300.0 up to 330.0	6

a. What is the class interval?   _____
b. How many homes were sold?   _____
c. How many homes sold for less than $210,000?   _____
d. What is the relative frequency of the 210 up to 240 class?   _____
e. What is the midpoint of the 150 up to 180 class?   _____
f. The selling prices range between what two amounts?   _____

3. A sample of eight college students revealed they owned the following number of CDs.

| 52   76   64   79   80   74   66   69 |

a. What is the mean number of CDs owned?   _____
b. What is the median number of CDs owned?   _____
c. What is the 40th percentile?   _____
d. What is the range of the number of CDs owned?   _____
e. What is the standard deviation of the number of CDs owned?   _____

4. An investor purchased 200 shares of the Blair Company for $36 each in July 2019, 300 shares at $40 each in September 2021, and 500 shares at $50 each in January 2022. What is the investor's weighted mean price per share?   _____

5. During the 50th Super Bowl, 30 million pounds of snack food were eaten. The chart depicts this information.

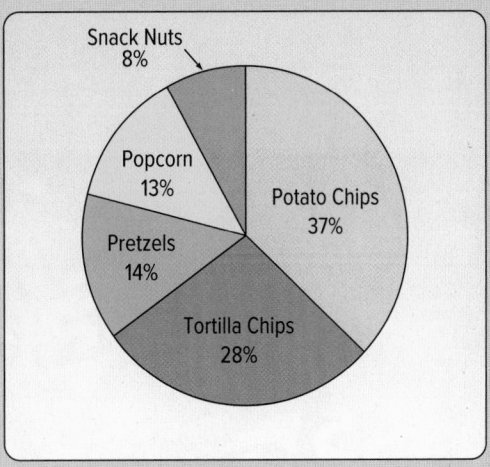

a. What is the name given to this graph?
b. Estimate, in millions of pounds, the amount of potato chips eaten during the game.
c. Estimate the relationship of potato chips to popcorn. (twice as much, half as much, three times, none of these—pick one)
d. What percent of the total do potato chips and tortilla chips comprise?

A Survey of Probability Concepts

Gabriel Petrescu/Shutterstock

▲ **FOR THE DAILY** lottery game in Illinois, participants select three numbers between 0 and 9. A number cannot be selected more than once, so a winning ticket could be, say, 307 but not 337. Purchasing one ticket allows you to select one set of numbers. The winning numbers are announced on TV each night. Suppose you purchase three tickets for tonight's drawing and select a different number for each ticket. What is the probability that you will not win with any of the tickets? (See Exercise 74, **LO5-2, LO5-6**.)

LEARNING OBJECTIVES

When you have completed this chapter, you will be able to:

LO5-1 Define the terms *probability, experiment, event,* and *outcome.*

LO5-2 Apply the classical approach to assign probabilities.

LO5-3 Determine the number of outcomes using principles of counting.

LO5-4 Apply the empirical approach to assign probabilities.

LO5-5 Apply the subjective approach to assign probabilities.

LO5-6 Calculate probabilities using the rules of addition.

LO5-7 Calculate probabilities using the rules of multiplication.

LO5-8 Compute probabilities using a contingency table.

LO5-9 Calculate probabilities using Bayes' theorem.

Introduction

The emphasis in Chapters 2, 3, and 4 is on ways to describe, summarize, and visualize data. In Chapter 2, we organize the profits of 180 vehicles sold by the Applewood Auto Group into a frequency distribution. This frequency distribution shows the smallest and the largest profits and where the largest concentration of data occurs. In Chapter 3, we use numerical measures of location, the mean, median, and mode, to find a typical

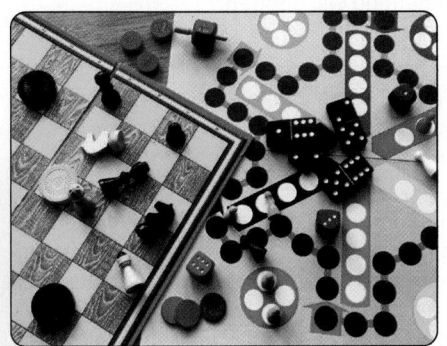

profit. We also describe and summarize the distribution of profits with measures of dispersion such as the range and the standard deviation. In Chapter 4, we develop charts and graphs, such as dot plots, box plots, and scatter diagrams, to graphically present and visualize the shape of the data's distribution.

For the most part, statistics are used to summarize data collected from current or past events. In this chapter, we focus on probability theory, often referred to as the science of uncertainty. Probability theory allows decision makers to estimate or compute the probability or likelihood of future, uncertain events. For example:

Ballda/Shutterstock

- Gaming Experience Inc., a gaming software company, recently developed a new sports trivia game. The company wants to find a good brand name to attract and sustain future sales. Two names under consideration are "The next great sports announcer" and "Ask me another sports question." To investigate, the president of Gaming Experience Inc. hired a market research firm. The firm selected a random sample of 800 consumers from the population and asked each respondent for a reaction to the new game and its proposed titles. Using the sample results, the company can estimate the probability a randomly selected consumer would favor each of the names. The results indicated that 60% of the sampled consumers preferred "The next great sports announcer," 30% liked "Ask me another sports question," and 10% did not like either name. The results indicate a 60% probability a random consumer would purchase "The next great sports announcer." The probability is also used to predict and estimate that 60% of the potential market of consumers would purchase a game with the preferred name.
- Financial decisions are often made based on the probabilities associated with future events. For example, a company uses corn and oats in the production of an organic breakfast cereal. The price of corn and oats is highly variable over time. If the probability that prices will increase next year is estimated as .75, then the company may decide to buy and inventory the corn and oats now. Hedging is another financial strategy to manage purchase decisions based on the probabilities of future events.
- Other decisions involving probability are: Should the popular television show, *The Bachelor,* be retained given the likelihood that its current ratings continue next year? Should a company sign an agreement with a foreign supplier based on the chance that the partnership will work? Should you look for another career option if there is a high probability that you will be promoted with a 20% increase in salary?

In Chapters 6 and 7, the concept of probability is extended to probability distributions. These distributions can be based on relative frequency distributions as presented in Chapter 2, or theoretical distributions as presented in Chapters 6 and 7. In Chapter 20, probability distributions provide the basis for decision making using expected values.

In statistics, probability is used to make decisions about rejecting hypotheses or propositions about a population based on empirical sample data. This is called statistical inference or inferential statistics. These topics are discussed starting in Chapter 8.

LO5-1
Define the terms
*probability, experiment,
event,* and *outcome.*

What Is a Probability?

No doubt you are familiar with terms such as *probability, chance,* and *likelihood.* They are often used interchangeably. For example, a weather forecast says there is a *70% chance* of rain during the Super Bowl on Sunday. Or a sample survey of consumers results in a *0.03 probability* that a randomly selected consumer prefers banana-flavored toothpaste. This means the *likelihood* that a consumer buys banana-flavored toothpaste is rather remote. What is a **probability**? In general, it is a numerical value that describes the chance or likelihood that something will happen.

> **PROBABILITY** A value between 0 and 1, inclusive, describing the relative possibility (chance or likelihood) an event will occur.

While a probability can assume any number from 0 to 1, inclusive, it can be communicated in three different ways: a decimal, a percent, or a fraction. For example, the probabilities 1.00, .70, .27, and .50 can also be expressed as percents such as 100%, 70%, 27%, or 50%, or fractions such as 10/10, 7/10, 27/100, or 1/2.

Probabilities close to 0 indicate that the chance of events happening are very unlikely. At the other end of the scale, probabilities close to 1 indicate that the chance of events happening is very likely. A probability of 0 indicates there is absolutely no chance of a particular event; a probability of 1 indicates that a particular event is certain to happen. The following diagram shows the relationship along with a few of our personal beliefs. You might, however, select a different probability for Slo Poke's chances to win the Kentucky Derby or for an increase in federal taxes.

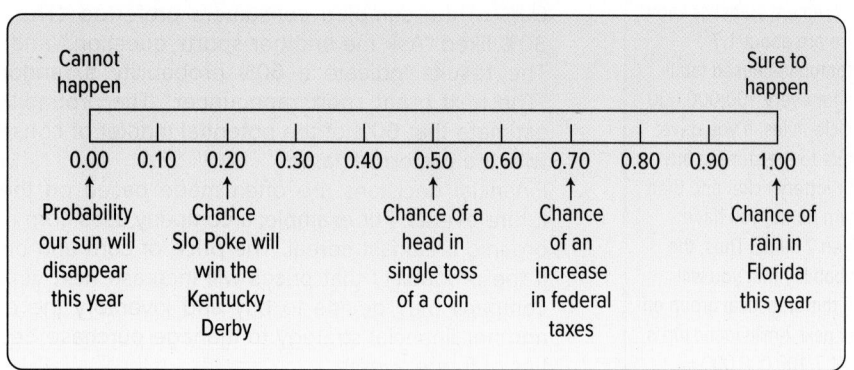

Sometimes, the likelihood of an event is expressed using the term *odds.* To explain, someone says the odds are "five to two" that an event will occur. This means that in a total of seven trials (5 + 2), the event will occur five times and not occur two times. Using odds, we can compute the probability that the event occurs as 5/(5 + 2) or 5/7. So, if the odds in favor of an event are *x* to *y,* the probability of the event is $x/(x + y)$.

Three key words are used in the study of probability: **experiment, outcome,** and **event.** These terms are used in our everyday language, but in statistics they have specific meanings.

> **EXPERIMENT** A process that leads to the occurrence of one and only one of several possible results.

This definition is more general than the one used in the physical sciences, where we picture someone manipulating test tubes or microscopes. In reference to probability, an experiment has two or more possible results, and it is uncertain which will occur.

> **OUTCOME** A particular result of an experiment.

For example, tossing a coin is an experiment. You are unsure if the outcome will be a head or a tail. Similarly, asking 500 college students if they would travel more than 100 miles to attend a Rolling Stones concert is an experiment. In this experiment, one possible outcome is that 273 students indicate they would travel more than 100 miles to attend the concert. Another outcome is that 317 students would attend the concert. Still another outcome is that 423 students indicate they would attend the concert.

When one or more of the experiment's outcomes are observed, we call this an event.

> **EVENT** A collection of one or more outcomes of an experiment.

If an experiment is defined as tossing a coin once and the outcome is recorded as a head, this outcome is the event. If an experiment is defined as tossing five coins once and the outcomes are recorded as head, head, tail, head, tail, these five outcomes are an event.

Examples to clarify the definitions of the terms *experiment, outcome,* and *event* are presented in the following figure. In the die-rolling experiment, there are six possible outcomes, but there are many possible events. When counting the number of members of the board of directors for Fortune 500 companies over 60 years of age, the number of possible outcomes can be anywhere from 0 to the total number of members. There are an even larger number of possible events in this experiment.

Experiment	Roll a die	Count the number of members of the board of directors for Fortune 500 companies who are over 60 years of age
All possible outcomes	Observe a 1	None is over 60
	Observe a 2	One is over 60
	Observe a 3	Two are over 60
	Observe a 4	...
	Observe a 5	29 are over 60
	Observe a 6	...
		...
		48 are over 60
		...
Some possible events	Observe an even number	More than 13 are over 60
	Observe a number greater than 4	Fewer than 20 are over 60
	Observe a number 3 or less	

SELF-REVIEW 5-1

RedLine Productions recently developed a new video game. Its playability is to be tested by 80 veteran game players.
(a)   What is the experiment?
(b)   What is one possible outcome?
(c)   Suppose 65 of the 80 players testing the new game said they liked it. Is 65 a probability?
(d)   The probability that the new game will be a success is computed to be −1.0. Comment.
(e)   Specify one possible event.

Approaches to Assigning Probabilities

There are three ways to assign a probability to an event: classical, empirical, and subjective. The classical and empirical methods are objective and are based on information and data. The subjective method is based on a person's belief or estimate of an event's likelihood.

LO5-2
Apply the classical approach to assign probabilities.

Classical Probability

Classical probability is based on the assumption that the outcomes of an experiment are *equally likely*. Using the classical viewpoint, the probability of an event happening is computed by dividing the number of favorable outcomes by the number of all possible outcomes.

CLASSICAL PROBABILITY	Probability of an event $= \dfrac{\text{Number of favorable outcomes}}{\text{Number of all possible outcomes}}$	(5–1)

▶ **EXAMPLE**

Consider an experiment of rolling a six-sided die once. What is the probability of the event "an even number of spots appear face up"?

SOLUTION

The possible outcomes are:

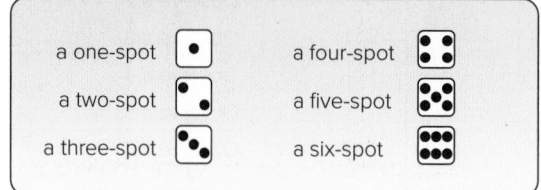

There are three "favorable" outcomes (a two, a four, and a six) in the collection of six equally likely possible outcomes. Therefore:

Probability of an even number $= \dfrac{3}{6}$ ←   Number of favorable outcomes
                                          ←   Number of all possible outcomes

$= .5$

The classical approach to probability can also be applied to lotteries. In South Carolina, one of the games of the Education Lottery is "Pick 3." A person buys a lottery ticket and selects three numbers between 0 and 9, say 243. Once per week, the lottery commission randomly selects three numbers from a machine that tumbles three containers each with balls numbered 0 through 9. To win, your number, 243, must match the numbers and order of the selections. Given that 1,000 possible outcomes exist (000 through 999), the probability of winning with any three-digit number, such as 243, is 0.001, or 1 in 1,000:

$$\text{Probability of 243} = \frac{\text{Number of favorable outcomes}}{\text{Number of all possible outcomes}} = \frac{1}{1,000} = 0.001$$

LO5-3

Determine the number of outcomes using principles of counting.

Principles of Counting

A challenge in computing classical probabilities is determining the values of the numerator and denominator. If the number of possible outcomes in an experiment is small, it is relatively easy to count them. For example, there are six possible outcomes, resulting from rolling a die once:

However, if the experiment is more complex, there are many more possible outcomes. For example, if an experiment is rolling three dice, how many outcomes are possible? A sample of three possible outcomes are: all 4s, one 4 and two 5s, and one 4, one 5, and one 6. There are many more. It would be tedious to list and count all the possibilities. To help determine the number of all possible outcomes, we describe three formulas: the multiplication formula (not to be confused with the multiplication rule described later in the chapter), the permutation formula, and the combination formula.

We begin with the **multiplication formula.**

> **MULTIPLICATION FORMULA**   Total number of arrangements = $(m)(n)$ **(5–2)**

where:

m = number of possibilities for an event
n = number of possibilities for another event

A simple experiment is tossing a coin twice. It is easy to list all four possible outcomes as TT, TH, HT, and HH. However, we know that there are two possible outcomes on the first toss or event, and two possible outcomes on the second toss or event. Therefore, using the multiplication formula:

Number of all possible outcomes = $(m)(n) = (2)(2) = 4$

Let's use the example of the "Pick 3" lottery. There are three tumblers, each with balls labeled 0 through 9. After the numbers are tumbled, one labeled ball is selected from each tumbler. What is the number of all possible outcomes? For each event, or picking a ball, there are 10 possible outcomes. Therefore, using the multiplication formula:

Number of all possible outcomes = $(m)(n)(o) = (10)(10)(10) = 1,000$

What if the experiment is tossing three dice, how many outcomes are possible? Each of the three events has six possible outcomes. So,

Number of all possible outcomes = $(m)(n)(o) = (6)(6)(6) = 216$

SELF-REVIEW 5–2

1. A customer browsing an online clothing site can dress a virtual model with various shirts and pants. If shirts come in five colors and pants are available in four colors, how many different possible outfits are there? What is the probability that the customer selects a red shirt and black pants?
2. During registration, a student typically selects five courses for the coming semester. The student must choose one course from each of the following five categories: 3 management courses, 2 math courses, 4 history courses, 1 statistics course, and 4 general elective courses. How many different possible course schedules are possible?

In the previous examples, the multiplication formula is applied to find the number of all possibilities when there are two or more groups. In contrast, when there is a single group or event and we want to determine the number of all possible arrangements of an outcome from the group, we use **permutations.**

> **PERMUTATION** Any arrangement of r objects selected from a single group of n possible objects.

An illustration follows:

- A group of three electronic components, a transistor, an LED, and a synthesizer, are assembled into a plug-in component for an HDTV. These parts can be assembled in any order. How many different ways can the three parts be assembled? A possible permutation is selecting the transistor first, the LED second, and the synthesizer third. Another permutation is selecting the LED first, the synthesizer second, and the transistor last. Note that the arrangements *A B C* and *B A C* are different permutations. The permutation formula to calculate the total number of different permutations without repeated objects is:

> **PERMUTATION FORMULA** $\qquad\qquad {}_nP_r = \dfrac{n!}{(n-r)!}$ $\qquad$ (5–3)

where:

n = the total number of objects
r = the number of objects selected

The permutation formula uses a notation called n factorial. It is written $n!$ Mathematically, it is computed as:

$$n! = n(n-1)(n-2)(n-3)\ldots(1)$$

If the total number of objects is five, then: $5! = (5)(4)(3)(2)(1) = 120$. Many of your calculators have a button with $x!$ that will perform this calculation for you. It will save you a great deal of time. In Excel, you can use the =FACT function to compute a factorial.

▶ **EXAMPLE**

Referring to the group of three electronic parts that are to be assembled in any order, in how many different ways can they be assembled?

SOLUTION

There are three electronic parts to be assembled, so $n = 3$. Because all three are to be inserted into the plug-in component, $r = 3$. Solving using formula (5–3) gives:

$$_nP_r = \frac{n!}{(n-r)!} = \frac{3!}{(3-3)!} = \frac{3!}{0!} = \frac{3!}{1} = 6$$

We can check the number of permutations arrived at by using the permutation formula. We determine how many "spaces" have to be filled and the possibilities for each "space." In the problem involving three electronic parts, there are three locations in the plug-in unit for the three parts. There are three possibilities for the first place, two for the second (one has been used up), and one for the third, as follows:

$$(3)(2)(1) = 6 \text{ permutations}$$

The six ways in which the three electronic parts, lettered *A, B, C,* can be arranged are:

ABC   BAC   CAB   ACB   BCA   CBA

In the previous example, we selected and arranged all the objects, that is $n = r$. In many cases, only some objects are selected and arranged from the n possible objects. We explain the details of this application in the following example.

▶ **EXAMPLE**

The Fast Media Company is producing a 1-minute video advertisement. In the production process, eight different video segments were made. To make the 1-minute ad, they can select only three of the eight segments. How many different ways can the eight video segments be arranged in the three spaces available in the ad?

SOLUTION

There are eight possibilities for the first available space in the ad, seven for the second space (one has been used up), and six for the third space. Thus:

$$(8)(7)(6) = 336$$

that is, there are a total of 336 different possible arrangements. This also could be found by using formula (5–3). If $n = 8$ video segments and $r = 3$ spaces available, the formula leads to

$$_nP_r = \frac{n!}{(n-r)!} = \frac{8!}{(8-3)!} = \frac{8!}{5!} = \frac{(8)(7)(6)5!}{5!} = 336$$

If the order of the selected objects is *not* important, any selection or arrangement is called a **combination.** Note that the arrangements *A B C* and *B A C* are the same and count as a single combination since *A, B,* and *C* are common to both arrangements. Logically, the number of combinations is always less than the number of permutations.

> **COMBINATION** An event of outcomes when the order of the outcomes does not matter.

The **combination formula** to count the number of r object combinations from a set of n objects is:

COMBINATION FORMULA	$$_nC_r = \frac{n!}{r!(n-r)!}$$	(5–4)

where:

$_nC_r$ = the notation for the number of combinations when selecting r objects from a total of n objects

n = the total number of objects

r = the number of objects selected

For example, if a company needs to form a committee by selecting two members from the executives, Able, Baker, and Chauncy, how many possible combinations are there? In this case, $n = 3$ and $r = 2$.

$$_nC_r = \frac{n!}{r!(n-r)!} = \frac{3!}{2!(3-1)!} = \frac{3 \cdot 2 \cdot 1}{2 \cdot 1(2 \cdot 1)} = \frac{6}{2} = 3$$

There are three possible combinations of the two committee members when selecting from a group of three.

► EXAMPLE

The Grand 16 movie theater uses teams of three employees to work the concession stand each evening. There are seven employees available to work each evening. How many different teams can be scheduled to staff the concession stand?

SOLUTION

According to formula (5–4), there are 35 combinations, found by

$$_7C_3 = \frac{n!}{r!(n-r)!} = \frac{7!}{3!(7-3)!} = \frac{7!}{3!4!} = 35$$

The seven employees taken three at a time would create the possibility of 35 different teams.

When the number of permutations or combinations is large, the calculations are tedious. Computer software and handheld calculators have "functions" to compute these numbers. The results using the PERMUT function in Excel applied to the selection of three video segments for the eight available at the Fast Media Company is shown next. There are a total of 336 arrangements.

Source: Microsoft Excel

Following is the result using the COMBIN function in Excel applied to the number of possible teams of three selected from seven employees at the Grand 16 movie theater. There are 35 possible teams of three.

Tutorial #30 in Connect

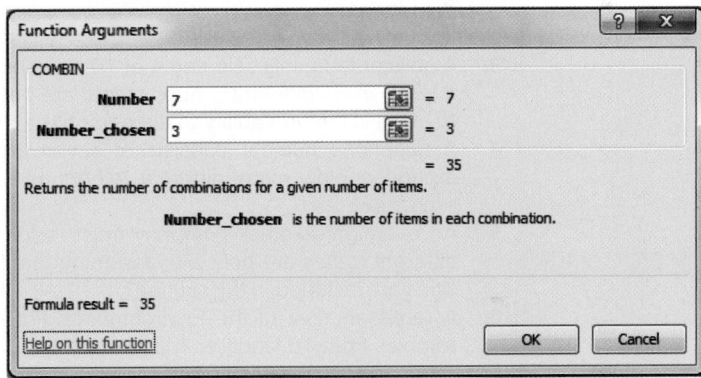

Source: Microsoft Excel

The Excel tutorial referenced to the left shows how to use the PERMUT and COMBIN functions.

SELF-REVIEW 5–3

1. A musician wants to write a score based on only five chords: B-flat, C, D, E, and G. However, only three chords out of the five will be used in succession, such as C, B-flat, and E. Repetitions, such as B-flat, B-flat, and E, will not be permitted.
   (a) How many permutations of the five chords, taken three at a time, are possible?
   (b) Using formula (5–3), how many permutations are possible?
2. A new clothing retailer would like to create its own inventory coding system. For example, a code of 1083 would identify a blue blouse, size medium; a code of 2031 would identify a pair of pants, size 18; and so on. Repetitions of numbers are not permitted. That is, the same number cannot be used more than once for a four-digit code. For example, 2256, 2562, or 5559 would not be permitted. How many different code groups can be created?

3. In the preceding Example/Solution involving the Grand 16 movie theater, there were 35 possible teams of three taken from seven employees.
    (a) Use formula (5–4) to show this is true.
    (b) The manager of the theater wants to plan for staffing the concession stand with teams of five employees on the weekends to serve the larger crowds. From the seven employees, how many teams of five employees are possible?
    (c) Charlie is one of the employees and wants to calculate the probability of membership on a weekend team. What is the probability that Charlie will be on a weekend team?
4. In a lottery game, three numbers are randomly selected from a tumbler of balls numbered 1 through 50. Balls are not returned to the tumbler.
    (a) How many permutations are possible?
    (b) How many combinations are possible?

EXERCISES

1. Solve the following:
    a. 40!/35!
    b. $_7P_4$
    c. $_5C_2$
2. Solve the following:
    a. 20!/17!
    b. $_9P_3$
    c. $_7C_2$
3. A pollster randomly selected 4 of 10 available people.
    a. How many different groups of four are possible.
    b. What is the probability that a person is a member of a group?
4. A telephone number consists of seven digits, the first three representing the exchange. How many different telephone numbers are possible within the 537 exchange?
5. An overnight express company must include five cities on its route. How many different routes are possible, assuming that it does not matter in which order the cities are included in the routing?
6. A representative of the Environmental Protection Agency (EPA) wants to select samples from 10 landfills. The director has 15 landfills from which she can collect samples. How many different samples are possible?
7. Sam Snead's restaurant in Conway, South Carolina, offers an early-bird special from 4 to 6 p.m. each weekday evening. If each patron selects a Starter Selection (four options), an Entrée (eight options), and a Dessert (three options), how many different meals are possible?
8. A company is creating three new divisions, and seven managers are eligible to be appointed head of a division. How many different ways could the three new heads be appointed? Hint: Assume the division assignment makes a difference.

LO5-4

Apply the empirical approach to assign probabilities.

Empirical Probability

Empirical probability is the second type of objective probability. It is based on the observation, counting, and recording of experimental outcomes. An empirical probability is based on relative frequencies as presented in Chapter 2. It is computed as the frequency of a particular outcome divided by the number of all possible experimental outcomes.

EMPIRICAL PROBABILITY The probability of an event based on a collection of observations or data.

The formula to determine an empirical probability is:

$$\text{Empirical probability} = \frac{\text{Number of times the event occurs}}{\text{Total number of observations}}$$

The empirical approach to probability is based on the **law of large numbers.** The key to establishing probabilities empirically is that more observations will provide a more accurate estimate of the probability.

> **LAW OF LARGE NUMBERS** Over a large number of trials, the empirical probability of an event will approach its true probability.

To explain the law of large numbers, suppose we toss a fair coin. The result of each toss is either a head or a tail. With just one toss of the coin, the empirical probability for heads is either 0 or 1. If we toss the coin a great number of times, the probability of the outcome of heads will approach .5. The following table reports the results of seven different experiments of flipping a fair coin 1, 10, 50, 100, 500, 1,000, and 10,000 times and then computing the relative frequency of heads. Note as we increase the number of trials, the empirical probability of a head appearing approaches .5, which is its value based on the classical approach to probability.

Number of Trials	Number of Heads	Relative Frequency of Heads
1	0	.00
10	3	.30
50	26	.52
100	52	.52
500	236	.472
1,000	494	.494
10,000	5,027	.5027

What have we demonstrated? Based on the classical definition of probability, the likelihood of obtaining a head in a single toss of a fair coin is .5. Based on the empirical or relative frequency approach to probability, the probability of the event happening approaches the same value based on the classical definition of probability.

This reasoning allows us to use the empirical or relative frequency approach to find a probability. Here are some examples.

- We want to estimate the likelihood a student at Scandia University will earn an A in Business Statistics 101. We apply the empirical approach to probability by collecting data from 80 students who completed the course last semester. The data show that 12 students earned an A. Based on this information, we compute a probability of 12/80 or .15 that a student registering for Business Statistics 101 will earn an A. Further, if next semester's class size is 100 students, then the probability predicts that 15%, or about 15 students, will earn an A.
- Chris Paul of the Phoenix Suns made 226 out of 246 free throw attempts during the 2020–2021 NBA season. Based on the empirical approach to probability, the likelihood that he makes his next free throw attempt is 0.93.

Life insurance companies rely on past data to determine the acceptability of an applicant as well as the premium to be charged. Mortality tables list the likelihood a person of a particular age will die within the upcoming year. For example, the likelihood a 20-year-old female will die within the next year is .00105.

The empirical concept is illustrated with the following example.

▶ **EXAMPLE**

The Standard & Poor's (S&P) 500 stock index finished up 24.04% in 2020. Based on the last 20 years, including 2020, the index was down four times. What is the probability that the index will be down for 2021?

SOLUTION

Using probability notation to simplify the equations, P stands for probability and A represents the event of a negative yearly return for the S&P 500 index. In this case $P(A)$ stands for the probability of a negative yearly return for the S&P 500 index:

$$P(A) = \frac{\text{Number of years of a negative annual return}}{\text{Total number of years}} = \frac{4}{20} = .20$$

This empirical probability estimates the probability of a negative return in future years for the S&P 500 index to be .20.

LO5-5

Apply the subjective approach to assign probabilities.

Subjective Probability

If there is little or no experience or information on which to base a probability, it is estimated subjectively. Essentially, this means an individual evaluates the available opinions and information and then estimates or assigns the probability. This probability is called a **subjective probability.**

> **SUBJECTIVE CONCEPT OF PROBABILITY** The likelihood (probability) of a particular event happening that is assigned by an individual based on whatever information is available.

Illustrations of subjective probability are:

1. Estimating the likelihood the New England Patriots will play in the Super Bowl next year
2. Estimating the likelihood you are involved in an automobile accident during the next 12 months
3. Estimating the likelihood the U.S. budget deficit will be reduced by half in the next 10 years

The types of probability are summarized in Chart 5–1. A probability statement always assigns a likelihood to an event that has not yet occurred. There is, of course, considerable latitude in the degree of uncertainty that surrounds this probability, based primarily on the knowledge possessed by the individual concerning the underlying process. Based on classical probability, an individual knows that the probability is .5 that a coin toss will result in a head, or that the probability is 1/6 or .167 that a one-spot will occur on a throw of a die. But we know very little concerning the acceptance in the marketplace of a new and untested product. For example, even though a market research director tests a newly developed product in 40 retail stores and states that there is a 70% chance that the product will have sales of more than 1 million units, she has limited knowledge of how consumers will react when it is marketed nationally. In both cases (the case of the person rolling a die and the testing of a new product), the individual is assigning a probability value to an event of interest, and a difference exists only in the predictor's confidence in the precision of the estimate. However, regardless of the viewpoint, the same laws of probability (presented in the following sections) will be applied.

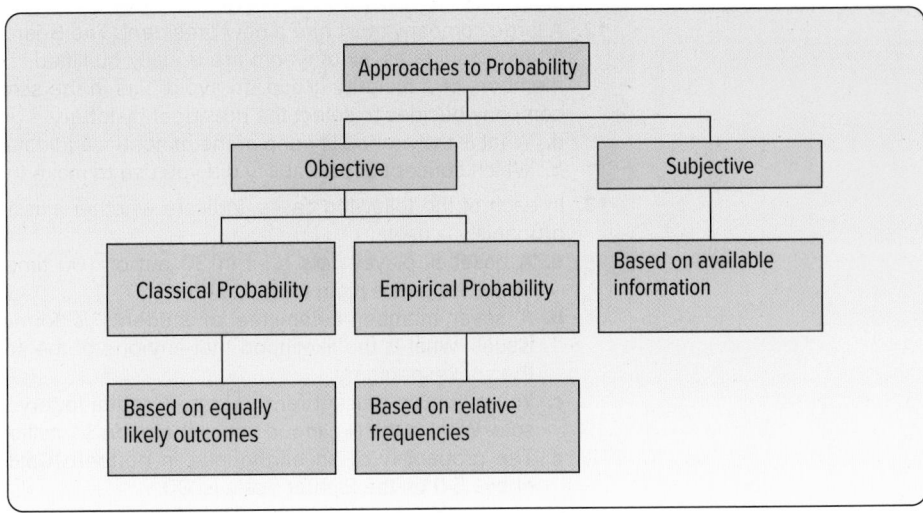

CHART 5–1 Summary of Approaches to Probability

SELF-REVIEW 5–4

1. One card will be randomly selected from a standard 52-card deck. What is the probability the card will be a queen? Which approach to probability did you use to answer this question?
2. The Center for Child Care reports on 539 children and the marital status of their parents. There are 333 married, 182 divorced, and 24 widowed parents. What is the probability a particular child chosen at random will have a parent who is divorced? Which approach did you use?
3. What is the probability you will save $1 million by the time you retire? Which approach to probability did you use to answer this question?

EXERCISES

9. Some people are in favor of reducing federal taxes to increase consumer spending and others are against it. Two persons are selected and their opinions are recorded. Assuming no one is undecided, list the possible outcomes. What is the probability that both people favor a tax increase? What is the probability that one of the two people favor a tax increase?
10. A quality control inspector selects a part to be tested. The part is then declared acceptable, repairable, or scrapped. Then another part is tested. List the possible outcomes of this experiment regarding two parts. What is the probability that both parts are scrapped? What is the probability that one of the two parts is scrapped?
11. **FILE** A survey of 34 students at the Wall College of Business showed the following majors:

Accounting	10
Finance	5
Economics	3
Management	6
Marketing	10

From the 34 students, suppose you randomly select a student.
a. What is the probability this student is a management major?
b. Which concept of probability did you use to make this estimate?

12. A large company must hire a new president. The Board of Directors prepares a list of five candidates, all of whom are equally qualified. Two of these candidates are members of a minority group. To avoid bias in the selection of the candidate, the company decides to select the president by lottery.
   a. What is the probability one of the minority candidates is hired?
   b. Which concept of probability did you use to make this estimate?

13. In each of the following cases, indicate whether classical, empirical, or subjective probability is used.
   a. A baseball player gets a hit in 30 out of 100 times at bat. The probability is .3 that he gets a hit in his next at bat.
   b. A seven-member committee of students is formed to study environmental issues. What is the likelihood that any one of the seven is randomly chosen as the spokesperson?
   c. You purchase a ticket for the Lotto Canada lottery. Over 5 million tickets were sold. What is the likelihood you will win the $1 million jackpot?
   d. The probability of an earthquake in northern California in the next 10 years above 5.0 on the Richter Scale is .80.

14. A firm will promote two employees out of a group of six men and three women.
   a. List all possible outcomes.
   b. What probability concept would be used to assign probabilities to the outcomes?

15. A sample of 40 oil industry executives was selected to test a questionnaire. One question about environmental issues required a yes-or-no answer.
   a. What is the experiment?
   b. List one possible event.
   c. Ten of the 40 executives responded yes. Based on these sample responses, what is the probability that an oil industry executive will respond yes?
   d. What concept of probability does this illustrate?

16. **FILE** A sample of 2,000 licensed drivers revealed the following number of speeding violations.

Number of Violations	Number of Drivers
0	1,910
1	46
2	18
3	12
4	9
5 or more	5
Total	2,000

   a. What is the experiment?
   b. List one possible event.
   c. What is the probability that a particular driver had exactly two speeding violations?
   d. What concept of probability does this illustrate?

17. Bank of America customers select their own four-digit personal identification number (PIN) for use at ATMs.
   a. Think of this as an experiment and list four possible outcomes.
   b. What is the probability that a customer will pick 2591 as their PIN?
   c. Which concept of probability did you use to answer (b)?

18. An investor buys 100 shares of AT&T stock and records its price change daily.
   a. List several possible events for this experiment.
   b. Which concept of probability did you use in (a)?

Rules of Addition for Computing Probabilities

There are two rules of addition, the special rule of addition and the general rule of addition. We begin with the special rule of addition.

Special Rule of Addition

When we use the **special rule of addition,** the events must be mutually exclusive. **Mutually exclusive** means that when one event occurs, none of the other events can occur at the same time. An illustration of mutually exclusive events in the die-tossing experiment is the events "a number 4 or larger" and "a number 2 or smaller." If the outcome is in the first group {4, 5, and 6}, then it cannot also be in the second group {1 and 2}. As another illustration, Hope Arbor Senior Care assigns residents to one of three care groups: independent living, assisted living, or skilled nursing. A resident can be assigned to only one of the three care groups. Hence the groups are said to be mutually exclusive.

> **MUTUALLY EXCLUSIVE** The occurrence of one event means that none of the other events can occur at the same time.

If two events A and B are mutually exclusive, the special rule of addition states that the probability of one *or* the other event's occurring equals the sum of their probabilities. This rule is expressed in the following formula:

> **SPECIAL RULE OF ADDITION** $\qquad P(A \text{ or } B) = P(A) + P(B)$ $\qquad$ **(5–5)**

For three mutually exclusive events designated A, B, and C, the rule is written:

$$P(A \text{ or } B \text{ or } C) = P(A) + P(B) + P(C)$$

An example will show the details.

▶ **EXAMPLE**

Ian Dagnall/Alamy Stock Photo

A machine fills plastic bags with a mixture of beans, broccoli, and other vegetables. Most of the bags contain the correct weight, but because of the variation in the size of the beans and other vegetables, a package might be underweight or overweight. A check of 4,000 packages filled in the past month revealed:

Weight	Event	Number of Packages	Probability of Occurrence	
Underweight	A	100	.025	← $\dfrac{100}{4{,}000}$
Satisfactory	B	3,600	.900	
Overweight	C	300	.075	
		4,000	1.000	

What is the probability that a particular package will be either underweight or overweight?

SOLUTION

The outcome "underweight" is the event *A*. The outcome "overweight" is the event *C*. Applying the special rule of addition:

$$P(A \text{ or } C) = P(A) + P(C) = .025 + .075 = .10$$

Note that the events are mutually exclusive, meaning that a package of mixed vegetables cannot be underweight, satisfactory, and overweight at the same time. The three classes of weight completely list the possible outcomes. When the list of outcomes is complete, it is also called **collectively exhaustive.** When the list of outcomes is mutually exclusive and collectively exhaustive, the sum of the probabilities should be 1.

> **COLLECTIVELY EXHAUSTIVE** At least one of the events must occur when an experiment is conducted.

English logician J. Venn (1834–1923) developed a diagram to portray graphically the outcome of an experiment. The *mutually exclusive* concept and various other rules for combining probabilities can be illustrated using this device. To construct a Venn diagram, a space is first enclosed representing the total of all possible outcomes. This space is usually in the form of a rectangle. An event is then represented by a circular area that is drawn inside the rectangle proportional to the probability of the event. The following Venn diagram represents the *mutually exclusive* concept. There is no overlapping of events, meaning that the events are mutually exclusive. In the following Venn diagram, the circles are equal in size and indicate that the events *A*, *B*, and *C* are equally likely.

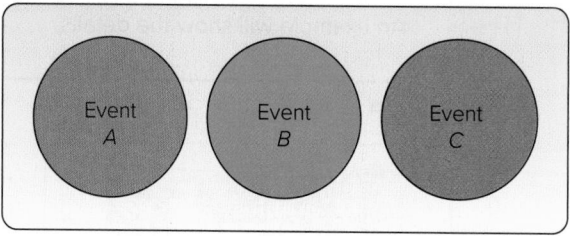

Complement Rule

One of the simplest and most important logical rules of probability is the **complement rule.** For example, the probability that a bag of mixed vegetables selected is underweight, expressed as *P(A)*, plus the probability that a bag of mixed vegetables selected is *not* underweight, expressed as *P(~A)*, must equal 1. This is written:

$$P(A) + P(\sim A) = 1$$

This can be revised to read:

> **COMPLEMENT RULE** $P(A) = 1 - P(\sim A)$ **(5–6)**

The complement rule is used to determine the probability of an event occurring by subtracting the probability of the event not occurring from 1. This rule is useful because sometimes it is easier to calculate the probability of an event happening by determining the probability of it not happening and subtracting the result from 1. Notice that the events A and $\sim A$ are mutually exclusive and collectively exhaustive. Therefore, the probabilities of A and $\sim A$ sum to 1. A Venn diagram illustrating the complement rule is shown as:

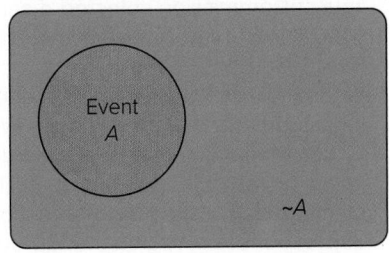

▶ **EXAMPLE**

Referring to the previous Example/Solution, the probability a bag of mixed vegetables is underweight is .025 and the probability of an overweight bag is .075. Use the complement rule to show the probability of a satisfactory bag is .900. Show the solution using a Venn diagram.

SOLUTION

The probability the bag is unsatisfactory equals the probability the bag is overweight plus the probability it is underweight. That is, $P(A \text{ or } C) = P(A) + P(C) = .025 + .075 = .100$. The bag is satisfactory if it is not underweight or overweight, so $P(B) = 1 - [P(A) + P(C)] = 1 - [.025 + .075] = 0.900$. The Venn diagram portraying this situation is:

SELF-REVIEW 5–5

A sample of employees of Worldwide Enterprises is surveyed about a new health care plan. The employees are classified as follows:

Classification	Event	Number of Employees
Supervisors	A	120
Maintenance	B	50
Production	C	1,460
Management	D	302
Secretarial	E	68

(a) What is the probability that the first person selected is:
   (i) either in maintenance or a secretary?
   (ii) not in management?
(b) Draw a Venn diagram illustrating your answers to part (a).
(c) Are the events in part (a)(i) complementary or mutually exclusive or both?

The General Rule of Addition

The outcomes of an experiment may not be mutually exclusive. For example, the Florida Tourist Commission selected a sample of 200 tourists who visited the state during the year. The survey revealed that 120 tourists went to Disney World and 100 went to Busch Gardens. What is the probability that a person selected visited either Disney World or Busch Gardens? If the special rule of addition is used, the probability of selecting a tourist who went to Disney World is .60, found by 120/200. Similarly, the probability of a tourist going to Busch Gardens is .50. The sum of these probabilities is 1.10. We know, however, that this probability cannot be greater than 1. The explanation is that many tourists visited both attractions and are being counted twice! A check of the survey responses revealed that 60 out of 200 sampled did, in fact, visit both attractions.

To answer our question, "What is the probability a selected person visited either Disney World or Busch Gardens?" (1) add the probability that a tourist visited Disney World and the probability a tourist visited Busch Gardens, and (2) subtract the probability of visiting both. Thus:

$$P(\text{Disney or Busch}) = P(\text{Disney}) + P(\text{Busch}) - P(\text{both Disney and Busch})$$
$$= .60 + .50 - .30 = .80$$

When two events both occur, the probability is called a **joint probability.** The probability (.30) that a tourist visits both attractions is an example of a joint probability.

Rostislav Glinsky/Shutterstock

The following Venn diagram shows two events that are not mutually exclusive. The two events overlap to illustrate the joint event that some people have visited both attractions.

> **JOINT PROBABILITY** A probability that measures the likelihood two or more events will happen concurrently.

So the general rule of addition, which is used to compute the probability of two events that are not mutually exclusive, is:

> **GENERAL RULE OF ADDITION** $P(A \text{ or } B) = P(A) + P(B) - P(A \text{ and } B)$ **(5–7)**

For the expression $P(A \text{ or } B)$, the word *or* suggests that A may occur or B may occur. This also includes the possibility that A and B may occur. This use of *or* is sometimes called an **inclusive.** You could also write $P(A \text{ or } B \text{ or both})$ to emphasize that the union of the events includes the intersection of A and B.

If we compare the general and special rules of addition, the important difference is determining if the events are mutually exclusive. If the events *are* mutually exclusive, then the joint probability $P(A \text{ and } B)$ is 0 and we could use the special rule of addition. Otherwise, we must account for the joint probability and use the general rule of addition.

▶ **EXAMPLE**

What is the probability that a card chosen at random from a standard deck of cards will be either a king or a heart?

SOLUTION

We may be inclined to add the probability of a king and the probability of a heart. But this creates a problem. If we do that, the king of hearts is counted with the kings and also with the hearts. So, if we simply add the probability of a king (there are 4 in a deck of 52 cards) to the probability of a heart (there are 13 in a deck of 52 cards) and report that 17 out of 52 cards meet the requirement, we have counted the king of hearts twice. We need to subtract 1 card from the 17 so the king of hearts is counted only once. Thus, there are 16 cards that are either hearts or kings. So the probability is 16/52 = .3077.

Card	Probability		Explanation
King	$P(A)$	= 4/52	4 kings in a deck of 52 cards
Heart	$P(B)$	= 13/52	13 hearts in a deck of 52 cards
King of Hearts	$P(A \text{ and } B)$ =	1/52	1 king of hearts in a deck of 52 cards

From formula (5–7):

$$P(A \text{ or } B) = P(A) + P(B) - P(A \text{ and } B)$$
$$= 4/52 + 13/52 - 1/52$$
$$= 16/52, \text{ or } .3077$$

A Venn diagram portrays these outcomes, which are not mutually exclusive.

SELF-REVIEW 5-6

Routine physical examinations are conducted annually as part of a health service program for General Concrete Inc. employees. It was discovered that 8% of the employees need corrective shoes, 15% need major dental work, and 3% need both corrective shoes and major dental work.

(a) What is the probability that an employee selected at random will need either corrective shoes or major dental work?

(b) Show this situation in the form of a Venn diagram.

EXERCISES

19. The events *A* and *B* are mutually exclusive. Suppose *P(A)* = .30 and *P(B)* = .20. What is the probability of either *A* or *B* occurring? What is the probability that neither *A* nor *B* will happen?

20. The events *X* and *Y* are mutually exclusive. Suppose *P(X)* = .05 and *P(Y)* = .02. What is the probability of either *X* or *Y* occurring? What is the probability that neither *X* nor *Y* will happen?

21. **FILE** A study of 200 advertising firms revealed their income after taxes:

Income after Taxes	Number of Firms
Under $1 million	102
$1 million to $20 million	61
$20 million or more	37

  a. What is the probability an advertising firm selected at random has under $1 million in income after taxes?

  b. What is the probability an advertising firm selected at random has either an income between $1 million and $20 million, or an income of $20 million or more? What rule of probability was applied?

22. The chairperson of the Board of Directors says, "There is a 50% chance this company will earn a profit, a 30% chance it will break even, and a 20% chance it will lose money next quarter."

  a. Use an addition rule to find the probability the company will not lose money next quarter.

  b. Use the complement rule to find the probability it will not lose money next quarter.

23. Suppose the probability you will get an A in this class is .25 and the probability you will get a B is .50. What is the probability your grade will be above a C?

24. Two coins are tossed. If *A* is the event "two heads" and *B* is the event "two tails," are *A* and *B* mutually exclusive? Are they complements?

25. The probabilities of the events *A* and *B* are .20 and .30, respectively. The probability that both *A* and *B* occur is .15. What is the probability of either *A* or *B* occurring?

26. Let $P(X) = .55$ and $P(Y) = .35$. Assume the probability that they both occur is .20. What is the probability of either X or Y occurring?

27. Suppose the two events A and B are mutually exclusive. What is the probability of their joint occurrence?

28. A student is taking two courses, history and math. The probability the student will pass the history course is .60, and the probability of passing the math course is .70. The probability of passing both is .50. What is the probability of passing at least one?

29. The aquarium at Sea Critters Depot contains 140 fish. Eighty of these fish are green swordtails (44 female and 36 male) and 60 are orange swordtails (36 female and 24 male). A fish is randomly captured from the aquarium:
   a. What is the probability the selected fish is a green swordtail?
   b. What is the probability the selected fish is male?
   c. What is the probability the selected fish is a male green swordtail?
   d. What is the probability the selected fish is either a male or a green swordtail?

30. A National Park Service survey of visitors to the Rocky Mountain region revealed that 50% visit Yellowstone, 40% visit the Tetons, and 35% visit both.
   a. What is the probability a vacationer will visit at least one of these parks?
   b. What is the probability .35 called?
   c. Are the events mutually exclusive? Explain.

LO5-7
Calculate probabilities using the rules of multiplication.

Rules of Multiplication to Calculate Probability

In this section, we discuss the rules for computing the likelihood that two events both happen, or their joint probability. For example, 16% of the 2022 tax returns were prepared by H&R Block and 75% of those returns showed a refund. What is the likelihood a person's tax form was prepared by H&R Block and the person received a refund? Venn diagrams illustrate this as the intersection of two events. To find the likelihood of two events happening, we use the rules of multiplication. There are two rules of multiplication: the special rule and the general rule.

Special Rule of Multiplication

The special rule of multiplication requires that two events A and B are **independent.** Two events are independent if the occurrence of one event does not alter the probability of the occurrence of the other event.

> **INDEPENDENCE** The occurrence of one event has no effect on the probability of the occurrence of another event.

One way to think about independence is to assume that events A and B occur at different times. For example, when event B occurs after event A occurs, does A have any effect on the likelihood that event B occurs? If the answer is no, then A and B are independent events. To illustrate independence, suppose two coins are tossed. The outcome of a coin toss (head or tail) is unaffected by the outcome of any other prior coin toss (head or tail).

For two independent events A and B, the probability that A and B will both occur is found by multiplying the two probabilities. This is the **special rule of multiplication** and is written symbolically as:

> **SPECIAL RULE OF MULTIPLICATION** $\qquad P(A \text{ and } B) = P(A)P(B) \qquad$ **(5–8)**

For three independent events, A, B, and C, the special rule of multiplication used to determine the probability that all three events will occur is:

$$P(A \text{ and } B \text{ and } C) = P(A)P(B)P(C)$$

▶ **EXAMPLE**

A survey by the American Automobile Association (AAA) revealed 60% of its members made airline reservations last year. Two members are selected at random. What is the probability both made airline reservations last year? What are the probabilities for the three other combinations?

SOLUTION

The probability the first member made an airline reservation last year is .60, written $P(R_1) = .60$, where R_1 refers to the fact that the first member made a reservation. The probability that the second member selected made a reservation is also .60, so $P(R_2) = .60$. Because the number of AAA members is very large, you may assume that R_1 and R_2 are independent. Consequently, using formula (5–8), the probability they both make a reservation is .36, found by:

$$P(R_1 \text{ and } R_2) = P(R_1)P(R_2) = (.60)(.60) = .36$$

To list all possible outcomes, R indicates that a reservation is made and $\sim R$ indicates no reservation is made. The complement rule is applied to compute the probability that a member does not make a reservation, $P(\sim R) = .40$. Using this information, the probability that neither member makes a reservation, $[P(\sim R1)P(\sim R2)] = (.40)(.40) = .16$. The probabilities for all possible combinations are listed here. The listing is collectively exhaustive, and each outcome is mutually exclusive. Since these conditions are true, the sum of the four probabilities must equal 1.00.

Outcomes	Joint Probability	
R_1 R_2	$(.60)(.60) =$	.36
R_1 $\sim R_2$	$(.60)(.40) =$	.24
$\sim R_1$ R_2	$(.40)(.60) =$	.24
$\sim R_1$ $\sim R_2$	$(.40)(.40) =$	.16
Total		1.00

SELF-REVIEW 5–7

From experience, Teton Tire knows the probability is .95 that a particular XB-70 tire will last 60,000 miles before it becomes bald or fails. An adjustment is made on any tire that does not last 60,000 miles. You purchase four XB-70s. What is the probability all four tires will last at least 60,000 miles?

General Rule of Multiplication

If two events are not independent, they are referred to as **dependent.** To illustrate dependency, suppose there are 10 cans of soda in a cooler; 7 are regular and 3 are diet. A can is selected from the cooler. The probability of selecting a can of diet soda is 3/10, and the probability of selecting a can of regular soda is 7/10. Then a second can is selected from the cooler, without returning the first. The probability the second is diet depends on whether the first one selected was diet or not. The probability that the second is diet is:

2/9, if the first can is diet. (Only two cans of diet soda remain in the cooler.)
3/9, if the first can selected is regular. (All three diet sodas are still in the cooler.)

The fraction 2/9 (or 3/9) is called a **conditional probability** because its value is conditional on (dependent on) whether a diet or regular soda was the first selection from the cooler.

> **CONDITIONAL PROBABILITY** The probability of a particular event occurring, given that another event has occurred.

In the general rule of multiplication, the conditional probability is required to compute the joint probability of two events that are not independent. For two events, A and B, that are not independent, the conditional probability is represented as $P(B|A)$, and expressed as the probability of B given A. Or the probability of B is conditional on the occurrence and effect of event A. Symbolically, the general rule of multiplication for two events that are not independent is:

> **GENERAL RULE OF MULTIPLICATION** $P(A \text{ and } B) = P(A)P(B|A)$ **(5–9)**

▶ **EXAMPLE**

A golfer has 12 golf shirts in the closet. Suppose nine of these shirts are white and the others blue. The golfer gets dressed in the dark and just grabs a shirt and puts it on. The shirt from the first day is not returned to the closet. The golfer plays the next day, and again randomly selects a shirt from the closet. What is the likelihood both shirts selected are white?

SOLUTION

The event that the first shirt selected is white is W_1. The probability is $P(W_1) = 9/12$ because 9 of the 12 shirts are white. The event that the second shirt selected is also white is identified as W_2. The conditional probability that the second shirt selected is white, given that the first shirt selected is also white, is $P(W_2|W_1) = 8/11$. Why is this so? Because after the first shirt is selected, there are only 11 shirts remaining in the closet and 8 of these are white. To determine the probability of two white shirts being selected, we use formula (5–9).

$$P(W_1 \text{ and } W_2) = P(W_1)P(W_2|W_1) = \left(\frac{9}{12}\right)\left(\frac{8}{11}\right) = .55$$

So the likelihood of selecting two shirts and finding them both to be white is .55.

We can extend the general rule of multiplication to more than two events. For three events A, B, and C, the formula is:

$$P(A \text{ and } B \text{ and } C) = P(A)P(B|A)P(C|A \text{ and } B)$$

In the case of the golf shirt example, the probability of selecting three white shirts without replacement is:

$$P(W_1 \text{ and } W_2 \text{ and } W_3) = P(W_1)P(W_2 \mid W_1)P(W_3 \mid W_1 \text{ and } W_2) = \left(\frac{9}{12}\right)\left(\frac{8}{11}\right)\left(\frac{7}{10}\right) = .38$$

So the likelihood of selecting three shirts without replacement and all being white is .38.

SELF-REVIEW 5–8

The board of directors of Tarbell Industries consists of eight men and four women. A four-member search committee is chosen at random to conduct a nationwide search for a new company president.
(a) What is the probability all four members of the search committee will be women?
(b) What is the probability all four members will be men?
(c) Does the sum of the probabilities for the events described in parts (a) and (b) equal 1? Explain.

LO5-8
Compute probabilities using a contingency table.

Contingency Tables

Often we tally the results of a survey in a two-way table and use the results of this tally to determine various probabilities. We described this idea in Chapter 4. To review, we refer to a two-way table as a **contingency table.**

> **CONTINGENCY TABLE** A table used to classify sample observations according to two or more identifiable categories or classes.

A contingency table is a cross-tabulation that simultaneously summarizes two variables of interest and their relationship. The level of measurement can be nominal. Following are several examples.

- One hundred fifty adults were asked if they were older than 50 years of age and the number of Meta accounts they used. The following table summarizes the results.

Meta Accounts	Over 50 years of age?		Total
	Yes	**No**	
0	20	40	60
1	40	30	70
2 or more	10	10	20
Total	70	80	150

- The American Coffee Producers Association reports the following information on age and the amount of coffee consumed in a month.

Age (Years)	Coffee Consumption			Total
	Low	**Moderate**	**High**	
Under 30	36	32	24	92
30 up to 40	18	30	27	75
40 up to 50	10	24	20	54
50 and over	26	24	29	79
Total	90	110	100	300

According to this table, each of the 300 respondents is classified according to two criteria: (1) age and (2) the amount of coffee consumed.

The following example shows how the rules of addition and multiplication are used when we employ contingency tables.

▶ **EXAMPLE**

Last month, the National Association of Theater Managers conducted a survey of 500 randomly selected adults. The survey asked respondents their age and the number of times they saw a movie in a theater. The results are summarized in Table 5–1.

TABLE 5–1 Number of Movies Attended per Month by Age

Movies per Month		Age			Total
		Less than 30 B_1	30 up to 60 B_2	60 or Older B_3	
0	A_1	15	50	10	75
1 or 2	A_2	25	100	75	200
3, 4, or 5	A_3	55	60	60	175
6 or more	A_4	5	15	30	50
Total		100	225	175	500

The association is interested in understanding the probabilities that an adult will see a movie in a theater, especially for adults 60 and older. This information is useful for making decisions regarding discounts on tickets and concessions for seniors.

Determine the probability of:

1. Selecting an adult who attended six or more movies per month.
2. Selecting an adult who attended two or fewer movies per month.
3. Selecting an adult who attended six or more movies per month **or** is 60 years of age or older.
4. Selecting an adult who attended six or more movies per month **given** the person is 60 years of age or older.
5. Selecting an adult who attended six or more movies per month **and** is 60 years of age or older.
    Determine the independence of:
6. Number of movies per month attended and the age of the adult.

SOLUTION

Table 5–1 is called a contingency table. In a contingency table, an individual or an object is classified according to two criteria. In this example, a sampled adult is classified by age and by the number of movies attended per month. The rules of addition [formulas (5–5) and (5–7)] and the rules of multiplication [formulas (5–8) and (5–9)] allow us to answer the various probability questions based on the contingency table.

1. To find the probability that a randomly selected adult attended six or more movies per month, focus on the row labeled "6 or more" (also labeled A_4)

in Table 5–1. The table shows that 50 of the total 500 adults are in this class. Using the empirical approach, the probability is computed:

$$P(6 \text{ or more}) = P(A_4) = \frac{50}{500} = .10$$

This probability indicates 10% of the 500 adults attend six or more movies per month.

2. To determine the probability of randomly selecting an adult who went to two or fewer movies per month, two outcomes must be combined: attending zero movies per month and attending one or two movies per month. These two outcomes are mutually exclusive. That is, a person can only be classified as attending zero movies per month, or one or two movies per month, not both. Because the two outcomes are mutually exclusive, we use the special rule of addition [formula (5–5)] by adding the probabilities of attending no movies and attending one or two movies:

$$P[(\text{attending } 0) \text{ or } (\text{attending } 1 \text{ or } 2)] = P(A_1) + P(A_2) = \left(\frac{75}{500} + \frac{200}{500} \right) = .55$$

So 55% of the adults in the sample attended two or fewer movies a month.

3. To determine the probability of randomly selecting an adult who went to "6 or more" movies per month or whose age is "60 or older," we again use the rules of addition. However, in this case the outcomes are **not** mutually exclusive. Why is this? Because a person can attend six or more movies per month, be 60 or older, or be both. So the two groups are not mutually exclusive because it is possible that a person would be counted in both groups. To determine this probability, the general rule of addition [formula (5–7)] is used.

$$P[(6 \text{ or more}) \text{ or } (60 \text{ or older})] = P(A_4) + P(B_3) - P(A_4 \text{ and } B_3)$$
$$= \left(\frac{50}{500} + \frac{175}{500} - \frac{30}{500} \right) = .39$$

So 39% of the adults are either 60 or older, attend six or more movies per month, or both.

4. To determine the probability of selecting a person who attends six or more movies per month given that the person is 60 or older, focus only on the column labeled B_3 in Table 5–1. That is, we are only interested in the 175 adults who are 60 or older. Of these 175 adults, 30 attended six or more movies.

$$P[(6 \text{ or more}) \text{ given } (60 \text{ or older})] = P(A_4|B_3) = \frac{30}{175} = .17$$

Of the 500 adults, 17% of adults who are 60 or older attend six or more movies per month. This is called a conditional probability because the probability is based on the "condition" of being the age of 60 or older. Recall that in part 1, 10% of all adults attend six or more movies per month; here we see that 17% of adults who are 60 or older attend movies. This is valuable information for theater managers regarding the characteristics of their customers. Older attendees are likely to attend more movies.

5. The probability a person attended six or more movies and is 60 or older is based on two conditions and they must both happen. That is, the two outcomes "6 or more movies" (A_4) and "60 or older" (B_3) must occur jointly. To find this joint probability we use the general rule of multiplication [formula (5–9)].

$$P[(6 \text{ or more movies}) \text{ and } (60 \text{ or older})] = P(A_4 \text{ and } B_3) = P(A_4)P(B_3|A_4)$$

To compute the joint probability, first compute the simple probability of the first outcome, A_4, randomly selecting a person who attends six or more movies.

To find the probability, refer to row A_4 in Table 5–1. There are 50 of 500 adults that attended six or more movies. So $P(A_4) = 50/500$.

Next, compute the conditional probability $P(B_3|A_4)$. This is the probability of selecting an adult who is 60 or older given that the person attended six or more movies. The conditional probability is:

$$P[(60 \text{ or older}) \text{ given } (6 \text{ or more movies})] = P(B_3|A_4) = 30/50$$

Using these two probabilities, the joint probability that an adult attends six or more movies and is 60 or older is:

$$P[(6 \text{ or more movies }) \text{ and } (60 \text{ or older})] = P(A_4 \text{ and } B_3) = P(A_4)P(B_3|A_4)$$
$$= (50/500)(30/50) = .06$$

Based on the sample information from Table 5–1, the probability that an adult is both over 60 and attended six or more movies is 6%. It is important to know that the 6% is relative to all 500 adults.

Is there another way to determine this joint probability without using the special rule of multiplication formula? Yes. Look directly at the cell where row A_4, attends 6 or more movies, and column B_3, 60 or older, intersect. There are 30 adults in this cell that meet both criteria, so $P(A_4 \text{ and } B_3) = 30/500 = .06$. This is the same as computed with the formula.

6.   Are the events independent? We can answer this question with the help of the results in part 4. In part 4 we found the probability of selecting an adult who was 60 or older given that the adult attended six or more movies was .17. If age is not a factor in movie attendance, then we would expect the probability of a person who is 30 or less that attended six or more movies to also be 17%. That is, the two conditional probabilities would be the same. The probability that an adult attends six or more movies per month given the adult is less than 30 years old is:

$$P[(6 \text{ or more}) \text{ given } (\text{less than } 30)] = \frac{5}{100} = .05$$

Because these two probabilities are not the same, the number of movies attended and age are not independent. To put it another way, for the 500 adults, age is related to the number of movies attended. In Chapter 15, we investigate this concept of independence in greater detail.

SELF-REVIEW 5–9

Refer to Table 5–1 on page 155 to find the following probabilities.
(a)   What is the probability of selecting an adult who is 30 up to 60 years old?
(b)   What is the probability of selecting an adult who is under 60 years of age?
(c)   What is the probability of selecting an adult who is less than 30 years old or attended no movies?
(d)   What is the probability of selecting an adult who is less than 30 years old and went to no movies?

Tree Diagrams

A tree diagram is a visual that is helpful in organizing and calculating probabilities for problems similar to the previous Example/Solution. This type of problem involves several stages, and each stage is illustrated with a branch of the tree. The branches of a tree diagram are labeled with probabilities. We will use the information in Table 5–1 to show the construction of a tree diagram.

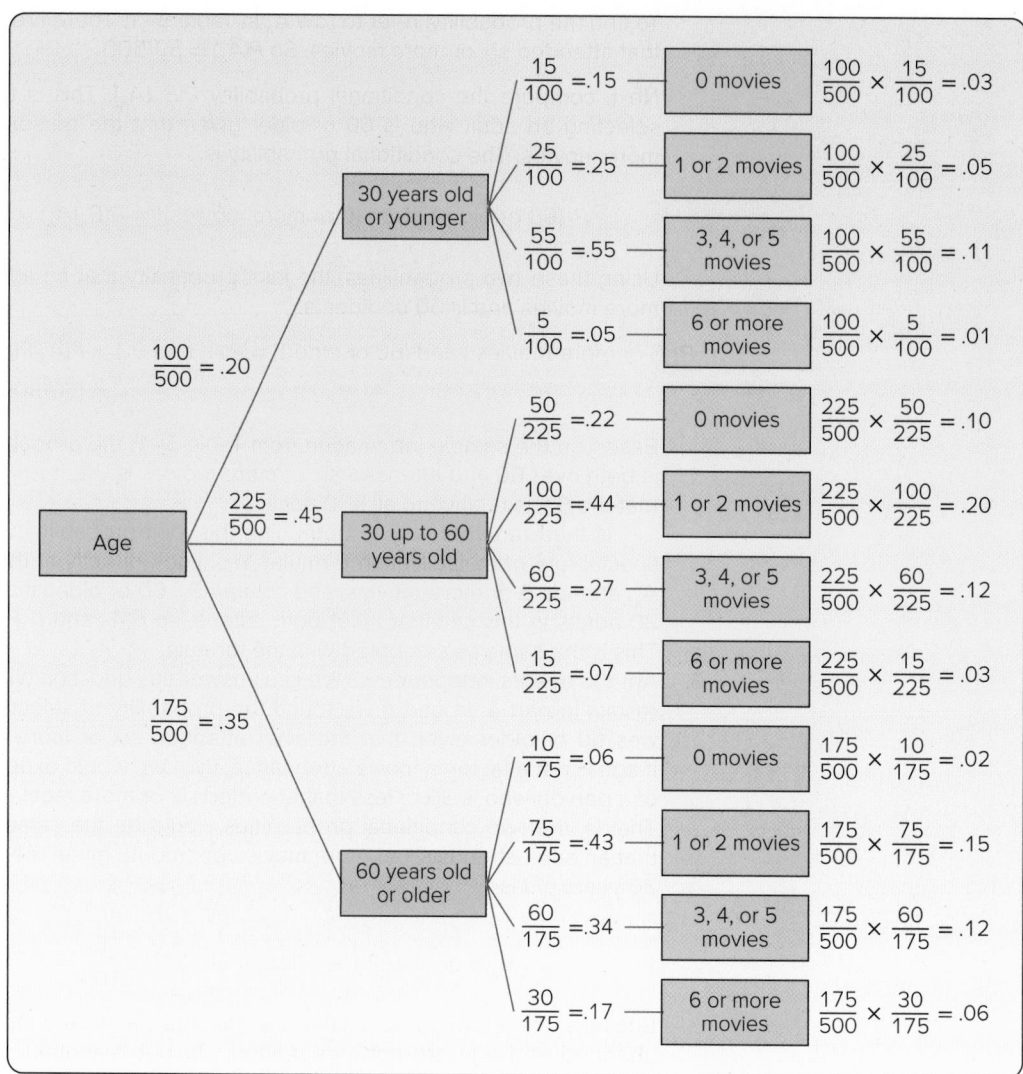

CHART 5–2 Tree Diagram Showing Age and Number of Movies Attended

1. We begin the construction by drawing a box with the variable, age, on the left to represent the root of the tree (Chart 5–2).
2. There are three main branches going out from the root. The upper branch represents the outcome that an adult is less than 30 years old. The branch is labeled with the probability, $P(B_1) = 100/500$. The next branch represents the outcome that adults are 30 up to 60 years old. This branch is labeled with the probability $P(B_2) = 225/500$. The remaining branch is labeled $P(B_3) = 175/500$.
3. Four branches "grow" out of each of the three main branches. These branches represent the four categories of movies attended per month—0; 1 or 2; 3, 4, or 5; and 6 or more. The upper branches of the tree represent the conditional probabilities that an adult did not attend any movies given they are less than 30 years old. These are written $P(A_1|B_1)$, $P(A_2|B_1)$, $P(A_3|B_1)$, and $P(A_4|B_1)$, where A_1 refers to attending no movies; A_2 attending one or two movies per month; A_3 attending

three, four, or five movies per month; and A_4 attending six or more movies per month.

For the upper branch of the tree, these probabilities are 15/100, 25/100, 55/100, and 5/100. We write the conditional probabilities in a similar fashion on the other branches.

4. Finally we determine the various joint probabilities. For the top branches, the events are an adult attends no movies per month and is 30 years old or younger; an adult attends one or two movies and is 30 years old or younger; an adult attends three, four, or five movies per month and is 30 years old or younger; and an adult attends six or more movies per month and is 30 years old or younger. These joint probabilities are shown on the right side of Chart 5–2. To explain, the joint probability that a randomly selected adult is less than 30 years old and attends zero movies per month is:

$$P(B_1 \text{ and } A_1) = P(B_1)P(A_1|B_1) = \left(\frac{100}{500}\right)\left(\frac{15}{100}\right) = .03$$

The tree diagram summarizes all the probabilities based on the contingency table in Table 5–1. For example, the conditional probabilities show that the 60-and-older group has the highest percentage, 17%, attending six or movies per month. The 30-to-60-year-old group has the highest percentage, 22%, of seeing no movies per month. Based on the joint probabilities, 20% of the adults sampled attend one or two movies per month and are 30 up to 60 years of age. As you can see, there are many observations that we can make based on the information presented in the tree diagram.

SELF-REVIEW 5–10

Consumers were surveyed on the relative number of visits (often, occasional, and never) to a Kohl's Department Store and if the store was located in an enclosed mall (yes and no). The contingency table summarizes the responses.

Visits	Enclosed Mall		Total
	Yes	No	
Often	60	20	80
Occasional	25	35	60
Never	5	50	55
	90	105	195

What is the probability of selecting a shopper who:
(a) visited a Kohl's store often?
(b) visited a Kohl's store in an enclosed mall?
(c) visited a Kohl's store in an enclosed mall or visited a Kohl's store often?
(d) visited a Kohl's store often, given that the shopper went to a Kohl's store in an enclosed mall?

In addition:

(e) Are the number of visits and the enclosed mall variables independent?
(f) What is the probability of selecting a shopper who visited a Kohl's store often and it was in an enclosed mall?
(g) Draw a tree diagram and determine the various joint probabilities.

EXERCISES

31. Suppose $P(A) = .40$ and $P(B|A) = .30$. What is the joint probability of A and B?

32. Suppose $P(X_1) = .75$ and $P(Y_2|X_1) = .40$. What is the joint probability of X_1 and Y_2?

33. A local bank reports that 80% of its customers maintain a checking account, 60% have a savings account, and 50% have both. If a customer is chosen at random, what is the probability the customer has either a checking or a savings account? What is the probability the customer does not have either a checking or a savings account?

34. All Seasons Plumbing has two service trucks that frequently need repair. If the probability the first truck is available is .75, the probability the second truck is available is .50, and the probability that both trucks are available is .30, what is the probability neither truck is available?

35. **FILE** Refer to the following table.

	First Event			
Second Event	A_1	A_2	A_3	Total
B_1	2	1	3	6
B_2	1	2	1	4
Total	3	3	4	10

    a. Determine $P(A_1)$.

    b. Determine $P(B_1|A_2)$.

    c. Determine $P(B_2 \text{ and } A_3)$.

36. Three defective electric toothbrushes were accidentally shipped to a drugstore by Cleanbrush Products along with 17 nondefective ones.

    a. What is the probability the first two electric toothbrushes sold will be returned to the drugstore because they are defective?

    b. What is the probability the first two electric toothbrushes sold will not be defective?

37. **FILE** Each salesperson at Puchett, Sheets, and Hogan Insurance Agency is rated either below average, average, or above average with respect to sales ability. Each salesperson also is rated with respect to his or her potential for advancement— either fair, good, or excellent. These traits for the 500 salespeople were cross-classified into the following table.

	Potential for Advancement		
Sales Ability	Fair	Good	Excellent
Below average	16	12	22
Average	45	60	45
Above average	93	72	135

    a. What is this table called?

    b. What is the probability a salesperson selected at random will have above average sales ability and excellent potential for advancement?

    c. Construct a tree diagram showing all the probabilities, conditional probabilities, and joint probabilities.

38. An investor owns three common stocks. Each stock, independent of the others, has equally likely chances of (1) increasing in value, (2) decreasing in value, or (3) remaining the same value. List the possible outcomes of this experiment. Estimate the probability at least two of the stocks increase in value.

39. **FILE** A survey of 545 college students asked: What is your favorite winter sport? And, what type of college do you attend? The results are summarized here:

College Type	Favorite Winter Sport			
	Snowboarding	Skiing	Ice Skating	Total
Junior College	68	41	46	155
Four-Year College	84	56	70	210
Graduate School	59	74	47	180
Total	211	171	163	545

Using these 545 students as the sample, a student from this study is randomly selected.
  a. What is the probability of selecting a student whose favorite sport is skiing?
  b. What is the probability of selecting a junior-college student?
  c. If the student selected is a four-year-college student, what is the probability that the student prefers ice skating?
  d. If the student selected prefers snowboarding, what is the probability that the student is in junior college?
  e. If a graduate student is selected, what is the probability that the student prefers skiing or ice skating?

40. If you ask three strangers about their birthdays, what is the probability of the following: (a) All were born on Wednesday? (b) All were born on different days of the week? (c) None were born on Saturday?

Bayes' Theorem

In the 18th century, Reverend Thomas Bayes, an English Presbyterian minister, pondered this question: Does God really exist? Being interested in mathematics, he attempted to develop a formula to arrive at the probability God does exist based on evidence available to him on earth. Later Pierre-Simon Laplace refined Bayes' work and gave it the name "Bayes' theorem." The formula for **Bayes' theorem** is:

BAYES' THEOREM	$$P(A_i|B) = \frac{P(A_1)P(B|A_1)}{P(A_1)P(B|A_1) + P(A_2)P(B|A_2)}$$	**(5–10)**

Assume in formula (5–10) that the events A_1 and A_2 are mutually exclusive and collectively exhaustive, and A_i refers to either event A_1 or A_2. Hence A_1 and A_2 are in this case complements. The meaning of the symbols used is illustrated by the following example.

Suppose 5% of the population of Umen, a fictional Third World country, have a disease that is peculiar to that country. We will let A_1 refer to the event "has the disease" and A_2 refer to the event "does not have the disease." Thus, we know that if we select a person from Umen at random, the probability the individual chosen has the disease is .05, or $P(A_1) = .05$. This probability, $P(A_1) = P(\text{has the disease}) = .05$, is called the **prior probability.** It is given this name because the probability is assigned before any empirical data are obtained.

PRIOR PROBABILITY The initial probability based on the present level of information.

LO5-9
Calculate probabilities using Bayes' theorem.

STATISTICS IN ACTION

A recent study by the National Collegiate Athletic Association (NCAA) reported that of 150,000 senior boys playing on their high school basketball team, 64 would make a professional team. To put it another way, the odds of a high school senior basketball player making a professional team are 1 in 2,344. From the same study:

1. The odds of a high school senior basketball player playing some college basketball are about 1 in 40.

2. The odds of a high school senior playing college basketball as a senior in college are about 1 in 60.

3. If you play basketball as a senior in college, the odds of making a professional team are about 1 in 37.5.

The prior probability a person is not afflicted with the disease is therefore .95, or $P(A_2) = .95$, found by $1 - .05$.

There is a diagnostic technique to detect the disease, but it is not very accurate. Let B denote the event "test shows the disease is present." Assume that historical evidence shows that if a person actually has the disease, the probability that the test will indicate the presence of the disease is .90. Using the conditional probability definitions developed earlier in this chapter, this statement is written as:

$$P(B|A_1) = .90$$

Assume the probability is .15 that for a person who actually does not have the disease the test will indicate the disease is present.

$$P(B|A_2) = .15$$

Let's randomly select a person from Umen and perform the test. The test results indicate the disease is present. What is the probability the person actually has the disease? In symbolic form, we want to know $P(A_1|B)$, which is interpreted as: P(has the disease | the test results are positive). The probability $P(A_1|B)$ is called a **posterior probability.**

> **POSTERIOR PROBABILITY** A revised probability based on additional information.

With the help of Bayes' theorem, formula (5–10), we can determine the posterior probability.

$$P(A_1|B) = \frac{P(A_1)P(B|A_1)}{P(A_1)P(B|A_1) + P(A_2)P(B|A_2)}$$

$$= \frac{(.05)(.90)}{(.50)(.90) + (.95)(.15)} = \frac{.045}{.1875} = .24$$

So the probability that a person has the disease, given a positive test, is .24. How is the result interpreted? If selected at random from the population, the probability that the person has the disease is .05. If the person is tested and the test result is positive, the probability that the person actually has the disease is increased about fivefold, from .05 to .24.

In the preceding problem, we had only two mutually exclusive and collectively exhaustive events, A_1 and A_2. If there are n such events, A_1, A_2, ..., A_n, Bayes' theorem, formula (5–10), becomes

$$P(A_i|B) = \frac{P(A_i)P(B|A_i)}{P(A_1)P(B|A_1) + P(A_2)P(B|A_2) + \cdots + P(A_n)P(B|A_n)}$$

With the preceding notation, the calculations for the Umen problem are summarized in the following table.

Event, A_i	Prior Probability, $P(A_i)$	Conditional Probability, $P(B\|A_i)$	Joint Probability, $P(A_i$ and $B)$	Posterior Probability, $P(A_i\|B)$
Disease, A_1	.05	.90	.0450	.0450/.1875 = .24
No disease, A_2	.95	.15	.1425	.1425/.1875 = .76
			$P(B) = .1875$	1.00

Another illustration of Bayes' theorem follows.

▶ EXAMPLE

A manufacturer of cell phones purchases a microchip, called the LS-24, from three suppliers: Hall Electronics, Schuller Sales, and Crawford Components. Forty-five percent of the LS-24 chips are purchased from Hall Electronics, 30% from Schuller Sales, and the remaining 25% from Crawford Components. The manufacturer has extensive histories on the three suppliers and knows that 3% of the LS-24 chips from Hall Electronics are defective, 6% of chips from Schuller Sales are defective, and 4% of the chips purchased from Crawford Components are defective.

When the LS-24 chips arrive from the three suppliers, they are placed directly in a bin and not inspected or otherwise identified by supplier. A worker selects a chip for installation and finds it defective. What is the probability that it was manufactured by Schuller Sales?

Mark Dierker/McGraw-Hill
Education

SOLUTION

As a first step, let's summarize some of the information given in the problem statement.

- There are three mutually exclusive and collectively exhaustive events, that is, three suppliers.

  A_1 The LS-24 was purchased from Hall Electronics.
  A_2 The LS-24 was purchased from Schuller Sales.
  A_3 The LS-24 was purchased from Crawford Components.

- The prior probabilities are:

  $P(A_1) = .45$ The probability the LS-24 was manufactured by Hall Electronics
  $P(A_2) = .30$ The probability the LS-24 was manufactured by Schuller Sales
  $P(A_3) = .25$ The probability the LS-24 was manufactured by Crawford Components

- The additional information can be either:

  B_1 The LS-24 is defective, or
  B_2 The LS-24 is not defective.

- The following conditional probabilities are given.

  $P(B_1|A_1) = .03$ The probability that an LS-24 chip produced by Hall Electronics is defective
  $P(B_1|A_2) = .06$ The probability that an LS-24 chip produced by Schuller Sales is defective
  $P(B_1|A_3) = .04$ The probability that an LS-24 chip produced by Crawford Components is defective

- A chip is selected from the bin. Because the chips are not identified by supplier, we are not certain which supplier manufactured the chip. We want to determine the probability that the defective chip was purchased from Schuller Sales. The probability is written $P(A_2|B_1)$.

Look at Schuller's quality record. It is the worst of the three suppliers. They supply 30% of the product, but 6% are defective. Now that we have found a defective LS-24 chip, we suspect that $P(A_2|B_1)$ is greater than the 30% of $P(A_2)$. That is, we expect the revised probability to be greater than .30. But how much greater? Bayes' theorem can give us the answer. As a first step, consider the tree diagram in Chart 5–3.

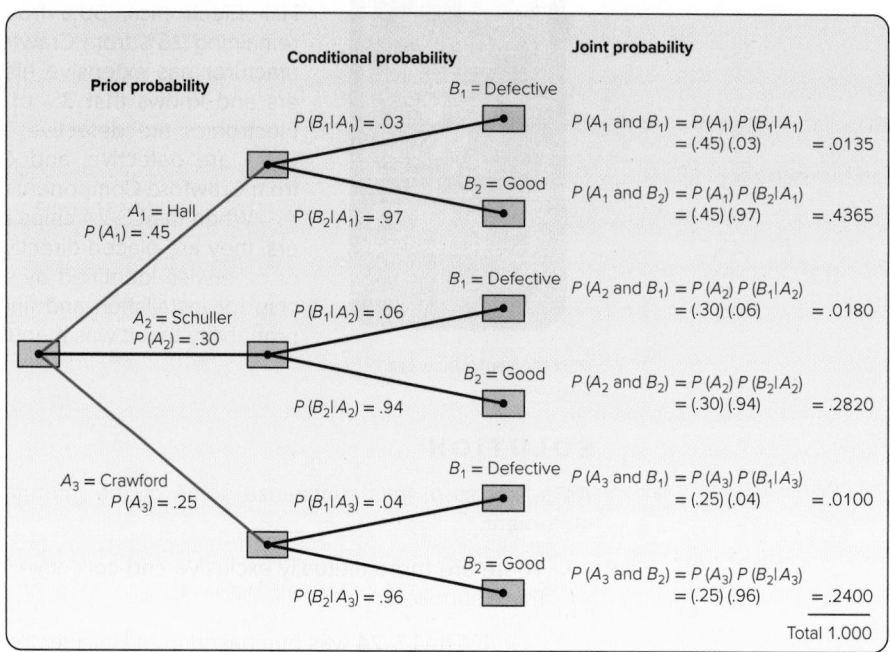

CHART 5–3 Tree Diagram of the Cell Phone Manufacturing Problem

REVISION OF CHART 5–3

The events are dependent, so the prior probability in the first branch is multiplied by the conditional probability in the second branch to obtain the joint probability. The joint probability is reported in the last column of Chart 5–3. To construct the tree diagram of Chart 5–3, we used a time sequence that moved from the supplier to the determination of whether the chip was defective.

What we need to do is reverse the time process. That is, instead of moving from left to right in Chart 5–3, we need to move from right to left. We have a defective chip, and we want to determine the likelihood that it was purchased from Schuller Sales. How is that accomplished? We first look at the joint probabilities as relative frequencies out of 10,000 cases. For example, the likelihood of a defective LS-24 chip that was produced by Hall Electronics is .0135. So of 10,000 cases, we would expect to find 135 defective chips produced by Hall Electronics. We observe that in 415 of 10,000 cases the LS-24 chip selected for assembly is defective, found by 135 + 180 + 100. Of these 415 defective chips, 180 were produced by Schuller Sales. Thus, the probability that the defective LS-24 chip was purchased from Schuller Sales is 180/415 = .4337. We have now determined the revised probability of $P(A_2|B_1)$. Before we found the defective chip, the likelihood that it was purchased from Schuller Sales was .30. This likelihood has been increased to .4337. What have we accomplished by using Bayes' theorem? Once we found the defective part, we conclude that it is much more likely it is a product of Schuller Sales. The increase in the probability is rather dramatic moving from .30 to .4337.

This information is summarized in the following table.

Event, A_i	Prior Probability, $P(A_i)$	Conditional Probability, $P(B_1 \mid A_i)$	Joint Probability, $P(A_i \text{ and } B_1)$	Posterior Probability, $P(A_i \mid B_1)$
Hall	.45	.03	.0135	.0135/.0415 = .3253
Schuller	.30	.06	.0180	.0180/.0415 = .4337
Crawford	.25	.04	.0100	.0100/.0415 = .2410
			$P(B_1) = .0415$	1.0000

The probability the defective LS-24 chip came from Schuller Sales can be formally found by using Bayes' theorem. We compute $P(A_2 \mid B_1)$, where A_2 refers to Schuller Sales and B_1 to the fact that the selected LS-24 chip was defective.

$$P(A_2 \mid B_1) = \frac{P(A_2)P(B_1 \mid A_2)}{P(A_1)P(B_1 \mid A_1) + P(A_2)P(B_1 \mid A_2) + P(A_3)(B_1 \mid A_3)}$$

$$= \frac{(.30)(.60)}{(.45)(.03) + (.30)(.60) + (.25)(.04)} = \frac{.0180}{.0415} = .4337$$

SELF-REVIEW 5–11

Refer to the preceding example and solution.
(a) Design a formula to find the probability the part selected came from Crawford Components, given that it was a good chip.
(b) Compute the probability using Bayes' theorem.

EXERCISES

41. $P(A_1) = .60$, $P(A_2) = .40$, $P(B_1 \mid A_1) = .05$, and $P(B_1 \mid A_2) = .10$. Use Bayes' theorem to determine $P(A_1 \mid B_1)$.

42. $P(A_1) = .20$, $P(A_2) = .40$, $P(A_3) = .40$, $P(B_1 \mid A_1) = .25$, $P(B_1 \mid A_2) = .05$, and $P(B_1 \mid A_3) = .10$. Use Bayes' theorem to determine $P(A_3 \mid B_1)$.

43. The Ludlow Wildcats baseball team, a minor league team in the Cleveland Indians organization, plays 70% of their games at night and 30% during the day. The team wins 50% of their night games and 90% of their day games. According to today's newspaper, they won yesterday. What is the probability the game was played at night?

44. Dr. Stallter has been teaching basic statistics for many years. She knows that 80% of the students will complete the assigned problems. She has also determined that among those who do their assignments, 90% will pass the course. Among those students who do not do their homework, 60% will pass. Mike Fishbaugh took statistics last semester from Dr. Stallter and received a passing grade. What is the probability that he completed the assignments?

45. The credit department of Lion's Department Store in Anaheim, California, reported that 30% of their sales are cash, 30% are paid with a credit card, and 40% with a debit card. Twenty percent of the cash purchases, 90% of the credit card purchases, and 60% of the debit card purchases are for more than $50. Ms. Tina Stevens just purchased a new dress that cost $120. What is the probability that she paid cash?

46. One-fourth of the residents of the Burning Ridge Estates leave their garage doors open when they are away from home. The local chief of police estimates that 5% of the garages with open doors will have something stolen, but only 1% of those closed will have something stolen. If a garage is robbed, what is the probability the doors were left open?

CHAPTER SUMMARY

I. A probability is a value between 0 and 1 inclusive that represents the likelihood a particular event will happen.
  A. An experiment is the observation of some activity or the act of taking some measurement.
  B. An outcome is a particular result of an experiment.
  C. An event is the collection of one or more outcomes of an experiment.
II. There are three definitions of probability.
  A. The classical definition applies when there are n equally likely outcomes to an experiment.
  B. The empirical definition occurs when the number of times an event happens is divided by the number of observations.
  C. A subjective probability is based on whatever information is available.
III. There are three counting rules that are useful in determining the number of outcomes in an experiment.
  A. The multiplication rule states that if there are m ways one event can happen and n ways another event can happen, then there are mn ways the two events can happen.

$$\text{Number of arrangements} = (m)(n) \qquad (5-2)$$

  B. A permutation is an arrangement in which the order of the objects selected from a specific pool of objects is important.

$$_nP_r = \frac{n!}{(n-r)!} \qquad (5-3)$$

  C. A combination is an arrangement where the order of the objects selected from a specific pool of objects is not important.

$$_nC_r = \frac{n!}{r!(n-r)!} \qquad (5-4)$$

IV. Two events are mutually exclusive if by virtue of one event happening the other cannot happen.
V. Events are independent if the occurrence of one event does not affect the occurrence of another event.
VI. The rules of addition refer to the probability that any of two or more events can occur.
  A. The special rule of addition is used when events are mutually exclusive.

$$P(A \text{ or } B) = P(A) + P(B) \qquad (5-5)$$

  B. The general rule of addition is used when the events are not mutually exclusive.

$$P(A \text{ or } B) = P(A) + P(B) - P(A \text{ and } B) \qquad (5-6)$$

  C. The complement rule is used to determine the probability of an event happening by subtracting the probability of the event not happening from 1.

$$P(A) = 1 - P(\sim A) \qquad (5-7)$$

VII. The rules of multiplication are applied when two or more events occur simultaneously.
  A. The special rule of multiplication refers to events that are independent.

$$P(A \text{ and } B) = P(A)P(B) \qquad (5-8)$$

  B. The general rule of multiplication refers to events that are not independent.

$$P(A \text{ and } B) = P(A)P(B|A) \qquad (5-9)$$

  C. A joint probability is the likelihood that two or more events will happen at the same time.
  D. A conditional probability is the likelihood that an event will happen, given that another event has already happened.

E. Bayes' theorem is a method of revising a probability, given that additional information is obtained. For two mutually exclusive and collectively exhaustive events:

$$P(A_1|B) = \frac{P(A_1)P(B|A_1)}{P(A_1)P(B|A_1) + P(A_2)P(B|A_2)}$$

(5–10)

CHAPTER EXERCISES

47. The marketing research department at PepsiCo plans a national survey of 2,500 teenagers regarding a newly developed soft drink. Each teenager will be asked to compare it with a favorite soft drink.
   a. What is the experiment?
   b. What is one possible event?

48. The number of times a particular event occurred in the past is divided by the number of occurrences. What is this approach to probability called?

49. The probability that the cause and the cure for all cancers will be discovered before the year 2030 is .20. What viewpoint of probability does this statement illustrate?

50. **FILE** Berdine's Chicken Factory has several stores in the Hilton Head, South Carolina, area. When interviewing applicants for server positions, the owner would like to include information on the amount of tip a server can expect to earn per check (or bill). A study of 500 recent checks indicated the server earned the following amounts in tips per 8-hour shift.

Amount of Tip	Number
$ 0 up to $ 20	200
20 up to 50	100
50 up to 100	75
100 up to 200	75
200 or more	50
Total	500

   a. What is the probability of a tip of $200 or more?
   b. Are the categories "$0 up to $20," "$20 up to $50," and so on considered mutually exclusive?
   c. If the probabilities associated with each outcome were totaled, what would that total be? Why?
   d. What is the probability of a tip of up to $50?
   e. What is the probability of a tip of less than $200?

51. Winning all three "Triple Crown" races is considered the greatest feat of a pedigree racehorse. After a successful Kentucky Derby, Corn on the Cob is a heavy favorite at 2-to-1 odds to win the Preakness Stakes.

    a. If he is a 2-to-1 favorite to win the Belmont Stakes as well, what is his probability of winning the Triple Crown?

    b. What do his chances for the Preakness Stakes have to be for him to be "even money" to earn the Triple Crown?

52. The first card selected from a standard 52-card deck is a king.

    a. If it is returned to the deck, what is the probability that a king will be drawn on the second selection?

    b. If the king is not replaced, what is the probability that a king will be drawn on the second selection?

    c. In part (b), are we assuming the card selections are independent? Justify your answer.

53. Armco, a manufacturer of traffic light systems, found that under accelerated-life tests, 95% of the newly developed systems lasted 3 years before failing to change signals properly.

    a. If a city purchased four of these systems, what is the probability all four systems would operate properly for at least 3 years?

    b. Which rule of probability does this illustrate?

    c. Using letters to represent the four systems, write an equation to show how you arrived at the answer to part (a).

54. Refer to the following picture.

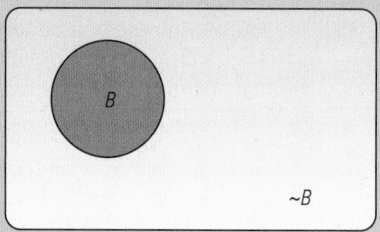

    a. What is the picture called?

    b. What rule of probability is illustrated?

    c. B represents the event of choosing a family that receives welfare payments. What does $P(B) + P(\sim B)$ equal?

55. In a management trainee program at Claremont Enterprises, 80% of the trainees are women and 20% men. Ninety percent of the women attended college, and 78% of the men attended college.

    a. A management trainee is selected at random. What is the probability that the person selected is a woman who did not attend college?

    b. Are gender and attending college independent? Why?

    c. Construct a tree diagram showing all the probabilities, conditional probabilities, and joint probabilities.

    d. Do the joint probabilities total 1.00? Why?

56. Assume the likelihood that any flight on Delta Airlines arrives within 15 minutes of the scheduled time is .90. We randomly selected a Delta flight on four different days.

    a. What is the likelihood all four of the selected flights arrived within 15 minutes of the scheduled time?

    b. What is the likelihood that none of the selected flights arrived within 15 minutes of the scheduled time?

    c. What is the likelihood at least one of the selected flights did not arrive within 15 minutes of the scheduled time?

57. There are 100 employees at Kiddie Carts International. Fifty-seven of the employees are hourly workers, 40 are supervisors, 2 are secretaries, and the remaining employee is the president. Suppose an employee is selected:

    a. What is the probability the selected employee is an hourly worker?

    b. What is the probability the selected employee is either an hourly worker or a supervisor?

c. Refer to part (b). Are these events mutually exclusive?

d. What is the probability the selected employee is neither an hourly worker nor a supervisor?

58. Trea Turner of the Los Angeles Dodgers had the highest batting average for the 2021 Major League Baseball season. His average was .328. So, the likelihood of his getting a hit is .328 for each time he bats. Assume he has four times at bat tonight in the Dodger-Giants game.

a. This is an example of what type of probability?

b. What is the probability of getting four hits in tonight's game?

c. Are you assuming his second at bat is independent or mutually exclusive of his first at bat? Explain.

d. What is the probability of not getting any hits in the game?

e. What is the probability of getting at least one hit?

59. Four women's college basketball teams are participating in a single-elimination holiday basketball tournament. If one team is favored in its semifinal match by odds of 2-to-1 and another squad is favored in its contest by odds of 3-to-1, what is the probability that:

a. both favored teams win their games?

b. neither favored team wins its game?

c. at least one of the favored teams wins its game?

60. On the trivia game show *Jeopardy,* three contestants select from a board of 30 clues; each clue is assigned a monetary value. Each correct answer adds to a contestant's monetary score, an incorrect answer results in a decrease in the score. A Daily Double is assigned to a clue or two on the board. A clue with a Daily Double allows the contestant to determine the monetary value up to the current score.

a. In the first round of the game show, 1 of the 30 clues is a Daily Double. What is the probability that a contestant finds the Daily Double on the first selection?

b. Given that 15 clues have been selected in the first round without a Daily Double, what is the probability a contestant finds the daily double?

c. The probabilities in parts (a) and (b) are conditional probabilities. What is the conditional common to each?

d. In the second round of *Jeopardy,* Daily Doubles are assigned to 2 of the 30 clues. On the first selection, what is the probability of finding a daily double?

e. In the second round, suppose that 15 clues were selected, and not one was a Daily Double. What is the probability a contestant finds a Daily Double?

f. The probabilities in parts (d) and (e) are conditional probabilities. What is the condition common to each?

61. Brooks Insurance Inc. wishes to offer life insurance to men aged 60 via the Internet. Mortality tables indicate the likelihood of a 60-year-old man surviving another year is .98. The policy is offered to five men aged 60.

a. What is the probability all five men survive the year?

b. What is the probability at least one does not survive?

62. Forty percent of the homes constructed in the Quail Creek area include a security system. Three homes are selected at random.

a. What is the probability all three of the selected homes have a security system?

b. What is the probability none of the three selected homes has a security system?

c. What is the probability at least one of the selected homes has a security system?

d. Did you assume the events to be dependent or independent?

63. Refer to Exercise 62, but assume there are 10 homes in the Quail Creek area and 4 of them have a security system. Three homes are selected at random.

a. What is the probability all three of the selected homes have a security system?

b. What is the probability none of the three selected homes has a security system?

c. What is the probability at least one of the selected homes has a security system?

d. Did you assume the events to be dependent or independent?

64. There are 20 families living in the Willbrook Farms Development. Of these families, 10 prepared their own federal income taxes for last year, seven had their taxes prepared by a local professional, and the remaining three by H&R Block.

a. What is the probability of selecting a family that prepared their own taxes?

b. What is the probability of selecting two families, both of which prepared their own taxes?

c. What is the probability of selecting three families, all of which prepared their own taxes?

d. What is the probability of selecting two families, neither of which had their taxes prepared by H&R Block?

65. The board of directors of Saner Automatic Door Company consists of 12 members, three of whom are women. A new policy and procedures manual is to be written for the company. A committee of three is randomly selected from the board to do the writing.

a. What is the probability that all members of the committee are men?

b. What is the probability that at least one member of the committee is a woman?

66. **FILE** A recent survey reported in *Bloomberg Businessweek* dealt with the salaries of CEOs at large corporations and whether company shareholders made money or lost money.

	CEO Paid More Than $1 Million	CEO Paid Less Than $1 Million	Total
Shareholders made money	2	11	13
Shareholders lost money	4	3	7
Total	6	14	20

If a company is randomly selected from the list of 20 studied, what is the probability:

a. the CEO made more than $1 million?

b. the CEO made more than $1 million or the shareholders lost money?

c. the CEO made more than $1 million given the shareholders lost money?

d. of selecting two CEOs and finding they both made more than $1 million?

67. Althoff and Roll, an investment firm in Augusta, Georgia, advertises extensively in the *Augusta Morning Gazette,* the newspaper serving the region. The *Gazette* marketing staff estimates that 60% of Althoff and Roll's potential market read the newspaper. It is further estimated that 85% of those who read the *Gazette* remember the Althoff and Roll advertisement.

a. What percent of the investment firm's potential market sees and remembers the advertisement?

b. What percent of the investment firm's potential market sees, but does not remember, the advertisement?

68. An Internet company located in Southern California has season tickets to the Los Angeles Lakers basketball games. The company president always invites one of the four vice presidents to attend games with him, and claims he selects the person to attend at random. One of the four vice presidents has not been invited to attend any of the last five Lakers home games. What is the likelihood this could be due to chance?

69. A computer-supply retailer purchased a batch of 1,000 micro-SD cards and attempted to format them for a particular application. There were 857 perfect cards, 112 cards were defective, and the remainder could not be used at all.

a. What is the probability a randomly chosen card is not perfect?

b. If the card is not perfect, what is the probability it cannot be used at all?

70. An investor purchased 100 shares of Fifth Third Bank stock and 100 shares of Santee Electric Cooperative stock. The probability the bank stock will appreciate over a year is .70. The probability the electric utility will increase over the same period is .60. Assume the two events are independent.

a. What is the probability both stocks appreciate during the period?

b. What is the probability the bank stock appreciates but the utility does not?

c. What is the probability at least one of the stocks appreciates?

71. Flashner Marketing Research Inc. specializes in providing assessments of the prospects for apparel shops in shopping malls. Finley Flashner, president, reports the prospects as good, fair, or poor. Records from previous assessments show that 60% of the time the prospects were rated as good, 30% of the time fair, and 10% of the time poor. Of those rated good, 80% made a profit the first year; of those rated fair, 60% made a profit the first year; and of those rated poor, 20% made a profit the first year. Tommie's Apparel was one of Flashner's clients. Tommie's Apparel made a profit last year. What is the probability that it was given an original rating of poor?

72. Two boxes of men's Old Navy shirts were received from the factory. Box 1 contained 25 mesh polo shirts and 15 Super-T shirts. Box 2 contained 30 mesh polo shirts and 10 Super-T shirts. One of the boxes was selected at random, and a shirt was chosen at random from that box to be inspected. The shirt was a mesh polo shirt. Given this information, what is the probability that the mesh polo shirt came from Box 1?

73. With each purchase of a large pizza at Ricci's Pizza, the customer receives a coupon that can be scratched to see if a prize will be awarded. The probability of winning a free soft drink is 0.10, and the probability of winning a free large pizza is 0.02. You plan to eat lunch tomorrow at Ricci's. What is the probability:
   a. that you will win either a large pizza or a soft drink?
   b. that you will not win a prize?
   c. that you will not win a prize on three consecutive visits to Ricci's?
   d. that you will win at least one prize on one of your next three visits to Ricci's?

74. For the daily lottery game in Illinois, participants select three numbers between 0 and 9. A number cannot be selected more than once, so a winning ticket could be, say, 307 but not 337. Purchasing one ticket allows you to select one set of numbers. The winning numbers are announced on TV each night.
   a. How many different outcomes (three-digit numbers) are possible?
   b. If you purchase a ticket for the game tonight, what is the likelihood you will win?
   c. Suppose you purchase three tickets for tonight's drawing and select a different number for each ticket. What is the probability that you will not win with any of the tickets?

75. Several years ago, Wendy's Hamburgers advertised that there are 256 different ways to order your hamburger. You may choose to have, or omit, any combination of the following on your hamburger: mustard, ketchup, onion, pickle, tomato, relish, mayonnaise, and lettuce. Is the advertisement correct? Show how you arrive at your answer.

76. Recent surveys indicate 60% of tourists to China visited the Forbidden City, the Temple of Heaven, the Great Wall, and other historical sites in or near Beijing. Forty percent visited Xi'an with its magnificent terra-cotta soldiers, horses, and chariots, which lay buried for over 2,000 years. Thirty percent of the tourists went to both Beijing and Xi'an. What is the probability that a tourist visited at least one of these places?

77. A new chewing gum has been developed that is helpful to those who want to stop smoking. If 60% of those people chewing the gum are successful in stopping smoking, what is the probability that in a group of four smokers using the gum at least one quits smoking?

78. The Swiftwater Construction Company has agreed not to build all "look-alike" homes in a new subdivision. Five exterior designs are offered to potential home buyers. The builder has standardized three interior plans that can be incorporated in any of the five exteriors. How many different ways can the exterior and interior plans be offered to potential home buyers?

79. A new sports car model has defective brakes 15% of the time and a defective steering mechanism 5% of the time. Let's assume (and hope) that these problems occur independently. If one or the other of these problems is present, the car is called a "lemon." If both of these problems are present, the car is a "hazard." Your instructor purchased one of these cars yesterday. What is the probability it is:
   a. a lemon?
   b. a hazard?

80. The state of Maryland has license plates with three numbers followed by three letters. How many different license plates are possible?

81. There are four people being considered for the position of chief executive officer of Dalton Enterprises. Three of the applicants are over 60 years of age. Two are female, of which only one is over 60.
   a. What is the probability that a candidate is over 60 and female?
   b. Given that the candidate is male, what is the probability he is less than 60?
   c. Given that the person is over 60, what is the probability the person is female?

82. Sora Kanzaki is the owner of Kanzaki Investment and Real Estate Company. The company recently purchased four tracts of land in Holly Farms Estates and six tracts in Newburg Woods. The tracts are all equally desirable and sell for about the same amount.
   a. What is the probability that the next two tracts sold will be in Newburg Woods?
   b. What is the probability that of the next four sold at least one will be in Holly Farms?
   c. Are these events independent or dependent?

83. A computer password consists of four characters. The characters can be one of the 26 letters of the alphabet. Each character may be used more than once. How many different passwords are possible?

84. A case of 24 cans contains one can that is contaminated. Three cans are to be chosen randomly for testing.
   a. How many different combinations of three cans could be selected?
   b. What is the probability that the contaminated can is selected for testing?

85. A puzzle in the newspaper presents a matching problem. The names of 10 U.S. presidents are listed in one column, and their vice presidents are listed in random order in the second column. The puzzle asks the reader to match each president with his vice president. If you make the matches randomly, how many matches are possible? What is the probability all 10 of your matches are correct?

86. Two components, A and B, operate in series. Being in series means that for the system to operate, both components A and B must work. Assume the two components are independent. What is the probability the system works under these conditions? The probability A works is .90 and the probability B functions is also .90.

87. Horwege Electronics Inc. purchases LED display screens from four different suppliers. Tyson Wholesale supplies 20% of the displays, Fuji Importers 30%, Kirkpatricks 25%, and Parts Inc. 25%. Tyson Wholesale tends to have the best quality, as only 3% of its displays arrive defective. Fuji Importers' displays are 4% defective, Kirkpatricks' 7%, and Parts Inc.'s are 6.5% defective.
   a. What is the overall percent defective?
   b. A defective display was discovered in the latest shipment. What is the probability that it came from Tyson Wholesale?

88. ABC Auto Insurance classifies drivers as good, medium, or poor risks. Drivers who apply to them for insurance fall into these three groups in the proportions 30%, 50%, and 20%, respectively. The probability a "good" driver will have an accident is .01, the probability a "medium" risk driver will have an accident is .03, and the probability a "poor" driver will have an accident is .10. The company sells Mr. Brophy an insurance policy and he has an accident. What is the probability Mr. Brophy is:
   a. a "good" driver?
   b. a "medium" risk driver?
   c. a "poor" driver?

89. You take a trip by air that involves three independent flights. If there is an 80% chance each specific leg of the trip is on time, what is the probability all three flights arrive on time?

90. A company uses three backup servers to secure its data. The probability that a server fails is 0.05. Assuming that the failure of a server is independent of the other servers, what is the probability that one or more of the servers is operational?

91. Twenty-two percent of all light-emitting diode (LED) displays are manufactured by Samsung. What is the probability that in a collection of three independent LED HDTV purchases, at least one is a Samsung?

DATA ANALYTICS

92. **FILE** Refer to the North Valley Real Estate data, which report information on homes sold during the last year.
   a. Sort the data into a table that shows the number of homes that have a pool versus the number that don't have a pool in each of the five townships. If a home is selected at random, compute the following probabilities.

    1. The home has a pool.

    2. The home is in Township 1 or has a pool.

    3. Given that it is in Township 3, that it has a pool.

    4. The home has a pool and is in Township 3.

  b. Sort the data into a table that shows the number of homes that have a garage attached versus those that don't in each of the five townships. If a home is selected at random, compute the following probabilities.

    1. The home has a garage attached.

    2. The home does not have a garage attached, given that it is in Township 5.

    3. The home has a garage attached and is in Township 3.

    4. The home does not have a garage attached or is in Township 2.

93. **FILE** The Baseball data set (in Appendix A and Connect) reports information on the 30 Major League Baseball (MLB) teams for the 2021 season.

  a. In the MLB, each team plays 162 games in a season. A rule-of-thumb is that 90 or more wins in a season qualify a team for the post-season playoffs. To summarize the 2021 season, create a frequency table of wins. Start the first class at 40 and use a class interval of 10.

    a. What is the probability that a team wins 90 or more games?

    b. In the playoffs, only 10 teams can enter the playoffs. Based on the 2021 season, what is the probability that a team that wins 90 or more games makes the playoffs?

    c. Make a statement based on your responses to parts (a) and (b).

  b. Presently the National League requires that all fielding players, including pitchers, take a turn to bat. In the American League, teams can use a designated hitter (DH) to take the pitcher's turn to bat. For each league, create a frequency distribution and a relative frequency distribution of teams based on the season total of home runs. For the frequency distributions, start the first class at 120 home runs and use a class interval of 30.

    a. In the American League, what is the probability that a team hits 180 or more home runs?

    b. In the National League, what is the probability that a team hits 180 or more home runs?

    c. Make statements comparing the two distributions.

94. **FILE** Refer to the Lincolnville school bus data. Set up a variable that divides the age of the buses into three groups: new (less than 5 years old), medium (5 but less than 10 years), and old (10 or more years). The median maintenance cost is $4,179. Based on this value, create a variable for those less than or equal to the median (low maintenance) and those more than the median (high maintenance cost). Finally, develop a table to show the relationship between maintenance cost and age of the bus.

  a. What percentage of the buses are less than 5 years old?

  b. What percentage of the buses less than 5 years old have low maintenance costs?

  c. What percentage of the buses 10 or more years old have high maintenance costs?

  d. Does maintenance cost seem to be related to the age of the bus? Hint: Compare the maintenance cost of the old buses with the cost of the new buses. Would you conclude maintenance cost is independent of the age?

6

Discrete Probability Distributions

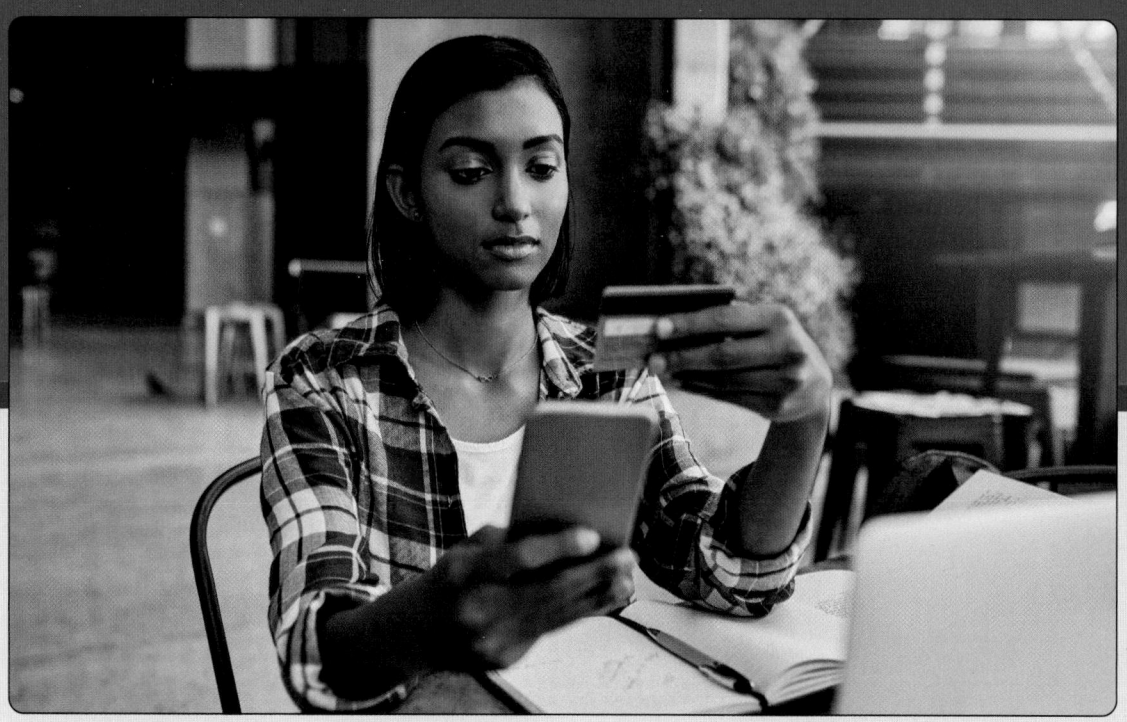

PeopleImages/Getty Images

▲ **THE PEW RESEARCH INSTITUTE** recently conducted a survey of adult Americans regarding Internet shopping. The survey found that 15% of the respondents made a retail purchase on the Internet last week. A retailer wished to verify this claim and surveyed a random sample of 16 adults. What is the likelihood that exactly three adults make an Internet purchase during a week? Of the 16 adults, how many are expected to make a purchase during a week? What is the likelihood that three or less of the 16 adults make an Internet purchase during a week? (See Exercise 49 and LO6-4.)

LEARNING OBJECTIVES

When you have completed this chapter, you will be able to:

LO6-1 Identify the characteristics of a probability distribution.

LO6-2 Distinguish between discrete and continuous random variables.

LO6-3 Compute the mean, variance, and standard deviation of a discrete probability distribution.

LO6-4 Explain the assumptions of the binomial distribution and apply it to calculate probabilities.

LO6-5 Explain the assumptions of the hypergeometric distribution and apply it to calculate probabilities.

LO6-6 Explain the assumptions of the Poisson distribution and apply it to calculate probabilities.

Introduction

Chapters 2 through 4 are devoted to descriptive statistics. We describe raw data by organizing the data into a frequency distribution and portraying the distribution in tables, graphs, and charts. Also, we compute a measure of location—such as the arithmetic mean, median, or mode—to locate a typical value near the center of the distribution. The range and the standard deviation are used to describe the spread in the data. These chapters focus on describing *something that has already happened*.

Starting with Chapter 5, the emphasis changes—we begin examining *something that could happen*. We note that this facet of statistics is called *statistical inference*. The objective is to make inferences (statements) about a population based on a number of observations, called a sample, selected from the population. In Chapter 5, we state that a probability is a value between 0 and 1 inclusive, and we examine how probabilities can be combined using rules of addition and multiplication.

This chapter begins the study of probability distributions. A probability distribution is like a relative frequency distribution. However, instead of describing the past, it is used to provide the likelihood of future events. Probability distributions can be described by measures of location and dispersion, so we show how to compute a distribution's mean, variance, and standard deviation.

In a much larger context, data scientists may explore data by using empirical probability distributions to summarize the likelihood of future outcomes. These probability distributions can then be used to support decision making with computer modeling. For example, decisions can be evaluated before they are made by testing alternatives given the likelihood of a particular outcome, and then, using a probability distribution, evaluate the decision again given the likelihood of another outcome. Data scientists often write computer code to conduct these complicated analyses. The result of the analysis would be a thorough assessment of all possible decisions and their predicted consequences.

In this chapter, we begin by describing the general characteristics of discrete probability distributions. These are called discrete probability distributions because the values of the random variable are discrete. We also discuss three frequently occurring discrete probability distributions: binomial, hypergeometric, and Poisson. These classical probability distributions were created based on observed patterns for very specific situations. Pay attention to the requirements or conditions that apply to each of these distributions.

What Is a Probability Distribution?

LO6-1
Identify the characteristics of a probability distribution.

A **probability distribution** defines or describes the likelihoods for a range of possible future outcomes. For example, Spalding Golf Products Inc. assembles golf clubs with three components: a club head, a shaft, and a grip. From experience, 5% of the shafts received from their Asian supplier are defective. As part of Spalding's statistical process control they inspect 20 shafts from each arriving shipment. From experience, we know that the probability of a defective shaft is 5%. Therefore, in a sample of 20 shafts, we would expect one shaft to be defective and the other 19 shafts to be acceptable. But, by using a probability distribution we can completely describe the range of possible outcomes. For example, we would know the probability that none of the 20 shafts are defective, or that two, or three, or four, or continuing up to 20 shafts in the sample are defective. Given the small probability of a defective shaft, the probability distribution would show that there is a very small probability of four or more defective shafts.

> **PROBABILITY DISTRIBUTION** A listing of all the outcomes of an experiment and the probability associated with each outcome.

The important characteristics of a probability distribution are:

> **CHARACTERISTICS OF A PROBABILITY DISTRIBUTION**
>
> 1. The probability of a particular outcome is between 0 and 1 inclusive.
> 2. The outcomes are mutually exclusive.
> 3. The list of outcomes is exhaustive. So the sum of the probabilities of the outcomes is equal to 1.

How can we generate a probability distribution? The following example will explain.

▶ **EXAMPLE**

Suppose we are interested in the number of heads showing face up on three tosses of a coin. This is the experiment. The possible results are zero heads, one head, two heads, and three heads. What is the probability distribution for the number of heads?

SOLUTION

This experiment applies the classical approach to probability. There are eight possible outcomes. A tail might appear face up on the first toss, another tail on the second toss, and another tail on the third toss of the coin. Or we might get a tail, tail, and head, in that order. We use the multiplication formula for counting outcomes (5-2). There are (2)(2)(2) or 8 possible results. These results are shown in the following table.

Possible Result	Coin Toss First	Coin Toss Second	Third	Number of Heads
1	T	T	T	0
2	T	T	H	1
3	T	H	T	1
4	T	H	H	2
5	H	T	T	1
6	H	T	H	2
7	H	H	T	2
8	H	H	H	3

The outcome "zero heads" occurred only once, "one head" occurred three times, "two heads" occurred three times, and the outcome "three heads" occurred only once. That is, "zero heads" happened one out of eight times. Thus, the probability of zero heads is one-eighth, the probability of one head is three-eighths, and so on. The probability distribution is shown in Table 6–1. Because one of these outcomes must happen, the total of the probabilities of all possible events is 1.000. This is always true. The same information is shown in Chart 6–1. In Chapter 2, we called Chart 6–1 a relative frequency distribution. Here we extend the relative frequencies to probabilities. The probabilities are used to predict the likelihood that a particular outcome will happen.

We write the probability of x as $P(x)$. So referring to Table 6–1 or Chart 6–1, the probability of zero heads is $P(0 \text{ heads}) = .125$, and the probability of one head is $P(1 \text{ head}) = .375$, and so forth. For these mutually exclusive and collectively exhaustive outcomes, the sum of their probabilities is 1; that is, from Table 6–1, $.125 + .375 + .375 + .125 = 1.00$.

TABLE 6–1 Probability Distribution for the Events of Zero, One, Two, and Three Heads Showing Face Up on Three Tosses of a Coin

Number of Heads, x	Probability of Outcome, P(x)
0	$\frac{1}{8} = .125$
1	$\frac{3}{8} = .375$
2	$\frac{3}{8} = .375$
3	$\frac{1}{8} = .125$
Total	$\frac{8}{8} = 1.000$

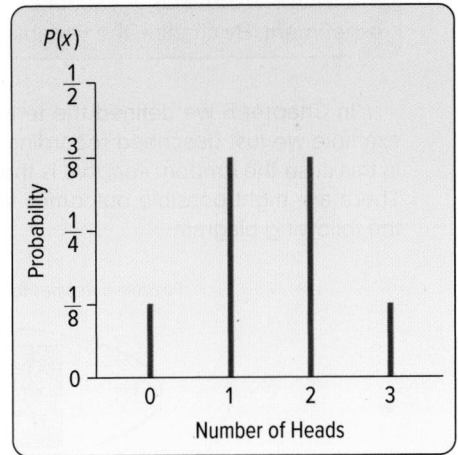

CHART 6–1 Graphical Presentation of the Number of Heads Resulting from Three Tosses of a Coin and the Corresponding Probability

---

SELF-REVIEW 6–1

The possible outcomes of an experiment involving the roll of a six-sided die are a one-spot, a two-spot, a three-spot, a four-spot, a five-spot, and a six-spot.

(a) Develop a probability distribution for the number of possible spots.
(b) Portray the probability distribution graphically.
(c) What is the sum of the probabilities?

LO6-2
Distinguish between discrete and continuous random variables.

Random Variables

In an experiment of chance, the outcomes occur randomly. So it is often called a **random variable.** For example, rolling a single die is an experiment. The random variable is the number of spots showing; the possible values of the random variable are 1, 2, 3, 4, 5, and 6. Any one of six possible outcomes can occur. Some experiments result in outcomes that are measured with quantitative variables (such as dollars, weight, or number of children), and other experimental outcomes are measured with qualitative variables (such as color or religious preference). A few examples will further illustrate what is meant by a random variable.

- The number of employees absent from the day shift on Monday, the number might be 0, 1, 2, 3, ... The number absent is the random variable.
- The hourly wage of a sample of 50 plumbers in Jacksonville, Florida. The hourly wage is the random variable.
- The number of defective lightbulbs produced in an hour at the Cleveland Electric Company Inc.
- The grade level (Freshman, Sophomore, Junior, or Senior) of the members of the St. James High School Varsity girls' basketball team. The grade level is the random variable, and notice that it is a qualitative variable.
- The number of participants in the 2022 New York City Marathon.
- The daily number of drivers charged with driving under the influence of alcohol in Brazoria County, Texas, last month.

A random variable is defined as follows:

> **RANDOM VARIABLE** A variable measured or observed as the result of an experiment. By chance, the variable can have different values.

In Chapter 5 we defined the terms *experiment, outcome,* and *event.* Consider the example we just described regarding the experiment of tossing a fair coin three times. In this case the *random variable* is the number of heads that appear in the three tosses. There are eight possible outcomes to this experiment. These outcomes are shown in the following diagram.

Possible *outcomes* for three coin tosses

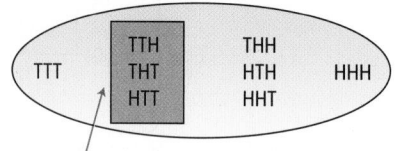

The *event* {one head} occurs and the *random variable* $x = 1$.

So, one possible outcome is that a tail appears on each toss: TTT. This single outcome would describe the event of zero heads appearing in three tosses. Another possible outcome is a head followed by two tails: HTT. If we wish to determine the event of exactly one head appearing in the three tosses, we must consider the three possible outcomes: TTH, THT, and HTT. These three outcomes describe the event of exactly one head appearing in three tosses.

In this experiment, the random variable is the number of heads in three tosses. The random variable can have four different values: 0, 1, 2, or 3. The outcomes of the experiment are unknown. But, we can compute the probability of a single head in three tosses as 3/8 or .375. As shown in Chart 6–1 and Table 6–1, the probability of each value of the random variable can be computed to create a probability distribution for the random variable, number of heads in three tosses of a coin.

There are two types of random variables: *discrete* and *continuous.*

Discrete Random Variable

A **discrete random variable** can assume only a certain number of separated values. For example, the Bank of the Carolinas counts the number of credit cards carried for a group of customers. The data are summarized with the following relative frequency table.

Number of Credit Cards	Relative Frequency
0	.03
1	.10
2	.18
3	.21
4 or more	.48
Total	1.00

In this frequency table, the number of cards carried is the discrete random variable.

DISCRETE RANDOM VARIABLE A random variable that can assume only certain clearly separated values.

A discrete random variable can, in some cases, assume fractional or decimal values. To be a discrete random variable, these values must be separated—that is, have distance between them. As an example, a department store offers coupons with discounts of 10%, 15%, and 25%. In terms of probability, we could compute the probability that a customer would use a 10% coupon versus a 15% or 25% coupon.

Continuous Random Variable

On the other hand, a **continuous random variable** can assume an infinite number of values within a given range. It is expressed as a rational number and measured with a ratio scale.

CONTINUOUS RANDOM VARIABLE A random variable that may assume an infinite number of values within a given range.

Examples of continuous random variables include:

- The times of commercial flights between Atlanta and Los Angeles are 4.67 hours, 5.13 hours, and so on. The random variable is time and is measured on a continuous scale of hours.
- The annual snowfall in Minneapolis, Minnesota. The random variable is the depth of snow, measured on a continuous scale of inches and feet, or centimeters and meters.

As with discrete random variables, the likelihood of a continuous random variable can be summarized with a *probability distribution*. For example, with a probability distribution for the flight time between Atlanta and Los Angeles, we could say that there is a probability of 0.90 that the flight will be less than 4.5 hours. This also implies that there is a probability of 0.10 that the flight will be more than 4.5 hours. With a probability of snowfall in Minneapolis, we could say that there is probability of 0.25 that the annual snowfall will exceed 48 inches. This also implies that there is a probability of 0.75 that annual snowfall will be less than 48 inches. Notice that these examples refer to a continuous range of values.

Sometimes, the measurement of a continuous random variable is rounded to simplify the analysis and presentation of the data. Suppose that we measure the distance an electric vehicle travels on one full battery charge. We find that the data are dispersed over the range of 190 to 205 miles. The data are measured with a precision of two decimal places, such as 195.56 or 201.04 miles. To construct a probability distribution for the random variable, distance, we decide to round each measurement to the nearest integer value. So, 195.56 would round up to 196, and 201.04 would round down to 201. Now, the data are defined by discrete integer values from 190 to 205, and the probability distribution would have 16 discrete classes that correspond to each of the 16 possible values. So, depending on the situation, a continuous variable can be transformed to a discrete variable.

LO6-3

Compute the mean, variance, and standard deviation of a discrete probability distribution.

The Mean, Variance, and Standard Deviation of a Discrete Probability Distribution

In Chapter 3, we discussed measures of location and variation for a frequency distribution. The mean reports the central location of the data, and the variance describes the spread in the data. In a similar fashion, a probability distribution is summarized by its mean and variance. We identify the mean of a probability distribution by the lowercase Greek letter mu (μ) and the standard deviation by the lowercase Greek letter sigma (σ).

Mean

The mean is a typical value of a random variable used to represent the central location of a probability distribution. It also is the long-run average value of the random variable. The mean of a probability distribution is also referred to as its expected value. It is a weighted average where the possible values of a random variable are weighted by their corresponding probabilities of occurrence.

The mean of a discrete probability distribution is computed by the formula:

MEAN OF A PROBABILITY DISTRIBUTION	$\mu = \Sigma[xP(x)]$	**(6–1)**

where $P(x)$ is the probability of a particular value x. In other words, multiply each value of a random variable, x, by its probability of occurrence, and then add these products.

Variance and Standard Deviation

The mean is a typical value used to summarize a discrete probability distribution. However, it does not describe the amount of spread (variation) in a distribution. The variance does this. The formula for the variance of a probability distribution is:

VARIANCE OF A PROBABILITY DISTRIBUTION	$\sigma^2 = \Sigma[(x - \mu)^2 P(x)]$	**(6–2)**

The computational steps are:

1. Subtract the mean from each value of the random variable, and square this difference.
2. Multiply each squared difference by its probability.
3. Sum the resulting products to arrive at the variance.

The standard deviation, σ, is found by taking the positive square root of σ^2; that is, $\sigma = \sqrt{\sigma^2}$.

An example will help explain the details of the calculation and interpretation of the mean and standard deviation of a probability distribution.

▶ **EXAMPLE**

Izzi Ahmed sells new cars for Pelican Ford. Izzi usually sells the largest number of cars on Saturday. He has developed the following probability distribution for the number of cars he expects to sell on a particular Saturday.

Number of Cars Sold, x	Probability, P(x)
0	.1
1	.2
2	.3
3	.3
4	.1
	1.0

1. What type of distribution is this?
2. On a typical Saturday, how many cars does Izzi expect to sell?
3. What is the variance of the distribution?

Thinkstock/JupiterImages

SOLUTION

1. This is a discrete probability distribution for the random variable called "number of cars sold." Note that Izzi expects to sell only within a certain range of cars; he does not expect to sell 5 cars or 50 cars. Further, he cannot sell half a car. He can sell only 0, 1, 2, 3, or 4 cars. Also, the outcomes are mutually exclusive—he cannot sell a total of both 3 and 4 cars on the same Saturday. The sum of the possible outcomes total 1. Hence, these circumstance qualify as a probability distribution.

2. The mean number of cars sold is computed by weighting the number of cars sold by the probability of selling that number and adding or summing the products, using formula (6–1):

$$\mu = \Sigma[xP(x)]$$
$$= 0(.1) + 1(.2) + 2(.3) + 3(.3) + 4(.1)$$
$$= 2.1$$

These calculations are summarized in the following table.

Number of Cars Sold, x	Probability, P(x)	x · P(x)
0	.1	0.0
1	.2	0.2
2	.3	0.6
3	.3	0.9
4	.1	0.4
	1.0	μ = 2.1

How do we interpret a mean of 2.1? This value indicates that, over a large number of Saturdays, Izzi Ahmed expects to sell a mean of 2.1 cars a day. Of course, it is not possible to sell *exactly* 2.1 cars on any particular Saturday.

However, the expected value can be used to predict the arithmetic mean number of cars sold on Saturdays in the long run. For example, if Izzi works 50 Saturdays during a year, Izzi can expect to sell (50) (2.1) or 105 cars just on Saturdays. Thus, the mean is sometimes called the expected value.

3. The following table illustrates the steps to calculate the variance using formula (6–2). The first two columns repeat the probability distribution. In column three, the mean is subtracted from each value of the random variable. In column four, the differences from column three are squared. In the fifth column, each squared difference in column four is multiplied by the corresponding probability. The variance is the sum of the values in column five.

Number of Cars Sold, x	Probability, $P(x)$	$(x - \mu)$	$(x - \mu)^2$	$(x - \mu)^2 P(x)$
0	.1	0 − 2.1	4.41	0.441
1	.2	1 − 2.1	1.21	0.242
2	.3	2 − 2.1	0.01	0.003
3	.3	3 − 2.1	0.81	0.243
4	.1	4 − 2.1	3.61	0.361
				$\sigma^2 = 1.290$

Recall that the standard deviation, σ, is the positive square root of the variance. In this example, $\sqrt{\sigma^2} = \sqrt{1.290} = 1.136$ cars. How do we apply a standard deviation of 1.136 cars? If salesperson Karsten Kirsch also sold a mean of 2.1 cars on Saturdays, and the standard deviation of Karsten's sales was 1.91 cars, we would conclude that there is more variability in Karsten's Saturday sales than in those of Izzi (because 1.91 > 1.136).

SELF-REVIEW 6-2

In The Pizza Palace offers three sizes of cola. The smallest size sells for $1.99, the medium for $2.49, and the large for $2.89. Thirty percent of the drinks sold are small, 50% are medium, and 20% are large. Create a probability distribution for the random variable price and answer the following questions.

(a) Is this a discrete probability distribution? Indicate why or why not.
(b) Compute the mean amount charged for a cola.
(c) What is the variance in the amount charged for a cola? The standard deviation?
(d) What is the probability that the next drink sold is a small size?
(e) What is the probability that the next drink sold is not a small size?

EXERCISES

1. **FILE** Using the following discrete probability distribution,

x	$P(x)$
0	.2
1	.4
2	.3
3	.1

a. What are the values of the random variable?
b. What is the mean of the distribution?

c. What is the standard deviation of the distribution?
d. What is the probability that the random variable is 2 or more?
e. What is the probability that the random variable is 1 or more? Apply the complement rule.

2. **FILE** Using the following discrete probability distribution,

x	P(x)
2	.5
8	.3
10	.2

a. What are the values of the random variable?
b. What is the mean of the distribution?
c. What is the standard deviation of the distribution?
d. What is the probability that the random variable is not equal to 2?
e. What is the probability that the random variable is not equal to 8?

3. **FILE** Using the following discrete probability distribution,

x	P(x)
5	.1
10	.3
15	.2
20	.4

a. What are the values of the random variable?
b. What is the mean of the distribution?
c. What is the standard deviation of the distribution?
d. What is the probability that the random variable is not equal to 5?
e. What is the probability that the random variable is 15 or less?

4. Which of these variables are discrete and which are continuous random variables?
a. The number of new accounts established by a salesperson in a year
b. The time between customer arrivals to a bank ATM
c. The number of customers in Big Nick's barber shop
d. The amount of fuel in your car's gas tank
e. The number of minorities on a jury
f. The outside temperature today

5. **FILE** The information provided is the number of daily emergency service calls made by the volunteer ambulance service of Walterboro, South Carolina, for the last 50 days. To explain, there were 22 days when there were two emergency calls, and 9 days when there were three emergency calls.

Number of Calls	Frequency
0	8
1	10
2	22
3	9
4	1
Total	50

a. Convert this information on the number of calls to a probability distribution.
b. Is this an example of a discrete or continuous probability distribution?
c. What is the probability that three or more calls are made in a day?
d. What is the mean number of emergency calls per day?
e. What is the standard deviation of the number of calls made daily?

6. **FILE** The director of admissions at Kinzua University in Nova Scotia estimated the distribution of student admissions for the fall semester on the basis of past experience. What is the expected number of admissions for the fall semester? Compute the variance and the standard deviation of the number of admissions.

Admissions	Probability
1,000	.6
1,200	.3
1,500	.1

7. **FILE** Belk Department Store is having a special sale this weekend. Customers charging purchases of more than $50 to their Belk credit card will be given a special Belk Lottery card. The customer will scratch off the card, which will indicate the amount to be taken off the total amount of the purchase. Listed are the amount of the prize and the percent of the time that amount will be deducted from the total amount of the purchase.

Prize Amount	Probability
$ 10	.50
25	.40
50	.08
100	.02

   a. What is the probability that the deducted amount is $50 or more?
   b. What is the mean amount deducted from the total purchase amount?
   c. What is the standard deviation of the amount deducted from the total purchase?

8. **FILE** The Downtown Parking Authority of Tampa, Florida, reported the following information for a sample of 250 customers on the number of hours cars are parked.

Number of Hours	Frequency
1	20
2	49
3	75
4	45
5	40
6	13
7	5
8	3
	250

   a. Convert the information on the number of hours parked to a probability distribution. Is this a discrete or a continuous probability distribution?
   b. Find the mean and the standard deviation of the number of hours parked. How would you answer the question: How long is a typical customer parked?
   c. What is the probability that a car would be parked for more than 6 hours? What is the probability that a car would be parked for 3 hours or less?

Binomial Probability Distribution

LO6-4

Explain the assumptions of the binomial distribution and apply it to calculate probabilities.

The **binomial probability distribution** is a widely occurring discrete probability distribution. To describe experimental outcomes with a binomial distribution, there are four requirements. The first requirement is there are only two possible outcomes on a particular experimental trial. For example, on an exam, a true/false question is either answered correctly or incorrectly. In a resort, a housekeeping supervisor reviews an employee's work and evaluates it as acceptable or unacceptable. A key characteristic of the two outcomes is that they must be mutually exclusive. This means that the answer to a true/false question must be either correct or incorrect but cannot be both correct and incorrect at the same time. Another example is the outcome of a sales call. Either a customer purchases or does not purchase the product, but the sale cannot result in both outcomes. Frequently, we refer to the two possible outcomes of a binomial experiment as a "success" and a "failure." However, this distinction does not imply that one outcome is good and the other is bad, only that there are two mutually exclusive outcomes.

The second binomial requirement is that the random variable is the number of successes for a fixed and known number of trials. For example, we flip a coin five times and count the number of times a head appears in the five flips, we randomly select 10 employees and count the number who are older than 50 years of age, or we randomly select 20 boxes of Kellogg's Raisin Bran and count the number that weigh more than the amount indicated on the package. In each example, we count the number of successes from the fixed number of trials.

A third requirement is that we know the probability of a success and it is the same for each trial. Three examples are:

- For an exam with 10 true/false questions, we know there are 10 trials and the probability of correctly guessing the answer for any of the 10 trials is 0.5. Or, for an exam with 20 multiple-choice questions with four options and only one correct answer, we know that there are 20 trials and the probability of randomly guessing the correct answer for each of the 20 trials is 0.25.
- Bones Albaugh is a Division I college basketball player who makes 70% of his free throws. If he has five opportunities in tonight's game, the likelihood he will be successful on each of the five attempts is 0.70.
- In a recent poll, 18% of adults indicated a Snickers bar was their favorite candy bar. We select a sample of 15 adults and ask each for their favorite candy bar. The likelihood a Snickers bar is the answer for each adult is 0.18.

David Madison/Digital Vision/Getty Images

The final requirement of a binomial probability distribution is that each trial is *independent* of any other trial. Independent means there is no pattern to the trials. The outcome of a particular trial does not affect the outcome of any other trial. Two examples are:

- A young family has two children, both boys. The probability of a third birth being a boy is still .50. That is, the sex of the third child is independent of the sex of the other two.
- Suppose 20% of the patients served in the emergency room at Waccamaw Hospital do not have insurance. If the second patient served on the afternoon shift today did not have insurance, that does not affect the probability the third, the tenth, or any of the other patients will or will not have insurance.

BINOMIAL PROBABILITY EXPERIMENT

1. An outcome on each trial of an experiment is classified into one of two mutually exclusive categories—a success or a failure.
2. The random variable is the number of successes in a fixed number of trials.
3. The probability of success is the same for each trial.
4. The trials are independent, meaning that the outcome of one trial does not affect the outcome of any other trial.

How Is a Binomial Probability Computed?

To construct a particular binomial probability, we use (1) the number of trials and (2) the probability of success on each trial. For example, if the Hannah Landscaping Company plants 10 Norfolk pine trees today knowing that 90% of these trees survive, we can compute the binomial probability that exactly 8 trees survive. In this case the number of trials is the 10 trees, the probability of success is .90, and the number of successes is eight. In fact, we can compute a binomial probability for any number of successes from 0 to 10 surviving trees. That is, using the binomial formula, we can construct the probability distribution of the number of surviving trees in 10 trials. The random variable is the number of surviving trees, 0, 1, 2, 3, ..., 9, 10.

A binomial probability is computed by the formula:

BINOMIAL PROBABILITY FORMULA	$P(x) = {}_nC_x\pi^x(1-\pi)^{n-x}$	**(6–3)**

where:

    C denotes a combination.
    n is the number of trials.
    x is the random variable defined as the number of successes.
    π is the probability of a success on each trial.

We use the Greek letter π (pi) to denote a binomial population parameter. Do not confuse it with the mathematical constant 3.1416.

▶ EXAMPLE

Debit and credit cards are widely used to make purchases. Recently, **www.creditcards .com** reported 28% of purchases at coffee shops were made with a debit card. For 10 randomly selected purchases at the Starbucks on the corner of 12th Street and Main, what is the probability exactly one of the purchases was made with a debit card? What is the probability distribution for the random variable, number of purchases made with a debit card? What is the probability that six or more purchases out of 10 are made with a debit card? What is the probability that five or fewer purchases out of 10 are made with a debit card?

SOLUTION

This example fits all the requirements for a binomial distribution. The probability of success, a purchase made with a debit card, is .28, so let $\pi = .28$. We determined the number of purchases to be 10, so the number of trials is 10 and $n = 10$. The trials are independent, and the probability of success is the same for each trial. The random variable, x, is the number of purchases with a debit card in 10 trials. The random variable, x, can be equal to 0, no purchases made with a debit card, 1, one purchase made with a debit card, or 2, 3, 4, or 10 purchases made with a debit card. To calculate the probability for each value of the random variable, apply formula 6–3. The probability that no purchases in 10 trials are made with a debit card is:

$$P(0) = {}_nC_x(\pi)^x(1-\pi)^{n-x} = {}_{10}C_0(.28)^0(1-.28)^{10-0} = (1)(1)(.0374) = .0374$$

The probability that exactly one of the 10 purchases is made with a debit card is .1456, found by:

$$P(1) = {}_nC_x(\pi)^x(1-\pi)^{n-x} = {}_{10}C_1(.28)^1(1-.28)^{10-1} = (10)(.28)(.0520) = .1456$$

Using statistical software, the entire binomial probability distribution with $\pi = .28$ and $n = 10$ is shown in the following bar chart and table.

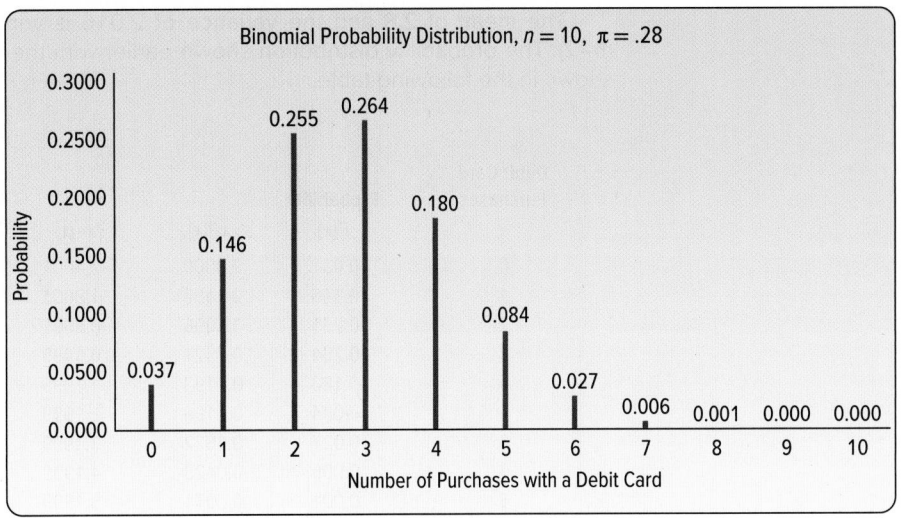

Number of Debit Card Purchases (x)	P(x)
0	0.037
1	0.146
2	0.255
3	0.264
4	0.180
5	0.084
6	0.027
7	0.006
8	0.001
9	0.000
10	0.000

Using the binomial probability distribution, the probability of six or more purchases out of 10 possible is only .034. Using the complement, there is a .966 probability that there will be five or fewer debit card purchases of the 10 trials.

The mean (μ) and the variance (σ^2) of a binomial distribution are computed in a "shortcut" fashion by:

MEAN OF A BINOMIAL DISTRIBUTION	$\mu = n\pi$	(6–4)

VARIANCE OF A BINOMIAL DISTRIBUTION	$\sigma^2 = n\pi(1 - \pi)$	(6–5)

For example, regarding the number of debit purchases in the sample of 10 customers, recall that $\pi = .28$ and n = 10. Hence:

$$\mu = n\pi = (10)(.28) = 2.8$$

$$\sigma^2 = n\pi(1 - \pi) = 10\,(.28)\,(1 -.28) = 2.016$$

$$\sigma = 1.420$$

The mean of 2.8 and the variance of 2.016 is verified from formulas (6–1) and (6–2). The probability distribution shown earlier with the details of the calculations are shown in the following table.

Debit Card Purchases x	Probability P(x)	xP(x)	(x–μ)	(x–μ)²	P(x)*(x–μ)²
0	0.037	0.0000	−2.8001	7.841	0.2935
1	0.146	0.1456	−1.8001	3.240	0.4718
2	0.255	0.5096	−0.8001	0.640	0.1631
3	0.264	0.7927	0.1999	0.040	0.0106
4	0.180	0.7193	1.1999	1.440	0.2589
5	0.084	0.4196	2.1999	4.840	0.4061
6	0.027	0.1632	3.1999	10.239	0.2785
7	0.006	0.0423	4.1999	17.639	0.1066
8	0.001	0.0071	5.1999	27.039	0.0238
9	0.000	0.0007	6.1999	38.439	0.0029
10	0.000	0.0000	7.1999	51.839	0.0002
Totals		2.8001			2.0160

Binomial Probability Tables

Formula (6–3) can be used to build a binomial probability distribution for any value of n and π. However, for a larger n, the calculations take more time. For convenience, the tables in Appendix B.1 show the result of using the formula for various values of n and π. Table 6–2 shows part of Appendix B.1 for $n = 6$ and various values of π.

TABLE 6–2 Binomial Probabilities for $n = 6$ and Selected Values of π

x\π	.05	.1	.2	.3	.4	.5	.6	.7	.8	.9	.95
0	.735	.531	.262	.118	.047	.016	.004	.001	.000	.000	.000
1	.232	.354	.393	.303	.187	.094	.037	.010	.002	.000	.000
2	.031	.098	.246	.324	.311	.234	.138	.060	.015	.001	.000
3	.002	.015	.082	.185	.276	.313	.276	.185	.082	.015	.002
4	.000	.001	.015	.060	.138	.234	.311	.324	.246	.098	.031
5	.000	.000	.002	.010	.037	.094	.187	.303	.393	.354	.232
6	.000	.000	.000	.001	.004	.016	.047	.118	.262	.531	.735

n = 6
Probability

▶ **EXAMPLE**

In the rural Southwest, 5% of all cell phone calls are dropped. What is the probability that out of six randomly selected calls, none was dropped? Exactly one? Exactly two? Exactly three? Exactly four? Exactly five? Exactly six out of six?

SOLUTION

The binomial conditions are met: (a) There are only two possible outcomes (a particular call is either dropped or not dropped), (b) there are a fixed number of trials (6), (c) there is a constant probability of success (.05), and (d) the trials are independent.

Refer to Table 6–2 for the probability of exactly zero dropped calls. Go down the left margin to an x of 0. Now move horizontally to the column headed by a π of .05 to find the probability. It is .735. The values in Table 6–2 are rounded to three decimal places.

The probability of exactly one dropped call in a sample of six calls is .232. The complete binomial probability distribution for $n = 6$ and $\pi = .05$ is:

Number of Dropped Calls, x	Probability of Occurrence, $P(x)$	Number of Dropped Calls, x	Probability of Occurrence, $P(x)$
0	.735	4	.000
1	.232	5	.000
2	.031	6	.000
3	.002		

Of course, there is a slight chance of getting exactly five dropped calls out of six random selections. It is .00000178, found by inserting the appropriate values in the binomial formula:

$$P(5) = {}_6C_5(.05)^5(.95)^1 = (6)(.05)_5(.95) = .00000178$$

For six out of the six, the exact probability is .000000016. Thus, the probability is very small that five or six calls will be dropped in six trials.

We can compute the mean or expected value and the variance of the distribution of the number defective:

$$\mu = n\pi = (6)(.05) = 0.30$$

$$\sigma^2 = n\pi(1 - \pi) = 6(.05)(.95) = 0.285$$

SELF-REVIEW 6-3

Ninety-five percent of the employees at the J. M. Smucker Company plant on Laskey Road have their bimonthly wages sent directly to their bank by electronic funds transfer. This is also called direct deposit. Suppose we select a random sample of seven employees.

(a) Does this situation fit the assumptions of the binomial distribution?
(b) What is the probability that all seven employees use direct deposit?
(c) Use formula (6–3) to determine the exact probability that four of the seven sampled employees use direct deposit.
(d) Use Excel to verify your answers to parts (b) and (c).

Tutorial #33
in Connect

Appendix B.1 is limited. It gives probabilities for n values from 1 to 15 and π values of .05, .10, . . . , .90, and .95. A software program can generate the probabilities for a specified number of successes, given n and π. The Excel output on the next page shows the probability when $n = 40$ and $\pi = .09$. Note that the number of successes stops at 15 because the probabilities for 16 to 40 are very close to 0. The Excel tutorials are available in Connect.

	A	B
1	Success	Probability
2	0	0.0230
3	1	0.0910
4	2	0.1754
5	3	0.2198
6	4	0.2011
7	5	0.1432
8	6	0.0826
9	7	0.0397
10	8	0.0162
11	9	0.0057
12	10	0.0017
13	11	0.0005
14	12	0.0001
15	13	0.0000
16	14	0.0000
17	15	0.0000

Source: Microsoft Excel

Several additional points should be made regarding the binomial probability distribution.

1. If n remains the same but π increases from .05 to .95, the shape of the distribution changes. Look at Table 6–3 and Chart 6–2. The distribution for a π of .05 is positively skewed. As π approaches .50, the distribution becomes symmetrical. As π goes beyond .50 and moves toward .95, the probability distribution becomes negatively skewed. Table 6–3 highlights probabilities for $n = 10$ and a π of .05, .10, .20, .50, and .70. The graphs of these probability distributions are shown in Chart 6–2.

TABLE 6–3 Probability of 0, 1, 2, … Successes for a π of .05, .10, .20, .50, and .70, and an n of 10

$x\backslash\pi$	.05	.1	.2	.3	.4	.5	.6	.7	.8	.9	.95
0	.599	.349	.107	.028	.006	.001	.000	.000	.000	.000	.000
1	.315	.387	.268	.121	.040	.010	.002	.000	.000	.000	.000
2	.075	.194	.302	.233	.121	.044	.011	.001	.000	.000	.000
3	.010	.057	.201	.267	.215	.117	.042	.009	.001	.000	.000
4	.001	.011	.088	.200	.251	.205	.111	.037	.006	.000	.000
5	.000	.001	.026	.103	.201	.246	.201	.103	.026	.001	.000
6	.000	.000	.006	.037	.111	.205	.251	.200	.088	.011	.001
7	.000	.000	.001	.009	.042	.117	.215	.267	.201	.057	.010
8	.000	.000	.000	.001	.011	.044	.121	.233	.302	.194	.075
9	.000	.000	.000	.000	.002	.010	.040	.121	.268	.387	.315
10	.000	.000	.000	.000	.000	.001	.006	.028	.107	.349	.599

CHART 6–2 Graphing the Binomial Probability Distribution for a π of .05, .10, .20, .50, and .70, and an n of 10

2. If π, the probability of success, remains the same but n becomes larger, the shape of the binomial distribution becomes more symmetrical. Chart 6–3 shows a situation where π remains constant at .10 but n increases from 7 to 40.

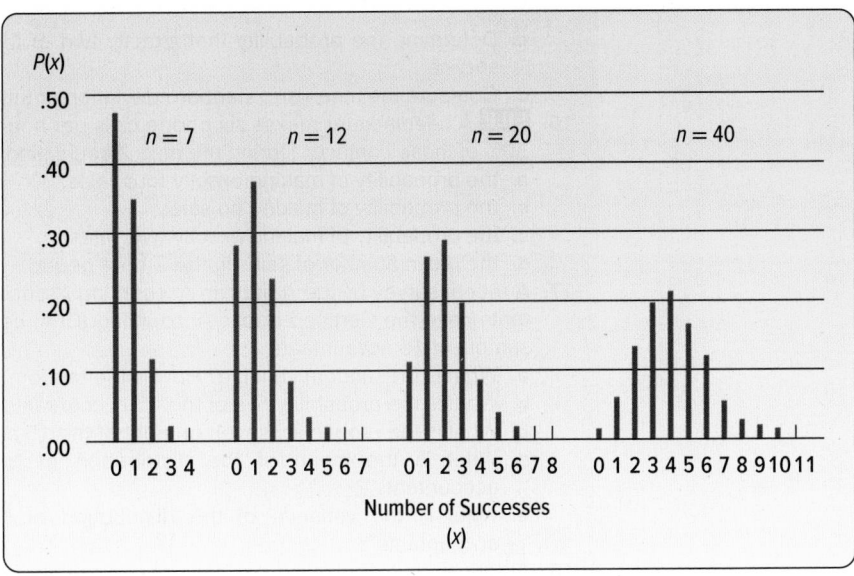

CHART 6–3 Chart Representing the Binomial Probability Distribution for a π of .10 and an *n* of 7, 12, 20, and 40

EXERCISES

9. In a binomial situation, $n = 4$ and $\pi = .20$. Find the probabilities for all possible values of the random variable, *x*.
10. In a binomial situation, $n = 5$ and $\pi = .40$. Find the probabilities for all possible values of the random variable, *x*.
11. Assume a binomial distribution where $n = 3$ and $\pi = .60$.
    a. Refer to Appendix B.1, and list the probabilities for values of *x* from 0 to 3.
    b. Determine the mean and standard deviation of the distribution from the general definitions given in formulas (6–1) and (6–2).
12. Assume a binomial distribution where $n = 5$ and $\pi = .30$.
    a. Refer to Appendix B.1 and list the probabilities for values of *x* from 0 to 5.
    b. Determine the mean and standard deviation of the distribution from the general definitions given in formulas (6–1) and (6–2).
13. An American Society of Investors survey found 30% of individual investors have used a discount broker. In a random sample of nine individuals, what is the probability of randomly selecting:
    a. exactly two individuals who used a discount broker?
    b. exactly four who used a discount broker?
    c. nine individuals when none used a discount broker?
14. **FILE** The U.S. Postal Service reports 95% of first-class mail within the same city is delivered within 2 days of the time of mailing. Six letters are randomly sent to different locations.
    a. What is the probability that all six arrive within 2 days?
    b. What is the probability that exactly five arrive within 2 days?
    c. Find the mean number of letters that will arrive within 2 days.
    d. Compute the variance and standard deviation of the number that will arrive within 2 days.
15. **FILE** Industry standards suggest that 10% of new vehicles require warranty service within the first year. Bauer Nissan in Sumter, South Carolina, sold 12 Nissans yesterday.
    a. What is the probability that none of these vehicles requires warranty service?
    b. What is the probability exactly one of these vehicles requires warranty service?

  c. Determine the probability that exactly two of these vehicles require warranty service.
  d. Compute the mean and standard deviation of this probability distribution.
16. **FILE** A telemarketer makes six phone calls per hour and is able to make a sale on 30% of these contacts. During the next 2 hours, find:
  a. the probability of making exactly four sales.
  b. the probability of making no sales.
  c. the probability of making exactly two sales.
  d. the mean number of sales in the 2-hour period.
17. A recent survey by the American Accounting Association revealed 52% of accountants have the Certified Public Accounting (CPA) certificate. Suppose we select a sample of 15 accountants.
  a. What is the random variable? How is the random variable distributed? Why?
  b. What is the probability five of the 15 accountants are CPAs?
  c. What is the probability seven or eight of the 15 accountants are CPAs?
  d. What is the mean of the distribution of "number of CPAs among 15 accountants"?
  e. What is the variance of the distribution of "number of CPAs among 15 accountants"?
18. American households increasingly rely on cell phones as their exclusive telephone service. It is reported that 49.2% of American households still have landline phone service. We decide to randomly call eight households and ask if the home has a landline phone.

  a. What is the random variable? How is the random variable distributed? Why?
  b. What is the probability that none of the households in the sampled group have landline phone service?
  c. What is the probability that exactly five of the households in the sampled group have a landline phone service?
  d. Given the probability distribution, what is the mean number of households with landline service?
  e. What is the variance of the probability distribution of the number of households with landline service?

Cumulative Binomial Probability Distributions

We may wish to know the probability of correctly guessing the answers to six *or more* true/false questions out of 10. Or we may be interested in the probability of *selecting less than two* defectives at random from production during the next hour. In these cases, we need cumulative frequency distributions similar to the ones developed in the Chapter 2, Cumulative Distribution section on page 40. The following example will illustrate.

▶ **EXAMPLE**

A study by the Illinois Department of Transportation concluded that 76.2% of front seat occupants used seat belts. That is, both occupants of the front seat were using their seat belts. Suppose we decide to compare that information with current usage. We select a sample of 12 vehicles.

1. What is the probability the front seat occupants in exactly 7 of the 12 vehicles selected are wearing seat belts?
2. What is the probability the front seat occupants in at least 7 of the 12 vehicles are wearing seat belts?

SOLUTION

This situation meets the binomial requirements.

- In a particular vehicle, both the front seat occupants are either wearing seat belts or they are not. There are only two possible outcomes.
- There are a fixed number of trials, 12 in this case, because 12 vehicles are checked.
- The probability of a "success" (occupants wearing seat belts) is the same from one vehicle to the next: 76.2%.
- The trials are independent. If the fourth vehicle selected in the sample has all the occupants wearing their seat belts, this does not have any effect on the results for the fifth or tenth vehicle.

To find the likelihood the occupants of *exactly* seven of the sampled vehicles are wearing seat belts, we use formula (6–3). In this case, $n = 12$ and $\pi = .762$.

$$P(x = 7) = {}_{12}C_7(.762)^7(1 - .762)^{12-7} = 792(.149171)(.000764) = .0902$$

So we conclude the likelihood that the occupants of exactly 7 of the 12 sampled vehicles will be wearing their seat belts is about 9%.

To find the probability that the occupants in 7 or more of the vehicles will be wearing seat belts, we use formula (6–3) from this chapter as well as the special rule of addition from the previous chapter. See formula (5-5) on page 145.

Because the events are mutually exclusive (meaning that a particular sample of 12 vehicles cannot have both a *total* of 7 and a *total* of 8 vehicles where the occupants are wearing seat belts), we find the probability of 7 vehicles where the occupants are wearing seat belts, the probability of eight, and so on up to the probability that occupants of all 12 sample vehicles are wearing seat belts. The probability of each of these outcomes is then totaled.

$$P(x \geq 7) = P(x = 7) + P(x = 8) + P(x = 9) + P(x = 10) + P(x = 11) + P(x = 12)$$
$$= .0902 + .1805 + .2569 + .2467 + .1436 + .0383$$
$$= .9562$$

So the probability of selecting 12 cars and finding that the occupants of 7 or more vehicles were wearing seat belts is .9562. This information is shown on the following Excel spreadsheet. There is a slight difference in the software answer due to rounding. See the Excel tutorial in Connect that shows how to compute a binomial distribution.

Tutorial #33 in Connect

	A	B	C	D
	Success	Probability		
1	Success	Probability		
2	0	0.0000		
3	1	0.0000		
4	2	0.0000		
5	3	0.0002		
6	4	0.0017		
7	5	0.0088		
8	6	0.0329		
9	7	0.0902		
10	8	0.1805		
11	9	0.2569	Sum of Probabilities	
12	10	0.2467	for 7 or more	
13	11	0.1436	successes	
14	12	0.0383		
15		0.9563		

Cumulative Binomial.xlsx

Source: Microsoft Excel

SELF-REVIEW 6-4

A recent study revealed that 40% of women in the San Diego metropolitan area who work full time also volunteer in the community. Suppose we randomly select eight women in the San Diego area.

(a) What are the values for n and π?
(b) What is the probability exactly three of the women volunteer in the community?
(c) What is the probability at least one of the women volunteers in the community?

EXERCISES

19. In a binomial distribution, $n = 8$ and $\pi = .30$. Find the probabilities of the following events.
   a. $x = 2$.
   b. $x \leq 2$ (the probability that x is equal to or less than 2).
   c. $x \geq 3$ (the probability that x is equal to or greater than 3).
20. In a binomial distribution, $n = 12$ and $\pi = .60$. Find the following probabilities.
   a. $x = 5$.
   b. $x \leq 5$.
   c. $x \geq 6$.
21. **FILE** In a recent study, 90% of the homes in the United States were found to have large-screen TVs. In a sample of nine homes, what is the probability that:
   a. all nine have large-screen TVs?
   b. less than five have large-screen TVs?
   c. more than five have large-screen TVs?
   d. at least seven homes have large-screen TVs?
22. **FILE** A manufacturer of window frames knows from long experience that 5% of the production will have some type of minor defect that will require an adjustment. What is the probability that in a sample of 20 window frames:
   a. none will need adjustment?
   b. at least one will need adjustment?
   c. more than two will need adjustment?
23. **FILE** The speed with which utility companies can resolve problems is very important. In the United Kingdom, Octopus Energy reports it can resolve customer problems the same day they are reported in 70% of the cases. Suppose the 15 cases reported today are representative of all complaints.
   a. How many of the problems would you expect to be resolved today? What is the standard deviation?
   b. What is the probability 10 of the problems can be resolved today?
   c. What is the probability 10 or 11 of the problems can be resolved today?
   d. What is the probability more than 10 of the problems can be resolved today?
24. Statistics from the Port Authority of New York and New Jersey show that 85% of the vehicles using the Lincoln Tunnel use E-ZPass to pay the toll rather than stopping at a toll booth. Twelve cars are randomly selected.
   a. How many of the 12 vehicles would you expect to use E-ZPass?
   b. What is the mode of the distribution? What is the probability associated with the mode?
   c. What is the probability seven or more of the sampled vehicles use E-ZPass?

LO6-5
Explain the assumptions of the hypergeometric distribution and apply it to calculate probabilities.

Hypergeometric Probability Distribution

For the binomial distribution to be applied, the probability of a success must stay the same for each trial. For example, the probability of guessing the correct answer to a true/false question is .50. This probability remains the same for each question on an examination. Likewise, suppose that 40% of the registered voters in a precinct are Republicans. If 27 registered voters are selected at random, the probability of choosing a Republican on the first selection is .40. The chance of choosing a Republican on the next selection is also .40, assuming that the sampling is done *with replacement,* meaning that the person selected is put back in the population before the next person is selected.

Most sampling, however, is done *without replacement.* Thus, if the population is small, the probability of a success will change for each observation. For example, if the population consists of 20 items, the probability of selecting a particular item from that population is 1/20. If the sampling is done without replacement, after the first selection there are only 19 items remaining; the probability of selecting a particular item on the second selection is only 1/19. For the third selection, the probability is 1/18, and so on. This assumes that the population is finite.

A population is said to be *finite* if the number in the population is known. Examples of a finite population include:

- The 45 undergraduate students in a sorority.
- The 25 Camrys available for purchase at Sparks Toyota.
- The 780 players currently on active rosters of Major League Baseball teams.
- The 150 residents at the Isle Senior Center.

The appropriate probability distribution is the **hypergeometric distribution.** It is used when (1) the sample is selected from a finite population without replacement and (2) if the size of the sample *n* is more than 5% of the size of the population *N.*

The formula for the hypergeometric distribution is:

| **HYPERGEOMETRIC DISTRIBUTION** | $P(x) = \dfrac{(_S C_x)(_{N-S} C_{n-x})}{_N C_n}$ | **[6–6]** |

where:

N is the size of the population.
S is the number of successes in the population.
x is the number of successes in the sample. It may be 0, 1, 2, 3, ...
n is the size of the sample or the number of trials.
C is the symbol for a combination.

In summary, a hypergeometric probability distribution has these characteristics:

HYPERGEOMETRIC PROBABILITY EXPERIMENT

1. An outcome on each trial of an experiment is classified into one of two mutually exclusive categories—a success or a failure.
2. The random variable is the number of successes in a fixed number of trials.
3. The trials are not independent.
4. We assume that we sample from a finite population without replacement and $n/N > 0.05$. So, the probability of a success *changes* for each trial.

The following example illustrates the details of determining a probability using the hypergeometric distribution.

▶ **EXAMPLE**

PlayTime Toys Inc. employs 50 people in the Assembly Department. Forty of the employees belong to a union and 10 do not. Five employees are selected at random to form a committee to meet with management regarding shift starting times. What is the probability that four of the five selected for the committee belong to a union?

Howard Berman/Getty Images

SOLUTION

The population in this case is the 50 Assembly Department employees. An employee can be selected for the committee only once. Hence, the sampling is done without replacement. Thus, the probability of selecting a union employee, for example, changes from one trial to the next. The hypergeometric distribution is appropriate for determining the probability. In this problem,

> N is 50, the number of employees.
> n is 5, the number of employees selected.
> S is 40, the number of union employees.
> x is 4, the number of union employees selected.

We wish to find the probability four of the five committee members belong to a union. Inserting these values into formula (6–6):

$$P(4) = \frac{(_{40}C_4)(_{50-40}C_{5-4})}{_{50}C_5} = \frac{(91,390)(10)}{2,118,760} = .431$$

Thus, the probability of selecting five assembly workers at random from the 50 workers and finding four of the five are union members is .431.

Table 6–4 shows the hypergeometric probabilities of finding 0, 1, 2, 3, 4, and 5 union members on the committee.

TABLE 6–4 Hypergeometric Probabilities ($N = 50$, $n = 5$, and $S = 40$) for the Number of Union Members on the Committee

Union Members	Probability
0	.000
1	.004
2	.044
3	.210
4	.431
5	.311
	1.000

Table 6–5 shows a comparison of the results using the binomial distribution and the hypergeometric distribution. Because 40 of the 50 Assembly Department employees belong to the union, we let $\pi = .80$ for the binomial distribution. The binomial probabilities for Table 6–5 come from the binomial distribution with $n = 5$ and $\pi = .80$.

TABLE 6–5 Hypergeometric and Binomial Probabilities for PlayTime Toys Inc. Assembly Department

Number of Union Members on Committee	Hypergeometric Probability, $P(x)$	Binomial Probability ($n = 5$ and $\pi = .80$)
0	.000	.000
1	.004	.006
2	.044	.051
3	.210	.205
4	.431	.410
5	.311	.328
	1.000	1.000

As Table 6–5 shows, when the binomial requirement of a constant probability of success cannot be met, the hypergeometric distribution should be used. There are clear differences between the probabilities.

However, under certain conditions the results of the binomial distribution can be used to approximate the hypergeometric. This leads to a rule of thumb: if selected items are not returned to the population, the binomial distribution can be used to closely approximate the hypergeometric distribution when $n < .05N$. In other words, the binomial will closely approximate the hypergeometric distribution if the sample is less than 5% of the population. For example, if the population, N, is 150, the number of successes in the population, S, is 120, and the sample size, n, is five, then the rule of thumb is true. That is, $5 < 0.05(150)$, or $5 < 7.5$. The sample size is less than 5% of the population. For this situation, Table 6–6 compares the hypergeometric and binomial probability distributions. The probabilities are very close.

TABLE 6–6 A Comparison of Hypergeometric and Binomial Probabilities When the Sample Size Is Less than 0.05(n)

Tutorial #34
in Connect

x	Hypergeometric Probability, $P(x)$	Binomial Probability ($n = 5$ and $\pi = .80 = (120/150)$)
0	.000	.000
1	.006	.006
2	.049	.051
3	.206	.205
4	.417	.410
5	.322	.328
	1.000	1.000

A hypergeometric distribution can be created using Excel. See the Excel tutorial in Connect that shows how to create a hypergeometric distribution.

SELF-REVIEW 6–5

Horwege Discount Brokers plans to hire five new financial analysts this year. There is a pool of 12 approved applicants, and George Horwege, the owner, decides to randomly select those who will be hired. There are eight men and four women among the approved applicants. What is the probability that three of the five hired are men?

EXERCISES

25. A youth basketball team has 12 players on the roster. Seven of the team members are boys and five are girls. The coach writes each player's name on a sheet of paper and places the names in a hat. The team captain shuffles the names, and the coach selects five slips of paper from the hat to determine the starting lineup.
   a. What is the probability the starting lineup consists of three boys and two girls?
   b. What is the probability the starting lineup is all boys?
   c. What is the probability there is at least one girl in the starting lineup?

26. A population consists of 15 items, 10 of which are acceptable. In a sample of four items, what is the probability that exactly three are acceptable? Assume the samples are drawn without replacement.

27. The Riverton Branch of the National Bank of Wyoming has 10 real estate loans over $1,000,000. Of these 10 loans, three are "underwater." A loan is underwater if the amount of the loan is greater than the value of the property. The chief loan officer decided to randomly select two of these loans to determine if they met all banking standards. What is the probability that neither of the selected loans is underwater?

28. The Computer Systems Department has eight faculty, six of whom are tenured. Dr. Vonder, the chairperson, wants to establish a committee of three department faculty members to review the curriculum. If she selects the committee at random:
   a. what is the probability all members of the committee are tenured?
   b. what is the probability that at least one member is not tenured? Hint: For this question, use the complement rule.

29. Jody's Florist has 15 delivery trucks, used mainly to deliver flowers and flower arrangements in the Greenville, South Carolina, area. Of these 15 trucks, six have brake problems. Five trucks are randomly selected. What is the probability that two of those tested have defective brakes?

30. The game called Lotto sponsored by the Louisiana Lottery Commission pays its largest prize when a contestant matches all six of the 40 possible numbers. Assume there are 40 ping-pong balls each with a single number between 1 and 40. Any number appears only once, and the winning balls are selected without replacement.
   a. The commission reports that the probability of matching all the numbers are 1 in 3,838,380. What is this in terms of probability?
   b. Use the hypergeometric formula to find this probability.
   The lottery commission also pays if a contestant matches four or five of the six winning numbers. Hint: Divide the 40 numbers into two groups, winning numbers and nonwinning numbers.
   c. Find the probability, again using the hypergeometric formula, for matching four of the six winning numbers.
   d. Find the probability of matching five of the six winning numbers.

LO6-6

Explain the assumptions of the Poisson distribution and apply it to calculate probabilities.

Poisson Probability Distribution

The **Poisson probability distribution** describes the number of times some event occurs during a specified interval. Examples of an interval may be time, distance, area, or volume.

The distribution is based on two assumptions. The first assumption is that the probability is proportional to the length of the interval. The second assumption is that the intervals are independent. To put it another way, the longer the interval, the larger the probability, and the number of occurrences in one interval does not affect the other intervals. This distribution is a limiting form of the binomial distribution when the probability of a success is very small and n is large. It is often referred to as the "law of improbable events," meaning that the probability, π, of a particular event's happening is quite small. The Poisson distribution is a discrete probability distribution because it is formed by counting.

The Poisson probability distribution has these characteristics:

POISSON PROBABILITY EXPERIMENT

1. The random variable is the number of times some event occurs during a defined interval.
2. The probability of the event is proportional to the size of the interval.
3. The intervals do not overlap and are independent.

This probability distribution has many applications. It is used as a model to describe the distribution of errors in data entry, the number of scratches and other imperfections in newly painted car panels, the number of defective parts in outgoing shipments, the number of customers waiting to be served at a restaurant or waiting to get into an attraction at Disney World, and the number of accidents on I–75 during a 3-month period.

The Poisson distribution is described mathematically by the formula:

POISSON DISTRIBUTION	$P(x) = \dfrac{\mu^x e^{-\mu}}{x!}$	(6–7)

where:

μ (mu) is the mean number of occurrences (successes) in a particular interval.
e is the constant 2.71828 (base of the Napierian logarithmic system).
x is the number of occurrences (successes).
$P(x)$ is the probability for a specified value of x.

The mean and variance of a Poisson distribution are both found by $n\pi$, where n is the total number of trials and π the probability of success. The standard deviation is, again, found as the square root of the variance.

MEAN OF A POISSON DISTRIBUTION	$\mu = n\pi$	(6–8)

VARIANCE OF A POISSON DISTRIBUTION	$\sigma^2 = n\pi$	(6–9)

The variance of the Poisson is equal to its mean. If, for example, the probability that a check cashed by a bank will bounce is .0003, and 10,000 checks are cashed, the mean and the variance for the number of bad checks are both 3.0, found by $\mu = n\pi = 10{,}000(.0003) = 3.0$. The standard deviation is 1.73.

Recall that for a binomial distribution there are a fixed number of trials. For example, for a four-question multiple-choice test there can only be zero, one, two, three, or four successes (correct answers). The random variable, x, for a Poisson distribution, however, can assume an *infinite number of values*—that is, 0, 1, 2, 3, 4, 5, ... However, *the probabilities become very small after the first few occurrences* (successes).

▶ **EXAMPLE**

Budget Airlines is a seasonal airline that operates flights from Myrtle Beach, South Carolina, to various cities in the northeast. The destinations include Boston, Pittsburgh, Buffalo, and both LaGuardia and JFK airports in New York City. Recently Budget has been concerned about the number of lost bags. Kendall Poston from the Analytics Department was asked to study the issue. Kendall randomly selected a sample of 500 flights and found that a total of 20 bags were lost on the sampled flights.

Show that this situation follows the Poisson distribution. What is the mean number of bags lost per flight? What is the likelihood that no bags are lost on a flight? What is the probability at least one bag is lost?

SOLUTION

To begin, let's confirm that the Budget Airlines situation follows a Poisson distribution. Refer to the highlighted box labeled Poisson Probability Experiment in this section. We count the number of bags lost on a particular flight. On most flights there were no bags lost, on a few flights one was lost, and perhaps in very rare circumstances more than one bag was lost. The continuum or interval is a particular flight. Each flight is assumed to be independent of any other flight.

Based on the sample information we can estimate the mean number of bags lost per flight. There were 20 bags lost in 500 flights so the mean number of bags lost per flight is .04, found by 20/500. Hence $\mu = .04$.

We use formula (6–7) to find the probability of any number of lost bags. In this case x, the number of lost bags is 0.

$$P(0) = \frac{\mu^x e^{-\mu}}{x!} = \frac{.04^0 e^{-0.04}}{0!} = .9608$$

The probability of exactly one lost bag is:

$$P(1) = \frac{\mu^x e^{-\mu}}{x!} = \frac{.04^0 e^{-0.04}}{1!} = .0384$$

The probability of one or more lost bags is:

$$1 - P(0) = 1 - \frac{\mu^x e^{-\mu}}{x!} = 1 - \frac{.04^0 e^{-0.04}}{0!} = 1 - .9608 = .0392$$

These probabilities also can be found as demonstrated in the Excel tutorial in Connect.

Tutorial #35
in Connect

	A	B
1	Success	Probability
2	0	0.9608
3	1	0.0384
4	2	0.0008
5	3	0.0000
6	4	0.0000
7	5	0.0000
8	6	0.0000
9	7	0.0000

Source: Microsoft Excel

Part of Appendix B.2 is repeated as Table 6–7. For certain values of μ, the mean of the Poisson distribution, we can read the probability directly from the table. Turning to another example, the NY-LA Trucking Company finds the mean number of breakdowns on the New York to Los Angeles route is 0.30. From Table 6–7 we can locate the probability of no breakdowns on a particular run. First find the column headed "0.30" then read down that column to the row labeled "0". The value at the intersection is .7408, so this value is the probability of no breakdowns on a particular run. The probability of one breakdown is .2222.

TABLE 6–7 Poisson Table for Various Values of μ (from Appendix B.2)

x	μ 0.1	0.2	0.3	0.4	0.5	0.6	0.7	0.8	0.9
0	0.9048	0.8187	0.7408	0.6703	0.6065	0.5488	0.4966	0.4493	0.4066
1	0.0905	0.1637	0.2222	0.2681	0.3033	0.3293	0.3476	0.3595	0.3659
2	0.0045	0.0164	0.0333	0.0536	0.0758	0.0988	0.1217	0.1438	0.1647
3	0.0002	0.0011	0.0033	0.0072	0.0126	0.0198	0.0284	0.0383	0.0494
4	0.0000	0.0001	0.0003	0.0007	0.0016	0.0030	0.0050	0.0077	0.0111
5	0.0000	0.0000	0.0000	0.0001	0.0002	0.0004	0.0007	0.0012	0.0020
6	0.0000	0.0000	0.0000	0.0000	0.0000	0.0000	0.0001	0.0002	0.0003
7	0.0000	0.0000	0.0000	0.0000	0.0000	0.0000	0.0000	0.0000	0.0000

Earlier in this section, we mentioned that the Poisson probability distribution is a limiting form of the binomial. That is, we could estimate a binomial probability using the Poisson. In the following example, we use the Poisson distribution to estimate a binomial probability when *n,* the number of trials, is large and π, the probability of a success, small.

▶ **EXAMPLE**

Coastal Insurance Company underwrites insurance for beachfront properties along the Virginia, North and South Carolina, and Georgia coasts. It uses the estimate that the probability of a named Category III hurricane with sustained winds of more than 110 miles per hour or higher striking a particular region of the coast (for example, St. Simons Island, Georgia) in any one year is .05. If a homeowner takes a 30-year mortgage on a recently purchased property in St. Simons, what is the likelihood that the owner will experience at least one hurricane during the mortgage period?

SOLUTION

To use the Poisson probability distribution, we begin by determining the mean or expected number of storms meeting the criterion hitting St. Simons during the 30-year period. That is:

$$\mu = n\pi = 30(.05) = 1.5$$

where:

    n is the number of years, 30 in this case.
    π is the probability a hurricane meeting the strength criteria comes ashore.
    μ is the mean or expected number of storms in a 30-year period.

To find the probability of at least one storm hitting St. Simons Island, Georgia, we first find the probability of no storms hitting the coast and subtract that value from 1.

$$P(x \geq 1) = 1 - P(x = 0) = 1 - \frac{\mu^0 e^{-1.5}}{0!} = 1 - .2231 = .7769$$

We conclude that the likelihood a hurricane meeting the strength criteria will strike the beachfront property at St. Simons during the 30-year period when the mortgage is in effect is .7769. To put it another way, the probability St. Simons will be hit by a Category III or higher hurricane during the 30-year period is a little more than 75%.

We should emphasize that the continuum, as previously described, still exists. That is, during a 30-year continuum, 1.5 storms are expected to hit St. Simons Island, Georgia.

In the preceding case, we are actually using the Poisson distribution as an estimate of the binomial. Note that we've met the binomial conditions outlined on page 185.

- There are only two possible outcomes: a hurricane hits the St. Simons area or it does not.
- There are a fixed number of trials, in this case 30 years.
- There is a constant probability of success; that is, the probability of a hurricane hitting the area is .05 each year.
- The years are independent. That means if a named storm strikes in the fifth year, that has no effect on any other year.

To find the probability of at least one storm striking the area in a 30-year period using the binomial distribution:

$$P(x \geq 1) = 1 - P(x = 0) = 1 - [_{30}C_0(.05)^0(.95)^{30}] = 1 - [(1)(1)(.2146)] = .7854$$

The probability of at least one hurricane hitting the St. Simons area during the 30-year period using the binomial distribution is .7854.

Which answer is correct? Why should we look at the problem both ways? The binomial is the more "technically correct" solution. The Poisson can be thought of as an approximation for the binomial, when n, the number of trials is large, and π, the probability of a success, is small. We look at the problem using both distributions to emphasize the convergence of the two discrete distributions. In some instances, using the Poisson may be the quicker solution, and as you see there is little practical difference in the answers. In fact, as n gets larger and π smaller, the difference between the two distributions gets smaller.

The Poisson probability distribution is always positively skewed and the random variable has no specific upper limit. In the lost bags example/solution, the Poisson distribution, with $\mu = 0.04$, is highly skewed. As μ becomes larger, the Poisson distribution becomes more symmetrical. For example, Chart 6–4 shows the distributions of the number of transmission services, muffler replacements, and oil changes per day at Avellino's Auto Shop. They follow Poisson distributions with means of 0.7, 2.0, and 6.0, respectively.

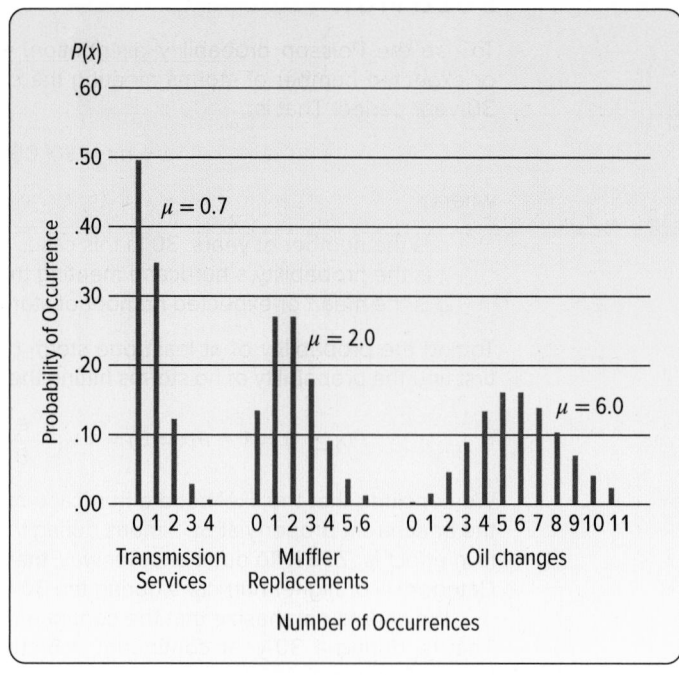

CHART 6–4 Poisson Probability Distributions for Means of 0.7, 2.0, and 6.0

In summary, the Poisson distribution is a family of discrete distributions. All that is needed to construct a Poisson probability distribution is the mean number of defects, errors, or other random variables, designated as μ.

SELF-REVIEW 6–6

From actuary tables, Washington Insurance Company determined the likelihood that a man age 25 will die within the next year is .0002. If Washington Insurance sells 4,000 policies to 25-year-old men this year, what is the probability they will pay on exactly one policy?

EXERCISES

31. In a Poisson distribution μ = 0.4.
   a. What is the probability that $x = 0$?
   b. What is the probability that $x > 0$?
32. In a Poisson distribution μ = 4.
   a. What is the probability that $x = 2$?
   b. What is the probability that $x \leq 2$?
   c. What is the probability that $x > 2$?
33. Ms. Bergen is a loan officer at Coast Bank and Trust. From her years of experience, she estimates that the probability is .025 that an applicant will not be able to repay an installment loan. Last month she made 40 loans.
   a. What is the probability that three loans will be defaulted?
   b. What is the probability that at least three loans will be defaulted?
34. Automobiles arrive at the Elkhart exit of the Indiana Toll Road at the rate of two per minute. The distribution of arrivals approximates a Poisson distribution.
   a. What is the probability that no automobiles arrive in a particular minute?
   b. What is the probability that at least one automobile arrives during a particular minute?
35. It is estimated that 0.5% of the callers to the Customer Service department of Dell Inc. will receive a busy signal. What is the probability that of today's 1,200 callers at least five received a busy signal?
36. In the past, schools in Los Angeles County have closed an average of 3 days each year for weather emergencies. What is the probability that schools in Los Angeles County will close for 4 days next year?

CHAPTER SUMMARY

I. A random variable is a numerical value determined by the outcome of an experiment.
II. A probability distribution is a listing of all possible outcomes of an experiment and the probability associated with each outcome.
   A. A discrete probability distribution can assume only certain values. The main features as follows:
      1. The sum of the probabilities is 1.00.
      2. The probability of a particular outcome is between 0.00 and 1.00.
      3. The outcomes are mutually exclusive.
   B. A continuous distribution can assume an infinite number of values within a specific range.
III. The mean and variance of a discrete probability distribution are computed as follows:
   A. The mean is:

$$\mu = \Sigma[xP(x)] \qquad (6\text{–}1)$$

   B. The variance is:

$$\sigma^2 = \Sigma[(x - \mu)^2 P(x)] \qquad (6\text{–}2)$$

IV. The binomial distribution has the following characteristics.
  A. Each outcome is classified into one of two mutually exclusive categories.
  B. The distribution results from a count of the number of successes in a fixed number of trials.
  C. The probability of a success remains the same from trial to trial.
  D. Each trial is independent.
  E. A binomial probability is determined as follows:

$$P(x) = {}_nC_x\pi^x(1-\pi)^{n-x}$$ **(6–3)**

  F. The mean is:

$$\mu = n\pi$$ **(6–4)**

  G. The variance is:

$$\sigma^2 = n\pi(1-\pi)$$ **(6–5)**

V. The hypergeometric distribution has the following characteristics.
  A. There are only two possible outcomes.
  B. The probability of a success is not the same on each trial.
  C. The distribution results from a count of the number of successes in a fixed number of trials.
  D. It is used when sampling without replacement from a finite population.
  E. A hypergeometric probability is computed from the following equation.

$$P(x) = \frac{({}_SC_x)({}_{N-S}C_{n-x})}{({}_NC_n)}$$ **(6–6)**

VI. The Poisson distribution has the following characteristics.
  A. It describes the number of times some event occurs during a specified interval.
  B. The probability of a "success" is proportional to the length of the interval.
  C. Nonoverlapping intervals are independent.
  D. It is a limiting form of the binomial distribution when n is large and π is small.
  E. A Poisson probability is determined from the following equation:

$$P(x) = \frac{\mu^x e^{-\mu}}{x!}$$ **(6–7)**

  F. The mean and the variance are:

$$\mu = n\pi$$ **(6–8)**

$$\sigma^2 = n\pi$$ **(6–9)**

CHAPTER EXERCISES

37. What is the difference between a random variable and a probability distribution?
38. For each of the following indicate whether the random variable is discrete or continuous.
  a. The length of time to get a haircut.
  b. The number of cars a jogger passes each morning while running.
  c. The number of hits for a team in a high school girls' softball game.
  d. The number of patients treated at the South Strand Medical Center between 6 and 10 p.m. each night.
  e. The distance your car traveled on the last fill-up.
  f. The number of customers at the Oak Street Wendy's who used the drive-through facility.
  g. The distance between Gainesville, Florida, and all Florida cities with a population of at least 50,000.
39. **FILE** An investment will be worth $1,000, $2,000, or $5,000 at the end of the year. The probabilities of these values are .25, .60, and .15, respectively. Determine the mean and variance of the investment's dollar value.

40. The following notice appeared in the golf shop at a Myrtle Beach, South Carolina, golf course.

> **Blackmoor Golf Club Members**
>
> The golf shop is holding a raffle to win a
> TaylorMade SiM Max 10.5° Regular Flex Driver
> ($300 value). Tickets are $5.00 each.
> Only 80 tickets will be sold.
> Please see the golf shop to get your tickets!

John Underpar buys a ticket.
- **a.** What are Mr. Underpar's possible monetary outcomes?
- **b.** What are the probabilities of the possible outcomes?
- **c.** Summarize Mr. Underpar's "experiment" as a probability distribution.
- **d.** What is the mean or expected value of the probability distribution? Explain your result.
- **e.** If all 80 tickets are sold, what is the expected return to the Club?

41. **FILE** Croissant Bakery Inc. offers special decorated cakes for birthdays, weddings, and other occasions. It also has regular cakes available in its bakery. The following table gives the total number of cakes sold per day and the corresponding probability. Compute the mean, variance, and standard deviation of the number of cakes sold per day.

Number of Cakes Sold in a Day	Probability
12	.25
13	.40
14	.25
15	.10

42. **FILE** The payouts for the Powerball lottery and their corresponding odds and probabilities of occurrence are shown. The price of a ticket is $1.00. Find the mean and standard deviation of the payout. Hint: Don't forget to include the cost of the ticket and its corresponding probability.

Divisions	Payout	Odds	Probability
Five plus Powerball	$50,000,000	146,107,962	0.000000006844
Match 5	200,000	3,563,609	0.000000280614
Four plus Powerball	10,000	584,432	0.000001711060
Match 4	100	14,255	0.000070145903
Three plus Powerball	100	11,927	0.000083836351
Match 3	7	291	0.003424657534
Two plus Powerball	7	745	0.001340482574
One plus Powerball	4	127	0.007812500000
Zero plus Powerball	3	69	0.014285714286

43. In a recent study, 35% of people surveyed indicated chocolate was their favorite flavor of ice cream. Suppose we select a sample of 10 people and ask them to name their favorite flavor of ice cream.
- **a.** How many of those in the sample would you expect to name chocolate?
- **b.** What is the probability exactly four of those in the sample name chocolate?
- **c.** What is the probability four or more name chocolate?

44. **FILE** Thirty percent of the population in a southwestern community are Spanish-speaking Americans. A Spanish-speaking person is accused of killing a non-Spanish-speaking American and goes to trial. Of the first 12 potential jurors, only two are Spanish-speaking Americans, and 10 are not. The defendant's lawyer challenges the jury selection, claiming bias against her client. The government lawyer disagrees, saying that the probability of this particular jury composition is common. Compute the probability and discuss the assumptions.

45. An auditor for Health Maintenance Services of Georgia reports 40% of policyholders 55 years or older submit a claim during the year. Fifteen policyholders are randomly selected for company records.

    a. How many of the policyholders would you expect to have filed a claim within the last year?

    b. What is the probability that 10 of the selected policyholders submitted a claim last year?

    c. What is the probability that 10 or more of the selected policyholders submitted a claim last year?

    d. What is the probability that more than 10 of the selected policyholders submitted a claim last year?

46. Tire and Auto Supply is considering a 2-for-1 stock split. Before the transaction is finalized, at least two-thirds of the 1,200 company stockholders must approve the proposal. To evaluate the likelihood the proposal will be approved, the CFO selected a sample of 18 stockholders. The CFO contacted each and found 14 approved of the proposed split. What is the likelihood of this event, assuming two-thirds of the stockholders approve?

47. A federal study reported that 7.5% of the U.S. workforce has a drug problem. A drug enforcement official for the state of Indiana wished to investigate this statement. In the official's sample of 20 employed workers:

    a. how many would you expect to have a drug problem? What is the standard deviation?

    b. what is the likelihood that *none* of the workers sampled has a drug problem?

    c. what is the likelihood *at least one* has a drug problem?

48. The Bank of Hawaii reports that 7% of its credit card holders will default at some time in their life. The Hilo branch just mailed out 12 new cards today.

    a. How many of these new cardholders would you expect to default? What is the standard deviation?

    b. What is the likelihood that *none* of the cardholders will default?

    c. What is the likelihood *at least one* will default?

49. The PEW Research Institute recently conducted a survey of adult Americans regarding Internet shopping. The survey found that 15% of the respondents made a retail purchase on the Internet last week. A retailer wished to verify this claim. In a random sample of 16 adults:

    a. what is the likelihood that exactly three adults make an Internet purchase during a week?

    b. how many are expected to make a purchase during a week?

    c. what is the likelihood that three or less of the 16 adults make an Internet purchase during a week?

50. In Chapter 19, we discuss *acceptance sampling*. Acceptance sampling is a statistical method used to monitor the quality of purchased parts and components. To ensure the quality of incoming parts, a purchaser or manufacturer normally samples 20 parts and allows one defect.

    a. What is the likelihood of accepting a lot that is 1% defective?

    b. If the quality of the incoming lot was actually 2%, what is the likelihood of accepting it?

    c. If the quality of the incoming lot was actually 5%, what is the likelihood of accepting it?

51. Unilever Inc. recently developed a new body wash with a scent of ginger. Their research indicates that 30% of men like the new scent. To further investigate, Unilever's marketing research group randomly selected 15 men and asked them if they liked the scent. What is the probability that six or more men like the ginger scent in the body wash?

52. Dr. Richmond, a psychologist, is studying the daytime television viewing habits of college students. She believes 45% of college students watch soap operas during the afternoon. To further investigate, she selects a sample of 10.

    a. Develop a probability distribution for the number of students in the sample who watch soap operas.

    b. Find the mean and the standard deviation of this distribution.

    c. What is the probability of finding exactly four students who watch soap operas?

    d. What is the probability less than half of the students selected watch soap operas?

53. **FILE** A recent study conducted by Penn, Shone, and Borland, on behalf of **LastMinute. com**, revealed that 52% of business travelers plan their trips less than 2 weeks before

departure. The study is to be replicated in the tri-state area with a sample of 12 frequent business travelers.
   a. Develop a probability distribution for the number of travelers who plan their trips within 2 weeks of departure.
   b. Find the mean and the standard deviation of this distribution.
   c. What is the probability exactly five of the 12 selected business travelers plan their trips within 2 weeks of departure?
   d. What is the probability five or fewer of the 12 selected business travelers plan their trips within 2 weeks of departure?

54. The Internal Revenue Service is studying the category of charitable contributions. A sample of 25 returns is selected from young couples between the ages of 20 and 35 who had an adjusted gross income of more than $100,000. Of these 25 returns, five had charitable contributions of more than $1,000. Four of these returns are selected for a comprehensive audit.
   a. Explain why the hypergeometric distribution is appropriate.
   b. What is the probability exactly one of the four audited had a charitable deduction of more than $1,000?
   c. What is the probability at least one of the audited returns had a charitable contribution of more than $1,000?

55. The law firm of Hagel and Hagel is located in downtown Cincinnati. There are 10 partners in the firm; seven live in Ohio and three in northern Kentucky. Wynne Hagel, the managing partner, wants to appoint a committee of three partners to look into moving the firm to northern Kentucky. If the committee is selected at random from the 10 partners, what is the probability that:
   a. one member of the committee lives in northern Kentucky and the others live in Ohio?
   b. at least one member of the committee lives in northern Kentucky?

56. Topten is a leading source on energy-efficient products. Their list of the top seven vehicles in terms of fuel efficiency for 2022 includes three Hondas.
   a. Determine the probability distribution for the number of Hondas in a sample of two cars chosen from the top seven.
   b. What is the likelihood that in the sample of two at least one Honda is included?

57. The position of chief of police in the city of Corry, Pennsylvania, is vacant. A search committee of Corry residents is charged with the responsibility of recommending a new chief to the city council. The search process results in 12 applicants. Four of the 12 applicants are minorities. To begin, they randomly select four applicants to be interviewed on the first day, and none of the four is a minority. The local newspaper, the *Corry Press,* suggests discrimination in an editorial. What is the likelihood of this occurrence?

58. **FILE** Listed are the 15 U.S. states with the largest populations. In addition, each state is classified with the variable, Coastline, based on whether a state borders the Gulf of Mexico, the Atlantic Ocean, or the Pacific Ocean. If four states are selected at random, what is the probability that:

Rank	State	Coastline
1	California	Yes
2	Texas	Yes
3	Florida	Yes
4	New York	Yes
5	Illinois	No
6	Pennsylvania	No
7	Ohio	No
8	Georgia	Yes
9	North Carolina	Yes
10	Michigan	No
11	New Jersey	Yes
12	Virginia	Yes
13	Washington	Yes
14	Massachusetts	Yes
15	Arizona	No

a. none of the states selected has any coastline?

b. exactly one of the selected states has a coastline?

c. one or more has a coastline?

59. The sales of Lexus automobiles in the Detroit area follow a Poisson distribution with a mean of three per day.

a. What is the probability that no Lexus is sold on a particular day?

b. What is the probability that for five consecutive days at least one Lexus is sold?

60. Suppose 1.5% of the antennas on new Nokia cell phones are defective. For a random sample of 200 antennas, find the probability that:

a. none of the antennas is defective.

b. three or more of the antennas are defective.

61. A study of the checkout lines at the Safeway Supermarket in the South Strand area revealed that between 4 and 7 p.m. on weekdays there is an average of four customers waiting in line. What is the probability that you visit Safeway today during this period and find:

a. no customers are waiting?

b. four customers are waiting?

c. four or fewer are waiting?

d. four or more are waiting?

62. An internal study by the Technology Services department at Lahey Electronics revealed company employees receive an average of two non-work-related emails per hour. Assume the arrival of these emails is approximated by the Poisson distribution.

a. What is the probability Linda Lahey, company president, received exactly one non-work-related email between 4 p.m. and 5 p.m. yesterday?

b. What is the probability she received five or more non-work-related emails during the same period?

c. What is the probability she did not receive any non-work-related emails during the period?

63. Recent crime reports indicate that 3.1 motor vehicle thefts occur each minute in the United States. Assume that the distribution of thefts per minute can be approximated by the Poisson probability distribution.

a. Calculate the probability exactly *four* thefts occur in a minute.

b. What is the probability there are *no* thefts in a minute?

c. What is the probability there is *at least one* theft in a minute?

64. Recent difficult economic times have caused an increase in the foreclosure rate of home mortgages. Statistics from the Penn Bank and Trust Company show their monthly foreclosure rate is now one loan out of every 136 loans. Last month the bank approved 300 loans.

a. How many foreclosures would you expect the bank to have last month?

b. What is the probability of exactly two foreclosures?

c. What is the probability of at least one foreclosure?

65. SpaceX is a private company that builds and launches rockets into space. Some are manned, some are not. NASA engineers estimate (through computer simulations and modeling) a probability of 1 in 276 that a manned mission would fail. For the next 20 manned SpaceX launches, what is the expected number of failures? What is the probability of no failed launches? What is the probability of one failed launch? What is the probability of one or more failed launches?

66. The 2009 RBC Canadian Open golf tournament was played at the Glen Abbey Golf Club in Oakville, Ontario. During the second round, Leif Olson, Arjun Atwal, Casey Wittenberg, and Briny Baird all aced the 132-yard par-3 15th hole. The odds of a professional golfer making a hole-in-one are estimated to be 2,500 to 1, so the probability is 1/2,501. There were 144 golfers participating in the second round that day.

a. What is the probability that no one gets a hole-in-one on the 15th hole?

b. What is the probability that exactly one golfer gets a hole-in-one on the 15th hole?

c. What is the probability that four golfers score a hole-in-one on the 15th hole?

67. According to the U.S. government, it costs more to make a penny, $0.0241, than a penny's value, $0.01. The U.S. government has considered eliminating pennies from its currency. Canada and Australia decided to eliminate pennies from their currencies.

As part of the decision, a survey of adult Americans found that two-thirds said that pennies should not be eliminated. If we randomly selected 12 adults:

a. how many would we expect to support continued use of the penny?

b. what is the likelihood that eight adults would support continued use of the penny?

c. what is the likelihood that the majority of the 12 people, that is seven or more adults, would support the continued use of the penny?

68. According to the "January theory," if the stock market is up at the end of January, it will be "up" for the year. If it is "down" at the end of January, it will be "down" for the year. Within the last 34 years, this theory proved to be true for 29 years. A different theory is that the market change at the end of January and the market change at the end of the year are unrelated. Specifically, for any market change in January, the probability that the market is "up" or "down" at the end of the year is equally likely—that is, the probability is 0.5. You will need a statistical software package to help you solve this problem.

a. Based on history, what is the probability that a year will end with an "up" market when January ends with an "up" market?

b. If the January market change and the yearend market change are unrelated, the probability that the market is "up" with an "up" January is 0.5. Using 0.5, what is the probability that the market would be up 29 or more years? What would be the mean number of years that the market is "up"?

c. Based on the result in part (b), what is your conclusion regarding the "January theory"?

69. In 2022, sales information shows that 30% of new cars and light trucks in the United States were leased. Zook Motors in Kane, Pennsylvania, sold 40 cars and light trucks last month, 10 of them were leased. Wallis Zook, the owner, wonders if the Zook Motors's results are similar to the national sales.

a. Based on the national sales information using 30%, what is the probability that 10 or more of the 40 cars and light trucks sold at Zook Motors were leased?

b. Using the response in part (a), decide if the Zook's sales data are similar to the national average. Explain.

DATA ANALYTICS

70. **FILE** Refer to the North Valley Real Estate data, which report information on homes sold in the area last year.

a. Create a probability distribution for the number of bedrooms. Compute the mean and the standard deviation of this distribution.

b. Create a probability distribution for the number of bathrooms. Compute the mean and the standard deviation of this distribution.

71. **FILE** Refer to the Baseball 2021 data. Compute the mean number of home runs per game. To do this, first find the mean number of home runs per team for 2021. Next, divide this value by 162 (a season comprises 162 games). Then multiply by 2 because there are two teams in each game. Use the Poisson distribution to estimate the number of home runs that will be hit in a game. Find the probability that there are:

a. no home runs in a game.

b. two home runs in a game.

c. at least four home runs in a game.

7

Continuous Probability Distributions

Shutterstock / Dusan Petkovic

▲ **BEST ELECTRONICS INC.** offers a "no hassle" return policy. The daily number of customers returning items follows the normal distribution. What is the probability that eight or less customers will return a product in a day? (See Exercise 51 and LO7-3.)

LEARNING OBJECTIVES

When you have completed this chapter, you will be able to:

LO7-1 Describe the uniform probability distribution and use it to calculate probabilities.

LO7-2 Describe the characteristics of a normal probability distribution.

LO7-3 Describe the standard normal probability distribution and use it to calculate probabilities.

LO7-4 Describe the exponential probability distribution and use it to calculate probabilities.

Introduction

Chapter 6 began our study of probability distributions. We consider three *discrete* probability distributions: binomial, hypergeometric, and Poisson. These distributions are based on discrete random variables, which can assume only clearly separated values. For example, we select for study 10 small businesses that began operations during the year 2020. The number still operating in 2026 can be 0, 1, 2, . . . , 10. There cannot be 3.7, 12, or −7 still operating in 2026. In this example, we are interested in a probability distribution of the number of the 10 businesses still operating in 2026. The discrete random variable is the number of successful businesses.

We continue our study of probability distributions by examining *continuous* probability distributions. A continuous probability distribution usually results from measuring something, such as the distance from the dormitory to the classroom, the weight of an individual, or the amount of bonus earned by CEOs. As an example, at Dave's Inlet Fish Shack flounder is the featured, fresh-fish menu item. The distribution of the amount of flounder sold per day has a mean of 10.0 pounds per day and a standard deviation of 3.0 pounds per day. This distribution is continuous because Dave, the owner, "measures" the amount of flounder sold each day. It is important to realize that a continuous random variable has an infinite number of values within a particular range. So, for a continuous random variable, probability is for a range of values. The probability for a specific value of a continuous random variable is 0.

This chapter shows how to use three continuous probability distributions: the uniform probability distribution, the normal probability distribution, and the exponential probability distribution.

The Family of Uniform Probability Distributions

LO7-1

Describe the uniform probability distribution and use it to calculate probabilities.

Why use a uniform distribution? The uniform distribution is used when we do not have any information regarding the shape of a random variable's probability distribution. When we have no information that any event is more likely than any other, then every event is equally likely, and we would use a uniform distribution. It has been called the "information-less distribution." To establish a uniform distribution, we only need to know or estimate the minimum and maximum values of the continuous random variable. Following are some examples.

- The sales of gasoline at the Kwik Fill in Medina, New York, varies between 2,000 and 5,000 gallons per day. The random variable is the number of gallons sold per day and is continuous within the interval between 2,000 gallons and 5,000 gallons. No other information about gasoline sales is known. So, we use a uniform probability distribution to describe gasoline sales.

- Volunteers at the Grand Strand Public Library prepare federal income tax forms. The time to prepare form 1040-EZ varies over the interval between 10 minutes and 30 minutes. The random variable is the number of minutes to complete the form, and the time to prepare can be equal to any value between 10 and 30 minutes. No other information about tax form preparation time is known. So, we use a uniform probability distribution to describe preparation times.

In a continuous probability distribution, probabilities are represented by areas within or under the distribution. We will use the uniform distribution to begin the process of determining these probabilities. A uniform distribution is shown in Chart 7–1. The distribution's shape is always rectangular with a base determined by the minimum value of *a* and a maximum of *b*.

Maksim Shchur/Shutterstock

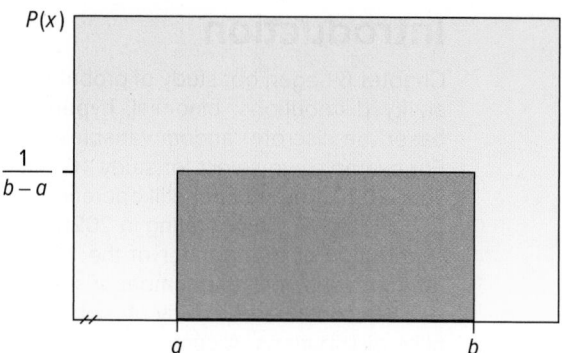

$P(x)$

$\dfrac{1}{b-a}$

a b

CHART 7–1 A Continuous Uniform Distribution

Also notice in Chart 7–1 the height of the distribution is constant or uniform for all values between a and b. The height is computed using the equation for the uniform probability distribution:

> **UNIFORM DISTRIBUTION** $P(x) = \dfrac{1}{b-a}$ if $a \leq x \leq b$ and 0 elsewhere   **(7–1)**

As we described in Chapter 6, probability distributions are useful for making probability statements about the values of a random variable. For distributions describing a continuous random variable, areas within the distribution represent probabilities. In the uniform distribution, its rectangular shape allows us to apply the area formula for a rectangle. Recall that we find the area of a rectangle by multiplying its base by its height. For the uniform distribution, the height of the rectangle is $P(x)$, which is $1/(b - a)$. The base of the distribution is $b - a$. So, if we multiply the height of the distribution by its entire range to find the area, the result is always 1.00. To put it another way, the total area within a continuous probability distribution is equal to 1.00. For a uniform probability distribution:

$$\text{Area} = (\text{height})(\text{base}) = \frac{1}{(b-a)}(b-a) = 1.00$$

So if a uniform distribution ranges from 10 to 15, the height is 0.20, found by $1/(15 - 10)$. The base is 5, found by $15 - 10$. The total area is:

$$\text{Area} = (\text{height})(\text{base}) = \frac{1}{(15-10)}(15-10) = 1.00$$

As with every probability distribution, the uniform distribution has a mean. Its value is located in the exact middle of the range between a and b. It is computed as:

> **MEAN OF THE UNIFORM DISTRIBUTION** $\mu = \dfrac{a+b}{2}$ **(7–2)**

In the uniform distribution, the standard deviation is also related to the interval between the minimum and maximum values. The standard deviation describes the dispersion of a distribution.

> **STANDARD DEVIATION OF THE UNIFORM DISTRIBUTION** $\sigma = \sqrt{\dfrac{(b-a)^2}{12}}$ **(7–3)**

The following example illustrates the features of a uniform distribution and how we use it to calculate probabilities.

▶ **EXAMPLE**

Southwest Arizona State University provides bus service to students while they are on campus. A bus arrives at the North Main Street and College Drive stop every 30 minutes between 6 a.m. and 11 p.m. during weekdays. Students arrive at the bus stop at random times. The time that a student waits is uniformly distributed from 0 to 30 minutes.

1. Draw a graph of this distribution.
2. Show that the probability of any value between 0 and 30 is equal to 1.0.
3. What is the mean of the distribution?
4. What is the standard deviation of the distribution?
5. What is the probability a student will wait more than 25 minutes?
6. What is the probability a student will wait between 10 and 20 minutes? Between 0 and 10 minutes?
7. What is the probability a student waits EXACTLY 15 minutes?

SOLUTION

In this case, the random variable is the length of time a student must wait. Time is measured on a continuous scale, and the wait times range from 0 minutes to 30 minutes.

1. The graph of the uniform distribution is shown in Chart 7–2. The horizontal line is drawn at a height of .0333, found by 1/(30 − 0). The range of this distribution is 30 minutes.

CHART 7–2 Uniform Probability Distribution of Student Wait Times

2. The times students must wait for the bus are uniform over the interval from 0 minutes to 30 minutes, so in this case a is 0 and b is 30.

$$\text{Probability} = (\text{height})(\text{base}) = \frac{1}{(30 - 0)}(30 - 0) = 1.00$$

3. To find the mean, we use formula (7–2).

$$\mu = \frac{a + b}{2} = \frac{0 + 30}{2} = 15$$

The mean of the distribution is 15 minutes. Knowing the mean, we can say that 50% of wait times are between 0 and 15 minutes, and 50% of wait times are between 15 and 30 minutes.

4. To find the standard deviation of the wait times, we use formula (7–3).

$$\sigma = \sqrt{\frac{(b-a)^2}{12}} = \sqrt{\frac{(30-0)^2}{12}} = 8.66$$

The standard deviation of the distribution is 8.66 minutes. This measures the variation in the student wait times.

5. The area within the distribution for the interval 25 to 30 represents this particular probability. From the area formula:

$$P(25 < \text{wait time} < 30) = (\text{height})(\text{base}) = \frac{1}{(30-0)}(5) = .1667$$

So the probability a student waits between 25 and 30 minutes is .1667. This conclusion is illustrated by the following graph.

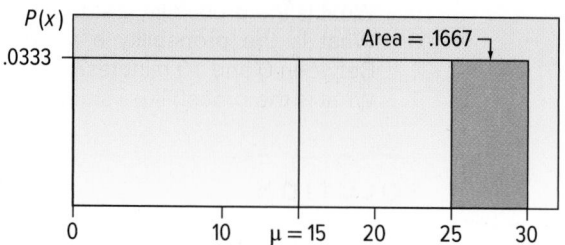

6. The area within the distribution for the interval 10 to 20 represents the probability.

$$P(10 < \text{wait time} < 20) = (\text{height})(\text{base}) = \frac{1}{(30-0)}(10) = .3333$$

We can illustrate this probability as follows:

7. The area of the distribution for the interval 0 to 10 is computed in the same way:

$$P(0 < \text{wait time} < 10) = (\text{height})(\text{base}) = \frac{1}{(30-0)}(10) = .3333$$

Notice that the probability a bus arrives in any 10-minute interval is exactly the same. The probability that a student waits between 0 and 10 minutes, 0.333, is exactly the same as the probability that a student waits between 12 and 22 minutes, 0.333. This is the idea of a uniform probability distribution. The area associated with exactly 15 minutes is zero; there is no interval or corresponding area. So, the probability that a student would wait 15 minutes, or any other specified time between 0 and 30 minutes, is zero.

SELF-REVIEW 7-1

The lifetime of a microwave oven follows a uniform distribution between 8 and 14 years.
(a) Draw this uniform distribution. What are the height and base values?
(b) Show the total area under the curve is 1.00.
(c) Calculate the mean and the standard deviation of this distribution.
(d) What is the probability a particular microwave oven lasts between 10 and 14 years?
(e) What is the probability a microwave oven will last less than 9 years?

EXERCISES

1. A uniform distribution is defined over the interval from 6 to 10.
    a. What are the values for a and b?
    b. What is the mean of this uniform distribution?
    c. What is the standard deviation?
    d. Show that the probability of any value between 6 and 10 is equal to 1.0.
    e. What is the probability that the random variable is more than 7?
    f. What is the probability that the random variable is between 7 and 9?
    g. What is the probability that the random variable is equal to 7.91?

2. A uniform distribution is defined over the interval from 2 to 5.
    a. What are the values for a and b?
    b. What is the mean of this uniform distribution?
    c. What is the standard deviation?
    d. Show that the probability of any value between 2 and 5 is equal to 1.0.
    e. What is the probability that the random variable is more than 2.6?
    f. What is the probability that the random variable is between 2.9 and 3.7?
    g. What is the probability that the random variable is equal to 4.25?

3. The closing price of Schnur Sporting Goods Inc. common stock is uniformly distributed between $20 and $30 per share. What is the probability that the stock price will be:
    a. more than $27?
    b. less than or equal to $24?

4. According to the Insurance Institute of America, a family of four spends between $400 and $3,800 per year on all types of insurance. Suppose the money spent is uniformly distributed between these amounts.
    a. What is the mean amount spent on insurance?
    b. What is the standard deviation of the amount spent?
    c. If we select a family at random, what is the probability they spend less than $2,000 per year on insurance per year?
    d. What is the probability a family spends more than $3,000 per year?

5. The April rainfall in Flagstaff, Arizona, follows a uniform distribution between 0.5 and 3.00 inches.
    a. What are the values for a and b?
    b. What is the mean amount of rainfall for the month? What is the standard deviation?
    c. What is the probability of less than an inch of rain for the month?
    d. What is the probability of *exactly* 1.00 inch of rain?
    e. What is the probability of more than 1.50 inches of rain for the month?

6. Customers experiencing technical difficulty with their Internet cable service may call an 800 number for technical support. It takes the technician between 30 seconds and 10 minutes to resolve the problem. The distribution of this support time follows the uniform distribution.
    a. What are the values for a and b in minutes?
    b. What is the mean time to resolve the problem? What is the standard deviation of the time?
    c. What percent of the problems take more than 5 minutes to resolve?
    d. Suppose we wish to find the middle 50% of the problem-solving times. What are the end points of these two times?

LO7-2
Describe the characteristics of a normal probability distribution.

STATISTICS IN ACTION

Many variables are approximately, normally distributed, such as IQ scores, life expectancies, and adult height. This implies that nearly all observations occur within 3 standard deviations of the mean. On the other hand, observations that occur beyond 3 standard deviations from the mean are extremely rare. For example, the mean adult male height is 68.2 inches (about 5 feet 8 inches) with a standard deviation of 2.74. This means that almost all males are between 60.0 inches (5 feet) and 76.4 inches (6 feet 4 inches). LeBron James, a professional basketball player with the Los Angeles Lakers, is 80 inches, or 6 feet 8 inches, which is clearly beyond 3 standard deviations from the mean. The height of a standard doorway is 6 feet 8 inches, and should be high enough for almost all adult males, except for a rare person like LeBron James.

As another example, the driver's seat in most vehicles is set to comfortably fit a person who is at least 159 cm (62.5 inches) tall. The distribution of heights of adult women is approximately a normal distribution with a mean of 161.5 cm and a standard deviation of 6.3 cm. Thus, about 35% of adult women will not fit comfortably in the driver's seat.

The Family of Normal Probability Distributions

Next we consider the normal probability distribution. Unlike the uniform distribution [see formula (7–1)] the normal probability distribution has a very complex formula.

> **NORMAL PROBABILITY DISTRIBUTION** $P(x) = \dfrac{1}{\sigma\sqrt{2\pi}}\, e^{-\left[\frac{(x-\mu)^2}{2\sigma^2}\right]}$ **(7–4)**

However, do not be bothered by how complex this formula looks. You are already familiar with many of the values. The symbols μ and σ refer to the mean and the standard deviation, as usual. The Greek symbol π is a constant and its value is approximately 22/7 or 3.1416. The letter e is also a constant. It is the base of the natural log system and is approximately equal to 2.718. x is the value of a continuous random variable. So a normal distribution is based on—that is, it is defined by—its mean and standard deviation.

You will not need to make calculations using formula (7–4). Instead you will use a table, given in Appendix B.3, to find various probabilities. These probabilities can also be calculated using software packages or online calculators.

The normal probability distribution has the following characteristics:

· It is **bell shaped** and has a single peak at the center of the distribution. The arithmetic mean, median, and mode are equal and located in the center of the distribution. The total area under the curve is 1.00. Half the area under the normal curve is to the right of this center line and the other half, to the left of it.
· It is **symmetrical** about the mean. If we cut the normal curve vertically at the center value, the shapes of the curves will be mirror images. Also, the area of each half is 0.5.
· It falls off smoothly in either direction from the central value. That is, the distribution is **asymptotic**: The curve gets closer and closer to the X-axis but never actually touches it. To put it another way, the tails of the curve extend indefinitely in both directions.
· The location of a normal distribution is determined by the mean, μ. The dispersion or spread of the distribution is determined by the standard deviation, σ.

These characteristics are shown graphically in Chart 7–3.

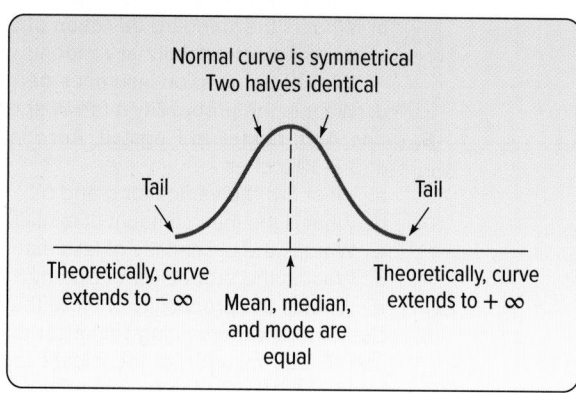

CHART 7–3 Characteristics of a Normal Distribution

There is not just one normal probability distribution, but rather a "family" of them. For example, in Chart 7–4 the probability distributions of length of employee service in three different plants are compared. In the Camden plant, the mean is 20 years and the standard deviation is 3.1 years. There is another normal probability distribution for the length of service in the Dunkirk plant, where $\mu = 20$ years and $\sigma = 3.9$ years. In the

Elmira plant, $\mu = 20$ years and $\sigma = 5.0$ years. Note that the means are the same but the standard deviations are different. As the standard deviation gets smaller, the distribution becomes more narrow and "peaked."

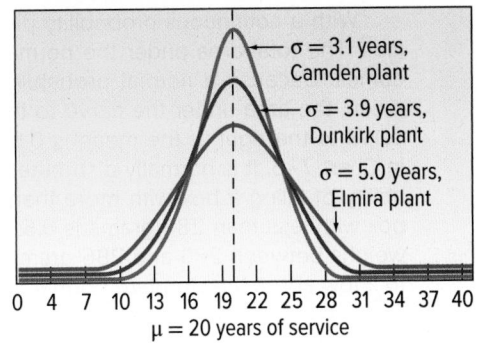

CHART 7–4 Normal Probability Distributions with Equal Means but Different Standard Deviations

Chart 7–5 shows the distribution of box weights of three different cereals. The weights follow a normal distribution with different means but identical standard deviations.

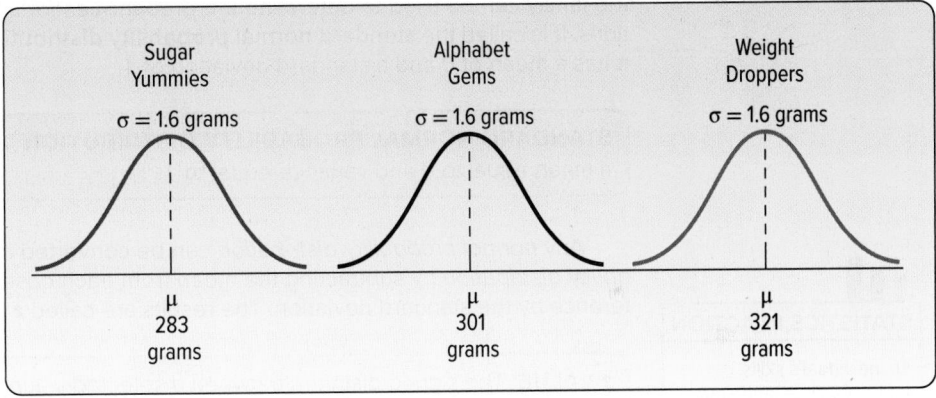

CHART 7–5 Normal Probability Distributions Having Different Means but Equal Standard Deviations

Finally, Chart 7–6 shows three normal distributions having different means and standard deviations. They show the distribution of tensile strengths, measured in pounds per square inch (psi), for three types of cables.

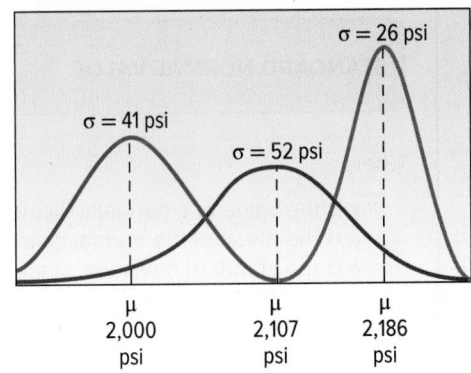

CHART 7–6 Normal Probability Distributions with Different Means and Standard Deviations

In Chapter 6, recall that discrete probability distributions show the specific likelihood a discrete value will occur. For example, on page 186 the binomial distribution is used to calculate the probability a specified number of customers will use a credit or debit card to pay for coffee at a Starbucks.

With a continuous probability distribution, areas below the curve define probabilities. The total area under the normal curve is 1.0. This accounts for all possible outcomes. Because a normal probability distribution is symmetric and centered on the mean, the area under the curve to the left of the mean is 0.5, and the area under the curve to the right of the mean is 0.5. Apply this to the distribution of Sugar Yummies in Chart 7–5. It is normally distributed with a mean of 283 grams. Therefore, the probability of filling a box with more than 283 grams is 0.5 and the probability of filling a box with less than 283 grams is 0.5. We also can determine the probability that a box weighs between 280 and 286 grams. However, to determine this probability we need to know about the standard normal probability distribution.

LO7-3

Describe the standard normal probability distribution and use it to calculate probabilities.

The Standard Normal Probability Distribution

The number of normal distributions is unlimited, each having a different mean (μ), standard deviation (σ), or both. While it is possible to provide a limited number of probability tables for discrete distributions such as the binomial and the Poisson, providing tables for the infinite number of normal distributions is impractical. Fortunately, one member of the family can be used to determine the probabilities for all normal probability distributions. It is called the **standard normal probability distribution,** and it is unique because it has a mean of 0 and a standard deviation of 1.

> **STANDARD NORMAL PROBABILITY DISTRIBUTION** A normal distribution with a mean equal to 0 and variance equal to 1.

Any *normal probability distribution* can be converted into a *standard normal probability distribution* by subtracting the mean from each observation and dividing this difference by the standard deviation. The results are called **z values** or **z scores.**

> **z VALUE** The signed distance between a selected value, designated x, and the mean, μ, divided by the standard deviation, σ.

So the z value calculates the distance between a value of the random variable, x, and the mean of the distribution, μ, in units of the standard deviation, σ. z values are also called **standard normal values.** The formula for this conversion is:

> **STANDARD NORMAL VALUE** $z = \dfrac{x - \mu}{\sigma}$ **(7–5)**

where:

    x is the value of a normally distributed random variable.
    μ is the mean of the normal distribution.
    σ is the standard deviation of the normal distribution.

As we noted in the preceding definition, a z value expresses the distance or difference between a particular value of x and the arithmetic mean in units of the standard deviation. Once the normally distributed observations are standardized, the z values are normally distributed with a mean of 0 and a standard deviation of 1. Therefore, the

STATISTICS IN ACTION

An individual's skills depend on a combination of many hereditary and environmental factors, each having about the same amount of weight or influence on the skills. Thus, much like a binomial distribution with a large number of trials, many skills and attributes follow the normal distribution. For example, the SAT Reasoning Test is the most widely used standardized test for college admissions in the United States. Scores are based on a normal distribution with a mean of 1,500 and a standard deviation of 300.

z distribution has all the characteristics of any normal probability distribution. It is bell shaped, symmetrical, and asymptotic.

The Standard Normal Distribution

We will use the standard normal distribution to find probabilities for any normal distribution. These probabilities are listed in Appendix B.3. A portion of Appendix B.3 is in Table 7–1. The table shows the computed probabilities in the body of the table. The *z* values are in the left and top margins of the table. To use the table, we first round computed *z* values to two decimal places. To find a particular *z* value in the table, say 1.12, the *z* value is split into two parts: 1.1 and 0.02. Find 1.1 in the left margin to locate the row with 1.1. Next go to the top margin and move horizontally starting with 0.00 and find the column headed 0.02. The probability we need is the intersection of the row of 1.1 and column 0.02. Table 7–1 highlights the row, column, and intersection. At the intersection, the probability associated with a *z* value of 1.12 is 0.3686.

TABLE 7–1 Areas under the Standard Normal Distribution

z	0.00	0.01	0.02	0.03	0.04	0.05	0.06	***	0.09
0.0	0.0000	0.0040	0.0080	0.0120	0.0160	0.0199	0.0239	•••	0.0359
0.1	0.0398	0.0438	0.0478	0.0517	0.0557	0.0596	0.0636	•••	0.0753
•	•	•	•	•	•	•	•	•••	•
•	•	•	•	•	•	•	•	•••	•
•	•	•	•	•	•	•	•	•••	•
0.9	0.3159	0.3186	0.3212	0.3238	0.3264	0.3289	0.3315	•••	0.3389
1.0	0.3413	0.3438	0.3461	0.3485	0.3508	0.3531	0.3554	•••	0.3621
1.1	0.3643	0.3665	0.3686	0.3708	0.3729	0.3749	0.3770	•••	0.3830
1.2	0.3849	0.3869	0.3888	0.3907	0.3925	0.3944	0.3962	•••	0.4015
1.3	0.4032	0.4049	0.4066	0.4082	0.4099	0.4115	0.4131	•••	0.4177
1.4	0.4192	0.4207	0.4222	0.4236	0.4251	0.4265	0.4279	•••	0.4319
1.5	0.4332	0.4345	0.4357	0.4370	0.4382	0.4394	0.4406	•••	0.4441
1.6	0.4452	0.4463	0.4474	0.4484	0.4495	0.4505	0.4515	•••	0.4545
1.7	0.4554	0.4564	0.4573	0.4582	0.4591	0.4599	0.4608	•••	0.4633
1.8	0.4641	0.4649	0.4656	0.4664	0.4671	0.4678	0.4686	•••	0.4706
1.9	0.4713	0.4719	0.4726	0.4732	0.4738	0.4744	0.4750	•••	0.4767
2.0	0.4772	0.4778	0.4783	0.4788	0.4793	0.4798	0.4803	•••	0.4817
2.1	0.4821	0.4826	0.4830	0.4834	0.4838	0.4842	0.4846	•••	0.4857
2.2	0.4861	0.4864	0.4868	0.4871	0.4875	0.4878	0.4881	•••	0.4890
•	•	•	•	•	•	•	•	•••	•
•	•	•	•	•	•	•	•	•••	•
•	•	•	•	•	•	•	•	•••	•

The following Example/Solution describes another application using the table.

▶ **EXAMPLE**

Rideshare services are available internationally where a customer uses a smartphone app to request a ride. Then, a driver receives the request, picks up the customer, and takes the customer to the desired location. No cash is involved; the payment for the transaction is handled digitally.

Suppose the weekly income of rideshare drivers follows the normal probability distribution with a mean of $1,000 and a standard deviation of $100. What is the *z* value of income for a driver who earns $1,100 per week? For a driver who earns $900 per week?

SOLUTION

Using formula (7–5), the z values corresponding to the two x values ($1,100 and $900) are:

For x = $1,100:

$$z = \frac{x - \mu}{\sigma}$$

$$= \frac{\$1,100 - \$1,000}{\$100}$$

$$= 1.00$$

For x = $900:

$$z = \frac{x - \mu}{\sigma}$$

$$= \frac{\$900 - \$1,000}{\$100}$$

$$= -1.00$$

The z of 1.00 indicates that a weekly income of $1,100 is 1 standard deviation above the mean, and a z of −1.00 shows that a $900 income is 1 standard deviation below the mean. Note that both incomes ($1,100 and $900) are the same distance ($100) from the mean.

SELF-REVIEW 7–2

A recent national survey concluded that the typical person consumes 48 ounces of water per day. Assume daily water consumption follows a normal probability distribution with a standard deviation of 12.8 ounces.
(a) What is the z value for a person who consumes 64 ounces of water per day? Based on this z value, how does this person compare to the national average?
(b) What is the z value for a person who consumes 32 ounces of water per day? Based on this z value, how does this person compare to the national average?

Applications of the Standard Normal Distribution

The following Example/Solution shows how to find the probability that a normally distributed variable is between the distribution's mean and a selected value of the random variable, x. To find the probability, we use the standard normal distribution.

▶ EXAMPLE

In the first Example/Solution described on page 219 in this section, we reported that the weekly income of rideshare drivers followed the normal distribution with a mean of $1,000 and a standard deviation of $100. That is, μ = $1,000 and σ = $100. What is the likelihood that a randomly selected driver earns between $1,000 and $1,100 per week?

SOLUTION

We have already converted $1,100 to a z value of 1.00 using formula (7–5). To repeat:

$$z = \frac{x - \mu}{\sigma} = \frac{\$1,100 - \$1,000}{\$100} = 1.00$$

That is, $1,100 is 1 standard deviation greater than the mean of $1,000.

The probability associated with a z of 1.00 is listed in Appendix B.3. A portion of Appendix B.3 follows in Table 7-2. To locate the probability, go down the left column to 1.0, and then move horizontally to the column headed .00. The value is .3413.

TABLE 7-2 Areas under the Standard Normal Distribution

z	0.00	0.01	0.02	0.03	0.04	0.05	0.06	•••	0.09
0.0	0.0000	0.0040	0.0080	0.0120	0.0160	0.0199	0.0239	•••	0.0359
0.1	0.0398	0.0438	0.0478	0.0517	0.0557	0.0596	0.0636	•••	0.0753
•	•	•	•	•	•	•	•	•••	•
•	•	•	•	•	•	•	•	•••	•
•	•	•	•	•	•	•	•	•••	•
0.9	0.3159	0.3186	0.3212	0.3238	0.3264	0.3289	0.3315	•••	0.3389
1.0	0.3413	0.3438	0.3461	0.3485	0.3508	0.3531	0.3554	•••	0.3621
1.1	0.3643	0.3665	0.3686	0.3708	0.3729	0.3749	0.3770	•••	0.3830
1.2	0.3849	0.3869	0.3888	0.3907	0.3925	0.3944	0.3962	•••	0.4015
1.3	0.4032	0.4049	0.4066	0.4082	0.4099	0.4115	0.4131	•••	0.4177
1.4	0.4192	0.4207	0.4222	0.4236	0.4251	0.4265	0.4279	•••	0.4319
1.5	0.4332	0.4345	0.4357	0.4370	0.4382	0.4394	0.4406	•••	0.4441
1.6	0.4452	0.4463	0.4474	0.4484	0.4495	0.4505	0.4515	•••	0.4545
1.7	0.4554	0.4564	0.4573	0.4582	0.4591	0.4599	0.4608	•••	0.4633
1.8	0.4641	0.4649	0.4656	0.4664	0.4671	0.4678	0.4686	•••	0.4706
1.9	0.4713	0.4719	0.4726	0.4732	0.4738	0.4744	0.4750	•••	0.4767
2.0	0.4772	0.4778	0.4783	0.4788	0.4793	0.4798	0.4803	•••	0.4817
2.1	0.4821	0.4826	0.4830	0.4834	0.4838	0.4842	0.4846	•••	0.4857
2.2	0.4861	0.4864	0.4868	0.4871	0.4875	0.4878	0.4881	•••	0.4890
•	•	•	•	•	•	•	•	•••	•
•	•	•	•	•	•	•	•	•••	•
•	•	•	•	•	•	•	•	•••	•

The area under the normal curve or probability that the random variable is between $1,000 and $1,100 is .3413. We could also say 34.13% of rideshare drivers earn between $1,000 and $1,100 weekly, or the likelihood of selecting a driver whose income is between $1,000 and $1,100 is .3413.

This information is summarized in the following diagram.

In the Example/Solution just completed, we are interested in the probability between the mean and a given value. Let's change the question. Instead of finding the probability of randomly selecting a driver who earned between $1,000 and $1,100, suppose we wanted the probability of selecting a driver who earned less than $1,100. In probability notation, we write this statement as P(weekly income < $1,100). The method of solution is the same. Using the standard normal probability table in Appendix B.3, we find the probability of selecting a driver who earns between $1,000, the mean, and $1,100. This probability is .3413. Next, recall that the normal distribution is symmetric and that half the area, or probability, is above the mean and half is below. So the probability of selecting a driver earning less than the mean of $1,000 is .5000. Finally, we add the two probabilities, so .3413 + .5000 = .8413. About 84% of rideshare drivers earn less than $1,100 per week. See the following diagram.

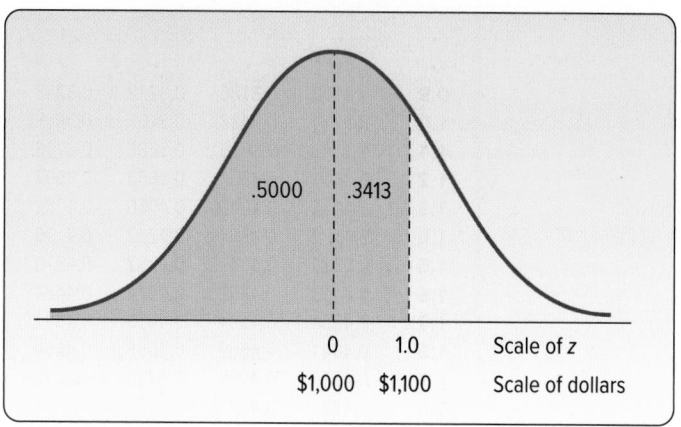

Excel can be used to calculate probabilities for a normal probability distribution. The Excel tutorial in Connect shows how to use the Excel function and dialogue box that follows.

Tutorial #37 in Connect

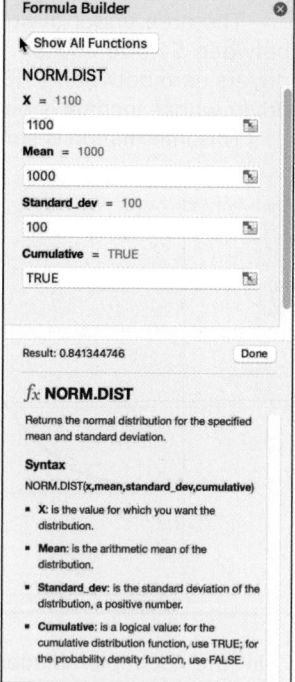

Source: Microsoft Excel

▶ EXAMPLE

Refer to the first Example/Solution discussed on page 219 in this section regarding the weekly income of rideshare drivers. The distribution of weekly incomes follows

the normal probability distribution, with a mean of $1,000 and a standard deviation of $100. What is the probability of selecting a driver whose income is:
1. between $790 and $1,000?
2. less than $790?

SOLUTION

We begin by finding the z value corresponding to a weekly income of $790. From formula (7–5):

$$z = \frac{x - \mu}{s} = \frac{\$790 - \$1,000}{\$100} = -2.10$$

That is, $790 is 2.10 standard deviations less (see the negative sign) than the mean of $1,000.

See a portion of Appendix B.3 in Table 7-3. Move down the left margin to the row 2.1 and across that row to the column headed 0.00. The value is .4821. So the area under the standard normal curve corresponding to a z value of 2.10 is .4821. However, because the normal distribution is symmetric, the area between 0 and a negative z value is the same as that between 0 and the corresponding positive z value. The likelihood of finding a driver earning between $790 and $1,000 is .4821. In probability notation, we write P ($790 < weekly income < $1,000) = .4821.

TABLE 7–3 Areas under the Standard Normal Distribution

z	0.00	0.01	0.02	0.03	0.04	0.05	0.06	...	0.09
0.0	0.0000	0.0040	0.0080	0.0120	0.0160	0.0199	0.0239	...	0.0359
0.1	0.0398	0.0438	0.0478	0.0517	0.0557	0.0596	0.0636	...	0.0753
•	•	•	•	•	•	•	•	...	•
•	•	•	•	•	•	•	•	...	•
•	•	•	•	•	•	•	•	...	•
0.9	0.3159	0.3186	0.3212	0.3238	0.3264	0.3289	0.3315	...	0.3389
1.0	0.3413	0.3438	0.3461	0.3485	0.3508	0.3531	0.3554	...	0.3621
1.1	0.3643	0.3665	0.3686	0.3708	0.3729	0.3749	0.3770	...	0.3830
1.2	0.3849	0.3869	0.3888	0.3907	0.3925	0.3944	0.3962	...	0.4015
1.3	0.4032	0.4049	0.4066	0.4082	0.4099	0.4115	0.4131	...	0.4177
1.4	0.4192	0.4207	0.4222	0.4236	0.4251	0.4265	0.4279	...	0.4319
1.5	0.4332	0.4345	0.4357	0.4370	0.4382	0.4394	0.4406	...	0.4441
1.6	0.4452	0.4463	0.4474	0.4484	0.4495	0.4505	0.4515	...	0.4545
1.7	0.4554	0.4564	0.4573	0.4582	0.4591	0.4599	0.4608	...	0.4633
1.8	0.4641	0.4649	0.4656	0.4664	0.4671	0.4678	0.4686	...	0.4706
1.9	0.4713	0.4719	0.4726	0.4732	0.4738	0.4744	0.4750	...	0.4767
2.0	0.4772	0.4778	0.4783	0.4788	0.4793	0.4798	0.4803	...	0.4817
2.1	0.4821	0.4826	0.4830	0.4834	0.4838	0.4842	0.4846	...	0.4857
2.2	0.4861	0.4864	0.4868	0.4871	0.4875	0.4878	0.4881	...	0.4890
•	•	•	•	•	•	•	•	...	•
•	•	•	•	•	•	•	•	...	•
•	•	•	•	•	•	•	•	...	•

The mean divides the normal curve into two identical halves. The area under the half to the left of the mean is .5000, and the area to the right is also .5000. Because the area under the curve between $790 and $1,000 is .4821, the area below $790 is .0179, found by .5000 − .4821. In probability notation, we write P(weekly income < $790) = .0179.

So we conclude that 48.21% of the rideshare drivers have weekly incomes between $790 and $1,000. Further, we can anticipate that 1.79% earn less than $790 per week. This information is summarized in the following diagram.

SELF-REVIEW 7-3

The temperature of coffee sold at the Coffee Bean Cafe follows the normal probability distribution, with a mean of 150 degrees. The standard deviation of this distribution is 5 degrees.
(a) What is the probability that the coffee temperature is between 150 degrees and 154 degrees?
(b) What is the probability that the coffee temperature is more than 164 degrees?

EXERCISES

7. A normal population has a mean of 20.0 and a standard deviation of 4.0.
   a. Compute the z value associated with 25.0.
   b. What proportion of the population is between 20.0 and 25.0?
   c. What proportion of the population is less than 18.0?
8. A normal population has a mean of 12.2 and a standard deviation of 2.5.
   a. Compute the z value associated with 14.3.
   b. What proportion of the population is between 12.2 and 14.3?
   c. What proportion of the population is less than 10.0?
9. The mean hourly pay of an American Airlines flight attendant is normally distributed with a mean of $29.81 per hour and a standard deviation of $9.31 per hour. What is the probability that the hourly pay of a randomly selected flight attendant is:
   a. between the mean and $35.00 per hour?
   b. more than $35.00 per hour?
   c. less than $20.00 per hour?
10. The mean of a normal probability distribution is 400 pounds. The standard deviation is 10 pounds.
    a. What is the area between 415 pounds and the mean of 400 pounds?
    b. What is the area between the mean and 395 pounds?
    c. What is the probability of selecting a value at random and discovering that it has a value of less than 395 pounds?

Another application of the normal distribution involves combining two areas, or probabilities. One of the areas is to the right of the mean and the other is to the left.

▶ **EXAMPLE**

Continuing the Example/Solution first discussed on page 219 using the weekly income of rideshare drivers, weekly income follows the normal probability distribution, with a mean of $1,000 and a standard deviation of $100. What is the probability that a randomly selected driver earns between $845 and $1,200 per week?

SOLUTION

The problem can be divided into two parts. For the area or probability between the mean and $845 we compute a z value:

$$z = \frac{\$845 - \$1,000}{\$100} = \frac{-\$155}{\$100} = -1.55$$

That is, $845 is 1.55 standard deviations less (notice the negative value) than the mean of $1,000.

For the area between the mean of $1,000 and $1,200:

$$z = \frac{\$1,200 - \$1,000}{\$100} = \frac{\$200}{\$100} = 2.00$$

The z value indicates that $1,200 is 2 standard deviations greater than the mean of $1,000. From the first step, the area under the curve for a z of −1.55 is .4394. From the second step, the area under the curve for a z of 2.00 is .4772. See Table 7-4 extracted from Appendix B.3.

TABLE 7–4 Areas under the Standard Normal Distribution

z	0.00	0.01	0.02	0.03	0.04	0.05	0.06	...	0.09
0.0	0.0000	0.0040	0.0080	0.0120	0.0160	0.0199	0.0239	...	0.0359
0.1	0.0398	0.0438	0.0478	0.0517	0.0557	0.0596	0.0636	...	0.0753
•	•	•	•	•	•	•	•	...	•
•	•	•	•	•	•	•	•	...	•
•	•	•	•	•	•	•	•	...	•
0.9	0.3159	0.3186	0.3212	0.3238	0.3264	0.3289	0.3315	...	0.3389
1.0	0.3413	0.3438	0.3461	0.3485	0.3508	0.3531	0.3554	...	0.3621
1.1	0.3643	0.3665	0.3686	0.3708	0.3729	0.3749	0.3770	...	0.3830
1.2	0.3849	0.3869	0.3888	0.3907	0.3925	0.3944	0.3962	...	0.4015
1.3	0.4032	0.4049	0.4066	0.4082	0.4099	0.4115	0.4131	...	0.4177
1.4	0.4192	0.4207	0.4222	0.4236	0.4251	0.4265	0.4279	...	0.4319
1.5	0.4332	0.4345	0.4357	0.4370	0.4382	0.4394	0.4406	...	0.4441
1.6	0.4452	0.4463	0.4474	0.4484	0.4495	0.4505	0.4515	...	0.4545
1.7	0.4554	0.4564	0.4573	0.4582	0.4591	0.4599	0.4608	...	0.4633
1.8	0.4641	0.4649	0.4656	0.4664	0.4671	0.4678	0.4686	...	0.4706
1.9	0.4713	0.4719	0.4726	0.4732	0.4738	0.4744	0.4750	...	0.4767
2.0	0.4772	0.4778	0.4783	0.4788	0.4793	0.4798	0.4803	...	0.4817
2.1	0.4821	0.4826	0.4830	0.4834	0.4838	0.4842	0.4846	...	0.4857
2.2	0.4861	0.4864	0.4868	0.4871	0.4875	0.4878	0.4881	...	0.4890
•	•	•	•	•	•	•	•	...	•
•	•	•	•	•	•	•	•	...	•
•	•	•	•	•	•	•	•	...	•

Adding the two areas: .4394 + .4772 = .9166. Thus, the probability of selecting an income between $845 and $1,200 is .9166. In probability notation, we write P($845 < weekly income < $1,200) = .4394 + .4772 = .9166. To summarize, 91.66% of the drivers have weekly incomes between $845 and $1,200. This is shown in the following diagram:

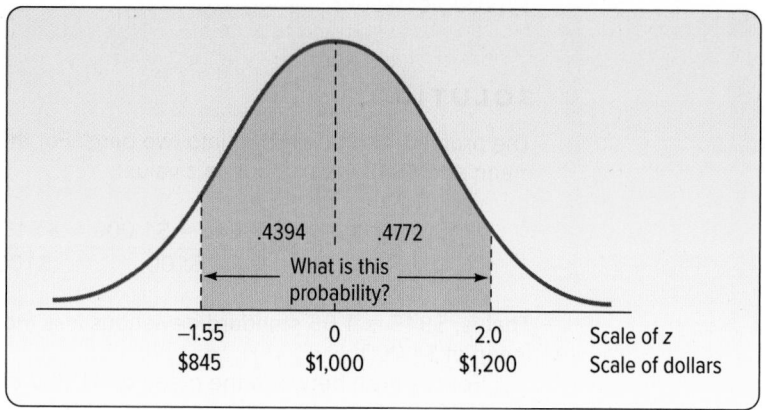

Another application of the normal distribution involves determining the area between values on the *same* side of the mean.

▶ **EXAMPLE**

Returning to the weekly income distribution of rideshare drivers (μ = $1,000, σ = $100), what is the probability that a driver earns between $1,150 and $1,215?

SOLUTION

The situation is again separated into two parts, and formula (7–5) is used. First, we find the z value associated with a weekly income of $1,215:

$$z = \frac{\$1,215 - \$1,000}{\$100} = 2.15$$

Next we find the z value for a weekly income of $1,150:

$$z = \frac{\$1,150 - \$1,000}{\$100} = 1.50$$

Using the following Table 7-5 which is extracted from Appendix B.3, the area associated with a z value of 2.15 is .4842. So, the probability of a weekly income between $1,000 and $1,215 is .4842. Similarly, the area associated with a z value of 1.50 is .4332, so the probability of a weekly income between $1,000 and $1,150 is .4332.

TABLE 7–5 Areas under the Standard Normal Distribution

z	0.00	0.01	0.02	0.03	0.04	0.05	0.06	...	0.09
0.0	0.0000	0.0040	0.0080	0.0120	0.0160	0.0199	0.0239	...	0.0359
0.1	0.0398	0.0438	0.0478	0.0517	0.0557	0.0596	0.0636	...	0.0753
•	•	•	•	•	•	•	•	...	•
•	•	•	•	•	•	•	•	...	•
•	•	•	•	•	•	•	•	...	•
0.9	0.3159	0.3186	0.3212	0.3238	0.3264	0.3289	0.3315	...	0.3389
1.0	0.3413	0.3438	0.3461	0.3485	0.3508	0.3531	0.3554	...	0.3621
1.1	0.3643	0.3665	0.3686	0.3708	0.3729	0.3749	0.3770	...	0.3830
1.2	0.3849	0.3869	0.3888	0.3907	0.3925	0.3944	0.3962	...	0.4015
1.3	0.4032	0.4049	0.4066	0.4082	0.4099	0.4115	0.4131	...	0.4177
1.4	0.4192	0.4207	0.4222	0.4236	0.4251	0.4265	0.4279	...	0.4319
1.5	0.4332	0.4345	0.4357	0.4370	0.4382	0.4394	0.4406	...	0.4441
1.6	0.4452	0.4463	0.4474	0.4484	0.4495	0.4505	0.4515	...	0.4545
1.7	0.4554	0.4564	0.4573	0.4582	0.4591	0.4599	0.4608	...	0.4633
1.8	0.4641	0.4649	0.4656	0.4664	0.4671	0.4678	0.4686	...	0.4706
1.9	0.4713	0.4719	0.4726	0.4732	0.4738	0.4744	0.4750	...	0.4767
2.0	0.4772	0.4778	0.4783	0.4788	0.4793	0.4798	0.4803	...	0.4817
2.1	0.4821	0.4826	0.4830	0.4834	0.4838	0.4842	0.4846	...	0.4857
2.2	0.4861	0.4864	0.4868	0.4871	0.4875	0.4878	0.4881	...	0.4890
•	•	•	•	•	•	•	•	...	•
•	•	•	•	•	•	•	•	...	•
•	•	•	•	•	•	•	•	...	•

Using the following diagram, the probability of a weekly income between $1,150 and $1,215 is found by subtracting the area associated with a z value of 1.50 (.4332) from that associated with a z of 2.15 (.4842). Thus, the probability of a weekly income between $1,150 and $1,215 or $P(\$1,150 < \text{weekly income} < \$1,215) = .4842 - .4332 = .0510$.

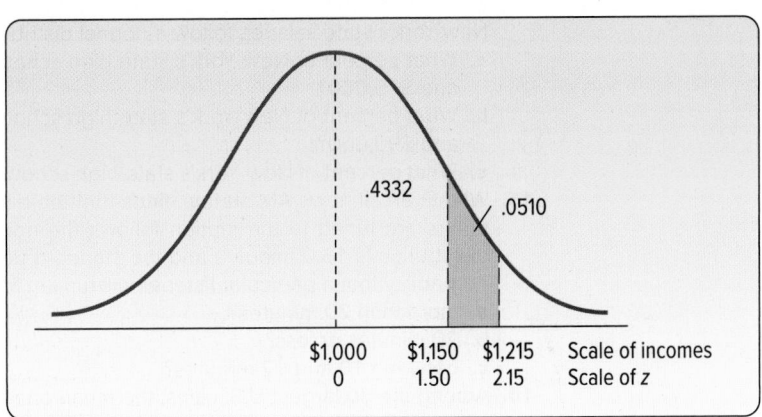

To summarize, there are four situations for finding the area under the standard normal probability distribution.

1. To find the area between 0 and z or (−z), look up the probability directly in the table.
2. To find the area beyond z or (−z), locate the probability of z in the table and subtract that probability from .5000.
3. To find the area between two points on different sides of the mean, determine the z values and add the corresponding probabilities.
4. To find the area between two points on the same side of the mean, determine the z values and subtract the smaller probability from the larger.

SELF-REVIEW 7−4

Refer to Self-Review 7–3. The temperature of coffee sold at the Coffee Bean Cafe follows the normal probability distribution with a mean of 150 degrees. The standard deviation of this distribution is 5 degrees.
(a) What is the probability the coffee temperature is between 146 and 156 degrees?
(b) What is the probability the coffee temperature is more than 156 but less than 162 degrees?

EXERCISES

11. A normal distribution has a mean of 50 and a standard deviation of 4.
    a. Compute the probability of a value between 44.0 and 55.0.
    b. Compute the probability of a value greater than 55.0.
    c. Compute the probability of a value between 52.0 and 55.0.
12. A normal population has a mean of 80.0 and a standard deviation of 14.0.
    a. Compute the probability of a value between 75.0 and 90.0.
    b. Compute the probability of a value of 75.0 or less.
    c. Compute the probability of a value between 55.0 and 70.0.
13. The Internal Revenue Service reported the average refund in 2022 was $3,401 with a standard deviation of 82.5. Assume the amount refunded is normally distributed.
    a. What percent of the refunds are more than $3,500?
    b. What percent of the refunds are more than $3,500 but less than $3,579?
    c. What percent of the refunds are more than $3,325 but less than $3,579?
14. In New York State, the mean salary for high school teachers in 2022 was $81,410 with a standard deviation of $9,500. Only Alaska's mean salary was higher! Assume New York's state salaries follow a normal distribution.
    a. What percent of New York's state high school teachers earn between $70,000 and $75,000?
    b. What percent of New York's state high school teachers earn between $75,000 and $90,000?
    c. What percent of New York's state high school teachers earn less than $60,000?
15. WNAE, an all-news AM station, finds that the distribution of the lengths of time listeners are tuned to the station follows the normal distribution. The mean of the distribution is 15.0 minutes and the standard deviation is 3.5 minutes. What is the probability that a particular listener will tune in for:
    a. more than 20 minutes?
    b. 20 minutes or less?
    c. between 10 and 12 minutes?
16. Among the 30 largest U.S. cities, the mean one-way commute time to work is 25.8 minutes. The longest one-way travel time is in New York City, where the mean time is 39.7 minutes. Assume the distribution of travel times in New York City follows the normal probability distribution and the standard deviation is 7.5 minutes.
    a. What percent of the New York City commutes are for less than 30 minutes?
    b. What percent are between 30 and 35 minutes?
    c. What percent are between 30 and 50 minutes?

In the previous Example/Solution we determined the probability associated with a specified range of a random variable, *x*. In the following Example/Solution we find the value of a random variable for a specified probability. For instance, we can determine the value of a random variable associated with the 90th percentile (that is, the value that separates the upper 10% of a distribution from the lower 90%).

▶ **EXAMPLE**

Continuing the rideshare services example on page 219, if the weekly income of rideshare drivers follows the normal probability distribution with a mean of $1,000 and a standard deviation of $100, what is the 97.5 percentile of weekly earnings? Or what is the earning that separates the upper 2.5% of weekly earnings from the lower 97.5% of earnings?

SOLUTION

From the diagram, the location of *x* is associated with the area in the right tail that represents the top 2.5%, or .025 of the distribution. The complement is the area to the left, which is .9750, or .5000 + .4750. See that all areas sum to 1.00.

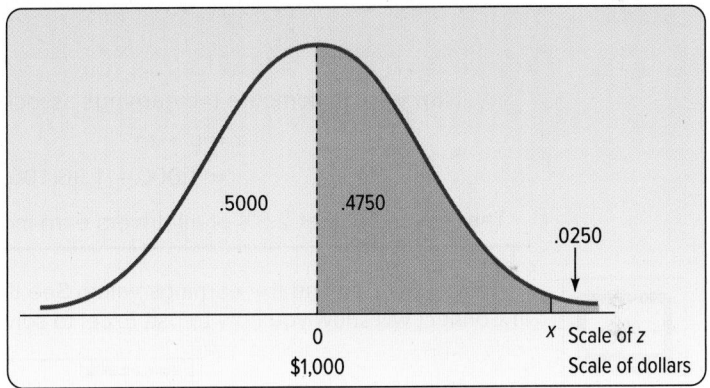

To find the value of the random variable, *x*, we will use the *z* value formula and rearrange it to compute *x*.

$$LC_z = \frac{x - \mu}{\sigma}$$

$$x = \mu + z\sigma$$

To find *x*, we know that $\mu = 1,000$ and $\sigma = 100$. We need to find the value of *z*. It will tell us the difference between the mean of $1,000 and the random variable, *x*, in terms of the number of standard deviations.

Using the standard normal probability table, we determine the area in the right half of the distribution that excludes the top .0250. This area is .5000 − .0250 = .4750. We search the body of the standard normal table for the value .4750. Finding this value is illustrated in the following Table 7-6. We are fortunate to find this exact value. In most cases you will need to approximate the value. Now, we need to find the *z* value for this area. We go to the left margin and find 1.9, then go to the top margin and find 0.06. The *z* value that corresponds with this area is 1.96.

TABLE 7–6 Areas under the Standard Normal Distribution

z	0.00	0.01	0.02	0.03	0.04	0.05	0.06	...	0.09
0.0	0.0000	0.0040	0.0080	0.0120	0.0160	0.0199	0.0239	...	0.0359
0.1	0.0398	0.0438	0.0478	0.0517	0.0557	0.0596	0.0636	...	0.0753
•	•	•	•	•	•	•	•	...	•
•	•	•	•	•	•	•	•	...	•
•	•	•	•	•	•	•	•	...	•
0.9	0.3159	0.3186	0.3212	0.3238	0.3264	0.3289	0.3315	...	0.3389
1.0	0.3413	0.3438	0.3461	0.3485	0.3508	0.3531	0.3554	...	0.3621
1.1	0.3643	0.3665	0.3686	0.3708	0.3729	0.3749	0.3770	...	0.3830
1.2	0.3849	0.3869	0.3888	0.3907	0.3925	0.3944	0.3962	...	0.4015
1.3	0.4032	0.4049	0.4066	0.4082	0.4099	0.4115	0.4131	...	0.4177
1.4	0.4192	0.4207	0.4222	0.4236	0.4251	0.4265	0.4279	...	0.4319
1.5	0.4332	0.4345	0.4357	0.4370	0.4382	0.4394	0.4406	...	0.4441
1.6	0.4452	0.4463	0.4474	0.4484	0.4495	0.4505	0.4515	...	0.4545
1.7	0.4554	0.4564	0.4573	0.4582	0.4591	0.4599	0.4608	...	0.4633
1.8	0.4641	0.4649	0.4656	0.4664	0.4671	0.4678	0.4686	...	0.4706
1.9	0.4713	0.4719	0.4726	0.4732	0.4738	0.4744	0.4750	...	0.4767
2.0	0.4772	0.4778	0.4783	0.4788	0.4793	0.4798	0.4803	...	0.4817
2.1	0.4821	0.4826	0.4830	0.4834	0.4838	0.4842	0.4846	...	0.4857
2.2	0.4861	0.4864	0.4868	0.4871	0.4875	0.4878	0.4881	...	0.4890
•	•	•	•	•	•	•	•	...	•
•	•	•	•	•	•	•	•	...	•
•	•	•	•	•	•	•	•	...	•

Now we can compute the earnings associated with the 97.5 percentile:

$$x = \mu + z\sigma$$
$$= 1,000 + 1.96(100) = \$1,196$$

The results say that 2.5% of all drivers earn more than $1,196; 97.5% earn less.

Tutorial #38
in Connect

Excel will also find the earnings value. See the following output. The Excel tutorial in Connect will show you how to use Excel to solve similar problems.

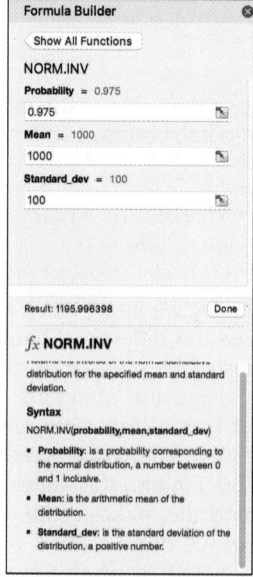

Source: Microsoft Excel

SELF-REVIEW 7–5

An analysis of the final test scores for Introduction to Business reveals the scores follow the normal probability distribution. The mean of the distribution is 75 and the standard deviation is 8. The professor wants to award an A to students whose score is in the highest 10%. What is the dividing point for those students who earn an A and those earning a B?

EXERCISES

17. A normal distribution has a mean of 50 and a standard deviation of 4. Determine the value below which 95% of the observations will occur.

18. A normal distribution has a mean of 80 and a standard deviation of 14. Determine the value above which 80% of the values will occur.

19. Assume that the hourly cost to operate a commercial airplane follows the normal distribution with a mean of $2,100 per hour and a standard deviation of $250. What is the operating cost for the lowest 3% of the airplanes?

20. The SAT Reasoning Test is perhaps the most widely used standardized test for college admissions in the United States. Scores are based on a normal distribution with a mean of 1,500 and a standard deviation of 300. Clinton College would like to offer an honors scholarship to students who score in the top 10% of this test. What is the minimum score that qualifies for the scholarship?

21. According to media research, the typical American listened to 195 hours of music in the last year. This is down from 290 hours 4 years earlier. Tatum Trythall is a big country and western music fan. Tatum listens to music while working around the house, reading, and driving a truck. Assume the number of hours spent listening to music follows a normal probability distribution with a standard deviation of 8.5 hours.
    a. If Tatum is in the top 1% in terms of listening time, how many hours did Tatum listen last year?
    b. Assume that the distribution of times 4 years earlier also follows the normal probability distribution with a standard deviation of 8.5 hours. How many hours did the 1% who listen to the *least* music actually listen?

22. For the most recent year available, the mean annual cost to attend a private university in the United States was $50,900. Assume the distribution of annual costs follows the normal probability distribution and the standard deviation is $4,500. Ninety-five percent of all students at private universities pay less than what amount?

23. In economic theory, a "hurdle rate" is the minimum return that people require before they will make an investment. A research report says that annual returns from a specific class of common equities are distributed according to a normal distribution with a mean of 12% and a standard deviation of 18%. A stock screener would like to identify a hurdle rate such that only one in 20 equities is above that value. Where should the hurdle rate be set?

24. The manufacturer of a laser printer reports the mean number of pages a cartridge will print before it needs replacing is 12,200. The distribution of pages printed per cartridge closely follows the normal probability distribution and the standard deviation is 820 pages. The manufacturer wants to provide guidelines to potential customers as to how long they can expect a cartridge to last. How many pages should the manufacturer advertise for each cartridge if it wants to be correct 99% of the time?

The Empirical Rule

The Empirical Rule is introduced on page 84 of Chapter 3. It states that if a random variable is normally distributed, then:

1. approximately 68% of the observations will lie within plus and minus 1 standard deviation of the mean.

2. about 95% of the observations will lie within plus and minus 2 standard deviations of the mean.
3. practically all, or 99.7% of the observations, will lie within plus and minus 3 standard deviations of the mean.

Now, knowing how to apply the standard normal probability distribution, we can verify the Empirical Rule. For example, 1 standard deviation from the mean is the same as a *z* value of 1.00. When we refer to the standard normal probability table (Appendix B.3), a *z* value of 1.00 corresponds to a probability of 0.3413. So what percent of the observations will lie within plus and minus 1 standard deviation of the mean? We multiply (2)(0.3413), which equals 0.6826, or approximately 68% of the observations are within plus and minus 1 standard deviation of the mean.

The Empirical Rule is summarized in the following graph.

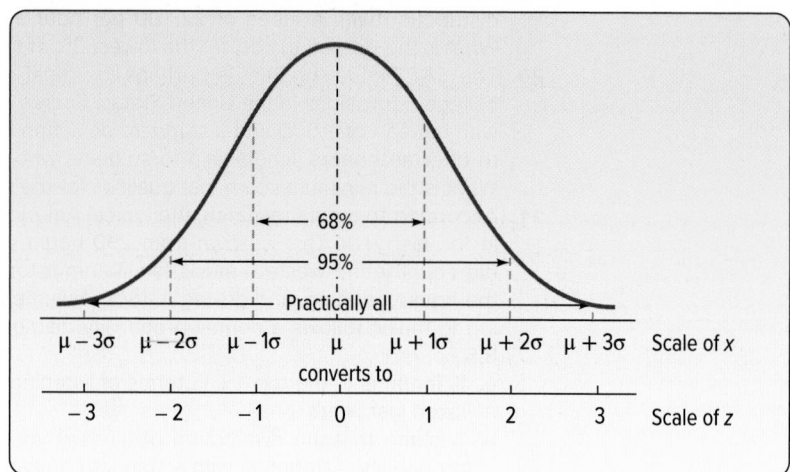

Transforming measurements to standard normal deviates changes the scale. The conversions are also shown in the graph. For example, $\mu + 1\sigma$ is converted to a *z* value of 1.00. Likewise, $\mu - 2\sigma$ is transformed to a *z* value of −2.00. Note that the center of the *z* distribution is zero, indicating no deviation from the mean, μ.

▶ **EXAMPLE**

As part of its quality assurance program, the Autolite Battery Company conducts tests on battery life. For a particular D-cell alkaline battery, the mean life is 19 hours. The useful life of the battery follows a normal distribution with a standard deviation of 1.2 hours. Answer the following questions.
1. About 68% of batteries have a life between what two values?
2. About 95% of batteries have a life between what two values?
3. Virtually all, or 99.7%, of batteries have a life between what two values?

SOLUTION

We can use the Empirical Rule to answer these questions.

1. We can expect about 68% of the batteries to last between 17.8 and 20.2 hours, found by 19.0 ± 1(1.2).
2. We can expect about 95% of the batteries to last between 16.6 and 21.4 hours, found by 19.0 ± 2(1.2).
3. We can expect about 99%, or practically all, of the batteries to last between 15.4 and 22.6 hours, found by 19.0 ± 3(1.2).

This information is summarized on the following chart.

SELF-REVIEW 7–6

Annual incomes for a group of middle-management employees at Compton Plastics is normally distributed with a mean of $47,200 and a standard deviation of $800.
(a) About 68% of the incomes lie between what two amounts?
(b) About 95% of the incomes lie between what two amounts?
(c) Virtually all of the incomes lie between what two amounts?
(d) What are the median and the modal incomes?
(e) Is the distribution of incomes symmetrical?

EXERCISES

25. Explain what is meant by this statement: "There is not just one normal probability distribution but a 'family' of them."
26. List the major characteristics of a normal probability distribution.
27. The mean of a normal probability distribution is 500; the standard deviation is 10.
    a. About 68% of the observations lie between what two values?
    b. About 95% of the observations lie between what two values?
    c. Practically all of the observations lie between what two values?
28. The mean of a normal probability distribution is 60; the standard deviation is 5.
    a. About what percent of the observations lie between 55 and 65?
    b. About what percent of the observations lie between 50 and 70?
    c. About what percent of the observations lie between 45 and 75?
29. The Kamp family has twins, Rob and Rachel. Both Rob and Rachel graduated from college 2 years ago, and each is now earning $70,000 per year. Rachel works in the retail industry, where the mean salary for executives with less than 5 years' experience is $55,000 with a standard deviation of $8,000. Rob is an engineer. The mean salary for engineers with less than 5 years' experience is $80,000 with a standard deviation of $5,000. Compute the z values for both Rob and Rachel and comment on your findings.
30. A recent article in the Cincinnati Enquirer reported that the mean labor cost to repair a heat pump is $90 with a standard deviation of $22. Monte's Plumbing and Heating Service completed repairs on two heat pumps this morning. The labor cost for the first was $75 and $100 for the second. Assume the distribution of labor costs follows the normal probability distribution. Compute z values for each and comment on your findings.

LO7-4
Describe the exponential probability distribution and use it to calculate probabilities.

The Family of Exponential Distributions

So far in this chapter, we have considered two continuous probability distributions, the uniform and the normal. The next continuous distribution we consider is the exponential distribution. This continuous probability distribution usually describes times between events in a sequence. The actions occur independently at a constant rate per unit of time or length. Because time is never negative, an exponential random variable is always positive. The exponential distribution usually describes situations such as the following:

- The service time for customers calling the Department of Motor Vehicles
- The time between "hits" on a website
- The lifetime of a kitchen appliance
- The time until the next phone call arrives in a customer service center

The exponential probability distribution is positively skewed. That differs from the uniform and normal distributions, which were both symmetric. Moreover, the distribution is described by only one parameter, which we will identify as λ (pronounced "lambda"). λ is often referred to as the "rate" parameter. The following chart shows the change in the shape of the exponential distribution as we vary the value of λ from 1/3 to 1 to 2. Observe that as we decrease λ, the shape of the distribution is "less skewed."

Another feature of the exponential distribution is its close relationship to the Poisson distribution. The Poisson is a discrete probability distribution and also has a single parameter, μ. We described the Poisson distribution starting in Chapter 6 on page 198. It, too, is a positively skewed distribution. To explain the relationship between the Poisson and the exponential distributions, suppose customers arrive at a family restaurant during the dinner hour at a rate of six per hour. The Poisson distribution would have a mean of 6. For a time interval of 1 hour, we can use the Poisson distribution to find the probability that one, or two, or ten customers arrive. But suppose instead of studying the number of customers *arriving in an hour,* we wish to study the time *between their arrivals.* The time between arrivals is a continuous distribution because time is measured as a continuous random variable. If customers arrive at a rate of six per hour, then logically the typical or mean time between arrivals is 1/6 of an hour, or 10 minutes. We need to be careful here to be consistent with our units, so let's stay with 1/6 of an hour. So in general, if we know customers arrive at a certain rate per hour, which we call μ, then we can expect the mean time between arrivals to be $1/\mu$. The rate parameter λ is equal to $1/\mu$. So in our restaurant arrival example, the mean time between customer arrivals is $\mu = 1/6$ of an hour.

Robert Cicchetti/Shutterstock

The graph of the exponential distribution starts at the value of λ when the random variable's (*x*) value is 0. The distribution declines steadily as we move to the right with increasing values of *x*. Formula (7–6) describes the exponential probability distribution with λ as rate parameter. As we described with the Poisson distribution on page 199, e is a mathematical constant equal to 2.71828. It is the base for the natural logarithm system. It is a pleasant surprise that both the mean and the standard deviation of the exponential probability distribution are equal to $1/\lambda$.

EXPONENTIAL DISTRIBUTION	$P(x) = \lambda e^{-\lambda x}$	**(7–6)**

With continuous distributions, we do not address the probability that a distinct value will occur. Instead, areas or regions below the graph of the probability distribution between two specified values give the probability the random variable is in that interval. A table, such as Appendix B.3 for the normal distribution, is not necessary for the exponential distribution. The area under the exponential probability distribution is found by a formula and the necessary calculations can be accomplished with a handheld calculator with an e^x key. Most statistical software packages will also calculate exponential probabilities by inputting the rate parameter, λ, only. The probability of obtaining an arrival value less than a particular value of x is:

FINDING A PROBABILITY USING THE EXPONENTIAL DISTRIBUTION	$P(\text{Arrival time} < x) = 1 - e^{-\lambda x}$	**(7–7)**

▶ **EXAMPLE**

Orders for prescriptions arrive at a pharmacy website according to an exponential probability distribution at a mean of one every 20 seconds. Find the probability the next order arrives in less than 5 seconds. Find the probability the next order arrives in more than 40 seconds.

SOLUTION

To begin, we determine the rate parameter λ, which in this case is 1/20. To find the probability, we insert 1/20 for λ and 5 for x in formula (7–7).

$$P(\text{Arrival time} < 5) = 1 - e^{-\frac{1}{20}(5)} = 1 - e^{-0.25} = 1 - .7788 = .2212$$

So we conclude there is a 22% chance the next order will arrive in less than 5 seconds. The region is identified as the colored area under the curve.

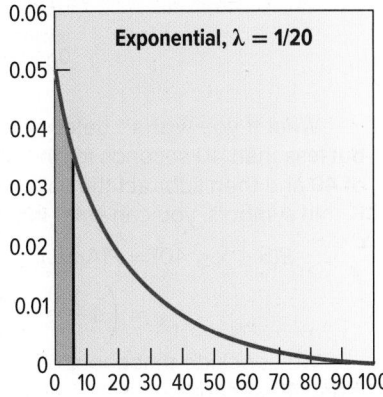

The preceding computations addressed the area in the left-tail area of the exponential distribution with $\lambda = 1/20$ and the area between 0 and 5—that is, the area that is below 5 seconds. What if you are interested in the right-tail area? It is found using the complement rule. See formula (5–6) in Chapter 5. To put it another way, to find the probability the next order will arrive in more than 40 seconds, we find the probability the order arrives in less than 40 seconds and subtract the result from 1.00. We show this in two steps.

1. Find the probability an order is received *in less than* 40 seconds.

$$P(\text{Arrival} < 40) = 1 - e^{-\frac{1}{20}(40)} = 1 - .1353 = .8647$$

2. Find the probability an order is received *in more than* 40 seconds.

$$P(\text{Arrival} > 40) = 1 - P(\text{Arrival} < 40) = 1 - .8647 = .1353$$

We conclude that the likelihood that it will be 40 seconds or more before the next order is received at the pharmacy is 13.5%.

In the preceding Example/Solution, when we apply the exponential probability distribution to compute the probability that the arrival time is greater than 40 seconds, you probably observed that there is some redundancy. In general, if we wish to find the likelihood of a time greater than some value x, such as 40, the complement rule is applied as follows:

$$P(\text{Arrival} > x) = 1 - P(\text{Arrival} < x) = 1 - (1 - e^{-\lambda x}) = e^{-\lambda x}$$

In other words, when we subtract formula (7–7) from 1 to find the area in the right tail, the result is $e^{-\lambda x}$. Thus, the probability that more than 40 seconds go by before the next order arrives is computed without the aid of the complement rule as follows:

$$P(\text{Arrival} > 40) = e^{-\frac{1}{20}(40)} = .1353$$

The result is shown in the following graph.

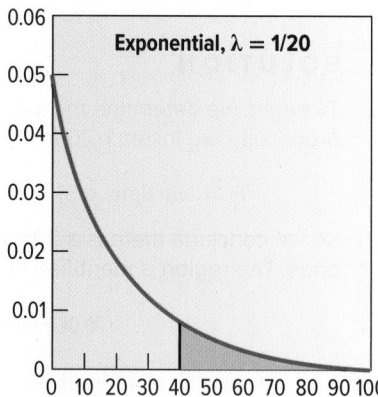

What if you wish to determine the probability that it will take more than 5 seconds but less than 40 seconds for the next order to arrive? Use formula (7–7) with an x value of 40 and then subtract the value of formula (7–7) when x is 5.

In symbols, you can write this as:

$$P(5 \leq x \leq 40) = P(\text{Arrival} \leq 40) - P(\text{Arrival} \leq 5)$$

$$= \left(1 - e^{-\frac{1}{20}(40)}\right) - \left(1 - e^{-\frac{1}{20}(5)}\right) = .8647 - .2212 = .6435$$

We conclude that about 64% of the time, the time between orders will be between 5 and 40 seconds.

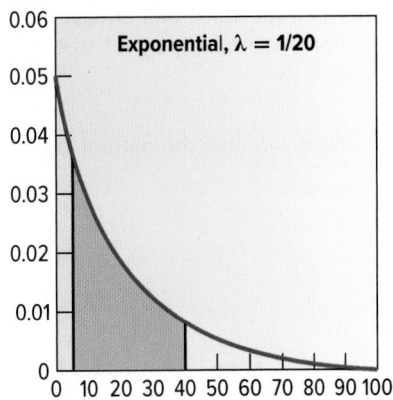

Previous examples require finding the percentage of the observations located between two values or the percentage of the observations above or below a particular value, *x*. We can also use formula (7–7) in "reverse" to find the value of the observation *x* when the percentage above or below the observation is given. The following Example/Solution illustrates this situation.

▶ EXAMPLE

Compton Computers wishes to set a minimum lifetime guarantee on its new power supply unit. Quality testing shows the time to failure follows an exponential distribution with a mean of 4,000 hours. Compton wants a warranty period such that only 5% of the power supply units fail during that period. What value should they set for the warranty period?

SOLUTION

Note that 4,000 hours is a mean and not a rate. Therefore, we must compute λ as 1/4,000, or 0.00025 failure per hour. A diagram of the situation is shown here, where *x* represents the minimum guaranteed lifetime.

We use formula (7–7) and essentially work backward for the solution. In this case, the rate parameter is 4,000 hours and we want the area, as shown in the diagram, to be .05.

$$P(\text{Arrival time} < x) = 1 - e^{(-\lambda x)}$$

$$= 1 - e^{-\frac{1}{4,000}(x)} = .05$$

Next, we solve this equation for x. So, we subtract 1 from both sides of the equation and multiply by −1 to simplify the signs. The result is:

$$.95 = e^{-\frac{1}{4,000}(x)}$$

Next, we take the natural log of both sides and solve for x:

$$\ln(.95) = -\frac{1}{4,000}x$$

$$-(.051293294) = -\frac{1}{4,000}x$$

$$x = 205.17$$

In this case, $x = 205.17$. Hence, Compton can set the warranty period at 205 hours and expect about 5% of the power supply units to be returned.

SELF-REVIEW 7–7

The time between ambulance arrivals at the Methodist Hospital emergency room follows an exponential distribution with a mean of 10 minutes.
(a) What is the likelihood the next ambulance will arrive in 15 minutes or less?
(b) What is the likelihood the next ambulance will arrive in more than 25 minutes?
(c) What is the likelihood the next ambulance will arrive in more than 15 minutes but less than 25?
(d) Find the 80th percentile for the time between ambulance arrivals. (This means only 20% of the runs are longer than this time.)

EXERCISES

31. Waiting times to receive food after placing an order at the local Subway sandwich shop follow an exponential distribution with a mean of 60 seconds. Calculate the probability a customer waits:
   a. less than 30 seconds.
   b. more than 120 seconds.
   c. between 45 and 75 seconds.
   d. Fifty percent of the patrons wait less than how many seconds? What is the median?
32. The lifetime of LCD TV sets follows an exponential distribution with a mean of 100,000 hours. Compute the probability a television set:
   a. fails in less than 10,000 hours.
   b. lasts more than 120,000 hours.
   c. fails between 60,000 and 100,000 hours of use.
   d. Find the 90th percentile. So 10% of the TV sets last more than what length of time?
33. The Bureau of Labor Statistics' *American Time Use Survey,* www.bls.gov/data, showed that the amount of time spent using a computer for leisure varied greatly by age. Individuals aged 75 and over averaged 31 minutes per day using a computer for leisure. Individuals ages 15 to 19 spend 113 minutes per day using a computer for leisure. If these times follow an exponential distribution, find the proportion of each group that spends:
   a. less than 15 minutes per day using a computer for leisure.
   b. more than 2 hours.
   c. between 30 minutes and 90 minutes using a computer for leisure.
   d. Find the 20th percentile. Eighty percent spend more than what amount of time?
34. The cost per item at a supermarket follows an exponential distribution. There are many inexpensive items and a few relatively expensive ones. The mean cost per item is $3.50. What is the percentage of items that cost:
   a. less than $1?
   b. more than $4?
   c. between $2 and $3?
   d. Find the 40th percentile. Sixty percent of the supermarket items cost more than what amount?

CHAPTER SUMMARY

I. The uniform distribution is a continuous probability distribution with the following characteristics.
   A. It is rectangular in shape.
   B. The mean and the median are equal.
   C. It is completely described by its minimum value a and its maximum value b.
   D. It is described by the following equation for the region from a to b:

$$P(x) = \frac{1}{b - a} \tag{7-1}$$

   E. The mean and standard deviation of a uniform distribution are computed as follows:

$$\mu = \frac{(a + b)}{2} \tag{7-2}$$

$$\sigma = \frac{\sqrt{(b - a)^2}}{12} \tag{7-3}$$

II. The normal probability distribution is a continuous distribution with the following characteristics.
   A. It is bell shaped and has a single peak at the center of the distribution.
   B. The distribution is symmetric.
   C. It is asymptotic, meaning the curve approaches but never touches the X-axis.
   D. It is completely described by its mean and standard deviation.
   E. There is a family of normal probability distributions.
      1. Another normal probability distribution is created when either the mean or the standard deviation changes.
      2. The normal probability distribution is described by the following formula.

$$P(x) = \frac{1}{\sigma \sqrt{2\pi}} e^{-\left[\frac{(x - \mu)^2}{2\sigma^2}\right]} \tag{7-4}$$

III. The standard normal probability distribution is a particular normal distribution.
   A. It has a mean of 0 and a standard deviation of 1.
   B. Any normal probability distribution can be converted to the standard normal probability distribution by the following formula.

$$z = \frac{x - \mu}{\sigma} \tag{7-5}$$

   C. By standardizing a normal probability distribution, we can report the distance of a value from the mean in units of the standard deviation.
IV. The exponential probability distribution describes times between events in a sequence.
   A. The actions occur independently at a constant rate per unit of time or length.
   B. The probabilities are computed using the formula:

$$P(x) = \lambda e^{-\lambda x} \tag{7-6}$$

   C. It is nonnegative, is positively skewed, declines steadily to the right, and is asymptotic.
   D. The area under the curve is given by the formula:

$$P(\text{Arrival time} < x) = 1 - e^{-\lambda x} \tag{7-7}$$

   E. The mean and variance are:

$$\mu = 1/\lambda$$
$$\sigma^2 = 1/\lambda$$

CHAPTER EXERCISES

35. If a continuous random variable, x, is uniformly distributed with a minimum value of 5 and a maximum value of 25, what is the probability that:
 a. x = 10? Why?
 b. x = 13.4? Why?

36. If a continuous random variable, x, is normally distributed with a mean of 100 and a standard deviation of 15, what is the probability that:
 a. x = 100? Why?
 b. x = 113.56? Why?

37. The amount of cola in a 12-ounce can is uniformly distributed between 11.96 ounces and 12.05 ounces.
 a. What is the mean amount per can?
 b. What is the standard deviation amount per can?
 c. What is the probability of selecting a can of cola and finding it has less than 12 ounces?
 d. What is the probability of selecting a can of cola and finding it has more than 11.98 ounces?
 e. What is the probability of selecting a can of cola and finding it has more than 11.00 ounces?

38. A tube of Listerine Tartar Control toothpaste contains 4.2 ounces. As people use the toothpaste, the amount remaining in any tube is random. Assume the amount of toothpaste remaining in the tube follows a uniform distribution. From this information, we can determine the following information about the amount remaining in a toothpaste tube without invading anyone's privacy.
 a. How much toothpaste would you expect to be remaining in the tube?
 b. What is the standard deviation of the amount remaining in the tube?
 c. What is the likelihood there is less than 3.0 ounces remaining in the tube?
 d. What is the probability there is more than 1.5 ounces remaining in the tube?

39. Many retail stores offer their own credit cards. At the time of the credit application, the customer is given a 10% discount on the purchase. The time required for the credit application process follows a uniform distribution with the times ranging from 4 minutes to 10 minutes.
 a. What is the mean time for the application process?
 b. What is the standard deviation of the process time?
 c. What is the likelihood a particular application will take less than 6 minutes?
 d. What is the likelihood an application will take more than 5 minutes?

40. Patrons of the Grande Dunes Hotel in the Bahamas spend time waiting for an elevator. The wait time follows a uniform distribution between 0 and 3.5 minutes.
 a. Show that the probability of any time between 0 and 3.5 minutes is equal to 1.0.
 b. How long does the typical patron wait for elevator service?
 c. What is the standard deviation of the wait time?
 d. What percent of the patrons wait for less than a minute?
 e. What percent of the patrons wait more than 2 minutes?

41. You visit a friend who lives in the suburbs of Chicago. You decide to take a commuter train into the city. Your friend says that a train stops at the station every 30 minutes. Without any more information, you logically apply the uniform probability distribution and determine that you will wait between 0 and 30 minutes for a train with a probability of 1.00. You arrive at the train station and start timing your wait time. A train arrives 35 minutes later. Given your friend's information, what was the probability that a train arrives in 35 minutes or more? What conclusion can you make about your friend's information?

42. The accounting department at Weston Materials Inc., a national manufacturer of unattached garages, reports that it takes two construction workers a mean of 32 hours and a standard deviation of 2 hours to erect the Red Barn model. Assume the assembly times follow the normal distribution.
 a. Determine the z values for 29 and 34 hours. What percent of the garages take between 32 hours and 34 hours to erect?
 b. What percent of the garages take between 29 hours and 34 hours to erect?

c. What percent of the garages take 28.7 hours or less to erect?

d. Of the garages, 5% take how many hours or more to erect?

43. In 2021, the U.S. Department of Agriculture issued a report https://www.fns.usda.gov/cnpp/usda-food-plans-cost-food-reports-monthly-reports indicating a family of four spent an average of $1,370.10 per month on food. This is for a family of four (two parents aged 19 to 50) and two children (one whose age is between 6 and 8 years and one between 9 and 11 years). Assume the distribution of food expenditures for a family of four follows the normal distribution with a standard deviation of $120 per month.

   a. What percent of the families spend more than $1,200 but less than $1,370.10 per month on food?

   b. What percent of the families spend less than $1,200 per month on food?

   c. What percent spend between $1,200 and $1,500 per month on food?

   d. What percent spend between $1,200 and $1,300 per month on food?

44. A study of phone calls made from General Electric Corporate Headquarters in Fairfield, Connecticut, revealed the length of the calls, in minutes, follows the normal probability distribution. The mean length of time per call was 4.2 minutes and the standard deviation was 0.60 minute.

   a. What is the probability that calls last between 4.2 and 5 minutes?

   b. What is the probability that calls last more than 5 minutes?

   c. What is the probability that calls last between 5 and 6 minutes?

   d. What is the probability that calls last between 4 and 6 minutes?

   e. As part of a report to the president, the director of communications would like to report the length of the longest (in duration) 4% of the calls. What is this time?

45. Shaver Manufacturing Inc. offers dental insurance to its employees. A review by the human resources director and staff revealed the annual cost per employee per year followed the normal probability distribution, with a mean of $1,280 and a standard deviation of $420 per year.

   a. What is the probability that annual dental expenses are more than $1,500?

   b. What is the probability that annual dental expenses are between $1,500 and $2,000?

   c. Estimate the probability that an employee had no annual dental expenses.

   d. What was the cost for the 10% of employees who incurred the highest dental expense?

46. The annual commissions earned by sales representatives of Machine Products Inc., a manufacturer of light machinery, follow the normal probability distribution. The mean yearly amount earned is $40,000 and the standard deviation is $5,000.

   a. What percent of the sales representatives earn more than $42,000 per year?

   b. What percent of the sales representatives earn between $32,000 and $42,000?

   c. What percent of the sales representatives earn between $32,000 and $35,000?

   d. The sales manager wants to award the sales representatives who earn the largest commissions a bonus of $1,000. The sales manager can award a bonus to 20% of the representatives. What is the cutoff point between those who earn a bonus and those who do not?

47. A recent study reported that Americans spend an average of 270 minutes per day watching TV. Assume the distribution of minutes per day watching TV follows a normal distribution with a standard deviation of 23 minutes.

   a. What percent of the population watch more than 300 minutes per day?

   b. What percent of the population watch more than 220 minutes per day?

   c. What percent of the population watch between 220 hours and 300 hours?

   d. Let's define a "binge watcher" as someone in the upper 15% of the distribution of minutes watching TV. How many minutes does a "binge watcher" spend per day watching TV?

48. According to a government study among adults in the 25- to 34-year age group, the mean amount spent per year on reading and entertainment is $1,994. Assume that the distribution of the amounts spent follows the normal distribution with a standard deviation of $450.

   a. What percent of the adults spend more than $2,500 per year on reading and entertainment?

   b. What percent spend between $2,500 and $3,000 per year on reading and entertainment?

   c. What percent spend less than $1,000 per year on reading and entertainment?

49. Management at Gordon Electronics is considering adopting a bonus system to increase production. One suggestion is to pay a bonus on the highest 5% of production based on past experience. Past records indicate weekly production follows the normal distribution. The mean of this distribution is 4,000 units per week and the standard deviation is 60 units per week. If the bonus is paid on the upper 5% of production, the bonus will be paid on how many units or more?

50. Fast Service Truck Lines uses the Ford Super Duty F-750 exclusively. Management made a study of the maintenance costs and determined the number of miles traveled during the year followed the normal distribution. The mean of the distribution was 60,000 miles and the standard deviation 2,000 miles.

   a. What percent of the Ford Super Duty F-750s logged 65,200 miles or more?

   b. What percent of the trucks logged more than 57,060 but less than 58,280 miles?

   c. What percent of the Fords traveled 62,000 miles or less during the year?

   d. Is it reasonable to conclude that any of the trucks were driven more than 70,000 miles? Explain.

51. Best Electronics Inc. offers a "no hassle" returns policy. The daily number of customers returning items follows the normal distribution. The mean number of customers returning items is 10.3 per day and the standard deviation is 2.25 per day.

   a. For any day, what is the probability that eight or fewer customers returned items?

   b. For any day, what is the probability that the number of customers returning items is between 12 and 14?

   c. Is there any chance of a day with no customer returns?

52. The funds dispensed at the ATM machine located near the checkout line at the Kroger's in Union, Kentucky, follows a normal probability distribution with a mean of $4,200 per day and a standard deviation of $720 per day. The machine is programmed to notify the nearby bank if the amount dispensed is very low (less than $2,500) or very high (more than $6,000).

   a. What percent of the days will the bank be notified because the amount dispensed is very low?

   b. What percent of the time will the bank be notified because the amount dispensed is high?

   c. What percent of the time will the bank not be notified regarding the amount of funds dispersed?

53. The weights of canned hams processed at Henline Ham Company follow the normal distribution, with a mean of 9.20 pounds and a standard deviation of 0.25 pounds. The label weight is given as 9.00 pounds.

   a. What proportion of the hams actually weigh less than the amount claimed on the label?

   b. The owner, Carter Henline, is considering two proposals to reduce the proportion of hams below label weight. One option is to increase the mean weight to 9.25 and leave the standard deviation the same, or leave the mean weight at 9.20 and reduce the standard deviation from 0.25 pounds to 0.15. Which change would you recommend?

54. The price of shares of Bank of Florida at the end of trading each day for the last year followed the normal distribution. Assume there were 240 trading days in the year. The mean price was $42.00 per share and the standard deviation was $2.25 per share.

   a. What is the probability that the end-of-day trading price is over $45.00? Estimate the number of days in a year when the trading price finished above $45.00.

   b. What percent of the days was the price between $38.00 and $40.00?

   c. What is the minimum share price for the top 15% of end-of-day trading prices?

55. A recent graduate from a business college is hired by a marketing firm in sales. Her first year's estimated income is $35,000. She did research on starting salaries for similar positions and found that starting salaries are normally distributed with a mean of $33,500 and a standard deviation of $2,000. One day, she called a fellow alumnus who had a very similar position with a different firm and reported that his annual income was more than $50,000. Based on the research, what is the probability that a person would have a starting salary of $50,000 or more? What can you conclude?

56. A carbon monoxide detector in the Wheelock household activates once every 200 days on average. Assume this activation follows the exponential distribution. What is the probability that:
   a. there will be an alarm within the next 60 days?
   b. at least 400 days will pass before the next alarm?
   c. it will be between 150 and 250 days until the next warning?
   d. Find the median time until the next activation.

57. "Boot time" (the time between the appearance of the Bios screen to the first file that is loaded in Windows) on Madison Gagnon's personal computer follows an exponential distribution with a mean of 27 seconds. What is the probability Madison's "boot" will require:
   a. less than 15 seconds?
   b. more than 60 seconds?
   c. between 30 and 45 seconds?
   d. What is the point below which only 10% of the boots occur?

58. The time between visits to a U.S. emergency room for a member of the general population follows an exponential distribution with a mean of 2.5 years. What proportion of the population will:
   a. visit an emergency room within the next 6 months?
   b. not visit the ER over the next 6 years?
   c. visit an ER next year, but not this year?
   d. Find the first and third quartiles of this distribution.

59. The times between failures on a personal computer follow an exponential distribution with a mean of 300,000 hours. What is the probability of:
   a. a failure in less than 100,000 hours?
   b. no failure in the next 500,000 hours?
   c. the next failure occurring between 200,000 and 350,000 hours?
   d. What are the mean and standard deviation of the time between failures?

DATA ANALYTICS

(The data for these exercises are available at the text website: **www.mhhe.com/lind19e.**)

60. Refer to the North Valley Real Estate data, which report information on homes sold during the last year.
   a. The mean selling price (in $ thousands) of the homes was computed earlier to be $357.0, with a standard deviation of $160.7. Use the normal distribution to estimate the percentage of homes selling for more than $500.000. Compare this to the actual results. Is price normally distributed? Try another test. If price is normally distributed, how many homes should have a price greater than the mean? Compare this to the actual number of homes. Construct a frequency distribution of price. What do you observe?
   b. The mean days on the market is 30 with a standard deviation of 10 days. Use the normal distribution to estimate the number of homes on the market more than 24 days. Compare this to the actual results. Try another test. If days on the market is normally distributed, how many homes should be on the market more than the mean number of days? Compare this to the actual number of homes. Does the normal distribution yield a good approximation of the actual results? Create a frequency distribution of days on the market. What do you observe?

61. Refer to the data set that reports information on the 30 Major League Baseball teams for 2021 the season.
   a. For the variable salary, compute the mean, median, range, standard deviation, and coefficient of skewness. Also, make a box plot for the variable, salary. Does it seem reasonable that salary is normally distributed? Explain.
   b. Compute a new variable, stadium age, by subtracting the year the stadium was built from 2022. For the variable stadium age, compute the mean, median, range, standard deviation, and coefficient of skewness. Also, make a box plot for the variable, stadium age. Does it seem reasonable that stadium age is normally distributed? Explain.

62. Refer to the Lincolnville School District bus data.
   a. Refer to the maintenance cost variable. The mean maintenance cost for last year is $4,552 with a standard deviation of $2,332. Estimate the number of buses with a maintenance cost of more than $6,000. Compare that with the actual number. Create a frequency distribution of maintenance cost. Is the distribution normally distributed?
   b. Refer to the variable on the number of miles driven since the last maintenance. The mean is 11,121 and the standard deviation is 617 miles. Estimate the number of buses traveling more than 11,500 miles since the last maintenance. Compare that number with the actual value. Create a frequency distribution of miles since maintenance cost. Is the distribution normally distributed?

A REVIEW OF CHAPTERS 5–7

The chapters in this section consider methods of dealing with uncertainty. In Chapter 5, we describe the concept of probability. A *probability* is a value between 0 and 1 that expresses the likelihood a particular event will occur. We also looked at methods to calculate probabilities using rules of addition and multiplication; presented principles of counting, including permutations and combinations; and described situations for using Bayes' theorem.

Chapter 6 describes *discrete* probability distributions. Discrete probability distributions list all possible outcomes of an experiment and the probability associated with each outcome. We describe three discrete probability distributions: the *binomial distribution,* the *hypergeometric distribution,* and the *Poisson distribution.* The requirements for the binomial distribution are there are only two possible outcomes for each trial, there is a constant probability of success, there are a fixed number of trials, and the trials are independent. The binomial distribution lists the probabilities for the number of successes in a fixed number of trials. The hypergeometric distribution is similar to the binomial, but the probability of success is not constant, so the trials are not independent. The Poisson distribution is characterized by a small probability of success in a large number of trials. It has the following characteristics: the random variable is the number of times some event occurs in a fixed interval, the probability of a success is proportional to the size of the interval, and the intervals are independent and do not overlap.

Chapter 7 describes three continuous probability distributions: the *uniform distribution,* the *normal distribution,* and the *exponential distribution.* The uniform probability distribution is rectangular in shape and is defined by minimum and maximum values. The mean and the median of a uniform probability distribution are equal, and it does not have a mode.

A normal probability distribution is the most widely used and widely reported distribution. Its major characteristics are that it is bell shaped and symmetrical, completely described by its mean and standard deviation, and asymptotic—that is, it falls smoothly in each direction from its peak but never touches the horizontal axis. There is a family of normal probability distributions, each with its own mean and standard deviation. There are an unlimited number of normal probability distributions.

To find the probabilities for any normal probability distribution, we convert a normal distribution to a *standard normal probability distribution* by computing z values. A z value is the distance between x and the mean in units of the standard deviation. The standard normal probability distribution has a mean of 0 and a standard deviation of 1. It is useful because the probability for any event from a normal probability distribution can be computed using standard normal probability tables (see Appendix B.3).

The exponential probability distribution describes the time between events in a sequence. These events occur independently at a constant rate per unit of time or length. The exponential probability distribution is positively skewed, with λ as the "rate" parameter. The mean and standard deviation are equal and are the reciprocal of λ.

PROBLEMS

1. Proactine, a new medicine for acne, is claimed by the manufacturer to be 80% effective. It is applied to the affected area of a sample of 15 people. What is the probability that:
   a. all 15 will show significant improvement?
   b. fewer than 9 of 15 will show significant improvement?
   c. 12 or more people will show significant improvement?

2. Customers at the Bank of Commerce of Idaho Falls, Idaho, default at a rate of .005 on small home-improvement loans. The bank has approved 400 small home-improvement loans. Assuming the Poisson probability distribution applies to this problem:
   a. what is the probability that no homeowners out of the 400 will default?
   b. how many of the 400 are expected not to default?
   c. what is the probability that three or more homeowners will default on their small home-improvement loans?

3. A study of the attendance at the University of Alabama's basketball games revealed that the distribution of attendance is normally distributed with a mean of 10,000 and a standard deviation of 2,000.
   a. What is the probability a particular game has an attendance of 13,500 or more?
   b. What percent of the games have an attendance between 8,000 and 11,500?
   c. Ten percent of the games have an attendance of how many or less?

4. FILE Daniel-James Insurance Company will insure an offshore ExxonMobil oil production platform against weather losses for 1 year. The president of Daniel-James estimates the following losses for that platform (in millions of dollars) with the accompanying probabilities:

Amount of Loss ($ millions)	Probability of Loss
0	.98
40	.016
300	.004

   a. What is the expected amount Daniel-James will have to pay to ExxonMobil in claims?
   b. What is the likelihood that Daniel-James will actually lose less than the expected amount?
   c. Given that Daniel-James suffers a loss, what is the likelihood that it is for $300 million?
   d. Daniel-James has set the annual premium at $2.0 million. Does that seem like a fair premium? Will it cover its risk?

5. FILE The distribution of the number of school-age children per family in the Sunset Park neighborhood of Brooklyn, New York, is:

Number of children	0	1	2	3	4
Percent of families	40	30	15	10	5

   a. Determine the mean and standard deviation of the number of school-age children per family in Sunset Park.
   b. A new school is planned in Sunset Park. An estimate of the number of school-age children is needed. There are 500 family units. How many children would you estimate?
   c. Some additional information is needed about only the families having children. Convert the preceding distribution to one for families with children. What is the mean number of children among families that have children?

6. The following table shows a breakdown of the 117th U.S. Congress by party affiliation. (There are two independent senators included in the count of Democratic senators. There are two vacant House seats.)

	Party				
	Dem	Reb	Ind	Vacant	Total
House	221	213	0	1	435
Senate	50	48	2	0	100
Total	271	261	2	1	535

   a. A member of Congress is selected at random. What is the probability of selecting a Republican?

b. Given that the person selected is a member of the House of Representatives, what is the probability this person is a Republican?

c. What is the probability of selecting a member of the House of Representatives or a Democrat?

CASES

A. Century National Bank

Refer to the Century National Bank data. Is it reasonable that the distribution of checking account balances approximates a normal probability distribution? Determine the mean and the standard deviation for the sample of 60 customers. Compare the actual distribution with the theoretical distribution. Cite some specific examples and comment on your findings.

Divide the account balances into three groups, of about 20 each, with the smallest third of the balances in the first group, the middle third in the second group, and those with the largest balances in the third group. Next, develop a table that shows the number in each of the categories of the account balances by branch. Does it appear that account balances are related to the branch? Cite some examples and comment on your findings.

B. Elections Auditor

An item such as an increase in taxes, recall of elected officials, or an expansion of public services can be placed on the ballot if a required number of valid signatures are collected on the petition. Unfortunately, many people will sign the petition even though they are not registered to vote in that particular district, or they will sign the petition more than once.

Dylan Kelly, the elections auditor in Venango County, must certify the validity of these signatures after the petition is officially presented. Not surprisingly, the staff is overloaded, so Dylan is considering using statistical methods to validate the pages of 200 signatures, instead of validating each individual signature. At a recent professional meeting, Dylan found that, in some communities in the state, election officials were checking only five signatures on each page and rejecting the entire page if two or more signatures were invalid. Some people are concerned that five may not be enough to make a good decision. They suggest that you should check 10 signatures and reject the page if three or more are invalid.

To investigate these methods, Dylan asks the staff to pull the results from the last election and sample 30 pages. It happens that the staff selected 14 pages from the Avondale district, nine pages from the Midway district, and seven pages from the Kingston district. Each page had 200 signatures, and the data provided show the number of invalid signatures on each.

Use the data to evaluate Dylan's two proposals. Calculate the probability of rejecting a page under each of the approaches. Would you get about the same results by examining every single signature? Offer a plan of your own, and discuss how it might be better or worse than the two plans proposed by Dylan.

Avondale	Midway	Kingston
9	19	38
14	22	39
11	23	41
8	14	39
14	22	41
6	17	39
10	15	39
13	20	
8	18	
8		
9		
12		
7		
13		

C. Kai Applies Data Analytics

Kai Denton is the manager for a small telemarketing firm and is evaluating the sales rate of experienced workers in order to set minimum standards for new hires. During the past few weeks, Kai has recorded the number of successful calls per hour for the staff. These data appear next along with some summary statistics he worked out with a statistical software package. Kai has been a student at the local community college and has heard of many different kinds of probability distributions (binomial, normal, hypergeometric, Poisson, etc.). Could you give Kai some advice on which distribution to use to fit these data as well as possible and how to decide when a probationary employee should be accepted as having reached full production status? This is important because it means a pay raise for the employee, and there have been some probationary employees in the past who have quit because of discouragement that they would never meet the standard.

Successful sales calls per hour during the week of August 14:

4	2	3	1	4	5	5	2	3	2	2	4	5	2	5	3	3	0
1	3	2	8	4	5	2	2	4	1	5	5	4	5	1	2	4	

Descriptive statistics:

N	MEAN	MEDIAN	STANDARD DEVIATION
35	3.229	3.000	1.682
MIN	MAX	1ST QUARTILE	3RD QUARTILE
0.0	8.0	2.0	5.0

Analyze the distribution of sales calls. Which distribution do you think Kai should use for his analysis? Support your recommendation with your analysis. What standard should be used to determine if an employee has reached "full production" status? Explain your recommendation.

D. CNP Bank Card

Before banks issue a credit card, they usually rate or score the customer in terms of the projected probability of being a profitable customer. A typical scoring table appears here:

Age	Under 25 (12 pts.)	25–29 (5 pts.)	30–34 (0 pts.)	35+ (18 pts.)	
Time at same address	<1 yr. (9 pts.)	1–2 yrs. (0 pts.)	3–4 yrs. (13 pts.)	5+ yrs. (20 pts.)	
Auto age	None (18 pts.)	0–1yr. (12 pts.)	2–4 yrs. (13 pts.)	5+ yrs. (3 pts.)	
Monthly car payment	None (15 pts.)	$1–$99 (6 pts.)	$100–$299 (4 pts.)	$300+ (0 pts.)	
Housing cost	$1–$199 (0 pts.)	$200–$399 (10 pts.)	Owns (12 pts.)	Lives with relatives (24 pts.)	
Checking/ savings accounts	Both (15 pts.)	Checking only (3 pts.)	Savings only (2 pts.)	Neither (0 pts.)	

The score is the sum of the points on the six items. For example, Tracy Wong is under 25 years old (12 pts.), has lived at the same address for 2 years (0 pts.), owns a 4-year-old car (13 pts.), with car payments of $75 (6 pts.), housing cost of $450 (10 pts.), and a checking account (3 pts.). She would score 44.

A second chart is then used to convert scores into the probability of being a profitable customer. A sample chart of this type follows:

Score	30	40	50	60	70	80	90
Probability	.70	.78	.85	.90	.94	.95	.96

Tracy's score of 44 would translate into a probability of being profitable of approximately .81. In other words, 81% of customers like Tracy will make money for the bank card operations.

Here are the interview results for three potential customers.

Name	David Born	Edward Brendan	Ann McLaughlin
Age	42	23	33
Time at same address	9	2	5
Auto age	2	3	7
Monthly car payment	$140	$99	$175
Housing cost	$450	$650	Owns clear
Checking/savings accounts	Both	Checking only	Neither

1. Score each of these customers and estimate their probability of being profitable.
2. What is the probability that all three are profitable?
3. What is the probability that none of them are profitable?
4. Find the entire probability distribution for the number of profitable customers among this group of three.
5. Write a brief summary of your findings.

PRACTICE TEST

Part 1—Objective

1. Under what conditions will a probability be greater than 1 or 100%?
2. An _____ is the observation of some activity or the act of taking some type of measurement.
3. An _____ is the collection of one or more outcomes to an experiment.
4. A _____ probability is the likelihood that two or more events will happen at the same time.
5. In a (5a) _____, the order in which the events are counted is important, but in a (5b) _____, it is not important.
6. In a discrete probability distribution, the sum of the possible outcomes is equal to _____.
7. Which of the following is NOT a requirement of the binomial distribution? (constant probability of success, three or more outcomes, the result of counts)
8. How many normal distributions are there? (1, 10, 30, 1,000, or infinite—pick one)
9. How many standard normal distributions are there? (1, 10, 30, 1,000, or infinite—pick one)
10. What is the probability of finding a z value between 0 and −0.76?
11. What is the probability of finding a z value greater than 1.67?
12. Two events are _____ if the occurrence of one event does not affect the occurrence of another event.
13. Two events are _____ if by virtue of one event happening the other cannot happen.

1. _____
2. _____
3. _____
4. _____
5. a. _____
5. b. _____
6. _____
7. _____
8. _____
9. _____
10. _____
11. _____
12. _____
13. _____

14. Which of the following is not true regarding the normal probability distribution? (asymptotic, family of distributions, only two outcomes, 50% of the observations greater than the mean)

14. _____

15. Which of the following statements best describes the shape of a normal probability distribution? (bell shaped, uniform, V shaped, no constant shape)

15. _____

Part 2—Problems

1. Fred Friendly, CPA, has 20 tax returns to prepare before the April 15th deadline. It is late at night so he decides to do two more before going home. In his stack of accounts, 12 are personal, five are businesses, and three are for charitable organizations. If he selects the two returns at random, what is the probability:
  a. both are businesses?
  b. at least one is a business?

2. The IRS reports that 15% of returns where the adjusted gross income is more than $1,000,000 will be subject to a computer audit. For the year 2022, Fred Friendly, CPA, completed 16 returns where the adjusted gross income was more than $1,000,000.
  a. What is the probability exactly one of these returns will be audited?
  b. What is the probability at least one will be audited?

3. Fred works in a tax office with five other CPAs. There are five parking spots beside the office. In how many different ways can the cars belonging to the CPAs be arranged in the five spots? Assume they all drive to work.

4. Fred decided to study the number of exemptions claimed on personal tax returns he prepared for 2022. The data are summarized in the following table.

Exemptions	Percent
1	20
2	50
3	20
4	10

  a. What is the mean number of exemptions per return?
  b. What is the variance of the number of exemptions per return?

5. In a 2022 report, the Internal Revenue Service indicated the mean refund was $2,750 with a standard deviation of $850. Assume the distribution of the refunds follows the normal distribution.
  a. What percent of the refunds was between $1,600 and $2,000?
  b. What percent of the refunds was between $900 and $3,000?
  c. Based on this information, what percent of the refunds was less than $0 (that is, the taxpayer owed the IRS)?

6. For the year 2022, Fred Friendly completed a total of 80 returns. He developed the following table summarizing the relationship between number of dependents and whether or not the client received a refund.

Refund	Dependents 1	2	3 or more	Total
Yes	20	20	10	50
No	10	20	0	30
Total	30	40	10	80

  a. What is the name given to this table?
  b. What is the probability of selecting a client who received a refund?
  c. What is the probability of selecting a client who received a refund or had one dependent?
  d. Given that the client received a refund, what is the probability the client had one dependent?
  e. What is the probability of selecting a client who did *not* receive a refund and had one dependent?

7. The IRS offers taxpayers the choice of allowing the IRS to compute the amount of their tax refund. During the busy filing season, the number of returns received at the Springfield Service Center that request this service follows a Poisson distribution with a mean of three per day. What is the probability that on a particular day:
  a. there are no requests?
  b. exactly three requests appear?
  c. five or more requests take place?
  d. there are no requests on two consecutive days?

Sampling, Sampling Methods, and the Central Limit Theorem

August_0802/Shutterstock

▲ **THE NIKE** annual report says that the average American buys 6.5 pairs of sports shoes per year. Suppose a sample of 81 customers is surveyed and the population standard deviation of sports shoes purchased per year is 2.1. What is the standard error of the mean in this experiment? (See Exercise 49 and **LO8-4**.)

LEARNING OBJECTIVES

When you have completed this chapter, you will be able to:

LO8-1   Explain why populations are sampled and describe four methods to sample a population.

LO8-2   Define sampling error.

LO8-3   Explain the sampling distribution of the sample mean.

LO8-4   Explain how the central limit theorem applies to the sampling distribution of the sample mean.

LO8-5   Apply the sampling distribution of the sample mean to compute probabilities.

LO8-6   Apply the central limit theorem to the sampling distribution of the sample proportion.

Introduction

Chapters 2 through 4 emphasize techniques to describe data. To illustrate these techniques, we organize the profits for the sale of 180 vehicles by the four dealers included in the Applewood Auto Group into a frequency distribution and compute measures of location and dispersion. Such measures as the mean and the standard deviation describe the typical profit and the spread in the profits. In these chapters, the emphasis is on describing the distribution of the data. That is, we describe something that has already happened.

In Chapter 5, we begin to lay the foundation for statistical inference with the study of probability. Recall that in statistical inference our goal is to determine something about a *population* based only on the *sample*. The population is the entire group of individuals or objects under consideration, and the sample is a part or subset of that population. Chapter 6 extends the probability concepts by describing three discrete probability distributions: the binomial, hypergeometric, and the Poisson. Chapter 7 describes three continuous probability distributions: the uniform, normal, and exponential distributions. Probability distributions encompass all possible outcomes of an experiment and the probability associated with each outcome. We use probability distributions to evaluate the likelihood something occurs in the future.

This chapter begins our study of sampling. Sampling is a process of selecting items from a population so we can use this information to make judgments or inferences about the population. We begin this chapter by discussing methods of selecting a sample from a population. Next, we construct distributions of the sample mean and sample proportion to understand how these estimates tend to cluster around their respective population parameters. Finally, we show that for any population the shape of this sampling distribution tends to follow the normal probability distribution.

LO8-1

Explain why populations are sampled and describe four methods to sample a population.

Research and Sampling

Research is the process of studying a problem, question, or hypothesis. Typically, data are collected on relevant variables by sampling from a clearly defined population. Then statistical and analytical techniques are applied to summarize and analyze the data. The analytical results are the basis for making inferences and stating conclusions about the population. The primary goal of sampling is that the sample is unbiased and hence a good representation of the population. Using unbiased sample information, valid inferences and conclusions about the research hypothesis can be made.

Sampling is also a matter of professional ethics. In its Ethical Guidelines for Statistical Practice, the American Statistical Association includes the following: "The ethical statistician applies statistical sampling and analysis procedures scientifically, without predetermining the outcome" (**www.amstat.org/ASA/Your-Career/Ethical -Guidelines-for-Statistical-Practice.aspx**). Selecting a sample that intentionally includes individuals or objects that support someone's belief or motivation is unethical, especially if the study does not communicate the intention. Another example where bias can be found is anecdotal, case study research. In this type of research, the sample is limited to a small number of hand-picked individuals or objects. For example, some studies have focused on the most successful businesses. A purpose is to find common practices among the businesses that result in their success. The studies then suggest that these practices can help other businesses to be successful. The small sample clearly does not represent the population of businesses. Consequently, generalizing these conclusions has proven unreliable.

Understanding if research conclusions are biased should begin with determining the purpose of the research study, defining the population, and knowing how a sample was selected from the population. For example, a researcher wished to study cell phone usage among college students. For convenience, the researcher selected 30 students who were eating lunch in the residence hall cafeteria. Appropriately, this sampling approach is called *convenience sampling.* The researcher then surveyed them on several variables, such as last month's bill, how long they owned their phone, and phone brand. Does the sample of students represent the population of college students? Probably not; to explain, the 30 sampled students are likely to be freshmen and sophomores. Older students and part-time students who work during the day are unlikely to be eating lunch in the residence hall cafeteria and are not represented in the sample. So, inferences and conclusions from the survey should be limited to the population represented by the characteristics of the sample, that is, college students who eat lunch in the residence hall cafeteria.

Given an ethical and honest approach to sampling, there are a variety of practical reasons to sample from a population primarily related to the time and cost needed to collect the data. Here are some of the practical reasons.

1. **To contact the whole population would be time consuming.** A candidate for a national office may wish to determine the chances for election. A sample poll using the regular staff and field interviews of a professional polling firm would take only 1 or 2 days. Using the same staff and interviewers and working 7 days a week, it would take nearly 200 years to contact all the voting population! Even if a large staff of interviewers could be assembled, the benefit of contacting all of the voters would probably not be worth the time.

2. **The cost of studying all the items in a population may be prohibitive.** Public opinion polls and consumer testing organizations, such as Harris Interactive Inc., CBS News Polls, and Zogby Analytics, usually contact fewer than 2,000 of the nearly 128.45 million families in the United States. One consumer panel–type organization charges $40,000 to mail samples and tabulate responses to test a product (such as breakfast cereal, cat food, or perfume). The same product test using all 128.45 million families would be too expensive to be worthwhile.

3. **The physical impossibility of checking all items in the population.** Some populations are infinite. It would be impossible to check all the water in Lake Erie for bacterial levels, so we select samples at various locations. The populations of fish, birds, snakes, deer, and the like are large and are constantly moving, being born, and dying. Instead of even attempting to count all the ducks in Canada or all the fish in Lake Pontchartrain, we make estimates using various techniques—such as counting all the ducks on a pond selected at random, tracking fish catches, or netting fish at predetermined places in a lake.

4. **The destructive nature of some tests.** If the wine tasters at the Sutter Home Winery in California drank all the wine to evaluate the vintage, they would consume the entire crop, and none would be available for sale. In the area of industrial production, steel plates, wires, and similar products must have a certain minimum tensile strength. To ensure that the product meets the minimum standard, the Quality Assurance Department selects a sample from the current production. Each piece is stretched until it breaks and the breaking point (usually measured in pounds per square inch) recorded. Obviously, if all the wire or all the plates were tested for tensile strength, none would be available for sale or use. For the same reason, only a few seeds are tested for germination by Burpee Seeds Inc. prior to the planting season.

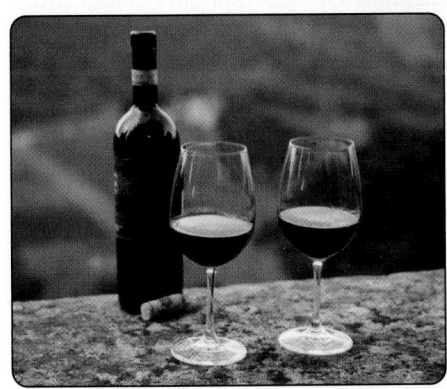

David Epperson/Getty Images

Sampling Methods

There are different sampling methods that can be used to select an unbiased sample.

Simple Random Sampling

The most widely used sampling method is a **simple random sampling.**

> **SIMPLE RANDOM SAMPLE** A sample selected so that each item or person in the population has the same probability or chance of being included.

To illustrate the selection process for a simple random sample, suppose the population of interest is the 780 Major League Baseball players on the active rosters of the 30 teams at the end of the last season. The president of the players' union wishes to form a committee of 10 players to study the issue of concussions. One way of ensuring that every player in the population has the same chance of being chosen to serve on the Concussion Committee is to write each name of the 780 players on a slip of paper and place all the slips of paper in a box. After the slips of paper have been thoroughly mixed, the first selection is made by drawing a slip of paper from the box identifying the first player. The slip of paper is not returned to the box. This process is repeated nine more times to form the committee. (Note that the probability of each selection does increase slightly because the slip is not replaced. However, the differences are very small because the sample of 10 is relatively small compared to the population of 780. The probability of each selection in a sample of 10 is about 0.0013, rounded to four decimal places.)

Of course, the process of writing all the players' names on a slip of paper is very time consuming. A more convenient method of selecting a random sample is to use a **table of random numbers** such as the one in Appendix B.4. In this case the union president would prepare a list of all 780 players and number each of the players from 1 to 780. Using a table of random numbers, we would randomly pick a starting place in the table, and then select 10 three-digit numbers between 001 and 780. These numbers would correspond with the 10 players in the list that will be asked to participate on the committee. As the name *simple random sampling* implies, the probability of selecting any number between 001 and 780 is the same. Thus, the probability of selecting the player assigned the number 131 is the same as the probability of selecting player 722 or player 382. Using random numbers to select players for the committee removes any bias from the selection process.

The way to select random numbers using a portion of a random number table is illustrated here. First, we choose a starting point in the table. One way of selecting the starting point is to close your eyes and point at a number in the table. Any starting point will do. Another way is to randomly pick a column and row. Suppose the time is 3:04. Using the hour, three o'clock, pick the third column and then, using the minutes, four, move down to the fourth row of numbers. The number is 03759. Because there are only 780 players, we will use the first three digits of a five-digit random number. Thus, 037 is the number of the first player to be a member of the sample. To continue selecting players, we could move in any direction. Suppose we move right. The first three digits of the number to the right of 03759 are 447. Player number 447 is the second player selected to be on the committee. The next three-digit number to the right is 961. You skip 961 as well as the next number 784 because there are only 780 players. The third player selected is number 189. We continue this process until we have 10 players.

50525	57454	28455	68226	34656	38884	39018
72507	53380	53827	42486	54465	71819	91199
34986	74297	00144	38676	89967	98869	39744
68851	27305	03759	44723	96108	78489	18910
06738	62879	03910	17350	49169	03850	18910
11448	10734	05837	24397	10420	16712	94496

Starting point   Second player   Third player

Tutorial #41 in Connect

Instead of using a random number table, statistical software often includes random number generators to compute a list of random numbers. The tutorial noted in the margin shows how to compute random numbers in Excel and is used in the following Example/Solution.

▶ **EXAMPLE**

Jane and Joe Miley operate the Foxtrot Inn, a bed and breakfast in Tryon, North Carolina. There are eight rooms available for rent at this B&B. For each day of June 2022, the number of rooms rented is listed. Use Excel to select a sample of five nights during the month of June.

June	Rentals	June	Rentals	June	Rentals
1	0	11	3	21	3
2	2	12	4	22	2
3	3	13	4	23	3
4	2	14	4	24	6
5	3	15	7	25	0
6	4	16	0	26	4
7	2	17	5	27	1
8	3	18	3	28	1
9	4	19	6	29	3
10	7	20	2	30	3

SOLUTION

Excel will compute five random numbers between 1 and 30 corresponding to the days in June. Sampling is done *with* replacement, so it is possible that a random number may appear more than once. Note that the probability of selecting any day is exactly the same, 1/30, or 0.0333. The probability that a particular day would be selected twice is (1/30)(1/30) or .0011. The random numbers are 20, 3, 4, 26, and 14. So, the days selected are June 3, 4, 14, 20, and 26. The corresponding number of day rentals are 3, 2, 4, 2, and 4. Based on this sample, the mean number of rentals per day in June is 3.

	A	B	C	D	E
1	Day of June	Rentals		Random Number Between 1 and 30	Rentals for Each Randomly Selected Day
2	1	0		20	2
3	2	2		3	3
4	3	3		4	2
5	4	2		26	4
6	5	3		14	4
7	6	4			
8	7	2			
9	8	3			
10	9	4			
11	10	7			
12	11	3			
13	12	4			
14	13	4			
15	14	4			
16	15	7			

Source: Microsoft Excel

SELF-REVIEW 8–1

The following roster lists the students enrolled in an introductory course in business statistics. Six students will be randomly selected and asked questions about course content and method of instruction.

(a) The numbers 00 through 45 are handwritten on slips of paper and placed in a bowl. The six numbers selected are 22, 10, 28, 6, 37, and 18. Which students are in the sample?

(b) Now use the table of random numbers (Appendix B.4) or statistical software to select your own sample.

(c) What would you do if you encountered the number 59 in the table of random digits?

STAT 264 BUSINESS STATISTICS
9:00 AM - 9:50 AM MW; 118 CARLSON HALL; PROFESSOR LIND

NUMBER	NAME	CLASS RANK	NUMBER	NAME	CLASS RANK
00	ANDERSON, RAYMOND	SO	23	MEDLEY, CHERYL ANN	SO
01	ANGER, CHERYL RENEE	SO	24	MITCHELL, GREG R	FR
02	BALL, CLAIRE JEANETTE	FR	25	MOLTER, KRISTI MARIE	SO
03	BERRY, CHRISTOPHER G	FR	26	MULCAHY, STEPHEN ROBERT	SO
04	BOBAK, JAMES PATRICK	SO	27	NICHOLAS, ROBERT CHARLES	JR
05	BRIGHT, M. STARR	JR	28	NICKENS, VIRGINIA	SO
06	CHONTOS, PAUL JOSEPH	SO	29	PENNYWITT, SEAN PATRICK	SO
07	DETLEY, BRIAN HANS	JR	30	POTEAU, KRIS E	JR
08	DUDAS, VIOLA	SO	31	PRICE, MARY LYNETTE	SO
09	DULBS, RICHARD ZALFA	JR	32	RISTAS, JAMES	SR
10	EDINGER, SUSAN KEE	SR	33	SAGER, ANNE MARIE	SO
11	FINK, FRANK JAMES	SR	34	SMILLIE, HEATHER MICHELLE	SO
12	FRANCIS, JAMES P	JR	35	SNYDER, LEISHA KAY	SR
13	GAGHEN, PAMELA LYNN	JR	36	STAHL, MARIA TASHERY	SO
14	GOULD, ROBYN KAY	SO	37	ST. JOHN, AMY J	SO
15	GROSENBACHER, SCOTT ALAN	SO	38	STURDEVANT, RICHARD K	SO
16	HEETFIELD, DIANE MARIE	SO	39	SWETYE, LYNN MICHELE	SO
17	KABAT, JAMES DAVID	JR	40	WALASINSKI, MICHAEL	SO
18	KEMP, LISA ADRIANE	FR	41	WALKER, DIANE ELAINE	SO
19	KILLION, MICHELLE A	SO	42	WARNOCK, JENNIFER MARY	SO
20	KOPERSKI, MARY ELLEN	SO	43	WILLIAMS, WENDY A	SO
21	KOPP, BRIDGETTE ANN	SO	44	YAP, HOCK BAN	SO
22	LEHMANN, KRISTINA MARIE	JR	45	YODER, ARLAN JAY	JR

Systematic Random Sampling

Simple random sampling may not be practical in some research situations. For example, Stood's Grocery Market needs to sample its customers to study the length of time customers spend in the store. Simple random sampling is not an effective method. Practically, we cannot list the population of all customers, so assigning random numbers to customers is impossible. Instead, we can use **systematic random sampling** to select a representative sample. Using this method for Stood's Grocery Market, we decide to select 100 customers over 4 days, Monday through Thursday. We will select 25 customers a day and begin the sampling at different times each day: 8 a.m., 11 a.m., 4 p.m., and 7 p.m. We write the four times and four days on slips of paper and put them in two hats—one hat for the days and the other hat for the times. We select one slip from each hat. This ensures that the time of day is randomly assigned for each day. Suppose we selected 4 p.m. for the starting time on Monday. Next, we select a random number between 1 and 10; it is 6. Our selection process begins on Monday at 4 p.m. by selecting the sixth customer to enter the store. Then, we select every 10th (16th, 26th, 36th) customer until we reach the goal of 25 customers. By systematically selecting every 10th customer, the sampling plan eliminates any bias in selecting customers. For each of these sampled customers, we measure the length of time the customer spends in the store.

> **SYSTEMATIC RANDOM SAMPLE** A random starting point is selected, and then every kth member of the population is selected.

Simple random sampling is used in the selection of the days, the times, and the starting point. But the systematic procedure is used to select the actual customer.

Before using systematic random sampling, we should carefully observe the physical order of the population. When the physical order is related to the population characteristic, then systematic random sampling should not be used because the sample could be biased. For example, if we wanted to audit the invoices in a file drawer that were ordered in increasing dollar amounts, systematic random sampling would not guarantee an unbiased random sample. Other sampling methods should be used.

Stratified Random Sampling

When a population can be clearly divided into groups based on some characteristic, we may use **stratified random sampling.** It guarantees each group is represented in the sample. The groups are called **strata.** For example, college students can be grouped as full time or part time, or as freshmen, sophomores, juniors, or seniors. Usually the strata are formed based on members' shared attributes or characteristics. A random sample from each stratum is taken in a number proportional to the stratum's size when compared to the population. Once the strata are defined, we apply simple random sampling within each group or stratum to collect the sample.

> **STRATIFIED RANDOM SAMPLE** A population is divided into subgroups, called strata, and a sample is randomly selected from each stratum.

For instance, we might study the advertising expenditures for the 352 largest companies in the United States. The objective of the study is to determine whether firms with high returns on equity (a measure of profitability) spend more on advertising than firms with low returns on equity. To make sure the sample is a fair representation of the 352 companies, the companies are grouped on percent return on equity. Table 8–1 shows the strata and the relative frequencies. If simple random sampling is used, observe that firms in the third and fourth strata have a high chance of selection

TABLE 8–1 Number Selected for a Stratified Random Sample

Stratum	Profitability (return on equity)	Number of Firms	Relative Frequency	Number Sampled
1	30% and over	8	0.02	1*
2	20 up to 30%	35	0.10	5*
3	10 up to 20%	189	0.54	27
4	0 up to 10%	115	0.33	16
5	Deficit	5	0.01	1
Total		352	1.00	50

*0.02 of 50 = 1, 0.10 of 50 = 5, etc.

(probability of .87) while firms in the other strata have a small chance of selection (probability of .13). We might not select any firms in stratum 1 or 5 *simply by chance.* However, stratified random sampling will guarantee that at least one firm in each of strata 1 and 5 is represented in the sample. Let's say that 50 firms are selected for intensive study. Then based on probability, one firm, or (.02)(50), should be randomly selected from stratum 1. We would randomly select five, or (.10)(50), firms from stratum 2. In this case, the number of firms sampled from each stratum is proportional to the stratum's relative frequency in the population. Stratified sampling has the advantage, in some cases, of more accurately reflecting the characteristics of the population than does simple random or systematic random sampling.

Cluster Sampling

Another common type of sampling is **cluster sampling.** It is often employed to reduce the cost of sampling a population scattered over a large geographic area.

> **CLUSTER SAMPLING** A population is divided into clusters using naturally occurring geographic or other boundaries. Then, clusters are randomly selected and a sample is collected by randomly selecting from each cluster.

Suppose you want to determine the views of residents in the greater Chicago, Illinois, metropolitan area about state and federal environmental protection policies. Selecting a random sample of residents in this region and personally contacting each one would be time consuming and very expensive. Instead, you could employ cluster sampling by subdividing the region into small units, perhaps by counties. These are often called *primary units.*

There are 12 counties in the greater Chicago metropolitan area. Suppose you randomly select three counties. The three chosen are LaPorte, Cook, and Kenosha (see Chart 8–1). Next, you select a random sample of the residents in each of these counties and interview them. This is also referred to as sampling through an *intermediate unit.* In this case, the intermediate unit is the county. (Note that this is a combination of cluster sampling and simple random sampling.)

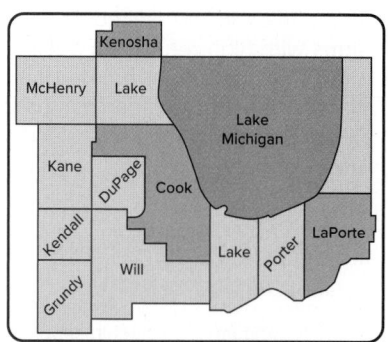

CHART 8–1 The Counties of the Greater Chicago, Illinois, Metropolitan Area

The discussion of sampling methods in the preceding sections did not include all the sampling methods available to a researcher. Should you become involved in a major research project in marketing, finance, accounting, or other areas, you would need to consult with experts and refer to books devoted solely to sampling theory and sample design.

SELF-REVIEW 8-2

Refer to Self-Review 8–1 and the class roster on page 254. Suppose a systematic random sample will select every ninth student enrolled in the class. Initially, the fourth student on the list was selected at random. That student is numbered 03. Remembering that the numbers start with 00, which students will be chosen to be members of the sample?

EXERCISES

1. **FILE** The following is a list of 24 Marco's Pizza stores in Lucas County. The stores are identified by numbering them 00 through 23. Also noted is whether the store is corporate owned (C) or manager owned (M). A sample of four locations is to be selected and inspected for customer convenience, safety, cleanliness, and other features.

ID No.	Address	Type	ID No.	Address	Type
00	2607 Starr Av	C	12	2040 Ottawa River Rd	C
01	309 W Alexis Rd	C	13	2116 N Reynolds Rd	C
02	2652 W Central Av	C	14	3678 Rugby Dr	C
03	630 Dixie Hwy	M	15	1419 South Av	C
04	3510 Dorr St	C	16	1234 W Sylvania Av	C
05	5055 Glendale Av	C	17	4624 Woodville Rd	M
06	3382 Lagrange St	M	18	5155 S Main	M
07	2525 W Laskey Rd	C	19	106 E Airport Hwy	C
08	303 Louisiana Av	C	20	6725 W Central	M
09	149 Main St	C	21	4252 Monroe	C
10	835 S McCord Rd	M	22	2036 Woodville Rd	C
11	3501 Monroe St	M	23	1316 Michigan Av	M

   a. The random numbers selected are 08, 18, 11, 54, 02, 41, and 54. Which stores are selected?

   b. Using a random number table (Appendix B.4) or statistical software, select your own sample of locations.

   c. Using systematic random sampling, every seventh location is selected starting with the third store in the list. Which locations will be included in the sample?

   d. Using stratified random sampling, select three locations. Two should be corporate owned and one should be manager owned.

2. **FILE** The following is a list of 29 hospitals in the Cincinnati, Ohio, and Northern Kentucky region. Each hospital is assigned a number, 00 through 28. The hospitals are classified by type, either a general medical/surgical hospital (M/S) or a specialty hospital (S). We are interested in estimating the average number of full- and part-time nurses employed in the area hospitals.

ID Number	Name	Address	Type	ID Number	Name	Address	Type
00	Bethesda North	10500 Montgomery Rd. Cincinnati, Ohio 45242	M/S	04	Mercy Hospital–Hamilton	100 Riverfront Plaza Hamilton, Ohio 45011	M/S
01	Ft. Hamilton–Hughes	630 Eaton Avenue Hamilton, Ohio 45013	M/S	05	Middletown Regional	105 McKnight Drive Middletown, Ohio 45044	M/S
02	Jewish Hospital–Kenwood	4700 East Galbraith Rd. Cincinnati, Ohio 45236	M/S	06	Clermont Mercy Hospital	3000 Hospital Drive Batavia, Ohio 45103	M/S
03	Mercy Hospital–Fairfield	3000 Mack Road Fairfield, Ohio 45014	M/S	07	Mercy Hospital–Anderson	7500 State Road Cincinnati, Ohio 45255	M/S

ID Number	Name	Address	Type	ID Number	Name	Address	Type
08	Bethesda Oak Hospital	619 Oak Street Cincinnati, Ohio 45206	M/S	19	St. Luke's Hospital West	7380 Turfway Drive Florence, Kentucky 41075	M/S
09	Children's Hospital Medical Center	3333 Burnet Avenue Cincinnati, Ohio 45229	M/S	20	St. Luke's Hospital East	85 North Grand Avenue Ft. Thomas, Kentucky 41042	M/S
10	Christ Hospital	2139 Auburn Avenue Cincinnati, Ohio 45219	M/S	21	Care Unit Hospital	3156 Glenmore Avenue Cincinnati, Ohio 45211	S
11	Deaconess Hospital	311 Straight Street Cincinnati, Ohio 45219	M/S	22	Emerson Behavioral Science	2446 Kipling Avenue Cincinnati, Ohio 45239	S
12	Good Samaritan Hospital	375 Dixmyth Avenue Cincinnati, Ohio 45220	M/S	23	Pauline Warfield Lewis Center for Psychiatric Treat.	1101 Summit Road Cincinnati, Ohio 45237	S
13	Jewish Hospital	3200 Burnet Avenue Cincinnati, Ohio 45229	M/S	24	Children's Psychiatric No. Kentucky	502 Farrell Drive Covington, Kentucky 41011	S
14	University Hospital	234 Goodman Street Cincinnati, Ohio 45267	M/S	25	Drake Center Rehab—Long Term	151 W. Galbraith Road Cincinnati, Ohio 45216	S
15	Providence Hospital	2446 Kipling Avenue Cincinnati, Ohio 45239	M/S	26	No. Kentucky Rehab Hospital—Short Term	201 Medical Village Edgewood, Kentucky	S
16	St. Francis–St. George Hospital	3131 Queen City Avenue Cincinnati, Ohio 45238	M/S	27	Shriners Burns Institute	3229 Burnet Avenue Cincinnati, Ohio 45229	S
17	St. Elizabeth Medical Center, North Unit	401 E. 20th Street Covington, Kentucky 41014	M/S	28	VA Medical Center	3200 Vine Street Cincinnati, Ohio 45220	S
18	St. Elizabeth Medical Center, South Unit	One Medical Village Edgewood, Kentucky 41017	M/S				

    a. A sample of five hospitals is to be randomly selected. The random numbers are 09, 16, 00, 49, 54, 12, and 04. Which hospitals are included in the sample?

    b. Using a random number table (Appendix B.4) or statistical software, develop your own sample of five hospitals.

    c. Using systematic random sampling, every fifth location is selected starting with the second hospital in the list. Which hospitals will be included in the sample?

    d. Using stratified random sampling, select five hospitals. Four should be medical and surgical hospitals and one should be a specialty hospital. Select an appropriate sample.

3. **FILE** Listed are the 35 members of the Metro Toledo Automobile Dealers Association. We would like to estimate the mean revenue from dealer service departments. The members are identified by numbering them 00 through 34.

ID Number	Dealer	ID Number	Dealer	ID Number	Dealer
00	Dave White Acura	12	Spurgeon Chevrolet Motor	24	Lexus of Toledo
01	Autofair Nissan	13	Dunn Chevrolet	25	Mathews Ford Oregon, Inc.
02	Autofair Toyota-Suzuki	14	Don Scott Chevrolet	26	Northtown Chevrolet
03	George Ball's Buick GMC	15	Dave White Chevrolet Co.	27	Quality Ford Sales, Inc.
04	York Automotive Group	16	Dick Wilson Infiniti	28	Rouen Chrysler Jeep Eagle
05	Bob Schmidt Chevrolet	17	Doyle Buick	29	Mercedes of Toledo
06	Bowling Green Lincoln	18	Franklin Park Lincoln	30	Ed Schmidt Jeep Eagle
07	Brondes Ford	19	Genoa Motors	31	Southside Lincoln Mercury
08	Brown Honda	20	Great Lakes Ford Nissan	32	Valiton Chrysler
09	Brown Mazda	21	Grogan Towne Chrysler	33	Vin Divers
10	Charlie's Dodge	22	Hatfield Motor Sales	34	Whitman Ford
11	Thayer Chevrolet/Toyota	23	Kistler Ford, Inc.		

    a. We want to select a random sample of five dealers. The random numbers are 05, 20, 59, 21, 31, 28, 49, 38, 66, 08, 29, and 02. Which dealers would be included in the sample?

b. Using a random number table (Appendix B.4) or statistical software, select your own sample of five dealers.

c. Using systematic random sampling, every seventh dealer is selected starting with the fourth dealer in the list. Which dealers are included in the sample?

4. **FILE** Listed are the 27 insurance agencies in the southern region of Texas. The agencies are numbered 00 through 26. We would like to estimate the mean number of years an agency has been in business.

ID Number	Agent	ID Number	Agent	ID Number	Agent
00	Richard Hernandez	08	Balmer Insurance Group Inc.	18	Insurance Analytics Group
01	Crossland & Co. Insurance Agency, Inc.	09	Cynthia Aguilar Insurance Agency Inc.	19	BIG Insurance Solutions
02	Victor F Nevarez	10	The Bernal Insurance Agency	20	Gonzalez Insurance & Financial
03	Hub International Texas Inc.	11	Ed Flores Insurance Agency, Inc.	21	Leal Insurance Services LLC
04	Usi Southwest Inc.	12	Main Street Independent Insurance	22	Reyes Insurance Agency
05	1st Trust Insurance Agency LLC	13	Grindell & Romero Insurance Inc.	23	Dakari Rose
06	Pinon & Associates Financial Corporation	14	All Seasons Insurance	24	H & H Risk Partners LLC
07	Commercial Insurance Brokers Inc.	15	Axcess Insurance LLC	25	Toubin Insurance Agency Inc.
		16	Financial LLC	26	Sogo Wealth & Risk Management LLC
		17	Ruben Saucedo Agency		

a. We want to select a random sample of four agencies. The random numbers are 02, 59, 51, 25, 14, 29, 77, 69, and 18. Which agencies would be included in the sample?

b. Using a random number table (Appendix B.4) or statistical software, select your own sample of four agencies.

c. Using systematic random sampling, every fifth agency is selected starting with the third agency in the list. Which agencies are included in the sample?

LO8-2
Define sampling error.

Sample Mean as a Random Variable

The result of sampling is a random selection of population objects or individuals. Data collected about the sampled objects are used to compute sample statistics, such as the mean and standard deviation. Because each sample is different, each sample will have a different mean and standard deviation. Therefore, sample statistics such as the sample mean and standard deviation are random variables that can be described with probability distributions. The following section develops the sampling distribution of the sample mean.

▶ **EXAMPLE**

Refer to the Example/Solution on page 253, where we studied the number of rooms rented at the Foxtrot Inn B&B in Tryon, North Carolina. The population is the number of rooms rented each of the 30 days in June 2022. Find the mean of the population. Select three random samples of 5 days. Calculate the mean rooms rented for each sample and compare it to the population mean. What is the sample mean in each case? Compare each to the population mean.

SOLUTION

In this case, the population is all days in June 2022. The random variable of interest is the number of rooms rented each day. To summarize the number of rooms rented, we compute the population mean number of rentals:

$$\mu = \frac{\Sigma x}{N} = \frac{0 + 2 + 3 + \cdots + 3}{30} = \frac{94}{30} = 3.13$$

If we needed a quick sample estimate of the population mean, we might randomly sample 5 days. The first random sample of 5 nights resulted in the following number of rooms rented: 4, 7, 4, 3, and 1. The mean of this sample is 3.80 rooms, which we designate as $\bar{x}_1$. The bar over the x reminds us that it is a sample mean and the subscript 1 indicates it is the mean of the first sample.

$$\bar{x}_1 = \frac{\Sigma x}{n} = \frac{4 + 7 + 4 + 3 + 1}{5} = \frac{19}{5} = 3.80$$

The sample mean of the first sample is different from the population mean: $(\bar{x}_1 - \mu) = 3.80 - 3.13 = 0.67$. This difference is called **sampling error.** Because the sample mean is an estimate of the population mean, the difference is expected.

> **SAMPLING ERROR** The difference between a sample statistic and its corresponding population parameter.

The second random sample of 5 days from the population of all 30 days in June shows the following number of rooms rented: 3, 3, 2, 3, and 6. The mean of this sample is 3.40.

$$\bar{x}_2 = \frac{\Sigma x}{n} = \frac{3 + 3 + 2 + 3 + 6}{5} = 3.40$$

The sampling error is $(\bar{x}_2 - \mu) = 3.40 - 3.13 = 0.27$. For the third sample, the mean is 1.80 and the sampling error is $(\bar{x}_3 - \mu) = 1.80 - 3.13 = -1.33$.

Each sample mean provides a different estimate of the population mean because it is based on a different random sample. Each estimate has a different sampling error. The sign of the sampling error is important because sample means can be either less than or greater than the population mean. The second sample provided the best estimate of the population mean; the third sample provided the worst estimate of the population mean.

June	Rentals	June	Rentals	June	Rentals			Sample 1	Sample 2	Sample 3
1	0	11	3	21	3			4	3	0
2	2	12	4	22	2			7	3	0
3	3	13	4	23	3			4	2	3
4	2	14	4	24	6			3	3	3
5	3	15	7	25	0			1	6	3
6	4	16	0	26	4		Total	19	17	9
7	2	17	5	27	1		Mean	3.80	3.40	1.80
8	3	18	3	28	1		Sampling Error	0.67	0.27	-1.33
9	4	19	6	29	3					
10	7	20	2	30	3					

Source: Microsoft Excel

This Example/Solution is only the beginning of understanding the sample mean as a random variable. To completely understand how the sample mean is distributed, the sample means from all possible 142,506 samples of five taken from the 30 days [computed with the combination formula (5–4)] would be calculated and summarized with a distribution. The following sections develop and explain why the sample mean is normally distributed.

LO8-3
Explain the sampling distribution of the sample mean.

Sampling Distribution of the Sample Mean

In the previous section, we explained why the sample mean is a random variable, and that, as an estimate of the population mean, the sample mean will be different from the population mean. This is the concept of sampling error.

In this section, we will show and demonstrate that the distribution of all possible sample means, calculated from all possible random samples, is normally distributed. This distribution is called the **sampling distribution of the sample mean.** With this knowledge, probability statements regarding the size of a specified sample error can be made. For example, knowing that the distribution of sample means is normally distributed, we can apply the empirical rule and state that approximately 68% of all sample means are within one standard error of the mean. Or, 95% of all sample means are within two standard errors of the mean. The complement of this probability statement is that 5% of all sample means are more than two standard errors distant from the mean. So, using sampling and knowing about the sampling distribution of the sample mean ensures that large sampling errors are unlikely. An earlier section in this chapter listed several practical reasons to prefer sampling over collecting information on a population. Here, we recognize that sampling results in a small probability, or risk, of a large sampling error.

> **SAMPLING DISTRIBUTION OF THE SAMPLE MEAN** A probability distribution of all possible sample means of a given sample size.

The following Example/Solution illustrates the construction of a sampling distribution of the sample mean. We have intentionally used a small population to highlight the relationship between the population mean and the various sample means.

▶ **EXAMPLE**

Tartus Industries has seven production employees (considered the population). The hourly earnings of each employee are given in Table 8–2.

TABLE 8–2 Hourly Earnings of the Production Employees of Tartus Industries

Employee	Hourly Earnings	Employee	Hourly Earnings
Joe	$14	Jan	$14
Sam	14	Art	16
Sue	16	Ted	18
Bob	16		

1. What is the population mean?
2. What is the sampling distribution of the sample mean for samples of size 2?
3. What is the mean of the sampling distribution?
4. What observations can be made about the population and the sampling distribution?

SOLUTION

Here are the solutions to the questions.

1. The population is small so it is easy to calculate the population mean. It is $15.43, found by:

$$\mu = \frac{\Sigma x}{N} = \frac{\$14 + \$14 + \$16 + \$16 + \$14 + \$16 + \$18}{7} = \$15.43$$

We identify the population mean with the Greek letter μ. Recall from earlier chapters, Greek letters represent population parameters.

2. To arrive at the sampling distribution of the sample mean, we need to select all possible samples of two without replacement from the population, then compute the mean of each sample. There are 21 possible samples, found by using formula (5–4) on page 138.

$$_NC_n = \frac{N!}{n!(N-n)!} = \frac{7!}{2!(7-2)!} = 21$$

where $N = 7$ is the number of items in the population and $n = 2$ is the number of items in the sample.

TABLE 8–3 Sample Means for All Possible Samples of Two Employees

Sample	Employees	Hourly Earnings	Sum	Mean	Sample	Employees	Hourly Earnings	Sum	Mean
1	Joe, Sam	$14, $14	$28	$14	12	Sue, Bob	$16, $16	$32	$16
2	Joe, Sue	14, 16	30	15	13	Sue, Jan	16, 14	30	15
3	Joe, Bob	14, 16	30	15	14	Sue, Art	16, 16	32	16
4	Joe, Jan	14, 14	28	14	15	Sue, Ted	16, 18	34	17
5	Joe, Art	14, 16	30	15	16	Bob, Jan	16, 14	30	15
6	Joe, Ted	14, 18	32	16	17	Bob, Art	16, 16	32	16
7	Sam, Sue	14, 16	30	15	18	Bob, Ted	16, 18	34	17
8	Sam, Bob	14, 16	30	15	19	Jan, Art	14, 16	30	15
9	Sam, Jan	14, 14	28	14	20	Jan, Ted	14, 18	32	16
10	Sam, Art	14, 16	30	15	21	Art, Ted	16, 18	34	17
11	Sam, Ted	14, 18	32	16					

The 21 sample means from all possible samples of two that can be drawn from the population of seven employees are shown in Table 8–3. These 21 sample means are used to construct a probability distribution. This is called the sampling distribution of the sample mean, and it is summarized in Table 8–4.

TABLE 8–4 Sampling Distribution of the Sample Mean for $n = 2$

Sample Mean	Number of Means	Probability
$14	3	.1429
15	9	.4285
16	6	.2857
17	3	.1429
	21	1.0000

3. Using the data in Table 8–3, the mean of the sampling distribution of the sample mean is obtained by summing the various sample means and dividing the sum by the number of samples. The mean of all the sample means is usually written $\mu_{\bar{x}}$. The μ reminds us that it is a population value because we have considered all possible samples of two employees from the population of seven employees. The subscript $\bar{x}$ indicates that it is the sampling distribution of the sample mean.

$$\mu_{\bar{x}} = \frac{\text{Sum of all sample means}}{\text{Total number of samples}} = \frac{\$14 + \$15 + \$15 + \cdots + \$16 + \$17}{21}$$

$$= \frac{\$324}{21} = \$15.43$$

4. Refer to Chart 8–2. It shows the population distribution based on the data in Table 8–2 and the distribution of the sample mean based on the data in Table 8–4. These observations can be made:

a. The mean of the distribution of the sample mean ($15.43) is equal to the mean of the population: $\mu = \mu_{\bar{x}}$.

b. The spread in the distribution of the sample mean is less than the spread in the population values. The sample means range from $14 to $17 while the population values vary from $14 up to $18. If we continue to increase the sample size, the spread of the distribution of the sample mean becomes smaller.

c. The shapes of the population distribution and the sampling distribution of the mean are different. The distribution of the sample mean tends to be more bell shaped and to approximate the normal probability distribution.

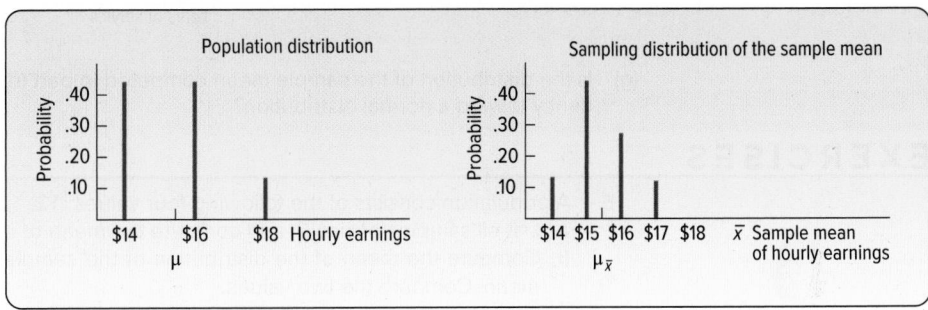

CHART 8–2 Distributions of Population Values and Sample Means

In summary, we took all possible random samples from a population and for each sample calculated a sample statistic (the mean amount earned). This example illustrates important relationships between the population distribution and the sampling distribution of the sample mean:

1. The mean of the sample means is exactly equal to the population mean.
2. The dispersion of the sampling distribution of the sample mean is narrower than the population distribution.
3. The sampling distribution of the sample mean tends to become bell shaped and to approximate the normal probability distribution.

Given a bell-shaped or normal probability distribution, we will be able to apply concepts from Chapter 7 to determine the probability of selecting a sample with a specified sample mean. In the next section, we will show the importance of sample size as it relates to the sampling distribution of the sample mean.

SELF-REVIEW 8–3

The years of service of the five executives employed by Standard Chemicals are:

Name	Years
Mr. Snow	20
Ms. Tolson	22
Mr. Kraft	26
Ms. Irwin	24
Mr. Jones	28

(a) Using the combination formula, how many samples of size 2 are possible?
(b) List all possible samples of two executives from the population and compute their means.

(c)   Organize the means into a sampling distribution.
(d)   Compare the population mean and the mean of the sample means.
(e)   Compare the dispersion in the population with that in the distribution of the sample mean.
(f)   A chart portraying the population values follows. Is the distribution of population values normally distributed (bell shaped)?

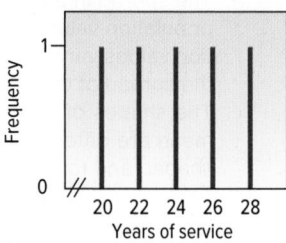

(g)   Is the distribution of the sample mean computed in part (c) starting to show some tendency toward a normal distribution?

EXERCISES

5.   A population consists of the following four values: 12, 12, 14, and 16.
   a. List all samples of size 2, and compute the mean of each sample.
   b. Compute the mean of the distribution of the sample mean and the population mean. Compare the two values.
   c. Compare the dispersion in the population with that of the sample mean.
6.   A population consists of the following five values: 2, 2, 4, 4, and 8.
   a. List all samples of size 2, and compute the mean of each sample.
   b. Compute the mean of the distribution of sample means and the population mean. Compare the two values.
   c. Compare the dispersion in the population with that of the sample means.
7.   A population consists of the following five values: 12, 12, 14, 15, and 20.
   a. List all samples of size 3, and compute the mean of each sample.
   b. Compute the mean of the distribution of sample means and the population mean. Compare the two values.
   c. Compare the dispersion in the population with that of the sample means.
8.   A population consists of the following five values: 0, 0, 1, 3, and 6.
   a. List all samples of size 3, and compute the mean of each sample.
   b. Compute the mean of the distribution of sample means and the population mean. Compare the two values.
   c. Compare the dispersion in the population with that of the sample means.
9.   In the law firm Tybo and Associates, there are six partners. Listed is the number of cases each partner actually tried in court last month.

Partner	Number of Cases
Ruud	3
Wu	6
Sass	3
Flores	3
Wilhelms	0
Schueller	1

   a. How many different samples of size 3 are possible?
   b. List all possible samples of size 3, and compute the mean number of cases in each sample.
   c. Compare the mean of the distribution of sample means to the population mean.
   d. On a chart similar to Chart 8–2, compare the dispersion in the population with that of the sample means.

10. There are five sales associates at Mid-Motors Ford. The five associates and the number of cars they sold last week are:

Sales Associate	Cars Sold
Peter Hankish	8
Connie Stallter	6
Juan Lopez	4
Ted Barnes	10
Peggy Chu	6

a. How many different samples of size 2 are possible?
b. List all possible samples of size 2, and compute the mean of each sample.
c. Compare the mean of the sampling distribution of the sample mean with that of the population.
d. On a chart similar to Chart 8–2, compare the dispersion in sample means with that of the population.

LO8-4

Explain how the central limit theorem applies to the sampling distribution of the sample mean.

The Central Limit Theorem

In this section, we examine the **central limit theorem.** Its application to the sampling distribution of the sample mean, introduced in the previous section, allows us to use the normal probability distribution to create confidence intervals for the population mean (described in Chapter 9) and perform tests of hypothesis (described in Chapter 10). The central limit theorem states that, for large random samples, the shape of the sampling distribution of the sample mean is close to the normal probability distribution. The approximation is more accurate for large samples than for small samples. This is one of the most useful conclusions in statistics. We can reason about the distribution of the sample mean with absolutely no information about the shape of the population distribution from which the sample is taken. In other words, the central limit theorem is true for all population distributions.

> **CENTRAL LIMIT THEOREM** If all samples of a particular size are selected from any population, the sampling distribution of the sample mean is approximately a normal distribution. This approximation improves with larger samples.

To further illustrate the central limit theorem, if the population follows a normal probability distribution, then for any sample size the sampling distribution of the sample mean will also be normal. If the population distribution is symmetrical (but not normal), you will see the normal shape of the distribution of the sample mean emerge with samples as small as 10. On the other hand, if you start with a distribution that is skewed or has thick tails, it may require samples of 30 or more to observe the normality feature.

This concept is summarized in Chart 8–3 for various population shapes. For example, in the first column, the population distribution can be described as having two modes at the extremes of the random variable, x. The next graph in the column shows the sampling distribution of sample means if all samples of size 2 were collected from the population. Clearly, the shapes of the population distribution and the distribution of sample means are different. The central limit theorem says that if sample size increases, the sampling distribution of sample means continues to approximate the normal distribution. The next graph in the column with samples of size 6 shows a stronger approximation of the normal distribution. The bottom graph in the column clearly shows the effect of larger sample sizes; the sampling distribution of the sample mean closely approximates a normal distribution. The other columns illustrate the same concept with

CHART 8–3 Results of the Central Limit Theorem for Several Populations

different population distributions. The second column starts with a triangular population distribution, the third column starts with a population described with a uniform distribution, and the fourth column starts with a positively skewed population distribution. Note that for each column, as sample size increases, the sampling distribution of sample means changes and evolves to a normal distribution. The following example/solution will provide more evidence to support the central limit theorem.

▶ **EXAMPLE**

Ed Spence began his sprocket business 20 years ago. The business has grown over the years and now employs 40 people. Spence Sprockets Inc. faces some major decisions regarding health care for these employees. Before making a final decision on what health care plan to purchase, Ed decides to form a committee of five representative employees. The committee will be asked to study the health care issue carefully and make a recommendation as to what plan best fits the employees' needs. Ed feels the views of newer employees toward health care may differ from those of more experienced employees. If Ed randomly selects this committee, what can he expect in terms of the mean years with Spence Sprockets for those on the committee? How does the shape of the distribution of years of service of all employees (the population) compare with the shape of the sampling distribution of the mean? The years of service (rounded to the nearest year) of the 40 employees currently on the Spence Sprockets Inc. payroll are as follows.

11	4	18	2	1	2	0	2	2	4
3	4	1	2	2	3	3	19	8	3
7	1	0	2	7	0	4	5	1	14
16	8	9	1	1	2	5	10	2	3

SOLUTION

Chart 8–4 shows a histogram for the frequency distribution of the years of service for the population of 40 current employees. This distribution is positively skewed. Why? Because the business has grown in recent years, the distribution shows that 29 of the 40 employees have been with the company less than 6 years. Also, there are 11 employees who have worked at Spence Sprockets for more than 6 years. In particular, four employees have been with the company 12 years or more (count the frequencies above 12). So there is a long tail in the distribution of service years to the right, that is, the distribution is positively skewed.

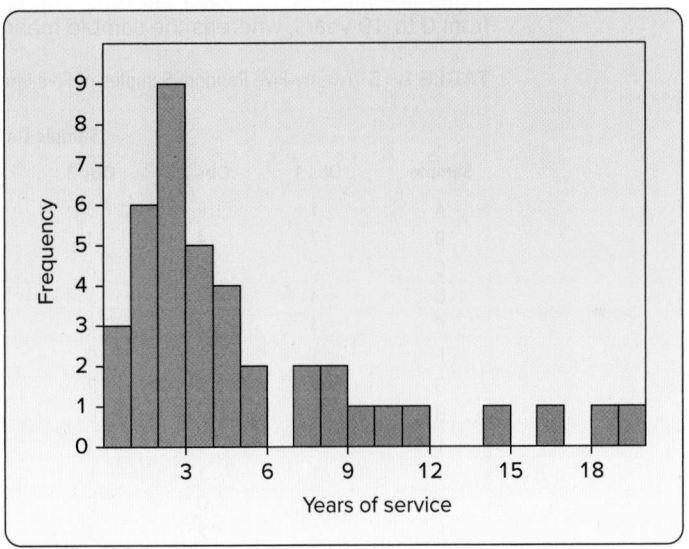

CHART 8–4 Years of Service for Spence Sprockets Inc. Employees

Let's consider the first of Ed Spence's problems. He would like to form a committee of five employees to look into the health care question and suggest what type of health care coverage would be most appropriate for the majority of workers. How should he select the committee? If he selects the committee randomly, what might he expect in terms of mean years of service for those on the committee?

To begin, Ed writes the years of service for each of the 40 employees on pieces of paper and puts them into an old baseball hat. Next, he shuffles the pieces of paper and randomly selects five slips of paper. The years of service for these five employees are 1, 9, 0, 19, and 14 years. Thus, the mean years of service for these five sampled employees is 8.60 years. How does that compare with the population mean? At this point, Ed does not know the population mean, but the number of employees in the population is only 40, so he decides to calculate the mean years of service for *all* his employees. It is 4.8 years, found by adding the years of service for *all* the employees and dividing the total by 40.

$$\mu = \frac{11 + 4 + 18 + \cdots + 2 + 3}{40} = 4.80$$

The difference between a sample mean ($\bar{x}$) and the population mean (μ) is called **sampling error.** In other words, the difference of 3.80 years between the sample mean of 8.60 and the population mean of 4.80 is the sampling error. It is due to chance. Thus, if Ed selected these five employees to constitute the committee, their mean years of service would be larger than the population mean.

What would happen if Ed put the five pieces of paper back into the baseball hat and selected another sample? Would you expect the mean of this second sample to be exactly the same as the previous one? He selects another sample of five employees and finds the years of service in this sample to be 7, 4, 4, 1, and 3. This sample mean is 3.80 years. The result of selecting 25 samples of five employees and computing the mean for each sample is shown in Table 8–5 and Chart 8–5. There are actually 658,008 possible samples of five from the population of 40 employees, found by the combination formula (5–4) for 40 things taken five at a time. Notice the difference in the shape of the population and the distribution of these sample means. The population of the years of service for employees (see Chart 8–4) is positively skewed, but the distribution of these 25 sample means does not reflect the same positive skew. There is also a difference in the range of the sample means versus the range of the population. The population ranged from 0 to 19 years, whereas the sample means range from 1.6 to 8.6 years.

TABLE 8–5 Twenty-Five Random Samples of Five Employees

Sample	Obs 1	Obs 2	Obs 3	Obs 4	Obs 5	Sum	Mean
			Sample Data				
A	1	9	0	19	14	43	8.6
B	7	4	4	1	3	19	3.8
C	8	19	8	2	1	38	7.6
D	4	18	2	0	11	35	7.0
E	4	2	4	7	18	35	7.0
F	1	2	0	3	2	8	1.6
G	2	3	2	0	2	9	1.8
H	11	2	9	2	4	28	5.6
I	9	0	4	2	7	22	4.4
J	1	1	1	11	1	15	3.0
K	2	0	0	10	2	14	2.8
L	0	2	3	2	16	23	4.6
M	2	3	1	1	1	8	1.6
N	3	7	3	4	3	20	4.0
O	1	2	3	1	4	11	2.2
P	19	0	1	3	8	31	6.2
Q	5	1	7	14	9	36	7.2
R	5	4	2	3	4	18	3.6
S	14	5	2	2	5	28	5.6
T	2	1	1	4	7	15	3.0
U	3	7	1	2	1	14	2.8
V	0	1	5	1	2	9	1.8
W	0	3	19	4	2	28	5.6
X	4	2	3	4	0	13	2.6
Y	1	1	2	3	2	9	1.8

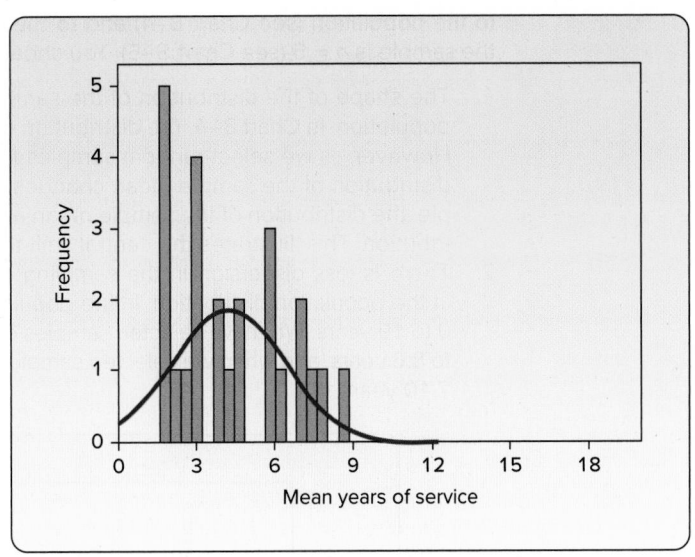

CHART 8–5 Histogram of Mean Years of Service for 25 Samples of Five Employees

Now let's change the example by increasing the size of each sample from 5 employees to 20. Table 8–6 reports the result of selecting 25 samples of 20 employees each and computing their sample means. The frequency distribution of these sample means is shown in Chart 8–6. Compare the shape of this distribution

TABLE 8–6 Twenty-Five Random Samples of 20 Employees

Sample Data							
Sample	**Obs 1**	**Obs 2**	**Obs 3**	**–**	**Obs 19**	**Obs 20**	**Sum**	**Mean**
A	3	8	3	–	4	16	79	3.95
B	2	3	8	–	3	1	65	3.25
C	14	5	0	–	19	8	119	5.95
D	9	2	1	–	1	3	87	4.35
E	18	1	2	–	3	14	107	5.35
F	10	4	4	–	2	1	80	4.00
G	5	7	11	–	2	4	131	6.55
H	3	0	2	–	16	5	85	4.25
I	0	0	18	–	2	3	80	4.00
J	2	7	2	–	3	2	81	4.05
K	7	4	5	–	1	2	84	4.20
L	0	3	10	–	0	4	81	4.05
M	4	1	2	–	1	2	88	4.40
N	3	16	1	–	11	1	95	4.75
O	2	19	2	–	2	2	102	5.10
P	2	18	16	–	4	3	100	5.00
Q	3	2	3	–	3	1	102	5.10
R	2	3	1	–	0	2	73	3.65
S	2	14	19	–	0	7	142	7.10
T	0	1	3	–	2	0	61	3.05
U	1	0	1	–	9	3	65	3.25
V	1	9	4	–	2	11	137	6.85
W	8	1	9	–	8	7	107	5.35
X	4	2	0	–	2	5	86	4.30
Y	1	2	1	–	1	18	101	5.05

to the population (see Chart 8–4) and to the distribution of sample means where the sample is $n = 5$ (see Chart 8–5). You should observe two important features:

1. The shape of the distribution of the sample mean is different from that of the population. In Chart 8–4, the distribution of all employees is positively skewed. However, as we select random samples from this population, the shape of the distribution of the sample mean changes. As we increase the size of the sample, the distribution of the sample mean approaches the normal probability distribution. This illustrates the central limit theorem.

2. There is less dispersion in the sampling distribution of the sample mean than in the population distribution. In the population, the years of service varied from 0 to 19 years. When we selected samples of 5, the sample means varied from 1.6 to 8.6 years, and when we selected samples of 20, the means varied from 3.05 to 7.10 years.

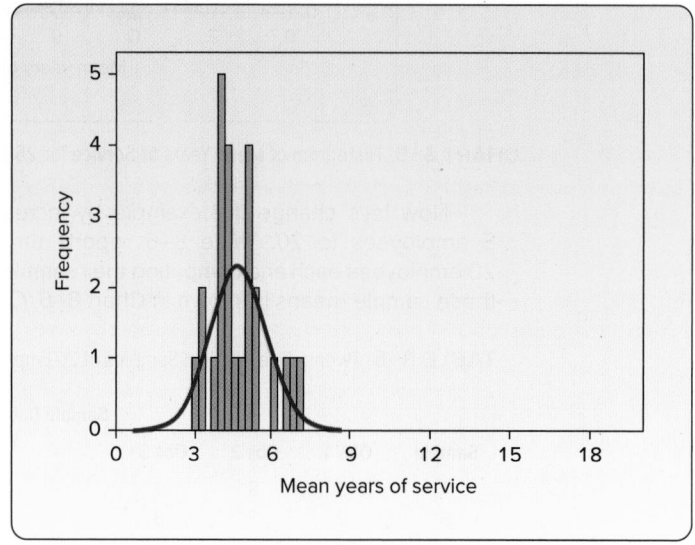

CHART 8–6 Histogram of Mean Years of Service for 25 Samples of 20 Employees

We can also compare the mean of the sample means to the population mean. The mean of the 25 samples of 20 employees reported in Table 8–6 is 4.676 years.

$$\mu_{\bar{x}} = \frac{3.95 + 3.25 + \cdots + 4.30 + 5.05}{25} = 4.676$$

We use the symbol $\mu_{\bar{x}}$ to identify the mean of the distribution of the sample mean. The subscript reminds us that the distribution is of the sample mean. It is read "mu sub x bar." We observe that the mean of the sample means, 4.676 years, is very close to the population mean of 4.80.

The Spence Sprockets Inc. example shows how the central limit theorem works. We began with a positively skewed population (see Chart 8–4). Next, we selected 25 random samples of five observations, computed the mean of each sample, and finally organized these 25 sample means into a histogram (see Chart 8–5). We observe that the shape of the sampling distribution of the sample mean is very different from that of the population. The population distribution is positively skewed compared to the nearly normal shape of the sampling distribution of the sample mean.

To further illustrate the effects of the central limit theorem, we increased the number of observations in each sample from 5 to 20. We selected 25 samples of 20 observations each and calculated the mean of each sample. Finally, we organized these sample means into a histogram (see Chart 8–6). The shape of the histogram in Chart 8–6 is clearly moving toward the normal probability distribution. In sum, each of the previous examples demonstrates the principle of the central limit theorem: As sample size increases, the distribution of sample means will approximate a normal distribution.

If you go back to Chapter 6 where several binomial distributions with a "success" proportion of .10 are shown in Chart 6–3 on page 191, you can see yet another demonstration of the central limit theorem. Observe as *n* increases from 7 through 12 and 20 up to 40 that the profile of the probability distributions moves closer and closer to a normal probability distribution. This again reinforces the fact that, as more observations are sampled from any population distribution, the shape of the sampling distribution of the sample mean will get closer and closer to a normal distribution.

Standard Error of the Mean

The *central limit theorem,* defined on page 265, does not say anything about the dispersion of the sampling distribution of the sample mean. However, in our Spence Sprockets example, we did observe that there was less dispersion in the distribution of the sample mean than in the population distribution by noting the difference in the range in the population and the range of the sample means. We observe that the mean of the sample means is close to the mean of the population. It can be demonstrated that the mean of the sampling distribution is exactly equal to the population mean (i.e., $\mu_{\bar{x}} = \mu$), and if the standard deviation in the population is σ, the standard deviation of the sample means is $\sigma/\sqrt{n}$ where *n* is the number of observations in each sample. We refer to $\sigma/\sqrt{n}$ as the **standard error of the mean.** Its longer name is actually the *standard deviation of the sampling distribution of the sample mean.*

STANDARD ERROR OF THE MEAN	$\sigma_{\bar{x}} = \dfrac{\sigma}{\sqrt{n}}$	(8–1)

In formula (8–1), note the relationship between the standard error and sample size, *n.* As the sample size increases, the dispersion of the sampling distribution of the mean decreases and the shape of the distribution narrows around the population mean. In Chapter 9, the relationship between sample size and the precision in estimating population parameters is presented.

SELF-REVIEW 8–4

Refer to the Spence Sprockets Inc. data on page 267. Select 10 random samples of five employees each. Use the methods described earlier in the chapter and the Table of Random Numbers (Appendix B.4) or statistical software to find the employees to include in the sample. Compute the mean of each sample and plot the sample means on a chart similar to Chart 8–4. What is the mean of your 10 sample means?

EXERCISES

11. **FILE** Appendix B.4 is a table of random numbers that are uniformly distributed. Hence, each digit from 0 to 9 has the same likelihood of occurrence.
    a. Draw a graph showing the population distribution of random numbers. What is the population mean?
    b. Following are the first 10 rows of five digits from the table of random numbers in Appendix B.4. Assume that these are 10 random samples of five values each. Determine the mean of each sample and plot the means on a chart similar to Chart 8–4. Compare the mean of the sampling distribution of the sample mean with the population mean.

0	2	7	1	1
9	4	8	7	3
5	4	9	2	1
7	7	6	4	0
6	1	5	4	5
1	7	1	4	7
1	3	7	4	8
8	7	4	5	5
0	8	9	9	9
7	8	8	0	4

12. **FILE** Scrapper Elevator Company has 20 sales representatives who sell its product throughout the United States and Canada. The number of units sold last month by each representative is listed here. Assume these sales figures to be the population values.

2	3	2	3	3	4	2	4	3	2	2	7	3	4	5	3	3	3	3	5

   a. Draw a graph showing the population distribution.
   b. Compute the mean of the population.
   c. Select five random samples of five each. Compute the mean of each sample. Use the methods described in this chapter. Using a random number table (Appendix B.4) or statistical software, select the items to be included in the sample.
   d. Compare the mean of the sampling distribution of the sample mean to the population mean. Would you expect the two values to be about the same?
   e. Draw a histogram of the sample means. Why are the two distributions different?

13. Collect a random assortment of at least 30 coins (pennies, nickels, dimes, quarters, etc.). Make a frequency table beginning with the current year and counting backward to record the ages (in years) of the coins. For example, if the current year is 2022, then a coin with 2020 stamped on it is 2 years old.
   a. Draw a histogram or other graph showing the population distribution.
   b. Randomly select five coins and record the mean age of the sampled coins. Repeat this sampling process 20 times. Now draw a histogram or other graph showing the distribution of the sample means.
   c. Compare the shapes of the two histograms. Why are the two distributions different?

14. Using a random number generator from statistical software, create five sets (columns) of 50 random numbers between 0 and 9.
   a. Create a frequency distribution and a histogram summarizing all 250 random numbers. What distribution best describes the histogram?
      1. What is the mean of this distribution?
      2. What is the standard deviation of this distribution?
   b. Now, identify each row as a sample with five observations.
      1. In a new column, compute the average of the first two observations in each row or sample. This is a sample size of 2, $n = 2$. In another column, compute the average of the first three observations ($n = 3$) in each row or sample. Continue this process for sample sizes of 4 ($n = 4$) and 5 ($n = 5$).
      2. For each sample size, summarize the sample means with a frequency distribution and histogram.
      3. For each sample size compute the mean of the means, the standard deviation of the means, and the range of the means.
      4. Write a report that compares the population distribution to the sampling distributions of the means.
      5. Write a report that compares the four sampling distributions of the mean.
      6. What statistical principle does this exercise demonstrate? How does your analysis support this principle?

Using the Sampling Distribution of the Sample Mean

The previous discussion is important because most business decisions are made on the basis of sample information. Here are some examples.

1. Arm & Hammer Company wants to ensure that its laundry detergent actually contains 100 fluid ounces, as indicated on the label. Historical summaries from the filling process indicate the mean amount per container is 100 fluid ounces and the standard deviation is 2 fluid ounces. At 10 a.m., a quality technician measures 40 containers and finds the mean amount per container is 99.8 fluid ounces. Should the technician shut down the filling operation?

2. In 2021, Elite Content Marketer (**https://elitecontentmarketer.com/screen-time-statistics/**) reported that American adults spend an average of 3 hours and 43 minutes (223 minutes) per day using their mobile devices. Suppose the standard deviation of mobile device time is 60 minutes. If we randomly selected 50 American adults, what is the probability their mobile device time is less than an average of 200 minutes per day?

3. Haughton Elevator Company wishes to develop specifications for the number of people who can ride in a new oversized elevator. Suppose the mean weight of an adult is 160 pounds and the standard deviation is 15 pounds. However, the distribution of weights does not follow the normal probability distribution. It is positively skewed. For a sample of 30 adults, what is the likelihood that their mean weight is 170 pounds or more?

We can answer the questions in each of these situations using the ideas discussed in the previous section. In each case, we have a population with information about its mean and standard deviation. Using this information and sample size, we can determine the distribution of sample means and compute the probability that a sample mean will fall within a certain range. The sampling distribution will be normally distributed under two conditions:

1. When the samples are taken from populations known to follow the normal distribution, the size of the sample is not a factor.

2. When the shape of the population distribution is not known, sample size is important. In general, the sampling distribution will be normally distributed as the sample size approaches infinity. In practice, a sampling distribution will be close to a normal distribution with samples of at least 30 observations.

We use formula (7–5) from the previous chapter to convert any normal distribution to the standard normal distribution. Using formula (7–5) to compute z-values, we can use the standard normal table, Appendix B.3, to find the probability that an observation is within a specific range. The formula for finding a z-value is:

$$z = \frac{x - \mu}{\sigma}$$

In this formula, x is the value of the random variable, μ is the population mean, and σ is the population standard deviation.

However, when we sample from populations, we are interested in the distribution of $\bar{x}$, the sample mean, instead of X, the value of one observation. That is the first change we make in formula (7–5). The second is that we use the standard error of the mean of n observations instead of the population standard deviation. That is, we use $\sigma/\sqrt{n}$ in the denominator rather than σ. Therefore, to find the likelihood of a sample mean within a specified range, we first use the following formula to find the corresponding z-value. Then we use Appendix B.3 or statistical software to determine the probability.

FINDING THE z-VALUE OF $\bar{x}$ WHEN THE POPULATION STANDARD DEVIATION IS KNOWN	$z = \dfrac{\bar{x} - \mu}{\sigma/\sqrt{n}}$	(8–2)

The following Example/Solution will show the application.

► EXAMPLE

The Quality Assurance Department for Cola Inc. maintains records regarding the amount of cola in its jumbo bottle. The actual amount of cola in each bottle is critical but varies from one bottle to the next. Cola Inc. does not wish to underfill the bottles because it will have a problem with truth in labeling. On the other hand, it cannot overfill each bottle because it would be giving cola away, hence reducing its profits. Records maintained by the Quality Assurance Department indicate that the amount of cola follows the normal probability distribution. The mean amount per bottle is 31.2 ounces and the population standard deviation is 0.4 ounce. At 8 a.m. today the quality technician randomly selected 16 bottles from the filling line. The mean amount of cola contained in the bottles is 31.38 ounces. Is this an unlikely result? Is it likely the process is putting too much soda in the bottles? To put it another way, is the sampling error of 0.18 ounce unusual?

SOLUTION

We use the results of the previous section to find the likelihood that we could select a sample of 16 (n) bottles from a normal population with a mean of 31.2 (μ) ounces and a population standard deviation of 0.4 (σ) ounce and find the sample mean to be 31.38 ($\bar{x}$) or more. We use formula (8–2) to find the value of z.

$$z = \frac{\bar{x}-\mu}{\sigma/\sqrt{n}} = \frac{31.38-31.20}{0.4/\sqrt{16}} = 1.80$$

The numerator of this equation, $\bar{x} - \mu = 31.38 - 31.20 = .18$, is the sampling error. The denominator, $\sigma/\sqrt{n} = 0.4/\sqrt{16} = 0.1$, is the standard error of the sampling distribution of the sample mean. So the z-values express the sampling error in standard units—in other words, the standard error.

Next, we compute the likelihood of a z-value greater than 1.80. In Appendix B.3, locate the probability corresponding to a z-value of 1.80. It is .4641. The likelihood of a z-value greater than 1.80 is .0359, found by .5000 − .4641.

What do we conclude? It is unlikely, less than a 4% chance, we could select a sample of 16 observations from a normal population with a mean of 31.2 ounces and a population standard deviation of 0.4 ounce and find the sample mean equal to or greater than 31.38 ounces. We conclude the process is putting too much cola in the bottles. The quality technician should see the production supervisor about reducing the amount of soda in each bottle. This information is summarized in Chart 8–7.

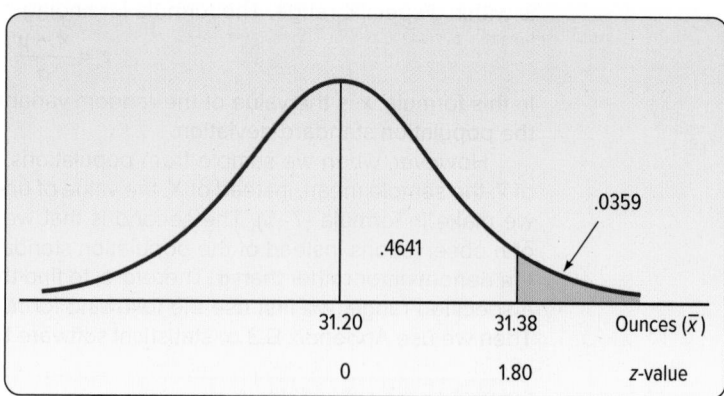

CHART 8–7 Sampling Distribution of the Mean Amount of Cola in a Jumbo Bottle

SELF-REVIEW 8–5

Refer to the Cola Inc. information. Suppose the quality technician selected a sample of 16 jumbo bottles that averaged 31.08 ounces. What can you conclude about the filling process?

EXERCISES

15. A normal population has a mean of $60 and standard deviation of $12. You select random samples of nine.
  a. Apply the central limit theorem to describe the sampling distribution of the sample mean with $n = 9$. With the small sample size, what condition is necessary to apply the central limit theorem?
  b. What is the standard error of the sampling distribution of sample means?
  c. What is the probability that a sample mean is greater than $63?
  d. What is the probability that a sample mean is less than $56?
  e. What is the probability that a sample mean is between $56 and $63?
  f. What is the probability that the sampling error $(\bar{x} - \mu)$ would be $9 or more? That is, what is the probability that the estimate of the population mean is less than $51 or more than $69?

16. A normal population has a mean of $75 and standard deviation of $5. You select random samples of 40.
  a. Apply the central limit theorem to describe the sampling distribution of the sample mean with $n = 40$. What condition is necessary to apply the central limit theorem?
  b. What is the standard error of the sampling distribution of sample means?
  c. What is the probability that a sample mean is less than $74?
  d. What is the probability that a sample mean is between $74 and $76?
  e. What is the probability that a sample mean is between $76 and $77?
  f. What is the probability that the sampling error $(\bar{x} - \mu)$ would be $1.50 or less?

17. In a certain section of Southern California, the distribution of monthly rent for a one-bedroom apartment has a mean of $2,200 and a standard deviation of $250. The distribution of the monthly rent does not follow the normal distribution. In fact, it is positively skewed. What is the probability of selecting a sample of 50 one-bedroom apartments and finding the mean to be at least $1,950 per month?

18. According to an IRS study, it takes a mean of 330 minutes for taxpayers to prepare, copy, and electronically file a 1040 tax form. This distribution of times follows the normal distribution and the standard deviation is 80 minutes. A consumer watchdog agency selects a random sample of 40 taxpayers.
  a. What is the standard error of the mean in this example?
  b. What is the likelihood the sample mean is greater than 320 minutes?
  c. What is the likelihood the sample mean is between 320 and 350 minutes?
  d. What is the likelihood the sample mean is greater than 350 minutes?
  e. What is the probability that the sampling error would be more than 20 minutes?

LO8-6

Apply the central limit theorem to the sampling distribution of the sample proportion.

The Sampling Distribution of the Sample Proportion

The central limit theorem is also applied to a statistic called the sample proportion. **Proportions** are used when measuring a random variable with the nominal scale of measurement and the outcomes are limited to two values. Observations are classified into one of two mutually exclusive groups. For example, we may be interested in the proportion of graduates from Southern Tech placed in a position related to their field of study. The outcome is limited to two values: placed in related field or not. The proportion would be the number placed in a related field relative to the total number of graduates.

> **PROPORTION** The fraction, ratio, or percent indicating the part of the sample or the population having a particular trait of interest.

As another example, a Burger King franchise would like to know the proportion of customers purchasing an order at the drive-thru window. In this case, the franchise would review all the receipts for a time period, count the total number of receipts, count the number of receipts from the drive-thru window, and determine the proportion of the total receipts that were recorded at the window. The sample proportion is computed as follows:

SAMPLE PROPORTION	$p = \dfrac{x}{n}$	(8–3)

where:

> p is the sample proportion
> x is the count or number of "successful" outcomes
> n is the sample size or the total count or number of outcomes

A recent survey asked 100 people if they favored the continued use of daylight saving time in the summer. In the survey, 92 of 100 people responded in favor. So, we compute the sample proportion as 92/100, or .92, or 92%. Thus, 92% of the sample favors the continued use of daylight saving time in the summer.

As a statistic, the sample proportion, p, estimates the true population proportion, π. The sample proportion is a random variable and is described with a probability distribution. If the sample size is large enough, we can apply the central limit theorem and say that the distribution of the sample proportion is approximately normal. The two requirements that determine if the sample size is large enough are:

$$n\pi \geq 5 \text{ and } n\pi(1 - \pi) \geq 5$$

For this normal distribution, the mean is equal to the population proportion, π, and the standard error of the sampling distribution of sample proportions is:

STANDARD ERROR OF THE PROPORTION	$\sigma_p = \sqrt{\dfrac{\pi(1-\pi)}{n}}$	(8–4)

Because the central limit theorem allows us to describe the probability distribution of the sample proportion with a normal distribution, we can make probability statements regarding the value of a sample proportion. To determine the probabilities, we will compute z-values and use the standard normal distribution table. For the sample proportion we compute z-values as:

FIND THE Z-VALUE FOR A SAMPLE PROPORTION	$z = \dfrac{p - \pi}{\sqrt{\dfrac{\pi(1 - \pi)}{n}}}$	(8–5)

▶ **EXAMPLE**

The population proportion for a distribution of sample proportions is .45. The sample size is 100. What is the probability that a sample proportion is more than 0.50?

SOLUTION

First, $n\pi = 100(.45) = 45$ and $n\pi(1 - \pi) = 100(.45)(.55) = 24.75$. Both values exceed 5 so the sample size is large enough to conclude that the distribution of sample proportions is approximately normal.

Next, compute the z-value for a p of 0.5.

$$z = \frac{.5 - .45}{\sqrt{\dfrac{.5(1 - .5)}{100}}} = \frac{.05}{.05} = 1.00$$

The following graph shows the normal curve using a z-value of 1.00. From the standard normal distribution table, we find the area between the population proportion of .45 and the sample proportion of .50. It is .3413. Using this information, we determine the area for proportions greater than .50: $.5000 - .3413 = .1587$. We would conclude that given a population proportion of .45, the probability of sample proportions greater than .5 is .1587.

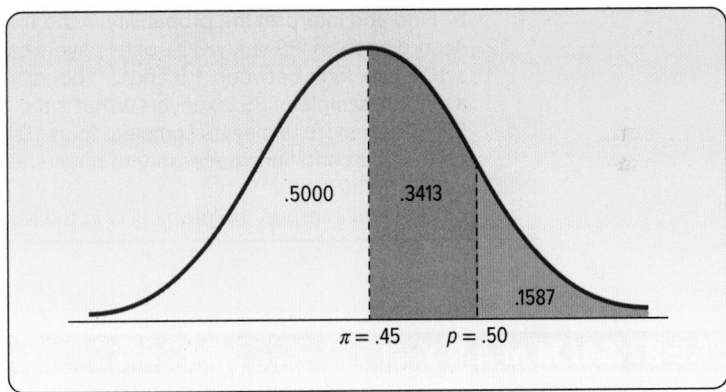

CHART 8–8 Sampling Distribution of the Sample Proportion, $\pi = .45$, $n = 100$

SELF-REVIEW 8–6

A bottling process is designed to fill bottles with 24 ounces of water. They expect the proportion of bottles with less than 24 ounces is 0.50. Every hour they sample 25 bottles. What is the probability that 20% of the sampled bottles have less than 24 ounces?

EXERCISES

19. A population proportion is 0.70. From this population you select random samples of 30.
    a. Test the conditions necessary to apply the central limit theorem. Are they satisfied? Why?
    b. What is the standard error of the sampling distribution of sample proportions?
    c. What is the probability that a sample proportion is greater than .75?
    d. What is the probability that a sample proportion is less than .45?
    e. What is the probability that a sample proportion is between .45 and .70?
    f. What is the probability that the sampling error $(p - \pi)$ would be .20 or more? That is, what is the probability that an estimate of a population proportion is less than .50 or more than .90?

20. A population proportion is 0.35. From this population you select random samples of 50.
    a. Test the conditions necessary to apply the central limit theorem. Are they satisfied? Why?
    b. What is the standard error of the sampling distribution of sample proportions?
    c. What is the probability that a sample proportion is more than .75?
    d. What is the probability that a sample proportion is less than .45?
    e. What is the probability that a sample proportion is between .45 and .75?
    f. What is the probability that the sampling error ($p - \pi$) would be .1 or less? That is, what is the probability that an estimate of a population proportion is between .25 and .45?

21. In a residential section of Southern California, a realtor believes that 80% of one-bedroom apartments rent between $1,950 and $2,450. What is the probability of selecting a random sample of 50 one-bedroom apartments and finding the proportion is less than 50%?
    a. Test the conditions necessary to apply the central limit theorem. Are they satisfied? Why?
    b. Find and interpret the probability in the exercise.

22. According to an IRS study, 30% of taxpayers can prepare, copy, and electronically file a 1040 tax form between 1.5 and 2.0 hours. A consumer watchdog agency selects a random sample of 25 taxpayers. What is the probability that, in a random sample of 25, 50% or more taxpayers complete form 1040 between 1.5 and 2.0 hours?
    a. Test the conditions necessary to apply the central limit theorem. Are they satisfied? Why?
    b. Find and interpret the probability in the exercise.

CHAPTER SUMMARY

I. There are many reasons for sampling a population.
   A. It may be too time consuming to contact all members of the population.
   B. It may be impossible to check or locate all the members of the population.
   C. The cost of studying all the items in the population may be prohibitive.
   D. Often testing destroys the sampled item and it cannot be returned to the population.
II. In an unbiased or probability sample, all members of the population have a chance of being selected for the sample. There are several probability sampling methods.
   A. In a simple random sample, all members of the population have the same chance of being selected for the sample.
   B. In a systematic sample, a random starting point is selected, and then every kth item thereafter is selected for the sample.
   C. In a stratified sample, the population is divided into several groups, called strata, and then a random sample is selected from each stratum.
   D. In cluster sampling, the population is divided into primary units, then samples are drawn from the primary units.
III. The sampling error is the difference between a population parameter and a sample statistic.
IV. The sampling distribution of the sample mean is a probability distribution of all possible sample means of the same sample size.
   A. For a given sample size, the mean of all possible sample means selected from a population is equal to the population mean.
   B. There is less variation in the distribution of the sample mean than in the population distribution.
   C. The standard error of the mean measures the variation in the sampling distribution of the sample mean. The standard error is found by:

$$\sigma_{\bar{x}} = \frac{\sigma}{\sqrt{n}} \qquad\qquad (8\text{--}1)$$

D. If the population follows a normal distribution, the sampling distribution of the sample mean will also follow the normal distribution for samples of any size. If the population is not normally distributed, the sampling distribution of the sample mean will approach a normal distribution when the sample size is at least 30. Assume the population standard deviation is known. To determine the probability that a sample mean falls in a particular region, use the following formula.

$$z = \frac{\bar{x} - \mu}{\sigma / \sqrt{n}} \qquad (8\text{–}2)$$

V. The sampling distribution of the sample proportion is a probability distribution of all possible sample proportions of the same sample size.
  A. The sample proportion is the number of "successful" outcomes relative to the total number of outcomes.

$$p = \frac{x}{n} \qquad (8\text{–}3)$$

  B. For a given sample size, the mean of all possible sample proportions selected from a population is equal to the population proportion, π.
  C. The standard error of the proportion measures the variation in the sampling distribution of the sample proportion. The standard error is found by:

$$\sigma_p = \sqrt{\frac{\pi(1-\pi)}{n}} \qquad (8\text{–}4)$$

  D. If the sample size is large enough, we can apply the central limit theorem. The two requirements are:

$$n\pi \geq 5 \text{ and } n\pi(1 - \pi) \geq 5$$

  If the two requirements are met, the distribution of sample proportions is approximately normally distributed.
  E. If the sample size is large enough, we use the standard normal distribution to determine the probability that a sample proportion falls in a particular range. We calculate the z-value using the following formula:

$$Z = \frac{p - \pi}{\sqrt{\frac{\pi(1 - \pi)}{n}}} \qquad (8\text{–}5)$$

PRONUNCIATION KEY

SYMBOL	MEANING	PRONUNCIATION
$\mu_{\bar{x}}$	Mean of the sampling distribution of the sample mean	*mu sub x bar*
$\sigma_{\bar{x}}$	Population standard error of the sample mean	*sigma sub x bar*
σ_p	Population standard error of the sample proportion	*sigma sub p*

CHAPTER EXERCISES

23. FILE The 24 retail stores located in the Mall of America numbered 00 through 23 are:

00	Tilly's	08	Zara	16	Impulse
01	Lids	09	Madewell	17	Perfumania
02	Aldo	10	Cariloha	18	Ragstock
03	Fabletics	11	Kiehl's	19	JJill
04	Windsor	12	Nike	20	Disney Store
05	Sephora	13	UNTUCKit	21	Soma
06	Banana Republic	14	H&M	22	Ecco
07	SoftMoc	15	Guess	23	Nordstrom

a. If the following random numbers are selected, which retail stores should be contacted for a survey? 11, 65, 86, 62, 06, 10, 12, 77, and 04

b. Using a random number table (Appendix B.4) or statistical software, select a random sample of four retail stores.

c. A systematic sampling procedure will be used. The first store will be selected and then every third store. Which stores will be in the sample?

24. **FILE** The Medical Assurance Company is investigating the cost of a routine office visit to family practice physicians in the Rochester, New York, area. The following is a list of 38 family practice physicians in the region. Physicians are to be randomly selected and contacted regarding their charges. The 38 physicians have been coded from 00 to 37. Also noted is whether they are in practice by themselves (S), have a partner (P), or are in a group practice (G).

Number	Physician	Type of Practice	Number	Physician	Type of Practice
00	John Missirian M.D.	S	19	David Samuel Rusen M.D.	P
01	Luke Flynn Bremner M.D.	P	20	Sumeet Bhinder M.D.	P
02	Francis Palmer Iii M.D.	P	21	Michael D. Molina M.D.	P
03	K. Alex Kim M.D.	P	22	Ronald Borchardt M.D.	P
04	Timothy Friederichs M.D.	P	23	David Ross Field M.D.	S
05	Ryan A. Stanton M.D.	P	24	Justin F. Weiss M.D.	S
06	Gregory Macdonell M.D.	S	25	Philip Chamberlain M.D.	S
07	Steven G. Farmer DPM.	S	26	Jackson Lee M.D.	G
08	Brenda N. Ikemoto O.D.	G	27	Robert Schoenberg O.D.	G
09	Rhonda Louise Carlson M.D.	S	28	Peter Panagotacos M.D.	G
10	Anita Gorwara-Dohad M.D.	S	29	Patricia Iorfino M.D.	P
11	John E. Padour M.D.	S	30	Heajin Kamalani M.D.	P
12	Stacey Le O.D.	P	31	Leslie J.Andrews M.D.	P
13	Gail D. Feinberg D.O.	P	32	Danny Phu M.D.	P
14	Randy Lee Stone O.D.	P	33	William Chunghun Sim M.D.	P
15	Bruce M. McCormack M.D.	P	34	Mark Clifford Goodwin M.D.	P
16	Richard Mark Shaw M.D.	G	35	Jeffrey Neal Stoneberg D.O.	S
17	Rebecca Sloan M.S., CCC-SLP.	G	36	Michalynn Marie Farley M.D.	P
18	Jacob Offenberger M.D.	S	37	Katrina E Woodhall M.D.	P

a. The random numbers obtained from Appendix B.4 are 31, 94, 43, 36, 03, 24, 17, and 09. Which physicians should be contacted?

b. Select a random sample of four physicians using a random number table (Appendix B.4) or statistical software.

c. Using systematic random sampling, every fifth physician is selected starting with the fourth physician in the list. Which physicians will be contacted?

d. Select a sample that includes two physicians in solo practice (S), two in partnership (P), and one in group practice (G). Explain your procedure.

25. A population consists of the following three values: 1, 2, and 3.

a. Sampling with replacement, list all possible samples of size 2 and compute the mean of every sample.

b. Compute the population mean and mean of the sample means. How do they compare?

c. Compare the dispersions of the population distribution and the sampling distribution of the sample mean.

d. Describe the shapes of the two distributions.

26. Based on all student records at Camford University, students spend an average of 5.5 hours per week playing organized sports. The population's standard deviation is 2.2 hours per week. Based on a sample of 121 students, Healthy Lifestyles Incorporated (HLI) would like to apply the central limit theorem to make various estimates.

a. Compute the standard error of the sampling distribution of sample means.

b. What is the chance HLI will find a sample mean between 5 and 6 hours?

c. Calculate the probability that the sample mean will be between 5.3 and 5.7 hours.

d. How strange would it be to obtain a sample mean greater than 6.5 hours?

27. eComputers Inc. recently completed the design for a new laptop model. Top management would like some assistance in pricing the new laptop. Two market research firms were contacted and asked to prepare a pricing strategy. Marketing-Gets-Results tested the new eComputers laptop with 50 randomly selected consumers who indicated they plan to purchase a laptop within the next year. The second marketing research firm, called Marketing-Reaps-Profits, test-marketed the new eComputers laptop with 200 current laptop owners. Which of the marketing research companies' test results will be more useful? Discuss why.

28. Answer the following questions in one or two well-constructed sentences.
   a. What happens to the standard error of the mean if the sample size is increased?
   b. What happens to the distribution of the sample means if the sample size is increased?
   c. When using sample means to estimate the population mean, what is the benefit of using larger sample sizes?

29. **FILE** There are 25 motels in Goshen, Indiana. The number of rooms in each motel follows:

> 90 72 75 60 75 72 84 72 88 74 105 115 68 74 80 64 104 82 48 58 60 80 48 58 100

   a. Using a random number table (Appendix B.4) or statistical software, select a random sample of five motels from this population.
   b. Obtain a systematic sample by selecting a random starting point among the first five motels and then select every fifth motel.
   c. Suppose the last five motels are "cut-rate" motels. Describe how you would select a random sample of three regular motels and two cut-rate motels.

30. As a part of their customer-service program, Global Airlines randomly selected 10 passengers from today's 9 a.m. Chicago–Tampa flight. Each sampled passenger will be interviewed about airport facilities, service, and so on. To select the sample, each passenger was given a number on boarding the aircraft. The numbers started with 001 and ended with 250.
   a. Select 10 usable numbers at random using a random number table (Appendix B.4) or statistical software.
   b. The sample of 10 could have been chosen using a systematic sample. Choose the first number using a random number table (Appendix B.4) or statistical software, and then list the numbers to be interviewed.
   c. Evaluate the two methods by giving the advantages and possible disadvantages.
   d. What other way could a random sample be selected from the 250 passengers?

31. Suppose your statistics instructor gave six examinations during the semester. You received the following exam scores (percent correct): 79, 64, 84, 82, 92, and 77. The instructor decided to randomly select two exam scores, compute their mean, and use this score to determine your final course grade.
   a. Compute the population mean.
   b. How many different samples of two test grades are possible?
   c. List all possible samples of size 2 and compute the mean of each.
   d. Compute the mean of the sample means and compare it to the population mean.
   e. If you were a student, would you like this arrangement? Would the result be different from dropping the lowest score? Write a brief report.

32. At the downtown office of First National Bank, there are five tellers. Last week, the tellers made the following number of errors each: 2, 3, 5, 3, and 5.
   a. How many different samples of two tellers are possible?
   b. List all possible samples of size 2 and compute the mean of each.
   c. Compute the mean of the sample means and compare it to the population mean.

33. The Quality Control Department employs five technicians during the day shift. Listed is the number of times each technician instructed the production foreman to shut down the manufacturing process last week.

Technician	Shutdowns	Technician	Shutdowns
Taylor	4	Rousche	3
Hurley	3	Huang	2
Gupta	5		

   a. How many different samples of two technicians are possible from this population?
   b. List all possible samples of two observations each and compute the mean of each sample.
   c. Compare the mean of the sample means with the population mean.
   d. Compare the shape of the population distribution with the shape of the distribution of the sample means.
34. The Appliance Center has six sales representatives at its North Jacksonville outlet. The following table lists the number of refrigerators sold by each representative last month.

Sales Representative	Number Sold	Sales Representative	Number Sold
Zina Craft	54	Jan Niles	48
Woon Junge	50	Molly Camp	50
Ernie DeBrul	52	Rachel Myak	52

   a. How many samples of size 2 are possible?
   b. Select all possible samples of size 2 and compute the mean number sold.
   c. Organize the sample means into a frequency distribution.
   d. What is the mean of the population? What is the mean of the sample means?
   e. What is the shape of the population distribution?
   f. What is the shape of the distribution of the sample mean?
35. Power + Inc. produces AA batteries used in remote-controlled toy cars. The mean life of these batteries follows the normal probability distribution with a mean of 35.0 hours and a standard deviation of 5.5 hours. As a part of its quality assurance program, Power +, Inc. tests samples of 25 batteries.
   a. What can you say about the shape of the distribution of the sample mean?
   b. What is the standard error of the distribution of the sample mean?
   c. What is the probability that the mean useful life will be more than 36 hours?
   d. What is the probability that the mean useful life will be greater than 34.5 hours?
   e. What is the probability that the mean useful life will be between 34.5 and 36.0 hours?
   f. What is the probability that the sampling error would be less than or more than 1 hour?
36. Majesty Video Production Inc. wants the mean length of its advertisements to be 30 seconds. Assume the distribution of ad length follows the normal distribution with a population standard deviation of 2 seconds. Suppose we select a sample of 16 ads produced by Majesty.
   a. What can we say about the shape of the distribution of the sample mean time?
   b. What is the standard error of the mean time?
   c. What percent of the sample means will be greater than 31.25 seconds?
   d. What percent of the sample means will be greater than 28.25 seconds?
   e. What percent of the sample means will be greater than 28.25 but less than 31.25 seconds?
   f. What is the probability that the sampling error would be less than or more than 1.5 seconds?
37. Recent studies indicate that the typical 50-year-old person spends $350 per year for personal-care products. The distribution of the amounts spent follows a normal distribution with a standard deviation of $45 per year. We select a random sample of 40 people. The mean amount spent for those sampled is $335. What is the likelihood of finding a sample mean this large or larger from the specified population?
38. Information from the American Institute of Insurance indicates the mean amount of life insurance per household in the United States is $165,000. This distribution follows the normal distribution with a standard deviation of $40,000.
   a. If we select a random sample of 50 households, what is the standard error of the mean?
   b. What is the expected shape of the distribution of the sample mean?
   c. What is the likelihood of selecting a sample with a mean of at least $167,000?
   d. What is the likelihood of selecting a sample with a mean of more than $155,000?
   e. Find the likelihood of selecting a sample with a mean of more than $155,000 but less than $167,000.

39. In the United States, the mean age of men when they marry for the first time follows the normal distribution with a mean of 29 years. The standard deviation of the distribution is 2.5 years. For a random sample of 60 men, what is the likelihood that the age when they were first married is less than 29.3. years?

40. A recent study by the Greater Los Angeles Taxi Drivers Association showed that the mean fare charged for service from Hermosa Beach to Los Angeles International Airport is $25 and the standard deviation is $3.50. We select a sample of 15 fares.
   a. What is the likelihood that the sample mean is between $24 and $27?
   b. What must you assume to make the calculation in (a)?

41. Crossett Trucking Company claims that the mean weight of its delivery trucks when they are fully loaded is 6,000 pounds and the standard deviation is 150 pounds. Assume that the population follows the normal distribution. Forty trucks are randomly selected and weighed. Within what limits will 95% of the sample means occur?

42. The mean amount purchased by a typical customer at Churchill's Grocery Store is $23.50, with a standard deviation of $5.00. Assume the distribution of amounts purchased follows the normal distribution. For a sample of 50 customers, answer the following questions.
   a. What is the likelihood the sample mean is at least $25.00?
   b. What is the likelihood the sample mean is greater than $22.50 but less than $25.00?
   c. Within what limits will 90% of the sample means occur?

43. The mean performance score on a physical fitness test for Division I student-athletes is 947 with a standard deviation of 205. If you select a random sample of 60 of these students, what is the probability the mean is below 900?

44. Suppose we roll a fair die two times.
   a. How many different samples are there?
   b. List each of the possible samples and compute the mean.
   c. On a chart similar to Chart 8–2, compare the distribution of sample means with the distribution of the population.
   d. Compute the mean and the standard deviation of each distribution and compare them.

45. FILE Following is a list of the 50 states with the numbers 0 through 49 assigned to them.

Number	State	Number	State
0	Alabama	25	Montana
1	Alaska	26	Nebraska
2	Arizona	27	Nevada
3	Arkansas	28	New Hampshire
4	California	29	New Jersey
5	Colorado	30	New Mexico
6	Connecticut	31	New York
7	Delaware	32	North Carolina
8	Florida	33	North Dakota
9	Georgia	34	Ohio
10	Hawaii	35	Oklahoma
11	Idaho	36	Oregon
12	Illinois	37	Pennsylvania
13	Indiana	38	Rhode Island
14	Iowa	39	South Carolina
15	Kansas	40	South Dakota
16	Kentucky	41	Tennessee
17	Louisiana	42	Texas
18	Maine	43	Utah
19	Maryland	44	Vermont
20	Massachusetts	45	Virginia
21	Michigan	46	Washington
22	Minnesota	47	West Virginia
23	Mississippi	48	Wisconsin
24	Missouri	49	Wyoming

a. You wish to select a sample of eight from this list. The selected random numbers are 45, 15, 81, 09, 39, 43, 90, 26, 06, 45, 01, and 42. Which states are included in the sample?

b. Select a systematic sample of every sixth item using the digit 02 as the starting point. Which states are included?

46. Human Resource Consulting (HRC) surveyed a random sample of 60 Twin Cities construction companies to find information on the costs of their health care plans. One of the items being tracked is the annual deductible that employees must pay. The Minnesota Department of Labor reports that historically the mean deductible amount per employee is $502 with a standard deviation of $100.

a. Compute the standard error of the sample mean for HRC.

b. What is the chance HRC finds a sample mean between $477 and $527?

c. Calculate the likelihood that the sample mean is between $492 and $512.

d. What is the probability the sample mean is greater than $550?

47. Over the past decade, the mean number of hacking attacks experienced by members of the Information Systems Security Association is 510 per year with a standard deviation of 14.28 attacks. The number of attacks per year is normally distributed. Suppose nothing in this environment changes.

a. What is the likelihood this group will suffer an average of more than 600 attacks in the next 10 years?

b. Compute the probability the mean number of attacks over the next 10 years is between 500 and 600.

c. What is the possibility they will experience an average of less than 500 attacks over the next 10 years?

48. An economist uses the price of a gallon of milk as a measure of inflation. She finds that the average price is $3.82 per gallon and the population standard deviation is $0.33. You decide to sample 40 convenience stores, collect their prices for a gallon of milk, and compute the mean price for the sample.

a. What is the standard error of the mean in this experiment?

b. What is the probability that the sample mean is between $3.78 and $3.86?

c. What is the probability that the difference between the sample mean and the population mean is less than $0.01?

d. What is the likelihood the sample mean is greater than $3.92?

49. Nike's annual report says that the average American buys 6.5 pairs of sports shoes per year. Suppose a sample of 81 customers is surveyed and the population standard deviation of sports shoes purchased per year is 2.1.

a. What is the standard error of the mean in this experiment?

b. What is the probability that the sample mean is between six and seven pairs of sports shoes?

c. What is the probability that the difference between the sample mean and the population mean is less than 0.25 pair?

d. What is the likelihood the sample mean is greater than seven pairs?

50. The population mean proportion is .30. We decide to sample the population by randomly selecting 25 items and computing sample proportions.

a. Can we use the normal distribution to approximate the distribution of sample proportions? Why?

b. What is the standard error of this distribution?

c. Applying the empirical rule, approximately 68% of sample proportions are between what values?

51. The population mean proportion is .80. We decide to sample the population by randomly selecting 40 items and computing sample proportions.

a. Can we use the normal distribution to approximate the distribution of sample proportions? Why?

b. What is the standard error of this distribution?

c. Applying the empirical rule, approximately 95% of sample proportions are between what values?

52. In Phoenix, a Rideshare company believes that 50% of all rides originate at the Sky Harbor International Airport. The company decides to sample 30 rides during a particular day.

a. Test the conditions necessary to apply the central limit theorem. Are they satisfied? Why?

   b. What is the standard error of the sampling distribution of sample proportions?
   c. What is the probability that a sample proportion is greater than .75?
   d. What is the probability that a sample proportion is less than .45?
   e. What is the probability that a sample proportion is between .45 and .70?
   f. What is the probability that the sampling error $(p - \pi)$ would be .20 or more? That is, what is the probability that an estimate of a population proportion is less than .30 or more than .70?

53. A population proportion is 0.90. From this population you select random samples of 60.
   a. Test the conditions necessary to apply the central limit theorem to the distribution of sample proportions. Are they satisfied? Why?
   b. What is the standard error of the sampling distribution of sample proportions?
   c. What is the probability that a sample proportion is more than .95?
   d. What is the probability that a sample proportion is less than .75?
   e. What is the probability that a sample proportion is between .75 and .95?
   f. What is the probability that the sampling error $(p - \pi)$ would be .1 or less? That is, what is the probability that an estimate of a population proportion is between .80 and 1.00?

54. At the Heathrow Airport in London, England, an airport administrator believes that the proportion of delayed flights is .15 per day. What is the probability of selecting a sample of 50 flights on a particular day and finding the proportion is more than .40?
   a. Test the conditions necessary to apply the central limit theorem. Are they satisfied? Why?
   b. Find and interpret the probability in the exercise.

55. A professor writes a statistics test and estimates that 90% of test takers will complete the test in 1 hour or less. She gives the test to a class of 100 students. What is the probability that 5 or less students do not complete the test in less than an hour?
   a. Test the conditions necessary to apply the central limit theorem. Are they satisfied? Why?
   b. Find and interpret the probability in the exercise.

DATA ANALYTICS

56. **FILE** Refer to the North Valley Real Estate data, which report information on the homes sold last year. Assume the 105 homes is a population. Compute the population mean and the standard deviation of price. Select a sample of 10 homes. Compute the mean. Determine the likelihood of a sample mean price this high or higher.

57. **FILE** Refer to the Baseball 2021 data, which report information on the 30 Major League Baseball teams for the 2021 season. Over the last decade, the mean attendance per team followed a normal distribution with a mean of 2.45 million per team and a standard deviation of 0.71 million. Compute the mean attendance per team for the 2021 season. Determine the likelihood of a sample mean attendance this large or larger from the population.

58. **FILE** Refer to the Lincolnville School District bus data. Information provided by manufacturers of school buses suggests the mean maintenance cost per year is $4,400 per bus with a standard deviation of $1,000. Compute the mean maintenance cost for the Lincolnville buses. Does the Lincolnville data seem to be in line with that reported by the manufacturer? Specifically, what is the probability of Lincolnville's mean annual maintenance cost, or greater, given the manufacturer's data?

9

Estimation and Confidence Intervals

MBI/Alamy Stock Photo

▲ **THE AMERICAN RESTAURANT ASSOCIATION** collected information on the number of meals eaten outside the home each week by young married couples. A survey of 60 couples showed the sample mean was 2.76 meals per week, with a standard deviation of 0.75 meal per week. Construct a 99% confidence interval for the population mean. (See Exercise 38 and **LO9-2**.)

LEARNING OBJECTIVES

When you have completed this chapter, you will be able to:

LO9-1 Compute and interpret a point estimate of a population mean.

LO9-2 Compute and interpret a confidence interval for a population mean.

LO9-3 Compute and interpret a confidence interval for a population proportion.

LO9-4 Adjust a confidence interval for finite populations.

LO9-5 Calculate the required sample size to estimate a population proportion or population mean.

Introduction

In Chapter 8, we began our discussion of conducting research. The first steps in the process are clearly stating the research question, defining the variables of interest, and collecting information and data from a defined population. In some situations, the entire population of items may be available. However, in most research, we collect samples from the population. In review, the reasons for sampling are as follows:

- Contacting the entire population is too time consuming.
- Studying all the items in the population is often too expensive.
- The sample results are usually adequate.
- Certain tests are destructive.
- Checking all the items is physically impossible.

An objective of sampling is to collect data and information that represent the population. That is, the sample is an unbiased selection of observations from the population. There are several methods of sampling that help to ensure unbiased sampling. Simple random sampling is the most widely used method. With this type of sampling, each member of the population has the same chance of being selected to be a part of the sample. Other methods of sampling include systematic sampling, stratified sampling, and cluster sampling.

Chapter 8 also introduced the central limit theorem. It is extremely important to the application of statistical methods because it says that, given adequate sample size, sample statistics, such as the sample mean and sample proportion, are normally distributed. To illustrate and apply the central limit theorem, the examples and exercises in Chapter 8 used values for the population mean, μ, population proportion, π, and population standard deviation, σ.

Starting in this chapter, we transition from population parameters to sample statistics. That is, we use sample information to estimate the values of unknown population parameters. We begin by studying point estimates. A point estimate is a single (point) value computed from sample information. Point estimates, such as the sample mean and sample proportion, estimate the population mean and population proportion. For example, we may be interested in a point estimate of the number of billable hours that consultants of Boston Consulting Group charge their clients in a week. Using simple random sampling, we select an unbiased sample of 50 consultants and ask how many hours they billed their clients during a particular week. The sample's mean—say, 26 weekly billable hours—is a point estimate of the unknown population mean.

From Chapter 8, we know that, given adequate sample size, the sample mean is a normally distributed random variable. In addition, we know that because we sample from a population, there will be sampling error. That is, the sample mean will most likely not equal the population mean and the sampling error, $(\bar{x} - \mu)$, will most likely not be zero. In this chapter, we account for sampling error by using the standard error of the sampling distribution to compute an interval estimate of a population parameter. For example, with sample data, we can say that the population mean weekly billable hours is between 22 and 30 billable hours. This range is called an interval estimate of the population mean. In addition, we will use the sampling distribution to determine a level of confidence that the population mean is within the interval. This is called a confidence interval.

Based on the application of the central limit theorem, we see that sample size is crucial in knowing the distribution of a sample statistic is normal. Sample size is also important in controlling the size of the standard error and the accuracy of an interval estimate. Larger sample sizes are related to smaller standard errors and increased accuracy of an estimate. That is, interval estimates will be narrower. This chapter shows how to determine the sample size for a specified sampling error.

LO9-1
Compute and interpret a point estimate of a population mean.

Point Estimate for a Population Mean

A point estimate is a single statistical value used to estimate a population parameter. Suppose Best Buy Inc. wants to estimate the mean age of people who purchase LCD

HDTV televisions. They select a random sample of 75 recent purchases, determine the age of each buyer, and compute the mean age of the buyers in the sample. The mean of this sample is a **point estimate** of the population mean.

> **POINT ESTIMATE** The statistic, computed from sample information, that estimates a population parameter.

The following examples illustrate point estimates of population means.

1. Tourism is a major source of income for many Caribbean countries, such as Barbados. Suppose the Bureau of Tourism for Barbados wants an estimate of the mean amount spent by tourists visiting the country. It would not be feasible to contact each tourist. Therefore, 500 tourists are randomly selected as they depart the country and asked in detail about their spending while visiting Barbados. The survey of the 500 sampled tourists showed mean spending of $168 per day. This sample mean is the point estimate of the population mean of spending per day.

2. Litchfield Home Builders Inc. builds homes in the southeastern region of the United States. One of the major concerns of new buyers is the date when the home will be completed. Recently, Litchfield has been telling customers, "Your home will be completed 45 working days from the date we begin installing drywall." The customer relations department at Litchfield wishes to compare this pledge with recent experience. A random sample of 50 homes completed this year revealed that the point estimate of the population mean is 46.7 working days from the start of drywall to the completion of the home. This point estimate is longer than the assumed population mean of 45 days. The company may need to change the expected completion time to a time longer than 45 days.

3. Recent medical studies indicate that exercise is an important part of a person's overall health. The director of human resources at OCF, a large glass manufacturer, wants an estimate of the number of hours per week employees spend exercising. A random sample of 70 employees reveals the mean number of hours of exercise last week is 3.3. This value is a point estimate of the unknown population mean.

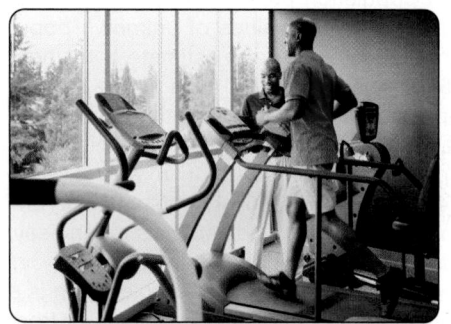

The sample mean, $\bar{x}$, is not the only point estimate of a population parameter. For example, p, a sample proportion, is a point estimate of π, the population proportion; and s, the sample standard deviation, is a point estimate of σ, the population standard deviation.

LO9-2
Compute and interpret a confidence interval for a population mean.

Confidence Intervals for a Population Mean

A point estimate, however, tells only part of the story. While we expect the point estimate to be close to the population parameter, we would like to measure how close it really is. A **confidence interval** serves this purpose. For example, we estimate the mean yearly income for construction workers in the New York–New Jersey area is $85,000. The range of this estimate might be from $81,000 to $89,000. We can describe how confident we are that the population parameter is in the interval. We might say, for instance, that we are 90% confident that the mean yearly income of construction workers in the New York–New Jersey area is between $81,000 and $89,000.

> **CONFIDENCE INTERVAL** A range of values constructed from sample data so that the population parameter is likely to occur within that range at a specified probability. The specified probability is called the *level of confidence.*

To compute a confidence interval for a population mean, we will consider two situations:

- We use sample data to estimate μ with $\bar{x}$ and the population standard deviation (σ) is known.
- We use sample data to estimate μ with $\bar{x}$ and the population standard deviation is unknown. In this case, we substitute the sample standard deviation (s) for the population standard deviation (σ).

There are important distinctions in the assumptions between these two situations. We first consider the case where σ is known.

Population Standard Deviation, Known σ

A confidence interval is computed using two statistics: the sample mean, $\bar{x}$, and the standard deviation. From previous chapters, you know that the standard deviation is an important statistic because it measures the dispersion, or variation, of a population or sampling distribution. In computing a confidence interval, the standard deviation is used to compute the standard error of the sampling distribution and the limits of the confidence interval.

Typically, we do not know the population standard deviation, σ. We estimate it with the standard deviation of a sample, s. However, to begin our presentation of confidence intervals, we assume that we know the value of the population standard deviation. This assumption allows us to simplify the introduction of confidence intervals by using the standard normal distribution as presented in Chapters 7 and 8.

Based on the central limit theorem, we know that the sampling distribution of the sample mean is normally distributed with a mean of μ and a standard deviation $\sigma/\sqrt{n}$. Also recall that this value is called the standard error. The results of the central limit theorem allow us to make the following general confidence interval statements using z-statistics:

1. Ninety-five percent of all confidence intervals computed from random samples selected from a population will contain the population mean. These intervals are computed using a z-statistic equal to 1.96.
2. Ninety percent of all confidence intervals computed from random samples selected from a population will contain the population mean. These confidence intervals are computed using a z-statistic equal to 1.65.

These confidence interval statements provide examples of *levels of confidence* and are called a **95% confidence interval** and a **90% confidence interval.** The *95%* and *90%* are the levels of confidence and refer to the percentage of similarly constructed intervals that would include the parameter being estimated—in this case, μ, the population mean.

How are the values of 1.96 and 1.65 obtained? First, let's look for the z-value for a 95% confidence interval. The following diagram and Table 9–1 will help explain.

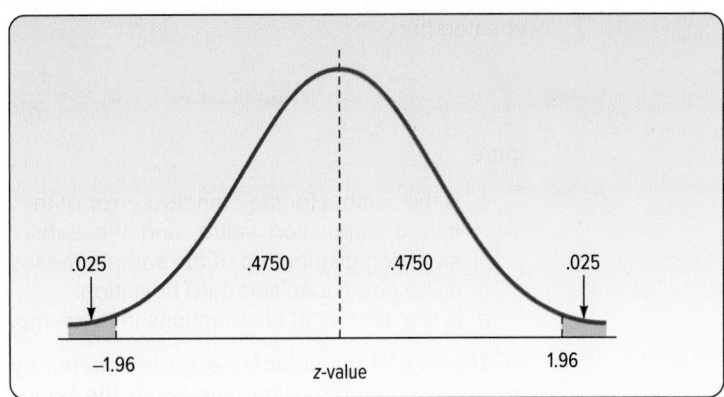

TABLE 9–1 The Standard Normal Table for Selected Values

z	0.00	0.01	0.02	0.03	0.04	0.05	0.06	0.07
⋮	⋮	⋮	⋮	⋮	⋮	⋮	⋮	⋮
1.5	0.4332	0.4345	0.4357	0.4370	0.4382	0.4394	0.4406	0.4418
1.6	0.4452	0.4463	0.4474	0.4484	0.4495	0.4505	0.4515	0.4525
1.7	0.4554	0.4564	0.4573	0.4582	0.4591	0.4599	0.4608	0.4616
1.8	0.4641	0.4649	0.4656	0.4664	0.4671	0.4678	0.4686	0.4693
1.9	0.4713	0.4719	0.4726	0.4732	0.4738	0.4744	0.4750	0.4756
2.0	0.4772	0.4778	0.4783	0.4788	0.4793	0.4798	0.4803	0.4808
2.1	0.4821	0.4826	0.4830	0.4834	0.4838	0.4842	0.4846	0.4850
2.2	0.4861	0.4864	0.4868	0.4871	0.4875	0.4878	0.4881	0.4884

Table 9–1 is a reproduction of the standard normal table in Appendix B.3. However, many rows and columns have been eliminated to allow us to better focus on particular rows and columns.

1. First, we divide the confidence level in half, so .9500/2 = .4750.
2. Next, we find the value .4750 in the body of Table 9–1. Note that .4750 is located in the table at the intersection of a row and a column.
3. Locate the corresponding row value in the left margin, which is 1.9, and the column value in the top margin, which is .06. Adding the row and column values gives us a z-value of 1.96.
4. Thus, the probability of finding a z-value between 0 and 1.96 is .4750.
5. Likewise, because the normal distribution is symmetric, the probability of finding a z-value between −1.96 and 0 is also .4750.
6. When we add these two probabilities, the probability that a z-value is between −1.96 and 1.96 is .9500.

For the 90% level of confidence, we follow the same steps. First, one-half of the desired confidence interval is .4500. A search of Table 9–1 does not reveal this exact value. However, it is between two values, .4495 and .4505. As in step 3, we locate each value in the table. The first, .4495, corresponds to a z-value of 1.64 and the second, .4505, corresponds to a z-value of 1.65. To be conservative, we will select the larger of the two z-values, 1.65, and the exact level of confidence is 90.1%, or 2(0.4505). Next, the probability of finding a z-value between −1.65 and 0 is .4505, and the probability that a z-value is between −1.65 and 1.65 is .9010.

How do we determine a 95% confidence interval? The width of the interval is determined by two factors: (1) the level of confidence, as described in the previous section, and (2) the size of the standard error of the mean. To find the standard error of the mean, recall from the previous chapter [see formula (8–1) on page 271] that the standard error of the mean reports the variation in the distribution of sample means. It is really the standard deviation of the distribution of sample means. The formula is repeated here:

$$\sigma_{\bar{x}} = \frac{\sigma}{\sqrt{n}}$$

where:

$\sigma_{\bar{x}}$ is the symbol for the standard error of the mean. We use a Greek letter because it is a population value, and the subscript $\bar{x}$ reminds us that it refers to a sampling distribution of the sample means.

σ is the population standard deviation.

n is the number of observations in the sample.

The size of the standard error is affected by two values. The first is the standard deviation of the population. The larger the population standard deviation, σ, the larger

$\sigma/\sqrt{n}$. If the population is homogeneous, resulting in a small population standard deviation, the standard error will also be small. However, the standard error is also affected by the number of observations in the sample. A large number of observations in the sample will result in a small standard error of estimate, indicating that there is less variability in the sample means.

We can summarize the calculation for a 95% confidence interval using the following formula:

$$\bar{x} \pm 1.96 \frac{\sigma}{\sqrt{n}}$$

Similarly, a 90.1% confidence interval is computed as follows:

$$\bar{x} \pm 1.65 \frac{\sigma}{\sqrt{n}}$$

The values 1.96 and 1.65 are z-values corresponding to the 95% and the 90.1% confidence intervals, respectively. However, we are not restricted to these values. We can select any confidence level between 0 and 100% and find the corresponding value for z. If the population standard deviation is known, we use a z-value and compute confidence intervals for the population mean as:

CONFIDENCE INTERVAL FOR A POPULATION MEAN WITH σ KNOWN	$\bar{x} \pm z \dfrac{\sigma}{\sqrt{n}}$	(9–1)

Denis Michaliov/denismart/ 123RF

To explain these ideas, consider the following example. Del Monte Foods distributes mandarin oranges in 4.5-ounce plastic cups. To ensure that each cup contains at least the required amount, Del Monte sets the filling operation to dispense 4.51 ounces of mandarin oranges and gel in each cup. Of course, not every cup will contain exactly 4.51 ounces of mandarin oranges and gel. Some cups will have more and others less. From data and information about the filling process, Del Monte knows that 0.04 ounce is the population standard deviation of the filling process and that the amount, in ounces, follows the normal probability distribution. The quality control technician selects a sample of 64 cups at the start of each shift, measures the amount in each cup, computes the mean fill amount, and then develops a 95% confidence interval for the population mean. Using the confidence interval, is the process filling the cups to the desired amount? This morning's sample of 64 cups had a sample mean of 4.507 ounces. Based on this information, the 95% confidence interval is:

$$\bar{x} \pm 1.96 \frac{\sigma}{\sqrt{n}} = 4.507 \pm 1.96 \frac{0.04}{\sqrt{64}} = 4.507 \pm 0.0098$$

The 95% confidence interval estimates that the population mean is between 4.4972 and 4.5168 ounces of mandarin oranges and gel. Recall that the process is set to fill each cup with 4.51 ounces. Because the desired fill amount of 4.51 ounces is in this interval, we conclude that the filling process is achieving the desired results. In other words, it is reasonable to conclude that the sample mean of 4.507 could have come from a population distribution with a mean of 4.51 ounces.

In this example, we observe that the population mean of 4.51 ounces is in the confidence interval. But this is not always the case. If we selected 100 samples of 64 cups from the population, calculated the sample mean, and developed a confidence interval based on each sample, we would expect to find the population mean in about 95 of the 100 intervals. Or, in contrast, about five of the intervals would not contain the population mean. From Chapter 8, this is called sampling error. The following Example/Solution details repeated sampling from a population.

▶ **EXAMPLE**

The American Management Association (AMA) is studying the income of store managers in the retail industry. A random sample of 49 managers reveals a sample mean of $63,400. The standard deviation of this population is $2,050. The association would like answers to the following questions:

1.   What is the population mean? What is an estimate of the population mean?
2.   What is a reasonable range of values for the population mean?
3.   How do we interpret these results?

SOLUTION

Generally, distributions of salary and income are positively skewed because a few individuals earn considerably more than others, thus the distribution has a long tail to the right. Fortunately, the central limit theorem states that the sampling distribution of the mean becomes a normal distribution as sample size increases. In this instance, a sample of 49 store managers is large enough that we can assume that the sampling distribution will follow the normal distribution. Now to answer the questions posed in the example.

1.   **What is the population mean? What is an estimate of the population mean?** In this case, we do not know the population mean. We do know the sample mean is $63,400. Hence, our best estimate of the unknown population value is the corresponding sample statistic. Thus, the sample mean of $63,400 is a *point estimate* of the unknown population mean.

2.   **What is a reasonable range of values for the population mean?** The AMA decides to use the 95% level of confidence. To determine the corresponding confidence interval, we use formula (9–1):

$$\bar{x} \pm z \frac{\sigma}{\sqrt{n}} = \$63,400 \pm 1.96 \frac{\$2,050}{\sqrt{49}} = \$63,400 \pm \$574$$

The confidence interval limits are $62,826 and $63,974 determined by subtracting $574 and adding $574 to the sample mean. The degree or level of confidence is 95% and the confidence interval is from $62,826 to $63,974. The value, $574, is called the margin of error.

3.   **How do we interpret these results?** Ninety-five percent of all confidence intervals computed from random samples selected from a population will contain the population mean. To illustrate, suppose we select many samples of 49 store managers, perhaps several hundred. For each sample, we compute the mean and then construct a 95% confidence interval, such as we did in the previous section. We could expect about 95% of these confidence intervals to contain the *population* mean. About 5% of the intervals would not contain the population mean annual income, which is μ. However, a particular confidence interval either contains the population parameter or it does not. The following diagram shows the results of selecting samples from the population of store managers in the retail industry, computing the mean of each,

and then, using formula (9–1), determining a 95% confidence interval for the population mean. Note that not all intervals include the population mean. Both the endpoints of the fifth sample are less than the population mean. We attribute this to sampling error, and it is the risk we assume when we select the level of confidence.

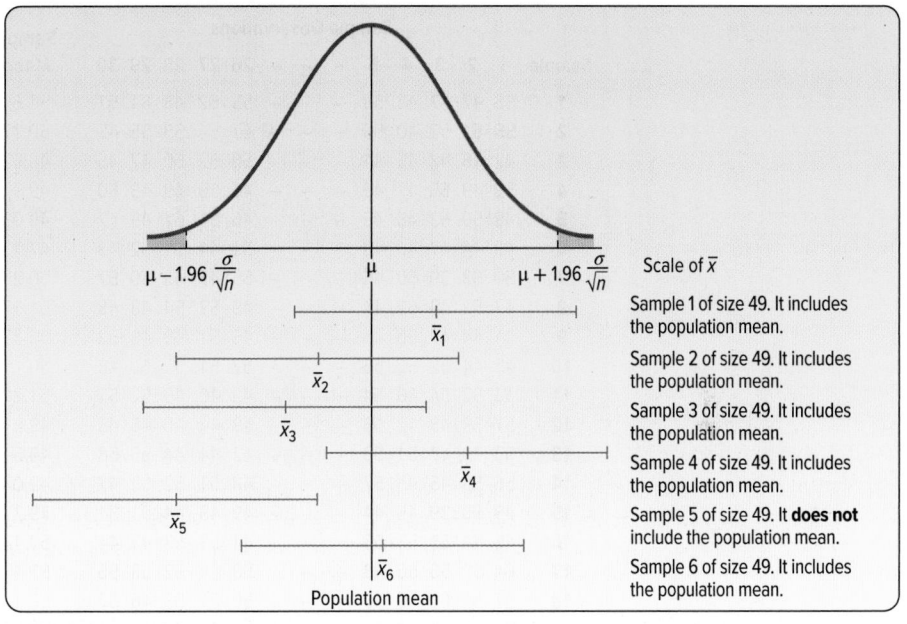

A Computer Simulation

With statistical software, we can create random samples of a desired sample size, *n*, from a population. For each sample of *n* observations with corresponding numerical values, we can calculate the sample mean. With the sample mean, population standard deviation, and confidence level, we can determine the confidence interval for each sample. Then, using all samples and the confidence intervals, we can find the frequency that the population mean is included in the confidence intervals. The following example does just that.

▶ **EXAMPLE**

From many years in the automobile leasing business, Town Bank knows that the mean distance driven on an automobile with a 4-year lease is 50,000 miles and the standard deviation is 5,000 miles. These are population values. Suppose Town Bank would like to experiment with the idea of sampling to estimate the population mean of 50,000 miles. Town Bank decides to choose a sample size of 30 observations and a 95% confidence interval to estimate the population mean. Based on the experiment, we want to count the number of confidence intervals that include the population mean of 50,000. We expect about 95%, or 57 of the 60 intervals, will include the population mean. To make the calculations easier to understand, we'll conduct the study in thousands of miles, instead of miles.

SOLUTION

Using statistical software, 60 random samples of 30 observations, $n = 30$, are generated and the sample means for each sample computed. Then, using the n of 30 and a standard error of 0.913 ($\sigma/\sqrt{n} = 5/\sqrt{30}$), a 95% confidence interval is computed for each sample. The results of the experiment are shown next.

	Sample Observations													Sample	95% Confidence Limits	
Sample	1	2	3	4	5	–	–	–	26	27	28	29	30	Mean	Lower Limit	Upper Limit
1	56	47	47	48	58	–	–	–	55	62	48	61	57	51.6	49.811	53.389
2	55	51	52	40	53	–	–	–	47	54	55	55	45	50.77	48.981	52.559
3	42	46	48	46	41	–	–	–	50	52	50	47	45	48.63	46.841	50.419
4	52	49	55	47	49	–	–	–	46	56	49	43	50	49.9	48.111	51.689
5	48	50	53	48	45	–	–	–	46	51	61	49	47	49.03	47.241	50.819
6	49	44	47	46	48	–	–	–	51	44	51	52	43	47.73	45.941	49.519
7	50	53	39	50	46	–	–	–	55	47	43	50	57	50.2	48.411	51.989
8	47	51	49	58	44	–	–	–	49	57	54	48	48	51.17	49.381	52.959
9	51	44	47	56	45	–	–	–	45	51	49	49	52	50.33	48.541	52.119
10	45	44	52	52	56	–	–	–	52	51	52	50	48	50	48.211	51.789
11	43	52	54	46	54	–	–	–	43	46	49	52	52	51.2	49.411	52.989
12	57	53	48	42	55	–	–	–	49	44	46	46	48	49.8	48.011	51.589
13	53	39	47	51	53	–	–	–	42	44	44	55	58	49.6	47.811	51.389
14	56	55	45	43	57	–	–	–	48	51	52	55	47	49.03	47.241	50.819
15	49	50	39	45	44	–	–	–	49	43	44	51	51	49.37	47.581	51.159
16	46	44	55	53	55	–	–	–	44	53	53	43	44	50.13	48.341	51.919
17	64	52	55	55	43	–	–	–	58	46	52	58	55	52.47	50.681	54.259
18	57	51	60	40	53	–	–	–	50	51	53	46	52	50.1	48.311	51.889
19	50	49	51	57	45	–	–	–	53	52	40	45	52	49.6	47.811	51.389
20	45	46	53	57	49	–	–	–	49	43	43	53	48	49.47	47.681	51.259
21	52	45	51	52	45	–	–	–	43	49	49	58	53	50.43	48.641	52.219
22	48	48	52	49	40	–	–	–	50	47	54	51	45	47.53	45.741	49.319
23	48	50	50	53	44	–	–	–	48	57	52	44	39	49.1	47.311	50.889
24	51	51	40	54	52	–	–	–	54	45	50	57	48	50.13	48.341	51.919
25	48	63	41	52	41	–	–	–	48	50	48	44	53	49.33	47.541	51.119
26	47	45	48	59	49	–	–	–	44	47	49	55	42	49.63	47.841	51.419
27	52	45	60	51	52	–	–	–	52	50	54	46	52	49.4	47.611	51.189
28	46	48	46	57	51	–	–	–	51	50	51	41	52	49.33	47.541	51.119
29	46	48	45	42	48	–	–	–	49	43	59	46	50	48.27	46.481	50.059
30	55	48	47	48	48	–	–	–	47	59	54	51	42	50.53	48.741	52.319
31	58	49	56	46	46	–	–	–	44	51	47	51	46	50.77	48.981	52.559
32	53	54	52	58	55	–	–	–	53	52	45	44	51	50	48.211	51.789
33	50	57	56	51	51	–	–	–	58	47	50	56	46	49.7	47.911	51.489
34	61	48	49	53	54	–	–	–	46	46	56	45	54	50.03	48.241	51.819
35	43	42	43	46	49	–	–	–	49	49	56	51	45	49.43	47.641	51.219
36	39	48	48	51	44	–	–	–	54	52	47	50	52	50.07	48.281	51.859
37	48	43	57	42	54	–	–	–	52	50	59	50	52	50.17	48.381	51.959
38	55	43	49	57	45	–	–	–	41	51	51	52	52	49.5	47.711	51.289
39	47	49	58	54	54	–	–	–	50	56	51	56	58	50.37	48.581	52.159
40	47	56	41	50	54	–	–	–	46	56	61	61	45	51.6	49.811	53.389
41	48	47	42	47	62	–	–	–	44	47	49	55	43	49.43	47.641	51.219
42	46	49	43	36	52	–	–	–	45	51	46	51	43	47.67	45.881	49.459
43	44	48	49	48	51	–	–	–	47	52	51	48	49	49.63	47.841	51.419
44	45	52	54	54	49	–	–	–	49	45	53	50	52	49.07	47.281	50.859

(continued)

| | Sample Observations | | | | | | | | | | | | | Sample | 95% Confidence Limits | |
Sample	1	2	3	4	5	–	–	–	26	27	28	29	30	Mean	Lower Limit	Upper Limit
45	54	46	54	45	48	–	–	–	55	38	56	50	62	49.53	47.741	51.319
46	48	50	49	52	51	–	–	–	53	57	58	46	50	49.9	48.111	51.689
47	54	55	46	55	50	–	–	–	56	54	50	55	51	50.5	48.711	52.289
48	45	47	47	63	44	–	–	–	45	53	42	53	50	50.1	48.311	51.889
49	47	47	48	54	56	–	–	–	50	48	54	49	51	49.93	48.141	51.719
50	45	61	51	45	54	–	–	–	55	52	47	45	53	51.03	49.241	52.819
51	49	62	43	49	48	–	–	–	49	58	42	58	52	51.07	49.281	52.859
52	54	52	62	43	54	–	–	–	51	57	49	58	55	50.17	48.381	51.959
53	46	50	59	56	46	–	–	–	50	51	52	54	53	50.47	48.681	52.259
54	52	50	48	48	58	–	–	–	58	52	43	61	54	51.77	49.981	53.559
55	45	44	46	56	46	–	–	–	43	45	63	48	56	49.37	47.581	51.159
56	60	50	56	51	43	–	–	–	45	43	49	59	54	50.37	48.581	52.159
57	59	56	43	47	52	–	–	–	49	54	50	50	57	49.53	47.741	51.319
58	52	55	48	51	40	–	–	–	53	51	51	52	47	49.77	47.981	51.559
59	53	50	44	53	52	–	–	–	47	50	55	46	51	50.07	48.281	51.859
60	55	54	50	52	43	–	–	–	57	50	48	47	53	52.07	50.281	53.859

To explain, in the first row, the statistical software computed 30 random observations from a population distribution with a mean of 50 and a standard deviation of 5. To conserve space, only observations 1 through 5 and 26 through 30 are listed. The first sample's mean is computed and listed as 51.6. In the next columns, the upper and lower limits of the 95% confidence interval for the first sample are shown. The confidence interval calculation for the first sample follows:

$$\bar{x} \pm 1.96 \frac{\sigma}{\sqrt{n}} = 51.6 \pm 1.96 \frac{5}{\sqrt{30}} = 51.6 \pm 1.789$$

This calculation is repeated for all samples. The results of the experiment show 91.67%, or 55 of the 60 confidence intervals, include the population mean of 50. Thus, 91.67% is close to the estimate that 95%, or 57, of the intervals will include the population mean. Using the complement, we expected 5%, or three, of the intervals would not include the population mean. The experiment resulted in 8.33%, or five, of the intervals that did not include the population mean. The particular intervals, 6, 17, 22, 42, and 60, are highlighted. This is another example of sampling error, or the possibility that a particular random sample may not be a good representation of the population. In each of these five samples, the mean of the sample is either much less or much more than the population mean. Because of random sampling, the mean of the sample is not a good estimate of the population mean, and the confidence interval based on the sample's mean does not include the population mean.

SELF-REVIEW 9–1

The Bun-and-Run is a franchise fast-food restaurant located in the Northeast specializing in half-pound hamburgers, fish sandwiches, and chicken sandwiches. Soft drinks and French fries also are available. The Marketing Department of Bun-and-Run Inc. reports that the distribution of daily sales for their restaurants follows the normal distribution and that the population standard deviation is $3,000. A sample of 40 franchises showed the mean daily sales to be $20,000.

(a) What is the population mean of daily sales for Bun-and-Run franchises?
(b) What is the best estimate of the population mean? What is this value called?
(c) Develop a 95% confidence interval for the population mean of daily sales.
(d) Interpret the confidence interval.

EXERCISES

1. A sample of 49 observations is taken from a normal population with a population standard deviation of 10. The sample mean is 55. Determine the 99% confidence interval for the population mean.

2. A sample of 81 observations is taken from a normal population with a population standard deviation of 5. The sample mean is 40. Determine the 95% confidence interval for the population mean.

3. A sample of 250 observations is selected from a normal population with a population standard deviation of 25. The sample mean is 20.
    a. Determine the standard error of the mean.
    b. Explain why we can use a z-value and formula (9–1) to determine the 95% confidence interval.
    c. Determine the 95% confidence interval for the population mean.

4. Suppose you want to compute an 85% confidence interval for the population mean. If you know σ, what z-value would you use in formula (9–1)? Hint: Use the standard normal distribution table.

5. A research firm surveyed 49 randomly selected Americans to determine the mean amount spent on coffee during 1 week. The sample mean was $20 per week. The population distribution is normal with a population standard deviation of $5.
    a. What is the point estimate of the population mean? Explain what it indicates.
    b. Using the 95% level of confidence, determine the confidence interval for μ. Explain what it indicates.

6. Refer to the previous exercise. Instead of 49, suppose that 64 Americans were surveyed about their weekly expenditures on coffee. Assume the sample mean remained the same.
    a. What is the 95% confidence interval estimate of μ?
    b. Explain why this confidence interval is narrower than the one determined in the previous exercise.

7. Bob Nale is the owner of Nale's Quick Fill. Bob would like to estimate the mean number of gallons of gasoline sold to his customers. Assume the number of gallons sold follows the normal distribution with a population standard deviation of 2.30 gallons. From his records, he selects a random sample of 60 sales and finds the mean number of gallons sold is 8.60.
    a. What is the point estimate of the population mean?
    b. Develop a 99% confidence interval for the population mean.
    c. Interpret the meaning of part (b).

8. Dr. Hume is a professor of English. Recently she counted the number of misspelled words in a group of student essays. She noted the distribution of misspelled words per essay followed the normal distribution with a population standard deviation of 2.44 words per essay. For her 10 a.m. section of 40 students, the mean number of misspelled words was 6.05. Construct a 95% confidence interval for the mean number of misspelled words in the population of student essays.

Population Standard Deviation, σ Unknown

In the previous section, we assumed the population standard deviation was known. In the case involving Del Monte 4.5-ounce cups of mandarin oranges, there would likely be a long history of measurements in the filling process. Therefore, it is reasonable to assume the standard deviation of the population is available. However, in most sampling situations the population standard deviation (σ) is not known. Here are some examples where we wish to estimate the population means and it is unlikely we would know the population standard deviations. Suppose each of these studies involves students at West Virginia University.

- The Dean of the Business College wants to estimate the mean number of hours full-time students work at paying jobs each week. He selects a sample of 30 students, contacts each student, and asks them how many hours they worked last week. From the sample information, he can calculate the sample mean, but it is not likely he would know or be able to find the *population* standard deviation (σ) required in formula (9–1).
- The Dean of Students wants to estimate the distance the typical commuter student travels to class. She selects a sample of 40 commuter students, contacts each, and determines the one-way distance from each student's home to the center of campus. From the sample data, she calculates the mean travel distance, that is, $\bar{x}$. It is unlikely the standard deviation of the population would be known or available, again making formula (9–1) unusable.
- The Director of Student Loans wants to estimate the mean amount owed on student loans at the time of graduation. The director selects a sample of 20 graduating students and contacts each to find the information. From the sample information, the director can estimate the mean amount. However, to develop a confidence interval using formula (9–1), the population standard deviation is necessary. It is not likely this information is available.

Fortunately we can use the sample standard deviation to estimate the population standard deviation. That is, we use *s*, the sample standard deviation, to estimate σ, the population standard deviation. But in doing so, we cannot use formula (9–1). Because we do not know σ, we cannot use the *z*-distribution. However, there is a remedy. We use the *t*-distribution.

The *t*-distribution is a continuous probability distribution, with many similar characteristics to the *z*-distribution. William Gosset, an English brewmaster, was the first to study the *t*-distribution. He was particularly interested in the behavior of the distribution of the following statistic:

$$t = \frac{\bar{x} - \mu}{s/\sqrt{n}}$$

where *s* is the sample standard deviation and the point estimate of the population standard deviation, σ. He noticed differences between the *z*- and *t*-distributions when estimating σ based on *s*, especially when *s* was calculated from a very small sample. The *t*-distribution and the standard normal distribution are shown graphically in Chart 9–1. Note particularly that the *t*-distribution is flatter, more spread out, than the standard normal distribution. This is because the standard deviation of the *t*-distribution is larger than that of the standard normal distribution.

The following characteristics of the *t*-distribution are based on the assumption that the population of interest is normal, or nearly normal.

- It is, like the *z*-distribution, a continuous distribution.
- It is, like the *z*-distribution, bell shaped and symmetrical.
- There is not one *t*-distribution, but rather a family of *t*-distributions. All *t*-distributions have a mean of 0, but their standard deviations differ according to the sample size, *n*. There is a *t*-distribution for a sample size of 20, another for a sample size of 22, and so on. The standard deviation for a *t*-distribution with 5 observations is larger than for a *t*-distribution with 20 observations.
- The *t*-distribution is more spread out and flatter at the center than the standard normal distribution (see Chart 9–1). As the sample size increases, however, the *t*-distribution approaches the standard normal distribution because the errors in using *s* to estimate σ decrease with larger samples.

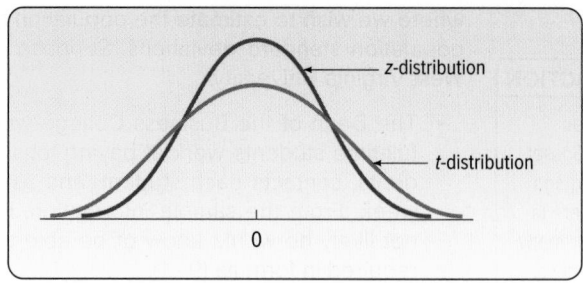

CHART 9–1 The Standard Normal Distribution and Student's *t*-Distribution

Because Student's *t*-distribution has a greater spread than the *z*-distribution, the absolute value of *t* for a given level of confidence is greater in magnitude than the absolute value of the corresponding *z*-value. Chart 9–2 shows the values of *z* for a 95% level of confidence and of *t* for the same level of confidence when the sample size is *n* = 5. How we obtained the actual value of *t* will be explained shortly. For now, observe that for the same level of confidence the *t*-distribution is flatter or more spread out than the standard normal distribution. Note that the margin of error for a 95% confidence interval using a *t*-statistic will be larger compared to using a *z*-statistic. The associated confidence interval using a *t*-statistic will be wider than an interval using a *z*-statistic.

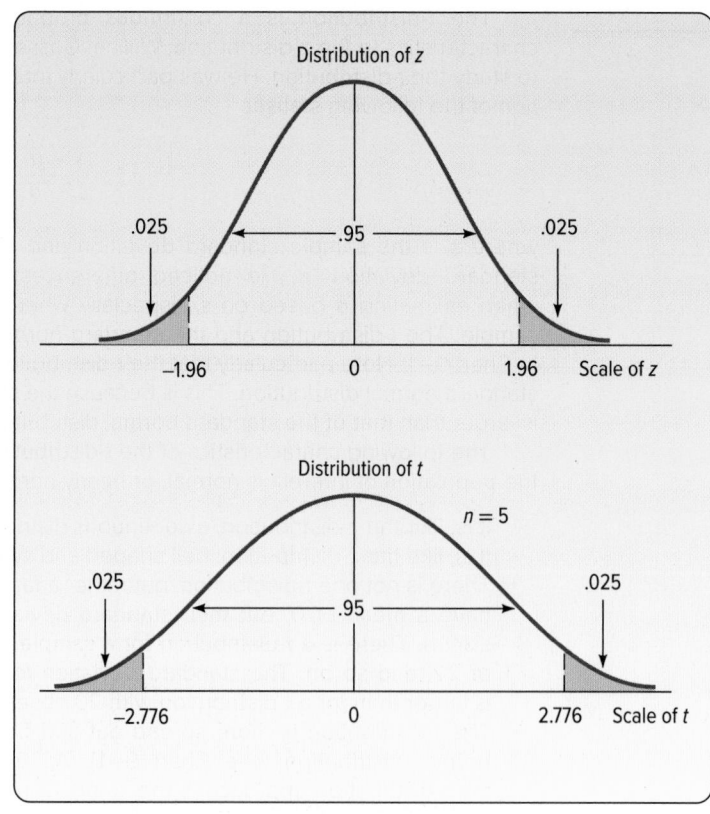

CHART 9–2 Values of *z* and *t* for the 95% Level of Confidence

To develop a confidence interval for the population mean using the *t*-distribution, we adjust formula (9–1) as follows.

CONFIDENCE INTERVAL FOR THE POPULATION MEAN, σ UNKNOWN	$\bar{x} \pm t \dfrac{s}{\sqrt{n}}$	(9–2)

To determine a confidence interval for the population mean with an unknown population standard deviation, we:

1. Assume the sampled population is normal or approximately normal. This assumption may be questionable for small sample sizes, but it becomes more valid with larger sample sizes.
2. Estimate the population standard deviation (σ) with the sample standard deviation (*s*).
3. Use the *t*-distribution rather than the *z*-distribution.

We should be clear at this point. We base the decision to use the *t* or the *z* on whether we know σ, the population standard deviation. If we know the population standard deviation, then we use *z*. If we do not know the population standard deviation, then we must use *t*. Chart 9–3 summarizes the decision-making process.

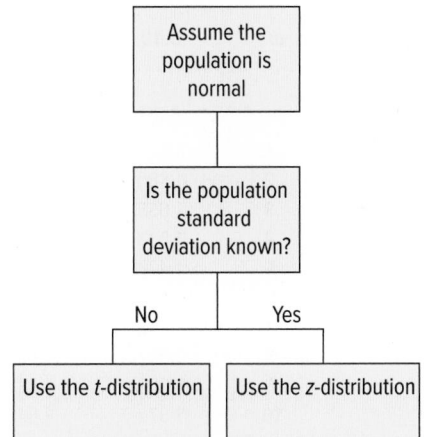

CHART 9–3 Determining When to Use the *z*-Distribution or the *t*-Distribution

The following Example/Solution will illustrate a confidence interval for a population mean when the population standard deviation is unknown and how to find the appropriate value of *t* in a table.

▶ **EXAMPLE**

A tire manufacturer wishes to investigate the tread life of its tires. A sample of 10 tires driven 50,000 miles revealed a sample mean of 0.32 inch of tread remaining with a standard deviation of 0.09 inch. Construct a 95% confidence interval for the population mean. Would it be reasonable for the manufacturer to conclude that after 50,000 miles the population mean amount of tread remaining is 0.30 inch?

SOLUTION

To begin, we assume the population distribution is normal. In this case, we don't have a lot of evidence, but the assumption is probably reasonable. We know the sample standard deviation is .09 inch. We use formula (9–2):

$$\bar{x} \pm t \frac{s}{\sqrt{n}}$$

From the information given, $\bar{x} = 0.32$, $s = 0.09$, and $n = 10$. To find the value of t, we use Appendix B.5, a portion of which is reproduced in Table 9–2. The first step for locating t is to move across the columns identified for "Confidence Intervals" to the level of confidence requested. In this case, we want the 95% level of confidence, so we move to the column headed "95%." The column on the left margin is identified as "*df.*" This refers to the degrees of freedom. The number of degrees of freedom is the number of observations in the sample minus the number of samples, written $n - 1$. In this case, it is $10 - 1 = 9$. Why did we decide there were 9 degrees of freedom? When sample statistics are being used, it is necessary to determine the number of values that are *free to vary*.

TABLE 9–2 A Portion of the *t*-Distribution

df	80%	90%	95%	98%	99%
	Level of Significance for One-Tailed Test				
	0.10	0.05	0.025	0.010	0.005
	Level of Significance for Two-Tailed Test				
	0.20	0.10	0.05	0.02	0.01
1	3.078	6.314	12.706	31.821	63.657
2	1.886	2.920	4.303	6.965	9.925
3	1.638	2.353	3.182	4.541	5.841
4	1.533	2.132	2.776	3.747	4.604
5	1.476	2.015	2.571	3.365	4.032
6	1.440	1.943	2.447	3.143	3.707
7	1.415	1.895	2.365	2.998	3.499
8	1.397	1.860	2.306	2.896	3.355
9	1.383	1.833	2.262	2.821	3.250
10	1.372	1.812	2.228	2.764	3.169

To illustrate the meaning of degrees of freedom: Assume that the mean of four numbers is known to be 5. The four numbers are 7, 4, 1, and 8. The deviations of these numbers from the mean must total 0. The deviations of +2, −1, −4, and +3 do total 0. If the deviations of +2, −1, and −4 are known, then the value of +3 is fixed (restricted) to satisfy the condition that the sum of the deviations must equal 0. Thus, 1 degree of freedom is lost in a sampling problem involving the standard deviation of the sample because one value in the sample can be determined based on the other sample information. Therefore, the degrees of freedom equal $(n - 1)$. For a 95% level of confidence and 9 degrees of freedom, we select the row with 9 degrees of freedom. The value of t is 2.262.

To determine the confidence interval, we substitute the values in formula (9–2).

$$\bar{x} \pm t \frac{s}{\sqrt{n}} = 0.32 \pm 2.262 \frac{0.09}{\sqrt{10}} = 0.32 \pm 0.064$$

The upper limit of the confidence interval, 0.384, is computed by adding the sample mean and the *margin of error,* 0.32 + 0.064. The lower limit of the confidence interval, 0.256, is computed by subtracting the *margin of error* from the sample mean, 0.32–0.064.

How do we interpret this result? If we repeated this study 200 times, calculating the 95% confidence interval with each sample's mean and the standard deviation, we expect 190, 95% of 200, of the intervals would include the population mean. Ten, or 5% of 200, of the intervals would not include the population mean. This is the effect of sampling error. The manufacturer can be reasonably sure (95% confident) that the mean remaining tread depth is between 0.256 and 0.384 inch. Because the value of 0.30 is in this interval, it is possible that the mean of the population is 0.30.

Here is another example to clarify the use of confidence intervals. Suppose an article in your local newspaper reported that the mean time to sell a residential property in the area is 60 days. You select a random sample of 20 homes sold in the last year and find the mean selling time is 65 days. Based on the sample data, you develop a 95% confidence interval for the population mean. You find that the endpoints of the confidence interval are 62 and 68 days. How do you interpret this result? You can be reasonably confident the population mean is within this range. The value proposed for the population mean, that is, 60 days, is not included in the interval. Based on the sample of 20 homes, it is not likely that the population mean is 60 days. The evidence indicates the statement by the local newspaper may not be correct. To put it another way, if the population mean was really 60 days, then it would be very unlikely that we would get our sample results. Therefore, the sample data indicate that we have reason to doubt the information reported in the paper.

The following Example/Solution will show additional details for determining and interpreting a confidence interval.

▶ EXAMPLE

The manager of the Inlet Square Mall, near Ft. Myers, Florida, wants to estimate the mean amount spent per shopping visit by customers. A sample of 20 customers reveals the following amounts spent.

$ 96.32	$ 83.72	$101.64	$122.92
84.44	109.72	93.88	102.70
93.64	75.84	123.66	105.36
102.90	105.28	123.38	117.68
47.56	97.18	98.34	87.76

What is the best estimate of the population mean? Determine a 95% confidence interval. Interpret the result. Would it be reasonable to conclude that the population mean is $100? What about $115?

SOLUTION

The mall manager assumes that the population of the amounts spent follows the normal distribution. This is a reasonable assumption and allows us to use the *t*-distribution. Additionally, the confidence interval technique is quite powerful and tends to commit any errors on the conservative side if the population is not normal. We should not make the normality assumption when the population is severely

Kumar Sriskandan/Alamy Stock Photo

skewed or when the distribution has "thick tails." In Chapter 16, we present methods for handling this issue if we cannot make the normality assumption. In this case, the normality assumption is reasonable.

The mall manager does not know the population mean or standard deviation. The best *point estimate* of the population mean is the sample mean. Using statistical software, the mean is $98.70. It is computed as:

$$\bar{x} = \frac{\Sigma x}{n} = \frac{\$96.32 + \$83.72 + \cdots + \$117.68 + \$87.76}{20} = \$98.696$$

The best point estimate of the population standard deviation is the sample standard deviation. Again, using statistical software, the sample standard deviation is $18.02. It is computed as:

$$s = \sqrt{\frac{\Sigma(x - \bar{x})^2}{n - 1}}$$

$$= \sqrt{\frac{(\$96.32 - \$98.696)^2 + (\$84.44 - \$98.696)^2 + \cdots + (\$87.76 - \$98.696)^2}{19}} = \$18.024$$

To compute the confidence interval, we use formula (9–2) with a *t*-statistic because we assumed that the population distribution is normal. We use the sample standard deviation as the point estimate of the unknown population standard deviation. The value of *t* is available from Appendix B.5. There are $n - 1 = 20 - 1 = 19$ degrees of freedom. We move across the row with 19 degrees of freedom to the column for the 95% confidence level. The value at this intersection is 2.093. We substitute these values into formula (9–2) to find the confidence interval.

$$\bar{x} \pm t\frac{s}{\sqrt{n}} = \$98.696 \pm 2.093\frac{\$18.024}{\sqrt{20}} = \$98.696 \pm \$8.436$$

The upper limit of the confidence interval, $107.132, is computed by adding the sample mean and the *margin of error,* $98.696 + $8.436. The lower limit of the confidence interval, $90.260, is computed by subtracting the *margin of error* from the sample mean, $98.696 − $8.436. So, we are 95% confident that the population mean of amount spent is in the interval between $90.260 and $107.132. See the Excel tutorial to learn how to compute the sample statistics, the margin of error, and the confidence interval.

The manager of Inlet Square wondered whether the population mean could have been $100 or $115. The value of $100 is within the confidence interval. It is reasonable that the population mean could be $100. The value of $115 is not in the confidence interval. Hence, we conclude that the population mean is unlikely to be $115.

Tutorial #48
in Connect

Before doing the confidence interval exercises, we would like to point out a useful characteristic of the *t*-distribution that will allow us to use the *t*-table to quickly find both *z* and *t*-values. Earlier in this section on page 297, we detailed the characteristics of the *t*-distribution. The last point indicated that as we increase the sample size the *t*-distribution approaches the *z*-distribution. In fact, when we reach an infinitely large sample, the *t*-distribution is exactly equal to the *z*-distribution.

To explain, Table 9–3 is a portion of Appendix B.5, with the degrees of freedom between 4 and 99 omitted. To find the appropriate z-value for a 95% confidence interval, we begin by going to the confidence interval section and selecting the column headed "95%." Move down that column to the last row, which is labeled "∞," or infinite degrees of freedom. The value reported is 1.960, the same value that we found using the standard normal distribution in Appendix B.3. This confirms the convergence of the t-distribution to the z-distribution.

TABLE 9–3 Student's t-Distribution

df (degrees of freedom)	Confidence Interval					
	80%	90%	95%	98%	99%	99.9%
	Level of Significance for One-Tailed Test, α					
	0.1	0.05	0.025	0.01	0.005	0.0005
	Level of Significance for Two-Tailed Test, α					
	0.2	0.1	0.05	0.02	0.01	0.001
1	3.078	6.314	12.706	31.821	63.657	636.619
2	1.886	2.920	4.303	6.965	9.925	31.599
3	1.638	2.353	3.182	4.541	5.841	12.924
⋮	⋮	⋮	⋮	⋮	⋮	⋮
100	1.290	1.660	1.984	2.364	2.626	3.390
120	1.289	1.658	1.980	2.358	2.617	3.373
140	1.288	1.656	1.977	2.353	2.611	3.361
160	1.287	1.654	1.975	2.350	2.607	3.352
180	1.286	1.653	1.973	2.347	2.603	3.345
200	1.286	1.653	1.972	2.345	2.601	3.340
∞	1.282	1.645	1.960	2.326	2.576	3.291

What does this mean for us? Instead of searching in the body of the z-table, we can go to the last row of the t-table and find the appropriate value to build a confidence interval. An additional benefit is that the values have three decimal places. So, using this table for a 90% confidence interval, go down the column headed "90%" and see the value 1.645, which is a more precise z-value that can be used for the 90% confidence level. Other z-values for 98% and 99% confidence intervals are also available with three decimals. Note that we will use the t-table, which is summarized in Table 9–3, to find the z-values with three decimals for all the following exercises and problems.

SELF-REVIEW 9–2

Dottie Kleman is the "Cookie Lady." She bakes and sells cookies at locations in the Philadelphia area. Ms. Kleman is concerned about absenteeism among her workers. The following information reports the number of days absent for a sample of 10 workers during the last 2-week pay period.

| 4 | 1 | 2 | 2 | 1 | 2 | 2 | 1 | 0 | 3 |

(a) Determine the mean and the standard deviation of the sample.
(b) What is the population mean? What is the best estimate of that value?
(c) Develop a 95% confidence interval for the population mean. Assume that the population distribution is normal.
(d) Explain why the t-distribution is used as a part of the confidence interval.
(e) Is it reasonable to conclude that the typical worker does not miss any days during a pay period?

EXERCISES

9. Use the *t*-distribution in Appendix B.5 to locate the value of *t* under the following conditions.
   a. The sample size is 12 and the level of confidence is 95%.
   b. The sample size is 20 and the level of confidence is 90%.
   c. The sample size is 8 and the level of confidence is 99%.

10. Use the *t*-distribution in Appendix B.5 to locate the value of *t* under the following conditions.
   a. The sample size is 15 and the level of confidence is 95%.
   b. The sample size is 24 and the level of confidence is 98%.
   c. The sample size is 12 and the level of confidence is 90%.

11. Use the *t*-distribution in Appendix B.5 to determine *z*-values, using three decimals, for a:
   a. 95% confidence interval.
   b. 90% confidence interval.
   c. 80% confidence interval.

12. In parts a, b, and c, use the *t*-distribution in Appendix B.5 to determine the margin of error in estimating the population mean with a 95% confidence interval if:
   a. $s = 10$ and $n = 10$.
   b. $s = 10$ and $n = 20$.
   c. $s = 10$ and $n = 30$.
   d. As sample size increases, how does the margin of error change? What would be the effect on a confidence interval as sample size increases?

13. The owner of Britten's Egg Farm wants to estimate the mean number of eggs produced per chicken. A sample of 20 chickens shows they produced an average of 20 eggs per month with a standard deviation of 2 eggs per month.
   a. What is the value of the population mean? What is the best estimate of this value?
   b. Explain why we need to use the *t*-distribution. What assumption do you need to make?
   c. For a 95% confidence interval, what is the value of *t*?
   d. What is the margin of error for a 95% confidence interval?
   e. Develop the 95% confidence interval for the population mean.
   f. Would it be reasonable to conclude that the population mean is 21 eggs? What about 25 eggs?

14. The U.S. Dairy Industry wants to estimate the mean yearly milk consumption. A sample of 16 people reveals the mean yearly consumption to be 45 gallons with a standard deviation of 20 gallons. Assume the population distribution is normal.
   a. What is the value of the population mean? What is the best estimate of this value?
   b. Explain why we need to use the *t*-distribution. What assumption do you need to make?
   c. For a 90% confidence interval, what is the value of *t*?
   d. What is the margin of error for a 90% confidence interval?
   e. Develop the 90% confidence interval for the population mean.
   f. Would it be reasonable to conclude that the population mean is 48 gallons?

15. **FILE** Merrill Lynch Securities and Health Care Retirement Inc. are two large employers in downtown Toledo, Ohio. They are considering jointly offering child care for their employees. As a part of the feasibility study, they wish to estimate the mean weekly child-care cost of their employees. A sample of 10 employees who use child care reveals the following amounts spent last week.

| $107 | $92 | $97 | $95 | $105 | $101 | $91 | $99 | $95 | $104 |

Develop a 90% confidence interval for the population mean. Interpret the result.

16. **FILE** The Buffalo, New York, Area Chamber of Commerce wants to estimate the mean time workers who are employed in the downtown area spend getting to work. A sample of 15 workers reveals the following number of minutes spent traveling.

14	24	24	19	24	7	31	20
26	23	23	28	16	15	21	

Develop a 98% confidence interval for the population mean. Interpret the result.

LO9-3

Compute and interpret a confidence interval for a population proportion.

A Confidence Interval for a Population Proportion

The material presented so far in this chapter uses the ratio scale of measurement. That is, we use such variables as incomes, weights, distances, and ages. We now want to consider situations that use the nominal scale of measurement:

Vytautas Kielaitis/Shutterstock

- The career services director at Southern Technical Institute reports that 80% of its graduates enter the job market in a position related to their field of study.
- A company representative claims that 60% of Burger King sales are made at the drive-thru window.
- A survey of homes in the Chicago area indicated that 85% of the new construction had central air conditioning.
- A recent survey of married men between the ages of 35 and 50 found that 63% felt that both partners should earn a living.

These examples illustrate the nominal scale of measurement when the outcome is limited to two values. In these cases, an observation is classified into one of two mutually exclusive groups. We can talk about the groups in terms of **proportions.**

> **PROPORTION** The fraction, ratio, or percent indicating the part of the sample or the population having a particular trait of interest.

As an example of a proportion, a recent survey indicated that 62 of 100 people surveyed favored Zoom meetings to in-person meetings. The sample proportion is 62/100, or .62, or 62%. If we let p represent the sample proportion, x the number of "successes," and n the number of items sampled, we can determine a sample proportion as follows.

SAMPLE PROPORTION	$p = \dfrac{x}{n}$	**(9–3)**

The population proportion is identified by π. Therefore, π refers to the percent of successes in the population. Recall from Chapter 6 that π is the proportion of "successes" in a binomial distribution. This continues our practice of using Greek letters to identify population parameters and Roman letters to identify sample statistics.

To develop a confidence interval for a proportion, we need to meet two requirements:

1. The binomial conditions, discussed in Chapter 6, have been met. These conditions are:
   a. The sample data are the number of successes in n trials.
   b. There are only two possible outcomes. (We usually label one of the outcomes a "success" and the other a "failure.")
   c. The probability of a success remains the same from one trial to the next.
   d. The trials are independent. This means the outcome on one trial does not affect the outcome on another.
2. The values $n\pi$ and $n(1 - \pi)$ should both be greater than or equal to 5. When these two conditions are met, the sample size, n, is large enough to apply the central limit theorem and infer that the distribution of the sample proportions is normal. Then, we can use z-values from the standard normal distribution to compute the margin of error for confidence intervals.

Developing a point estimate for a population proportion and a confidence interval for a population proportion is similar to doing so for a mean. To illustrate, John Gail is running for Congress from the 3rd District of Nebraska. From a random sample of 100 voters in the district, 60 indicate they plan to vote for him in the upcoming election. The sample proportion is .60, but the population proportion is unknown. That is, we do not know what proportion of voters in the *population* will vote for Mr. Gail. The sample value, .60, is the best estimate we have of the unknown population parameter. So we let p, which is .60, be an estimate of π, which is not known.

To develop a confidence interval for a population proportion, we use:

CONFIDENCE INTERVAL FOR A POPULATION PROPORTION	$p \pm z\sqrt{\dfrac{p(1 - p)}{n}}$	**(9–4)**

Note that the standard error of the sample proportion is:

$$\sqrt{\frac{p(1 - p)}{n}}$$

And the margin of error for the confidence interval is:

$$z\sqrt{\frac{p(1 - p)}{n}}$$

The following Example/Solution explains the details of determining a confidence interval for a population proportion and interpreting the result.

▶ EXAMPLE

The union representing the Bottle Blowers of America (BBA) is considering a proposal to merge with the Teamsters Union. According to BBA union bylaws, at least three-fourths of the union membership must approve any merger. A random sample of 2,000 current BBA members reveals 1,600 plan to vote for the merger proposal. What is the estimate of the population proportion? Develop a 95% confidence interval for the population proportion. Based on this sample information, can you conclude that the necessary proportion of BBA members favor the merger? Why?

SOLUTION

First, calculate the sample proportion from formula (9–3). It is .80, found by

$$p = \frac{x}{n} = \frac{1,600}{2,000} = .80$$

Thus, we estimate that 80% of the population favor the merger proposal. We determine the 95% confidence interval using formula (9–4). The z-value corresponding to the 95% level of confidence is 1.96.

$$p \pm z\sqrt{\frac{p(1-p)}{n}} = .80 \pm 1.96\sqrt{\frac{.80(1-.80)}{2,000}} = .80 \pm .018$$

The upper limit of the confidence interval, .818, is computed by adding the sample proportion and the *margin of error,* .80 + .018. The lower limit of the confidence interval, .782, is computed by subtracting the *margin of error* from the sample mean, .80 − .018. Therefore, we estimate that the population proportion is between .782 and .818 with 95% confidence. Hence, we conclude that the merger proposal will likely pass because the interval estimate includes only values greater than 75% of the union membership.

STATISTICS IN ACTION

The results of many surveys include confidence intervals. For example, a recent survey of 800 TV viewers in Toledo, Ohio, found 44% watched the evening news on the local CBS affiliate. The article also reported a margin of error of 3.4%. The margin of error is actually the amount that is added and subtracted from the point estimate to find the endpoints of a confidence interval. For a 95% level of confidence, the margin of error is:

$$z\sqrt{\frac{p(1-p)}{n}}$$

$$= 1.96\sqrt{\frac{.44(1-.44)}{800}}$$

$$= 0.034$$

The estimate of the proportion of all TV viewers in Toledo who watch the local news on CBS is between (.44 − .034) and (.44 + .034) or 40.6% and 47.4%.

To review the interpretation of the confidence interval: If the poll was conducted 100 times with 100 different samples, we expect the confidence intervals constructed from 95 of the samples would contain the true population proportion. In addition, the interpretation of a confidence interval can be very useful in decision making and play a very important role especially on election night. For example, Cliff Obermeyer is running for Congress from the 6th District of New Jersey. Suppose 500 voters are contacted upon leaving the polls and 275 indicate they voted for Mr. Obermeyer. We will assume that the exit poll of 500 voters is a random sample of those voting in the 6th District. That means that 55% of those in the sample voted for Mr. Obermeyer. Based on formula (9–3):

$$p = \frac{x}{n} = \frac{275}{500} = .55$$

Now, to be assured of election, he must earn *more than* 50% of the votes in the population of those voting. At this point, we know a point estimate, which is .55, of the population of voters that will vote for him. But we do not know the percent in the population that will ultimately vote for the candidate. So the question is: Could we take a sample of 500 voters from a population where 50% or less of the voters support Mr. Obermeyer and find that 55% of the sample support him? To put it another way, could the sampling error, which is $p - \pi = .55 - .50 = .05$, be due to chance, or is the population of voters who support Mr. Obermeyer greater than .50? If we develop a confidence interval for the sample proportion and find that the lower endpoint is greater than .50, then we conclude that the proportion of voters supporting Mr. Obermeyer is greater than .50. What does that mean? Well, it means he should be elected! What if .50 is in the interval? Then we conclude that he is not assured of a majority and we cannot conclude he will be elected. In this case, using the 95% significance level and formula (9–4):

$$p \pm z\sqrt{\frac{p(1-p)}{n}} = .55 \pm 1.96\sqrt{\frac{.55(1-.55)}{500}} = .55 \pm .044$$

The endpoints of the confidence interval are $.55 - .044 = .506$ and $.55 + .044 = .594$. The value of .50 is not in this interval. So our conclusion is that we are 95% confident that between 50.6% and 59.4% of voters support Mr. Obermeyer. That is enough to get him elected.

Is this procedure ever used? Yes! It is exactly the procedure used by polling organizations, television networks, and surveys of public opinion on election night.

SELF-REVIEW 9–3

A market research consultant was hired to estimate the proportion of households that associate the brand name of a laundry detergent with the container's shape and color. The consultant randomly selected 1,400 households. From the sample, 420 were able to identify the brand by name based only on the shape and color of the container.
(a) Estimate the value of the population proportion.
(b) Develop a 99% confidence interval for the population proportion.
(c) Interpret your findings.

EXERCISES

17. The owner of the West End Kwick Fill Gas Station wishes to determine the proportion of customers who pay at the pump using a credit card or debit card. He surveys 100 customers and finds that 85 paid at the pump.
   a. Estimate the population proportion.
   b. Develop a 95% confidence interval for the population proportion.
   c. Interpret your findings.
18. Ms. Malika Wilson is considering running for mayor of Bear Gulch, Montana. Before completing the petitions, she decides to conduct a survey of voters in Bear Gulch. A sample of 400 voters reveals that 300 would support her in the November election.
   1. Estimate the population proportion.
   2. Develop a 99% confidence interval for the population proportion.
   3. Interpret your findings.
19. Netflix is considering a new romantic comedy series. Before making a final decision, the producers design an experiment to estimate the proportion of viewers who would watch the series. A random sample of 400 viewers was selected and asked to watch the first two episodes. After viewing the episodes, 250 viewers indicated they would watch the new series.
   a. Estimate the proportion of people in the population who would watch the new series.
   b. Develop a 99% confidence interval for the proportion of people in the population who would watch the new series.
   c. Interpret your findings.
20. Schadek Silkscreen Printing Inc. purchases plastic cups and imprints them with logos for sporting events, proms, birthdays, and other special occasions. Vardon Schadek, the owner, received a large shipment this morning. To ensure the quality of the shipment, Vardon inspected a random sample of 300 cups and found 15 to be defective.
   a. What is the estimated proportion defective in the population?
   b. Develop a 95% confidence interval for the proportion defective.
   c. Vardon has an agreement with his supplier that if 10% or more of the cups are defective, he can return the order. Should he return this lot? Explain your decision.

LO9-4
Adjust a confidence interval for finite populations.

Finite-Population Correction Factor

The populations we have sampled so far have been very large or infinite. What if the sampled population is not very large? We need to make some adjustments in the way we compute the standard error of the sample means and the standard error of the sample proportions.

A population that has a fixed upper bound is *finite*. For example, there are 5,957 students enrolled at Eastern Illinois University, there are 40 employees at Spence Sprockets, there were 917 Jeep Wranglers assembled at the Alexis Avenue plant yesterday, or there were 65 surgical patients at St. Rose Memorial Hospital in Sarasota yesterday. A finite population can be rather small; it could be all the students registered for your statistics class. It can also be very large, such as all senior citizens living in Florida.

For a finite population, where the total number of objects or individuals is N and the number of objects or individuals in the sample is n, we need to adjust the margin of error in the confidence interval formulas. To put it another way, to find the confidence interval for the mean, we adjust the margin of error in formulas (9–1) and (9–2). If we are determining the confidence interval for a proportion, then we need to adjust the margin of error of the proportion in formula (9–4).

This adjustment is called the **finite-population correction factor.** It is often shortened to *FPC* and is:

$$FPC = \sqrt{\frac{N-n}{N-1}}$$

Why is it necessary to apply a factor, and what is its effect? Logically, if the sample is a substantial percentage of the population, the estimate of the population parameter is more precise. Note the effect of the term $(N-n)/(N-1)$. Suppose the population is 1,000 and the sample is 100. Then this ratio is $(1,000-100)/(1,000-1)$, or 900/999. Taking the square root gives the correction factor, .9492. Applying the correction factor *reduces* the margin of error by about 5% $(1 - .9492 = .0508)$. This reduction in the margin of error yields a smaller range of values in estimating the population mean or the population proportion. If the sample is 200, the correction factor is .8949, meaning that the margin of error has been reduced by more than 10%. Table 9–4 shows the effects of various sample sizes.

TABLE 9–4 Finite-Population Correction Factor for Selected Samples When the Population Is 1,000

Sample Size	Fraction of Population	Correction Factor
10	.010	.9955
25	.025	.9879
50	.050	.9752
100	.100	.9492
200	.200	.8949
500	.500	.7075

So if we wished to develop a confidence interval for the mean from a finite population and the population standard deviation was unknown, we would adjust formula (9–2) as follows:

$$\bar{x} \pm t\frac{s}{\sqrt{n}}\left(\sqrt{\frac{N-n}{N-1}}\right)$$

We would make a similar adjustment to formula (9–4) in the case of a proportion.

The following Example/Solution summarizes the steps to find a confidence interval for the mean.

▶ **EXAMPLE**

There are 250 families residing in Scandia, Pennsylvania. A random sample of 40 of these families revealed the mean annual church contribution was $450 and the standard deviation of this was $75.

1. What is the population mean? What is the best estimate of the population mean?
2. Develop a 90% confidence interval for the population mean. What are the endpoints of the confidence interval?
3. Using the confidence interval, explain why the population mean could be $445. Could the population mean be $425? Why?

SOLUTION

First, note the population is finite. That is, we can identify and list all families residing in Scandia. There are a total of 250 families

1. We do not know the population mean. This is the value we wish to estimate using our random sample of 40 families. The best estimate we have of the population mean is the sample mean, which is $450.
2. The formula to find the confidence interval for a population mean follows:

$$\bar{x} \pm t \frac{s}{\sqrt{n}} \left(\sqrt{\frac{N-n}{N-1}} \right)$$

In this case, we know $\bar{x} = 450$, $s = 75$, $N = 250$, and $n = 40$. We do not know the population standard deviation, so we use the t-distribution. To find the appropriate value of t, we use Appendix B.5, and move across the top row to the column headed 90%. The degrees of freedom are $df = n - 1 = 40 - 1 = 39$, so we move to the cell where the df row of 39 intersects with the column headed 90%. The value is 1.685. Inserting these values in the formula:

$$\bar{x} + t \frac{s}{\sqrt{n}} \left(\sqrt{\frac{N-n}{N-1}} \right)$$

$$= \$450 \pm 1.685 \frac{\$75}{\sqrt{40}} \left(\sqrt{\frac{250-40}{250-1}} \right) = \$450 \pm \$19.98 \sqrt{.8434} = \$450 \pm \$18.35$$

The endpoints of the confidence interval are $431.65 and $468.35.

3. It is likely that the population mean is more than $431.65 but less than $468.35. To put it another way, could the population mean be $445? Yes, but it is not likely that it is $425. Why is this so? Because the value $445 is within the confidence interval and $425 is not within the confidence interval.

SELF-REVIEW 9-4

The same study of church contributions in Scandia revealed that 15 of the 40 families sampled attend church regularly. Construct the 95% confidence interval for the proportion of families attending church regularly.

EXERCISES

21. Thirty-six items are randomly selected from a population of 300 items. The sample mean is 35 and the sample standard deviation 5. Develop a 95% confidence interval for the population mean.

22. Forty-nine items are randomly selected from a population of 500 items. The sample mean is 40 and the sample standard deviation 9. Develop a 99% confidence interval for the population mean.

23. The attendance at the Savannah Colts minor league baseball game last night was 400. A random sample of 50 of those in attendance revealed that the mean number of soft drinks consumed per person was 1.86, with a standard deviation of 0.50. Develop a 99% confidence interval for the mean number of soft drinks consumed per person.

24. There are 300 welders employed at Maine Shipyards Corporation. A sample of 30 welders revealed that 18 graduated from a registered welding course. Construct the 95% confidence interval for the proportion of all welders who graduated from a registered welding course.

LO9-5

Calculate the required sample size to estimate a population proportion or population mean.

Choosing an Appropriate Sample Size

When working with confidence intervals, one important variable is sample size. However, in practice, sample size is not a variable. It is a decision we make so that our estimate of a population parameter is a good one. Our decision is based on three factors:

1. The margin of error the researcher will tolerate
2. The level of confidence desired, for example, 95%
3. The variation or dispersion of the population being studied

The first factor is the *margin of error*. It is designated as E and is the amount that is added and subtracted to the sample mean (or sample proportion) to determine the endpoints of the confidence interval. For example, in a study of wages, we decide to estimate the mean wage of the population with a margin of error of plus or minus $1,000. Or, in an opinion poll, we may decide that we want to estimate the population proportion with a margin of error of plus or minus 3.5%. The margin of error is the amount of error we are willing to tolerate in estimating a population parameter. You may wonder why we do not choose small margins of error. There is a trade-off between the margin of error and sample size. A small margin of error will require a larger sample and more money and time to collect the sample. A larger margin of error will permit a smaller sample and result in a wider confidence interval.

The second factor is the *level of confidence*. In working with confidence intervals, we logically choose relatively high levels of confidence such as 95% and 99%. To compute the sample size, we need the z-value that corresponds to the chosen level of confidence. The 95% level of confidence corresponds to a z-value of 1.96, and a 90% level of confidence corresponds to a z-value of 1.645 (using the t-table). Notice that larger sample sizes (and more time and money to collect the sample) correspond with higher levels of confidence. Also, notice that we use a z-statistic.

The third factor to determine the sample size is the *population standard deviation*. If the population is widely dispersed, a large sample is required to get a good estimate. On the other hand, if the population is concentrated (homogeneous), the required sample size to get a good estimate will be smaller. Often, we do not know the population standard deviation. Here are three suggestions to estimate the population standard deviation.

1. **Conduct a pilot study.** This is the most common method. Suppose we want an estimate of the number of hours per week worked by students enrolled in the College of Business at the University of Texas. To test the validity of our questionnaire,

we use it on a small sample of students. From this small sample, we compute the standard deviation of the number of hours worked and use this value as the population standard deviation.

2. **Use a comparable study.** Use this approach when there is an estimate of the standard deviation from another study. Suppose we want to estimate the number of hours worked per week by refuse workers. Information from certain state or federal agencies that regularly study the workforce may provide a reliable value to use for the population standard deviation.

3. **Use a range-based approach.** To use this approach, we need to know or have an estimate of the largest and smallest values in the population. Recall from Chapter 3, the Empirical Rule states that virtually all the observations could be expected to be within plus or minus 3 standard deviations of the mean, assuming that the distribution follows the normal distribution. Thus, the distance between the largest and the smallest values is 6 standard deviations. We can estimate the standard deviation as one-sixth of the range. For example, the director of operations at University Bank wants to estimate the number of ATM transactions per month made by college students. She believes that the distribution of ATM transactions follows the normal distribution. The minimum and maximum of ATM transactions per month are 2 and 50, so the range is 48, found by (50 − 2). Then the estimated value of the population standard deviation would be eight ATM transactions per month, 48/6.

Sample Size to Estimate a Population Mean

To estimate a population mean, we can express the interaction among these three factors and the sample size in the following formula. Notice that this formula is the margin of error used to calculate the endpoints of confidence intervals to estimate a population mean! See formula (9–1).

$$E = z\frac{\sigma}{\sqrt{n}}$$

Solving this equation for n yields the following result.

SAMPLE SIZE FOR ESTIMATING THE POPULATION MEAN	$n = \left(\dfrac{z\sigma}{E}\right)^2$	(9–5)

where:

  n is the size of the sample.
  z is the standard normal z-value corresponding to the desired level of confidence.
  σ is the population standard deviation.
  E is the maximum allowable error.

The result of this calculation is not always a whole number. When the outcome is not a whole number, the usual practice is to round up *any* fractional result to the next whole number. For example, 201.21 would be rounded up to 202.

▶ **EXAMPLE**

A student in public administration wants to estimate the mean monthly earnings of city council members in large cities. She can tolerate a margin of error of $100 in estimating the mean. She would also prefer to report the interval estimate with a 95% level of confidence. The student found a report by the Department of Labor that reported a standard deviation of $1,000. What is the required sample size?

SOLUTION

The stated margin of error for the confidence interval, E, is \$100. The value of z for a 95% level of confidence is 1.96, and the value of the standard deviation is \$1,000. Substituting these values into formula (9–5) gives the required sample size as:

$$n = \left(\frac{z\sigma}{E}\right)^2 = \left(\frac{(1.96)(\$1,000)}{\$100}\right)^2 = (19.6)^2 = 384.16$$

The computed value of 384.16 is rounded up to 385. A sample of 385 is required to meet the specifications.

If the student wants to increase the level of confidence, for example to 99%, this will require a larger sample. Using the t-table with infinite degrees of freedom, the z-value for a 99% level of confidence is 2.576.

$$n = \left(\frac{z\sigma}{E}\right)^2 = \left(\frac{(2.576)(\$1,000)}{\$100}\right)^2 = (25.76)^2 = 663.58$$

We recommend a sample of 664. Observe how much the change in the confidence level changed the size of the sample. An increase from the 95% to the 99% level of confidence resulted in an increase of 279 observations, or 72% [(664/385) × 100]. This would greatly increase the cost of the study, in terms of both time and money. Hence, the level of confidence should be considered carefully.

Sample Size to Estimate a Population Proportion

To determine the sample size to estimate a population proportion, the same three factors need to be specified:

1. The margin of error
2. The desired level of confidence
3. The variation or dispersion of the population being studied

For the binomial distribution, the margin of error is:

$$E = z\sqrt{\frac{\pi(1-\pi)}{n}}$$

Solving this equation for n yields the following equation

SAMPLE SIZE FOR THE POPULATION PROPORTION	$n = \pi(1-\pi)\left(\dfrac{z}{E}\right)^2$	**(9–6)**

where:

   n is the size of the sample.
   z is the standard normal z-value corresponding to the desired level of confidence.
   π is the population proportion.
   E is the maximum allowable error.

As before, the z-value is associated with our choice of confidence level. We also decide the margin of error, E. However, the population variance of the binomial distribution is represented by $\pi(1-\pi)$. To estimate the population variance, we need a value of the population proportion. If a reliable value cannot be determined with a pilot study or found in a comparable study, then a value of .50 is used for π. Note that π(1 − π) has the largest value using 0.50 and, therefore, without a good estimate of the population proportion, using 0.50 as an estimate of π overstates the sample size. Using a larger sample size will not hurt the estimate of the population proportion.

▶ **EXAMPLE**

The student in the previous example also wants to estimate the proportion of cities that have private refuse collectors. The student wants to estimate the population proportion with a margin of error of .10, prefers a level of confidence of 90%, and has no estimate for the population proportion. What is the required sample size?

SOLUTION

The stated margin of error for the confidence interval is .10, so $E = .10$. The desired level of confidence is .90, which corresponds to a z-value of 1.645, using the t-table with infinite degrees of freedom. Because no estimate of the population proportion is available, we use .50. The suggested number of observations is

$$n = (.5)(1 - .5)\left(\frac{1.645}{.10}\right)^2 = 67.65$$

The student needs a random sample of 68 cities.

SELF-REVIEW 9–5

A university's office of research wants to estimate the arithmetic mean grade point average (GPA) of all graduating seniors during the past 10 years. GPAs range between 2.0 and 4.0. The estimate of the population mean GPA should be within plus or minus .05 of the population mean. Based on prior experience, the population standard deviation is 0.279. Using a 99% level of confidence, how many student records need to be selected?

EXERCISES

Note: Use the t-table with infinite degrees of freedom to select z-values with three decimal places.

25. A population's standard deviation is 10. We want to estimate the population mean with a margin of error of 2, with a 95% level of confidence. How large a sample is required?

26. We want to estimate the population mean within 5, with a 95% level of confidence. The population standard deviation is estimated to be 15. How large a sample is required?

27. The estimate of the population proportion should be within plus or minus .05, with a 99% level of confidence. The best estimate of the population proportion is .15. How large a sample is required?

28. The estimate of the population proportion should have a margin of error of 0.10, with a 99% level of confidence. The best estimate of the population proportion is .45. How large a sample is required?

29. A large on-demand, video streaming company is designing a large-scale survey to determine the mean amount of time corporate executives watch on-demand television. A small pilot survey of 10 executives indicated that the mean time per week is 12 hours, with a standard deviation of 3 hours. The estimate of the mean

viewing time should be within 0.25 hour. The 80% level of confidence is to be used. How many executives should be surveyed?

30. A processor of carrots cuts the green top off each carrot, washes the carrots, and inserts six to a package. Twenty packages are inserted in a box for shipment. Each box of carrots should weigh 20.4 pounds. The processor knows that the standard deviation of box weight is 0.5 pound. The processor wants to know if the current packing process meets the 20.4 weight standard. How many boxes must the processor sample to be 98% confident that the estimate of the population mean is within 0.2 pound?

31. Suppose the U.S. president wants to estimate the proportion of the population that supports proposed revisions to voting rights legislation. The president wants the margin of error to be 0.04. Assume a 95% level of confidence. The president's political advisors found a similar survey from 2 years ago that reported that 60% of people supported revisions to voting rights legislation.
   a. How large of a sample is required?
   b. How large of a sample would be necessary if no estimate were available for the proportion supporting revised legislation?

32. Past surveys reveal that 30% of tourists going to Las Vegas to gamble spend more than $1,000. The Visitor's Bureau of Las Vegas wants to update this percentage.
   a. How many tourists should be randomly selected to estimate the population proportion with a 99.9% confidence level and a 1% margin of error?
   b. The Bureau feels the sample size determined above is too large. What can be done to reduce the sample? Based on your suggestion, recalculate the sample size.

CHAPTER SUMMARY

I. A point estimate is a single value (statistic) used to estimate a population value (parameter).

II. A confidence interval is a range of values within which the population parameter is expected to occur.
   A. The factors that determine the width of a confidence interval for a mean are:
      1. The number of observations in the sample, n.
      2. The variability in the population, usually estimated by the sample standard deviation, s.
      3. The level of confidence.
         a. To determine the confidence limits when the population standard deviation is known, we use the z-distribution. The formula is

$$\bar{x} \pm z \frac{\sigma}{\sqrt{n}} \tag{9-1}$$

         b. To determine the confidence limits when the population standard deviation is unknown, we use the t-distribution. The formula is

$$\bar{x} \pm t \frac{s}{\sqrt{n}} \tag{9-2}$$

III. The major characteristics of the t-distribution are:
   A. It is a continuous distribution.
   B. It is mound shaped and symmetrical.
   C. It is flatter, or more spread out, than the standard normal distribution.
   D. There is a family of t-distributions, depending on the number of degrees of freedom.

IV. A proportion is a ratio, fraction, or percent that indicates the part of the sample or population that has a particular characteristic.
   A. A sample proportion, p, is found by x, the number of successes, divided by n, the number of observations.

B. We construct a confidence interval for a sample proportion from the following formula.

$$p \pm z\sqrt{\frac{p(1-p)}{n}} \qquad (9\text{--}4)$$

V. For a finite population, the standard error is adjusted by the factor:

$$\sqrt{\frac{N-n}{N-1}}$$

VI. We can determine an appropriate sample size for estimating both means and proportions.
   A. There are three factors that determine the sample size when we wish to estimate the mean.
      1. The margin of error, E
      2. The desired level of confidence
      3. The variation in the population
         The formula to determine the sample size for the mean is

$$n = \left(\frac{z\sigma}{E}\right)^2 \qquad (9\text{--}5)$$

   B. There are three factors that determine the sample size when we wish to estimate a proportion.
      1. The margin of error, E
      2. The desired level of confidence
      3. A value for π to calculate the variation in the population
         The formula to determine the sample size for a proportion is

$$n = \pi(1-\pi)\left(\frac{z}{E}\right)^2 \qquad (9\text{--}6)$$

CHAPTER EXERCISES

33. A random sample of 85 group leaders, supervisors, and similar personnel at General Motors revealed that, on average, they spent 6.5 years in a particular job before being promoted. The standard deviation of the sample was 1.7 years. Construct a 95% confidence interval.

34. A state meat inspector in Iowa would like to estimate the mean net weight of packages of ground chuck labeled "3 pounds." Of course, the inspector realizes that the weights cannot always be precisely 3 pounds. A sample of 36 packages reveals the mean weight to be 3.01 pounds, with a standard deviation of 0.03 pound.
   a. What is the point estimate of the population mean?
   b. What is the margin of error for a 95% confidence interval estimate?
   c. Determine a 95% confidence interval for the population mean.

35. As part of their business promotional package, the Milwaukee Chamber of Commerce would like an estimate of the mean cost per month to lease a one-bedroom apartment. The mean cost per month for a random sample of 40 apartments currently available for lease is $1,147. The standard deviation of the sample is $50.
   a. What is the point estimate of the population mean?
   b. What is the point estimate of the population standard deviation?
   c. What is the margin of error for a 98% confidence interval estimate?
   d. Based on a 98% confidence interval, would it be reasonable to conclude that the population mean is $1,250 per month?

36. A recent survey of 50 executives who were laid off during a recent recession revealed it took a mean of 26 weeks for them to find another position. The standard deviation of the sample was 6.2 weeks. Construct a 95% confidence interval for the population mean. Is it reasonable that the population mean is 28 weeks? Justify your answer.

37. Marty Rowatti recently assumed the position of director of the YMCA of South Jersey. He would like some current data on how long current members of the YMCA have been

members. To investigate, suppose he selects a random sample of 40 current members. The mean length of membership for the sample is 8.32 years and the standard deviation is 3.07 years.
   a. What is the point estimate of the population mean?
   b. Develop a 90% confidence interval for the population mean.
   c. A summary report prepared by the previous director indicated the mean length of membership was now "almost 10 years." Does the sample information substantiate this claim? Cite evidence.

38. The American Restaurant Association collected information on the number of meals eaten outside the home per week by young married couples. A survey of 60 couples showed the sample mean number of meals eaten outside the home was 2.76 meals per week, with a standard deviation of 0.75 meal per week. Construct a 99% confidence interval for the population mean.

39. The National Collegiate Athletic Association (NCAA) reported that college football assistant coaches spend a mean of 70 hours per week coaching players, recruiting, and game planning during the season. A random sample of 50 assistant coaches showed the sample mean to be 68.6 hours, with a standard deviation of 8.2 hours.
   a. Using the sample data, construct a 99% confidence interval for the population mean.
   b. Does the 99% confidence interval include the value suggested by the NCAA? Interpret this result.
   c. Suppose you decided to switch from a 99% to a 95% confidence interval. Without performing any calculations, will the interval increase, decrease, or stay the same? Explain your choice.

40. The Human Resources Department of Electronics Inc. would like to include a dental plan as part of the benefits package. The question is: How much does a typical employee and his or her family spend per year on dental expenses? A sample of 45 employees reveals the mean amount spent last year was $1,820, with a standard deviation of $660.
   a. Construct a 95% confidence interval for the population mean.
   b. The information from part (a) was given to the president of Electronics Inc. He indicated he could afford $1,700 of dental expenses per employee. Is it possible that the population mean could be $1,700? Justify your answer.

41. A student conducted a study and reported that the 95% confidence interval for the mean ranged from 46 to 54. He was sure that the mean of the sample was 50, that the standard deviation of the sample was 16, and that the sample size was at least 30, but could not remember the exact number. Can you help him out?

42. A recent study by the American Automobile Dealers Association surveyed a random sample of 20 dealers. The data revealed a mean amount of profit per car sold was $290, with a standard deviation of $125. Develop a 95% confidence interval for the population mean of profit per car.

43. A study of 25 graduates of 4-year public colleges revealed the mean amount owed by a student in student loans was $55,051. The standard deviation of the sample was $7,568.
   a. Compute a 90% confidence interval for the population mean.
   b. Is it reasonable to conclude that the population mean is $55,000? Why?

44. An important factor in selling a residential property is the number of times real estate agents show a home. A sample of 15 homes recently sold in the Buffalo, New York, area revealed the mean number of times a home was shown was 24 and the standard deviation of the sample was 5.
   a. What is the margin of error for a 98% confidence interval?
   b. What is the 98% confidence interval for the population mean?

45. **FILE** In 2003, the Accreditation Council for Graduate Medical Education (ACGME) implemented new rules limiting work hours for all residents. A key component of these rules is that residents should work no more than 80 hours per week. The following is the number of weekly hours worked in 2022 by a sample of residents at the Tidelands Medical Center.

84	86	84	86	79	82	87	81	84	78	74	86

a. What is the point estimate of the population mean for the number of weekly hours worked at the Tidelands Medical Center?

b. What is the point estimate of the population standard deviation?

c. What is the margin of error for a 90% confidence interval estimate?

d. Develop a 90% confidence interval for the population mean.

e. Is the Tidelands Medical Center within the ACGME guideline? Why?

46. **FILE** PrintTech Inc. is introducing a new line of ink-jet printers and would like to promote the number of pages a user can expect from a print cartridge. A sample of 10 cartridges revealed the following number of pages printed.

| 2,698 | 2,028 | 2,474 | 2,395 | 2,372 | 2,475 | 1,927 | 3,006 | 2,334 | 2,379 |

a. What is the point estimate of the population mean?

b. What is the point estimate of the population standard deviation?

c. What is the margin of error for a 95% confidence interval estimate?

d. Develop a 95% confidence interval for the population mean.

47. **FILE** Dr. Kendi Sadek is an industrial psychologist. She is currently studying stress among executives of Internet companies. She has developed a questionnaire that she believes measures stress. A score above 80 indicates stress at a dangerous level. A random sample of 15 executives revealed the following stress level scores.

| 94 | 78 | 83 | 90 | 78 | 99 | 97 | 90 | 97 | 90 | 93 | 94 | 100 | 75 | 84 |

a. Find the point estimate of the population mean.

b. Construct a 95% confidence level for the population mean.

c. According to Dr. Sadek's test, is it reasonable to conclude that the mean stress level of Internet executives is 80? Explain.

48. Pharmaceutical companies promote their prescription drugs using television advertising. In a survey of 80 randomly sampled television viewers, 10 indicated that they asked their physician about using a prescription drug they saw advertised on TV.

a. What is the point estimate of the population proportion?

b. What is the margin of error for a 95% confidence interval estimate?

c. Compute the 95% confidence interval for the population proportion.

d. Is it reasonable to conclude that 25% of the viewers discuss an advertised drug with their physician? Why?

49. HighTech Inc. randomly drug tests its employees. Last year in the 400 random tests conducted, 14 employees failed the test.

a. What is the point estimate of the population proportion?

b. What is the margin of error for a 99% confidence interval estimate?

c. Compute the 99% confidence interval for the population proportion.

d. Is it reasonable to conclude that 5% of the employees cannot pass a drug test? Why?

50. During a national debate on changes to health care, a cable news service performs an opinion poll of 500 small-business owners. It shows that 65% of small-business owners do not approve of the changes.

a. Compute the 95% confidence interval for the population proportion.

b. Comment on the result.

51. There are 20,000 eligible voters in York County, South Carolina. A random sample of 500 York County voters revealed 350 plan to vote to return Louella Miller to the state senate.

a. Compute the 99% confidence interval for the proportion of voters who plan to vote for Ms. Miller.

b. Can we conclude that it is likely that Ms. Miller will receive a majority of the votes?

52. In a poll to estimate presidential popularity, each person in a random sample of 1,000 voters was asked to agree with one of the following statements:

1. The president is doing a good job.

2. The president is doing a poor job.

3. I have no opinion.

A total of 560 respondents selected the first statement, indicating they thought the president was doing a good job.

a. Construct a 95% confidence interval for the proportion of respondents who feel the president is doing a good job.

b. Based on your interval in part (a), is it reasonable to conclude that a majority of the population believes the president is doing a good job?

53. Police Chief Dannie Wilkin of River City reports 500 traffic citations were issued last month. A sample of 35 of these citations showed the mean amount of the fine was $54, with a standard deviation of $4.50.

a. What is the margin of error for a 95% confidence interval for the population mean?

b. What is the 95% confidence interval for the population mean?

54. The First National Bank of Wilson has 650 checking account customers. A recent sample of 50 of these customers showed 26 have a Visa card with the bank.

a. What is the margin of error for a 99% confidence interval for the population proportion?

b. What is the 99% confidence interval for the population proportion?

55. It is estimated that 60% of U.S. households subscribe to cable TV. You would like to verify this statement for your class in mass communications. If you want your estimate to be within 5 percentage points, with a 95% level of confidence, how many households should you sample?

56. You wish to estimate the mean number of travel days per year for salespeople. The mean of a small pilot study was 150 days, with a standard deviation of 14 days. If you want to estimate the population mean with 90% confidence and a margin of error of 2 days, how many salespeople should you sample?

57. You want to estimate the mean family income in a rural area of central Indiana. The question is, how many families should be sampled? In a pilot sample of 10 families, the standard deviation of family income was $500. How many families should be interviewed to estimate the population mean income with 95% confidence and a margin of error of $100?

58. *Families USA*, a monthly magazine that discusses issues related to health and health costs, randomly surveyed 20 of its subscribers. It found that the annual health insurance premiums for a family with coverage through an employer averaged $10,979. The standard deviation of the sample was $1,000.

a. Based on this sample information, develop a 90% confidence interval for the population mean yearly premium.

b. How large a sample is needed to find the population mean within $250 at 99% confidence?

59. Passenger comfort is influenced by the amount of pressurization in an airline cabin. Higher pressurization permits a closer-to-normal environment and a more relaxed flight. A study by an airline user group recorded the equivalent air pressure on 30 randomly chosen flights. The study revealed a mean equivalent air pressure of 8,000 feet with a standard deviation of 300 feet.

a. Develop a 99% confidence interval for the population mean equivalent air pressure.

b. How large a sample is needed to find the population mean within 25 feet at 95% confidence?

60. A survey of 25 randomly sampled judges employed by the state of Florida found that they earned an average wage (including benefits) of $65.00 per hour. The sample standard deviation was $6.25 per hour.

a. What is the population mean? What is the point estimate of the population mean?

b. Develop a 99% confidence interval for the population mean wage (including benefits) for these employees.

c. How many judges should be selected to estimate the population mean wage with 95% confidence and a margin of error of $1.00?

61. Based on a sample of 50 U.S. citizens, the American Film Institute found that a typical American spent 78 hours watching movies last year. The standard deviation of this sample was 9 hours.

a. Develop a 95% confidence interval for the population mean number of hours spent watching movies last year.

b. How large a sample should be used to be 90% confident the sample mean is within 1.0 hour of the population mean?

62. Dylan Jones, who owns a car, keeps careful records of the car's fuel efficiency. Based on a sample of nine measurements, the mean was 23.4 miles per gallon (mpg) with a sample standard deviation of 0.9 mpg.
   a. Compute the 95% confidence interval of mpg.
   b. How many measurements should be collected to compute a confidence interval with a 0.1 mpg margin of error?

63. A survey of 36 randomly selected iPhone owners showed that the purchase price has a mean of $650 with a sample standard deviation of $24.
   a. What is the point estimate of the population mean?
   b. What is the point estimate of the population standard deviation?
   c. What is the standard error of the sample mean?
   d. Compute the 95% confidence interval to estimate the population mean.
   e. How many users need to be sampled to estimate the population mean price with 95% confidence and a $10 margin of error?

64. You plan to conduct a survey to find what proportion of the workforce has two or more jobs. You decide on the 95% confidence level and a margin of error of 2%. A pilot survey reveals that 5 of the 50 sampled hold two or more jobs. How many in the workforce should be interviewed to meet your requirements?

65. A study conducted several years ago reported that 21% of public accountants changed companies within 3 years. The American Institute of CPAs would like to update the study. They would like to estimate the population proportion of public accountants who changed companies within 3 years with a margin of error of 3% and a 95% level of confidence.
   a. To update this study, how many public accountants should be contacted?
   b. How many public accountants should be contacted if no previous estimates of the population proportion are available?

66. As part of an annual review of its accounts, a discount brokerage selected a random sample of 36 customers and reviewed the value of their accounts. The mean was $32,000 with a sample standard deviation of $8,200. What is a 90% confidence interval to estimate the mean account value of the population of customers?

67. The National Weight Control Registry tries to mine secrets of success from people who lost at least 30 pounds and kept it off for at least a year. It reports that out of 2,700 registrants, 459 were on a low-carbohydrate diet (less than 90 grams a day).
   a. Develop a 95% confidence interval for the proportion of people on a low-carbohydrate diet.
   b. Is it possible that the population percentage is 18%? Why?
   c. How large a sample is needed to estimate the proportion within 0.5%?

68. Near the time of an election, a cable news service performs an opinion poll of 1,000 probable voters. It shows that the Republican contender has an advantage of 52% to 48%.
   a. Develop a 95% confidence interval for the proportion favoring the Republican candidate.
   b. Estimate the probability that the Democratic candidate is actually leading.
   c. Repeat the above analysis based on a sample of 3,000 probable voters.

69. A sample of 352 subscribers to *Wired* magazine shows the mean time spent using the Internet is 13.4 hours per week, with a sample standard deviation of 6.8 hours. Find the 95% confidence interval for the mean time *Wired* subscribers spend on the Internet.

70. The Tennessee Tourism Institute (TTI) plans to sample information center visitors entering the state to learn the fraction of visitors who plan to camp in the state. Current estimates are that 35% of visitors are campers. How many visitors would you sample to estimate the population proportion of campers with a 95% confidence level and an error of 2%?

DATA ANALYTICS

71. **FILE** Refer to the North Valley Real Estate data, which reports information on homes sold in the area during the last year. Select a random sample of 20 homes.
   a. Based on your random sample of 20 homes, develop a 95% confidence interval for the mean selling price of the homes.
   b. Based on your random sample of 20 homes, develop a 95% confidence interval for the mean days on the market.

    c. Based on your random sample of 20 homes, develop a 95% confidence interval for the proportion of homes with a pool.

    d. Suppose that North Valley Real Estate employs several agents. Each agent will be randomly assigned 20 homes to sell. The agents are highly motivated to sell homes based on the commissions they earn. They are also concerned about the 20 homes they are assigned to sell. Using the confidence intervals you created, write a general memo informing the agents about the characteristics of the homes they may be assigned to sell.

    e. What would you do if your confidence intervals did not include the mean of all 105 homes? How could this happen?

72. **FILE** Refer to the Baseball 2021 data, which report information on the 30 Major League Baseball teams for the 2021 season. Assume the 2021 data represents a sample.

    a. Develop a 95% confidence interval for the mean number of home runs per team.

    b. Develop a 95% confidence interval for the mean batting average by each team.

    c. Develop a 95% confidence interval for the mean earned run average (ERA) for each team.

73. **FILE** Refer to the Lincolnville School District bus data.

    a. Develop a 95% confidence interval for the mean bus maintenance cost.

    b. Develop a 95% confidence interval for the mean bus odometer miles.

    c. Write a business memo to the state transportation official to report your results.

A REVIEW OF CHAPTERS 8–9

We began Chapter 8 by describing the reasons sampling is necessary. We sample because it is often impossible to study every item, or individual, in some populations. For example, to contact all U.S. bank officers and record their annual incomes would be too expensive and time consuming. Also, sampling often destroys the product. A drug manufacturer cannot test the properties of each vitamin tablet manufactured because there would be none left to sell. Therefore, to estimate a population parameter, we select a sample from the population. A sample is a part of the population. Care must be taken to ensure that every member of our population has a chance of being selected; otherwise, the conclusions might be biased. A number of probability-type sampling methods can be used, including *simple random, systematic, stratified,* and *cluster sampling.*

Regardless of the sampling method selected, a sample statistic is seldom equal to the corresponding population parameter. For example, the mean of a sample is seldom exactly the same as the mean of the population. The difference between this sample statistic and the population parameter is the *sampling error.*

In Chapter 8, we demonstrated that, if we select all possible samples of a specified size from a population and calculate the mean of these samples, the result will be exactly equal to the population mean. We also showed that the dispersion in the distribution of the sample means is equal to the population standard deviation divided by the square root of the sample size. This result is called the standard error of the mean. There is less dispersion in the distribution of the sample means than in the population. In addition, as we increase the number of observations in each sample, we decrease the variation in the sampling distribution.

The central limit theorem is the foundation of statistical inference. It states that, if the population from which we select the samples follows the normal probability distribution, the distribution of the sample means will also follow the normal distribution. If the population is not normal, the sampling distribution of sample means will approach the normal probability distribution as we increase the size of the sample. The central limit theorem also applies to the sampling distribution of the sample proportion.

Our focus in Chapter 9 was point estimates and interval estimates. A point estimate is a single value used to estimate a population parameter. An interval estimate is a range of values within which we expect the population parameter to occur. For example, based on a sample, we estimate that the mean annual income of all professional house painters in Atlanta, Georgia (the population), is $45,300. That estimate is called a *point estimate.* If we state that the population mean is probably in the interval between $45,200 and $45,400, that estimate is called an *interval estimate.* The two endpoints ($45,200 and $45,400) are the *confidence limits* for the population mean. We also described procedures for establishing a confidence interval for a population mean when the population standard deviation is not known and for a population proportion. In this chapter, we also provided a method to determine the necessary sample size based on the dispersion in the population, the level of confidence desired, and the desired precision of the estimate or margin of error.

PROBLEMS

1. A recent study indicated that women took an average of 8.6 weeks of unpaid leave from their jobs after the birth of a child. Assume that this distribution follows the normal probability distribution with a standard deviation of 2.0 weeks. We select a sample of 35 women who recently returned to work after the birth of a child. What is the likelihood that the mean of this sample is at least 8.8 weeks?

2. The manager of Tee Shirt Emporium reports that the mean number of shirts sold per week is 1,210, with a standard deviation of 325. The distribution of sales follows the normal distribution. What is the likelihood of selecting a sample of 25 weeks and finding the sample mean to be 1,100 or less?

3. The owner of the Gulf Stream Café wished to estimate the mean number of lunch customers per day. A sample of 40 days revealed a mean of 160 per day, with a standard deviation of 20 per day. Develop a 98% confidence interval for the mean number of customers per day.

4. The manager of the local Hamburger Express wishes to estimate the mean time customers spend at the drive-thru window. A sample of 20 customers experienced a mean waiting time of 2.65 minutes, with a standard deviation of 0.45 minute. Develop a 90% confidence interval for the mean wait time.

5. Defiance Tool and Die has 293 sales offices throughout the world. The VP of Sales is studying the usage of its copy machines. A random sample of six of the sales offices revealed the following number of copies made in each selected office last week.

| 826 | 931 | 1,126 | 918 | 1,011 | 1,101 |

Develop a 95% confidence interval for the mean number of copies per week.

6. John Kleman is the host of KXYZ Radio 55 AM drive-time news in Denver. During his morning program, John asks listeners to call in and discuss current local and national news. This morning, John was concerned with the number of hours children under 12 years of age watch TV per day. The last five callers reported that their children watched the following number of hours of TV last night.

| 3.0 | 3.5 | 4.0 | 4.5 | 3.0 |

Would it be reasonable to develop a confidence interval from these data to show the mean number of hours of TV watched? If yes, construct an appropriate confidence interval and interpret the result. If no, why would a confidence interval not be appropriate?

7. Historically, Widgets Manufacturing Inc. produces 250 widgets per day. Recently the new owner bought a new machine to produce more widgets per day. A sample of 16 days' production revealed a mean of 240 units with a standard deviation of 35. Construct a confidence interval for the mean number of widgets produced per day. Does it seem reasonable to conclude that the mean daily widget production has changed? Justify your conclusion.

8. A manufacturer of cell phone batteries wants to estimate the useful life of its battery (in thousands of hours). The estimate is to be within 0.10 (100 hours). Assume a 95% level of confidence and that the standard deviation of the useful life of the battery is 0.90 (900 hours). Determine the required sample size.

9. The manager of a home improvement store wishes to estimate the mean amount of money spent in the store. The estimate is to be within $4.00 with a 95% level of confidence. The manager does not know the standard deviation of the amounts spent. However, he does estimate that the range is from $5.00 up to $155.00. How large of a sample is needed? (Hint: To estimate the standard deviation, remember that the Empirical Rule estimates that 99.9% of a normal distribution is within ± 3 standard deviations of the mean.)

10. In a sample of 200 residents of Georgetown County, 120 reported they believed the county real estate taxes were too high. Develop a 95% confidence interval for the proportion of residents who believe the tax rate is too high. Does it seem reasonable to conclude that 50% of the voters believe that taxes are too high?

11. In recent times, the percent of buyers purchasing a new vehicle via the Internet has been large enough that local automobile dealers are concerned about its impact on their business. The information needed is an estimate of the proportion of purchases via the Internet. How large of a sample of purchasers is necessary for the estimate to be within 2 percentage points with a 98% level of confidence? Current thinking is that about 30% of the vehicles are purchased via the Internet.

12. Historically, the proportion of adults over the age of 24 who smoke has been .30. In recent years, much information has been published and aired on radio and TV that smoking is not good for one's health. A sample of 500 adults revealed only 25% of those sampled smoked. Develop a 98% confidence interval for the proportion of adults who currently smoke. Does it seem reasonable to conclude that the proportion of adults who smoke has changed?

13. The auditor of the state of Ohio needs an estimate of the proportion of residents who regularly play the state lottery. Historically, about 40% regularly play, but the auditor would like some current information. How large a sample is necessary for the estimate to be within 3 percentage points, with a 98% level of confidence?

CASES

Century National Bank

Refer to the description of Century National Bank at the end of the Review of Chapters 1–4 on page 126. When Mr. Selig took over as president of Century several years ago, the use of debit cards was just beginning. He would like an update on the use of these cards. Develop a 95% confidence interval for the proportion of customers using these cards. On the basis of the confidence interval, is it reasonable to conclude that more than half of the customers use a debit card? Write a brief report interpreting the results.

PRACTICE TEST

Part 1—Objective

1. If each item in the population has the same chance of being selected, this is called a _____.   1. _____
2. The difference between the population mean and the sample mean is called the _____.   2. _____
3. The _____ is the standard deviation of the distribution of sample means.   3. _____
4. If the sample size is increased, the variance of the sample means will _____. (become smaller, become larger, not change)   4. _____
5. A single value used to estimate a population parameter is called a _____.   5. _____
6. A range of values within which the population parameter is expected to occur is called a _____.   6. _____
7. Which of the following does not affect the width of a confidence interval? (sample size, variation in the population, level of confidence, size of population)   7. _____
8. The fraction of a population that has a particular characteristic is called a _____.   8. _____
9. Which of the following is not a characteristic of the t-distribution? (positively skewed, continuous, mean of zero, based on degrees of freedom)   9. _____
10. To determine the required sample size of a proportion when no estimate of the population proportion is available, what value is used?   10. _____

Part 2—Problems

1. Americans spend an average (mean) of 12.2 minutes (per day) in the shower. The distribution of times follows the normal distribution with a population standard deviation of 2.3 minutes. What is the likelihood that the mean time per day for a sample of 12 Americans was 11 minutes or less?

2. A recent study of 26 Conway, South Carolina, residents revealed they had lived at their current address an average of 9.3 years. The standard deviation of the sample was 2 years.

   a. What is the population mean?
   b. What is the best estimate of the population mean?
   c. What is the standard error of estimate?
   d. Develop a 90% confidence interval for the population mean.

3. A recent federal report indicated that 27% of children ages 2 to 5 ate a vegetable at least five times a week. How large a sample is needed to estimate the true population proportion within 2% with a 98% level of confidence? Be sure to use the information contained in the federal report.

4. The Philadelphia Area Transit Authority wishes to estimate the proportion of central city workers that use public transportation to get to work. A sample of 100 workers revealed that 64 used public transportation. Develop a 95% confidence interval for the population proportion.

One-Sample Tests of Hypothesis 10

Franco Salmoiraghi/Photo Resource Hawaii/Alamy Stock Photo

▲ **DOLE PINEAPPLE INC.** is concerned that the 16-ounce can of sliced pineapple is being overfilled. Assume the standard deviation of the process is 0.03 ounce. The quality control department took a random sample of 50 cans and found that the arithmetic mean weight was 16.05 ounces. At the 5% level of significance, can we conclude that the mean weight is greater than 16 ounces? Determine the *p*-value. (See Exercise 34 and LO10-4.)

LEARNING OBJECTIVES

When you have completed this chapter, you will be able to:

LO10-1 Explain the process of testing a hypothesis.

LO10-2 Apply the six-step procedure for testing a hypothesis.

LO10-3 Distinguish between a one-tailed and a two-tailed test of hypothesis.

LO10-4 Conduct a test of a hypothesis about a population mean.

LO10-5 Compute and interpret a *p*-value.

LO10-6 Use a *t*-statistic to test a hypothesis.

LO10-7 Compute the probability of a Type II error.

LO10-8 Test a hypothesis about a population proportion.

Introduction

Chapter 8 began our study of sampling and statistical inference. We described how we could select a random sample to estimate the value of a population parameter. For example, we selected a sample of five employees at Spence Sprockets, found the number of years of service for each sampled employee, computed the mean years of service, and used the sample mean to estimate the mean years of service for the population of all employees. In other words, we estimated a population parameter from a sample statistic.

Chapter 9 continued the study of statistical inference by developing a confidence interval. A confidence interval is a range of values within which we expect the population parameter to occur. In this chapter, rather than computing confidence intervals, we introduce a procedure that uses statistical inference to test statements about population parameters. Some examples of statements we might want to test are:

Russell Illig/Photodisc/Getty Images

- The West Virginia highway patrol reports the mean speed of automobiles passing milepost 150 on the West Virginia Turnpike is 68 miles per hour.
- General Motors Inc. reports the mean number of miles driven by those leasing a Chevy Trailblazer for 3 years is 32,000 miles.
- The Federal Housing Administration reports the mean time an American family lives in a particular single-family dwelling is 11.8 years.
- In 2022, an online job site reports the mean starting salary for a graduate from a 4-year business program is $56,720.
- According to Kelley Blue Book (**www.kbb.com**), a 2021 Ford Edge averages 24 combined miles per gallon.
- Home Depot reports the mean cost to remodel a kitchen is $20,000.

In this chapter, we continue to apply statistics and statistical inference to the research process. In the research process, we often start with a hypothetical statement. Then we define a population to sample, collect data on the variables of interest, and then conduct statistical analysis. This analysis performs statistical tests of the hypothesis using the sample data. The results of the analysis provide the evidence used to make inferences about the population. Next, we prescribe the procedure to conduct statistical hypothesis testing. The procedure is applied to hypotheses about population means and population proportions. The chapter also discusses two types of decision-making errors that originate with sampling error.

LO10-1
Explain the process of testing a hypothesis.

What Is Hypothesis Testing?

The terms *hypothesis testing* and *testing a hypothesis* are used interchangeably. Hypothesis testing starts with a statement, or assumption, about a population parameter— such as the population mean. This statement is referred to as a **hypothesis.**

> **HYPOTHESIS** A statement about a population parameter subject to verification.

For example, a new marketing graduate is interested in a sales position with an office supply company and is collecting information about pay and compensation. One store, Staples, says that their employees' monthly commission averages $2,000. This statement becomes our hypothesis, $\mu = \$2,000$. We would like to analyze sample data to see if this statement is false. So, we apply a **hypothesis testing** procedure.

> **HYPOTHESIS TESTING** A procedure based on sample evidence and probability theory to determine whether the hypothesis is a reasonable statement.

To test the validity of the hypothesis ($\mu = \$2{,}000$), we select a sample from the population of all Staples sales associates, request their monthly commission, and calculate the monthly commission sample statistics. We use the statistics to conduct a hypothesis test about the population mean, $\mu = \$2{,}000$. Based on the sample evidence, we decide to either reject or fail to reject this statement regarding the population mean commission.

LO10-2

Apply the six-step procedure for testing a hypothesis.

Six-Step Procedure for Testing a Hypothesis

There is a six-step procedure that systematizes hypothesis testing; when we get to step 6 we are ready to interpret the results of the test based on the decision to reject or not reject the hypothesis. However, hypothesis testing as used by statisticians does not provide proof that something is true, in the manner in which a mathematician "proves" a statement. It does provide a kind of "proof beyond a reasonable doubt," in the manner of the court system. Hence, there are specific rules of evidence, or procedures, that are followed. The steps are shown in the following diagram. We will discuss in detail each of the steps.

Step 1	Step 2	Step 3	Step 4	Step 5	Step 6
State null and alternate hypotheses	Select a level of significance	Identify the test statistic	Formulate a decision rule	Take a sample, arrive at decision	Interpret the result

Step 1: State the Null Hypothesis (H_0) and the Alternate Hypothesis (H_1)

The first step is to state the null hypothesis, designated H_0, and read "*H sub zero.*" The capital letter H stands for hypothesis, and the subscript zero implies "no difference." In a written statement of the null hypothesis, words such as "not different," "no change," or "equal to" are often used. For example, a quality assurance department determines that the tensile strength of window glass is 70 psi (pounds per square inch). To test this statement, it is rewritten as a null hypothesis: H_0: $\mu = 70$. We test the null hypothesis with sample data. If the sample data provide convincing evidence that it is false, then the null hypothesis is rejected. If the sample data does not provide convincing evidence, then we fail to reject the null hypothesis.

Often, the *null hypothesis* begins by stating, "There is no *significant* difference between . . ." or "The mean strength of the glass is not *significantly* different from. . . ." When we select a sample from a population, the sample statistic is usually numerically different from the hypothesized population parameter. The size of this difference is the basis of the hypothesis test. As an illustration, suppose the hypothesized strength of window glass is 70 psi, and the mean strength of a sample of 12 window glass sections is 69.5 psi. Using the sample data, we need to decide if the difference between the hypothesized strength and the sample mean strength, 0.5 psi, provides enough evidence to reject the assertion that the population strength is 70 psi. That is, is the difference of 0.5 psi large enough to say that the strength is probably not equal to 70 psi? To answer this question, we start the hypothesis testing procedure by stating the **null hypothesis.**

> **NULL HYPOTHESIS** A statement about the value of a population parameter developed for the purpose of testing with sample data.

If the null hypothesis is rejected, we conclude that the **alternate hypothesis** is supported by the sample data. It is written H_1 and is read "*H sub one.*" It is also referred to as the research hypothesis.

> **ALTERNATE HYPOTHESIS** An inference about a population parameter based on sample data when the null hypothesis is rejected.

The following example will help clarify what is meant by the null hypothesis and the alternate hypothesis. A recent article indicated the mean age of U.S. commercial aircraft is 15 years. To conduct a statistical test regarding this statement, the first step is to determine the null and the alternate hypotheses. The null hypothesis represents the current or reported condition. It is written H_0: $\mu = 15$. The alternate hypothesis, or counterargument, is that the null hypothesis is not true, that is, H_1: $\mu \neq 15$. It is important to remember that no matter how the problem is stated, *the null hypothesis will always contain the equal sign.* The equal sign (=) will never appear in the alternate hypothesis. Why? Because the null hypothesis is the statement being tested, and we need a specific value to include in our calculations. We turn to the alternate hypothesis only if the data suggest the null hypothesis is untrue.

Step 2: Select a Level of Significance

After setting up the null hypothesis and alternate hypothesis, the next step is to state the **level of significance.**

> **LEVEL OF SIGNIFICANCE** The probability of rejecting the null hypothesis when it is true.

Because we sample from a population, a researcher assumes a risk that the sample results may indicate that the null hypothesis is false, when it is, in fact, true. The risk, designated by the Greek letter alpha, α, is the probability of making this error. The researcher gets to assign this probability before proceeding with the hypothesis testing procedure.

There is no one level of significance that is applied to all tests. A decision is made to use the .05 level (often stated as the 5% level), the .01 level, the .10 level, or any other level between 0 and 1. Traditionally, the .05 level is selected for consumer research projects, .01 for quality assurance, and .10 for political polling.

Step 3: Select the Test Statistic

There are many **test statistics.** In this chapter, we use both z and t as the test statistics. In later chapters, we will use test statistics such as F and χ^2, called chi-square.

> **TEST STATISTIC** A value, computed from sample information, used to determine whether to reject the null hypothesis.

In hypothesis testing for the mean (μ) when σ is known, the test statistic z is computed by:

> **TESTING A MEAN, σ KNOWN** $$z = \frac{\bar{x} - \mu}{\sigma/\sqrt{n}}$$ **(10–1)**

As in Chapter 9, we will assume that σ is known so that we can use z-values. Please note that we use z-values with three decimals by using the t-table assuming infinite degrees of freedom.

The z-value can be used because the central limit theorem says that the sampling distribution of the sample mean, $\bar{x}$, is normally distributed. The mean of the sample means, $\mu_{\bar{x}}$, is equal to the population mean, μ. The dispersion of the distribution is measured by the standard error of the distribution of sample means, $\sigma/\sqrt{n}$. Using the distribution of sample means, we can calculate a z-value for any sample mean. The z-value is the number of standard errors that separate the sample mean, $\bar{x}$, and the population mean, μ. Note that the numerator of the z-value is *sampling error*.

Using the z-value, we can determine probabilities that a sample mean is within a specified number of standard errors of the population mean. For example, applying the Empirical Rule, about 95% of all sample means will be within 2 standard errors ($z = 2$) of the population mean; 5% of all sample means will be more than 2 standard errors distant from the population mean.

Step 4: Formulate the Decision Rule

A decision rule is a statement of the specific conditions under which the null hypothesis is rejected and the conditions under which it is not rejected. The region or area of rejection defines the location of all those values that are so large or so small that the probability of their occurrence under a true null hypothesis is rather remote.

Chart 10–1 portrays the rejection region for a test of significance that will be conducted later in the chapter.

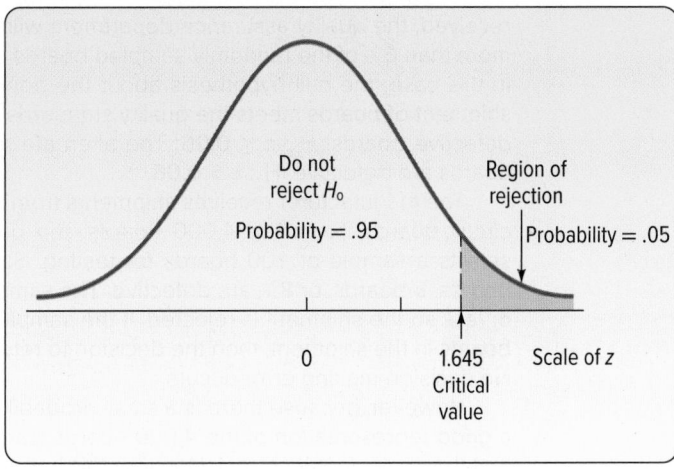

CHART 10–1 The Standard Normal Distribution Showing a Right-Tailed Test with a .05 Level of Significance

Note in the chart that:

- The area where the null hypothesis is not rejected is to the left of 1.645. We will explain how to get the 1.645 value shortly.
- The area of rejection is to the right of 1.645.
- A one-tailed test is being applied. (This will also be explained later.)
- The .05 level of significance was chosen.
- The value 1.645 separates the regions where the null hypothesis is rejected and where it is not rejected.
- The value 1.645 is the **critical value.**

CRITICAL VALUE The dividing point between the region where the null hypothesis is rejected and the region where it is not rejected.

Step 5: Make a Decision

The fifth step in hypothesis testing is to compute the value of the test statistic, compare its value to the critical value, and make a decision to reject or fail to reject the null hypothesis. Referring to Chart 10–1, if, based on sample information, z is computed to be 2.34, the null hypothesis is rejected at the .05 level of significance. The decision to reject H_0 was made because 2.34 lies in the region of rejection, that is, beyond 1.645. We reject the null hypothesis, reasoning that it is highly improbable that a computed z-value this large is due to sampling error (chance).

Had the computed value been 1.645 or less, say 0.71, the null hypothesis is not rejected. It is reasoned that such a small computed value could be attributed to chance, that is, sampling error. As we have emphasized, only one of two decisions is possible in hypothesis testing—either reject or do not reject the null hypothesis.

However, because the decision is based on a sample, it is always possible to make either of two decision errors. It is possible to make a Type I error when the null hypothesis is rejected when it should not be rejected. Or it is also possible to make a Type II error when the null hypothesis is not rejected and it should have been rejected.

To illustrate the possibility that sampling error can lead to rejecting a true null hypothesis, suppose a firm manufactures personal computers and purchases a large number of printed circuit boards. Suppliers competitively bid on a contract to supply the boards, and the supplier with the lowest bid is awarded the contract. Suppose the contract specifies that the computer manufacturer's quality assurance department requires that the proportion of defective boards must be 6% or less. When a shipment is received, the quality assurance department will randomly sample 100 circuit boards. If more than 6% of the randomly sampled boards are defective, the shipment is returned. In this case, the null hypothesis about the population proportion is that the incoming shipment of boards meets the quality standards of the contract and contains 6% or less defective boards, H_0: $\pi \leq 0.06$. The alternate hypothesis is that more than 6% of the boards are defective, H_1: $\pi > 0.06$.

The manufacturer receives shipments from Allied Electronics in quantities of 4,000 circuit boards. From the 4,000 boards, the quality assurance department randomly selects a sample of 100 boards for testing. Suppose that in a sample of 100 circuit boards, 8 boards, or 8%, are defective. The sample proportion exceeds the required 6% or less so the shipment is rejected. If the sample is a good representation of the 4,000 boards in the shipment, then the decision to return the boards to the supplier is correct. No decision-making error occurs.

However, because there is a small probability that the sample of 100 boards is not a good representation of the 4,000 boards (sampling error) there is a small probability that the decision is incorrect. How can this happen? Suppose that only 120 of the 4,000 boards, or 3%, are defective, which is well under the 6% threshold. Suppose also, that somehow when the sample of 100 boards is randomly picked from the 4,000 boards, 8 of the 120 defective boards are selected. The sample data result in a sample proportion defective of 8% (8 of 100). Based on this evidence, we reject the null hypothesis and return the shipment. But, in fact, of the 4,000 boards, the proportion defective is only 3%. Because of sampling error, that is, the sample is not a good representation of the population, an incorrect decision is made. We rejected the null hypothesis when we should have failed to reject the null hypothesis. In statistics, rejecting a true null hypothesis is called a **Type I error.** In the hypothesis testing procedure the researcher must select or assign this probability. In statistics, it is represented by the Greek letter alpha (α).

> **TYPE I ERROR** Rejecting the null hypothesis, H_0, when it is true.

> α The probability of making a Type I error, represented by the Greek letter alpha.

In comparison, the firm would commit a Type II error if the quality assurance department accepted an incoming shipment that exceeded the requirement that 6% or fewer are defective. How could this happen? Suppose that, in fact, 15% of the 4,000 boards are defective. Somehow, in the process of selecting a random sample of 100 boards from this defective shipment, only 4 (4%) of the sampled boards are defective. According to the stated procedure, because the sample contained less than 6% defective boards, we fail to reject the null hypothesis and incorrectly decide to accept the shipment. This is a **Type II error.** After a hypothesis testing procedure is completed, we can use the sample statistics to compute the probability of a Type II error. It is represented by the Greek letter beta (β).

> **TYPE II ERROR** Not rejecting the null hypothesis when it is false.

> β The probability of making a Type II error, represented by the Greek letter beta.

Another illustration of inference and decision-making errors occurs in the U.S. judicial system. In this system, a person is presumed innocent until proven guilty. A trial starts with a null hypothesis that the individual is innocent. The prosecuting attorneys provide evidence used to reject the null hypothesis and convict the individual. Defense attorneys defend the individual against false and misleading evidence. If, in the opinion of the judge or jury, the trial did not provide sufficient evidence to reject the presumption of innocence, the individual is presumed innocent and is free to leave the courtroom. It is still possible that a Type II error is committed; based on the evidence, the jury fails to reject the presumption of innocence when the individual is, in fact, guilty. In the judicial system, Type I errors also occur, that is, a jury or judge decides that the evidence leads to a rejection of innocence when, in fact, the person is innocent.

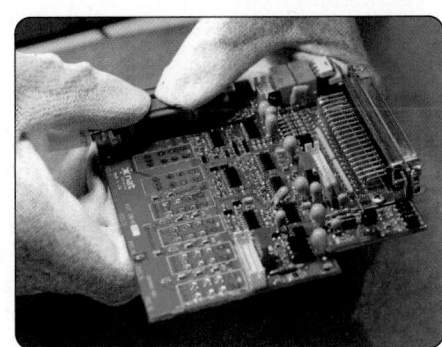
Jim Stern/Bloomberg/Getty Images

We often refer to the probability of these two possible errors as *alpha,* α, and *beta,* β. Alpha (α) is the probability of making a Type I error, and beta (β) is the probability of making a Type II error. The following table summarizes the decisions you could make and the possible consequences.

Null Hypothesis	Researcher	
	Does Not Reject H_0	Rejects H_0
H_0 is true	Correct decision	Type I error
H_0 is false	Type II error	Correct decision

Step 6: Interpret the Result

The final step in the hypothesis testing procedure is to interpret the results. The process does not end with the value of a sample statistic or the decision to reject or not reject the null hypothesis. How do we interpret these results in the context of the hypothesis statement? Here are two examples:

- The following is an example when we fail to reject the null hypothesis. An investigative reporter for a Colorado newspaper reports that the mean monthly income of convenience stores in the state is $130,000. You believe that the report is incorrect and decide to evaluate the report. Following the hypothesis testing procedure, the null and alternate hypotheses are:

$$H_0: \mu = \$130,000$$

$$H_1: \mu \neq \$130,000$$

You select a sample of convenience stores and collect data on monthly income. Based on the sample's statistics, you compare the hypothesized income to the sample mean income by computing the test statistic. The test statistic is not in the rejection region, so the decision is to fail to reject the null hypothesis.

When failing to reject the null hypothesis, be careful with the interpretation. This result does not prove or demonstrate anything. The result is a *null* result. The difference between the sample mean and hypothesized population mean was not large enough to reject the null hypothesis. In different words, the sample data simply do not support the inference, as stated in the alternate hypothesis, that the population mean is not equal to $130,000.

- The following is an example when we reject the null hypothesis. In a recent speech to students, the dean of the College of Business reported that the mean credit card debt for college students is $3,000. You decide to investigate the statement's truth. The null hypothesis and the alternate hypothesis are:

$$H_0: \mu = \$3,000$$

$$H_1: \mu \neq \$3,000$$

A random sample of college students provides a sample mean and standard deviation, and you compute a *z*-statistic. The hypothesis test results in a decision to reject the null hypothesis.

How do you interpret the result? The sample evidence does not support the dean's statement. Based on the sample data, the mean amount of student credit card debt is different from $3,000. The null hypothesis is rejected with a stated probability, α, of a Type I error. That is, there is a small probability that the decision to reject the null hypothesis is an error due to random sampling.

STATISTICS IN ACTION

LASIK is a 15-minute surgical procedure that uses a laser to reshape an eye's cornea with the goal of improving eyesight. Research shows that about 5% of all surgeries involve complications such as glare, corneal haze, overcorrection or undercorrection of vision, and loss of vision. In a statistical sense, the research tests a null hypothesis that the surgery will not improve eyesight with the alternative hypothesis that the surgery will improve eyesight. The sample data of LASIK surgery shows that 5% of all cases result in complications. The 5% represents a Type I error rate. When deciding to have the surgery, a person expects to reject the null hypothesis. In 5% of future cases, this expectation will not be met. (Source: *American Academy of Ophthalmology Journal*, Vol. 16, no. 43.)

> **SUMMARY OF THE STEPS IN HYPOTHESIS TESTING**
> 1. Establish the null hypothesis (H_0) and the alternate hypothesis (H_1).
> 2. Select the level of significance, that is, α.
> 3. Select an appropriate test statistic.
> 4. Formulate a decision rule based on steps 1, 2, and 3.
> 5. Make a decision regarding the null hypothesis based on the sample information.
> 6. Interpret the results of the test.

Before demonstrating a test of hypothesis, we describe the difference between a one-tailed and a two-tailed hypothesis test.

LO10-3

Distinguish between a one-tailed and a two-tailed test of hypothesis.

One-Tailed and Two-Tailed Hypothesis Tests

Refer to Chart 10–1. It shows a one-tailed test. It is called a one-tailed test because the rejection region is only in one tail of the curve. In this case, it is in the right, or upper, tail of the curve. To illustrate, suppose that the packaging department at General Foods Corporation is concerned that some boxes of Grape Nuts are significantly overweight. The cereal is packaged in 453-gram boxes, so the null hypothesis is H_0: $\mu \leq 453$. This is read, "The population mean (μ) is equal to or less than 453." The alternate hypothesis is, therefore, H_1: $\mu > 453$. This is read, "μ is greater than 453." Note that the inequality sign in the alternate hypothesis (>) points to the region of rejection in the upper tail. (See Chart 10–1.) Also observe that the null hypothesis includes the equal sign. That is, H_0: $\mu \leq 453$. The equality condition always appears in H_0, never in H_1.

Chart 10–2 portrays a situation where the rejection region is in the left (lower) tail of the standard normal distribution. As an illustration, consider the problem of automobile manufacturers, large automobile leasing companies, and other organizations that purchase large quantities of tires. They want the tires to average, say, 60,000 miles of wear under normal usage. They will, therefore, reject a shipment of tires if tests reveal that the mean life of the tires is significantly below 60,000 miles. They gladly accept a shipment if the mean life is greater than 60,000 miles! They are not concerned with this possibility, however. They are concerned only if they have sample evidence to conclude that the tires will average less than 60,000 miles of useful life. Thus, the test is set up to satisfy the concern of the automobile manufacturers that *the mean life of the tires is not less than 60,000 miles*. This statement appears in the null hypothesis. The null and alternate hypotheses in this case are written H_0: $\mu \geq 60,000$ and H_1: $\mu < 60,000$.

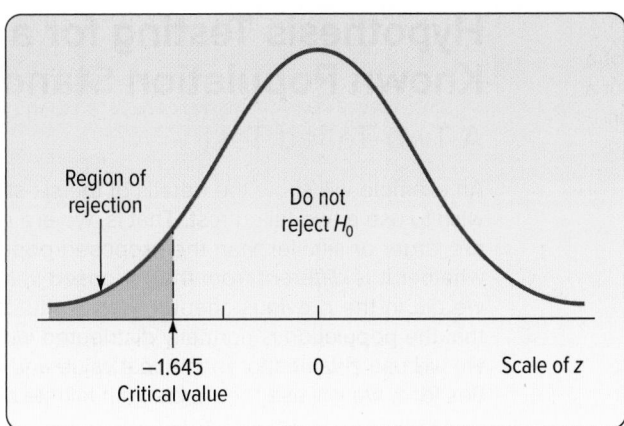

CHART 10–2 Sampling Distribution for the Statistic *z*, Left-Tailed Test, .05 Level of Significance

One way to determine the location of the rejection region is to look at the direction in which the inequality sign in the alternate hypothesis is pointing (either < or >). In the tire wear problem, it is pointing to the left, and the rejection region is therefore in the left tail.

In summary, a test is *one-tailed* when the alternate hypothesis, H_1, states a direction, such as:

H_0: The mean income of female stockbrokers is *less than or equal to* $65,000 per year.
H_1: The mean income of female stockbrokers is *greater than* $65,000 per year.

If no direction is specified in the alternate hypothesis, we use a *two-tailed* test. Changing the previous problem to illustrate, we can say:

H_0: The mean income of female stockbrokers is $65,000 per year.
H_1: The mean income of female stockbrokers is *not equal to* $65,000 per year.

If the null hypothesis is rejected in the two-tailed case, the mean income could be significantly greater than $65,000 per year or it could be significantly less than $65,000 per year. To accommodate these two possibilities, the 5% area of rejection is divided equally into the two tails of the sampling distribution (2.5% each). Chart 10–3 shows the two areas and the critical values. Note that the total area in the normal distribution is 1.0000, found by .9500 + .0250 + .0250.

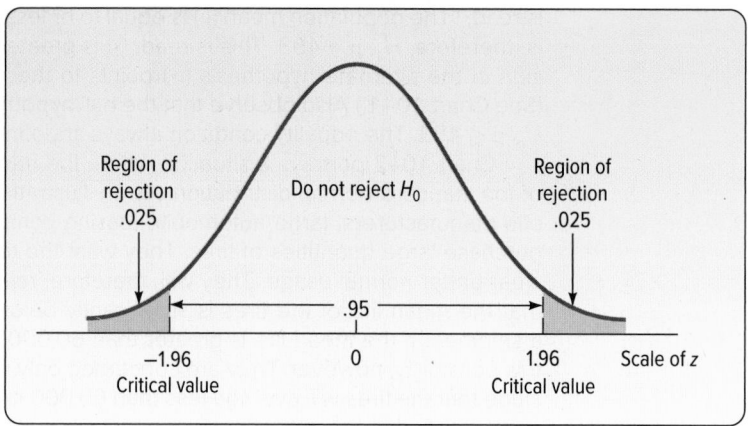

CHART 10–3 Regions of Nonrejection and Rejection for a Two-Tailed Test, .05 Level of Significance

LO10-4
Conduct a test of a hypothesis about a population mean.

Hypothesis Testing for a Population Mean: Known Population Standard Deviation

A Two-Tailed Test

An example will show the details of the six-step hypothesis testing procedure. We also wish to use a two-tailed test. That is, we are *not* concerned whether the sample results are larger or smaller than the proposed population mean. Rather, we are interested in whether it is *different from* the proposed value for the population mean. We begin, as we did in the previous chapter, with a situation where we have historical information that the population is normally distributed with a known standard deviation. Therefore, we will use z-values for the critical value and test statistic. To determine the critical values for z, we will use the *t*-table with infinite degrees of freedom.

▶ **EXAMPLE**

Jamestown Steel Company manufactures and assembles desks and other office equipment at several plants in western New York State. The weekly production of the Model A325 desk at the Fredonia Plant follows a normal probability distribution with a mean of 200 desks and a standard deviation of 16 desks. Recently, because of market expansion, new production methods have been introduced and new employees hired. The vice president of manufacturing would like to investigate whether there has been a *change* in the weekly production of the Model A325 desk. Is the mean number of desks produced at the Fredonia Plant *different from* 200? The vice president decides to test the hypothesis using a .01 level of significance. By randomly sampling desks from the population, the vice president will accept a small risk, $\alpha = 0.01$, of making a Type I error, that is, rejecting the null hypothesis when it is true.

Robert Nicholas/OJO Images/Getty Images

SOLUTION

In this example, we know two important pieces of information: (1) The population of weekly production follows the normal distribution, and (2) the standard deviation of this normal distribution is 16 desks per week. So it is appropriate to use the *z*-statistic. We use the statistical hypothesis testing procedure to investigate whether the production rate has changed from 200 per week.

Step 1: State the null hypothesis and the alternate hypothesis. The null hypothesis is "The population mean is 200 desks per week." The alternate hypothesis is "The mean is different from 200 desks per week" or "The mean is not 200 desks per week." These two hypotheses are written:

$$H_0: \mu = 200$$

$$H_1: \mu \neq 200$$

This is a *two-tailed test* because the alternate hypothesis does not state a direction. In other words, it does not state whether the mean production is greater than 200 or less than 200. The vice president wants only to find out whether the production rate is different from 200.

Before moving to step 2, we wish to emphasize two points.

- The null hypothesis has the equal sign. Why? Because the value we are testing is always in the null hypothesis. Logically, the alternate hypothesis never contains the equal sign.
- Both the null hypothesis and the alternate hypothesis contain Greek letters—in this case μ, which is the symbol for the population mean. Tests of hypothesis **always** refer to population parameters, never to sample statistics. To put it another way, you will never see the symbol $\bar{x}$ as part of the null hypothesis or the alternate hypothesis.

Step 2: Select the level of significance. In the example description, the significance level selected is .01. This is α, the probability of committing a Type I error by rejecting a true null hypothesis.

Step 3: Select the test statistic. The test statistic is z when the population standard deviation is known. Transforming the production data to standard units (z-values) permits their use not only in this problem but also in other hypothesis-testing problems. Formula (10–1) for z is repeated next with the various letters identified.

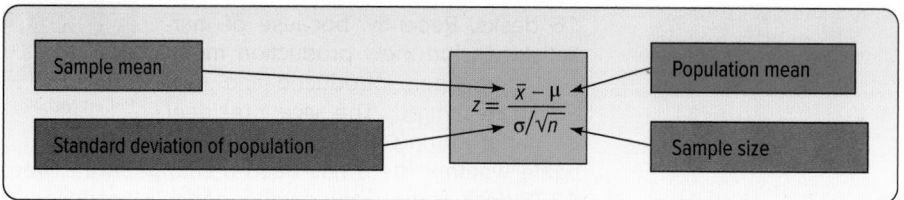

Step 4: Formulate the decision rule. We formulate the decision rule by first determining the critical values of z. Because this is a two-tailed test, half of .01, or .005, is placed in each tail. The area where H_0 is not rejected, located between the two tails, is therefore .99. Using the Student's t-Distribution table in Appendix B.5, move to the top margin called "Level of Significance for Two-Tailed Tests, α," select the column with $\alpha = .01$, and move to the last row, which is labeled ∞, or infinite degrees of freedom. The z-value in this cell is 2.576. All the facets of this problem are shown in Chart 10–4.

CHART 10–4 Decision Rule for the .01 Significance Level

The decision rule is: If the computed value of z is not between −2.576 and 2.576, reject the null hypothesis. If z falls between −2.576 and 2.576, do not reject the null hypothesis.

Step 5: Make a decision. Take a sample from the population (weekly production), compute a test statistic, apply the decision rule, and arrive at a decision to reject H_0 or not to reject H_0. The mean number of desks produced last year (50 weeks because the plant was shut down 2 weeks for vacation) is 203.5. The standard deviation of the population is 16 desks per week. Computing the z-value from formula (10–1):

$$z = \frac{\bar{x} - \mu}{\sigma/\sqrt{n}} = \frac{203.5 - 200}{16/\sqrt{50}} = 1.547$$

Because 1.547 is between -2.576 and 2.576, we do not reject H_0.

Step 6: Interpret the result. We fail to reject the null hypothesis, so we did not show that the population mean has changed from 200 desks per week. To put it another way, the difference between the population mean of 200 per week and the sample mean of 203.5 could simply be due to chance. What should we tell the vice president? The sample information fails to indicate that the new production methods resulted in a change in the 200-desks-per-week production rate.

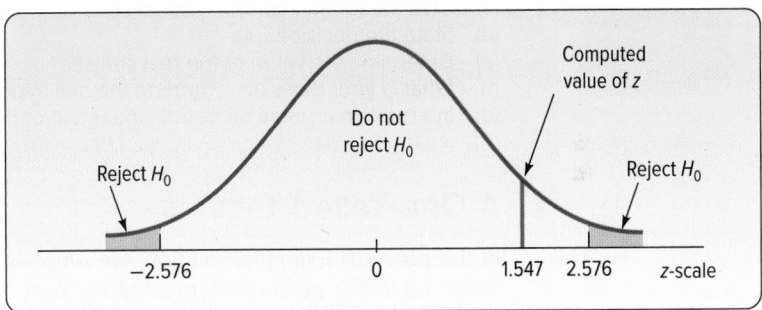

In failing to reject the null hypothesis, did we prove that the assembly rate is still 200 per week? Absolutely not. In failing to reject the hypothesis that the population mean is 200, we did NOT prove it was true. The result does not support any conclusion about the null hypothesis. Another point of view is to consider the sample results in terms of the alternative hypothesis. The sample data simply do not support the inference, as stated in the alternate hypothesis, that the population mean is not equal to 200 desks.

We selected the significance level, .01 in this case, before setting up the decision rule and sampling the population. This is the appropriate strategy. The significance level should be set by the investigator *before* gathering the sample evidence and not changed based on the sample evidence.

How does the hypothesis testing procedure just described compare with that of confidence intervals discussed in the previous chapter? When we conducted the test of hypothesis regarding the production of desks, we changed the units from desks per week to a z-value. Then we compared the computed value of the test statistic (1.547) to that of the critical values (-2.576 and 2.576). Because the computed value of the test statistic was in the region where the null hypothesis was not rejected, we concluded that the population mean could be 200. To use the confidence interval approach, on the other hand, we would develop a confidence interval, based on formula (9–1). See page 291. The interval would be from 197.671 to 209.329, found by $203.5 \pm 2.576(16/\sqrt{50})$. Note that the proposed population value, 200, is within this interval. Hence, we would conclude that the population mean could reasonably be 200.

In general, H_0 is rejected if the confidence interval does not include the hypothesized value. If the confidence interval includes the hypothesized value, then H_0 is not rejected. So the "do not reject region" for a test of hypothesis is equivalent to the proposed population value occurring in the confidence interval.

STATISTICS IN ACTION

There is a difference between *statistically significant* and *practically significant*. To explain, suppose we develop a new diet pill and test it on 100,000 people. We conclude that the typical person taking the pill for 2 years lost 1 pound. Do you think many people would be interested in taking the pill to lose 1 pound? The results of using the new pill were statistically significant but not practically significant.

SELF-REVIEW 10–1

Heinz fills 16-ounce containers with ketchup using a filling machine. From many years of experience with the machine, Heinz knows that the amount dispensed in each container follows a normal distribution, with a mean of 16 ounces and a standard deviation of 0.15 ounce. A sample of 50 containers filled last hour revealed the mean amount per container was 16.017 ounces. Does this evidence suggest that the mean amount dispensed is different from 16 ounces? Use the .05 significance level.

Kevin Lorenzi/Bloomberg/Getty Images

(a) State the null hypothesis and the alternate hypothesis.
(b) What is the probability of a Type I error?
(c) Give the formula for the test statistic.
(d) State the decision rule.
(e) Determine the value of the test statistic.
(f) What is your decision regarding the null hypothesis?
(g) Interpret, in a single sentence, the result of the statistical test.

A One-Tailed Test

In the previous Example/Solution, we emphasized that we were concerned only with reporting to the vice president whether there had been a change in the mean number of desks assembled at the Fredonia Plant. We were not concerned with whether the change was an increase or a decrease in the production.

To illustrate a one-tailed test, let's change the problem. Suppose the vice president wants to know whether there has been an *increase* in the number of units assembled. Can we conclude, because of the improved production methods, that the mean number of desks assembled in the last 50 weeks was more than 200? Look at the difference in the way the problem is formulated. In the first case, we wanted to know whether there was a *difference* in the mean number assembled, but now we want to know whether there has been an *increase*. Because we are investigating different questions, we will set our hypotheses differently. The biggest difference occurs in the alternate hypothesis. Earlier, we stated the alternate hypothesis as "different from"; now we want to state it as "greater than." In symbols:

A two-tailed test:	A one-tailed test:
$H_0: \mu = 200$	$H_0: \mu \leq 200$
$H_1: \mu \neq 200$	$H_1: \mu > 200$

The critical values for a one-tailed test are different from a two-tailed test at the same significance level. In the previous Example/Solution, we split the significance level in half and put half in the lower tail and half in the upper tail. In a one-tailed test, we put all the rejection region in one tail. See Chart 10–5.

For the one-tailed test, the critical value of z is 2.326. Using the Student's t-Distribution table in Appendix B.5, move to the top heading called "Level of Significance for One-Tailed Tests, α," select the column with $\alpha = .01$, and move to the last row, which is labeled ∞, or infinite degrees of freedom. The z-value in this cell is 2.326.

CHART 10-5 Rejection Regions for Two-Tailed and One-Tailed Tests, $\alpha = .01$

p-Value in Hypothesis Testing

In testing a hypothesis, we compare the test statistic to a critical value. A decision is made to either reject or not reject the null hypothesis. So, for example, if the critical value is 1.96 and the computed value of the test statistic is 2.19, the decision is to reject the null hypothesis.

The critical value approach to evaluating a hypothesis provides a good description of the hypothesis testing procedure. However the hypothesis decision can also be based on the probability of the sample outcome assuming that the null hypothesis is true. This probability is called a **p-value.** To make a decision about the null hypothesis, the *p*-value is compared to the level of significance. If the *p*-value is less than α, then we reject the null hypothesis.

> **p-VALUE** The probability of observing a sample value as extreme as, or more extreme than, the value observed, given that the null hypothesis is true.

How do we find the *p*-value? To calculate *p*-values, we will need to use the *z*-table (Appendix B.3) and, to use this table, we will round *z* test statistics to two decimals. To illustrate how to compute a *p*-value, we will use the example where we tested the null hypothesis that the mean number of desks produced per week at Fredonia was 200.

Recall that the sample mean, 203.5, corresponds with a *z*-value of 1.547. That is, the difference between the sample mean and the population mean, $203.5 - 200.0 = 3.5$, is 1.547 standard errors. Rounding the *z*-value to 1.55, we use the standard normal *z*-table to find the probability that the difference exceeds 1.55. This probability is .0606. Because the null hypothesis is two tailed, the *p*-value must also recognize the possibility that a sample mean is 1.55 standard errors less than the population mean. So, the two-tailed *p*-value is .1212, found by 2(.0606). To find *p*-values, be aware that many *p*-value calculators are available online. Simply search "*p*-value calculators." The primary information required for the calculators is the value of the test statistic.

The *p*-value of .1212 is greater than the significance level of .01 decided upon initially, so H_0 is not rejected. The details are shown in the following graph. Notice for the two-tailed hypothesis test, the *p*-value is represented by areas in both tails of the distribution. Then the *p*-value can easily be compared with the significance level. The same decision rule is used in a one-sided test.

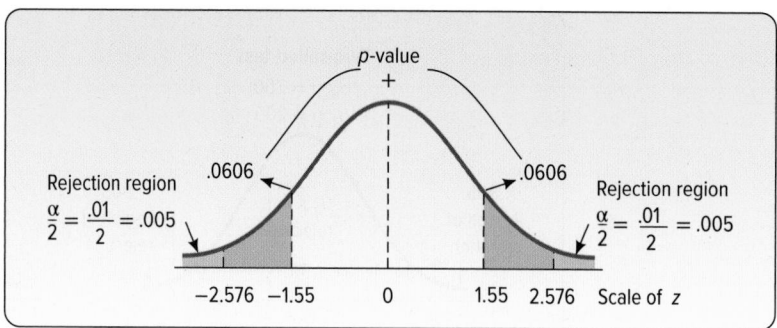

A p-value provides a basis for deciding if H_0 should be rejected. How do we interpret a p-value? A very small p-value—say, .001—indicates that the sampling error, or the difference between the sample and population means, is extremely unlikely. Therefore, the sample information is not consistent with the hypothesis and provides evidence that the null hypothesis should be rejected. For comparison, if the p-value were 0.20, the sampling error, or the difference between the sample and population means, is possible, and the sample information may be consistent with the hypothesis. Therefore, the sample information does not provide enough evidence to reject the null hypothesis. The following box summarizes the interpretation of different p-values.

INTERPRETING THE WEIGHT OF EVIDENCE AGAINST H_0

If the p-value is less than

(a) .10, we have *some* evidence that H_0 is not true.

(b) .05, we have *strong* evidence that H_0 is not true.

(c) .01, we have *very strong* evidence that H_0 is not true.

(d) .001, we have *extremely strong* evidence that H_0 is not true.

SELF-REVIEW 10–2

Refer to Self-Review 10–1.

(a) Suppose the next to the last sentence is changed to read: Does this evidence suggest that the mean amount dispensed is *more than* 16 ounces? State the null hypothesis and the alternate hypothesis under these conditions.

(b) What is the decision rule under the new conditions stated in part (a)?

(c) A second sample of 50 filled containers revealed the mean to be 16.040 ounces. What is the sampling error for this sample?

(d) Convert the sampling error to a test statistic.

(e) What is your decision regarding the null hypothesis?

(f) Interpret, in a single sentence, the result of the statistical test.

(g) What is the p-value? What is your decision regarding the null hypothesis based on the p-value? Is this the same conclusion reached in part (e)?

EXERCISES

For Exercises 1–4, answer the questions: (a) Is this a one- or two-tailed test? (b) What is the decision rule? (c) What is the value of the test statistic? (d) What is the p-value? (e) What is your decision regarding H_0? Interpret the result.

1. A sample of 36 observations is selected from a normal population. The sample mean is 49, and the population standard deviation is 5. Conduct the following test of hypothesis using the .05 significance level.

$$H_0: \mu = 50$$
$$H_1: \mu \neq 50$$

2. A sample of 36 observations is selected from a normal population. The sample mean is 12, and the population standard deviation is 3. Conduct the following test of hypothesis using the .01 significance level.

$$H_0: \mu \leq 10$$
$$H_1: \mu > 10$$

3. A sample of 36 observations is selected from a normal population. The sample mean is 21, and the population standard deviation is 5. Conduct the following test of hypothesis using the .05 significance level.

$$H_0: \mu \leq 20$$
$$H_1: \mu > 20$$

4. A sample of 64 observations is selected from a normal population. The sample mean is 215, and the population standard deviation is 15. Conduct the following test of hypothesis using the .025 significance level.

$$H_0: \mu \geq 220$$
$$H_1: \mu < 220$$

For Exercises 5–8: (a) State the null hypothesis and the alternate hypothesis. (b) State the decision rule. (c) Compute the value of the test statistic. (d) What is the *p*-value? (e) What is your decision regarding H_0? Interpret the result.

5. The manufacturer of the X-15 steel-belted radial truck tire claims that the mean mileage the tire can be driven before the tread wears out is 60,000 miles. Assume the mileage wear follows the normal distribution and the standard deviation of the distribution is 5,000 miles. Crosset Truck Company bought 48 tires and found that the mean mileage for its trucks is 59,500 miles. Is Crosset's experience different from that claimed by the manufacturer at the .05 significance level?

6. The waiting time for customers at MacBurger Restaurants follows a normal distribution with a population standard deviation of 1 minute. At the Warren Road MacBurger, the quality-assurance department sampled 50 customers and found that the mean waiting time was 2.75 minutes. At the .05 significance level, can we conclude that the mean waiting time is less than 3 minutes?

7. A recent national survey found that high school students watched an average (mean) of 6.8 movies per month with a population standard deviation of 1.8. The distribution of number of movies watched per month follows the normal distribution. A random sample of 36 college students revealed that the mean number of movies watched last month was 6.2. At the .05 significance level, can we conclude that college students watch fewer movies per month than high school students?

8. At the time she was hired as a server at the Grumney Family Restaurant, Beth Brigden was told, "You can average $80 a day in tips." Assume the population of daily tips is normally distributed with a standard deviation of $9.95. Over the first 35 days she was employed at the restaurant, the mean daily amount of her tips was $84.85. At the .01 significance level, can Ms. Brigden conclude that her daily tips average more than $80?

Hypothesis Testing for a Population Mean: Population Standard Deviation Unknown

LO10-6

Use a *t*-statistic to test a hypothesis.

In the preceding examples, we assumed that σ, the population standard deviation, was known, and that the population followed the normal distribution. In most cases, however, the population standard deviation is unknown and σ is estimated with the sample standard deviation, *s*. In this case, we use the *t*-distribution to calculate the test statistic. Formula (10–1) is revised as follows:

TESTING A MEAN, σ UNKNOWN	$t = \dfrac{\bar{x} - \mu}{s/\sqrt{n}}$	(10–2)

with *n* − 1 degrees of freedom, where:

$\bar{x}$ is the sample mean.
μ is the hypothesized population mean. Refer to the null hypothesis for this value.
s is the sample standard deviation.
n is the number of observations in the sample.

We encountered this same situation when constructing confidence intervals in the previous chapter. See pages 296–299 in Chapter 9. We summarized this problem in Chart 9–3 on page 299. Under these conditions, the correct statistical procedure is to replace the standard normal distribution with the *t*-distribution. To review, the major characteristics of the *t*-distribution are:

- It is a continuous distribution.
- It is bell shaped and symmetrical.
- There is a family of *t*-distributions. Each time the degrees of freedom change, a new distribution is created.
- As the number of degrees of freedom increases, the shape of the *t*-distribution approaches that of the standard normal distribution.
- The *t*-distribution is flatter, or more spread out, than the standard normal distribution.

The following Example/Solution shows the details.

▶ **EXAMPLE**

The Myrtle Beach International Airport provides a cell phone parking lot where people can wait for a message to pick up arriving passengers. To decide if the cell phone lot has enough parking places, the manager of airport parking needs to know if the mean time in the lot is more than 15 minutes. A sample of 12 recent customers showed they were in the lot the following lengths of time, in minutes.

| 30 | 24 | 28 | 22 | 14 | 2 | 39 | 23 | 23 | 28 | 12 | 31 |

At the .05 significance level, is it reasonable to conclude that the mean time in the lot is more than 15 minutes?

SOLUTION

We continue to use the six-step hypothesis testing procedure.

Step 1: State the null and alternate hypotheses. We begin by stating the null hypothesis and the alternate hypothesis. In this case, the question is whether the population mean could be more than 15 minutes. It is a one-tailed test. Note that the question does not include or consider the possibility that the population mean is equal to 15 minutes. So, the question is stated as the alternate hypothesis. We state the two hypotheses as follows:

$$H_0: \mu \leq 15$$

$$H_1: \mu > 15$$

Step 2: Select the level of significance. We decided to use the .05 significance level.

Step 3: Select the test statistic. We would use t as a test statistic for the following reasons: We presume that the population distribution of times is normally distributed; we also do not know the population standard deviation and estimate it with the sample standard deviation.

Step 4: Formulate the decision rule. There are 11 degrees of freedom, found by $n - 1 = 12 - 1 = 11$. The critical t-value is 1.796, found by referring to Appendix B.5 for a one-tailed test. See a portion of the t-table in Table 10–1.

TABLE 10–1 A Portion of the t-Distribution

	Confidence Intervals				
	80%	**90%**	**95%**	**98%**	**99%**
	Level of Significance for One-Tailed Test				
df	**0.10**	**0.05**	**0.025**	**0.010**	**0.005**
	Level of Significance for Two-Tailed Test				
	0.20	**0.10**	**0.05**	**0.02**	**0.01**
1	3.078	6.314	12.706	31.321	63.657
2	1.886	2.920	4.303	6.965	9.925
3	1.638	2.353	3.182	4.541	5.841
4	1.533	2.132	2.776	3.747	4.604
5	1.476	2.015	2.571	3.365	4.032
6	1.440	1.943	2.447	3.143	3.707
7	1.415	1.895	2.365	2.998	3.499
8	1.397	1.860	2.306	2.896	3.355
9	1.383	1.833	2.262	2.821	3.250
10	1.372	1.812	2.228	2.764	3.169
11	1.363	1.796	2.201	2.718	3.106
12	1.356	1.782	2.179	2.681	3.055

Using $\alpha = .05$ with 11 degrees of freedom, the decision rule is: Reject the null hypothesis if the computed t is greater than 1.796. This information is summarized in Chart 10–6.

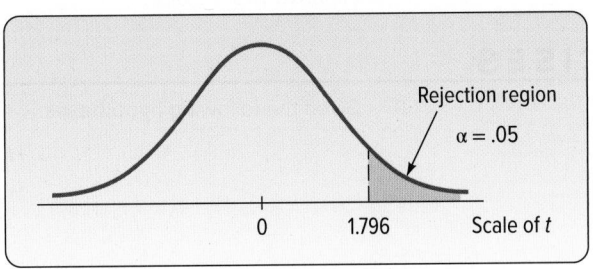

CHART 10–6 Rejection Region, One-Tailed Test, Student's t-Distribution, $\alpha = .05$

Step 5: Make a decision. We calculate the sample mean using formula (3–2) and the sample standard deviation using formula (3–10). The sample mean is 23 minutes, and the sample standard deviation is 9.835 minutes. The details of the calculations are shown in Table 10–2.

TABLE 10–2 Calculations of Sample Mean and Standard Deviation Parking Times

Customer	x, Minutes	$(x - \bar{x})^2$
Chmura	30	49
Will	24	1
Crompton	28	25
Craver	22	1
Cao	14	81
Nowlin	2	441
Esposito	39	256
Colvard	23	0
Hoefle	23	0
Lawler	28	25
Trask	12	121
Grullon	31	64
Total	276	1064

$$\bar{x} = \frac{\Sigma x}{n} = \frac{276}{12} = 23$$

$$s = \sqrt{\frac{\Sigma(x - \bar{x})^2}{n - 1}} = \sqrt{\frac{1064}{12 - 1}} = 9.835$$

Now we are ready to compute the value of the test statistic, t, using formula (10–2).

$$t = \frac{\bar{x} - \mu}{s/\sqrt{n}} = \frac{23 - 15}{9.835/\sqrt{12}} = 2.818$$

Step 6: Interpret the results. The null hypothesis that the population mean is less than or equal to 15 minutes is rejected because the computed t-value of 2.818 lies in the area to the right of 1.796. We conclude that the mean time customers spend in the lot is more than 15 minutes. This result indicates that the airport may need to add more parking places.

SELF-REVIEW 10-3

The mean life of a battery used in a digital clock is 305 days. The lives of the batteries follow the normal distribution. The battery was recently modified to last longer. A sample of 20 of the modified batteries had a mean life of 311 days with a standard deviation of 12 days. Did the modification increase the mean life of the battery?
(a) State the null hypothesis and the alternate hypothesis.
(b) Show the decision rule graphically. Use the .05 significance level.
(c) Compute the value of t. What is your decision regarding the null hypothesis? Briefly summarize your results.

EXERCISES

9. Given the following hypotheses:

$$H_0: \mu \leq 10$$
$$H_1: \mu > 10$$

A random sample of 10 observations is selected from a normal population. The sample mean was 12 and the sample standard deviation 3. Using the .05 significance level:
a. state the decision rule.
b. compute the value of the test statistic.
c. what is your decision regarding the null hypothesis?

10. Given the following hypotheses:

$$H_0: \mu = 400$$
$$H_1: \mu \neq 400$$

A random sample of 12 observations is selected from a normal population. The sample mean was 407 and the sample standard deviation 6. Using the .01 significance level:
a. state the decision rule.
b. compute the value of the test statistic.
c. what is your decision regarding the null hypothesis?

11. The Rocky Mountain district sales manager of Rath Publishing Inc., a college textbook publishing company, claims that the sales representatives make an average of 40 sales calls per week on professors. Several reps say that this estimate is too low. To investigate, a random sample of 28 sales representatives reveals that the mean number of calls made last week was 42. The standard deviation of the sample is 2.1 calls. Using the .05 significance level, can we conclude that the mean number of calls per salesperson per week is more than 40?

12. The management of GoGo Carts is considering a new method of assembling its golf cart. The present method requires a mean time of 42.3 minutes to assemble a cart. The mean assembly time for a random sample of 24 carts, using the new method, was 40.6 minutes, and the standard deviation of the sample was 2.7 minutes. Using the .10 level of significance, can we conclude that the assembly time using the new method is faster?

13. The mean income per person in the United States is $60,000, and the distribution of incomes follows a normal distribution. A random sample of 10 residents of Wilmington, Delaware, had a mean of $70,000 with a standard deviation of $10,000. At the .05 level of significance, is that enough evidence to conclude that residents of Wilmington, Delaware, have more income than the national average?

14. **FILE** Most air travelers now use e-tickets. Electronic ticketing allows passengers to not worry about a paper ticket, and it costs the airline companies less to handle than paper ticketing. However, in recent times the airlines have received complaints from passengers regarding their e-tickets, particularly when connecting flights and a change of airlines were involved. To investigate the problem, an independent watchdog agency contacted a random sample of 20 airports and collected information on the number of complaints the airport had with e-tickets for the month of March. The information is reported here.

14	14	16	12	12	14	13	16	15	14
12	15	15	14	13	13	12	13	10	13

At the .05 significance level, can the watchdog agency conclude the mean number of complaints per airport is less than 15 per month?
a. What assumption is necessary before conducting a test of hypothesis?
b. Plot the number of complaints per airport in a frequency distribution or a dot plot. Is it reasonable to conclude that the population follows a normal distribution?
c. Conduct a test of hypothesis and interpret the results.

A Statistical Software Solution

The following Example/Solution applies statistical software to compute the statistics for a hypothesis test. See the reference to the Excel tutorial in Connect.

▶ **EXAMPLE**

FILE The McFarland Insurance Company Claims Department reports the mean cost to process a claim is $60. An industry comparison showed this amount to be larger than most other insurance companies, so the company instituted cost-cutting measures. To evaluate the effect of the cost-cutting measures, the supervisor of the Claims Department selected a random sample of 26 claims processed last month and recorded the cost to process each claim. The sample information is reported as follows:

$45	$49	$62	$40	$43	$61
48	53	67	63	78	64
48	54	51	56	63	69
58	51	58	59	56	57
38	76				

Tutorial #52
in Connect

Using statistical software to compute a *p*-value and applying the .01 significance level, is it reasonable to conclude that the mean cost to process a claim is now less than $60? The tutorial referenced to the left demonstrates the process in Excel.

SOLUTION

We will use the six-step hypothesis testing procedure.

Step 1: **State the null hypothesis and the alternate hypothesis.** The null hypothesis is that the population mean is at least $60. The alternate hypothesis is that the population mean is less than $60. We can express the null and alternate hypotheses as follows:

$$H_0: \mu \geq \$60$$
$$H_1: \mu < \$60$$

The test is *one-tailed* because we want to determine whether there has been a *reduction* in the cost. The inequality in the alternate hypothesis points to the region of rejection in the left tail of the distribution.

Step 2: **Select the level of significance.** We decided on the .01 significance level.

Step 3: **Select the test statistic.** The test statistic in this situation is the *t*-distribution. Why? First, it is reasonable to conclude that the distribution of the cost per claim follows the normal distribution. Also, we do not know the standard deviation of the population. So we substitute the sample standard deviation. The test statistic is computed by formula (10–2):

$$t = \frac{\bar{x} - \mu}{s/\sqrt{n}}$$

Step 4: **Formulate the decision rule.** Applying statistical software, the test statistic and its associated *p*-value will be computed. The decision rule is: If the *p*-value is less than the significance level, .01, reject the null hypothesis.

Step 5: **Make a decision.** The statistical software in Excel provides the following output. Please follow the tutorial in Connect to replicate these results.

t-Test: One Sample	
	Claim Cost
Mean	56.4230769
Variance	100.813846
Observations	26
Hypothesized mean difference	60
df	25
t-statistic	−1.8165033
P(T<=t) one-tail	0.04065164
t Critical one-tail	1.70814076
P(T<=t) two-tail	0.08130327
t Critical two-tail	2.05953855

We can insert these values into formula (10–2) to confirm the software results.

$$t = \frac{\bar{x} - \mu}{s/\sqrt{n}} = \frac{\$56.423 - \$60}{\$10.041/\sqrt{26}} = -1.816$$

The statistical software reports a one-tail *p*-value of .041. The *p*-value is greater than .01. Therefore, we fail to reject the null hypothesis. Chart 10–7 illustrates the solution.

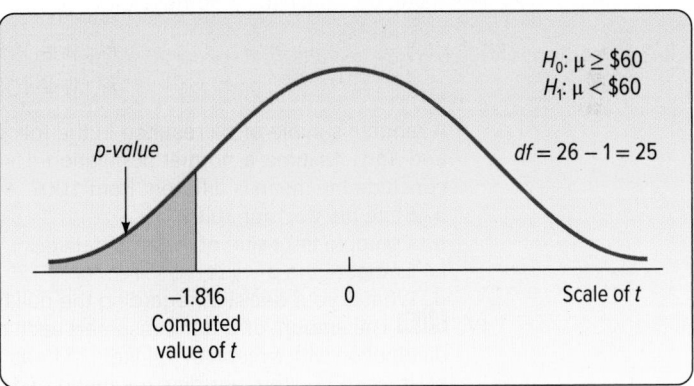

CHART 10–7 Rejection Region, *t*-Distribution, .01 Significance Level

Step 6: **Interpret the result.** We failed to reject the null hypothesis. The sample of claims could have been selected from a population with a mean cost of $60 per claim. To put it another way, the difference of $3.577 ($56.423 − $60.00) between the sample mean and the population mean could be due to sampling error. The test results do not allow the claims department manager to conclude that the cost-cutting measures have been effective.

SELF-REVIEW 10-4

A machine is set to fill a small bottle with 9.0 grams of medicine. A sample of eight bottles revealed the following amounts (grams) in each bottle.

| 9.2 | 8.7 | 8.9 | 8.6 | 8.8 | 8.5 | 8.7 | 9.0 |

At the .01 significance level, can we conclude that the mean weight is less than 9.0 grams?
(a) State the null hypothesis and the alternate hypothesis.
(b) How many degrees of freedom are there?
(c) Give the decision rule.
(d) Using statistical software, compute the value of t. What is your decision regarding the null hypothesis?
(e) Using statistical software, compute the p-value.
(f) What is the conclusion?

EXERCISES

15. Given the following hypotheses:

$$H_0: \mu \geq 20$$
$$H_1: \mu < 20$$

A random sample of five resulted in the following values: 18, 15, 12, 19, and 21. Assume a normal population. Using the .01 significance level, can we conclude the population mean is less than 20?
a. State the decision rule.
b. Compute the value of the test statistic.
c. Compute the p-value.
d. What is your decision regarding the null hypothesis?

16. Given the following hypotheses:

$$H_0: \mu = 100$$
$$H_1: \mu \neq 100$$

A random sample of six resulted in the following values: 118, 105, 112, 119, 105, and 111. Assume a normal population. Using the .05 significance level, can we conclude the mean is different from 100?
a. State the decision rule.
b. Compute the value of the test statistic.
c. Compute the p-value.
d. What is your decision regarding the null hypothesis?

17. **FILE** The amount of water consumed each day by a healthy adult follows a normal distribution with a mean of 1.4 liters. A health campaign promotes the consumption of at least 2.0 liters per day. A sample of 10 adults after the campaign shows the following consumption in liters:

| 1.5 | 1.6 | 1.5 | 1.4 | 1.9 | 1.4 | 1.3 | 1.9 | 1.8 | 1.7 |

Calculate and interpret the p-value. At the .01 significance level, can we conclude that water consumption has increased?

18. **FILE** The liquid chlorine added to swimming pools to combat algae has a relatively short shelf life before it loses its effectiveness. Records indicate that the mean shelf life of a 5-gallon jug of chlorine is 2,160 hours (90 days). As an experiment, Holdlonger was added to the chlorine to find whether it would increase the shelf life. A sample of nine jugs of chlorine had these shelf lives (in hours):

| 2,159 | 2,170 | 2,180 | 2,179 | 2,160 | 2,167 | 2,171 | 2,181 | 2,185 |

Compute the p-value. At the .025 level, has Holdlonger increased the shelf life of the chlorine?

19. **FILE** A Washington, D.C., "think tank" announces the typical teenager sent 67 text messages per day in 2022. To update that estimate, you phone a sample of 12 teenagers and ask them how many text messages they sent the previous day. Their responses were:

| 51 | 175 | 47 | 49 | 44 | 54 | 145 | 203 | 21 | 59 | 42 | 100 |

Compute the p-value and describe what it tells you. At the .05 level, can you conclude that the mean number is greater than 67?

20. **FILE** Hugger Polls contends that an agent conducts a mean of 53 in-depth home surveys every week. A streamlined survey form has been introduced, and Hugger wants to evaluate its effectiveness. The number of in-depth surveys conducted during a week by a random sample of 15 agents are:

| 53 | 57 | 50 | 55 | 58 | 54 | 60 | 52 | 59 | 62 | 60 | 60 | 51 | 59 | 56 |

Compute the p-value. At the .05 level of significance, can we conclude that the mean number of interviews conducted by the agents is more than 53 per week?

LO10-7

Compute the probability of a Type II error.

Type II Error

Recall that the level of significance, identified by the symbol α, is the probability that the null hypothesis is rejected when it is true. This is called a Type I error. The most common levels of significance are .05 and .01 and are set by the researcher at the outset of the test.

In a hypothesis-testing situation there is also the possibility that a null hypothesis is not rejected when it is actually false. This is called a Type II error. The probability of a Type II error is identified by the Greek letter beta (β). In contrast to selecting a value for α in the hypothesis testing procedure, the value of β is calculated after the hypothesis testing procedure is finished. The following Example/Solution illustrates the details of determining the value of β.

▶ **EXAMPLE**

Western Wire Products purchases steel bars to make cotter pins. Past experience indicates that the mean tensile strength of all incoming shipments is 10,000 psi and that the standard deviation, σ, is 400 psi. To monitor the quality of the cotter pins, samples of 100 pins are randomly selected and tested for their strength. In our hypothesis testing procedure the hypotheses are:

$$H_0: \mu = 10,000$$

$$H_1: \mu \neq 10,000$$

To determine if a shipment of steel bars meets the quality standard, Western Wire Products sets up a rule for the quality-control inspector to follow: "Take a sample of 100 steel bars. Test each of the bars for tensile strength. Using a .05 significance level, accept the shipment if the sample mean ($\bar{x}$) strength falls between 9,922 psi and 10,078 psi." These values are the critical values for the hypothesis test. If the sample mean is more than 10,078 or less than 9,922, the hypothesis is rejected and we conclude that the shipment does not meet the quality standard.

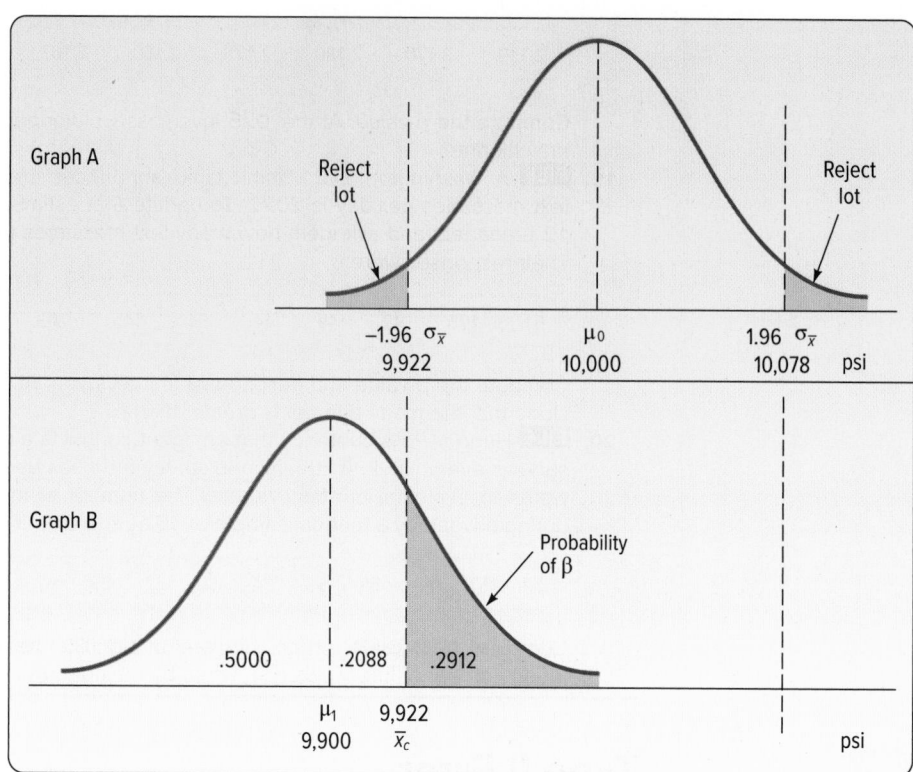

CHART 10–8 Charts Showing Type I and Type II Errors

Refer to Chart 10–8, Graph A. Given that the population mean is 10,000 psi, designated μ_0, with a standard deviation of 400, the distribution shows the regions where the hypothesis is rejected and where it is not rejected, that is, whether the shipment meets the quality standard for tensile strength.

Suppose that the result of testing 100 bars results in a sample mean of 9,900 psi. Clearly, based on Graph A, the shipment does not meet the quality standard and is rejected with a .05 probability of a Type I error, a small chance of rejecting the shipment in error. To calculate the Type II error, we assume that the sample mean of 9,900 psi is the true population mean. Compare Graph A and Graph B. Graph A represents the company's distribution of tensile strength centered on 10,000 psi. Graph B, based on the sample data, suggests that the distribution is centered on 9,900 psi.

Now, let's use Graph B to determine the probability of a Type II error, β. From the quality standards we know that 9,922 psi is used to reject the null hypothesis. Any sample mean greater than 9,922 and less than 10,078 is accepted. If the distribution is really centered on 9,900 psi, it is possible to find sample means more than 9,922, and we would fail to reject the null hypothesis, $\mu = 10,000$. This is the area in Graph B labeled "Probability of β" where the null hypothesis would not be rejected. The graph indicates that the probability of a Type II error is .2912. We can also calculate the power of the test as $(1 - \beta)$. The power is the probability of not making a Type II error, rejecting the null hypothesis correctly. Here, the power of the test is .7088.

SOLUTION

The probability of committing a Type II error is represented by the shaded area in Chart 10–8, Graph B. It is computed by determining the area under the normal curve that lies above 9,922 psi. The calculation of the areas under the normal curve was discussed in Chapter 7. Reviewing briefly, first determine the probability of the sample mean falling between 9,900 and 9,922. Then this probability is subtracted from .5000 (which represents all the area to the right of the mean of 9,900) to arrive at the probability of making a Type II error.

The number of standard errors (z-value) between the mean of the incoming lot (9,900), designated by μ_1, and $\bar{x}_c$, representing the critical value for 9,922, is computed by:

TYPE II ERROR	$$z = \dfrac{\bar{x}_c - \mu_1}{\sigma/\sqrt{n}}$$	(10–3)

With $n = 100$ and $\sigma = 400$, the value of z is 0.55:

$$z = \frac{\bar{x}_c - \mu_1}{\sigma/\sqrt{n}} = \frac{9{,}922 - 9{,}900}{400/\sqrt{100}} = \frac{22}{40} = 0.55$$

The area under the curve between 9,900 and 9,922 (a z-value of 0.55) is .2088. The area under the curve beyond 9,922 psi is .5000 − .2088, or .2912; this is the probability of making a Type II error—that is, accepting an incoming lot of steel bars, based on the company's standard of 10,000 psi, when the sample suggests that the population mean is 9,900 psi and the shipment should be rejected.

Let's use another example, illustrated in Chart 10–9. Suppose the testing of a sample of 100 bars results in a mean of 10,120 psi. Based on the company's standards, represented in Graph A, the shipment should be rejected. The sample mean of 10,120 is more than the critical value of 10,078. Based on the sample mean, Graph C shows the distribution of sample means based on the distribution centered on the sample mean, 10,120.

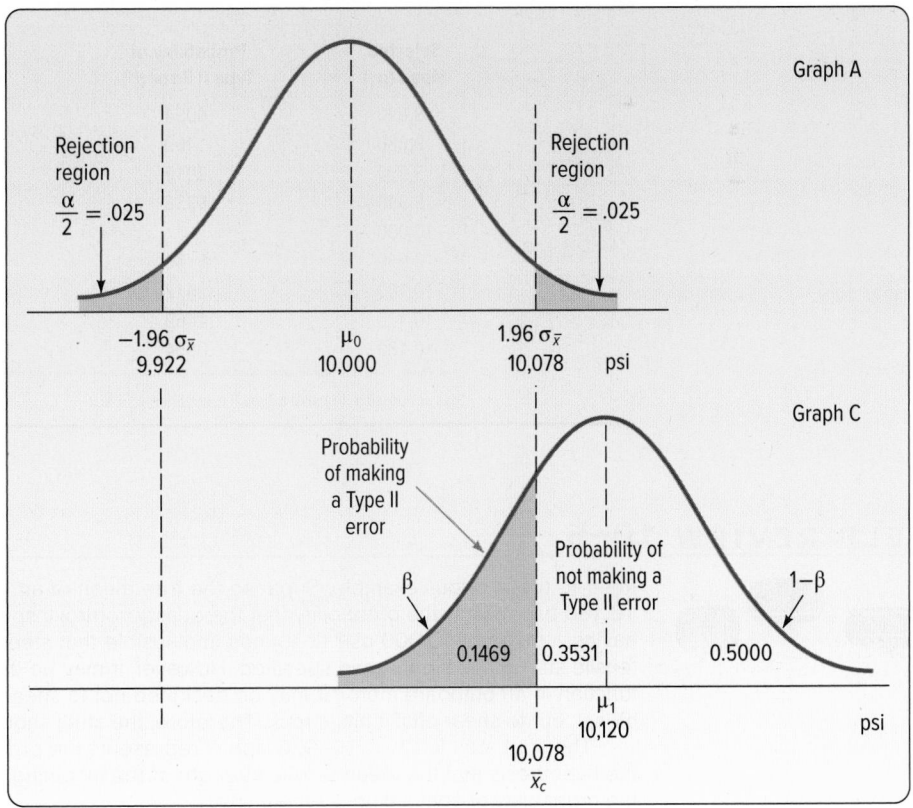

CHART 10–9 Type I and Type II Errors (Another Example)

If the distribution is centered on the sample mean of 10,120, there is a probability that a sample mean could be less than the upper critical value of 10,078. In Graph C, this is labeled β. To find the probability, we calculate the z-value of 10,078 in Graph C:

$$z = \frac{\bar{x}_c - \mu_1}{\sigma/\sqrt{n}} = \frac{10{,}078 - 10{,}120}{400/\sqrt{100}} = -1.05$$

The probability that z is less than -1.05 is .1469, found by .5000 $-$ .3531. Therefore, β, or the probability of a Type II error, is .1469. The power of the test is 1.000 $-$ .1469 or .8531. Caution: If the difference between μ_0 and μ_1 is relatively small, the probability of a Type II error may occur in both tails. This eventuality is not considered here.

Using the methods illustrated by Chart 10–8, Graph B and Chart 10–9, Graph C, the probability of a Type II error can be determined for any sample mean used as an estimate of μ_1.

To review, in hypothesis testing, we select the probability of making a Type I error, α. Naturally, we pick small probabilities, typically less than 0.10. The probability of a Type II error depends on the sample result. The larger the difference between the hypothesized mean and the sample mean, the smaller the probability of a Type II error, failing to reject the null hypothesis when it should have been rejected.

For this Example/Solution, Table 10–3 shows the probabilities of a Type II error and the power of the test for selected values of μ_1. The right column gives the probability of not making a Type II error, which is also known as the power of a test.

TABLE 10–3 Probabilities of a Type II Error for $\mu_0 = 10{,}000$ psi and Selected Alternative Means, .05 Level of Significance

Selected Mean (μ_1)	Probability of Type II Error (β)	Power of a Test ($1 - \beta$)
9,820	.0054	.9946
9,880	.1469	.8531
9,900	.2912	.7088
9,940	.6736	.3264
10,000	— *	—
10,060	.6736	.3264
10,100	.2912	.7088
10,120	.1469	.8531
10,180	.0054	.9946

*It is not possible to make a Type II error when $\mu_1 = \mu_0$.

SELF-REVIEW 10–5

Refer to the previous example. Suppose the true mean of an incoming lot of steel bars is 10,180 psi. What is the probability that the quality control inspector will accept the bars as having a mean of 10,000 psi? (It sounds implausible that steel bars will be rejected if the tensile strength is higher than specified. However, it may be that the cotter pin has a dual function in an outboard motor. It may be designed not to shear off if the motor hits a small object, but to shear off if it hits a rock. Therefore, the steel should not be *too* strong.)

The light area in Chart 10–9, Graph C represents the probability of falsely accepting the hypothesis that the mean tensile strength of the incoming steel is 10,000 psi. What is the probability of committing a Type II error?

EXERCISES

21. Refer to Table 10–3 and the example just completed. With $n = 100$, $\sigma = 400$, $\bar{x}_c = 9{,}922$, and $\mu_1 = 9{,}880$, verify that the probability of a Type II error is .1469.

22. Refer to Table 10–3 and the example just completed. With $n = 100$, $\sigma = 400$, $\bar{x}_c = 10{,}078$, and $\mu_1 = 10{,}100$, verify that the probability of a Type II error is .2912.

23. The management of KSmall Industries is considering a new method of assembling a computer. The current assembling method requires a mean time of 60 minutes with a standard deviation of 2.7 minutes. Using the new method, the mean assembly time for a random sample of 24 computers was 58 minutes. Using the .10 level of significance, can we conclude that the assembly time using the new method is faster? What is the probability of a Type II error?

24. A recent national survey found that parents read an average (mean) of 10 books per month to their children under 5 years old. The population standard deviation is 5. The distribution of books read per month follows the normal distribution. A random sample of 25 households revealed that the mean number of books read last month was 12. At the .01 significance level, can we conclude that parents read more than the average number of books to their children? What is the probability of a Type II error?

Test a Hypothesis of a Population Proportion

LO10-8

Test a hypothesis about a population proportion.

Beginning on page 305 in Chapter 9, we discussed confidence intervals for proportions. We can also conduct a test of hypothesis for a proportion. Recall that a proportion is the ratio of the number of successes to the number of observations. We let X refer to the number of successes and n the number of observations, so the proportion of successes in a fixed number of trials is X/n. Thus, the formula for computing a sample proportion, p, is $p = X/n$. Consider the following potential hypothesis-testing situations.

- Historically, General Motors reports that 70% of leased vehicles are returned with less than 36,000 miles. A recent sample of 200 vehicles returned at the end of their lease showed 158 had less than 36,000 miles. Has the proportion increased?
- The American Association of Retired Persons (AARP) reports that 60% of retired people under the age of 65 would return to work on a full-time basis if a suitable job were available. A sample of 500 retirees under 65 revealed 315 would return to work. Can we conclude that more than 60% would return to work?
- Able Moving and Storage Inc. advises its clients for long-distance residential moves that their household goods will be delivered in 3 to 5 days from the time they are picked up. Able's records show it is successful 90% of the time with this claim. A recent audit revealed it was successful 190 times out of 200. Can the company conclude its success rate has increased?

Some assumptions must be made and conditions met before testing a population proportion. To test a hypothesis about a population proportion, a random sample is chosen from the population. It is assumed that the binomial assumptions discussed in Chapter 6 are met: (1) The sample data collected are the result of counts; (2) the outcome of an experiment is classified into one of two mutually exclusive categories—a "success" or a "failure"; (3) the probability of a success is the same for each trial; and (4) the trials are independent, meaning the outcome of one trial does not affect the outcome of any other trial. This test is appropriate when the sample size meets the following two requirements: $n\pi$ and $n(1 - \pi)$ are at least 5. n is the sample size, and π is the population proportion. When both are true, the normal distribution is a good approximation of the binomial distribution. Therefore, we use the z-distribution and the z-statistic.

▶ **EXAMPLE**

A Republican governor of a western state is thinking about running for reelection. Historically, to be reelected, a Republican candidate needs to earn at least 80% of the vote in the northern section of the state. The governor hires a polling organization to survey the voters in the northern section of the state and determine what percent would vote for him. The polling organization will survey 2,000 voters. Use a statistical hypothesis-testing procedure to assess the governor's chances of reelection.

SOLUTION

This situation regarding the governor's reelection meets the binomial conditions.

- There are only two possible outcomes. That is, a sampled voter will either vote or not vote for the governor.
- The probability of a success is the same for each trial. In this case, the likelihood a particular sampled voter will support reelection is .80.
- The trials are independent. This means, for example, the likelihood the 23rd voter sampled will support reelection is not affected by what the 24th or 52nd voter does.
- The sample data are the result of counts. We are going to count the number of voters who support reelection in the sample of 2,000.

We can use a normal approximation to the binomial distribution if both $n\pi$ and $n(1 - \pi)$ exceed 5. In this case, $n = 2,000$ and $\pi = 0.80$. (π is the proportion of the vote in the northern part of the state, or 80%, needed to be elected.) Thus, $n\pi = 2,000(.80) = 1,600$ and $n(1 - \pi) = 2,000(1 - .80) = 400$. Both 1,600 and 400 are clearly greater than 5.

Step 1: State the null hypothesis and the alternate hypothesis. The null hypothesis, H_0, is that the population proportion π is .80 or larger. The alternate hypothesis, H_1, is that the proportion is less than .80. From a practical standpoint, the incumbent governor is concerned only when the proportion is less than .80. If it is equal to or greater than .80, he will have no problem; that is, the sample data would indicate he will be reelected. These hypotheses are written symbolically as:

$$H_0: \pi \geq .80$$

$$H_1: \pi < .80$$

H_1 states a direction. Thus, as noted previously, the test is one-tailed with the inequality sign pointing to the tail of the distribution containing the region of rejection.

Step 2: Select the level of significance. The level of significance is .05. This is the likelihood that a true hypothesis will be rejected.

Step 3: Select the test statistic. z is the appropriate statistic, found by:

TEST OF HYPOTHESIS, ONE PROPORTION	$z = \dfrac{p - \pi}{\sqrt{\dfrac{\pi(1 - \pi)}{n}}}$	**(10-4)**

where:
    π is the population proportion.
    p is the sample proportion.
    n is the sample size.

Step 4: Formulate the decision rule. The critical value or values of z form the dividing point or points between the regions where H_0 is rejected and where it is not rejected. Because the alternate hypothesis states a direction, this is a one-tailed test. The sign of the inequality points to the left, so only the left side of the curve is used. (See Chart 10–10.) The significance level is .05. This probability is in the left tail and determines the region of rejection. The area between zero and the critical value is .4500, found by .5000 − .0500. Referring to Appendix B.5, go to the column indicating a .05 significance level for a one-tailed test, find the row with infinite degrees of freedom, and read the z-value of 1.645. The decision rule is, therefore: Reject the null hypothesis and accept the alternate hypothesis if the computed value of z falls to the left of −1.645; otherwise do not reject H_0.

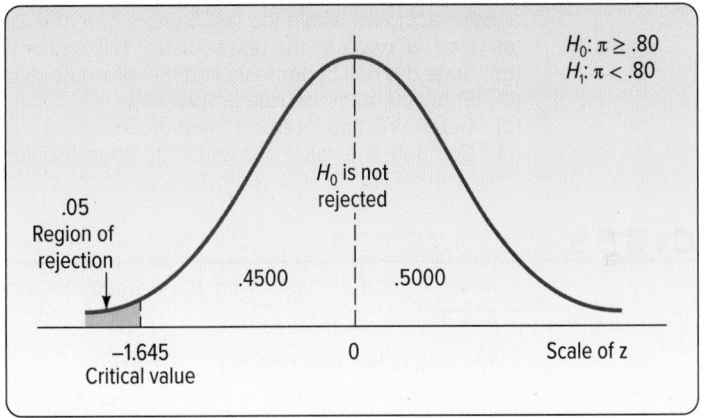

CHART 10–10 Rejection Region for the .05 Level of Significance, One-Tailed Test

Step 5: Make a decision. Select a sample and make a decision about H_0. A sample survey of 2,000 potential voters in the northern part of the state revealed that 1,550 planned to vote for the incumbent governor. Is the sample proportion of .775 (found by 1,550/2,000) close enough to .80 to conclude that the difference is due to sampling error? In this case:

p is .775, the proportion in the sample who plan to vote for the governor.
n is 2,000, the number of voters surveyed.
π is .80, the hypothesized population proportion.
z is a normally distributed test statistic. We can use it because the normal approximation assumptions are true.

Using formula (10–4)

$$z = \frac{p - \pi}{\sqrt{\dfrac{\pi(1 - \pi)}{n}}} = \frac{\dfrac{1,550}{2,000} - .80}{\sqrt{\dfrac{.80(1 - .80)}{2,000}}} = \frac{.775 - .80}{\sqrt{.00008}} = -2.80$$

The computed value of z (−2.80) is less than the critical value, so the null hypothesis is rejected at the .05 level. The difference of 2.5 percentage points between the sample percent (77.5%) and the hypothesized population percent in the northern part of the state necessary to carry the state (80%) is statistically significant. From Appendix B.3, the probability of a z-value between zero and −2.80 is .4974. So the p-value is .0026, found by .5000 − .4974. Because the p-value is less than the significance level, the null hypothesis is rejected.

Step 6: **Interpret the result.** The governor can conclude that he does not have the necessary support in the northern section of the state to win reelection. To put it another way, the evidence at this point does not support the claim that the incumbent governor will return to the governor's mansion for another 4 years.

SELF-REVIEW 10–6

A recent insurance industry report indicated that 40% of those persons involved in minor traffic accidents this year have been involved in at least one other traffic accident in the last 5 years. An advisory group decided to investigate this claim, believing it was too large. A sample of 200 traffic accidents this year showed 74 persons were also involved in another accident within the last 5 years. Use the .01 significance level.
(a) Can we use z as the test statistic? Tell why or why not.
(b) State the null hypothesis and the alternate hypothesis.
(c) Show the decision rule graphically.
(d) Determine and interpret the p-value.
(e) Compute the value of z and state your decision regarding the null hypothesis.

EXERCISES

Note: *To find z-values with three decimals, use the t-table with infinite degrees of freedom.*

25. The following hypotheses are given.

$$H_0: \pi \le .70$$
$$H_1: \pi > .70$$

A sample of 100 observations revealed that $p = .75$. At the .05 significance level, can the null hypothesis be rejected?
a. State the decision rule.
b. Compute the value of the test statistic.
c. What is your decision regarding the null hypothesis?

26. The following hypotheses are given.

$$H_0: \pi = .40$$
$$H_1: \pi \ne .40$$

A sample of 120 observations revealed that $p = .30$. At the .05 significance level, can the null hypothesis be rejected?
a. State the decision rule.
b. Compute the value of the test statistic.
c. What is your decision regarding the null hypothesis?

Note: It is recommended that you use the six-step hypothesis testing procedure to solve the following problems.

27. The U.S. Department of Transportation estimates that 10% of Americans carpool. Does that imply that 10% of cars will have two or more occupants? A sample of 300 cars traveling southbound on the New Jersey Turnpike yesterday revealed that 63 had two or more occupants. At the .01 significance level, can we conclude that 10% of cars traveling on the New Jersey Turnpike have two or more occupants?
28. A recent article reported that a job awaits only one in three new college graduates. The major reasons given were an overabundance of college graduates and a weak economy. A survey of 200 recent graduates from your school revealed that 80 students had jobs. At the .01 significance level, can we conclude that a larger proportion of students at your school have jobs?

29. Chicken Delight claims that 90% of its orders are delivered within 10 minutes of the time the order is placed. A sample of 100 orders revealed that 82 were delivered within the promised time. At the .10 significance level, can we conclude that less than 90% of the orders are delivered in less than 10 minutes?

30. Research at the University of Toledo indicates that 50% of students change their major area of study after their first year in a program. A random sample of 100 students in the College of Business revealed that 48 had changed their major area of study after their first year of the program. Has there been a significant decrease in the proportion of students who change their major after the first year in this program? Test at the .05 level of significance.

CHAPTER SUMMARY

I. The objective of hypothesis testing is to verify the validity of a statement about a population parameter.

II. The steps to conduct a test of hypothesis are:

  A. State the null hypothesis (H_0) and the alternate hypothesis (H_1).

  B. Select the level of significance.

    1. The level of significance is the likelihood or probability of rejecting a true null hypothesis.

    2. The most frequently used significance levels are .01, .05, and .10. As a probability, any value between 0 and 1.00 is possible, but we prefer small probabilities of making a Type I error.

  C. Select the test statistic.

    1. A test statistic is a value calculated from sample information used to determine whether to reject the null hypothesis.

    2. Two test statistics were considered in this chapter.

      a. The standard normal distribution (the z-distribution) is used when the population follows the normal distribution and the population standard deviation is known.

      b. The t-distribution is used when the population follows the normal distribution and the population standard deviation is unknown.

  D. State the decision rule.

    1. The decision rule indicates the condition or conditions when the null hypothesis is rejected.

    2. In a two-tailed test, the rejection region is evenly split between the upper and lower tails.

    3. In a one-tailed test, all of the rejection region is in either the upper or the lower tail.

  E. Select a sample, compute the value of the test statistic, and make a decision regarding the null hypothesis.

  F. Interpret the results of your decision.

III. A p-value is the probability that the value of the test statistic is as extreme as the value computed, when the null hypothesis is true.

IV. When testing a hypothesis about a population mean:

  A. If the population standard deviation, σ, is known, the test statistic is the standard normal distribution and is determined from:

$$z = \frac{\bar{x} - \mu}{\sigma/\sqrt{n}} \tag{10–1}$$

  B. If the population standard deviation is not known, s is substituted for σ. The test statistic is the t-distribution, and its value is determined from:

$$t = \frac{\bar{x} - \mu}{s/\sqrt{n}} \tag{10–2}$$

The major characteristics of the *t*-distribution are as follows:
  1. It is a continuous distribution.
  2. It is mound shaped and symmetrical.
  3. It is flatter, or more spread out, than the standard normal distribution.
  4. There is a family of *t*-distributions, depending on the number of degrees of freedom.
V. There are two types of errors that can occur in a test of hypothesis.
  A. A Type I error occurs when a true null hypothesis is rejected.
    1. The probability of making a Type I error is equal to the level of significance.
    2. This probability is designated by the Greek letter α.
  B. A Type II error occurs when a false null hypothesis is not rejected.
    1. The probability of making a Type II error is designated by the Greek letter β.
    2. The likelihood of a Type II error must be calculated comparing the hypothesized distribution to an alternate distribution based on sample results.
VI. When we sample from a single population and the variable of interest has only two possible outcomes, we call this a test of proportion.
  A. The binomial conditions must be met.
  B. Both $n\pi$ and $n(1 - \pi)$ must be at least 5.
  C. The test statistic is

$$z = \frac{p - \pi}{\sqrt{\dfrac{\pi(1 - \pi)}{n}}}$$ (10–4)

PRONUNCIATION KEY

SYMBOL	MEANING	PRONUNCIATION
H_0	Null hypothesis	*H sub zero*
H_1	Alternate hypothesis	*H sub one*
$\alpha/2$	Two-tailed significance level	*Alpha divided by 2*
$\bar{x}_c$	Limit of the sample mean	*x bar sub c*
μ_0	Assumed population mean	*mu sub zero*

CHAPTER EXERCISES

31. According to the local union president, the mean gross income of plumbers in the Salt Lake City area follows the normal probability distribution with a mean of $45,000 and a population standard deviation of $3,000. A recent investigative reporter for KYAK TV found, for a sample of 120 plumbers, the mean gross income was $45,500. At the .10 significance level, is it reasonable to conclude that the mean income is not equal to $45,000? Determine the *p*-value.

32. **FILE** Rutter Nursery Company packages its pine bark mulch in 50-pound bags. From a long history, management knows that the distribution of bag weights is normally distributed with a population standard deviation of 3 pounds per bag. At the end of each day, Jeff Rutter, the production manager, weighs 10 bags and computes the mean weight of the sample. Following are the weights of 10 bags from today's production.

45.6	47.7	47.6	46.3	46.2	47.4	49.2	55.8	47.5	48.5

  a. Can Mr. Rutter conclude that the mean weight of the bags is less than 50 pounds? Use the .01 significance level.
  b. In a brief report, tell why Mr. Rutter can use the *z*-distribution as the test statistic.
  c. Compute the *p*-value.

33. A new weight-watching company, Weight Reducers International, advertises that those who join will lose an average of 10 pounds after the first 2 weeks. The population standard deviation is 2.8 pounds. A random sample of 50 people who joined the weight reduction program revealed a mean loss of 9 pounds. At the .05 level of significance, can we conclude that those joining Weight Reducers will lose less than 10 pounds? Determine the *p*-value.

34. Dole Pineapple Inc. is concerned that the 16-ounce can of sliced pineapple is being overfilled. Assume the population standard deviation of the process is 0.03 ounce. The quality-control department took a random sample of 50 cans and found that the arithmetic mean weight was 16.05 ounces. At the 5% level of significance, can we conclude that the mean weight is greater than 16 ounces? Determine the *p*-value.

35. According to a recent survey, Americans get a mean of 7 hours of sleep per night. A random sample of 50 students at West Virginia University revealed the mean length of time slept last night was 6 hours and 48 minutes (6.8 hours). The standard deviation of the sample was 0.9 hour. At the 5% level of significance, is it reasonable to conclude that students at West Virginia sleep less than the typical American? Compute the *p*-value.

36. A statewide real estate sales agency, Farm Associates, specializes in selling farm property in the state of Nebraska. Its records indicate that the mean selling time of farm property is 90 days. Because of recent drought conditions, the agency believes that the mean selling time is now greater than 90 days. A statewide survey of 100 recently sold farms revealed a mean selling time of 94 days, with a standard deviation of 22 days. At the .10 significance level, has there been an increase in selling time?

37. According to the Census Bureau, 3.13 people reside in the typical American household. A sample of 25 households in Arizona retirement communities showed the mean number of residents per household was 2.86 residents. The standard deviation of this sample was 1.20 residents. At the .05 significance level, is it reasonable to conclude the mean number of residents in the retirement community household is less than 3.13 persons?

38. A recent article in *Vitality* magazine reported that the mean amount of leisure time per week for American men is 40.0 hours. You believe this figure is too large and decide to conduct your own test. In a random sample of 60 men, you find the mean is 37.8 hours of leisure per week and the standard deviation of the sample is 12.2 hours. Can you conclude that the information in the article is untrue? Use the .05 significance level. Determine the *p*-value and explain its meaning.

39. **FILE** A 2022 survey of American households with two or more children indicated the mean annual interest paid on household debt was $8,000. A sample of 12 households reported the following annual paid interest. At the .05 significance level is it reasonable to conclude that these households paid less than $8,000 of interest per year?

| 7077 | 5744 | 6753 | 7381 | 7625 | 6636 | 7164 | 7348 | 8060 | 5848 | 9275 | 7052 |

40. **FILE** According to ValuePenguin.com, the current 30-year mortgage rate is now less than 5%. A sample of eight small banks in the Midwest revealed the following rates (in percent):

| 3.6 | 4.1 | 5.3 | 3.6 | 4.9 | 4.6 | 5.0 | 4.4 |

At the .01 significance level, can we conclude that the 30-year mortgage rate for small banks is less than 5%? Compute the *p*-value.

41. **FILE** A recent study revealed the typical American coffee drinker consumes an average of 3.1 cups per day. A sample of 12 senior citizens revealed they consumed the following amounts of coffee, reported in cups, yesterday.

| 3.1 | 3.3 | 3.5 | 2.6 | 2.6 | 4.3 | 4.4 | 3.8 | 3.1 | 4.1 | 3.1 | 3.2 |

At the .05 significance level, do these sample data suggest there is a difference between the national average and the sample mean from senior citizens?

42. **FILE** The postanesthesia care area (recovery room) at St. Luke's Hospital in Maumee, Ohio, was recently enlarged. The hope was that the change would increase the mean number of patients served per day to more than 25. A random sample of 15 days revealed the following numbers of patients.

| 25 | 27 | 25 | 26 | 25 | 28 | 28 | 27 | 24 | 26 | 25 | 29 | 25 | 27 | 24 |

At the .01 significance level, can we conclude that the mean number of patients per day is more than 25? Compute the *p*-value and interpret it.

43. **FILE** An Etsy store receives an average of 6.5 returns per day from online shoppers. For a sample of 12 days, it received the following number of returns.

| 0 | 4 | 3 | 4 | 9 | 4 | 5 | 9 | 1 | 6 | 7 | 10 |

At the .01 significance level, can we conclude the mean number of returns is less than 6.5?

44. **FILE** During recent seasons, Major League Baseball has been criticized for the length of the games. A report indicated that the average game lasts 3 hours and 30 minutes. A sample of 17 games revealed the following times to completion. (Note that the minutes have been changed to fractions of hours, so that a game that lasted 2 hours and 24 minutes is reported at 2.40 hours.)

| 2.98 | 2.40 | 2.70 | 2.25 | 3.23 | 3.17 | 2.93 | 3.18 | 2.80 |
| 2.38 | 3.75 | 3.20 | 3.27 | 2.52 | 2.58 | 4.45 | 2.45 | |

Can we conclude that the mean time for a game is less than 3.50 hours? Use the .05 significance level.

45. **FILE** Watch Corporation of Switzerland claims that its watches on average will neither gain nor lose time during a week. A sample of 18 watches provided the following gains (+) or losses (−) in seconds per week.

| −0.38 | −0.20 | −0.38 | −0.32 | +0.32 | −0.23 | +0.30 | +0.25 | −0.10 |
| −0.37 | −0.61 | −0.48 | −0.47 | −0.64 | −0.04 | −0.20 | −0.68 | +0.05 |

Is it reasonable to conclude that the mean gain or loss in time for the watches is 0? Use the .05 significance level. Compute the *p*-value.

46. **FILE** Listed is the annual rate of return (reported in percent) for a sample of 12 taxable mutual funds.

| 4.63 | 4.15 | 4.76 | 4.70 | 4.65 | 4.52 | 4.70 | 5.06 | 4.42 | 4.51 | 4.24 | 4.52 |

Using the .05 significance level, is it reasonable to conclude that the mean rate of return is more than 4.50%?

47. **FILE** Many grocery stores and large retailers such as Kroger and Walmart use self-checkout systems so shoppers can scan their own items and cash out themselves. Listed is the number of customers using the service for a sample of 15 days at a Walmart location.

| 120 | 108 | 120 | 114 | 118 | 91 | 118 | 92 | 104 | 104 |
| 112 | 97 | 118 | 108 | 117 | | | | | |

Is it reasonable to conclude that the mean number of customers using the self-checkout system is more than 100 per day? Use the .05 significance level.

48. **FILE** For a recent year, the mean fare to fly from Charlotte, North Carolina, to Chicago, Illinois, on a discount ticket was $267. A random sample of 13 round-trip discount fares on this route last month shows:

| $321 | $286 | $290 | $330 | $310 | $250 | $270 | $280 | $299 | $265 | $291 | $275 | $281 |

At the .01 significance level, can we conclude that the mean fare has increased? What is the *p*-value?

49. The publisher of *Celebrity Living* claims that the mean sales for personality magazines that feature people such as Beyoncé or Jennifer Lawrence are 1.5 million copies per week. A sample of 10 comparable titles shows a mean weekly sales last week of 1.3 million copies with a standard deviation of 0.9 million copies. Do these data contradict the publisher's claim? Use the 0.01 significance level.

50. A United Nations report shows the mean family income for Mexican migrants to the United States is $27,000 per year. A FLOC (Farm Labor Organizing Committee) evaluation of 25 Mexican family units reveals a mean to be $30,000 with a sample standard deviation of $10,000. Does this information disagree with the United Nations report? Apply the 0.01 significance level.

51. **FILE** The number of "destination weddings" has skyrocketed in recent years. For example, many couples are opting to have their weddings in the Caribbean. A Caribbean vacation resort recently advertised in *Bride Magazine* that the cost of a Caribbean wedding was less than $30,000. Listed is a total cost in $000 for a sample of eight Caribbean weddings.

| 29.7 | 29.4 | 31.7 | 29.0 | 29.1 | 30.5 | 29.1 | 29.8 |

At the .05 significance level, is it reasonable to conclude the mean wedding cost is less than $30,000 as advertised?

52. The American Water Works Association reports that the per capita water use in a single-family home is 69 gallons per day. Legacy Ranch is a relatively new housing development. The builders installed more efficient water fixtures, such as low-flush toilets, and subsequently conducted a survey of the residences. Thirty-six owners responded, and the sample mean water use per day was 64 gallons with a standard deviation of 8.8 gallons per day. At the .10 level of significance, is that enough evidence to conclude that residents of Legacy Ranch use less water on average?

53. A cola-dispensing machine is set to dispense 9.00 ounces of cola per cup, with a standard deviation of 1.00 ounce. The manufacturer of the machine would like to set the control limit in such a way that, for samples of 36, 5% of the sample means will be greater than the upper control limit, and 5% of the sample means will be less than the lower control limit.
   a. At what value should the control limit be set?
   b. If the population mean shifts to 8.6, what is the probability of detecting the change?
   c. If the population mean shifts to 9.6, what is the probability of detecting the change?

54. The owners of the Westfield Mall wished to study customer shopping habits. From earlier studies, the owners were under the impression that a typical shopper spends 0.75 hour at the mall, with a standard deviation of 0.10 hour. Recently the mall owners added some specialty restaurants designed to keep shoppers in the mall longer. The consulting firm, Brunner and Swanson Marketing Enterprises, was hired to evaluate the effects of the restaurants. A sample of 45 shoppers by Brunner and Swanson revealed that the mean time spent in the mall had increased to 0.80 hour.
   a. Develop a hypothesis test to determine if the mean time spent in the mall changed. Use the .10 significance level.
   b. Suppose the mean shopping time actually increased from 0.75 hour to 0.79 hour. What is the probability of making a Type II error?
   c. When Brunner and Swanson reported the information in part (b) to the mall owners, the owners believed that the probability of making a Type II error was too high. How could this probability be reduced?

55. The following null and alternate hypotheses are given.

$$H_0: \mu \leq 50$$
$$H_1: \mu > 50$$

Suppose the population standard deviation is 10. The probability of a Type I error is set at .01 and the probability of a Type II error at .30. Assume that the population mean shifts from 50 to 55. How large a sample is necessary to meet these requirements?

56. An insurance company, based on past experience, estimates the mean damage for a natural disaster in its area is $5,000. After introducing several plans to prevent loss, it randomly samples 200 policyholders and finds the mean amount per claim was $4,800 with a standard deviation of $1,300. Does it appear the prevention plans were effective in reducing the mean amount of a claim? Use the .05 significance level.

57. A coin toss is used to decide which team gets the ball first in most sports. It involves little effort and is believed to give each side the same chance. In 55 Super Bowl games, the coin toss resulted in 26 heads and 29 tails. However, the National Football Conference has correctly called the coin flip 37 times. Meanwhile, the American Football Conference has correctly called the flip only 18 times. Use the six-step hypothesis-testing procedure at the .01 significance level to test whether these data suggest that the National Football Conference has an advantage in calling the coin flip.
  a. State the null and alternate hypotheses.
  b. Do the data satisfy the binomial conditions for approximating a normal distribution?
  c. What is the decision rule?
  d. What is your decision regarding the null hypothesis?
  e. What is the p-value and what does it imply?

58. According to a study by the American Pet Food Dealers Association, 63% of U.S. households own pets. A report is being prepared for an editorial in the *San Francisco Chronicle*. As a part of the editorial, a random sample of 300 households showed 210 own pets. Do these data disagree with the Pet Food Dealers Association's data? Use a .05 level of significance.

59. Marlee Singh is the comptroller for Meek Industries. Marlee believes that the current cash-flow problem at Meek is due to the slow collection of accounts and that more than 60% of the accounts are more than 3 months in arrears. A random sample of 200 accounts showed that 140 were more than 3 months old. At the .01 significance level, can Marlee conclude that more than 60% of the accounts are in arrears for more than 3 months?

60. The policy of the Suburban Transit Authority is to add a bus route if more than 55% of the potential commuters indicate they would use the particular route. A sample of 70 commuters revealed that 42 would use a proposed route from Bowman Park to the downtown area. Does the Bowman-to-downtown route meet the STA criterion? Use the .05 significance level.

61. Past experience at the Crowder Travel Agency indicated that 44% of those persons who wanted the agency to plan a vacation for them wanted to go to Europe. During the most recent season, a sampling of 1,000 persons was selected at random from the files. It was found that 480 persons wanted to go to Europe on vacation. Has there been a significant shift upward in the percentage of persons who want to go to Europe? Test at the .05 significance level.

62. Research in the gaming industry showed that 10% of all slot machines in the United States stop working each year. Short's Game Arcade has 60 slot machines and only 3 failed last year. At the .05 significance level, test whether these data contradict the research report.
  a. Why can you use a z-statistic as the test statistic?
  b. State the null and alternate hypotheses.
  c. Evaluate the test statistic and make the decision.
  d. What is the p-value and what does that imply?

63. An urban planner claims that, nationally, 20% of all families renting condominiums move during a given year. A random sample of 200 families renting condominiums in the Dallas Metroplex revealed that 56 moved during the past year. At the .01 significance level, does this evidence suggest that a larger proportion of condominium owners moved in the Dallas area? Determine the p-value.

64. After a losing season, there is a great uproar to fire the head football coach. In a random sample of 200 college alumni, 80 favor keeping the coach. Test at the .05 level of significance whether the proportion of alumni who support the coach is less than 50%.

65. During the 1990s, the fatality rate for lung cancer was 80 per 100,000 people. After the turn of the century and the establishment of newer treatments and adjustment in public health advertising, a random sample of 10,000 people exhibits only six deaths due to lung cancer. Using the .05 significance level, does the sample data indicate a reduced rate of lung cancer in the population?

DATA ANALYTICS

66. **FILE** The North Valley Real Estate data report information on the homes sold last year.
  a. Adam Marty recently joined North Valley Real Estate and was assigned 20 homes to market and show. When he was hired, North Valley assured him that the 20 homes would be fairly assigned to him. When he reviewed the selling prices of his assigned homes, he thought that the prices were much below the average of $357,000. Adam was able to find the data of how the other agents in the firm were assigned to the homes. Use statistical inference to analyze the "fairness" that homes were assigned to the agents.

67. **FILE** Refer to the Baseball 2021 data, which report information on the 30 Major League Baseball teams for the 2021 season.
  a. Conduct a test of hypothesis to determine whether the mean salary of the teams was different from $130.0 million. Use the .05 significance level.
  b. Using a 5% significance level, conduct a test of hypothesis to determine whether the mean attendance was more than 2 million per team.

68. **FILE** Refer to the Lincolnville School District bus data.
  a. Select the variable for the number of miles traveled last month. Conduct a hypothesis test to determine whether the mean miles traveled last month equals 10,000. Use the .01 significance level. Find the p-value and explain what it means.
  b. A study of school bus fleets reports that the average per bus maintenance cost is $4,000 per year. Using the maintenance cost variable, conduct a hypothesis test to determine whether the mean maintenance cost for Lincolnville's bus fleet is more than $4,000 at the .05 significance level. Determine the p-value and report the results.

11

Two-Sample Tests of Hypothesis

Niran Movie/Shutterstock

▲ **GIBBS BABY FOOD COMPANY** wishes to compare the weight gain of infants using its brand versus its competitor's. A sample of 40 babies using the Gibbs products revealed a mean weight gain of 7.6 pounds in the first 3 months after birth. For the Gibbs brand, the population standard deviation of the sample is 2.3 pounds. A sample of 55 babies using the competitor's brand revealed a mean increase in weight of 8.1 pounds. The population standard deviation is 2.9 pounds. At the .05 significance level, can we conclude that babies using the Gibbs brand gained less weight? (See Exercise 9 and **LO11-2**.)

LEARNING OBJECTIVES

When you have completed this chapter, you will be able to:

LO11-1 Apply the *F*-distribution to test a hypothesis that two population variances are equal.

LO11-2 Test a hypothesis that two independent population means are equal, assuming that the population standard deviations are known.

LO11-3 Test a hypothesis that two independent population means are equal, with estimated population standard deviations.

LO11-4 Test a hypothesis about the mean population difference between paired or dependent observations.

LO11-5 Explain the difference between dependent and independent samples.

LO11-6 Test a hypothesis about two population proportions.

364

Introduction

Chapter 10 began our study of hypothesis testing. We described the nature of hypothesis testing and conducted tests of a hypothesis in which we compared the results of a single sample to a population value. That is, we selected a single random sample from a population and conducted a test of whether the proposed population value was reasonable. Recall in Chapter 10 that we selected a sample of the number of desks assembled per week at Jamestown Steel Company to determine whether there

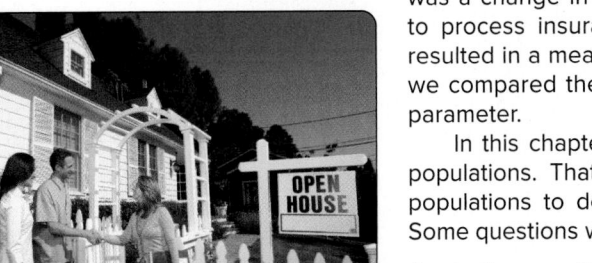

John Lund/Drew Kelly/Blend Images

was a change in the production rate. Similarly, we sampled the cost to process insurance claims to determine if cost-cutting measures resulted in a mean less than the current $60 per claim. In both cases, we compared the results of a *single* sample statistic to a population parameter.

In this chapter, we expand the idea of hypothesis testing to two populations. That is, we select random samples from two different populations to determine whether the population means are equal. Some questions we might want to test are:

1. Is there a difference in the mean value of residential real estate sold by male agents and female agents in south Florida?
2. At Grabit Software Inc., do customer service employees receive more calls for assistance during the morning or afternoon?
3. In the fast-food industry, is there a difference in the mean number of days absent between young workers (under 21 years of age) and older workers (more than 60 years of age)?
4. Is there an increase in the production rate if music is piped into the production area?

When testing hypotheses that compare two population means, the analyses differ based on the equality of the population variances. In the next section, we introduce the hypothesis testing procedure to determine if two population variances are equal.

LO11-1

Apply the *F*-distribution to test a hypothesis that two population variances are equal.

Comparing Two Population Variances

In this chapter, we test hypotheses that two population means are equal. The test differs based on assumptions regarding the equality of the population variances. In this section, we introduce the *F*-distribution and use it to test the assumption or hypothesis that two population variances are equal.

The *F*-Distribution

The probability distribution used in this chapter is the *F*-distribution. It was named to honor Sir Ronald Fisher, one of the founders of modern-day statistics. The test statistic for several situations follows this probability distribution. It is used to test whether two samples are from populations having equal variances, and it is also applied when we want to compare several population means simultaneously. This is the topic of Chapter 12. In both of these situations, the populations must follow a normal distribution, and the data must be at least interval scale.

What are the characteristics of the *F*-distribution?

1. **There is a family of *F*-distributions.** A particular member of the family is determined by two parameters: the degrees of freedom in the numerator and the degrees of freedom in the denominator. The shape of the distribution is illustrated by the following graph. There is one *F*-distribution for the combination of 29 degrees of freedom in the numerator (*df*) and 28 degrees of freedom in the denominator. There is another *F*-distribution for 19 degrees of freedom in the numerator and 6 degrees

of freedom in the denominator. The final distribution shown has 6 degrees of freedom in the numerator and 6 degrees of freedom in the denominator. Note that the shapes of the distributions change as the degrees of freedom change.

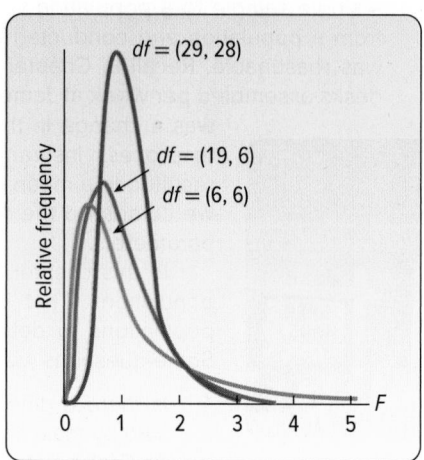

2. **The *F*-distribution is continuous.** This means that the value of F can assume an infinite number of values between zero and positive infinity.
3. **The *F*-statistic cannot be negative.** The smallest value F can assume is zero.
4. **The *F*-distribution is positively skewed.** The long tail of the distribution is to the right-hand side. As the number of degrees of freedom increases in both the numerator and denominator, the distribution approaches a normal distribution.
5. **The *F*-distribution is asymptotic.** As the values of F increase, the distribution approaches the horizontal axis but never touches it. This is similar to the behavior of the normal probability distribution, described in Chapter 7.

Testing a Hypothesis of Equal Population Variances

The first application of the *F*-distribution that we describe occurs when we test the hypothesis that the variance of one normal population equals the variance of another normal population. The following examples show the use of the test:

- A health services corporation manages two hospitals in Knoxville, Tennessee: St. Mary's North and St. Mary's South. In each hospital, the mean waiting time in the Emergency Department is 42 minutes. The hospital administrator believes that the St. Mary's North Emergency Department has more variation in waiting time than St. Mary's South.
- The mean rate of return on two types of common stock may be the same, but there may be more variation in the rate of return in one than the other. A sample of 10 technology and 10 utility stocks shows the same mean rate of return, but there is likely more variation in the technology stocks.
- An online newspaper found that men and women spend about the same amount of time per day accessing news apps. However, the same report indicated the times of men had nearly twice as much variation compared to the times of women.

To compare two population variances, we first state the null hypothesis. The null hypothesis is that the variance of one normal population, σ_1^2, equals the variance of another normal population, σ_2^2.

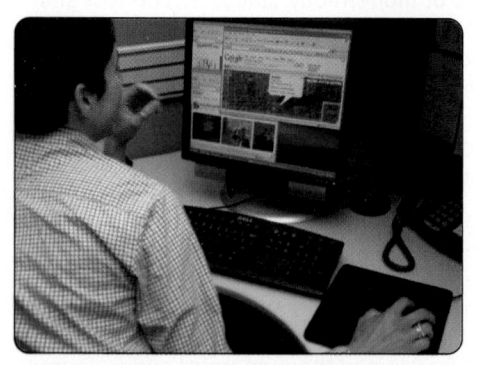

The alternate hypothesis is that the variances differ. In this instance, the null hypothesis and the alternate hypothesis are:

$$H_0: \sigma_1^2 = \sigma_2^2$$
$$H_1: \sigma_1^2 \neq \sigma_2^2$$

To conduct the test, we select a random sample of observations, n_1, from one population and a random sample of observations, n_2, from the second population. The test statistic is defined as follows:

TEST STATISTIC FOR COMPARING TWO VARIANCES	$F = \dfrac{s_1^2}{s_2^2}$	(11–1)

The terms s_1^2 and s_2^2 are the respective sample variances. If the null hypothesis is true, the test statistic follows the F-distribution with $n_1 - 1$ and $n_2 - 1$ degrees of freedom. To reduce the size of the table of critical values, the *larger* sample variance is placed in the numerator; hence, the tabled F-ratio is always larger than 1.00. Thus, the right-tail critical value is the only one required. The critical value of F for a two-tailed test is found by dividing the significance level in half ($\alpha/2$) and then referring to the appropriate degrees of freedom in Appendix B.6. An Example/Solution will illustrate.

▶ **EXAMPLE**

Lammers Limos offers limousine service from Government Center in downtown Toledo, Ohio, to Metro Airport in Detroit. Sean Lammers, president of the company, is considering two routes. One is via U.S. 25 and the other via I-75. He wants to study the time it takes to drive to the airport using each route and then compare the results. He collected the following sample data, reported in minutes. Using the .10 significance level, is there a difference in the variation in the driving times for the two routes?

Shutterstock / egd

U.S. Route 25	Interstate 75
52	59
67	60
56	61
45	51
70	56
54	63
64	57
	65

SOLUTION

The mean driving times along the two routes are nearly the same. The mean time is 58.29 minutes for the U.S. 25 route and 59.0 minutes along the I-75 route. However, in evaluating travel times, Mr. Lammers is also concerned about the variation in the travel times. The first step is to compute the two sample variances. We'll use formula (3–10) to compute the sample standard deviations. To obtain the sample variances, we square the standard deviations.

U.S. ROUTE 25

$$\bar{x} = \frac{\Sigma x}{n} = \frac{408}{7} = 58.29 \qquad s = \sqrt{\frac{\Sigma(x - \bar{x})^2}{n - 1}} = \sqrt{\frac{485.43}{7 - 1}} = 8.9947$$

INTERSTATE 75

$$\bar{x} = \frac{\Sigma x}{n} = \frac{472}{8} = 59.00 \qquad s = \sqrt{\frac{\Sigma(x - \bar{x})^2}{n - 1}} = \sqrt{\frac{134}{8 - 1}} = 4.3753$$

There is more variation, as measured by the standard deviation, in the U.S. 25 route than in the I-75 route. This is consistent with his knowledge of the two routes; the U.S. 25 route contains more stoplights, whereas I-75 is a limited-access interstate highway. However, the I-75 route is several miles longer. It is important that the service offered be both timely and consistent, so he decides to conduct a statistical test to determine if there is a real, statistically significant, difference in the variation of the two routes.

We use the six-step hypothesis test procedure.

Step 1: We begin by stating the null hypothesis and the alternate hypothesis. The test is two-tailed because we are looking for a difference in the variation of the two routes. We are *not* trying to show that one route has more variation than the other. For this Example/Solution, the subscript 1 indicates information for U.S. 25; the subscript 2 indicates information for I-75.

$$H_0: \sigma_1^2 = \sigma_2^2$$
$$H_1: \sigma_1^2 \neq \sigma_2^2$$

Step 2: We decide on a .10 significance level. This also sets the probability of a Type I error to .10.

Step 3: The appropriate test statistic follows the *F*-distribution.

Step 4: The critical value is obtained from Appendix B.6A, a portion of which is reproduced as Table 11–1. Because we are conducting a two-tailed test, the tabled significance level is .05, found by $\alpha/2 = .10/2 = .05$. There are $n_1 - 1 = 7 - 1 = 6$ degrees of freedom in the numerator and $n_2 - 1 = 8 - 1 = 7$ degrees of freedom in the denominator. To find the critical value, move horizontally across the top portion of the *F*-table (Table 11–1 or Appendix B.6A) for the .05 significance level to 6 degrees of freedom in the numerator. Then move down that column to the critical value opposite 7 degrees of freedom in the denominator. The critical value is 3.87. Thus, the decision rule is: Reject the null hypothesis if the ratio of the sample variances exceeds 3.87.

TABLE 11–1 Critical Values of the *F*-Distribution, $\alpha = .05$ in the Right Tail

Degrees of Freedom for Denominator	Degrees of Freedom for Numerator			
	5	6	7	8
1	230.16	233.99	236.77	238.88
2	19.30	19.33	19.35	19.37
3	9.01	8.94	8.89	8.85
4	6.26	6.16	6.09	6.04
5	5.05	4.95	4.88	4.82
6	4.39	4.28	4.21	4.15
7	3.97	3.87	3.79	3.73
8	3.69	3.58	3.50	3.44
9	3.48	3.37	3.29	3.23
10	3.33	3.22	3.14	3.07

Step 5: Next we compute the ratio of the two sample variances, determine the value of the test statistic, and make a decision regarding the null hypothesis. Note that formula (11–1) refers to the sample *variances,* but we calculated the sample *standard deviations.* We need to square the standard deviations to determine the variances.

$$F = \frac{s_1^2}{s_2^2} = \frac{(8.9947)^2}{(4.3753)^2} = 4.23$$

The decision is to reject the null hypothesis because the computed *F*-value (4.23) is larger than the critical value (3.87).

Step 6: We conclude there is a difference in the variation in the time to travel the two routes. Mr. Lammers will want to consider this in his scheduling.

The usual practice is to determine the *F*-ratio by putting the larger of the two sample variances in the numerator. This will force the *F*-ratio to be at least 1.00. This allows us to always use the right tail of the *F*-distribution, thus avoiding the need for more extensive *F*-tables.

A logical question arises: Is it possible to conduct one-tailed tests? For example, suppose in the previous example we suspected that the variance of the times using the U.S. 25 route, σ_1^2, is larger than the variance of the times along the I-75 route, σ_2^2. We would state the null and the alternate hypothesis as

$$H_0: \sigma_1^2 \le \sigma_2^2$$
$$H_1: \sigma_1^2 > \sigma_2^2$$

The test statistic is computed as s_1^2/s_2^2. Notice that we labeled the population with the larger sample variance as population 1. So s_1^2 appears in the numerator. The *F*-ratio will be larger than 1.00, so we can use the upper tail of the *F*-distribution. Under these conditions, it is not necessary to divide the significance level in half. Because Appendix B.6A gives us only the .05 and .01 significance levels, we are restricted to these levels for one-tailed tests and .10 and .02 for two-tailed tests unless we consult a more complete table or use statistical software to compute the *F*-statistic.

The Excel software has a procedure to perform a test of variances. Following is the output. The computed value of *F* is the same as that determined by using formula (11–1).

The result of the one-tail hypothesis test is to reject the null hypothesis. The F of 4.23 is greater than the critical value of 3.87. Also, the p-value is less than 0.05. We conclude the variance of travel times on U.S. 25 is greater than the variance of travel times on I-75. See the tutorial link in the margin for a demonstration of the analysis.

Tutorial #58
in Connect

⬛ Variance Test							
◢	A	B	C	D	E	F	G
1	**U.S. 25**	**Interstate 75**		**F-Test Two-Sample for Variances**			
2	52	59			*U.S. 25*	*Interstate 75*	
3	67	60		Mean	58.29	59.00	
4	56	61		Variance	80.90	19.14	
5	45	51		Observations	7.00	8.00	
6	70	56		df	6.00	7.00	
7	54	63		F	4.23		
8	64	57		P(F<=f) one-tail	0.04		
9		65		F Critical one-tail	3.87		
10							

Source: Microsoft Excel

SELF-REVIEW 11–1

Steele Electric Products Inc. assembles cell phones. For the last 10 days, Avery Nagy completed a mean of 39 phones per day, with a standard deviation of 2 per day. Delilah Richmond completed a mean of 38.5 phones per day, with a standard deviation of 1.5 per day. At the .05 significance level, can we conclude that there is more variation in Avery's daily production?

EXERCISES

1. What is the critical F-value when the sample size for the numerator is six and the sample size for the denominator is four? Use a two-tailed test and the .10 significance level.

2. What is the critical F-value when the sample size for the numerator is four and the sample size for the denominator is seven? Use a one-tailed test and the .01 significance level.

3. The following hypotheses are given.

$$H_0: \sigma_1^2 = \sigma_2^2$$
$$H_1: \sigma_1^2 \neq \sigma_2^2$$

A random sample of eight observations from the first population resulted in a standard deviation of 10. A random sample of six observations from the second population resulted in a standard deviation of 7. At the .02 significance level, is there a difference in the variation of the two populations?

4. The following hypotheses are given.

$$H_0: \sigma_1^2 \leq \sigma_2^2$$
$$H_1: \sigma_1^2 > \sigma_2^2$$

A random sample of five observations from the first population resulted in a standard deviation of 12. A random sample of seven observations from the second population showed a standard deviation of 7. At the .01 significance level, is there more variation in the first population?

5. Arbitron Media Research Inc. conducted a study of podcast listening habits of men and women. One facet of the study involved the mean listening time. It was discovered that the mean listening time for a sample of 10 men was 35 minutes per day. The standard deviation was 10 minutes per day. The mean listening time for a sample of 12 women was also 35 minutes, but the standard deviation of the sample was 12 minutes. At the .10 significance level, can we conclude that there is a difference in the variation in the listening times for men and women?
   a. State the null and alternate hypotheses.
   b. State the decision rule.
   c. Compute the value of the test statistic.
   d. Compute the *p*-value.
   e. What is your decision regarding H_0?
   f. Interpret the result.

6. A stockbroker at Critical Securities reported that the mean rate of return on a sample of 10 oil stocks was 12.6% with a standard deviation of 3.9%. The mean rate of return on a sample of 8 utility stocks was 10.9% with a standard deviation of 3.5%. At the .05 significance level, can we conclude that there is more variation in the oil stocks?
   a. State the null and alternate hypotheses.
   b. State the decision rule.
   c. Compute the value of the test statistic.
   d. Compute the *p*-value.
   e. What is your decision regarding H_0?
   f. Interpret the result.

LO11-2
Test a hypothesis that two independent population means are equal, assuming that the population standard deviations are known.

Two-Sample Tests of Hypothesis: Independent Samples

A city planner in Tampa, Florida, wishes to know whether there is a difference in the mean hourly wage rate of plumbers and electricians in central Florida. A financial accountant wishes to know whether the mean rate of return for U.S. stock mutual funds is different from the mean rate of return on international stock mutual funds. In each of these cases, there are two independent populations. In the first case, the plumbers represent one population and the electricians, the other. In the second case, U.S. stock mutual funds are one population and international stock mutual funds, the other.

To investigate each of these cases, we would hypothesize that the two population means are equal, select a random sample from each population, compute the means of each sample, compute a test statistic that compares the two sample means, and decide if the sample evidence is sufficient to reject the null hypothesis. If the two population means are the same, that is, the mean hourly rate is the same for the plumbers and the electricians, we would expect the *difference* between the two sample means to be zero. But what if our sample results yield a difference other than zero? Is that difference due to chance or is it because there is a real difference in the hourly earnings? A two-sample test of means will help to answer this question.

We can illustrate this theory in terms of the city planner in Tampa, Florida. To begin, let's assume some information that is not usually available. Suppose that the population of plumbers has a mean of $30.00 per hour and a standard deviation of $5.00 per hour. The population of electricians has a mean of $29.00 and a standard deviation of $4.50. Now, from this information it is clear that the two population means are not the same. The plumbers actually earn $1.00 per hour more than the electricians. But we cannot expect to uncover this difference each time we sample the two populations.

Suppose we select a random sample of 40 plumbers and a random sample of 35 electricians and compute the mean of each sample. Then, we determine the difference between the sample means. It is this difference between the sample means that holds our interest. If the populations have the same mean, then we would expect the difference between the two sample means to be zero. If there is a difference between the population means, then we expect to find a difference between the sample means.

To understand the theory, we need to take several pairs of samples, compute the mean of each, determine the difference between the sample means, and study the distribution of the differences in the sample means. Recall in Chapter 8, the central limit theorem states that the sampling distribution of the sample mean is normally distributed as sample size increases. The central limit theorem can be extended to show that the sampling distribution of the difference between two sample means is also normally distributed. Therefore, we will continue to use the z-value to test hypotheses about the difference between two population means. This is the first hurdle.

The second hurdle refers to the mean of this distribution of differences. If we find the mean of this distribution is zero, that implies there is no difference in the two populations. On the other hand, if the mean of the distribution of differences is equal to some value other than zero, either positive or negative, then we conclude that the two populations do not have the same mean.

To report some concrete results, let's return to the city planner in Tampa, Florida. Table 11–2 shows the result of selecting 20 different samples of 40 plumbers and 35 electricians, computing the mean of each sample, and finding the difference between the two sample means. In the first case, the sample of 40 plumbers has a mean of $29.80, and for the 35 electricians the mean is $28.76. The difference between the sample means is $1.04. This process was repeated 19 more times. Observe that in 17 of the 20 cases, the differences are positive because the mean of the plumbers is larger than the mean of the electricians. In two cases, the differences are negative because the mean of the electricians is larger than the mean of the plumbers. In one case, the means are equal.

TABLE 11–2 The Mean Hourly Earnings of 20 Random Samples of Plumbers and Electricians and the Differences between the Means

Sample	Plumbers	Electricians	Difference
1	$29.80	$28.76	$1.04
2	30.32	29.40	0.92
3	30.57	29.94	0.63
4	30.04	28.93	1.11
5	30.09	29.78	0.31
6	30.02	28.66	1.36
7	29.60	29.13	0.47
8	29.63	29.42	0.21
9	30.17	29.29	0.88
10	30.81	29.75	1.06
11	30.09	28.05	2.04
12	29.35	29.07	0.28
13	29.42	28.79	0.63
14	29.78	29.54	0.24
15	29.60	29.60	0.00
16	30.60	30.19	0.41
17	30.79	28.65	2.14
18	29.14	29.95	−0.81
19	29.91	28.75	1.16
20	28.74	29.21	−0.47

Our final hurdle is that we need to know something about the *variability* of the distribution of differences. To put it another way, what is the standard deviation of this distribution of differences? Statistical theory shows that when we have independent populations, as in this case, the distribution of the differences has a variance (standard deviation squared) equal to the sum of the two individual variances. So, we can add the variances of the two sampling distributions. To put it another way, the variance of the difference in sample means ($\bar{x}_1 - \bar{x}_2$) is equal to the sum of the variance for the plumbers and the variance for the electricians.

VARIANCE OF THE DISTRIBUTION OF DIFFERENCES IN MEANS	$\sigma^2_{\bar{x}_1 - \bar{x}_2} = \dfrac{\sigma^2_1}{n_1} + \dfrac{\sigma^2_2}{n_2}$	(11–2)

The term $\sigma^2_{\bar{x}_1 - \bar{x}_2}$ looks complex but need not be difficult to interpret. The σ^2 portion reminds us that it is a variance, and the subscript $\bar{x}_1 - \bar{x}_2$ that it is a distribution of differences in the sample means.

We can put this equation in a more usable form by taking the square root, so that we have the standard deviation or "standard error" of the distribution of differences. Finally, we standardize the distribution of the differences. The result is the following equation.

TWO-SAMPLE TEST OF MEANS—KNOWN σ	$z = \dfrac{\bar{x}_1 - \bar{x}_2}{\sqrt{\dfrac{\sigma^2_1}{n_1} + \dfrac{\sigma^2_2}{n_2}}}$	(11–3)

Before we present an example, let's review the assumptions necessary for using formula (11–3).

- The two populations follow normal distributions.
- The two samples are unrelated, that is, independent.
- The standard deviations for both populations are known.

The following Example/Solution shows the details of the test of hypothesis for two population means and shows how to interpret the results.

▶ **EXAMPLE**

Customers at the FoodTown Supermarket have a choice when paying for their groceries. They may check out and pay using the standard cashier-assisted checkout, or they may use the new Fast Lane procedure. In the standard procedure, a FoodTown employee scans each item and puts it on a short conveyor, where another employee puts it in a bag and then into the grocery cart. In the Fast Lane procedure, the customer scans each item, bags it, and places the bags

adriaticfoto/Shutterstock

in the cart. The Fast Lane procedure is designed to reduce the time a customer spends in the checkout line.

The Fast Lane facility was recently installed at the Byrne Road FoodTown location. The store manager would like to know if the mean checkout time using the standard checkout method is longer than using the Fast Lane. She gathered the following sample information. The time is measured from when the customer enters the line until all bags are in the cart. Hence, the time includes both waiting in line and checking out. What is the *p*-value?

Customer Type	Sample Size	Sample Mean	Population Standard Deviation
Standard	50	5.50 minutes	0.40 minute
Fast Lane	100	5.30 minutes	0.30 minute

SOLUTION

We use the six-step hypothesis testing procedure to investigate the question.

Step 1: State the null hypothesis and the alternate hypothesis. The null hypothesis is that the mean standard checkout time is less than or equal to the mean Fast Lane checkout time. In other words, the difference of 0.20 minute between the mean checkout time for the standard method and the mean checkout time for Fast Lane is due to chance. The alternate hypothesis, or research question, is that the mean checkout time is longer for those using the standard method. We will let μ_S refer to the mean checkout time for the population of standard customers and μ_F the mean checkout time for the Fast Lane customers. The null and alternative hypotheses are:

$$H_0: \mu_S \leq \mu_F$$
$$H_1: \mu_S > \mu_F$$

Step 2: Select the level of significance. The significance level is the probability that we reject the null hypothesis when it is actually true. In a research situation, you get to determine this probability. You must select it prior to collecting or reviewing the data. As a probability, the significance level must be between 0 and 1. However, the reasonable decision is to choose probabilities that are small. The .05 and .01 significance levels are the most common, but other values, such as .02 and .10, are also used. In this case, we selected the .01 significance level.

Step 3: Determine the test statistic. In Chapter 10, we used the standard normal distribution (that is, *z*) and *t* as test statistics. In this case, we use the *z*-distribution as the test statistic because we assume the two population distributions are both normal and the standard deviations of both populations are known.

Step 4: Formulate a decision rule. The decision rule is based on the null and the alternate hypotheses (i.e., one-tailed or two-tailed test), the level of significance, and the test statistic used. We selected the .01 significance level and the *z*-distribution as the test statistic, and we wish to determine whether the mean checkout time is longer using the standard method. We set the alternate hypothesis to indicate that the mean checkout time is longer for those using the standard method than the Fast Lane method. Hence, the rejection region is in the upper tail of the standard normal distribution (a one-tailed test).

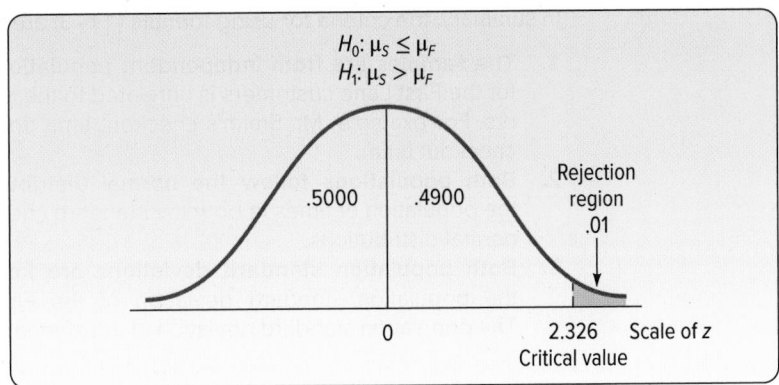

$H_0: \mu_S \leq \mu_F$
$H_1: \mu_S > \mu_F$

.5000 | .4900

Rejection
region
.01

0

2.326   Scale of z
Critical value

CHART 11–1 Decision Rule for One-Tailed Test at .01 Significance Level

To find the critical value, go to Student's t-distribution (Appendix B.5). In the table headings, find the row labeled "Level of Significance for One-Tailed Test" and select the column for an alpha of .01. Go to the bottom row with infinite degrees of freedom. The z critical value is 2.326. So the decision rule is to reject the null hypothesis if the value of the test statistic exceeds 2.326. Chart 11–1 depicts the decision rule.

Step 5: **Make the decision regarding H_0.** FoodTown randomly selected 50 customers using the standard checkout and computed a sample mean checkout time of 5.5 minutes, and 100 customers using the Fast Lane checkout and computed a sample mean checkout time of 5.3 minutes. We assume that the population standard deviations for the two methods is known. We use formula (11–3) to compute the value of the test statistic.

$$z = \frac{\bar{x}_S - \bar{x}_F}{\sqrt{\dfrac{\sigma_S^2}{n_S} + \dfrac{\sigma_F^2}{n_F}}} = \frac{5.5 - 5.3}{\sqrt{\dfrac{0.40^2}{50} + \dfrac{0.30^2}{100}}} = \frac{0.2}{0.064031} = 3.123$$

The computed value of 3.123 is larger than the critical value of 2.326. Our decision is to reject the null hypothesis and accept the alternate hypothesis.

Step 6: **Interpret the result.** The difference of .20 minute between the mean checkout times is too large to have occurred by chance. We conclude the Fast Lane method is quicker.

What is the p-value for the test statistic? Recall that the p-value is the probability of finding a value of the test statistic this extreme when the null hypothesis is true. To calculate the p-value, we need the probability of a z-value larger than 3.123. From Appendix B.3, we cannot find the probability associated with 3.123. The largest value available is 3.09. The area corresponding to 3.09 is .4990. In this case, we can report that the p-value is less than .0010, found by .5000 − .4990. We conclude that if the population difference was really zero, the probability of getting our sample evidence that the difference is .20 is very, very low. So, the sample evidence is sufficient to reject the null hypothesis. The checkout time is less using the Fast Lane.

In summary, the criteria for using formula (11–3) are:

1. **The samples are from independent populations.** This means the checkout time for the Fast Lane customers is unrelated to the checkout time for the other customers. For example, Mr. Smith's checkout time does not affect any other customer's checkout time.
2. **Both populations follow the normal distribution.** In the FoodTown example, the population of times in both the standard checkout line and the Fast Lane follow normal distributions.
3. **Both population standard deviations are known.** In the FoodTown example, the population standard deviation of the Fast Lane times was 0.30 minute. The population standard deviation of the standard checkout times was 0.40 minute.

SELF-REVIEW 11–2

Rory Sevits is the owner of the Appliance Patch. Recently Rory observed a difference in the dollar value of sales between the men and women he employs as sales associates. A sample of 40 days revealed the men sold a mean of $1,400 worth of appliances per day. For a sample of 50 days, the women sold a mean of $1,500 worth of appliances per day. Assume the population standard deviation for men is $200 and for women $250. At the .05 significance level, can the owner conclude that the mean amount sold per day is larger for the women?
(a)   State the null hypothesis and the alternate hypothesis.
(b)   What is the decision rule?
(c)   What is the value of the test statistic?
(d)   What is your decision regarding the null hypothesis?
(e)   What is the p-value?
(f)   Interpret the result.

EXERCISES

7. A sample of 40 observations is selected from one population with a population standard deviation of 5. The sample mean is 102. A sample of 50 observations is selected from a second population with a population standard deviation of 6. The sample mean is 99. Conduct the following test of hypothesis using the .04 significance level.

$$H_0: \mu_1 = \mu_2$$
$$H_1: \mu_1 \neq \mu_2$$

a. Is this a one-tailed or a two-tailed test?
b. State the decision rule.
c. Compute the value of the test statistic.
d. What is your decision regarding H_0?
e. What is the p-value?

8. A sample of 65 observations is selected from one population with a population standard deviation of 0.75. The sample mean is 2.67. A sample of 50 observations is selected from a second population with a population standard deviation of 0.66. The sample mean is 2.59. Conduct the following test of hypothesis using the .08 significance level.

$$H_0: \mu_1 \leq \mu_2$$
$$H_1: \mu_1 > \mu_2$$

   a. Is this a one-tailed or a two-tailed test?
   b. State the decision rule.
   c. Compute the value of the test statistic.
   d. What is your decision regarding H_0?
   e. What is the *p*-value?

Note: Use the six-step hypothesis testing procedure to solve the following exercises.

9. Gibbs Baby Food Company wishes to compare the weight gain of infants using its brand versus its competitor's. A sample of 40 babies using the Gibbs products revealed a mean weight gain of 7.6 pounds in the first 3 months after birth. For the Gibbs brand, the population standard deviation of the sample is 2.3 pounds. A sample of 55 babies using the competitor's brand revealed a mean increase in weight of 8.1 pounds. The population standard deviation is 2.9 pounds. At the .05 significance level, can we conclude that babies using the Gibbs brand gained less weight? Compute the *p*-value and interpret it.

10. As part of a study of corporate employees, the director of human resources for PNC Inc. wants to compare the distance traveled to work by employees at its office in downtown Cincinnati with the distance for those in downtown Pittsburgh. A sample of 35 Cincinnati employees showed they travel a mean of 370 miles per month. A sample of 40 Pittsburgh employees showed they travel a mean of 380 miles per month. The population standard deviations for the Cincinnati and Pittsburgh employees are 30 and 26 miles, respectively. At the .05 significance level, is there a difference in the mean number of miles traveled per month between Cincinnati and Pittsburgh employees?

11. Do married and unmarried women spend the same amount of time per week using Facebook? A random sample of 45 married women who use Facebook spent an average of 4.0 hours per week on this social media website. A random sample of 39 unmarried women who regularly use Facebook spent an average of 4.4 hours per week. Assume that the weekly Facebook time for married women has a population standard deviation of 1.2 hours, and the population standard deviation for unmarried, regular Facebook users is 1.1 hours per week. Using the .05 significance level, do married and unmarried women differ in the amount of time per week spent on Facebook? Find the *p*-value and interpret the result.

12. Sydney Fitzpatrick is the vice president for Nursing Services at St. Luke's Memorial Hospital. Recently Sydney noticed in the job postings for nurses that those who are unionized seem to offer higher wages. Sydney decided to investigate and gathered the following information.

Group	Sample Size	Sample Mean Wage	Population Standard Deviation
Union	40	$20.75	$2.25
Nonunion	45	$19.80	$1.90

Would it be reasonable to conclude that union nurses earn more? Use the .02 significance level. What is the *p*-value?

LO11-3

Test a hypothesis that two independent population means are equal, with estimated population standard deviations.

Comparing Population Means with Estimated Population Standard Deviations

In the previous section, we used the standard normal distribution and *z* as the test statistic to test a hypothesis that two population means from independent populations were equal. The hypothesis tests presumed that the populations were normally distributed and that we knew the population standard deviations. However, in most cases, we do not know the population standard deviations. We can overcome this problem, as we did in the one-sample case in the previous chapter, by using the sample standard deviation (s) to estimate the population standard deviation (σ).

Two-Sample Pooled Test

Next, we describe the methoddology to test the hypothesis that the means of two independent populations are equal. This method requires that we estimate population standard deviations with sample standard deviations. This gives us a great deal more flexibility when investigating the difference between sample means. There are three differences in this test and the test described in the previous section of this chapter.

1. First, we test the hypothesis that the population variances are equal as described in the first section of this chapter.
2. If we fail to reject the hypothesis that the population variances are equal, then we assume the variances are equal and average or "pool" the sample variances.
3. We use the t-distribution as the test statistic.

The formula for computing the value of the test statistic t is similar to formula (11–3), but an additional calculation is necessary. The two sample variances are pooled to form a single estimate of the unknown population variance. In essence, we compute a weighted mean of the two sample variances and use this value as an estimate of the unknown population variance. The weights are the degrees of freedom that each sample provides. Why do we need to pool the sample variances? Because we assume that the two populations have equal variances, the best estimate we can make of that value is to combine or pool all the sample information we have about the value of the population variance.

The following formula is used to pool the sample variances. Notice that two factors are involved: the number of observations in each sample and the sample variances themselves.

POOLED VARIANCE	$$s_p^2 = \frac{(n_1 - 1)s_1^2 + (n_2 - 1)s_2^2}{n_1 + n_2 - 2}$$	**(11–4)**

where:

s_1^2 is the variance of the first sample.
s_2^2 is the variance of the second sample.
n_1 is the number of observations in the first sample.
n_2 is the number of observations in the second sample.

The value of t is computed using the following equation.

TWO-SAMPLE TEST OF MEANS— UNKNOWN σ'S	$$t = \frac{\bar{x}_1 - \bar{x}_2}{\sqrt{s_p^2\left(\frac{1}{n_1} + \frac{1}{n_2}\right)}}$$	**(11–5)**

where:

$\bar{x}_1$ is the mean of the first sample.
$\bar{x}_2$ is the mean of the second sample.

n_1 is the number of observations in the first sample.

n_2 is the number of observations in the second sample.

s_p^2 is the pooled estimate of the population variance.

The number of degrees of freedom in the test is the total number of items sampled minus the total number of samples. Because there are two samples, there are $n_1 + n_2 - 2$ degrees of freedom.

To summarize, there are three requirements or assumptions for the test.

1. The sampled populations are approximately normally distributed.
2. The sampled populations are independent.
3. The standard deviations of the two populations are equal.

The following Example/Solution explains the details of the test.

▶ **EXAMPLE**

Owens Lawn Care Inc. manufactures and assembles lawnmowers that are shipped to dealers throughout the United States and Canada. Two different procedures have been proposed for mounting the engine on the frame of the lawnmower. The question is: Is there a difference in the mean time to mount the engines on the frames of the lawnmowers? The first procedure was developed by longtime Owens employee Herb Welles (designated as procedure W), and the other procedure was developed by Owens Vice President of Engineering William Atkins (designated as procedure A). To evaluate the two methods, we conduct a time and motion study. A sample of five employees is timed using the Welles method and six using the Atkins method. The results, in minutes, are shown in the following table. Is there a difference in the mean mounting times? Use the .10 significance level.

Welles (minutes)	Atkins (minutes)
2	3
4	7
9	5
3	8
2	4
	3

SOLUTION

Following the six steps to test a hypothesis, the null hypothesis states that there is no difference in mean mounting times between the two procedures. The alternate hypothesis indicates that there is a difference.

$$H_0: \mu_W = \mu_A$$
$$H_1: \mu_W \neq \mu_A$$

The required assumptions are:

- The observations in the Welles sample are *independent* of the observations in the Atkins sample.
- The two populations follow the normal distribution.
- The two populations are assumed to have equal standard deviations, but these standard deviations are not known.

Is there a difference between the mean assembly times using the Welles and the Atkins methods? The degrees of freedom are equal to the total number of items sampled minus the number of samples. In this case, that is $n_W + n_A - 2$. Five assemblers used the Welles method and six the Atkins method. Thus, there are 9 degrees of freedom, found by $5 + 6 - 2$. The critical values of t, from Appendix B.5 for $df = 9$, a two-tailed test, and the .10 significance level, are -1.833 and 1.833. The decision rule is portrayed graphically in Chart 11–2. We do not reject the null hypothesis if the computed value of t falls between -1.833 and 1.833.

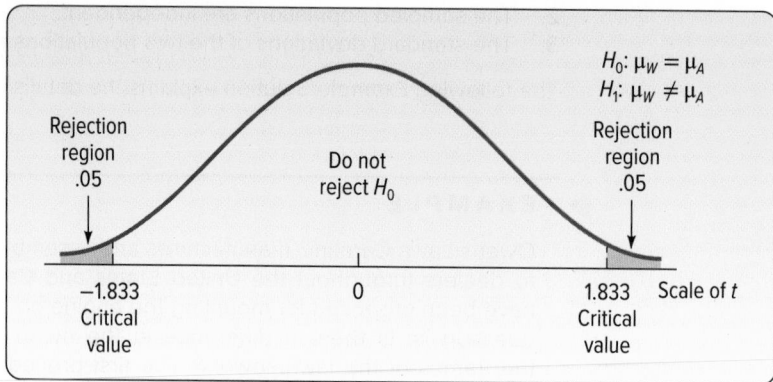

CHART 11–2 Regions of Rejection, Two-Tailed Test, $df = 9$, and .10 Significance Level

We use three steps to compute the value of t.

Step 1: **Calculate the sample standard deviations.** To compute the sample standard deviations, we use formula (3–10). See the details to come.

Welles Method		Atkins Method	
x_W	$(x_W - \bar{x}_W)^2$	x_A	$(x_A - \bar{x}_A)^2$
2	$(2 - 4)^2 = 4$	3	$(3 - 5)^2 = 4$
4	$(4 - 4)^2 = 0$	7	$(7 - 5)^2 = 4$
9	$(9 - 4)^2 = 25$	5	$(5 - 5)^2 = 0$
3	$(3 - 4)^2 = 1$	8	$(8 - 5)^2 = 9$
2	$(2 - 4)^2 = 4$	4	$(4 - 5)^2 = 1$
20	34	3	$(3 - 5)^2 = 4$
		30	22

$$\bar{x}_W = \frac{\Sigma x_W}{n_W} = \frac{20}{5} = 4 \qquad \bar{x}_A = \frac{\Sigma x_A}{n_A} = \frac{30}{6} = 5$$

$$s_W = \sqrt{\frac{\Sigma(x_W - \bar{x}_W)^2}{n_W - 1}} = \sqrt{\frac{34}{5 - 1}} = 2.9155 \quad s_A = \sqrt{\frac{\Sigma(X_A - \bar{x}_A)}{n_A - 1}} = \sqrt{\frac{22}{6 - 1}} = 2.0976$$

Step 2: We test the assumption or hypothesis that the population variances are equal.

$$H_0: \sigma_w^2 = \sigma_a^2$$
$$H_1: \sigma_w^2 \neq \sigma_a^2$$

This a two-tail test. To use the F-table in the text, we select a significance level, α, of .10 and divide by 2 to use the F-table with a right tail area of .05. With 4 degrees of freedom in the numerator and 5 degrees of freedom in the denominator, the F critical value is 5.19.

Using the sample standard deviations, we calculate the F-statistic.

$$F = \frac{s_w^2}{s_a^2} = \frac{2.9155^2}{2.0976^2} = 1.93$$

The calculated F-statistic is less than 5.19. We fail to reject the null hypothesis. The sample data are not sufficient to conclude that the population variances are different. We will use the pooled sample variances as the best estimate of the population variance.

Step 3: Pool the sample variances. We use formula (11–4) to pool the sample variances (standard deviations squared).

$$s_p^2 = \frac{(n_w - 1)s_w^2 + (n_A - 1)s_A^2}{n_w + n_A - 2} = \frac{(5 - 1)(2.9155)^2 + (6 - 1)(2.0976)^2}{5 + 6 - 2} = 6.2222$$

Step 4: Determine the value of t. The mean mounting time for the Welles method is 4.00 minutes, found by $\bar{x}_w = 20/5$. The mean mounting time for the Atkins method is 5.00 minutes, found by $\bar{x}_A = 30/6$. We use formula (11–5) to calculate the value of t.

$$t = \frac{\bar{x}_w - \bar{x}_A}{\sqrt{s_p^2\left(\frac{1}{n_w} + \frac{1}{n_A}\right)}} = \frac{4.00 - 5.00}{\sqrt{6.2222\left(\frac{1}{5} + \frac{1}{6}\right)}} = -0.662$$

The decision is not to reject the null hypothesis because -0.662 falls in the region between -1.833 and 1.833. Our conclusion is that the sample data failed to show a difference between the mean assembly times of the two methods.

We also can estimate the p-value using Appendix B.5. Locate the row with 9 degrees of freedom, and use the two-tailed test column. Find the t-value, without regard to the sign, that is closest to our computed value of 0.662. It is 1.383, corresponding to a significance level of .20. Thus, even had we used the 20% significance level, we would not have rejected the null hypothesis of equal means. We can report that the p-value is greater than .20.

Tutorial #54
in Connect

Excel has a procedure called "t-Test: Two Sample Assuming Equal Variances" that will perform the calculations of formulas (11–4) and (11–5) as well as find the sample means, sample variances, and pooled variance. The hypothesis test is demonstrated in the tutorial link in the margin. The data are input in the first two columns of the spreadsheet. They are labeled "Welles" and "Atkins." The output follows. The value of t, called the "t Stat," is -0.662, and the two-tailed p-value is .525. As we would expect, the computed p-value is larger than the significance level of .10. So the conclusion is not to reject the null hypothesis.

⊞ welles and atkins.xlsx						
◢	A	B	C	D	E	F
1	Welles	Atkins		t-Test: Two-Sample Assuming Equal Variances		
2	2	3				
3	4	7			Welles	Atkins
4	9	5		Mean	4.000	5.000
5	3	8		Variance	8.500	4.400
6	2	4		Observations	5.000	6.000
7		3		Pooled Variance	6.222	
8				Hypothesized Mean Difference	0.000	
9				df	9.000	
10				t Stat	-0.662	
11				P(T<=t) one-tail	0.262	
12				t Critical one-tail	1.833	
13				P(T<=t) two-tail	0.525	
14				t Critical two-tail	2.262	

Source: Microsoft Excel

SELF-REVIEW 11–3

The production manager at Bellevue Steel, a manufacturer of wheelchairs, wants to compare the number of defective wheelchairs produced on the day shift with the number on the afternoon shift. A sample of the production from six day shifts and eight afternoon shifts revealed the following number of defects.

Day	5	8	7	6	9	7		
Afternoon	8	10	7	11	9	12	14	9

At the .10 significance level, test the assumption that the population variances are equal. At the .05 significance level, is there a difference in the mean number of defects per shift?
(a)   State the null hypothesis and the alternate hypothesis.
(b)   What is the decision rule?
(c)   What is the value of the test statistic?
(d)   What is your decision regarding the null hypothesis?
(e)   What is the p-value?
(f)   Interpret the result.
(g)   What are the assumptions necessary for this test?

EXERCISES

For Exercises 7 and 8: Test the hypothesis that the population variances are equal with a .10 significance level. Then test the hypothesis that the population means are equal by (a) stating the decision rule, (b) computing the pooled estimate of the population variance, (c) computing the test statistic, (d) estimating or computing the p-value, and (e) stating your decision about the null hypothesis.

13. The null and alternate hypotheses are:

$$H_0: \mu_1 = \mu_2$$
$$H_1: \mu_1 \neq \mu_2$$

A random sample of 10 observations from one population revealed a sample mean of 23 and a sample standard deviation of 4. A random sample of 8 observations from another population revealed a sample mean of 26 and a sample standard deviation of 5. At the .05 significance level, is there a difference between the population means?

14. The null and alternate hypotheses are:

$$H_0: \mu_1 = \mu_2$$
$$H_1: \mu_1 \neq \mu_2$$

A random sample of 15 observations from the first population revealed a sample mean of 350 and a sample standard deviation of 12. A random sample of 16 observations from the second population revealed a sample mean of 342 and a sample standard deviation of 15. At the .10 significance level, is there a difference in the population means?

Note: Use the six-step hypothesis testing procedure for the following exercises.

15. FILE Following are the 28 players on the opening-day roster of the 2021 Boston Red Sox Major League Baseball team, their salaries, and fielding positions.

Player	Position	Salary ($millions)
Chris Sale	Pitcher	30.0000
Xander Bogaerts	Infielder	20.0000
J.D. Martinez	Outfield	19.3500
Nathan Eovaldi	Pitcher	17.0000
Garrett Richards	Pitcher	8.5000
Eduardo Rodriguez	Pitcher	8.3000
Adam Ottavino	Pitcher	7.1500
Christian Vazquez	Catcher	6.2500
Rafael Devers	Infielder	4.5750
Enrique Hernandez	Infielder	6.0000
Matt Barnes	Pitcher	4.5000
Martin Perez	Pitcher	4.5000
Hunter Renfroe	Outfield	3.1000
Kyle Schwarber	Outfield	7.0000
Kevin Plawecki	Catcher	1.6000
Hirokazu Sawamura	Pitcher	1.2000
Ryan Brasier	Pitcher	1.2500
Hansel Robles	Pitcher	2.0000
Alex Verdugo	Outfield	0.6495
Nick Pivetta	Pitcher	0.6135
Christian Arroyo	Infielder	0.5815
Darwinzon Hernandez	Pitcher	0.5785
Bobby Dalbec	Infielder	0.5750
Garrett Whitlock	Pitcher	0.5705
Travis Shaw	Infielder	1.5000
Austin Davis	Pitcher	0.5880
Tanner Houck	Pitcher	0.5770
Jose Iglesias	Infielder	0.5705

Sort the players into two groups, all pitchers (relief and starting) and position players (all others). Test the assumption that the pitcher and position player population variances are equal. Test the hypothesis that mean salaries of pitchers and position players are equal using the .01 significance level.

16. A recent study compared the time watching television by single- and dual-earner households. Based on a sample of 15 single-earner households, the mean amount of time watching television was 61 minutes per day, with a standard deviation of 15.5 minutes. Based on a sample of 12 dual-earner households, the mean number of minutes watching television was 48.4 minutes, with a standard deviation of 18.1 minutes.

a. Using the .10 level of significance, verify the assumption that the variances are equal.
b. Using the .01 significance level, can we conclude that the single-earner households spend more time watching television?

17. **FILE** Ms. Lisa Monnin is the budget director for Nexus Media Inc. She would like to compare the daily travel expenses for the sales staff and the audit staff. She collected the following sample information.

Sales ($)	131	135	146	165	136	142	
Audit ($)	130	102	129	143	149	120	139

a. Verify the assumption that the variances are equal. Use the .10 significance level.
b. At the .10 significance level, can Lisa conclude that the mean daily expenses are greater for the sales staff than the audit staff? What is the p-value?

18. **FILE** The Tampa Bay (Florida) Area Chamber of Commerce wanted to know whether the mean weekly salary of nurses was larger than that of school teachers. To investigate, they collected the following information on the amounts earned last week by a sample of school teachers and a sample of nurses.

School Teachers ($)	1,095	1,076	1,077	1,125	1,034	1,059	1,052	1,070	1,079	1,080	1.092	1,082
Nurses ($)		1,091	1,140	1,071	1,021	1,100	1,109	1,075	1,079			

a. Verify the assumption that the variances are equal. Use the .10 significance level.
b. Is it reasonable to conclude that the mean weekly salary of nurses is higher? Use the .01 significance level. What is the p-value?

Unequal Population Standard Deviations

In the previous section, the hypothesis testing procedure was dependent on equal population variances. We tested this assumption with the F-distribution. In this section, if we test for equal population variances and reject the hypothesis, the procedure to test the equality of two population means is different. Specifically, the sample variances are NOT pooled, and the degrees of freedom are adjusted downward by a rather complex formula. The effect is to reduce the degrees of freedom and use a larger critical value for the hypothesis test.

The formula for the t-statistic is:

TEST STATISTIC FOR NO DIFFERENCE IN MEANS, UNEQUAL VARIANCES	$t = \dfrac{\bar{x}_1 - \bar{x}_2}{\sqrt{\dfrac{s_1^2}{n_1} + \dfrac{s_2^2}{n_2}}}$	**(11–6)**

The degrees of freedom statistic is found by:

DEGREES OF FREEDOM FOR UNEQUAL VARIANCE TEST	$df = \dfrac{[(s_1^2/n_1) + (s_2^2/n_2)]^2}{\dfrac{(s_1^2/n_1)^2}{n_1 - 1} + \dfrac{(s_2^2/n_2)^2}{n_2 - 1}}$	**(11–7)**

where n_1 and n_2 are the respective sample sizes and s_1 and s_2 are the respective sample standard deviations. If necessary, this fraction is rounded down to an integer value. An Example/Solution will explain the details.

▶ **EXAMPLE**

Personnel in a consumer testing laboratory are evaluating the absorbency of paper towels. They wish to compare a set of store brand towels to a similar group of name brand ones. For each brand they dip a ply of the paper into a tub of fluid, allow the paper to drain back into the vat for 2 minutes, and then evaluate the amount of liquid the paper has taken up from the vat. A random sample of nine store brand paper towels absorbed the following amounts of liquid in milliliters.

| 8 | 8 | 3 | 1 | 9 | 7 | 5 | 5 | 12 |

An independent random sample of 12 name brand towels absorbed the following amounts of liquid in milliliters.

| 12 | 11 | 10 | 6 | 8 | 9 | 9 | 10 | 11 | 9 | 8 | 10 |

Use the .10 significance level and test if there is a difference in the mean amount of liquid absorbed by the two types of paper towels.

SOLUTION

Tutorial #27
in Connect

To begin, let's assume that the amounts of liquid absorbed follow the normal probability distribution for both the store brand and the name brand towels. We do not know either of the population variances, so we are going to use the *t*-distribution as the test statistic. The assumption of equal population variances does not appear reasonable. The amount of absorption in the store brand ranges from 1 ml to 12 ml. For the name brand, the amount of absorption ranges from 6 ml to 12 ml. That is, there is considerably more variation in the amount of absorption in the store brand than in the name brand. We observe the difference in the variation in the following box plots. The link in the margin shows how to create box plots.

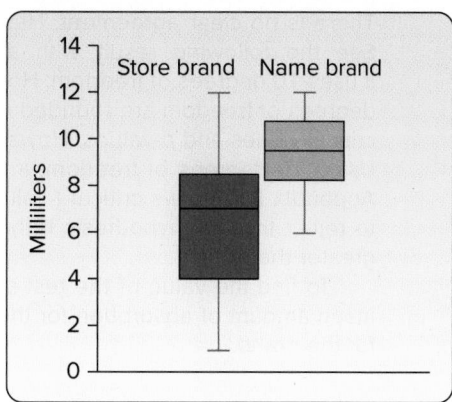

To statistically verify our observations of the box plots, we can test the hypothesis that the two variances are equal.

$$H_0: \sigma_s^2 = \sigma_n^2$$
$$H_1: \sigma_s^2 \neq \sigma_n^2.$$

This a two-tail test. To use the *F*-table in the text, we select a significance level, α, of .10 and divide by 2 to use the *F*-table with a right tail area of .05. With 8 degrees of freedom in the numerator and 11 degrees of freedom in the denominator, the *F* critical value is 2.95.

Using the sample standard deviations as presented in the following table,

Variable	n	Mean	Standard Deviation
Store	9	6.444	3.321
Name	12	9.417	1.621

we calculate the F-statistic.

$$F = \frac{s_s^2}{s_n^2} = \frac{3.321^2}{1.621^2} = 4.1950$$

The calculated F-statistic is greater than 2.95. We reject the null hypothesis. The sample data are sufficient to conclude that the population variances are different.

To test the null hypothesis that there is no difference in the mean amount of liquid absorbed between the two types of paper towels,

$$H_0: \mu_s = \mu_n$$
$$H_1: \mu_s \neq \mu_n$$

we will adjust the degrees of freedom to account for the differences in the population variances with formula (11–7):

$$df = \frac{[(s_1^2/n_1) + (s_2^2/n_2)]^2}{\dfrac{(s_1^2/n_1)^2}{n_1 - 1} + \dfrac{(s_2^2/n_2)^2}{n_2 - 1}} = \frac{[(3.321^2/9) + (1.621^2/12)]^2}{\dfrac{(3.321^2/9)^2}{9 - 1} + \dfrac{(1.621^2/12)^2}{12 - 1}} = \frac{1.4444^2}{.1877 + .0044} = 10.86$$

Tutorial #56
in Connect

Usually, degrees of freedom are integer values. However, you see that using a formula to adjust the degrees of freedom for unequal variances can result in a decimal value. Now, the decision is whether to round the value up or down. There is no clear agreement. Here we round down to 10 degrees of freedom. See the following result with a statistical software product called Minitab; it uses 10 degrees of freedom. However, as in the Excel tutorial in the margin, the degrees of freedom are rounded up to 11. Each value results in slightly different critical values and p-values. However, both values result in the same conclusion. Using 10 degrees of freedom, a two-tailed test, and the .10 significance level, Appendix B.5 shows critical t-values of −1.812 and 1.812. Our decision rule is to reject the null hypothesis if the computed value of t is less than −1.812 or greater than 1.812.

To find the value of the test statistic, we use formula (11–6). Recall that the mean amount of absorption for the store paper towels is 6.444 ml and 9.417 ml for the brand.

$$t = \frac{\bar{x}_1 - \bar{x}_2}{\sqrt{\dfrac{s_1^2}{n_1} + \dfrac{s_2^2}{n_2}}} = \frac{6.444 - 9.417}{\sqrt{\dfrac{3.321^2}{9} + \dfrac{1.621^2}{12}}} = -2.474$$

The computed value of t is less than the lower critical value, so our decision is to reject the null hypothesis. We conclude that the mean absorption rate for the two towels is not the same.

For this analysis there are many calculations. Statistical software often provides an option to compare two population means with different standard deviations. The Minitab output for this example follows.

Source: Minitab

SELF-REVIEW 11–4

It is often useful for companies to know who their customers are and how they became customers. A credit card company is interested in whether owners of the card applied for the card on their own or were contacted by a sales associate. The company obtained the following sample information regarding end-of-the-month balances for the two groups.

Source	Sample Size	Mean	Standard Deviation
Applied	10	$1,568	$356
Contacted	8	1,967	857

Using the .10 level of significance, test the hypothesis that the population variances are equal. Is it reasonable to conclude the mean balance is larger for the credit card holders who were contacted by sales associates than for those who applied on their own for the card?

(a) State the null hypothesis and the alternate hypothesis.
(b) How many degrees of freedom are there? Round your result down to the nearest integer value.
(c) Using the .05 significance level, what is the decision rule?
(d) What is the value of the test statistic?
(e) What is your decision regarding the null hypothesis?
(f) Interpret the result.

EXERCISES

For Exercises 19 through 21, test the assumption that the population variances are equal with a .10 significance level. Then, using a .05 significance level, test the hypothesis that the population means are equal by (a) stating the decision rule, (b) computing degrees of freedom, (c) computing the test statistic, (d) reporting the *p*-value, and (e) stating your decision about the null hypothesis.

19. The null and alternate hypotheses are:

$$H_0: \mu_1 = \mu_2$$
$$H_1: \mu_1 \neq \mu_2$$

A random sample of 15 items from the first population showed a mean of 50 and a standard deviation of 5. A sample of 12 items for the second population showed a mean of 46 and a standard deviation of 15.

20. The null and alternate hypotheses are:

$$H_0: \mu_1 \leq \mu_2$$
$$H_1: \mu_1 > \mu_2$$

A random sample of 20 items from the first population showed a mean of 100 and a standard deviation of 15. A sample of 16 items for the second population showed a mean of 94 and a standard deviation of 8. Use the .05 significance level.

21. A recent survey compared the costs of adoption through public and private agencies. For a sample of 16 adoptions through a public agency, the mean cost was $21,045, with a standard deviation of $835. For a sample of 18 adoptions through a private agency, the mean cost was $22,840, with a standard deviation of $1,545.

22. **FILE** Suppose you are an expert on the fashion industry and wish to gather information to compare the amount earned per month by models featuring Liz Claiborne attire with those of Calvin Klein. The following is the amount ($000) earned per month by a sample of 15 Claiborne models:

| $4.3 | $4.5 | $3.4 | $3.4 | $5.2 | $3.3 | $4.5 | $4.6 | $3.5 | $5.0 |
| 4.8 | 4.4 | 4.6 | 3.6 | 4.5 | | | | | |

The following is the amount ($000) earned by a sample of 12 Klein models.

| $2.8 | $3.7 | $3.6 | $4.5 | $2.5 | $3.8 | $5.9 | $4.9 | $6.0 | $3.6 |
| 2.3 | 4.0 | | | | | | | | |

a. Test the assumption that the population variances are equal.
b. Using the .05 significance level, is it reasonable to conclude that Claiborne models earn more?

LO11-4

Test a hypothesis about the mean population difference between paired or dependent observations.

Two-Sample Tests of Hypothesis: Dependent Samples

In the Owens Lawn Care Example/Solution on page 379, we tested the difference between the means from two independent populations. We compared the mean time required to mount an engine using the Welles method to the time to mount the engine using the Atkins method. The samples were *independent,* meaning that the sample of assembly times using the Welles method was in no way related to the sample of assembly times using the Atkins method.

There are situations, however, in which the samples are not independent. To put it another way, the samples are *dependent* or *related.* As an example, Nickel Savings and Loan employs two firms, Schadek Appraisals and Bowyer Real Estate, to appraise the value of the real estate properties on which it makes loans. It is important that these two firms be similar in their appraisal values. To review the consistency of the two appraisal firms, Nickel Savings randomly selects 10 homes and has both Schadek Appraisals and Bowyer Real Estate appraise the values of the selected homes. For each home, there will be a pair of appraisal values. That is, for each home there will be an appraised value from both Schadek Appraisals and Bowyer Real Estate. The appraised values depend on, or are related to, the home selected. This is also referred to as a **paired sample.**

For hypothesis testing, we are interested in the distribution of the *differences* in the appraised value of each home. Hence, there is only one sample. To put it more formally, we are investigating whether the mean of the distribution of differences in the appraised values is 0. The sample is made up of the *differences* between the appraised values determined by Schadek Appraisals and the values from Bowyer Real Estate. If the two appraisal firms are reporting similar estimates, then sometimes Schadek Appraisals will be the higher value and sometimes Bowyer Real Estate will have the higher value. However, the mean of the distribution of differences will be 0. On the other hand, if one of the firms consistently reports larger appraisal values, then the mean of the distribution of the differences will not be 0.

We will use the symbol μ_d to indicate the population mean of the distribution of differences. We assume the distribution of the population of differences is approximately normally distributed. The test statistic follows the *t*-distribution and we calculate its value from formula (11–8).

PAIRED *t*-TEST	$$t = \frac{\bar{d}}{s_d/\sqrt{n}}$$	**(11–80)**

There are $n - 1$ degrees of freedom and

$\bar{d}$ is the mean of the differences between the paired or related observations.
s_d is the standard deviation of the differences between the paired or related observations.
n is the number of paired observations.

The standard deviation of the differences is computed by the familiar formula for the standard deviation [see formula (3–10)], except d is substituted for *x*. The formula is:

$$s_d = \sqrt{\frac{\Sigma(d - \bar{d})^2}{n - 1}}$$

The following Example/Solution illustrates this test.

▶ **EXAMPLE**

Recall that Nickel Savings and Loan wishes to compare the two companies it uses to appraise the value of residential homes. Nickel Savings selected a sample of 10 residential properties and scheduled both firms for an appraisal. The results, reported in $000, are:

Home	Schadek	Bowyer
A	235	228
B	210	205
C	231	219
D	242	240
E	205	198
F	230	223
G	231	227
H	210	215
I	225	222
J	249	245

At the .05 significance level, can we conclude there is a difference between the firms' mean appraised home values?

SOLUTION

The first step is to state the null and the alternate hypotheses. In this case, a two-tailed alternative is appropriate because we are interested in determining whether there is a *difference* in the firms' appraised values. We are not interested in showing whether one particular firm appraises property at a higher value than the other. The question is whether the sample differences in the appraised values could have come from a population with a mean of 0. If the population mean of the differences is 0, then we conclude that there is no difference between the two firms' appraised values. The null and alternate hypotheses are:

$$H_0: \mu_d = 0$$
$$H_1: \mu_d \neq 0$$

There are 10 homes appraised by both firms, so $n = 10$, and $df = n - 1 = 10 - 1 = 9$. We have a two-tailed test, and the significance level is .05. To determine the critical value, go to Appendix B.5 and move across the row with 9 degrees of freedom to the column for a two-tailed test and the .05 significance level. The value at the intersection is 2.262. This value appears in Table 11–3. The decision rule is to reject the null hypothesis if the computed value of t is less than -2.262 or greater than 2.262. Here are the computational details.

Home	Schadek	Bowyer	Difference, d	$(d - \bar{d})$	$(d - \bar{d})^2$
A	235	228	7	2.4	5.76
B	210	205	5	0.4	0.16
C	231	219	12	7.4	54.76
D	242	240	2	−2.6	6.76
E	205	198	7	2.4	5.76
F	230	223	7	2.4	5.76
G	231	227	4	−0.6	0.36
H	210	215	−5	−9.6	92.16
I	225	222	3	−1.6	2.56
J	249	245	4	−0.6	0.36
			46	0	174.40

$$\bar{d} = \frac{\Sigma d}{n} = \frac{46}{10} = 4.60$$

$$s_d = \sqrt{\frac{\Sigma(d - \bar{d})^2}{n - 1}} = \sqrt{\frac{174.4}{10 - 1}} = 4.402$$

Using formula (11–8), the value of the test statistic is 3.305, found by

$$t = \frac{\bar{d}}{s_d/\sqrt{n}} = \frac{4.6}{4.402/\sqrt{10}} = \frac{4.6}{1.3920} = 3.305$$

Because the computed t falls in the rejection region, the null hypothesis is rejected. The population distribution of differences does not have a mean of 0. We conclude that there is a difference between the firms' mean appraised home values. The largest difference of $12,000 is for Home 3. Perhaps that would be an appropriate place to begin a more detailed review.

To estimate the p-value, we use Appendix B.5 and the section for a two-tailed test. Move along the row with 9 degrees of freedom and find the values of t that are closest to our calculated value. For a .01 significance level, the value of t is 3.250. The computed value is larger than this value, but smaller than the value of 4.781 corresponding to the .001 significance level. Hence, the p-value is between .01 and .001. This information is highlighted in Table 11–3.

TABLE 11–3 A Portion of the *t*-Distribution from Appendix B.5

	Confidence Intervals					*p*-value between 0.01 and 0.001
	80%	90%	95%	98%	99%	
	Level of Significance for One-Tailed Test					
df	0.10	0.05	0.025	0.01	0.005	
	Level of Significance for Two-Tailed Test					
	0.20	0.10	0.05	0.02	0.01	0.001
1	3.078	6.314	12.706	31.821	63.657	636.619
2	1.886	2.920	4.303	6.965	9.925	31.599
3	1.638	2.353	3.182	4.541	5.841	12.924
		2.132	2.776	3.747	4.604	8.610
		2.015	2.571	3.365	4.032	6.869
6	1.440	1.943	2.447	3.143	3.707	5.959
7	1.415	895	2.365	2.998	3.499	5.408
8	1.397	1.860	2.306	2.896	3.355	5.041
9	1.383	1.833	2.262	2.821	3.250	4.781
10	1.372	1.812	2.228	2.764	3.169	4.587

Critical *t*-statistic for 0.05

Tutorial #57
in Connect

Excel's statistical analysis software has a procedure called "*t*-Test: Paired Two-Sample for Means" to perform the calculations of formula (11–8). A link to a tutorial demonstrating the procedure is in the margin. The output from this procedure follows.

The computed value of *t* is 3.305, and the two-tailed *p*-value is .009. Because the *p*-value is less than .05, we reject the hypothesis that the mean of the distribution of the differences between the appraised values is zero.

	A	B	C	D	E	F	G
1	Home	Schadek	Bowyer		t-Test: Paired Two-Sample for Means		
2	A	235	228				
3	B	210	205			Schadek	Bowyer
4	C	231	219		Mean	226.800	222.200
5	D	242	240		Variance	208.844	204.178
6	E	205	198		Observations	10.000	10.000
7	F	230	223		Pearson Correlation	0.953	
8	G	231	227		Hypothesized Mean Difference	0.000	
9	H	210	215		df	9.000	
10	I	225	222		t Stat	3.305	
11	J	249	245		P(T<=t) one-tail	0.005	
12					t Critical one-tail	1.833	
13					P(T<=t) two-tail	0.009	
14					t Critical two-tail	2.262	
15							

Source: Microsoft Excel

LO11-5

Explain the difference between dependent and independent samples.

Comparing Dependent and Independent Samples

Sometimes there is confusion about whether a study is comparing means from two independent or two dependent samples. How do we tell the difference between the two? We focus on two situations involving dependent samples.

The first situation illustrating dependent samples is characterized by a sequence of events. First, a variable of interest is measured for sampled individuals. Then, the individuals experience a treatment. Finally, the same individuals are measured on the same variable and the difference for each individual is calculated. This could be called a "before" and "after" study. Suppose we want to know if placing speakers in an office area and playing soothing music increases productivity. We begin by randomly selecting a sample of employees and measuring their productivity under the current conditions. Then, speakers are installed in the office. After a period of time, we again measure the productivity of the same employees. Now, for each employee, there are two measurements, one before playing the music in the office area and another measurement after the treatment. The two samples of productivity measures are dependent because the productivity of the same employee was measured before and after the treatment, and a difference for the employee is calculated.

Another example of dependent samples is evaluating the effect of an SAT test preparation course. Suppose a school decides to offer such a course and would like to know if it increases SAT scores. To begin, each student takes the SAT in the junior year in high school. Between the junior and senior year, these students take the course and learn tips on taking the SAT. During the fall of their senior year, the same students retake the SAT. Now, the difference in the two SAT scores for each student can be compared. Therefore, the two sets of SAT scores are dependent samples. The effect of the course is determined by comparing the "before" and "after" SAT scores and calculating difference scores for each student.

The second situation illustrating dependent samples does not involve treatments or time. However, each individual in a sample is measured twice. The Example/Solution regarding Nickel Savings and Loan illustrates dependent samples. We wanted to know if different firms appraise a property the same. The samples are dependent because both firms appraise the same property and the difference in the appraisals for each property would be computed. Notice the samples are dependent because each difference refers to the same property. Another example is a study to know if the intelligence of newly married couples is similar. A random sample of newlywed couples is selected. Next, both partners take a standard intelligence test. Then, the difference in the scores for each couple would be computed. Notice the samples are dependent because each difference score refers to the same couple.

Why do we prefer dependent samples to independent samples? By using dependent samples, we are able to reduce the variation in the sampling distribution. To illustrate, we will use the Nickel Savings and Loan Example/Solution just completed. Suppose we mistakenly decide that the two samples are independent. So, we conduct a two-sample hypothesis test assuming equal variances. See formulas (11–4) and (11–5). The null and alternate hypotheses are:

$$H_0: \mu_1 = \mu_2$$
$$H_1: \mu_1 \neq \mu_2$$

Tutorial #54 in Connect

There are now two independent samples of 10 each. So the number of degrees of freedom is 10 + 10 − 2 = 18. From Appendix B.5, for the .05 significance level, H_0 is rejected if t is less than −2.101 or greater than 2.101.

We use statistical software to do the analysis. See the link in the margin that demonstrates the test of hypothesis comparing the means of two independent samples, variances assumed equal. The results of the analysis follow.

	A	B	C	D	E	F	G	H
1	Home	Schadek	Bowyer		t-Test: Two-Sample Assuming Equal Variances			
2	A	235	228					
3	B	210	205			Schadek	Bowyer	
4	C	231	219		Mean	226.800	222.200	
5	D	242	240		Variance	208.844	204.178	
6	E	205	198		Observations	10.000	10.000	
7	F	230	223		Pooled Variance	206.511		
8	G	231	227		Hypothesized Mean Difference	0.000		
9	H	210	215		df	18.000		
10	I	225	222		t Stat	0.716		
11	J	249	245		P(T<=t) one-tail	0.242		
12					t Critical one-tail	1.734		
13	Mean =	226.80	222.20		P(T<=t) two-tail	0.483		
14	S =	14.45	14.29		t Critical two-tail	2.101		
15								

Source: Microsoft Excel

The mean of the appraised value of the 10 properties by Schadek is $226,800, and the standard deviation is $14,500. For Bowyer Real Estate, the mean appraised value is $222,200, and the standard deviation is $14,290. To make the calculations easier, we use $000 instead of $. The value of the pooled estimate of the variance from formula (11–4) is

$$s_p^2 = \frac{(n_1 - 1)s_1^2 + (n_2 - 1)s_2^2}{n_1 + n_2 - 2} = \frac{(10 - 1)(14.45^2) + (10 - 1)(14.29)^2}{10 + 10 - 2} = 206.50$$

From formula (11–5), t is 0.716.

$$t = \frac{\bar{x}_1 - \bar{x}_2}{\sqrt{s_p^2\left(\frac{1}{n_1} + \frac{1}{n_2}\right)}} = \frac{226.8 - 222.2}{\sqrt{206.50\left(\frac{1}{10} + \frac{1}{10}\right)}} = \frac{4.6}{6.4265} = 0.716$$

The computed t (0.716) is less than 2.101; the p-value is .483. So, the null hypothesis is not rejected. We cannot show that there is a difference in the mean appraisal value. That is not the same conclusion that we got before!

Why does this happen? The numerator is the same in the paired observations test (4.6). However, the denominator is smaller. In the paired test, the denominator is 1.3920 (see the calculations on page 390 in the previous section). In the case of the independent samples, the denominator is 6.4265. There is more variation or uncertainty. This accounts for the difference in the t-values and the difference in the statistical decisions. The denominator measures the standard error of the statistic. When the samples are *not* paired, two kinds of variation are present: differences between the two appraisal firms and the difference in the value of the real estate. Properties numbered 4 and 10 have relatively high values, whereas number 5 is relatively low. These data show how different the values of the property are, but we are really interested in the difference between the two appraisal firms.

So, when we can pair or match observations that measure differences for a common variable, a hypothesis test based on dependent samples is more sensitive to detecting a significant difference than a hypothesis test based on independent samples. In the case of comparing the property valuations by Schadek Appraisals and Bowyer Real Estate, the hypothesis test based on dependent samples eliminates the variation between the values of the properties and focuses only on the differences in the two appraisals for each property. There is a bit of bad news here. In the dependent samples test, the degrees of freedom are half of what they are if the samples are not paired. For the real estate example, the degrees of freedom drop from 18 to 9 when the observations are paired. However, in most cases, this is a small price to pay for a better test.

SELF-REVIEW 11–5

Advertisements by Core Fitness Center claim that completing its course will result in losing weight. A random sample of eight recent participants showed the following weights before and after completing the course. At the .01 significance level, can we conclude the students lost weight?

Name	Before	After
Hunter	155	154
Cashman	228	207
Mervine	141	147
Massa	162	157
Creola	211	196
Peterson	164	150
Redding	184	170
Poust	172	165

(a) State the null hypothesis and the alternate hypothesis.
(b) What is the critical value of *t?*
(c) What is the computed value of *t?*
(d) What is the *p*-value?
(e) Interpret the result.
(f) What assumption needs to be made about the distribution of the differences?

EXERCISES

23. The null and alternate hypotheses are:

$$H_0: \mu_d \leq 0$$
$$H_1: \mu_d > 0$$

The following sample information shows the number of defective units produced on the day shift and the afternoon shift for a sample of 4 days last month.

	Day			
	1	2	3	4
Day shift	10	12	15	19
Afternoon shift	8	9	12	15

a. What is the *p*-value?
b. Is the null hypothesis rejected?
c. What is the conclusion indicated by the analysis?

24. The null and alternate hypotheses are:

$$H_0: \mu_d = 0$$
$$H_1: \mu_d \neq 0$$

The following paired observations show the number of traffic citations given for speeding by Officer Dhondt and Officer Meredith of the South Carolina Highway Patrol for the last 5 months.

	Number of Citations Issued				
	May	June	July	August	September
Officer Dhondt	30	22	25	19	26
Officer Meredith	26	19	20	15	19

At the .05 significance level, is there a difference in the mean number of citations given by the two officers?
a. What is the *p*-value?
b. Is the null hypothesis rejected?
c. What is the conclusion indicated by the analysis?

Note: Use the six-step hypothesis testing procedure to solve the following exercises.

25. **FILE** The management of Discount Furniture, a chain of discount furniture stores in the Northeast, designed an incentive plan for salespeople. To evaluate this innovative plan, 12 salespeople were selected at random, and their weekly incomes before and after the plan were recorded.

Salesperson	Before	After
Sid Mahone	$320	$340
Carol Quick	290	285
Tom Jackson	421	475
Andy Jones	510	510
Jean Sloan	210	210
Jack Walker	402	500
Peg Mancuso	625	631
Anita Loma	560	560
John Cuso	360	365
Carl Utz	431	431
A. S. Kushner	506	525
Fern Lawton	505	619

Was there a significant increase in the typical salesperson's weekly income due to the innovative incentive plan? Use the .05 significance level.
a. State the null and alternate hypotheses.
b. What is the p-value?
c. Is the null hypothesis rejected?
d. What is the conclusion indicated by the analysis?

26. **FILE** The federal government recently granted funds for a special program designed to reduce crime in high-crime areas. A study of the results of the program in eight high-crime areas of Miami, Florida, yielded the following results.

	Number of Crimes by Area							
	A	B	C	D	E	F	G	H
Before	14	7	4	5	17	12	8	9
After	2	7	3	6	8	13	3	5

Has there been a decrease in the number of crimes since the inauguration of the program? Use the .01 significance level.
a. State the null and alternate hypotheses.
b. What is the p-value?
c. Is the null hypothesis rejected?
d. What is the conclusion indicated by the analysis?

LO11-6

Test a hypothesis about two population proportions.

Two-Sample Tests about Proportions

In the previous section, we considered a test of a single population proportion. However, we are often interested also in whether two sample proportions come from populations that are equal. Here are several examples.

- The vice president of human resources wishes to know whether there is a difference in the proportion of hourly employees who miss more than 5 days of work per year at the Atlanta and the Houston plants.
- General Motors is considering a new design for the Chevy Malibu. The design is shown to a group of millennials and another group of baby-boomers. General Motors wishes to know whether there is a difference in the proportion of the two groups who like the new design.
- A consultant to the airline industry is investigating the fear of flying among adults. Specifically, the consultant wishes to know whether there is a difference in the proportion of men versus women who are fearful of flying.

In these cases, each sampled item or individual can be classified as a "success" or a "failure." That is, in the Chevy Malibu example, each potential buyer is classified as "liking the new design" or "not liking the new design." We then compare the proportion in the millennial group with the proportion in the baby-boomer group who indicated they liked the new design. Can we conclude that the differences are due to chance? In this study, there is no measurement obtained, only classifying the individuals or objects.

To conduct the test, we assume each sample is large enough that the normal distribution will serve as a good approximation of the binomial distribution. The test statistic follows the standard normal distribution. We compute the value of z from formula (11–9).

TWO-SAMPLE TEST OF PROPORTIONS

$$z = \frac{p_1 - p_2}{\sqrt{\dfrac{p_c(1 - p_c)}{n_1} + \dfrac{p_c(1 - p_c)}{n_2}}}$$

(11–9)

where:

n_1 is the number of observations in the first sample.
n_2 is the number of observations in the second sample.
p_1 is the proportion in the first sample possessing the trait.
p_2 is the proportion in the second sample possessing the trait.
p_c is the pooled proportion possessing the trait in the combined samples. It is called the pooled estimate of the population proportion and is computed from formula (11–10).

POOLED PROPORTION

$$p_c = \frac{x_1 + x_2}{n_1 + n_2}$$

(11–10)

where:

x_1 is the number possessing the trait in the first sample.
x_2 is the number possessing the trait in the second sample.

The following Example/Solution will illustrate the two-sample test of proportions.

▶ **EXAMPLE**

A business researcher is studying online shopping and would like to know if there is a difference in the proportion of men and women who made an online purchase last year. The researcher sampled 100 women and 200 men. The results of the sample follow:

Purchase Decision	Sex	
	Women	Men
Made a purchase	81	138
Did not make a purchase	19	62
Total	100	200

At the .05 significance level, is there a difference in the proportion of men and women who made an online purchase?

SOLUTION

We will use the usual six-step hypothesis testing procedure.

Step 1: **State H_0 and H_1.** In this case, we designate π_w as the proportion of women who made an online purchase and π_m as the proportion of men who made an online purchase. The null hypothesis is: "There is no difference in the proportions of women and men who made online purchases." The alternate hypothesis is: "The two proportions are not equal." They are written as follows:

$$H_0: \pi_w = \pi_m$$
$$H_1: \pi_w \neq \pi_m$$

Step 2: **Select the level of significance.** In this example, we decide to use a .05 significance level.

Step 3: **Identify the test statistic.** The two samples are sufficiently large, so we use the standard normal distribution as the test statistic. The z-score is computed using formula (11–9).

Step 4: **Formulate the decision rule.** Recall that the alternate hypothesis from step 1 does not indicate a direction, so this is a two-tailed test. To find the critical z-value, go to Student's t-distribution (Appendix B.5). In the table headings, find the row labeled "Level of Significance for Two-Tailed Test" and select the column for a significance level of .05. Go to the bottom row with infinite degrees of freedom. The z-critical value is 1.960, so the critical values are -1.960 and 1.960. As before, if the computed test statistic is less than -1.960 or greater than 1.960, the null hypothesis is rejected. This information is summarized in Chart 11–3.

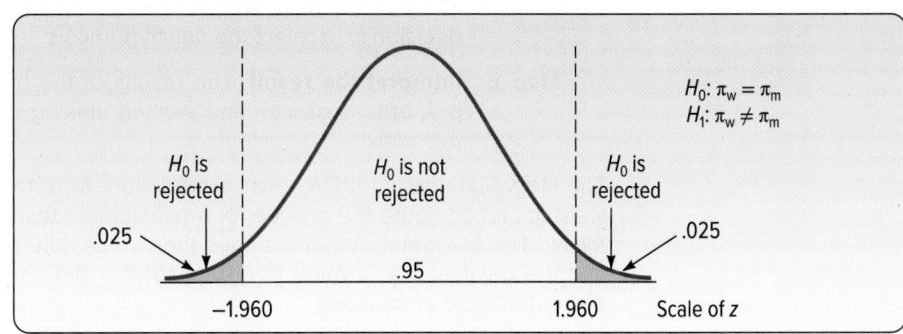

CHART 11–3 Decision Rules for Online Purchasing Test, .05 Significance Level

Step 5: **Select a sample and make a decision.** A random sample of 100 women revealed 81 made an online purchase in the last year. Similarly, a sample of 200 men revealed 138 made an online purchase in the last year. Let p_w refer to the proportion of women who made online purchases and p_m refer to the proportion of men who made online purchases.

$$p_w = \frac{x_w}{n_w} = \frac{81}{100} = .81$$

$$p_m = \frac{x_m}{n_m} = \frac{138}{200} = .69$$

The statistical question is whether the difference in the two sample proportions, .12, found by $p_w - p_m = .81 - .69 = .12$, is large enough to reject the null hypothesis.

Next, we combine or pool the sample proportions, using formula (11–10).

$$p_c = \frac{x_w + x_m}{n_w + n_m} = \frac{81 + 38}{100 + 200} = \frac{219}{300} = .73$$

Note that the pooled proportion, .73, is closer to .69 than to .81. Why? There are more men in the survey than women.

We use formula (11–9) to find the value of the test statistic.

$$z = \frac{p_w - p_m}{\sqrt{\dfrac{p_c(1 - p_c)}{n_1} + \dfrac{p_c(1 - p_c)}{n_2}}} = \frac{.81 - .69}{\sqrt{\dfrac{.73(1 - .73)}{100} + \dfrac{.73(1 - .73)}{200}}} = 2.207$$

Referring to Chart 11–3, the computed test statistic, 2.207, is in the rejection region to the right of 1.960. Therefore, the null hypothesis is rejected at the .05 significance level. We conclude that the proportion of men who made a purchase online last year is not the same as the proportion of women.

To locate the p-value in the standard normal distribution table, Appendix B.3, we need to round the z-test statistic from −2.207 to −2.21. In the table, find the probability of a z-value less than −2.21 or greater than 2.21. The probability corresponding to 2.21 is .4864, so the likelihood of finding the value of the test statistic to be less than −2.21 or greater than 2.21 is:

$$p\text{-value} = 2(.5000 - .4864) = 2(.0136) = .0272$$

The p-value of .0272 is less than the significance level of .05, so our decision is to reject the null hypothesis.

Step 6: Interpret the result. The results of the hypothesis test indicate the proportions of men and women making an online purchase are not the same.

The MegaStat add-in for Excel has a procedure to determine the value of the test statistic and compute the p-value for a two-sample test of proportions. The results follow. The MegaStat output includes the two sample proportions, the value of z, and the p-value. The p-value from MegaStat is different from the one calculated earlier because of rounding.

Hypothesis test for two independent proportions

p1	p2	p_c	
.81	.69	.73	p (as decimal)
81/100	138/200	219/300	p (as fraction)
81	138	219	X
100	200	300	n
	0.12		difference
		0.	hypothesized difference
	0.0544		std. error
	2.21		z
	.0273		p-value (two-tailed)

SELF-REVIEW 11–6

Of 150 adults who tried a new peach-flavored Peppermint Pattie, 87 rated it excellent. Of 200 children sampled, 123 rated it excellent. Using the .10 level of significance, can we conclude that there is a significant difference in the proportion of adults and the proportion of children who rate the new flavor excellent?

(a)   State the null hypothesis and the alternate hypothesis.
(b)   What is the probability of a Type I error?
(c)   Is this a one-tailed or a two-tailed test?
(d)   What is the decision rule?
(e)   What is the value of the test statistic?
(f)   What is your decision regarding the null hypothesis?
(g)   What is the p-value? Explain what it means in terms of this problem.

EXERCISES

27. The null and alternate hypotheses are:

$$H_0: \pi_1 \leq \pi_2$$
$$H_1: \pi_1 > \pi_2$$

A sample of 100 observations from the first population indicated that x_1 is 70. A sample of 150 observations from the second population revealed x_2 to be 90. Use the .05 significance level to test the hypothesis.
  a. State the decision rule.
  b. Compute the pooled proportion.
  c. Compute the value of the test statistic.
  d. What is your decision regarding the null hypothesis?

28. The null and alternate hypotheses are:

$$H_0: \pi_1 = \pi_2$$
$$H_1: \pi_1 \neq \pi_2$$

A sample of 200 observations from the first population indicated that x_1 is 170. A sample of 150 observations from the second population revealed x_2 to be 110. Use the .05 significance level to test the hypothesis.
  a. State the decision rule.
  b. Compute the pooled proportion.
  c. Compute the value of the test statistic.
  d. What is your decision regarding the null hypothesis?

Note: Use the six-step hypothesis testing procedure in solving the following exercises.

29. The Damon family owns a large grape vineyard in western New York along Lake Erie. The grapevines must be sprayed at the beginning of the growing season to protect against various insects and diseases. Two new insecticides have just been marketed: Pernod 5 and Action. To test their effectiveness, three long rows were selected and sprayed with Pernod 5, and three others were sprayed with Action. When the grapes ripened, 400 of the vines treated with Pernod 5 were checked for infestation. Likewise, a sample of 400 vines sprayed with Action were checked. The results are:

Insecticide	Number of Vines Checked (sample size)	Number of Infested Vines
Pernod 5	400	24
Action	400	40

At the .05 significance level, can we conclude that there is a difference in the proportion of vines infested using Pernod 5 as opposed to Action?

30. GfK Research North America conducted identical surveys 5 years apart. One question asked of women was "Are most men basically kind, gentle, and thoughtful?" The earlier survey revealed that, of the 3,000 women surveyed, 2,010 said that they were. The later revealed 1,530 of the 3,000 women surveyed thought that men were kind, gentle, and thoughtful. At the .05 level, can we conclude that women think men are less kind, gentle, and thoughtful in the later survey compared with the earlier one?

31. A nationwide sample of influential Republicans and Democrats was asked as a part of a comprehensive survey whether they favored lowering environmental standards so that high-sulfur coal could be burned in coal-fired power plants. The results were:

	Republicans	Democrats
Number sampled	1,000	800
Number in favor	200	168

At the .02 level of significance, can we conclude that there is a larger proportion of Democrats in favor of lowering the standards? Determine the p-value.

32. The research department at the home office of New Hampshire Insurance conducts ongoing research on the causes of automobile accidents, the characteristics of the drivers, and so on. A random sample of 400 policies written on single persons revealed 120 had at least one accident in the previous 3-year period. Similarly, a sample of 600 policies written on married persons revealed that 150 had been in at least one accident. At the .05 significance level, is there a significant difference in the proportions of single and married persons having an accident during a 3-year period? Determine the p-value.

CHAPTER SUMMARY

I. The characteristics of the F-distribution are as follows:
   A. It is continuous.
   B. Its values cannot be negative.
   C. It is positively skewed.
   D. There is a family of F-distributions. Each time the degrees of freedom in either the numerator or the denominator change, a new distribution is created.

II. The F-distribution is used to test whether two population variances are the same.
   A. The sampled populations must follow the normal distribution.
   B. The larger of the two sample variances is placed in the numerator, forcing the ratio to be at least 1.00.
   C. The value of F is computed using the following equation:

$$F = \frac{s_1^2}{s_2^2} \tag{11–1}$$

III. In comparing two population means, we wish to know whether they could be equal.
   A. We are investigating whether the distribution of the difference between the means could have a mean of 0.
   B. The test statistic follows the standard normal distribution if the population standard deviations are known.
      1. The two populations follow normal distributions.
      2. The samples are from independent populations.

3. The formula to compute the value of z is

$$z = \frac{\bar{x}_1 - \bar{x}_2}{\sqrt{\dfrac{\sigma_1^2}{n_1} + \dfrac{\sigma_2^2}{n_2}}} \qquad (11\text{–}3)$$

IV. The test statistic to compare two means is the t-distribution if the population standard deviations are not known.
  A. Both populations are approximately normally distributed.
  B. The populations must have equal standard deviations.
  C. The samples are independent.
  D. Finding the value of t requires two steps.
  1. The first step is to pool the standard deviations according to the following formula.

$$s_p^2 = \frac{(n_1 - 1)s_1^2 + (n_2 - 1)s_2^2}{n_1 + n_2 - 2} \qquad (11\text{–}4)$$

  2. The value of t is computed from the following formula.

$$t = \frac{\bar{x}_1 - \bar{x}_2}{\sqrt{s_p^2 \left(\dfrac{1}{n_1} + \dfrac{1}{n_2} \right)}} \qquad (11\text{–}5)$$

  3. The degrees of freedom for the test are $n_1 + n_2 - 2$.
V. If we cannot assume the population standard deviations are equal, we adjust the degrees of freedom and the formula for finding t.
  A. We determine the degrees of freedom based on the following formula.

$$df = \frac{[(s_1^2/n_1) + (s_2^2/n_2)]^2}{\dfrac{(s_1^2/n_1)^2}{n_1 - 1} + \dfrac{(s_2^2/n_2)^2}{n_2 - 1}} \qquad (11\text{–}7)$$

  B. The value of the test statistic is computed from the following formula.

$$t = \frac{\bar{x}_1 - \bar{x}_2}{\sqrt{\dfrac{s_1^2}{n_1} + \dfrac{s_2^2}{n_2}}} \qquad (11\text{–}6)$$

VI. For dependent samples, we assume the population distribution of the paired differences has a mean of 0.
  A. We first compute the mean and the standard deviation of the sample differences.
  B. The value of the test statistic is computed from the following formula.

$$t = \frac{\bar{d}}{s_d/\sqrt{n}} \qquad (11\text{–}8)$$

VII. We can also test whether two samples came from populations with an equal proportion of successes.
  A. The two sample proportions are pooled using the following formula.

$$p_c = \frac{x_1 + x_2}{n_1 + n_2} \qquad (11\text{–}10)$$

  B. We compute the value of the test statistic from the following formula.

$$z = \frac{p_1 - p_2}{\sqrt{\dfrac{p_c(1 - p_c)}{n_1} + \dfrac{p_c(1 - p_c)}{n_2}}} \qquad (11\text{–}9)$$

PRONUNCIATION KEY

SYMBOL	MEANING	PRONUNCIATION
s_p^2	Pooled sample variance	s squared sub p
$\bar{x}_1$	Mean of the first sample	x bar sub 1
$\bar{x}_2$	Mean of the second sample	x bar sub 2
$\bar{d}$	Mean of the difference between dependent observations	d bar
s_d	Standard deviation of the difference between dependent observations	s sub d

CHAPTER EXERCISES

33. A real estate agent in the coastal area of Georgia wants to compare the variation in the selling price of homes on the oceanfront with those one to three blocks from the ocean. A sample of 21 oceanfront homes sold within the last year revealed the standard deviation of the selling prices was $45,600. A sample of 18 homes, also sold within the last year, that were one to three blocks from the ocean revealed that the standard deviation was $21,330. At the .01 significance level, can we conclude that there is more variation in the selling prices of the oceanfront homes?

34. One variable that Google uses to rank pages on the Internet is page speed, the time it takes for a Web page to load into your browser. A source for women's clothing is redesigning their page to improve the images that show its products and to reduce its load time. The new page is clearly faster, but initial tests indicate there is more variation in the time to load. A sample of 16 different load times showed that the standard deviation of the load time was 22 hundredths of a second for the new page and 12 hundredths of a second for the current page. At the .05 significance level, can we conclude that there is more variation in the load time of the new page?

35. A recent study focused on the number of times men and women who live alone buy take-out dinner in a month. Assume that the distributions follow the normal probability distribution and the population standard deviations are equal. The information is summarized in the following table.

Statistic	Men	Women
Sample mean	24.51	22.69
Population standard deviation	4.48	3.86
Sample size	35	40

At the .01 significance level, is there a difference in the mean number of times men and women order take-out dinners in a month?
  a. State the null and alternate hypotheses.
  b. Compute the test statistic.
  c. Compute the *p*-value.
  d. What is your decision regarding the null hypothesis?
  e. Interpret the result.

36. Clark Heter is an industrial engineer at Lyons Products. He would like to determine whether there are more units produced on the night shift than on the day shift. The mean number of units produced by a sample of 54 day-shift workers was 345. The mean number of units produced by a sample of 60 night-shift workers was 351. Assume the population standard deviation of the number of units produced on the day shift is 21 and 28 on the night shift. Using the .05 significance level, is the number of units produced on the night shift larger?

a. State the null and alternate hypotheses.
b. Compute the test statistic.
c. Compute the *p*-value.
d. What is your decision regarding the null hypothesis?
e. Interpret the result.

37. Fry Brothers Heating and Air Conditioning Inc. employs Gael Clark and Leslie Murnen to make service calls to repair furnaces and air-conditioning units in homes. Tom Fry, the owner, would like to know whether there is a difference in the mean number of service calls they make per day. A random sample of 40 days last year showed that Gael Clark made an average of 4.77 calls per day. For a sample of 50 days Leslie Murnen made an average of 5.02 calls per day. Assume the population standard deviation for Gael Clark is 1.05 calls per day and 1.23 calls per day for Leslie Murnen. At the .05 significance level, is there a difference in the mean number of calls per day between the two employees?
a. State the null and alternate hypotheses.
b. Compute the test statistic.
c. Compute the *p*-value.
d. What is your decision regarding the null hypothesis?
e. Interpret the result.

38. A coffee manufacturer is interested in whether the mean daily consumption of regular-coffee drinkers is less than that of decaffeinated-coffee drinkers. Assume the population standard deviation for those drinking regular coffee is 1.20 cups per day and 1.36 cups per day for those drinking decaffeinated coffee. A random sample of 50 regular-coffee drinkers showed a mean of 4.35 cups per day. A sample of 40 decaffeinated-coffee drinkers showed a mean of 5.84 cups per day. Use the .01 significance level.
a. State the null and alternate hypotheses.
b. Compute the test statistic.
c. Compute the *p*-value.
d. What is your decision regarding the null hypothesis?
e. Interpret the result.

39. A cell phone company offers two plans to its subscribers. At the time new subscribers sign up, they are asked to provide some demographic information. The mean yearly income for a sample of 31 subscribers to Plan A is $57,000 with a standard deviation of $9,200. For a sample of 26 subscribers to Plan B, the mean income is $61,000 with a standard deviation of $6,500. At the .05 significance level, is it reasonable to conclude the mean income of those selecting Plan B is larger?
a. Test the assumption that the population variances are equal using a .10 significance level.
b. What are the null and alternate hypotheses?
c. Compute the test statistic.
d. Compute the *p*-value.
e. What is your decision regarding the null hypothesis?
f. Interpret the result.

40. A computer manufacturer offers technical support that is available 24 hours a day, 7 days a week. Timely resolution of these calls is important to the company's image. For 16 calls that were related to software, technicians resolved the issues in a mean time of 18 minutes with a standard deviation of 4.2 minutes. For 26 calls related to hardware, technicians resolved the problems in a mean time of 15.5 minutes with a standard deviation of 3.9 minutes. At the .05 significance level, does it take longer to resolve software issues?
a. Test the assumption that the population variances are equal using a .10 significance level.
b. What are the null and alternate hypotheses?
c. Compute the test statistic.
d. Compute the *p*-value.
e. What is your decision regarding the null hypothesis?
f. Interpret the result.

41. Music streaming services are the most popular way to listen to music. Data gathered over the last 12 months show Apple Music was used by an average of 1.65 million households with a sample standard deviation of 0.56 million family units. Over the same 12 months Spotify was used by an average of 2.2 million families with a sample standard deviation of 0.30 million. Assume the population standard deviations are not the same. Using a significance level of .05, test the hypothesis of no difference in the mean number of households picking either service.
   a. Test the assumption that the population variances are equal using a .10 significance level.
   b. What are the null and alternate hypotheses?
   c. Compute the test statistic.
   d. Compute the *p*-value.
   e. What is your decision regarding the null hypothesis?
   f. Interpret the result.

42. Businesses such as General Mills, Kellogg's, and Betty Crocker regularly use coupons to build brand allegiance and stimulate sales. Marketers believe that the users of paper coupons are different from the users of e-coupons accessed through the Internet. One survey recorded the age of each person who redeemed a coupon along with the type of coupon (either paper or electronic). The sample of 25 traditional paper-coupon clippers had a mean age of 39.5 with a standard deviation of 4.8. The sample of 31 e-coupon users had a mean age of 33.6 years with a standard deviation of 10.9. Assume the population standard deviations are not the same. Using a significance level of .01, test the hypothesis of no difference in the mean ages of the two groups of coupon clients.
   a. Test the assumption that the population variances are equal using a .10 significance level.
   b. What are the null and alternate hypotheses?
   c. Compute the test statistic.
   d. Compute the *p*-value.
   e. What is your decision regarding the null hypothesis?
   f. Interpret the result.

43. The owner of Bun 'N' Run Hamburgers wishes to compare the sales per day at two locations. The mean number sold for 10 randomly selected days at the Northside site was 83.55, and the standard deviation was 10.50. For a random sample of 12 days at the Southside location, the mean number sold was 78.80 and the standard deviation was 14.25. At the .05 significance level, is there a difference in the mean number of hamburgers sold at the two locations?
   a. Test the assumption that the population variances are equal using a .10 significance level.
   b. What are the null and alternate hypotheses?
   c. Compute the test statistic.
   d. Compute the *p*-value.
   e. What is your decision regarding the null hypothesis?
   f. Interpret the result.

44. **FILE** Educational Technology Inc. sells software to provide guided homework problems for a statistics course. The company would like to know if students who use the software score better on exams. A sample of students who used the software had the following exam scores: 86, 78, 66, 83, 84, 81, 84, 109, 65, and 102. Students who did not use the software had the following exam scores: 91, 71, 75, 76, 87, 79, 73, 76, 79, 78, 87, 90, 76, and 72. At the .10 significance level, can we conclude that there is a difference in the mean exam scores for the two groups of students?
   a. Test the assumption that the population variances are equal using a .10 significance level.
   b. What are the null and alternate hypotheses?
   c. Compute the test statistic.
   d. Compute the *p*-value.
   e. What is your decision regarding the null hypothesis?
   f. Interpret the result.

45. **FILE** The Willow Run Outlet Mall has two Haggar Outlet Stores, one located on Peach Street and the other on Plum Street. The two stores are laid out differently, but both store managers claim their layout maximizes the amounts customers will purchase on impulse. A sample of 10 customers at the Peach Street store revealed they spent the following amounts on impulse purchases: $17.58, $19.73, $12.61, $17.79, $16.22, $15.82, $15.40, $15.86, $11.82, and $15.85. A sample of 14 customers at the Plum Street store revealed they spent the following amounts on impulse purchases: $18.19, $20.22, $17.38, $17.96, $23.92, $15.87, $16.47, $15.96, $16.79, $16.74, $21.40, $20.57, and $19.79. At the .01 significance level, is there a difference in the mean amounts purchased on impulse at the two stores?
  a. Test the assumption that the population variances are equal using a .10 significance level.
  b. What are the null and alternate hypotheses?
  c. Compute the test statistic.
  d. Compute the *p*-value.
  e. What is your decision regarding the null hypothesis?
  f. Interpret the result.

46. **FILE** Grand Strand Family Medical Centers treat minor medical emergencies for visitors to the Myrtle Beach area. There are two facilities, one in the Little River Area and the other in Murrells Inlet. The Quality Assurance Department wishes to compare the mean waiting time for patients at the two locations. Samples of the waiting times for each location, reported in minutes, follow:

Location				Waiting Time							
Little River	31	28	29	22	29	18	32	25	29	26	
Murrells Inlet	22	23	26	27	26	25	30	29	23	23	27	25

At the .05 significance level, is there a difference in the mean waiting time?
  a. Test the assumption that the population variances are equal using a .10 significance level.
  b. What are the null and alternate hypotheses?
  c. Compute the test statistic.
  d. Compute the *p*-value.
  e. What is your decision regarding the null hypothesis?
  f. Interpret the result.

47. **FILE** Commercial Bank and Trust Company is studying the use of its automatic teller machines (ATMs). Of particular interest is whether young adults (under 25 years) use the machines more than senior citizens. To investigate further, samples of customers under 25 years of age and customers over 60 years of age were selected. The number of ATM transactions last month was determined for each selected individual, and the results are shown in the table. At the .01 significance level, can bank management conclude that younger customers use the ATMs more?

Under 25	10	10	11	15	7	11	10	9		
Over 60	4	8	7	7	4	5	1	7	4	10	5

  a. Test the assumption that the population variances are equal using a .10 significance level.
  b. What are the null and alternate hypotheses?
  c. Compute the test statistic.
  d. Compute the *p*-value.
  e. What is your decision regarding the null hypothesis?
  f. Interpret the result.

48. **FILE** Two of the teams competing in the *America's Cup* race are American Magic and Australia II. They race their boats over a part of the course several times. Following are a sample of times in minutes for each boat. Assume the population standard deviations are not the same. At the .05 significance level, can we conclude that there is a difference in their mean times?

Boat	Time (minutes)										
Australia II	12.9	12.5	11.0	13.3	11.2	11.4	11.6	12.3	14.2	11.3	
American Magic	14.1	14.1	14.2	17.4	15.8	16.7	16.1	13.3	13.4	13.6	10.8	19.0

    a. Test the assumption that the population variances are equal using a .10 significance level.
    b. What are the null and alternate hypotheses?
    c. Compute the test statistic.
    d. Compute the p-value.
    e. What is your decision regarding the null hypothesis?
    f. Interpret the result.

49. **FILE** The manufacturer of an bluetooth speaker wanted to know whether a 10% reduction in price is enough to increase the sales of its product. To investigate, the owner randomly selected eight outlets and sold the bluetooth speaker at the reduced price. At seven randomly selected outlets, the bluetooth speaker was sold at the regular price. Reported in the table is the number of units sold last month at the regular and reduced prices at the randomly selected outlets. At the .01 significance level, can the manufacturer conclude that the price reduction resulted in an increase in sales?

Regular price	138	121	88	115	141	125	96	
Reduced price	128	134	152	135	114	106	112	120

    a. Test the assumption that the population variances are equal using a .10 significance level.
    b. What are the null and alternate hypotheses?
    c. Compute the test statistic.
    d. Compute the p-value.
    e. What is your decision regarding the null hypothesis?
    f. Interpret the result.

50. **FILE** A number of minor automobile accidents occur at various high-risk intersections in Teton County despite traffic lights. The Traffic Department claims that a modification in the type of light will reduce these accidents. The county commissioners have agreed to a proposed experiment. Eight intersections were chosen at random, and the lights at those intersections were modified. The numbers of minor accidents during a 6-month period before and after the modifications were:

	Number of Accidents							
	A	**B**	**C**	**D**	**E**	**F**	**G**	**H**
Before modification	5	7	6	4	8	9	8	10
After modification	3	7	7	0	4	6	8	2

At the .01 significance level, is it reasonable to conclude that the modification reduced the number of traffic accidents?
    a. What are the null and alternate hypotheses?
    b. Compute the test statistic.
    c. Compute the p-value.
    d. What is your decision regarding the null hypothesis?
    e. Interpret the result.

51. **FILE** Lester Hollar is vice president for human resources for a large manufacturing company. In recent years, he has noticed an increase in absenteeism that he thinks is related to the general health of the employees. Four years ago, in an attempt to improve the situation, he began a fitness program in which employees exercise during their lunch hour. To evaluate the program, he selected a random sample of eight participants and found the number of days each was absent in the 6 months before the exercise program began and in the 6 months following the exercise program. Following are the results. At the .05 significance level, can he conclude that the number of absences has declined?

Employee	Before	After
Bauman	6	5
Briggs	6	2
Dottellis	7	1
Lee	7	3
Perralt	4	3
Rielly	3	6
Steinmetz	5	3
Stoltz	6	7

a. What are the null and alternate hypotheses?
b. Compute the test statistic.
c. Compute the p-value.
d. What is your decision regarding the null hypothesis?
e. Interpret the result.

52. **FILE** The president of the American Insurance Institute wants to compare the yearly costs of auto insurance offered by two leading companies. He selects a sample of 15 families, some with only a single insured driver, others with several teenage drivers, and pays each family a stipend to contact the two companies and ask for a price quote. To make the data comparable, certain features, such as the deductible amount and limits of liability, are standardized. The data for the sample of families and their two insurance quotes are reported in the table. At the .10 significance level, can we conclude that there is a difference in the amounts quoted?

Family	Midstates Car Insurance	Gecko Mutual Insurance
Becker	$2,090	$1,610
Berry	1,683	1,247
Cobb	1,402	2,327
Debuck	1,830	1,367
DuBrul	930	1,461
Eckroate	697	1,789
German	1,741	1,621
Glasson	1,129	1,914
King	1,018	1,956
Kucic	1,881	1,772
Meredith	1,571	1,375
Obeid	874	1,527
Price	1,579	1,767
Phillips	1,577	1,636
Tresize	860	1,188

a. What are the null and alternate hypotheses?
b. Compute the test statistic.
c. Compute the p-value.
d. What is your decision regarding the null hypothesis?
e. Interpret the result.

53. Fairfield Homes is developing two parcels near Pigeon Fork, Tennessee. To test different advertising approaches, Fairfield uses different media to reach potential buyers. The mean annual family income for 12 people making inquiries at the first development is $150,000, with a standard deviation of $40,000. A corresponding sample of 25 people at the second development had a mean of $180,000, with a standard deviation of $30,000. Assume the population standard deviations are the same. At the .05 significance level, can Fairfield conclude that the population means are different?
  a. Test the assumption that the population variances are equal using a .10 significance level.
  b. What are the null and alternate hypotheses?
  c. Compute the test statistic.
  d. Compute the p-value.
  e. What is your decision regarding the null hypothesis?
  f. Interpret the result.

54. A candy company taste-tested two chocolate bars, one with almonds and one without almonds. A panel of testers rated the bars on a scale of 0 to 5, with 5 indicating the highest taste rating. A hypothesis test fails to reject the equality of the variances. At the .05 significance level, do the ratings show a difference between chocolate bars with or without almonds?

With Almonds	Without Almonds
3	0
1	4
2	4
3	3
1	4
1	
2	

  a. What are the null and alternate hypotheses?
  b. Compute the test statistic.
  c. Compute the p-value.
  d. What is your decision regarding the null hypothesis?
  e. Interpret the result.

55. **FILE** An investigation of the effectiveness of an antibacterial soap in reducing operating room contamination resulted in the accompanying table. The new soap was tested in a sample of eight operating rooms in the greater Seattle area during the last year. The following table reports the contamination levels before and after the use of the soap for each operating room.

	Operating Room							
	A	**B**	**C**	**D**	**E**	**F**	**G**	**H**
Before	6.6	6.5	9.0	10.3	11.2	8.1	6.3	11.6
After	6.8	2.4	7.4	8.5	8.1	6.1	3.4	2.0

At the .05 significance level, can we conclude the contamination measurements are lower after use of the new soap?
  a. What are the null and alternate hypotheses?
  b. Compute the test statistic.
  c. Compute the p-value.
  d. What is your decision regarding the null hypothesis?
  e. Interpret the result.

56. **FILE** The following data on annual rates of return were collected from 11 randomly selected stocks listed on the New York Stock Exchange ("the big board") and

12 randomly selected stocks listed on NASDAQ. A hypothesis test fails to reject the equality of the population variances. At the .10 significance level, can we conclude that the annual rates of return are higher on "the big board"?

NYSE	NASDAQ
15.0	8.8
10.7	6.0
20.2	14.4
18.6	19.1
19.1	17.6
8.7	17.8
17.8	15.9
13.8	17.9
22.7	21.6
14.0	6.0
26.1	11.9
	23.4

   a. What are the null and alternate hypotheses?
   b. Compute the test statistic.
   c. Compute the p-value.
   d. What is your decision regarding the null hypothesis?
   e. Interpret the result.

57. FILE The city of Laguna Beach operates two public parking lots. The Ocean Drive parking lot can accommodate up to 125 cars and the Rio Rancho parking lot can accommodate up to 130 cars. City planners are considering increasing the size of the lots and changing the fee structure. To begin, the Planning Office would like some information on the number of cars in the lots at various times of the day. A junior planner officer is assigned the task of visiting the two lots at random times of the day and evening and counting the number of cars in the lots. The study lasted over a period of 1 month. Following is the number of cars in the lots for 25 visits of the Ocean Drive lot and 28 visits of the Rio Rancho lot. A hypothesis test fails to reject the equality of the population variances.

Ocean Drive

89	115	93	79	113	77	51	75	118	105	106	91	54
63	121	53	81	115	67	53	69	95	121	88	64	

Rio Rancho

128	110	81	126	82	114	93	40	94	45	84	71	74
92	66	69	100	114	113	107	62	77	80	107	90	129
105	124											

Is it reasonable to conclude that there is a difference in the mean number of cars in the two lots? Use the .05 significance level.
   a. What are the null and alternate hypotheses?
   b. Compute the test statistic.
   c. Compute the p-value.
   d. What is your decision regarding the null hypothesis?
   e. Interpret the result.

58. FILE The amount of income spent on housing is an important component of the cost of living. The total costs of housing for homeowners might include mortgage payments, property taxes, and utility costs (water, heat, electricity). An economist selected a sample of 20 homeowners in New England and then calculated these total housing costs as a percent of monthly income, 5 years ago and now. The information is reported in the table. Is it reasonable to conclude the percent is less now than 5 years ago?

Homeowner	Five Years Ago	Now	Homeowner	Five Years Ago	Now
Holt	17%	10%	Lozier	35%	32%
Loman	20	39	Cieslinski	16	32
Merenick	29	37	Rowatti	23	21
Lanoue	43	27	Koppel	33	12
Fagan	36	12	Rumsey	44	40
Bobko	43	41	McGinnis	44	42
Kippert	45	24	Pierce	28	22
San Roman	19	26	Roll	29	19
Kurimsky	49	28	Lang	39	35
Davison	49	26	Miller	22	12

a. What are the null and alternate hypotheses?
b. Compute the test statistic.
c. Compute the *p*-value.
d. What is your decision regarding the null hypothesis?
e. Interpret the result.

59. **FILE** The CVS Pharmacy located on US 17 in Murrells Inlet has been one of the busiest pharmaceutical retail stores in South Carolina for many years. To try and capture more business in the area, CVS top management opened another store about 6 miles west on SC 707. After a few months, CVS management decided to compare the business volume at the two stores. One way to measure business volume is to count the number of cars in the store parking lots on random days and times. The results of the survey from the last 3 months of the year are reported in the table. To explain, the first observation was on October 2 at 20:52 military time (8:52 p.m.). At that time there were four cars in the US 17 lot and nine cars in the SC 707 lot. At the .05 significance level, is it reasonable to conclude that, based on vehicle counts, the US 17 store has more business volume than the SC 707 store?

		Vehicle Count	
Date	Time	US 17	SC 707
Oct 2	20:52	4	9
Oct 11	19:30	5	7
Oct 15	22:08	9	12
Oct 19	11:42	4	5
Oct 25	15:32	10	8
Oct 26	11:02	9	15
Nov 3	11:22	13	7
Nov 5	19:09	20	3
Nov 8	15:10	15	14
Nov 9	13:18	15	11
Nov 15	22:38	13	11
Nov 17	18:46	16	12
Nov 21	15:44	17	8
Nov 22	15:34	15	3
Nov 27	21:42	20	6
Nov 29	9:57	17	13
Nov 30	17:58	5	9
Dec 3	19:54	7	13
Dec 15	18:20	11	6
Dec 16	18:25	14	15
Dec 17	11:08	8	8
Dec 22	21:20	10	3
Dec 24	15:21	4	6
Dec 25	20:21	7	9
Dec 30	14:25	19	4

a. What are the null and alternate hypotheses?
b. Compute the test statistic.
c. Compute the *p*-value.
d. What is your decision regarding the null hypothesis?
e. Interpret the result.

60. **FILE** A goal of financial literacy for children is to learn how to manage money wisely. One question is: How much money do children have to manage? A recent study by Schnur Educational Research Associates randomly sampled 15 children between 8 and 10 years old and 18 children between 11 and 14 years old and recorded their monthly allowance. Is it reasonable to conclude that the mean allowance received by children between 11 and 14 years is more than the allowance received by children between 8 and 10 years? Use the .01 significance level.

8–10 Years	11–14 Years
$26	$49
33	44
30	42
26	38
34	39
26	41
27	39
27	38
30	38
26	41
25	38
27	44
29	39
34	50
32	49
	41

a. Test the assumption that the population variances are equal using a .10 significance level.
b. What are the null and alternate hypotheses?
c. Compute the test statistic.
d. Compute the *p*-value.
e. What is your decision regarding the null hypothesis?
f. Interpret the result.

61. As part of a recent survey among dual-wage-earner couples, an industrial psychologist found that 990 men out of the 1,500 surveyed believed the division of household duties was fair. A sample of 1,600 women found 970 believed the division of household duties was fair. At the .01 significance level, is it reasonable to conclude that the proportion of men who believe the division of household duties is fair is larger? What is the *p*-value?

62. There are two major cell phone providers in the Colorado Springs, Colorado area, one called HTC and the other, Mountain Communications. We want to investigate the "churn rate" for each provider. Churn is the number of customers or subscribers who cut ties with a company during a given time period. At the beginning of the month, HTC had 10,000 customers; at the end of the month, HTC had 9,810 customers for a loss of 190. For the same month, Mountain Communications started with 12,500 customers and ended the month with 12,285 customers, for a loss of 215. At the .01 significance level, is there a difference in the churn rate for the two providers?

63. The Consumer Confidence Survey is a monthly review that measures consumer confidence in the U.S. economy. It is based on a sample of 5,000 U.S. households. Last month 9.1% of consumers said conditions were "good." In the prior month, only 8.5% said they were "good." Use the six-step hypothesis testing method at the .05 level

of significance to see whether you can determine if there is an increase in the share asserting conditions are "good." Find the p-value and explain what it means.

64. A study was conducted to determine if there was a difference in the humor content in British and American trade magazine advertisements. In an independent random sample of 270 American trade magazine advertisements, 56 were humorous. An independent random sample of 203 British trade magazines contained 52 humorous ads. Do these data provide evidence at the .05 significance level that there is a difference in the proportion of humorous ads in British versus American trade magazines?

65. The AP-Petside.com poll contacted 300 married women and 200 married men. All owned pets. One hundred of the women and 36 of the men replied that their pets are better listeners than their spouses. At the .05 significance level, is there a difference between the responses of women and men?

66. Each month the National Association of Purchasing Managers surveys purchasing managers and publishes the NAPM index. One of the questions asked on the survey is: Do you think the economy is contracting? Last month, of the 300 responding managers, 160 answered yes to the question. This month, 170 of the 290 managers indicated they felt the economy was contracting. At the .05 significance level, can we conclude that a larger proportion of the purchasing managers believe the economy is contracting this month?

DATA ANALYTICS

67. **FILE** The North Valley Real Estate data reports information on the homes sold last year.
    a. At the .05 significance level, can we conclude that there is a difference in the mean selling price of homes with a pool and homes without a pool?
    b. At the .05 significance level, can we conclude that there is a difference in the mean selling price of homes with an attached garage and homes without an attached garage?
    c. At the .05 significance level, can we conclude that there is a difference in the mean selling price of homes that are in default on the mortgage?

68. **FILE** Refer to the Baseball 2021 data, which report information on the 30 Major League Baseball teams for the 2021 season.
    a. At the .05 significance level, can we conclude that there is a difference in the mean salary of teams in the American League versus teams in the National League?
    b. At the .05 significance level, can we conclude that there is a difference in the mean home attendance of teams in the American League versus teams in the National League?
    c. Compute the mean and the standard deviation of the number of wins for the 10 teams with the highest salaries. Do the same for the 10 teams with the lowest salaries. At the .05 significance level, is there a difference in the mean number of wins for the two groups? At the .05 significance level, is there a difference in the mean attendance for the two groups?

69. **FILE** Refer to the Lincolnville School District bus data. Is there a difference in the mean maintenance cost for the diesel versus the gasoline buses? Use the .05 significance level.

Analysis of Variance 12

MBI/Alamy Stock Photo

▲ **A HEALTH CARE AGENCY** is studying differences between three hospitals in Tulsa, Oklahoma: Saint Francis Hospital, Oklahoma Surgical Hospital, and Hillcrest Hospital South. The agency is interested in comparing the number of outpatient surgeries among the three hospitals. In addition, the agency would like to know if differences in the number of outpatient surgeries exist by the day of the week: Monday, Tuesday, Wednesday, Thursday, and Friday. The agency collected data from last week. At the .05 significance level, can we conclude there is a difference in the mean number of surgeries performed by hospital or by day of the week? (See Exercise 12 and LO12-3.)

LEARNING OBJECTIVES

When you have completed this chapter, you will be able to:

LO12-1 Use ANOVA to test a hypothesis that three or more population means are equal.

LO12-2 Use confidence intervals to test and interpret differences between pairs of population means.

LO12-3 Use a blocking variable in a two-way ANOVA to test a hypothesis that three or more population means are equal.

LO12-4 Perform a two-way ANOVA with interaction and describe the results.

Introduction

In this chapter, we continue our discussion of hypothesis testing. Recall that in Chapter 10 and 11 we examined a statistical approach to hypothesis testing. We described the case where a sample was selected from the population. We used the z-distribution (the standard normal distribution) or the t-distribution to determine whether it was reasonable to conclude that the population mean was equal to a specified value. We tested whether two population means are the same. In this chapter, we expand our idea of hypothesis tests. We describe a test that simultaneously compares several population means to determine if they are equal.

ANOVA: Analysis of Variance

LO12-1

Use ANOVA to test a hypothesis that three or more population means are equal.

When testing the equality of three or more population means, the analysis of variance (ANOVA) technique is used and the F-statistic is used as the test statistic.

ANOVA Assumptions

The ANOVA to test the equality of three or more population means requires that three assumptions are true:

1. The populations follow the normal distribution.
2. The populations have equal standard deviations (σ).
3. The populations are independent.

When these conditions are met, F is used as the distribution of the test statistic.

Why do we need to study ANOVA? Why can't we just use the test of differences in population means discussed in the previous chapter? We could compare the population means two at a time. The major reason is the unsatisfactory buildup of Type I error. To explain further, suppose we have four different methods (A, B, C, and D) of training new recruits to be firefighters. We randomly assign each of the 40 recruits in this year's class to one of the four methods. At the end of the training program, we administer a test to measure understanding of firefighting techniques to the four groups. The question is: Is there a difference in the mean test scores among the four groups? An answer to this question will allow us to compare the four training methods.

Using the t-distribution to compare the four population means, we would have to conduct six different t-tests. That is, we would need to compare the mean scores for the four methods as follows: A versus B, A versus C, A versus D, B versus C, B versus D, and C versus D. For each t-test, suppose we choose an $\alpha = .05$. Therefore, the probability of a Type I error, rejecting the null when it is true, is .05. The complement is the probability of .95 that we do not reject the null when it is true. Because we conduct six separate (independent) tests, the probability that all six tests result in correct decisions is:

$$P(All\ correct) = (.95)(.95)(.95)(.95)(.95)(.95) = .735$$

To find the probability of at least one error due to sampling, we subtract this result from 1. Thus, the probability of at least one incorrect decision due to sampling is $1 - .735 = .265$. So, if we conduct six independent tests using the t-distribution, the likelihood of rejecting a true null hypothesis because of sampling error is an unsatisfactory .265. The ANOVA technique allows us to compare population means simultaneously at a selected significance level. It avoids the buildup of Type I error associated with testing many hypotheses.

ANOVA was first developed for applications in agriculture, and many of the terms related to that context remain. In particular, the term *treatment* identifies the different populations being examined. For example, treatment refers to how a plot of ground was treated with a particular type of fertilizer. The following illustration will clarify the term *treatment* and demonstrate an application of ANOVA.

▶ **EXAMPLE**

Jordan Kuhlman manages a regional financial center. Jordan wishes to compare the productivity, as measured by the number of customers served, among three employees. Four days are randomly selected and the number of customers served by each employee is recorded. The results are:

Wolfe	White	Korosa
55	66	47
54	76	51
59	67	46
56	71	48

SOLUTION

Is there a difference in the mean number of customers served? Chart 12–1 illustrates how the populations would appear if there were a difference in the treatment means. Note that the populations follow the normal distribution and the variation in each population is the same. However, the means are *not* the same.

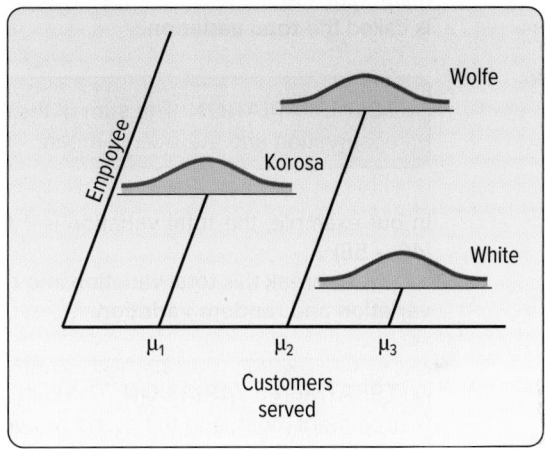

CHART 12–1 Case Where Treatment Means Are Different

Suppose there is no difference in the treatment means. This would indicate that the population means are the same. This is shown in Chart 12–2. Note again that the populations follow the normal distribution and the variation in each of the populations is the same.

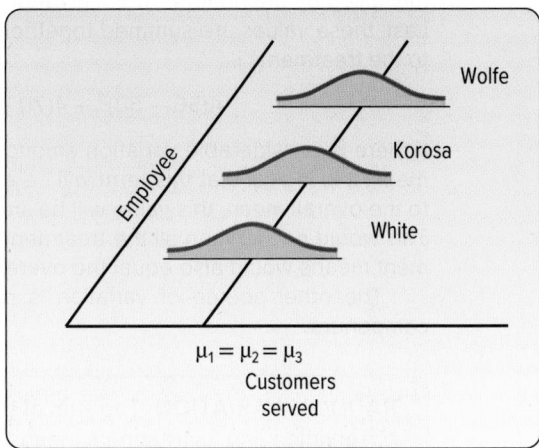

CHART 12–2 Case Where Treatment Means Are the Same

The ANOVA Test

How does the ANOVA test work? Recall that we want to determine whether the various sample means come from a single population or populations with different means. We actually compare these sample means through their variances. To explain, on page 414 we listed the assumptions required for ANOVA. One of those assumptions was that the standard deviations of the various normal populations had to be the same. We take advantage of this requirement in the ANOVA test. The underlying strategy is to estimate the population variance (standard deviation squared) two ways and then compute an *F*-test statistic to find the ratio of these two estimates. If this ratio is about 1, then logically the two estimates are the same, and we conclude that the population means are the same. If the ratio is quite different from 1, then we conclude that the population means are not the same. The *F*-distribution serves as a referee by indicating when the ratio of the sample variances is significantly greater than 1 to have occurred by chance.

Refer to the previous Example/Solution. The manager wants to determine whether there is a difference in the mean number of customers served. To begin, find the overall mean of the 12 observations. It is 58, found by $(55 + 54 + \cdots + 48)/12$. Next, for each of the 12 observations find the difference between the particular value and the overall mean. Each of these differences is squared and these squares are summed. This term is called the **total variation.**

> **TOTAL VARIATION** The sum of the squared differences between each observation and the overall mean.

In our example, the total variation is 1,082, found by $(55 - 58)^2 + (54 - 58)^2 + \cdots + (48 - 58)^2$.

Next, break this total variation into two components: variation due to the **treatment variation** and **random variation.**

> **TREATMENT VARIATION** The sum of the squared differences between each treatment mean and the grand or overall mean.

The variation due to treatments is also called variation between treatment means. In this example, we first square the difference between each treatment mean and the overall mean. The mean for Wolfe is 56 customers, found by $(55 + 54 + 59 + 56)/4$. The other means are 70 and 48, respectively. Then, each of the squared differences is multiplied by the number of observations in each treatment. In this case, the value is 4. Last, these values are summed together. This term is 992. The sum of the squares due to the treatments is:

$$4(56 - 58)^2 + 4(70 - 58)^2 + 4(48 - 58)^2 = 992$$

If there is considerable variation among the treatment means compared to the overall mean, it is logical that this term will be a large value. If the treatment means are similar to the overall mean, this value will be small. The smallest possible value would be zero. This would occur when all the treatment means are the same. In this case, all the treatment means would also equal the overall mean.

The other source of variation is referred to as **random variation,** or the error component.

> **RANDOM VARIATION** The sum of the squared differences between each observation and its treatment mean.

In the example, this term is the sum of the squared differences between each value and the mean for each treatment or employee. This is also called the variation within the treatments. The error variation is 90.

$$(55 - 56)^2 + (54 - 56)^2 + \cdots + (48 - 48)^2 = 90$$

We determine the test statistic, which is the ratio of the two estimates of the population variance, from the following equation.

$$F = \frac{\text{Estimate of the population variance based on the differences between the treatment means}}{\text{Estimate of the population variance based on the variation within the treatments}}$$

Our first estimate of the population variance is based on the treatments, that is, the difference *between* the means. It is 992/2. Why did we divide by 2? Recall from Chapter 3, to find a sample variance [see formula (3–9)], we divide by the number of observations minus 1. In this case, there are three treatments, so we divide by 2. Our first estimate of the population variance is 992/2.

The variance estimate *within* the treatments is the random variation divided by the total number of observations less the number of treatments—that is, 90/(12 − 3). Hence, our second estimate of the population variance is 90/9.

The last step is to take the ratio of these two estimates.

$$F = \frac{992/2}{90/9} = 49.6$$

Because this ratio is much greater than 1, we can conclude that the treatment means are not the same. There is a difference in the mean number of customers served by the three employees.

Here's another Example/Solution, which deals with samples of different sizes.

▶ **EXAMPLE**

Recently airlines cut services, such as meals and snacks during flights, and started charging for checked luggage. A group of four carriers hired Brunner Marketing Research Inc. to survey passengers regarding their level of satisfaction with a recent flight. The survey included questions on ticketing, boarding, in-flight service, baggage handling, pilot communication, and so forth. Twenty-five questions offered a range of possible answers: excellent, good, fair, or poor. A response of excellent was given a score of 4, good a 3, fair a 2, and poor a 1. These responses were then totaled, so the total score was an indication of the satisfaction with the flight. The greater the score, the higher the level of satisfaction with the service. The highest possible score was 100.

Brunner randomly selected and surveyed passengers from the four airlines. Following is the sample information. Is there a difference in the mean satisfaction level among the four airlines? Use the .01 significance level.

Northern	WTA	Pocono	Branson
94	75	70	68
90	68	73	70
85	77	76	72
80	83	78	65
	88	80	74
		68	65
		65	

SOLUTION

We will use the six-step hypothesis testing procedure.

Step 1: **State the null hypothesis and the alternate hypothesis.** The null hypothesis is that the mean scores are the same for the four airlines.

$$H_0: \mu_N = \mu_W = \mu_P = \mu_B$$

The alternate hypothesis is that the mean scores are not all the same for the four airlines.

H_1: The mean scores are not all equal.

We can also think of the alternate hypothesis as "at least two mean scores are not equal."

If the null hypothesis is not rejected, we conclude that there is no difference in the mean scores for the four airlines. If H_0 is rejected, we conclude that there is a difference in at least one pair of mean scores, but at this point we do not know which pair or how many pairs differ.

Step 2: **Select the level of significance.** We selected the .01 significance level.

Step 3: **Determine the test statistic.** The test statistic follows the F-distribution.

Step 4: **Formulate the decision rule.** To determine the decision rule, we need the critical value. The critical value for the F-statistic is found in Appendix B.6B. To use this table, we need to know the degrees of freedom in the numerator and the denominator. The degrees of freedom in the numerator equals the number of treatments, designated as k, minus 1. The degrees of freedom in the denominator are the total number of observations, n, minus the number of treatments. For this problem, there are four treatments and a total of 22 observations.

Degrees of freedom in the numerator $= k - 1 = 4 - 1 = 3$
Degrees of freedom in the denominator $= n - k = 22 - 4 = 18$

Refer to Appendix B.6B and the .01 significance level. Move horizontally across the top of the page to 3 degrees of freedom in the numerator. Then move down that column to the row with 18 degrees of freedom. The value at this intersection is 5.09. So the decision rule is to reject H_0 if the computed value of F exceeds 5.09.

Step 5: **Select the sample, perform the calculations, and make a decision.** It is convenient to summarize the calculations of the F-statistic in an **ANOVA table.** The format for an ANOVA table is as follows. Statistical software packages also use this format.

ANOVA Table				
Source of Variation	**Sum of Squares**	**Degrees of Freedom**	**Mean Square**	**F**
Treatments	SST	$k - 1$	$SST/(k - 1) = MST$	MST/MSE
Error	SSE	$n - k$	$SSE/(n - k) = MSE$	
Total	SS total	$n - 1$		

There are three values, or sum of squares, used to compute the test statistic F. You can determine these values by obtaining SS total and SSE, then finding SST by subtraction. The SS total term is the total variation, SST is the variation due to the treatments, and SSE is the variation within the treatments or the random error.

We usually start the process by finding SS total. This is the sum of the squared differences between each observation and the overall mean. The formula for finding SS total is:

$$\text{SS total} = \Sigma(x - \bar{x}_G)^2 \tag{12–1}$$

where:

x is each sample observation.

$\bar{x}_G$ is the overall or grand mean.

Next determine SSE or the sum of the squared errors. This is the sum of the squared differences between each observation and its respective treatment mean. The formula for finding SSE is:

$$\text{SSE} = \Sigma(x - \bar{x}_c)^2 \tag{12–2}$$

where:

$\bar{x}_c$ is the sample mean for treatment c.

The SSE is calculated:

$$\text{SSE} = \Sigma(x - \bar{x}_N)^2 + \Sigma(x - \bar{x}_W)^2 + \Sigma(x - \bar{x}_P)^2 + \Sigma(x - \bar{x}_B)^2$$

The detailed calculations of SS total and SSE for this example follow. To determine the values of SS total and SSE we start by calculating the overall or grand mean. There are 22 observations and the total is 1,664, so the grand mean is 75.64.

$$\bar{x}_G = \frac{1,664}{22} = 75.64$$

	Northern	WTA	Pocono	Branson	Total
	94	75	70	68	
	90	68	73	70	
	85	77	76	72	
	80	83	78	65	
		88	80	74	
			68	65	
			65	Grand Mean	
Column total	349	391	510	414	1,664
n	4	5	7	6	22
Mean	87.25	78.20	72.86	69.00	75.64

Next we find the deviation of each observation from the grand mean, square those deviations, and sum this result for all 22 observations. For example, the first sampled passenger had a score of 94 and the overall or grand mean is 75.64. So $(x - \bar{x}_G) = 94 - 75.64 = 18.36$. For the last passenger, $(x - \bar{x}_G) = 65 - 75.64 = -10.64$. The calculations for all other passengers follow:

Northern	WTA	Pocono	Branson
18.36	−0.64	−5.64	−7.64
14.36	−7.64	−2.64	−5.64
9.36	1.36	0.36	−3.64
4.36	7.36	2.36	−10.64
	12.36	4.36	−1.64
		−7.64	−10.64
		−10.64	

Then square each of these differences and sum all the values. Thus, for the first passenger:

$$(x - \bar{x}_G)^2 = (94 - 75.64)^2 = (18.36)^2 = 337.09$$

Finally, sum all the squared differences as formula (12–1) directs. Our SS total value is 1,485.10.

	Northern	WTA	Pocono	Branson	Total
	337.09	0.41	31.81	58.37	
	206.21	58.37	6.97	31.81	
	87.61	1.85	0.13	13.25	
	19.01	54.17	5.57	113.21	
		152.77	19.01	2.69	SS Total
			58.37	113.21	
			113.21		
Total	649.92	267.57	235.07	332.54	1,485.10

To compute the term SSE, find the deviation between each observation and its treatment mean. In the example, the mean of the first treatment (that is, the passengers on Northern Airlines) is 87.25, found by $\bar{x}_N = 349/4$. The subscript N refers to Northern Airlines.

The first passenger rated Northern a 94, so $(x - \bar{x}_N) = (94 - 87.25) = 6.75$. The first passenger in the WTA group responded with a total score of 75, so $(x - \bar{x}_W) = (75 - 78.20) = -3.2$. The detail for all the passengers follows:

Northern	WTA	Pocono	Branson
6.75	−3.2	−2.86	−1
2.75	−10.2	0.14	1
−2.25	−1.2	3.14	3
−7.25	4.8	5.14	−4
	9.8	7.14	5
		−4.86	−4
		−7.86	

Each of these values is squared and then summed for all 22 observations. The four column totals can also be summed to find SSE. The values are shown in the following table.

	Northern	WTA	Pocono	Branson	Total
	45.5625	10.24	8.18	1	
	7.5625	104.04	0.02	1	
	5.0625	1.44	9.86	9	
	52.5625	23.04	26.42	16	
		96.04	50.98	25	
			23.62	16	SSE
			61.78		
Total	110.7500	234.80	180.86	68	594.41

So the SSE value is 594.41. That is, $\Sigma(x - \bar{x}_c)^2 = 594.41$.

Finally, we determine SST, the sum of the squares due to the treatments, by subtraction.

$$SST = SS\ total - SSE \qquad \textbf{(12–3)}$$

For this example:

$$SST = SS\ total - SSE = 1{,}485.10 - 594.41 = 890.69$$

To find the computed value of F, work your way across the ANOVA table. The degrees of freedom for the numerator and the denominator are the same as in step 4 on page 418 when we were finding the critical value of F. The term **mean square** is another expression for an estimate of the variance. The mean square for treatments is SST divided by its degrees of freedom. The result is the **mean square for treatments** and is written MST. Compute the **mean square error** in a similar fashion. To be precise, divide SSE by its degrees of freedom. To complete the process, compute F by dividing MST by MSE.

Insert the particular values of F into an ANOVA table and compute the value of F as follows:

Source of Variation	Sum of Squares	Degrees of Freedom	Mean Square	F
Treatments	890.69	3	296.90	8.99
Error	594.41	18	33.02	
Total	1,485.10	21		

The computed value of F is 8.99, which is greater than the critical value of 5.09, so the null hypothesis is rejected.

Step **6: Interpret the result.** We conclude the population means are not all equal. At this point, the results of the ANOVA only show that at least one pair of mean satisfaction scores are not the same among the four airlines. We cannot statistically show which airlines differ in satisfaction or which airlines have the highest or lowest satisfaction scores. The techniques for determining how the airlines differ are presented in the next section.

Tutorial #59
in Connect

The calculations in the previous Example/Solution are tedious. Most statistical software packages will perform the calculations and output the results. See the tutorial link in the margin for a demonstration of Excel's ANOVA analysis.

In the following illustration, Excel is used to calculate the descriptive statistics and ANOVA for the previous Example/Solution involving airlines and passenger ratings. There are some slight differences between the output and the previous calculations due to rounding.

	A	B	C	D	E	F	G	H	I	J	K	L	M
	Northern	WTA	Pocono	Branson		Anova: Single Factor							
1	Northern	WTA	Pocono	Branson		Anova: Single Factor							
2	94	75	70	68									
3	90	68	73	70		SUMMARY							
4	85	77	76	72		Groups	Count	Sum	Average	Variance			
5	80	83	78	65		Northern	4	349	87.250	36.917			
6		88	80	74		WTA	5	391	78.200	58.700			
7			68	65		Pocono	7	510	72.857	30.143			
8			65			Branson	6	414	69.000	13.600			
9													
10						ANOVA							
11						Source of Variation	SS	df	MS	F	P-value	F crit	
12						Between Groups	890.684	3	296.895	8.99	0.0007	3.160	
13						Within Groups	594.407	18	33.023				
14													
15						Total	1485.091	21					
16													

Microsoft Excel

Notice Excel uses the term "Between Groups" for treatments and "Within Groups" for error. They have the same meanings. The p-value is .0007. This is the probability of finding a value of the test statistic this large or larger when the null hypothesis is true. To put it another way, the likelihood of an F-value larger than 8.99 with 3 degrees of freedom in the numerator and 18 degrees of freedom in the denominator is very small. So, we reject the null hypothesis; the probability of committing a Type I error is very small!

SELF-REVIEW 12–1

Citrus Clean is a new all-purpose cleaner being test-marketed by placing displays in three different locations within various supermarkets. The number of 12-ounce bottles sold from each location within the supermarket is reported here:

Near Bread Cleaners	Near Beer	With
18	12	26
14	18	28
19	10	30
17	16	32

At the .05 significance level, is there a difference in the mean number of bottles sold at the three locations?
(a)   State the null hypothesis and the alternate hypothesis.
(b)   What is the decision rule?
(c)   Compute the values of SS total, SST, and SSE.
(d)   Develop an ANOVA table. What is the value of the test statistic?
(e)   What is your decision regarding the null hypothesis? Interpret the result.

EXERCISES

1. The following are four observations collected from each of three treatments. Test the hypothesis that the treatment means are equal. Use the .05 significance level.

Treatment 1	Treatment 2	Treatment 3
8	3	3
6	2	4
10	4	5
9	3	4

   a. State the null and the alternate hypotheses.
   b. What is the decision rule?
   c. Compute SST, SSE, and SS total.
   d. Complete an ANOVA table.
   e. State your decision regarding the null hypothesis.

2. The following are six observations collected from treatment 1, four observations collected from treatment 2, and five observations collected from treatment 3. Test the hypothesis at the .05 significance level that the treatment means are equal.

Treatment 1	Treatment 2	Treatment 3
9	13	10
7	20	9
11	14	15
9	13	14
12		15
10		

   a. State the null and the alternate hypotheses.
   b. What is the decision rule?
   c. Compute SST, SSE, and SS total.
   d. Complete an ANOVA table.
   e. State your decision regarding the null hypothesis.

3. **FILE** A real estate developer is considering investing in a shopping mall on the outskirts of Atlanta, Georgia. Three parcels of land are being evaluated. Of particular importance is the income in the area surrounding the proposed mall. A random sample of four families is selected near each proposed mall. Following are the sample results. At the .05 significance level, can the developer conclude there is a difference in the mean income?

Southwyck Area ($000)	Franklin Park ($000)	Old Orchard ($000)
64	74	75
68	71	80
70	69	76
60	70	78

   a. What are the null and alternate hypotheses?
   b. What is the critical value?
   c. Compute the test statistic.
   d. Compute the p-value.
   e. What is your decision regarding the null hypothesis?
   f. Interpret the result.

4. **FILE** The manager of a computer software company wishes to study the number of hours per week senior executives by type of industry spend at their desktop computers. The manager selected a sample of five executives from each of three industries. At the .05 significance level, can the manager conclude there is a difference in the mean number of hours spent per week by industry?

Banking	Retail	Insurance
32	28	30
30	28	28
30	26	26
32	28	28
30	30	30

a. What are the null and alternate hypotheses?
b. What is the critical value?
c. Compute the test statistic.
d. Compute the p-value.
e. What is your decision regarding the null hypothesis?
f. Interpret the result.

LO12-2

Use confidence intervals to test and interpret differences between pairs of population means.

Inferences about Pairs of Treatment Means

Suppose we carry out the ANOVA procedure, make the decision to reject the null hypothesis, and conclude that all the treatment means are not the same. Sometimes we may be satisfied with this conclusion, but in other instances we may want to know which treatment means differ. This section provides the details for this analysis.

Recall in the previous Example/Solution regarding airline passenger ratings, we concluded that there was a difference in the treatment means. That is, the null hypothesis was rejected and the alternate hypothesis accepted. The conclusion is that at least one of the airline's mean level of satisfaction is different for the others. Now, the question is which of the four airlines differ?

Several procedures are available to answer this question. The simplest is through the use of confidence intervals as presented in Chapter 9. From the computer output of the example on page 422, the sample mean score for those passengers rating Northern's service is 87.25, and for those rating Branson's service, the sample mean score is 69.00. Is there enough disparity to justify the conclusion that there is a significant difference in the mean satisfaction scores of the two airlines?

The t-distribution, described in Chapters 10 and 11, is the test statistic. Recall that one of the assumptions of ANOVA is that the population variances are the same for all treatments. This common population value is the **mean square error,** or MSE, and is determined by SSE/$(n - k)$. A confidence interval for the difference between two populations is found by:

CONFIDENCE INTERVAL FOR THE DIFFERENCE IN TREATMENT MEANS	$(\bar{x}_1 - \bar{x}_2) \pm t\sqrt{MSE\left(\dfrac{1}{n_1} + \dfrac{1}{n_2}\right)}$	**(12–4)**

where:

$\bar{x}_1$ is the mean of the first sample.
$\bar{x}_2$ is the mean of the second sample.

t is obtained from Appendix B.5. The degrees of freedom are equal to $n - k$.
MSE is the mean square error term obtained from the ANOVA table [SSE/$(n - k)$].
n_1 is the number of observations in the first sample.
n_2 is the number of observations in the second sample.

How do we decide whether there is a difference in the treatment means? If the confidence interval includes zero, there is *not* a difference between the treatment means. For example, if the left endpoint of the confidence interval has a negative sign and the right endpoint has a positive sign, the interval includes zero and the two means do not differ. So if we develop a confidence interval from formula (12–4) and find the difference in the sample means was 5.00—that is, if $\bar{x}_1 - \bar{x}_2 = 5$ and $t\sqrt{\text{MSE}\left(\dfrac{1}{n_1} + \dfrac{1}{n_2}\right)} = 12$—the confidence interval would range from −7.00 up to 17.00. To put it in symbols:

$$(\bar{x}_1 - \bar{x}_2) \pm t\sqrt{\text{MSE}\left(\frac{1}{n_1} + \frac{1}{n_2}\right)} = 5.00 \pm 12.00 = -7.00 \text{ up to } 17.00$$

Note that zero is in this interval. Therefore, we conclude that there is no significant difference in the selected treatment means.

On the other hand, if the endpoints of the confidence interval have the same sign, this indicates that the treatment means differ. For example, if $\bar{x}_1 - \bar{x}_2 = -.35$ and $t\sqrt{\text{MSE}\left(\dfrac{1}{n_1} + \dfrac{1}{n_2}\right)} = .25$, the confidence interval would range from −.60 up to −.10. Because −.60 and −.10 have the same sign, both negative, zero is not in the interval and we conclude that these treatment means differ.

Using the previous airline example, let us compute the confidence interval for the difference between the mean scores of passengers on Northern and Branson. With a 95% level of confidence, the endpoints of the confidence interval are 10.457 and 26.043.

$$(\bar{x}_N - \bar{x}_B) \pm t\sqrt{\text{MSE}\left(\frac{1}{n_N} + \frac{1}{n_B}\right)} = (87.25 - 69.00) \pm 2.101\sqrt{33.023\left(\frac{1}{4} + \frac{1}{6}\right)}$$

$$= 18.25 \pm 7.793$$

where:

$\bar{x}_N$ is 87.25.
$\bar{x}_B$ is 69.00.
t is 2.101: from Appendix B.5 with $(n - k) = 22 - 4 = 18$ degrees of freedom.
MSE is 33.023: from the ANOVA table with SSE/$(n - k) = 594.4/18$.
n_N is 4.
n_B is 6.

The 95% confidence interval ranges from 10.457 up to 26.043. Both endpoints are positive; hence, we can conclude these treatment means differ significantly. That is, passengers on Northern Airlines rated service significantly different from those on Branson Airlines.

The confidence intervals for the differences between each pair of means can be obtained directly using statistical software. The following confidence intervals were computed using the one-way ANOVA in Minitab. In this case, Minitab is presented instead of Excel because Minitab directly computes the confidence intervals to compare the sample means. It also provides a graphical presentation of the analysis. Minitab also provides a choice of different methods to control Type I error when making multiple comparisons. The following analysis used Fisher's method to compare means.

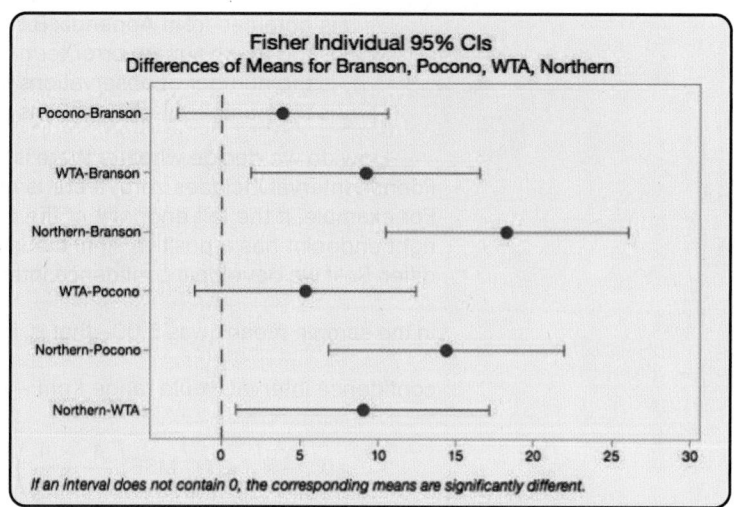

Minitab

The Minitab output on the left shows the confidence intervals for the difference between each pair of treatment means. The first row shows the confidence interval that compares WTA and Northern. It shows a confidence interval that does not include zero. It also shows the p-value for a hypothesis test that the means of WTA and Northern are equal. The hypothesis is rejected because a p-value of .031 is less than an assumed α of .05. Both results indicate that the WTA and Northern means are significantly different. Reviewing the entire table, only two pairs of means are not significantly different: Pocono and WTA, and Branson and Pocono. All other confidence intervals do not include zero and have p-values less than .05. Therefore, all other pairs of means are significantly different.

The graphic illustrates the results of the confidence interval analysis. Each confidence interval is represented by its endpoints and treatment mean. Note that a difference of zero is illustrated with the vertical dotted line. Two of the intervals include zero, Pocono and WTA, and Branson and Pocono. The others do not include zero so the means are significantly different. The following pairs of means are different: WTA and Northern, Pocono and Northern, Branson and Northern, and Branson and WTA.

We should emphasize that this investigation is a step-by-step process. The initial step is to conduct the ANOVA test. Only if the null hypothesis that the treatment means are equal is rejected should any analysis of the individual treatment means be attempted.

SELF-REVIEW 12-2

The following data are the semester tuition charges ($000) for a sample of five private colleges in the Northeast region of the United States, four in the Southeast region, and five in the West region. At the .05 significance level, can we conclude there is a difference in the mean tuition rates for the various regions?

Northeast ($000)	Southeast ($000)	West ($000)
40	38	37
41	39	38
42	40	36
40	38	37
42		36

(a) State the null and the alternate hypotheses.
(b) What is the decision rule?
(c) Develop an ANOVA table. What is the value of the test statistic?

(d) What is your decision regarding the null hypothesis?
(e) Could there be a significant difference between the mean tuition in the Northeast and that of the West? Compute the 95% confidence interval for the difference. Is the difference statistically significant? Why?

EXERCISES

5. **FILE** The following are three observations collected from treatment 1, five observations collected from treatment 2, and four observations collected from treatment 3. Test the hypothesis that the treatment means are equal at the .05 significance level.

Treatment 1	Treatment 2	Treatment 3
8	3	3
11	2	4
10	1	5
	3	4
	2	

   a. State the null hypothesis and the alternate hypothesis.
   b. What is the decision rule?
   c. Compute SST, SSE, and SS total.
   d. Complete an ANOVA table.
   e. Based on the value of the test statistic, state your decision regarding the null hypothesis.
   f. If H_0 is rejected, can we conclude that treatment 1 and treatment 2 differ? Use the 95% level of confidence.

6. **FILE** The following are six observations collected from treatment 1, ten observations collected from treatment 2, and eight observations collected from treatment 3. Test the hypothesis that the treatment means are equal at the .05 significance level.

Treatment 1	Treatment 2	Treatment 3
3	9	6
2	6	3
5	5	5
1	6	5
3	8	5
1	5	4
	4	1
	7	5
	6	
	4	

   a. State the null hypothesis and the alternate hypothesis.
   b. What is the decision rule?
   c. Compute SST, SSE, and SS total.
   d. Complete an ANOVA table.
   e. Based on the value of the test statistic, state your decision regarding the null hypothesis.
   f. If H_0 is rejected, can we conclude that treatment 2 and treatment 3 differ? Use the 95% level of confidence.

7. A senior accounting major at Midsouth State University has job offers from four CPA firms. To explore the offers further, she asked a sample of recent trainees from each firm: How many months did you work before receiving a raise in salary? Using the following ANOVA table, is there a difference in the mean number of months before receiving a raise among the four firms? Use the .05 level of significance.

```
Analysis of Variance
Source    DF      SS       MS       F        P
Factor     3    32.33    10.78    2.36    0.133
Error     10    45.67     4.57
Total     13    78.00
```

    a. What are the null and alternate hypotheses?
    b. What is the test statistic?
    c. What is the *p*-value?
    d. What is your decision regarding the null hypothesis?
    e. Interpret the result.

8. **FILE** A stock analyst wants to determine whether there is a difference in the mean return on equity for three types of stock: utility, retail, and banking stocks. The following output is obtained.

Analysis of Variance

Source	DF	Adj SS	Adj MS	F-Value	P-Value
Factor	2	303.697	151.848	5.50	0.0202
Error	12	331.381	27.615		
Total	14	635.077			

Means

Factor	N	Mean	StDev	95% CI
bank	5	5.318	3.904	(0.198, 10.438)
utility	5	9.3160	1.5376	(4.1956, 14.4364)
retail	5	16.212	8.077	(11.092, 21.332)

Pooled StDev = 5.25500

Fisher Individual Tests for Differences of Means

Difference of Levels	Difference of Means	SE of Difference	95% CI	T-Value	Adjusted P-Value
utility-bank	3.998	3.324	(-3.243, 11.239)	1.20	0.2522
retail-bank	10.894	3.324	(3.653, 18.135)	3.28	0.0066
retail-utility	6.896	3.324	(-0.345, 14.137)	2.07	0.0602

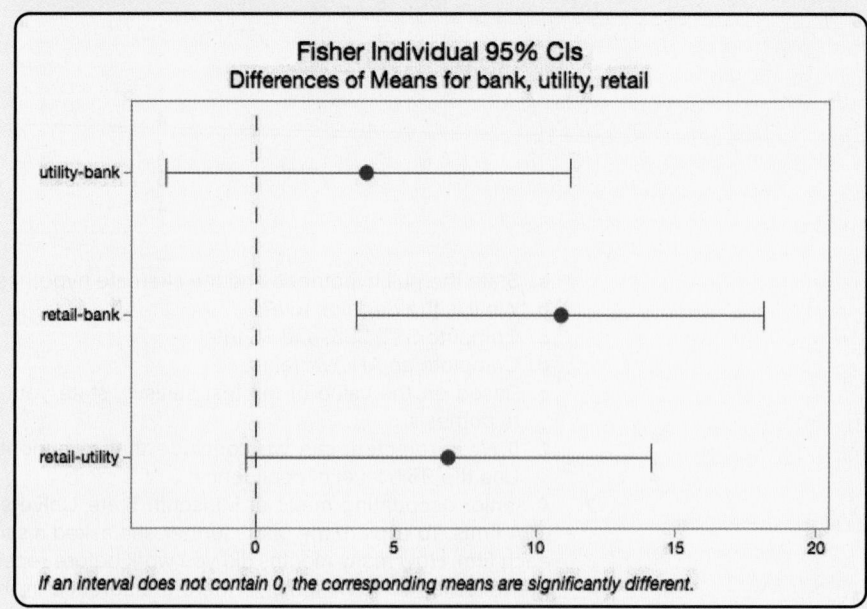

Fisher Individual 95% CIs
Differences of Means for bank, utility, retail

If an interval does not contain 0, the corresponding means are significantly different.

a. Using the .05 level of significance, is there a difference in the mean return on equity among the three types of stock? What evidence supports your answer?

b. Can the analyst conclude there is a difference between the mean return on equity for utility and retail stocks? For utility and banking stocks? For banking and retail stocks? Explain.

LO12-3
Use a blocking variable in a two-way ANOVA to test a hypothesis that three or more population means are equal.

Two-Way Analysis of Variance

In the Example/Solution in the previous section, we divided the total variation in passenger ratings of the airlines into two categories: the variation between the treatments and the variation within the treatments. We also called the variation within the treatments the error or the random variation. To put it another way, we considered only two sources of variation: that due to the treatments and the random differences. In the airline passenger ratings example, there may be other causes of variation. These factors might include, for example, the season of the year, the particular airport, or the number of passengers on the flight.

The benefit of considering other factors is that we can reduce the error variance. That is, if we can reduce the denominator of the F-statistic (reducing the error variance or, more directly, the SSE term), the value of F will be larger, causing us to reject the hypothesis of equal treatment means. In other words, if we can explain more of the variation, then there is less "error." An example will clarify the reduction in the error variance.

▶ **EXAMPLE**

WARTA, the Warren Area Regional Transit Authority, is expanding bus service from the suburb of Starbrick into the central business district of Warren. There are four routes being considered from Starbrick to downtown Warren: (1) via U.S. 6, (2) via the West End, (3) via the Hickory Street Bridge, and (4) via Route 59. WARTA conducted several tests to determine whether there was a difference in the mean travel times along the four routes. Because there will be many different drivers, the test was set up so each

John A. Rizzo/Getty Images

driver drove along each of the four routes. Following is the travel time, in minutes, for each driver–route combination.

	Travel Time from Starbrick to Warren (minutes)			
Driver	U.S. 6	West End	Hickory St.	Rte. 59
Deans	18	17	21	22
Snaverly	16	23	23	22
Ormson	21	21	26	22
Zollaco	23	22	29	25
Filbeck	25	24	28	28

At the .05 significance level, is there a difference in the mean travel time along the four routes? If we remove the effect of the drivers, is there a difference in the mean travel time?

SOLUTION

To begin, we conduct a test of hypothesis using a one-way ANOVA. That is, we consider only the four routes. Under this condition, differences in travel times are due to either treatment or random variation. In this Example/Solution, the subscripts correspond to the treatments or routes: 1 for U.S. 6, 2 for West End, 3 for Hickory Street, and 4 for Route 59. The null hypothesis and the alternate hypothesis for comparing the mean travel time along the four routes are:

$$H_0: \mu_1 = \mu_2 = \mu_3 = \mu_4$$
$$H_1: \text{Not all treatment means are the same.}$$

There are four routes, so the numerator degrees of freedom is $(k - 1) = (4 - 1) = 3$. There are 20 observations, so the degrees of freedom in the denominator is $(n - k) = (20 - 4) = 16$. From Appendix B.6A, at the .05 significance level, the critical value of F is 3.24. The decision rule is to reject the null hypothesis if the computed F-test statistic's value is greater than 3.24.

We use Excel to perform the calculations and output the results. The computed value of F is 2.483, so we decide to not reject the null hypothesis. We conclude there is no difference in the mean travel time along the four routes. There is no evidence to conclude that any one of the routes is faster than any other.

Microsoft Excel

From the previous Excel output, the mean travel times along the routes were 20.6 minutes along U.S. 6, 21.4 minutes along the West End route, 25.4 minutes using Hickory Street, and 23.8 minutes using Route 59. We conclude these differences could reasonably be attributed to chance. From the ANOVA table, we note SST is 72.8, SSE is 156.4, and SS total is 229.2.

In this example, we only considered the variation due to the treatments (routes) and took all the remaining variation to be random. If we include the effect or variance of the drivers, this would allow us to reduce the SSE term, and the computed values of the F-statistics would be larger.

In this case, we let the drivers be the **blocking variable.** To include the variance due to the drivers, we need to determine the sum of squares due to the blocks. In a two-way ANOVA, the sum of squares due to blocks is found by the following formula.

> **BLOCKING VARIABLE** A second treatment variable that when included in the ANOVA analysis will have the effect of reducing the SSE term.

$$SSB = k\Sigma(\bar{x}_b - \bar{x}_G)^2 \tag{12-5}$$

where:

> k is the number of treatments.
> b is the number of blocks.
> $\bar{x}_b$ is the sample mean of block b.
> $\bar{x}_G$ is the overall or grand mean.

From the calculations that follow, the means for the respective drivers are 19.5, 21, 22.5, 24.75, and 26.25 minutes. The overall mean is 22.8 minutes, found by adding the travel time for all 20 drives (456 minutes) and dividing by 20.

	Travel Time from Starbrick to Warren (minutes)					
Driver	**U.S. 6**	**West End**	**Hickory St.**	**Rte. 59**	**Driver Sums**	**Driver Means**
Deans	18	17	21	22	78	19.50
Snaverly	16	23	23	22	84	21.00
Ormson	21	21	26	22	90	22.50
Zollaco	23	22	29	25	99	24.75
Filbeck	25	24	28	28	105	26.25

Substituting this information into formula (12–5) we determine SSB, the sum of squares due to the drivers (the blocking variable), is 119.7.

$$\begin{aligned} SSB &= k\Sigma(\bar{x}_b - \bar{x}_G)^2 \\ &= 4(19.5 - 22.8)^2 + 4(21.0 - 22.8)^2 + 4(22.5 - 22.8)^2 \\ &\quad +4(24.75 - 22.8)^2 + 4(26.25 - 22.8)^2 \\ &= 119.7 \end{aligned}$$

The SSE term is found by subtraction.

> **SUM OF SQUARES ERROR, TWO-WAY** $SSE = SS\ total - SST - SSB$ **(12–6)**

The same format is used in the two-way ANOVA table as in the one-way case, except there is an additional row for the blocking variable. SS total and SST are calculated as before, and SSB is found from formula (12–5). The values for the various components of the ANOVA table are computed as follows:

Source of Variation	Sum of Squares	Degrees of Freedom	Mean Square	F
Treatments	SST	$k - 1$	$SST/(k - 1) = MST$	MST/MSE
Blocks	SSB	$b - 1$	$SSB/(b - 1) = MSB$	MSB/MSE
Error	SSE	$(k - 1)(b - 1)$	$SSE/[(k - 1)(b - 1)] = MSE$	
Total	SS total	$n - 1$		

SSE is found by formula (12–6).

$$SSE = SS\ total - SST - SSB = 229.2 - 72.8 - 119.7 = 36.7$$

Source of Variation	(1) Sum of Squares	(2) Degrees of Freedom	(3) Mean Square (1)/(2)
Treatments	72.8	3	24.27
Blocks	119.7	4	29.93
Error	36.7	12	3.06
Total	229.2	19	

There is disagreement at this point. If the purpose of the blocking variable (the drivers in this example) was only to reduce the error variation, we should not conduct a test of hypothesis for the difference in block means. That is, if our goal was to reduce the MSE term, then we should not test a hypothesis regarding the blocking variable. On the other hand, we may wish to give the blocks the same status as the treatments and conduct a hypothesis test. In the latter case, when the blocks are important enough to be considered as a second factor, we refer to this as a **two-factor experiment.** In many cases the decision is not clear. In our example we are concerned about the difference in the travel time for the different drivers, so we will conduct the hypothesis test of equal block means. The subscripts are the first letter of each driver's name. The two sets of hypotheses are:

1. H_0: The treatment means are equal ($\mu_1 = \mu_2 = \mu_3 = \mu_4$).
    H_1: At least one treatment mean is different.
2. H_0: The block means are equal ($\mu_D = \mu_S = \mu_O = \mu_Z = \mu_F$).
    H_1: At least one block mean is different.

First, we will test the hypothesis concerning the treatment means. There are $(k - 1) = (4 - 1) = 3$ degrees of freedom in the numerator and $(b - 1)(k - 1) = (5 - 1)(4 - 1) = 12$ degrees of freedom in the denominator. Using the .05 significance level, the critical value of F is 3.49. The null hypothesis that the mean times for the four routes are the same is rejected if the F ratio exceeds 3.49.

$$F = \frac{MST}{MSE} = \frac{24.27}{3.06} = 7.93$$

The null hypothesis is rejected and we conclude that at least one of the route's mean travel times is different from the other routes. WARTA will want to conduct some tests to determine which treatment means differ.

Next, we test to find whether the travel times for the various drivers are equal. The degrees of freedom in the numerator for blocks are $(b - 1) = (5 - 1) = 4$. The degrees of freedom for the denominator are the same as before: $(b - 1)(k - 1) = (5 - 1)(4 - 1) = 12$. The null hypothesis that the block means are the same is rejected if the F-ratio exceeds 3.26.

$$F = \frac{MSB}{MSE} = \frac{29.93}{3.06} = 9.78$$

The null hypothesis about the block means is rejected, and we conclude that at least one driver's mean travel time is different from the other drivers. Thus, WARTA management can conclude, based on the sample results, that there is a difference in the mean travel times of drivers.

The Excel spreadsheet has a two-factor ANOVA procedure. The output for the WARTA example just completed follows. This output also includes the p-values. The p-value for the null hypothesis regarding the drivers is .001 and .004 for the routes. These p-values confirm that the null hypotheses for treatments and blocks should both be rejected because the p-values are less than the significance level. See the tutorial link in the margin for a demonstration of the analysis.

Tutorial #61
in Connect

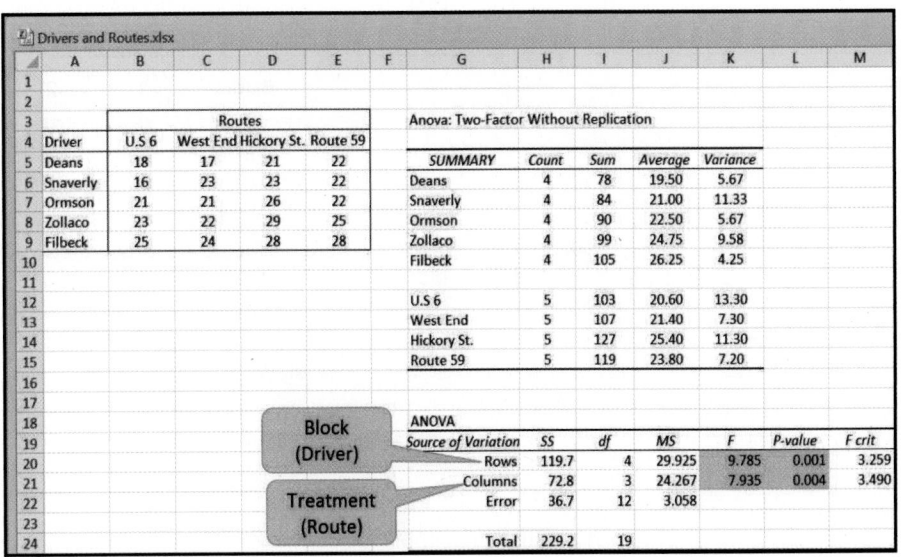

Microsoft Excel

SELF-REVIEW 12–3

Vive Shampoo sells three shampoos, one each for dry, normal, and oily hair. Sales, in millions of dollars, for the past 5 months are given in the following table. Using the .05 significance level, test whether the mean sales differ for the three types of shampoo or by month.

Month	Sales ($ million)		
	Dry	Normal	Oily
June	7	9	12
July	11	12	14
August	13	11	8
September	8	9	7
October	9	10	13

(a) What are the null and alternate hypotheses?
(b) What is the test statistic?
(c) Compute the ANOVA table.
(d) What is your decision regarding the null hypothesis?
(e) Interpret the result.

EXERCISES

For Exercises 9 through 12, conduct a test of hypothesis to determine whether the block or the treatment means differ. Using the .05 significance level: (a) state the null and alternate hypotheses for treatments; (b) state the decision rule for treatments; and (c) state the null and alternate hypotheses for blocks. Also, state the decision rule for blocks, then: (d) compute SST, SSB, SS total, and SSE; (e) complete an ANOVA table; and (f) give your decision regarding the two sets of hypotheses and interpret the results.

9. The following data were collected for a two-factor ANOVA with two treatments and three blocks.

	Treatment	
Block	**1**	**2**
A	46	31
B	37	26
C	44	35

10. The following data were collected for a two-factor ANOVA with three treatments and three blocks.

	Treatment		
Block	**1**	**2**	**3**
A	12	14	8
B	9	11	9
C	7	8	8

11. **FILE** Chapin Manufacturing Company operates 24 hours a day, 5 days a week. The workers rotate shifts each week. Management is interested in whether there is a difference in the number of units produced when the employees work on various shifts. A sample of five workers is selected and their output recorded on each shift. At the .05 significance level, can we conclude there is a difference in the mean production rate by shift or by employee?

	Units Produced		
Employee	**Day**	**Afternoon**	**Night**
Skaff	31	25	35
Lum	33	26	33
Clark	28	24	30
Treece	30	29	28
Morgan	28	26	27

12. A health care agency is studying differences between three hospitals in Tulsa, Oklahoma: Saint Francis Hospital, Oklahoma Surgical Hospital, and Hillcrest Hospital South. The agency is interested in comparing the number of outpatient surgeries between the three hospitals. In addition, the agency would like to know if differences in the number of outpatient surgeries exist by the day of the week: Monday, Tuesday, Wednesday, Thursday, and Friday. The agency collected data from last week. At the .05 significance level, can we conclude there is a difference in the mean number of surgeries performed by hospital or by day of the week?

	Number of Surgeries Performed		
Day	**Saint Francis**	**Oklahoma Surgical**	**Hillcrest**
Monday	14	18	24
Tuesday	20	24	14
Wednesday	16	22	14
Thursday	18	20	22
Friday	20	28	24

LO12-4

Perform a two-way ANOVA with interaction and describe the results.

Two-Way ANOVA with Interaction

In the previous section, we studied the separate or independent effects of two variables, or factors, on a response variable, travel time. In the Example/Solution, the two factors were the bus routes and the drivers and the response was travel time.

The analysis shows two significant results. First, the mean travel times between routes, averaged over all drivers, are different. Second, the mean travel times between the five drivers, averaged over all the routes, are different. What could explain these differences? The differences between routes may simply be related to differences in the distance of the routes. We really didn't study the distance of the various routes. Perhaps the differences are explained by how fast, on average, the drivers drive regardless of the route.

There is another effect that may influence travel time that we have not considered. This is called the **interaction effect** between route and driver on travel time. That is, differences in travel time may depend on both the driver and the route. For example, it is possible that one of the drivers is especially good at driving one of the routes. Perhaps one driver knows how to effectively time the traffic lights or how to avoid heavily congested intersections for one or more of the routes. In this case, differences in mean travel time may depend on the combined effect of driver and route. The results of the interaction of driver and route can provide interesting information.

> **INTERACTION EFFECT** The effect of one factor on a response variable differs depending on the value of another factor.

Interaction Plots

An illustration of interaction is the effect of diet and exercise on body weight. It is generally agreed that body weight (the response variable) can be affected by two factors, diet and exercise. However, research shows there is also a combined or *interaction effect* of diet and exercise on weight loss. That is, the amount of weight loss will be different and depend on diet AND whether people exercise.

The following graph, or interaction plot, illustrates the interaction of diet and exercise. First, for people who do not exercise, the mean weight losses for Diet 1 and Diet 2 are plotted. These are connected with the blue line. Clearly, there is a difference in weight loss for the two diets. Second, for people who did exercise, the mean weight losses for Diet 1 and Diet 2 are plotted. These are connected with the green line. Again, there is a clear difference in weight loss between Diet 1 and Diet 2 for people who exercise. The plot also shows an interaction effect between diet and exercise on weight loss. Notice the two lines are not parallel to each other. For Diet 1, the mean weight loss is more when people also exercise. For Diet 2, the mean weight loss is also more when people also exercise, but the weight loss is much greater than for Diet 1. So, what is the effect of diet and exercise on weight loss? It depends on the combined, or interaction, effects of diet and exercise.

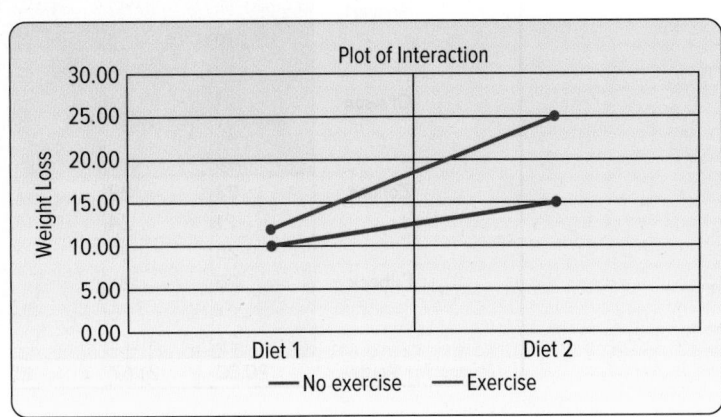

How would the interaction plot look if there were no interaction? The following graph shows an analysis of diet and exercise with no interaction.

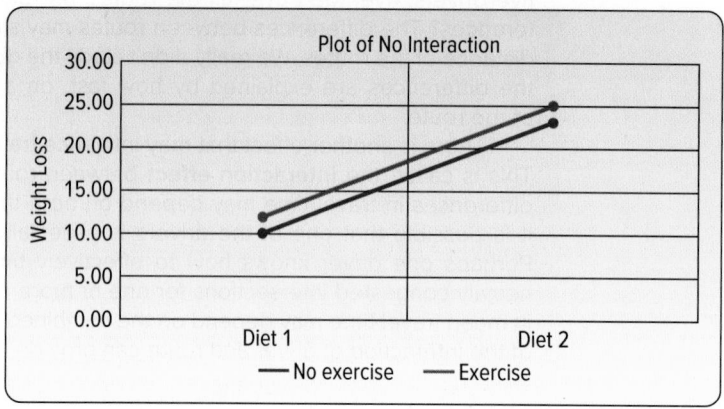

In this case the lines are parallel. Comparing the means, the effect of exercise on weight loss for Diet 1 and Diet 2 is the same. The estimated weight loss is about 2 pounds. In addition, the effect of diet is the same whether people exercise or not. It is about 13 pounds.

Testing for Interaction

To test for an interaction effect, we use a two-way ANOVA with interaction. To illustrate, we return to the previous WARTA Example/Solution. Restating the issue facing WARTA management: They want to expand bus service from downtown Warren to Starbrick. So far they have concluded, based on statistical analysis, that there is a difference in the mean travel time along the four proposed routes and a difference in the mean travel times of the five drivers. But it is possible that the combination, or the interaction between routes and drivers, has a significant effect on mean travel time.

In this analysis, we call the two variables, route and driver, **factors.** We refer to the variable, travel time, as the **response** variable. To test for interaction, the sample data must be replicated for each route. In this case, each driver drives each route three times so there are three observed times for each route/driver combination. This information is summarized in the following Excel spreadsheet.

		Routes				Means for
		US 6	West End	Hickory St	Route 59	Drivers
Deans		18	17	21	22	
		15	14	20	19	
		21	20	22	25	19.50
Snaverly		16	23	23	22	
		19	19	24	20	
		13	25	22	24	20.83
Ormson		21	21	26	22	
		19	23	24	24	
		14	25	28	20	22.25
Zollaco		23	22	29	25	
		21	24	30	20	
		25	20	28	26	24.42
Filbeck		25	24	28	28	
		24	25	29	30	Grand Mean
		26	23	27	26	26.25
Means for Routes		20.00	21.67	25.40	23.53	22.65

To evaluate interaction effects, a useful first step is to plot the means for each driver/route combination. For the driver/route combination Driver Deans using Route 6, the mean is 18 minutes, found by $(18 + 15 + 21)/3$. For the driver/route combination Driver Filbeck using Route 59, the mean is 28 minutes, found by $(28 + 30 + 26)/3$. Similarly, we calculate the means for the other cells and summarize the results in the following table.

Drivers	Routes			
	US 6	West End	Hickory St	Route 59
Deans	18	17	21	22
Snaverly	16	22.33	23	22
Ormson	18	23	26	22
Zollaco	23	22	29	23.67
Filbeck	25	24	28	28

The following graph shows the interaction plot using the information in the previous table. The vertical axis is the travel time in minutes. The four routes are labeled on the horizontal axis and each line plots the mean travel times for each driver for all four routes. For example, the green line reports average travel times for Deans for each of the four routes.

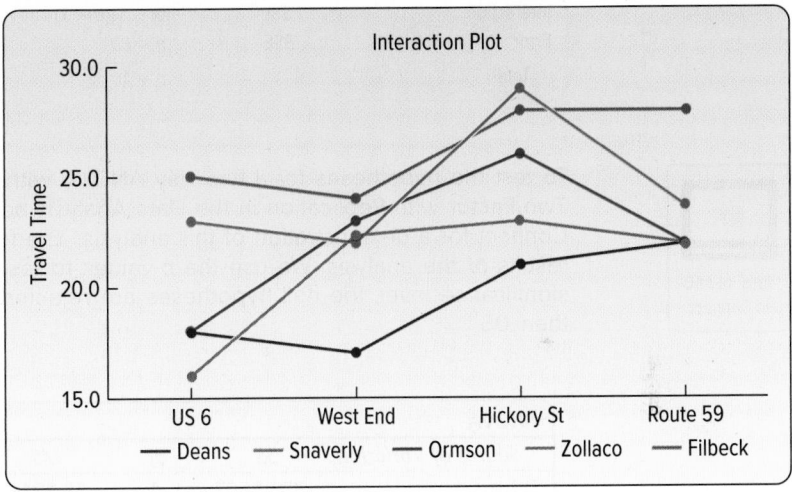

From the graph, what observations can be made about the interaction of driver and route on travel time? Most importantly, the lines are not parallel. Because the five lines are clearly not parallel, there is an interaction effect of driver and route on travel time; that is, travel time depends on the combined effect of driver and route.

Note the differences in travel times. For the U.S. 6 route, Snaverly has the lowest or fastest mean travel time. Deans has the lowest mean travel time for the West End and Hickory Street routes. Zollaco has the slowest average time for the Hickory Street route. There are many other observations that lead to the general observation that travel time is related to the combined effects of driver AND route. The critical question is whether the observed interactions are significant or the differences are due to chance.

Hypothesis Tests for Interaction

The next step is to conduct statistical tests to further investigate the possible interaction effects. In summary, our study of travel times has several questions:

- Is there an interaction effect of routes and drivers on mean travel times?
- Are the mean travel times for drivers the same?
- Are the mean travel times for the routes the same?

Of the three questions, we are most interested in the test for interactions.

We formalize these ideas into three sets of hypotheses:

1. H_0: There is no interaction between drivers and routes.
   H_1: There is interaction between drivers and routes.
2. H_0: The driver means are equal.
   H_1: At least one driver travel time mean is different.
3. H_0: The route means are equal.
   H_1: At least one route travel time mean is different.

We test each of these hypotheses as we did in the previous section using the F-distribution. The tests are summarized with the following ANOVA table. It is similar to the two-way ANOVA in the previous section with the addition of the Interaction source of variation. In addition, we refer to the driver effect as Factor A and the route effect as Factor B. Each of these hypotheses is tested using the familiar F-statistic.

Source of Variation	Sum of Squares	df	Mean Square	F
Factor A (driver)	SSA	$k - 1$	$MSA = SSA/(k - 1)$	MSA/MSE
Factor B (route)	SSB	$b - 1$	$MSB = SSA/(b - 1)$	MSB/MSE
Interaction	SSI	$(k - 1)(b - 1)$	$MSI = SSI/[(k - 1)(b - 1)]$	MSI/MSE
Error	SSE	$n - kb$	$MSE = SSE/(n - kb)$	
Total		$n - 1$		

Tutorial #60
in Connect

To test the hypotheses for a two-way ANOVA with interaction, we use the ANOVA: Two-Factor with Replication in the Data Analysis add-in for Excel. See the tutorial in Connect for a demonstration of this analysis. The following ANOVA table shows the results of the analysis. We use the p-values to test each hypothesis. Using the .05 significance level, the null hypotheses are rejected if the computed p-value is less than .05.

ANOVA						
Source of Variation	SS	df	MS	F	P-value	F crit
Drivers	353.5667	4	88.39167	17.21916	0.0000	2.605975
Routes	244.9833	3	81.66111	15.90801	0.0000	2.838745
Interaction	125.7667	12	10.48056	2.041667	0.0456	2.003459
Error	205.3333	40	5.133333			
Total	929.65	59				

Reviewing the results of the ANOVA, the p-value for the interaction effect of .0456 is less than our significance level of .05, so our decision is to reject the null hypothesis of no interaction and conclude that the combination of route and driver has a significant effect on the response variable, travel time.

A significant interaction effect provides important information about the combined effects of the variables. If interaction is present, then a test of differences in the factor means using a one-way ANOVA for each level of the other factor is the next step. This analysis requires some time and work to complete, but the results are usually enlightening.

We will continue the analysis by conducting a one-way ANOVA for each route by testing the hypothesis H_0: Driver travel times are equal. The results follow:

US 6; H_0 **: Driver times are equal**

Source of Variation	SS	df	MS	F	P-value	F crit
Between Groups	174	4	43.5	6.04167	0.010	3.478
Within Groups	72	10	7.2			
Total	246	14				

West End; H_0 **: Driver times are equal**

Source of Variation	SS	df	MS	F	P-value	F crit
Between Groups	88.6667	4	22.1667	4.05488	0.033	3.478
Within Groups	54.6667	10	5.46667			
Total	143.333	14				

Hickory; H_0 **: Driver times are equal**

Source of Variation	SS	df	MS	F	P-value	F crit
Between Groups	135.6	4	33.9	21.1875	0.000	3.478
Within Groups	16	10	1.6			
Total	151.6	14				

Route 59; H_0 **: Driver times are equal**

Source of Variation	SS	df	MS	F	P-value	F crit
Between Groups	81.0667	4	20.2667	3.23404	0.060	3.478
Within Groups	62.6667	10	6.26667			
Total	143.733	14				

The results of the one-way ANOVA show there are significant differences in the mean travel times among the drivers for every route, except Route 59 with a p-value of .06. A review of the interaction plot may reveal some of the differences. For example, for the West End route, the graph suggests that Deans has the best mean travel time. Further statistical analysis would test pairs of mean travel times to determine the significant differences between driver travel times for each route that has a significant p-value.

SELF-REVIEW 12–4

See the following ANOVA table.

	ANOVA				
Source of Variation	SS	df	MS	F	p-value
Factor A	6.41	3	2.137	3.46	0.0322
Factor B	5.01	2	2.507	4.06	0.0304
Interaction	33.15	6	5.525	8.94	0.0000
Error	14.83	24	0.618		
Total	59.41	35			

Use the .05 significance level to answer the following questions.
(a) How many levels does Factor A have? Is there a significant difference among the Factor A means? How do you know?

(b) How many levels does Factor B have? Is there a significant difference among the Factor B means? How do you know?

(c) How many observations are there in each cell? Is there a significant interaction between Factor A and Factor B on the response variable? How do you know?

EXERCISES

13. **FILE** Consider the following sample data for a two-factor ANOVA analysis. There are two levels (heavy and light) of factor A (weight), and three levels (small, medium, and large) of factor B (size). For each combination of size and weight, there are three observations.

		Size		
		Small	Medium	Large
		23	20	11
	Heavy	21	32	20
		25	26	20
Weight				
		13	20	11
	Light	32	17	23
		17	15	8

Compute an ANOVA with statistical software, and use the .05 significance level to answer the following questions.

a. Is there a difference in the Size means?
b. Is there a difference in the Weight means?
c. Is there a significant interaction between Weight and Size?

14. Consider the following partially completed two-way ANOVA table. Suppose there are four levels of Factor A and three levels of Factor B. The number of replications per cell is 5. Complete the table and test to determine if there is a significant difference in Factor A means, Factor B means, or the interaction means. Use the .05 significance level. (Hint: Estimate the values from the F-table.)

ANOVA				
Source	SS	df	MS	F
Factor A	75			
Factor B	25			
Interaction	300			
Error	600			
Total	1000			

15. **FILE** A vending machine company sells its packaged foods in a variety of different machines. The company is considering three types of new vending machines. Management wants to know if the different machines affect sales. These vending machines are designated as J-1000, D-320, and UV-57. Management also wants to know if the position of the machines indoors or outdoors affects sales. Each of six similar locations was randomly assigned a machine and position combination. The following data are the number of purchases over 4 days.

Position/Machine	J-1000	D-320	UV-57
Inside	33, 40, 30, 31	29, 28, 33, 33	47, 39, 39, 45
Outside	43, 36, 41, 40	48, 45, 40, 44	37, 32, 36, 35

a. Draw the interaction graph. Based on your observations, is there an interaction effect? Based on the graph, describe the interaction effect of machine and position.

b. Compute an ANOVA with statistical software, and use the .05 level to test for position, machine, and interaction effects on sales. Report the statistical results.

c. Compare the inside and outside mean sales for each machine using statistical techniques. What do you conclude?

16. **FILE** A large company is organized into three functional areas: manufacturing, marketing, and research and development. The employees claim that the company pays women less than men for similar jobs. The company randomly selected four males and four females in each area and recorded their weekly salaries in dollars.

Area/Sex	Female	Male
Manufacturing	1016, 1007, 875, 968	978, 1056, 982, 748
Marketing	1045, 895, 848, 904	1154, 1091, 878, 876
Research and Development	770, 733, 844, 771	926, 1055, 1066, 1088

a. Draw the interaction graph. Based on your observations, is there an interaction effect? Based on the graph, describe the interaction effect of sex and area on salary.

b. Compute an ANOVA with statistical software, and use the .05 level to test for sex, area, and interaction effects on salary. Report the statistical results.

c. Compare the male and female mean salary for each area using statistical techniques. What do you recommend to the distributor?

CHAPTER SUMMARY

I. A one-way ANOVA is used to compare several treatment means.
   A. A treatment is a source of variation.
   B. The assumptions underlying ANOVA are as follows:
      1. The samples are from populations that follow the normal distribution.
      2. The populations have equal standard deviations.
      3. The populations are independent.
   C. The information for finding the value of F is summarized in an ANOVA table.
      1. The formula for SS total, the sum of squares total, is:

$$\text{SS total} = \Sigma(\bar{x} - \bar{x}_G)^2 \tag{12–1}$$

      2. The formula for SSE, the sum of squares error, is:

$$\text{SSE} = \Sigma(\bar{x} - \bar{x}_c)^2 \tag{12–2}$$

      3. The formula for the SST, the sum of squares treatment, is found by subtraction.

$$\text{SST} = \text{SS total} - \text{SSE} \tag{12–3}$$

      4. This information is summarized in the following ANOVA table and the value of F is determined.

Source of Variation	Sum of Squares	Degrees of Freedom	Mean Square	F
Treatments	SST	$k - 1$	$\text{SST}/(k-1) = \text{MST}$	MST/MSE
Error	SSE	$n - k$	$\text{SSE}/(n-k) = \text{MSE}$	
Total	SS total	$n - 1$		

II. If a null hypothesis of equal treatment means is rejected, we can identify the pairs of means that differ from the following confidence interval.

$$(\bar{x}_1 - \bar{x}_2) \pm t\sqrt{MSE\left(\frac{1}{n_1} + \frac{1}{n_2}\right)} \tag{12–4}$$

III. In a two-way ANOVA, we consider a second treatment variable.
   A. The second treatment variable is called the blocking variable.
   B. It is determined using the following equation.

$$SSB = k\Sigma(\bar{x}_b - \bar{x}_G)^2 \tag{12–5}$$

   C. The SSE term, or sum of squares error, is found from the following equation.

$$SSE = SS\ total - SST - SSB \tag{12–6}$$

   D. The F-statistics for the treatment variable and the blocking variable are determined in the following table.

Source of Variation	Sum of Squares	Degrees of Freedom	Mean Square	F
Treatments	SST	$k - 1$	$SST/(k - 1) = MST$	MST/MSE
Blocks	SSB	$b - 1$	$SSB/(b - 1) = MSB$	MSB/MSE
Error	SSE	$(k - 1)(b - 1)$	$SSE/[(k - 1)(b - 1)] = MSE$	
Total	SS total	$n - 1$		

IV. In a two-way ANOVA with repeated observations, we consider two treatment variables and the possible interaction between the variables. The complete ANOVA table including interactions is:

Source	Sum of Squares	df	Mean Square	F
Factor A	SSA	$k - 1$	$SSA/(k - 1) = MSA$	MSA/MSE
Factor B	SSB	$b - 1$	$SSB/(b - 1) = MSB$	MSB/MSE
Interaction	SSI	$(k - 1)(b - 1)$	$SSI/[(k - 1)(b - 1)] = MSI$	MSI/MSE
Error	SSE	$n - kb$	$SSE/(n - kb) = MSE$	
Total	SS total	$n - 1$		

PRONUNCIATION KEY

SYMBOL	MEANING	PRONUNCIATION
SS total	Sum of squares total	S S total
SST	Sum of squares treatment	S S T
SSE	Sum of squares error	S S E
MSE	Mean square error	M S E
SSB	Block sum of squares	S S B
SSI	Sum of squares interaction	S S I

CHAPTER EXERCISES

17. In an ANOVA table, the MSE is equal to 10. Random samples of six were selected from each of four populations, where the sum of squares total was 250.
   a. Set up the null hypothesis and the alternate hypothesis.
   b. What is the decision rule? Use the .05 significance level.
   c. Create the ANOVA table. What is the value of F?
   d. What is your decision regarding the null hypothesis?

18. The following is a partial ANOVA table.

Source	Sum of Squares	df	Mean Square	F
Treatment		2		
Error			20	
Total	500	11		

Complete the table and answer the following questions. Use the .05 significance level.
a. How many treatments are there?
b. What is the total sample size?
c. What is the critical value of F?
d. Write out the null and alternate hypotheses.
e. What is your conclusion regarding the null hypothesis?

19. **FILE** A consumer organization wants to know whether there is a difference in the price of a particular toy at three different types of stores. The price of the toy was checked in a sample of five discount stores, five variety stores, and five department stores. The results are shown here. Use the .05 significance level.

Discount	Variety	Department
$12	$15	$19
13	17	17
14	14	16
12	18	20
15	17	19

a. What are the null and alternate hypotheses?
b. Compute the ANOVA table.
c. What is the test statistic?
d. What if the p-value?
e. What is your decision regarding the null hypothesis?
f. Interpret the result.

20. **FILE** Jacob Lee is a frequent traveler between Los Angeles and San Diego. For the past month, he recorded the flight times in minutes on three different airlines. The results are:

Goust	Jet Red	Cloudtran
51	50	52
51	53	55
52	52	60
42	62	64
51	53	61
57	49	49
47	50	49
47	49	
50	58	
60	54	
54	51	
49	49	
48	49	
48	50	

a. Use the .05 significance level and the six-step hypothesis testing process to check if there is a difference in the mean flight times among the three airlines.
b. Develop a 95% confidence interval for the difference in the means between Goust and Cloudtran.

21. **FILE** The City of Maumee comprises four districts. Chief of Police Jeri Hall wants to determine whether there is a difference in the mean number of crimes committed among the four districts. Chief Hall examined the records from six randomly selected days and recorded the number of crimes. At the .05 significance level, can Chief Hall conclude that there is a difference in the mean number of crimes among the four districts?

Number of Crimes			
Rec Center	Key Street	Monclova	Whitehouse
13	21	12	16
15	13	14	17
14	18	15	18
15	19	13	15
14	18	12	20
15	19	15	18

a. What are the null and alternate hypotheses?
b. Compute the ANOVA table.
c. What is the test statistic?
d. What if the p-value?
e. What is your decision regarding the null hypothesis?
f. Interpret the result.

22. **FILE** A study of the effect of television commercials on 12-year-old children measured their attention span, in seconds. The commercials were for clothes, food, and toys.
At the .05 significance level, is there a difference in the mean attention span of the children for the various commercials? Are there significant differences between pairs of means? Would you recommend dropping one of the three commercial types?

Clothes	Food	Toys
26	45	60
21	48	51
43	43	43
35	53	54
28	47	63
31	42	53
17	34	48
31	43	58
20	57	47
	47	51
	44	51
	54	

a. What are the null and alternate hypotheses?
b. Compute the ANOVA table.
c. What is the test statistic?
d. What is the p-value?
e. What is your decision regarding the null hypothesis?
f. Interpret the result.
g. Compute the 95% confidence intervals that estimate the difference between each pair of means.
h. Which pairs of means are statistically different?

23. **FILE** When only two treatments are involved, ANOVA and the Student's t-test (Chapter 11) result in the same conclusions. Also, for computed test statistics, $t^2 = F$.

To demonstrate this relationship, use the following example. Fourteen randomly selected students enrolled in a history course were divided into two groups, one consisting of six students who took the course in the normal lecture format. The other group of eight students took the course in a distance format. At the end of the course, each group was examined with a 50-item test. The following is a list of the number correct for each of the two groups.

Traditional Lecture	Distance
37	50
35	46
41	49
40	44
35	41
34	42
	45
	43

a. Using analysis of variance techniques, test H_0 that the two mean test scores are equal; $\alpha = .05$.
b. Using the *t*-test from Chapter 11, compute *t*.
c. Interpret the results.

24. There are four auto body shops in Bangor, Maine, and all claim to promptly repair cars. To check if there is any difference in repair times, customers are randomly selected from each repair shop and their repair times in days are recorded. The output from a statistical software package is:

Summary				
Groups	**Sample Size**	**Sum**	**Average**	**Variance**
Ray's Auto Body	3	15.4	5.133333	0.323333
Downeast Auto Body	4	32	8	1.433333
East Coast Auto Body	5	25.2	5.04	0.748
Maine Collision Center	4	25.9	6.475	0.595833

ANOVA					
Source of Variation	**SS**	**df**	**MS**	**F**	**p-value**
Between Groups	23.37321	3	7.791069	9.612506	0.001632
Within Groups	9.726167	12	0.810514		
Total	33.09938	15			

Is there evidence to suggest a difference in the mean repair times at the four body shops? Use the .05 significance level.
a. What are the null and alternate hypotheses?
b. What is the test statistic?
c. What is the *p*-value?
d. What is your decision regarding the null hypothesis?
e. Interpret the result.

25. The fuel efficiencies for a sample of 27 compact, midsize, and large cars are entered into a statistical software package. Analysis of variance is used to investigate if there is

a difference in the mean miles per gallon of the three car sizes. What do you conclude? Use the .01 significance level. The results of the analysis follow:

Summary				
Groups	Sample Size	Sum	Average	Variance
Compact	12	268.3	22.35833	9.388106
Midsize	9	172.4	19.15556	7.315278
Large	6	100.5	16.75	7.303

ANOVA					
Source of Variation	SS	df	MS	F	p-value
Between Groups	136.4803	2	68.24014	8.258752	0.001866
Within Groups	198.3064	24	8.262766		
Total	334.7867	26			

a. What are the null and alternate hypotheses?
b. What is the test statistic?
c. What is the *p*-value?
d. What is your decision regarding the null hypothesis?
e. Interpret the result.

26. Three assembly lines are used to produce a certain component for an airliner. To examine the production rate, a random sample of six hourly periods is chosen for each assembly line and the number of components produced during these periods for each line is recorded. The output from a statistical software package is:

Summary				
Groups	Sample Size	Sum	Average	Variance
Line A	6	250	41.66667	0.266667
Line B	6	260	43.33333	0.666667
Line C	6	249	41.5	0.7

ANOVA					
Source of Variation	SS	df	MS	F	p-value
Between Groups	12.33333	2	6.166667	11.32653	0.001005
Within Groups	8.166667	15	0.544444		
Total	20.5	17			

a. What are the null and alternate hypotheses?
b. What is the test statistic?
c. What is the *p*-value?
d. Using a .01 significance level, what is your decision regarding the null hypothesis?
e. Interpret the result.
f. Compute 99% confidence intervals that estimate the difference between each pair of means.
g. Which pairs of means are statistically different?

27. **FILE** The postal service sorts mail as Priority Mail Express, Priority Mail, First-Class Mail, or Standard Mail. Over a period of 3 weeks, 18 of each type were mailed from

the Network Distribution Center in Atlanta, Georgia, to Des Moines, Iowa. The total delivery time in days was recorded. Minitab was used to perform the ANOVA. The results follow:

Analysis of Variance

Source	DF	Adj SS	Adj MS	F-Value	P-Value
Factor	3	35.7678	11.9226	13.62	<0.0001
Error	68	59.5167	0.8752		
Total	71	95.2844			

Model Summary

S	R-sq	R-sq(adj)	R-sq(pred)
0.935545	37.54%	34.78%	29.97%

Means

Factor	N	Mean	StDev	95% CI
Priority Mail Express	18	1.2556	0.6271	(0.8155, 1.6956)
Priority Mail	18	1.9944	0.9434	(1.5544, 2.4345)
First-Class Mail	18	2.8611	1.0600	(2.4211, 3.3011)
Standard Mail	18	3.0000	1.0460	(2.5600, 3.4400)

Pooled StDev = 0.935545

Fisher Individual Tests for Differences of Means

Difference of Levels	Difference of Means	SE of Difference	95% CI	T-Value	Adjusted P-Value
Priority Mail-Priority Mail Express	0.7389	0.3118	(0.1166, 1.3612)	2.37	0.0207
First-Class Mail-Priority Mail Express	1.6056	0.3118	(0.9833, 2.2278)	5.15	<0.0001
Standard Mail-Priority Mail Express	1.7444	0.3118	(1.1222, 2.3667)	5.59	<0.0001
First-Class Mail-Priority Mail	0.8667	0.3118	(0.2444, 1.4890)	2.78	0.0070
Standard Mail-Priority Mail	1.0056	0.3118	(0.3833, 1.6278)	3.22	0.0019
Standard Mail-First-Class Mail	0.1389	0.3118	(-0.4834, 0.7612)	0.45	0.6575

Simultaneous confidence level = 80.02%

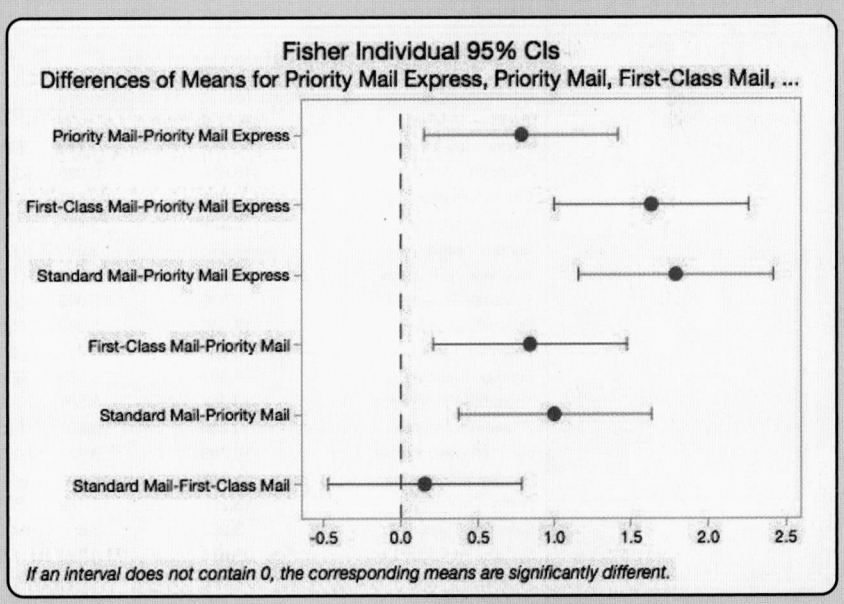

Fisher Individual 95% CIs
Differences of Means for Priority Mail Express, Priority Mail, First-Class Mail, ...

If an interval does not contain 0, the corresponding means are significantly different.

Using the ANOVA results, compare the average delivery times of the four different types of mail.

28. **FILE** To prevent spam from entering your email inbox, you use a filter. You are interested in knowing if the number of spam emails differs by day of the week. The number of spam emails by day of week is counted and recorded. Minitab is used to perform the data analysis. Here are the results:

Analysis of Variance

Source	DF	Adj SS	Adj MS	F-Value	P-Value
Factor	6	2266.92	377.820	9.29	<0.0001
Error	48	1952.43	40.676		
Total	54	4219.35			

Means

Factor	N	Mean	StDev	95% CI
Monday	10	76.400	4.452	(72.345, 80.455)
Tuesday	9	60.444	4.333	(56.170, 64.719)
Wednesday	7	74.286	4.231	(69.439, 79.132)
Thursday	8	60.750	6.251	(56.216, 65.284)
Friday	8	74.000	7.838	(69.466, 78.534)
Saturday	5	64.000	7.036	(58.265, 69.735)
Sunday	8	69.125	9.372	(64.591, 73.659)

Pooled StDev = 6.37774

Grouping Information Using the Fisher LSD Method and 95% Confidence

Factor	N	Mean	Grouping			
Monday	10	76.400	A			
Wednesday	7	74.286	A	B		
Friday	8	74.000	A	B		
Sunday	8	69.125		B	C	
Saturday	5	64.000			C	D
Thursday	8	60.750				D
Tuesday	9	60.444				D

Means that do not share a letter are significantly different.

Fisher Individual Tests for Differences of Means

Difference of Levels	Difference of Means	SE of Difference	95% CI	T-Value	Adjusted P-Value
Tuesday-Monday	-15.956	2.930	(-21.847, -10.064)	-5.44	<0.0001
Wednesday-Monday	-2.114	3.143	(-8.434, 4.205)	-0.67	0.5044
Thursday-Monday	-15.650	3.025	(-21.733, -9.567)	-5.17	<0.0001
Friday-Monday	-2.400	3.025	(-8.483, 3.683)	-0.79	0.4315
Saturday-Monday	-12.400	3.493	(-19.424, -5.376)	-3.55	0.0009
Sunday-Monday	-7.275	3.025	(-13.358, -1.192)	-2.40	0.0201
Wednesday-Tuesday	13.841	3.214	(7.379, 20.304)	4.31	<0.0001
Thursday-Tuesday	0.306	3.099	(-5.925, 6.537)	0.10	0.9219
Friday-Tuesday	13.556	3.099	(7.325, 19.787)	4.37	<0.0001
Saturday-Tuesday	3.556	3.557	(-3.597, 10.708)	1.00	0.3226
Sunday-Tuesday	8.681	3.099	(2.450, 14.912)	2.80	0.0073
Thursday-Wednesday	-13.536	3.301	(-20.172, -6.899)	-4.10	0.0002
Friday-Wednesday	-0.286	3.301	(-6.922, 6.351)	-0.09	0.9314
Saturday-Wednesday	-10.286	3.734	(-17.794, -2.777)	-2.75	0.0083
Sunday-Wednesday	-5.161	3.301	(-11.797, 1.476)	-1.56	0.1245
Friday-Thursday	13.250	3.189	(6.838, 19.662)	4.16	0.0001
Saturday-Thursday	3.250	3.636	(-4.060, 10.560)	0.89	0.3759
Sunday-Thursday	8.375	3.189	(1.963, 14.787)	2.63	0.0115
Saturday-Friday	-10.000	3.636	(-17.310, -2.690)	-2.75	0.0084
Sunday-Friday	-4.875	3.189	(-11.287, 1.537)	-1.53	0.1329
Sunday-Saturday	5.125	3.636	(-2.185, 12.435)	1.41	0.1651

Simultaneous confidence level = 57.84%

Using the ANOVA results, compare the average number of spam emails for each day of the week.

29. **FILE** Shank's Inc., a nationwide advertising firm, wants to know whether the size of an advertisement and the color of the advertisement make a difference in the response of magazine readers. A random sample of readers is shown ads of four different colors and three different sizes. Each reader is asked to give the particular combination of size and color a score between 1 and 10. Assume that the ratings follow the normal distribution. The score for each combination is shown in the following table (for example, the rating for a small red ad is 2).

Size of Ad	Color of Ad			
	Red	Blue	Orange	Green
Small	2	3	3	8
Medium	3	5	6	7
Large	6	7	8	8

Is there a difference in the effectiveness of an advertisement by color and by size?
a. What are the null and alternate hypotheses?
b. What are the test statistics?
c. What are the p-values?
d. Using a .05 significance level, what is your decision regarding the null hypotheses?
e. Interpret the result.

30. **FILE** There are four McBurger restaurants in the Columbus, Georgia, area. The numbers of burgers sold at the respective restaurants for each of the last 6 weeks are shown here. Is there a difference in the mean number sold among the four restaurants when the factor of week is considered?

Week	Restaurant			
	Metro	Interstate	University	River
1	124	160	320	190
2	234	220	340	230
3	430	290	290	240
4	105	245	310	170
5	240	205	280	180
6	310	260	270	205

a. What are the null and alternate hypotheses?
b. What are the test statistics?
c. What are the p-values?
d. Using a .05 significance level, what is your decision regarding the null hypotheses?
e. Interpret the result.

31. **FILE** The city of Tucson, Arizona, employs people to assess the value of homes for the purpose of calculating real estate tax. The city manager sends each assessor to the same five homes and then compares the results. The information is given here, in thousands of dollars. Can we conclude that there is a difference in the assessors?

Home	Assessor			
	Zawodny	Norman	Cingle	Holiday
A	$53.0	$55.0	$49.0	$45.0
B	50.0	51.0	52.0	53.0
C	48.0	52.0	47.0	53.0
D	70.0	68.0	65.0	64.0
E	84.0	89.0	92.0	86.0

a. What are the null and alternate hypotheses?
b. What are the test statistics?
c. What are the p-values?
d. Using a .05 significance level, what is your decision regarding the null hypotheses?
e. Interpret the result.

32. **FILE** A task requires the completion of four activities. A teacher would like to know if differences in the sequence of the four activities results in different task completion times. The teacher selects three students and demonstrates the activities in random order to the students. Then each student completes the task with each of the activity sequences. The completion times are recorded. The following table shows the minutes for each student to complete each task.

Sequence	Time (minutes)		
	Oakley	Sam	Hayden
A	22.4	20.8	21.5
B	17.0	19.4	20.7
C	19.2	20.2	21.2
D	20.3	18.6	20.4

a. What are the null and alternate hypotheses?
b. What are the test statistics?
c. What are the p-values?
d. Using a .05 significance level, what is your decision regarding the null hypotheses?
e. Interpret the result.

33. **FILE** A research firm wants to compare the miles per gallon of unleaded regular, mid-grade, and super premium gasolines. Because of differences in the performance of different automobiles, seven different automobiles were selected and treated as blocks. Therefore, each brand of gasoline was tested with each type of automobile. The results of the trials, in miles per gallon, are shown in the following table.

Automobile	Regular	Mid-grade	Super Premium
1	21	23	26
2	23	22	25
3	24	25	27
4	24	24	26
5	26	26	30
6	26	24	27
7	28	27	32

a. What are the null and alternate hypotheses?
b. What are the test statistics?
c. What are the p-values?
d. Using a .05 significance level, what is your decision regarding the null hypotheses?
e. Interpret the result.

34. **FILE** Each of three supermarket chains in the Denver, Colorado, area claims to have the lowest overall prices. As part of an investigative study on supermarket advertising, a local television station conducted a study by randomly selecting nine grocery items. Then, on the same day, an intern was sent to each of the three stores to purchase the nine items. From the receipts, the following data were recorded.

Item	Super$	Ralph's	Lowblaws
1	$1.12	$1.02	$1.07
2	1.14	1.10	1.21
3	1.72	1.97	2.08
4	2.22	2.09	2.32
5	2.40	2.10	2.30
6	4.04	4.32	4.15
7	5.05	4.95	5.05
8	4.68	4.13	4.67
9	5.52	5.46	5.86

a. What are the null and alternate hypotheses?
b. What are the test statistics?
c. What are the p-values?
d. Using a .05 significance level, what is your decision regarding the null hypotheses?
e. Interpret the result.

35. **FILE** Following are the weights (in grams) of a sample of M&M's Plain candies, classified according to color. Use a statistical software system to determine whether there is a difference in the mean weights of candies of different colors.

Red	Orange	Yellow	Brown	Tan	Green
0.946	0.902	0.929	0.896	0.845	0.935
1.107	0.943	0.960	0.888	0.909	0.903
0.913	0.916	0.938	0.906	0.873	0.865
0.904	0.910	0.933	0.941	0.902	0.822
0.926	0.903	0.932	0.838	0.956	0.871
0.926	0.901	0.899	0.892	0.959	0.905
1.006	0.919	0.907	0.905	0.916	0.905
0.914	0.901	0.906	0.824	0.822	0.852
0.922	0.930	0.930	0.908		0.965
1.052	0.883	0.952	0.833		0.898
0.903		0.939			
0.895		0.940			
		0.882			
		0.906			

a. What are the null and alternate hypotheses?
b. What is the test statistic?
c. What is the p-value?
d. Using a .05 significance level, what is your decision regarding the null hypothesis?
e. Interpret the result.

36. There are four radio stations in Midland, Texas. The stations have different formats (hard rock, classical, country/western, and easy listening), but each is concerned with the number of minutes of music played per hour. From a sample of 10 randomly selected hours from each station, the sum of squared differences between each observation and the mean for its respective radio station, $\Sigma(x - \bar{x}_c)^2$ are:

Hard rock station:	126.29	Country/western station:	166.79
Classical station:	233.34	Easy listening station:	77.57

The total sum of squares for the data is: SS total = 1,099.61.
a. Determine SSE.
b. Determine SST.
c. Complete an ANOVA table.
d. At the .05 significance level, is there a difference in the treatment means?
e. If the mean for the hard rock station is 51.32 and the mean for the country/western station is 50.85, determine if there is a difference using the .05 significance level.

37. **FILE** The American Accounting Association recently conducted a study to compare the weekly wages of males and females employed in either the public or private sector of accounting. Random samples of five males and five females were selected in each group.

Sex	Sector	
	Public	Private
Male	$ 978	$1,335
	1,035	1,167
	964	1,236
	996	1,317
	1,117	1,192
Female	$ 863	$1,079
	975	1,160
	999	1,063
	1,019	1,110
	1,037	1,093

a. Draw an interaction plot of male and female means by sector.
b. Compute an ANOVA with statistical software and, using the .05 significance level, test the interaction effect of sex and sector on wages.
c. Based on your results in part (b), conduct the appropriate tests of hypotheses for differences in factor means.
d. Interpret the results in a brief report.

38. **FILE** Robert Altoff is vice president of engineering for a manufacturer of household washing machines. As part of a new product development project, he wishes to determine the optimal length of time for the washing cycle. Included in the project is a study of the relationship between the detergent used (four brands) and the length of the washing cycle (18, 20, 22, or 24 minutes). To run the experiment, 32 standard household laundry loads (having equal amounts of dirt and the same total weights) are randomly assigned to the 16 detergent–washing cycle combinations. The results (in pounds of dirt removed) are shown here:

Detergent Brand	Cycle Time (min)			
	18	20	22	24
A	0.13	0.12	0.19	0.15
	0.11	0.11	0.17	0.18
B	0.14	0.15	0.18	0.20
	0.10	0.14	0.17	0.18
C	0.16	0.15	0.18	0.19
	0.17	0.14	0.19	0.21
D	0.09	0.12	0.16	0.15
	0.13	0.13	0.16	0.17

a. Draw an interaction plot of the detergent means by cycle time.
b. Compute the ANOVA with statistical software and, using the .05 significance level, test the interaction effect of brand and cycle time on "dirt removed."
c. Based on your results in part (b), conduct the appropriate tests of hypotheses for differences in factor means.
d. Interpret the results in a brief report.

DATA ANALYTICS

39. **FILE** The North Valley Real Estate data report information on the homes sold last year.
    a. At the .02 significance level, is there a difference in the variability of the selling prices of the homes that have a pool versus those that do not have a pool?
    b. At the .02 significance level, is there a difference in the variability of the selling prices of the homes with an attached garage versus those that do not have an attached garage?
    c. At the .05 significance level, is there a difference in the mean selling price of the homes among the five townships?
    d. Adam Marty recently joined North Valley Real Estate and was assigned 20 homes to market and show. When he was hired, North Valley assured him that the 20 homes would be fairly assigned to him. When he reviewed the selling prices of his assigned homes, he thought that the prices were much below the average of $357,000. Adam was able to find the data of the homes assigned to agents in the firm. Use statistical inference to compare the mean price of homes assigned to him to the mean price of homes assigned to the other agents. What do the results indicate? How is your analysis defining fairness?
    e. Home buyers finance the purchase of their home with a mortgage. In these data, the mortgages are either a fixed rate mortgage paid over 30 years or an adjustable rate mortgage. The adjustable rate mortgage provides a lower introductory interest rate for the first 5 years of occupancy. Then, in the fifth year, the rate is adjusted to the current rate plus an additional percent. Usually, the adjusted rate is higher than the "introductory" rate. With this information, we may predict that the average years of occupancy would be different for homeowners based on the type of mortgage and whether they defaulted on the mortgage. Use the data to evaluate this prediction.

40. **FILE** Refer to the Baseball 2021 data, which report information on the 30 Major League Baseball teams for the 2021 season.
    a. At the .10 significance level, is there a difference in the variation in team salary among the American and National League teams?
    b. Create a variable that classifies a team's total attendance into three groups: less than 2.0 (million), 2.0 up to 3.0, and 3.0 or more. At the .05 significance level, is there a difference in the mean number of games won among the three groups?
    c. Using the same attendance variable developed in part (b), is there a difference in the mean number of home runs hit per team? Use the .05 significance level.
    d. Using the same attendance variable developed in part (b), is there a difference in the mean salary of the three groups? Use the .05 significance level.

41. **FILE** Refer to the Lincolnville School District bus data.
    a. Conduct a test of hypothesis to reveal whether the mean maintenance cost is equal for each of the bus manufacturers. Use the .01 significance level.
    b. Conduct a test of hypothesis to determine whether the mean miles traveled since the last maintenance is equal for each bus manufacturer. Use the .05 significance level.

A REVIEW OF CHAPTERS 10–12

This section is a review of the major concepts and terms introduced in Chapters 10, 11, and 12. Chapter 10 began our study of hypothesis testing. A hypothesis is an assumption about a characteristic of a population. In statistical hypothesis testing, we begin by making a statement about the value of the population parameter in the null hypothesis. We establish the null hypothesis for the purpose of testing. When we complete the testing, our decision is either to reject or to fail to reject the null hypothesis. If we reject the null hypothesis, we conclude that the alternate hypothesis is true. The alternate hypothesis is "accepted" only if we show that the null hypothesis is false. We also refer to the alternate hypothesis as the research hypothesis. Most of the time we want to prove the alternate hypothesis.

In Chapter 10, we selected random samples from a single population and tested whether it was reasonable that the population parameter under study equaled a particular value. For example, we wish to investigate whether the mean tenure of those holding the position of CEO in large firms is 12 years. We select a sample of CEOs, compute the sample mean, and compare the mean of the sample to the population. The single population under consideration is the length of tenure of CEOs of large firms. We described methods for conducting the test when the population standard deviation was available and when it was not available.

In Chapter 11, we extended the idea of hypothesis testing to whether two independent random samples came from populations having equal population means. For example, St. Mathews Hospital operates an urgent care facility on both the north and south sides of Knoxville, Tennessee. The research question is: Is the mean waiting time for patients visiting the two facilities the same? To investigate, we select a random sample from each of the facilities and compute the sample means. We test the null hypothesis that the mean waiting time is the same at the two facilities. The alternate hypothesis is that the mean waiting time is not the same for the two facilities. If the population standard deviations are known, we use the z-distribution as the test statistic. If the population standard deviations are estimated with sample standard deviations, the test statistic follows the t-distribution. If the sample standard deviations are estimated, we presented a way to test the equality of population variances using the F-distribution. The hypothesis testing procedure comparing two population means differs depending on the hypothesized equality of the population variances. The chapter also shows the procedure to compare two population proportions.

Our discussion in Chapter 11 also concerned dependent samples. The test statistic is the t-distribution and we assume that the distribution of differences follows the normal distribution. One typical paired sample problem calls for recording an individual's blood pressure before administering medication and then again afterward to evaluate the effectiveness of the medication. We also considered the case of testing two population proportions. For example, the production manager wished to compare the proportion of defects on the day shift with that of the second shift.

Chapter 11 dealt with the difference between two population means. Chapter 12 presented tests for variances and a procedure called the *analysis of variance,* or *ANOVA.* ANOVA is used to simultaneously determine whether several independent normal populations have the same mean. This is accomplished by comparing the variances of the random samples selected from these populations. We apply the usual hypothesis testing procedure, but we use the F-distribution as the test statistic. Often the calculations are tedious, so a statistical software package is recommended.

As an example of analysis of variance, a test could be conducted to resolve whether there is any difference in effectiveness among five fertilizers on the weight of popcorn ears. This type of analysis is referred to as *one-factor ANOVA* because we are able to draw conclusions about only one factor, called a *treatment.* If we want to draw conclusions about the simultaneous effects of more than one factor or variable, we use the *two-factor ANOVA* technique. Both the one-factor and two-factor tests use the *F-distribution* as the distribution of the test statistic. The F-distribution is also the distribution of the test statistic used to find whether one normal population has more variation than another.

An additional feature of the two-factor ANOVA is the possibility that interactions may exist between the factors. There is an *interaction* if the response to one of the factors depends on the level of the other factor. Fortunately, the ANOVA is easily extended to include a test for interactions.

PROBLEMS

For Problems 1–6, state: (a) the null and the alternate hypotheses, (b) the decision rule, (c) the decision regarding the null hypothesis, and (d) then interpret the result.

1. A machine is set to produce tennis balls so the mean bounce is 36 inches when the ball is dropped from a platform of a certain height. The production supervisor suspects that the mean bounce has changed and is less than 36 inches. As an experiment, a sample of 12 balls was dropped from the platform and the mean height of the bounce was 35.5 inches, with a standard deviation of .9 inches. At the .05 significance level, can the supervisor conclude that the mean bounce height is less than 36 inches?

2. **FILE** It was hypothesized that road construction workers, on the average, spend 20 minutes of each hour not engaged in productive work. Some claimed the nonproductive time is greater than 20 minutes. An actual study conducted at a construction site used a stopwatch and other ways of checking the work habits. A random check of workers revealed the following unproductive times, in minutes, during a 1-hour period (exclusive of regularly scheduled breaks):

| 10 | 25 | 17 | 20 | 28 | 30 | 18 | 23 | 18 |

Using the .05 significance level, is it reasonable to conclude the mean unproductive time is greater than 20 minutes?

3. Stiktite Inc. plans a test of the mean holding power of two glues designed for plastic. First, a small plastic hook was coated at one end with Epox glue and fastened to a sheet of plastic. After it dried, weight was added to the hook until it separated from the sheet of plastic. The weight was then recorded. This was repeated until 12 hooks were tested. The same procedure was followed for Holdtite glue, but only 10 hooks were used. The sample results, in pounds, were:

	Epox	Holdtite
Sample size	12	10
Sample mean	250	252
Sample standard deviation	5	8

First, test the assumption that the population variances are equal. Then, at the .01 significance level, is there a difference between the mean holding power of Epox and that of Holdtite?

4. **FILE** Pittsburgh Paints wishes to test an additive formulated to increase the life of paints used in the hot and arid conditions of the Southwest. The top half of a piece of wood was painted using the regular paint. The bottom half was painted with the paint including the additive. The same procedure was followed for a total of 10 pieces. Then each piece was subjected to brilliant light. The data, the number of hours each piece lasted before it faded beyond a certain point, follow:

	Number of Hours by Sample									
	A	B	C	D	E	F	G	H	I	J
Without additive	325	313	320	340	318	312	319	330	333	319
With additive	323	313	326	343	310	320	313	340	330	315

Using the .05 significance level, determine whether the additive is effective in prolonging the life of the paint.

5. **FILE** A Buffalo, New York, cola distributor is featuring a special sale on 12-packs. She wonders where in the grocery store to place the cola for maximum attention. Should it be near the front door of the grocery stores, in the cola section, at the checkout registers, or near the milk and other dairy products? Four stores with similar total sales cooperated in an experiment. In one store, the 12-packs were stacked near the front door, in another they were placed near the checkout registers, and so on. The number of cases sold during randomly selected hours were recorded at each store. The results are:

Cola at the Door	In Soft Drink Section	Near Registers	Dairy Section
6	5	7	10
8	10	10	9
3	12	9	6
7	4	4	11
	9	5	
		7	

The Buffalo distributor wants to find out whether there is a difference in the mean number of cases sold based on the four locations in the store. Use the .05 significance level.

6. **FILE** Williams Corporation is investigating the effects of educational background on employee performance. A potential relevant variable, in this case, is the self-rated social status of the employee. The company has recorded the annual sales volumes (in $000) achieved by sales employees in each of the categories shown. Perform a complete two-way analysis of variance (including the possibility of interactions) on the data and describe what your results suggest.

Self-Rated Social Status	School Type		
	Ivy League	State-supported	Small Private
Low	62, 61	68, 64	70, 70
Medium	68, 64	74, 68	62, 65
High	70, 71	57, 60	57, 56

7. A school supervisor is reviewing initial wages of former students (in $000). Samples were taken over 3 years for four different majors (accounting, administration, finance, and marketing). For each combination of major and year, three former students were sampled.

Major/Year	2014	2015	2016
Accounting	75.4, 69.8, 62.3	73.9, 78.8, 62.0	64.2, 80.8, 68.2
Administration	61.5, 59.9, 62.1	63.9, 57.6, 66.5	74.2, 67.5, 58.1
Finance	63.6, 70.2, 72.2	69.2, 72.5, 67.2	74.7, 66.4, 77.9
Marketing	71.3, 69.2, 66.4	74.0, 67.6, 61.7	60.0, 61.3, 62.5

a. Here is an interaction plot of the information. What does it reveal?

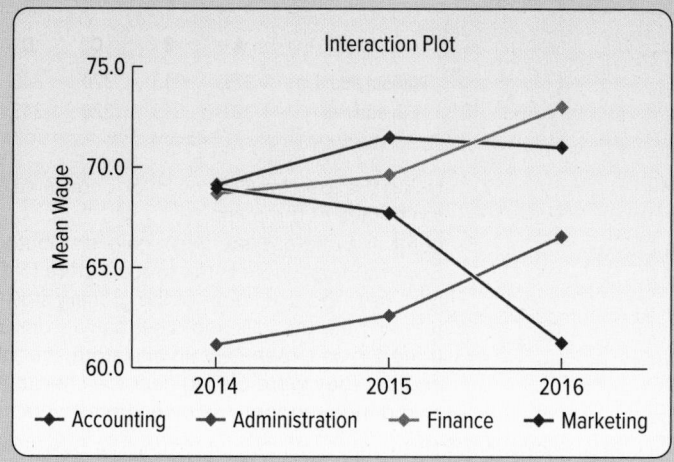

b. Write out all of the pairs of null and alternative hypotheses you would apply for a two-way ANOVA.

c. Here is the statistical software output. Use the .05 level to check for interactions.

```
Source        DF        SS        MS        F        P
Major          3    329.20   109.732     3.39    0.034
Year           2      7.32     3.659     0.11    0.894
Interaction    6    183.57    30.595     0.94    0.482
Error         24    777.29    32.387
Total         35   1297.37
```

d. If proper, test the other hypotheses at the .05 significance level. If it is not appropriate, describe why you should not do the tests.

CASES

A. Century National Bank

Refer to the description of Century National Bank on page 126 at the end of the Review of Chapters 1–4.

With many other options available, customers no longer let their money sit in a checking account. For many years the mean checking balance has been $1,600. Do the sample data indicate that the mean account balance has declined from this value?

Recent years have also seen an increase in the use of ATM machines. When Mr. Selig took over the bank, the mean number of transactions per month per customer was 8; now he believes it has increased to more than 10. In fact, the advertising agency that prepares TV commercials for Century would like to use this on the new commercial being designed. Is there sufficient evidence to conclude that the mean number of transactions per customer is more than 10 per month? Could the advertising agency say the mean is more than 9 per month?

The bank has branch offices in four different cities: Cincinnati, Ohio; Atlanta, Georgia; Louisville, Kentucky; and Erie, Pennsylvania. Mr. Selig would like to know whether there is a difference in the mean checking account balances among the four branches. If there are differences, between which branches do these differences occur?

Mr. Selig is also interested in the bank's ATMs. Is there a difference in ATM use among the branches? Also, do customers who have debit cards tend to use ATMs differently from those who do not have debit cards? Is there a difference in ATM use by those with checking accounts that pay interest versus those that do not? Prepare a report for Mr. Selig answering these questions.

B. Bell Grove Medical Center

Ms. Gene Dempsey manages the emergency care center at Bell Grove Medical Center. One of her responsibilities is to have enough nurses so that incoming patients needing service can be handled promptly. It is stressful for patients to wait a long time for emergency care even when their care needs are not life threatening. Ms. Dempsey gathered the following information regarding the number of patients over the last several weeks. The center is not open on weekends. Does it appear that there are any differences in the number of patients served by the day of the week? If there are differences, which days seem to be the busiest? Write a brief report summarizing your findings.

Date	Day	Patients
9-29-22	Monday	38
9-30-22	Tuesday	28
10-1-22	Wednesday	28
10-2-22	Thursday	30
10-3-22	Friday	35
10-6-22	Monday	35
10-7-22	Tuesday	25
10-8-22	Wednesday	22
10-9-22	Thursday	21
10-10-22	Friday	32
10-13-22	Monday	37
10-14-22	Tuesday	29
10-15-22	Wednesday	27
10-16-22	Thursday	28
10-17-22	Friday	35
10-20-22	Monday	37
10-21-22	Tuesday	26
10-22-22	Wednesday	28
10-23-22	Thursday	23
10-24-22	Friday	33

PRACTICE TEST

Part 1—Objective

1. A statement about the value of a population parameter that always includes the equal sign is called the _____.

2. The likelihood of rejecting a true null hypothesis is called the _____.

3. Assuming the null hypothesis is true, the likelihood of finding a value of the test statistic at least as extreme as the one found in the sample is called the _____.

4. When conducting a test of hypothesis about a single population mean, the z-distribution is used as the test statistic only when the _____ is known.

5. In a two-sample test of hypothesis for means, if the population standard deviations are not known, *what must we assume about the shape of the populations?*

6. A value calculated from sample information used to determine whether to reject the null hypothesis is called the _____.

7. In a two-tailed test, the rejection region is _____. (all in the upper tail, all in the lower tail, split evenly between the two tails, none of these—pick one)

8. Which of the following is not a characteristic of the F-distribution? (continuous, positively skewed, range from $-\infty$ to ∞, family of distributions)

1. _____

2. _____

3. _____

4. _____

5. _____

6. _____

7. _____

8. _____

9. To perform a one-way ANOVA, the treatments must be _____.
(independent, mutually exclusive, continuous)

9. _____

10. In a one-way ANOVA, there are four treatments and six observations in each treatment. What are the degrees of freedom for the *F*-distribution?

10. _____

Part 2—Problems

For Problems 1 and 2, state the null and alternate hypotheses and the decision rule, make a decision regarding the null hypothesis, and interpret the result.

1. The Park Manager at Fort Fisher State Park in North Carolina believes the typical summer visitor spends more than 90 minutes in the park. A sample of 18 visitors during the months of June, July, and August revealed the mean time in the park for visitors was 96 minutes, with a standard deviation of 12 minutes. At the .01 significance level, is it reasonable to conclude the mean time in the park is greater than 90 minutes?

2. Is there a difference in the mean miles traveled per week by each of two taxicab companies operating in the Grand Strand area? The *Sun News*, the local paper, is investigating and obtained the following sample information. At the .05 significance level, is it reasonable to conclude there is a difference in the mean miles traveled? Test the assumption that the population variances are equal.

Variable	Yellow Cab	Horse and Buggy Cab Company
Sample size	14	12
Mean miles	837	797
Standard deviation	30	40

3. The results of a one-way ANOVA are reported here. Use the .05 significance level.

ANOVA				
Source of Variation	SS	df	MS	F
Between groups	6.892202	2	3.446101	4.960047
Within groups	12.50589	18	0.694772	
Total	19.3981	20		

Answer the following questions.
a. How many treatments are in the study?
b. What is the total sample size?
c. What is the critical value of *F*?
d. Write out the null hypothesis and the alternate hypothesis.
e. What is your decision regarding the null hypothesis?
f. Why can we conclude the treatment means differ?

Correlation and Linear Regression

13

Ingram Publishing/SuperStock

▲ **TRAVELAIR.COM** would like to know if there is a correlation between airfare and flight distance. If there is a correlation, what percentage of the variation in airfare is accounted for by distance? How much does each additional mile add to the fare? (See Exercise 61 and LO13-2, LO13-3, and LO13-5.)

LEARNING OBJECTIVES

When you have completed this chapter, you will be able to:

LO13-1 Explain the purpose of correlation analysis.

LO13-2 Calculate a correlation coefficient to test and interpret the relationship between two variables.

LO13-3 Apply regression analysis to estimate the linear relationship between two variables.

LO13-4 Evaluate the significance of the slope of the regression equation.

LO13-5 Evaluate a regression equation's ability to predict using the standard error of the estimate and the coefficient of determination.

LO13-6 Calculate and interpret confidence and prediction intervals.

LO13-7 Use a log function to transform a nonlinear relationship.

Introduction

Chapters 2 through 4 presented *descriptive statistics.* We organized raw data into a frequency distribution and computed several measures of location and measures of dispersion to describe the major characteristics of the distribution. In Chapters 5 through 7, we described probability, and from probability statements, we created probability distributions. In Chapters 8 through 12, we studied *statistical inference,* where we collected a sample to estimate a population parameter such as the population mean or population proportion. In addition, we used the sample data to test a hypothesis about a population mean or a population proportion, the difference between two population means, or the equality of several population means. Each of these tests involved just *one* interval- or ratio-level variable, such as the profit made on a car sale, the income of bank presidents, or the number of patients admitted each month to a particular hospital.

In this chapter, we shift the emphasis to the study of relationships between two interval- or ratio-level variables. In all business fields, identifying and studying relationships between variables can provide information on ways to increase profits, methods to decrease costs, or variables to predict demand. In marketing products, many firms use price reductions through coupons and discount pricing to increase sales. In this example, we are interested in the relationship between two variables: price reductions and sales. To collect the data, a company can test-market a variety of price reduction methods and observe sales. We hope to confirm a relationship that decreasing price leads to increased sales. In economics, you will find many relationships between two variables that are the basis of economics, such as price and demand.

As another familiar example, recall in Chapter 4 we used the Applewood Auto Group data to show the relationship between two variables with a scatter diagram. We plotted the profit for each vehicle sold on the vertical axis and the age of the buyer on the horizontal axis. See page 113. In that graph, we observed that as the age of the buyer increased, the profit for each vehicle also increased.

Other examples of relationships between two variables are:

- Does the amount Healthtex spends per month on training its sales force affect its monthly sales?
- Is the number of square feet in a home related to the cost to heat the home in January?
- In a study of fuel efficiency, is there a relationship between miles per gallon and the weight of a car?
- Does the number of hours that students study for an exam influence the exam score?

In this chapter, we carry this idea further. That is, we develop numerical measures to express the relationship between two variables. Is the relationship strong or weak? Is it direct or inverse? In addition, we develop an equation to express the relationship between variables. This will allow us to estimate one variable on the basis of another.

To begin our study of relationships between two variables, we examine the meaning and purpose of **correlation analysis.** We continue by developing an equation that will allow us to estimate the value of one variable based on the value of another. This is called **regression analysis.** We will also evaluate the ability of the equation to accurately make estimations.

LO13-1
Explain the purpose of correlation analysis.

What Is Correlation Analysis?

When we study the relationship between two interval- or ratio-scale variables, we often start with a scatter diagram. This procedure provides a visual representation of the relationship between the variables. The next step is usually to calculate the correlation coefficient. It provides a quantitative measure of the strength of the relationship between two variables. As an example, the sales manager of North American Copier Sales, which has a large sales force throughout the United States and Canada, wants to determine whether there is a relationship between the number of sales calls made in a month and the number of copiers sold that month. The manager selects a random sample of 15

TABLE 13–1 Number of Sales Calls and Copiers Sold for 15 Salespeople

Sales Representative	Sales Calls	Copiers Sold
Brian Virost	96	41
Carlos Ramirez	40	41
Carol Saia	104	51
Greg Fish	128	60
Jeff Hall	164	61
Mark Reynolds	76	29
Meryl Rumsey	72	39
Mike Kiel	80	50
Ray Snarsky	36	28
Rich Niles	84	43
Ron Broderick	180	70
Sal Spina	132	56
Soni Jones	120	45
Susan Welch	44	31
Tom Keller	84	30

representatives and determines, for each representative, the number of sales calls made and the number of copiers sold. This information is reported in Table 13–1.

By reviewing the data, we observe that there does seem to be some relationship between the number of sales calls and the number of units sold. That is, the salespeople who made the most sales calls sold the most units. However, the relationship is not "perfect" or exact. For example, Mark Reynolds made 36 more sales calls than Carlos Ramirez but sold 12 fewer copiers.

Discriminating against people based on their physical appearance is ethically wrong, and in many cases legally wrong. However, studies indicate that for both men and women, those who are perceived as good looking earn higher wages than those who are not. For example, for men there is a correlation between height and salary. For each additional inch of height, a man can expect to earn an additional $789 per year. So, a man 6′0″ tall receives nearly a $5,000 "stature" bonus over his 5′6″ counterpart. Being overweight or underweight is also related to earnings, particularly among women. A study showed that women who wear makeup can earn 30% more than non-makeup-wearing workers. **https://www.salary.com/passages/ways-your-looks-affect-your-pay/1/**

In addition to the graphical techniques in Chapter 4, we will develop numerical measures to precisely describe the relationship between the two variables, sales calls and copiers sold. This group of statistical techniques is called **correlation analysis.**

> **CORRELATION ANALYSIS** A group of techniques to measure the relationship between two variables.

The basic idea of correlation analysis is to report the relationship between two variables. The usual first step is to plot the data in a **scatter diagram.** An Example/Solution will show how a scatter diagram is used.

▶ **EXAMPLE**

North American Copier Sales sells copiers to businesses of all sizes throughout the United States and Canada. Ms. Marcy Bancer was recently promoted to the position of national sales manager. At the upcoming sales meeting, sales representatives from all over the country will be in attendance. She would like to impress upon them the importance of making that extra sales call each day. She decides to gather some information on the relationship between the number of sales calls and the number of copiers sold. She selects a random sample of

15 sales representatives and determines the number of sales calls they made last month and the number of copiers they sold. The sample information is reported in Table 13–1. What observations can you make about the relationship between the number of sales calls and the number of copiers sold? Develop a scatter diagram to display the information.

SOLUTION

Based on the information in Table 13–1, Ms. Bancer suspects there is a relationship between the number of sales calls made in a month and the number of copiers sold. Ron Broderick sold the most copiers last month and made 180 sales calls. On the other hand, Ray Snarsky, Carlos Ramirez, and Susan Welch made the fewest calls: 36, 40, and 44. They also had the lowest number of copiers sold among the sampled representatives.

The implication is that the number of copiers sold is related to the number of sales calls made. As the number of sales calls increases, it appears the number of copiers sold also increases. We refer to number of sales calls as the **independent variable** and number of copiers sold as the **dependent variable.**

The independent variable provides the basis for estimating or predicting the dependent variable. For example, we would like to predict the expected number of copiers sold if a salesperson makes 100 sales calls. In the randomly selected sample data, the independent variable—sales calls—is a random number.

The dependent variable is the variable that is being predicted or estimated. It can also be described as the result or outcome for a particular value of the independent variable. The dependent variable is random. That is, for a given value of the independent variable, there are many possible outcomes for the dependent variable.

It is common practice to scale the dependent variable (copiers sold) on the vertical or Y-axis and the independent variable (number of sales calls) on the horizontal or X-axis. To develop the scatter diagram of the North American Copier Sales information, we begin with the first sales representative, Brian Virost. Brian made 96 sales calls last month and sold 41 copiers, so $x = 96$ and $y = 41$. To plot this point, move along the horizontal axis to $x = 96$, then go vertically to $y = 41$ and place a dot at the intersection. This process is continued until all the paired data are plotted, as shown in Chart 13–1.

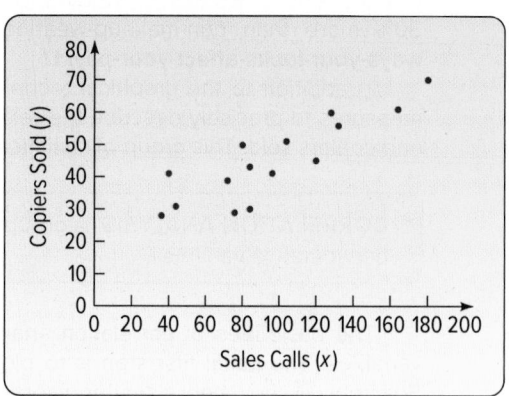

CHART 13–1 Scatter Diagram Showing Sales Calls and Copiers Sold

The scatter diagram shows graphically that the sales representatives who make more calls tend to sell more copiers. It is reasonable for Ms. Bancer, the national sales manager, to tell her salespeople that the more sales calls they make, the more copiers they can expect to sell. Note that, while there appears to be a positive relationship between the two variables, all the points do not fall on a straight line. In the following section, you will measure the strength and direction of this relationship between two variables by determining the correlation coefficient.

LO13-2
Calculate a correlation
coefficient to test and
interpret the relationship
between two variables.

The Correlation Coefficient

Originated by Karl Pearson about 1900, the **correlation coefficient** describes the strength of the relationship between two sets of interval-scaled or ratio-scaled variables. Designated *r*, it is often referred to as *Pearson's r* and as the *Pearson product-moment correlation coefficient*. It can assume any value from −1.00 to +1.00 inclusive. A correlation coefficient of −1.00 or +1.00 indicates *perfect correlation*. For example, a correlation coefficient for the preceding example computed to be +1.00 would indicate that the number of sales calls and the number of copiers sold are perfectly related in a positive linear sense. A computed value of −1.00 would reveal that sales calls and the number of copiers sold are perfectly related in an inverse linear sense. How the scatter diagram would appear if the relationship between the two variables were linear and perfect is shown in Chart 13–2.

> **CORRELATION COEFFICIENT** A measure of the strength of the linear relationship between two variables.

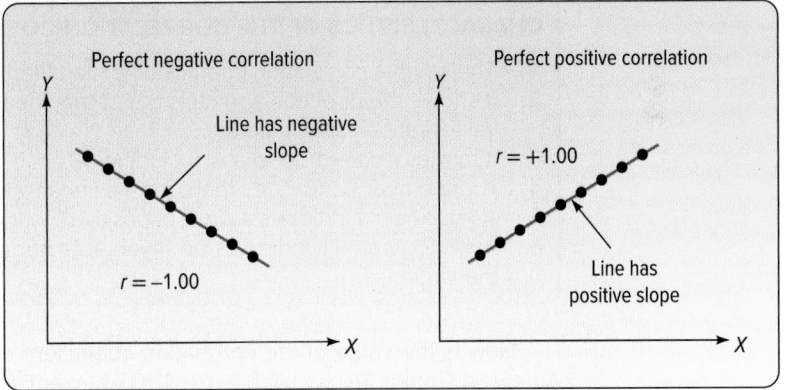

CHART 13–2 Scatter Diagrams Showing Perfect Negative Correlation and Perfect Positive Correlation

If there is absolutely no relationship between the two sets of variables, Pearson's *r* is zero. A correlation coefficient *r* close to 0 (say, .08) shows that the linear relationship is quite weak. The same conclusion is drawn if *r* = −.08. Coefficients of −.91 and +.91 have equal strength; both indicate very strong correlation between the two variables. Thus, *the strength of the correlation does not depend on the direction (either − or +).*

Scatter diagrams for *r* = 0, a weak *r* (say, −.23), and a strong *r* (say, +.87) are shown in Chart 13–3. Note that, if the correlation is weak, there is considerable scatter about a line drawn through the center of the data. For the scatter diagram representing a strong relationship, there is very little scatter about the line. This indicates, in the example shown on the chart, that hours studied is a good predictor of exam score.

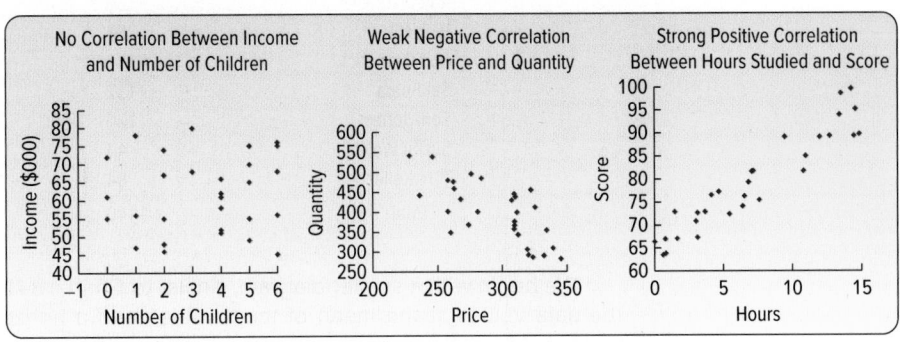

CHART 13–3 Scatter Diagrams Depicting Zero, Weak, and Strong Correlation

The following drawing summarizes the strength and direction of the correlation coefficient.

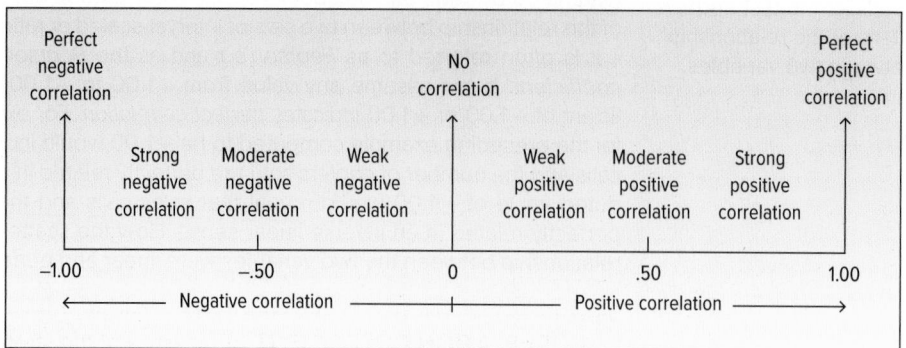

The characteristics of the correlation coefficient are summarized as follows:

CHARACTERISTICS OF THE CORRELATION COEFFICIENT

1. The sample correlation coefficient is identified by the lowercase letter r.
2. It shows the direction and strength of the linear relationship between two interval- or ratio-scale variables.
3. It ranges from −1 up to and including +1.
4. A value near 0 indicates there is little linear relationship between the variables.
5. A value near 1 indicates a direct or positive linear relationship between the variables.
6. A value near −1 indicates an inverse or negative linear relationship between the variables.

How is the value of the correlation coefficient determined? We will use the North American Copier Sales in Table 13–1 as an example. It is replicated in Table 13–2 for your convenience.

TABLE 13–2 Number of Sales Calls and Copiers Sold for 15 Salespeople

Sales Representative	Sales Calls	Copiers Sold
Brian Virost	96	41
Carlos Ramirez	40	41
Carol Saia	104	51
Greg Fish	128	60
Jeff Hall	164	61
Mark Reynolds	76	29
Meryl Rumsey	72	39
Mike Kiel	80	50
Ray Snarsky	36	28
Rich Niles	84	43
Ron Broderick	180	70
Sal Spina	132	56
Soni Jones	120	45
Susan Welch	44	31
Tom Keller	84	30
Total	1440	675

We begin with a scatter diagram, similar to Chart 13–2. Draw a vertical line through the data values at the mean of the x-values and a horizontal line at the mean of the *y*-values. In Chart 13–4, we've added a vertical line at 96 calls ($\bar{x} = \Sigma x/n = 1440/15 = 96$) and a horizontal line at 45 copiers ($\bar{y} = \Sigma y/n = 675/15 = 45$). These lines pass through the "center" of the data and divide the scatter diagram into four quadrants. Think of moving the origin from (0, 0) to (96, 45).

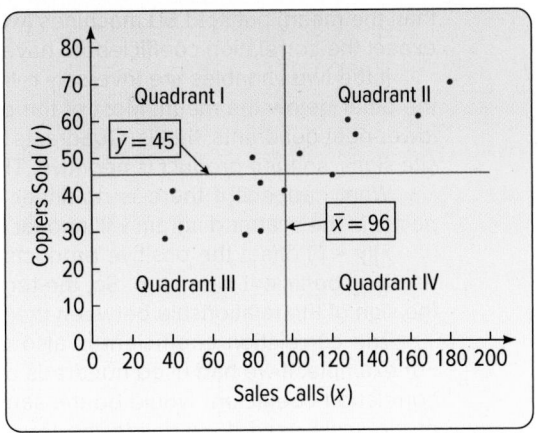

CHART 13–4 Computation of the Correlation Coefficient

Two variables are positively related when the number of copiers sold is above the mean and the number of sales calls is also above the mean. These points appear in the upper-right quadrant (labeled Quadrant II) of Chart 13–4. Similarly, when the number of copiers sold is less than the mean, so is the number of sales calls. These points fall in the lower-left quadrant of Chart 13–4 (labeled Quadrant III). For example, the third person on the list in Table 13–2, Carol Saia, made 104 sales calls and sold 51 copiers. These values are above their respective means, so this point is located in Quadrant II, which is in the upper-right quadrant. She made 8 more calls than the mean number of sales calls and sold 6 more than the mean number sold. Tom Keller, the last name on the list in Table 13–2, made 84 sales calls and sold 30 copiers. Both of these values are less than their respective means, hence this point is in the lower-left quadrant. Tom made 12 fewer sales calls and sold 15 fewer copiers than the respective means. The deviations from the mean number of sales calls and the mean number of copiers sold are summarized in Table 13–3 for

TABLE 13–3 Deviations from the Mean and Their Products

Sales Representative	Sales Calls (x)	Copiers Sold (y)	x − x̄	y − ȳ	(x − x̄)(y − ȳ)
Brian Virost	96	41	0	−4	0
Carlos Ramirez	40	41	−56	−4	224
Carol Saia	104	51	8	6	48
Greg Fish	128	60	32	15	480
Jeff Hall	164	61	68	16	1,088
Mark Reynolds	76	29	−20	−16	320
Meryl Rumsey	72	39	−24	−6	144
Mike Kiel	80	50	−16	5	−80
Ray Snarsky	36	28	−60	−17	1,020
Rich Niles	84	43	−12	−2	24
Ron Broderick	180	70	84	25	2,100
Sal Spina	132	56	36	11	396
Soni Jones	120	45	24	0	0
Susan Welch	44	31	−52	−14	728
Tom Keller	84	30	−12	−15	180
Totals	1440	675	0	0	6,672

the 15 sales representatives. The sum of the products of the deviations from the respective means is 6672. That is, the term $\Sigma(x - \bar{x})(y - \bar{y}) = 6{,}672$.

In both the upper-right and the lower-left quadrants, the product of $(x - \bar{x})(y - \bar{y})$ is positive because both of the factors have the same sign. In our example, this happens for all sales representatives except Mike Kiel. Mike made 80 sales calls (which is less than the mean) but sold 50 machines (which is more than the mean). We can therefore expect the correlation coefficient to have a positive value.

If the two variables are inversely related, one variable will be above the mean and the other below the mean. Most of the points, in this case, occur in the upper-left and lower-right quadrants, that is, Quadrants I and IV. Now $(x - \bar{x})$ and $(y - \bar{y})$ will have opposite signs, so their product is negative. The resulting correlation coefficient is negative.

What happens if there is no linear relationship between the two variables? The points in the scatter diagram will appear in all four quadrants. The negative products of $(x - \bar{x})(y - \bar{y})$ offset the positive products, so the sum is near zero. This leads to a correlation coefficient near zero. So, the term $\Sigma(x - \bar{x})(y - \bar{y})$ drives the strength as well as the sign of the relationship between the two variables.

The correlation coefficient is also unaffected by the units of the two variables. For example, if we had used hundreds of copiers sold instead of the number sold, the correlation coefficient would be the same. The correlation coefficient is independent of the scale used if we divide the term $\Sigma(x - \bar{x})(y - \bar{y})$ by the sample standard deviations. It is also made independent of the sample size and bounded by the values $+1.00$ and -1.00 if we divide by $(n - 1)$.

This reasoning leads to the following formula.

CORRELATION COEFFICIENT	$r = \dfrac{\Sigma(x - \bar{x})(y - \bar{y})}{(n - 1)s_x s_y}$	(13–1)

Tutorial #20
in Connect

To compute the correlation coefficient, we use the standard deviations of the sample of 15 sales calls and 15 copiers sold. We could use formula (3–10) to calculate the sample standard deviations or we could use a statistical software package. The link in the margin is a tutorial showing how to compute a variable's descriptive statistics using Excel. The following output from Excel shows the standard deviation of the number of sales calls is 42.76 and of the number of copiers sold 12.89.

⊿	A	B	C	D	E	F	G	H
1		Sales Representative	Sales Calls (x)	Copiers Sold (y)			Sales Calls (x)	Copiers Sold (y)
2		Brian Virost	96	41		Mean	96.00	45.00
3		Carlos Ramirez	40	41		Standard Error	11.04	3.33
4		Carol Saia	104	51		Median	84.00	43.00
5		Greg Fish	128	60		Mode	84.00	41.00
6		Jeff Hall	164	61		Standard Deviation	42.76	12.89
7		Mark Reynolds	76	29		Sample Variance	1828.57	166.14
8		Meryl Rumsey	72	39		Kurtosis	-0.32	-0.73
9		Mike Kiel	80	50		Skewness	0.46	0.36
10		Ray Snarsky	36	28		Range	144.00	42.00
11		Rich Niles	84	43		Minimum	36.00	28.00
12		Ron Broderick	180	70		Maximum	180.00	70.00
13		Sal Spina	132	56		Sum	1440.00	675.00
14		Soni Jones	120	45		Count	15.00	15.00
15		Susan Welch	44	31				
16		Tom Keller	84	30				
17		Total	1440	675				

Microsoft Excel

We now insert these values into formula (13–1) to determine the correlation coefficient.

$$r = \frac{\Sigma(x - \bar{x})(y - \bar{y})}{(n - 1)s_x s_y} = \frac{6672}{(15 - 1)(42.76)(12.89)} = .865$$

How do we interpret a correlation of .865? First, it is positive, so we conclude there is a direct relationship between the number of sales calls and the number of copiers sold. This confirms our reasoning based on the scatter diagram, Chart 13–4. The value of .865 is fairly close to 1.00, so we conclude that the association is strong.

We must be careful with the interpretation. The correlation of .865 indicates a strong positive linear association between the variables. Ms. Bancer would be correct to encourage the sales personnel to make that extra sales call because the number of sales calls made is related to the number of copiers sold. However, does this mean that more sales calls *cause* more sales? No, we have not demonstrated cause and effect here, only that the two variables—sales calls and copiers sold—are statistically related.

If there is a strong relationship (say, .97) between two variables, we are tempted to assume that an increase or decrease in one variable *causes* a change in the other variable. For example, historically, the consumption of Georgia peanuts and the consumption of aspirin have a strong correlation. However, this does not indicate that an increase in the consumption of peanuts *caused* the consumption of aspirin to increase. Likewise, the incomes of professors and the number of inmates in mental institutions have increased proportionately. Further, as the population of donkeys has decreased, there has been an increase in the number of doctoral degrees granted. Relationships such as these are called **spurious correlations.** What we can conclude when we find two variables with a strong correlation is that there is a relationship or association between the two variables, not that a change in one causes a change in the other.

▶ **EXAMPLE**

The Applewood Auto Group's marketing department believes younger buyers purchase vehicles on which lower profits are earned and the older buyers purchase vehicles on which higher profits are earned. They would like to use this information as part of an upcoming advertising campaign to try to attract older buyers, for whom the profits tend to be higher. Develop a scatter diagram depicting the relationship between vehicle profits and age of the buyer. Use statistical software to determine the correlation coefficient. Would this be a useful advertising feature?

SOLUTION

Using the Applewood Auto Group example, the first step is to graph the data using a scatter plot. It is shown in Chart 13–5.

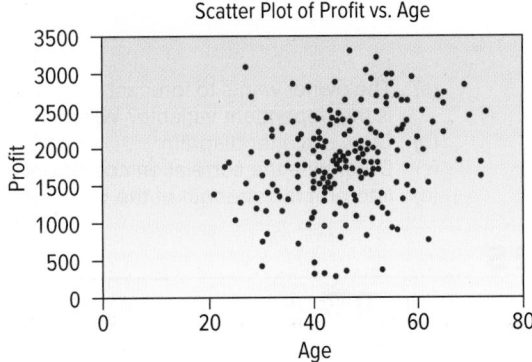

CHART 13–5 Scatter Diagram of Profit versus Age for the Applewood Auto Group Data

The scatter diagram suggests that a positive relationship exists between age and profit; however, that relationship does not appear strong.

Tutorial #62
in Connect

The next step is to calculate the correlation coefficient to evaluate the relative strength of the relationship. Statistical software provides an easy way to calculate the value of the correlation coefficient. The link in the margin is a tutorial demonstrating how to perform correlation analysis in Excel. The Excel output follows:

◢	A	B	C
1		*Age*	*Profit*
2	Age	1	
3	Profit	0.262	1

Microsoft Excel

For these data, $r = .262$. To evaluate the relationship between a buyer's age and the profit on a car sale:

1. The relationship is positive or direct. Why? Because the sign of the correlation coefficient is positive. This confirms that as the age of the buyer increases, the profit on a car sale also increases.
2. The correlation coefficient is $r = .262$. It is much closer to 0 than 1. Therefore, the relationship between the two variables is weak. We would observe that the relationship between the age of a buyer and the profit of the buyer's purchase is not very strong.

For Applewood Auto Group, the data do not support a business decision to create an advertising campaign to attract older buyers.

SELF-REVIEW 13–1

Haverty's Furniture is a family business that has been selling to retail customers in the Chicago area for many years. The company advertises extensively on radio, TV, and the Internet, emphasizing low prices and easy credit terms. The owner would like to review the relationship between sales and the amount spent on advertising. Following is information on sales and advertising expense for the last 4 months.

Month	Advertising Expense ($ million)	Sales Revenue ($ million)
July	2	7
August	1	3
September	3	8
October	4	10

(a) The owner wants to forecast sales on the basis of advertising expense. Which variable is the dependent variable? Which variable is the independent variable?
(b) Draw a scatter diagram.
(c) Determine the correlation coefficient.
(d) Interpret the strength of the correlation coefficient.

EXERCISES

1. **FILE** The following sample of observations was randomly selected.

x	4	5	3	6	10
y	4	6	5	7	7

Determine the correlation coefficient and interpret the relationship between *x* and *y*.

2. **FILE** The following sample of observations was randomly selected.

x	5	3	6	3	4	4	6	8
y	13	15	7	12	13	11	9	5

Determine the correlation coefficient and interpret the relationship between x and y.

3. **FILE** Bi-lo Appliance Super-Store has outlets in several large metropolitan areas in New England. The general sales manager aired a commercial for a digital camera on selected local TV stations prior to a sale starting on Saturday and ending Sunday. The manager obtained the information for Saturday–Sunday digital camera sales at the various outlets and paired it with the number of times the advertisement was shown on the local TV stations. The purpose is to find whether there is any relationship between the number of times the advertisement was aired and digital camera sales. The pairings are:

Location of TV Station	Number of Airings	Saturday–Sunday Sales ($ thousands)
Providence	4	15
Springfield	2	8
New Haven	5	21
Boston	6	24
Hartford	3	17

a. What is the dependent variable?
b. Draw a scatter diagram.
c. Determine the correlation coefficient.
d. Interpret the correlation coefficient.

4. **FILE** The production department of Celltronics International wants to explore the relationship between the number of employees who assemble a subassembly and the number produced. As an experiment, two employees were assigned to assemble the subassemblies. They produced 15 during a 1-hour period. Then four employees assembled them. They produced 25 during a 1-hour period. The complete set of paired observations follows:

Number of Assemblers	One-Hour Production (units)
2	15
4	25
1	10
5	40
3	30

The dependent variable is production; that is, it is assumed that different levels of production result from a different number of employees.

a. Draw a scatter diagram.
b. Based on the scatter diagram, does there appear to be any relationship between the number of assemblers and production? Explain.
c. Compute and interpret the correlation coefficient.

5. **FILE** The city council of Pine Bluffs is considering increasing the number of police in an effort to reduce crime. Before making a final decision, the council asked the chief of police to survey other cities of similar size to determine the relationship between the number of police and the number of crimes reported. The chief gathered the following sample information.

City	Police	Number of Crimes	City	Police	Number of Crimes
Oxford	15	17	Holgate	17	7
Starksville	17	13	Carey	12	21
Danville	25	5	Whistler	11	19
Athens	27	7	Woodville	22	6

  a. Which variable is the dependent variable and which is the independent variable? Hint: Which of the following makes better sense: Cities with more police have fewer crimes, or cities with fewer crimes have more police? Explain your choice.

  b. Draw a scatter diagram.

  c. Determine the correlation coefficient.

  d. Interpret the correlation coefficient. Does it surprise you that the correlation coefficient is negative?

6. **FILE** The owner of Maumee Ford-Volvo wants to study the relationship between the age of a car and its selling price. Listed is a random sample of 12 used cars sold at the dealership during the last year.

Car	Age (years)	Selling Price ($000)	Car	Age (years)	Selling Price ($000)
1	9	8.1	7	8	7.6
2	7	6.0	8	11	8.0
3	11	3.6	9	10	8.0
4	12	4.0	10	12	6.0
5	8	5.0	11	6	8.6
6	7	10.0	12	6	8.0

  a. Draw a scatter diagram.

  b. Determine the correlation coefficient.

  c. Interpret the correlation coefficient. Does it surprise you that the correlation coefficient is negative?

Testing the Significance of the Correlation Coefficient

Recall that the sales manager of North American Copier Sales found the correlation between the number of sales calls and the number of copiers sold was .865. This indicated a strong positive association between the two variables. However, only 15 salespeople were sampled. Could it be that the correlation in the population is actually 0? This would mean the correlation of .865 was due to chance, or sampling error. The population in this example is all the salespeople employed by the firm.

    Resolving this dilemma requires a test to answer the question: Could there be zero correlation in the population from which the sample was selected? To put it another way, did the computed r come from a population of paired observations with zero correlation? To continue our convention of allowing Greek letters to represent a population parameter, we will let ρ represent the correlation in the population. It is pronounced "rho."

    We will continue with the illustration involving sales calls and copiers sold. We employ the same hypothesis testing steps described in Chapter 10. The null hypothesis and the alternate hypothesis are:

H_0: $\rho = 0$ (The correlation in the population is zero.)
H_1: $\rho \neq 0$ (The correlation in the population is different from zero.)

This is a two-tailed test. The null hypothesis can be rejected with either large or small sample values of the correlation coefficient.

The formula for t is:

---

t-TEST FOR THE CORRELATION COEFFICIENT

$$t = \frac{r\sqrt{n-2}}{\sqrt{1-r^2}} \text{ with } n-2 \text{ degrees of freedom}$$

(13–2)

Using the .05 level of significance, the decision rule states that if the computed t falls in the area between plus 2.160 and minus 2.160, the null hypothesis is not rejected. To locate the critical value of 2.160, refer to Appendix B.5 for $df = n - 2 = 15 - 2 = 13$. See Chart 13–6.

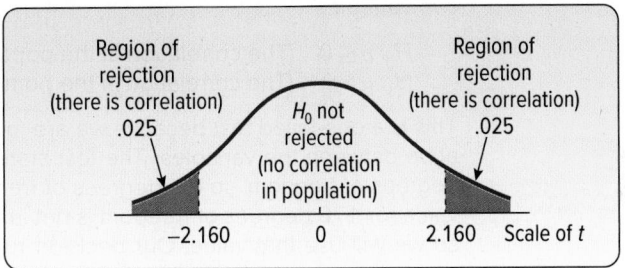

CHART 13–6 Decision Rule for Test of Hypothesis at .05 Significance Level and 13 df

Applying formula (13–2) to the example regarding the number of sales calls and units sold:

$$t = \frac{r\sqrt{n-2}}{\sqrt{1-r^2}} = \frac{.865\sqrt{15-2}}{\sqrt{1-.865^2}} = 6.216$$

The computed t is in the rejection region. Thus, H_0 is rejected at the .05 significance level. Hence we conclude the correlation in the population is not zero. This indicates to the sales manager that there is correlation with respect to the number of sales calls made and the number of copiers sold in the population of salespeople.

We can also interpret the test of hypothesis in terms of p-values. A p-value is the likelihood of finding a value of the test statistic more extreme than the one computed, when H_0 is true. To determine the p-value, go to the t-distribution in Appendix B.5 and find the row for 13 degrees of freedom. The value of the test statistic is 6.216, so in the row for 13 degrees of freedom and a two-tailed test, find the value closest to 6.216. For a two-tailed test at the .001 significance level, the critical value is 4.221. Because 6.216 is greater than 4.221, we conclude that the p-value is less than .001.

Many p-value calculators are available on the Internet. Simply search "p-value calculators." The primary information required to calculate a p-value for a t-statistic is the value of the t-statistic and the degrees of freedom. The two-tailed p-value for a t equal to 6.216 with 13 degrees of freedom is .000013.

▶ **EXAMPLE**

In the Applewood Auto Group example on page 468, we found that the correlation coefficient between the profit on the sale of a vehicle by the Applewood Auto Group and the age of the person who purchased the vehicle was .262. The sign of the correlation coefficient was positive, so we concluded there was a direct relationship between the two variables. However, because the value of the correlation coefficient was small—that is, near zero—we concluded that an advertising campaign directed toward the older buyers was not warranted. We can test our conclusion by conducting a hypothesis test that the correlation coefficient is greater than zero using the .05 significance level.

SOLUTION

To test the hypothesis, we need to clarify the sample and population issues. Let's assume that the data collected on the 180 vehicles sold by the Applewood Group are a sample from the population of *all* vehicles sold over many years by the Applewood Auto Group. The Greek letter ρ is the correlation coefficient in the population and r the correlation coefficient in the sample.

Our next step is to set up the null hypothesis and the alternate hypothesis. We test the null hypothesis that the correlation coefficient is equal to or less than zero. The alternate hypothesis is that there is positive correlation between the two variables.

$H_0: \rho \leq 0$ (The correlation in the population is negative or equal to zero.)
$H_1: \rho > 0$ (The correlation in the population is positive.)

This is a one-tailed test because we are interested in confirming a positive association between the variables. The test statistic follows the t-distribution with $n - 2$ degrees of freedom, so the degrees of freedom are $180 - 2 = 178$. However, the value for 178 degrees of freedom is not in Appendix B.5. The closest value is 180, so we will use that value. Our decision rule is to reject the null hypothesis if the computed value of the test statistic is greater than 1.653.

We use formula (13–2) to find the value of the test statistic.

$$t = \frac{r\sqrt{n-2}}{\sqrt{1-r^2}} = \frac{.262\sqrt{180-2}}{\sqrt{1-.262^2}} = 3.622$$

Comparing the value of our test statistic of 3.622 to the critical value of 1.653 and, using a *p*-value calculator, the one-tailed *p*-value with 178 degrees of freedom is .000191. We reject the null hypothesis. We conclude that the sample correlation coefficient of .262 is too large to have come from a population with no correlation. To put our results another way, there is a positive correlation between profits and age in the population.

This result is confusing and seems contradictory. On one hand, we observed that the correlation coefficient did not indicate a very strong relationship and that the Applewood Auto Group marketing department should not use this information for its promotion and advertising decisions. On the other hand, the hypothesis test indicated that the correlation coefficient is not equal to zero and that a positive relationship between age and profit exists. How can this be? We must be very careful about the application of the hypothesis test results. The hypothesis test shows a statistically significant result. However, this result does not necessarily support a practical decision to start a new marketing and promotion campaign to older purchasers. In fact, the relatively low correlation coefficient is an indication that the outcome of a new marketing and promotion campaign to older potential purchasers is, at best, uncertain.

SELF-REVIEW 13–2

A sample of 25 mayoral campaigns in medium-sized cities with populations between 50,000 and 250,000 showed that the correlation between the percent of the vote received and the amount spent on the campaign by the candidate was .43. At the .05 significance level, is there a positive association between the variables?

EXERCISES

7. The following hypotheses are given.

$$H_0: \rho \le 0$$
$$H_1: \rho > 0$$

A random sample of 12 paired observations indicated a correlation of .32. Can we conclude that the correlation in the population is greater than zero? Use the .05 significance level.

8. The following hypotheses are given.

$$H_0: \rho \ge 0$$
$$H_1: \rho < 0$$

A random sample of 15 paired observations has a correlation of −.46. Can we conclude that the correlation in the population is less than zero? Use the .05 significance level.

9. Pennsylvania Refining Company is studying the relationship between the pump price of gasoline and the number of gallons sold. For a sample of 20 stations last Tuesday, the correlation was .78. At the .01 significance level, is the correlation in the population greater than zero?

10. A study of 20 worldwide financial institutions showed the correlation between their assets and pretax profit to be .86. At the .05 significance level, can we conclude that there is positive correlation in the population?

11. The Airline Passenger Association studied the relationship between the number of passengers on a particular flight and the cost of the flight. It seems logical that more passengers on the flight will result in more weight and more luggage, which in turn will result in higher fuel costs. For a sample of 15 flights, the correlation between the number of passengers and total fuel cost was .667. Is it reasonable to conclude that there is positive association in the population between the two variables? Use the .01 significance level.

12. **FILE** The Student Government Association at Middle Carolina University wanted to demonstrate the relationship between the number of beers a student drinks and his or her blood alcohol content (BAC). A random sample of 18 students participated in a study in which each participating student was randomly assigned a number of 12-ounce cans of beer to drink. Thirty minutes after they consumed their assigned number of beers, a member of the local sheriff's office measured their BAC. The sample information is reported here:

Student	Beers	BAC	Student	Beers	BAC
Charles	6	0.10	Jaime	3	0.07
Ellis	7	0.09	Shannon	3	0.05
Harriet	7	0.09	Nellie	7	0.08
Marlene	4	0.10	Jeanne	1	0.04
Tara	5	0.10	Michele	4	0.07
Kerry	3	0.07	Seth	2	0.06
Vera	3	0.10	Gilberto	7	0.12
Pat	6	0.12	Lillian	2	0.05
Marjorie	6	0.09	Becky	1	0.02

Use a statistical software package to answer the following questions.

a. Develop a scatter diagram for the number of beers consumed and BAC. Comment on the relationship. Does it appear to be strong or weak? Does it appear to be positive or inverse?

b. Determine the correlation coefficient.
c. At the .01 significance level, is it reasonable to conclude that there is a positive relationship in the population between the number of beers consumed and the BAC? What is the *p*-value?

LO13-3

Apply regression analysis to estimate the linear relationship between two variables.

Regression Analysis

In the previous sections of this chapter, we evaluated the direction and the significance of the linear relationship between two variables by finding the correlation coefficient. Regression analysis is another method to examine a linear relationship between two variables. This analysis uses the basic concepts of correlation but provides much more information by expressing the linear relationship between two variables in the form of an equation. Using this equation, we will be able to estimate the value of the dependent variable *Y* based on a selected value of the independent variable *X*. The technique used to develop the equation and provide the estimates is called **regression analysis.**

In Table 13–1, we reported the number of sales calls and the number of units sold for a sample of 15 sales representatives employed by North American Copier Sales.

Image Source/Getty Images

Chart 13–1 portrayed this information in a scatter diagram. Recall that we tested the significance of the correlation coefficient (*r* = .865) and concluded that a significant relationship exists between the two variables. Now we want to develop a linear equation that expresses the relationship between the number of sales calls, the independent variable, and the number of units sold, the dependent variable. The equation for the line used to estimate *Y* on the basis of *X* is referred to as the **regression equation.**

> **REGRESSION EQUATION** An equation that expresses the linear relationship between two variables.

STATISTICS IN ACTION

In finance, investors are interested in the trade-off between returns and risk. One technique to quantify risk is a regression analysis of a company's stock price (dependent variable) and an average measure of the stock market (independent variable). Often the Standard and Poor's (S&P) 500 Index is used to estimate the market. The regression coefficient, called beta in finance, shows the change in a company's stock price for a one-unit change in the S&P Index. For example, if a stock has a beta of 1.5, then when the S&P index increases by 1%, the stock price will increase by 1.5%. The opposite is also true. If the S&P decreases by 1%, the stock price will decrease by 1.5%. If the beta is 1.0, then a 1% change in the index should show a 1% change in a stock price. If the beta is less than 1.0, then a 1% change in the index shows less than a 1% change in the stock price.

Least Squares Principle

In regression analysis, our objective is to use the data to position a line that best represents the relationship between the two variables. Our first approach is to use a scatter diagram to visually position the line.

The scatter diagram in Chart 13–1 is reproduced in Chart 13–7, with a line drawn with a ruler through the dots to illustrate that a line would probably fit the data. However, the line drawn using a straight edge has one disadvantage: Its position is based in part on the judgment of the person drawing the line. The hand-drawn lines in Chart 13–8 represent the judgments of four people. All the lines except line A seem to be reasonable. That is, each line is centered among the graphed data. However, each would result in a different estimate of units sold for a particular number of sales calls.

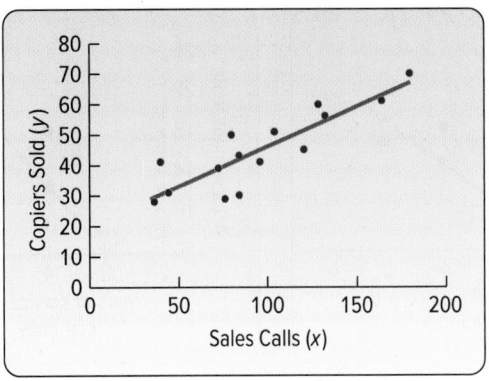

CHART 13–7 Sales Calls and Copiers Sold for 15 Sales Representatives

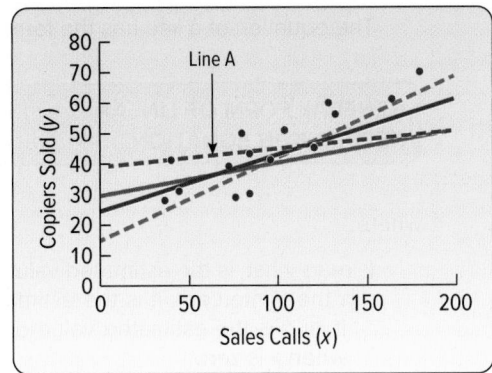

CHART 13–8 Four Lines Superimposed on the Scatter Diagram

We prefer a method that results in a single, best regression line. This method is called the **least squares principle.** It gives what is commonly referred to as the "best-fitting" line.

> **LEAST SQUARES PRINCIPLE** A mathematical procedure that uses the data to position a line with the objective of minimizing the sum of the squares of the vertical distances between the actual y-values and the predicted values of y.

To illustrate this concept, the same data are plotted in the three charts that follow. The dots are the actual values of y, and the asterisks are the predicted values of y for a given value of x. The regression line in Chart 13–9 was determined using the least squares method. It is the best-fitting line because the sum of the squares of the vertical deviations about it is at a minimum. The first plot ($x = 3$, $y = 8$) deviates by 2 from the line, found by $10 - 8$. The deviation squared is 4. The squared deviation for the plot $x = 4$, $y = 18$ is 16. The squared deviation for the plot $x = 5$, $y = 16$ is 4. The sum of the squared deviations is 24, found by $4 + 16 + 4$.

Assume that the lines in Charts 13–10 and 13–11 were drawn with a straight edge. The sum of the squared vertical deviations in Chart 13–10 is 44. For Chart 13–11, it is 132. Both sums are greater than the sum for the line in Chart 13–9, found by using the least squares method.

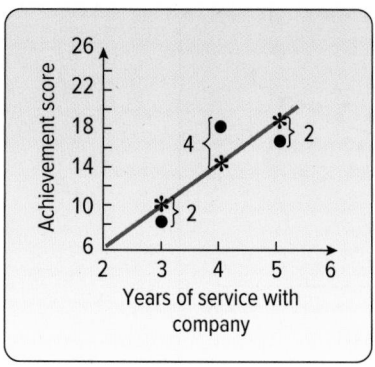

CHART 13–9 The Least Squares Line

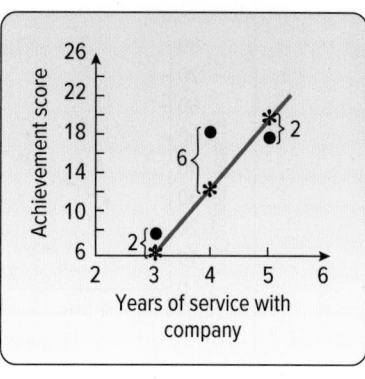

CHART 13–10 Line Drawn with a Straight Edge

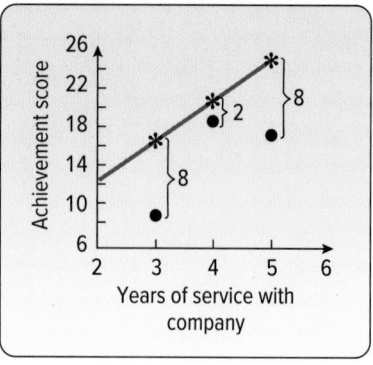

CHART 13–11 Different Line Drawn with a Straight Edge

The equation of a line has the form

GENERAL FORM OF LINEAR REGRESSION EQUATION	$\hat{y} = a + bx$	**(13–3)**

where:

$\hat{y}$, read y hat, is the estimated value of the y-variable for a selected x-value.

a is the y-intercept. It is the estimated value of Y when x = 0. Another way to put it is: a is the estimated value of y where the regression line crosses the Y-axis when x is zero.

b is the slope of the line, or the average change in $\hat{y}$ for each change of one unit (either increase or decrease) in the independent variable x.

x is any value of the independent variable that is selected.

The general form of the linear regression equation is exactly the same form as the equation of any line. a is the y-intercept and b is the slope. The purpose of regression analysis is to calculate the values of a and b to develop a linear equation that best fits the data.

The formulas for a and b are:

SLOPE OF THE REGRESSION LINE	$b = r\left(\dfrac{s_y}{s_x}\right)$	**(13–4)**

where:

r is the correlation coefficient.

s_y is the standard deviation of y (the dependent variable).

s_x is the standard deviation of x (the independent variable).

Y-INTERCEPT	$a = \bar{y} - b\bar{x}$	**(13–5)**

where:

$\bar{y}$ is the mean of y (the dependent variable).

$\bar{x}$ is the mean of x (the independent variable).

▶ **EXAMPLE**

Recall the example involving North American Copier Sales. The sales manager gathered information on the number of sales calls made and the number of copiers sold for a random sample of 15 sales representatives. As a part of her presentation at the upcoming sales meeting, Ms. Bancer, the sales manager, would like to offer specific information about the relationship between the number of sales calls and the number of copiers sold. Use the least squares method to determine a linear equation to express the relationship between the two variables. What is the expected number of copiers sold by a representative who made 100 calls?

SOLUTION

The first step in determining the regression equation is to find the slope of the least squares regression line. That is, we need the value of b. In the previous section on page 466, we determined the correlation coefficient r (.865). In the Excel output on page 466, we determined the standard deviation of the independent variable x (42.76) and the standard deviation of the dependent variable y (12.89). The values are inserted in formula (13–4).

$$b = r\left(\frac{s_y}{s_x}\right) = .865\left(\frac{12.89}{42.76}\right) = .2608$$

Next, we need to find the value of a. To do this, we use the value for b that we just calculated as well as the means for the number of sales calls and the number of copiers sold. These means are also available in the Excel worksheet on page 466. From formula (13–5):

$$a = \bar{y} - b\bar{x} = 45 - .2608(96) = 19.9632$$

Thus, the regression equation is

$$\hat{y} = 19.9632 + .2608x.$$

So if a salesperson makes 100 calls, the salesperson can expect to sell 46.0432 copiers, found by

$$\hat{y} = 19.9632 + .2608x = 19.9632 + .2608(100) = 46.0432$$

The b value of .2608 indicates that for each additional sales call, the sales representative can expect to increase the number of copiers sold by about .2608. To put it another way, 20 additional sales calls in a month will result in about five more copiers being sold, found by .2608 (20) = 5.216.

The a value of 19.9632 is the point where the equation crosses the Y-axis. A literal translation is that if no sales calls are made, that is $x = 0$, 19.9632 copiers will be sold. Note that $x = 0$ is outside the range of values included in the sample and, therefore, should not be used to estimate the number of copiers sold. The sales calls ranged from 36 to 180, so estimates should be limited to that range.

Drawing the Regression Line

The least squares equation $\hat{y} = 19.9632 + .2608x$ can be drawn on the scatter diagram. The fifth sales representative in the sample is Jeff Hall. He made 164 calls. His estimated number of copiers sold is $\hat{y} = 19.9632 + .2608(164) = 62.7344$. The plot $x = 164$ and $\hat{y} = 62.7344$ is located by moving to 164 on the X-axis and then going vertically to 62.7344. The other points on the regression equation are

CHART 13–12 The Line of Regression Drawn on the Scatter Diagram

determined by substituting a particular value of x into the regression equation and cal-culating $\hat{y}$. All the points are connected to give the line. See Chart 13–12.

Sales Representative	Sales Calls (x)	Copiers Sold (y)	Estimated Sales ($\hat{y}$)
Brian Virost	96	41	45.0000
Carlos Ramirez	40	41	30.3952
Carol Saia	104	51	47.0864
Greg Fish	128	60	53.3456
Jeff Hall	164	61	62.7344
Mark Reynolds	76	29	39.7840
Meryl Rumsey	72	39	38.7408
Mike Kiel	80	50	40.8272
Ray Snarsky	36	28	29.3520
Rich Niles	84	43	41.8704
Ron Broderick	180	70	66.9072
Sal Spina	132	56	54.3888
Soni Jones	120	45	51.2592
Susan Welch	44	31	31.4384
Tom Keller	84	30	41.8704

The least squares regression line has some interesting and unique features. First, it will always pass through the point ($\bar{x}$, $\bar{y}$). To show this is true, we can use the mean number of sales calls to predict the number of copiers sold. In this example, the mean number of sales calls is 96, found by $\bar{x} = 1440/15$. The mean number of copiers sold is 45.0, found by $\bar{y} = 675/15$. If we let $x = 96$ and then use the regression equation to find the estimated value for the result is:

$$\hat{y} = 19.9632 + .2608(96) = 45$$

The estimated number of copiers sold is exactly equal to the mean number of copiers sold. This simple example shows the regression line will pass through the point repre-sented by the two means. In this case, the regression equation will pass through the point $x = 96$ and $y = 45$.

Second, as we discussed earlier in this section, there is no other line through the data where the sum of the squared deviations is smaller. To put it another way, the term $\Sigma(y - \hat{y})^2$ is smaller for the least squares regression equation than for any other equa-tion. We use the Excel system to demonstrate this result in the following printout.

◢	A	B	C	D	E	F	G	H	I	J
1	**Sales Rep**	**Sales Calls (x)**	**Copiers Sold (y)**	**Estimated Sales**	$(y - \hat{y})$	$(y - \hat{y})^2$	y^*	$(y - y^*)^2$	y^{**}	$(y - y^{**})^2$
2	Brian Virost	96	41	45.0000	−4.0000	16.0000	44.4000	11.5600	41.6000	0.3600
3	Carlos Ramirez	40	41	30.3952	10.6048	112.4618	29.0000	144.0000	29.0000	144.0000
4	Carol Saia	104	51	47.0864	3.9136	15.3163	46.6000	19.3600	43.4000	57.7600
5	Greg Fish	128	60	53.3456	6.6544	44.2810	53.2000	46.2400	48.8000	125.4400
6	Jeff Hall	164	61	62.7344	−1.7344	3.0081	63.1000	4.4100	56.9000	16.8100
7	Mark Reynolds	76	29	39.7840	−10.7840	116.2947	38.9000	98.0100	37.1000	65.6100
8	Meryl Rumsey	72	39	38.7408	0.2592	0.0672	37.8000	1.4400	36.2000	7.8400
9	Mike Kiel	80	50	40.8272	9.1728	84.1403	40.0000	100.0000	38.0000	144.0000
10	Ray Snarsky	36	28	29.3520	−1.3520	1.8279	27.9000	0.0100	28.1000	0.0100
11	Rich Niles	84	43	41.8704	1.1296	1.2760	41.1000	3.6100	38.9000	16.8100
12	Ron Broderick	180	70	66.9072	3.0928	9.5654	67.5000	6.2500	60.5000	90.2500
13	Sal Spina	132	56	54.3888	1.6112	2.5960	54.3000	2.8900	49.7000	39.6900
14	Soni Jones	120	45	51.2592	−6.2592	39.1776	51.0000	36.0000	47.0000	4.0000
15	Susan Welch	44	31	31.4384	−0.4384	0.1922	30.1000	0.8100	29.9000	1.2100
16	Tom Keller	84	30	41.8704	−11.8704	140.9064	41.1000	123.2100	38.9000	79.2100
17	**Total**				0.0000	587.1108		597.8000		793.0000

Microsoft Excel

In columns A, B, and C of this Excel spreadsheet, we duplicated the sample information on sales and copiers sold from Table 13–1. In column D, we provide the estimated sales values, the $\hat{y}$-values, as calculated earlier.

In column E, we calculate the **residuals,** or the error values. This is the difference between the actual values and the predicted values. That is, column E is $(y - \hat{y})$. For Soni Jones,

$$\hat{y} = 19{,}9632 + .2608(120) = 51.2592$$

Her actual value is 45. So the residual, or error of estimate, is

$$(y - \hat{y}) = (45 - 51.2592) = -6.2592$$

This value reflects the amount the predicted value of sales is "off" from the actual sales value.

Next, in column F, we square the residuals for each of the sales representatives and total the result. The total is 587.1108.

$$\Sigma(y - \hat{y})^2 = 16.0000 + 112.4618 + \cdots + 140.9064 = 587.1108$$

This is the sum of the squared differences or the least squares value. There is no other line through these 15 data points where the sum of the squared differences is smaller.

We can demonstrate the least squares criterion by choosing two arbitrary equations that are close to the least squares equation and determining the sum of the squared differences for these equations. In column G, we use the equation $y^* = 18 + .275x$ to find the predicted value. Notice this equation is very similar to the least squares equation. In column H, we determine the residuals and square these residuals. For the first sales representative, Brian Virost,

$$y^* = 18 + .275(96) = 44.4$$
$$(y - y^*)^2 = (41 - 44.4)^2 = 11.56$$

This procedure is continued for the other 14 sales representatives and the squared residuals totaled. The result is 597.8. This is a larger value (597.8 is more than 587.1108) than the residuals for the least squares line.

In columns I and J on the output, we repeat the previous process for yet another equation $y^{**} = 20 + .225x$. Again, this equation is similar to the least squares equation. The details for Brian Virost are:

$$y^{**} = 20 + .225x = 20 + .225(96) = 41.6$$
$$(y - y^{**})^2 = (41 - 41.6)^2 = .36$$

This procedure is continued for the other 14 sales representatives and the residuals totaled. The result is 793, which is also larger than the least squares values.

What have we shown with the example? The sum of the squared residuals $[\Sigma(y - \hat{y})^2]$ for the least squares equation is smaller than for other selected lines. The bottom line is you will not be able to find a line passing through these data points where the sum of the squared residuals is smaller.

SELF-REVIEW 13–3

Refer to Self-Review 13–1, where the owner of Haverty's Furniture Company was studying the relationship between sales and the amount spent on advertising. The advertising expense and sales revenue, both in millions of dollars, for the last 4 months are repeated here:

Month	Advertising Expense ($ million)	Sales Revenue ($ million)
July	2	7
August	1	3
September	3	8
October	4	10

(a)   Determine the regression equation.
(b)   Interpret the values of a and b.
(c)   Estimate sales when $3 million is spent on advertising.

EXERCISES

13. **FILE** The following sample of observations was randomly selected.

x:	4	5	3	6	10
y:	4	6	5	7	7

a. Determine the regression equation.
b. Determine the value of $\hat{y}$ when x is 7.

14. **FILE** The following sample of observations was randomly selected.

x:	5	3	6	3	4	4	6	8
y:	13	15	7	12	13	11	9	5

a. Determine the regression equation.
b. Determine the value of $\hat{y}$ when x is 7.

15. **FILE** Bradford Electric Illuminating Company is studying the relationship between kilowatt-hours (thousands) used and the number of rooms in a private single-family residence. A random sample of 10 homes yielded the following:

Number of Rooms	Kilowatt-Hours (thousands)	Number of Rooms	Kilowatt-Hours (thousands)
12	9	8	6
9	7	10	8
14	10	10	10
6	5	5	4
10	8	7	7

a. Determine the regression equation.
b. Determine the number of kilowatt-hours, in thousands, for a six-room house.

16. **FILE** Mr. James McWhinney, president of Daniel-James Financial Services, believes there is a relationship between the number of client contacts and the dollar amount of sales. To document this assertion, Mr. McWhinney gathered the following sample information. The *x* column indicates the number of client contacts last month and the *y* column shows the value of sales ($ thousands) last month for each client sampled.

Number of Contacts, *x*	Sales ($ thousands), *y*	Number of Contacts, *x*	Sales ($ thousands), *y*
14	24	23	30
12	14	48	90
20	28	50	85
16	30	55	120
46	80	50	110

  a. Determine the regression equation.
  b. Determine the estimated sales if 40 contacts are made.

17. **FILE** Bloomberg Intelligence listed 50 companies to watch in 2022 (**www.bloomberg.com/features/companies-to-watch-2022**). Twelve of the companies are listed here with their market value and 3-year annualized return.

Company	Market Value ($ billions)	3-Year Annualized Return (%)
Abrdn	7.1	6.6
Barclays	42.1	9.8
FedEx	68.7	19.8
Freshpet	4.1	43.7
ING	55.1	14.4
Lululemon	50.0	45.9
Netflix	265.1	30.2
Pfizer	322.2	17.4
Roku	31.3	97.7
SK Innovation	19.2	14.9
T-Mobile US	144.2	21.1
Volkswagen	131.0	28.5

Let 3-year return be the dependent variable and market value the independent variable.
  a. Draw a scatter diagram.
  b. Compute the correlation coefficient.
  c. Determine the regression equation.
  d. For a company with $100 billion of market value, predict the 3-year annualized return.

18. **FILE** We are studying mutual bond funds for the purpose of investing in several funds. For this particular study, we want to focus on the assets of a fund and its 5-year performance. The question is: Can the 5-year rate of return be estimated based on the assets of the fund? Nine mutual funds were selected at random, and their assets and rates of return are as follows:

Fund	Assets ($ millions)	Return (%)	Fund	Assets ($ millions)	Return (%)
AARP High Quality Bond	$622.2	10.8	MFS Bond A	$494.5	11.6
Babson Bond L	160.4	11.3	Nichols Income	158.3	9.5
Compass Capital Fixed Income	275.7	11.4	T. Rowe Price Short-term	681.0	8.2
Galaxy Bond Retail	433.2	9.1	Thompson Income B	241.3	6.8
Keystone Custodian B-1	437.9	9.2			

a. Draw a scatter diagram.
b. Compute the correlation coefficient.
c. Write a brief report of your findings for parts (a) and (b).
d. Determine the regression equation. Use assets as the independent variable.
e. For a fund with $400.0 million in sales, determine the 5-year rate of return (in percent).

19. **FILE** Refer to Exercise 5. Assume the dependent variable is number of crimes.
a. Determine the regression equation.
b. Estimate the number of crimes for a city with 20 police officers.
c. Interpret the regression equation.

20. **FILE** Refer to Exercise 6.
a. Determine the regression equation.
b. Estimate the selling price of a 10-year-old car.
c. Interpret the regression equation.

LO13-4

Evaluate the significance of the slope of the regression equation.

Testing the Significance of the Slope

In the prior section, we described how to find the equation of the regression line that best fits the data. The method for finding the equation is based on the *least squares principle*. The purpose of the regression equation is to quantify a linear relationship between two variables.

The next step is to analyze the regression equation by conducting a test of hypothesis to see if the slope of the regression line is different from zero. Why is this important? If we can show that the slope of the line in the population is different from zero, then we can conclude that using the regression equation adds to our ability to predict or forecast the dependent variable based on the independent variable. If we cannot demonstrate that this slope is different from zero, then we conclude there is no merit to using the independent variable as a predictor. To put it another way, if we cannot show the slope of the line is different from zero, we might as well use the mean of the dependent variable as a predictor, rather than use the regression equation.

Following from the hypothesis testing procedure in Chapter 10, the null and alternative hypotheses to test if the slope is zero are:

$$H_0: \beta = 0$$
$$H_1: \beta \neq 0$$

We use β (the Greek letter beta) to represent the population slope for the regression equation. This is consistent with our policy to identify population parameters by Greek letters. We assumed the information regarding North American Copier Sales, Table 13–2, is a sample. Be careful here. Remember, this is a single sample of 15 salespeople, but when we selected a particular salesperson we identified two variables or pieces of information: how many customers they called on and how many copiers they sold.

We identified the slope value as b. So b is our computed slope based on a sample and is an estimate of the population's slope, identified as β. The null hypothesis is that the slope of the regression equation in the population is zero. If this is the case, the regression line is horizontal and there is no relationship between the independent variable, X, and the dependent variable, Y. In other words, the value of the dependent variable is the same for any value of the independent variable and does not offer us any help in estimating the value of the dependent variable.

What if the null hypothesis is rejected? If the null hypothesis is rejected in favor of the alternate hypothesis, we conclude that the slope of the regression line for the population is not equal to zero. To put it another way, a significant relationship exists between the two variables. Knowing the value of the independent variable allows us to estimate the value of the dependent variable.

Before we test the hypothesis, we use statistical software to determine the needed regression statistics. We continue to use the North American Copier Sales data from

Table 13–2 and use Excel to perform the necessary calculations. The link in the margin is a tutorial demonstrating how to perform regression analysis in Excel. The following spreadsheet shows three tables to the right of the sample data.

Tutorial #63
in Connect

	A	B	C	D	E	F	G	H	I	J
1	Sales Representative	Sales calls (x)	Copiers Sold (y)		SUMMARY OUTPUT					
2	Brian Virost	96	41							
3	Carlos Ramirez	40	41		*Regression Statistics*					
4	Carol Saia	104	51		Multiple R	0.865				
5	Greg Fish	128	60		R Square	0.748				
6	Jeff Hall	164	61		Adjusted R Square	0.728				
7	Mark Reynolds	76	29		Standard Error	6.720				
8	Meryl Rumsey	72	39		Observations	15				
9	Mike Kiel	80	50							
10	Ray Snarsky	36	28		ANOVA					
11	Rich Niles	84	43			df	SS	MS	F	Significance F
12	Ron Broderick	180	70		Regression	1	1738.89	1738.89	38.5031	3.19277E-05
13	Sal Spina	132	56		Residual	13	587.11	45.1623		
14	Sani Jones	120	45		Total	14	2326			
15	Susan Welch	44	31							
16	Tom Keller	84	30			Coefficients	Standard Error	t Stat	P-value	
17					Intercept	19.9800	4.389675533	4.55159	0.00054	
18					Sales calls (x)	0.2606	0.042001817	6.20509	3.2E-05	

Microsoft Excel

1. Starting on the top are the *Regression Statistics*. We will use this information later in the chapter, but notice that the "Multiple R" value is familiar. It is .865, which is the correlation coefficient we calculated using formula (13–1).
2. Next is an ANOVA table. This is a useful table for summarizing regression information. We will refer to it later in this chapter and use it extensively in the next chapter when we study multiple regression.
3. At the bottom, highlighted in blue, is the information needed to conduct our test of hypothesis regarding the slope of the line. It includes the value of the slope, which is .2606, and the intercept, which is 19.98. (Note that these values for the slope and the intercept are slightly different from those computed in the Example/ Solution on page 477. These small differences are due to rounding.) To the right of the regression coefficient is a column labeled "Standard Error." This is a value similar to the standard error of the mean. Recall that the standard error of the mean reports the variation in the sample means. In a similar fashion, these standard errors report the possible variation in slope and intercept values. The standard error of the slope coefficient is .0420.

To test the null hypothesis, we use the *t*-distribution with $(n - 2)$ degrees of freedom, and the following formula.

TEST FOR THE SLOPE $\qquad t = \dfrac{b - 0}{s_b} \qquad$ with $n - 2$ degrees of freedom $\qquad$ **(13–6)**

where:

b is the estimate of the regression line's slope calculated from the sample information.

s_b is the standard error of the slope estimate, also determined from sample information.

Our first step is to set the null and the alternative hypotheses. They are:

$$H_0: \beta \leq 0$$
$$H_1: \beta > 0$$

Notice that we have a one-tailed test. If we do not reject the null hypothesis, we conclude that the slope of the regression line in the population could be zero. This means the independent variable is of no value in improving our estimate of the dependent variable. In our case, this means that knowing the number of sales calls made by a representative does not help us predict the sales.

If we reject the null hypothesis, then we conclude the slope of the line is greater than zero. Hence, the independent variable is an aid in predicting the dependent variable. Thus, if we know the number of sales calls made by a salesperson, we can predict or forecast their sales. We also know, because we have demonstrated that the slope of the line is greater than zero—that is, positive—that more sales calls will result in the sale of more copiers.

The t-distribution is the test statistic; there are 13 degrees of freedom, found by $n - 2 = 15 - 2$. We use the .05 significance level. From Appendix B.5, the critical value is 1.771. Our decision rule is to reject the null hypothesis if the value computed from formula (13–6) is greater than 1.771. We apply formula (13–6) to find t.

$$t = \frac{b - 0}{s_b} = \frac{.2606 - 0}{.042} = 6.205$$

The computed value of 6.205 exceeds our critical value of 1.771, so we reject the null hypothesis and conclude that the slope of the line is greater than zero. The independent variable, number of sales calls, is useful in estimating copier sales.

The table also provides us information on the p-value of this test. This cell is highlighted in purple. So we could select a significance level, say .05, and compare that value with the p-value. In this case, the calculated p-value in the table is reported in exponential notation and is equal to .0000319, so our decision is to reject the null hypothesis. An important caution is that the p-values reported in the statistical software are usually for a two-*tailed test.*

Before moving on, here is an interesting note. If we compute formula (13-2) without rounding and use $r = .864632$, we compute the same t-statistic when using formula (13-6), $t = 6.205$. Actually, when comparing the results of simple linear regression and correlation analysis, the two tests are equivalent and will always yield exactly the same values of t and the same p-values.

SELF-REVIEW 13–4

Refer to Self-Review 13–1, where the owner of Haverty's Furniture Company studied the relationship between the amount spent on advertising in a month and sales revenue for that month. The amount of sales is the dependent variable and advertising expense, the independent variable. The regression equation in that study was $\hat{y} = 1.5 + 2.2x$ for a sample of 5 months. Conduct a test of hypothesis to show there is a positive relationship between advertising and sales. From statistical software, the standard error of the regression coefficient is .42. Use the .05 significance level.

EXERCISES

21. **FILE** Refer to Exercise 5. The regression equation is $\hat{y} = 29.29 - .96x$, the sample size is 8, and the standard error of the slope is .22. Use the .05 significance level. Can we conclude that the slope of the regression line is less than zero?

22. **FILE** Refer to Exercise 6. The regression equation is $\hat{y} = 11.18 - .49x$, the sample size is 12, and the standard error of the slope is .23. Use the .05 significance level. Can we conclude that the slope of the regression line is less than zero?

23. **FILE** Refer to Exercise 17. The regression equation is $\hat{y} = 32.7613 - .038x$, the sample size is 12, and the standard error of the slope is .075. Use the .05 significance level. Can we conclude that the slope of the regression line is *different from zero?*

24. **FILE** Refer to Exercise 18. The regression equation is $\hat{y} = 9.9198 - .00039x$, the sample size is 9, and the standard error of the slope is .0032. Use the .05 significance level. Can we conclude that the slope of the regression line is less than zero?

LO13-5
Evaluate a regression equation's ability to predict using the standard error of the estimate and the coefficient of determination.

Evaluating a Regression Equation's Ability to Predict

The Standard Error of Estimate

The results of the regression analysis for North American Copier Sales show a significant relationship between number of sales calls and the number of sales made. By substituting the names of the variables into the equation, it can be written as:

Number of copiers sold = 19.9632 + .2608 (Number of sales calls)

The equation can be used to estimate the number of copiers sold for any given "number of sales calls" within the range of the data. For example, if the number of sales calls is 84, then we can predict the number of copiers sold. It is 41.8704, found by 19.9632 + .2608(84). However, the data show two sales representatives with 84 sales calls and 30 and 43 copiers sold. So, is the regression equation a good predictor of "Number of copiers sold"?

Perfect prediction, which is finding the exact outcome, is practically impossible in almost all disciplines, including economics and business. For example:

- A large electronics firm, with production facilities throughout the United States, has a stock option plan for employees. Suppose there is a relationship between the number of years employed and the number of shares owned. This relationship is likely because, as number of years of service increases, the number of shares an employee earns also increases. If we observe all employees with 20 years of service, they would most likely own different numbers of shares.
- A real estate developer in the southwest United States studied the relationship between the income of buyers and the size, in square feet, of the home they purchased. The developer's analysis shows that as the income of a purchaser increases, the size of the home purchased will also increase. However, all buyers with an income of $70,000 will not purchase a home of exactly the same size.

What is needed, then, is a measure that describes how precise the prediction of Y is based on X or, conversely, how inaccurate the estimate might be. This measure is called the **standard error of estimate.** The standard error of estimate is symbolized by $s_{y \cdot x}$. The subscript, $y \cdot x$, is interpreted as the standard error of y for a given value of x. It is the same concept as the standard deviation discussed in Chapter 3. The standard deviation measures the dispersion around the mean. The standard error of estimate measures the dispersion about the regression line for a given value of x.

> **STANDARD ERROR OF ESTIMATE** A measure of the dispersion, or scatter, of the observed values around the line of regression for a given value of x.

The standard error of estimate is found using formula (13–7):

> **STANDARD ERROR OF ESTIMATE**
> $$s_{y \cdot x} = \sqrt{\frac{\Sigma (y - \hat{y})^2}{n - 2}}$$
> **(13–7)**

The calculation of the standard error of estimate requires the sum of the squared differences between each observed value of y and the predicted value of y, which is identified as $\hat{y}$ in the numerator. This calculation is illustrated in the following spreadsheet. See the highlighted cell in the lower right corner.

◢	A	B	C	D	E	F
1	**Sales Rep**	**Sales Calls (x)**	**Copiers Sold (y)**	**Estimated Sales**	**$(y - \hat{y})$**	**$(y - \hat{y})^2$**
2	Brian Virost	96	41	45.0000	−4.0000	16.0000
3	Carlos Ramirez	40	41	30.3952	10.6048	112.4618
4	Carol Saia	104	51	47.0864	3.9136	15.3163
5	Greg Fish	128	60	53.3456	6.6544	44.2810
6	Jeff Hall	164	61	62.7344	−1.7344	3.0081
7	Mark Reynolds	76	29	39.7840	−10.7840	116.2947
8	Meryl Rumsey	72	39	38.7408	0.2592	0.0672
9	Mike Kiel	80	50	40.8272	9.1728	84.1403
10	Ray Snarsky	36	28	29.3520	−1.3520	1.8279
11	Rich Niles	84	43	41.8704	1.1296	1.2760
12	Ron Broderick	180	70	66.9072	3.0928	9.5654
13	Sal Spina	132	56	54.3888	1.6112	2.5960
14	Soni Jones	120	45	51.2592	−6.2592	39.1776
15	Susan Welch	44	31	31.4384	−0.4384	0.1922
16	Tom Keller	84	30	41.8704	−11.8704	140.9064
17	**Total**				**0.0000**	**587.1108**

Microsoft Excel

The calculation of the standard error of estimate is:

$$s_{y \cdot x} = \sqrt{\frac{\Sigma (y - \hat{y})^2}{n - 2}} = \sqrt{\frac{587.1108}{15 - 2}} = 6.720$$

The standard error of estimate can be calculated using statistical software such as Excel. It is included in Excel's regression analysis on page 483 and highlighted in yellow. Its value is 6.720.

    If the standard error of estimate is small, this indicates that the data are relatively close to the regression line and the regression equation can be used to predict y with little error. If the standard error of estimate is large, this indicates that the data are widely scattered around the regression line and the regression equation will not provide a precise estimate of y.

The **Coefficient of Determination**

Using the standard error of estimate provides a relative measure of a regression equation's ability to predict. We will use it to provide more specific information about a prediction in the next section. In this section, another statistic is explained that will provide a more interpretable measure of a regression equation's ability to predict. It is called the coefficient of determination, or R-square.

> **COEFFICIENT OF DETERMINATION** The proportion of the total variation in the dependent variable Y that is explained, or accounted for, by the variation in the independent variable X.

    The coefficient of determination is easy to compute. It is the correlation coefficient squared. Therefore, the term R-square is also used. With the North American Copier Sales data, the correlation coefficient for the relationship between the number of copiers sold and the number of sales calls is .865. If we compute $(.865)^2$, the coefficient of determination is .748. See the blue (Multiple R) and green (R-square) highlighted cells in the spreadsheet on page 483. To better interpret the coefficient of determination, convert it to a percentage. Hence, we say that 74.8% of the variation in the number of copiers sold is explained, or accounted for, by the variation in the number of sales calls.

How well can the regression equation predict number of copiers sold with number of sales calls made? If it were possible to make perfect predictions, the coefficient of determination would be 100%. That would mean that the independent variable, number of sales calls, explains or accounts for all the variation in the number of copiers sold. A coefficient of determination of 100% is associated with a correlation coefficient of +1.0 or − 1.0. Refer to Chart 13–2, which shows that a perfect prediction is associated with a perfect linear relationship where all the data points form a perfect line in a scatter diagram. Our analysis shows that only 74.8% of the variation in copiers sold is explained by the number of sales calls. Clearly, these data do not form a perfect line. Instead, the data are scattered around the best-fitting, least squares regression line, and there will be error in the predictions. In the next section, the standard error of estimate is used to provide more specific information regarding the error associated with using the regression equation to make predictions.

SELF-REVIEW 13–5

Refer to Self-Review 13–1, where the owner of Haverty's Furniture Company studied the relationship between the amount spent on advertising in a month and sales revenue for that month. The amount of sales is the dependent variable, and advertising expense is the independent variable.
(a) Determine the standard error of estimate.
(b) Determine the coefficient of determination.
(c) Interpret the coefficient of determination.

EXERCISES

(You may wish to use a statistical software package such as Excel, Minitab, or Megastat to assist in your calculations.)

25. Refer to Exercise 5. Determine the standard error of estimate and the coefficient of determination. Interpret the coefficient of determination.
26. Refer to Exercise 6. Determine the standard error of estimate and the coefficient of determination. Interpret the coefficient of determination.
27. Refer to Exercise 15. Determine the standard error of estimate and the coefficient of determination. Interpret the coefficient of determination.
28. Refer to Exercise 16. Determine the standard error of estimate and the coefficient of determination. Interpret the coefficient of determination.

Relationships among the Correlation Coefficient, the Coefficient of Determination, and the Standard Error of Estimate

In formula (13-7) shown on page 485, we described the standard error of estimate. Recall that it measures how close the actual values are to the regression line. When the standard error is small, it indicates that the two variables are closely related. In the calculation of the standard error, the key term is

$$\Sigma(y - \hat{y})^2$$

If the value of this term is small, then the standard error will also be small.

The correlation coefficient measures the strength of the linear association between two variables. When the points on the scatter diagram appear close to the line, we note that the correlation coefficient tends to be large. Therefore, the correlation coefficient and the standard error of the estimate are inversely related. As the strength of a linear relationship between two variables increases, the correlation coefficient increases and the standard error of the estimate decreases.

We also noted that the square of the correlation coefficient is the coefficient of determination. The coefficient of determination measures the percentage of the variation in Y that is explained by the variation in X.

A convenient vehicle for showing the relationship among these three measures is an ANOVA table. See the highlighted portion of the following spreadsheet. This table is similar to the analysis of variance table developed in Chapter 12. In that chapter, the total variation was divided into two components: variation due to the *treatments* and variation due to *random error*. The concept is similar in regression analysis. The total variation is divided into two components: (1) variation explained by the *regression* (explained by the independent variable) and (2) the *error*, or *residual*. This is the unexplained variation. These three sources of variance (total, regression, and residual) are identified in the first column of the spreadsheet ANOVA table. The column headed "*df*" refers to the degrees of freedom associated with each category. The total number of degrees of freedom is $n - 1$. The number of degrees of freedom in the regression is 1 because there is only one independent variable. The number of degrees of freedom associated with the error term is $n - 2$. The term SS located in the middle of the ANOVA table refers to the sum of squares. You should note that the total degrees of freedom are equal to the sum of the regression and residual (error) degrees of freedom, and the total sum of squares is equal to the sum of the regression and residual (error) sum of squares. This is true for any ANOVA table.

◢	A	B	C	D	E	F	G	H	I	J
1	Sales Representative	Sales Calls (x)	Copiers Sold (y)		SUMMARY OUTPUT					
2	Brian Virost	96	41		*Regression Statistics*					
3	Carlos Ramirez	40	41		Multiple R	0.865				
4	Carol Saia	104	51		R Square	0.748				
5	Greg Fish	128	60		Adjusted R Square	0.728				
6	Jeff Hall	164	61		Standard Error	6.720				
7	Mark Reynolds	76	29		Observations	15				
8	Meryl Rumsey	72	39							
9	Mike Kiel	80	50		ANOVA					
10	Ray Snarsky	36	28			df	SS	MS	F	Significance F
11	Rich Niles	84	43		Regression	1	1738.890	1738.890	38.503	0.000
12	Ron Broderick	180	70		Residual	13	587.110	45.162		
13	Sal Spina	132	56		Total	14	2326			
14	Sani Jones	120	45							
15	Susan Welch	44	31			Coefficients	Standard Error	t Stat	P-value	
16	Tom Keller	84	30		Intercept	19.980	4.390	4.552	0.001	
17					Sales Calls (x)	0.261	0.042	6.205	0.000	

Microsoft Excel

The ANOVA sum of squares are:

Regression Sum of Squares = SSR = $\Sigma(\hat{y} - \bar{y})^2 = 1738.89$

Residual or Error Sum of Squares = SSE = $\Sigma(y - \hat{y})^2 = 587.11$

Total Sum of Squares = SS Total = $\Sigma(y - \bar{y})^2 = 2326.0$

Recall that the coefficient of determination is defined as the percentage of the total variation (SS Total) explained by the regression equation (SSR). Using the ANOVA table, the reported value of R-square can be validated.

COEFFICIENT OF DETERMINATION	$r^2 = \dfrac{\text{SSR}}{\text{SS Total}} = 1 - \dfrac{\text{SSE}}{\text{SS Total}}$	**(13–8)**

Using the values from the ANOVA table, the coefficient of determination is 1738.89/2326.0 = .748. Therefore, the more variation of the dependent variable (SS Total) explained by the independent variable (SSR), the higher the coefficient of determination.

We can also express the coefficient of determination in terms of the error or residual variation:

$$r^2 = 1 - \frac{SSE}{SS\ Total} = 1 - \frac{587.11}{2326.0} = 1 - .252 = .748$$

As illustrated in formula (13–8), the coefficient of determination and the residual or error sum of squares are inversely related. The higher the unexplained or error variation as a percentage of the total variation, the lower is the coefficient of determination. In this case, 25.2% of the total variation in the dependent variable is error or residual variation.

The final observation that relates the correlation coefficient, the coefficient of determination, and the standard error of estimate is to show the relationship between the standard error of estimate and SSE. By substituting [SSE Residual or Error Sum of Squares = SSE = $\Sigma(y - \hat{y})^2$] into the formula for the standard error of estimate, we find:

STANDARD ERROR OF ESTIMATE	$s_{y \cdot x} = \sqrt{\dfrac{SSE}{n - 2}}$	(13–9)

Note that $s_{y \cdot x}$ can also be computed using the residual mean square from the ANOVA table.

STANDARD ERROR OF THE ESTIMATE	$s_{y \cdot x} = \sqrt{Residual\ mean\ square}$	(13–10)

In sum, regression analysis provides two statistics to evaluate the predictive ability of a regression equation: the standard error of the estimate and the coefficient of determination. When reporting the results of a regression analysis, the findings must be clearly explained, especially when using the results to make predictions of the dependent variable. The report must always include a statement regarding the coefficient of determination so that the relative precision of the prediction is known to the reader of the report. Objective reporting of statistical analysis is required so that the readers can make their own decisions.

EXERCISES

29. Given the following ANOVA table:

Source	DF	SS	MS	F
Regression	1	1000.0	1000.0	26.00
Error	13	500.0	38.46	
Total	14	1500.0		

  a. Determine the coefficient of determination.
  b. Assuming a direct relationship between the variables, what is the correlation coefficient?
  c. Determine the standard error of estimate.
30. On the first statistics exam, the coefficient of determination between the hours studied and the grade earned was 80%. The standard error of estimate was 10. There were 20 students in the class. Develop an ANOVA table for the regression analysis of hours studied as a predictor of the grade earned on the first statistics exam.

Interval Estimates of Prediction

The standard error of estimate and the coefficient of determination are two statistics that provide an overall evaluation of the ability of a regression equation to predict a dependent variable. Another way to report the ability of a regression equation to predict is specific to a stated value of the independent variable. For example, we can predict the number of copiers sold (y) for a selected value of number of sales calls made (x). In fact, we can calculate a confidence interval for the predicted value of the dependent variable for a selected value of the independent variable.

Assumptions Underlying Linear Regression

Before we present the confidence intervals, let's review the necessary regression assumptions. Chart 13–13 illustrates these assumptions.

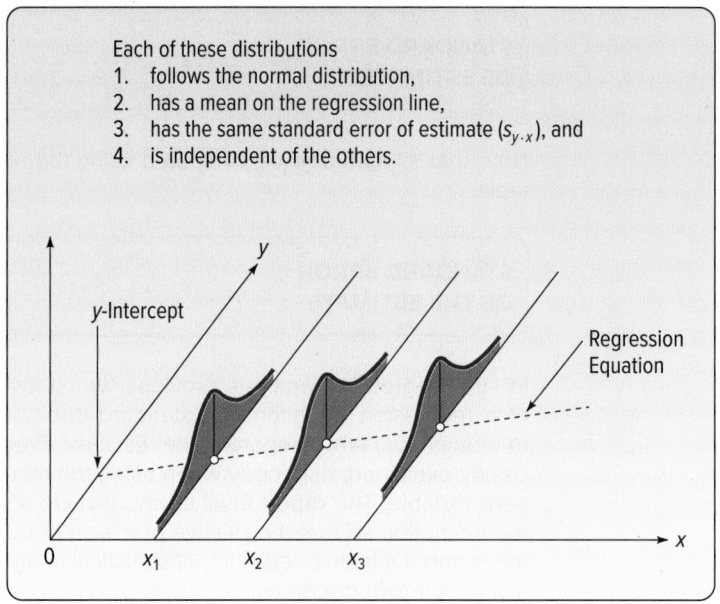

CHART 13–13 Regression Assumptions Shown Graphically

1. For each value of x, there are corresponding y-values. These y-values follow the normal distribution.
2. The means of these normal distributions lie on the regression line.
3. The standard deviations of these normal distributions are all the same. The best estimate we have of this common standard deviation is the standard error of estimate ($s_{y \cdot x}$).
4. The y-values are statistically independent. This means that in selecting a sample, a particular x does not depend on any other value of x. This assumption is particularly important when data are collected over a period of time. In such situations, the errors for a particular time period are often correlated with those of other time periods.

Recall from Chapter 7 that if the values follow a normal distribution, then the mean plus or minus 1 standard deviation will encompass 68% of the observations, the mean plus or minus 2 standard deviations will encompass 95% of the observations, and the mean plus or minus 3 standard deviations will encompass virtually all of the observations. The same relationship exists between the predicted values $\hat{y}$ and the standard error of estimate $(s_{y \cdot x})$.

1. $\hat{y} \pm s_{y \cdot x}$ will include the middle 68% of the observations.
2. $\hat{y} \pm 2s_{y \cdot x}$ will include the middle 95% of the observations.
3. $\hat{y} \pm 3s_{y \cdot x}$ will include virtually all the observations.

We can now relate these assumptions to North American Copier Sales, where we studied the relationship between the number of sales calls and the number of copiers sold. If we drew a parallel line 6.72 units above the regression line and another 6.72 units below the regression line, about 68% of the points would fall between the two lines. Similarly, a line 13.44 [$2s_{y \cdot x} = 2\,(6.72)$] units above the regression line and another 13.44 units below the regression line should include about 95% of the data values.

As a rough check, refer to column E in the Excel spreadsheet appearing on page 486. Four of the 15 deviations exceed one standard error of estimate. That is, the deviations of Carlos Ramirez, Mark Reynolds, Mike Keil, and Tom Keller all exceed 6.72 (one standard error). All values are less than 13.44 units away from the regression line. In short, 11 of the 15 deviations are within one standard error and all are within two standard errors. That is a fairly good result for a relatively small sample.

Constructing Confidence and Prediction Intervals

When using a regression equation, two different predictions can be made for a selected value of the independent variable. The differences are subtle but very important and are related to the assumptions stated in the last section. Recall that for any selected value of the independent variable (X), the dependent variable (Y) is a random variable that is normally distributed with a mean $\hat{y}$. Each distribution of Y has a standard deviation equal to the regression analysis's standard error of estimate.

The first interval estimate is called a **confidence interval.** This is used when the regression equation is used to predict the mean value of Y for a given value of x. For example, we would use a confidence interval to estimate the mean salary of all executives in the retail industry based on their years of experience. To determine the confidence interval for the mean value of y for a given x, the formula is:

CONFIDENCE INTERVAL FOR THE MEAN OF Y, GIVEN X	$\hat{y} \pm ts_{y \cdot x}\sqrt{\dfrac{1}{n} + \dfrac{(x - \bar{x})^2}{\Sigma(x - \bar{x})^2}}$	**(13–11)**

The second interval estimate is called a prediction interval. This is used when the regression equation is used to predict an individual y for a given value of x. For example, we would estimate the salary of a particular retail executive who has 20 years of experience. To calculate a prediction interval, formula (13-11) is modified by adding a 1 under the radical. To determine the prediction interval for an estimate of an individual for a given x, the formula is:

PREDICTION INTERVAL FOR Y, GIVEN X	$\hat{y} \pm ts_{y \cdot x}\sqrt{1 + \dfrac{1}{n} + \dfrac{(x - \bar{x})^2}{\Sigma(x - \bar{x})^2}}$	**(13–12)**

▶ **EXAMPLE**

We return to the North American Copier Sales illustration. Determine a 95% confidence interval for all sales representatives who make 50 calls, and determine a prediction interval for Sheila Baker, a West Coast sales representative who made 50 calls.

SOLUTION

We use formula (13–11) to determine a confidence level. Table 13–4 includes the necessary totals and a repeat of the information of Table 13–2.

TABLE 13–4 Determining Confidence and Prediction Intervals

Sales Representative	Sales Calls (x)	Copiers Sold (y)	($x - \bar{x}$)	($x - \bar{x}$)^2
Brian Virost	96	41	0	0
Carlos Ramirez	40	41	−56	3,136
Carol Saia	104	51	8	64
Greg Fish	128	60	32	1,024
Jeff Hall	164	61	68	4,624
Mark Reynolds	76	29	−20	400
Meryl Rumsey	72	39	−24	576
Mike Kiel	80	50	−16	256
Ray Snarsky	36	28	−60	3,600
Rich Niles	84	43	−12	144
Ron Broderick	180	70	84	7,056
Sal Spina	132	56	36	1,296
Sani Jones	120	45	24	576
Susan Welch	44	31	−52	2,704
Tom Keller	84	30	−12	144
Total	1440	675	0	25,600

The first step is to determine the number of copiers we expect a sales representative to sell if the representative makes 50 calls. It is 33.0032, found by

$$\hat{y} = 19.9632 + .2608x = 19.9632 + .2608(50) = 33.0032$$

To find the t-value, we need to first know the number of degrees of freedom. In this case, the degrees of freedom are $n - 2 = 15 - 2 = 13$. We set the confidence level at 95%. To find the value of t, move down the left-hand column of Appendix B.5 to 13 degrees of freedom, then move across to the column with the 95% level of confidence. The value of t is 2.160.

In the previous section, we calculated the standard error of estimate to be 6.720. We let $x = 50$, and from Table 13–4, the mean number of sales calls is 96.0 (1440/15) and $\Sigma(x - \bar{x})^2 = 25,600$. Inserting these values in formula (13–11), we can determine the confidence interval.

$$\text{Confidence Interval} = \hat{y} \pm ts_{y \cdot x}\sqrt{\frac{1}{n} + \frac{(x - \bar{x})^2}{\Sigma(x - \bar{x})^2}}$$

$$= 33.0032 \pm 2.160(6.720)\sqrt{\frac{1}{15} + \frac{(50 - 96)^2}{25,600}}$$

$$= 33.0032 \pm 5.6090$$

Thus, the 95% confidence interval for all sales representatives who make 50 calls is from 27.3942 up to 38.6122. To interpret, let's round the values. If a sales representative makes 50 calls, the representative can expect to sell 33 copiers. It is likely the sales will range from 27.4 to 38.6 copiers.

Suppose we want to estimate the number of copiers sold by Sheila Baker, who made 50 sales calls. Using formula (13–12), the 95% prediction interval is determined as follows:

$$\text{Prediction Interval} = \hat{y} \pm ts_{y \cdot x}\sqrt{1 + \frac{1}{n} + \frac{(x - \bar{x})^2}{\Sigma(x - \bar{x})^2}}$$

$$= 33.0032 \pm 2.160(6.720)\sqrt{1 + \frac{1}{15} + \frac{(50 - 96)^2}{25{,}600}}$$

$$= 33.0032 \pm 5.6090$$

Thus, the interval is from 17.442 up to 48.5644 copiers. We conclude that the number of office machines sold will be between about 17.4 and 48.6 for a particular sales representative, such as Sheila Baker, who makes 50 calls. This interval is quite large. It is much larger than the confidence interval for all sales representatives who made 50 calls. It is logical, however, that there should be more variation in the sales estimate for an individual than for a group.

The following graph shows the relationship between the least squares regression line (in the center), the confidence interval (shown in crimson), and the prediction interval (shown in green). The bands for the prediction interval are always further from the regression line than those for the confidence interval. Also, as the values of *x* move away from the mean number of calls (96) in either direction, the confidence interval and prediction interval bands widen. This is caused by the numerator of the right-hand term under the radical in formulas (13–11) and (13–12). That is, as the term increases, the widths of the confidence interval and the prediction interval also increase. To put it another way, there is less precision in our estimates as we move away, in either direction, from the mean of the independent variable. This graph was created with a statistical software package called Minitab, one of many available statistical software packages.

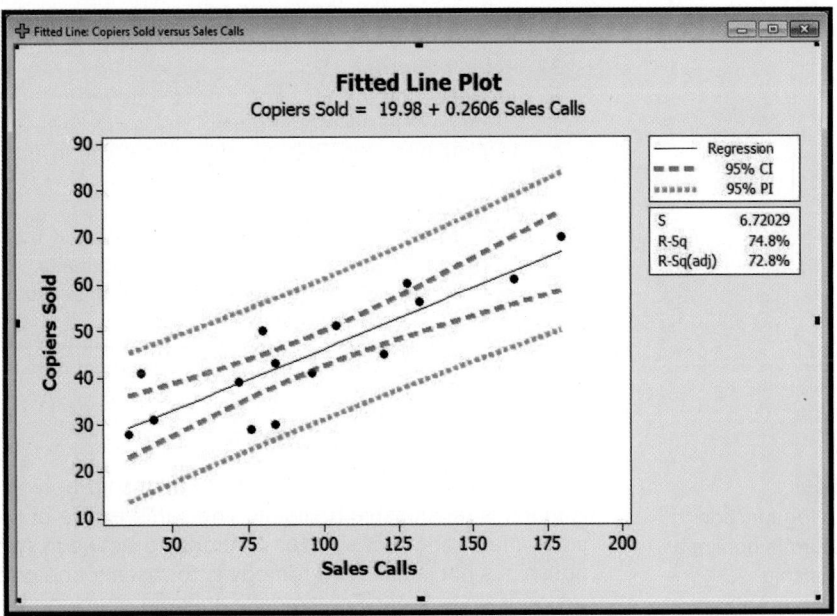

Minitab

We wish to emphasize again the distinction between a confidence interval and a prediction interval. A confidence interval refers to the mean of all cases for a given value of x and is computed by formula (13–11). A prediction interval refers to a particular, single case for a given value of x and is computed using formula (13–12). The prediction interval will always be wider because of the extra 1 under the radical in the second equation.

SELF-REVIEW 13–6

Refer to the sample data in Self-Review 13–1, where the owner of Haverty's Furniture was studying the relationship between sales and the amount spent on advertising. The advertising expense and sales revenue, both in millions of dollars, for the last 4 months are repeated here:

Month	Advertising Expense ($ million)	Sales Revenue ($ million)
July	2	7
August	1	3
September	3	8
October	4	10

The regression equation was computed to be $\hat{y} = 1.5 + 2.2x$ and the standard error .9487. Both variables are reported in millions of dollars. Determine the 90% confidence interval for the typical month in which $3 million was spent on advertising.

EXERCISES

31. Refer to Exercise 13.
   a. Determine the 95% confidence interval for the mean predicted when $x = 7$.
   b. Determine the 95% prediction interval for an individual predicted when $x = 7$.
32. Refer to Exercise 14.
   a. Determine the 95% confidence interval for the mean predicted when $x = 7$.
   b. Determine the 95% prediction interval for an individual predicted when $x = 7$.
33. Refer to Exercise 15.
   a. Determine the 95% confidence interval, in thousands of kilowatt-hours, for the mean of all six-room homes.
   b. Determine the 95% prediction interval, in thousands of kilowatt-hours, for a particular six-room home.
34. Refer to Exercise 16.
   a. Determine the 95% confidence interval, in thousands of dollars, for the mean of all sales personnel who make 40 contacts.
   b. Determine the 95% prediction interval, in thousands of dollars, for a particular salesperson who makes 40 contacts.

Transforming Data

LO13-7

Use a log function to transform a nonlinear relationship.

Regression analysis describes the relationship between two variables. A requirement is that this relationship be linear. The same is true of the correlation coefficient. It measures the strength of a linear relationship between two variables. But what if the relationship is not linear? The remedy is to rescale one or both of the variables so the new relationship is linear. For example, instead of using the actual values of the dependent variable, y, we would create a new dependent variable by computing the log to the base 10 of *y*, Log(*y*). This calculation is called a transformation. Other common transformations include taking the square root, taking the reciprocal, or squaring one or both of the variables.

Thus, two variables could be closely related, but their relationship is not linear. Be cautious when you are interpreting the correlation coefficient or a regression equation. These statistics may indicate there is no linear relationship, but there could be a relationship of some other nonlinear or curvilinear form. The following Example/Solution explains the details.

▶ **EXAMPLE**

GroceryLand Supermarkets is a regional grocery chain with over 300 stores located in the midwestern United States. The corporate director of marketing for GroceryLand wishes to study the effect of price on the weekly sales of 2-liter bottles of their private-brand diet cola. Sales is the quantity of 2-liter bottles of diet cola sold in a week. The objectives of the study are:

1. To determine whether there is a relationship between selling price and weekly sales. Is this relationship direct or indirect? Is it strong or weak?
2. To determine the effect of price increases or decreases on sales. Can we effectively forecast sales based on the price?

SOLUTION

To begin the project, the marketing director meets with the vice president of sales and other company staff members. They decide that it would be reasonable to price the 2-liter bottle of their private-brand diet cola from $.50 up to $2.00. To collect the data needed to analyze the relationship between price and sales, the marketing director selects a random sample of 20 stores and then randomly assigns a selling price for the 2-liter bottle of diet cola between $.50 and $2.00 to each selected store. The director contacts each of the 20 store managers included in the study to tell them the selling price and ask them to report the sales for the product at the end of the week. The results are reported in the following table. For example, store number A-17 sold 181 of the 2-liter bottles of diet cola at $.50 each.

GroceryLand Sales and Price Data			GroceryLand Sales and Price Data		
Store Number	Price	Sales	Store Number	Price	Sales
A-17	0.50	181	A-30	0.76	91
A-121	1.35	33	A-127	1.79	13
A-227	0.79	91	A-266	1.57	22
A-135	1.71	13	A-117	1.27	34
A-6	1.38	34	A-132	0.96	74
A-282	1.22	47	A-120	0.52	164
A-172	1.03	73	A-272	0.64	129
A-296	1.84	11	A-120	1.05	55
A-143	1.73	15	A-194	0.72	107
A-66	1.62	20	A-105	0.75	119

To examine the relationship between Price and Sales, we use regression analysis setting *Price* as the independent variable and *Sales* as the dependent variable.

The analysis will provide important information about the relationship between the variables. The analysis is summarized in the following Minitab output.

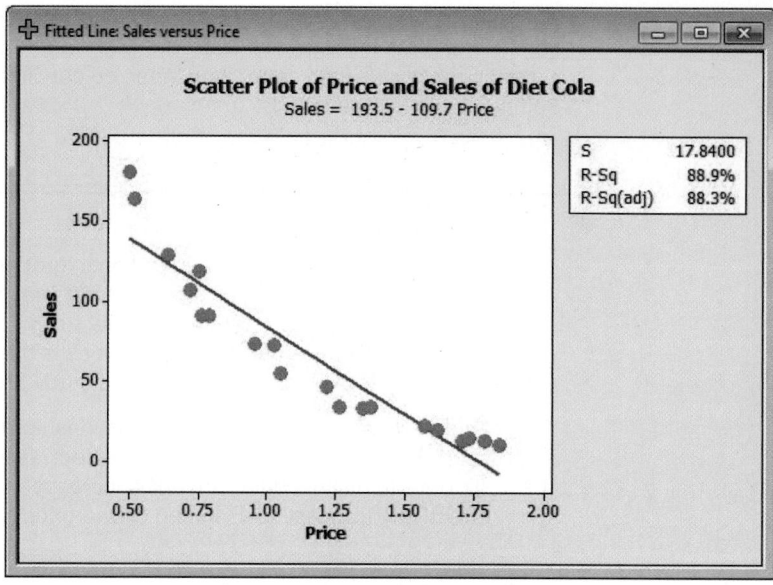

Minitab

From the output, we can make these conclusions:

1.   The relationship between the two variables is inverse or indirect. As the *Price* of the cola increases, the *Sales* of the product decreases. Given basic economic theory of price and demand, this is expected.

2.   There is a strong relationship between the two variables. The coefficient of determination is 88.9%. So 88.9% of the variation in *Sales* is accounted for by the variation in *Price*. From the coefficient of determination, we can compute the correlation coefficient as the square root of the coefficient of determination. The correlation coefficient is the square root of .889, or .943. The sign of the correlation coefficient is negative because sales are inversely related to price. Therefore, the correlation coefficient is −.943.

3.   Before continuing our summary of conclusions, we should look carefully at the scatter diagram and the plot of the regression line. The assumption of a linear relationship is tenuous. If the relationship is linear, the data points should be distributed both above and below the line over the entire range of the independent variable. However, for the highest and lowest prices, the data points are above the regression line. For the selling prices in the middle, most of the data points are below the regression line. So the linear regression equation does not effectively describe the relationship between *Price* and *Sales*. A transformation of the data is needed to create a linear relationship.

By transforming one of the variables, we may be able to change the nonlinear relationship between the variables to a linear relationship. Of the possible choices, the director of marketing decides to transform the dependent variable,

Sales, by taking the logarithm to the base 10 of each *Sales* value. Note the new variable, *Log-Sales,* in the following analysis. Now, the regression analysis uses *Log-Sales* as the dependent variable and *Price* as the independent variable. This analysis is reported here:

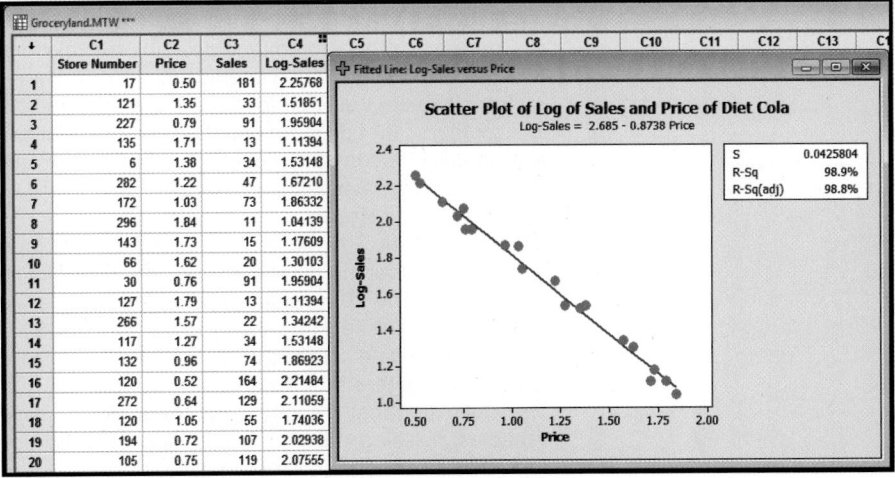

Minitab

What can we conclude from the regression analysis using the transformation of the dependent variable *Sales?*

1. By transforming the dependent variable, *Sales,* we increase the coefficient of determination from .889 to .989. So *Price* now explains nearly all of the variation in *Log-Sales.*

2. Compare this result with the scatter diagram before we transformed the dependent variable. The transformed data seem to fit the linear relationship requirement much better. Observe that the data points are both above and below the regression line over the range of *Price.*

3. The regression equation is $\hat{y} = 2.685 - .8738x$. The sign of the slope value is negative, confirming the inverse association between the variables. We can use the new equation to estimate sales and study the effect of changes in price. For example, if we decided to sell the 2-liter bottle of diet cola for $1.25, the predicted *Log-Sales* is:

$$\hat{y} = 2.685 - .8738x = 2.685 - .8738(1.25) = 1.593$$

Remember that the regression equation now predicts the log, base10, of *Sales.* Therefore, we must undo the transformation by taking the antilog of 1.593, which is $10^{1.593}$, or 39.174. So, if we price the 2-liter diet cola product at $1.25, the predicted weekly sales are 39 bottles. If we increase the price to $2.00, the regression equation would predict a value of .9374. Taking the antilog, $10^{.9374}$, the predicted sales decrease to 8.658, or, rounding, 9 of the 2-liter bottles per week. Clearly, as price increases, sales decrease. This relationship will be very helpful to GroceryLand when making pricing decisions for this product.

EXERCISES

35. **FILE** Using the following data with x as the independent variable and y as the dependent variable, answer the items.

x	−8	−16	12	2	18
y	58	247	153	3	341

a. Create a scatter diagram and describe the relationship between x and y.
b. Compute the correlation coefficient.
c. Transform the x variable by squaring each value, x^2.
d. Create a scatter diagram and describe the relationship between x^2 and y.
e. Compute the correlation coefficient between x^2 and y.
f. Compare the relationships between x and y, and x^2 and y.
g. Interpret your results.

36. **FILE** Every April, The Masters—one of the most prestigious golf tournaments on the PGA golf tour—is played in Augusta, Georgia. In 2021, 54 players received prize money. The 2021 winner, Hideki Matsuyama, earned a prize of $2,070,000. Will Zalatoris finished in second place earning $1,242,000. Jordan Spieth and Xander Schauffele finished tied for third each earning $667,000. Three amateur players entered the tournament but did not qualify for the final two rounds. The data are briefly summarized here. Each player has three corresponding variables: finishing position, score, and prize (in dollars). We want to study the relationship between score and prize.

Place	Name	Score	Prize
1	Hideki Matsuyama	278	$2,070,000
2	Will Zalatoris	279	$1,242,000
Tied 3	Jordan Spieth	281	$ 667,000
Tied 3	Xander Schauffele	281	$ 667,000
Tied 5	Jon Rahm	282	$ 437,000
Tied 5	Marc Leishman	282	$ 437,000
7	Justin Rose	283	$ 385,250
49	Jason Kokrak	295	$ 29,900
Tied 50	Jose Maria Olazabal	296	$ 28,635
Tied 50	Billy Horschel	296	$ 28,635
52	Francesco Molinari	297	$ 27,600
53	Jim Herman	298	$ 27,140
54	Adam Scott	299	$ 26,680

a. Using *Score* as the independent variable and *Prize* as the dependent variable, develop a scatter diagram. Does the relationship appear to be linear? Does it seem reasonable that as *Score* increases the *Prize* decreases?
b. What percentage of the variation in the dependent variable, *Prize*, is accounted for by the independent variable, *Score*?
c. Calculate a new variable, *Log-Prize*, computing the log to the base 10 of *Prize*. Draw a scatter diagram with *Log-Prize* as the dependent variable and *Score* as the independent variable.
d. Develop a regression equation and compute the coefficient of determination using *Log-Prize* as the dependent variable.
e. Compare the coefficient of determination in parts (b) and (d). What do you conclude?
f. Write out the regression equation developed in part (d). If a player shot an even par score of 288 for the four rounds, how much would you expect that player to earn?

CHAPTER SUMMARY

I. A scatter diagram is a graphic tool used to portray the relationship between two variables.
 A. The dependent variable is scaled on the *Y*-axis and is the variable being estimated.
 B. The independent variable is scaled on the *X*-axis and is the variable used as the predictor.

II. The correlation coefficient measures the strength of the linear association between two variables.
 A. Both variables must be at least the interval scale of measurement.
 B. The correlation coefficient can range from −1.00 to 1.00.
 C. If the correlation between the two variables is 0, there is no association between them.
 D. A value of 1.00 indicates perfect positive correlation, and a value of −1.00 indicates perfect negative correlation.
 E. A positive sign means there is a direct relationship between the variables, and a negative sign means there is an inverse relationship.
 F. It is designated by the letter *r* and found by the following equation:

$$r = \frac{\Sigma(x - \bar{x})(y - \bar{y})}{(n - 1)s_x s_y} \qquad\qquad \textbf{(13–1)}$$

 G. To test a hypothesis that a population correlation is different from 0, we use the following statistic:

$$t = \frac{r\sqrt{n - 2}}{\sqrt{1 - r^2}} \qquad \text{with } n - 2 \text{ degrees of freedom} \qquad \textbf{(13–2)}$$

III. In regression analysis, we estimate one variable based on another variable.
 A. The variable being estimated is the dependent variable.
 B. The variable used to make the estimate or predict the value is the independent variable.
  1. The relationship between the variables is linear.
  2. Both the independent and the dependent variables must be interval or ratio scale.
  3. The least squares criterion is used to determine the regression equation.

IV. The least squares regression line is of the form $\hat{y} = a + bx$.
 A. $\hat{y}$ is the estimated value of *y* for a selected value of *x*.
 B. *a* is the constant or intercept.
  1. It is the value of $\hat{y}$ when $x = 0$.
  2. *a* is computed using the following equation.

$$a = \bar{y} - b\bar{x} \qquad\qquad \textbf{(13–5)}$$

 C. *b* is the slope of the fitted line.
  1. It shows the amount of change in $\hat{y}$ for a change of one unit in *x*.
  2. A positive value for *b* indicates a direct relationship between the two variables. A negative value indicates an inverse relationship.
  3. The sign of *b* and the sign of *r*, the correlation coefficient, are always the same.
  4. *b* is computed using the following equation.

$$b = r\left(\frac{s_y}{s_x}\right) \qquad\qquad \textbf{(13–4)}$$

 D. *x* is the value of the independent variable.

V. For a regression equation, the slope is tested for significance.
 A. We test the hypothesis that the slope of the line in the population is 0.
  1. If we do not reject the null hypothesis, we conclude there is no relationship between the two variables.
  2. The test is equivalent to the test for the correlation coefficient.

B. When testing the null hypothesis about the slope, the test statistic is with $n - 2$ degrees of freedom:

$$t = \frac{b - 0}{s_b} \qquad (13\text{--}6)$$

VI. The standard error of estimate measures the variation around the regression line.
   A. It is in the same units as the dependent variable.
   B. It is based on squared deviations from the regression line.
   C. Small values indicate that the points cluster closely about the regression line.
   D. It is computed using the following formula.

$$s_{y \cdot x} = \sqrt{\frac{\Sigma(y - \hat{y})^2}{n - 2}} \qquad (13\text{--}7)$$

VII. The coefficient of determination is the proportion of the variation of a dependent variable explained by the independent variable.
   A. It ranges from 0 to 1.0.
   B. It is the square of the correlation coefficient.
   C. It is found from the following formula.

$$r^2 = \frac{SSR}{SS\ Total} = 1 - \frac{SSE}{SS\ Total} \qquad (13\text{--}8)$$

VIII. Inference about linear regression is based on the following assumptions.
   A. For a given value of x, the values of Y are normally distributed about the line of regression.
   B. The standard deviation of each of the normal distributions is the same for all values of x and is estimated by the standard error of estimate.
   C. The deviations from the regression line are independent, with no pattern to the size or direction.
IX. There are two types of interval estimates.
   A. In a confidence interval, the mean value of y is estimated for a given value of x.
      1. It is computed from the following formula.

$$\hat{y} \pm t s_{y \cdot x} \sqrt{\frac{1}{n} + \frac{(x - \bar{x})^2}{\Sigma(x - \bar{x})^2}} \qquad (13\text{--}11)$$

   2. The width of the interval is affected by the level of confidence, the size of the standard error of estimate, and the size of the sample, as well as the value of the independent variable.
   B. In a prediction interval, the individual value of y is estimated for a given value of x.
      1. It is computed from the following formula.

$$\hat{y} \pm t s_{y \cdot x} \sqrt{1 + \frac{1}{n} + \frac{(x - \bar{x})^2}{\Sigma(x - \bar{x})^2}} \qquad (13\text{--}12)$$

   2. The difference between formulas (13–11) and (13–12) is the 1 under the radical.
      a. The prediction interval will be wider than the confidence interval.
      b. The prediction interval is also based on the level of confidence, the size of the standard error of estimate, the size of the sample, and the value of the independent variable.

PRONUNCIATION KEY

SYMBOL	MEANING	PRONUNCIATION
Σxy	Sum of the products of x and y	Sum x y
ρ	Correlation coefficient in the population	Rho
$\hat{y}$	Estimated value of Y	y hat
$s_{y \cdot x}$	Standard error of estimate	s sub y dot x
r^2	Coefficient of determination	r square

CHAPTER EXERCISES

37. A regional commuter airline selected a random sample of 25 flights and found that the correlation between the number of passengers and the total weight, in pounds, of luggage stored in the luggage compartment is .94. Using the .05 significance level, can we conclude that there is a positive association between the two variables?

38. A sociologist claims that the success of students in college (measured by their GPA) is related to their family's income. For a sample of 20 students, the correlation coefficient is .40. Using the .01 significance level, can we conclude that there is a positive correlation between the variables?

39. An Environmental Protection Agency study of 12 automobiles revealed a correlation of .47 between engine size and emissions. Compute the *p*-value. At the .01 significance level, can we conclude that there is a positive association between these variables?

40. **FILE** A suburban hotel derives its revenue from its hotel and restaurant operations. The owners are interested in the relationship between the number of rooms occupied on a nightly basis and the revenue per day in the restaurant. Following is a sample of 25 days (Monday through Thursday) from last year showing the restaurant income and number of rooms occupied.

Day	Revenue	Occupied
1	$1,452	23
2	1,361	47
3	1,426	21
4	1,470	39
5	1,456	37
6	1,430	29
7	1,354	23
8	1,442	44
9	1,394	45
10	1,459	16
11	1,399	30
12	1,458	42
13	1,537	54
14	1,425	27
15	1,445	34
16	1,439	15
17	1,348	19
18	1,450	38
19	1,431	44
20	1,446	47
21	1,485	43
22	1,405	38
23	1,461	51
24	1,490	61
25	1,426	39

Use a statistical software package to answer the following questions.
  a. Draw a scatter diagram. Describe the relationship between revenue and number of occupied rooms.
  b. Determine the correlation coefficient between the two variables. Interpret the value.
  c. Is it reasonable to conclude that there is a positive relationship between revenue and occupied rooms? Use the .10 significance level.
  d. What percent of the variation in revenue in the restaurant is accounted for by the number of rooms occupied?

41. **FILE** For each of the 32 National Football League teams, the numbers of points scored and allowed during the 2021 season are shown here:

Team	Wins	Points Scored	Points Allowed	Team	Wins	Points Scored	Points Allowed
Buffalo Bills	11	483	289	Dallas Cowboys	12	530	358
New England Patriots	10	462	303	Philadelphia Eagles	9	444	385
Miami Dolphins	9	341	373	Washington Football Team	7	335	434
New York Jets	4	310	504	New York Giants	4	258	416
Cincinnati Bengals	10	460	376	Green Bay Packers	13	450	371
Pittsburgh Steelers	9	343	398	Minnesota Vikings	8	425	426
Cleveland Browns	8	349	371	Chicago Bears	6	311	407
Baltimore Ravens	8	387	392	Detroit Lions	3	325	467
Tennessee Titans	12	419	354	Tampa Bay Buccaneers	13	511	353
Indianapolis Colts	9	451	365	New Orleans Saints	9	364	335
Houston Texans	4	280	452	Atlanta Falcons	7	313	459
Jacksonville Jaguars	3	253	457	Carolina Panthers	5	304	404
Kansas City Chiefs	12	480	364	Los Angeles Rams	12	460	372
Las Vegas Raiders	10	374	439	Arizona Cardinals	11	449	366
Los Angeles Chargers	9	474	459	San Francisco 49ers	10	427	365
Denver Broncos	7	335	322	Seattle Seahawks	7	395	366

Assuming these are sample data, answer the following questions. You will need to use statistical software to assist you.

a. What is the correlation coefficient between "points scored" and "points allowed"? Interpret your results.

b. At the .05 significance level, can you conclude there is a negative association between "points scored" and "points allowed"?

42. For a sample of 40 large U.S. cities, the correlation between the mean number of square feet per office worker and the mean monthly rental rate in the central business district is −.363. At the .05 significance level, can we conclude that there is a negative association between the two variables?

43. Refer to the data in Exercise 41. First compute a new variable by subtracting "points scored" − "points allowed." Call this new variable "point differential." For the following questions, "wins" is the dependent variable and "point differential" is the independent variable. Note that during the National Football League season, each team plays 17 games.

a. Create a scatterplot of "wins" versus "point differential." What do you observe?

b. Calculate the correlation coefficient for "wins" and "point differential." Interpret the result.

c. Complete a regression analysis of the relationship. Report and interpret the coefficient of determination.

d. Write the regression equation that predicts "wins."

e. For a "point differential" of 100 points, how many games would you expect a team to win? Interpret this finding.

f. Using the slope of the regression line, in a season, what is the increase in the point differential that corresponds to an increase of one win?

44. **FILE** The Cotton Mill is an upscale chain of women's clothing stores, located primarily in the southwest United States. As a result of recent success, The Cotton Mill's top management is planning to expand by locating new stores in other regions of the country. The director of planning has been asked to study the relationship between yearly sales and the store size. As part of the study, the director selects a sample of 25 stores and determines the size of the store in square feet and the sales for last year. The sample data follow. The use of statistical software is suggested.

Store Size (thousands of square feet)	Sales (millions $)	Store Size (thousands of square feet)	Sales (millions $)
3.7	9.18	0.4	0.55
2.0	4.58	4.2	7.56
5.0	8.22	3.1	2.23
0.7	1.45	2.6	4.49
2.6	6.51	5.2	9.90
2.9	2.82	3.3	8.93
5.2	10.45	3.2	7.60
5.9	9.94	4.9	3.71
3.0	4.43	5.5	5.47
2.4	4.75	2.9	8.22
2.4	7.30	2.2	7.17
0.5	3.33	2.3	4.35
5.0	6.76		

a. Draw a scatter diagram. Use store size as the independent variable. Does there appear to be a relationship between the two variables? Is it positive or negative?
b. Determine the correlation coefficient and the coefficient of determination. Is the relationship strong or weak? Why?
c. At the .05 significance level, can we conclude there is a significant positive correlation?

45. **FILE** The manufacturer of Cardio Glide exercise equipment wants to study the relationship between the number of months since the glide was purchased and the time, in hours, the equipment was used last week.

Person	Months Owned	Hours Exercised	Person	Months Owned	Hours Exercised
Rupple	12	4	Massa	2	8
Hall	2	10	Sass	8	3
Bennett	6	8	Karl	4	8
Longnecker	9	5	Malrooney	10	2
Phillips	7	5	Veights	5	5

a. Plot the information on a scatter diagram. Let hours of exercise be the dependent variable. Comment on the graph.
b. Determine the correlation coefficient and interpret it.
c. At the .01 significance level, can we conclude that there is a negative association between the variables?

46. The following regression equation was computed from a sample of 20 observations:

$$\hat{y} = 15 - 5x$$

SSE was found to be 100 and SS total, 400.
a. Determine the standard error of estimate.
b. Determine the coefficient of determination.
c. Determine the correlation coefficient. (Caution: Watch the sign!)

47. **FILE** City planners believe that larger cities are populated by older residents. To investigate the relationship, data on population and median age in 10 large cities were collected.

City	Population City (in millions)	Median Age	City	Population City (in millions)	Median Age
Chicago, IL	2.833	31.5	Philadelphia, PA	1.448	34.2
Dallas, TX	1.233	30.5	Phoenix, AZ	1.513	30.7
Houston, TX	2.144	30.9	San Antonio, TX	1.297	31.7
Los Angeles, CA	3.849	31.6	San Diego, CA	1.257	32.5
New York, NY	8.214	34.2	San Jose, CA	0.930	32.6

a. Create a scatter plot of the data. What do you observe?
b. Calculate the correlation coefficient. What does it indicate about the relationship between median age and population?
c. Complete a regression analysis of the relationship. Report and interpret the coefficient of determination.
d. Write the regression equation that predicts median age.
e. Is the slope of the regression line significantly different from zero? Why?
f. Summarize the results of this analysis.

48. **FILE** Jaime Mendoza decides to buy a fuel-efficient used car. Here are several vehicles Jaime is considering, with the estimated cost to purchase and the age of the vehicle.

Vehicle	Estimated Cost	Age
Honda Insight	$5,555	8
Toyota Prius	$17,888	3
Toyota Prius	$9,963	6
Toyota Echo	$6,793	5
Honda Civic Hybrid	$10,774	5
Honda Civic Hybrid	$16,310	2
Chevrolet Cruz	$2,475	8
Mazda3	$2,808	10
Toyota Corolla	$7,073	9
Acura Integra	$8,978	8
Scion xB	$11,213	2
Scion xA	$9,463	3
Mazda3	$15,055	2
Mini Cooper	$20,705	2

a. Create a scatter plot of the data. What do you observe?
b. Calculate the correlation coefficient. What does it indicate about the relationship between cost and age?
c. Complete a regression analysis of the relationship. Report and interpret the coefficient of determination.
d. Write the regression equation that predicts cost.
e. Is the slope of the regression line significantly different from zero? Why?
f. Estimate the cost of a 5-year-old car.

49. **FILE** The National Highway Association is studying the relationship between the number of bidders on a highway project and the winning (lowest) bid for the project. Of particular interest is whether the number of bidders increases or decreases the amount of the winning bid.

Project	Number of Bidders, x	Winning Bid ($ millions), y	Project	Number of Bidders, x	Winning Bid ($ millions), y
1	9	5.1	9	6	10.3
2	9	8.0	10	6	8.0
3	3	9.7	11	4	8.8
4	10	7.8	12	7	9.4
5	5	7.7	13	7	8.6
6	10	5.5	14	7	8.1
7	7	8.3	15	6	7.8
8	11	5.5			

a. Create a scatter plot of the data. What do you observe?
b. Calculate the correlation coefficient. What does it indicate about the relationship between number of bidders and the winning bid?

   c. Complete a regression analysis of the relationship. Report and interpret the coefficient of determination.
   d. Write the regression equation that predicts the winning bid.
   e. Is the slope of the regression line significantly different from zero? Why?
   f. Estimate the winning bid if there were seven bidders.
   g. Compute the 95% prediction interval for a winning bid if there are seven bidders.

50. **FILE** Mr. Keagan Profit is studying companies going public for the first time. He is particularly interested in the relationship between the size of the offering and the price per share. A sample of 15 companies that recently went public revealed the following information.

Company	Size ($ millions), x	Price per Share, y	Company	Size ($ millions), x	Price per Share, y
1	9.0	10.8	9	160.7	11.3
2	94.4	11.3	10	96.5	10.6
3	27.3	11.2	11	83.0	10.5
4	179.2	11.1	12	23.5	10.3
5	71.9	11.1	13	58.7	10.7
6	97.9	11.2	14	93.8	11.0
7	93.5	11.0	15	34.4	10.8
8	70.0	10.7			

   a. Determine the regression equation.
   b. Conduct a test to determine whether the slope of the regression line is positive.
   c. Determine the coefficient of determination. Do you think Mr. Profit should use the regression equation to accurately predict price per share? Why?

51. **FILE** Bardi Trucking Co., located in Cleveland, Ohio, makes deliveries in the Great Lakes region, the Southeast, and the Northeast. Jim Bardi, the president, is studying the relationship between the distance a shipment must travel and the length of time, in days, it takes the shipment to arrive at its destination. To investigate, Mr. Bardi selected a random sample of 20 shipments made last month. Shipping distance is the independent variable and shipping time is the dependent variable. The results are as follows:

Shipment	Distance (miles)	Shipping Time (days)	Shipment	Distance (miles)	Shipping Time (days)
1	656	5	11	862	7
2	853	14	12	679	5
3	646	6	13	835	13
4	783	11	14	607	3
5	610	8	15	665	8
6	841	10	16	647	7
7	785	9	17	685	10
8	639	9	18	720	8
9	762	10	19	652	6
10	762	9	20	828	10

   a. Draw a scatter diagram. Based on these data, does it appear that there is a relationship between how many miles a shipment has to go and the time it takes to arrive at its destination?
   b. Determine the correlation coefficient. Can we conclude that there is a positive correlation between distance and time? Use the .05 significance level.
   c. Determine and interpret the coefficient of determination.
   d. Determine the standard error of estimate.
   e. Would you recommend using the regression equation to accurately predict shipping time? Why or why not?

52. **FILE** Super Markets Inc. is considering expanding into the Scottsdale, Arizona, area. You, as director of planning, must present an analysis of the proposed expansion to the operating committee of the board of directors. As a part of your proposal, you need to include information on the amount people in the region spend per month for grocery items. You would also like to include information on the relationship between the amount spent for grocery items and income. Your assistant gathered the following sample information.

Household	Amount Spent	Monthly Income
1	$ 555	$4,388
2	489	4,558
⋮	⋮	⋮
39	1,206	9,862
40	1,145	9,883

a. Draw a scatter diagram. Based on these data, does it appear that there is a relationship between monthly income and amount spent?
b. Determine the correlation coefficient. Can we conclude that there is a positive correlation between monthly income and amount spent? Use the .05 significance level.
c. Determine and interpret the coefficient of determination.
d. Determine the standard error of estimate.
e. Would you recommend using the regression equation to predict amount spent with monthly income? Why or why not?

53. **FILE** Following is information on the price per share and the dividend for a sample of 30 companies.

Company	Price per Share	Dividend
1	$20.00	$ 3.14
2	22.01	3.36
⋮	⋮	⋮
29	77.91	17.65
30	80.00	17.36

a. Calculate the regression equation that predicts price per share based on the annual dividend.
b. Test the significance of the slope.
c. Determine the coefficient of determination. Interpret its value.
d. Determine the correlation coefficient. Can you conclude that it is greater than 0 using the .05 significance level?
e. If the dividend is $10, what is the predicted price per share?
f. What is the 95% prediction interval of price per share if the dividend is $10?

54. A highway employee performed a regression analysis of the relationship between the number of construction work-zone fatalities and the number of unemployed people in a state. The regression equation is Fatalities = 12.7 + .000114 (Unemp). Some additional output is:

```
Predictor            Coef        SE Coef        T       P
Constant           12.726          8.115     1.57   0.134
Unemp          0.00011386    0.00002896     3.93   0.001
Analysis of Variance
Source               DF       SS        MS       F       P
Regression            1    10354     10354   15.46   0.001
Residual Error       18    12054       670
Total                19    22408
```

a. How many states were in the sample?
b. Determine the standard error of estimate.
c. Determine the coefficient of determination.
d. Determine the correlation coefficient.
e. At the .05 significance level, does the evidence suggest there is a positive associa-tion between fatalities and the number unemployed? Why?

55. A regression analysis relating the current market value in dollars to the size in square feet of homes in Greene County, Tennessee, follows. The regression equation is: Value = −37,186 + 65.0 Size.

Predictor	Coef	SE Coef	T	P		
Constant	−37186	4629	−8.03	0.000		
Size	64.993	3.047	21.33	0.000		
Analysis of Variance						
Source	DF	SS	MS		F	P
Regression	1	13548662082	13548662082		454.98	0.000
Residual Error	33	982687392	29778406			
Total	34	14531349474				

a. How many homes were in the sample?
b. Compute the standard error of estimate.
c. Compute the coefficient of determination.
d. Compute the correlation coefficient.
e. At the .05 significance level, does the evidence suggest a positive association between the market value of homes and the size of the home in square feet? Why?

56. **FILE** The following table shows the mean annual percent return on capital (profitabil-ity) and the mean annual percentage sales growth for eight aerospace and defense companies.

Company	Profitability	Growth
Alliant Techsystems	23.1	8.0
Boeing	13.2	15.6
General Dynamics	24.2	31.2
Honeywell	11.1	2.5
L-3 Communications	10.1	35.4
Northrop Grumman	10.8	6.0
Rockwell Collins	27.3	8.7
United Technologies	20.1	3.2

a. Compute the correlation coefficient. Conduct a test of hypothesis to determine if it is reasonable to conclude that the population correlation is greater than zero. Use the .05 significance level.
b. Develop the regression equation for profitability based on growth. Can we conclude that the slope of the regression line is negative? Why?

57. **FILE** The following data show the retail price for 12 randomly selected laptop comput-ers along with their corresponding processor speeds in gigahertz.

Computer	Speed	Price	Computer	Speed	Price
1	2.0	1008.50	7	2.0	1098.50
2	1.6	461.00	8	1.6	693.50
3	1.6	532.00	9	2.0	1057.00
4	1.8	971.00	10	1.6	1001.00
5	2.0	1068.50	11	1.0	468.50
6	1.2	506.00	12	1.4	434.50

a. Compute the correlation coefficient between the two variables. At the .05 significance level, conduct a test of hypothesis to determine if the population correlation is greater than zero.

b. Develop a regression equation that can be used to describe how the price depends on the processor speed.

c. Based on your regression equation, is there one machine that seems particularly over- or underpriced?

58. **FILE** A consumer buying cooperative tested the effective heating area of 20 different electric space heaters with different wattages. Here are the results.

Heater	Wattage	Area	Heater	Wattage	Area
1	1,500	205	11	1,250	116
2	750	70	12	500	72
3	1,500	199	13	500	82
4	1,250	151	14	1,500	206
5	1,250	181	15	2,000	245
6	1,250	217	16	1,500	219
7	1,000	94	17	750	63
8	2,000	298	18	1,500	200
9	1,000	135	19	1,250	151
10	1,500	211	20	500	44

a. Compute the correlation between the wattage and heating area. Is there a direct or an indirect relationship?

b. Conduct a test of hypothesis to determine if it is reasonable that the coefficient is greater than zero. Use the .05 significance level.

c. Develop the regression equation for effective heating based on wattage.

d. What heating area corresponds with a 1,500-watt heater?

e. What is the 95% confidence interval of heating the area if the wattage is 1,500?

59. **FILE** A dog trainer is exploring the relationship between the dog's weight and its daily food consumption (measured in standard cups). Following is the result of a sample of 18 observations.

Dog	Weight	Consumption	Dog	Weight	Consumption
1	41	3	10	91	5
2	148	8	11	109	6
3	79	5	12	207	10
4	41	4	13	49	3
5	85	5	14	113	6
6	111	6	15	84	5
7	37	3	16	95	5
8	111	6	17	57	4
9	41	3	18	168	9

a. Compute the correlation coefficient. Is it reasonable to conclude that the correlation in the population is greater than zero? Use the .05 significance level.

b. Develop a regression equation that predicts a dog's weight based on the cups of food per day. How much does each additional cup change the estimated weight of the dog?

c. Using the residuals, identify the dogs that are relatively overweight or underweight.

60. Waterbury Insurance Company wants to study the relationship between the amount of fire damage and the distance between the burning house and the nearest fire station. This information will be used in setting rates for insurance coverage. For a sample of 30 claims for the last year, the director of the actuarial department determined the distance from the fire station (x) and the amount of fire damage, in thousands of dollars (y). The MegaStat output is reported here:

```
ANOVA table
Source              SS        df        MS         F
Regression    1,864.5782     1     1,864.5782   38.83
Residual      1,344.4934    28       48.0176
Total         3,209.0716    29
Regression output
Variables    Coefficients   Std. Error   t(df = 28)
Intercept       12.3601       3.2915        3.755
Distance-X       4.7956       0.7696        6.231
```

Answer the following questions.

a. Write out the regression equation. Is there a direct or indirect relationship between the distance from the fire station and the amount of fire damage?

b. How much damage would you estimate for a fire 5 miles from the nearest fire station?

c. Determine and interpret the coefficient of determination.

d. Determine the correlation coefficient. Interpret its value. How did you determine the sign of the correlation coefficient?

e. Conduct a test of hypothesis to determine if there is a significant relationship between the distance from the fire station and the amount of damage. Use the .01 significance level and a two-tailed test.

61. TravelAir.com would like to know if there is a correlation between airfare and flight distance. If there is a correlation, what percentage of the variation in airfare is accounted for by distance? How much does each additional mile add to the fare? The data follow:

Origin	Destination	Distance	Fare
Detroit, MI	Myrtle Beach, SC	636	$109
Baltimore, MD	Sacramento, CA	2,395	252
Las Vegas, NV	Philadelphia, PA	2,176	221
Sacramento, CA	Seattle, WA	605	151
Atlanta, GA	Orlando, FL	403	138
Boston, MA	Miami, FL	1,258	209
Chicago, IL	Covington, KY	264	254
Columbus, OH	Minneapolis, MN	627	259
Fort Lauderdale, FL	Los Angeles, CA	2,342	215
Chicago, IL	Indianapolis, IN	177	128
Philadelphia, PA	San Francisco, CA	2,521	348
Houston, TX	Raleigh/Durham, NC	1,050	224
Houston, TX	Midland/Odessa, TX	441	175
Cleveland, OH	Dallas/Ft.Worth, TX	1,021	256
Baltimore, MD	Columbus, OH	336	121
Boston, MA	Covington, KY	752	252
Kansas City, MO	San Diego, CA	1,333	206
Milwaukee, WI	Phoenix, AZ	1,460	167
Portland, OR	Washington, DC	2,350	308
Phoenix, AZ	San Jose, CA	621	152
Baltimore, MD	St. Louis, MO	737	175
Houston, TX	Orlando, FL	853	191
Houston, TX	Seattle, WA	1,894	231
Burbank, CA	New York, NY	2,465	251
Atlanta, GA	San Diego, CA	1,891	291
Minneapolis, MN	New York, NY	1,028	260
Atlanta, GA	West Palm Beach, FL	545	123
Kansas City, MO	Seattle, WA	1,489	211
Baltimore, MD	Portland, ME	452	139
New Orleans, LA	Washington, DC	969	243

a. Draw a scatter diagram with *Distance* as the independent variable and *Fare* as the dependent variable. Is the relationship direct or indirect?

b. Compute the correlation coefficient. At the .05 significance level, is it reasonable to conclude that the correlation coefficient is greater than zero?

c. What percentage of the variation in *Fare* is accounted for by *Distance* of a flight?

d. Determine the regression equation. How much does each additional mile add to the fare? Estimate the fare for a 1,500-mile flight.

e. A traveler is planning to fly from Atlanta to London Heathrow. The distance is 4,218 miles. The traveler wants to use the regression equation to estimate the fare. Explain why it would not be a good idea to estimate the fare for this international flight with the regression equation.

DATA ANALYTICS

62. **FILE** The North Valley Real Estate data reports information on homes on the market.

a. Let selling price be the dependent variable and size of the home the independent variable. Determine the regression equation. Estimate the selling price for a home with an area of 2,200 square feet. Determine the 95% confidence interval for all 2,200-square-foot homes and the 95% prediction interval for the selling price of a home with 2,200 square feet.

b. Let days-on-the-market be the dependent variable and price be the independent variable. Determine the regression equation. Estimate the days-on-the-market of a home that is priced at $300,000. Determine the 95% confidence interval of days-on-the-market for homes with a mean price of $300,000, and the 95% prediction interval of days-on-the-market for a home priced at $300,000.

c. Can you conclude that the independent variables "days on the market" and "selling price" are positively correlated? Are the size of the home and the selling price positively correlated? Use the .05 significance level. Report the *p*-value of the test. Summarize your results in a brief report.

63. **FILE** Refer to the Baseball 2021 data, which reports information on the 2021 Major League Baseball season. Let attendance be the dependent variable and total team salary be the independent variable. Determine the regression equation and answer the following questions.

a. Draw a scatter diagram. From the diagram, does there seem to be a direct relationship between the two variables?

b. What is the expected attendance for a team with a salary of $100.0 million?

c. If the owners pay an additional $30 million, how many more people could they expect to attend?

d. At the .05 significance level, can we conclude that the slope of the regression line is positive? Conduct the appropriate test of hypothesis.

e. What percentage of the variation in attendance is accounted for by salary?

f. Determine the correlation between attendance and team batting average and between attendance and team ERA. Which is stronger? Conduct an appropriate test of hypothesis for each set of variables.

64. **FILE** Refer to the Lincolnville School bus data. Develop a regression equation that expresses the relationship between age of the bus and maintenance cost. The age of the bus is the independent variable.

a. Draw a scatter diagram. What does this diagram suggest as to the relationship between the two variables? Is it direct or indirect? Does it appear to be strong or weak?

b. Develop a regression equation. How much does an additional year add to the maintenance cost. What is the estimated maintenance cost for a 10-year-old bus?

c. Conduct a test of hypothesis to determine whether the slope of the regression line is greater than zero. Use the .05 significance level. Interpret your findings from parts (a), (b), and (c) in a brief report.

Multiple Regression Analysis

14

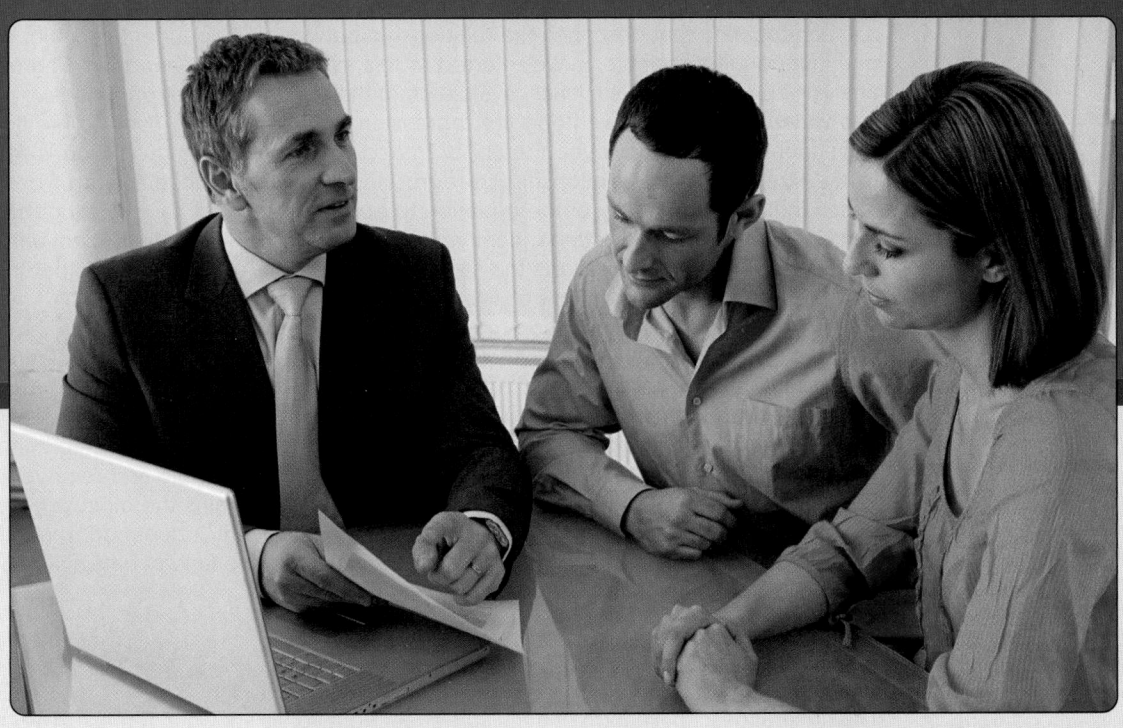

Image Source/Getty Images

▲ **THE MORTGAGE DEPARTMENT** of the Bank of New England is studying data from recent loans. Of particular interest is how such factors as the value of the home being purchased, education level of the head of the household, age of the head of the household, current monthly mortgage payment, and sex of the head of the household relate to the family income. Are the proposed variables effective predictors of the dependent variable family income? (See the Example/Solution within the Review of Multiple Regression section.)

LEARNING OBJECTIVES

When you have completed this chapter, you will be able to:

LO14-1 Use multiple regression analysis to describe and interpret a relationship between several independent variables and a dependent variable.

LO14-2 Evaluate how well a multiple regression equation fits the data.

LO14-3 Test hypotheses about the relationships inferred by a multiple regression model.

LO14-4 Evaluate the assumptions of multiple regression.

LO14-5 Use and interpret a qualitative, dummy variable in multiple regression.

LO14-6 Include and interpret an interaction effect in multiple regression analysis.

LO14-7 Apply stepwise regression to develop a multiple regression model.

LO14-8 Apply multiple regression techniques to develop a linear model.

Introduction

In Chapter 13, we discussed correlation and regression methods that analyze the relationship between a pair of interval- or ratio-scaled variables. We began the chapter by studying the correlation coefficient that measures the strength of the relationship. A coefficient near plus or minus 1.00 (−.88 or .78, for example) indicates a very strong linear relationship, whereas a value near 0 (−.12 or .18, for example) indicates the relationship is weak. Next, we presented regression analysis. Regression analysis results in a linear equation that describes the relationship between a dependent variable, *y,* and one independent variable, *x.* We referred to this as a *regression equation.* Regression analysis also provides a statistical evaluation of the relationship's strength between the two variables. Typically, we hope the regression equation can be used to predict the dependent variable. However, the ability to accurately make this prediction is related to the strength of the relationship. In regression analysis, the coefficient of determination indicates the ability of the equation to accurately predict by indicating the percent of the variation in the dependent variable explained by the independent variable. Regression analysis also reports the standard error of the estimate as another indication of the regression equation's ability to predict.

Chapter 13 is an introduction to regression analysis using only a single independent variable. In multiple linear regression, we expand the discussion by relating the dependent variable to more than one, or multiple, independent variables. With multiple regression, we can simultaneously explore the relationship of a dependent variable to a set of independent variables. Based on the analysis, we can determine the variables that are not statistically related to the dependent variable and remove these from the analysis. The result is a regression model that explains the most variance in the dependent variable with a set of statistically significant independent variables. Multiple regression is one of many statistical tools used in the field of data science and the application of machine learning.

Multiple Regression Analysis

LO14-1
Use multiple regression analysis to describe and interpret a relationship between several independent variables and a dependent variable.

The general descriptive form of a multiple linear equation is shown in formula (14–1). We use *k* to represent the number of independent variables. So *k* can be any positive integer.

GENERAL MULTIPLE REGRESSION EQUATION	$\hat{y} = a + b_1 x_1 + b_2 x_2 + b_3 x_3 + \ldots + b_k x_k$	(14–1)

where:

a is the intercept, the value of $\hat{y}$ when all the *x*'s are zero.

b_j is the amount by which $\hat{y}$ changes when that particular x_j increases by one unit, with the values of all other independent variables held constant. The subscript *j* is simply a label that helps to identify each independent variable; it is not used in any calculations. Usually the subscript is an integer value between 1 and *k,* which is the number of independent variables. However, the subscript can also be a short or abbreviated label. For example, "age" could be used as a subscript to identify the independent variable, age.

In Chapter 13, the regression analysis described and tested the relationship between a dependent variable, $\hat{y}$, and a single independent variable, *x.* The relationship between $\hat{y}$ and *x* was graphically portrayed in two dimensions by a line. When there are two independent variables, the regression equation is:

$$\hat{y} = a + b_1 x_1 + b_2 x_2$$

Because there are two independent variables, this relationship is graphically portrayed as a plane in a three-dimensional space and is shown in Chart 14–1. The chart shows the residuals as the difference between the actual y and the fitted $\hat{y}$ on the plane. If a multiple regression analysis includes more than two independent variables, we cannot use a graph to illustrate the analysis since graphs are limited to three dimensions.

To illustrate the interpretation of the intercept and the two regression coefficients, suppose the selling price of a home is directly related to the number of rooms and *inversely* related to its age. We let x_1 refer to the number of rooms, x_2 to the age of the home in years, and y to the selling price of the home in thousands of dollars ($000).

CHART 14–1 Regression Plane with 10 Sample Points

Suppose the regression equation, calculated using statistical software, is:

$$\hat{y} = 21.2 + 18.7x_1 - .25x_2$$

The intercept value of 21.2 indicates the regression equation (plane) intersects the Y-axis at 21.2. This happens when both the number of rooms and the age of the home are zero. We could say that $21,200 is the average value of a property without a house.

The first regression coefficient, 18.7, indicates that for each increase of one room in the size of a home, the selling price will increase by $18.7 thousand ($18,700), regardless of the age of the home. The second regression coefficient, −.25, indicates that for each increase of one year in age, the selling price will *decrease* by $.25 thousand ($250), regardless of the number of rooms. As an example, a seven-room home that is 30 years old is expected to sell for $144,600.

$$\hat{y} = 21.2 + 18.7x_1 - .25x_2 = 21.2 + 18.7(7) - .25(30) = 144.6$$

The values for the coefficients in the multiple linear equation are found by using the method of least squares. Recall from the previous chapter that the least squares method makes the sum of the squared differences between the fitted and actual values of y as small as possible, that is, the term $\Sigma(y - \hat{y})^2$ is minimized. The calculations are very tedious, so they are usually performed by a statistical software package.

In the following Example/Solution, we show a multiple regression analysis with three independent variables using Excel's regression analysis. Other statistical software such as Minitab and MegaStat provide advanced regression analysis techniques.

EXAMPLE

Salsberry Realty sells homes along the East Coast of the United States. One of the questions most frequently asked by prospective buyers is: If we purchase this home, how much can we expect to pay to heat it during the winter? The research department at Salsberry has been asked to develop some guidelines regarding heating costs for single-family homes. Three variables are thought to relate to the heating costs: (1) the mean daily outside temperature, (2) the number of inches of insulation in the attic, and (3) the age in years of the furnace. To investigate, Salsberry's research department selected a random sample of 20 recently sold homes.

It determined the cost to heat each home last January, as well as the January outside temperature in the region, the number of inches of insulation in the attic, and the age of the furnace. The sample information is reported in Table 14–1.

TABLE 14–1 Factors in January Heating Cost for a Sample of 20 Homes

Home	Heating Cost ($)	Mean Outside Temperature (°F)	Attic Insulation (inches)	Age of Furnace (years)
1	$250	35	3	6
2	360	29	4	10
3	165	36	7	3
4	43	60	6	9
5	92	65	5	6
6	200	30	5	5
7	355	10	6	7
8	290	7	10	10
9	230	21	9	11
10	120	55	2	5
11	73	54	12	4
12	205	48	5	1
13	400	20	5	15
14	320	39	4	7
15	72	60	8	6
16	272	20	5	8
17	94	58	7	3
18	190	40	8	11
19	235	27	9	8
20	139	30	7	5

Determine the multiple regression equation. Which variables are the independent variables? Which variable is the dependent variable? Discuss the regression coefficients. What does it indicate if some coefficients are positive and some coefficients are negative? What is the intercept value? What is the estimated heating cost for a home if the mean outside temperature is 30 degrees, there are 5 inches of insulation in the attic, and the furnace is 10 years old?

The data in Table 14–1 are available in Excel worksheet format at the textbook website, **www.mhhe.com/Lind19e**. The link in the margin is a tutorial showing how to use Excel to perform multiple regression analysis.

Tutorial #65
in Connect

SOLUTION

We begin the analysis by defining the dependent and independent variables. The dependent variable is the January heating cost. It is represented by y. There are three independent variables:

- The mean outside temperature in January, represented by x_1.
- The number of inches of insulation in the attic, represented by x_2.
- The age in years of the furnace, represented by x_3.

Given these definitions, the general form of the multiple regression equation follows. The value $\hat{y}$ is used to estimate the value of y.

$$\hat{y} = a + b_1 x_1 + b_2 x_2 + b_3 x_3$$

Now that we have defined the regression equation, we are ready to use Excel to compute all the statistics needed for the analysis. The output from Excel is shown on the following page.

	A	B	C	D	E	F	G	H	I	J	K
1	Cost	Temp	Insul	Age		SUMMARY OUTPUT					
2	250	35	3	6							
3	360	29	4	10		*Regression Statistics*					
4	165	36	7	3		Multiple R	0.897				
5	43	60	6	9		R Square	0.804				
6	92	65	5	6		Adjusted R Square	0.767				
7	200	30	5	5		Standard Error	51.049				
8	355	10	6	7		Observations	20				
9	290	7	10	10							
10	230	21	9	11		ANOVA					
11	120	55	2	5			*df*	*SS*	*MS*	*F*	*Significance F*
12	73	54	12	4		Regression	3	171220.473	57073.491	21.901	0.000
13	205	48	5	1		Residual	16	41695.277	2605.955		
14	400	20	5	15		Total	19	212915.750			
15	320	39	4	7							
16	72	60	8	6			*Coefficients*	*Standard Error*	*t Stat*	*P-value*	
17	272	20	5	8		Intercept	427.194	59.601	7.168	0.000	
18	94	58	7	3		Temp	-4.583	0.772	-5.934	0.000	
19	190	40	8	11		Insul	-14.831	4.754	-3.119	0.007	
20	235	27	9	8		Age	6.101	4.012	1.521	0.148	
21	139	30	7	5							

Source: Microsoft Excel

To use the regression equation to predict the January heating cost, we need to know the values of the regression coefficients: b_1, b_2, and b_3. These are highlighted in the software reports. The software uses the variable names or labels associated with each independent variable. The regression equation intercept, a, is labeled "intercept" in the Excel output.

In this case, the estimated regression equation is:

$$\hat{y} = 427.194 - 4.583x_1 - 14.831x_2 + 6.101x_3$$

We can now estimate or predict the January heating cost for a home if we know the mean outside temperature, the inches of insulation, and the age of the furnace. For an example home, the mean outside temperature for the month is 30 degrees (x_1), there are 5 inches of insulation in the attic (x_2), and the furnace is 10 years old (x_3). By substituting the values for the independent variables:

$$\hat{y} = 427.194 - 4.583(30) - 14.831(5) + 6.101(10) = 276.56$$

The estimated January heating cost is $276.56.

The regression coefficients, and their algebraic signs, also provide information about their individual relationships with the January heating cost. The regression coefficient for mean outside temperature is −4.583. The coefficient is negative and shows an inverse relationship between heating cost and temperature. This is not surprising. As the outside temperature increases, the cost to heat the home decreases. The numeric value of the regression coefficient provides more information. If the outside temperature increases by 1 degree and the other two independent variables remain constant, we can estimate a decrease of $4.583 in monthly heating cost. So if the mean temperature in Boston is 25 degrees and it is 35 degrees in Philadelphia, all other things being the same (insulation and age of furnace), we expect the heating cost would be $45.83 less in Philadelphia.

The attic insulation variable also shows an inverse relationship: the more insulation in the attic, the less the cost to heat the home. So the negative sign for this coefficient is logical. For each additional inch of insulation, we expect the cost to heat the home to decline $14.83 per month, holding the outside temperature and the age of the furnace constant.

The age of the furnace variable shows a direct relationship. With an older furnace, the cost to heat the home increases. Specifically, for each additional year older the furnace is, we expect the cost to increase $6.10 per month.

STATISTICS IN ACTION

Many studies indicate a woman will earn about 70% of what a man would for the same work. Researchers at the University of Michigan Institute for Social Research found that about one-third of the difference can be explained by such social factors as differences in education, seniority, and work interruptions. The remaining two-thirds is not explained by these social factors.

SELF-REVIEW 14–1

There are many restaurants in northeastern South Carolina. They serve beach vacationers in the summer, golfers in the fall and spring, and snowbirds in the winter. Bill and Joyce Tuneall manage several restaurants in the North Jersey area and are considering moving to Myrtle Beach, SC, to open a new restaurant. Before making a final decision, they wish to investigate existing restaurants and what variables seem to be related to profitability. They gather sample information where profit (reported in $000) is the dependent variable and the independent variables are:

x_1 the number of parking spaces near the restaurant.
x_2 the number of hours the restaurant is open per week.
x_3 the distance from the SkyWheel, a landmark in Myrtle Beach.
x_4 the number of servers employed.
x_5 the number of years the current owner operated the restaurant.

The following is part of the output obtained using statistical software.

Predictor	Coefficient	SE Coefficient	t
Constant	2.50	1.50	1.667
x_1	3.00	1.50	2.000
x_2	4.00	3.00	1.333
x_3	-3.00	0.20	-15.000
x_4	0.20	0.05	4.000
x_5	1.00	1.50	0.667

(a) What is the amount of profit for a restaurant with 40 parking spaces that is open 72 hours per week, is 10 miles from the SkyWheel, has 20 servers, and has been operated by the current owner for 5 years?

(b) Interpret the values of b_2 and b_3 in the multiple regression equation.

EXERCISES

1. The director of marketing at Reeves Wholesale Products is studying monthly sales. Three independent variables were selected as estimators of sales:

   x_1 = regional population
   x_2 = per capita income (dollars)
   x_3 = regional unemployment rate (%)

   The following regression equation was computed to predict sales dollars:

   $$\hat{y} = 64{,}100 + .394x_1 + 9.6x_2 - 11{,}600x_3$$

   a. Why is this analysis called multiple regression analysis?
   b. Interpret the regression coefficient, 9.6.
   c. Interpret the regression coefficient, −11,600.
   d. What are the estimated monthly sales for a particular region with a population of 796,000, per capita income of $6,940, and an unemployment rate of 6.0%?

2. Thompson Photo Works purchased several new, highly sophisticated processing machines. The production department asked for guidance with respect to qualifications needed by an operator. Is age a factor? Is the length of service as an operator (in years) important? To evaluate the factors needed to estimate performance on the new processing machines, four variables were selected:

   x_1 = Length of time an employee was in the industry
   x_2 = Mechanical aptitude test score
   x_3 = Prior on-the-job rating
   x_4 = Age

   Performance on the new machine is designated y.

Thirty employees were randomly selected and data were collected for each of the variables. A few results follow:

Name	Performance on New Machine, y	Length of Time in Industry, x_1	Mechanical Aptitude Score, x_2	Prior on-the-Job Performance, x_3	Age, x_4
Mike Miraglia	112	12	312	121	52
Sue Trythall	113	2	380	123	27

The equation is:

$$\hat{y} = 11.6 + .4x_1 + .286x_2 + .112x_3 + .002x_4$$

a. What is this equation called?
b. How many dependent variables are there? Independent variables?
c. What is the number .286 called?
d. As age increases by one year, how much does estimated performance on the new machine increase?
e. Carl Knox applied for a job at Photo Works. He has been in the business for 6 years and scored 280 on the mechanical aptitude test. Carl's prior on-the-job performance rating is 97, and he is 35 years old. Estimate Carl's performance on the new machine.

3. A consulting group was hired by the Human Resources Department at General Mills Inc. to survey company employees regarding their degree of satisfaction with their quality of life. A special index, called the index of satisfaction, was used to measure satisfaction. Six factors were studied, namely, age at the time of first marriage (x_1), annual income (x_2), number of children living (x_3), value of all assets (x_4), status of health in the form of an index (x_5), and the average number of social activities per week—such as bowling and dancing (x_6). Suppose the multiple regression equation is:

$$\hat{y} = 16.24 + .017x_1 + .0028x_2 + 42x_3 + .0012x_4 + .19x_5 + 26.8x_6$$

a. What is the estimated index of satisfaction for a person who first married at 18, has an annual income of $26,500, has three children living, has assets of $156,000, has an index of health status of 141, and has 2.5 social activities each week on the average?
b. Which would add more to satisfaction, an additional income of $10,000 a year or two more social activities a week?

4. Cellulon, a manufacturer of home insulation, wants to develop guidelines for builders and consumers on how the thickness of the insulation in the attic of a home and the outdoor temperature affect natural gas consumption. In the laboratory, it varied the insulation thickness and temperature. A few of the findings are:

Monthly Natural Gas Consumption (cubic feet), y	Thickness of Insulation (inches), x_1	Outdoor Temperature (°F), x_2
30.3	6	40
26.9	12	40
22.1	8	49

On the basis of the sample results, the regression equation is:

$$\hat{y} = 62.65 - 1.86x_1 - .52x_2$$

a. How much natural gas can homeowners expect to use per month if they install 6 inches of insulation and the outdoor temperature is 40 degrees F?

> **b.** What effect would installing 7 inches of insulation instead of 6 have on the monthly natural gas consumption (assuming the outdoor temperature remains at 40 degrees F)?
>
> **c.** Why are the regression coefficients b_1 and b_2 negative? Is this logical?

LO14-2

Evaluate how well a multiple regression equation fits the data.

Evaluating a Multiple Regression Equation

Many statistics and statistical methods are used to evaluate the relationship between a dependent variable and more than one independent variable. Our first step was to write the relationship in terms of a multiple regression equation. The next step follows on the concepts presented in Chapter 13 by using the information in an ANOVA table to evaluate how well the equation fits the data.

The ANOVA Table

As in Chapter 13, the statistical analysis of a multiple regression equation is summarized in an ANOVA table. To review, the total variation of the dependent variable, y, is divided into two components: (1) *regression,* or the variation of y explained by all the independent variables, and (2) *the error or residual,* or unexplained variation of y. These two categories are identified in the first column of the ANOVA table here. The column headed "*df*" refers to the degrees of freedom associated with each category. The total number of degrees of freedom is $n - 1$. The number of degrees of freedom in the regression is equal to the number of independent variables in the multiple regression equation. We call the regression degrees of freedom k. The number of degrees of freedom associated with the error term is equal to the total degrees of freedom, $n - 1$, minus the regression degrees of freedom, k. So, the residual or error degrees of freedom is $(n - 1) - k$, and is the same as $n - (k + 1)$.

Source	df	SS	MS	F
Regression	k	SSR	$MSR = SSR/k$	MSR/MSE
Residual or error	$n - (k + 1)$	SSE	$MSE = SSE/[n - (k + 1)]$	
Total	$n - 1$	SS total		

In the ANOVA table, the column headed "SS" lists the sum of squares for each source of variation: regression, residual or error, and total. The sum of squares is the amount of variation attributable to each source.

The total variation of the dependent variable, y, is summarized in "SS total." You should note that this is simply the numerator of the usual formula to calculate any variation—in other words, the sum of the squared deviations from the mean. It is computed as:

$$\text{Total Sum of Squares} = \text{SS total} = \Sigma(y - \bar{y})^2$$

As we have seen, the total sum of squares is the sum of the regression and residual sum of squares. The regression sum of squares is the sum of the squared differences between the estimated or predicted values, $\hat{y}$, and the overall mean of y. The regression sum of squares is found by:

$$\text{Regression Sum of Squares} = \text{SSR} = \Sigma(\hat{y} - \bar{y})^2$$

The residual sum of squares is the sum of the squared differences between the observed values of the dependent variable, y, and their corresponding estimated or predicted values, $\hat{y}$. Notice that this difference is the error of estimating or predicting the dependent variable with the multiple regression equation. It is calculated as:

$$\text{Residual or Error Sum of Squares} = \text{SSE} = \Sigma(y - \hat{y})^2$$

We use the ANOVA table information from the previous Example/Solution to evaluate the regression equation to estimate January heating costs.

	A	B	C	D	G	H	I	J	K	L	M
1	Cost	Temp	Insul	Age		SUMMARY OUTPUT					
2	250	35	3	6							
3	360	29	4	10		*Regression Statistics*					
4	165	36	7	3		Multiple R	0.897				
5	43	60	6	9		R Square	0.804				
6	92	65	5	6		Adjusted R Square	0.767				
7	200	30	5	5		Standard Error	51.049				
8	355	10	6	7		Observations	20				
9	290	7	10	10							
10	230	21	9	11		ANOVA					
11	120	55	2	5			*df*	*SS*	*MS*	*F*	*Significance F*
12	73	54	12	4		Regression	3	171220.473	57073.491	21.901	0.000
13	205	48	5	1		Residual	16	41695.277	2605.955		
14	400	20	5	15		Total	19	212915.750			
15	320	39	4	7							
16	72	60	8	6			*Coefficients*	*Standard Error*	*t Stat*	*P-value*	
17	272	20	5	8		Intercept	427.194	59.601	7.168	0.000	
18	94	58	7	3		Temp	-4.583	0.772	-5.934	0.000	
19	190	40	8	11		Insul	-14.831	4.754	-3.119	0.007	
20	235	27	9	8		Age	6.101	4.012	1.521	0.148	

Source: Microsoft Excel

Multiple Standard Error of Estimate

We begin with the **multiple standard error of estimate.** Recall that the standard error of estimate is comparable to the standard deviation. To explain the details of the standard error of estimate, refer to the first sampled home in row 2 in the Excel spreadsheet above. The actual heating cost for the first observation, y, is \$250; the outside temperature, x_1, is 35 degrees; the depth of insulation, x_2, is 3 inches; and the age of the furnace, x_3, is 6 years. Using the regression equation developed in the previous section, the estimated heating cost for this home is:

$$\hat{y} = 427.194 - 4.583x_1 - 14.831x_2 + 6.101x_3$$
$$= 427.194 - 4.583(35) - 14.831(3) + 6.101(6)$$
$$= 258.90$$

So we would estimate that a home with a mean January outside temperature of 35 degrees, 3 inches of insulation, and a 6-year-old furnace would cost \$258.90 to heat. The actual heating cost was \$250, so the residual—which is the difference between the actual value and the estimated value—is $y - \hat{y} = 250 - 258.90 = -8.90$. This difference of \$8.90 is the random or unexplained error for the first home sampled. Our next step is to square this difference—that is, find $(y - \hat{y})^2 = (250 - 258.90)^2 = (-8.90)^2 = 79.21$.

If we repeat this calculation for the other 19 observations and sum all 20 squared differences, the total will be the residual or error sum of squares from the ANOVA table. Using this information, we can calculate the multiple standard error of the estimate as:

MULTIPLE STANDARD ERROR OF ESTIMATE $\quad S_{y.123...k} = \sqrt{\dfrac{\Sigma(y - \hat{y})^2}{n - (k + 1)}} = \sqrt{\dfrac{SSE}{n - (k + 1)}}$	**(14–2)**

where:

y is the actual observation.
$\hat{y}$ is the estimated value computed from the regression equation.
n is the number of observations in the sample.
k is the number of independent variables.
SSE is the Residual Sum of Squares from an ANOVA table.

There is more information in the ANOVA table that can be used to compute the multiple standard error of estimate. The column headed "MS" reports the mean squares for the regression and residual variation. These values are calculated as the sum of squares divided by the corresponding degrees of freedom. The multiple standard error of estimate is equal to the square root of the residual MS, which is also called the mean square error (MSE).

$$s_{y.123...k} = \sqrt{\text{MSE}} = \sqrt{2605.995} = \$51.05$$

How do we interpret the standard error of estimate of 51.05? It is the typical "error" when we use this equation to predict the cost. First, the units are the same as the dependent variable, so the standard error is in dollars, $51.05. Second, we expect the residuals to be approximately normally distributed, so about 68% of the residuals will be within ± $51.05 and about 95% within ± 2(51.05), or ± $102.10. As before with similar measures of dispersion, such as the standard error of estimate in Chapter 13, a smaller multiple standard error indicates a better or more effective predictive equation.

Coefficient of Multiple Determination

Next, let's look at the coefficient of multiple determination. Recall from the previous chapter the coefficient of determination is defined as the percent of variation in the dependent variable explained, or accounted for, by the independent variable. In the multiple regression case, we extend this definition as follows:

> **COEFFICIENT OF MULTIPLE DETERMINATION** The percent of variation in the dependent variable, y, explained by the set of independent variables, $x_1, x_2, x_3, \ldots x_k$.

The characteristics of the coefficient of multiple determination are:

1. **It is symbolized by a capital R squared.** In other words, it is written as R^2 because it is calculated as the square of a correlation coefficient.
2. **It can range from 0 to 1.** A value near 0 indicates little association between the set of independent variables and the dependent variable. A value near 1 means a strong association.
3. **It cannot assume negative values.** Any number that is squared or raised to the second power cannot be negative.
4. **It is easy to interpret.** Because R^2 is a value between 0 and 1, it is easy to interpret, compare, and understand.

We can calculate the coefficient of determination from the information found in the ANOVA table. We look in the sum of squares column, which is labeled SS in the Excel output, and use the regression sum of squares, SSR, then divide by the total sum of squares, SS total.

> **COEFFICIENT OF MULTIPLE DETERMINATION** $\qquad R^2 = \dfrac{\text{SSR}}{\text{SS total}} \qquad$ **(14–3)**

We can use the regression and the total sum of squares from the ANOVA table highlighted in the Excel output appearing earlier in this section and compute the coefficient of determination.

$$R^2 = \frac{\text{SSR}}{\text{SS total}} = \frac{171,220.473}{212,915.750} = .804$$

How do we interpret this value? We conclude that the independent variables (outside temperature, amount of insulation, and age of furnace) explain, or account for, 80.4% of the variation in heating cost. To put it another way, 19.6% of the variation is due to other sources, such as random error or variables not included in the analysis. Using the

ANOVA table, 19.6% is the error sum of squares divided by the total sum of squares. Knowing that the SSR + SSE = SS total, the following relationship is true.

$$1 - R^2 = 1 - \frac{SSR}{SS\ total} = \frac{SSE}{SS\ total} = \frac{41,695.277}{212,915.750} = .196$$

Adjusted Coefficient of Determination

The coefficient of determination tends to increase as more independent variables are added to the multiple regression model. Each new independent variable causes the predictions to be more accurate. That, in turn, makes SSE smaller and SSR larger. Hence, R^2 increases only because the total number of independent variables increases and not because the added independent variable is a good predictor of the dependent variable. In fact, if the number of variables, k, and the sample size, n, are equal, the coefficient of determination is 1.0. In practice, this situation is rare and would also be ethically questionable. To balance the effect that the number of independent variables has on the coefficient of multiple determination, statistical software packages use an *adjusted* coefficient of multiple determination.

ADJUSTED COEFFICIENT OF DETERMINATION	$R^2_{adj} = 1 - \dfrac{\dfrac{SSE}{n-(k+1)}}{\dfrac{SS\ total}{n-1}}$	**(14–4)**

The error and total sum of squares are divided by their degrees of freedom. Notice especially the degrees of freedom for the error sum of squares include k, the number of independent variables. For the cost of heating example, the adjusted coefficient of determination is:

$$R^2_{adj} = 1 - \frac{\dfrac{41,695.277}{20-(3+1)}}{\dfrac{212,915.750}{20-1}} = 1 - \frac{2,605.955}{11,206.092} = 1 - .233 = .767$$

If we compare the R^2 (.80) to the adjusted R^2 (.767), the difference in this case is small.

SELF-REVIEW 14–2

Refer to Self-Review 14–1 on the subject of restaurants in Myrtle Beach. The ANOVA portion of the regression output is presented here.

```
                    Analysis of Variance
          Source            DF      SS    MS
          Regression         5     100    20
          Residual Error    20      40     2
          Total             25     140
```

(a) How large was the sample?
(b) How many independent variables are there?
(c) How many dependent variables are there?
(d) Compute the standard error of estimate. About 95% of the residuals will be between what two values?
(e) Determine the coefficient of multiple determination. Interpret this value.
(f) Find the coefficient of multiple determination, adjusted for the degrees of freedom.

EXERCISES

5. Consider the ANOVA table that follows:

```
Analysis of Variance
Source            DF        SS        MS       F        P
Regression         2    77.907    38.954    4.14    0.021
Residual Error    62   583.693     9.414
Total             64   661.600
```

   a. Determine the standard error of estimate. About 95% of the residuals will be between what two values?
   b. Determine the coefficient of multiple determination. Interpret this value.
   c. Determine the coefficient of multiple determination, adjusted for the degrees of freedom. Interpret the value. Why is this answer less than the unadjusted coefficient of multiple determination?

6. Consider the ANOVA table that follows:

```
Analysis of Variance
Source            DF        SS        MS       F
Regression         5   3710.00    742.00    12.89
Residual Error    46   2647.38     57.55
Total             51   6357.38
```

   a. Determine the standard error of estimate. About 95% of the residuals will be between what two values?
   b. Determine the coefficient of multiple determination. Interpret this value.
   c. Determine the coefficient of multiple determination, adjusted for the degrees of freedom. Interpret the value. Why is this answer less than the unadjusted coefficient of multiple determination?

LO14-3

Test hypotheses about the relationships inferred by a multiple regression model.

Inferences in Multiple Linear Regression

Thus far, multiple regression analysis has been viewed only as a way to describe the relationship between a dependent variable and several independent variables. However, the least squares method also has the ability to draw inferences or generalizations about the relationship for an entire population. Recall that when you create confidence intervals or perform hypothesis tests as a part of inferential statistics, you view the data as a random sample taken from some population.

In the multiple regression setting, we assume there is an unknown population regression equation that relates the dependent variable to the k independent variables. This is sometimes called a **model** of the relationship. In symbols we write:

$$Y = \alpha + \beta X_1 + \beta_2 X_2 + \cdots + \beta_k X_k$$

This equation is analogous to formula (14–1) except the coefficients are now reported as Greek letters. We use the Greek letters to denote *population parameters*. Then under a certain set of assumptions, which will be discussed shortly, the computed values of a and b_j are sample statistics. These sample statistics are point estimates of the corresponding population parameters α and β_j. For example, the sample regression coefficient b_2 is a point estimate of the population parameter β_2. The sampling distribution of these point estimates follows the normal probability distribution. These sampling distributions are each centered at their respective parameter values. To put it another way, the means of the sampling distributions are equal to the parameter values to be estimated. Thus, by using the properties of the sampling distributions of these statistics, inferences about the population parameters are possible.

Global Test: Testing the Multiple Regression Model

We can test the ability of the independent variables $X_1, X_2, ..., X_k$ to explain the behavior of the dependent variable Y. To put this in question form: Can the dependent variable be estimated without relying on the independent variables? The test used is referred to as the **global test.** This test investigates whether it is possible that all the independent variables have zero regression coefficients.

To relate this question to the heating cost example, we will test whether the three independent variables (amount of insulation in the attic, mean daily outside temperature, and age of furnace) effectively estimate home heating costs. In testing the hypothesis, we first state the null hypothesis and the alternate hypothesis in terms of the three population parameters, β_1, β_2, and β_3. Recall that b_1, b_2, and b_3 are sample regression coefficients and are not used in the hypothesis statements. In the null hypothesis, we test whether the regression coefficients in the population are all zero. The null hypothesis is:

$$H_0: \beta_1 = \beta_2 = \beta_3 = 0$$

The alternate hypothesis is:

$$H_1: \text{At least one } \beta_i \text{ is not equal to 0.}$$

If the hypothesis test fails to reject the null hypothesis, then the data provides no evidence that any regression coefficient differs from 0. In other words, none of the independent variables are statistically related to the dependent variable. If the null hypothesis is rejected, then at least one regression coefficient differs from 0. At least one of the dependent variables is statistically related to the dependent variable.

To test the null hypothesis that the multiple regression coefficients are all zero, we employ the *F*-distribution introduced in Chapter 11. We will use the .05 level of significance. Recall these characteristics of the *F*-distribution:

1. **There is a family of *F*-distributions.** Each time the degrees of freedom in either the numerator or the denominator change, a new *F*-distribution is created.
2. **The *F*-distribution cannot be negative.** The smallest possible value is 0.
3. **It is a continuous distribution.** The distribution can assume an infinite number of values between 0 and positive infinity.
4. **It is positively skewed.** The long tail of the distribution is to the right-hand side. As the number of degrees of freedom increases in both the numerator and the denominator, the distribution approaches the normal probability distribution. That is, the distribution will move toward a symmetric distribution.
5. **It is asymptotic.** As the values of *X* increase, the *F*-curve will approach the horizontal axis but will never touch it.

The *F*-statistic to test the global hypothesis follows. As in Chapter 11, it is the ratio of two variances. In this case, the numerator is the regression sum of squares divided by its degrees of freedom, *k*. The denominator is the residual sum of squares divided by its degrees of freedom, $n - (k + 1)$. The formula follows:

GLOBAL TEST	$$F = \frac{SSR/k}{SSE/[n - (k + 1)]}$$	**(14–5)**

Using the values from the ANOVA table on page 519, the *F*-statistic is:

$$F = \frac{SSR/k}{SSE/[n - (k + 1)]} = \frac{171{,}220.473/3}{41{,}695.277/[20 - (3 + 1)]} = 21.90$$

Remember that the *F*-statistic tests the basic null hypothesis that two variances or, in this case, two mean squares are equal. In our global multiple regression hypothesis test, we will reject the null hypothesis, H_0, that all regression coefficients are zero when the regression mean square is larger in comparison to the residual mean square. If this is true, the *F*-statistic will be relatively large and in the far right tail of the *F*-distribution, and the *p*-value will be small, that is, less than our choice of significance level of .05. Thus, we will reject the null hypothesis.

As with other hypothesis-testing methods, the decision rule can be based on either of two methods: (1) comparing the test statistic to a critical value or (2) calculating a p-value based on the test statistic and comparing the p-value to the significance level. The critical value method using the F-statistic requires three pieces of information: (1) the numerator degrees of freedom, (2) the denominator degrees of freedom, and (3) the significance level. The degrees of freedom for the numerator and the denominator are reported in the Excel ANOVA table that follows. The ANOVA output is highlighted in green. The top number in the column marked "df" is 3, indicating there are 3 degrees of freedom in the numerator. This value corresponds to the number of independent variables. The middle number in the "df" column (16) indicates there are 16 degrees of freedom in the denominator. The number 16 is found by $n - (k + 1) = 20 - (3 + 1) = 16$.

	A	B	C	D	G	H	I	J	K	L	M
1	Cost	Temp	Insul	Age		SUMMARY OUTPUT					
2	250	35	3	6							
3	360	29	4	10		*Regression Statistics*					
4	165	36	7	3		Multiple R	0.897				
5	43	60	6	9		R Square	0.804				
6	92	65	5	6		Adjusted R Square	0.767				
7	200	30	5	5		Standard Error	51.049				
8	355	10	6	7		Observations	20				
9	290	7	10	10							
10	230	21	9	11		ANOVA					
11	120	55	2	5			*df*	*SS*	*MS*	*F*	*Significance F*
12	73	54	12	4		Regression	3	171220.473	57073.491	21.901	0.000
13	205	48	5	1		Residual	16	41695.277	2605.955		
14	400	20	5	15		Total	19	212915.750			
15	320	39	4	7							
16	72	60	8	6			*Coefficients*	*Standard Error*	*t Stat*	*P-value*	
17	272	20	5	8		Intercept	427.194	59.601	7.168	0.000	
18	94	58	7	3		Temp	-4.583	0.772	-5.934	0.000	
19	190	40	8	11		Insul	-14.831	4.754	-3.119	0.007	
20	235	27	9	8		Age	6.101	4.012	1.521	0.148	

Source: Microsoft Excel

The critical value of F is found in Appendix B.6A. Using the table for the .05 significance level, move horizontally to 3 degrees of freedom in the numerator, then down to 16 degrees of freedom in the denominator, and read the critical value. It is 3.24. The region where H_0 is not rejected and the region where H_0 is rejected are shown in the following diagram.

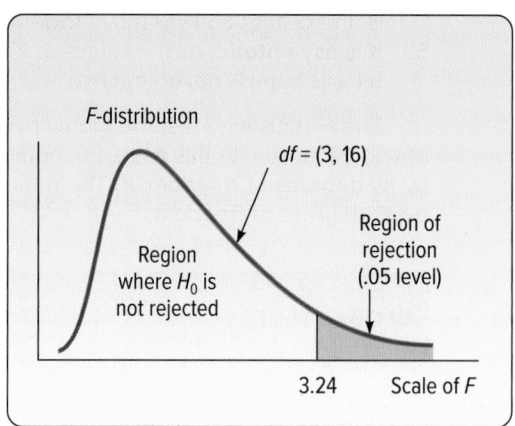

Continuing with the global test, the decision rule is: Do not reject the null hypothesis, H_0, that all the regression coefficients are 0 if the computed value of F is less than or equal to 3.24. If the computed F is greater than 3.24, reject H_0 and accept the alternate hypothesis, H_1.

The computed value of F is 21.90, which is in the rejection region. The null hypothesis that all the multiple regression coefficients are zero is therefore rejected. This indicates that at least one of the independent variables has the ability to explain the variation in the dependent variable (heating cost). We expected this decision. Logically, the outside temperature, the amount of insulation, or the age of the furnace has a great bearing on heating costs. The global test assures us they do.

Testing the null hypothesis can also be based on a *p*-value, which is reported in the statistical software output for all hypothesis tests. In the case of the *F*-statistic, the *p*-value is defined as the probability of observing an *F*-value as large or larger than the *F*-test statistic, assuming the null hypothesis is true. If the *p*-value is less than our selected significance level, then we decide to reject the null hypothesis. The ANOVA shows the *F*-statistic's *p*-value is equal to .000. It is clearly less than our significance level of .05. Therefore, we decide to reject the global null hypothesis and conclude that at least one of the regression coefficients is not equal to zero.

Evaluating Individual Regression Coefficients

So far we have shown that at least one, but not necessarily all, of the regression coefficients is not equal to zero and thus useful for predictions. The next step is to test the independent variables *individually* to determine which regression coefficients may be 0 and which are not.

Why is it important to know if any of the β_i's equal 0? If a β could equal 0, it implies that this particular independent variable is of no value in explaining any variation in the dependent value. If there are coefficients for which H_0 cannot be rejected, we may want to eliminate them from the regression equation.

Our strategy is to use three sets of hypotheses: one for temperature, one for insulation, and one for age of the furnace.

For temperature	For insulation	For furnace age:
$H_0: \beta_1 = 0$	$H_0: \beta_2 = 0$	$H_0: \beta_3 = 0$
$H_1: \beta_1 \neq 0$	$H_1: \beta_2 \neq 0$	$H_1: \beta_3 \neq 0$

We will test the hypotheses at the .05 level. Note that these are two-tailed tests.

The test statistic follows Student's *t*-distribution with $n - (k + 1)$ degrees of freedom. The number of sample observations is *n*. There are 20 homes in the study, so $n = 20$. The number of independent variables is *k*, which is 3. Thus, there are $n - (k + 1) = 20 - (3 + 1) = 16$ degrees of freedom.

The critical value for *t* is in Appendix B.5. For a two-tailed test with 16 degrees of freedom using the .05 significance level, H_0 is rejected if *t* is less than −2.120 or greater than 2.120.

Refer to the Excel output earlier in this section. The column highlighted in orange, headed "Coefficients," shows the values for the multiple regression equation:

$$\hat{y} = 427.194 - 4.583x_1 - 14.831x_2 + 6.101x_3$$

Interpret the term $-4.583x_1$ in the equation: For each degree increase in temperature, we predict that heating cost will decrease $4.58, holding the insulation and age of the furnace variables constant.

The column in the Excel output labeled "Standard Error" shows the standard error of the sample regression coefficients. Recall that Salsberry Realty selected a sample of 20 homes along the East Coast of the United States. If Salsberry Realty selected a second random sample and computed the regression coefficients for that sample, the values would not be exactly the same. If the sampling process was repeated many times, we could construct a sampling distribution for each of these regression coefficients. The column labeled "Standard Error" estimates the variability for each of these regression coefficients. The sampling distributions of the coefficients follow the *t*-distribution with $n - (k + 1)$ degrees of freedom. Hence, we are able to test the independent variables individually to determine whether the regression coefficients differ from zero. The formula is:

TESTING INDIVIDUAL REGRESSION COEFFICIENTS	$t = \dfrac{b_i - 0}{s_{b_i}}$	**(14–6)**

The b_i refers to any one of the regression coefficients, and s_b refers to the standard deviation of that distribution of the regression coefficient. We include 0 in the equation because the null hypothesis is $\beta_i = 0$.

To illustrate this formula, refer to the test of the regression coefficient for the independent variable temperature. From the output earlier in this section, the regression coefficient for temperature is −4.583. The standard deviation of the sampling distribution of the regression coefficient for the independent variable temperature is .772. Inserting these values in formula (14–6):

$$t = \frac{b_1 - 0}{s_{b_1}} = \frac{-4.583 - 0}{.772} = -5.937$$

The computed value of t is −5.937 for temperature (the small difference between the computed value and that shown on the Excel output is due to rounding) and −3.119 for insulation. Both of these t-values are in the rejection region to the left of −2.120. Thus, we conclude that the regression coefficients for the temperature and insulation variables are *not* zero. The computed t for the age of the furnace is 1.521, so we conclude that the coefficient could equal 0. The independent variable age of the furnace is not a significant predictor of heating cost. The results of these hypothesis tests indicate that the analysis should focus on temperature and insulation as predictors of heating cost.

We can also use p-values to test the individual regression coefficients. Again, these are commonly reported in statistical software output. The computed value of t for temperature on the Excel output is −5.934 and has a p-value of .000. Because the p-value is less than .05, the regression coefficient for the independent variable temperature is not equal to zero and should be included in the equation to predict heating costs. For insulation, the value of t is −3.119 and has a p-value of .007. As with temperature, the p-value is less than .05, so we conclude that the insulation regression coefficient is not equal to zero and should be included in the equation to predict heating cost. In contrast to temperature and insulation, the p-value to test the "age of the furnace" regression coefficient is .148. It is clearly greater than .05, so we conclude that the "age of furnace" regression coefficient could equal 0. Further, as an independent variable it is not a significant predictor of heating cost. Thus, age of furnace should not be included in the equation to predict heating costs.

At this point, we need to develop a strategy for deleting independent variables. In the Salsberry Realty case, there were three independent variables. For the age of the furnace variable, we failed to reject the null hypothesis that the regression coefficient was zero. It is clear that we should drop that variable and rerun the regression equation. Following is the Excel output where heating cost is the dependent variable and outside temperature and amount of insulation are the independent variables.

	A	B	C	D	E	F	G	H	I	J	K
1	Cost	Temp	Insul	Age		SUMMARY OUTPUT					
2	250	35	3	6							
3	360	29	4	10		*Regression Statistics*					
4	165	36	7	3		Multiple R	0.881				
5	43	60	6	9		R Square	0.776				
6	92	65	5	6		Adjusted R Square	0.749				
7	200	30	5	5		Standard Error	52.982				
8	355	10	6	7		Observations	20				
9	290	7	10	10							
10	230	21	9	11		ANOVA					
11	120	55	2	5			*df*	*SS*	*MS*	*F*	*Significance F*
12	73	54	12	4		Regression	2	165194.521	82597.261	29.424	0.000
13	205	48	5	1		Residual	17	47721.229	2807.131		
14	400	20	5	15		Total	19	212915.750			
15	320	39	4	7							
16	72	60	8	6			*Coefficients*	*Standard Error*	*t Stat*	*P-value*	
17	272	20	5	8		Intercept	490.286	44.410	11.040	0.000	
18	94	58	7	3		Temp	-5.150	0.702	-7.337	0.000	
19	190	40	8	11		Insul	-14.718	4.934	-2.983	0.008	
20	235	27	9	8							

Source: Microsoft Excel

Summarizing the results from this new output:

1. The new regression equation is:

$$\hat{y} = 490.286 - 5.150x_1 - 14.718x_2$$

Notice that the regression coefficients for outside temperature (x_1) and amount of insulation (x_2) are similar to but not exactly the same as when we included the independent variable age of the furnace. Compare the previous equation to that in the Excel output earlier in this section. Both of the regression coefficients are negative as in the earlier equation.

2. The details of the global test are as follows:

$$H_0: \beta_1 = \beta_2 = 0$$
$$H_1: \text{Not all of the } \beta_i\text{'s} = 0$$

The F-distribution is the test statistic and there are $k = 2$ degrees of freedom in the numerator and $n - (k + 1) = 20 - (2 + 1) = 17$ degrees of freedom in the denominator. Using the .05 significance level and Appendix B.6A, the decision rule is to reject H_0 if F is greater than 3.59. We compute the value of F as follows:

$$F = \frac{\text{SSR}/k}{\text{SSE}/[n - (k + 1)]} = \frac{165{,}194.521/2}{47{,}721.229/[20 - (2 + 1)]} = 29.424$$

Because the computed value of F (29.424) is greater than the critical value (3.59), the null hypothesis is rejected and the alternate accepted. We conclude that at least one of the regression coefficients is different from 0.

Using the p-value, the F-test statistic (29.424) has a p-value (.000), which is clearly less than .05. Therefore, we reject the null hypothesis and accept the alternate. We conclude that at least one of the regression coefficients is different from 0.

3. The next step is to conduct a test of the regression coefficients individually. We want to determine if one or both of the regression coefficients are different from 0. The null and alternate hypotheses for each of the independent variables are:

Outside Temperature	Insulation
$H_0: \beta_1 = 0$	$H_0: \beta_2 = 0$
$H_1: \beta_1 \neq 0$	$H_1: \beta_2 \neq 0$

The test statistic is the t-distribution with $n - (k + 1) = 20 - (2 + 1) = 17$ degrees of freedom. Using the .05 significance level and Appendix B.5, the decision rule is to reject H_0 if the computed value of t is less than -2.110 or greater than 2.110.

Outside Temperature	Insulation
$t = \dfrac{b_1 - 0}{s_{b_1}} = \dfrac{-5.150 - 0}{.702} = -7.337$	$t = \dfrac{b_2 - 0}{s_{b_2}} = \dfrac{-14.718 - 0}{4.934} = -2.983$

In both tests, we reject H_0 and accept H_1. We conclude that each of the regression coefficients is different from 0. Both outside temperature and amount of insulation are useful variables in explaining the variation in heating costs.

Using p-values, the p-value for the temperature t-statistic is .000 and the p-value for the insulation t-statistic is .008. Both p-values are less than .05, so in both tests we reject the null hypothesis and conclude that each of the regression coefficients is different from 0. Both outside temperature and amount of insulation are useful variables in explaining the variation in heating costs.

In the heating cost example, it was clear which independent variable to delete. However, in some instances which variable to delete may not be as clear-cut. To explain, suppose we develop a multiple regression equation based on five independent variables. We conduct the global test and find that some of the regression coefficients are different from zero. Next, we test the regression coefficients individually and find that three are significant and two are not. The preferred procedure is to drop the single independent variable with the *smallest absolute* t-*value* or *largest* p-*value* and rerun the regression equation with the four remaining variables; then, on the new regression equation with four independent variables, conduct the individual tests. If there are still regression coefficients that are not significant, again drop the variable with the smallest absolute t-value or the largest, nonsignificant p-value. To describe the process in another way, we should delete only one variable at a time. Each time we delete a variable, we need to rerun the regression equation and check the remaining variables.

This process of selecting variables to include in a regression model can be automated, using Minitab, MegaStat, or other statistical software. Most of the software systems include methods to sequentially remove and/or add independent variables and at the same time provide estimates of the percentage of variation explained (the R-square term). Two of the common methods are **stepwise regression** and **best subset regression.** It may take a long time, but in the extreme we could compute every regression between the dependent variable and any possible subset of the independent variables.

Unfortunately, on occasion, the software may work "too hard" to find an equation that fits all the quirks of your particular data set. The suggested equation may not represent the relationship in the population. Judgment is needed to choose among the equations presented. Consider whether the results are logical. They should have a simple interpretation and be consistent with your knowledge of the application under study.

SELF-REVIEW 14–3

The regression output about eating places in Myrtle Beach is repeated here (see earlier Self-Reviews).

Predictor	Coefficient	SE Coefficient	t	p-value	
Constant	2.50	1.50	1.667	0.111	
x_1	3.00	1.50	2.000	0.056	
x_2	4.00	3.00	1.333	0.194	
x_3	-3.00	0.20	-15.000	0.000	
x_4	0.20	0.05	4.000	0.000	
x_5	1.00	1.50	0.667	0.511	
Analysis of Variance					
Source	DF	SS	MS	F	p-value
Regression	5	100	20	10	0.000
Residual Error	20	40	2		
Total	25	140			

(a) Perform a global test of hypothesis to check if any of the regression coefficients are different from 0. What do you decide? Use the .05 significance level.
(b) Perform an individual test of each independent variable. Which variables would you consider eliminating? Use the .05 significance level.
(c) Outline a plan for possibly removing independent variables.

EXERCISES

7. Given the following regression output,

Predictor	Coefficient	SE Coefficient	t	p-value	
Constant	84.998	1.863	45.62	0.000	
x_1	2.391	1.200	1.99	0.051	
x_2	-0.409	0.172	-2.38	0.021	
Analysis of Variance					
Source	DF	SS	MS	F	p-value
Regression	2	77.907	38.954	4.138	0.021
Residual Error	62	583.693	9.414		
Total	64	661.600			

answer the following questions:

a. Write the regression equation.

b. If x_1 is 4 and x_2 is 11, what is the expected or predicted value of the dependent variable?

c. How large is the sample? How many independent variables are there?

d. Conduct a global test of hypothesis to see if any of the set of regression coefficients could be different from 0. Use the .05 significance level. What is your conclusion?

e. Conduct a test of hypothesis for each independent variable. Use the .05 significance level. Which variable would you consider eliminating?

f. Explain why one of the independent variables could be removed from the regression equation.

8. The following regression output is from a study of architectural firms. The dependent variable is the total amount of fees in millions of dollars.

Predictor	Coefficient	SE Coefficient	t	p-value
Constant	7.987	2.967	2.690	0.010
x_1	0.122	0.031	3.920	0.000
x_2	-1.220	0.053	-2.270	0.028
x_3	-0.063	0.039	-1.610	0.114
x_4	0.523	0.142	3.690	0.001
x_5	-0.065	0.040	-1.620	0.112

Analysis of Variance					
Source	DF	SS	MS	F	p-value
Regression	5	371000	742	12.89	0.000
Residual Error	46	2647.38	57.55		
Total	51	6357.38			

x_1 is the number of architects employed by the company.

x_2 is the number of engineers employed by the company.

x_3 is the number of years involved with health care projects.

x_4 is the number of states in which the firm operates.

x_5 is the percent of the firm's work that is health care related.

a. Write out the regression equation.

b. How large is the sample? How many independent variables are there?

c. Conduct a global test of hypothesis to see if any of the set of regression coefficients could be different from 0. Use the .05 significance level. What is your conclusion?

d. Conduct a test of hypothesis for each independent variable. Use the .05 significance level. Which variable would you consider eliminating first?

e. Explain how to decide which independent variables could be removed from the regression equation.

LO14-4

Evaluate the assumptions of multiple regression.

Evaluating the Assumptions of Multiple Regression

In the previous section, we described the methods to statistically evaluate the multiple regression equation. The results of the test let us know if at least one of the coefficients was not equal to zero and we described a procedure of evaluating each regression coefficient. We also discussed the decision-making process for including and excluding independent variables in the multiple regression equation.

It is important to know that the validity of the statistical global and individual tests rely on several assumptions. So if the assumptions are not true, the results might be biased or misleading. However, strict adherence to the following assumptions is not always possible. Fortunately, the statistical techniques discussed in this chapter are robust enough to work effectively even when one or more of the assumptions are violated. Even if the values in the multiple regression equation are "off" slightly, our estimates using a multiple regression equation will be closer than any that could be made otherwise.

In Chapter 13, we listed the necessary assumptions for regression when we considered only a single independent variable. The assumptions for multiple regression are similar.

1. **There is a linear relationship.** That is, there is a straight-line relationship between the dependent variable and the set of independent variables.
2. **The variation in the residuals is the same for both large and small values of $\hat{y}$.** To put it another way, $(y - \hat{y})$ is unrelated to whether $\hat{y}$ is large or small.
3. **The residuals follow the normal probability distribution.** Recall the residual is the difference between the actual value of y and the estimated value $\hat{y}$. So the term $(y - \hat{y})$ is computed for every observation in the data set. These residuals should approximately follow a normal probability distribution with a mean of 0.
4. **The independent variables should not be correlated.** That is, we would like to select a set of independent variables that are not themselves correlated.
5. **The residuals are independent.** This means that successive observations of the dependent variable are not correlated. This assumption is often violated when time is involved with the sampled observations.

In this section, we present a brief discussion of each of these assumptions. In addition, we provide methods to validate these assumptions and indicate the consequences if these assumptions cannot be met. For those interested in additional discussion, search the term "Applied Linear Models."

Linear Relationship

Let's begin with the linearity assumption. The idea is that the relationship between the set of independent variables and the dependent variable is linear. If we are considering two independent variables, we can visualize this assumption. The two independent variables and the dependent variable would form a three-dimensional space. The regression equation would then form a plane as shown on page 513. We can evaluate this assumption with scatter diagrams and residual plots.

Using Scatter Diagrams   The evaluation of a multiple regression equation should always include a scatter diagram that plots the dependent variable against each independent variable. These graphs help us to visualize the relationships and provide some initial information about the direction (positive or negative), linearity, and strength of the relationship. For example, the scatter diagrams for the home heating example follow. The plots suggest a fairly strong negative, linear relationship between heating cost and temperature, and a negative relationship between heating cost and insulation.

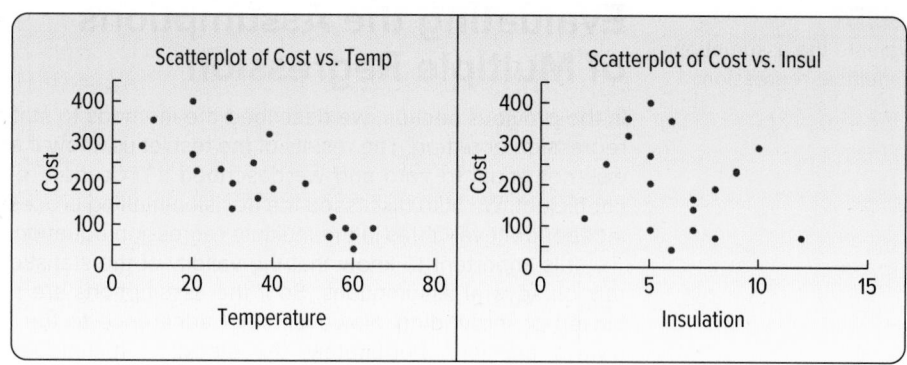

Using Residual Plots   Recall that a residual $(y - \hat{y})$ is computed using the multiple regression equation for each observation in a data set. In Chapter 13, we discussed the idea that the best regression line passed through the center of the data in a scatter plot. In this case, you would find a good number of the observations above the regression line (these residuals would have a positive sign) and a good number of the observations below the line (these residuals would have a negative sign). Further, the observations would be scattered above and below the line over the entire range of the independent variable.

The same concept is true for multiple regression, but we cannot graphically portray the multiple regression. However, plots of the residuals can help us evaluate the linearity of the multiple regression equation. To investigate, the residuals are plotted on the vertical axis against the predicted variable, $\hat{y}$. In the following graphs, the left graph shows the residual plots for the home heating cost example. Notice the following:

- The residuals are plotted on the vertical axis and are centered around zero. There are both positive and negative residuals.
- The residual plots show a random distribution of positive and negative values across the entire range of the variable plotted on the horizontal axis.
- The points are scattered and there is no obvious pattern, so there is no reason to doubt the linearity assumption.

The plot on the right shows nonrandom residuals. See that the residual plot does *not* show a random distribution of positive and negative values across the entire range of the variable plotted on the horizontal axis. In fact, the graph shows a nonlinear pattern of the residuals. This indicates the relationship is probably not linear. In this case, we would evaluate different transformations of the variables in the equation as discussed in Chapter 13.

Variation in Residuals Same for Large and Small $\hat{y}$ Values

This requirement indicates that the variation in the residuals is constant, regardless of whether the predicted values are large or small. To cite a specific example that may violate the assumption, suppose we use the single independent variable age to explain variation in monthly income. We suspect that as age increases so does income, but it also seems reasonable that as age increases there may be more variation around the regression line. That is, there will likely be more variation in income for 50-year-olds than for 35-year-olds. The requirement for constant variation around the regression line is called **homoscedasticity.**

> **HOMOSCEDASTICITY** The variation around the regression equation is the same for all of the values of the independent variables.

To check for homoscedasticity, the residuals are plotted against $\hat{y}$. This is the same graph we used to evaluate the assumption of linearity. Based on the scatter diagram, it is reasonable to conclude that this assumption has not been violated.

Distribution of Residuals

To be sure that the inferences we make in the global and individual hypothesis tests are valid, we evaluate the distribution of residuals. Ideally, the residuals should follow a normal probability distribution.

To evaluate this assumption, we can organize the residuals into a frequency distribution. The Histogram of Residuals graph is shown on the left for the home heating cost example. Although it is difficult to show that the residuals follow a normal distribution with only 20 observations, it does appear the normality assumption is reasonable.

Another graph that helps to evaluate the assumption of normally distributed residuals is called a Normal Probability Plot and is shown to the right of the histogram. This graphical analysis is often included in statistical software. If the plotted points are fairly close to a straight line drawn from the lower left to the upper right of the graph, the normal probability plot supports the assumption of normally distributed residuals This plot supports the assumption of normally distributed residuals.

In this case, both graphs support the assumption that the residuals follow the normal probability distribution. Therefore, the inferences that we made based on the global and individual hypothesis tests are supported with the results of this evaluation.

Multicollinearity

Multicollinearity exists when independent variables are correlated. Correlated independent variables make it difficult to make inferences about the individual regression coefficients and their individual effects on the dependent variable. In practice, it is nearly impossible to select variables that are completely unrelated. To put it another way, it is nearly impossible to create a set of independent variables that are not correlated to some degree. However, a general understanding of the issue of multicollinearity is important.

First, multicollinearity does not affect a multiple regression equation's ability to predict the dependent variable. However, when we are interested in evaluating the relationship between each independent variable and the dependent variable, multicollinearity may show unexpected results.

For example, if we use two highly correlated independent variables, high school GPA and high school class rank, to predict the GPA of incoming college freshmen (dependent variable), we would expect that both independent variables would be positively related to the dependent variable. However, because the independent variables are highly correlated, one of the independent variables may have an unexpected and inexplicable negative sign. In essence, these two independent variables are redundant in that they explain the same variation in the dependent variable.

A second reason to avoid correlated independent variables is they may lead to erroneous results in the hypothesis tests for the individual independent variables.

This is due to the instability of the standard error of estimate. Several clues that indicate problems with multicollinearity include the following:

1. An independent variable known to be an important predictor ends up having a regression coefficient that is not significant.
2. A regression coefficient that should have a positive sign turns out to be negative, or vice versa.
3. When an independent variable is added or removed, there is a drastic change in the values of the remaining regression coefficients.

In our evaluation of a multiple regression equation, an approach to reducing the effects of multicollinearity is to carefully select the independent variables that are included in the regression equation. A general rule is if the correlation between two independent variables is between −.70 and .70, there likely is not a problem using both of the independent variables. A more precise test is to use the **variance inflation factor.** It is usually written *VIF.* The value of *VIF* is found as follows:

VARIANCE INFLATION FACTOR	$VIF = \dfrac{1}{1 - R_j^2}$	**(14–7)**

The term R_j^2 refers to the coefficient of determination, where the selected *independent variable* is used as a dependent variable and the remaining independent variables are used as independent variables. If the *VIF* is between 4 and 10, multicollinearity is present and careful consideration in the selection of the independent variables is warranted. A *VIF* greater than 10 is considered unsatisfactory, indicating that the independent variable should be removed from the analysis. The following Example/Solution will explain the details of finding the *VIF.*

▶ **EXAMPLE**

Refer to the data in Table 14–1, which relate the heating cost to the independent variables: outside temperature, amount of insulation, and age of furnace. Develop a correlation matrix for all the independent variables. Does it appear there is a problem with multicollinearity? Find and interpret the variance inflation factor for each of the independent variables.

SOLUTION

We begin by finding the correlation matrix for the dependent variable and the three independent variables. A correlation matrix shows the correlation between all pairs of the variables. A portion of that output follows:

	Cost	Temp	Insul	Age
Cost	1.000			
Temp	−0.812	1.000		
Insul	−0.257	−0.103	1.000	
Age	0.537	−0.486	0.064	1.000

The highlighted area indicates the correlation among the independent variables. Because all of the correlations are between −.70 and .70, we do not suspect problems with multicollinearity. The largest correlation among the independent variables is −.486 between age and temperature.

To confirm this conclusion, we compute the *VIF* for each of the three independent variables. We will consider the independent variable temperature first. We use the Regression Analysis in Excel to find the multiple coefficient of determination with temperature as the *dependent variable* and amount of insulation and age of the furnace as independent variables. The relevant regression output follows:

SUMMARY OUTPUT					
Regression Statistics					
Multiple R	0.491				
R Square	0.241				
Adjusted R Square	0.152				
Standard Error	16.031				
Observations	20				
ANOVA					
	df	*SS*	*MS*	*F*	*Significance F*
Regression	2	1390.291	695.145	2.705	0.096
Residual	17	4368.909	256.995		
Total	19	5759.200			

The coefficient of determination is .241, so inserting this value into the *VIF* formula:

$$VIF = \frac{1}{1 - R_1^2} = \frac{1}{1 - .241} = 1.32$$

The *VIF* value of 1.32 is less than the upper limit of 10. This indicates that the independent variable temperature is not strongly correlated with the other independent variables.

Again, to find the *VIF* for insulation we would develop a regression equation with insulation as the *dependent variable* and temperature and age of furnace as independent variables. For this equation, the R^2 is .011 and, using formula (14–7), the *VIF* for insulation would be 1.011. To find the *VIF* for age, we would develop a regression equation with age as the dependent variable and temperature and insulation as the independent variables. For this equation, the R^2 is .236 and, using formula (14–7), the *VIF* for age would be 1.310. All the *VIF* values are less than 10. Hence, we conclude there is not a problem with multicollinearity in this Example/Solution.

Independent Observations

The fifth assumption about regression and correlation analysis is that successive residuals should be independent. This means that there is not a pattern to the residuals, the residuals are not highly correlated, and there are not long runs of positive or negative residuals. When successive residuals are correlated, we refer to this condition as **autocorrelation.**

Autocorrelation frequently occurs when the data are collected over a period of time. For example, we wish to predict yearly sales of Agis Software Inc. based on the time and the amount spent on advertising. The dependent variable is yearly sales and the independent variables are time and amount spent on advertising. It is likely that for a period of time the actual points will be above the regression plane (remember there are two independent variables) and then for a period of time the points will be below the regression plane. The following graph shows the residuals plotted on the vertical axis and the fitted values $\hat{y}$ on the horizontal axis. Note the run of residuals above the mean of the residuals, followed by a run below the mean. A scatter plot such as this would indicate possible autocorrelation.

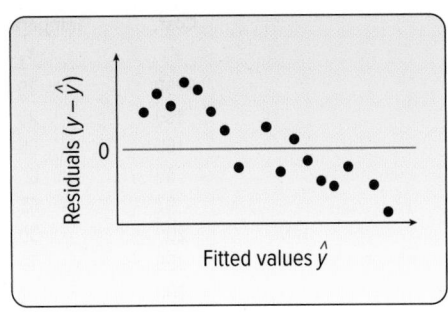

There is a test for autocorrelation, called the Durbin-Watson. It is discussed in Chapter 18.

Qualitative Independent Variables

In the previous Example/Solution regarding heating cost, the two independent variables outside temperature and insulation were quantitative; that is, numerical in nature. Frequently we wish to use nominal-scale variables—such as a variable to indicate if a home has a swimming pool or a variable indicating if a sports team is playing at home or visiting—in our analysis. These are called **qualitative variables** because they describe a particular quality or attribute. To use a qualitative variable in regression analysis, we use a scheme of **dummy variables** in which one of the two possible conditions is coded 0 and the other 1.

> **DUMMY VARIABLE** A variable in which there are only two possible outcomes. For analysis, one of the outcomes is coded a 1 and the other a 0.

For example, we are interested in estimating an executive's salary on the basis of years of job experience and whether the executive graduated from college. "Graduation from college" can take on only one of two conditions: yes or no. Thus, it is considered a qualitative variable.

Suppose in the Salsberry Realty example that the independent variable garage is added. For those homes without an attached garage, 0 is used; for homes with an attached garage, a 1 is used. We will refer to the garage variable as x_4. The data from Table 14–2 are entered into an Excel worksheet. Recall that the variable age of the furnace is not included in the analysis because we determined that it was not significantly related to heating cost.

The output from Excel is:

	A	B	C	D	E	F	G	H	I	J	K
1	Cost	Temp	Insul	Garage		SUMMARY OUTPUT					
2	250	35	3	0							
3	360	29	4	1		*Regression Statistics*					
4	165	36	7	0		Multiple R	0.933				
5	43	60	6	0		R Square	0.870				
6	92	65	5	0		Adjusted R Square	0.845				
7	200	30	5	0		Standard Error	41.618				
8	355	10	6	1		Observations	20				
9	290	7	10	1							
10	230	21	9	0		ANOVA					
11	120	55	2	0			df	SS	MS	F	Significance F
12	73	54	12	0		Regression	3	185202.269	61734.090	35.641	0.000
13	205	48	5	1		Residual	16	27713.481	1732.093		
14	400	20	5	1		Total	19	212915.750			
15	320	39	4	1							
16	72	60	8	0			Coefficients	Standard Error	t Stat	P-value	
17	272	20	5	1		Intercept	393.666	45.001	8.748	0.000	
18	94	58	7	0		Temp	-3.963	0.653	-6.072	0.000	
19	190	40	8	1		Insul	-11.334	4.002	-2.832	0.012	
20	235	27	9	0		Garage	77.432	22.783	3.399	0.004	

Source: Microsoft Excel

TABLE 14–2 Home Heating Costs, Temperature, Insulation, and Presence of a Garage for a Sample of 20 Homes

Cost, y	Temperature, x_1	Insulation, x_2	Garage, x_4
$250	35	3	0
360	29	4	1
165	36	7	0
43	60	6	0
92	65	5	0
200	30	5	0
355	10	6	1
290	7	10	1
230	21	9	0
120	55	2	0
73	54	12	0
205	48	5	1
400	20	5	1
320	39	4	1
72	60	8	0
272	20	5	1
94	58	7	0
190	40	8	1
235	27	9	0
139	30	7	0

What is the effect of the garage variable? Should it be included in the analysis? To show the effect of the variable, suppose we have two homes exactly alike next to each other in Buffalo, New York; one has an attached garage and the other does not. Both homes have 3 inches of insulation, and the mean January temperature in Buffalo is 20 degrees. For the house without an attached garage, a 0 is substituted for x_4 in the regression equation. The estimated heating cost is $280.404, found by:

$$\hat{y} = 393.666 - 3.963x_1 - 11.334x_2 + 77.432x_4$$
$$= 393.666 - 3.963(20) - 11.334(3) + 77.432(0) = 280.404$$

For the house with an attached garage, a 1 is substituted for x_4 in the regression equation. The estimated heating cost is $357.836, found by:

$$\hat{y} = 393.666 - 3.963x_1 - 11.334x_2 + 77.432x_4$$
$$= 393.666 - 3.963(20) - 11.334(3) + 77.432(1) = 357.836$$

The difference between the estimated heating costs is $77.432 ($357.836 − $280.404). Hence, we can expect the cost to heat a house with an attached garage to be $77.432 more than the cost for an equivalent house without a garage.

We have shown the difference between the two types of homes to be $77.432, but is the difference significant? We conduct the following test of hypothesis.

$$H_0: \beta_4 = 0$$
$$H_1: \beta_4 \neq 0$$

The information necessary to answer this question is in the output at the bottom of the previous page. The regression coefficient for the independent variable garage is $77.432, and the standard deviation of the sampling distribution is 22.783. We identify this as the fourth independent variable, so we use a subscript of 4. (Remember we dropped age of the furnace, the third independent variable.) Finally, we insert these values in formula (14–6).

$$t = \frac{b_4 - 0}{s_{b_4}} = \frac{77.432 - 0}{22.783} = 3.399$$

There are three independent variables in the analysis, so there are $n - (k + 1) = 20 - (3 + 1) = 16$ degrees of freedom. The critical value from Appendix B.5 is 2.120. The decision rule, using a two-tailed test and the .05 significance level, is to reject H_0 if the computed t is to the left of -2.120 or to the right of 2.120. Because the computed value of 3.399 is to the right of 2.120, the null hypothesis is rejected. We conclude that the regression coefficient is not zero. The independent variable garage should be included in the analysis.

Using the p-value approach, the computed t-value of 3.399 has a p-value of .004. This value is less than the .05 significance level. Therefore, we reject the null hypothesis. We conclude that the regression coefficient is not zero and the independent variable garage should be included in the analysis.

Is it possible to use a qualitative variable with more than two possible outcomes? Yes, but the coding scheme becomes more complex and will require a series of dummy variables. To explain, suppose a company is studying its sales as they relate to advertising expense by quarter for the last 5 years. Let sales be the dependent variable and advertising expense be the first independent variable, x_1. To include the qualitative information regarding the quarter, we use three additional independent variables. For the variable x_2, the five observations referring to the first quarter of each of the 5 years are coded 1 and the other quarters 0. Similarly, for x_3 the five observations referring to the second quarter are coded 1 and the other quarters 0. For x_4, the five observations referring to the third quarter are coded 1 and the other quarters 0. An observation that does not refer to any of the first three quarters must refer to the fourth quarter, so a distinct independent variable referring to this quarter is not necessary.

SELF-REVIEW 14–4

A study by the National Association of Health Underwriters investigated the relationship between commissions earned by insurance agents last year and the number of months since the agents earned their licenses. Also of interest in the study is the sex of the agent. Following is a portion of the regression output. The dependent variable is commissions, which is reported in $000, and the independent variables are months since the license was earned and sex (female = 1 and male = 0).

Regression Analysis

Regression Statistics

Multiple R	0.801
R Square	0.642
Adjusted R Square	0.600
Standard Error	3.219
Observations	20

ANOVA

	df	SS	MS	F	p-value
Regression	2	315.9291	157.9645	15.2468	0.0002
Residual	17	176.1284	10.36049		
Total	19	492.0575			

	Coefficients	Standard Error	t Stat	p-value
Intercept	15.7625	3.0782	5.121	.0001
Months	0.4415	0.0839	5.262	.0001
Sex	3.8598	1.4724	2.621	.0179

(a) Write out the regression equation. How much commission would you expect a female agent to make who earned her license 30 months ago?

(b) Do the female agents on the average make more or less than the male agents? How much more?

(c) Conduct a test of hypothesis to determine if the independent variable sex should be included in the analysis. Use the .05 significance level. What is your conclusion?

LO14-6
Include and interpret an interaction effect in a multiple regression analysis.

Regression Models with Interaction

In Chapter 12, we discussed interaction among independent variables. To explain, suppose we are studying weight loss and assume, as the current literature suggests, that diet and exercise are related. So the dependent variable is amount of change in weight and the independent variables are diet (yes or no) and exercise (none, moderate, significant). We are interested in whether there is interaction among the independent variables. That is, if those studied maintain their diet and exercise significantly, will that increase the mean amount of weight lost? Is total weight loss more than the sum of the loss due to the diet effect and the loss due to the exercise effect?

We can expand on this idea. Instead of having two nominal-scale variables, diet and exercise, we can examine the effect (interaction) of several ratio-scale variables. For example, suppose we want to study the effect of room temperature (68, 72, 76, or 80 degrees Fahrenheit) and noise level (60, 70, or 80 decibels) on the number of units produced. To put it another way, does the combination of noise level in the room and the temperature of the room have an effect on the productivity of the workers? Would workers produce more units in a quiet, cool room compared to a hot, noisy room?

In regression analysis, interaction is examined as a separate independent variable. An interaction prediction variable is developed by multiplying the data values of one independent variable by the values of another independent variable, thereby creating a new independent variable. A two-variable model that includes an interaction term is:

$$Y = \alpha + \beta_1 X_1 + \beta_2 X_2 + \beta_3 X_1 X_2$$

The term $X_1 X_2$ is the *interaction term*. We create this variable by multiplying the values of X_1 and X_2 to create a third independent variable. We then develop a regression equation using the three independent variables and test the significance of the third independent variable using the individual test for independent variables, described earlier in the chapter. An Example/Solution will illustrate the details.

▶ EXAMPLE

Refer to the heating cost example and the data in Table 14–1. Is there an interaction between the outside temperature and the amount of insulation? If both variables are increased, is the effect on heating cost greater than the sum of savings from warmer temperature and the savings from increased insulation separately?

SOLUTION

The information from Table 14–1 for the independent variables temperature and insulation is repeated here. We create the interaction variable by multiplying the value of temperature by the value insulation for each observation in the data set. For the first sampled home, the value temperature is 35 degrees and insulation is 3 inches so the value of the interaction variable is $35 \times 3 = 105$. The values of the other interaction products are found in a similar fashion.

◢	A	B	C	D	E	F	G	H	I	J	K
1	Cost	Temp	Insul	Temp X Insul		SUMMARY OUTPUT					
2	250	35	3	105							
3	360	29	4	116		*Regression Statistics*					
4	165	36	7	252		Multiple R	0.893				
5	43	60	6	360		R Square	0.798				
6	92	65	5	325		Adjusted R Square	0.760				
7	200	30	5	150		Standard Error	51.846				
8	355	10	6	60		Observations	20				
9	290	7	10	70							
10	230	21	9	189		ANOVA					
11	120	55	2	110			*df*	*SS*	*MS*	*F*	*Significance F*
12	73	54	12	648		Regression	3	169908.452	56636.151	21.070	0.000
13	205	48	5	240		Residual	16	43007.298	2687.956		
14	400	20	5	100		Total	19	212915.750			
15	320	39	4	156							
16	72	60	8	480			*Coefficients*	*Standard Error*	*t Stat*	*P-value*	
17	272	20	5	100		Intercept	598.070	92.265	6.482	0.000	
18	94	58	7	406		Temp	-7.811	2.124	-3.678	0.002	
19	190	40	8	320		Insul	-30.161	12.621	-2.390	0.030	
20	235	27	9	243		Temp X Insul	0.385	0.291	1.324	0.204	
21	139	30	7	210							

Source: Microsoft Excel

We find the multiple regression using temperature, insulation, and the interaction of temperature and insulation as independent variables. The regression equation is reported here:

$$\hat{y} = 598.070 - 7.811x_1 - 30.161x_2 + .385x_1x_2$$

The question we wish to answer is whether the interaction variable is significant. Note we use the subscript, 1×2, to indicate the coefficient of the interaction of variables 1 and 2. We will use the .05 significance level. In terms of a hypothesis:

$$H_0: \beta_{1\times2} = 0$$
$$H_1: \beta_{1\times2} \neq 0$$

There are $n - (k + 1) = 20 - (3 + 1) = 16$ degrees of freedom. Using the .05 significance level and a two-tailed test, the critical values of t are -2.120 and 2.120. We reject the null hypothesis if t is less than -2.120 or t is greater than 2.120. From the output, $b_{1\times2} = .385$ and $s_{b_{1\times2}}$ Using the values from the table above in formula (14-6), the t-value is.

$$t = \frac{b_{1\times2} - 0}{s_{b_{1\times2}}} = \frac{.385 - 0}{.291} = 1.323$$

Because the computed value of 1.323 is less than the critical value of 2.120, we do not reject the null hypothesis. In addition, the p-value of .204 exceeds .05. We conclude that there is not a significant interaction effect of temperature and insulation on home heating costs. Note that a hand calculation of the formula above yields a t-value of 1.323. The difference is the result of rounding.

There are other situations that can occur when studying interaction among independent variables.

1. It is possible to have a three-way interaction among the independent variables. In our heating example, we might have considered the three-way interaction between temperature, insulation, and age of the furnace.
2. It is possible to have an interaction where one of the independent variables is nominal scale. In our heating cost example, we could have studied the interaction between temperature and garage.

Studying all possible interactions can become very complex. However, careful consideration to possible interactions among independent variables can often provide useful insight into the regression models.

LO14-7
Apply stepwise
regression to develop
a multiple regression
model.

Stepwise Regression

In our heating cost example (see sample information in Table 14–1), we considered three independent variables: the mean outside temperature, the amount of insulation in the home, and the age of the furnace. To obtain the equation, we first ran a global or "all at once" test to determine if any of the regression coefficients were significant. When we found at least one to be significant, we tested the regression coefficients individually to determine which were important. We kept the independent variables that had significant regression coefficients and left the others out. By retaining the independent variables with significant coefficients, we found the regression equation that used the fewest independent variables. This made the regression equation easier to interpret. Then we considered the qualitative variable garage and found that it was significantly related to heating cost. The variable garage was added to the equation.

Deciding the set of independent variables to include in a multiple regression equation can be accomplished using a technique called **stepwise regression.** This technique efficiently builds an equation that only includes independent variables with significant regression coefficients.

> **STEPWISE REGRESSION** A step-by-step method to determine a regression equation that begins with a single independent variable and adds or deletes independent variables one by one. Only independent variables with nonzero regression coefficients are included in the final regression equation.

In the stepwise method, we develop a sequence of equations. The first equation contains only one independent variable. However, this independent variable is the one from the set of proposed independent variables that explains the most variation in the dependent variable. Stated differently, if we compute all the simple correlations between each independent variable and the dependent variable, the stepwise method first selects the independent variable with the strongest correlation with the dependent variable.

Next, the stepwise method reviews the remaining independent variables and selects the one that will explain the largest percentage of the variation yet unexplained. We continue this process until all the independent variables with significant regression coefficients are included in the regression equation. Advantages to the stepwise method are as follows:

1. Only independent variables with significant regression coefficients are entered into the equation.
2. The steps involved in building the regression equation are clear.
3. It is efficient in finding the regression equation with only significant regression coefficients.
4. The changes in the multiple standard error of estimate and the coefficient of determination are shown.

Stepwise regression procedures are included in many statistical software packages. For example, Minitab's stepwise regression analysis for the home heating cost problem follows. Note that the final equation, which is reported in column 3 (C3), includes the three independent variables temperature, garage, and insulation. These are the same independent variables that were included in our equation using the global test and the test for individual independent variables. The independent variable age, indicating the furnace's age, is not included because it is not a significant predictor of cost.

	C1	C2	C3	C4
	Cost	Temp	Insul	Garage
1	250	35	3	0
2	360	29	4	1
3	165	36	7	0
4	43	60	6	0
5	92	65	5	0
6	200	30	5	0
7	355	10	6	1
8	290	7	10	1
9	230	21	9	0
10	120	55	2	0
11	73	54	12	0
12	205	48	5	1
13	400	20	5	1
14	320	39	4	1
15	72	60	8	0
16	272	20	5	1
17	94	58	7	0
18	190	40	8	1
19	235	27	9	0
20	139	30	7	0

Stepwise Regression: Cost versus Temp, Insul, Garage

Alpha-to-Enter: 0.15   Alpha-to-Remove: 0.15

Response is Cost on 3 predictors, with N = 20

Step	1	2	3
Constant	388.8	300.3	393.7
Temp	-4.93	-3.56	-3.96
T-Value	-5.89	-4.70	-6.07
P-Value	0.000	0.000	0.000
Garage		93	77
T-Value		3.56	3.40
P-Value		0.002	0.004
Insul			-11.3
T-Value			-2.83
P-Value			0.012
S	63.6	49.5	41.6
R-Sq	65.85	80.46	86.98
R-Sq(adj)	63.96	78.16	84.54
Mallows Cp	26.0	10.0	4.0

Source: Minitab

Reviewing the steps and interpreting output:

1. The stepwise procedure selects the independent variable temperature first. This variable explains more of the variation in heating cost than any of the other three proposed independent variables. Temperature explains 65.85% of the variation in heating cost. The regression equation is:

$$\hat{y} = 388.8 - 4.93x_1$$

There is an inverse relationship between heating cost and temperature. For each degree the temperature increases, heating cost is reduced by $4.93.

2. The next independent variable to enter the regression equation is garage. When this variable is added to the regression equation, the coefficient of determination is increased from 65.85% to 80.46%. That is, by adding garage as an independent variable, we increase the coefficient of determination by 14.61 percentage points. The regression equation after step 2 is:

$$\hat{y} = 300.3 - 3,56x_1 + 93.0x_2$$

Usually the regression coefficients will change from one step to the next. In this case, the coefficient for temperature retained its negative sign, but it changed from −4.93 to −3.56. This change is reflective of the added influence of the independent variable garage. Why did the stepwise method select the independent variable garage instead of either insulation or age? The increase in R^2, the coefficient of determination, is larger if garage is included rather than either of the other two variables.

3. At this point, there are two unused variables remaining, insulation and age. Notice on the third step the procedure selects insulation and then stops. This indicates the variable insulation explains more of the remaining variation in heating cost than the age variable does. After the third step, the regression equation is:

$$\hat{y} = 393.7 - 3.96x_1 + 77.0x_2 - 11.3x_3$$

At this point, 86.98% of the variation in heating cost is explained by the three independent variables temperature, garage, and insulation. This is the same R^2-value and regression equation we found on page 535 except for rounding differences.

4. Here, the stepwise procedure stops. This means the independent variable age does not add significantly to the coefficient of determination.

The stepwise method developed the same regression equation, selected the same independent variables, and found the same coefficient of determination as the global and individual tests described earlier in the chapter. The advantage to the stepwise method is that it is more direct than using a combination of the global and individual procedures.

Other methods of variable selection are available. The stepwise method is also called the **forward selection method** because we begin with no independent variables and add one independent variable to the regression equation at each iteration. There is also the **backward elimination method,** which begins with the entire set of variables and eliminates one independent variable at each iteration.

The methods described so far look at one variable at a time and decide whether to include or eliminate that variable. Another approach is the **best-subset regression.** With this method, we look at the best model using one independent variable, the best model using two independent variables, the best model with three, and so on. The criterion is to find the model with the largest R^2-value, regardless of the number of independent variables. Also, each independent variable does not necessarily have a nonzero regression coefficient. Since each independent variable could either be included or not included, there are $2^k - 1$ possible models, where k refers to the number of independent variables. In our heating cost example, we considered four independent variables so there are 15 possible regression models, found by $2^4 - 1 = 16 - 1 = 15$. We would examine all regression models using one independent variable, all combinations using two variables, all combinations using three independent variables, and the possibility of using all four independent variables. The advantages to the best-subset method is it may examine combinations of independent variables not considered in the stepwise method. Many of these selection methods are available in Minitab, MegaStat, and other statistical software packages.

EXERCISES

9.   **FILE** The manager of High Point Sofa and Chair, a large furniture manufacturer located in North Carolina, is studying the job performance ratings of a sample of 15 electrical technicians employed by the company. An aptitude test is required by the human resources department to become an electrical technician. The manager was able to get the score for each technician in the sample. In addition, the manager determined which of the technician were union members (code = 1) and which were not (code = 0). The sample information is reported here:

Technician	Job Performance Score	Aptitude Test Score	Union Membership
Abbott	58	5	0
Anderson	53	4	0
Bender	33	10	0
Bush	97	10	0
Center	36	2	0
Coombs	83	7	0
Eckstine	67	6	0
Gloss	84	9	0
Herd	98	9	1
Householder	45	2	1
Lori	97	8	1
Lindstrom	90	6	1
Mason	96	7	1
Pierse	66	3	1
Rohde	82	6	1

a. Use a statistical software package to develop a multiple regression equation using the job performance score as the dependent variable and aptitude test score and union membership as independent variables.

b. Summarize the results of the regression analysis by interpreting the coefficient of determination and explaining the significance of the independent variables in predicting job performance.

c. Conduct a test of hypothesis to determine if union membership should be included as an independent variable.

d. Repeat the analysis by adding a variable to the regression equation that represents the interaction of aptitude and union membership. Summarize the results of adding an interaction effect.

10. **FILE** Cincinnati Paint Company sells quality brands of paints through hardware stores throughout the United States. The company maintains a large sales force who call on existing customers and look for new business. The national sales manager is investigating the relationship between the number of sales calls made and the miles driven by the sales representative. Also, do the sales representatives who drive the most miles and make the most calls necessarily earn the most in sales commissions? To investigate, the vice president of sales selected a sample of 25 sales representatives and determined the following:

- The amount earned in commissions last month (y)
- The number of miles driven last month (x_1)
- The number of sales calls made last month (x_2)

The information is reported here:

Commissions ($000)	Calls	Driven
22	139	2,371
13	132	2,226
33	144	2,731
⋮	⋮	⋮
25	127	2,671
43	154	2,988
34	147	2,829

a. Use a statistical software package to develop a multiple regression equation with commissions as the dependent variable and number of miles driven and number of sales calls as independent variables. Also include a variable representing the interaction of miles driven and sales calls.

b. Should the interaction term be included in the regression equation? Explain.

c. Rerun and report the regression analysis without the interaction term.

d. Summarize the results of the regression equation without interaction by writing the equation, reporting and interpreting the adjusted R^2, and reporting the significance of the independent variables.

11. **FILE** An art collector is studying the relationship between the selling price of a painting and two independent variables. The two independent variables are the number of bidders at the particular auction and the age of the painting, in years. A sample of 25 paintings revealed the following sample information.

Painting	Auction Price	Bidders	Age
1	3,470	10	67
2	3,500	8	56
3	3,700	7	73
⋮	⋮	⋮	⋮
23	4,660	5	94
24	4,710	3	88
25	4,880	1	84

a. Develop a multiple regression equation using the independent variables number of bidders and age of painting to estimate the dependent variable auction price. Discuss the equation. Does it surprise you that there is an inverse relationship between the number of bidders and the price of the painting?

b. Create an interaction variable and include it in the regression equation. Explain the meaning of the interaction. Is this variable significant?

c. What is the final result of this regression analysis? Report and interpret the coefficient of determination.

12. **FILE** A real estate developer wishes to study the relationship between the size of home a client will purchase (in square feet) and other variables. Possible independent variables include the family income, family size, whether there is a senior adult parent living with the family (1 for yes, 0 for no), and the total years of education beyond high school for the buyers. The sample information is reported here:

Family	Square Feet	Income (000s)	Family Size	Senior Parent	Education
1	2,240	60.8	2	0	4
2	2,380	68.4	2	1	6
3	3,640	104.5	3	0	7
4	3,360	89.3	4	1	0
5	3,080	72.2	4	0	2
6	2,940	114	3	1	10
7	4,480	125.4	6	0	6
8	2,520	83.6	3	0	8
9	4,200	133	5	0	2
10	2,800	95	3	0	6

a. Using stepwise regression, create a regression model to predict the square feet of a purchased house.

b. Report the regression model.

c. Report and interpret the adjusted R^2.

d. Interpret each of the independent variables as it relates to square feet.

LO14-8

Apply multiple regression techniques to develop a linear model.

Review of Multiple Regression

We described many topics involving multiple regression in this chapter. In this section of the chapter, we focus on a single Example/Solution that reviews the procedure and guides your application of multiple regression analysis.

▶ **EXAMPLE**

The Bank of New England is a large financial institution serving the New England states as well as New York and New Jersey. The mortgage department of the Bank of New England is studying data from recent loans. Of particular interest is how such factors as the value of the home being purchased ($000), education level of the head of the household (number of years, beginning with first grade), age of the head of the household, current monthly mortgage payment (in dollars), and sex of the head of the household (male = 1, female = 0) relate to the family income. The mortgage department would like to know whether these variables are effective predictors of family income.

SOLUTION

FILE Consider a random sample of 25 loan applications submitted to the Bank of New England last month. A portion of the sample information is shown in Table 14–3. The entire data set is available at the website (**www.mhhe.com/Lind19e**) and is identified as Bank of New England.

TABLE 14–3 Information on Sample of 25 Loans by the Bank of New England

Loan	Income ($000)	Value ($000)	Education	Age	Mortgage	Sex
1	100.7	190	14	53	230	1
2	99.0	121	15	49	370	1
3	102.0	161	14	44	397	1
⋮	⋮	⋮	⋮	⋮	⋮	⋮
23	102.3	163	14	46	142	1
24	100.2	150	15	50	343	0
25	96.3	139	14	45	373	0

We begin by calculating the correlation matrix shown. It shows the relationship between each of the independent variables and the dependent variable. It helps to identify the independent variables that are more closely related to the dependent variable (family income). The correlation matrix also reveals the independent variables that are highly correlated and possibly redundant.

	Income	Value	Education	Age	Mortgage	Sex
Income	1					
Value	0.720	1				
Education	0.188	−0.144	1			
Age	0.243	0.220	0.621	1		
Mortgage	0.116	0.358	−0.210	−0.038	1	
Sex	0.486	0.184	0.062	0.156	−0.129	1

What can we learn from this correlation matrix?

1. The first column shows the correlations between each of the independent variables and the dependent variable family income. Observe that each of the independent variables is positively correlated with family income. The value of the home has the strongest correlation with family income. The level of education of the person applying for the loan and the current mortgage payment have a weak correlation with family income. These two variables are candidates to be dropped from the regression equation.
2. All possible correlations among the independent variables are identified with the green background. Our standard is to look for correlations that exceed an absolute value of .700. Using this standard, none of the independent variables are strongly correlated with each other. This indicates that multicollinearity is not likely.

Next, we compute the multiple regression equation using all the independent variables. The software output follows:

SUMMARY OUTPUT					
Regression Statistics					
Multiple R	0.866				
R Square	0.750				
Adjusted R Square	0.684				
Standard Error	1.478				
Observations	25				
ANOVA					
	df	SS	MS	F	p-value
Regression	5	124.3215	24.8643	11.3854	0.0000
Residual	19	41.4936	2.1839		
Total	24	165.8151			
	Coefficients	Standard Error	t Stat	P-value	
Intercept	70.6061	7.4644	9.4591	0.0000	
Value	0.0717	0.0124	5.7686	0.0000	
Years	1.6242	0.6031	2.6930	0.0144	
Age	-0.1224	0.0781	-1.5661	0.1338	
Mortgage	-0.0010	0.0032	-0.3191	0.7531	
Sex	1.8066	0.6228	2.9007	0.0092	

Source: Microsoft Excel

The coefficients of determination, that is, both R^2 and adjusted R^2, are reported at the top of the summary output and highlighted in yellow. The R^2-value is 75.0%, so the five independent variables account for three-quarters of the variation in family income. The adjusted R^2 measures the strength of the relationship between the set of independent variables and family income and also accounts for the number of variables in the regression equation. The adjusted R^2 indicates that the five variables account for 68.4% of the variance of family income. Both of these suggest that the proposed independent variables are useful in predicting family income.

The output also includes the regression equation.

$$\hat{y} = 70.606 + .072(Value) + 1.624(Education) - .122(Age)$$
$$- .001(Mortgage) + 1.807(Sex)$$

Be careful in this interpretation. Both income and the value of the home are in thousands of dollars. Here is a summary:

1. An increase of $1,000 in the value of the home suggests an increase of $72 in family income. An increase of 1 year of education increases income by $1,624, another year older reduces income by $122, and an increase of $1,000 in the mortgage reduces income by $1.
2. If a male is head of the household, the value of family income will increase by $1,807. Remember that "female" was coded 0 and "male" was coded 1, so a male head of household is positively related to home value.
3. The age of the head of household and monthly mortgage payment are inversely related to family income. This is true because the sign of the regression coefficient is negative.

Next we conduct the global hypothesis test. Here we check to see if any of the regression coefficients are different from 0. We use the .05 significance level.

$$H_0: \beta_1 = \beta_2 = \beta_3 = \beta_4 = \beta_5 = 0$$
$$H_1: \text{Not all the } \beta\text{'s are 0}$$

The p-value from the table is .000. Because the p-value is less than the significance level, we reject the null hypothesis and conclude that at least one of the regression coefficients is not equal to zero.

Next we evaluate the individual regression coefficients. The p-values to test each regression coefficient are reported in the software output on the previous page. The null hypothesis and the alternate hypothesis are:

$$H_0: \beta_i = 0$$
$$H_1: \beta_i \neq 0$$

The subscript i represents any particular independent variable. Again using .05 significance levels, the p-values for the regression coefficients for home value, years of education, and sex are all less than .05. We conclude that these regression coefficients are not equal to zero and are significant predictors of family income. The p-value for age and mortgage amount are greater than the significance level of .05, so we do not reject the null hypotheses for these variables. The regression coefficients are not different from zero and are not related to family income.

Based on the results of testing each of the regression coefficients, we conclude that the variables age and mortgage amount are not effective predictors of family income. Thus, they should be removed from the multiple regression equation. Remember that we must remove one independent variable at a time and redo the analysis to evaluate the overall effect of removing the variable. Our strategy is to remove the variable with the smallest t-statistic or the largest p-value. This variable is mortgage amount. The result of the regression analysis without the mortgage variable follows:

SUMMARY OUTPUT					
Regression Statistics					
Multiple R	0.865				
R Square	0.748				
Adjusted R Square	0.698				
Standard Error	1.444				
Observations	25				
ANOVA					
	df	*SS*	*MS*	*F*	*P-value*
Regression	4	124.099	31.025	14.874	0.000
Residual	20	41.716	2.086		
Total	24	165.815			
	Coefficients	*Standard Error*	*t Stat*	*P-value*	
Intercept	70.159	7.165	9.791	0.000	
Value ($000)	0.070	0.011	6.173	0.000	
Education	1.647	0.585	2.813	0.011	
Age	-0.122	0.076	-1.602	0.125	
Sex	1.846	0.596	3.096	0.006	

Source: Microsoft Excel

Observe that the R^2 and adjusted R^2 change very little without the mortgage variable. Also observe that the p-value associated with age is greater than the .05 significance level. So next we remove the age variable and redo the analysis. The regression output with the variables age and mortgage amount removed follows:

SUMMARY OUTPUT					
Regression Statistics					
Multiple R	0.846				
R Square	0.716				
Adjusted R Square	0.676				
Standard Error	1.497				
Observations	25				
ANOVA					
	df	*SS*	*MS*	*F*	*P-value*
Regression	3	118.743	39.581	17.658	0.000
Residual	21	47.072	2.242		
Total	24	165.815			
	Coefficients	*Standard Error*	*t Stat*	*P-value*	
Intercept	74.527	6.870	10.849	0.000	
Value ($000)	0.063	0.011	5.803	0.000	
Education	1.016	0.449	2.262	0.034	
Sex	1.770	0.616	2.872	0.009	

Source: Microsoft Excel

From this output, we conclude:

1. The R^2 and adjusted R^2-values have declined but only slightly. Using all five independent variables, the R^2-value was .750. With the two nonsignificant variables removed, the R^2 and adjusted R^2-values are .716 and .676, respectively. We prefer the equation with the fewer number of independent variables. It is easier to interpret.
2. In ANOVA, we observe that the p-value is less than .05. Hence, at least one of the regression coefficients is not equal to zero.
3. Reviewing the significance of the individual coefficients, the p-values associated with each of the remaining independent variables are less than .05. We conclude that all the regression coefficients are different from zero. Each independent variable is a useful predictor of family income.

Our final step is to examine the regression assumptions (Evaluating the Assumptions of Multiple Regression section on page 529) with our regression model. The first assumption is that there is a linear relationship between each independent variable and the dependent variable. It is not necessary to review the dummy variable sex because there are only two possible outcomes. Following are the scatter plots of family income versus home value and family income versus years of education.

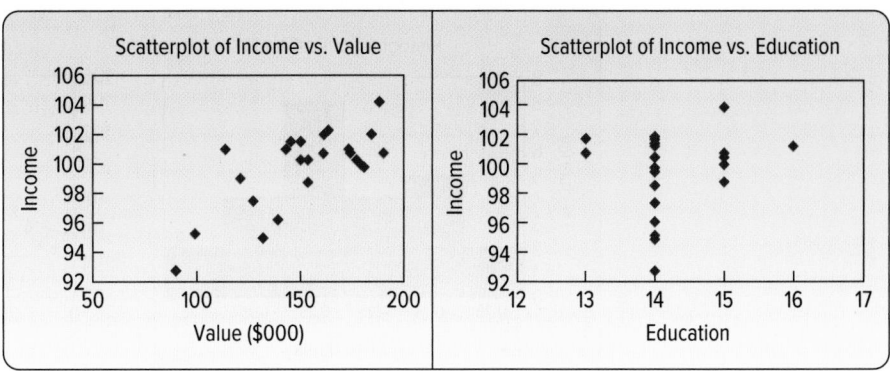

The scatter plot of income versus home value shows a general increasing trend. As the home value increases, so does family income. The points appear to be linear. That is, there is no observable nonlinear pattern in the data. The scatter plot on the right, of income versus years of education, shows that the data are measured to the nearest year. The measurement is to the nearest year and is a discrete variable. Given the measurement method, it is difficult to determine if the relationship is linear or not.

A plot of the residuals is also useful to evaluate the overall assumption of linearity. Recall that a residual is $(y - \hat{y})$, the difference between the actual value of the dependent variable (y) and the predicted value of the dependent variable $(\hat{y})$. Assuming a linear relationship, the distribution of the residuals should show about an equal proportion of negative residuals (points above the line) and positive residuals (points below the line) centered on zero. There should be no observable pattern to the plots. The graph follows:

There is no discernable pattern to the plot, so we conclude that the linearity assumption is reasonable.

If the linearity assumption is valid, then the distribution of residuals should follow the normal probability distribution with a mean of zero. To evaluate this assumption, we will use a histogram and a normal probability plot.

In general, the histogram on the left shows the major characteristics of a normal distribution, that is, a majority of observations in the middle and centered on the mean of zero, with lower frequencies in the tails of the distribution. The normal probability plot on the right is based on a cumulative normal probability distribution. The line shows the standardized cumulative normal distribution. The green dots show the cumulative distribution of the residuals. To confirm the normal distribution of the residuals, the green dots should be close to the line. This is true for most of the plot. However, we would note that there are departures and even perhaps a nonlinear pattern in the residuals. As before, we are looking for serious departures from linearity and these are not indicated in these graphs.

The final assumption refers to multicollinearity. This means that the independent variables should not be highly correlated. We suggested a rule of thumb that multicollinearity would be a concern if the correlations among independent variables were close to .7 or −.7. There are no violations of this guideline.

Recall the statistic that is used to more precisely evaluate multicollinearity, the variance inflation factor (*VIF*). To calculate the *VIF*s, we need to do a regression analysis for each independent variable as a function of the other independent variables. From each of these regression analyses, we need the R^2 to compute the *VIF* using formula (14–7). The following table shows the R^2 for each regression analysis and the computed *VIF*. If the *VIF*s are less than 10, then multicollinearity is not a concern. In this case, the *VIF*s are all less than 10, so multicollinearity among the independent variables is not a concern.

Dependent Variable	Independent Variables	*R*-square	*VIF*
Value	Education and Sex	0.058	1.062
Education	Sex and Value	0.029	1.030
Sex	Value and Education	0.042	1.044

To summarize, the multiple regression equation is

$$\hat{y} = 74.527 + .063(Value) + 1.016(Education) + 1.770(Sex)$$

This equation explains 71.6% of the variation in family income. There are no major departures from the multiple regression assumptions of linearity, normally distributed residuals, and multicollinearity.

CHAPTER SUMMARY

I. The general form of a multiple regression equation is:

$$\hat{y} = a + b_1 x_1 + b_2 x_2 + \ldots + b_k x_k \qquad \textbf{(14–1)}$$

where a is the Y-intercept when all x's are zero, b_j refers to the sample regression coefficients, and x_j refers to the value of the various independent variables.
   A. There can be any number of independent variables.
   B. The least squares criterion is used to develop the regression equation.
   C. A statistical software package is needed to perform the calculations.

II. An ANOVA table summarizes the multiple regression analysis.
   A. It reports the total amount of the variation in the dependent variable and divides this variation into that explained by the set of independent variables and that not explained.
   B. It reports the degrees of freedom associated with the independent variables, the error variation, and the total variation.

III. There are two measures of the effectiveness of the regression equation.
   A. The multiple standard error of estimate is similar to the standard deviation.
      1. It is measured in the same units as the dependent variable.
      2. It is based on squared deviations between the observed and predicted values of the dependent variable.
      3. It ranges from 0 to plus infinity.
      4. It is calculated from the following equation.

$$s_{y.123\ldots k} = \sqrt{\frac{\Sigma(y - \hat{y})^2}{n - (k + 1)}} \qquad \textbf{(14–2)}$$

   B. The coefficient of multiple determination reports the percent of the variation in the dependent variable explained by the variation in the set of independent variables.
      1. It may range from 0 to 1.
      2. It is also based on squared deviations from the regression equation.
      3. It is found by the following equation.

$$R^2 = \frac{SSR}{SS\ total} \qquad \textbf{(14–3)}$$

      4. When the number of independent variables is large, we adjust the coefficient of determination for the degrees of freedom as follows:

$$R_{adj}^2 = 1 - \frac{\dfrac{SSE}{n - (k + 1)}}{\dfrac{SS\ total}{n - 1}} \qquad \textbf{(14–4)}$$

IV. A global test is used to investigate whether any of the independent variables have a regression coefficient that differs significantly from zero.
   A. The null hypothesis is: All the regression coefficients are zero.
   B. The alternate hypothesis is: At least one regression coefficient is not zero.
   C. The test statistic is the F-distribution with k (the number of independent variables) degrees of freedom in the numerator and $n - (k + 1)$ degrees of freedom in the denominator, where n is the sample size.
   D. The formula to calculate the value of the test statistic for the global test is:

$$F = \frac{SSR/k}{SSE/[n - (k + 1)]} \qquad \textbf{(14–5)}$$

V. The test for individual variables determines which independent variables have regression coefficients that differ significantly from zero.
   A. The variables that have zero regression coefficients are usually dropped from the analysis.
   B. The test statistic is the t-distribution with $n - (k + 1)$ degrees of freedom.

C. The formula to calculate the value of the test statistic for the individual test is:

$$t = \frac{b_i - 0}{s_{b_i}}$$
(14–6)

VI. There are five assumptions to use multiple regression analysis.
   A. The relationship between the dependent variable and the set of independent variables must be linear.
      1. To verify this assumption, develop a scatter diagram and plot the residuals on the vertical axis and the fitted values on the horizontal axis.
      2. If the plots appear random, we conclude the relationship is linear.
   B. The variation is the same for both large and small values of $\hat{y}$.
      1. Homoscedasticity means the variation is the same for all fitted values of the dependent variable.
      2. This condition is checked by developing a scatter diagram with the residuals on the vertical axis and the fitted values on the horizontal axis.
      3. If there is no pattern to the plots—that is, they appear random—the residuals meet the homoscedasticity requirement.
   C. The residuals follow the normal probability distribution.
      1. This condition is checked by developing a histogram of the residuals or a normal probability plot.
      2. The mean of the distribution of the residuals is 0.
   D. The independent variables are not correlated.
      1. A correlation matrix will show all possible correlations among independent variables. Signs of trouble are correlations larger than .70 or less than −.70.
      2. Signs of correlated independent variables include when an important predictor variable is found insignificant, when an obvious reversal occurs in signs in one or more of the independent variables, or when a variable is removed from the solution, there is a large change in the regression coefficients.
      3. The variance inflation factor is used to identify correlated independent variables.

$$VIF = \frac{1}{1 - R_j^2}$$
(14–7)

   E. Each residual is independent of other residuals.
      1. Autocorrelation occurs when successive residuals are correlated.
      2. When autocorrelation exists, the value of the standard error will be biased and will return poor results for tests of hypothesis regarding the regression coefficients.
VII. Several techniques help build a regression model.
   A. A dummy or qualitative independent variable can assume one of two possible outcomes.
      1. A value of 1 is assigned to one outcome and 0 to the other.
      2. Use formula (14–6) to determine if the dummy variable should remain in the equation.
   B. Interaction is the case in which one independent variable (such as x_2) affects the relationship with another independent variable (x_1) and the dependent variable (y).
   C. Stepwise regression is a step-by-step process to find the regression equation.
      1. Only independent variables with nonzero regression coefficients enter the equation.
      2. Independent variables are added one at a time to the regression equation.

PRONUNCIATION KEY

SYMBOL	MEANING	PRONUNCIATION
b_1	Regression coefficient for the first independent variable	b sub 1
b_k	Regression coefficient for any independent variable	b sub k
$s_{y.123...k}$	Multiple standard error of estimate	s sub y dot 1, 2, 3 . . . k

CHAPTER EXERCISES

13. A multiple regression analysis yields the following partial results.

Source	Sum of Squares	df
Regression	750	4
Error	500	35

    a. What is the total sample size?
    b. How many independent variables are being considered?
    c. Compute the coefficient of determination.
    d. Compute the standard error of estimate.
    e. Test the hypothesis that at least one of the regression coefficients is not equal to zero. Let $\alpha = .05$.

14. In a multiple regression analysis, two independent variables are considered, and the sample size is 25. The regression coefficients and the standard errors are as follows:

$$b_1 = 2.676 \quad s_{b_1} = .56$$
$$b_2 = -.880 \quad s_{b_2} = .71$$

    a. Using a .05 significance level, conduct a test of hypothesis to determine whether either independent variable has a coefficient equal to zero.
    b. Would you consider deleting either variable from the regression equation? Why?

15. Refer to the following multiple regression analysis.

Analysis of Variance			
Source	DF	SS	MS
Regression	5	100	20
Residual Error	20	40	2
Total	25	140	

Predictor	Coefficient	SE Coefficient	t
Constant	3.00	1.50	2.00
x_1	4.00	3.00	1.33
x_2	3.00	0.20	15.00
x_3	0.20	0.05	4.00
x_4	-2.50	1.00	-2.50
x_5	3.00	4.00	0.75

    a. What is the sample size?
    b. Compute the value of R^2.
    c. Compute the multiple standard error of estimate.
    d. Conduct a global test of hypothesis to determine whether any of the regression coefficients are significant. Use the .05 significance level.
    e. Test the regression coefficients individually. Would you consider omitting any variable(s)? If so, which one(s)? Use the .05 significance level.

16. In a multiple regression analysis, $k = 5$ and $n = 20$, the MSE value is 5.10, and SS total is 519.68. At the .05 significance level, can we conclude that any of the regression coefficients are not equal to 0? Hint: Build the ANOVA table.

17. The district manager of Jasons, a large discount electronics chain, is investigating why certain stores in her region are performing better than others. She believes that three factors are related to total sales: the number of competitors in the region, the population in the surrounding area, and the amount spent on advertising. From her district, consisting of several hundred stores, she selects a random sample of 30 stores. For each store, she gathered the following information.

    y = total sales last year (in \$ thousands)
    x_1 = number of competitors in the region
    x_2 = population of the region (in millions)
    x_3 = advertising expense (in \$ thousands)

The results of a multiple regression analysis follow:

Analysis of Variance			
Source	DF	SS	MS
Regression	3	3050	1016.67
Residual Error	26	2200	84.62
Total	29	5250	
Predictor	Coefficient	SE Coefficient	t
Constant	14.00	7.00	2.00
x_1	-1.00	0.70	-1.43
x_2	30.00	5.20	5.77
x_3	0.20	0.08	2.50

a. What are the estimated sales for the Bryne store, which has four competitors, a regional population of .4 (400,000), and an advertising expense of 30 ($30,000)?

b. Compute the R^2-value.

c. Compute the multiple standard error of estimate.

d. Conduct a global test of hypothesis to determine whether any of the regression coefficients are not equal to zero. Use the .05 level of significance.

e. Conduct tests of hypothesis to determine which of the independent variables have significant regression coefficients. Which variables would you consider eliminating? Use the .05 significance level.

18. The sales manager of a large automotive parts distributor wants to estimate the total annual sales for each of the company's regions. Five factors appear to be related to regional sales: the number of retail outlets in the region, the number of automobiles in the region registered as of April 1, the total personal income recorded in the first quarter of the year, the average age of the automobiles (years), and the number of sales supervisors in the region. The data for each region were gathered for last year. For example, see the following table. In region 1 there were 1,739 retail outlets stocking the company's automotive parts, there were 9,270,000 registered automobiles in the region as of April 1, and so on. The region's sales for that year were $37,702,000.

Annual Sales ($ millions), y	Number of Retail Outlets, x_1	Number of Automobiles Registered (millions), x_2	Personal Income ($ billions), x_3	Average Age of Automobiles (years), x_4	Number of Supervisors, x_5
37.702	1,739	9.27	85.4	3.5	9.0
24.196	1,221	5.86	60.7	5.0	5.0
32.055	1,846	8.81	68.1	4.4	7.0
3.611	120	3.81	20.2	4.0	5.0
17.625	1,096	10.31	33.8	3.5	7.0
45.919	2,290	11.62	95.1	4.1	13.0
29.600	1,687	8.96	69.3	4.1	15.0
8.114	241	6.28	16.3	5.9	11.0
20.116	649	7.77	34.9	5.5	16.0
12.994	1,427	10.92	15.1	4.1	10.0

a. Consider the following correlation matrix. Which single variable has the strongest correlation with the dependent variable? The correlations between the independent variables outlets and income and between outlets and number of automobiles are fairly strong. Could this be a problem? What is this condition called?

```
              sales      outlets      cars     income      age
outlets       0.899
automobiles   0.605      0.775
income        0.964      0.825      0.409
age          -0.323     -0.489     -0.447     -0.349
bosses        0.286      0.183      0.395      0.155      0.291
```

b. The regression analysis using all five variables follows. Compute and interpret the R^2 for the regression equation.

```
The regression equation is
Sales = -19.7 - 0.00063 outlets + 1.74 autos + 0.410 income
        + 2.04 age - 0.034 bosses

        Predictor          Coef      SE Coef          T          P
        Constant        -19.672        5.422      -3.63      0.022
        outlets        -0.000629     0.002638      -0.24      0.823
        automobiles      1.7399       0.5530       3.15      0.035
        income          0.40994      0.04385       9.35      0.001
        age             2.0357       0.8779        2.32      0.081
        bosses         -0.0344       0.1880       -0.18      0.864

Analysis of Variance
        SOURCE            DF          SS          MS          F          P
        Regression         5     1593.81      318.76     140.36      0.000
        Residual Error     4        9.08        2.27
        Total              9     1602.89
```

c. Conduct a global test of hypothesis to determine whether any of the regression coefficients are not zero. Use the .05 significance level.

d. Conduct a test of hypothesis on each of the independent variables. Would you consider eliminating the variables outlets and bosses? Use the .05 significance level.

e. The regression has been rerun here with the variables outlets and bosses eliminated. Compute the coefficient of determination. How much has R^2 changed from the previous analysis?

```
The regression equation is
Sales = -18.9 + 1.61 autos + 0.400 income + 1.96 age

        Predictor          Coef      SE Coef          T          P
        Constant        -18.924        3.636      -5.20      0.002
        automobiles      1.6129       0.1979       8.15      0.000
        income          0.40031      0.01569      25.52      0.000
        age             1.9637       0.5846        3.36      0.015

Analysis of Variance
        SOURCE            DF          SS          MS          F          P
        Regression         3     1593.66      531.22     345.25      0.000
        Residual Error     6        9.23        1.54
        Total              9     1602.89
```

f. Following is a histogram of the residuals. Does the normality assumption appear reasonable? Why?

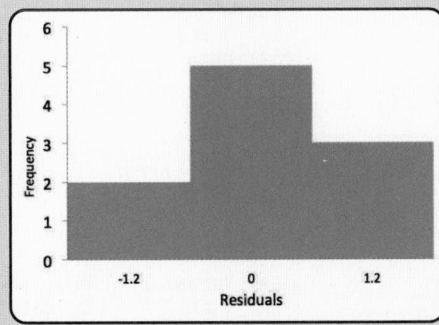

g. Following is a plot of the fitted values of y (i.e., $\hat{y}$) and the residuals. What do you observe? Do you see any violations of the assumptions?

19. **FILE** The administrator of a new paralegal program at Seagate Technical College wants to predict the grade point average (GPA) of students in the program. The administrator thought that high school GPA, the verbal score on the Scholastic Aptitude Test (SAT), and the mathematics score on the SAT would be good predictors of paralegal GPA. The data on nine students are:

Student	High School GPA	SAT Verbal	SAT Math	Paralegal GPA
1	3.25	480	410	3.21
2	1.80	290	270	1.68
3	2.89	420	410	3.58
4	3.81	500	600	3.92
5	3.13	500	490	3.00
6	2.81	430	460	2.82
7	2.20	320	490	1.65
8	2.14	530	480	2.30
9	2.63	469	440	2.33

a. Use statistical software to replicate the following correlation matrix. Which variable has the strongest correlation with the dependent variable? Some of the correlations among the independent variables are strong. Does this appear to be a problem?

```
                  Paralegal    High School
                     GPA          GPA      SAT Verbal
High School GPA     0.911
SAT Verbal          0.616        0.609
SAT Math            0.487        0.636       0.599
```

b. Use statistical software to replicate the following regression analysis with all the independent variables. Report and interpret the coefficient of multiple determination.

```
The regression equation is
Paralegal GPA = -0.411 + 1.20 HSGPA + 0.00163 SAT_Verbal - 0.00194
SAT_Math

Predictor            Coef         SE Coef           T          P
Constant          -0.4111         0.7823        -0.53      0.622
HSGPA              1.2014         0.2955         4.07      0.010
SAT_Verbal         0.001629       0.002147       0.76      0.482
SAT_Math          -0.001939       0.002074      -0.94      0.393

Analysis of Variance
SOURCE            DF          SS          MS          F          P
Regression         3      4.3595      1.4532      10.33      0.014
Residual Error     5      0.7036      0.1407
Total              8      5.0631

SOURCE      DF      Seq SS
HSGPA        1      4.2061
SAT_Verbal   1      0.0303
SAT_Math     1      0.1231
```

c. Conduct a global test of hypothesis from the preceding output. Does it appear that any of the regression coefficients are not equal to zero?

d. Conduct a test of hypothesis on each independent variable. Would you consider eliminating the variables SAT_Verbal and SAT_Math? Let $\alpha = .05$.

e. Use statistical software to replicate the following regression analysis without the SAT Math and SAT Verbal independent variables. Report the coefficient of determination. How much has R^2 changed from the previous analysis?

```
The regression equation is
Paralegal GPA = -0.454 + 1.16 HSGPA

Predictor        Coef      SE Coef         T        P
Constant       -0.4542      0.5542      -0.82     0.439
HSGPA           1.1589      0.1977       5.86     0.001

Analysis of Variance
SOURCE          DF        SS         MS        F        P
Regression       1      4.2061     4.2061    34.35    0.001
Residual Error   7      0.8570     0.1224
Total            8      5.0631
```

f. Following is a histogram of the residuals. Does the normality assumption for the residuals seem reasonable?

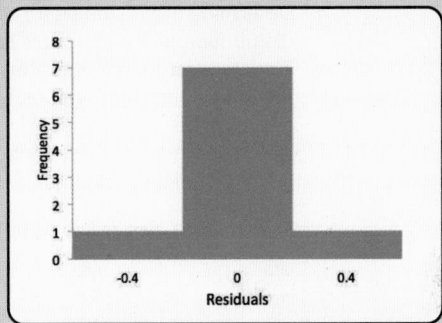

g. Following is a plot of the residuals and the $\hat{y}$ values. Do you see any violation of the assumptions?

20. **FILE** Mike Wilde is president of the teachers' union for Otsego School District. In preparing for upcoming negotiations, he is investigating the salary structure of classroom teachers in the district. He believes there are three factors that affect a teacher's salary: years of experience, a teaching effectiveness rating given by the principal, and whether the teacher has a master's degree. A random sample of 20 teachers resulted in the following data.

Salary ($ thousands), y	Years of Experience, x_1	Principal's Rating, x_2	Master's Degree,* x_3
31.1	8	35	0
33.6	5	43	0
29.3	2	51	1
⋮	⋮	⋮	⋮
30.7	4	62	0
32.8	2	80	1
42.8	8	72	0

*1 = yes, 0 = no.

a. Develop a correlation matrix. Which independent variable has the strongest correlation with the dependent variable? Does it appear there will be any problems with multicollinearity?

b. Determine the regression equation. What salary would you estimate for a teacher with 5 years' experience, a rating by the principal of 60, and no master's degree?

c. Conduct a global test of hypothesis to determine whether any of the regression coefficients differ from zero. Use the .05 significance level.

d. Conduct a test of hypothesis for the individual regression coefficients. Would you consider deleting any of the independent variables? Use the .05 significance level.

e. If your conclusion in part (d) was to delete one or more independent variables, run the analysis again without those variables.

f. Determine the residuals for the equation of part (e). Use a histogram to verify that the distribution of the residuals is approximately normal.

g. Plot the residuals computed in part (f) in a scatter diagram with the residuals on the Y-axis and the $\hat{y}$ values on the X-axis. Does the plot reveal any violations of the assumptions of regression?

21. **FILE** A video media consultant collected the following data on popular LED televisions sold through online retailers.

Manufacturer	Screen Size (in.)	Price	Manufacturer	Screen Size (in.)	Price
Sharp	46	$ 736.50	Sharp	37	$ 657.25
Samsung	52	1150.00	Sharp	32	426.75
Samsung	46	895.00	Sharp	52	1389.00
Sony	40	625.00	Samsung	40	874.75
Sharp	42	773.25	Sharp	32	517.50
Samsung	46	961.25	Samsung	52	1475.00
Samsung	40	686.00	Sony	40	954.25
Sharp	37	574.75	Sony	52	1551.50
Sharp	46	1000.00	Sony	46	1303.00
Sony	40	722.25	Sony	46	1430.50
Sony	52	1307.50	Sony	52	1717.00
Samsung	32	373.75			

a. Does there appear to be a linear relationship between the screen size and the price?

b. Which variable is the dependent variable?

c. Using statistical software, determine the regression equation. Interpret the value of the slope in the regression equation.

d. Include the manufacturer in a multiple linear regression analysis using a dummy variable. Does it appear that some manufacturers can command a premium price? Hint: You will need to use a set of dummy variables.

e. Test each of the individual coefficients to see if they are significant.

f. Make a plot of the residuals and comment on whether they appear to follow a normal distribution.

g. Plot the residuals versus the fitted values. Do they seem to have the same amount of variation?

22. FILE A regional planner is studying the demographics of nine counties in the eastern region of an Atlantic seaboard state. The planner has gathered the following data.

County	Median Income	Median Age	Coastal
A	$48,157	57.7	1
B	48,568	60.7	1
C	46,816	47.9	1
D	34,876	38.4	0
E	35,478	42.8	0
F	34,465	35.4	0
G	35,026	39.5	0
H	38,599	65.6	0
J	33,315	27.0	0

a. Is there a linear relationship between the median income and median age?
b. Which variable is the dependent variable?
c. Use statistical software to determine the regression equation based on only median age. Interpret the value of the slope.
d. Include the aspect that the county is coastal or not in a multiple linear regression analysis using a dummy variable. Does it appear to be a significant influence on incomes?
e. Using a .05 significance level, test each of the individual coefficients to see if they are significant.
f. Make a plot of the residuals and comment on whether they appear to follow a normal distribution.
g. Plot the residuals versus the fitted values. Do they seem to have the same amount of variation?

23. FILE Great Plains Distributors Inc. sells roofing and siding products to home improvement retailers, such as Lowe's and Home Depot, and commercial contractors. The owner is interested in studying the effects of several variables on the sales volume of fiber-cement siding products.

The company has 26 marketing districts across the United States. In each district, it collected information on the following variables: sales volume (in thousands of dollars), advertising dollars (in thousands), number of active accounts, number of competing brands, and a rating of market potential.

Sales (000s)	Advertising Dollars (000s)	Number of Accounts	Number of Competitors	Market Potential
$79.3	$5.5	31	10	8
200.1	2.5	55	8	6
163.2	8.0	67	12	9
200.1	3.0	50	7	16
146.0	3.0	38	8	15
177.7	2.9	71	12	17
⋮	⋮	⋮	⋮	⋮
93.5	4.2	26	8	3
259.0	4.5	75	8	19
331.2	5.6	71	4	9

Conduct a multiple regression analysis to find the best predictors of sales.
a. Draw a scatter diagram comparing sales volume with each of the independent variables. Comment on the results.
b. Develop a correlation matrix. Do you see any problems? Does it appear there are any redundant independent variables?
c. Develop a regression equation. Conduct the global test. Can we conclude that some of the independent variables are useful in explaining the variation in the dependent variable?

d. Conduct a test of each of the independent variables. Are there any that should be dropped?

e. Conduct a stepwise regression analysis based on the information in part (d).

f. Develop a histogram of the residuals and a normal probability plot. Are there any problems?

g. What is the variance inflation factor for the independent variables? Is there evidence of multicollinearity?

24. **FILE** A marketing executive is studying online services, and is researching the effect of web page hits, advertising budget, and price on a service's number of subscriptions. A sample of 25 online services is collected. The variable definitions and an overview of the data follow.

$$Sub = \text{Number of subscriptions (in thousands)}$$
$$\text{Web page hits} = \text{Average monthly count (in thousands)}$$
$$Adv = \text{The advertising budget of the service (in \$ hundreds)}$$
$$Price = \text{Average monthly subscription price (\$)}$$

Service	Sub	Web Page Hits	Adv	Price
1	37.95	588.9	$13.2	$35.1
2	37.66	585.3	13.2	34.7
3	37.55	566.3	19.8	34.8
⋮	⋮	⋮	⋮	⋮
23	38.83	629.6	22.0	35.3
24	38.33	680.0	24.2	34.7
25	40.24	651.2	33.0	35.8

a. Conduct a regression analysis using all independent variables. Report the regression equation.

b. Conduct a global test of hypothesis to determine whether any of the regression coefficients are not equal to zero.

c. Conduct a test for the individual coefficients. Would you consider deleting any coefficients?

d. Determine the residuals and plot them against the fitted values. Do you see any problems?

e. Develop a histogram of the residuals. Do you see any problems with the normality assumption?

25. **FILE** Fred G. Hire is the manager of human resources at Crescent Custom Steel Products. As part of his yearly report to the CEO, he is required to present an analysis of the salaried employees. For each of the 30 salaried employees, he records monthly salary; service at Crescent, in months; age; sex (1 = male, 0 = female); and whether the employee has a management or engineering position. Those employed in management are coded 0, and those in engineering are coded 1.

Sampled Employee	Monthly Salary	Length of Service	Age	Sex	Job
1	$1,769	93	42	1	0
2	1,740	104	33	1	0
3	1,941	104	42	1	1
⋮	⋮	⋮	⋮	⋮	⋮
28	1,791	131	56	0	1
29	2,001	95	30	1	1
30	1,874	98	47	1	0

a. Determine the regression equation, using salary as the dependent variable and the other four variables as independent variables.

b. What is the value of R^2? Comment on this value.

c. Conduct a global test of hypothesis to determine whether any of the independent variables are different from 0.

d. Conduct an individual test to determine whether any of the independent variables can be dropped.

e. Rerun the regression equation, using only the independent variables that are significant. How much more does a male earn per month than a female? Does it make a difference whether the employee has a management or engineering position?

26. FILE Many regions in North and South Carolina and Georgia have experienced rapid population growth over the last 10 years. It is expected that the growth will continue over the next 10 years. This has motivated many of the large grocery store chains to build new stores in the region. The Kelley's Super Grocery Stores Inc. chain is no exception. The director of planning for Kelley's Super Grocery Stores wants to study adding more stores in this region. The director believes there are two main factors that indicate the amount families spend on groceries. The first is their income and the other is the number of people in the family. The director gathered the following sample information.

Family	Food	Income	Size
1	$5.04	$73.98	4
2	4.08	54.90	2
3	5.76	94.14	4
⋮	⋮	⋮	⋮
23	4.56	38.16	3
24	5.40	43.74	7
25	4.80	48.42	5

Food and income are reported in thousands of dollars per year, and the variable size refers to the number of people in the household.

a. Develop a correlation matrix. Do you see any problems with multicollinearity?

b. Conduct and report the regression analysis predicting dollars spent on food with family income and size. Conduct and report the global hypothesis test of significance. Determine the regression equation. Discuss the regression equation. How much does an additional family member add to the amount spent on food?

c. Report and interpret the R^2.

d. Would you consider deleting either of the independent variables? Why?

e. Plot the residuals in a histogram. Is there any problem with the normality assumption?

f. Plot the fitted values against the residuals. Does this plot indicate any problems with homoscedasticity?

27. FILE An investment advisor is studying the relationship between a common stock's price to earnings (P/E) ratio and factors that would influence it. The advisor has the following data on the earnings per share (EPS) and the dividend percentage (Yield) for a sample of 20 stocks.

Stock	P/E	EPS	Yield
1	20.79	$2.46	1.42
2	3.03	2.69	4.05
3	44.46	−0.28	4.16
⋮	⋮	⋮	⋮
18	30.21	1.71	3.07
19	32.88	0.35	2.21
20	15.19	5.02	3.50

a. Compute and report the correlation matrix. Review the correlation coefficients for the independent variables. Do they indicate multicollinearity? Why?

b. Compute and report a multiple regression equation with P/E as the dependent variable.

c. Apply the stepwise procedure to remove insignificant independent variables. Report the regression equation.

d. Interpret the relationship between the dependent and independent variables in part (c).

e. Plot the fitted values against the residuals. Does the graph display evidence of homoscedasticity?

f. Would you use this regression equation to accurately predict the price to earnings ratio? Why?

28. **FILE** The Conch Café, located in Gulf Shores, Alabama, features casual lunches with a great view of the Gulf of Mexico. To accommodate the increase in business during the summer vacation season, Fuzzy Conch, the owner, hires a large number of servers as seasonal help. When he interviews a prospective server, he would like to provide data on the amount a server can earn in tips. He believes that the amount of the bill and the number of diners are both related to the amount of the tip. He gathered the following sample information.

Customer	Amount of Tip	Amount of Bill	Number of Diners
1	$7.00	$48.97	5
2	4.50	31.23	4
3	1.00	10.65	1
⋮	⋮	⋮	⋮
28	2.50	26.25	2
29	9.25	56.81	5
30	8.25	50.65	5

a. Compute and report the correlation matrix for all the variables. Review the correlation coefficients for the independent variables. Do they suggest multicollinearity?

b. Conduct and report the regression analysis that predicts amount of tip with both independent variables. Summarize the significance of each independent variable. Is there evidence of multicollinearity?

c. Compute and interpret the variance inflation factor for the two independent variables.

d. Based on the information in parts (a), (b), and (c), explain why a regression analysis with only one independent variable is logical. Conduct and report the regression analysis based on your analysis.

e. Using the regression equations from part (d), predict the tip based on a bill amount of $100.

f. Plot the residuals versus the fitted values. Does the plot satisfy the assumption of randomness?

29. **FILE** The president of Blitz Sales Enterprises sells kitchen products through cable television infomercials. The president gathered data from the last 15 weeks of sales to determine the relationship between sales and the number of infomercials.

Infomercials	Sales ($000s)	Infomercials	Sales ($000s)
20	3.2	22	2.5
15	2.6	15	2.4
25	3.4	25	3.0
10	1.8	16	2.7
18	2.2	12	2.0
18	2.4	20	2.6
15	2.4	25	2.8
12	1.5		

a. Determine the regression equation. Are the sales predictable from the number of commercials?

b. Determine the residuals and plot a histogram. Does the normality assumption seem reasonable?

30. **FILE** The director of special events for Sun City believed that the amount of money spent on fireworks displays for the Fourth of July was predictive of attendance at the Fall Festival held in October. The director gathered the following data to test the suspicion.

4th of July ($000)	Fall Festival (000)	4th of July ($000)	Fall Festival (000)
10.6	8.8	9.0	9.5
8.5	6.4	10.0	9.8
12.5	10.8	7.5	6.6
9.0	10.2	10.0	10.1
5.5	6.0	6.0	6.1
12.0	11.1	12.0	11.3
8.0	7.5	10.5	8.8
7.5	8.4		

a. Compute and report the regression equation that predicts fall festival attendance with amount spent on Fourth of July fireworks. Report the coefficient of determination. Interpret the regression coefficient.

b. Evaluate the regression assumptions based on an analysis of the residuals.

31. **FILE** You are a new hire at Laurel Woods Real Estate, which specializes in selling foreclosed homes via public auction. Your boss has asked you to use the following data (mortgage/loan balance, monthly payments, payments made before default, and final auction price) on a random sample of recent sales to estimate what the actual auction price will be.

Loan	Monthly Payments	Payments Made	Auction Price
$ 85,600	$ 985.87	1	$16,900
115,300	902.56	33	75,800
103,100	736.28	6	43,900
⋮	⋮	⋮	⋮
119,400	1,021.23	58	69,000
90,600	836.46	3	35,600
104,500	1,056.37	22	63,000

a. Conduct the requested regression analysis. Carry out a global test of hypothesis to verify if any of the regression coefficients are different from zero.

b. Perform an individual test of the independent variables. Would you remove any of the variables?

c. If one or more of the independent variables is not needed, report the revised regression analysis and report and interpret the results.

32. **FILE** Review the analysis from Exercise 31. Add a new variable that describes the potential interaction between the loan amount and the number of payments made. Then do a test of hypothesis to check if the interaction is significant.

DATA ANALYTICS

(The data for these exercises are available at the text website: **www.mhhe.com/Lind19e.**)

33. The North Valley Real Estate data report information on homes on the market. Use the selling price of the home as the dependent variable and determine the regression equation using the size of the house, number of bedrooms, days on the market, and number of bathrooms as independent variables.

a. Develop a correlation matrix. Which independent variables have strong or weak correlations with the dependent variable? Do you see any problems with multicollinearity?

b. Use a statistical software package to determine the multiple regression equation. How did you select the variables to include in the equation? How did you use the information from the correlation analysis? Show that your regression equation shows a significant relationship. Write out the regression equation and interpret its practical application. Report and interpret the R-square.

c. Using your results from part (b), evaluate the addition of the variables: pool or garage. Report your results and conclusions.

d. Develop a histogram of the residuals from the final regression equation developed in part (c). Is it reasonable to conclude that the normality assumption has been met?

e. Plot the residuals against the fitted values from the final regression equation developed in part (c). Plot the residuals on the vertical axis and the fitted values on the horizontal axis.

34. Refer to the Baseball 2021 data, which report information on the 30 Major League Baseball teams for the 2021 season. Let the number of games won be the dependent variable and the following variables be independent variables: team batting average, team earned run average (ERA), number of home runs, and whether the team plays in the American or the National League.

a. Develop a correlation matrix. Which independent variables have strong or weak correlations with the dependent variable? Do you see any problems with multicollinearity? Are you surprised that the correlation coefficient for ERA is negative?

b. Use a statistical software package to determine the multiple regression equation. How did you select the variables to include in the equation? How did you use the information from the correlation analysis? Show that your regression equation shows a significant relationship. Write out the regression equation and interpret its practical application. Report and interpret the R-square. Is the number of wins affected by whether the team plays in the National or the American League?

c. Conduct a global test on the set of independent variables. Interpret.

d. Conduct a test of hypothesis on each of the independent variables. Would you consider deleting any of the variables? If so, which ones? Report the final regression equation.

e. Develop a histogram of the residuals from the final regression equation developed in part (d). Is it reasonable to conclude that the normality assumption has been met?

f. Plot the residuals against the fitted values from the final regression equation developed in part (d). Plot the residuals on the vertical axis and the fitted values on the horizontal axis. What regression assumption is supported?

35. Refer to the Lincolnville School District bus data. First, add a variable to change the type of engine (diesel or gasoline) to a qualitative variable. If the engine type is diesel, then set the qualitative variable to 0. If the engine type is gasoline, then set the qualitative variable to 1. Develop a regression equation using statistical software with maintenance cost as the dependent variable and age, odometer miles, miles since last maintenance, and engine type as the independent variables.

a. Develop a correlation matrix. Which independent variables have strong or weak correlations with the dependent variable? Do you see any problems with multicollinearity?

b. Use a statistical software package to determine the multiple regression equation. How did you select the variables to include in the equation? How did you use the information from the correlation analysis? Show that your regression equation shows a significant relationship. Write out the regression equation and interpret its practical application. Report and interpret the R-square.

c. Develop a histogram of the residuals from the final regression equation developed in part (b). Is it reasonable to conclude that the normality assumption has been met?

d. Plot the residuals against the fitted values from the final regression equation developed in part (b) against the fitted values of Y. Plot the residuals on the vertical axis and the fitted values on the horizontal axis.

A REVIEW OF CHAPTERS 13–14

This section is a review of the major concepts and terms introduced in Chapters 13 and 14. Chapter 13 noted that the strength of the relationship between the independent variable and the dependent variable is measured by the *correlation coefficient*. The correlation coefficient is designated by the letter *r*. It can assume any value between −1.00 and +1.00 inclusive. Coefficients of −1.00 and +1.00 indicate a perfect relationship, and 0 indicates no relationship. A value near 0, such as −.14 or .14, indicates a weak relationship. A value near −1 or +1, such as −.90 or +.90, indicates a strong relationship. The *coefficient of determination,* also called R^2, measures the proportion of the total variation in the dependent variable explained by the independent variable. It can be computed as the square of the correlation coefficient.

Likewise, the strength of the relationship between several independent variables and a dependent variable is measured by the *coefficient of multiple determination*, R^2. It measures the proportion of the variation in y explained by two or more independent variables.

The linear relationship in the simple case involving one independent variable and one dependent variable is described by the equation $\hat{y} = a + bx$. For k independent variables, $x_1, x_2, \ldots x_k$, the same multiple regression equation is:

$$\hat{y} = a + b_1 x_1 + b_2 x_2 + \ldots + b_k x_k$$

Solving for $b_1, b_2, \ldots, b_k$ would involve tedious calculations. Fortunately, this type of problem can be quickly solved using one of the many statistical software packages and spreadsheet packages. Various measures, such as the coefficient of determination, the multiple standard error of estimate, the results of the global test, and the test of the individual variables, are reported in the output of most statistical software programs.

PROBLEMS

1. The accounting department at Box and Go Apparel wishes to estimate the net profit for each of the chain's many stores on the basis of the number of employees in the store, overhead costs, average markup, and theft loss. The data from two stores are:

Store	Net Profit ($ thousands) $\hat{y}$	Number of Employees x_1	Overhead Cost ($ thousands) x_2	Average Markup (percent) x_3	Theft Loss ($ thousands) x_4
1	$846	143	$79	69%	$52
2	513	110	64	50	45

   a. The dependent variable is _____.
   b. The general equation for this problem is _____.
   c. The multiple regression equation was computed to be $\hat{y} = 67 + 8x_1 - 10x_2 + .004x_3 - 3x_4$. What are the predicted sales for a store with 112 employees, an overhead cost of $65,000, a markup rate of 50%, and a loss from theft of $50,000?
   d. Suppose R^2 was computed to be .86. Explain.
   e. Suppose that the multiple standard error of estimate was 3 (in $ thousands). Explain what this means in this problem.

2. Quick-print firms in a large downtown business area spend most of their advertising dollars on displays on bus benches. A research project involves predicting monthly sales based on the annual amount spent on placing ads on bus benches. A sample of quick-print firms revealed these advertising expenses and sales:

Firm	Annual Bus Bench Advertising ($ thousands)	Monthly Sales ($ thousands)
A	2	10
B	4	40
C	5	30
D	7	50
E	3	20

   a. Draw a scatter diagram.
   b. Determine the correlation coefficient.
   c. What is the coefficient of determination?
   d. Compute the regression equation.
   e. Estimate the monthly sales of a quick-print firm that spends $4,500 on bus bench advertisements.
   f. Summarize your findings.

3. The following ANOVA output is given.

Analysis of Variance			
Source	DF	SS	MS
Regression	4	1050.8	262.70
Residual Error	20	83.8	4.19
Total	24	1134.6	
Predictor	Coefficient	SE Coefficient	t
Constant	70.06	2.13	32.89
x_1	0.42	0.17	2.47
x_2	0.27	0.21	1.29
x_3	0.75	0.30	2.50
x_4	0.42	0.07	6.00

a. Compute the coefficient of determination.
b. Compute the multiple standard error of estimate.
c. Conduct a test of hypothesis to determine whether any of the regression coefficients are different from zero.
d. Conduct a test of hypothesis on the individual regression coefficients. Can any of the variables be deleted?

CASES

A. The Century National Bank

Refer to the Century National Bank data. Using checking account balance as the dependent variable and using as independent variables the number of ATM transactions, the number of other services used, whether the individual has a debit card, and whether interest is paid on the particular account, write a report indicating which of the variables seem related to the account balance and how well they explain the variation in account balances. Should all of the independent variables proposed be used in the analysis or can some be dropped?

B. Terry and Associates: The Time to Deliver Medical Kits

FILE Terry and Associates is a specialized medical testing center in Denver, Colorado. One of the firm's major sources of revenue is a kit used to test for elevated amounts of lead in the blood. Workers in auto body shops, those in the lawn care industry, and commercial house painters are exposed to large amounts of lead and thus must be randomly tested. It is expensive to conduct the test, so the kits are delivered on demand to a variety of locations throughout the Denver area.

Kai Terry, the owner, is concerned about setting appropriate costs for each delivery. To investigate, Kai gathered information on a random sample of 50 recent deliveries. Factors thought to be related to the cost of delivering a kit were:

Prep   The time in minutes between when the customized order is phoned into the company and when it is ready for delivery.

Delivery The actual travel time in minutes from Kia's plant to the customer.

Mileage   The distance in miles from Kia's plant to the customer.

Sample Number	Cost	Prep	Delivery	Mileage	Sample Number	Cost	Prep	Delivery	Mileage
1	$32.60	10	51	20	6	$22.63	9	20	11
2	23.37	11	33	12	7	22.63	9	39	11
3	31.49	6	47	19	8	21.53	10	23	10
4	19.31	9	18	8	9	21.16	13	20	8
5	28.35	8	88	17	10	21.53	10	32	10

Sample Number	Cost	Prep	Delivery	Mileage	Sample Number	Cost	Prep	Delivery	Mileage
11	$28.17	5	35	16	31	$24.29	7	35	13
12	20.42	7	23	9	32	19.56	2	12	6
13	21.53	9	21	10	33	22.63	8	30	11
14	27.55	7	37	16	34	21.16	5	13	8
15	23.37	9	25	12	35	21.16	11	20	8
16	17.10	15	15	6	36	19.68	5	19	8
17	27.06	13	34	15	37	18.76	5	14	7
18	15.99	8	13	4	38	17.96	5	11	4
19	17.96	12	12	4	39	23.37	10	25	12
20	25.22	6	41	14	40	25.22	6	32	14
21	24.29	3	28	13	41	27.06	8	44	16
22	22.76	4	26	10	42	21.96	9	28	9
23	28.17	9	54	16	43	22.63	8	31	11
24	19.68	7	18	8	44	19.68	7	19	8
25	25.15	6	50	13	45	22.76	8	28	10
26	20.36	9	19	7	46	21.96	13	18	9
27	21.16	3	19	8	47	25.95	10	32	14
28	25.95	10	45	14	48	26.14	8	44	15
29	18.76	12	12	5	49	24.29	8	34	13
30	18.76	8	16	5	50	24.35	3	33	12

1. Develop a multiple linear regression equation that describes the relationship between the cost of delivery and the other variables. Do these three variables explain a reasonable amount of the variation in the dependent variable?
2. Test to determine if one or more regression coefficients differ from zero. Also test to see whether any of the variables can be dropped from the analysis. If some of the variables can be dropped, rerun the regression equation until only significant variables are included.
3. Write a brief report interpreting the final regression equation. Estimate the delivery cost for a kit that must cover a distance of 14 miles.

PRACTICE TEST

Part 1—Objective

1. In a scatter diagram, the dependent variable is always scaled on which axis? 1. _____
2. What level of measurement is required to compute the correlation coefficient? 2. _____
3. If there is no correlation between two variables, what is the value of the correlation coefficient? 3. _____
4. Which of the following values indicates the strongest correlation between two variables? (.65, −.77, 0, −.12) 4. _____
5. Under what conditions will the coefficient of determination assume a value greater than 1? 5. _____

Given the following regression equation, $\hat{y} = 7 - .5x$, and that the coefficient of determination is .81, answer questions 6, 7, and 8.

6. At what point does the regression equation cross the Y-axis? 6. _____
7. An increase of 1 unit in the independent variable will result in what amount of an increase or decrease in the dependent variable? 7. _____
8. What is the correlation coefficient? (Be careful of the sign.) 8. _____
9. If all the data points in a scatter diagram were on the regression line, what would be the value of the standard error of estimate? 9. _____
10. In a multiple regression equation, what is the maximum number of independent variables allowed? (2, 10, 30, unlimited) 10. _____
11. In multiple regression analysis, we assume what type of relationship between the dependent variable and the set of independent variables? (linear, multiple, curved, none of these) 11. _____

12. The difference between y and $\hat{y}$ is called a _____.   12. _____

13. Typically, how many values does a dummy variable have?   13. _____

14. What is the term given to a table that shows all possible correlation coefficients between the dependent variable and all the independent variables and among all the independent variables?   14. _____

15. If there is a linear relationship between the dependent variable and the set of independent variables, a graph of the residuals will show what type of distribution?   15. _____

Part 2—Problems

1. Given the following regression analysis output:

ANOVA Table					
Source	SS	df	MS	F	p-value
Regression	129.7275	1	129.7275	14.50	.0007
Residual	250.4391	28	8.9443		
Total	380.1667	29			

Regression Output			
Variables	Coefficients	Standard Error	t (df = 28)
Intercept	90.6190	1.5322	59.141
Slope	−0.9401	0.2468	−3.808

   a. What is the sample size?

   b. Write out the regression equation. Interpret the slope and intercept values.

   c. If the value of the independent variable is 10, what is the value of the dependent variable?

   d. Calculate the coefficient of determination. Interpret this value.

   e. Calculate the correlation coefficient. Conduct a test of hypothesis to determine if there is a significant negative association between the variables.

2. Given the following regression analysis output:

ANOVA Table					
Source	SS	df	MS	F	p-value
Regression	227.0928	4	56.7732	9.27	0.000
Residual	153.0739	25	6.1230		
Total	380.1667	29			

Regression Output				
Variables	Coefficients	Standard Error	t (df = 25)	p-value
Intercept	68.3366	8.9752	7.614	0.000
x_1	0.8595	0.3087	2.784	0.010
x_2	−0.3380	0.8381	−0.403	0.690
x_3	−0.8179	0.2749	−2.975	0.006
x_4	−0.5824	0.2541	−2.292	0.030

   a. What is the sample size?

   b. How many independent variables are in the study?

   c. Determine the coefficient of determination.

   d. Conduct a global test of hypothesis. Can you conclude at least one of the independent variables does not equal zero? Use the .01 significance level.

   e. Conduct an individual test of hypothesis on each of the independent variables. Would you consider dropping any of the independent variables? If so, which variable(s) would you drop? Use the .01 significance level.

Nonparametric Methods

NOMINAL LEVEL HYPOTHESIS TESTS

metamorworks/Shutterstock

15

▲ **TELEVISION VIEWING** habits are changing. In a recent survey, viewers were asked: "Which network or source would you keep if you could only keep one?" Using this information, in the top four choices, 35% of all viewers would keep Netflix, 23% would keep CBS, 21% would keep ABC, and 21% would keep NBC. A random sample of 120 viewers who were 35 years or older showed that 30 would keep ABC, 32 would keep CBS, 30 would keep NBC, and 28 would keep Netflix. At the .05 significance level, can we conclude that the viewing habits of viewers who are 35 years or older are the same when compared to all age groups? (See Exercise 12 and LO15-1.)

LEARNING OBJECTIVES

When you have completed this chapter, you will be able to:

LO15-1 Test a hypothesis comparing an observed set of frequencies to an expected frequency distribution.

LO15-2 Explain the limitations of using the chi-square statistic in goodness-of-fit tests.

LO15-3 Test a hypothesis that an observed frequency distribution is normally distributed.

LO15-4 Perform a chi-square test for independence on a contingency table.

Introduction

In Chapters 10 through 12, we present hypothesis tests about a single population mean (Chapter 10), about two population means (Chapter 11), and about three or more population means (Chapter 12). For these tests we use interval or ratio data. Examples of interval- and ratio-scale data include scores on the first statistics examination in your class, incomes of corporate executive officers in technology companies, or years of employment for production workers at the BMW plant in Greer, South Carolina.

In this chapter, we present hypothesis tests for variables measured with a nominal scale. In these tests, the nominal variable is used to classify the data into two or more mutually exclusive categories. Examples include the colors of M&M Plain Candies (red, green, blue, yellow, orange, and brown), brand of peanut butter purchased (Peter Pan, Jif, Skippy, and others), or days of the workweek (Monday, Tuesday, Wednesday, Thursday, and Friday). The data are summarized with counts or frequencies. For analyses using two nominal-scale categories, we introduce the chi-square distribution as a new test statistic.

LO 15-1
Test a hypothesis comparing an observed set of frequencies to an expected frequency distribution.

Goodness-of-Fit Tests: Comparing Observed and Expected Frequency Distributions

To begin, we discuss goodness-of-fit tests that compare an observed frequency distribution to an expected frequency distribution for variables measured on a nominal or ordinal scale. For example, a life insurance company classifies its policies into four categories using a nominal variable, policy type. Policy type has four categories: whole life, level term, decreasing term, and others. The following table shows the historical relative frequency distribution of the policy types. These would be the expected frequencies.

Policy Type	Percent
Whole life	40
Level term	25
Decreasing term	15
Other	20

The insurance company wishes to compare this historical distribution with an observed distribution of policy types for a sample of 2,000 current policies. The goodness-of-fit test determines if the current distribution of policies "fits" the historical distribution or if it has changed. A goodness-of-fit test is one of the most commonly used statistical tests.

Hypothesis Test of Equal Expected Frequencies

In our first illustration of a goodness-of-fit test, we test a hypothesis that the frequencies of each category are the same. That is, the frequency distribution is uniform. To test the hypothesis, we compute a test statistic that compares a set of observed frequencies to a set of equal expected frequencies. If the null hypothesis is rejected, we conclude that the distribution of observed frequencies is not uniform. That is, the observed frequencies are not equal.

▶ **EXAMPLE**

Bubba's Fish and Pasta is a chain of restaurants located along the Gulf Coast of Florida. Bubba, the owner, is considering adding steak to his menu. Before doing so, he decides to hire Magnolia Research LLC to conduct a survey of adults as to their favorite meal when eating out. Magnolia selected a sample 120 adults and asked them all to indicate their favorite meal when dining out. The results are reported in Table 15–1.

TABLE 15–1 Favorite Entrée as Selected by a Sample of 120 Adults

Favorite Entrée	Frequency
Chicken	32
Fish	24
Ham	35
Pasta	29
Total	120

Is it reasonable to conclude there is no preference among the four entrées?

SOLUTION

If there is no difference in the popularity of the four entrées, we would expect the observed frequencies to be equal—or nearly equal. To put it another way, we would expect as many adults to indicate they preferred chicken as fish. Thus, any discrepancy in the observed and expected frequencies is attributed to chance.

What is the level of measurement in this problem? Notice that when a person is selected, we can only classify the selected adult as to the entrée preferred. We do not get a reading or a measurement of any kind. The "measurement" or "classification" is based on the selected entrée. In addition, there is no natural order to the favorite entrée. No one entrée is assumed better than another. Therefore, the nominal scale is appropriate.

EQRoy/Shutterstock

If the entrées are equally popular, we would expect 30 adults to select each meal. Why is this so? If there are 120 adults in the sample and four categories, we expect that one-fourth of those surveyed would select each entrée. So 30, found by 120/4, is the expected frequency for each category, assuming there is no preference for any of the entrées. This information is summarized in Table 15–2. An examination of the data indicates Ham is the entrée selected most frequently (35 of 120) and fish is selected least frequently (24 of 120). Is the difference in the number

TABLE 15–2 Observed and Expected Frequencies for Survey of 120 Adults

Favorite Meal	Observed Frequency, f_o	Expected Frequency, f_e
Chicken	32	30
Fish	24	30
Ham	35	30
Pasta	29	30
Total	120	120

of times each entrée is selected due to chance, or should we conclude that the entrées are not equally preferred?

To investigate the issue, we use the six-step hypothesis-testing procedure.

Step 1: **State the null hypothesis and the alternate hypothesis.** The null hypothesis, H_0, is that there is no difference between the set of observed frequencies and the set of expected frequencies. In other words, any difference between the two sets of frequencies is attributed to sampling error. The alternate hypothesis, H_1, is that there is a difference between the observed and expected sets of frequencies. If the null hypothesis is rejected and the alternate hypothesis is accepted, we conclude the preferences are not equally distributed among the four categories.

H_0: There is no difference in the proportion of adults selecting each entrée.

H_1: There is a difference in the proportion of adults selecting each entrée.

Step 2: **Select the level of significance.** We selected the .05 significance level. The probability is .05 that a true null hypothesis is rejected.

Step 3: **Select the test statistic.** The test statistic follows the chi-square distribution, designated by χ^2.

CHI-SQUARE TEST STATISTIC	$\chi^2 = \Sigma \left[\dfrac{(f_o - f_e)^2}{f_e} \right]$	**(15–1)**

with $k - 1$ degrees of freedom, where:

k is the number of categories.

f_o is an observed frequency in a particular category.

f_e is an expected frequency in a particular category.

We will examine the characteristics of the chi-square distribution in more detail shortly.

Step 4: **Formulate the decision rule.** Recall that the decision rule in hypothesis testing is the value that separates the region where we do not reject H_0 from the region where H_0 is rejected. This number is called the *critical value*. As we will soon see, the chi-square distribution is really a family of distributions. Each distribution has a slightly different shape, depending on the number of degrees of freedom. The number of degrees of freedom is $k - 1$, where k is the number of categories. In this particular problem, there are four categories, the four meal entrées. Because there are four categories, there are $k - 1 = 4 - 1 = 3$ degrees of freedom. The critical value for 3 degrees of freedom and the .05 level of significance is found in Appendix B.7. A portion of that table is shown in Table 15–3. The critical value is 7.815, found by locating 3 degrees of freedom in the left margin and then moving horizontally (to the right) and reading the critical value in the .05 column.

STATISTICS IN ACTION

Many state governments operate lotteries to help fund education. In many lotteries, numbered balls are mixed and selected by a machine. In a Select Three game, numbered balls are selected randomly from three groups of balls numbered 0 through 9. Randomness would predict that the frequency of each number is equal. How would you test if the machine ensured a random selection process? A chi-square, goodness-of-fit test could be used to investigate this question.

TABLE 15–3 A Portion of the Chi-Square Table

Degrees of Freedom *df*	Right-Tail Area			
	.10	**.05**	**.02**	**.01**
1	2.706	3.841	5.412	6.635
2	4.605	5.991	7.824	9.210
3	6.251	7.815	9.837	11.345
4	7.779	9.488	11.668	13.277
5	9.236	11.070	13.388	15.086

The decision rule is to reject the null hypothesis if the computed value of chi-square is greater than 7.815. If it is less than or equal to 7.815, we fail to reject the null hypothesis. Chart 15–1 shows the decision rule.

CHART 15–1 Chi-Square Probability Distribution for 3 Degrees of Freedom, Showing the Region of Rejection, .05 Level of Significance

The decision rule indicates that if there are large differences between the observed and expected frequencies, resulting in a computed χ^2 of more than 7.815, the null hypothesis should be rejected. However, if the differences between f_o and f_e are small, the computed χ^2 will be 7.815 or less, and the null hypothesis should not be rejected. The reasoning is that small differences between the observed and expected frequencies are due to chance. Remember, the 120 observations are a sample of the population.

Step 5: **Compute the value of chi-square and make a decision.** Of the 120 adults in the sample, 32 indicated their favorite entrée was chicken. The counts were reported in Table 15–1. The calculations for chi-square follow. (Note again that the expected frequencies are the same for each cell.)

Column D: Determine the differences between each f_o and f_e. That is, $f_o - f_e$. The sum of these differences is 0.

Column E: Square the difference between each observed and expected frequency, that is, $(f_o - f_e)^2$.

Column F: Divide the result for each observation by the expected frequency, that is, $(f_o - f_e)^2/f_e$. Finally, sum these values. The result is the value of χ^2, which is 2.20.

STATISTICS IN ACTION

For many years, researchers and statisticians believed that all variables were normally distributed. In fact, it was generally assumed to be a universal law. However, Karl Pearson, an English mathematician born in 1857, observed that experimental data were not always normally distributed, but there was no way to prove his observations were correct. To solve this problem, Pearson discovered the chi-square statistic that basically compares an observed frequency distribution with an assumed or expected normal distribution. His discovery proved that all variables were not normally distributed.

	A	B	C	D	E	F	G
1	Favorite Entrée	f_o	f_e	$(f_o - f_e)$	$(f_o - f_e)^2$	$(f_o - f_e)^2/f_e$	
2	Chicken	32	30	2	4	0.133	
3	Fish	24	30	-6	36	1.200	
4	Ham	35	30	5	25	0.833	χ^2 Value
5	Pasta	29	30	-1	1	0.033	
6	Total	120	120			2.200	

Microsoft Excel

The computed χ^2 of 2.20 is not in the rejection region. It is less than the critical value of 7.815. The decision, therefore, is to not reject the null hypothesis.

Tutorial #66
in Connect

Step 6:   Interpret the results. We conclude that the differences between the observed and the expected frequencies could be due to chance. That is, the data do not suggest that the preferences among the four entrées are different.

Several functions in Excel can be applied to easily perform this analysis. See the tutorial on Connect.

The chi-square distribution has many applications in statistics. Its characteristics are:

1. **Chi-square values are always greater than or equal to zero.** This is because the difference between f_o and f_e is squared, that is, $(f_o - f_e)^2$.
2. **There is a family of chi-square distributions.** There is a chi-square distribution for 1 degree of freedom, another for 2 degrees of freedom, another for 3 degrees of freedom, and so on. For a chi-square distribution, the number of degrees of freedom is determined by $k - 1$, where k is the number of categories. Therefore, the shape of the chi-square distribution does *not* depend on the size of the sample but on the number of categories. For example, if 200 employees of an airline were classified into one of three categories—flight personnel, ground support, and administrative personnel—there would be $k - 1 = 3 - 1 = 2$ degrees of freedom.
3. **The chi-square distribution is positively skewed.** As the number of degrees of freedom increases, the distribution begins to approximate the normal probability distribution. Chart 15–2 shows the distributions for selected degrees of freedom. Notice that as the degrees of freedom increases to 10, the curve approaches a normal distribution.

CHART 15–2 Chi-Square Distributions for Selected Degrees of Freedom

SELF-REVIEW 15–1

The human resources director at Georgetown Paper Inc. is concerned about absenteeism among hourly workers, and decides to sample the company records to determine whether absenteeism is distributed evenly throughout the 6-day workweek. The hypotheses are:

H_0: Absenteeism is evenly distributed throughout the workweek.
H_1: Absenteeism is *not* evenly distributed throughout the workweek.

The sample results are:

	Number Absent		Number Absent
Monday	12	Thursday	10
Tuesday	9	Friday	9
Wednesday	11	Saturday	9

(a) What are the numbers 12, 9, 11, 10, 9, and 9 called?
(b) How many categories are there?
(c) What is the *expected* frequency for each day?
(d) How many degrees of freedom are there?
(e) What is the chi-square critical value at the 1% significance level?
(f) Compute the chi-square test statistic.
(g) What is the decision regarding the null hypothesis?
(h) Specifically, what does this indicate to the human resources director?

EXERCISES

1. In a particular chi-square goodness-of-fit test, there are four categories and 200 observations. Use the .05 significance level.
    a. How many degrees of freedom are there?
    b. What is the critical value of chi-square?
2. In a particular chi-square goodness-of-fit test, there are six categories and 500 observations. Use the .01 significance level.
    a. How many degrees of freedom are there?
    b. What is the critical value of chi-square?
3. The null hypothesis and the alternate hypothesis are:

    H_0: The frequencies are equal.
    H_1: The frequencies are not equal.

Category	f_o
A	10
B	20
C	30

    a. State the decision rule, using the .05 significance level.
    b. Compute the value of chi-square.
    c. What is your decision regarding H_0?
4. The null hypothesis and the alternate hypothesis are:

    H_0: The frequencies are equal.
    H_1: The frequencies are not equal.

Category	f_o
A	10
B	20
C	30
D	20

a. State the decision rule, using the .05 significance level.
b. Compute the value of chi-square.
c. What is your decision regarding H_0?

5. A six-sided die is rolled 30 times and the numbers 1 through 6 appear as shown in the following frequency distribution. At the .10 significance level, can we conclude that the die is fair?

Outcome	Frequency	Outcome	Frequency
1	3	4	3
2	6	5	9
3	2	6	7

6. Classic Golf Inc. manages five courses in the Jacksonville, Florida, area. The director of golf wishes to study the number of rounds of golf played per weekday at the five courses, and so gathered the following sample information. At the .05 significance level, is there a difference in the number of rounds played by day of the week?

Day	Rounds
Monday	124
Tuesday	74
Wednesday	104
Thursday	98
Friday	120

7. **FILE** A group of 240 retail store buyers reviewed a new line of apparel. Each buyer rated the new line in one of six classes.

Opinion	Number of Buyers	Opinion	Number of Buyers
Outstanding	47	Good	39
Excellent	45	Fair	35
Very good	40	Undesirable	34

Because the largest number (47) indicated the new line is outstanding, the head designer thinks that this is a mandate to go into mass production of the dresses. The head sweeper (who somehow became involved in this) believes that there is not a clear mandate and claims that the opinions are evenly distributed among the six categories. The sweeper further states that the slight differences among the various counts are probably due to chance. Test the null hypothesis that there is no significant difference among the opinions of the buyers at the .01 level of significance.

8. **FILE** The safety director of a large steel mill took samples at random from company records of minor work-related accidents and classified them according to the time the accident took place.

Time	Number of Accidents	Time	Number of Accidents
8 up to 9 a.m.	6	1 up to 2 p.m.	7
9 up to 10 a.m.	6	2 up to 3 p.m.	8
10 up to 11 a.m.	20	3 up to 4 p.m.	19
11 up to 12 p.m.	8	4 up to 5 p.m.	6

Using the goodness-of-fit test and the .01 level of significance, determine whether the accidents are evenly distributed throughout the day. Write a brief explanation of your conclusion.

Hypothesis Test of Unequal Expected Frequencies

The expected frequencies (f_e) in the previous Example/Solution involving preferred entrées were all equal. According to the null hypothesis, it was expected that of the 120 adults in the study, an equal number would select each of the four entrées. So we expect 30 to select chicken, 30 to select fish, and so on. The chi-square test can also be used if the expected frequencies are not equal.

The following Example/Solution illustrates the case of unequal expected frequencies and gives a practical use of the chi-square goodness-of-fit test—namely, to find whether a local experience differs from the national experience.

▶ **EXAMPLE**

The American Hospital Administrators Association (AHAA) reports the following information concerning the number of times senior citizens are admitted to a hospital during a 1-year period. Forty percent are not admitted; 30% are admitted once; 20% are admitted twice, and the remaining 10% are admitted three or more times.

A survey of 150 residents of Bartow Estates, a community devoted to active seniors located in central Florida, revealed 55 residents were not admitted during the last year, 50 were admitted to a hospital once, 32 were admitted twice, and the rest of those in the survey were admitted three or more times. Can we conclude the survey at Bartow Estates is consistent with the information reported by the AHAA? Use the .05 significance level.

SOLUTION

We begin by organizing this information into Table 15–4. Clearly, we cannot compare the percentages given in the AHAA study to the counts or frequencies reported for Bartow Estates residents. However, we can use the AHAA information to compute expected frequencies, f_e, for the Bartow Estates residents. According to AHAA, 40% of the seniors do not require hospitalization. Thus, if there is no difference between the national experience and the Bartow Estates' study, then the expectation is that 40% of the 150 Bartow seniors surveyed, or $f_e = 60$, would not have been hospitalized. Further, based on the AHAA information, 30% of the 150 Bartow seniors, or $f_e = 45$, would be expected to be admitted once, and so on. The observed and expected frequencies for Bartow residents are given in Table 15–4.

TABLE 15–4 Summary of Study by AHAA and a Survey of Bartow Estates

Number of Times Admitted	AHAA Relative Frequencies	Observed Frequency of Bartow Residents (f_o)	Expected Frequency of Bartow Residents (f_e)
0	40%	55	$60 = (.40)(150)$
1	30%	50	$45 = (.30)(150)$
2	20%	32	$30 = (.20)(150)$
3 or more	10%	13	$15 = (.10)(150)$
Total	100	150	

The null hypothesis and the alternate hypothesis are:

H_0: There is no difference between local and national experience for hospital admissions.

H_1: There is a difference between local and national experience for hospital admissions.

To find the decision rule, we use Appendix B.7 and the .05 significance level. There are four admitting categories, so the degrees of freedom are $df = 4 - 1 = 3$. The critical value is 7.815. Therefore, the decision rule is to reject the null hypothesis if $\chi^2 > 7.815$. The decision rule is portrayed in Chart 15–3.

CHART 15–3 Decision Criteria for the Bartow Estates Research Study

Now to compute the chi-square test statistic:

Tutorial #66
in Connect

Number of Times Admitted	f_o	f_e	$(f_o - f_e)$	$(f_o - f_e)^2$	$(f_o - f_e)^2/f_e$
0	55	60	−5	25	0.4167
1	50	45	5	25	0.5556
2	32	30	2	4	0.1333
3 or more	13	15	−2	4	0.2667
Total	150				1.3723

χ^2 value

The computed value of χ^2 (1.3723) lies to the left of 7.815. Thus, we cannot reject the null hypothesis. We conclude that the survey results do not provide evidence of a difference between the local and national experience for hospital admissions. See the Excel tutorial on Connect to learn how to perform this analysis. When you replicate this analysis with statistical software, you will find the same test statistic, 1.3723, and a corresponding *p*-value of .712.

LO 15-2

Explain the limitations of using the chi-square statistic in goodness-of-fit tests.

Limitations of Chi-Square

If there is an unusually small expected frequency for a category, chi-square (if applied) might result in an erroneous conclusion. Why? Because f_e is in the denominator, and dividing by a very small number makes the quotient quite large! Two generally accepted policies regarding small category frequencies are:

1. If there are only two cells, the *expected* frequency in each category should be at least 5. The computation of chi-square would be permissible in the following problem, involving a minimum f_e of 6.

Individual	f_o	f_e
Literate	641	642
Illiterate	7	6

2. For more than two categories, chi-square should *not* be used if more than 20% of the categories have expected frequencies less than 5. According to this policy, it would not be appropriate to use the goodness-of-fit test on the following data. The sample data are the number of credit applications per day in a large retail chain of clothing stores. Three of the seven categories, or 43%, have expected frequencies (f_e) of less than 5.

Number of Applications	f_o	f_e
0	30	32
1	110	113
2	86	87
3	23	24
4	5	2
5	5	4
6	4	1
Total	263	263

To show the reason for the 20% policy, we conducted the goodness-of-fit test on the data. The output from a statistical software package called MegaStat follows:

Goodness-of-Fit Test

Observed	Expected	O - E	$(O - E)^2/E$	% of chisq
30	32.000	−2.000	0.125	0.89
110	113.000	−3.000	0.080	0.57
86	87.000	−1.000	0.011	0.08
23	24.000	−1.000	0.042	0.30
5	2.000	3.000	4.500	32.12
5	4.000	1.000	0.250	1.78
4	1.000	3.000	9.000	64.25
263	263.000	0.000	14.008	100.00

14.01 chi-square
6 df
.0295 p-value

For this test at the .05 significance level, H_0 is rejected if the computed value of chi-square is greater than 12.592. The computed value is 14.01, so we reject the null hypothesis that the observed and expected frequency distributions are the same. However, examine the MegaStat output critically. More than 98% of the computed chi-square value is accounted for by the categories where there are 4, 5, or 6 applications [(4.500 + .250 + 9.000)/14.008 = .9815]. Logically, too much weight is being given to these categories.

The issue is resolved by combining the frequencies for the categories: 4, 5, and 6 applications. The new category of 4, 5, or 6 applications now has a frequency of 7. See the following table. Combining these three categories satisfies the 20% requirement. None of the categories has a frequency less than 5. Because the number of categories is now 5, the degrees of freedom for the goodness-of-fit test changes from 6 to 4.

Number of Applications	f_o	f_e
0	30	32
1	110	113
2	86	87
3	23	24
4, 5, or 6	14	7
Total	263	263

The computed value of chi-square with the revised categories is 7.26. See the following MegaStat output. This value is less than the critical value of 9.488 (based on 4 degrees of freedom) for the .05 significance level. The null hypothesis is, therefore, not rejected at the .05 significance level. This indicates there is not a significant difference between the observed and expected distributions.

Goodness-of-Fit Test

Observed	Expected	O - E	$(O - E)^2/E$	% of chisq
30	32.000	−2.000	0.125	1.72
110	113.000	−3.000	0.080	1.10
86	87.000	−1.000	0.011	0.16
23	24.000	−1.000	0.042	0.57
14	7.000	7.000	7.000	96.45
263	263.000	0.000	7.258	100.00

7.26 chi-square
4 df
.1229 p-value

SELF-REVIEW 15–2

The American Accounting Association classifies accounts receivable as "current," "late," and "not collectible." Industry figures show that 60% of accounts receivable are current, 30% are late, and 10% are not collectible. Massa and Barr, a law firm in Greenville, Ohio, has 500 accounts receivable: 320 are current, 120 are late, and 60 are not collectible. Are these numbers in agreement with the industry distribution? Use the .05 significance level.

EXERCISES

9. For a particular population, a hypothesis states:

H_0: Forty percent of the observations are in category A, 40% are in B, and 20% are in C.

H_1: The distribution of the observations is not as described in H_0.

We took a sample of 60 observations from the population with the following results.

Category	f_o
A	30
B	20
C	10

a. For the hypothesis test, state the decision rule using the .01 significance level.

b. Compute the value of chi-square.

c. What is your decision regarding H_0?

10. The chief of security for the Mall of the Dakotas directed a study of theft. He selected a sample of 100 boxes that had been tampered with and ascertained that, for 60 of the boxes, the missing pants, shoes, and so on were attributed to shoplifting. For 30 boxes, employees had stolen the goods, and for the remaining 10 boxes he blamed poor inventory control. In his report to the mall management, can he conclude or infer that shoplifting is *twice* as likely to be the cause of the loss as compared with either employee theft or poor inventory control and that employee theft and poor inventory control are equally likely? Use the .02 significance level.

11. From experience, the bank credit card department of Carolina Bank knows that 5% of its card holders have had some high school, 15% have completed high school, 25% have had some college, and 55% have completed college. Of the 500 card holders whose cards have been called in for failure to pay their charges this month, 50 had some high school, 100 had completed high school, 190 had some college, and 160 had completed college. Can we conclude that the distribution of card holders who do not pay their charges is different from all others? Use the .01 significance level.

12. Television viewing habits are changing. In a recent study, viewers were asked: "Which network or source would you keep if you could only keep one?" Using this information, in the top four choices, 35% of all viewers would keep Netflix, 23% would keep CBS, 21% would keep ABC, and 21% would keep NBC. A random sample of 120 viewers who were 35 years or older showed that 30 would keep ABC, 32 would keep CBS, 30 would keep NBC, and 28 would keep Netflix. At the .05 significance level, can we conclude that the viewing habits of viewers who are 35 years or older are the same when compared to all age groups?

LO 15-3

Test a hypothesis that an observed frequency distribution is normally distributed.

Testing the Hypothesis That a Distribution Is Normal

We use a goodness-of-fit test to compare an observed frequency distribution to an expected frequency distribution. In the Example/Solution regarding Bubba's Fish and Pasta, the observed frequencies are the count of each entrée selected for a sample of 120 adults. We determine the expected frequencies by assuming there is no preference for any of the four entrées, so we expect that one-fourth of the sample, or 30 adults, selects each entrée. In this section, we want to test a hypothesis that a distribution is normal by using the goodness-of-fit test to compare an observed frequency distribution to an expected frequency distribution that is normal. Why is this test important? In Chapter 11, when we tested for differences in two population means, we assumed the two populations followed the normal distribution. We made the same assumption in Chapter 12 when we tested if several population means were equal. In Chapter 13 we assume the distribution of the residuals in a least squares regression analysis follow the normal probability distribution.

The following Example/Solution provides the details of a goodness-of-fit test to investigate the reasonableness of the normality assumption.

▶ **EXAMPLE**

In Chapter 2 we use a frequency distribution to organize the profits from the Applewood Auto Group's sale of 180 vehicles. The frequency distribution is repeated in Table 15–5.

TABLE 15–5 Frequency Distribution of Profits for Vehicles Sold Last Month by Applewood Auto Group

Profit	Frequency
$ 200 up to $ 600	8
600 up to 1,000	11
1,000 up to 1,400	23
1,400 up to 1,800	38
1,800 up to 2,200	45
2,200 up to 2,600	32
2,600 up to 3,000	19
3,000 up to 3,400	4
Total	180

Blend Images/Getty Images

Using statistical software, on page 64 in Chapter 3 we determined that the mean profit on a vehicle for the Applewood Auto Group was $1,843.17 and that the standard deviation was $643.63. Is it reasonable to conclude that the profit data are a sample obtained from a normal population? To put it another way, do the profit data follow a normal population? We use the .05 significance level.

SOLUTION

To test for a normal distribution, we need to find the expected frequencies for each class in the distribution, assuming that the expected distribution follows a normal probability distribution. We start with the normal distribution by calculating probabilities for each class. Then we use these probabilities to compute the expected frequencies for each class.

To begin, we find the area, or probability, for each of the eight classes in Table 15–5, assuming a normal population with a mean of $1,843.17 and a standard deviation of $643.63. To find this probability, we adapt formula (7–5) from Chapter 7, replacing μ with $\bar{x}$ and σ with s. So we use the following formula to determine the various values of z.

$$z = \frac{x - \bar{x}}{s}$$

In this case, z is the value of the standard normal statistic; $\bar{x}$, $1,843.17, is the sample mean; and s, $643.63, is the sample standard deviation. We select class $200 up to $600 from Table 15–5. We want to determine the expected frequency in this class, assuming the distribution of profits follows a normal distribution. First, we find the z-value corresponding to $200.

$$z = \frac{x - \bar{x}}{s} = \frac{\$200 - \$1,843.17}{\$643.63} = -2.55$$

This indicates that the lower limit of this class is 2.55 standard deviations below the mean. From Appendix B.3, the probability of finding a z-value less than -2.55 is $.5000 - .4946 = .0054$.

For the upper limit of the $200 up to $600 class:

$$z = \frac{x - \bar{x}}{s} = \frac{\$600 - \$1,843.17}{\$643.63} = -1.93$$

The area to the left of $600 is the probability of a z-value less than -1.93. To find this value, we again use Appendix B.3 and reason that $.5000 - .4732 = .0268$.

Finally, to find the area between $200 and $600:

$$P(\$200 < x < \$600) = P(-2.55 < z < -1.93) = .0268 - .0054 = .0214$$

That is, about 2.14% of the vehicles sold will result in a profit of between $200 and $600.

There is a chance that the profit earned is less than $200. To find this probability:

$$P(x < \$200) = P(z < -2.55) = .5000 - .4946 = .0054$$

We enter these two probabilities in the first and second rows of column 3 in Table 15–6.

TABLE 15–6 Profits at Applewood Auto Group, z-Values, Areas under the Normal Distribution, and Expected Frequencies

Profit	z-Values	Area	Found by	Expected Frequency
Under $200	Under -2.55	.0054	$0.5000 - 0.4946$	0.97
$ 200 up to $ 600	-2.55 up to -1.93	.0214	$0.4946 - 0.4732$	3.85
600 up to 1,000	-1.93 up to -1.31	.0683	$0.4732 - 0.4049$	12.29
1,000 up to 1,400	-1.31 up to -0.69	.1500	$0.4049 - 0.2549$	27.00
1,400 up to 1,800	-0.69 up to -0.07	.2270	$0.2549 - 0.0279$	40.86
1,800 up to 2,200	-0.07 up to 0.55	.2367	$0.0279 + 0.2088$	42.61
2,200 up to 2,600	0.55 up to 1.18	.1722	$0.3810 - 0.2088$	31.00
2,600 up to 3,000	1.18 up to 1.80	.0831	$0.4641 - 0.3810$	14.96
3,000 up to 3,400	1.80 up to 2.42	.0281	$0.4922 - 0.4641$	5.06
3,400 or more	2.42 or more	.0078	$0.5000 - 0.4922$	1.40
Total		1.0000		180.00

Logically, if we sold 180 vehicles, we would expect to earn a profit of between $200 and $600 on 3.85 vehicles, found by .0214(180). We would expect to sell .97 vehicle with a profit of less than $200, found by 180(.0054). We continue this process for the remaining classes. This information is summarized in Table 15–7. Don't be concerned that we are reporting fractional vehicles.

TABLE 15–7 Computations of the Chi-Square Statistic

Profit	f_o	f_e	$(f_o - f_e)$	$(f_o - f_e)^2$	$(f_o - f_e)^2/f_e$
Under $600	8	4.82	3.18	10.1124	2.098
$ 600 up to $1,000	11	12.29	-1.29	1.6641	.135
1,000 up to 1,400	23	27.00	-4.00	16.0000	.593
1,400 up to 1,800	38	40.86	-2.86	8.1796	.200
1,800 up to 2,200	45	42.61	2.39	5.7121	.134
2,200 up to 2,600	32	31.00	1.00	1.0000	.032
2,600 up to 3,000	19	14.96	4.04	16.3216	1.091
3,000 and over	4	6.46	-2.46	6.0516	.937
Total	180	180.00	0		5.220

Before continuing, we should emphasize one of the limitations of tests using chi-square as the test statistic. The second limitation on page 578 indicates that if more than 20% of the categories have *expected frequencies* of less than 5, some of the categories should be combined. In Table 15–6, the expected frequencies in 3 of the 10 classes, or 30%, are less than 5. So, we combine the "Under $200" class with the "$200 up to $600" class and the "$3,400 or more" class with the

"$3,000 up to $3,400" class. So the expected frequency in the "Under $600" class is now 4.82, found by .97 + 3.85. We do the same for the "$3,000 and over" class: 5.06 + 1.40 = 6.46. The results are shown in Table 15–7. The computed value of chi-square is 5.220.

Now let's put this information into the formal hypothesis-testing format. The null and alternate hypotheses are:

H_0: The population of profits follows the normal distribution.
H_1: The population of profits does not follow the normal distribution.

To determine the critical value of chi-square, we need to know the degrees of freedom. In this case, there are eight categories, or classes, so the degrees of freedom are $k - 1 = 8 - 1 = 7$. In addition, the values $1,843.17, the mean profit, and $643.63, the standard deviation of the Applewood Auto Group profits, were computed from a sample. When we estimate population parameters from sample data, we lose a degree of freedom for each estimate. So we lose two more degrees of freedom for estimating the population mean and the population standard deviation. Thus, the number of degrees of freedom in this problem is 5, found by $k - 2 - 1 = 8 - 2 - 1 = 5$.

From Appendix B.7, using the .05 significance level, the critical value of chi-square is 11.070. Our decision rule is to reject the null hypothesis if the computed value of chi-square is more than 11.070.

Now, to compute the value of chi-square, we use formula (15–1):

$$\chi^2 = \Sigma \frac{(f_o - f_e)^2}{f_e} = \frac{(8 - 4.82)^2}{4.82} + \cdots + \frac{(4 - 6.46)^2}{6.46} = 5.220$$

The values for each class are shown in the right-hand column of Table 15–7, as well as the column total, which is 5.220. Because the computed value of 5.220 is less than the critical value, we do not reject the null hypothesis. We conclude the evidence does not suggest the distribution of profits is other than normal.

To expand on the calculation of the number of degrees of freedom, if we know the mean and the standard deviation of a population and wish to find whether some sample data conform to a normal, the degrees of freedom are $k - 1$. On the other hand, suppose we have sample data grouped into a frequency distribution, but we do not know the value of the population mean and the population standard deviation. In this case, the degrees of freedom are $k - 2 - 1$. In general, when we use sample statistics to estimate population parameters, we lose a degree of freedom for each parameter we estimate.

EXERCISES

13. **FILE** The IRS is interested in the number of individual tax forms prepared by small accounting firms. To investigate, they sampled 50 public accounting firms with 10 or fewer employees in the Dallas–Fort Worth area. The following frequency table reports the results of the study. Assume the sample mean is 44.8 clients and the sample standard deviation is 9.37 clients. Is it reasonable to conclude that the sample data are from a population that follows a normal probability distribution? Use the .05 significance level.

Number of Clients	Frequency
20 up to 30	1
30 up to 40	15
40 up to 50	22
50 up to 60	8
60 up to 70	4

14. FILE Advertising expenses are a significant component of the cost of goods sold. Listed is a frequency distribution showing the advertising expenditures for 60 manufacturing companies located in the Southwest. The mean expense is $52.0 million and the standard deviation is $11.32 million. Is it reasonable to conclude the sample data are from a population that follows a normal probability distribution? Use the .05 significance level.

Advertising Expense ($ Million)	Number of Companies
25 up to 35	5
35 up to 45	10
45 up to 55	21
55 up to 65	16
65 up to 75	8
Total	60

LO15-4

Perform a chi-square test for independence on a contingency table.

Contingency Table Analysis

In Chapter 4, we discussed bivariate data, where we studied the relationship between two variables. We described a contingency table, which simultaneously summarizes two nominal-scale variables of interest. For example, a sample of students enrolled in the School of Business is classified by sex (male or female) and major (accounting, management, finance, marketing, or business analytics). This classification is based on the nominal scale because there is no natural order to the classifications.

We discussed contingency tables in Chapter 5. On page 155, we illustrated the relationship between the number of movies attended per month and the age of the attendee. We can use the chi-square distribution to test whether two nominal-scaled variables are related. To put it another way, is one variable *independent* of the other?

Here are some examples where we are interested in testing whether two nominal-scaled variables are related.

- Ford Motor Company operates an assembly plant in Dearborn, Michigan. The plant operates three shifts per day, 5 days a week. The quality control manager wishes to compare the quality level on the three shifts. Vehicles are classified by quality level (acceptable, unacceptable) and shift (day, afternoon, night). Is there a difference in the quality level on the three shifts? That is, is the quality of the product related to the shift when it was manufactured? Or is the quality of the product independent of the shift on which it was manufactured?
- A sample of 100 drivers who were stopped for speeding violations was classified by sex and whether the driver was wearing a seat belt. For this sample, is wearing a seatbelt related to sex?
- Does a male released from federal prison make a different adjustment to civilian life if he returns to his hometown or if he goes elsewhere to live? The two variables are adjustment to civilian life and place of residence. Note that both variables are measured on the nominal scale.

The following Example/Solution provides the details of the analysis and possible conclusions.

▶ **EXAMPLE**

Rainbow Chemical Inc. employs hourly and salaried employees. The vice president of human resources surveyed 380 employees about their satisfaction level with the current health care benefits program. The employees were then classified according to the pay type (i.e., salary or hourly). The results are shown in Table 15–8.

TABLE 15–8 Health Care Satisfaction Level for Rainbow Chemical Employees

Pay Type	Satisfied	Neutral	Dissatisfied	Total
Salary	30	17	8	55
Hourly	140	127	58	325
Total	170	144	66	380

At the .05 significance level, is it reasonable to conclude that pay type and level of satisfaction with the health care benefits are related?

SOLUTION

The first step is to state the null hypothesis and the alternate hypothesis.

H_0: There is no relationship between level of satisfaction and pay type.
H_1: There is a relationship between level of satisfaction and pay type.

The significance level, as requested by the HR vice president, is .05. The level of measurement for pay type is the nominal scale. The satisfaction level with health benefits is actually the ordinal scale, but we use it as a nominal-scale variable. Each sampled employee is classified by two criteria: the level of satisfaction with benefits and pay type. The information is tabulated into Table 15–8, which is called a contingency table.

We use the chi-square distribution as the test statistic. To determine the critical value of chi-square, we calculate the degrees of freedom (df) as:

$$df = (\text{Number of rows} - 1)(\text{Number of columns} - 1) = (r - 1)(c - 1)$$

In this Example/Solution there are 2 rows and 3 columns, so there are 2 degrees of freedom.

$$df = (r - 1)(c - 1) = (2 - 1)(3 - 1) = 2$$

To find the critical value for 2 degrees of freedom and the .05 level, refer to Appendix B.7. Move down the degrees of freedom column in the left margin to the row with 2 degrees of freedom. Move across this row to the column headed .05. At the intersection, the chi-square critical value is 5.991. The decision rule is to reject the null hypothesis if the computed value of χ^2 is greater than 5.991. See Chart 15–4.

CHART 15–4 Chi-Square Distribution for 2 Degrees of Freedom

Next we compute the chi-square value χ^2, using formula (15–1). The observed frequencies, f_o, are shown in Table 15–9. How are the corresponding expected frequencies, f_e, determined? To begin, notice from Table 15–8 that 55 of the 380 Rainbow Chemical employees sampled are salaried. So the fraction of salaried employees in the sample is 55/380 = .14474. *If there is no relationship* between pay type and level of satisfaction with the health care benefits program, we would expect about the same fraction of the employees who are satisfied with the health care to be salaried. There are 170 employees who are satisfied with the health care program, so the expected number of satisfied employees who are salaried is 24.61, found by (.14474)(170). Thus, the expected frequency for the upper-left cell is 24.61. Likewise, if there were no relationship between satisfaction level and pay type, we would expect .14474 of the 144 employees, or 20.84, who were neutral about the health care program to be salaried. We continue this process, filling in the remaining cells. It is not necessary to calculate each of these cell values. In fact we only need to calculate two cells. We can find the others by subtraction.

The expected frequency for any cell is determined by:

EXPECTED FREQUENCY $\qquad f_e = \dfrac{\text{(Row total)(Column total)}}{\text{(Grand total)}}$ $\qquad$ **(15–2)**

From this formula, the expected frequency for the upper-left cell in Table 15–8 is:

$$f_e = \frac{\text{(Row total)(Column total)}}{\text{(Grand total)}} = \frac{(55)(170)}{380} = 24.61$$

The observed frequencies, f_o, and the expected frequencies, f_e, for all of the cells in the contingency table are listed in Table 15–9. Note there are slight differences due to rounding.

TABLE 15–9 Observed and Expected Frequencies

	Satisfaction Level with Health Care					
	Satisfied		Neutral		Dissatisfied	
Pay Type	f_o	f_e	f_o	f_e	f_o	f_e
Salary	30	24.61	17	20.84	8	9.55
Hourly	140	145.39	127	123.16	58	56.45
Total	170	170.00	144	144.00	66	66.00

We use formula (15–1) to determine the value of chi-square. Starting with the upper-left cell:

$$\chi^2 = \Sigma \frac{(f_o - f_e)^2}{f_e} = \frac{(30 - 24.61)^2}{24.61} + \frac{(17 - 20.84)^2}{20.84} + \cdots + \frac{(58 - 56.45)^2}{56.45}$$

$$= 1.181 + .708 + \cdots + .043 = 2.506$$

Because the computed value of chi-square (2.506) lies in the region to the left of 5.991, the null hypothesis is not rejected at the .05 significance level. What do we conclude? The sample data do not provide evidence that pay type and satisfaction level with health care benefits are related.

The following output is from the MegaStat Excel add-in.

Chi-square Contingency Table Test for Independence

Pay Type		Satisfied	Neutral	Dissatisfied	Total
		Satisfaction Level with Health Care			
Salary	Observed	**30**	**17**	**8**	55
	Expected	24.61	20.84	9.55	55.00
Hourly	Observed	**140**	**127**	**58**	325
	Expected	145.39	123.16	56.45	325.00
Total	Observed	170	144	66	380
	Expected	170.00	144.00	66.00	380.00

2.506 chi-square
2 df
0.286 p-value

Tutorial #67
in Connect

Observe that the value of chi-square is the same as that computed earlier, 2.506. In addition, the p-value, .286, is reported. So the probability of finding a value of the test statistic as large or larger, assuming the null hypothesis is true, is .286. The p-value also results in the same decision: Do not reject the null hypothesis. To perform this analysis in Excel, please see the tutorial on Connect.

SELF-REVIEW 15–3

A social scientist sampled 140 people and classified them according to income level and whether they played a state lottery in the last month. The sample information is reported here. Is it reasonable to conclude that playing the lottery is related to income level? Use the .05 significance level.

	Low	Middle	High	Total
	Income			
Played	46	28	21	95
Did not play	14	12	19	45
Total	60	40	40	140

(a) What is this table called?
(b) State the null hypothesis and the alternate hypothesis.
(c) What is the decision rule?
(d) Determine the value of chi-square.
(e) Make a decision on the null hypothesis. Interpret the result.

EXERCISES

15. FILE The director of advertising for the *Carolina Sun Times,* the largest newspaper in the Carolinas, is studying the relationship between the type of community in which a subscriber resides and the section of the newspaper the subscriber reads first. For a sample of readers, the director collected the sample information in the following table.

	National News	Sports	Food
City	170	124	90
Suburb	120	112	100
Rural	130	90	88

At the .05 significance level, can we conclude there is a relationship between the type of community where the person resides and the section of the paper read first?

16. **FILE** Four brands of lightbulbs are being considered for use in the final assembly area of the Ford F-150 truck plant in Dearborn, Michigan. The director of purchasing asked for samples of 100 from each manufacturer. The numbers of acceptable and unacceptable bulbs from each manufacturer are shown here. At the .05 significance level, is there a difference in the quality of the bulbs?

	Manufacturer			
	A	**B**	**C**	**D**
Unacceptable	12	8	5	11
Acceptable	88	92	95	89
Total	100	100	100	100

17. **FILE** The quality control department at Food Town Inc., a grocery chain in upstate New York, conducts a monthly check on the comparison of scanned prices to posted prices. The following chart summarizes the results of a sample of 500 items last month. Company management would like to know whether there is any relationship between error rates on regularly priced items and specially priced items. Use the .01 significance level.

	Scanned Price	Posted Price
Undercharge	20	10
Overcharge	15	30
Correct price	200	225

18. **FILE** The owner of the Liberty Movie Theater Group wishes to investigate the relationship between purchasing a snack and the type of movie. During a 1-month period, the owner gathered the following sample information.

Movie Type	No Snack	Snack	Total
Comedy	88	162	250
Family	32	48	80
Action	42	78	120
Horror	15	35	50
Total	177	323	500

At the .05 significance level, can we conclude there is a relationship between the type of movie playing and whether a patron purchases a snack?

CHAPTER SUMMARY

I. This chapter considered tests of hypothesis for nominal level data.
II. The characteristics of the chi-square distribution are as follows:
   A. The value of chi-square is never negative.
   B. The chi-square distribution is positively skewed.
   C. There is a family of chi-square distributions.
      1. Each time the degrees of freedom change, a new distribution is formed.
      2. As the degrees of freedom increase, the distribution approaches a normal distribution.

III. The goodness-of-fit test shows whether an observed set of frequencies resulted from a hypothesized population distribution.

    A. The degrees of freedom are $k - 1$, where k is the number of categories.

    B. The formula for computing the value of chi-square is

$$\chi^2 = \Sigma \frac{(f_o - f_e)^2}{f_e} \qquad \textbf{(15–1)}$$

IV. A goodness-of-fit test is also used to determine whether a sample of observations is from a normal population.

    A. First, calculate the mean and standard deviation of the sample data.

    B. Group the data into a frequency distribution.

    C. Convert the class limits to z-values and find the standard normal probability distribution for each class.

    D. For each class, find the expected normally distributed frequency by multiplying the standard normal probability distribution by the class frequency.

    E. Calculate the chi-square goodness-of-fit statistic based on the observed and expected class frequencies.

    F. Find the expected frequency in each cell by determining the product of the probability of finding a value in each cell by the total number of observations.

    G. If we use the information on the sample mean and the sample standard deviation from the sample data, the degrees of freedom are $k - 3$.

V. A contingency table is used to test whether two traits or characteristics are related.

    A. Each observation is classified according to two traits.

    B. The expected frequency is determined as follows:

$$f_e = \frac{(\text{Row total})(\text{Column total})}{\text{Grand total}} \qquad \textbf{(15–2)}$$

    C. The degrees of freedom are found by:

$$df = (\text{Rows} - 1)(\text{Columns} - 1)$$

    D. The usual hypothesis testing procedure is used.

PRONUNCIATION KEY

SYMBOL	MEANING	PRONUNCIATION
χ^2	Chi-square statistic	*ki square*
f_o	Observed frequency	*f sub oh*
f_e	Expected frequency	*f sub e*

CHAPTER EXERCISES

19. Vehicles heading west on Front Street may turn right, turn left, or continue straight ahead on Front Street. The city traffic engineer believes that half of the vehicles will continue straight through the intersection. Of the remaining half, equal proportions will turn right and left. Two hundred vehicles were observed, with the following sample results. Can we conclude that the traffic engineer is correct? Use the .10 significance level.

Direction	Frequency
Straight	112
Right turn	48
Left turn	40
Total	200

20. The publisher of a sports magazine plans to offer new subscribers one of three gifts: a sweatshirt with the logo of their favorite team, a coffee cup with the logo of their favorite team, or a pair of earrings also with the logo of their favorite team. In a sample of 500 new subscribers, the number selecting each gift is reported here. At the .05 significance level, is there a preference for the gifts or should we conclude that the gifts are equally well liked?

Gift	Frequency
Sweatshirt	183
Coffee cup	175
Earrings	142

21. In a particular metro area, there are three commercial television stations, each with its own news program from 6:00 to 6:30 p.m. According to a report in this morning's local newspaper, a random sample of 150 viewers last night revealed 53 watched the news on WNAE (channel 5), 64 watched on WRRN (channel 11), and 33 on WSPD (channel 13). At the .05 significance level, is there a difference in the proportion of viewers watching the three channels?

22. **FILE** There are four entrances to the Government Center Building in downtown Philadelphia. The building maintenance supervisor would like to know if the entrances are equally utilized. To investigate, 400 people were observed entering the building. The number using each entrance is reported here. At the .01 significance level, is there a difference in the use of the four entrances?

Entrance	Frequency
Main Street	140
Broad Street	120
Cherry Street	90
Walnut Street	50
Total	400

23. **FILE** The owner of a mail-order catalog would like to compare her sales with the geographic distribution of the population. According to the U.S. Bureau of the Census, 21% of the population lives in the Northeast, 24% in the Midwest, 35% in the South, and 20% in the West. Listed is a breakdown of a sample of 400 orders randomly selected from those shipped last month. At the .01 significance level, does the distribution of the orders reflect the population?

Region	Frequency
Northeast	68
Midwest	104
South	155
West	73
Total	400

24. **FILE** Banner Mattress and Furniture Company wishes to study the number of credit applications received per day for the last 300 days. The sample information is reported here:

Number of Credit Applications	Frequency (Number of Days)
0	50
1	77
2	81
3	48
4	31
5 or more	13

To interpret, there were 50 days on which no credit applications were received, 77 days on which only one application was received, and so on. Would it be reasonable to conclude that the population distribution is Poisson with a mean of 2.0? Use the .05 significance level. (Hint: To find the expected frequencies use the Poisson distribution with a mean of 2.0. Find the probability of exactly one success given a Poisson distribution with a mean of 2.0. Multiply this probability by 300 to find the expected frequency for the number of days in which there was exactly one application. Determine the expected frequency for the other days in a similar manner.)

25. **FILE** A lottery that picks 5 balls from 10 balls numbered 0 through 9 is played once weekly. Over many weeks, the following table shows the frequency of each digit selected in the lottery. If the lottery is fair, each number should be equally likely. That is, the distribution should be uniform. Perform the chi-square test to see if you reject the hypothesis at the .05 significance level that the digits are from a uniform population.

Digit	Frequency	Digit	Frequency
0	44	5	24
1	32	6	31
2	23	7	27
3	27	8	28
4	23	9	21

26. **FILE** A recent national survey of patient visits found that 53% of patient visits were to primary care physicians, 19% to medical specialists, 17% to surgical specialists, and 11% to emergency departments.

Isaac Inc. is a designer and installer of industrial signs in the Denver, Colorado, area. The human resources director at Isaac wishes to compare employee visits with the national experience. A sample of 60 employee visits, during the past year, revealed the following distribution. At the .01 significance level, do Isaac employees seem to mirror the national survey data?

Visit Type	Number of Visits
Primary care	29
Medical specialist	11
Surgical specialist	16
Emergency	4

Tutorial #21 in Connect

27. **FILE** The Eckel Manufacturing Company believes that its hourly wages follow a normal probability distribution. To confirm this, 270 employees were sampled and the results organized into the following frequency distribution. (In the margin, see the link to a tutorial on Connect that reviews the calculation of the mean and standard deviation for grouped data.) At the .10 significance level, is it reasonable to conclude that the distribution of hourly wages follows a normal distribution?

Hourly Wage	Frequency
$5.50 up to $ 6.50	20
6.50 up to 7.50	24
7.50 up to 8.50	130
8.50 up to 9.50	68
9.50 up to 10.50	28
Total	270

28. **FILE** The National Cable and Telecommunications Association recently reported that the mean number of HDTVs per household in the United States is 2.30 with a standard deviation of 1.474 sets. A sample of 100 homes in Boise, Idaho, revealed the following sample information.

Number of HDTVs	Number of Households
0	7
1	27
2	28
3	18
4	10
5 or more	10
Total	100

At the .05 significance level, is it reasonable to conclude that the number of HDTVs per household follows a normal distribution? (Hint: Use limits such as .5 up to 1.5, 1.5 up to 2.5, and so on.)

29. Suppose we randomly contact 300 married women and 200 married men, who all own dogs. One hundred of the women and 36 of the men replied that their pets are better listeners than their spouses. Organize this information into a contingency table. At the .05 significance level, is there a difference between the responses of women and men?

30. More than 34 million people took a cruise last year, spending more than $60 billion. One of the most profitable parts of a cruise for the cruise companies is shore excursions. However, recent data indicate that about one-third of passengers never leave the ship! Swedish Cruise Lines, one of the major lines, operates in both the Caribbean and the Mediterranean regions. They wish to compare customer participation in shore excursions in the two regions. They collect the following sample information.

	Cruise Region	
	Caribbean	Mediterranean
Went on an excursion	414	462
Stayed on the ship	186	238

At the .01 significance level, is there a difference in the proportion of customers who remain on board in the two regions?

31. **FILE** A survey investigated the public's attitude toward the federal deficit. Each sampled citizen was classified as to whether the individual felt the government should reduce the deficit or increase the deficit, or had no opinion. The sample results of the study by sex are reported here.

Sex	Reduce the Deficit	Increase the Deficit	No Opinion
Female	244	194	68
Male	305	114	25

At the .05 significance level, is it reasonable to conclude that sex is independent of a person's position on the deficit?

32. **FILE** A study regarding the relationship between age and the amount of pressure sales personnel feel in relation to their jobs revealed the following sample information. At the .01 significance level, is there a relationship between job pressure and age?

	Degree of Job Pressure		
Age (years)	Low	Medium	High
Less than 25	20	18	22
25 up to 40	50	46	44
40 up to 60	58	63	59
60 and older	34	43	43

33. **FILE** The claims department at Wise Insurance Company believes that younger drivers have more accidents and, therefore, should be charged higher insurance rates. Investigating a sample of 1,200 Wise policyholders revealed the following breakdown on whether a claim had been filed in the last 3 years and the age of the policyholder. Is it reasonable to conclude that there is a relationship between the age of the policyholder and whether the person filed a claim? Use the .05 significance level.

Age Group	No Claim	Claim
16 up to 25	170	74
25 up to 40	240	58
40 up to 55	400	44
55 or older	190	24
Total	1,000	200

34. **FILE** A sample of employees at a large chemical plant was asked to indicate a preference for one of three pension plans. The results are given in the following table. Does it seem that there is a relationship between the pension plan selected and the job classification of the employees? Use the .01 significance level.

Job Class	Pension Plan		
	Plan A	Plan B	Plan C
Supervisor	10	13	29
Clerical	19	80	19
Labor	81	57	22

35. **FILE** Did you ever purchase a bag of M&M's candies and wonder about the distribution of colors? Did you know in the beginning they were all brown? Now, peanut M&M's are 12% brown, 15% yellow, 12% red, 23% blue, 23% orange, and 15% green. The author purchased a 19.20-ounce bag at the nearby Walmart. There were 192 candies in the bag with the following breakdown by color.

Color	Observed
Red	9
Brown	26
Green	44
Yellow	41
Orange	40
Cyan Blue	32
Total	192

Is it reasonable to conclude that the actual distribution agrees with the expected distribution? Use the .05 significance level.

DATA ANALYTICS

(The data for these exercises are available at the text website: **www.mhhe.com/Lind19e.**)

36. The North Valley Real Estate data report information on homes on the market.
   a. Develop a contingency table that shows whether a home has a pool and the township in which the house is located. Is there an association between the variables pool and township? Use the .05 significance level.
   b. Develop a contingency table that shows whether a home has an attached garage and the township in which the home is located. Is there an association between the variables attached garage and township? Use the .05 significance level.

37. Refer to the Baseball 2021 data, which report information on the 30 Major League Baseball teams for the 2021 season. Set up a variable that divides the teams into two groups, those that had a winning season and those that did not. There are 162 games in the season, so define a winning season as having won 81 or more games. Next, find the median team salary and divide the teams into two salary groups. Let the 15 teams with the largest salaries be in one group and the 15 teams with the lowest salaries be in the other. At the .05 significance level, is there a relationship between salaries and winning?

38. Refer to the Lincolnville School District bus data.

   a. Find the median maintenance cost and the median age of the buses. Organize the data into a two-by-two contingency table, with buses above and below the median of each variable. Determine whether the age of the bus is related to the amount of the maintenance cost. Use the .05 significance level.

   b. Is there a relationship between the maintenance cost and the manufacturer of the bus? Use the breakdown in part (a) for the buses above and below the median maintenance cost and the bus manufacturers to create a contingency table. Use the .05 significance level.

16

Nonparametric Methods:

ANALYSIS OF ORDINAL DATA

Asia File/Alamy Stock Photo

▲ **EMPLOYEES OF TRANSPACIFIC INC.** build a computer by inserting several subassemblies into a computer frame. Testing of the computer is completed in a different department. Executives of TransPacific think that employees would have more pride in their work if they performed both assembly and testing tasks. A sample of 25 employees was selected to test the idea. Twenty indicated higher job satisfaction when assembling and testing the computer; five employees rated their work as less satisfying. At the .10 level, can we conclude that employee job satisfaction increased? (See Exercise 4 and LO16-1.)

LEARNING OBJECTIVES

When you have completed this chapter, you will be able to:

LO16-1 Use the sign test to compare two dependent populations.

LO16-2 Test a hypothesis about a median.

LO16-3 Test a hypothesis of dependent populations using the Wilcoxon signed-rank test.

LO16-4 Test a hypothesis of independent populations using the Wilcoxon rank-sum test.

LO16-5 Test a hypothesis of several independent populations using the Kruskal-Wallis test.

LO16-6 Test and interpret a nonparametric hypothesis test of correlation.

Introduction

In Chapter 15, we introduced tests of hypothesis for *nominal-scale* variables. Recall from Chapter 1 that the nominal level of measurement implies the data can only be classified into categories, and there is no particular order to the categories. The purpose of these tests is to determine whether an observed set of frequencies, f_o, is significantly different from a corresponding set of expected frequencies, f_e. Likewise, if you are interested in the relationship between two characteristics—such as job satisfaction and job title—you would tally the data into a contingency table and use the chi-square distribution as the test statistic. For both these types of problems, no assumptions need to be made about the shape of the population. We do not have to assume, for example, that the population of interest follows the normal distribution, as we did with the tests of hypotheses in Chapters 10 through 12.

This chapter continues our discussion of hypothesis tests designed especially for nonparametric data. For these tests, we do not need to assume anything about the shape of the population distribution. Sometimes, we use the term *distribution-free tests*. These tests require that the variables in the data can be sorted and ranked. The variables must be measured with an ordinal, interval, or ratio scale. An example of an ordinal scale is executive title. Corporate executives can be ranked as assistant vice president, vice president, senior vice president, and president. A vice president is ranked higher than an assistant vice president, a senior vice president is ranked higher than a vice president, and so on.

In this chapter, we consider five distribution-free tests and the Spearman coefficient of rank correlation. The tests are the sign test, the median test, the Wilcoxon signed-rank test, the Wilcoxon rank-sum test, and the Kruskal-Wallis analysis of variance by ranks.

The Sign Test

LO 16-1
Use the sign test to compare two dependent populations.

The **sign test** is based on the sign of a difference between two related observations. We usually designate a plus sign for a positive difference and a minus sign for a negative difference. For example, a dietitian wishes to see if a person's cholesterol level decreases if the diet is supplemented by a certain mineral. The dietitian selects a sample of 20 production workers over the age of 40 and measures the workers' cholesterol level. After the 20 subjects take the mineral for 6 weeks, they are tested again. If the cholesterol level has dropped, a plus sign is recorded. If it has increased, a negative sign is recorded. If there is no change, a zero is recorded (and that person is dropped from the study). For the sign test, we are not concerned with the magnitude of the difference, only the direction of the difference.

The sign test has many applications. One is for "before/after" experiments. To illustrate, an auto repair shop wants to evaluate a new tune-up program for automobiles. We record the number of miles traveled per gallon of gasoline before the tune-up and again after the tune-up. If the tune-up is not effective—that is, it had no effect on performance—then about half of the automobiles tested would show an increase in miles per gallon and the other half a decrease. A "plus" sign is assigned to an increase, and a "minus" sign to a decrease.

A product-preference experiment illustrates another use of the sign test. Taster's Choice markets two kinds of coffee: decaffeinated and regular. Its market research department wants to determine whether coffee drinkers prefer decaffeinated or regular coffee. Coffee drinkers are given two small, unmarked cups of coffee, and each is asked about preference. Preference for decaffeinated could be coded "+" and preference for regular "−." In a sense, the data are ordinal level because the coffee drinkers give their preferred coffee the higher rank; they rank the other kind below it. Here again, if the population of consumers do not have a preference, we would expect half of the sample of coffee drinkers to prefer decaffeinated and the other half regular coffee.

digitalreflections/Shutterstock

We can best show the application of the sign test by an Example/Solution. We will use a "before/after" experiment.

▶ **EXAMPLE**

The director of information systems at Samuelson Chemicals recommended that an in-plant training program be instituted for certain managers. The objective is to improve the technology knowledge base in the Payroll, Accounting, and Production Planning departments.

A sample of 15 managers is randomly selected from the three departments. The managers are rated on their technology knowledge based on an assessment of how they use technology to solve problems. Based on the results, they were rated as outstanding, excellent, good, fair, or poor. (See Table 16–1.) After the 3-month training program, the same assessment rated each manager's technology knowledge again. The two ratings (before and after) are shown along with the sign of the difference. A "+" indicates improvement, and "−" indicates that the manager's competence using technology had declined after the training program.

TABLE 16–1 Competence Before and After the Training Program

	Name	Before	After	Sign of Difference
	Petr Kellner	Good	Outstanding	+
	Indra Nooyi	Fair	Excellent	+
	Andrea Jung	Excellent	Good	−
Dropped from analysis	Akta Kapoor	Poor	Good	+
	~~Jerry Yang~~	~~Excellent~~	~~Excellent~~	~~0~~
	Richard Li	Good	Outstanding	+
	Susanne Klatten	Poor	Fair	+
	Alex Chung	Excellent	Outstanding	+
	Galen Weston	Good	Poor	−
	Vera Wang	Poor	Good	+
	Steve Kim	Good	Outstanding	+
	Analjit Singh	Fair	Excellent	+
	Garrett Camp	Good	Fair	−
	Georg Schaeffler	Good	Outstanding	+
	Micky Jagtiani	Poor	Good	+

We are interested in whether the in-plant training program increased the managers' technology knowledge. That is, are the managers more knowledgeable after the training program than before?

SOLUTION

We will use the six-step hypothesis-testing procedure.

Step 1: State the null hypothesis and the alternate hypothesis.

$H_0: \pi \leq .50$ There has been no change in the technology knowledge base of the managers as a result of the training program.

$H_1: \pi > .50$ There has been an increase in the technology knowledge base of the managers as a result of the training program.

The symbol π refers to the proportion in the population with a particular characteristic. If we *do not reject* the null hypothesis, it will indicate the training program has produced no change in the knowledge base, or that knowledge actually decreased. If we *reject* the null hypothesis, it will indicate that the knowledge of the managers has increased as a result of the training program.

The test statistic follows the binomial probability distribution. It is appropriate because the sign test meets all the binomial assumptions, namely:

1. There are only two outcomes: a "success" and a "failure." A manager either increased one's knowledge (a success) or did not.
2. For each trial, the probability of success is assumed to be .50. Thus, the probability of a success is the same for all trials (managers in this case).
3. The total number of trials is fixed (15 in this experiment).
4. Each trial is independent. This means, for example, that Susanne Klatten's performance in the 3-month course is unrelated to Steve Kim's performance.

Step 2: **Select a level of significance.** We chose the .10 level.

Step 3: **Decide on the test statistic.** It is the *number of plus signs* resulting from the experiment.

Step 4: **Formulate a decision rule.** Fifteen managers were enrolled in the training course, but Jerry Yang showed no change in technology knowledge. (See Table 16–1.) He was, therefore, eliminated from the study because he could not be assigned to either group, so $n = 14$. From the binomial probability distribution table in Appendix B.1, for an n of 14 and a probability of .50, we copied the binomial probability distribution in Table 16–2. The number of successes is in column 1, the probabilities of success in column 2, and the cumulative probabilities in column 3. To arrive at the cumulative probabilities, we *add* the probabilities of success in column 2 from the bottom. For illustration, to get the cumulative probability of 11 or more successes, we add $.000 + .001 + .006 + .022 = .029$.

This is a one-tailed test because the alternate hypothesis gives a direction. The inequality (>) points to the right. Thus, the region of rejection is in the upper tail. If the inequality sign pointed toward the left tail (<), the region of rejection would be in the lower tail. If that were the case, we would add the probabilities in column 2 *from the top down* to get the cumulative probabilities in column 3.

Recall that we selected the .10 level of significance. To arrive at the decision rule for this problem, we go to the cumulative probabilities in Table 16–2, column 3. We sum from the bottom until we reach the *cumulative probability nearest to but not exceeding the level of significance* (.10). That cumulative probability is .090. The number of successes (plus signs) corresponding to .090 in column 1 is 10. Therefore, the decision rule is: If the number of pluses in the sample is 10 or more, the null hypothesis is rejected and the alternate hypothesis accepted.

To put it another way, we sum the probabilities from the bottom-up because the direction of the inequality (>) is toward the right, indicating that the region of rejection is in the upper tail. If the number of plus signs in the sample is 10 or more, we reject the null hypothesis; otherwise, we do not reject H_0. The region of rejection is portrayed in Chart 16–1.

TABLE 16–2 Binomial Probability Distribution for $n = 14$, $\pi = .50$

Number of Successes	Probability of Success		Cumulative Probability
0	0.000		1.000
1	0.001		0.999
2	0.006		0.998
3	0.022		0.992
4	0.061		0.970
5	0.122		0.909
6	0.183		0.787
7	0.209	**Add up**	0.604
8	0.183		0.395
9	0.122		0.212
10	0.061		0.090
11	0.022		0.029
12	0.006		0.007
13	0.001		0.001
14	0.000		0.000

$.000 + .001 + .006 + .022 + .061$

CHART 16–1 Binomial Distribution, $n = 14$, $\pi = .50$

$H_0: \pi \leq .50$
$H_1: \pi > .50$

Rejection region
10 or more + signs

Step 5: **Make a decision regarding the null hypothesis.** Eleven of the 14 managers in the training course increased their technology knowledge. The number 11 is in the rejection region, which starts at 10, so H_0 is rejected.

Step 6: **Interpret the results.** We conclude that the 3-month training course was effective. It increased the managers' level of technology knowledge.

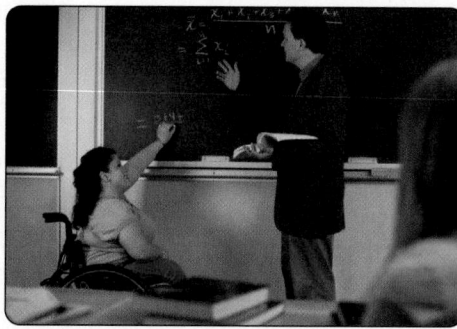

Design Pics Inc/Alamy Stock Photo

What procedure is followed for a two-tailed test? We combine (sum) the probabilities of success in the two tails until we come as close to the desired level of significance (α) as possible without exceeding it. In this example, α is .10. The probability of 3 or fewer successes is .029, found by .000 + .001 + .006 + .022. The probability of 11 or more successes is also .029. Adding the two probabilities gives .058. This is the closest we can come to .10 without exceeding it. Had we included the probabilities of 4 and 10 successes, the total would be .180, which exceeds .10. Hence, the decision rule for a two-tailed test would be to reject the null hypothesis if there are 3 or fewer plus signs, or 11 or more plus signs.

SELF-REVIEW 16–1

Recall the Taster's Choice example described on page 597, involving a consumer test to determine the preference for decaffeinated versus regular coffee. Use the .10 significance level. The null and alternate hypotheses are:

$$H_0: \pi = .50 \quad n = 12$$
$$H_1: \pi \neq .50$$

(a) Is this a one-tailed or a two-tailed test of hypothesis?
(b) Show the decision rule in a chart.
(c) Letting consumer preference for decaffeinated coffee be "+" and preference for regular coffee "−," it was found that two customers preferred decaffeinated. What is your decision? Explain.

EXERCISES

1. The following hypothesis-testing situation is given: $H_0: \pi \leq .50$ and $H_1: \pi > .50$. The significance level is .10, and the sample size is 12.
   a. What is the decision rule?
   b. There were nine successes. What is your decision regarding the null hypothesis? Explain.
2. The following hypothesis-testing situation is given: $H_0: \pi = .50$ and $H_1: \pi \neq .50$. The significance level is .05, and the sample size is 9.
   a. What is the decision rule?
   b. There were five successes. What is your decision regarding the null hypothesis?
3. Calorie Watchers has low-calorie breakfasts, lunches, and dinners. If you join the club, you receive two packaged meals a day. Calorie Watchers claims that you can eat anything you want for the third meal and still lose at least 5 pounds in the first month. Members of the club are weighed before commencing the program and again at the end of the first month. The experiences of a random sample of 11 enrollees are:

Name	Weight Change	Name	Weight Change
Foster	Lost	Hercher	Lost
Taoka	Lost	Camder	Lost
Lange	Gained	Hinckle	Lost
Rousos	Lost	Hinkley	Lost
Stephens	No change	Justin	Lost
Cantrell	Lost		

We are interested in whether there has been a weight loss as a result of the Calorie Watchers program.
   a. State H_0 and H_1.
   b. Using the .05 level of significance, what is the decision rule?
   c. What is your conclusion about the Calorie Watchers program?
4. Employees of TransPacific Inc. build a computer by inserting several subassemblies into a computer frame. Testing of the computer is completed in a different department. Executives of TransPacific think that employees would have more

pride in their work if they performed both assembly and testing tasks. A sample of 25 employees was selected to test the idea. Twenty indicated higher job satisfaction when assembling and testing the computer; five employees rated their work as less satisfying. At the .10 level, can we conclude that employee job satisfaction increased?

a. State the null and alternate hypotheses.
b. State the decision rule.
c. What is the result of the analysis?
d. Interpret the results.

LO 16-2

Test a hypothesis about a median.

Testing a Hypothesis About a Median

Most of the tests of hypothesis we have conducted so far involved the population mean or a proportion. The sign test is one of the few tests that can be used to test the value of a median. Recall from Chapter 3 that the median is the value above which half of the observations lie and below which the other half lie. For hourly wages of $7, $9, $11, and $18, the median is $10. Half of the wages are above $10 an hour and the other half below $10.

To conduct a test of hypothesis, a value above the median is assigned a plus sign, and a value below the median is assigned a minus sign. If a value is the same as the median, it is dropped from further analysis.

▶ **EXAMPLE**

In September 2021, the U.S. Bureau of Labor Statistics reported that the median income for a family unit is $84,352. The business editor of the *Portland (Oregon) Tribune* wishes to know if the median income of Portland families differs from the national median income. The editor selected a random sample of 20 families and found that 15 earned more than $84,352 last year, and 5 earned less than $84,352. At the .05 significance level, can we conclude the median income for a family unit in Portland differs from the national median income?

SOLUTION

If the population median is $84,352, then we expect that half of the 20 sampled families earned more than $84,352 last year and half less than $84,352. So, of 20 families sampled we would expect 10 to be above the median and 10 to be below the median. Is the difference between the 15 families that earned more than $84,352 and the expected number to earn more than $84,352 attributable to chance? To put it another way, based on the data, is the median for the Portland families a value different than $84,352? The statistical test for the median will help answer this question.

The null and the alternate hypotheses are:

$$H_0: \text{Median} = \$84,352$$
$$H_1: \text{Median} \neq \$84,352$$

This is a two-tailed test because the alternate hypothesis does not indicate a direction. That is, we are not interested in whether the median is less than or greater than $84,352, only that it is *different from* $84,352. The test statistic meets the binomial assumptions. That is:

1. Each family's income is either larger or smaller than the proposed median, so there are only two possible outcomes.

2. Under the null hypothesis, the probability of a success is .50. That is, $\pi = .50$.
3. The random selection of the families represents independent trials.
4. We count the number of successes in a fixed number of trials. In this case, we found that 15 of the 20 sampled families earned more than $84,352 annually.

The strategy here resembles the sign test. That is:

1. We use the binomial distribution as the test statistic.
2. The number of trials is 20.
3. The hypothesized probability of a success is .50.

Using statistical software, we can create the entire binomial distribution when $n = 20$ and $\pi = .50$. Table 16–3 and Chart 16–2 show this distribution. Determining the decision rule is the next step. For the two-tailed hypothesis test, we selected the .05 significance level. The chart shows how to determine the rule for rejecting the null hypothesis. Using the probabilities in the tails of the distribution, we sum the most extreme probabilities from each tail until the sum is as close as possible to .05 without exceeding it. Note that the probabilities in each tail are the same because the binomial distribution is symmetric when $\pi = .50$.

$$P(x \leq 5) = .0000 + .0000 + .0002 + .0011 + .0046 + .0148 = .0207$$
$$P(x \geq 15) = .0000 + .0000 + .0002 + .0011 + .0046 + .0148 = .0207$$

$$P(x \leq 5) + P(x \geq 15) = .0414$$

The result is a probability of .0414, and the decision rule is to reject the null hypothesis that the median is $84,352 if the count is 5 or less, or 15 or more. If we had included $P(x = 6)$ and $P(x = 14)$ in the sum of the probabilities, the chart shows that the result is .071, which exceeds the .05 significance level.

TABLE 16–3 Binomial Probability Distribution for $n = 20$, $\pi = .50$

Success	Probability	One-Tail Probability	Two-Tail Probability
0	0.0000		
1	0.0000		
2	0.0002	0.0207	
3	0.0011		
4	0.0046		
5	0.0148		
6	0.0370		
7	0.0739		
8	0.1201		
9	0.1602		
10	0.1762		0.0414
11	0.1602		
12	0.1201		
13	0.0739		
14	0.0370		
15	0.0148		
16	0.0046		
17	0.0011	0.0207	
18	0.0002		
19	0.0000		
20	0.0000		

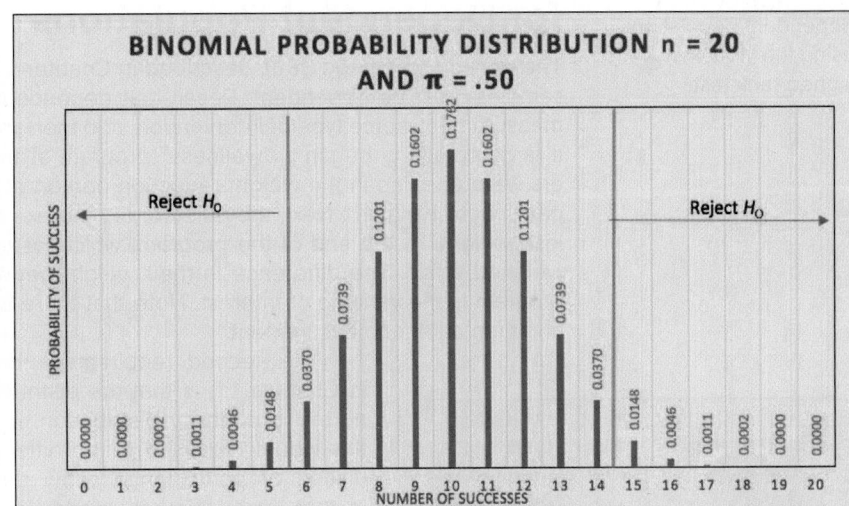

CHART 16–2 Binomial Probability Distribution for $n = 20$, $\pi = .50$

In the business editor's sample, 15 families earned more than $84,352. Fifteen is in the rejection region, so the null hypothesis is rejected. The sample evidence indicates that the median amount earned annually in Portland is not equal to $84,352.

SELF-REVIEW 16-2

After reading the results of the Portland, Oregon, study, the business editor of the *Tampa Times* decided to conduct a similar study. The Tampa business editor decides to alter the study slightly by investigating whether families in the region earn *more than* a median amount of $84,352. A sample of 20 Tampa couples revealed 13 earned more than $84,352 per year. Using the .05 significance level, what should the business editor conclude?

EXERCISES

5. According to the U.S. Department of Labor, the median salary for a chiropractor in the United States is $70,720 per year. A group of recent graduates employed in the state of Colorado believe this amount is too low. In a random sample of 18 chiropractors who recently graduated, 13 began with a salary of more than $70,720. Is it reasonable to conclude that the starting salary in Colorado is more than $70,720?
   a. State the null and alternate hypotheses.
   b. State the decision rule. Use the .05 significance level.
   c. Test the hypothesis and interpret the results.

6. Central Airlines claims that the median price of a round-trip ticket from Chicago, Illinois, to Jackson Hole, Wyoming, is $603. This claim is being challenged by the Association of Travel Agents, who believe the median price is less than $603. A random sample of 25 round-trip tickets from Chicago to Jackson Hole revealed 11 tickets were below $603. None of the tickets was exactly $603.
   a. State the null and alternate hypotheses.
   b. State the decision rule. Use the .05 significance level.
   c. Test the hypothesis and interpret the results.

LO 16-3

Test a hypothesis of dependent populations using the Wilcoxon signed-rank test.

Wilcoxon Signed-Rank Test for Dependent Populations

The paired *t*-test (page 388), described in Chapter 11, has two requirements. First, the samples must be dependent. Recall that dependent samples are characterized by a measurement, some type of intervention, and then another measurement. For example, a large company began a "wellness" program at the start of the year. Twenty workers were enrolled in the weight-reduction portion of the program. To begin, all participants were weighed. Next, they dieted, did the exercise, and so forth in an attempt to lose weight. At the end of the program, which lasted 6 months, all participants were weighed again. The difference in their weight between the start and the end of the program is the variable of interest. Note that there is a measurement, an intervention, and then another measurement.

The second requirement for the paired *t*-test, as described in Chapter 11, is that the distribution of the differences follow the normal probability distribution. In the company wellness example, this would require that the differences in the weights of the population of participants follow the normal probability distribution. In that case, this assumption is reasonable. However, there are instances when we want to study the differences between dependent observations where we cannot assume that the distribution of the differences approximates a normal distribution. Frequently, we encounter a problem with the normality assumption when the level of measurement in the samples is ordinal, rather than interval or ratio. For example, suppose there are 10 surgical patients on 3 East today. The nursing supervisor asks Nurse Benner and Nurse Jurris to rate each of the 10 patients on a scale of 1 to 10,

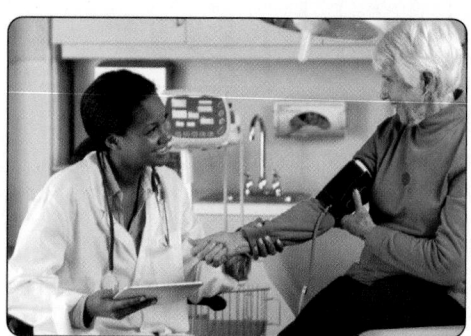

Monkey Business Images/Shutterstock

according to the difficulty of patient care. The distribution of the differences in the ratings probably would not approximate the normal distribution, and, therefore, the paired *t*-test would not be appropriate.

In 1945, Frank Wilcoxon developed a nonparametric test, based on the differences in dependent samples, where the normality assumption is not required. This test is called the **Wilcoxon signed-rank test.** The following Example/Solution details its application.

▶ **EXAMPLE**

Fricker's is a family restaurant chain located primarily in the southeastern part of the United States. It offers a full dinner menu, but its specialty is chicken. Recently, Bernie Frick, the owner and founder, developed a new spicy flavor for the batter in which the chicken is cooked. Before replacing the current flavor, he wants to be sure that patrons will like the spicy flavor better.

To begin his taste test, Bernie selects a random sample of 15 customers. Each sampled customer is given a small piece of the current chicken and asked to rate its overall taste on a scale of 1 to 20. A value near 20 indicates the participant liked the flavor, whereas a rating near 0 indicates they did not like the flavor. Next, the same 15 participants are given a sample of the new chicken with the spicier flavor and again asked to rate its taste on a scale of 1 to 20. The results are reported here. Is it reasonable to conclude that the spicy flavor is preferred? Use the .05 significance level.

Participant	Spicy Flavor Rating	Current Flavor Rating
Arquette	14	12
Lavigne	8	16
Laurent	6	2
Wagner	18	4
Badenhop	20	12
Dubois	16	16
Lyon	14	5
Virost	6	16
Garcia	19	10
Sundar	18	10
Bacho	16	13
Ghaffari	18	2
Boggart	4	13
Hein	7	14
Habib	16	4

SOLUTION

Each participant is asked to rate both flavors of chicken. So the ratings are dependent or related and, for each participant, we compute the difference between the ratings for the spicy flavor and the current flavor. The resulting value shows the amount the participants favor one flavor over the other. If we choose to subtract the current flavor rating from the spicy flavor rating, a positive result is the "amount" the participant favors the spicy flavor. Negative differences indicate the participant favored the current flavor. Because of the subjective nature of the ratings, we are not confident that the distribution of the differences follows the normal distribution. So, we use the nonparametric Wilcoxon signed-rank test.

As usual, we will use the six-step hypothesis-testing procedure. The null hypothesis is that there is no difference in the rating of the chicken flavors by the participants. The alternate hypothesis is that the ratings are higher for the spicy flavor. More formally:

H_0: There is no difference in the ratings of the two flavors.
H_1: The spicy ratings are higher.

This is a one-tailed test. Why? Because Bernie Frick, the owner of Fricker's, will want to change his chicken flavor only if the sample participants show that the population of customers like the new flavor better. The significance level is .05, as stated earlier.

The steps to conduct the Wilcoxon signed-rank test are as follows.

1. Compute the difference between the spicy flavor rating and the current flavor rating for each participant. For example, Arquette's spicy flavor rating was 14 and the current flavor rating was 12, so the amount of the difference is 2. For Lavigne, the difference is −8, found by 8 − 16, and for Laurent it is 4, found by 6 − 2. The differences for all participants are shown in column D of Table 16−4.

TABLE 16−4 Flavor Rating for Current and Spicy Flavors

A	B	C	D	E	F	G	H	
	Spicy	Current				Signed		
	Flavor	Flavor	Difference	Absolute		Rank		
Participant	Rating	Rating	in Ratings	Difference	Rank	R⁺	R⁻	
Arquette	14	12	2	2	1	1		
Lavigne	8	16	−8	8	6		6	
Laurent	6	2	4	4	3	3		
Wagner	18	4	14	14	13	13		
Badenhop	20	12	8	8	6	6		
Dubois	16	16	0	*	*			
Lyon	14	5	9	9	9	9		
Virost	6	16	−10	10	11		11	
Garcia	19	10	9	9	9	9		
Sundar	18	10	8	8	6	6		
Bacho	16	13	3	3	2	2		
Ghaffari	18	2	16	16	14	14		
Boggart	4	13	−9	9	9		9	
Hein	7	14	−7	7	4		4	
Habib	16	4	12	12	12	12		
					Sum	75	30	Smaller rank sum

2. Only the positive and negative differences are considered further. That is, if the difference in flavor ratings is 0, that participant is dropped from further analysis and the number in the sample reduced. From Table 16−4, Dubois, the sixth participant, rated both the spicy and the current flavor a 16. Hence, Dubois is dropped from the study and the usable sample size reduced from 15 to 14.

3. Determine the absolute differences for the values computed in column D. Recall that in an absolute difference we disregard the sign of the difference

and focus on the magnitude of the differences in ratings. The absolute differences are shown in column E.

4. Next, rank the absolute differences from smallest to largest. Arquette, the first participant, rated the spicy chicken a 14 and the current a 12. The difference of 2 in the two taste ratings is the smallest absolute difference, so it is given a ranking of 1. The next largest difference is 3, given by Bacho, so it is given a rank of 2. The other differences are ranked in a similar manner. There are three participants who rated the difference in the flavor as 8. To resolve this issue, we average the ranks involved and report the average rank for each. This situation involves the ranks 5, 6, and 7, so all three participants are assigned the rank of 6. The same situation occurs for the three participants with a difference of 9. The ranks involved are 8, 9, and 10, so those participants are assigned a rank of 9.

5. Each assigned rank in column F is then given the same sign as the original difference, and the results are reported in column G or H. For example, the second participant has a difference of −8 and a rank of 6. So the value of 6 is recorded for Lavigne in the R^- section of column H.

6. Finally, the R^+ and R^- columns are totaled. The sum of the positive ranks is 75 and the sum of the negative ranks is 30. The smaller of the two rank sums is used as the test statistic and referred to as T.

The critical values for the Wilcoxon signed-rank test are located in Appendix B.8. A portion of that table is shown here. The α row is used for one-tailed tests and the 2α row for two-tailed tests. In this case, we want to show that customers like the spicy taste better, which is a one-tailed test, so we select the α row. We chose the .05 significance level, so move to the right to the column headed .05. Go down that column to the row where n is 14. (Recall that one person in the study rated the chicken flavors the same and was dropped from the study, making the usable sample size 14.) The value at the intersection is 25, so the critical value is 25. The decision rule is to reject the null hypothesis if the *smaller* of the rank sums is 25 or less. The value obtained from Appendix B.8 is the *largest value in the rejection region*. To put it another way, our decision rule is to reject H_0 if the smaller of the two rank sums is 25 or less. In this case, the smaller rank sum is 30, so the decision is not to reject the null hypothesis. We cannot conclude there is a difference in the flavor ratings between the current and the spicy. The study has failed to show that customers prefer the new flavor. Mr. Frick should stay with the current flavor of chicken.

n	2α .15 α .075	.10 .05	.05 .025	.04 .02	.03 .015	.02 .01	.01 .005
4	0						
5	1	0					
6	2	2	0	0			
7	4	3	2	1	0	0	
8	7	5	3	3	2	1	0
9	9	8	5	5	4	3	1
10	12	10	8	7	6	5	3
11	16	13	10	9	8	7	5
12	19	17	13	12	11	9	7
13	24	21	17	16	14	12	9
14	28	25	21	19	18	15	12
15	33	30	25	23	21	19	15

SELF-REVIEW 16–3

The assembly area of Gotrac Products was recently redesigned. Installing a new lighting system and purchasing new workbenches were two features of the redesign. The production supervisor would like to know if the changes resulted in improved worker productivity. To investigate, the supervisor selected a sample of 11 workers and determined the production rate before and after the changes. The sample information is reported as follows:

Operator	Production Before	Production After	Operator	Production Before	Production After
S. M.	17	18	U. Z.	10	22
D. J.	21	23	Y. U.	20	19
M. D.	25	22	U. T.	17	20
B. B.	15	25	Y. H.	24	30
M. F.	10	28	Y. Y.	23	26
A. A.	16	16			

(a) How many usable pairs are there? That is, what is *n*?
(b) Use the Wilcoxon signed-rank test to determine whether the new procedures actually increased production. Use the .05 level and a one-tailed test.
(c) What assumption are you making about the distribution of the differences in production before and after redesign?

EXERCISES

7. **FILE** An industrial psychologist selected a random sample of seven young urban professional couples who own their homes. The size of their home (square feet) is compared with that of their parents. At the .05 significance level, can we conclude that the professional couples live in larger homes than their parents?

Couple Name	Professional	Parent	Couple Name	Professional	Parent
Gordon	1,725	1,175	Kuhlman	1,290	1,360
Sharkey	1,310	1,120	Welch	1,880	1,750
Uselding	1,670	1,420	Anderson	1,530	1,440
Bell	1,520	1,640			

8. **FILE** Toyota USA is studying the effect of regular versus high-octane gasoline on the fuel economy of its new high-performance, 3.5-liter, V6 engine. Ten executives are selected and asked to maintain records on the number of miles traveled per gallon of gas. The results are:

	Miles per Gallon			Miles per Gallon	
Executive	Regular	High-Octane	Executive	Regular	High-Octane
Bowers	25	28	Rau	38	40
Demars	33	31	Greolke	29	29
Grasser	31	35	Burns	42	37
DeToto	45	44	Snow	41	44
Kleg	42	47	Lawless	30	44

At the .05 significance level, is there a difference in the number of miles traveled per gallon between regular and high-octane gasoline?

9. **FILE** A new assembly-line procedure to increase production has been suggested. To test whether the new procedure is superior to the old procedure, a random sample of 15 assembly-line workers was selected. The number of units produced in an hour under the old procedure was determined, then the new procedure was

introduced. After an appropriate break-in period, their production was measured again using the new procedure. The results are as follows:

Employee	Procedure Old	New	Employee	Procedure Old	New
A	60	64	I	87	84
B	40	52	J	80	80
C	59	58	K	56	57
D	30	37	L	21	21
E	70	71	M	99	108
F	78	83	N	50	56
G	43	46	O	56	62
H	40	52			

At the .05 significance level, can we conclude the production is greater using the new procedure?
  a. State the null and alternate hypotheses.
  b. State the decision rule.
  c. Arrive at a decision regarding the null hypothesis.

10. **FILE** It has been suggested that daily production of a subassembly would be increased if better lighting were installed and background music and free coffee and doughnuts were provided during the day. Management agreed to try the scheme for a limited time. A listing of the number of subassemblies produced per week before and after the new work environment for each employee follows:

Employee	Past Production Record	Production after Installing Lighting, Music, etc.	Employee	Past Production Record	Production after Installing Lighting, Music, etc.
JD	23	33	WWJ	21	25
SB	26	26	OP	25	22
MD	24	30	CD	21	23
RCF	17	25	PA	16	17
MF	20	19	RRT	20	15
UHH	24	22	AT	17	9
IB	30	29	QQ	23	30

Using the Wilcoxon signed-rank test, determine whether the suggested changes are worthwhile.
  a. State the null hypothesis.
  b. You decide on the alternate hypothesis.
  c. You decide on the level of significance.
  d. State the decision rule.
  e. Compute T and arrive at a decision.
  f. What did you assume about the distribution of the differences?

LO 16-4
Test a hypothesis of independent populations using the Wilcoxon rank-sum test.

Wilcoxon Rank-Sum Test for Independent Populations

One test specifically designed to determine whether two *independent* samples came from equivalent populations is the **Wilcoxon rank-sum test.** This test is an alternative to the two-sample *t*-test described starting on page 377 in Chapter 11. Recall that the *t*-test requires the two populations follow the normal distribution and have equal population variances. These conditions are not required for the Wilcoxon rank-sum test.

The Wilcoxon rank-sum test is based on the sum of ranks. The data are ranked as if the observations were from a single population. If the null hypothesis is true, then the ranks will be about evenly distributed between the two samples, and the sum of the ranks for the two samples will be about the same. That is, the low, medium, and high ranks should be about equally divided between the two samples. If the alternate hypothesis is true, one of the samples will have more of the lower ranks and, thus, a smaller rank sum. The other sample will have more of the higher ranks and, therefore, a larger rank sum. If each of the samples contains *at least eight observations,* the standard normal distribution is used as the test statistic. We use the following formula to find the value of the test statistic.

WILCOXON RANK-SUM TEST
$$z = \frac{W - \dfrac{n_1(n_1 + n_2 + 1)}{2}}{\sqrt{\dfrac{n_1 n_2(n_1 + n_2 + 1)}{12}}}$$
(16–1)

where:

n_1 is the number of observations from the first population.
n_2 is the number of observations from the second population.
W is the sum of the ranks from the first population.

▶ **EXAMPLE**

Dan Thompson, the president of OTG Airlines, recently noted an increase in the number of bags that were checked at the gate (gate-checked bags) in Atlanta. He is particularly interested in determining whether there are more gate-checked bags from Atlanta compared with flights leaving Chicago. A sample of nine flights from Atlanta and eight from Chicago are reported in Table 16–5. At the .05 significance level, can we conclude that there are more gate-checked bags for flights originating in Atlanta?

TABLE 16–5 Number of Bags Checked at the Gate

Atlanta	Chicago
11	13
15	14
10	10
18	8
11	16
20	9
24	17
22	21
25	

SOLUTION

If the population frequency distributions of gate-checked bags follow the normal probability distribution and have equal variances, the two-sample *t*-test is appropriate. However, Mr. Thompson believes these two conditions cannot be met. Therefore, a nonparametric test, the Wilcoxon rank-sum test, is appropriate.

If the number of gate-checked bags is the same for Atlanta and Chicago, then we expect the sum of the ranks for the two samples to be about the same.

Or to put it another way, the sum of the ranks of the two groups will be about the same. If the number of gate-checked bags is not the same, we expect the sum of the ranks to be quite different.

Mr. Thompson believes there are more gate-checked bags for Atlanta flights. Thus, a one-tailed test is appropriate. The null and alternate hypotheses are:

H_0: The number of gate-checked bags for Atlanta is the same or less than the number of gate-checked bags for Chicago.

H_1: The number of gate-checked bags for Atlanta is more than the number of gate-checked bags for Chicago.

The test statistic follows the standard normal distribution. At the .05 significance level, we find from the last row in Appendix B.5 the critical value of z is 1.645. The null hypothesis is rejected if the computed value of z is greater than 1.645.

The alternate hypothesis is that there are more gate-checked bags in Atlanta, which means that the Atlanta distribution is located to the right of the Chicago distribution. The details of rank assignment are shown in Table 16–6. We rank the observations from *both* samples as if they were a single group. The Chicago flight with only 8 gate-checked bags had the fewest, so it is assigned a rank of 1. The Chicago flight with 9 gate-checked bags is ranked 2, and so on. The Atlanta flight with 25 gate-checked bags is the highest, so it is assigned the largest rank, 17. There are also two instances of tied ranks. There are Atlanta and Chicago flights that each have 10 gate-checked bags. There are also two Atlanta flights with 11 gate-checked bags. How do we handle these ties? The solution is to average the ranks involved and assign the average rank to both flights. In the case involving 10 gate-checked bags, the ranks involved are 3 and 4. The mean of these ranks is 3.5, so a rank of 3.5 is assigned to both the Atlanta and the Chicago flights with 10 gate-checked bags.

TABLE 16–6 Ranked Number of Gate-checked Bags

Atlanta		Chicago	
Gate-Checked Bags	**Rank**	**Gate-Checked Bags**	**Rank**
11	5.5	13	7
15	9	14	8
10	3.5	10	3.5
18	12	8	1
11	5.5	16	10
20	13	9	2
24	16	17	11
22	15	21	14
25	17		
	96.5		56.5

Atlanta Rank Sum

The sum of the ranks for the Atlanta flights is 96.5. This is the value of W in formula (16–1). From Table 16–6, there are nine flights originating in Atlanta and eight in Chicago, so $n_1 = 9$ and $n_2 = 8$. Computing z from formula (16–1) gives:

$$z = \frac{W - \dfrac{n_1(n_1 + n_2 + 1)}{2}}{\sqrt{\dfrac{n_1 n_2(n_1 + n_2 + 1)}{12}}} = \frac{96.5 - \dfrac{9(9 + 8 + 1)}{2}}{\sqrt{\dfrac{9(8)(9 + 8 + 1)}{12}}} = 1.49$$

Because the computed z-value (1.49) is less than 1.645, the null hypothesis is not rejected. The evidence does not show a difference in the distributions of the number of gate-checked bags. That is, it appears that the number of gate-checked bags is the same in Atlanta as in Chicago. The p-value of .0681, found by determining the area to the right of 1.49 (.5000 − .4319), indicates the same result.

The Wilcoxon-Mann/Whitney test is available in MegaStat. It provides the following results. The p-value, .0679, is slightly different as the software corrects for ties.

Wilcoxon-Mann/Whitney Test

n	sum of ranks	
9	96.5	Atlanta
8	56.5	Chicago
17	153	total

81.000	expected value
10.392	standard deviation
1.491	z
.0679	p-value (one-tailed, upper)

In using the Wilcoxon rank-sum test, you may number the two populations in either order. However, once you have made a choice, W must be the sum of the ranks identified as population 1. If, in the gate-checked bags example, the population of Chicago was identified as number 1, the direction of the alternate hypothesis would be changed. The value of z would be the same but have the opposite sign.

H_0: The population distribution of gate-checked bags is the same or larger for Chicago than for Atlanta.

H_1: The population distribution of gate-checked bags is smaller for Chicago than for Atlanta.

The computed value of z is −1.49, found by:

$$z = \frac{W - \dfrac{n_1(n_1 + n_2 + 1)}{2}}{\sqrt{\dfrac{n_1 n_2(n_1 + n_2 + 1)}{12}}} = \frac{56.5 - \dfrac{8(8 + 9 + 1)}{2}}{\sqrt{\dfrac{8(9)(8 + 9 + 1)}{12}}} = -1.49$$

Our conclusion is the same as described earlier. There is no difference in the typical number of gate-checked bags for Chicago and Atlanta.

SELF-REVIEW 16–4

Suppose the director of golf research at TaylorMade Inc. wants to know whether there is a difference in the distribution of the distances traveled by two of the company's golf balls. Eight of its XL-5000 brand and eight of its D2 brand balls were hit by an automatic fairway metal. The distances (in yards) were as follows:

XL-5000:	252, 263, 279, 273, 271, 265, 257, 280
D2:	262, 242, 256, 260, 258, 243, 239, 265

Do not assume the distributions of the distances traveled follow the normal probability distribution. At the .05 significance level, is there a difference between the two distributions?

EXERCISES

11. **FILE** Using the following data, apply a two-tailed Wilcoxon rank-sum test to determine if the two populations are different. Use the .05 significance level.

| Population A | 38, 45, 56, 57, 61, 69, 70, 79 |
| Population B | 26, 31, 35, 42, 51, 52, 57, 62 |

12. **FILE** Using the following data, apply a two-tailed Wilcoxon rank-sum test to determine if the two populations are different. Use the .05 significance level.

| Population A | 12, 14, 15, 19, 23, 29, 33, 40, 51 |
| Population B | 13, 16, 19, 21, 22, 33, 35, 43 |

13. **FILE** Tucson State University offers two MBA programs. In the first program, the students meet two nights per week at the university's main campus in downtown Tucson. In the second program, students only communicate remotely with the instructor. The director of the MBA experience at Tucson wishes to compare the number of hours studied last week by the two groups of students. A sample of 10 on-campus students and 12 online students revealed the following information.

| Campus | 28, 16, 42, 29, 31, 22, 50, 42, 23, 25 |
| Online | 26, 42, 65, 38, 29, 32, 59, 42, 27, 41, 46, 18 |

Do not assume the two distributions of study times (in hours) follow a normal distribution. At the .05 significance level, can we conclude the online students spend more time studying?

14. **FILE** In recent times, with mortgage rates at low levels, financial institutions have had to provide more customer convenience. One of the innovations offered by Coastal National Bank and Trust is online mortgage applications. Listed are the times, in minutes, for eight customers to complete the application process for a 15-year fixed-rate mortgage and the times for nine customers to complete an application for a 30-year fixed-rate mortgage.

| 15 years, fixed-rate | 41, 36, 42, 39, 36, 48, 49, 38 |
| 30 years, fixed-rate | 21, 27, 36, 20, 19, 21, 39, 24, 22 |

At the .05 significance level, is it reasonable to conclude that it takes less time for those customers applying for the 30-year fixed-rate mortgage? Do not assume the distribution times follow a normal distribution for either group.

LO 16-5

Test a hypothesis of several independent populations using the Kruskal-Wallis test.

Kruskal-Wallis Test: Analysis of Variance by Ranks

The analysis of variance (ANOVA) procedure discussed in Chapter 12 tests the hypothesis that several population means are equal. The data were interval or ratio level. Also, it was assumed the populations followed the normal probability distribution and their standard deviations were equal. What if the data are ordinal scale and/or the populations do not follow a normal distribution? Then we would use the **Kruskal-Wallis one-way analysis of variance by ranks.** It requires ordinal-, interval-, or ratio-scaled variables that can be ranked. The analysis makes no assumptions about the shape of the population distributions.

For the Kruskal-Wallis test to be applied, the populations must be *independent*. For example, if samples from three populations—executives, staff, and supervisors—are selected and interviewed, the responses of one group (say, the executives) must in no way influence the responses of the others.

To compute the Kruskal-Wallis test statistic, (1) all the samples are combined, (2) the combined values are ordered from low to high, and (3) the ordered values are *replaced by ranks, starting with 1 for the smallest value.* An Example/Solution will clarify the details of the procedure.

▶ **EXAMPLE**

The Hospital Systems of the Carolinas operate three hospitals in the Greater Charlotte area: St. Luke's Memorial on the west side of the city, Swedish Medical Center to the south, and Piedmont Hospital on the east side of town. The director of administration is concerned about the waiting time of patients with non-life-threatening injuries that arrive during weekday evenings at the three hospitals. Specifically, is there a difference in the waiting times at the three hospitals?

SOLUTION

To investigate, the director selected random samples of patients at the three locations and determined the time, in minutes, between entering the facility and when treatment was completed. The times in minutes are reported in Table 16–7.

TABLE 16–7 Waiting Times for Emergency Treatment at Hospital Systems of the Carolinas

St. Luke's Memorial	Swedish Medical Center	Piedmont Hospital
56	103	42
39	87	38
48	51	89
38	95	75
73	68	35
60	42	61
62	107	
	89	

From Table 16–7, we observe that the shortest waiting time is 35 minutes for the fifth sampled patient at Piedmont Hospital. The longest waiting time is 107 minutes by the seventh patient at the Swedish Medical Center.

Likely the first thought for comparing the waiting times is to determine whether there is a difference in the mean waiting time at the three hospitals, that is, use the one-way ANOVA described on page 414 of Chapter 12. However, there are three requirements for this test:

1. The samples are from independent populations.
2. The population variances must be equal.
3. The samples are from normal populations.

In this instance the samples are from independent populations, the three different hospitals. However, assumptions 2 and 3 may not be true. Specifically, the variances of the three samples are:

Sample variances		
St. Luke's Memorial	Swedish Medical Center	Piedmont Hospital
163.57	577.36	486.67

Notice that the variance for the Swedish Medical Center and Piedmont Hospital are more than twice that of St. Luke's. The equal variance assumption is tenuous. Also, with the small number of observations in each sample it would be difficult to support the assumption of normally distributed populations. Clearly, all the assumptions required for ANOVA techniques are not supported. So, we should use the Kruskal-Wallis test. It does not require these assumptions.

The first step in conducting the Kruskal-Wallis test is to state the null and the alternate hypotheses.

H_0: The population distributions of waiting times are the same for the three hospitals.

H_1: The population distributions are not all the same for the three hospitals.

The director of administration selected the .05 significance level.

The test statistic used for the Kruskal-Wallis test is designated H. Its formula is:

KRUSKAL-WALLIS TEST

$$H = \frac{12}{n(n+1)}\left[\frac{(\Sigma R_1)^2}{n_1} + \frac{(\Sigma R_2)^2}{n_2} + \cdots + \frac{(\Sigma R_k)^2}{n_k}\right] - 3(n+1) \qquad \textbf{(16–2)}$$

---

with $k - 1$ degrees of freedom (k is the number of populations), where:

$\Sigma R_1, \Sigma R_2, \ldots, \Sigma R_k$,	are the sums of the ranks of samples 1, 2, . . . , k, respectively.
$n_1, n_2, \ldots, n_k$	are the sizes of samples 1, 2, . . . , k, respectively.
n	is the combined number of observations for all samples.

The distribution of the sample H-statistic approximates the chi-square distribution with $k - 1$ degrees of freedom. So, the decision rule is formulated using the chi-square distribution. It requires that the number of observations in each sample is at least 5. In this example, there are three populations—a population of waiting times for patients at St. Luke's Memorial, another for patients at the Swedish Medical Center, and a third for Piedmont Hospital patients. Thus, there are $k - 1$, or $3 - 1 = 2$ degrees of freedom. Refer to the chi-square table of critical values in Appendix B.7. The critical value for 2 degrees of freedom and the .05 level of significance is 5.991. So our decision rule is: Do not reject the null hypothesis if the computed value of the test statistic H is less than or equal to 5.991. If the computed value of H is greater than 5.991, reject the null hypothesis and accept the alternate hypothesis.

The next step is to determine the value of the test statistic. We assign the waiting times at the three hospitals with the corresponding ranks. Considering the waiting times as a single group, the Piedmont patient with a waiting time of 35 minutes waited the shortest time and hence is given the lowest rank of 1. There are two patients that waited 38 minutes, one at St. Luke's and one at Piedmont. To resolve this tie, each patient is given a rank of 2.5, found by $(2 + 3)/2$. This process is continued for all waiting times. The longest waiting time is 107 minutes, and that Swedish Medical Center patient is given a rank of 21. The scores, the ranks, and the sum of the ranks for each of the three hospitals are given in Table 16–8.

Solving for H gives

$$H = \frac{12}{n(n+1)}\left[\frac{(\Sigma R_1)^2}{n_1} + \frac{(\Sigma R_2)^2}{n_2} + \frac{(\Sigma R_3)^2}{n_3}\right] - 3(n+1)$$

$$= \frac{12}{21(21+1)}\left[\frac{58.5^2}{7} + \frac{120^2}{8} + \frac{52.5^2}{6}\right] - 3(21+1) = 5.38$$

Because the computed value of H (5.38) is less than the critical value of 5.991, we do not reject the null hypothesis. There is not enough evidence to conclude that there is a difference among the distributions of waiting times at the three hospitals.

TABLE 16–8 Waiting Times for Emergency Treatment at Hospital Systems of the Carolinas

St. Luke's Memorial		Swedish Medical Center		Piedmont Hospital	
Time	Rank	Time	Rank	Time	Rank
56	9	103	20	42	5.5
39	4	87	16	38	2.5
48	7	51	8	89	17.5
38	2.5	95	19	75	15
73	14	68	13	35	1
60	10	42	5.5	61	11
62	12	107	21		
		89	17.5		
$\Sigma R_1 = 58.5$		$\Sigma R_2 = 120$		$\Sigma R_3 = 52.5$	

Waiting time rank sums

The Kruskal-Wallis procedure can be done using the MegaStat add-in for Excel. Output for the example regarding the hospital waiting time follows. The computed value of H is 5.39 and the p-value is .067. The values are slightly different because of rounding. Based on these results, the decision and conclusion are the same.

Kruskal-Wallis Test				
	Median	n	Avg. Rank	
	56.00	7	8.36	St. Luke's
	88.00	8	15.00	Swedish
	51.50	6	8.75	Piedmont
	61.00	21		Total
			5.39	H (corrected for ties)
			2	d.f.
			0.067	p-value

Recall from Chapter 12 that, for the analysis of variance technique to apply, we assume (1) the populations are normally distributed, (2) these populations have equal standard deviations, and (3) the samples are selected from independent populations. If these assumptions are met in the hospital waiting time example, we use the F-distribution as the test statistic. If these assumptions cannot be met, we apply the distribution-free test by Kruskal-Wallis. To highlight the differences between the two approaches, we will solve the hospital waiting time example using the ANOVA technique.

To begin, we state the null and the alternate hypotheses for the three hospitals.

H_0: $\mu_1 = \mu_2 = \mu_3$
H_1: The treatment means are not all the same.

For the .05 significance level, with $k - 1 = 3 - 1 = 2$ degrees of freedom in the numerator and $n - k = 21 - 3 = 18$ degrees of freedom in the denominator, the critical value of F is 3.55. The decision rule is to reject the null hypothesis if the computed value of F is greater than 3.55. The output using Excel follows:

▲	A	B	C	D	E	F	G	H	I	J	K
1	St. Luke's	Swedish	Piedmont		Anova: Single Factor						
2	56	103	42								
3	39	87	38		SUMMARY						
4	48	51	89		Groups	Count	Sum	Average	Variance		
5	38	95	75		St. Luke's	7	376	53.714	163.571		
6	73	68	35		Swedish	8	642	80.250	577.357		
7	60	42	61		Piedmont	6	340	56.667	486.667		
8	62	107									
9		89									
10					ANOVA						
11					Source of Variation	SS	df	MS	F	P-value	F crit
12					Between Groups	3166.4	2	1583.202	3.822	0.041	3.555
13					Within Groups	7456.26	18	414.24			
14											
15					Total	10622.7	20				

Microsoft Excel

Using the one-way ANOVA test, the computed value of F is 3.822 and the p-value is .041. Our decision is to reject the null hypothesis and conclude that the treatment means are not the same. That is, the mean waiting times at the three Hospital Systems of the Carolinas hospitals are different.

This comparison of the Kruskal-Wallis and ANOVA analyses shows important differences. The result of the Kruskal-Wallis test is to fail to reject the hypothesis that the samples are from identical populations. Remember that this test does not require any assumptions about the variances or distributions of the populations. The result of the ANOVA test is to reject the hypothesis and conclude that the population means are different. However, the assumption of equal population variances is probably not true, and the assumption of normally distributed populations is difficult to validate. Therefore, we should suspect that the ANOVA results are not valid. Comparing the results of the Kruskal-Wallis and ANOVA serves to show the importance of validating the assumptions required for ANOVA. If the ANOVA assumptions are not supported, the results are not reliable. In this case, the Kruskal-Wallis analysis should be used.

SELF-REVIEW 16–5

The regional bank manager of Statewide Financial Bank is interested in the number of transactions occurring in personal checking accounts at four of the bank's branches. Each branch randomly samples a number of personal checking accounts and records the number of transactions made in each account over the last 6 months. The results are in the following table. Using the .01 level and the Kruskal-Wallis test, determine whether there is a difference in the number of personal checking account transactions among the four branches.

Englewood Branch	West Side Branch	Great Northern Branch	Sylvania Branch
208	91	302	99
307	62	103	116
199	86	319	189
142	91	340	103
91	80	180	100
296			131

EXERCISES

15. Under what conditions should the Kruskal-Wallis test be used instead of ANOVA?
16. Under what conditions should the Kruskal-Wallis test be used instead of the Wilcoxon rank-sum test?

17. **FILE** The following sample data were obtained from three populations that did not follow a normal distribution.

Sample 1	Sample 2	Sample 3
50	48	39
54	49	41
59	49	44
59	52	47
65	56	51
	57	

    a. State the null hypothesis.
    b. Using the .05 level of risk, state the decision rule.
    c. Compute the value of the test statistic.
    d. What is your decision on the null hypothesis?

18. **FILE** The following sample data were obtained from three populations where the variances were not equal, and you wish to compare the populations.

Sample 1	Sample 2	Sample 3
21	15	38
29	17	40
35	22	44
45	27	51
56	31	53
71		

    a. State the null hypothesis.
    b. Using the .01 level of risk, state the decision rule.
    c. Compute the value of the test statistic.
    d. What is your decision on the null hypothesis?

19. **FILE** Davis Outboard Motors Inc. recently developed an epoxy painting process to protect exhaust components from corrosion. Bill Davis, the owner, wishes to determine whether the durability of the paint was equal for three different conditions: saltwater, freshwater without weeds, and freshwater with a heavy concentration of weeds. Accelerated-life tests were conducted in the laboratory, and the number of hours the paint lasted before peeling was recorded. Five boats were tested for each condition.

Saltwater	Freshwater	Freshwater with Weeds
167.3	160.6	182.7
189.6	177.6	165.4
177.2	185.3	172.9
169.4	168.6	169.2
180.3	176.6	174.7

Use the Kruskal-Wallis test and the .01 level to determine whether the number of hours the paint lasted is the same for the three water conditions.

20. **FILE** The National Turkey Association wants to experiment with the effects of three different feed mixtures on weight gain in poults. Because no experience exists regarding the three mixtures, no assumptions regarding the population distribution of weights exist. To study the effects of the three mixtures, five poults were given feed A, six were given feed B, and five were given feed C over a 3-week period. Test at the .05 level the hypothesis that there is no effect of feed mixture on weight.

Weight (in pounds)		
Feed Mixture A	**Feed Mixture B**	**Feed Mixture C**
11.2	12.6	11.3
12.1	10.8	11.9
10.9	11.3	12.4
11.3	11.0	10.6
12.0	12.0	12.0
	10.7	

LO16-6

Test and interpret a nonparametric hypothesis test of correlation.

Rank-Order Correlation

In Chapter 13 we described the correlation coefficient. Recall that it measures the association between two interval- or ratio-scaled variables. For example, the correlation coefficient reports the association between the salary of executives and their years of experience, or the association between the number of miles a shipment had to travel and the number of days it took to arrive at its destination. The correlation coefficient is a versatile measure of association. However, there are several conditions when it is not appropriate or can be misleading. Those conditions include:

1. When the scale of measurement of one of the two variables is ordinal (ranked).
2. When the relationship between the variables is not linear.
3. When one or more of the data points are quite different from the others.

Charles Spearman, a British statistician, introduced a measure of correlation for ranked data. This measure allows us to describe the relationship between sets of ranked data. For example, two staff members in the Office of Research at the University of the Valley are asked to rank 10 faculty research proposals for funding purposes. We want to study the association between the ratings of the two staff members. That is, do the two staff members rate the same proposals as the most worthy and the least worthy of funding?

This coefficient of rank correlation is also applied to conditions 2 and 3 just listed. Instead of using the actual values in the data set, we rank the sample data and compute a correlation between the rankings. Like Pearson's coefficient of correlation described in Chapter 13, it can range from -1.00 up to 1.00. Values of -1.00 or 1.00 indicate perfect association between the ranks. A value of 0 indicates no association between the two variables. Values of $-.84$ and $.84$ both exhibit the same amount of association but $-.84$ indicates an inverse relationship and $.84$ a direct relationship. We denote Spearman's coefficient of rank correlation as r_s. Formula (16–3) is used to compute it. Note that rankings can begin by assigning the largest value a rank of 1 or the smallest value with a rank of 1. Use the same ranking method for both variables. The resulting rank correlation is the same. In this text, we assign the smallest values with a rank of 1.

SPEARMAN'S COEFFICIENT OF RANK CORRELATION	$r_s = 1 - \dfrac{6\Sigma d^2}{n(n^2 - 1)}$	**[16–3]**

where:

d is the difference between the ranks for each pair.
n is the number of paired observations.

The following Example/Solution provides the details of computing the coefficient of rank correlation.

▶ **EXAMPLE**

A recent study investigated the relationship between the age of a licensed driver and the number of miles driven last week. Table 16–9 reports the information from this study for a sample of 15 drivers.

TABLE 16–9 Age and Miles Driven for a Sample of 15 Drivers

Name	Age	Miles	Name	Age	Miles
Spina, Sal	28	412	Koppel, Marty	21	410
Gordon, Ray	50	151	Rowatti, Marty	45	203
Schnur, Roberta	44	146	Monahan, Joyce	52	266
Alvear, Jose	32	108	Lanoue, Bernie	33	289
Myers, Tom	55	672	Roll, Judy	19	586
Lyons, George	60	91	Goodall, Jody	17	472
Harbin, Joe	38	222	Broderick, Ron	21	299
Bobko, Jack	22	169			

1. Draw a scatter diagram. Plot age on the horizontal axis and miles driven on the vertical axis.
2. What type of association do the sample data suggest—strong or weak, direct or inverse?
3. Do you see any issues with the relationship between the variables?
4. Find the coefficient of rank correlation.
5. Conduct a test of hypothesis to determine if there is a statistically significant negative association between the ranks.

SOLUTION

Our first step is to create a scatter diagram, shown in Chart 16–3, to better understand the relationship between the two variables.

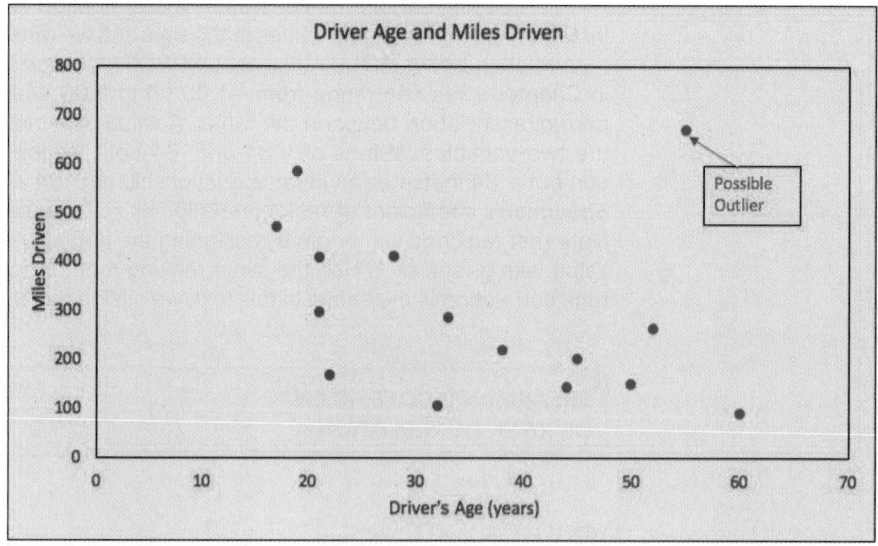

CHART 16–3 Scatter Diagram of Miles Driven Versus Driver's Age

The graph suggests an inverse relationship between the driver's age and the miles driven. That is, as the variable age increases, the miles driven decrease. We can confirm this observation by using statistical software to determine the coefficient of correlation as described in Chapter 13. The correlation coefficient is −.305, which indicates a moderate inverse relationship. But there is a potential problem. Tom Meyers is 55 years old, but he drove 672 miles! He appears to be different from the others in the sample. An outlier observation such as this can affect the correlation coefficient. An appropriate remedy is to use ranks instead of the actual values. So, we rank the driver's age from youngest to oldest and rank the miles driven from smallest to largest, then compute the correlation between the ranked values. The effect of this strategy is to reduce the impact of the one apparent outlier observation.

To calculate the coefficient of rank correlation, we first rank the individuals by age. Jody Goodall is the youngest, she is 17, so she is ranked 1. The next youngest is Judy Roll, so she is ranked 2. There are two drivers, Marty Koppel and Ron Broderick, who are 21 years old. This tie is resolved by giving each a rank of 3.5, which is the average of ranks 3 and 4. The oldest driver in the sample is George Lyons; he is given a rank of 15. The same ranking strategy is used for miles driven. George Lyons drove the fewest miles, so he has the rank of 1. Jose Alvear is next with 108 minutes, so he has a driving distance rank of 2. All the ranking data are shown in Table 16–10.

Moving to the right, column d is the difference for each observation in the ranked data. So, for Sal Spina he has a rank of 6 for age and 12 for miles driven. Subtracting the miles driven rank from the age rank results in a d-value of −6. This difference is squared, hence 36 is in column d^2. This procedure is done for each row and the d^2 column is totaled. The result is 812.5, which is needed to compute the coefficient of rank correlation [formula (16–3)].

TABLE 16–10 Age and Driving Distance, Ranks, Rank Differences, and Differences Squared

Name	Age	Miles	Age Rank	Miles Rank	Difference in Ranks d	Difference Squared d^2
Spina, Sal	28	412	6	12	−6	36
Gordon, Ray	50	151	12	4	8	64
Schnur, Roberta	44	146	10	3	7	49
Alvear, Jose	32	108	7	2	5	25
Myers, Tom	55	672	14	15	−1	1
Lyons, George	60	91	15	1	14	196
Harbin, Joe	38	222	9	7	2	4
Bobko, Jack	22	169	5	5	0	0
Koppel, Marty	21	410	3.5	11	−7.5	56.25
Rowatti, Marty	45	203	11	6	5	25
Monahan, Joyce	52	266	13	8	5	25
Lanoue, Bernie	33	289	8	9	−1	1
Roll, Judy	19	586	2	14	−12	144
Goodall, Jody	17	472	1	13	−12	144
Broderick, Ron	21	299	3.5	10	−6.5	42.25
					Sum $d^2 =$	812.5

The coefficient of rank correlation is −.451, found by using formula (16-3):

$$r_s = 1 - \frac{6\Sigma d^2}{n(n^2 - 1)} = 1 - \frac{6(812.5)}{15(15^2 - 1)} = 1 - 1.451 = -.451$$

The coefficient of rank correlation is −.451 and it indicates an inverse relationship between the ranks of the two variables. It also indicates that there is a stronger correlation among the ranks than the actual data, −.305 versus −.451. The effect of the outlier point has been reduced.

Testing the Significance of r_s

Next, based on the ranks, we test the hypothesis that there is no relationship between age and miles driven. The null and the alternate hypotheses are:

H_0: The rank correlation in the population is zero.
H_1: There is a negative association among the ranks.

The sampling distribution of r_s follows the t-distribution with $n - 2$ degrees of freedom. Notice that the alternate hypothesis states a one-tailed test. We decide to use the .05 significance level. The rejection region is in the left tail. Using the t-table in Appendix B.5 with $n - 2 = 15 - 2 = 13$ degrees of freedom, the decision rule is to reject the null hypothesis if the computed t-value is less than -1.771. We use formula (16–4) to compute the t-test statistic:

HYPOTHESIS TEST, RANK CORRELATION	$t = r_s \sqrt{\dfrac{n - 2}{1 - r_s^2}}$	**(16–4)**

Using the values for n and r_s, the test statistic is computed as:

$$t = r_s \sqrt{\frac{n - 2}{1 - r_s^2}} = -.451 \sqrt{\frac{15 - 2}{1 - (-.451)^2}} = -1.822$$

The computed t-statistic of -1.822 is less than -1.771; the p-value is .0458 and is less than .05. Therefore, the null hypothesis is rejected, and the alternate hypothesis is accepted. There is evidence of a statistically significant inverse association between driver's age and miles driven.

SELF-REVIEW 16–6

A sample of individuals applying for manufacturing jobs at Davis Enterprises revealed the following scores on an eye perception test (X) and a mechanical aptitude test (Y):

Subject	Eye Perception	Mechanical Aptitude	Subject	Eye Perception	Mechanical Aptitude
001	805	23	006	810	28
002	777	62	007	805	30
003	820	60	008	840	42
004	682	40	009	777	55
005	777	70	010	820	51

(a) Compute the coefficient of rank correlation between eye perception and mechanical aptitude.
(b) At the .05 significance level, can we conclude that the correlation in the population is different from 0?

EXERCISES

21. **FILE** At the Warren County Fair, one of the animal events was evaluating hogs on several criteria. Based on the criteria the hogs were rank ordered. Wally Sedwick, director of the Warren County Fair, and Denise Heban, a member of a high school 4-H club, evaluated and ranked the same hogs. Following are the results. Using correlation analysis, evaluate the consistency of the two raters by answering the following items.

Hog	Ranks Director	Ranks 4-H Member
Lois	7	3
Eddie	5	9
Ralph	6	5
Charley	10	7
Gert	14	13
Francis	4	1
Willie	3	10
Homer	1	6
Winston	9	4
Wanda	2	12
Walter	12	2
Connie	13	11
Doris	8	8
George	15	14
Bonnie	11	15

a. Explain why Spearman's rank correlation is the appropriate measure of association.
b. Draw a scatter diagram. Place Director's ranking on the horizontal axis and 4-H Member's ranking on the vertical axis. Do any of the points seem to be outliers?
c. Compute the coefficient of rank correlation.
d. At the .05 significance level, can we conclude there is agreement between the raters?

22. **FILE** Far West University offers both day and evening classes in business administration. A survey of students inquires how they perceive the prestige associated with eight careers. A day student was asked to rank the careers from 1 to 8, with 1 having the most prestige and 8 the least prestige. An evening student was asked to do the same. The results follow:

Carrer	Ranking by Day Student	Ranking by Evening Student	Carrer	Ranking by Day Student	Ranking by Evening Student
Accountant	6	3	Business analytics	1	7
Computer programmer	7	2	Marketing researcher	4	8
Branch bank manager	2	6	Stock analyst	3	5
Hospital administrator	5	4	Production manager	8	1

Find Spearman's coefficient of rank correlation.

23. **FILE** Ten new sales representatives for Clark Sprocket and Chain Inc. were required to attend a training program before being assigned to a regional sales office. At the end of the program, the representatives took a series of tests and the scores were ranked. For example, Arden had the lowest test score and is ranked 1; Arbuckle had the highest test score and is ranked 10. At the end of the first sales year, the representatives' ranks based on test scores were paired with their first-year sales.

Representative	Annual Sales ($ thousands)	Ranking in Training Program	Representative	Annual Sales ($ thousands)	Ranking in Training Program
Kitchen	319	8	Arden	300	1
Bond	150	2	Crane	280	6
Gross	175	5	Arthur	200	9
Arbuckle	460	10	Keene	190	4
Greene	348	7	Knopf	300	3

a. Compute and interpret the coefficient of rank correlation between first-year sales and class rank after the training program.

b. At the .05 significance level, can we conclude that there is a positive association between first-year sales dollars and ranking in the training program?

24. **FILE** Suppose Texas A & M University—Commerce has five scholarships available for the women's basketball team. The head coach provided the two assistant coaches with the names of 10 high school players with potential to play at the university. The coaches attended three games and evaluated each player's defense, dribbling, passing, rebounding, shooting, and court sense. Each coach computed an overall score for each player. Then each coach ranked the players based on the overall score. The data follow:

Player	Rank, by Assistant Coach Jean Cann	John Cannelli	Player	Rank, by Assistant Coach Jean Cann	John Cannelli
Mia Seiple	7	5	Desiray Cooke	3	1
Chania Jones	2	4	Rita Schott	5	7
Lele Staley	10	10	Dyani Lockes	4	2
Chania Hall	1	3	Destanni Henderson	8	9
Carmalita Boston	6	6	Jordyn Beal	9	8

a. For the rankings, compute Spearman's rank correlation coefficient. At the .05 significance level, test the hypothesis that the correlation is less than or equal to zero, that is, there is no agreement between the coach's rankings.

b. Based on the hypothesis test, do the coaches agree on the player rankings?

CHAPTER SUMMARY

I. The sign test is based on the sign difference between two related observations.
   A. No assumptions need to be made about the shape of the two populations.
   B. It is based on paired or dependent samples.
   C. For small samples, find the number of plus or minus signs and refer to the binomial distribution for the critical value.

II. The median test is used to test a hypothesis about a population median.
   A. The binomial distribution is the test statistic.
   B. Use the number of observations and .50 as the probability of a success to determine the values of the binomial distribution.

III. The Wilcoxon signed-rank test is a nonparametric test for differences between two dependent populations.
   A. The assumption of normally distributed populations is not required.
   B. The steps to conduct the test are:
      1. Rank absolute differences between the related observations.
      2. Apply the sign of the differences to the ranks.
      3. Sum negative ranks and positive ranks.
      4. The smaller of the two sums is the computed T-value.
      5. Refer to Appendix B.8 for the critical value, and make a decision regarding H_0.

IV. The Wilcoxon rank-sum test is used to test a hypothesis that two independent samples were collected from the same population.
   A. The assumption of normally distributed populations is not required.
   B. The data must be at least ordinal scale.
   C. Each sample must contain at least eight observations.
   D. To determine the value of the test statistic W, the sample observations are ranked from low to high as if they were from a single group.
   E. The sum of ranks for each of the two samples is determined.

F. W is used to compute z, where W is the sum of the ranks for population 1.

$$z = \frac{W - \dfrac{n_1(n_1 + n_2 + 1)}{2}}{\sqrt{\dfrac{n_1 n_2 (n_1 + n_2 + 1)}{12}}} \qquad (16\text{--}1)$$

G. The standard normal distribution, found in Appendix B.3, is the test statistic.

V. The Kruskal-Wallis one-way ANOVA by ranks is used to test whether several population distributions are the same.

  A. The assumption of normally distributed populations is not required.

  B. The populations must be independent and at least ordinal scale.

  C. The sample observations are ranked from smallest to largest as though they were a single group.

  D. The test statistic follows the chi-square distribution, provided there are at least five observations in each sample.

  E. The value of the test statistic is computed from the following:

$$H = \frac{12}{n(n+1)}\left[\frac{(\Sigma R_1)^2}{n_1} + \frac{(\Sigma R_2)^2}{n_2} + \cdots + \frac{(\Sigma R_k)^2}{n_k}\right] - 3(n+1) \qquad (16\text{--}2)$$

VI. Spearman's coefficient of rank correlation is a measure of the association between two ordinal-scale variables.

  A. It can range from -1 up to 1.

  1. A value of 0 indicates there is no association between the variables.

  2. A value of -1 indicates perfect negative correlation, and 1 indicates perfect positive correlation.

  B. The value of r_s is computed from the following formula.

$$r_s = 1 - \frac{6\Sigma d^2}{n(n^2 - 1)} \qquad (16\text{--}3)$$

  C. Provided the sample size is at least 10, we can conduct a test of hypothesis using the following formula:

$$t = r_s \sqrt{\frac{n-2}{1 - r_s^2}} \qquad (16\text{--}4)$$

  1. The test statistic follows the t-distribution.

  2. There are $n - 2$ degrees of freedom.

PRONUNCIATION KEY

SYMBOL	MEANING	PRONUNCIATION
$(\Sigma R_1)^2$	Square of the total of the first column ranks	*Sigma R sub 1 squared*
r_s	Spearman's coefficient of rank correlation	*r sub s*

CHAPTER EXERCISES

25. The vice president of programming at NBC is finalizing the prime-time schedule for the fall and has decided to include a hospital drama but is unsure which of the two possibilities to select. The VP has a pilot called *The Surgeon* and another called *Critical Care*. To help the VP make a final decision, a sample of 20 viewers from throughout the United States was asked to watch the two pilots and indicate which show they prefer. The results were that 12 liked *The Surgeon*, 7 liked *Critical Care*, and 1 had no preference. Is there a preference for one of the two shows? Use the .10 significance level.

26. A large corporation is going to award a contract for fine-line pens to be used nationally in its offices. Two suppliers, Bic and Pilot, have submitted bids. To determine the preference of office personnel, a preference test was conducted using a randomly selected sample of 20 employees. The .05 level of significance is to be used.
    a. If the alternate hypothesis states that Bic is preferred over Pilot, is the sign test to be conducted as a one-tailed or a two-tailed test? Explain.
    b. As each of the sampled employees told the researchers his or her preference, a "+" was recorded if it was Bic and a "−" if it was the Pilot fine-line pen. A count of the pluses revealed that 12 employees preferred Bic, 5 preferred Pilot, and 3 were undecided. What is n?
    c. What is the decision rule in words?
    d. What conclusion did you reach regarding pen preference? Explain.

27. Cornwall and Hudson, a large retail department store, wants to handle just one brand of MP3 player. The list has been narrowed to two brands: TIMMKOO and Dyzeryk. To help make a decision, a panel of 16 audio experts met. A music track using the TIMMKOO player was played. Then the same track was played using the Dyzeryk player. A "+" in the following table indicates an individual's preference for the TIMMKOO player, a "−" indicates preference for the Dyzeryk player, and a 0 signifies no preference.

Expert															
1	2	3	4	5	6	7	8	9	10	11	12	13	14	15	16
+	−	+	−	+	+	−	0	−	+	−	+	+	−	+	−

Conduct a test of hypothesis at the .10 significance level to determine whether there is a difference in preference between the two brands.

28. The Greater Jacksonville, Florida, Real Estate Association claims that the median rental for three-bedroom condominiums is more than $1,200 a month. A random sample of 30 units showed 5 rented for exactly $1,200 a month, and 18 rented for more than $1,200. At the .05 level, can we conclude that the median rental is more than $1,200?
    a. State H_0 and H_1.
    b. Give the decision rule.
    c. Do the necessary calculations and arrive at a decision.

29. The Citrus Council of America wants to determine whether consumers prefer orange juice with or without pulp. A random sample of 22 consumers was selected. Each member of the sample tasted a small, unlabeled cup of orange juice with pulp and a cup of orange juice without pulp. Of the 22 consumers, 2 said they had no preference, 5 preferred juice with pulp, and the remainder liked the juice without pulp better. Test at the .05 level that the preferences for orange juice with pulp and orange juice without pulp are equal.

30. **FILE** The objective of a community research project is to determine whether women are more community conscious before marriage or after 5 years of marriage. A test designed to measure community consciousness was administered to a sample of nine women before marriage, and the same test was given to them 5 years after marriage. The test scores are:

Name	Before Marriage	After Marriage	Name	Before Marriage	After Marriage
Beth	110	114	Sawyer	186	196
Ari	157	159	Landry	116	116
Blake	121	120	Ezra	160	140
Chandler	96	103	Milan	149	142
Quinn	130	139			

Test at the .05 level. H_0 is: There is no difference in community consciousness before and after marriage. H_1 is: There is a difference.

31. **FILE** Is there a difference in the annual divorce rates in rural counties among three geographic regions, namely, the Southwest, the Southeast, and the Northwest?

Test at the .05 level. Annual divorce rates per 1,000 population for five randomly selected counties in the Southwest, six counties in the Southeast, and five counties in the Northwest are:

Southwest:	5.9, 6.2, 7.9, 8.6, 4.6
Southeast:	5.0, 6.4, 7.3, 6.2, 8.1, 5.1
Northwest:	6.7, 6.2, 4.9, 8.0, 5.5

32. **FILE** The production manager of MPS Audio Systems Inc. is concerned about the idle time of workers. In particular, the manager would like to know if there is a difference in the idle minutes for workers on the day shift and the evening shift. The table shows the number of idle minutes yesterday for the five day-shift workers and the six evening-shift workers. Use the .05 significance level.

Day Shift	Evening Shift
92	96
103	114
116	80
81	82
89	88
	91

33. **FILE** Drs. Trythall and Kerns are studying the mobility of executives in selected industries. Their research measures mobility using a score based on the number of times an executive has moved, changed companies, or changed jobs within a company over the last 10 years. The highest number of points is awarded for moving and changing companies; the fewest, for changing jobs within a company and not moving. They randomly sampled five executives in the chemical industry, six in the retail industry, five in the Internet industry, and five in the aerospace industry. The distribution of scores does not follow the normal probability distribution. Develop an appropriate test to determine if there is a difference in the mobility scores in the four industries. Use the .05 significance level.

Chemical	Retail	Internet	Aerospace
4	3	62	30
17	12	40	38
8	40	81	46
20	17	96	40
16	31	76	21
	19		

34. **FILE** A series of questions on sports and world events was asked of 14 randomly selected young adult naturalized citizens. The results were translated into sports and world events "knowledge" scores. The scores were:

Citizen	Sports	World Events	Citizen	Sports	World Events
J. C. Garcia	47	49	L. M. Zaugg	87	75
A. N. Baker	12	10	J. B. Simon	59	86
B. B. Beebe	62	76	J. Goulden	40	61
L. D. Li	81	92	A. A. Fernandez	87	18
C. A. Diaz	90	86	A. M. Carbo	16	75
J. N. McLeod	35	42	A. O. Smithy	50	51
A. F. Bertrand	61	61	J. J. Pascal	60	61

a. Determine the degree of association between how the citizens ranked with respect to knowledge of sports and how they ranked on world events.

b. At the .05 significance level, is the rank correlation between the sports and world events "knowledge" scores greater than zero?

35. **FILE** Early in the basketball season, 12 college teams appeared to be outstanding. A panel of sportswriters and a panel of college basketball coaches were asked to rank the 12 teams. Their composite rankings were as follows:

Team	Coaches	Sportswriters	Team	Coaches	Sportswriters
Duke	1	1	Syracuse	7	10
UNLV	2	5	Georgetown	8	11
Indiana	3	4	Villanova	9	7
North Carolina	4	6	LSU	10	12
Louisville	5	3	St. Johns	11	8
Ohio State	6	2	Michigan	12	9

Determine the correlation between the rankings of the coaches and the sportswriters. At the .05 significance level, can we conclude there is a positive correlation between the rankings?

36. **FILE** Professor Bert Forman believes the students who complete his examinations in the shortest time receive the highest grades and those who take the longest to complete them receive the lowest grades. To verify his suspicion, he assigns a rank to the order of finish and then grades the examinations. The results are as follows:

Student	Order of Completion	Score (50 possible)	Student	Order of Completion	Score (50 possible)
Gromney	1	48	Smythe	7	39
Bates	2	48	Arquette	8	30
MacDonald	3	43	Govito	9	37
Sosa	4	49	Gankowski	10	35
Harris	5	50	Bonfigilo	11	36
Cribb	6	47	Matsui	12	33

Convert the test scores to a rank and find the coefficient of rank correlation between the order of completion and the rank of the test score. At the .05 significance level, can Professor Forman conclude there is a positive association between the order of finish and the test scores?

DATA ANALYTICS

(The data for these exercises are available at the text website: **www.mhhe.com/Lind19e.**)

37. The North Valley Real Estate data report information on homes on the market.

a. Use an appropriate nonparametric test to determine whether there is a difference in the typical selling price of the homes among the townships. Assume the selling prices are not normally distributed. Use the .05 significance level.

b. Combine the homes with six or more bedrooms into one group and determine whether there is a difference according to the number of bedrooms in the typical selling prices of the homes. Use the .05 significance level and assume the distribution of selling prices is not normally distributed.

c. Compare the distribution of FICO scores for fixed and variable mortgages. FICO scores are people's credit rating. Higher ratings indicate better credit. Can we conclude there is a difference in the distributions of FICO scores based on the type of mortgage? Use the .05 significance level.

38. Refer to the Baseball 2021 data, which report information on the 2021 Major League Baseball season.

    a. Rank the teams by the number of wins and their total team salary. Compute the coefficient of rank correlation between the two variables. At the .01 significance level, can you conclude that it is greater than zero?

    b. Assume that the distributions of team salaries for the American League and National League do not follow the normal distribution. Conduct a test of hypothesis to see whether there is a difference in the two distributions.

    c. Rank the 30 teams by attendance and by team salary. Determine the coefficient of rank correlation between these two variables. At the .05 significance level, is it reasonable to conclude the ranks of these two variables are related?

39. Refer to the Lincolnville School District school bus data.

    a. Assume the distribution of the maintenance cost for the bus capacities does not follow a normal distribution. Conduct a test of hypothesis at the .05 significance level to determine whether the distributions differ.

    b. Assume the distribution of the maintenance cost for the fuel types, diesel or gasoline, does not follow a normal distribution. Conduct a test of hypothesis at the .05 significance level to determine whether the distributions differ.

    c. Assume the distribution of the maintenance cost for the three bus manufacturers does not follow a normal distribution. Conduct a test of hypothesis at the .05 significance level to determine whether the distributions differ.

A REVIEW OF CHAPTERS 15–16

In Chapters 15 and 16, we describe statistical methods to study data that are either the nominal or the ordinal scale of measurement. These methods are referred to as *nonparametric* or *distribution-free* statistics. They do not require assumptions regarding the shape of the population. Recall, for example, in Chapter 12 when investigating the means of several populations, we assume the populations follow the normal probability distribution.

We begin Chapter 15 by using the chi-square distribution to compare an observed set of frequencies with the corresponding set of expected frequencies. The level of measurement is either the nominal or ordinal scale. We use the chi-square distribution to investigate an instance where there are several possible nominal-scale outcomes. A gasoline purchaser can buy regular, midgrade, or premium. Recall that when data are measured at the nominal level, the observations can only be classified according to some label, name, or characteristic.

In Chapter 15, we also explore the relationship between two variables in a contingency table. That is, we observe two characteristics of each sampled individual or object. For example, is there a relationship between the quality of the product (acceptable or unacceptable) and the shift when it was manufactured (day, afternoon, or night)? The chi-square distribution is the test statistic.

In Chapter 16, we describe five nonparametric tests of hypothesis and the coefficient of rank correlation. Each of these tests requires at least the ordinal scale of measurement. That is, we are able to rank, or order, the variables of interest.

The *sign test* for dependent samples is based on the sign of the difference between related observations. The binomial distribution is the test statistic. The binomial distribution is also used when testing a *hypothesis about the median* of a distribution.

The *Wilcoxon signed-rank test* requires dependent samples. It is an extension of the sign test in that it makes use of both the direction and the magnitude of the difference between related values. It has its own sampling distribution, which is reported in Appendix B.8.

The *Wilcoxon ranked-sum test* assumes independent populations, but does not require the populations to follow the normal probability distribution. It is an alternative to the *t*-test for independent samples described in Chapter 11. When there are at least eight observations in each sample, the test statistic is the standard normal distribution.

The *Kruskal-Wallis test* is an extension of the Wilcoxon ranked-sum test in that it handles more than two populations. It is an alternative to the one-way ANOVA method described in Chapter 12. It does not require the populations to follow the normal probability distribution or to have equal standard deviations. The chi-square distribution is used as the test statistic.

The statistic *Spearman's coefficient of rank correlation* is a special case of the Pearson coefficient of correlation, described in Chapter 13. It is based on the correlation between the *ranks* of related observations. It may range from −1.00 to 1.00, with 0 indicating no association between the ranks.

PROBLEMS

1. The owner of Beach Front Snow Cones Inc. believes the median number of snow cones sold per day between Memorial Day and Labor Day is 60. The table shows the number of snowcones sold on 20 randomly selected days. Is it reasonable to conclude that the median is actually greater than 60? Use the .05 significance level.

65	70	65	64	66	54	68	61	62	67
65	50	64	55	74	57	67	72	66	65

2. The manufacturer of children's raincoats wants to know if there is a preference among children for blue, red, green, or yellow raincoats. The table shows color preference for a sample of 50 children between the ages of 6 and 10. Use the .05 significance level to investigate.

Color	Frequency
Blue	17
Red	8
Green	12
Yellow	13

3. Is there a difference in the length of suspension bridges in the northeast, southeast, and far west parts of the United States? The following table shows the lengths (in feet) of seven randomly sampled bridges in the northeast, nine bridges in the southeast, and eight bridges in the far west. Conduct an appropriate test of hypothesis on the following data. Do not assume the bridge lengths follow a normal probability distribution. Use the .05 significance level.

Northeast	Southeast	Far West
3,645	3,502	3,547
3,727	3,645	3,636
3,772	3,718	3,659
3,837	3,746	3,673
3,873	3,758	3,728
3,882	3,845	3,736
3,894	3,940	3,788
	4,070	3,802
	4,081	

4. Research by the First Bank of Illinois revealed that 8% of its customers wait more than 5 minutes for a teller in a bank lobby. Management considers this reasonable and will not add more tellers unless the proportion of those waiting longer than 5 minutes becomes larger than 8%. The branch manager at the Litchfield Branch believes that the wait is longer than the standard at her branch and requested additional part-time tellers. To support her request, she found that, in a sample of 100 customers, 10 waited more than 5 minutes. At the .01 significance level, is it reasonable to conclude that the 8% assumption is not correct at the Litchfield Branch?

CASES

A. Century National Bank

Is there a relationship between the location of the branch bank and whether the customer has a debit card? Based on the information available, develop a table that shows the relationship between these two variables. At the .05 significance level, can we conclude there is a relationship between the branch location and whether the customer uses a debit card?

B. Thomas Testing Labs

John Thomas, the owner of Thomas Testing, has for some time done contract work for insurance companies regarding drunk driving. To improve his research capabilities, he recently purchased the Rupple Driving Simulator. This device will allow a subject to take a "road test" and provide a score indicating the number of driving errors committed during the test drive. Higher scores indicate more driving errors. Driving errors would include not coming to a complete stop at a stop sign, not using turning signals, not exercising caution on wet or snowy pavement, and so on. During the road test, problems appear at random and not all problems appear in each road test. These are major advantages to the Rupple Driving Simulator because subjects do not gain any advantage by taking the test several times.

With the new driving simulator, Mr. Thomas would like to study in detail the problem of drunk driving. He begins by selecting a random sample of 25 drivers. He asks each of the selected individuals to take the test drive on the Rupple Driving Simulator. The number of errors for each driver is recorded. Next, he has each of the individuals in the group drink three 16-ounce cans of beer in a 60-minute period and return to the Rupple

Driving Simulator for another test drive. The number of driving errors after drinking the beer is also shown. The research question is: Does alcohol impair the driver's ability and, therefore, increase the number of driving errors?

Mr. Thomas believes the distribution of scores on the test drive does not follow a normal distribution and, therefore, a nonparametric test should be used. Because the observations are paired, he decides to use both the sign test and the Wilcoxon signed-rank test.

	Driving Errors			Driving Errors	
Subject	Without Alcohol	With Alcohol	Subject	Without Alcohol	With Alcohol
1	75	89	14	72	106
2	78	83	15	83	89
3	89	80	16	99	89
4	100	90	17	75	77
5	85	84	18	58	78
6	70	68	19	93	108
7	64	84	20	69	69
8	79	104	21	86	84
9	83	81	22	97	86
10	82	88	23	65	92
11	83	93	24	96	97
12	84	92	25	85	94
13	80	103			

a. Compare the results using these two procedures. Conduct an appropriate test of hypothesis to determine if alcohol is related to driving errors.
b. Write a report that summarizes your findings.

PRACTICE TEST

Part 1—Objective

1. The _____ level of measurement is required for the chi-square goodness-of-fit test.   1. _____
2. Which of the following is *not* a characteristic of the chi-square distribution? (positively skewed, based on degrees of freedom, cannot be negative, at least 30 observations)   2. _____
3. In a contingency table, how many traits are considered for each observation?   3. _____
4. In a contingency table, there are four rows and three columns. How many degrees of freedom are there?   4. _____
5. In a goodness-of-fit test, the critical value of chi-square is based on _____. (sample size, number of categories, number of variables, none of these)   5. _____
6. In a sign test, are the samples dependent or independent?   6. _____
7. In a sign test of eight paired observations, the test statistic is the _____ distribution. (binomial, *z, t,* chi-square)   7. _____
8. What is the major difference between the Kruskal-Wallis test and the Wilcoxon rank-sum test? (one is based on dependent samples and the other independent samples, one is for comparing two independent samples and the other two or more independent samples)   8. _____
9. Under what conditions can the coefficient of rank correlation be less than −1.00?   9. _____
10. The Kruskal-Wallis test is used in place of ANOVA when which two of the following criteria are not met? (normal population, equal standard deviations, more than 12 items in the sample, the populations are independent)   10. _____

Part 2—Problems

Use the standard six-step hypothesis testing procedure.

1. A recent census report indicated that 65% of families have two parents present, 20% have only a mother present, 10% have only a father present, and 5% have no parent present. A random sample of 200 children from a large rural school district revealed the following frequencies of children with two parents, mother only, father only, no parent, and the total of 200.

Two Parents	Mother Only	Father Only	No Parent	Total
120	40	30	10	200

Is there sufficient evidence to conclude that the proportion of families by type of parent present in this particular school district differs from those reported in the recent census?

2. A book publisher wants to investigate the type of book selected for recreational reading by males and females. A random sample of 540 males and 500 females provided the following information regarding their preferences for mystery, romance, or self-help books. At the .05 significance level, should we conclude that sex is related or unrelated to type of book selected?

	Mystery	Romance	Self-Help	Total
Male	250	100	190	540
Female	130	170	200	500

3. An instructor has three sections of basic statistics: 8:00 a.m., 10:00 a.m., and 1:30 p.m. Listed are the grades on the first exam for each section. Assume that the distributions do not follow the normal probability distribution. At the .05 significance level, is there a difference in the distributions of scores?

8 a.m.	10 a.m.	1:30 p.m.
68	59	67
84	59	69
75	63	75
78	62	76
70	78	79
77	76	83
88	80	86
71		86
		87

4. According to a study in *Health Magazine,* one in three children in the United States is obese. A health practitioner in Louisiana sampled 600 children and found 230 who were obese or overweight. Does this evidence suggest that the actual frequency of obese children is different from one out of three? Use the .01 significance level.

Index Numbers

17

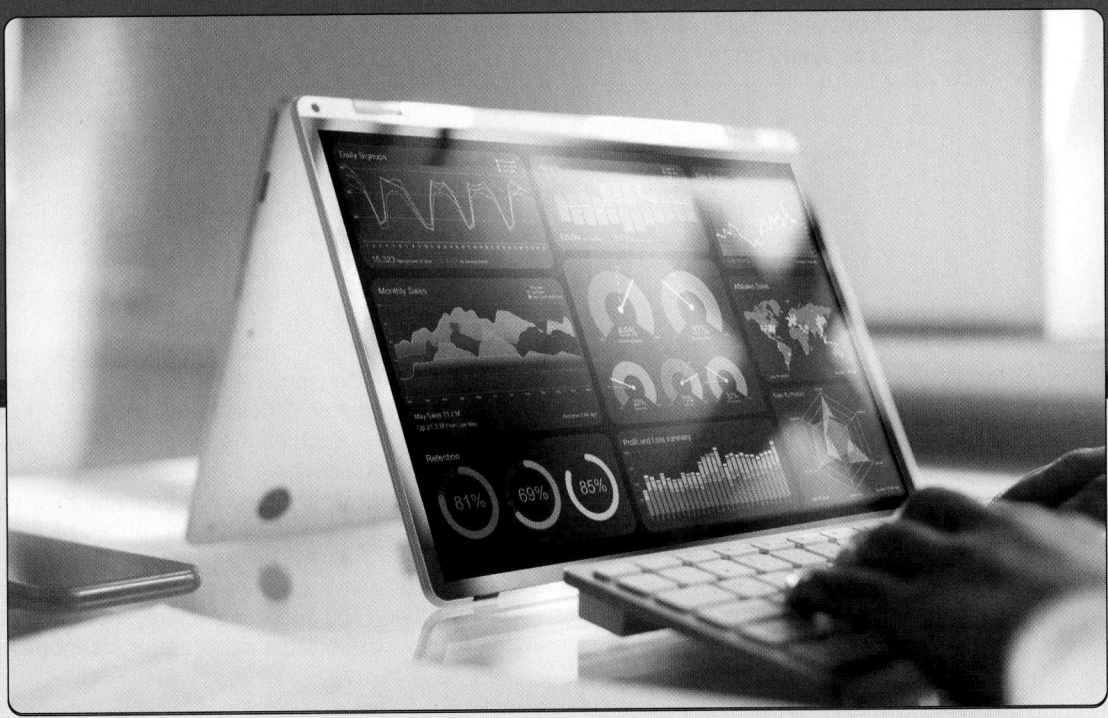

Andrey_Popov/Shutterstock12

▲ **INFORMATION ON PRICES** and quantities for margarine, shortening, milk, and potato chips for 2012 and 2022 is provided in Exercise 27. Compute a simple price index for each of the four items, using 2012 as the base period. (See Exercise 27 and **LO17-1**.)

LEARNING OBJECTIVES

When you have completed this chapter, you will be able to:

LO17-1 Compute and interpret a simple, unweighted index.

LO17-2 Compute and interpret an unweighted aggregate index.

LO17-3 Compute and interpret a weighted aggregate index.

LO17-4 List and describe special-purpose indexes.

LO17-5 Apply the Consumer Price Index.

Introduction

In this chapter, we will examine a useful descriptive tool called an **index.** An index expresses the relative change in a value from one period to another. No doubt you are familiar with indexes such as the **Consumer Price Index,** which is released monthly by the U.S. Department of Labor. There are many other indexes, such as the **Dow Jones Industrial Average** (DJIA), **NASDAQ, NIKKEI 225,** and **Standard & Poor's 500 Stock Average.** Indexes are published on a regular basis by the federal government, by business publications such as *Bloomberg Businessweek* and *Forbes,* in most daily newspapers, and on the Internet.

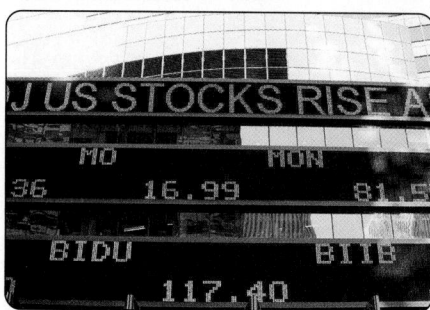

Image Source/Getty Images

Of what importance is an index? Why is the Consumer Price Index so important and so widely reported? As the name implies, it measures the change in the price of a large group of items consumers purchase. The Federal Reserve Board, consumer groups, unions, management, senior citizens organizations, and others in business and economics are concerned about changes in prices. These groups closely monitor the Consumer Price Index as well as the **Producer Price Index,** which measures price fluctuations at all stages of production. To combat sharp price increases, the Federal Reserve often raises the interest rate to "cool down" the economy. Likewise, the DJIA which is updated continuously during the business day, describes the overall change in common stock prices of 30 large companies.

A few stock market indexes appear daily in the financial section of most news papers. Many are also reported in real time. The following figure shows the DJIA, NASDAQ, and other indexes from the MSN website (**https.msn.com/en-us/money**).

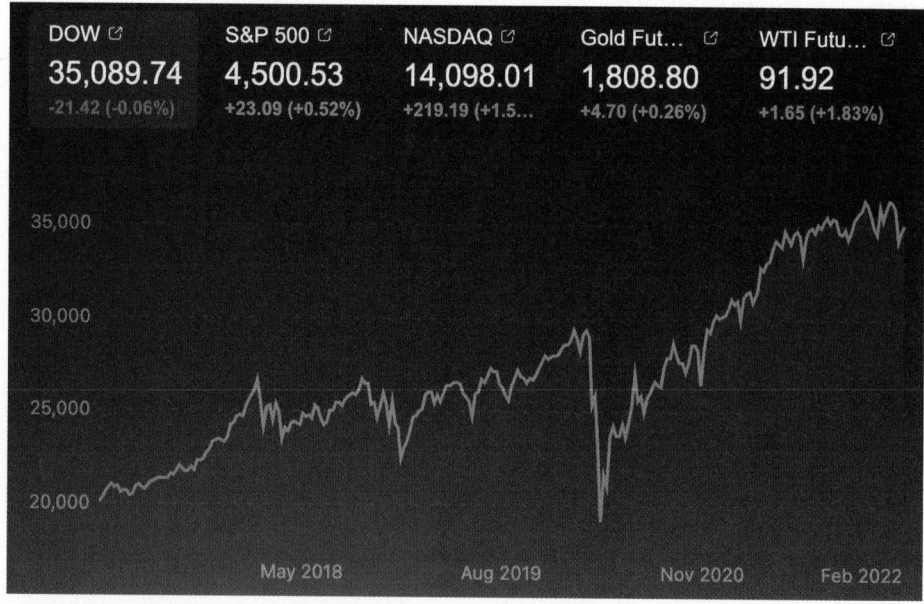

Dow Jones & Company

LO17-1

Compute and interpret a simple, unweighted index.

Simple Index Numbers

What is an **index number?** An index or index number measures the change in a particular item (typically a product or service) between two time periods.

> **INDEX NUMBER** A number that expresses the relative change in price, quantity, or value compared to a base period.

If the index number is used to measure the relative change in just one variable, such as hourly wages in manufacturing, we refer to this as a simple index. It is the ratio of two variables converted to a percentage. The following Example/Solutions illustrate the use of index numbers. As noted in the definition, the main use of an index number in business is to show the percent change in one or more items from one time period to another.

▶ **EXAMPLE**

According to the Bureau of Labor Statistics, the average hourly earnings of production workers in August 2011 was $23.07. In August 2021, the preliminary estimate of hourly wages increased to $30.73. What is the index of hourly earnings of production workers for August 2021 based on 2011 data?

SOLUTION

It is 133.20, found by:

$$P = \frac{\text{Average hourly wage August 2021}}{\text{Average hourly wage August 2011}} = \frac{\$30.73}{\$23.07}(100) = 133.2$$

Based on the index, hourly earnings in August 2021 were 133.20% of the average hourly wage in August 2011. This means there was a 33.2% increase in hourly earnings during the period, found by $133.20 - 100.0 = 33.20$. We conclude hourly earnings of production workers increased by one-third during the period.

You can check the latest information on wages, the Consumer Price Indexes, and other business-related values at the Bureau of Labor Statistics (BLS). Go to **http://www .bls.gov** and search for "Latest Numbers." The following chart shows some statistics from the BLS.

LATEST NUMBERS 🔊 RSS

Consumer Price Index (CPI):
+0.5% in Dec 2021

Unemployment Rate:
4.0% in Jan 2022

Payroll Employment:
+467,000(p) in Jan 2022

Average Hourly Earnings:
+$0.23(p) in Jan 2022

Producer Price Index - Final Demand:
+0.2%(p) in Dec 2021

Employment Cost Index (ECI):
+1.0% in 4th Qtr of 2021

Productivity:
+6.6% in 4th Qtr of 2021

U.S. Import Price Index:
-0.2% in Dec 2021

U.S. Export Price Index:
-1.8% in Dec 2021

Historical Data
News Release
p - preliminary

Source: U.S. Bureau of Labor Statistics

▶ **EXAMPLE**

An index can also compare two items. Suppose we would like to compare the population of two Canadian provinces: British Columbia and Ontario. At the end of the second quarter of 2021, the population of British Columbia was 5,174,724. At the same time, the population of Ontario was 14,789,778. Compute and interpret an index to compare the populations of British Columbia and Ontario.

SOLUTION

The index to compare the populations of British Columbia and Ontario is 35.0, found by:

$$p = \frac{\text{Population of British Columbia}}{\text{Population of Ontario}}(100) = \frac{5,174,724}{14,789,778}(100) = 35.0$$

This indicates that the population of British Columbia is 35.0% (about one-third) of the population of Ontario, or the population of British Columbia is 65.0% less than the population of Ontario (100 − 35.0 = 65.0).

Statistics Canada. Table 17-10-0009-01 Population estimates, quarterly

---

▶ ### EXAMPLE

The following chart shows the number of passengers for the 15 busiest airports in the world for 2020 (**https://en.wikipedia.org/wiki/List_of_busiest_airports_by_passenger_traffic**). Using the Los Angeles International Airport as the base, compute indexes of passengers for the other airports. How do the airports compare to Los Angeles?

Number of Passengers at the 15 Busiest Airports in the World				
Rank	Airport	Country	Passengers	Index
1	Guangzhou Baiyun International Airport	China	43,760,427	152.1
2	Hartsfield–Jackson Atlanta International Airport	United States	42,918,685	149.1
3	Chengdu Shuangliu International Airport	China	40,741,509	141.6
4	Dallas/Fort Worth International Airport	United States	39,364,990	136.8
5	Shenzhen Bao'an International Airport	China	37,916,059	131.7
6	Chongqing Jiangbei International Airport	China	34,937,789	121.4
7	Beijing Capital International Airport	China	34,513,827	119.9
8	Denver International Airport	United States	33,741,129	117.2
9	Kunming Changshui International Airport	China	32,989,127	114.6
10	Shanghai Hongqiao International Airport	China	31,165,641	108.3
11	Xi'an Xianyang International Airport	China	31,073,884	108.0
12	Tokyo Haneda Airport	Japan	30,965,027	107.6
13	O'Hare International Airport	United States	30,860,251	107.2
14	Shanghai Pudong International Airport	China	30,476,531	105.9
15	Los Angeles International Airport	United States	28,779,527	100.0

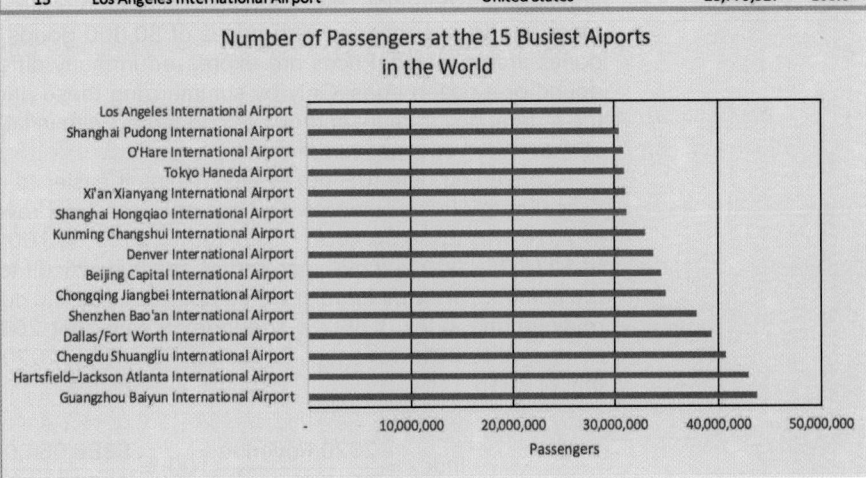

Number of Passengers at the 15 Busiest Airports in the World

SOLUTION

To find the 15 indexes, we divide the number of passengers for each airport by the number of passengers traveling through Los Angeles. So, the index for Guangzhou is 152.1, found by (43,760,427/28,779,527) (100). The table reports the actual data, and the chart summarizes the indexes. We observe the following:

1. The 15 busiest airports are in three countries: China, the United States, and Japan. There are 9 in China, 5 in the United States, and 1 in Japan.
2. Guangzhou is 52.1% busier than Los Angeles.
3. Atlanta and Dallas are the busiest airports in the United States. The numbers of passengers flowing through Atlanta and Dallas are 49.1% and 36.8% more than Los Angeles International.
4. The Tokyo Haneda Airport is 7.6% busier compared to Los Angeles.

Note from the previous discussion that:

1. The index of average hourly earnings of production workers (133.20) is a percentage, but the percent symbol is usually omitted.
2. Indexes have either a **base** or a **base period.** In the Example/Solution regarding the average hourly earnings of production workers, we used 2011 as the base period. In contrast, the Consumer Price Index uses 1982–84 as the base period. The Example/Solution about airport passengers uses the Los Angeles International Airport as the base for comparison.
3. Most business and economic indexes are reported to the nearest whole number, such as 214 or 96, or to the nearest tenth of a percent, such as 83.4 or 118.7.

Why Convert Data to Indexes?

Compiling index numbers is not a recent innovation. An Italian, G. R. Carli, is credited with originating index numbers in 1764. They were incorporated in a report he made regarding price fluctuations in Europe from 1500 to 1750. No systematic approach to collecting and reporting data in index form was evident in the United States until about 1900. The cost-of-living index (now called the Consumer Price Index) was introduced in 1913, and a long list of indexes has been compiled since then.

Why convert data to indexes? An index is a convenient way to express a change in a diverse group of items. The Consumer Price Index, for example, encompasses 200 categories of items summarized by eight groups—food and beverages, housing, apparel, transportation, medical care, recreation, education and communication, and other goods and services. The prices of 80,000 goods and services in the 200 categories are collected. Prices are expressed in many different units such as dollars per pound or a dozen eggs. Only by summarizing these prices with an index number can the federal government and others concerned with inflation keep informed of the overall movement of consumer prices.

Converting data to indexes also makes it easier to assess the trend in a series of exceptionally large numbers. For example, the total revenue for Amazon Corporation in 2020 was $386,064,000 compared to $107,006,000 in 2015. This is an increase of $279,058,000 in the 5-year period, but it is difficult to realize the increase because the numbers are very large. If we compute an index to compare 2020 revenue to 2015 revenue, the index is 360.8. The index means that 2020 revenue increased 360.8% compared to 2015 revenue. To put it another way, 2020 revenue was about 3.6 times that of 2015.

$$\text{Index} = \frac{2020 \text{ Revenue}}{2015 \text{ Revenue}}(100) = \frac{\$386,064,000}{\$107,006,000}(100) = 360.8$$

Construction of Index Numbers

We already discussed the construction of a simple price index. The price in a selected year (such as 2021) is divided by the price in the base year. The base-period price is designated as p_0, and a price other than the base period is often referred to as the *given period* or *selected period* and designated p_t. To calculate the simple price index P using 100 as the base value for any given period, use the formula:

SIMPLE INDEX	$P = \dfrac{p_t}{p_0} \times 100$	**(17–1)**

Suppose the price of a fall weekend package (including lodging and all meals) at Tryon Mountain Lodge in western North Carolina in 2010 was $450. The price rose to $795 in 2022. What is the price index for 2022 using 2010 as the base period and 100 as the base value? It is 176.7, found by:

$$P = \frac{p_t}{p_0}(100) = \frac{\$795}{\$450}(100) = 176.7$$

Interpreting this result, the price of the fall weekend package increased 76.7% from 2010 to 2022.

The base period need not be a single year. Note in Table 17–1 that if we use 2019–2020 = 100, the base price for the stapler would be $21 [found by determining the mean price of 2019–2020, ($20 + $22)/2 = $21]. The prices $20, $22, and $23 are averaged if 2019–2021 is selected as the base. The mean price would be $21.67. The indexes constructed using the three different base periods are presented in Table 17–1. (Note that when 2019–2021 = 100, the index numbers for 2019, 2020, and 2021 average 100.0, as we would expect.) Logically, the index numbers for 2022 using the three different bases are not the same.

TABLE 17–1 Prices of a Benson Automatic Stapler, Model 3, Converted to Indexes Using Three Different Base Periods

Year	Price of Stapler	Price Index (2019 = 100)	Price Index (2019–20 = 100)	Price Index (2019–21 = 100)
2014	$18	90.0	$\frac{18}{21} \times 100 = 85.7$	$\frac{18}{21.67} \times 100 = 83.1$
2019	20	100.0	$\frac{20}{21} \times 100 = 95.2$	$\frac{20}{21.67} \times 100 = 92.3$
2020	22	110.0	$\frac{22}{21} \times 100 = 104.8$	$\frac{22}{21.67} \times 100 = 101.5$
2021	23	115.0	$\frac{23}{21} \times 100 = 109.5$	$\frac{23}{21.67} \times 100 = 106.1$
2022	38	190.0	$\frac{38}{21} \times 100 = 181.0$	$\frac{38}{21.67} \times 100 = 175.4$

SELF-REVIEW 17–1

1. Listed are the top steel-producing countries for the year 2021 (**http://www.worldsteel.org**). Express the amount produced by China, India, Japan, and Russia as an index, using the United States as a base. What percent more steel does China produce than the United States?

Country	Amount (millions of tons)
China	1,032
India	119
Japan	96
United States	86
Russia	76

2. The median annual wages in the United States (**https://www.ssa.gov/oact/cola/central.html**) for selected years are given in the accompanying table.

Year	Median Annual Wage
2016	$30,533.31
2017	31,561.49
2018	32,828.05
2019	34,248.45
2020	34,612.04

(a) Using 2016 as the base period and 100 as the base value, determine the indexes for the other years. Interpret the index.
(b) Use the average of 2016 and 2017 as the base and determine indexes for the other years. Interpret the index.

EXERCISES

1. **FILE** Amazon.com Inc. reported the following stock price at the beginning of each year since 2012. Using 2012 as the base year, develop a simple index for stock prices. What is the percentage increase in price over the 10-year period?

Year	Stock Price to Open Year	Year	Stock Price to Open Year
2012	$175.89	2017	$ 757.92
2013	256.08	2018	1,172.00
2014	398.80	2019	1,465.20
2015	312.58	2020	1,875.00
2016	656.29	2021	3,270.00

2. **FILE** The table reports the earnings per share of common stock for Home Depot Inc. for 2011 through 2020. Develop an index, with 2011 as the base, for earnings per share for years 2012 through 2020.

Year	Earnings per Share	Year	Earnings per Share
2011	2.01	2016	6.45
2012	2.47	2017	7.29
2013	3.76	2018	9.73
2014	4.71	2019	10.25
2015	5.46	2020	11.94

3. **FILE** Listed are the net sales for a San Francisco–area mail-order retailer for the years 2011 to 2020. Use the mean sales for the earliest 3 years to determine a base and then find the index for 2019 and 2020. By how much have net sales increased from the base period?

Year	Sales (millions)	Year	Sales (millions)
2011	$486.6	2016	$568.5
2012	506.8	2017	581.9
2013	522.2	2018	496.1
2014	574.6	2019	456.6
2015	580.7	2020	433.3

4. According to the National Chicken Council (**www.nationalchickencouncil.org/about-the-industry/statistics/wholesale-and-retail-prices-for-chicken-beef-and-pork**), the mean retail price per pound of chicken in 2010 was $1.753. In 2020, the retail price for chicken was $1.908 per pound. Use the 2010 price as the base period and 100 as the base value to compute a simple index. What is the percentage change in the per pound retail price of chicken during the period?

LO 17-2

Compute and interpret an unweighted aggregate index.

Unweighted Indexes

In many situations, we wish to combine several items and develop an index to compare the cost of this aggregation of items in two different time periods. For example, we might be interested in an index for items that relate to the expense of operating and maintaining an automobile. The items in the index might include tires, oil changes, and gasoline prices. Or we might be interested in a college student index. This index might include the cost of books, tuition, housing, meals, and entertainment. There are several ways we can combine the items to determine the index.

Simple Average of the Price Indexes

Table 17–2 reports the prices for several food items for 2011 and 2021 (**www.bls.gov**). We would like to develop an index for this group of food items for 2021, using the 2011 prices as the base. This is written in the abbreviated code 2011 = 100.

TABLE 17–2 Computation of the Index for Various Food Item, 2011 = 100

Item	2011 (January) Price	2021 (January) Price	Simple Index
Bread, white, per pound	$1.401	$1.546	110.3
Eggs, dozen	1.806	1.466	81.2
Milk, gallon, white	3.301	3.468	105.1
Bananas, 1 pound	0.596	0.597	100.2
Orange juice, 12 oz, concentrate	2.461	2.341	95.1
Bacon, sliced, 1 pound	4.250	5.831	137.2
Total	$13.815	$15.249	

We could begin by computing a **simple average** of the price indexes for each item using 2011 as the base. The simple index for bread is 110.3, found by using formula (17–1).

$$P = \frac{p_t}{p_0}(100) = \frac{1.546}{1.401}(100) = 110.3$$

We compute the simple index for the other items in Table 17–2 similarly. The largest price increase was 37.2% for bacon. The largest decrease was 18.8% for eggs.

We can also determine the percentage change in the group of foods by averaging the simple indexes. The formula is:

SIMPLE AVERAGE OF THE PRICE RELATIVES	$P = \dfrac{\Sigma P_i}{n}$	(17–2)

where P_i refers to the simple index for each of the items and n the number of items. In our example, the index is 104.9, found by:

$$P = \frac{\Sigma P_i}{n} = \frac{110.3 + \cdots + 137.2}{6} = \frac{629.1}{6} = 104.9$$

This indicates that the mean price of the group of food items increased 4.9% from 2011 to 2021.

A positive feature of the simple average of price indexes is that we would obtain the same value for the index regardless of the units of measure. In the previous index, if bananas were priced in tons, instead of pounds, the impact of bananas on the combined index would not change. That is, the commodity "bananas" represents one of six items in the index, so the impact of the item is not related to the units. A negative feature of this index is that it fails to consider the relative importance of the items included in the index. For example, milk and eggs receive the same weight, even though a typical family might spend far more over the year on milk than on eggs.

Simple Aggregate Index

A second possibility is to sum the prices (rather than the indexes) for the two periods and then determine the index based on the totals. The formula is:

SIMPLE AGGREGATE INDEX	$P = \dfrac{\Sigma p_t}{\Sigma p_0} \times 100$	(17–3)

This is called a **simple aggregate index.** The index for the food items in Table 17–2 is found by dividing the sum of the prices in 2021 by the sum of the prices in 2011. The sum of the prices for the base period, 2011, is 13.815 and for 2021 the sum is 15.249. The simple aggregate index is 110.4. This means that the aggregate price for the group of items increased 10.4% over the time period.

$$P = \frac{\Sigma p_t}{\Sigma p_0} 100 = \frac{15.249}{13.815}(100) = 110.4$$

Because the value of a simple aggregate index can be influenced by the units of measurement, it is not used frequently. In our example, the value of the index would differ significantly if we were to report the price of bananas in tons rather than pounds. Also, note the effect of coffee on the total index. For both the current year and the base year, coffee is a significant contributor to the total index, so the current price of coffee will drive the index much more than any other item. Therefore, we need a way to appropriately "weight" the items according to their relative importance.

Weighted Indexes

LO17-3
Compute and interpret a weighted aggregate index.

Two methods of computing a **weighted price index** are the **Laspeyres** method and the **Paasche** method. They differ only in the period used for weighting. The Laspeyres method uses *base-period weights;* that is, the original prices and quantities of the purchased items are used to find the percent change over a period of time in either price or quantity consumed, depending on the problem. The Paasche method uses *current-year weights.*

Laspeyres Price Index

Etienne Laspeyres, a German economist, developed a method in the latter part of the 18th century to determine a weighted price index using base-period quantities as weights. Applying his method, a weighted price index is computed by:

LASPEYRES PRICE INDEX	$P = \dfrac{\Sigma p_t q_0}{\Sigma p_0 q_0} \times 100$	(17–4)

where:

P is the price index.
p_t is the current price.
p_0 is the price in the base period.
q_0 is the quantity used in the base period.

▶ **EXAMPLE**

The prices for the six food items from Table 17–2 are repeated in Table 17–3. Also included is the typical number of units consumed by a family in 2011 and 2021.

TABLE 17–3 Price and Quantity of Food Items in 2011 and 2021

Item	2011 (January) Price	2011 (January) Quantity	2021 (January) Price	2021 (January) Quantity
Bread, white, per pound	1.401	50	1.546	55
Eggs, dozen	1.806	26	1.466	20
Milk, gallon, white	3.301	102	3.468	130
Bananas, 1 pound	0.596	30	0.597	40
Orange juice, 12 oz, concentrate	2.461	40	2.341	41
Bacon, sliced, 1 pound	4.25	12	5.831	12

Determine a weighted price index using the Laspeyres method. Interpret the result.

SOLUTION

First, we determine the total amount spent for the six items in the base period, 2011. To find this value we multiply the base period price for bread, $1.401, by the base period quantity, 50. The result is $70.05. This indicates that a typical family spent $70.05 on bread in 2011. We continue with the same calculation for the remaining items in the base period. For each item in the current period, we multiply the current period price by the base period quantity. For example, the current period price for bread, $1.546, is multiplied by the base period quantity, 50, which results in a value of $77.30. The total of the 2011 weighted prices is $621.03; the total of the 2021 weighted prices is $650.67.

	Laspeyres Index					
	2011 (January)		2021 (January)			
Item	Price	Quantity	Price	Quantity	(2011 Price)(2011 Quantity)	(2021 Price)(2011 Quantity)
Bread, white, per pound	1.401	50	1.546	55	77.05	77.30
Eggs, dozen	1.806	26	1.466	20	46.96	38.12
Milk, gallon, white	3.301	102	3.468	130	336.70	353.74
Bananas, 1 pound	0.596	30	0.597	40	17.88	17.91
Orange juice, 12 oz, concentrate	2.461	40	2.341	41	98.44	93.64
Bacon, sliced, 1 pound	4.25	12	5.831	12	51.00	69.97
Totals					621.03	650.67

The Laspeyres weighted price index for the 2011–2021 time period is 104.8 found by

$$P = \frac{\Sigma p_t q_0}{\Sigma p_0 q_0} 100 = \frac{\$650.67}{621.03}(100) = 104.8$$

Based on this analysis, we conclude that the price of this group of items increased 4.8% during the time period. The advantage of the Laspeyres method over the simple aggregate index is that each price is weighted by quantity consumed by a typical family. Using the Laspeyres method, milk consumption makes the largest contribution to the totals and has the largest effect on the index.

Paasche Price Index

The major disadvantage of the Laspeyres index is it assumes that the base-period quantities are still realistic in the given period. That is, the quantities used for the six items are about the same in 2011 as 2021. In this case, the quantity of eggs purchased declined by 23%, the quantity of milk increased by nearly 28%, and the quantity of bananas increased by 33%.

The Paasche index, developed by the German economist Hermann Paasche, is an alternative. The procedure is similar, but instead of using base-period quantities as weights, we use current-period quantities as weights. We use the sum of the products of the 2011 prices and 2021 quantities. This has the advantage of using the more recent quantities. If there has been a change in the quantities consumed since the base period, such a change is reflected in the Paasche index.

PAASCHE PRICE INDEX	$P = \dfrac{\Sigma p_t q_t}{\Sigma p_0 q_t} \times 100$	(17–5)

▶ **EXAMPLE**

Use the information from Table 17–3 to determine the Paasche index. Discuss which of the indexes should be used.

SOLUTION

The following table shows the calculations to determine the Paasche index. Because of the repetitive calculations, a spreadsheet is very useful to compute the index.

					Paasche Index		
	2011 (January)		**2021 (January)**			
Item	Price	Quantity	Price	Quantity	(2011 Price)(2011 Quantity)	(2021 Price)(2011 Quantity)
Bread, white, per pound	1.401	50	1.546	55	77.06	85.03
Eggs, dozen	1.806	26	1.466	20	36.12	29.32
Milk, gallon, white	3.301	102	3.468	130	429.13	450.84
Bananas, 1 pound	0.596	30	0.597	40	23.84	23.88
Orange juice, 12 oz, concentrate	2.461	40	2.341	41	100.90	95.98
Bacon, sliced, 1 pound	4.25	12	5.831	12	51.00	69.97
Totals					718.05	755.02

The Paasche index is 105.1, found by

$$P = \frac{\Sigma p_t q_t}{\Sigma p_0 q_t} 100 = \frac{\$755.02}{\$718.05}(100) = 105.1$$

This result indicates that there was an increase of 5.1% in the price of this "market basket" of goods between 2011 and 2021. That is, it costs 5.1% more to purchase these items in 2021 than it did in 2011.

How do we decide which index to use? When is Laspeyres most appropriate and when is Paasche the better choice?

Laspeyres

Advantages — Requires quantity data from only the base period. This allows a more meaningful comparison over time. The changes in the index can be attributed to changes in the price.

Disadvantages — Does not reflect changes in buying patterns over time. Also, it may overweight goods whose prices increase.

Paasche

Advantages — Because it uses quantities from the current period, it reflects current buying habits.

Disadvantages — It requires quantity data for the current year. Because different quantities are used each year, it is impossible to attribute changes in the index to changes in price alone. It tends to overweight the goods whose prices have declined. It requires the product of prices and quantities to be recomputed each year.

Fisher's Ideal Index

As noted earlier, the Laspeyres index tends to overweight goods whose prices have increased. The Paasche index, on the other hand, tends to overweight goods whose prices have decreased. In an attempt to offset these shortcomings, Irving Fisher, in his book *The Making of Index Numbers,* published in 1922, proposed an index called **Fisher's ideal index.** It is the geometric mean of the Laspeyres and Paasche indexes. We described the geometric mean in Chapter 3. It is determined by taking the *k*th root of the product of *k* positive numbers.

$$\text{Fisher's ideal index} = \sqrt{(\text{Laspeyres index})(\text{Paasche index})} \qquad \textbf{(17–6)}$$

Fisher's index seems to be theoretically ideal because it combines the best features of the Laspeyres and Paasche indexes. That is, it balances the effects of the two indexes. However, it is rarely used because it has the same basic set of problems as the Paasche index. It requires that a new set of quantities be determined for each period.

▶ **EXAMPLE**

Determine Fisher's ideal index for the data in Table 17–3.

SOLUTION

Fisher's ideal index is 105.0.

$$\text{Fisher's ideal index} = \sqrt{(\text{Laspeyres index})(\text{Paasche index})}$$
$$= \sqrt{(104.8)(105.1)} = 105.0$$

SELF-REVIEW 17-2

Construct an index of clothing prices for 2022 based on 2012. The clothing items considered are shoes and dresses. The prices and quantities for both years are given here. Use 2012 as the base period and 100 as the base value.

| Item | 2012 | | 2022 | |
	Price	Quantity	Price	Quantity
Dress (each)	$75	500	$85	520
Shoes (pair)	40	1,200	45	1,300

(a)   Determine the simple average of the price indexes.
(b)   Determine the aggregate price index for the 2 years.
(c)   Determine the Laspeyres price index.
(d)   Determine the Paasche price index.
(e)   Determine Fisher's ideal index.

EXERCISES

For Exercises 5 through 8:
  a. Determine the simple price indexes.
  b. Determine the simple aggregate price index for the 2 years.
  c. Determine the Laspeyres price index.
  d. Determine the Paasche price index.
  e. Determine Fisher's ideal index.

5.   **FILE** Following are the prices of toothpaste (9 oz.), shampoo (7 oz.), cough tablets (package of 100), and antiperspirant (2 oz.) for August 2012 and August 2022. Also included are the quantity purchased. Use August 2012 as the base.

| Item | August 2012 | | August 2022 | |
	Price	Quantity	Price	Quantity
Toothpaste	$2.49	6	$3.35	6
Shampoo	3.29	4	4.49	5
Cough drops	1.59	2	4.19	3
Antiperspirant	1.79	3	2.49	4

6.   **FILE** Fruit prices and the amounts consumed for 2012 and 2022 are shown. Use 2012 as the base.

| Fruit | 2012 | | 2022 | |
	Price	Quantity	Price	Quantity
Bananas (pound)	$0.23	100	$0.69	120
Grapefruit (each)	0.29	50	1.00	55
Apples (pound)	0.35	85	1.89	85
Strawberries (basket)	1.02	8	3.79	10
Oranges (bag)	0.89	6	2.99	8

7.   **FILE** The prices and the numbers of various items produced by a small machine and stamping plant are reported in the table. Use 2012 as the base.

	2012		2022	
Item	Price	Quantity	Price	Quantity
Washer	$0.07	17,000	$0.10	20,000
Cotter pin	0.04	125,000	0.03	130,000
Stove bolt	0.15	40,000	0.15	42,000
Hex nut	0.08	62,000	0.10	65,000

8. **FILE** Following are the quantities and prices for the years 2012 and 2022 for Kinzua Valley Geriatrics. Use 2012 as the base period.

	2012		2022	
Item	Price	Quantity	Price	Quantity
Syringes (dozen)	$ 6.10	1,500	$ 6.83	2,000
Thermometers	8.10	10	9.35	12
Advil (bottle)	4.00	250	4.62	250
Patient record forms (box)	6.00	1,000	6.85	900
Copier paper (box)	12.00	30	13.65	40

Value Index

A **value index** measures changes in both the price and quantities involved. A value index, such as the index of department store sales, considers the base-year prices, the base-year quantities, the present-year prices, and the present-year quantities for its construction. Its formula is:

VALUE INDEX	$$V = \frac{\Sigma p_t q_t}{\Sigma p_0 q_0} \times 100$$	**(17–7)**

▶ **EXAMPLE**

The prices and quantities sold at the Waleska Clothing Emporium for ties, suits, and shoes for May 2018 and May 2022 are:

	2018		2022	
Item	Price p_o	Quantity q_o	Price p_t	Quantity q_t
Ties (each)	$ 1.00	1,000	$ 2	900
Suits (each)	30.00	100	40	120
Shoes (pair)	10.00	500	8	500

What is the index of value for May 2022 using May 2018 as the base period?

SOLUTION

Total sales in May 2022 were $10,600 and the comparable figure for 2018 is $9,000. (See Table 17–4.) Thus, the value index for May 2022 using 2018 = 100 is 117.8. The value of apparel sales in 2022 was 117.8% of the 2018 sales.

To put it another way, the value of apparel sales increased 17.8% from May 2018 to May 2022.

$$V = \frac{\Sigma p_t q_t}{\Sigma p_0 q_0}(100) = \frac{\$10,600}{\$9,000}(100) = 117.8$$

TABLE 17–4 Construction of Value Index for 2022 (2018 = 100)

	2018			2022		
	Price	Quantity	$	Price	Quantity	$
Item	p_0	q_0	$p_0 q_0$	p_t	q_t	$p_t q_t$
Ties (each)	$ 1.00	1,000	$1,000	$ 2.00	900	$ 1,800.00
Suits (each)	30.00	100	3,000	40.00	120	4,800.00
Shoes (pair)	10.00	500	5,000	8.00	500	4,000.00
Total			$9,000	Index = 117.8		$10,600.00

SELF-REVIEW 17–3

The number of items produced by Houghton Products for 2015 and 2022 and the wholesale prices for the two periods are:

	Price		Number Produced	
Item Produced	2015	2022	2015	2022
Shear pins (box)	$ 3	$4	10,000	9,000
Cutting compound (pound)	1	5	600	200
Tie rods (each)	10	8	3,000	5,000

(a)   Find the value index of production for 2022 using 2015 as the base period.
(b)   Interpret the index.

EXERCISES

9.   The year-end price and production of grains for 2015 and 2020 are listed. (**https://www.fsa.usda.gov/Assets/USDA-FSA-Public/usdafiles/arc-plc/2019/pdf/2019_MYA.pdf**)

	2015		2020	
Grain	Price/Bushel	Production (1,000 MT)	Price/Bushel	Production (1,000 MT)
Oats	$3.21	1,298	$2.82	949
Wheat	5.99	56,117	4.58	49,691
Corn	3.70	345,506	3.56	360,252
Barley	5.30	4,750	4.69	3,600

Using 2015 as the base period, find the value index for grains produced in 2020.

10.   **FILE** Johnson Wholesale Company manufactures a variety of products. The prices and quantities produced for April 2018 and April 2022 are:

Product	2018 Price	2022 Price	2018 Quantity Produced	2022 Quantity Produced
Small motor (each)	$23.60	$28.80	1,760	4,259
Scrubbing compound (gallon)	2.96	3.08	86,450	62,949
Nails (pound)	0.40	0.48	9,460	22,370

Using April 2018 as the base period, find the value index of goods produced for April 2022.

LO17-4

List and describe special-purpose indexes.

Special-Purpose Indexes

Many important indexes are prepared and published by private organizations. J. D. Power & Associates surveys automobile purchasers to determine how satisfied customers are with their vehicle after 90 days of ownership. This special index is called the *Consumer Satisfaction Index*. Financial institutions, utility companies, and university research centers often prepare indexes on employment, factory hours and wages, and retail sales for the regions they serve. Many trade associations prepare indexes of price and quantity that are vital to their particular area of interest. How are these special indexes prepared? An Example/Solution will explain the details.

▶ EXAMPLE

The Seattle Chamber of Commerce wants to develop a measure of general business activity for the northwest portion of the United States. The director of economic development is assigned the task of creating the index. It will be called the *General Business Activity Index of the Northwest*.

SOLUTION

After considerable thought and research, the director concluded that four factors should be considered: the regional department store sales (which are reported in $ millions), the regional employment index (which has a 2010 base and is reported by the State of Washington), the freight car loadings (reported in millions), and exports for the Seattle Harbor (reported in thousands of tons). Table 17–5 shows this information for years 2010, 2015, and 2022.

TABLE 17–5 Data for Computation of the General Business Activity Index of the Northwest

Year	Department Store Sales	Index of Employment	Freight Car Loadings	Exports
2010	20	100	50	500
2015	41	110	30	900
2022	44	125	18	700

After review and consultation, the director assigned weights of 40% to department store sales, 30% to employment, 10% to freight car loadings, and 20% to exports. To develop the General Business Activity Index of the Northwest for 2022 using 2010 = 100, each 2022 value is expressed as a percentage, with the base-period value as the denominator. For illustration, department store sales for 2022 are converted to a percentage by ($44/$20)(100) = 220. This means that department store sales have increased 120% in the period. This percentage is then multiplied by the appropriate weight. For the department store sales, this is (220)(.40) = 88.0. The details of the calculations for the years 2015 and 2022 are shown here.

	2015	**2022**
Department store sales	[($41)/($20)][100][.40] = 82.0	[($44)/($20)][100][.40] = 88.0
Index of employment	[(110)/(100)][100][.30] = 33.0	[(125)/(100)][100][.30] = 37.5
Freight car loadings	[(30)/(50)][100][.10] = 6.0	[(18)/(50)][100][.10] = 3.6
Experts	[(900)/(500)][100][.20] = 36.0	[(700)/(500)][100][.20] = 28.0
Total	157.0	157.1

The General Business Activity Index of the Northwest for 2015 is 157.0 and for 2022 it is 157.1. Interpreting, business activity has increased 57.0% from 2010 to 2015 and 57.1% from the base period of 2010 to 2022.

As we stated at the start of the section, there are many special-purpose indexes. Here are a few examples.

Consumer Price Index

The U.S. Bureau of Labor Statistics reports this index monthly. It describes the changes in prices from one period to another for a "market basket" of goods and services. We discuss its history and present some applications in the next section. You can access this information by going to **http://www.bls.gov,** then under **Data Tools** select **Top Picks, One screen, etc., then Inflation and prices.** Continue by selecting **Top Picks and U.S. city average all items.** You may elect to include different periods. Following is a recent summary report.

U.S. Bureau of Labor Statistics

Producer Price Index

Formerly called the Wholesale Price Index, it dates back to 1890 and is also published by the U.S. Bureau of Labor Statistics. It reflects the prices of over 3,400 commodities. Price data are collected from the sellers of the commodities, and it usually refers to the first large-volume transaction for each commodity. It is a Laspeyres-type index. To access this information, go to **http://www.bls.gov**, then **Data Tools.** Select **Top Picks, One Screen, etc.** and select **Commodity Data including "headline" FD-ID indexes.** Continue by selecting **Top Picks** and **Final demand.**

U.S. Bureau of Labor Statistics

Dow Jones Industrial Average (DJIA)

This is an index of stock prices, but perhaps it would be better to say it is an "indicator" rather than an index. It is supposed to be the mean price of 30 specific industrial stocks.

Kris Yeager/Shutterstock

However, summing the 30 stock prices and dividing by 30 does not yield its value. Why? Because over time stocks split, companies merge, and stocks are added or removed from the list. When changes in the 30 selected stocks occur, adjustments are made in the denominator used to compute the average. Today the DJIA is more of a psychological indicator than a representation of the general price movement on the New York Stock Exchange. The lack of representativeness of the stocks on the DJIA is one of the reasons for the development of the **New York Stock Exchange Index.** This index is the average price of *all* stocks on the New York Stock Exchange. More information about the DJIA is available by going to the website: **www.dowjones .com.** You can find the current value of the DJIA by going to **www .marketwatch.com.**

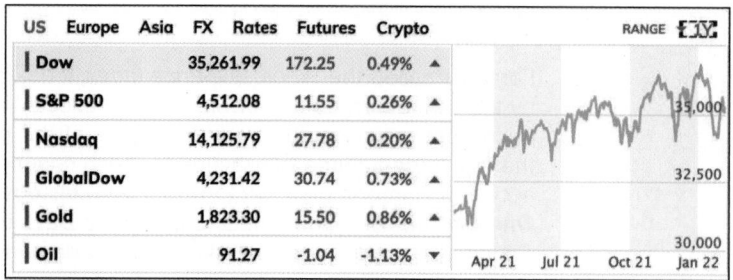

MarketWatch, Inc.

By clicking on **DOW** you can find additional detail on changes. You can change the horizontal scale to show the changes for a day, 5 days, and so on up to 5 years. In this case we changed the scale to show the changes for a year. Information on the NASDAQ and the S&P 500 is available by clicking on them as well.

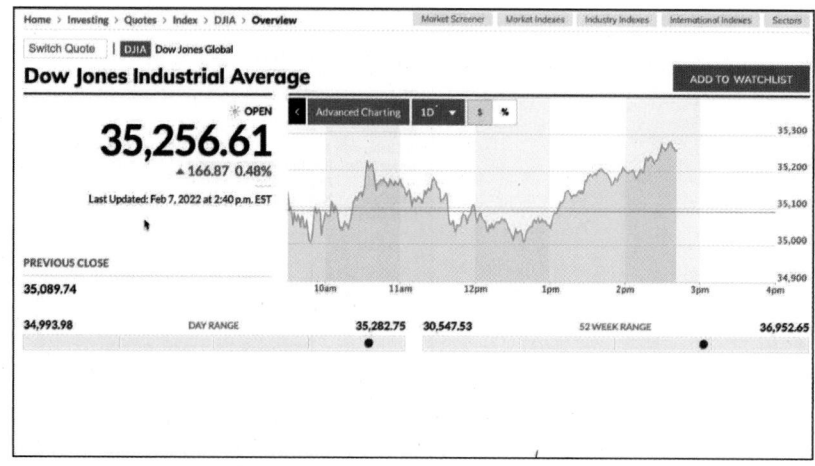

Dow Jones & Company

SELF-REVIEW 17–4

As an intern in the Fulton County Economic Development Office, you have been tasked to develop a special-purpose index for your county. Three economic series seem to hold promise as the basis of an index. These data are the price of cotton (per pound), the number of new automobiles sold in the county, and the rate of money turnover (published by the local bank). You decide that money turnover should have a weight of .60, the number of new automobiles sold a weight of .30, and the cotton price a weight of .10. The base period is 2019.

Year	Cotton Price	Automobiles Sold	Money Turnover
2019	$0.20	1,000	80
2020	0.25	1,200	90
2021	0.50	900	75

(a) Construct the index for 2020 and 2021.
(b) Interpret the index for 2020 and 2021.

EXERCISES

11. **FILE** The index of leading economic indicators, compiled and published by the U.S. National Bureau of Economic Research, is composed of 12 time series, such as the average work hours of production in manufacturing, manufacturers' new orders, and money supply. This index and similar indexes are designed to move up or down before the economy begins to move the same way. Thus, an economist has statistical evidence to forecast future trends.

You want to construct a leading indicator for Erie County in upstate New York. The index is to be based on 2010 data. Because of the time and work involved, you decide to use only four time series. Suppose you select these four series: unemployment in the county, a composite index of county stock prices, the County Price Index, and retail sales. Here are the figures for January 2010 and January 2022.

	2010	2022
Unemployment rate (%)	9.4	7.8
Composite county stocks	265.88	362.26
County Price Index (1982 = 100)	109.6	125.0
Retail sales ($ millions)	529,917.0	622,864.0

The weights you assign are unemployment rate 20%, stock prices 40%, County Price Index 25%, and retail sales 15%.
a. Using 2010 as the base period, construct a leading economic indicator for 2022.
b. Interpret your leading index.

12. **FILE** Aliyah Edwards is employed by the state bureau of economic development. There is a demand for a leading economic index to review past economic activity and to forecast future economic trends in the state. Aliyah decides that several key factors should be included in the index: number of new businesses started during the year, number of business failures, state income tax receipts, college enrollment, and the state sales tax receipts. Here are the data for 2010 and 2022.

	Weights	2010	2022
New businesses	.15	1,088	1,162
Business failures	.10	627	520
State income tax receipts ($ millions)	.40	191.7	162.6
College student enrollment	.10	242,119	290,841
State sales tax ($ millions)	.25	41.6	39.9

a. Compute the leading economic indicator for 2022.
b. Interpret the indexes.

LO17-5
Apply the Consumer Price Index.

Consumer Price Index

Frequent mention has been made of the Consumer Price Index (CPI) in the preceding pages. It measures the change in price of a fixed market basket of goods and services from one period to another. In January 1978, the Bureau of Labor Statistics began publishing CPIs for two groups of the population. One index, called the Consumer Price Index—All Urban Consumers, covers about 87% of the total population. The other index is for urban wage earners and clerical workers and covers about 32% of the population.

The CPI serves several major functions. It allows consumers to determine the degree to which their purchasing power is being eroded by price increases. In that respect, it is a yardstick for revising wages, pensions, and other income payments to keep pace with changes in prices. Equally important, it is an economic indicator of the rate of inflation in the United States.

The index is based on the prices of 80,000 items collected monthly. Prices are collected from thousands of U.S. retail stores, service establishments, rental units, and doctors' offices (**http://stats.bls.gov/cgi-bin/surveymost**). Bread, beer, gasoline, haircuts, mortgage interest rates, physicians' fees, taxes, and operating-room charges are just a few of the items included in what is often termed a "market basket" of goods and services that a typical consumer purchases.

The CPI originated in 1913 and has been published regularly since 1921. The standard reference period (the base period) has been updated periodically. The current base period is 1982–84. The earlier base periods were 1967, 1957–59, 1947–49, 1935–39, and 1925–29. Why is it necessary to change the base? Our purchasing patterns that determine the market basket of goods and services change dramatically, and these changes must be reflected in the base period prices.

The CPI is actually not just one index. There are Consumer Price Indexes for New York, Chicago, Seattle, and Atlanta, as well as a number of other large cities. There are also price indexes for food, apparel, medical care, and other items. A few of them are shown here, 1982–84 = 100, for September 2021.

Item	CPI-U
All items	274.138
Food and beverage	280.608
Apparel	120.779
Medical care	525.585
Housing	283.244

A review of this list shows that a weighted index of all items has increased 174.138% since 1982–84; medical care has increased 425.585%; and apparel went up the least, 20.779%.

Special Uses of the Consumer Price Index

In addition to measuring changes in the prices of goods and services, both consumer price indexes have a number of other applications. The CPI is used to determine real disposable personal income, to deflate sales or other variables, to find the purchasing power of the dollar, and to establish cost-of-living increases. We first discuss the use of the CPI in determining **real income.**

Real Income   As an example of the meaning and computation of *real income,* assume the Consumer Price Index is presently 200 with 1982–84 = 100. Also, assume that Ms. Watts earned $20,000 per year in the base period of 1982, 1983, and 1984. She has a current income of $40,000. Note that although her *money income* has doubled since the base period of 1982–84, the prices she paid for food, gasoline, clothing, and other items have also doubled. Thus, Ms. Watts's standard of living has remained the same from the base period to the present time. Price increases have exactly offset an increase in income, so her present buying power (real income) is still $20,000. (See Table 17–6 for computations.) In general:

REAL INCOME	$\text{Real income} = \dfrac{\text{Money income}}{\text{CPI}} \times 100$	**(17–8)**

TABLE 17–6 Computation of Real Income for 1982–84 and Present Year

Year	Annual Money Income	Consumer Price Index (1982–84 = 100)	Computation of Real Income	Real Income
1982–84	$20,000	100	$\dfrac{\$20,000}{100}(100)$	$20,000
Present year	40,000	200	$\dfrac{\$40,000}{200}(100)$	20,000

The concept of real income is sometimes called *deflated income,* and the CPI is called the *deflator.* Also, a popular term for deflated income is *income expressed in constant dollars.* Thus, in Table 17–6, to determine whether Ms. Watts's standard of living changed, her money income was converted to constant dollars. We found that her purchasing power, expressed in 1982–84 dollars (constant dollars), remained at $20,000.

SELF-REVIEW 17–5

The following reports Jodie Lind's take-home pay for 2000 and 2021. The CPI for these years is also reported.

Year	Take-Home Pay	CPI (1982–84 = 100)
2000	$25,000	172.2
2021	60,000	270.97

(a) What was Jodie's real income in 2000?
(b) What was Jodie's real income in 2021?
(c) Interpret your findings.

Deflating Sales A price index can also be used to "deflate" sales or similar money series. Deflated sales are determined by

USING AN INDEX AS A DEFLATOR	$\text{Deflated sales} = \dfrac{\text{Actual sales}}{\text{An appropriate index}} \times 100$	**(17–9)**

▶ **EXAMPLE**

The sales of Hill Enterprises, a small injection molding company in Upstate New York, increased from 2015 to 2021. The following table shows the increase.

Year	$ Sales ($000)
2015	$ 875
2016	1,482
2017	1,491
2018	1,502
2019	1.515
2020	1,596
2021	1,697

The owner, Harry Hill, realizes that the price of raw materials used in the process also has increased over the period, so Mr. Hill wants to deflate sales to account for the increase in raw material prices. What are the deflated sales for the selected years expressed in constant 1982 dollars?

SOLUTION

The Producer Price Index (PPI) is an index released every month and published in the *Monthly Labor Review;* it is also available at the Bureau of Labor Statistics website. The prices included in the PPI reflect the prices the manufacturer pays for the metals, rubber, and other purchased raw materials. So the PPI seems an appropriate index to use to deflate the manufacturer's sales. The manufacturer's sales are listed in the second column of Table 17–7, and the PPI for each year is in the third column. The next column shows sales divided by the PPI. The right-hand column details the calculations.

TABLE 17–7 Calculation of Deflated Sales for Hill Enterprises

Year	Sales Dollar $000	PPI	Constant Dollar $000	Found by
2015	$ 875	110.5	$ 791.86	(875/110.5)*100
2016	1,482	110.5	1,341.18	(1,482/110.5)*100
2017	1,491	112.7	1,322.98	(1,491/112.7)*100
2018	1,502	116.5	1,289.27	(1,502/116.5)*100
2019	1,515	118.5	1,278.48	(1,515/118.5)*100
2020	1,596	118.2	1,350.25	(1,596/118.2)*100
2021	1,697	127.3	1,333.07	(1,697/127.3)*100

Sales increased from 2015 through 2021; in fact they increased by 93.9%, found by:

$$\% \text{ increase} = \frac{\$1{,}697}{\$875}(100) - 100 = 93.9$$

However, if we review the sales adjusted for inflation using the PPI, sales from 2016 to 2021 are fairly constant. When sales are adjusted for inflation, the sales picture is different.

Purchasing Power of the Dollar The Consumer Price Index is also used to determine the *purchasing power of the dollar.*

USING AN INDEX TO FIND PURCHASING POWER	Purchasing power of dollar $= \dfrac{\$1}{\text{CPI}} \times 100$	**(17–10)**

▶ **EXAMPLE**

Suppose the Consumer Price Index this month is 200.0 (1982–84 = 100). What is the purchasing power of the dollar?

SOLUTION

From formula (17–10), it is 50 cents, found by:

$$\text{Purchasing power of dollar} = \frac{\$1}{200.0}(100) = \$.50$$

The CPI of 200.0 indicates that prices have doubled from the years 1982–84 to this month. Thus, the purchasing power of a dollar has been cut in half. That is, a

1982–84 dollar is worth only 50 cents this month. To put it another way, if you lost $1,000 in the period 1982–84 and just found it, the $1,000 could only buy half of what it could have bought in the years 1982, 1983, and 1984.

Cost-of-Living Adjustments The Consumer Price Index is also the basis for cost-of-living adjustments, or COLAs, in many management–union contracts. The specific clause in the contract is often referred to as the "escalator clause." About 31 million Social Security beneficiaries, 2.5 million retired military and federal civil service employees and survivors, and 600,000 postal workers have their incomes or pensions pegged to the CPI.

The CPI is also used to adjust alimony and child support payments; attorneys' fees; workers' compensation payments; rentals on apartments, homes, and office buildings; welfare payments; and so on. A retiree receives a pension of $500 a month and the CPI increases 5 points from 165 to 170. Suppose for each percentage point the CPI increases, the pension benefits increase 1%, so the monthly increase in benefits will be $15.15, found by $[(170 - 165)/165] \times 500$. Now the retiree will receive $515.15 per month.

SELF-REVIEW 17–6

The Consumer Price Index for the latest month is 274.138 (1982–84 = 100). What is the purchasing power of the dollar? Interpret.

Shifting the Base

If two or more time series have the same base period, they can be compared directly. As an example, suppose we are interested in the trend in the prices of food and beverages, housing, and medical care since the base period, 1982–84. Note in Table 17–8 that all of the consumer price indexes use the same base.

TABLE 17–8 Trend in Consumer Price to 2021 (1982–84 = 100)

Year	All Items	Food and Beverages	Housing	Medical Care
1982–84	100.0	100.0	100.0	100.0
1995	152.4	148.9	148.5	220.5
2000	172.2	168.4	169.6	260.8
2005	195.3	191.2	195.7	323.2
2010	218.056	219.984	216.256	388.436
2015	237.017	246.804	238.060	446.752
2018	251.107	253.350	258.479	484.715
2021 (December)	278.802	285.556	287.551	530.026

Table 17–8 shows that the price of all consumer items combined increased 178.802% from the base period (1982–84) to the year 2021. (Beginning with January 2007, the CPI is reported to three decimal places instead of one.) Likewise, food and beverage prices increased 185.556%, housing prices increased 187.551%, and medical care increased 430.026%.

A problem arises, however, when comparing two or more series that do not have the same base period. The following Example/Solution compares the two most widely reported stock market indexes, the DJIA and NASDAQ.

▶ **EXAMPLE**

We want to compare the opening prices of the DJIA and the NASDAQ Composite on the first trading day of the year for 2015 through 2021.

Year	Opening Price DJIA	Opening Price NASDAQ
2015	$17,832.99	$4.726.81
2016	17,148.94	4,903.09
2017	19,881.76	5,429.08
2018	24,824.01	7,006.90
2019	23,346.24	6,665.94
2020	28,634.88	9,092.19
2021	30,223.89	12,698.45

SOLUTION

A direct comparison of the DJIA and NASDAQ opening prices is not appropriate. Because we want to compare changes in the opening prices for the two markets, a logical approach is to compute indexes for each market using the 2015 opening price as the base. For the DJIA, the base is $17,832.99, and for the NASDAQ it is $4,726.81.

The calculation of the index for the DJIA in 2021 is:

$$\text{Index} = \frac{\$30,223.89}{\$17,832.99}(100) = 169.5$$

The following table reports the complete set of indexes.

Year	DIJA Open	DIJA Index	NASDAQ Open	NASDAQ Index
2015	$17,832.99	100.00	$ 4,726.81	100.0
2016	17,148.94	96.16	4,903.09	103.7
2017	19,881.76	111.49	5,429.08	114.9
2018	24,824.01	139.20	7,006.90	148.2
2019	23,346.24	130.92	6,665.94	141.0
2020	28,634.88	160.57	9,092.19	192.4
2021	30,223.89	169.48	12,698.45	268.6

We conclude that both indexes have increased over the period. The DJIA has increased 69.48% and the NASDAQ 168.6%.

The following chart shows the DJIA indexes in blue and NASDAQ indexes in brown. The graph shows the changes for both indexes starting from the base of 2015. In general, the two indexes seem to mirror each other rather closely until 2019 when the NASDAQ increases more rapidly. We should point out that if we select different periods as the base, the results may not be exactly the same. One should always be cautious of the base period selected for a chart or a graph.

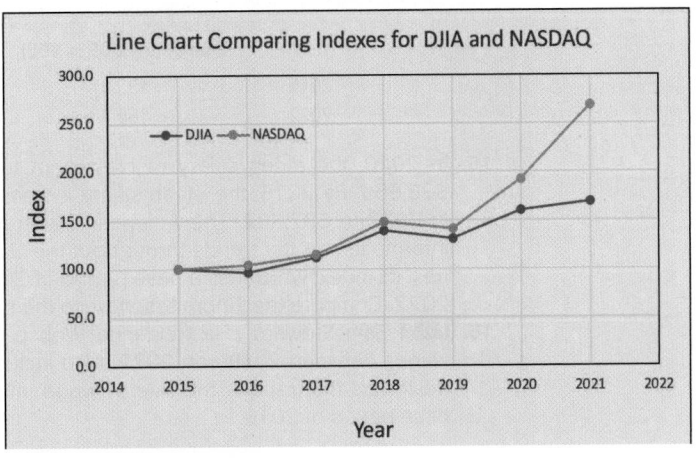

McGraw Hill LLC

SELF-REVIEW 17–7

The number of traffic fatalities for selected states for the 5-year period from 2016 to 2020 are:

Year	Florida	New York	Illinois	California
2016	3,176	1,041	1,078	3,837
2017	3,116	1,006	1,090	3,884
2018	3,135	964	1,035	3,798
2019	3,183	913	1,009	3,606
2020	2,915	943	1,031	3,568

a. Using 2016 as the base year for each state, convert the number of fatalities to index numbers.
b. For California, by what percent did the number of fatalities change from 2016 to 2017?
c. For New York, by what percent did the number of fatalities change from 2016 to 2019?
d. For Florida, by what percent did fatalities change from 2019 to 2020?
e. What is the general change in fatalities over the 5-year period? Explain your answer.

EXERCISES

13. In 2021, the mean salary for a nurse manager with a bachelor's degree was $106,100. The Consumer Price Index for 2021 was 270.97 (1982–84 = 100). The mean annual salary for a nurse in the base period of 1982–84 was $19,800. What was the real income of the nurse in 2021? How much did the mean salary increase?
14. The Trade Union Association of Orlando, Florida, maintains indexes on the hourly wages for a number of the trades. Unfortunately, the indexes do not all have the same base periods. Listed is information on plumbers and electricians. Shift the

base periods to 2015 and compare the hourly wage increases for the period from 2015 to 2022.

Year	Plumbers (2005 = 100)	Electricians (2008 = 100)
2015	133.8	126.0
2022	159.4	158.7

15. In 2010, the mean salary of classroom teachers in Tinora School District was $28,650. By 2015, the mean salary increased to $33,972, and further increased in 2022 to $37,382. The American Federation of Classroom Teachers maintains information on the trends throughout the United States in classroom teacher salaries. Its index, which has a base period of 2010, was 122.5 for 2015 and 136.9 for 2022. Compare the Tinora teachers to the national trends.

16. **FILE** Sam Steward is a freelance Web page designer. Listed are Sam's yearly wages between 2019 and 2022. Also included is an industry index for Web page designers that reports the rate of wage inflation in the industry. This index has a base period of 2010.

Year	Wage ($000)	Index (2010 = 100)
2019	134.8	160.6
2020	145.2	173.6
2021	156.6	187.9
2022	168.8	203.3

Compute Sam's real income for the selected years during the 4-year period. Did his wages keep up with inflation, or did Sam lose ground?

CHAPTER SUMMARY

I. An index number measures the relative change from one period to another.
 A. The major characteristics of an index are:
  1. It is a percentage, but the percent sign is usually omitted.
  2. It has a base period.
 B. The reasons for computing an index are:
  1. It facilitates the comparison of unlike series.
  2. If the numbers are very large, often it is easier to comprehend the change of the index than the actual numbers.
II. There are two types of price indexes, unweighted and weighted.
 A. In an unweighted index, we do not consider the quantities.
  1. In a simple index, we compare the base period to the given period.

$$P = \frac{p_t}{p_0} \times 100 \qquad (17\text{--}1)$$

where p_t refers to the price in the current period and p_0 is the price in the base period.
  2. In the simple average of price indexes, we add the simple indexes for each item and divide by the number of items.

$$P = \frac{\Sigma P_i}{n} \qquad (17\text{--}2)$$

  3. In a simple aggregate price index, the price of the items in the group are totaled for both periods and compared.

$$P = \frac{\Sigma p_t}{\Sigma p_0} \times 100 \qquad (17\text{--}3)$$

B. In a weighted index, the quantities are considered.
  1. In the Laspeyres method, the base-period quantities are used in both the base period and the given period.

$$P = \frac{\Sigma p_t q_0}{\Sigma p_0 q_0} \times 100 \qquad\qquad \textbf{(17–4)}$$

  2. In the Paasche method, current-period quantities are used.

$$P = \frac{\Sigma p_t q_t}{\Sigma p_0 q_t} \times 100 \qquad\qquad \textbf{(17–5)}$$

  3. Fisher's ideal index is the geometric mean of the Laspeyres and Paasche indexes.

$$\text{Fisher's ideal index} = \sqrt{(\text{Laspeyres index})(\text{Paasche index})} \qquad \textbf{(17–6)}$$

C. A value index uses both-base period and current-period prices and quantities.

$$V = \frac{\Sigma p_t q_t}{\Sigma p_0 q_0} \times 100 \qquad\qquad \textbf{(17–7)}$$

III. The most widely reported index is the Consumer Price Index (CPI).
  A. It is often used to show the rate of inflation in the United States.
  B. It is reported monthly by the U.S. Bureau of Labor Statistics.
  C. The current base period is 1982–84.
  D. CPI is used to compute "real" income and purchasing power and to adjust pensions and tax brackets.

CHAPTER EXERCISES

Johnson & Johnson is the world's largest and most broadly based healthcare company, with corporate offices in New Brunswick, New Jersey. Its common stock is listed on the New York Stock Exchange using the symbol JNJ. For Exercises 17 through 22, use the following information taken from Johnson & Johnson's annual reports.

Year	Domestic Sales ($ million)	International Sales ($ million)	Employees (thousands)
2016	$37,811	$34,079	126.4
2017	39,863	36,587	134.0
2018	41,884	39,697	135.1
2019	39,962	42,097	132.2
2020	43,133	39,451	135.5

17. `FILE` Using 2016 as the base period, compute a simple index of domestic sales for each year from 2017 until 2020. Interpret the trend in domestic sales.

18. `FILE` Using the period 2016–17 as the base period, compute a simple index of domestic sales for each year from 2018 to 2020.

19. `FILE` Using 2016 as the base period, compute a simple index of international sales for each year from 2017 until 2022. Interpret the trend in international sales.

20. `FILE` Using the period 2016–17 as the base period, compute a simple index of international sales for each year from 2018 to 2020.

21. `FILE` Using 2016 as the base period, compute a simple index of the number of employees for each year from 2017 until 2020. Interpret the trend in the number of employees.

22. `FILE` Using the period 2016–17 as the base period, compute a simple index of the number of employees for each year from 2018 to 2020.

General Electric Company (GE) is a high-tech industrial company that operates world-wide through its four industrial segments, Power, Renewable Energy, Aviation, and Healthcare, and its financial services segment, Capital (2020 General Electric Form 10-K). For Exercises 23 through 26, use the following information from General Electric Corporation's annual reports.

General Electric		
Year	Revenue ($ Billion)	Employees (thousands)
2015	94.49	333
2016	103.3	295
2017	99.28	313
2018	97.01	283
2019	95.21	205
2020	79.62	174

23. **FILE** Compute a simple index for GE's revenue. Use 2015 as the base period. What can you conclude about the change in revenue over the period?

24. **FILE** Compute a simple index for GE's revenue using the period 2015–16 as the base. What can you conclude about the change in revenue over the period?

25. **FILE** Compute a simple index for GE's number of employees. Use 2015 as the base period. What can you conclude about the change in the number of employees over the period?

26. **FILE** Compute a simple index for GE's number of employees. Use 2015-16 as the base period. What can you conclude about the change in the number of employees over the period?

For Exercises 27 through 32, use the following information on food items for the years 2012 and 2022.

Item	2012		2022	
	Price	Quantity	Price	Quantity
Margarine (pound)	$0.81	18	$2.00	27
Shortening (pound)	0.84	5	1.88	9
Milk (½ gallon)	1.44	70	2.89	65
Potato chips	2.91	27	3.99	33

27. **FILE** Compute a simple price index for each of the four items. Use 2012 as the base period.

28. **FILE** Compute a simple aggregate price index. Use 2012 as the base period.

29. **FILE** Compute the Laspeyres price index for 2022 using 2012 as the base period.

30. **FILE** Compute the Paasche index for 2022 using 2012 as the base period.

31. **FILE** Determine Fisher's ideal index using the values for the Laspeyres and Paasche indexes computed in the two previous problems.

32. **FILE** Determine a value index for 2022 using 2012 as the base period.

For Exercises 33 through 38, use the following information. Betts Electronics purchases three replacement parts for robotic machines used in its manufacturing process. Information on the price of the replacement parts and the quantity purchased is given here.

Part	Price		Quantity	
	2015	2022	2015	2022
RC-33	$0.50	$0.60	320	340
SM-14	1.20	0.90	110	130
WC50	0.85	1.00	230	250

33. **FILE** Compute a simple price index for each of the three items. Use 2015 as the base period.

34. FILE Compute a simple aggregate price index for 2022. Use 2015 as the base period.
35. FILE Compute the Laspeyres price index for 2022 using 2015 as the base period.
36. FILE Compute the Paasche index for 2022 using 2015 as the base period.
37. FILE Determine Fisher's ideal index using the values for the Laspeyres and Paasche indexes computed in the two previous problems.
38. FILE Determine a value index for 2022 using 2015 as the base period.

For Exercises 39 through 44, use the following price information for selected foods for 2015 and 2022 given in the table.

	Price		Quantity	
Item	2015	2022	2015	2022
Cabbage (pound)	$0.06	$0.05	2,000	1,500
Carrots (bunch)	0.10	0.12	200	200
Peas (quart)	0.20	0.18	400	500
Endive (bunch)	0.15	0.15	100	200

39. FILE Compute a simple price index for each of the four items. Use 2015 as the base period.
40. FILE Compute a simple aggregate price index. Use 2015 as the base period.
41. FILE Compute the Laspeyres price index for 2022 using 2015 as the base period.
42. FILE Compute the Paasche index for 2022 using 2015 as the base period.
43. FILE Determine Fisher's ideal index using the values for the Laspeyres and Paasche indexes computed in the two previous problems.
44. FILE Determine a value index for 2022 using 2015 as the base period.

For Exercises 45 through 50, use the following price information for selected items for 2015 and 2022. Production figures for those two periods are also given.

	Price		Quantity	
Item	2015	2022	2015	2022
Aluminum (cents per pound)	$ 0.82	$ 0.86	1,000	1,200
Natural gas $ per million BLA	4.37	2.99	5,000	4,000
Petroleum (barrel)	71.21	58.15	60,000	60,000
Platinum (troy ounce)	1,743.60	1,292.53	500	600

45. FILE Compute a simple price index for each of the four items. Use 2015 as the base period.
46. FILE Compute a simple aggregate price index. Use 2015 as the base period.
47. FILE Compute the Laspeyres price index for 2022 using 2015 as the base period.
48. FILE Compute the Paasche index for 2022 using 2015 as the base period.
49. FILE Determine Fisher's ideal index using the values for the Laspeyres and Paasche indexes computed in the two previous problems.
50. FILE Determine a value index for 2022 using 2015 as the base period.

51. FILE A special-purpose index is to be designed to monitor the overall economy of the Southwest. Four key series were selected. After considerable deliberation, it was decided to weight retail sales 20%, total bank deposits 10%, industrial production in the area 40%, and nonagricultural employment 30%. The data for 2000 and 2022 are:

Year	Retail Sales ($ millions)	Bank Deposits ($ billions)	Industrial Production (1990 = 100)	Employment
2000	1,159.0	87	110.6	1,214,000
2022	1,971.0	91	114.7	1,501,000

Construct a special-purpose index for 2022 using 2000 as the base period and interpret.

52. **FILE** We are making a historical study of the American economy from 1950 to 1980. Data on prices, the labor force, productivity, and the GNP were collected. Note in the following table that the CPI has a base period of 1967, employment is in millions of persons, and so on. A direct comparison, therefore, is not feasible.
   a. Make whatever calculations are necessary to compare the trend in the four series from 1950 to 1980.
   b. Interpret.

Year	Consumer Price Index (1967 = 100)	Total Labor Force (millions)	Index of Productivity in Manufacturing (1967 = 100)	Gross National Product ($ billions)
1950	72.1	64	64.9	286.2
1967	100.0	81	100.0	789.6
1971	121.3	87	110.3	1,063.4
1975	161.2	95	114.9	1,516.3
1980	246.8	107	146.6	2,626.0

53. **FILE** The management of Pharmacie Mutualiste Thiers in Paris wants to construct an index of economic activity for the metropolitan area. Management contends that, if the index reveals that the economy is slowing down, inventory should be kept at a low level.

   Three series seem to hold promise as predictors of economic activity–area retail sales, bank deposits, and employment. All of these data can be secured monthly from the government. Retail sales is to be weighted 40%, bank deposits 35%, and employment 25%. Seasonally adjusted data for the first 3 months of the year are:

Month	Retail Sales (EUR millions)	Bank Deposits (EUR millions)	Employment (thousands)
January	8.0	20	300
February	6.8	23	303
March	6.4	21	297

   Construct an index of economic activity for each of the 3 months, using January as the base period.

54. **FILE** The following table gives information on the Consumer Price Index (Base = 1982–84) and the monthly take-home pay of Bill Martin, an employee at Ford Motor Corporation.

Year	Consumer Price Index (1982–84 = 100)	Mr. Martin's Monthly Take-Home Pay
1982–84	100.0	$ 600
2020	258.811	7,000

   a. What is the purchasing power of the dollar in 2020, based on the period 1982–84?
   b. Determine Mr. Martin's "real" monthly income for 2020.

55. Suppose that the Producer Price Index (Base = 1984) and the sales of Hoskin's Wholesale Distributors for January 2015 and January 2020 are:

Year	Producer Price Index	Sales
2015	185.5	$2,400,000
2020	192.7	3,500,000

What are Hoskin's real sales (also called deflated sales) for each of the 2 years?

DATA ANALYTICS

(The data for this exercise is available at the text website: **www.mhhe.com/lind19e.**)

56. Refer to the average annual baseball player salary data in the 2021 Major League Baseball data set. The data also include the CPI from 2010 to 2021. The CPI base is $1982 - 84 = 100$.

    a. Develop a graph that shows the mean player salary from 2010 to 2021. What do you observe about the graph? Are the salaries increasing, decreasing, or staying the same over the period?

    b. Using the annual CPI, adjust the mean salaries for each year between 2010 and 2021. Graph the adjusted mean annual player salaries. Are the adjusted salaries increasing, decreasing, or staying the same over the period? Compare this graph to the graph in part (a). Write a paragraph summarizing your findings. Cite specific evidence.

18 Forecasting with Time Series Analysis

kali9/Getty Images

▲ **OVER THE YEARS,** the U.S. grocery distribution and sales industry has grown. Today, the total industry sales are in the tens of billions of dollars. Major retailers, such as Walmart and Target, added food to complement their merchandise sales and Amazon recently purchased Whole Foods. For many companies, forecasts of industry sales are necessary information to plan for short- and long-term decisions. Using historical data, compute forecasts of annual industry sales using time series analysis. (See Exercise 15 and **LO18-5.**)

LEARNING OBJECTIVES

When you have completed this chapter, you will be able to:

LO18-1 Identify and describe time series patterns.

LO18-2 Compute forecasts using simple moving averages.

LO18-3 Compute and interpret the Mean Absolute Deviation and Mean Absolute Percent Error.

LO18-4 Compute forecasts using exponential smoothing.

LO18-5 Compute a forecasting model using regression analysis.

LO18-6 Apply the Durban-Watson statistic to test for autocorrelation.

LO18-7 Compute seasonal indexes and use the indexes to make seasonally adjusted forecasts.

Introduction

Forecasts of the future produce information that is essential to every individual and organization. For example, we rely on weather forecasts to make decisions about how we dress, whether to postpone a scheduled event, or evacuate a coastal city for a hurricane. Businesses and organizations rely on forecasts of economic indicators, often produced by the U.S. government, such as the gross domestic product (GDP), the price of oil, or interest rates to make short- and long-term plans. Usually, more than one methodology or technique is used to make forecasts.

In this chapter, we focus on a forecasting technique called **time series analysis.** A time series data set is a collection of historical observations recorded over time. So, time series data are always presented in chronological order. For a time series, it is important to know the time period that corresponds to each observation. For example, a particular time series may be recorded in weeks, months, quarters, or years. Examples include:

- Microsoft Corporation's sales by quarter since 1985
- The daily reports of the Dow Jones Industrial Average over the last 3 months
- For the last 5 years, the number of students enrolled at Indiana University in Bloomington for the Fall, Spring, and Summer semesters
- The monthly quantity of bananas sold at Kroger over the last 12 months.

To make forecasts, time series analysis examines historical data for patterns that can be modeled, or explained, with mathematical equations. Then, forecasts are developed using these equations to project the historical patterns into the future. An important assumption of forecasts using time series data is that the future will replicate the past historical patterns. This assumption is not always true. Therefore, a constant monitoring of the environment for events that may disrupt the pattern is essential. Examples of disruptions include hurricanes, earthquakes, financial market disruptions, or international political events.

In the next section, we present typical patterns that may be present in a time series. The subsequent sections describe the mathematical modeling of the time series patterns.

LO18-1

Identify and describe time series patterns.

Time Series Patterns

There are three patterns that may be present in a time series: trend, seasonality, and cycles. In addition, we account for an irregular or random component in the data. To detect the presence of these patterns the usual first step is to draw a line graph. This graph is similar to the scatter diagram used in Chapter 13 because it has a horizontal *X*-axis and a vertical *Y*-axis. However, in a line graph, time is always plotted on the horizontal axis and the time series variable on the vertical axis.

Trend

A **trend pattern** describes the change of a variable over time. The trend could be a positive or upward trend, a negative or downward trend, or no observable trend. We describe a trend with no trend as a stationary time series. The trend might be fairly linear or it may be nonlinear and change exponentially.

> **TREND PATTERN** The change of a variable over time.

The following are examples of time series data that show trend.

- Home Depot Inc. was founded in 1978 and is the world's largest home improvement retailer. Chart 18–1 shows a line graph of the number of associates working for Home Depot Inc. (The data are reported in the Home Depot Inc. annual reports: **https://ir.homedepot.com/financial-reports/annual-reports/recent**). You can observe a steady increase or upward trend in the number of associates over the 26 years from 1995 to 2020. Between 2006 and 2010 the number of associates declined. The Great Recession that began in late 2007 and ended in mid-2009 likely interrupted the upward trend pattern. After 2013 the trend in the number of associates began increasing again. However, the rate of increase was slower until the spike in 2020.

Year	Associates	Year	Associates
1995	80.8	2008	322.0
1996	98.1	2009	317.0
1997	124.4	2010	321.0
1998	156.7	2011	331.0
1999	201.4	2012	340.0
2000	227.3	2013	365.0
2001	256.3	2014	371.0
2002	280.9	2015	385.0
2003	298.8	2016	406.0
2004	323.1	2017	413.0
2005	344.8	2018	413.0
2006	364.4	2019	415.0
2007	331.0	2020	504.0

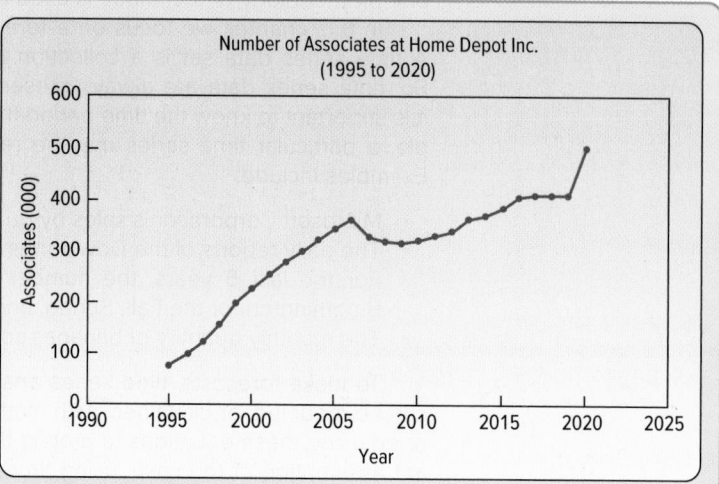

CHART 18–1 Number of Associates at Home Depot Inc.

- The price of gasoline affects each of us and is closely followed in the media. Chart 18–2 shows a line graph of the average price per gallon since 1998. The time series graph shows an increasing trend between 1998 and 2007. Then, the time series pattern was interrupted by the Great Recession. Over the last 10 years, the pattern is fairly stationary with no clear trends. Over the most recent 10 years, the average price per gallon was $2.79.

Year	Cost/Gallon	Year	Cost/Gallon
1998	$1.03	2010	$2.78
1999	$1.14	2011	$3.52
2000	$1.48	2012	$3.62
2001	$1.42	2013	$3.49
2002	$1.35	2014	$3.36
2003	$1.56	2015	$2.42
2004	$1.85	2016	$2.14
2005	$2.27	2017	$2.42
2006	$2.57	2018	$2.72
2007	$2.80	2019	$2.60
2008	$3.25	2020	$2.17
2009	$2.35	2021	$3.01

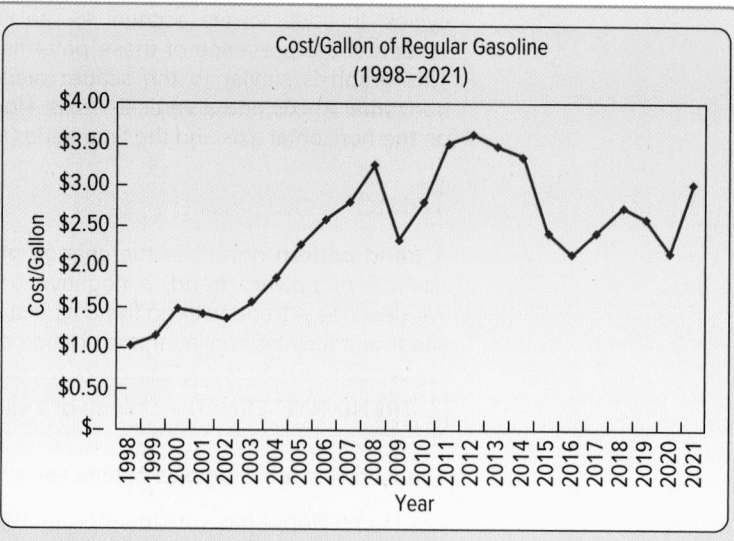

CHART 18–2 Price per Gallon of Regular Gasoline

Seasonality

A seasonal pattern describes changes in a time series that recur every calendar year. Many industries are driven by seasonal effects.

- In the fashion industry, the demand for swimsuits has a peak demand in the spring and summer months and low demand during the fall and winter months.
- In the food industry, the demand for soups is high during colder months and low during warm months.
- In the resort/vacation industry, ski resorts do most of their business during the winter season, while golf and tennis resorts do most of their business during the summer season.

While these examples show **seasonality** in terms of months, many organizations use the concept of seasonality on a weekly or even daily basis. In the hospitality industry, resorts experience seasonal effects on a weekly basis that often show peaks in demand for weeks that include holidays. Think about hotels in South Bend, Indiana, on the weekends when Notre Dame has a home football game!

> **SEASONALITY** Patterns of highs and lows in a time series within a calendar year. These patterns tend to repeat each year.

A seasonal pattern is illustrated in Chart 18–3. Shown is a line graph of quarterly sales, in millions of dollars, at Hercher Sporting Goods Inc. The sporting goods company specializes in selling baseball and softball equipment to high schools, colleges, and youth leagues in the greater Chicago area. They also have several retail outlets in some of the larger shopping malls. The time series graph shows a distinct seasonal pattern in sales. The highest sales always occur in the second quarter of the year (see the red squares) when schools and organizations are purchasing equipment for the upcoming summer season. In every calendar year, the third quarter (the green circles) shows the lowest sales. The graph also shows an overall positively increasing trend in sales dollars.

Year	Quarter	Code	Sales (mil)
2020	Q_1	1	$ 9.0
	Q_2	2	10.2
	Q_3	3	3.5
	Q_4	4	5.0
2021	Q_1	5	12.0
	Q_2	6	14.1
	Q_3	7	4.4
	Q_4	8	7.3
2022	Q_1	9	16.0
	Q_2	10	18.3
	Q_3	11	4.6
	Q_4	12	8.6

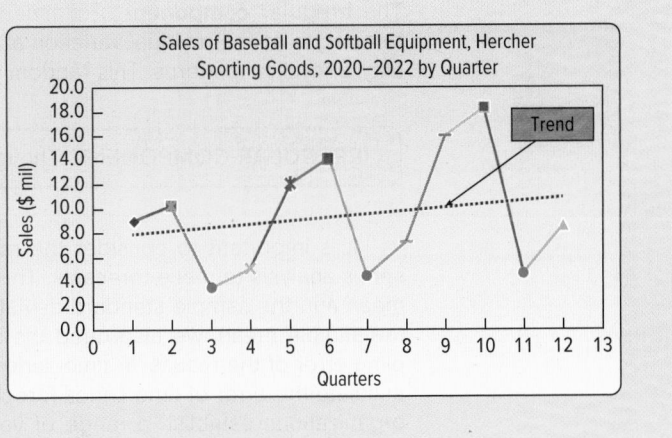

CHART 18–3 Seasonal Sales of Baseball and Softball Equipment

Cycles

Over a period of many years, time series can also display a **cyclical pattern.** For instance, national or regional economies may show recurring patterns of prosperity followed by periods of recession, depression, and then recovery.

> **CYCLICAL PATTERN** A pattern of highs and lows occurring over periods of many years.

Chart 18–4 shows the annual unit sales of batteries sold by National Battery Retailers Inc. from 2002 through 2022. The cyclical nature of the business is highlighted. There are periods of recovery, followed by prosperity, then contraction, and finally the cycle bottoms out with depression.

Year	Battery Sales (000)	Year	Battery Sales (000)
2002	24.0	2013	41.0
2003	30.0	2014	42.0
2004	31.0	2015	38.0
2005	26.5	2016	39.0
2006	27.0	2017	46.0
2007	27.5	2018	52.0
2008	34.0	2019	53.5
2009	35.0	2020	47.0
2010	31.0	2021	51.0
2011	32.0	2022	48.0
2012	35.5		

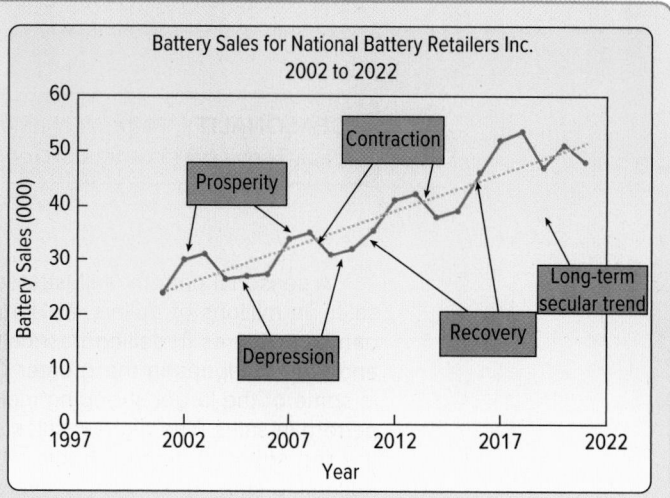

CHART 18–4 Battery Sales for National Battery Retailers Inc.

Irregular Component

The **irregular component** of a time series is the random variation of the data. It is referred to as the residual variation after a time series is summarized by trend, seasonality, or cyclical patterns. This random pattern is also called the residual or noise.

> **IRREGULAR COMPONENT** The random variation in a time series.

It is important to consider the random or irregular component when using time series analysis to make forecasts. This idea is analogous to reporting both the sample mean and the sample standard deviation. When we estimate the population mean via the sample mean, we also need the sample standard deviation to evaluate the sampling error of the results. In time series forecasting, the irregular component is used to estimate the error of time series forecasts. Knowing the forecast error, businesses and organizations establish a range of values that can reasonably be expected. By analyzing the irregular component in time series analysis, we can provide this important information.

The remainder of the chapter describes time series analysis techniques used to model, or explain, the patterns of a time series. We will focus on trend, seasonality, and irregular patterns. In the next section, we focus on time series analysis for the simplest of time series patterns: a time series with no trend or seasonality.

EXERCISES

1. Draw and label graphs of a stationary trend, a positive trend, and a negative trend.
2. Draw and label a graph that shows seasonality.
3. What is the irregular component of a time series?
4. What are the similarities and differences between the seasonal and cyclical patterns of a time series?

LO18-2
Compute forecasts using simple moving averages.

Modeling Stationary Time Series: Forecasts Using Simple Moving Averages

The simplest time series pattern is one with no trend or seasonality. This pattern is described as stationary. Examples of products that have a relatively stable demand pattern are staples of consumption, such as laundry detergent, toilet paper, and infant diapers.

When a time series is stationary, the appropriate forecasting technique is an average of recent observations. This type of forecasting technique is called a simple moving average. The number of past observations to include in the average affects the forecasts. When fewer observations are included in the average, the forecast will be more reactive to recent observations—that is, the variability of the time series will be evident in the forecasts. When more observations are included in the moving average, the forecast will be smoother and less reactive—that is, the variability of the time series will be "averaged" out. To put it another way, the forecast will not "bounce around." The following Example/Solution illustrates forecasting with a simple moving average.

▶ **EXAMPLE**

FILE Shown is a time series of the total annual enrollment for a university from 2014 to 2021. Use a three-period and a four-period simple moving average to forecast the total enrollment for 2022.

Year	Enrollment
2014	9,976
2015	10,263
2016	10,479
2017	10,663
2018	10,641
2019	10,484
2020	10,118
2021	10,473

SOLUTION

With any time series data set, the first task is to graph the data with a line graph as shown in Figure 18–1.

We observe from the graph that enrollment was fairly stable over the 8-year period. Also, over the 8 years a cyclical pattern is not evident. Therefore, using a simple moving average is a good choice to forecast enrollment for 2022.

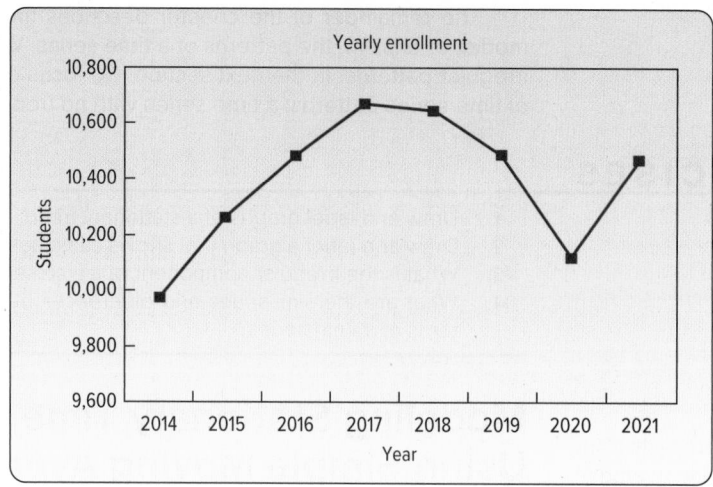

FIGURE 18–1 Student Enrollment

Using a three-period simple moving average, the forecast for 2022 would be the average of the enrollments from the most recent 3 years (2019, 2020, and 2021). The forecast is computed as follows:

$$\text{Enrollment for 2022} = \frac{10{,}484 + 10{,}118 + 10{,}473}{3} = 10{,}358$$

Using a three-period simple moving average, the value 10,358 is the forecast enrollment for 2022.

Using a four-period simple moving average, the forecast for 2022 would be the average enrollment from the most recent 4 years (2018, 2019, 2020, and 2021). The forecast is computed as follows:

$$\text{Enrollment for 2022} = \frac{10{,}641 + 10{,}484 + 10{,}118 + 10{,}473}{4} = 10{,}429$$

Using a four-period simple moving average, the value 10,429 is the forecast of total enrollment for 2022.

In this Example/Solution, a simple moving average forecasting technique was used to make a forecast using the most recent 3 years, and another forecast using the most recent 4 years. Which one is better? In the next section, we will develop the concept of forecasting error to help decide on the number of periods to include in a simple moving average.

LO 18–3

Compute and interpret the Mean Absolute Deviation and Mean Absolute Percent Error.

Forecasting Error

Any estimate or forecast is likely to be imprecise. The error, or lack of precision, is the difference between the actual observation and the forecast. Forecast error is found as:

Forecast Error = Actual − Forecast	**(18–1)**

This difference is called a deviation of the forecast from the actual value. The smaller the forecast error the better. The forecast error is also referred to as a residual. We will use "residual" in a later section of the chapter.

The previous Example/Solution concluded with two forecasts of university enrollment for 2022. If it were possible, the forecast with the smallest error would be the best. However, the actual enrollment for 2022 is unknown. So, we cannot compute the forecast errors. However, with the data, we can find the average error for each of the simple moving average models.

To find the forecasting error for the three-period moving average model, we begin by computing the forecast for 2017 by averaging the first 3 years: 2014, 2015, and 2016.

$$\text{Forecast } 2017 = (9{,}976 + 10{,}263 + 10{,}479)/3 = 10{,}239$$

Hence the forecast enrollment for 2017 is 10,239 students, and we know the actual enrollment for 2017 is 10,663. So, the forecast error for 2017 is 424.

$$\text{Forecast Error} = 10{,}663 - 10{,}239 = 424$$

This process starts in 2017 and moves through the time series to 2021. Now with the actual observed enrollment and the forecast for each year, we can calculate the error for each forecast. Chart 18–5 shows these results.

CHART 18–5 Three-Period Moving Average with Error

Year	Enrollment	3-Period Moving Average	Error	Absolute Value of Error	Absolute Percent Error
2014	9,976				
2015	10,263				
2016	10,479				
2017	10,663	10,239	424	424	3.97%
2018	10,641	10,468	173	173	1.62%
2019	10,484	10,594	(110)	110	1.05%
2020	10,118	10,596	(478)	478	4.72%
2021	10,473	10,414	59	59	0.56%
2022		10,358		Sum=1244	Sum=11.92%

We wish to summarize the yearly errors to determine the forecasting error using the three-period simple moving average model. As in Chapter 3, the best estimate of an unknown population parameter is a sample statistic. So, an average of the errors would be logical. But an issue remains. In some cases, the error is a positive value and in others, a negative value. If we simply summed the errors the negative values would tend to cancel out the positive values. This would lead to a misleading and likely understated forecasting error. The solution is to use the absolute value of each error term. That is, we make the error positive in all cases. We refer to this value as the absolute value of the error. The absolute value reports how much the forecast deviated from the actual value. These values are shown in Chart 18–5.

Logically, the mean of these absolute errors provides a good estimate of the typical error in the forecasted values. The mean of the absolute errors is called the **Mean Absolute Deviation** or **MAD.** It is calculated as follows:

$$\text{MAD} = \frac{\Sigma|\text{Error}|}{n} \qquad\qquad \textbf{(18–2)}$$

The MAD for the three-period moving average is:

$$\text{MAD} = \frac{\Sigma|\text{Error}|}{n} = \frac{1{,}244}{5} = 248.8$$

We interpret the MAD of 248.8, rounding to 249, as the average variability of forecast error using a three-period moving average forecasting model.

The MAD expresses forecasting error in absolute terms, 249 students. It is also helpful to express forecasting error in relative terms. In this case, we convert each of the absolute errors to absolute percent errors. In the previous example using the year 2017,

$$\text{Absolute Percent Error} = \frac{|\text{Error}|}{\text{Observed value}} = \frac{424}{10{,}663} = 0.0398 = 3.98\%.$$

So, the three-period moving average forecast for 2017 misses the observed value by 3.98%. Similar to the MAD, we calculate the absolute percent error for each period. Chart 18–5 shows these values. Then, the absolute percent errors are averaged to compute the **Mean Absolute Percent Error** or **MAPE.**

$$\text{MAPE} = \frac{\Sigma|\text{Percent Error}|}{n} \qquad\qquad \textbf{(18–3)}$$

The MAPE for the three-period moving average is:

$$\text{MAPE} = \frac{\Sigma|\text{Percent Error}|}{n} = \frac{11.92\%}{5} = 2.38\%$$

We interpret the MAPE of 2.38% as the average relative variability of forecast error using a three-period moving average forecasting model. Finally, we report that the forecast for 2022 is 10,358 students with a MAD equal to 249 and MAPE of 2.38%. Using a three-period simple moving average, we can expect the forecast of 2022 student enrollment is between 10,109 students (found by 10,358 − 249) and 10,607 students (found by 10,358 + 249). In relative terms, the estimate of forecast error is 2.38%.

▶ **EXAMPLE**

From the prior Example/Solution, find the MAD and MAPE when a four-period simple moving average is used to forecast enrollment for 2022. How does this MAD and MAPE compare to the MAD and MAPE for the three-period moving average?

SOLUTION

First, compute all possible four-period moving averages. Then compute the absolute value and absolute percent value of error for each period starting in 2018.

See Chart 18–6 for the results. Now compute forecast errors for 2018 through 2021. Next, apply the absolute value to all errors and compute the absolute percent errors. Finally, find the MAD and MAPE by averaging the absolute values of error and the absolute percent errors. The MAD is 193.88 rounded to 194 and the MAPE is 1.88%.

CHART 18–6 Six-Period Moving Average with Error

Year	Enrollment	4-Period Moving Average	Error	Absolute Value of Error	Absolute Percent Error
2014	9,976				
2015	10,263				
2016	10,479				
2017	10,663				
2018	10,641	10,345	296	296	2.78%
2019	10,484	10,512	(28)	28	0.26%
2020	10,118	10,567	(449)	449	4.44%
2021	10,473	10,477	(4)	4	0.03%
2022		10,429		MAD=194.25	MAPE=1.88%

Using a four-period moving average model, the MAD or the average variability of forecast error is 194.25, rounding to 194. The MAPE or the average relative variability of forecast error is 1.88%. Recalling that the four-period moving average forecast for 2022 is 10,429, we can expect the forecasted 2022 enrollment to be between 10,235 (found by 10,429 − 194) and 10,623 (found by 10,429 + 194). The relative error is 1.88%.

When using a simple moving average, we must choose the number of past periods to include in the average. The decision can be based on the choice that results in the smallest MAD and MAPE. The four-period MAD and MAPE are smaller, and therefore preferred to the three-period moving average. Caution: Do not make any general conclusions about the relationship between the number of periods and the error based on this single example.

Another outcome of using more periods in a simple moving average is its effect on the variation of the forecasts. Recall that calculating a mean or average essentially estimates the center or middle value of a data set. And the variance of the means is inversely related to the number of observations used to compute the mean. This relationship is important in time series analysis. Variation in the forecasts is related to the number of observations in a simple moving average. More periods will reduce variation in the forecasts. See Figure 18–2. It shows the actual prices and the 3- and 6-month moving average price forecasts. You can see that the range of forecast values for the 6-month averages is smaller than the range of forecasts for the 3-month averages.

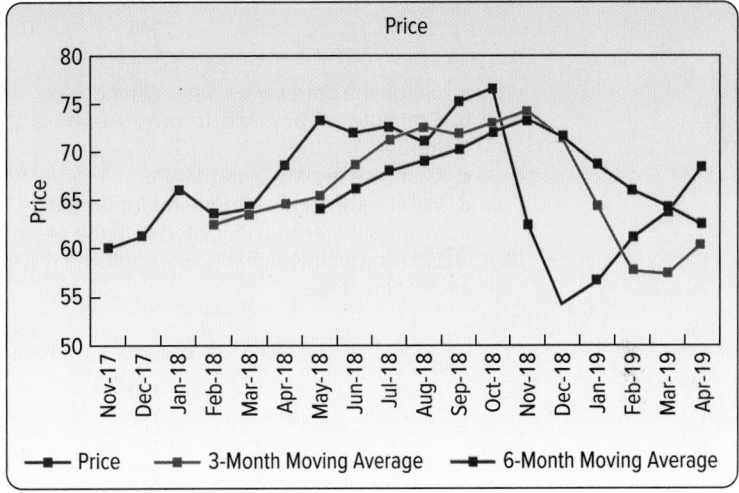

FIGURE 18–2 Comparing 3- and 6-Month Moving Average Forecasts

SELF-REVIEW 18–1

John is interested in analyzing the last 17 months of total revenue data for his Etsy store that features hand-crafted jewelry. The times series data follow:

Month	Revenue	Month	Revenue
March	$5,874	December	$5,192
April	7,651	January	7,177
May	5,546	February	7,693
June	7,594	March	7,232
July	6,450	April	7,742
August	5,580	May	7,142
September	6,560	June	6,227
October	7,209	July	6,639
November	7,679		

(a)   Graph the data.
(b)   Based on the graph, describe the time series.
(c)   For this time series, why is forecasting with a simple moving average appropriate?
(d)   Evaluate a simple moving average forecast model based on four periods. What are the MAD and MAPE?
(e)   Make a forecast using the four-period model.
(f)   Repeat parts (d) and (e), using an eight-period simple moving average model.
(g)   Would you recommend a four-period or an eight-period simple moving average model? Why?

EXERCISES

5.   **FILE** Using simple moving averages and the following time series data, respond to each of the items.

Period	Demand	Period	Demand
1	104	6	150
2	132	7	101
3	143	8	126
4	137	9	116
5	146	10	115

   a. Graph the time series data. What do you observe?
   b. Compute all possible forecasts using a three-period simple moving average model.
   c. Compute the MAD and MAPE.
   d. What is the forecast demand for period 11?
   e. What is the error associated with the eleventh-period forecast?

6.   **FILE** Using simple moving averages and the following time series data, respond to each of the items.

Period	Demand	Period	Demand
1	130	6	105
2	122	7	116
3	121	8	118
4	112	9	142
5	141	10	125

   a. Graph the time series data. What do you observe?
   b. Compute all possible forecasts using a six-period simple moving average model.
   c. Compute the MAD and MAPE.
   d. What is the forecast demand for period 11?
   e. What is the error associated with the eleventh-period forecast?

7.   **FILE** Using simple moving averages and the following time series data, respond to each of the items.

Period	Demand	Period	Demand
1	126	6	101
2	112	7	132
3	135	8	141
4	145	9	110
5	106	10	131

a. Graph the time series data. What do you observe?
b. Compute all possible forecasts using a four-period simple moving average model.
c. Compute all possible forecasts using a six-period simple moving average model.
d. Compute the MAD and MAPE for each forecast.
e. Which forecast has less error?

8. **FILE** Using simple moving averages and the following time series data, respond to each of the items.

Period	Demand	Period	Demand
1	72	8	28
2	60	9	53
3	27	10	50
4	52	11	57
5	26	12	87
6	46	13	22
7	52	14	56

a. Graph the time series data. What do you observe?
b. Compute all possible forecasts using a four-period simple moving average model.
c. Compute all possible forecasts using an eight-period simple moving average model.
d. Compute the MAD and MAPE for each forecast.
e. Which forecast has less error?

LO18-4
Compute forecasts using exponential smoothing.

Modeling Stationary Time Series: Simple Exponential Smoothing

When using a simple moving average, observe that each of the past observations is equally weighted. In a six-period simple moving average, this means that the observed value from six periods in the past and the most recent observation have the same weight or importance in computing the forecast.

Another time series model used to forecast a stationary pattern is simple exponential smoothing. It differs from a simple moving average because it applies unequal weights to past observations. The simple exponential smoothing equation is:

$$\text{Forecast}_{t+1} = \alpha(\text{Observed Value}_t) + (1 - \alpha)(\text{Forecast}_t) \tag{18–4}$$

The idea of forecasting is expressed using subscripts in the equation. The subscript t refers to a time period. So, the subscript $t + 1$ indicates the next time period. Using the subscripts with formula (18–4), the forecast for the next period, Forecast_{t+1}, is computed using the *Observed Value* and the *Forecast* from the current period, t. This again is the concept of time series forecasting using past data to predict the future.

Alpha (α) is called a **smoothing constant.**

SMOOTHING CONSTANT A value applied in exponential smoothing to determine the weights assigned to past observations. Smoothing constants are limited to values between 0 and 1.

When using exponential smoothing models, the smoothing constant is limited to values between 0 and 1.

Smoothing Constant: $0 \leq \alpha \leq 1$

As we decide the number of periods to include in a simple moving average, exponential smoothing requires us to select a value of α. The value of α determines the relative size of the weights applied to the past observed values in computing the weighted average. If we select a value near 1, recent data will receive more weight than older data. Suppose we assign .80 to α. Then, in the weighted average forecast, the most recent period's value is given a weight of 80%. The remaining 20% is distributed over all older values. On the other hand, if α is .10, the most recent period's value is given a weight of 10%. The remaining 90% of the weight is distributed over all older values.

To compute simple exponential smoothing forecasts, formula (18–4) can be restated as follows:

$$\text{Forecast}_{t+1} = \alpha(\text{Observed Value}_t) + (\text{Forecast}_t) - \alpha(\text{Forecast}_t)$$

$$\text{Forecast}_{t+1} = \text{Forecast}_t + \alpha(\text{Observed Value}_t - \text{Forecast}_t)$$

$$\text{Forecast}_{t+1} = \text{Forecast}_t + \alpha(\text{Error}_t) \qquad \textbf{(18–5)}$$

Formula (18–5) is a simpler way to compute forecasts. The next Example/Solution uses this equation.

▶ EXAMPLE

Using the time series of annual university enrollment, compute forecasts using simple exponential smoothing with a smoothing constant equal to 0.1. Include an estimate of forecasting error using the MAD and MAPE.

SOLUTION

Using the same data from the simple moving average Example/Solution, we replicate the line graph in Figure 18–1 here. As before, the graph indicates that the time series is relatively stationary and indicates that averaging past data is an appropriate way to compute forecasts.

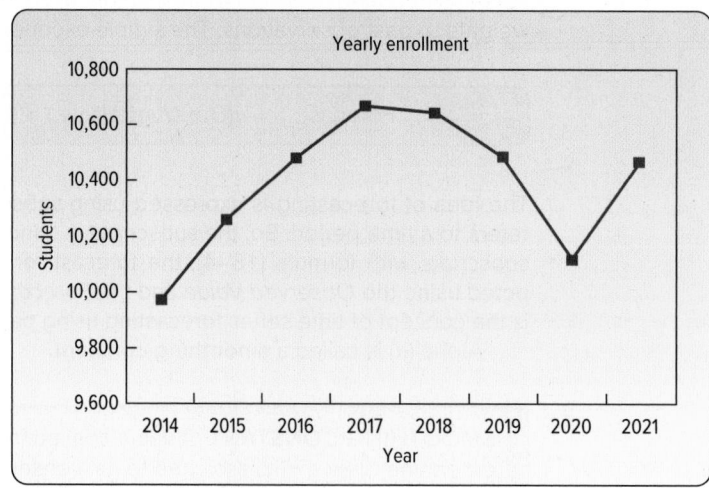

FIGURE 18–1 Student Enrollment (repeated)

Using simple exponential smoothing with a smoothing constant of 0.1, the exponential smoothing equation would be:

$$\text{Forecast}_{t+1} = \text{Forecast}_t + 0.1(\text{Error}_t)$$

The forecasting formula is applied in Chart 18–7. To begin the simple exponential smoothing equation, we need to recognize two issues. First, we cannot make a forecast for the first time period, year 2014, because there is no prior period. Second, to begin the series of forecasts we must assign a value to the forecast in the second period, year 2015. The preferred method is to set the forecast value in the second period to the observed enrollment from the first time period. In this case, the forecast value for the second period is 9,976. With this value, the forecast error for 2015 is 287, found by 10,263 − 9,976. Now we can begin using the simple exponential smoothing equation, period by period.

The forecast for 2016 is:

$$\text{Forecast}_{2016} = \text{Forecast}_{2015} + 0.1(\text{Error})_{2015}$$
$$\text{Forecast}_{2016} = 9,976 + 0.1(287) = 10,005$$
$$\text{Forecast Error}_{2016} = 10,479 - 10,005 = 474$$

Using the forecast and error values from 2016, now we can use the equation to estimate a forecast for the next year, 2017.

$$\text{Forecast}_{2017} = \text{Forecast}_{2016} + 0.1(\text{Error})_{2016}$$
$$\text{Forecast}_{2017} = 10,005 + 0.1(474) = 10,052$$

The smoothing formula is applied through the time series data until the last possible forecast for 2022 is made, which is 10,218. As we move through the time series, we compute the forecast errors, and apply the absolute value to all errors, and finally compute the MAD and the MAPE:

$$\text{MAD} = \frac{\Sigma|\text{Error}|}{n} = \frac{2,581}{7} = 369$$

$$\text{MAPE} = \frac{\Sigma|\text{Percent Error}|}{n} = \frac{24.54}{7} = 3.51\%$$

Year	Enrollment	Forecast $\alpha = 0.1$	Error	Absolute Error	Absolute Percent Error
2014	9,976	9,976	–	–	–
2015	10,263	9,976	287	287	2.80%
2016	10,479	10,005	474	474	4.53%
2017	10,663	10,052	611	611	5.73%
2018	10,641	10,113	528	528	4.96%
2019	10,484	10,166	318	318	3.03%
2020	10,118	10,198	(80)	80	0.79%
2021	10,473	10,190	283	283	2.70%
2022		10,218		MAD = 369	MAPE = 3.51%

CHART 18–7 Exponential Smoothing with a Smoothing Constant of 0.1

When using simple exponential smoothing, we must choose a value for the smoothing constant. Similar to simple moving averaging, the decision can be based on the smoothing constant that results in the smallest error. With the university enrollment time series, larger smoothing constants result in the smaller MADs and MAPEs. You can verify this result by using Excel to design a worksheet and substituting different values of α.

Another outcome of using different smoothing constant values is the effect on the variation of the forecasts. Refer to Figure 18–3. Recall that simple exponential smoothing places relative weights on past observations. The weights are determined by the smoothing constant value. If we select a relatively large value of α, such as 0.9, 90% of the weight is placed on the most recent observation. The forecasts are mostly determined by the price from the prior period. The remaining 10% of the weight is applied to the past observations. In this case, the forecast is very responsive to the most recent observed value. In contrast, a relatively small value of α, such as 0.1, places only 10% of the weight on the most recent observation and then distributes the remaining 90% of the weight more evenly over the past observations. The result is forecasts with less variability. A comparison of the two models is illustrated in Figure 18–3. The forecast with the high α-value, the green line graph, is very responsive to the most recent price; the forecast with the low α-value, the red line graph, is much smoother and follows the average of prices over time.

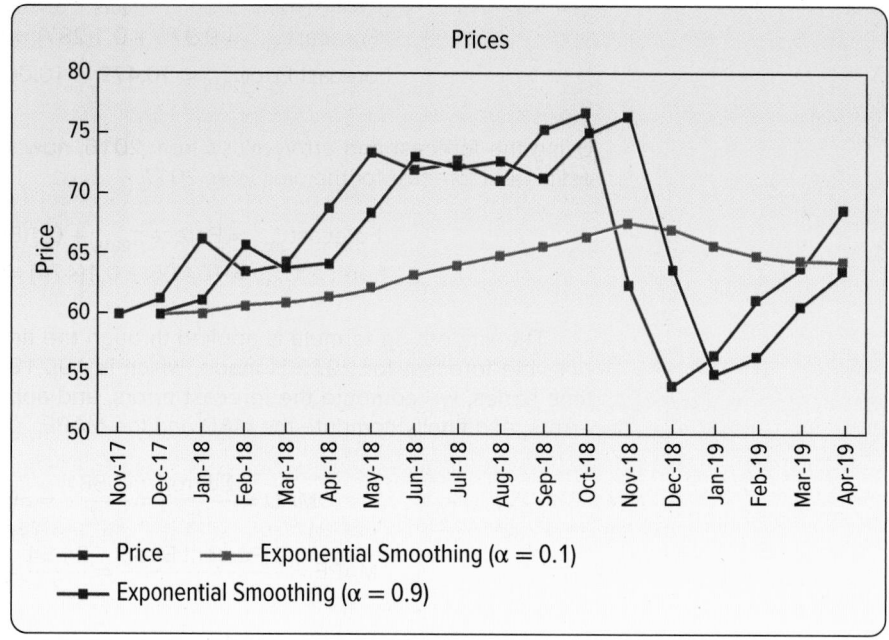

FIGURE 18–3 Forecasting Price with Different Smoothing Constants

SELF-REVIEW 18–2

FILE John is interested in analyzing the last 17 months of total revenue data for his Etsy store that features hand-crafted jewelry. The times series data follows:

Month	Revenue	Month	Revenue
March	$5,874	December	$5,192
April	7,651	January	7,177
May	5,546	February	7,693
June	7,594	March	7,232
July	6,450	April	7,742
August	5,580	May	7,142
September	6,560	June	6,227
October	7,209	July	6,639
November	7,679		

(a) Graph the data.
(b) Based on the graph, describe the time series.
(c) For this time series, why is forecasting with simple exponential smoothing appropriate?
(d) Evaluate a simple exponential smoothing forecast model with a smoothing constant of 0.2. What is the forecasting error?
(e) Make a forecast using simple exponential smoothing with a smoothing constant of 0.2.
(f) Repeat parts (d) and (e) using a smoothing constant of 0.7.
(g) Would you recommend using the simple exponential smoothing model with a constant of 0.2 or 0.7? Why?

EXERCISES

9. **FILE** Using simple exponential smoothing and the following time series data, respond to each of the items. (Note the data are the same as Exercise 5.)

Period	Demand	Period	Demand
1	104	6	150
2	132	7	101
3	143	8	126
4	137	9	116
5	146	10	115

a. Graph the time series data. What do you observe?
b. Compute all possible forecasts using a smoothing coefficient (α) of 0.3.
c. Compute the MAD and MAPE.
d. What is the forecast demand for period 11?
e. What is the error associated with period 11's forecast?

10. **FILE** Using simple exponential smoothing and the following time series data, respond to each of the items. (Note the data are the same as Exercise 6.)

Period	Demand
1	130
2	122
3	121
4	112
5	141
6	105
7	116
8	118
9	142
10	125

a. Graph the time series data. What do you observe?
b. Compute all possible forecasts using a smoothing coefficient (α) of 0.8.
c. Compute the MAD and MAPE.
d. What is the forecast demand for period 11?
e. What is the error associated with period 11's forecast?

11. **FILE** Using simple exponential smoothing and the following time series data, respond to each of the items. (Note the data are the same as Exercise 7.)

Period	Demand
1	126
2	112
3	135
4	145
5	106
6	101
7	132
8	141
9	110
10	131

  a. Graph the time series data. What do you observe?
  b. Compute all possible forecasts using a smoothing coefficient (α) of 0.35.
  c. Compute all possible forecasts using a smoothing coefficient (α) of 0.85.
  d. Compute the MAD and MAPE for each moving average forecast.
  e. Which forecast model would you choose? Why?

12. **FILE** Using simple exponential smoothing and the following time series data, respond to each of the items. (Note the data are the same as Exercise 8.)

Period	Demand	Period	Demand
1	72	8	28
2	60	9	53
3	27	10	50
4	52	11	57
5	26	12	87
6	46	13	22
7	52	14	56

  a. Graph the time series data. What do you observe?
  b. Compute all possible forecasts using a smoothing coefficient (α) of 0.4.
  c. Compute all possible forecasts using a smoothing coefficient (α) of 0.9.
  d. Compute the MAD and MAPE for each moving average forecast.
  e. Which forecast model would you choose? Why?

LO18-5

Compute a forecasting model using regression analysis.

Modeling Time Series with Trend: Regression Analysis

Rather than a stationary pattern, time series data may have an increasing upward trend or a decreasing downward trend. When we observe a line graph of a time series with a trend pattern, the trend may be linear or nonlinear. If the trend is linear, regression analysis is used to fit a linear trend model to the time series. If the trend is not linear, the data are rescaled with mathematical transformations or other approaches before using regression analysis. In this section, we focus on linear trend patterns and the application of simple linear regression. In Chapter 13 we described linear regression techniques. Here, we extend the use of regression to analyze time series data with a linear trend.

To illustrate trend analysis, we use the accompanying time series data that are available as a file in Connect. The time series is 2 years of monthly demand data. Each observation is labeled with the month. In addition, each observation is sequentially numbered with the variable, time period. The variable, time period, is very important because it is the *X*-axis variable in the line graph of the data and the independent variable in the regression analysis.

First Year		
Month	**Time Period**	**Demand**
January	1	40
February	2	22
March	3	48
April	4	72
May	5	75
June	6	64
July	7	64
August	8	53
September	9	65
October	10	97
November	11	71
December	12	80
Second Year		
Month	**Time Period**	**Demand**
January	13	97
February	14	83
March	15	107
April	16	124
May	17	128
June	18	114
July	19	133
August	20	142
September	21	153
October	22	135
November	23	132
December	24	132

To begin, we create a line graph of the data. It is the top graph in Figure 18–4 and shows a positive upward trend pattern of demand over time. If we apply an averaging technique such as simple moving averaging or exponential smoothing, these models do not fit the trend pattern. The lower left graph in Figure 18–4 shows that a 6-month moving average forecast model does not fit the trending time series; the averaging technique consistently underestimates the trend. The appropriate choice is to model the trend pattern with simple linear regression. The lower right graph shows the regression result; the trend line effectively fits the time series.

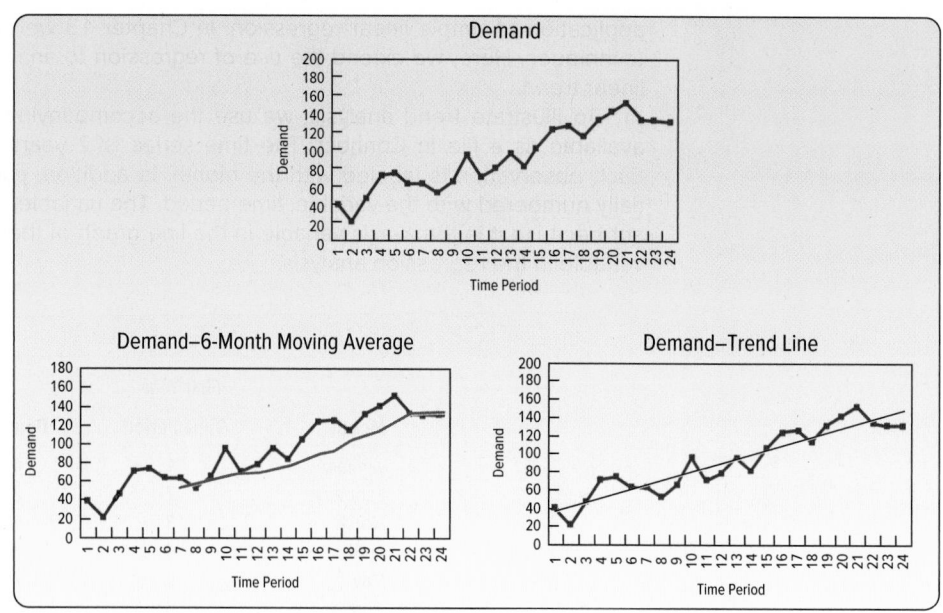

FIGURE 18–4 Time Series with Trend Pattern, 6-Month Moving Average Model, and Trend Line Model

Regression Analysis

To use simple linear regression analysis, the data must be presented in terms of a dependent variable and an independent variable. The independent variable, time period, is numbered consecutively as time periods 1 through 24, which are plotted on the horizontal axis. The dependent variable, demand, is plotted on the vertical axis.

By applying regression analysis, our objective is to find the equation of the trend line shown in the lower right graph of Figure 18–4. The line is represented by the following equation:

> Time Series Variable = Intercept + Slope (Time Period)   **(18–6)**

Using regression analysis in Excel yields the following results. The intercept and slope of the linear trend equation are highlighted in the output. The tutorial referenced in the margin demonstrates how to perform regression analysis in Excel.

Tutorial #63
in Connect

SUMMARY OUTPUT

Regression Statistics	
Multiple R	0.934
R Square	0.872
Adjusted R Square	0.866
Standard Error	13.384
Observations	24

ANOVA

	df	SS	MS	F	Significance F
Regression	1	26779.957	26779.957	149.495	0.000
Residual	22	3941.002	179.136		
Total	23	30720.958			

	Coefficients	Standard Error	t Stat	P-value
Intercept	32.63768	5.639	5.787	0.000
Time Period	4.82565	0.395	12.227	0.00

Applying the results to the regression equation, the trend forecasting model is:

$$\text{Demand} = 32.63768 + 4.82565 \text{ (Time Period)}$$

This result indicates that over the past 24 months, demand increased an average rate of 4.82565 units per month. Using the assumption of time series forecasting that the future will be similar to the past, the forecast is that demand will continue to increase at a rate of 4.82565 units for each future month. Applying the trend equation, the forecasts for months 25 and 26 (January and February of year 3) are:

$$\text{Demand (Time Period 25)} = 32.63768 + 4.82565 \text{ (25)} = 153.2789$$
$$\text{Demand (Time Period 26)} = 32.63768 + 4.82565 \text{ (26)} = 158.1046$$

To complete the forecasts for periods 25 and 26, we estimate the forecast error. As before, we use the MAD and MAPE. Chart 18–8 shows an abbreviated table of the MAD and MAPE calculation. First, we use the trend equation to compute a trend forecast for every time period. For instance, the trend forecast for the first time period is:

$$\text{Demand (Time Period 1)} = 32.63768 + 4.82565 \text{ (1)} = 37.4633$$

Month	Time Period	Demand	Trend Forecast	|Error|	|Percent error|
January	1	40	37.4633	2.5367	6.34%
February	2	22	42.2890	20.2890	92.22%
March	3	48	47.1146	0.8854	1.84%
.	.	.	.	.	.
.	.	.	.	.	.
.	.	.	.	.	.
October	22	135	138.8020	3.8020	2.82%
November	23	132	143.6276	11.6276	8.81%
December	24	132	148.4533	16.4533	12.46%
				Sum = 263.7248	Sum = 365.08

CHART 18–8 Calculation of Absolute Errors Using a Trend Equation

Then for each month, the absolute value of error is computed. The absolute value of error for the first time period is:

$$\text{Absolute Value of Forecast Error} = |40 - 37.4633| = 2.5367$$

The absolute percent error for the first time period is:

$$\text{Absolute Percent Error} = 2.5367/40 \text{ (100)} = 6.34\%$$

By summing all absolute values of error and dividing by the number of observations, the MAD is:

$$\text{MAD} = \frac{\Sigma|\text{Error}|}{n} = \frac{263.7248}{24} = 10.99$$

By summing all the absolute percent values and dividing by the number of observations, the MAPE is:

$$\text{MAPE} = \frac{\Sigma|\text{Percent Error}|}{n} = \frac{365.08}{24} = 15.21\%$$

If a trend forecasting model is used to compute forecasts beyond the next period, the forecast is more uncertain and will have more error. In the next Example/Solution, we illustrate the application of regression analysis when analyzing a time series with trend.

▶ **EXAMPLE**

FILE Shown are monthly total sales (in millions of dollars) for the retail and food service industry sourced from the U.S. Census data. (On the site **https://www.census. gov/retail/index.html#mrts**, find "Monthly Retail Trade Report," then select "Time Series/Trend Charts" to find the data for many retail sectors of the U.S. economy.)

Forecast total sales for the next 4 months. The variable, time period, is included in the data as the independent variable.

Retail and Food Service Dollars (millions)			
Year	Month	Time Period	Sales
1	January	1	$416,542
	February	2	420,654
	March	3	416,983
	April	4	417,151
	May	5	419,491
	June	6	421,678
	July	7	424,000
	August	8	423,225
	September	9	423,776
	October	10	426,522
	November	11	428,205
	December	12	427,827
2	January	13	423,937
	February	14	427,554
	March	15	434,018
	April	16	436,730
	May	17	438,605
	June	18	440,328
	July	19	441,829
	August	20	444,377

SOLUTION

The first task is to graph the time series data as shown with time period on the X-axis and sales on the Y-axis. It shows a positive increasing trend of sales over time. When this time series pattern occurs, regression analysis is appropriate to find the equation of a line that best fits the trend.

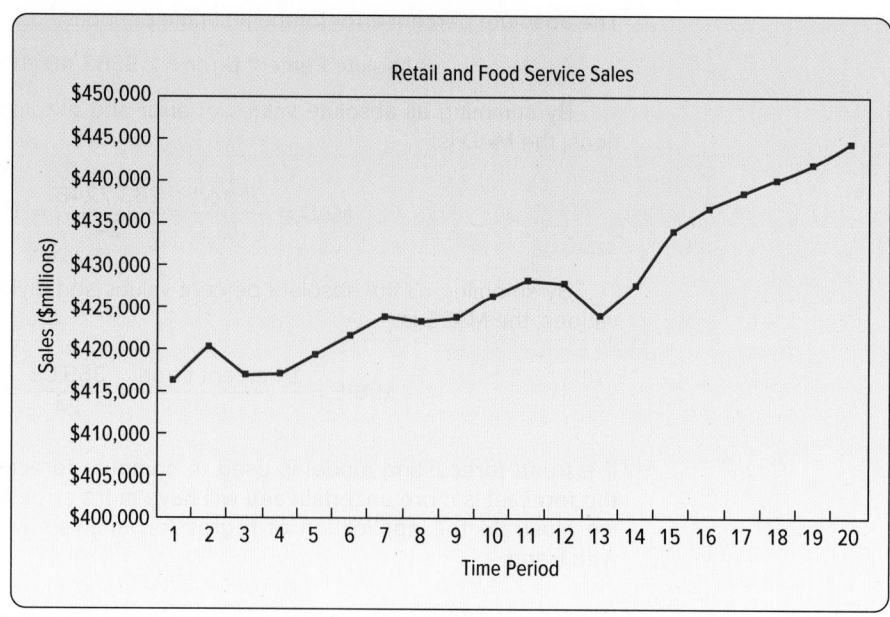

Regression analysis is usually performed using statistical software. Most, if not all, packages will ask you to input the data for dependent and independent variables. For this Example/Solution, the dependent variable is retail and food service sales and the independent variable is time period. Using regression analysis in Excel, the highlighted information in the following output shows an intercept of 412,980.44 and a slope of 1,399.16.

SUMMARY OUTPUT

Regression Statistics	
Multiple R	0.95
R Square	0.90
Adjusted R S	0.89
Standard Error	2334.65
Observations	20.00

ANOVA

	df	SS	MS	F	Significance F
Regression	1	1301832471.58	1301832471.58	162.02	0.00
Residual	18	144634259.22	8035236.62		
Total	19	1446466730.80			

	Coefficients	Standard Error	t Stat	P-value
Intercept	412,980.44	1316.78	313.63	0.00
Time Period	1,399.16	109.92	12.73	0.00

Therefore, the trend equation is:

Monthly Retail and Food Service Sales = 412,980.44 + 1,399.16 (Time Period)

Based on the historical pattern, the slope indicates that retail and food service sales are forecast to increase $1,399.16 million per year. The linear trend equation is illustrated with the time series data in the following graph.

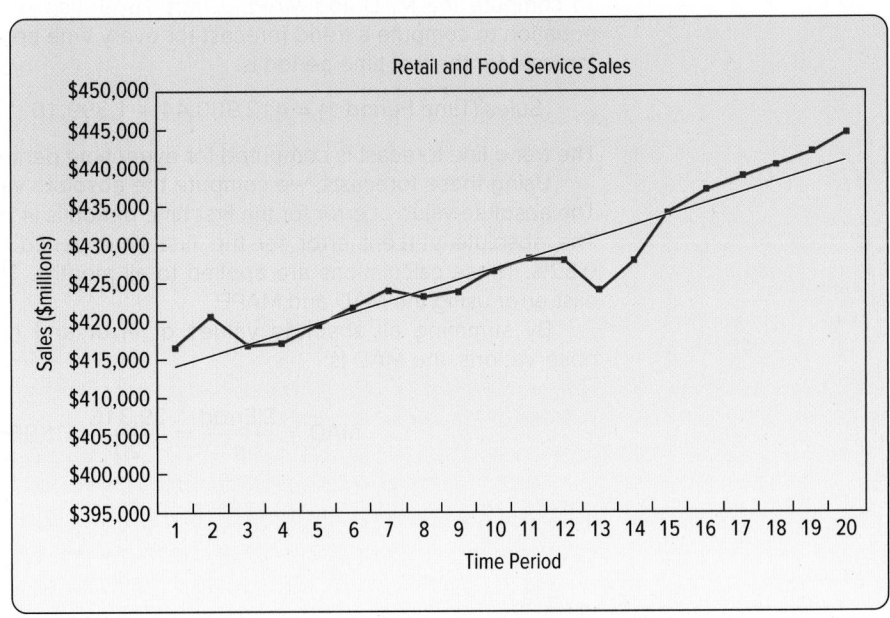

In Chart 18–9, forecasts are calculated for the future months of September through December. For example, the forecast for September of the second year (time period 21) is:

Sales (Time Period 21) = 412,980.44 + 1,399.16 (21) = $442,363 (Million)

Retail and Food Service Dollars (millions)						
Year	Month	Time Period	Sales	Forecast	|Error|	|Percent error|
1	January	1	$416,542	$414,380	2,162	0.52%
	February	2	420,654	415,779	4,875	1.16%
	March	3	416,983	417,178	195	0.05%
	April	4	417,151	418,577	1,426	0.34%
	May	5	419,491	419,976	485	0.12%
	June	6	421,678	421,375	303	0.07%
	July	7	424,000	422,775	1,225	0.29%
	August	8	423,225	424,174	949	0.22%
	September	9	423,776	425,573	1,797	0.42%
	October	10	426,522	426,972	450	0.11%
	November	11	428,205	428,371	166	0.04%
	December	12	427,827	429,770	1,943	0.45%
2	January	13	423,937	431,169	7,232	1.71%
	February	14	427,554	432,569	5,015	1.17%
	March	15	434,018	433,968	50	0.01%
	April	16	436,730	435,367	1,363	0.31%
	May	17	438,605	436,766	1,839	0.42%
	June	18	440,328	438,165	2,163	0.49%
	July	19	441,829	439,564	2,265	0.51%
	August	20	444,377	440,964	3,413	0.77%
	September	21		442,363		
	October	22		443,762		
	November	23		445,161		
	December	24		446,560		
				Sum	$39,316	Sum = 9.18%

CHART 18–9 Trend Forecasts and Errors for Retail and Food Services

To compute the MAD and MAPE, Chart 18–9 also shows that we use the trend equation to compute a trend forecast for every time period. For instance, the trend forecast for the first time period is:

Sales (Time Period 1) = 412,980.44 + 1,399.16 (1) = $414,380 (Million)

The trend line forecast is computed for every time period from 1 to 24.

Using these forecasts, we compute the absolute value for each month's error. The absolute value of error for the first time period is |416,542 − 414,380| = 2,162. The absolute percent error for the first time period is (2,162/416,542)(100) = 0.52%. These calculations are applied to all months. Then, find the model's forecast error using the MAD and MAPE.

By summing all absolute values of error and dividing by the number of observations, the MAD is:

$$MAD = \frac{\Sigma|Error|}{n} = \frac{39,316}{20} = 1,965.80$$

By summing all absolute percent errors and dividing by the number of observations, the MAPE is:

$$\text{MAPE} = \frac{\Sigma|\text{Percent Error}|}{n} = \frac{9.18}{20} = 0.46\%$$

So, the forecast for September of year 2 is 442,363 with an estimated error of 1,965.80. On average, the percentage error is only 0.46%. Similar statements can be made for October, November, and December of year 2.

To review, regression analysis is used to model a time series that shows either a positive increasing trend or a negative decreasing trend. You should note that we did not conduct any hypothesis tests about a relationship between the independent and dependent variables, or hypothesis tests about the significance of the intercept or slope. These tests require that the values of the dependent variable are uncorrelated over the range of the independent variable. The next section presents a method to statistically test for correlation in a time series, otherwise known as autocorrelation. If the values are autocorrelated, regression analysis can only be used as a tool to fit a line to time series data; we cannot test any hypothesis regarding statistical significance of the regression results.

SELF-REVIEW 18–3

FILE The table shows the total U.S. grocery store annual sales, in millions of dollars, from 1996 to 2021. (On the site **https://www.census.gov/retail/index.html#mrts**, find "Monthly Retail Trade Report," then select "Time Series/Trend Charts" to find the data for many retail sectors of the economy.)

Year	Sales ($millions)	Year	Sales ($millions)
1996	$365,547	2009	$510,033
1997	372,570	2010	520,750
1998	378,188	2011	547,476
1999	394,250	2012	563,645
2000	402,515	2013	574,547
2001	418,127	2014	599,603
2002	419,813	2015	613,159
2003	427,987	2016	625,295
2004	441,136	2017	639,161
2005	457,667	2018	661,785
2006	471,699	2019	693,015
2007	491,360	2020	773,741
2008	511,222	2021	803,041

Using this data, respond to the following items:
(a) Graph the data.
(b) Based on the graph, describe the time series pattern.
(c) For this time series, why is forecasting with a trend model appropriate?
(d) Evaluate a trend forecasting model using simple linear regression. What are the MAD and MAPE?
(e) What is the predicted annual change of industry sales?
(f) Forecast the annual industry sales for the next 3 years.

EXERCISES

13. **FILE** Using the time series data in the table, respond to the following items.

Period	Sales	Period	Sales
1	$1001	10	$686
2	1129	11	909
3	841	12	469
4	1044	13	566
5	1012	14	488
6	703	15	688
7	682	16	675
8	712	17	303
9	646	18	381

  a. Graph the data.
  b. Based on the graph, describe the time series pattern.
  c. For this time series, why is forecasting with a trend model appropriate?
  d. Evaluate a trend forecasting model using simple linear regression. What are the MAD and MAPE?
  e. What is the predicted annual change of industry sales?
  f. Predict sales for the next three periods.

14. **FILE** Using the time series data in the table, respond to the following items.

Period	Sales	Period	Sales
1	$615	10	$1115
2	676	11	1231
3	761	12	1259
4	710	13	1495
5	784	14	1229
6	801	15	1652
7	852	16	1337
8	698	17	1673
9	1193	18	1613

  a. Graph the data.
  b. Based on the graph, describe the time series pattern.
  c. For this time series, why is forecasting with a trend model appropriate?
  d. Evaluate a trend forecasting model using simple linear regression. What are the MAD and MAPE?
  e. What is the predicted annual change of industry sales?
  f. Predict sales for the next three periods.

15. **FILE** Over the years the U.S. grocery distribution and sales industry has grown. Today, the total industry sales are in the billions of dollars. Major retailers, such as Walmart and Target, added food to complement their merchandise sales and Amazon recently purchased Whole Foods. For many companies, forecasts of industry sales are necessary information to plan for short- and long-term decisions. Using the total U.S. grocery store annual sales in millions of dollars (**https://www.census.gov/retail/index.html#mrts**) in the following table, respond to the following items.

Year	Sales	Year	Sales
2012	$563,645	2017	$639,161
2013	574,547	2018	661,785
2014	599,603	2019	693,015
2015	613,159	2020	773,741
2016	625,295	2021	803,041

a. Graph the data.
b. Based on the graph, describe the time series pattern.
c. For this time series, why is forecasting with a trend model appropriate?
d. Evaluate a trend forecasting model using simple linear regression. What are the MAD and MAPE?
e. What is the predicted annual change of industry sales?
f. Using the trend model, forecast the next 3 years of grocery sales.

16. **FILE** The table shows the total annual sales of U.S. gasoline in millions of dollars from 2010 to 2021. (On the site **https://www.census.gov/retail/index.html#mrts**, find "Monthly Retail Trade Report," then select "Time Series/Trend Charts" to find the data for total U.S. sales of gasoline.)

Year	Annual Sales	Year	Annual Sales
2010	$335,528	2016	$280,241
2011	380,405	2017	372,429
2012	408,833	2018	521,453
2013	401,500	2019	512,377
2014	390,098	2020	430,116
2015	312,808	2021	588,140

a. Graph the data.
b. Based on the graph, describe the time series pattern.
c. For this time series, why is forecasting with a trend model appropriate?
d. Evaluate a trend forecasting model using simple linear regression. What are the MAD and MAPE?
e. What is the predicted annual change of industry sales?
f. Using the trend model, forecast the next 3 years of gasoline sales.

LO18-6

Apply the Durbin-Watson statistic to test for autocorrelation

The Durbin-Watson Statistic

As stated, time series analysis attempts to quantify patterns in the data and then use these patterns to make forecasts for the future. In these patterns, successive observations can be correlated. Successive residuals are correlated in time series data if an event in one time period influences the event in the next period. To explain, the owner of a furniture store decides to spend a large amount of money advertising a sale. We would expect to see an increase in this month's sales and increases in sales in future months. It is likely that some of the effect of the advertising carries over into future months. Therefore, we expect correlation among the subsequent monthly sales.

When using regression, correlation among observations presents a particular difficulty. This is called autocorrelation. To determine if a time series has autocorrelation, the analysis focuses on forecast errors, or the residuals. Note the term *residual* is the same as forecast error.

Residual or Forecast Error = Actual − Forecast

Residual values can be either positive or negative. If a forecasting model fits the time series data, the residuals would vary above and below zero.

To evaluate autocorrelation, we first graph the residuals scaled on the vertical axis and time period along the horizontal axis. If there is no autocorrelation, the graph would show a random scatter of observations. In Chart 18–10, the residuals are not randomly scattered. Notice there are nonrandom "runs" of residuals above and below the 0 line. If we computed the correlation between successive residuals, it is likely the correlation would be strong. This condition is called **autocorrelation**.

CHART 18–10 Plot of Residuals with a Nonrandom Pattern

AUTOCORRELATION Successive residuals are correlated.

If the residuals are correlated, hypothesis test results about the regression coefficients are unreliable. Also, a confidence interval or a prediction interval, which is based on the standard error of estimate, may not yield reliable results.

To determine if the data are autocorrelated, we use the Durbin-Watson statistic. The **Durbin-Watson statistic,** identified by the letter d, is computed by first determining the residual, e_t, for each time period, t. That is,

$$e_t = \text{Actual}_t - \text{Forecast}_t$$

Next, we compute d using the following equation.

DURBIN-WATSON STATISTIC	$d = \dfrac{\sum\limits_{t=2}^{n}(e_t - e_{t-1})^2}{\sum\limits_{t=1}^{n}(e_t)^2}$	(18–7)

To determine the numerator of formula (18–7), we lag each of the residuals one period. Then, in each time period, starting in period 2, we square the difference between the period's residual, e_t, and the lagged residual, e_{t-1}. Then sum these squared differences. In the denominator, we square the residuals and sum over all n observations.

The value of the Durbin-Watson statistic can range from 0 to 4. If the value of d is 2.00, then there is no autocorrelation among the residuals. When the value of d is close to 0, this indicates positive autocorrelation. Values of d greater than 2 indicate negative autocorrelation. To occur, successive residuals would tend to be large but would have opposite signs. Negative autocorrelation is rarely found in actual data. To conduct a test for autocorrelation, the null and alternate hypotheses are:

$$H_0: \text{No autocorrelation}$$

$$H_1: \text{Positive autocorrelation}$$

The critical values for d are reported in Appendix B.9. To determine the critical values, we need to know the significance level, α, the sample size, n, and the number of independent variables, k. Then, we can find the Durbin-Watson critical values, d_l and d_u. The subscript l refers to the lower limit of d and the subscript u the upper limit. The decision rule for the Durbin-Watson hypothesis test is different because it includes the possibility that the results are inconclusive. As usual, there is a range of d values where the null hypothesis is rejected and a range of d values where the null hypothesis is not rejected. However, there is also a range of d values where the null hypothesis is neither rejected nor not rejected. To state this more formally:

- For computed d values less than d_l, reject the null hypothesis.
- For computed d values greater than d_u, fail to reject the null hypothesis.
- For computed values of d between d_l and d_u, the result is inconclusive.

How do we interpret the various decisions for the autocorrelation test? If the null hypothesis is not rejected, the data provide no evidence that autocorrelation exists in the data. The results of the regression analysis hypothesis tests should not be influenced by autocorrelation. If the null hypothesis is rejected, then we conclude that autocorrelation is present and the results of the regression hypothesis tests may not be reliable—that is, the conclusions based on the p-values may be incorrect.

A possible remedy for autocorrelation is to transform the dependent variable or include another predictor variable that captures time order. We might use the square root of the dependent variable. Then we would repeat the regression analysis and compute the Durbin-Watson statistic to determine the effect of the transformation. If the Durbin-Watson result using a transformation falls in the inconclusive range, more sophisticated tests are needed, or conservatively, we treat the conclusion as rejecting the null hypothesis. The next Example/Solution shows the details of the Durbin-Watson test and how the results are interpreted.

▶ **EXAMPLE**

Using the same data from the previous Example/Solution, total monthly sales of retail and food services (in millions of dollars) from the U.S. Census, evaluate the regression results for autocorrelation using the Durbin-Watson statistic.

SOLUTION

See Chart 18–11 for all calculations. To examine the residuals, we first calculate forecasts for all time periods using the trend equation. Recall that the trend forecast model is:

Monthly retail and Food Service Sales = 412,980.44 + 1399.16 (Time Period)

By substituting the time period values 1 through 20 into this equation, we can compute the forecast for each period. In Chart 18–11, these are calculated in the column labeled $\hat{y}$. Then using the observed sales, y_t, and forecast, $\hat{y}_t$, we can calculate a residual, e_t, for each period.

$$e_t = y_t - \hat{y}_t$$

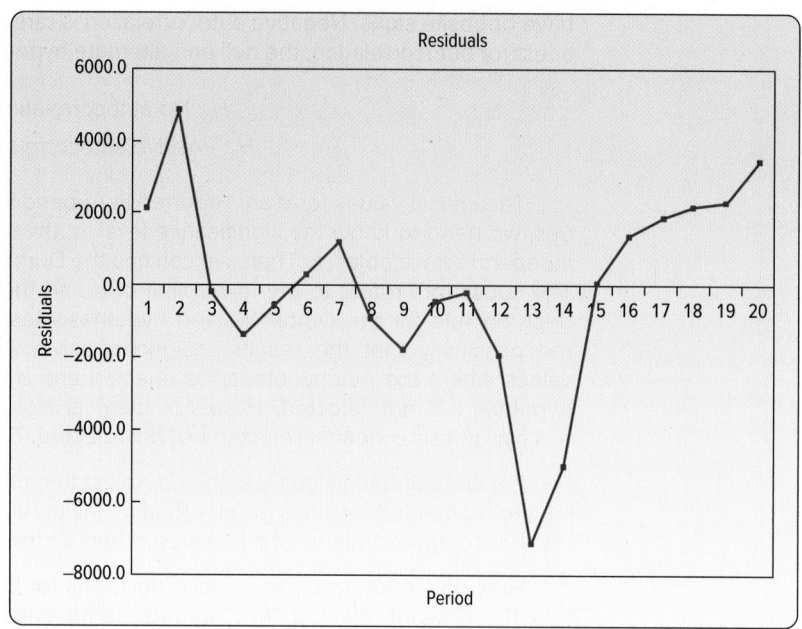

The graph shows the residuals versus time period. Notice that the residuals do not show a random pattern distributed around the expected value of zero. In the graph, autocorrelation is indicated by a non-random, downward trend followed by an upward trend. This pattern shows a strong case for autocorrelation.

To calculate the Durbin-Watson statistic, review Chart 18–11. There is a column of residuals, e_t, and a column of lagged residuals, e_{t-1}. Notice that the lagged values are the residual values from the previous period $(t-1)$. In the right two columns, we calculate the values needed for the numerator and denominator of the statistic.

Year	Month	Period	Sales y	Forecast $\hat{y}$	Residuals $e_t = y_t - \hat{y}_t$	Lagged Residuals (e_{t-1})	Squared Difference $(e_t - e_{t-1})^2$	Squared Residual $(e_t)^2$
1	January	1	$416,542	414,379.6000	2162.4000			4675973.8
	February	2	420,654	415,778.7579	4875.2421	2162.4000	7359512.3	23767985.5
	March	3	416,983	417,177.9158	−194.9158	4875.2421	25706501.1	37992.2
	April	4	417,151	418,577.0737	−1426.0737	−194.9158	1515749.8	2033686.2
	May	5	419,491	419,976.2316	−485.2316	−1426.0737	885183.9	235449.7
	June	6	421,678	421,375.3895	302.6105	−485.2316	620695.2	91573.1
	July	7	424,000	422,774.5474	1225.4526	302.6105	851637.5	1501734.1
	August	8	423,225	424,173.7053	−948.7053	1225.4526	4726962.6	900041.7
	September	9	423,776	425,572.8632	−1796.8632	−948.7053	719371.8	3228717.4
	October	10	426,522	426,972.0211	−450.0211	−1796.8632	1813983.6	202519.0
	November	11	428,205	428,371.1789	−166.1789	−450.0211	80566.4	27615.4
	December	12	427,827	429,770.3368	−1943.3368	−166.1789	3158290.2	3776557.9
2	January	13	423,937	431,169.4947	−7232.4947	−1943.3368	27975191.3	52308979.6
	February	14	427,554	432,568.6526	−5014.6526	−7232.4947	4918823.6	25146740.7
	March	15	434,018	433,967.8105	50.1895	−5014.6526	25652625.5	2519.0
	April	16	436,730	435,366.9684	1363.0316	50.1895	1723554.4	1857855.1
	May	17	438,605	436,766.1263	1838.8737	1363.0316	226425.7	3381456.5
	June	18	440,328	438,165.2842	2162.7158	1838.8737	104873.7	4677339.6
	July	19	441,829	439,564.4421	2264.5579	2162.7158	10371.8	5128222.5
	August	20	444,377	440,963.6000	3413.4000	2264.5579	1319838.2	11651299.6
							109370158.5	139958284.8

$$\sum_{t=1}^{n}(e_t)^2$$

$$\sum_{t=2}^{n}(e_t - e_{t-1})^2$$

CHART 18–11 Calculation of the Durbin-Watson Statistic

For example, the period 2 squared difference is calculated as:

$$(e_t - e_{t-1})^2 = (4{,}875.2421 - 2{,}162.4000)^2 = 7{,}359{,}512.3$$

In the right-most column, the residuals are simply squared. After completing the calculations for every time period, we have the information to calculate the Durbin-Watson statistic. Using the sums of the two right-most columns, the Durbin-Watson statistic is:

$$d = \frac{\sum_{t=2}^{n} (e_t - e_{t-1})^2}{\sum_{t=1}^{n} (e_t)^2} = \frac{109{,}370{,}158.5}{139{,}958{,}284.8} = 0.78$$

To test for autocorrelation, the null and the alternate hypotheses are stated as follows:

H_0: No autocorrelation
H_1: Positive autocorrelation

The critical values of d are found in Appendix B.9. A portion of the tables is shown here. To find the d's, we will use a .05 level of significance. The sample size, n, is 20, and there is one independent variable, so $k = 1$, We move to the .05 table, the column where $k = 1$, and the row where $n = 20$. The reported values are $d_l = 1.20$ and $d_u = 1.41$. The null hypothesis is rejected if $d < 1.20$ and not rejected if $d > 1.41$. No conclusion is reached if d is between 1.20 and 1.41.

n	k = 1		k = 2	
	d_l	d_u	d_l	d_u
7	0.70	1.36	0.47	1.90
8	0.76	1.33	0.56	1.78
9	0.82	1.32	0.63	1.70
10	0.88	1.32	0.70	1.64
11	0.93	1.32	0.76	1.60
12	0.97	1.33	0.81	1.58
13	1.01	1.34	0.86	1.56
14	1.04	1.35	0.91	1.55
15	1.08	1.36	0.95	1.54
16	1.11	1.37	0.98	1.54
17	1.13	1.38	1.02	1.54
18	1.16	1.39	1.05	1.54
19	1.18	1.40	1.07	1.54
20	1.20	1.41	1.10	1.54

N.E. Savin and K.J. White, "The Durbin-Watson Test for Serial Correlation with Extreme Sample Sizes or Many Regressors," *Econometrica* 45, 1977, pp. 1989–1996.

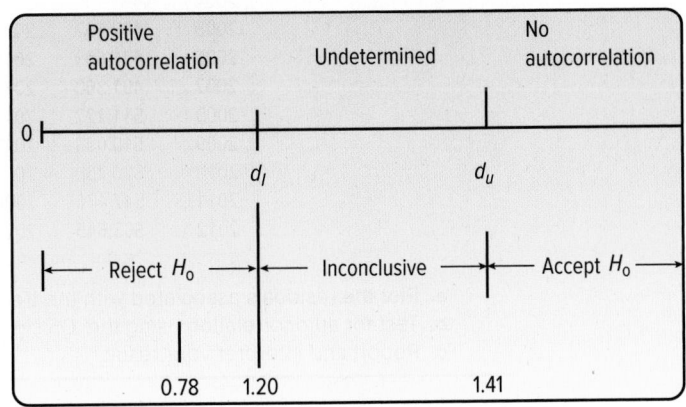

Because the computed value of d is 0.78, which is less than the d_l, we reject the null hypothesis and accept the alternate hypothesis. We conclude that the residuals are autocorrelated. The trend equation does not satisfy the regression assumption that the residuals are normally and randomly distributed. It is possible that we can reduce the autocorrelation by adding one or more independent variables that have a time-ordered effect on the dependent variable. The simplest independent variables represent lagged time periods.

More sophisticated statistical methods, such as autoregressive (AR), autoregressive moving average (ARMA), and autoregressive integrated moving average (ARIMA) techniques, account for autocorrelation. Information on these methods is available in other textbooks and online.

When we model the trend component of a time series, we expect that autocorrelation exists. Using the Durbin-Watson statistic helps us know that there are limitations to our interpretation and use of the regression results. Specifically, if autocorrelation exists, we can use the regression equation to model trend, but we cannot reliably report the significance of the equation or the regression coefficients.

EXERCISES

17. **FILE** Using the same time series data and trend forecast model as in Exercise 13, respond to the following items.

Period	Sales	Period	Sales
1	$1001	10	$686
2	1129	11	909
3	841	12	469
4	1044	13	566
5	1012	14	488
6	703	15	688
7	682	16	675
8	712	17	303
9	646	18	381

a. Plot the residuals associated with the trend model for this data.
b. Test for autocorrelation using the .05 significance level.
c. Report and interpret your result.

18. **FILE** Using the data, respond to the following items. (The data are sourced from **https://www.census.gov/retail/index.html#mrts**, find "Monthly Retail Trade Report," and select "Time Series/Trend Charts" to find the data for many retail sectors of the economy.)

Year	Sales	Year	Sales
2004	$441,136	2013	$574,547
2005	457,667	2014	599,603
2006	471,699	2015	613,159
2007	491,360	2016	625,295
2008	511,222	2017	639,161
2009	510,033	2018	671,330
2010	520,750	2019	693,015
2011	547,476	2020	773,741
2012	563,645	2021	803,041

a. Plot the residuals associated with the trend model for these data.
b. Test for autocorrelation using the .05 significance level.
c. Report and interpret your result.

LO18-7

Compute seasonal indexes and use the indexes to make seasonally adjusted forecasts.

Modeling Time Series with Seasonality: Seasonal Indexing

In addition to trend, a time series may also show seasonality. In a time series graph, seasonality is displayed by a recurring pattern of high and low values corresponding to specific time periods. In Chart 18–12, a line graph shows a sample of monthly bookings (room nights) from hotels, motels, and guest houses in Victoria, Australia. The data span 3 years, or 36 months. The line graph of the time series shows two distinct patterns. First, it shows an increasing, positive trend in bookings over the 36 months. Second, it shows seasonality. For example, the graph shows the highest bookings in the months of October and March, and the lowest bookings in December and June. For the most part, these observations are the basis for concluding that the time series displays seasonality or a seasonal pattern. The graph displays other recurring seasonal patterns as well. Observe the bookings for January.

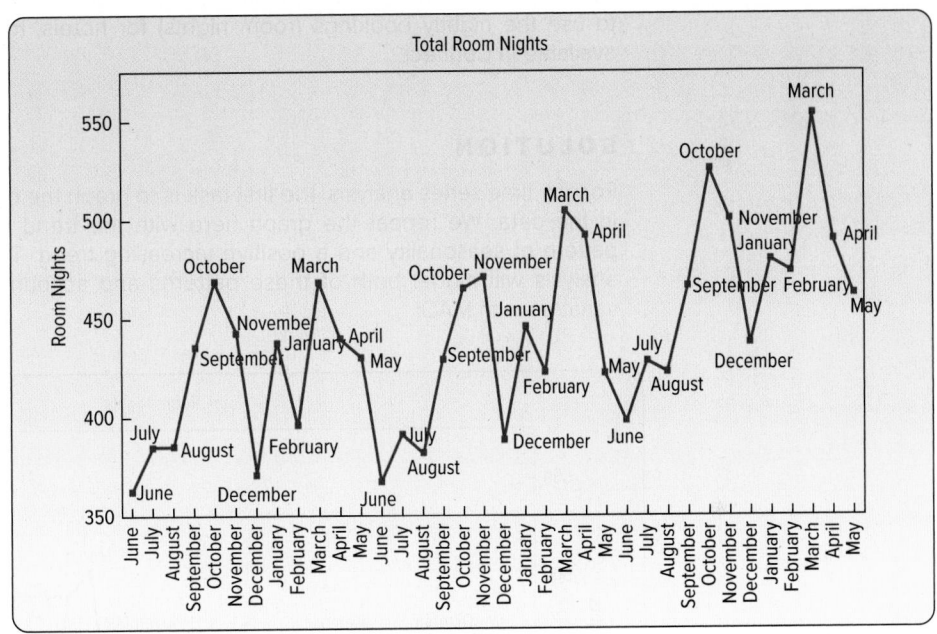

CHART 18–12 Monthly Total Bookings in Resorts over 3 Years

(Makridakis, Wheelwright and Hyndman, Wiley, 1998, 3rd edition)

When a seasonal pattern occurs, a forecast model should include a seasonal component. While there are other methods to quantify seasonality, our approach will focus on using seasonal indexes. An index is a quantitative way to compare two values. A commonly discussed index is the Consumer Price Index. It compares today's prices of a select group of items to the prices of the same items between 1982 and 1984. These prices are called the "base." The comparison is computed by dividing "today's prices" by the "base prices." The result is an index. If the index is equal to 1.0, then the numerator, the actual value, and the denominator, the base value, are equal and we would conclude that prices have not changed. If the index is less than 1.0, then prices have decreased. The index also allows us to quantify the change. If an index is 0.80, then today's prices are 20% less than the base prices. If the index is more than 1.0, then prices increased. If an index is 1.15, then today's prices are 15% more than the base prices. For some items such as medical care and higher education, the index may exceed 2.00. This means that the prices of medical care and higher education are 100% higher than the base period; the costs have doubled.

To quantify a seasonal pattern in a time series, we apply the concept of an index. First, we need to establish the base for the index. For a time series, we will define the base as the "average" over the range of the time series. To establish this average, we will fit the time series with a regression line as we did earlier in the chapter. Then for each time period in the time series, we will compare the observed value to the value or base predicted by the regression equation. For the periods with the highest recurring values, the seasonal index will be greater than 1.0; for periods with the lowest recurring values, the seasonal index will be less than 1.0. The following Example/Solution will illustrate the use of seasonal indexes.

▶ EXAMPLE

FILE Forecast monthly accommodation bookings for the next 12 months. Continue to use the nightly bookings (room nights) for hotels, motels, and guest houses available in Connect.

SOLUTION

For any time series analysis, the first task is to graph the data and observe patterns in the data. We repeat the graph here with the trend line. The graph shows a pattern of seasonality and a positive increasing trend. Therefore, our time series analysis will model both of these patterns and account for the randomness or variation with MAD.

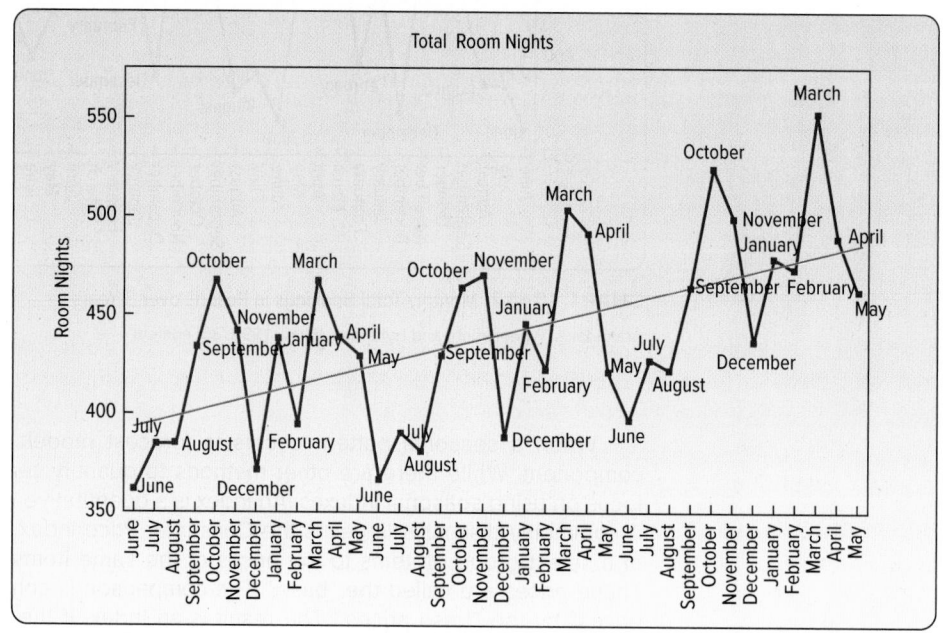

The first step is to fit the time series with a trend line using regression analysis. We use regression analysis in Excel to find the equation of the regression line.

SUMMARY OUTPUT

Regression Statistics	
Multiple R	0.591
R Square	0.349
Adjusted R Square	0.330
Standard Error	38.383
Observations	36

ANOVA

	df	SS	MS	F	p-value
Regression	1	26834.823	26834.823	18.215	0.000
Residual	34	50090.953	1473.263		
Total	35	76925.776			

	Coefficients	Standard Error	t Stat	P-value
Intercept	391.098	13.066	29.933	0.000
Time Period	2.628	0.616	4.268	0.000

See the highlighted part of the regression analysis output to find the slope and intercept of the trend line. The trend line is:

Total Monthly Bookings = 391.098 + 2.628 (Time Period)

The regression equation shows that total monthly bookings increase, on average, 2.628 per month. It is important to understand that the regression equation represents the average bookings over the range of the time series. Further, we can use the regression equation to calculate the "average" bookings for each time period in the time series. The "average" bookings for period 1 in the time series is:

Total Monthly Bookings (Period 1) = 391.098 + 2.628 (Time Period)
= 391.098 + 2.628 (1) = 393.726

Another example is the "average" bookings for period 5 in the time series. It is:

Total Monthly Bookings (Period 5) = 391.098 + 2.628 (Time Period)
= 391.098 + 2.628 (5) = 404.238

The "average" booking is emphasized because each of these values for the range of the time series will be the base for calculating the seasonal effect for each time period. For period 5, the observed bookings are 468.9. To calculate the seasonal effect or index for period 5, we compare the observed value to the "average" or base value:

$$\text{Seasonal Effect for Period 5} = \frac{468.9}{404.238} = 1.16$$

The result is an index of 1.16; it means the monthly bookings for October of year 1 are above the average. In fact, the monthly bookings are 116% of the expected value, 404.238. Another interpretation is that the monthly bookings are about 16% more than the average.

We calculate an index for every month in the data. For example, the seasonal effect or index for period 2 is:

$$\text{Seasonal Effect for Period 2} = \frac{384.9}{396.354} = 0.97$$

The result is an index of 0.97; it means the monthly bookings for July (period 2) are below the average. In fact, the monthly bookings are 3% less than the expected value, 396.354.

These calculations are completed for every time period in the time series. See Chart 18–13. Now you can see that every month in the time series has an estimated seasonal effect. In fact, for this time series of 36 months, each month has three indexes. These are presented in Chart 18–14. Next, the three indexes for each month are averaged. Chart 18–14 shows the monthly indexes. January's index is 1.03; our analysis indicates that the bookings for January will be 3% above the average predicted by the trend line equation.

Month	Time Period	Total Bookings	Base Value	Index
June	1	362.7	393.726	0.92
July	2	384.9	396.354	0.97
August	3	385.3	398.982	0.97
September	4	432.3	401.610	1.08
October	5	468.9	404.238	1.16
November	6	442.7	406.866	1.09
December	7	370.2	409.494	0.90
January	8	439.4	412.122	1.07
February	9	393.9	414.750	0.95
March	10	468.7	417.378	1.12
April	11	438.8	420.006	1.04
May	12	430.1	422.634	1.02
June	13	366.3	425.262	0.86
July	14	391	427.890	0.91
August	15	380.9	430.518	0.88
September	16	431.4	433.146	1.00
October	17	465.4	435.774	1.07
November	18	471.5	438.402	1.08
December	19	387.5	441.030	0.88
January	20	446.4	443.658	1.01
February	21	421.5	446.286	0.94
March	22	504.8	448.914	1.12
April	23	492.1	451.542	1.09
May	24	421.3	454.170	0.93
June	25	396.7	456.798	0.87
July	26	428	459.426	0.93
August	27	421.9	462.054	0.91
September	28	465.6	464.682	1.00
October	29	525.8	467.310	1.13
November	30	499.9	469.938	1.06
December	31	435.3	472.566	0.92
January	32	479.5	475.194	1.01
February	33	473	477.822	0.99
March	34	554.4	480.450	1.15
April	35	489.6	483.078	1.01
May	36	462.2	485.706	0.95

CHART 18–13 Monthly Indexes of Bookings

Month	Index 1	Index 2	Index 3	Monthly Index
January	1.07	1.01	1.01	1.03
February	0.95	0.94	0.99	0.96
March	1.12	1.12	1.15	1.13
April	1.04	1.09	1.01	1.05
May	1.02	0.93	0.95	0.97
June	0.92	0.86	0.87	0.88
July	0.97	0.91	0.93	0.94
August	0.97	0.88	0.91	0.92
September	1.08	1.00	1.00	1.03
October	1.16	1.07	1.13	1.12
November	1.09	1.08	1.06	1.08
December	0.90	0.88	0.92	0.90

CHART 18–14 Summary of Monthly Indexes

The monthly seasonal indexes show that March has the highest seasonal effect with an index of 1.13. This indicates that total bookings are 13% higher than the average demand. October is also a month with a high seasonal effect, 1.12. Based on the seasonal indexes, June is the month with the lowest index, 0.88, and therefore the lowest number of total bookings; the bookings are 12% lower than the average predicted bookings.

We must also calculate an estimate of the forecasting error by computing the MAD. To compute the MAD, we will use the trend line equation and the monthly indexes to make forecasts for time periods 1 through 36. This analysis follows. As examples, the forecast for period 1, June, and period 5, October, are:

Period 1 (June) Bookings = [391.098 + 2.628 (Time Period)] (Month Index for June)
Total Monthly Bookings (Period 1) = [391.098 + 2.628 (1)](0.88) = 346.479
Period 5 (October) Bookings = [391.098 + 2.628 (Time Period)] (Month Index for October)
Total Monthly Bookings (Period 5) = [391.098 + 2.628 (5)](1.12) = 452.747

This calculation is applied to all 36 months, as shown in Chart 18–15. Using these monthly forecasts, the absolute value of error is computed for every month. The MAD is:

$$\text{MAD} = \frac{\Sigma|\text{Error}|}{n} = \frac{374.04}{36} = 10.39$$

Then compute all absolute percent errors and compute the MAPE:

$$\text{MAPE} = \frac{\Sigma|\text{Percent Error}|}{n} = \frac{86.22}{36} = 2.40\%.$$

Now to make forecasts of total monthly bookings for the next 12 months, we use the trend or regression equation to predict the total bookings for each time period. Then, we adjust the prediction using the corresponding monthly index. For example, the forecast for June of the next year is time period 37. Using the trend or regression model, the predicted, average total bookings for period 37 are:

Total Bookings (Period 37) = 391.098 + 2.628 (Time Period)
= 391.098 + 2.628 (37) = 488.334

This prediction must be adjusted for seasonality using the index for June, which is 0.88. So, the seasonally adjusted forecast for June is:

Seasonally adjusted forecast (Period 37) = (488.334)(0.88) = 429.734

Month	Time Period	Total Bookings	Trend	Seasonally Adjusted Forecast	Absolute Error	Absolute Percent Error
June	1	362.7	393.726	346.479	16.22	4.47%
July	2	384.9	396.354	372.573	12.33	3.20%
August	3	385.3	398.982	367.063	18.24	4.73%
September	4	432.3	401.610	409.642	22.66	5.24%
October	5	468.9	404.238	452.747	16.15	3.44%
November	6	442.7	406.866	439.415	3.28	0.74%
December	7	370.2	409.494	368.545	1.66	0.45%
January	8	439.4	412.122	424.486	14.91	3.39%
February	9	393.9	414.750	398.160	4.26	1.08%
March	10	468.7	417.378	471.637	2.94	0.63%
April	11	438.8	420.006	441.006	2.21	0.50%
May	12	430.1	422.634	409.955	20.15	4.68%
June	13	366.3	425.262	374.231	7.93	2.16%
July	14	391	427.890	402.217	11.22	2.87%
August	15	380.9	430.518	396.077	15.18	3.99%
September	16	431.4	433.146	441.809	10.41	2.41%
October	17	465.4	435.774	488.067	22.67	4.87%
November	18	471.5	438.402	473.474	1.97	0.42%
December	19	387.5	441.030	396.927	9.43	2.43%
January	20	446.4	443.658	456.968	10.57	2.37%
February	21	421.5	446.286	428.435	6.93	1.64%
March	22	504.8	448.914	507.273	2.47	0.49%
April	23	492.1	451.542	474.119	17.98	3.65%
May	24	421.3	454.170	440.545	19.24	4.57%
June	25	396.7	456.798	401.982	5.28	1.33%
July	26	428	459.426	431.860	3.86	0.90%
August	27	421.9	462.054	425.090	3.19	0.76%
September	28	465.6	464.682	473.976	8.38	1.80%
October	29	525.8	467.310	523.387	2.41	0.46%
November	30	499.9	469.938	507.533	7.63	1.53%
December	31	435.3	472.566	425.309	9.99	2.29%
January	32	479.5	475.194	489.450	9.95	2.08%
February	33	473	477.822	458.709	14.29	3.02%
March	34	554.4	480.450	542.909	11.49	2.07%
April	35	489.6	483.078	507.232	17.63	3.60%
May	36	462.2	485.706	471.135	8.93	1.93%
					Sum = 374.04	Sum = 86.22

CHART 18–15 Computing Absolute Errors

For time period 38 (the following July), the seasonally adjusted forecast is:

Total Bookings (Period 38) = 391.098 + 2.628 (Time Period)
= 391.098 + 2.628 (38) = 490.962
Seasonally adjusted forecast (Period 38) = (490.962)(.94) = 461.504

Chart 18–16 shows the seasonally adjusted forecasts for the next 12 months. In practice, this information is used by resorts to plan for a variety of decisions such as pricing, the number of people to staff a resort, and the quantities of inventories to hold. All forecasts must include the average forecasting error or the MAD. All forecasts incorporate an average error of 10.39. The MAPE is 2.40%.

Forecasts for the Next Twelve Months				
Month	Time Period	Trend	Seasonal Indexes	Seasonally adjusted Forecast
June	37	488.334	0.88	429.734
July	38	490.962	0.94	461.504
August	39	493.590	0.92	454.103
September	40	496.218	1.03	506.142
October	41	498.846	1.12	558.708
November	42	501.474	1.08	541.592
December	43	504.102	0.90	453.692
January	44	506.730	1.03	521.932
February	45	509.358	0.97	488.984
March	46	511.986	1.14	578.544
April	47	514.614	1.06	540.345
May	48	517.242	0.97	501.725

CHART 18–16 Forecasts for the Next 12 Months

The basic requirement of a time series approach to forecasting is that historical data follow a pattern. For every example and exercise in this chapter, the time series data has a historical pattern. In each case, it is important to describe the pattern in terms of trend (stationary, positive, or negative) and seasonality (present or not). If the graph shows a pattern, then we can create a model of the pattern, and then use the model to replicate the pattern into the future.

The accompanying graph of the bookings data clearly shows a pattern: a clear upward trend and clear seasonality. This section demonstrates how to create models to replicate this pattern. First, the trend equation is modeled with regression analysis. It tells us the average increase in bookings per month. Second, using the trend equation as the basis for comparison, we compute indexes for each month. This set of indexes shows the seasonal pattern. Each index indicates how bookings will vary from the overall average. The bookings for some months are always less than average, and some months are always more than average. The graph of the bookings analysis shows the results of the time series analysis. The graph shows the remarkable ability of the forecasting model to replicate the trend and seasonal patterns. Compare the line graph of actual bookings (in blue) to the line graph of the forecast bookings (in green). Also, see that the graph shows the forecasts (in green) for the next year, periods 37 through 48.

From the graph we observe that time series analysis performed well in replicating the time series pattern.

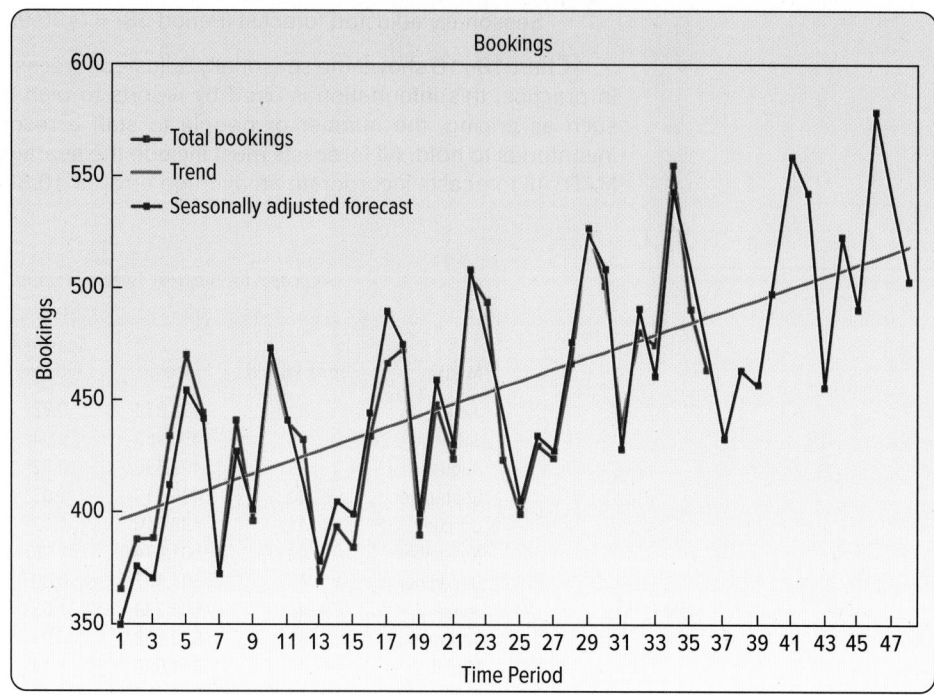

Finally, while the results of a time series forecasting analysis can be very good, every time series forecast must include an important disclaimer: A time series forecast assumes that the patterns in the historical data will continue into the future. In other words, the future will replicate the past. Hopefully, consumers of time series forecasts understand that many events can disrupt a time series pattern. These include weather events such as hurricanes, industry and market fluctuations such as changes in supply and demand, or international trade policies such as tariffs. All organizations should monitor their environments for events that might affect their forecasts and plans.

SELF-REVIEW 18–4

Teton Village, Wyoming, near Grand Teton Park and Yellowstone Park, contains shops, restaurants, and motels. The village has two peak seasons: winter, for skiing on the 10,000-foot slopes, and summer, for tourists visiting the parks. The number of visitors (in thousands) by quarter for 5 years, 2018 through 2022, follows:

| Year | Quarter | | | |
	Winter	Spring	Summer	Fall
2018	117.0	80.7	129.6	76.1
2019	118.6	82.5	121.4	77.0
2020	114.0	84.3	119.1	75.0
2021	120.7	79.6	129.9	69.5
2022	125.2	80.2	127.6	72.0

(a) Graph the time series.
(b) Based on the graph, describe the time series pattern.
(c) The average number of visitors per quarter is 100,000. Explain why 100,000 would be a reasonable base to calculate seasonal indexes.
(d) Compute the seasonal indexes.
(e) Interpret the four indexes.

EXERCISES

19. **FILE** Using the following time series data, respond to the following items.

Period	Quarter	Sales	Period	Quarter	Sales
1	1	$ 812	9	1	$ 965
2	2	920	10	2	844
3	3	1,268	11	3	961
4	4	1,280	12	4	1,160
5	1	832	13	1	751
6	2	791	14	2	674
7	3	1,071	15	3	828
8	4	1,109	16	4	1,033

a. Graph the time series.
b. Based on the graph, describe the time series pattern.
c. For this time series, why is forecasting with a seasonally adjusted trend model appropriate?
d. Evaluate a seasonally adjusted trend forecasting model. What are the MAD and MAPE?
e. What are the quarterly indexes?
f. Forecast sales for future periods 17 through 20.

20. **FILE** Using the following time series data, respond to the following items.

Period	Quarter	Sales	Period	Quarter	Sales
1	1	$ 867	9	1	$1,206
2	2	895	10	2	988
3	3	742	11	3	936
4	4	689	12	4	677
5	1	970	13	1	1,304
6	2	834	14	2	1,040
7	3	788	15	3	1,078
8	4	793	16	4	938

a. Graph the data.
b. Based on the graph, describe the time series pattern.
c. For this time series, why is forecasting with a seasonally adjusted trend model appropriate?
d. Evaluate a seasonally adjusted trend forecasting model. What are the MAD and MAPE?
e. What are the quarterly indexes?
f. Forecast sales for future periods 17 through 20.

21. **FILE** The following data report total, monthly, U.S. grocery store sales in millions of dollars from January 2020 to December 2021. (On the site **https://www.census. gov/retail/index.html#mrts**, find "Monthly Retail Trade Report," then select "Time Series/Trend Charts" to find the data for many retail sectors of the economy.)

Year	Month	Sales ($ millions)	Year	Month	Sales ($ millions)
2020	Jan	$58,722	2021	Jan	$64,785
2020	Feb	55,870	2021	Feb	59,018
2020	Mar	73,901	2021	Mar	64,734
2020	Apr	64,383	2021	Apr	63,749
2020	May	68,436	2021	May	68,015
2020	Jun	63,973	2021	Jun	66,531
2020	Jul	66,892	2021	Jul	68,923
2020	Aug	64,500	2021	Aug	68,259
2020	Sep	62,100	2021	Sep	66,939
2020	Oct	64,017	2021	Oct	69,523
2020	Nov	63,920	2021	Nov	68,948
2020	Dec	67,027	2021	Dec	73,617

a. Graph the data.
b. Based on the graph, describe the time series pattern.
c. For this time series, why is forecasting with a seasonally adjusted trend model appropriate?
d. Evaluate a seasonally adjusted trend forecasting model. What are the MAD and MAPE?
e. What are the monthly indexes?
f. Forecast sales for January, February, March, and April of 2022.

22. **FILE** The following data report total, monthly U.S. gasoline sales in millions of dollars from January 2020 to December 2021. (To find the data, go to the site **https://www.census.gov/retail/index.html#mrts**, find "Monthly Retail Trade Report," then select "Time Series/Trend Charts.")

Year	Month	Sales ($ millions)	Year	Month	Sales ($ millions)
2020	Jan	$39,696	2021	Jan	$37,214
2020	Feb	36,963	2021	Feb	36,295
2020	Mar	34,261	2021	Mar	46,360
2020	Apr	26,810	2021	Apr	47,274
2020	May	32,045	2021	May	50,180
2020	Jun	36,314	2021	Jun	51,303
2020	Jul	38,876	2021	Jul	53,489
2020	Aug	38,730	2021	Aug	53,272
2020	Sep	37,231	2021	Sep	52,459
2020	Oct	38,161	2021	Oct	55,248
2020	Nov	34,394	2021	Nov	52,738
2020	Dec	36,635	2021	Dec	52,308

a. Graph the data.
b. Based on the graph, describe the time series pattern.
c. For this time series, why is forecasting with a seasonally adjusted trend model appropriate?
d. Evaluate a seasonally adjusted trend forecasting model. What are the MAD and MAPE?
e. What are the monthly indexes?
f. Forecast sales for January, February, March, and April of 2022.

CHAPTER SUMMARY

I. A time series is a collection of data ordered over time.
  A. A stationary time series pattern shows no form or pattern.
  B. A time series may show a trend that may increase or decrease over time.
  C. A time series may show a seasonal pattern that repeats from year to year.
  D. A time series may show a cyclical pattern that repeats over the span of many years.
  E. A time series has an irregular pattern that is random and unpredictable.
    1. The randomness in a time series is measured as forecasting error.

$$\text{Forecast Error} = \text{Actual} - \text{Forecast} \qquad \text{(18--1)}$$

  2. One way to compute the average forecasting error is the Mean Absolute Deviation (MAD).

$$\text{MAD} = \frac{\Sigma|\text{Error}|}{n} \qquad \text{(18--2)}$$

  3. The Mean Absolute Percent Error (MAPE) expresses forecasting error as the average of the absolute percent errors.

$$\text{MAPE} = \frac{\Sigma|\text{Percent Error}|}{n} \qquad \text{(18--3)}$$

II. Averaging techniques are used to model a stationary time series.
  A. Moving averages compute a forecast by averaging past data.
  B. Simple exponential smoothing computes a forecast with a weighted average of past data.

$$\text{Forecast}_{t+1} = \alpha(\text{Observed Value}_t) + (1 - \alpha)(\text{Forecast}_t) \qquad \text{(18--4)}$$

$$\text{Forecast}_{t+1} = \text{Forecast}_t + \alpha(\text{Error}_t) \qquad \text{(18--5)}$$

III. Linear regression analysis is used to model time series with trend.

$$\text{Time Series Variable} = \text{Intercept} + \text{Slope (Time Period)} \qquad \text{(18--6)}$$

IV. When using regression analysis, the Durbin-Watson statistic is used to test for autocorrelation.

$$d = \frac{\sum_{t=2}^{n}(e_t - e_{t-1})^2}{\sum_{t=1}^{n}(e_t)^2} \qquad \text{(18--7)}$$

V. Seasonality can be computed using indexes.
  A. A seasonal index divides an observed value with seasonality by a base value without seasonality.
  B. A seasonal index greater than 1.0 indicates that the seasonality is more than the base value.
  C. A seasonal index less than 1.0 indicates that the seasonality is less than the base value.

CHAPTER EXERCISES

23. Compare and contrast forecasting with a simple moving average and simple exponential smoothing.
24. For a time series,
  a. What are the possible trend patterns?
  b. For each, what forecasting model would be applied?
25. If a time series analysis reports that the seasonal indexes are all equal to 1.0, what is true about the time series pattern?
26. Respond to the following questions:
  a. A time series with seasonality reports quarterly demand for the past 10 years. How many indexes would be reported?

b. A time series with seasonality reports monthly demand for the past 6 years. How many indexes would be reported?

c. A time series with seasonality reports semiannual demand for the past 20 years. How many indexes would be reported?

27. **FILE** Respond to each of the items using the following time series data.

   a. Graph the time series data. What do you observe?

Period	Demand	Period	Demand
1	104	9	109
2	132	10	143
3	117	11	142
4	120	12	109
5	104	13	113
6	141	14	124
7	120	15	113
8	136	16	104

   b. Compute all possible forecasts using a five-period moving average.
   c. Compute the MAD and MAPE.
   d. What is the forecast demand for period 17?
   e. What is the error associated with the period 17 forecast?

28. **FILE** Respond to each of the items using the following time series data.

Period	Demand	Period	Demand
1	104	9	329
2	207	10	143
3	383	11	285
4	183	12	188
5	181	13	378
6	212	14	373
7	167	15	101
8	262	16	103

   a. Graph the time series data. What do you observe?
   b. Compute all possible forecasts using a three-period moving average and compute the MAD and MAPE.
   c. Compute all possible forecasts using a six-period moving average and compute the MAD and MAPE.
   d. Compute the forecast demand for period 17 for each model.
   e. Comparing the two forecast models, explain which model you would choose to make forecasts.

29. **FILE** Respond to each of the items using the following time series data.

Period	Demand	Period	Demand
1	138	8	103
2	131	9	142
3	149	10	122
4	110	11	121
5	175	12	130
6	194	13	126
7	166	14	140

   a. Graph the time series data. What do you observe?
   b. Compute all possible forecasts using exponential smoothing with a smoothing coefficient (α) of 0.4.
   c. Compute all possible forecasts using exponential smoothing with a smoothing coefficient (α) of 0.9.

d. Compute the MAD and MAPE for each forecast model.
e. Which forecast model would you choose? Why?

30. **FILE** Respond to each of the items using the following time series data.

Period	Demand	Period	Demand
1	20	8	34
2	46	9	39
3	20	10	4
4	9	11	30
5	17	12	23
6	8	13	10
7	19	14	27

a. Graph the time series data. What do you observe?
b. Compute all possible forecasts using exponential smoothing with a smoothing coefficient (α) of 0.3.
c. Compute all possible forecasts using exponential smoothing with a smoothing coefficient (α) of 0.7.
d. Compute the MAD and MAPE for each forecast model.
e. Which forecast model would you choose? Why?

31. **FILE** Using the following time series sales data, respond to the following items.

Period	Sales	Period	Sales
1	988	10	604
2	990	11	670
3	859	12	703
4	781	13	550
5	691	14	427
6	776	15	493
7	677	16	524
8	690	17	563
9	605	18	471

a. Graph the data.
b. Based on the graph, describe the time series pattern.
c. For this time series, why is forecasting with a trend model appropriate?
d. Evaluate a trend forecasting model using simple linear regression. What are the MAD and MAPE?
e. What is the predicted annual change of industry sales?
f. Predict sales for the next three periods.
g. In your judgment, are the forecasts "good"? What disclaimer would you include with your forecast?

32. **FILE** Using the following time series data of U.S. new car sales ($ millions), respond to the following items. (The data are sourced from **https://www.census.gov/retail/index .html#mrts**. Find "Monthly Retail Trade Report," then select "Time Series/Trend Charts" to find the data for U.S. new car sales.)

Year	$ Sales (Millions)	Year	$ Sales (Millions)
2012	$672,550	2017	$ 911,157
2013	735,374	2018	943,538
2014	785,142	2019	944,324
2015	842,120	2020	931,212
2016	877,743	2021	1,131,310

a. Graph the data.
b. Based on the graph, describe the time series pattern.
c. For this time series, why is forecasting with a trend model appropriate?

d. Evaluate a trend forecasting model using simple linear regression. What are the MAD and MAPE?

e. What is the predicted annual change in industry sales?

f. Predict sales for the next 3 years.

g. In your judgment, are the forecasts "good"? What disclaimer would you include with your forecast?

33. **FILE** After completing Exercise 31, use the same data and your regression results to test for autocorrelation with the Durbin-Watson statistic by completing the following items.

Period	Sales	Period	Sales
1	988	10	604
2	990	11	670
3	859	12	703
4	781	13	550
5	691	14	427
6	776	15	493
7	677	16	524
8	690	17	563
9	605	18	471

a. Plot the residuals associated with the trend model for this data

b. Test for autocorrelation using the .05 significance level.

c. Report and interpret your result.

34. **FILE** After completing Exercise 32, use the same data and your regression results to test for autocorrelation with the Durbin-Watson statistic by completing the following items.

Year	$ Sales (Millions)	Year	$ Sales (Millions)
2012	$672,550	2017	$ 911,157
2013	735,374	2018	943,538
2014	785,142	2019	944,324
2015	842,120	2020	931,212
2016	877,743	2021	1,131,310

a. Plot the residuals associated with the trend model for this data.

b. Test for autocorrelation using the .05 significance level.

c. Report and interpret your result.

35. **FILE** The following data report total, monthly U.S. book-store sales in millions of dollars from January 2019 to December 2021. (Go to **https://www.census.gov/retail/index .html#mrts**, find "Monthly Retail Trade Report," then select "Time Series/Trend Charts" to find the data for the total U.S. bookstore sales.)

	Year		
Month	2019	2020	2021
January	$1,029	$990	$820
February	585	593	459
March	603	406	547
April	650	169	514
May	696	275	632
June	613	388	703
July	591	437	712
August	1,124	770	1,154
September	871	620	883
October	650	455	697
November	640	496	708
December	1,074	900	1,203

a. Graph the data.
b. Based on the graph, describe the time series pattern.
c. For this time series, why is forecasting with a seasonally adjusted trend model appropriate?
d. Evaluate a seasonally adjusted trend forecasting model. What are the MAD and MAPE?
e. What is the average monthly trend in book-store sales?
f. What are the monthly indexes? When are book sales the highest? When are book sales the lowest?
g. Predict book sales for the next 9 months.
h. In your judgment, are the forecasts "good"? What disclaimer would you include with your forecast?

36. **FILE** The following data report total, monthly, U.S. new car sales in millions of dollars from January 2019 to December 2021. (To find the data, go to **https://www.census .gov/retail/index.html#mrts**, find "Monthly Retail Trade Report," then select "Time Series/Trend Charts.")

	Year		
Month	**2019**	**2020**	**2021**
January	$67,012	$72,074	$79,954
February	67,456	74,360	77,194
March	82,564	59,487	107,329
April	76,907	50,131	105,362
May	83,937	77,773	105,868
June	78,207	81,593	100,052
July	82,550	84,691	98,633
August	88,148	86,015	93,126
September	76,300	85,909	89,210
October	79,728	87,522	90,324
November	78,776	79,269	88,409
December	82,739	92,388	95,849

a. Graph the data.
b. Based on the graph, describe the time series pattern.
c. For this time series, why is forecasting with a seasonally adjusted trend model appropriate?
d. What is the average monthly trend in new car sales?
e. Evaluate a seasonally adjusted trend forecasting model. What are the MAD and MAPE?
f. What are the monthly seasonal indexes? When are new car sales the highest? When are new car sales the lowest?
g. Forecast new car sales with error for the next 9 months.
h. In your judgment, are the forecasts "good"? What disclaimer would you include with your forecast?

DATA ANALYTICS

(The data for this exercise are available at the text website: **www.mhhe.com/lind19e.**)

Use the following information obtained from annual reports of Home Depot to do Exercises 37, 38, and 39. You will need the help of a software package such as Excel and perhaps a companion package such as MegaStat. For the years 1993 through 2020, the data include a coded time variable (1 through 26), the number of associates in thousands, net sales in millions of dollars, the average ticket sale, and the Consumer Price Index (CPI) for each year.

Year	Time	Associates	Net Sales ($Millions)	Average Ticket Sale	CPI
1993	1	50.6	9239	39.13	144.5
1994	2	67.3	12477	41.29	148.2
1995	3	80.8	15470	41.78	152.4
1996	4	98.1	19535	42.09	156.9
1997	5	124.4	24156	43.63	160.5
1998	6	156.7	30219	45.05	163
1999	7	201.4	38454	47.87	166
2000	8	227.3	45738	48.65	172.2
2001	9	256.3	53553	48.64	177.1
2002	10	280.9	58247	49.43	179.9
2003	11	298.8	64816	51.15	184
2004	12	323.1	73094	54.89	188.9
2005	13	344.8	81511	57.98	195.3
2006	14	364.4	79022	58.9	201.6
2007	15	331	77349	57.48	207.342
2008	16	322	71288	55.61	215.303
2009	17	317	66176	51.76	214.537
2010	18	321	67997	51.93	218.056
2011	19	331	70395	53.28	224.939
2012	20	340	74754	54.89	229.594
2013	21	365	78812	56.76	232.957
2014	22	371	83176	57.87	236.736
2015	23	385	88519	58.77	237.017
2016	24	406	94595	60.35	240.007
2017	25	413	100904	63.06	245.12
2018	26	413	108203	65.74	251.107
2019	27	415	110225	67.30	255.657
2020	28	504	132110	74.32	258.811

37. Develop a trend equation for the net sales ($ million) for Home Depot. Consider both a linear trend and a nonlinear trend. Which one would you select and why? Given the trend equation you selected, forecast the net sales for 2021 and 2022.

38. Consider the variable average ticket sale in the Home Depot data presented here. This variable indicates, for example, that customers spent an average of $39.13 on goods during a store visit in 1993. By 2020 this amount increased to $74.32. During that same period the CPI as reported by the Bureau of Labor Statistics increased from 144.5 to 258.811. Convert the CPI to a 1993 base, as described on page 657 in Chapter 17 and convert the average ticket sale to 1993 dollars. Develop a linear trend equation for the constant 1993 dollars of the average ticket sale. Is it reasonable that the trend is linear? Can we conclude that the value of the amount the customer spent is less?

39. Use the variables average ticket sale and number of associates to forecast net sales. Are these two independent variables reasonable predictors of net sales? (Hints: What is the R^2 value? Is it large? Look at the p-values for each of the independent variables. Is this value less than .05 for each?) Because all of these variables are associated with time, it may be that there is autocorrelation. Conduct the appropriate test of hypothesis to determine if there is autocorrelation present. What is your conclusion? Again, use the .05 significance level.

40. Refer to the Baseball 2021 data, which includes information on the 2021 Major League Baseball season. The data include the mean player salary since 2010. Plot the information and develop a linear trend equation. Write a brief report on your findings.

A REVIEW OF CHAPTERS 17–18

Chapter 17 presents index numbers. An *index number* describes the relative change in value from one period, called the base period, to another called the given period. It is actually a percent, but the percent sign is usually omitted. Indexes are used to compare the change in unlike series over time. For example, a company might wish to compare the change in sales with the change in the number of sales representatives employed over the same period of time. A direct comparison is not meaningful because the units for one set of data are dollars and the other people. Index numbers also facilitate the comparison of very large values, where the amount of change in the actual values is very large and therefore difficult to interpret.

There are two types of price indexes. In an *unweighted price index,* the quantities are not considered. To form an unweighted index, we divide the base period value into the current period (also called the given period) and report the percent change. So if sales were $12,000,000 in 2013 and $18,600,000 in 2019, the simple unweighted price index for 2019 is:

$$p = \frac{p_t}{p_0}(100) = \frac{\$18,600,000}{\$12,000,000}(100) = 155.0$$

We conclude there is a 55% increase in sales during the 6-year period.

In a *weighted price index, quantities* are considered. The most widely used weighted index is the *Laspeyres price index.* It uses the base period quantities as weights to compare changes in prices. It is computed by multiplying the base period quantities by the base period price for each product considered and summing the result. This result is the denominator of the fraction. The numerator of the fraction is the product of the base period quantities and the current price. For example, an appliance store sold 50 computers at $1,000 and 200 DVDs at $150 each in year 2013. In 2019, the same store sold 60 computers at $1,200 and 230 DVDs at $175. The Laspeyres price index is:

$$p = \frac{\Sigma p_t q_0}{\Sigma p_0 q_0}(100) = \frac{\$1,200 \times 50 + \$175 \times 200}{\$1,000 \times 50 + \$150 \times 200}(100) = \frac{\$95,000}{\$80,000}(100) = 118.75$$

Notice the same base period quantities are used as weights in both the numerator and the denominator. The index indicates there has been an 18.75% increase in the value of sales during the 6-year period.

The most widely used and reported index is the *Consumer Price Index (CPI).* The CPI is a Laspeyres-type index. It is reported monthly by the U.S. Department of Labor and is often used to report the rate of inflation in the prices of goods and services in the United States. The current base period is 1982–1984.

In Chapter 18, we studied time series and forecasting. A *time series* is a collection of data over a period of time. The earnings per share of General Electric common stock over the last 10 years is an example of a time series. There are four possible patterns to a time series: trend, seasonality, cyclical, and irregular patterns.

Trend is the long-term direction of the time series. It can be either increasing or decreasing.

Seasonal variation is the recurring pattern of the time series within a year. The consumption of many products and services is seasonal. Beach homes along the Gulf Coast are seldom rented during the winter and ski lodges in Wyoming are not used in the summer months. Hence, we say the rentals of beachfront properties and ski lodges are seasonal.

The *cyclical component* is the fluctuation above and below the trend line over a period of several years. Economic cycles are examples of the cyclical component. Most businesses shift between relative expansion and reduction periods over a cycle of several years.

The *irregular component* includes any unpredictable events. In other words, the irregular component includes events that cannot be forecast. There are two types of irregular components. Episodic variations are unpredictable, but can usually be identified. The COVID pandemic that started in 2020 is an example. The residual variation is random in nature and not predicted or identified.

The linear trend for a time series is given by the equation $\hat{y} = a + bt$, where $\hat{y}$ is the estimated trend value, a is the intercept with the Y-axis, b is the slope of the trend line (the rate of change), and t refers to the coded values for the time periods. We use the least squares method described in Chapter 13 to determine the trend line. Autocorrelation is often a problem when using the trend equation. Autocorrelation means that successive values of the time series are correlated.

PROBLEMS

1. Listed are the net sales (in millions of euros) for the Adidas Group from 2014 to 2021.

Year	Net Sales
2014	14,534
2015	16,915
2016	18,483
2017	21,218
2018	21,915
2019	23,640
2020	19,844
2021	22,448

   a. Determine the index for 2021 using 2014 as the base period.
   b. Use the period 2014 to 2016 as the base period and find the index for 2021.
   c. Use regression analysis to find the trend equation. What is the estimated net sales for 2022 and 2023? What is the rate of increase per year?

2. The table shows the labor force and the unemployment rate for three counties in northwest Pennsylvania for 2010 and 2019.

| | 2010 | | 2019 | |
County	Labor Force	Percent Unemployment	Labor Force	Percent Unemployment
Erie	141,800	4.8	128,251	3.4
Warren	21,300	4.7	18,871	2.7
McKean	20,900	4.9	17,685	3.7

   a. In 2010, the national unemployment rate was 9.3%. For 2010, compute a simple average unemployment index for the region using the national unemployment rate as the base. Interpret the simple average index.
   b. In 2019, the national unemployment rate was 3.6%. For 2019, compute a simple average unemployment index for the region using the national unemployment rate as the base. Interpret the simple average index.
   c. Use the data for this region of northwest Pennsylvania to create a weighted unemployment index using the Laspeyres method. Use 2010 as the base period. Interpret the index.

3. Based on 5 years of monthly data (the period from January 2018 to December 2022), the trend equation for a small company is $\hat{y} = 3.5 + 0.7t$. The seasonal index for January is 120 and for June it is 90. What are the seasonally adjusted sales forecasts for January 2023 and June 2023?

PRACTICE TEST

Part 1—Objective

1. To compute an index, the base period _____. (is always in the numerator, is always in the denominator, can be in either the numerator or denominator, is always 100)

2. A number that measures the relative change from one period to another is called a/an _____.

3. In a weighted index, both the price and the _____ are considered.

4. In a Laspeyres index, the _____ quantities are used in both the numerator and denominator. (base period, given period, oldest, newest—pick one)

5. The current base period for the Consumer Price Index is _____.

6. The long-term direction of a time series is called the _____.

7. A method to compute a forecast based on a weighted average of past data is _____.

8. When successive residuals are correlated, this condition is called _____.

9. Irregular pattern in a time series that is random in nature is called _____.

10. In a 3-year simple moving average, the weights given to each period are _____. (the same, oldest year has the most weight, oldest year has the least weight)

1. _____

2. _____

3. _____

4. _____
5. _____
6. _____

7. _____
8. _____
9. _____

10. _____

Part 2—Problems

1. Listed are the sales at Roberta's Ice Cream Stand for the last 5 years, 2018 through 2022.

Year	Sales
2018	$130,000
2019	145,000
2020	120,000
2021	170,000
2022	190,000

   a. Find the simple index for each year using 2018 as the base year.
   b. Find the simple index for each year using 2018–2019 as the base year.

2. Listed are the price and quantity of several golf items purchased by members of the men's golf league at Indigo Creek Golf and Tennis Club for 2018 and 2022.

	2018		2022	
	Price	Quantity	Price	Quantity
Driver	$250.00	5	$275.00	6
Putter	60.00	12	75.00	10
Irons	700.00	3	750.00	4

   a. Determine the simple aggregate price index, with 2018 as the base period.
   b. Determine a Laspeyres price index.
   c. Determine the Paasche price index.
   d. Determine a value index.

3. The trend model to predict monthly sales for the Hoopes ABC Beverage Store is:

$$\text{Sales} = 5.50 + 1.25t$$

The equation is based on 4 years of monthly sales data and is reported in thousands of dollars. The index for January is 105.0 and for February it is 98.3. Determine the seasonally adjusted sales forecast for January and February of the fifth year.

19

Statistical Process Control and Quality Management

EMMANUEL DUNAND/AFP/
Getty Images

▲ **A BICYCLE MANUFACTURER** randomly selects 10 frames each day and tests for defects. The numbers of defective frames found over the last 14 days are 3, 2, 1, 3, 2, 2, 8, 2, 0, 3, 5, 2, 0, and 4. Construct a control chart for this process and comment on whether the process is "in control." (See Exercise 11 and **LO19-6**.)

LEARNING OBJECTIVES

When you have completed this chapter, you will be able to:

LO19-1 Explain the purpose of quality control in production and service operations.

LO19-2 Define the two sources of process variation and explain how they are used to monitor quality.

LO19-3 Explain the use of charts to investigate the sources of process variation.

LO19-4 Compute control limits for mean and range control charts for a variable measure of quality.

LO19-5 Evaluate control charts to determine if a process is out of control.

LO19-6 Compute control limits of control charts for an attribute measure of quality.

LO19-7 Explain the process of acceptance sampling.

Introduction

Throughout this text, we present many applications of hypothesis testing. In Chapter 10, we describe methods for testing a hypothesis regarding a single population value. In Chapter 11, we describe methods for testing a hypothesis about two populations. In this chapter, we present another, somewhat different application of hypothesis testing, called **statistical process control** or **SPC.**

Statistical process control is a collection of strategies, techniques, and actions taken by an organization to ensure it is producing a quality product or providing a quality service. SPC begins at the product planning stage, when we specify the attributes of the product or service. It continues through the production stage. Each attribute throughout the process contributes to the overall quality of the product. To effectively use quality control, measurable attributes and specifications are developed against which the actual attributes of the product or service are compared.

A Brief History of Quality Control

LO19-1

Explain the purpose of quality control in production and service operations.

Prior to the 1900s, U.S. industry was largely characterized by small shops making relatively simple products, such as candles or furniture. In these small shops, the individual worker was generally a craftsman who was completely responsible for the quality of the work. The worker could ensure the quality through the personal selection of the materials, skillful manufacturing, and selective fitting and adjustment.

In the early 1900s, factories sprang up where people with limited training were formed into large assembly lines. Products became much more complex. The individual worker no longer had complete control over the quality of the product. A semiprofessional staff, usually called the Inspection Department, became responsible for the quality of the product. The quality responsibility was usually fulfilled by a 100% inspection of all the important characteristics. If there were any discrepancies noted, these problems were handled by the manufacturing department supervisor. In essence, quality was attained by "inspecting the quality into the product."

During the 1920s, Dr. Walter A. Shewhart, of Bell Telephone Laboratories, developed the concepts of statistical quality control. He introduced the concept of "controlling" the quality of a product as it was being manufactured, rather than inspecting the quality into the product after it was manufactured. For the purpose of controlling quality, Shewhart developed charting techniques for controlling in-process manufacturing operations. In addition, he introduced the concept of statistical sample inspection to estimate the quality of a product as it was being manufactured. This replaced the old method of inspecting each part after it was completed in the production operation.

Statistical quality control came into its own during World War II. The need for mass-produced war-related items, such as bomb sights, accurate radar, and other electronic equipment, at the lowest possible cost hastened the use of statistical sampling and quality control charts. Since World War II, these statistical techniques have been refined and sharpened. The use of computers has also widened the use of these techniques.

World War II virtually destroyed the Japanese production capability. Rather than retool their old production methods, the Japanese enlisted the aid of the late Dr. W. Edwards Deming, of the U.S. Department of Agriculture, to help them develop an overall plan. In a series of seminars with Japanese planners, he stressed a philosophy that is known today as Deming's 14 points. These 14 points are listed on the following page. He emphasized that quality originates from improving the process, not from inspection, and that quality is determined by the customers. The manufacturer must be able, via market research, to anticipate the needs of customers. Senior management has the responsibility for long-term improvement. Another of his points, and one that the Japanese strongly endorsed, is that every member of the company must contribute to long-term improvement. To achieve this improvement, ongoing education and training are necessary.

Deming had some ideas that did not mesh with contemporary management philosophies in the United States. Two areas where Deming's ideas differed from U.S. management philosophy were with production quotas and merit ratings. He believed these two practices, which are both common in the United States, are not productive and should be eliminated. He also pointed out that U.S. managers are mostly interested in good news. Good news, however, does not provide an opportunity for improvement. On the other hand, bad news opens the door for new products and allows for company improvement.

Following, in a condensed form, are Dr. Deming's 14 points. He was adamant that the 14 points needed to be adopted as a package to be successful. The underlying theme is cooperation, teamwork, and the belief that workers want to do their jobs in a quality fashion.

DEMING'S 14 POINTS

1. Create constancy of purpose for the continual improvement of products and service to society.
2. Adopt a philosophy that we can no longer live with commonly accepted levels of delays, mistakes, defective materials, and defective workmanship.
3. Eliminate the need for mass inspection as the way to achieve quality. Instead, achieve quality by building the product correctly in the first place.
4. End the practice of awarding business solely on the basis of price. Instead, require meaningful measures of quality along with the price.
5. Improve constantly and forever every process for planning, production, and service.
6. Institute modern methods of training on the job for all employees, including managers. This will lead to better utilization of each employee.
7. Adopt and institute leadership aimed at helping people do a better job.
8. Encourage effective two-way communication and other means to drive out fear throughout the organization so that everyone may work more effectively and more productively for the company.
9. Break down barriers between departments and staff areas.
10. Eliminate the use of slogans, posters, and exhortations demanding zero defects and new levels of productivity without providing methods.
11. Eliminate work standards that prescribe quotas for the workforce and numerical goals for people in management. Substitute aids and helpful leadership in order to achieve continual improvement in quality and productivity.
12. Remove the barriers that rob hourly workers and the people in management of their right to pride of workmanship.
13. Institute a vigorous program of education and encourage self-improvement for everyone. What an organization needs is good people and people who are improving with education. Advancement to a competitive position will have its roots in knowledge.
14. Define clearly management's permanent commitment to ever-improving quality and productivity to implement all of these principles.

Deming's 14 points did not ignore statistical quality control, which is often abbreviated as SQC. The objective of statistical quality control is to monitor production through many stages of manufacturing. We use the tools of statistical quality control, such as X-bar and R charts, to monitor the quality of many processes and services. Control charts allow us to identify when a process or service is "out of control," that is, when an excessive number of defective units are being produced.

The American Society for Quality (ASQ) (**www.asq.org**) estimates that the cost of poor quality in a thriving company will be about 10 to 15% of sales revenue. These costs are incurred through internal product or service failure costs such as waste, scrap, rework, and failure analysis. Poor quality costs are also incurred after the product or service is purchased and used by customers. These costs include repairs and servicing, warranty claims, complaints, and returns. Companies are interested in reducing these costs through quality improvement programs such as zero defects and six sigma.

Courtesy of Awarding You.

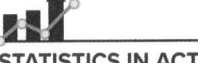

STATISTICS IN ACTION

Does excellence in quality management lead to higher financial performance? Recent research compared the financial performance of companies that received the Baldrige National Quality Award to similar companies that did not receive the award. The research showed that the companies receiving the award had an average of 39% higher operating income and 26% higher sales, and were 1.22% lower in their cost per sales dollar.

In recent years, companies have been motivated to improve quality by the challenge of being recognized for their quality achievements. The Malcolm Baldrige National Quality Award, established in 1988, is awarded annually to U.S. companies that demonstrate excellence in quality achievement and management. The award categories include manufacturing, service, small business, health care, and education. Past winners include Xerox, IBM, the University of Wisconsin–Stout, Ritz-Carlton Hotel Corporation, Federal Express, and Cadillac. Summary descriptions of the 2020 winners follow:

- AARP, located in Washington, D.C., is dedicated to improving the lives of people over age 50 and their families. In pursuit of this goal, AARP doubled its reach from 32 million people in 2015 to more than 60 million in 2019. To spur breakthrough products and services in the marketplace, AARP created the $40 million AARP Innovation Fund that provides capital to innovative companies focused on improving the lives of people aged 50 or older. It has also been recognized as a "Top Workplace" by *The Washington Post,* and, based on studies by the market research firm GfK, *AARP The Magazine* has been the most widely read publication in the United States for 3 years.
- Elevations Credit Union, located in Boulder, Colorado, won a Baldrige Award in 2014 and is the first two-time winner in the nonprofit category. In addition to offering a broad portfolio of consumer and business banking services, Elevations is the No. 1 credit union mortgage lender in Colorado. This member-owned, nonprofit financial institution serves more than 147,000 members via 14 branches. Based on Gallup's Employee Engagement Survey, Elevations ranked in the top 95% of U.S. organizations for overall employee engagement.
- GBMC HealthCare System is in Baltimore, Maryland. In 2020, it achieved the highest five-star rating from the Centers for Medicare and Medicaid Services. Among other performance measures, GBMC achieved the following: 100% of their stroke patients received antithrombotic therapy at discharge, 100% of high-risk mothers received antenatal steroids which accelerate the maturation of an infant's lungs, and 100% of patients diagnosed with breast cancer received combination chemotherapy. GBMC's Nurse Residency Program is one of only 61 worldwide to achieve the highest level of recognition from the American Nurses Credentialing Center.
- MESA, located in Tulsa, Oklahoma, won Baldrige Awards in 2006 and 2012, and is the first three-time winner of the award in the small business category. MESA specializes in corrosion control of pipelines and related equipment. Since 2015, the company's overall revenue increased nearly $30 million. During its journey to a Baldrige award recognition, the company has achieved a 10% average annual revenue growth, retained 100% of key customers in its services segment, and since 2017, retained 97% of key customers in its materials segment. In addition, 95% of its employees agree that maintaining a culture of operational safety is a top organizational priority.
- Wellstar Paulding Hospital (WPH) is in Hiram, Georgia. WPH is a community hospital providing inpatient and outpatient care and emergency services through an acute care hospital and two connected medical office buildings. It is part of Wellstar Health System (WHS), one of the largest and most integrated health systems in Georgia. From 2018 to 2020, outpatient ratings of "doctors courteous and respectful" increased 87% to 99%, ratings of "nurses listened carefully" increased 87% to 92%, ratings of "trust staff with care" increased 87% to 91%.

You can obtain more information on these and other winners by visiting the website **http://www.nist.gov/baldrige.**

Six Sigma

Many service, manufacturing, and nonprofit organizations are committed to improving the quality of their services and products. "Six Sigma" is a name given to an organization-wide program designed to improve quality and performance throughout an organization. The focus of the program is to reduce the variation in any process used to produce and deliver services and products to customers. Six Sigma programs apply to production processes as well as accounting and other organizational support processes. The ultimate outcomes of a Six Sigma program are to reduce the costs of defects and errors, increase customer satisfaction and sales of products and services, and increase profits.

Six Sigma gets its name from the normal distribution. The term *sigma* means standard deviation, and "plus or minus" 3 standard deviations gives a total range of 6 standard deviations. So Six Sigma means that a process should not generate more than 3.4 defects per million for any product or service. Many companies strive for even fewer defects.

To attain this goal, a Six Sigma program trains every organization member in processes to identify sources of process variation that significantly affect quality. The process includes identifying and defining problems, collecting and analyzing data to investigate and become knowledgeable about the problem, making process improvements to reduce process variation, and implementing procedures for improving the process.

Six Sigma uses many statistical techniques to collect and analyze the data needed to reduce process variation. The following are included in this text: histograms, analysis of variation, chi-square test of independence, regression, and correlation.

Bank of America, Caterpillar Inc., Honeywell Internationa Inc., General Electric, and 3M are large companies that have used Six Sigma methods and achieved significant quality improvement and cost savings. Even cities like Fort Wayne, Indiana, have used Six Sigma techniques to improve their operations. For example, the city reduced missed trash pickups by 50% and cut the response time to repair potholes from 21 to 3 hours. You can learn more about Six Sigma ideas, methods, and training at **http://www.6sigma.us.**

LO19-2

Define the two sources of process variation and explain how they are used to monitor quality.

Sources of Variation

No two products are *exactly* the same. There is always some variation. The weight of each McDonald's Quarter Pounder is not exactly .25 pound. Some will weigh more than 0.25 pound, others less. The standard time for the TARTA (Toledo Area Regional Transit Authority) bus run from downtown Toledo, Ohio, to Perrysburg is 25 minutes. However, each run does not take *exactly* 25 minutes. Some runs take longer. Other times the TARTA driver must wait in Perrysburg before returning to Toledo. In some cases, there is a reason for the bus being late, an accident on the expressway or a snowstorm, for example. In other cases, the driver may not "hit" the green lights or the traffic is unusually heavy and slow for no apparent reason. There are two general sources of variation in a process—chance and assignable.

Internal machine friction, slight variations in material or process conditions (such as the temperature of the mold being used to make glass bottles), atmospheric conditions (such as temperature, humidity, and the dust content of the air), and vibrations transmitted to a machine from a passing forklift are a few examples of sources of **chance variation.**

> **CHANCE VARIATION** Variation that is random in nature. This type of variation cannot be completely eliminated unless there is a major change in the techniques, technologies, methods, equipment, or materials used in the process.

If the hole drilled in a piece of steel is too large due to a dull drill, the drill may be sharpened or a new drill inserted. An operator who continually sets up the machine incorrectly can be replaced or retrained. If the roll of steel to be used in the process does not have the correct tensile strength, it can be rejected. These are examples of **assignable variation.**

> **ASSIGNABLE VARIATION** Variation that is not random. It can be eliminated or reduced by investigating the problem and finding the cause.

There are several reasons why we should be concerned with variation. Two follow:

1. It will change the shape, dispersion, and central location of the distribution of the product characteristic being measured.
2. Assignable variation is usually correctable, whereas chance variation usually cannot be corrected or stabilized economically.

LO19-3

Explain the use of charts to investigate the sources of process variation.

Diagnostic Charts

There are a variety of diagnostic techniques available to investigate quality problems. Two of the more prominent of these techniques are **Pareto charts** and **fishbone diagrams.**

Pareto Charts

Pareto analysis is a technique for tallying the number and type of defects that happen within a product or service. The chart is named after a 19-century Italian scientist, Vilfredo Pareto. He noted that most of the "activity" in a process is caused by relatively few of the "factors." His concept, often called the 80–20 rule, is that 80% of the activity is caused by 20% of the factors. By concentrating on 20% of the factors, managers can attack 80% of the problem. For example, Emily's Family Restaurant, located at the junction of Interstates 75 and 70, is investigating "customer complaints." The five complaints heard most frequently are discourteous service, cold food, long wait for seating, few menu choices, and unruly young children. Suppose discourteous service was mentioned most frequently and cold food second. The data show these two factors are more than 85% of the total complaints. Addressing these two complaints first will yield the largest reduction in complaints and the largest increase in customer satisfaction.

To develop a Pareto chart, we begin by tallying the type of defects. Next, we rank the defects in terms of frequency of occurrence from largest to smallest. Finally, we produce a vertical bar chart, with the height of the bars corresponding to the frequency of each defect. The following Example/Solution illustrates these ideas.

▶ **EXAMPLE**

The city manager of Grove City, Utah, is concerned with water usage, particularly in single-family homes and would like to develop a plan to reduce the water usage in Grove City. To investigate, the data on typical daily water usage from a sample of 100 homes is collected. These sample results are:

Reasons for Water Usage	Gallons per Day
Laundering	24.9
Watering lawn	143.7
Personal bathing	106.7
Cooking	5.1
Swimming pool	28.3
Dishwashing	12.3
Car washing	10.4
Drinking	7.9

What is the area of greatest usage? Where should efforts to reduce water usage be focused?

SOLUTION

A Pareto chart is useful for identifying the major areas of water usage and focusing on those areas where the greatest reduction can be achieved. The first step is to convert each of the activities to a percent and then to order them from largest to smallest. The total water usage per day is 339.3 gallons, found by totaling the gallons used in the eight activities. The activity with the largest use is watering lawns. It accounts for 143.7 gallons of water per day, or 42.4% of the amount of water used. The next largest category is personal bathing, which accounts for 31.4% of the water used. These two activities account for 73.8% of the water usage.

Reasons for Water Usage	Gallons per Day	Percent
Laundering	24.9	7.3
Watering lawn	143.7	42.4
Personal bathing	106.7	31.4
Cooking	5.1	1.5
Swimming pool usage	28.3	8.3
Dishwashing	12.3	3.6
Car washing	10.4	3.1
Drinking	7.9	2.3
Total	339.3	100.0

To draw the Pareto chart, we begin by scaling the number of gallons used on the left vertical axis and the corresponding percent on the right vertical axis. Next we draw a vertical bar with the height of the bar corresponding to the activity with the largest number of occurrences. In the Grove City example, we draw a vertical bar for the activity watering lawns to a height of 143.7 gallons. (We call this the count.) We continue this procedure for the other activities, as shown in the Minitab output in Chart 19–1.

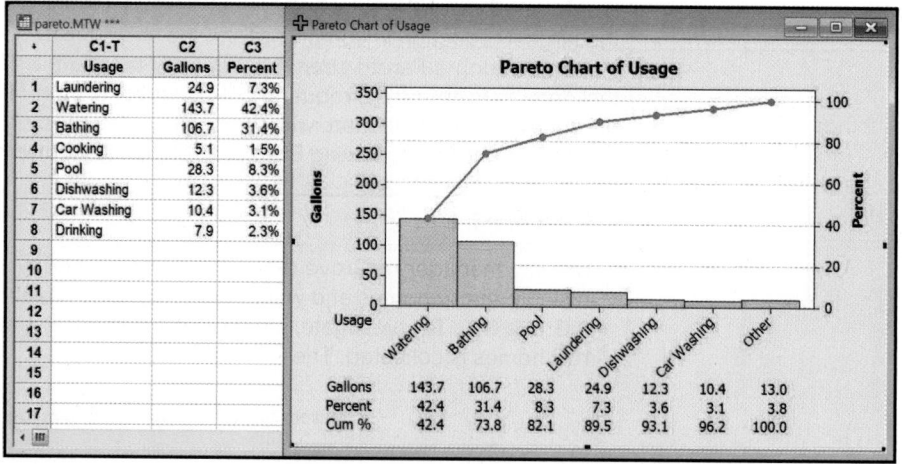

CHART 19–1 Pareto Chart for Water Usage in Grove City, Utah Minitab, Inc.

Below the chart, we list the activities, their frequency of occurrence, and the percent of the time each activity occurs. In the last row, we list the cumulative percentage. This cumulative row will allow us to quickly determine which set of activities account for most of the activity. These cumulative percents are plotted above the vertical bars. In the Grove City example, the activities of watering lawn, personal bathing, and pools account for 82.1% of the water usage. The city manager can attain the greatest gain by looking to reduce the water usage in these three areas.

Fishbone Diagrams

Another diagnostic chart is a **cause-and-effect diagram** or a **fishbone diagram.** It is called a cause-and-effect diagram to emphasize the relationship between an effect and a set of possible causes that produce the particular effect. This diagram is useful to help organize ideas and to identify relationships. It is a tool that encourages open brainstorming for ideas. By identifying these relationships, we can determine factors that are the cause of variability in our process. The name *fishbone* comes from the manner in which the various causes and effects are organized on the diagram. The effect is usually a particular problem, or perhaps a goal, and it is shown on the right-hand side of the diagram. The major causes are listed on the left-hand side of the diagram.

The usual approach to a fishbone diagram is to consider four problem areas, namely, methods, materials, equipment, and personnel. The problem, or the effect, is the head of the fish. See Chart 19–2.

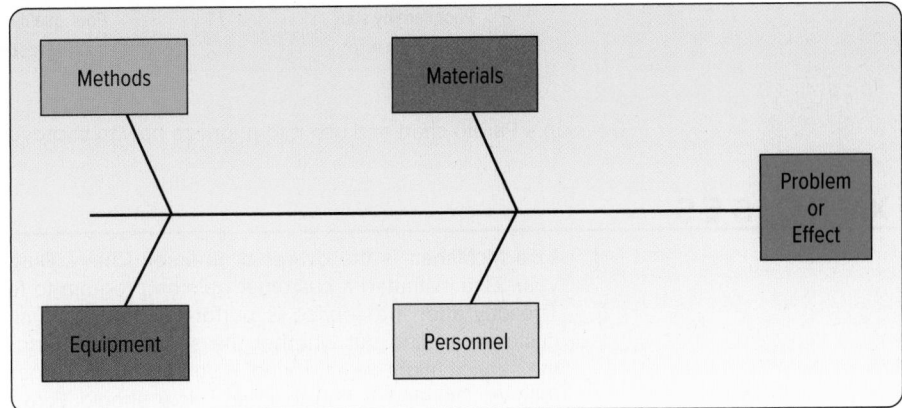

CHART 19–2 Fishbone Diagram

Under each of the possible causes are subcauses that are identified and investigated. The subcauses are factors that may be producing the particular effect. Information is gathered about the problem and used to fill in the fishbone diagram. Each of the subcauses is investigated and those that are not important eliminated, until the real cause of the problem is identified.

To illustrate a fishbone diagram, we investigate the causes of cold food served at Emily's Family Restaurant. Recall that a Pareto analysis showed that cold food was one of the top two complaints. In Chart 19–3, notice that each of the subcauses is

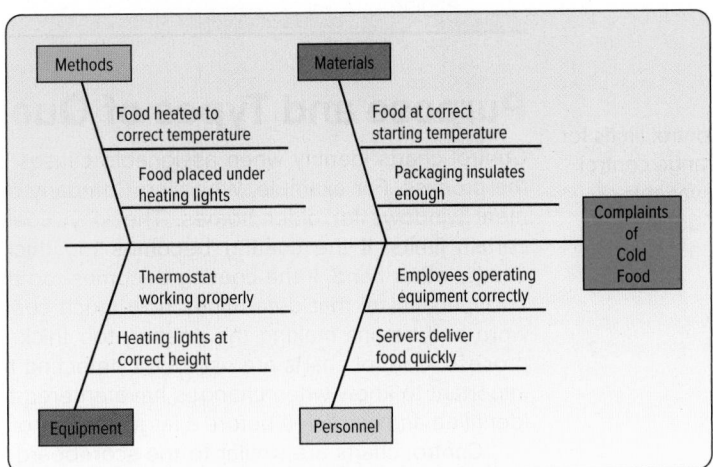

CHART 19–3 Fishbone Diagram for a Restaurant Investigation of Cold Food Complaints

listed as an assumption. Each of these subcauses must be investigated to find the real problem regarding the cold food. In a fishbone diagram, there is no weighting of the subcauses.

SELF-REVIEW 19–1

The Rouse Home, located on the south side of Chicago, is a mental health facility. Recently there have been complaints regarding conditions at the home. When a patient or a patient's relative has a complaint, it is documented by completing a complaint form. Listed is a summary of the complaints received during the last 12 months.

Complaint	Number	Complaint	Number
Nothing to do	45	Dirty conditions	63
Poor care by staff	71	Poor quality of food	84
Medication error	2	Lack of respect by staff	35

Develop a Pareto chart and use it to prioritize how to improve patient care.

EXERCISES

1. Ezra McMahan is the owner of Sharkey Chevy, Buick, GMC. At the start of the year, Ezra instituted a customer opinion program to find ways to improve service. The day after the service is performed, Ezra's administrative assistant calls the customer to find out whether the service was performed satisfactorily and how the service might be improved. A summary of the complaints for the first 6 months follows. Develop a Pareto chart. How should Ezra prioritize the complaints to improve the quality of service?

Complaint	Frequency	Complaint	Frequency
Problem not corrected	38	Price too high	23
Error on invoice	8	Wait too long for service	10
Unfriendly atmosphere	12		

2. Out of 110 diesel engines tested, a rework and repair facility found 9 had leaky water pumps, 15 had faulty cylinders, 4 had ignition problems, 52 had oil leaks, and 30 had cracked blocks. Draw a Pareto chart to identify the key problem in the engines.

LO19-4

Compute control limits for mean and range control charts for a variable measure of quality.

Purpose and Types of Quality Control Charts

Control charts identify when assignable causes of variation or changes have entered the process. For example, Wheeling Company makes vinyl-coated aluminum replacement windows for older homes. The vinyl coating must have a thickness between certain limits. If the coating becomes too thick, it will cause the windows to jam. On the other hand, if the coating becomes too thin, the window will not seal properly. The mechanism that determines how much coating is put on each window becomes worn and begins making the coating too thick. Thus, a change has occurred in the process. Control charts are useful for detecting the change in process conditions. It is important to know when changes have entered the process, so that the cause may be identified and corrected before a large number of unacceptable windows are produced.

Control charts are similar to the scoreboard in a baseball game. By looking at the scoreboard, the fans, coaches, and players can tell which team is winning the game.

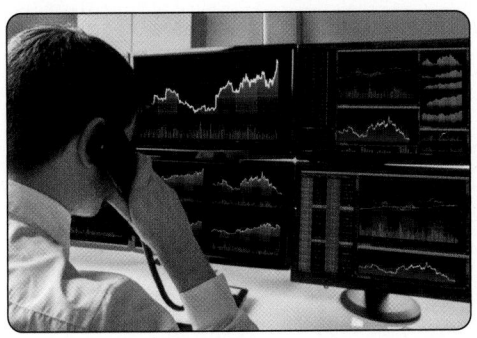

Andrey Popov/Shutterstock

However, the scoreboard can do nothing to win or lose the game. Control charts provide a similar function. These charts indicate to the workers, group leaders, quality control engineers, production supervisor, and management whether the production of the part or service is "in control" or "out of control." If the production is "out of control," the control chart will not fix the situation; it is just a piece of paper with numbers and dots on it. Instead, the person responsible must adjust the machine manufacturing the part or do what is necessary to return production to "in control."

There are two types of control charts. A **variable control chart** portrays measurements, such as the amount of cola in a 2-liter bottle or the outside diameter of a piece of pipe. A variable control chart requires the interval or the ratio scale of measurement. An **attribute control chart** classifies a product or service as either acceptable or unacceptable. It is based on the nominal scale of measurement. The Marines stationed at Camp Lejeune are asked to rate the meals served as acceptable or unacceptable; bank loans are either repaid or defaulted.

Control Charts for Variables

To develop control charts for variables, we rely on the sampling theory discussed in connection with the central limit theorem in Chapter 8. Suppose a sample of five pieces is selected each hour from the production process and the mean of each sample computed. The sample means are $\bar{x}_1$, $\bar{x}_2$, $\bar{x}_3$, and so on. The mean of these sample means is denoted as $\bar{\bar{x}}$. We use k to indicate the number of sample means. The overall or grand mean is found by:

$$\textbf{GRAND MEAN} \qquad \bar{\bar{x}} = \frac{\Sigma \text{ of the sample means}}{\text{Number of sample means}} = \frac{\Sigma \bar{x}}{k} \qquad \textbf{(19–1)}$$

The standard error of the distribution of the sample means is designated by $s_{\bar{x}}$. It is found by:

$$\textbf{STANDARD ERROR OF THE MEAN} \qquad s_{\bar{x}} = \frac{s}{\sqrt{n}} \qquad \textbf{(19–2)}$$

These relationships allow us to establish limits for the sample means to show how much variation can be expected for a given sample size. These expected limits are called the **upper control limit** (*UCL*) and the **lower control limit** (*LCL*). An Example/Solution will illustrate the use of control limits and how the limits are determined.

▶ **EXAMPLE**

Statistical Software Inc. offers a toll-free number where customers can call with problems involving the use of their products from 7 a.m. until 11 p.m. daily. It is impossible to have every call answered immediately by a technical representative. The company knows that the length of waiting time is related to a customer's perception of service quality. To understand its service-call process, Statistical Software decides to develop a control chart describing the total time from when a call is received until the representative answers the call and resolves the issue raised by the caller. Yesterday, for the 16 hours of operation, five calls were sampled each hour and the total time to resolve a customer's problem, in minutes, recorded. This information is reported here:

Time		Sample Number				
		1	2	3	4	5
a.m.	7	8	9	15	4	11
	8	7	10	7	6	8
	9	11	12	10	9	10
	10	12	8	6	9	12
	11	11	10	6	14	11
p.m.	12	7	7	10	4	11
	1	10	7	4	10	10
	2	8	11	11	7	7
	3	8	11	8	14	12
	4	12	9	12	17	11
	5	7	7	9	17	13
	6	9	9	4	4	11
	7	10	12	12	12	12
	8	8	11	9	6	8
	9	10	13	9	4	9
	10	9	11	8	5	11

Based on this information, develop a control chart for the mean duration of the call. Does there appear to be a trend in the calling times? Is there any period in which it appears that customers wait longer than others?

SOLUTION

A mean chart has two limits, an upper control limit (UCL) and a lower control limit (LCL). These upper and lower control limits are computed by:

CONTROL LIMITS FOR THE MEAN	$UCL = \bar{\bar{x}} + 3\dfrac{s}{\sqrt{n}}$ and $LCL = \bar{\bar{x}} - 3\dfrac{s}{\sqrt{n}}$	**(19–3)**

where s is an estimate of the standard deviation of the population, σ. Notice that in the calculation of the upper and lower control limits the number 3 appears. It represents the 99.74% confidence limits. The limits are often called the 3-sigma limits. However, other levels of confidence (such as 90 or 95%) can be used.

This application was developed before computers were widely available, and computing standard deviations was difficult. Rather than calculate the standard deviation from each sample as a measure of variation, it is easier to use the range. For fixed-sized samples, there is a constant relationship between the range and the standard deviation, so we can use the following formulas to determine the 99.74% control limits for the mean. It can be demonstrated that the term $3(s/\sqrt{n})$ from formula (19–3) is equivalent to $A_2\bar{R}$ in the following formula.

CONTROL LIMITS FOR THE MEAN	$UCL = \bar{\bar{x}} + A_2\bar{R} \qquad LCL = \bar{\bar{x}} - A_2\bar{R}$	**(19–4)**

where:

A_2 is a constant used in computing the upper and the lower control limits. It is based on the average range, $\overline{R}$. The factors for various sample sizes are available in Appendix B.10. (*Note: n* in this table refers to the number of items in the sample.) A portion of Appendix B.10 is shown here. To locate the A_2 factor for this problem, find the sample size for *n* in the left margin. It is 5. Then move horizontally to the A_2 column and read the factor. It is 0.577.

n	A_2	d_2	D_3	D_4
2	1.880	1.128	0	3.267
3	1.023	1.693	0	2.575
4	0.729	2.059	0	2.282
5	0.577	2.326	0	2.115
6	0.483	2.534	0	2.004

$\overline{\overline{x}}$ is the mean of the sample means, computed by $\Sigma\overline{x}/k$, where *k* is the number of samples selected. In this problem, a sample of five observations is taken each hour for 16 hours, so *k* = 16.

$\overline{R}$ is the mean of the ranges of the sample. It is $\Sigma R/k$. Remember the range is the difference between the largest and the smallest value in each sample. It describes the variability occurring in that particular sample. (See Table 19–1.)

TABLE 19–1 Sixteen Samples of Call Duration Data for Statistical Software Inc.

Time		1	2	3	4	5	Mean	Range
a.m.	7	8	9	15	4	11	9.4	11
	8	7	10	7	6	8	7.6	4
	9	11	12	10	9	10	10.4	3
	10	12	8	6	9	12	9.4	6
	11	11	10	6	14	11	10.4	8
p.m.	12	7	7	10	4	11	7.8	7
	1	10	7	4	10	10	8.2	6
	2	8	11	11	7	7	8.8	4
	3	8	11	8	14	12	10.6	6
	4	12	9	12	17	11	12.2	8
	5	7	7	9	17	13	10.6	10
	6	9	9	4	4	11	7.4	7
	7	10	12	12	12	12	11.6	2
	8	8	11	9	6	8	8.4	5
	9	10	13	9	4	9	9.0	9
	10	9	11	8	5	11	8.8	6
Total							150.6	102

The centerline for the chart is $\overline{\overline{x}}$. It is 9.413 minutes, found by 150.6/16. The mean of the ranges $(\overline{R})$ is 6.375 minutes, found by 102/16. Thus, the upper control limit of the mean chart is:

$$UCL = \overline{\overline{x}} + A_2\overline{R} = 9.413 + 0.577(6.375) = 13.091$$

The lower control limit of the mean chart is:

$$LCL = \overline{\overline{x}} - A_2\overline{R} = 9.413 - 0.577(6.375) = 5.735$$

$\overline{\overline{x}}$, *UCL, LCL,* and the sample means are portrayed in Chart 19–4. The mean, $\overline{\overline{x}}$, is 9.413 minutes, the upper control limit is located at 13.091 minutes, and the lower control limit is located at 5.735. There is some variation in the duration of the calls, but all sample means are within the control limits. Thus, based on 16 samples of five calls, we conclude that 99.74% of the time the mean length of a sample of five calls will be between 5.735 minutes and 13.091 minutes.

CHART 19–4 Control Chart for Mean Call Duration for Statistical Software Inc. Minitab, Inc.

Because the statistical theory is based on the normality of large samples, control charts should be based on a stable process, that is, a fairly large sample, taken over a long period of time. Before using control charts in practice, at least 25 samples need to be collected to establish control chart limits.

Range Charts

In addition to the central location in a sample, we must also monitor the amount of variation from sample to sample. A **range chart** shows the variation in the sample ranges. If the points representing the ranges fall between the upper and the lower limits, it is concluded that the operation is in control. According to chance, about 997 times out of 1,000 the range of the samples will fall within the limits. If the range should fall above the limits, we conclude that an assignable cause affected the operation and an adjustment to the process is needed. Why are we not as concerned about the lower control limit of the range? For small samples, the lower limit is often zero. Actually, for any sample of six or less, the lower control limit is 0. If the range is zero, then logically all the parts are the same and there is not a problem with the variability of the operation.

The upper and lower control limits of the range chart are determined from the following equations.

CONTROL CHART FOR RANGES	$UCL = D_4\bar{R}$ $LCL = D_3\bar{R}$	**(19–5)**

The values for D_3 and D_4, which reflect the usual three (sigma) limits for various sample sizes, are found in Appendix B.10 or in the table on page 727.

> **EXAMPLE**

The length of time customers of Statistical Software Inc. waited from the time their call was answered until a technical representative answered their question or solved their problem is recorded in Table 19–1. Develop a control chart for the range. Does it appear that there is any time when there is too much variation in the operation?

SOLUTION

The first step is to find the mean of the sample ranges. The range for the five calls sampled in the 7 a.m. hour is 11 minutes. The longest call selected from that hour was 15 minutes and the shortest 4 minutes; the difference in the lengths is 11 minutes. In the 8 a.m. hour, the range is 4 minutes. The total of the 16 ranges is 102 minutes, so the average range is 6.375 minutes, found by $\bar{R} = 102/16$. Referring to Appendix B.10 or the partial table on page 727, D_3 and D_4 are 0 and 2.115, respectively. The lower and upper control limits are 0 and 13.483.

$$UCL = D_4\bar{R} = 2.115(6.375) = 13.483$$

$$LCL = D_3\bar{R} = 0(6.375) = 0$$

The range chart with the 16 sample ranges plotted is shown in Chart 19–5. This chart shows all the ranges are well within the control limits. Hence, we conclude the variation in the time to service the customers' calls is within normal limits, that is, "in control." Of course, we should be determining the control limits based on one set of data and then applying them to evaluate future data, not the data we already know.

CHART 19–5 Control Chart for Ranges of Length of Customer Calls to Statistical Software Inc.

Statistical software packages will compute all the statistics and draw control charts. The following is the Minitab analysis for the Statistical Software example showing the mean and range charts. The minor differences in the control limits are due to rounding.

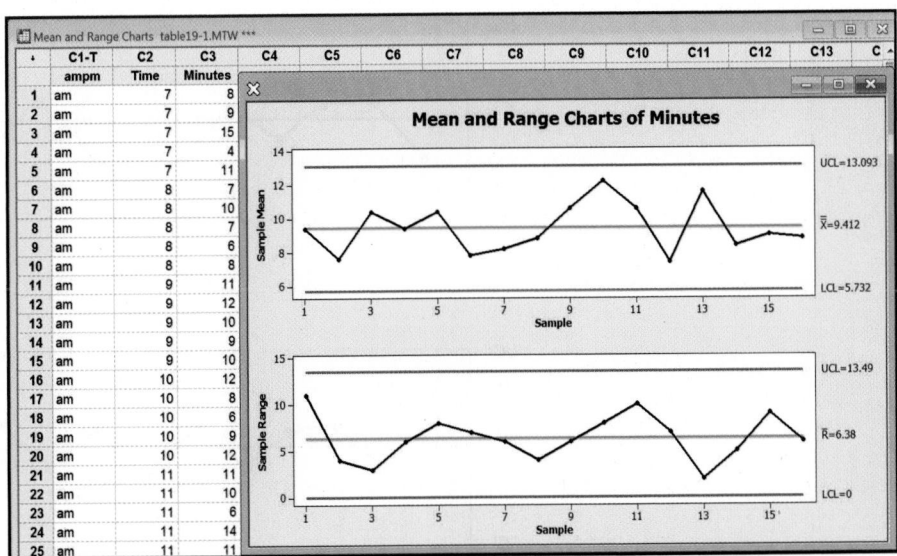

LO19-5

Evaluate control charts to determine if a process is out of control.

In-Control and Out-of-Control Situations

Three illustrations of in-control and out-of-control processes follow:

1. The mean chart and the range chart together indicate that the process is in control. Note the sample means and sample ranges are clustered close to the centerlines. Some are above and some below the centerlines, indicating the process is quite stable. That is, there is no visible tendency for the means and ranges to move toward the out-of-control areas.

2. The sample means are in control, but the ranges of the last two samples are out of control. This indicates there is considerable variation in the samples. Some sample ranges are large; others are small. An adjustment in the process is probably necessary.

3. The mean is in control for the first samples, but there is an upward trend toward the *UCL*. The last two sample means are out of control. An adjustment in the process is indicated.

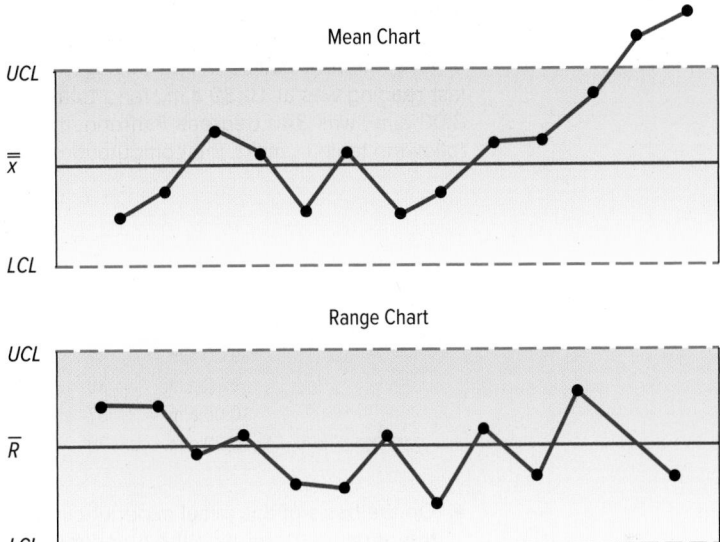

The preceding chart for the mean is an example of a control chart that offers some additional information. Note the direction of the last five observations of the mean. They are all above $\overline{\overline{x}}$ and increasing, and, in fact, the last two observations are out of control. The fact that the sample means were increasing for six consecutive observations is very improbable and another indication that the process is out of control.

SELF-REVIEW 19–2

The manager of River City McDonald's randomly selects four customers during 3 hours of the day: 9 a.m., 10 a.m., and 11 a.m. For these selected customers, the manager determines the time, in minutes, between order entry and order delivery. The results follow:

	Sample Times			
Time	**1**	**2**	**3**	**4**
9 a.m.	1	4	5	2
10 a.m.	2	3	2	1
11 a.m.	1	7	3	5

(a) Compute the mean service time and the mean range of service time, determine the control limits for the mean and the range, and create control charts.
(b) Are the measurements within the control limits? Interpret the chart.

EXERCISES

3. Describe the difference between assignable variation and chance variation.
4. Describe the difference between an attribute control chart and a variable control chart.
5. Samples of size $n = 4$ are selected from a production line.
   a. What is the value of the A_2 factor used to determine the upper and lower control limits for the mean?
   b. What are the values of the D_3 and D_4 factors used to determine the lower and upper control limits for the range?

6. Samples of size 5 are selected from a manufacturing process. The mean of the sample ranges is .50. What is the estimate of the standard deviation of the population?

7. **FILE** A new industrial oven has just been installed at Piatt Bakery. To develop experience regarding the oven temperature, an inspector reads the temperature at four different places inside the oven each half hour starting at 8:00 a.m. The last reading was at 10:30 a.m., for a total of six samples. The first reading, taken at 8:00 a.m., was 340 degrees Fahrenheit. (Only the last two digits are given in the following table to make the computations easier.)

Time	Reading			
	1	**2**	**3**	**4**
8:00 a.m.	40	50	55	39
8:30 a.m.	44	42	38	38
9:00 a.m.	41	45	47	43
9:30 a.m.	39	39	41	41
10:00 a.m.	37	42	46	41
10:30 a.m.	39	40	39	40

   a. On the basis of this initial experience, determine the control limits for the mean temperature. Determine the grand mean. Plot the results on a control chart.

   b. Interpret the chart. Does there seem to be a time when the temperature is out of control?

8. **FILE** Refer to Exercise 7.

   a. On the basis of this initial experience, determine the control limits for the range. Plot the plot results on a control chart.

   b. Does there seem to be a time when there is too much variation in the temperature?

LO19-6

Compute control limits of control charts for an attribute measure of quality.

Attribute Control Charts

Often the data we collect are the result of counting rather than measuring. That is, we observe the presence or absence of some attribute. For example, the screw top on a bottle of shampoo either fits onto the bottle and does not leak (an "acceptable" condition) or does not seal and a leak results (an "unacceptable" condition), or a bank makes a loan to a customer and the loan is either repaid or not repaid. In other cases, we are interested in the number of defects in a sample. British Airways might count the number of its flights arriving late per day at Gatwick Airport in London. In this section, we discuss two types of attribute charts: the *p*-chart (proportion defective) and the *c*-bar chart (number of defectives per unit).

p-Charts

If the item recorded is the proportion of unacceptable parts made in a larger batch of parts, the appropriate control chart is the **p-chart.** This chart is based on the binomial distribution, discussed in Chapter 6, and proportions, discussed in Chapters 10 and 11. The centerline is at p, the mean proportion defective. The p replaces the $\bar{\bar{x}}$ of the variable control chart. The mean proportion defective is found by:

MEAN PROPORTION DEFECTIVE	$p = \dfrac{\text{Total number defective}}{\text{Total number of items sampled}}$	**(19–6)**

The variation in the sample proportion is described by the standard error of a proportion. It is found by:

STANDARD ERROR OF THE SAMPLE PROPORTION	$s_p = \sqrt{\dfrac{p(1-p)}{n}}$	(19–7)

Hence, the upper control limit (*UCL*) and the lower control limit (*LCL*) are computed as the mean proportion defective plus or minus three times the standard error of the proportions. The formula for the control limits is:

CONTROL LIMITS FOR PROPORTIONS	$LCL, UCL = p \pm 3\sqrt{\dfrac{p(1-p)}{n}}$	(19–8)

An Example/Solution will show the details of the calculations and the conclusions.

▶ **EXAMPLE**

Jersey Glass Company Inc. produces small hand mirrors. Jersey Glass runs day and evening shifts each weekday. The quality assurance department (QA) monitors the quality of the mirrors twice during the day shift and twice during the evening shift. QA selects and carefully inspects a random sample of 50 mirrors once every 4 hours. Each mirror is classified as either acceptable or unacceptable. Finally, QA counts the number of mirrors in the sample that do not conform to quality specifications. Listed next are the results of these checks over the last 10 business days.

Date	Number Sampled	Defects	Date	Number Sampled	Defects
10-Oct	50	1	17-Oct	50	7
	50	0		50	9
	50	9		50	0
	50	9		50	8
11-Oct	50	4	18-Oct	50	6
	50	4		50	9
	50	5		50	6
	50	3		50	1
12-Oct	50	9	19-Oct	50	4
	50	3		50	5
	50	10		50	2
	50	2		50	5
13-Oct	50	2	20-Oct	50	0
	50	4		50	0
	50	9		50	4
	50	4		50	7
14-Oct	50	6	21-Oct	50	5
	50	9		50	1
	50	2		50	9
	50	4		50	9

Construct a *p*-chart for this process. What are the upper and lower control limits? Interpret the results. Does it appear the process is out of control during the period?

SOLUTION

The first step is to determine the overall proportion defective. We use formula (19–6).

$$p = \frac{\text{Total number defective}}{\text{Total number of items sampled}} = \frac{196}{2{,}000} = .098$$

So we estimate that .098 of the mirrors produced during the period do not meet specifications.

Date	Number Sampled	Defects	Proportion Defective	Date	Number Sampled	Defects	Proportion Defective
10-Oct	50	1	0.02	13-Oct	50	2	0.04
	50	0	0.00		50	4	0.08
	50	9	0.18		50	9	0.18
	50	9	0.18		50	4	0.08
11-Oct	50	4	0.08	14-Oct	50	6	0.12
	50	4	0.08		50	9	0.18
	50	5	0.10		50	2	0.04
	50	3	0.06		50	4	0.08
12-Oct	50	9	0.18	17-Oct	50	7	0.14
	50	3	0.06		50	9	0.18
	50	10	0.20		50	0	0.00
	50	2	0.04		50	8	0.16
18-Oct	50	6	0.12	20-Oct	50	0	0.00
	50	9	0.18		50	0	0.00
	50	6	0.12		50	4	0.08
	50	1	0.02		50	7	0.14
19-Oct	50	4	0.08	21-Oct	50	5	0.10
	50	5	0.10		50	1	0.02
	50	2	0.04		50	9	0.18
	50	5	0.10		50	9	0.18
				Total	**2,000**	**196**	

The upper and lower control limits are computed by using formula (19–8).

$$LCL,\ UCL = p \pm 3\sqrt{\frac{p(1-p)}{n}} = .098 \pm 3\sqrt{\frac{.098(1-.098)}{50}} = .098 \pm .1261$$

From these calculations, the upper control limit is .2241, found by .098 + .1261. The lower control limit is 0. Why? The lower limit by the formula is .098 − .1261 = −0.0281. However, a negative proportion defective is not possible, so the smallest value is 0. We set the control limits at 0 and 0.2241. Any sample outside these limits indicates the quality level of the process has changed.

This information is summarized in Chart 19–6, which is output from the Minitab system.

CHART 19–6 *p*-Chart for Mirrors at Jersey Glass Minitab, Inc.

After establishing the limits, the process is monitored for the next week—5 days, two shifts per day—with two quality checks per shift. The results are as follows:

Date	Number Sampled	Defects	Proportion Defective	Date	Number Sampled	Defects	Proportion Defective
24-Oct	50	1	0.02	27-Oct	50	2	0.04
	50	13	0.26		50	1	0.02
	50	10	0.20		50	7	0.14
	50	7	0.14		50	12	0.24
25-Oct	50	4	0.08	28-Oct	50	5	0.10
	50	5	0.10		50	5	0.10
	50	6	0.12		50	10	0.20
	50	10	0.20		50	9	0.18
26-Oct	50	6	0.12				
	50	1	0.02				
	50	8	0.16				
	50	4	0.08				

The process was out of control on two occasions, on October 24 when the proportion of defects was 0.26 and again on October 27 when the proportion of defects was 0.24. QA should report this information to the production department for the appropriate action. The Minitab output follows:

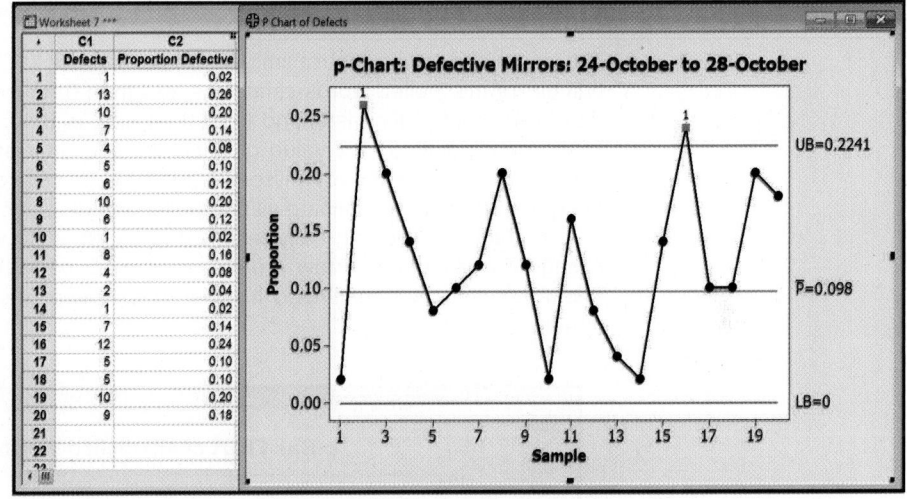

Minitab, Inc.

c-Bar Charts

The c-bar chart plots the number of defects or failures per unit. It is based on the Poisson distribution discussed in Chapter 6. The number of bags mishandled on a flight by Blue Sky Airlines might be monitored by a c-bar chart. The "unit" under consideration is the flight. On most flights, there are no bags mishandled. On others, there may be only one, on others two, and so on. The Internal Revenue Service might count and develop a control chart for the number of errors in arithmetic per tax return. Most returns will not have any errors, some returns will have a single error, others will have two, and so on. We let $\bar{c}$ be the mean number of defects per unit. Thus, $\bar{c}$ is the mean number of bags mishandled by Blue Sky Airlines per flight or the mean number of arithmetic errors per tax return. Recall from Chapter 6 that the standard deviation of a Poisson distribution is the square root of the mean. Thus, we can determine the 3-sigma, or 99.74%, limits on a c-bar chart by:

CONTROL LIMITS FOR THE NUMBER OF DEFECTS PER UNIT	$LCL, UCL = \bar{c} \pm 3\sqrt{\bar{c}}$	(19–9)

▶ **EXAMPLE**

The publisher of the *Oak Harbor Daily Telegraph* is concerned about the number of misspelled words in the daily newspaper. In an effort to control the problem and promote the need for correct spelling, a control chart will be used. The numbers of misspelled words found in the final edition of the paper for the last 10 days are 5, 6, 3, 0, 4, 5, 1, 2, 7, and 4. Determine the appropriate control limits and interpret the chart. Were there any days during the period that the number of misspelled words was out of control?

SOLUTION

During the 10-day period, there were a total of 37 misspelled words. The mean number of misspelled words per edition is 3.7. The number of misspelled words per edition follows the Poisson probability distribution. The standard deviation is the square root of the mean.

$$\bar{c} = \frac{\Sigma x}{n} = \frac{5 + 6 + \cdots + 4}{10} = \frac{37}{10} = 3.7 \qquad s = \sqrt{\bar{c}} = \sqrt{3.7} = 1.924$$

To find the upper control limit, we use formula (19–9). The lower control limit is zero.

$$UCL = \bar{c} + 3\sqrt{\bar{c}} = 3.7 + 3\sqrt{3.7} = 3.7 + 5.77 = 9.47$$

The computed lower control limit would be $3.7 - 3(1.924) = -2.07$. However, the number of misspelled words cannot be less than 0, so we use 0 as the lower limit. The lower control limit is 0 and the upper limit is 9.47. When we compare each of the data points to the value of 9.47, we see they are all less than the upper control limit; the number of misspelled words is "in control." Of course, newspapers are going to strive to eliminate all misspelled words, but control charting techniques offer a means of tracking daily results and determining whether there has been a change. For example, a new proofreader's work could be compared with others. These results are summarized in Chart 19–7, which is output from the Minitab system.

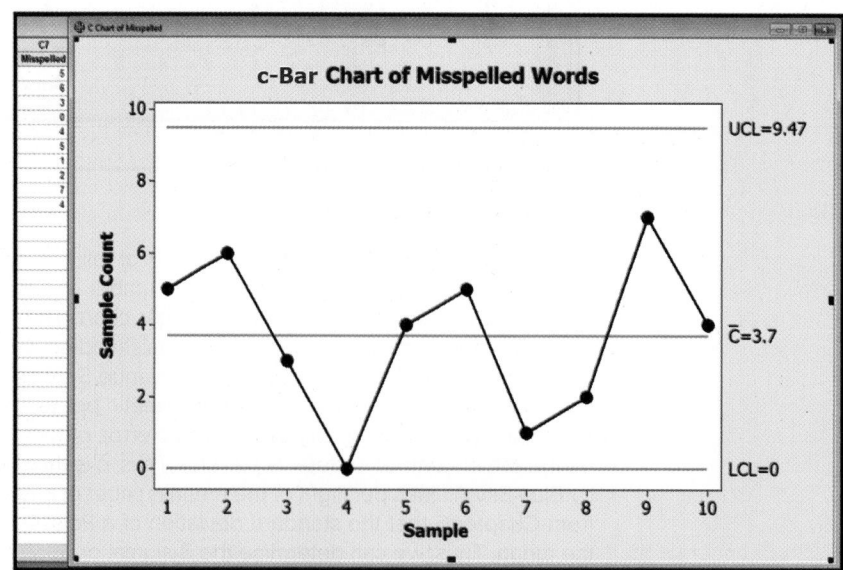

CHART 19–7 *c*-Bar Chart for Number of Misspelled Words per Edition of the *Oak Harbor Daily Telegraph* Minitab, Inc.

SELF-REVIEW 19–3

Auto-Lite Company manufactures car batteries. At the end of each shift, the quality assurance department selects a sample of batteries and tests them. The numbers of defective batteries found over the last 12 shifts are 2, 1, 0, 2, 1, 1, 7, 1, 1, 2, 6, and 1. Construct a control chart for the process and comment on whether the process is in control.

EXERCISES

9. Following is a *p*-chart for a manufacturing process.

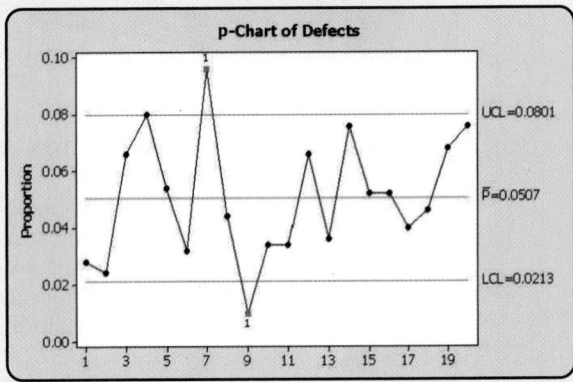

p-Chart of Defects

a. What is the mean proportion defective? What are the upper and lower control limits?
b. Are there any sample observations that indicate the process is out of control? Which sample numbers are they?
c. Does there seem to be any trend in the process? That is, does the process seem to be getting better, getting worse, or staying the same?

10. **FILE** Inter-State Moving and Storage Company wishes to establish a control chart to monitor the proportion of residential moves that result in written complaints due to late delivery, lost items, or damaged items. A sample of 50 moves is selected for each of the last 12 months. The number of written complaints in each sample is 8, 7, 4, 8, 2, 7, 11, 6, 7, 6, 8, and 12.
a. Design a *p*-chart and label the mean proportion defective, *UCL,* and *LCL.*
b. Plot the proportion of written complaints in the last 12 months.
c. Interpret the chart. Does it appear that the number of complaints is out of control for any of the months?

11. **FILE** A bicycle manufacturer randomly selects 10 frames each day and tests for defects. The numbers of defective frames found over the last 14 days are 3, 2, 1, 3, 2, 2, 8, 2, 0, 3, 5, 2, 0, and 4. Construct a control chart for this process and comment on whether the process is "in control."

12. **FILE** During the process of producing toilet paper, Scott Paper randomly selects a toilet paper roll five times throughout the day and subjects each roll to a stress test to see how often the paper tears. Over a 3-day period, the testing of 15 rolls found the following number of defectives in each roll: 2, 3, 1, 2, 2, 1, 3, 2, 2, 1, 2, 2, 1, 0, and 0. Construct a control chart for the process and comment on whether the process is "in control."

13. **FILE** Sam's Supermarkets monitors the checkout scanners by randomly examining the receipts for scanning errors. On October 27, they recorded the following number of scanner errors on each receipt: 0, 1, 1, 0, 0, 1, 1, 0, 1, 1, 0. Construct a control chart for this process and comment on whether the process is "in control."

14. **FILE** Liam Chu runs a car wash chain with outlets scattered throughout Chicago. He is concerned that some local managers are giving away free washes to their friends. He decides to collect data on the number of "voided" sales receipts. Of course, some of them are legitimate voids. Would the following data indicate a reasonable number of voided receipts: 3, 8, 3, 4, 6, 5, 0, 1, 2, 4? Construct a control chart for this process and comment on whether the process is "in control."

LO19-7

Explain the process of acceptance sampling.

Acceptance Sampling

Vstock LLC/Getty Images

The previous section was concerned with maintaining the *quality of the product as it is being produced.* In many business situations, we are also concerned with the *quality of the incoming finished product.* What do the following cases have in common?

- Sims Software Inc. purchases DVDs from DVD International. The normal purchase order is for 100,000 DVDs, packaged in lots of 1,000. Blair Sims, president, does not expect each DVD to be perfect. In fact, he has agreed to accept lots of 1,000 with up to 10% defective. He would like to develop a plan to inspect incoming lots, to ensure that the quality standard is met. The purpose of the inspection procedure is to separate the acceptable from the unacceptable lots.
- Zenith Electric purchases thermostats from Bono Electronics for use in its new microwave oven. The thermostats are shipped to Zenith in lots of 10,000. Zenith allows the incoming lots to contain up to 5% defective thermostats. It would like to develop a sampling plan to determine which lots meet the criterion and which do not.
- General Motors purchases windshields from many suppliers. GM insists that the windshields be in lots of 1,000, and is willing to accept 50 or fewer defects in each lot, that is, 5% defective. They would like to develop a sampling procedure to verify that incoming shipments meet the criterion.

The common thread in these cases is a need to verify that an incoming product meets the stipulated requirements. The situation can be likened to a screen door, which allows the warm summer air to enter the room while keeping the bugs out. Acceptance sampling lets the lots of acceptable quality into the manufacturing area and screens out lots that are not acceptable.

Of course, the situation in modern business is more complex. The buyer wants protection against accepting lots that are below the quality standard. The best protection against inferior quality is 100% inspection. Unfortunately, the cost of 100% inspection is often prohibitive. Another problem with checking each item is that the test may be destructive. If all lightbulbs were tested until burning out before they were shipped, there would be none left to sell. Also, 100% inspection may not lead to the identification of all defects because boredom might cause a loss of perception on the part of the inspectors. Thus, complete inspection is rarely employed in practical situations.

To evaluate the quality of incoming parts, we use a statistical sampling plan. According to this plan, a sample of n units is randomly selected from the lots of N units (the population). This is called **acceptance sampling.** The inspection will determine the number of defects in the sample. This number is compared with a predetermined number called the **critical number** or the **acceptance number.** The acceptance number is usually designated c. If the number of defects in the sample of size n is less than or equal to c, the lot is accepted. If the number of defects exceeds c, the lot is rejected and returned to the supplier, or perhaps submitted to 100% inspection.

Acceptance sampling is a decision-making process. There are two possible decisions: accept or reject the lot. In addition, there are two situations under which the decision is made: the lot is good or the lot is bad. These are the states of nature. If the lot is good and the sample inspection reveals the lot to be good, or if the lot is bad and the sample inspection indicates it is bad, then a correct decision is made. However, there are two other possibilities. The lot may actually contain more defects than it should, but it is accepted. This is called **consumer's risk.** Similarly, the lot may be within the agreed-upon limits, but it is rejected during the sample inspection. This is called the **producer's risk.** The following summary table for acceptance decisions shows these possibilities. Notice how this discussion is very similar to the ideas of Type I and Type II errors discussed in Chapter 10.

| | States of Nature | |
Decision	Good Lot	Bad Lot
Accept lot	Correct	Consumer's risk
Reject lot	Producer's risk	Correct

To evaluate a sampling plan and determine that it is fair to both the producer and the consumer, the usual procedure is to develop an **operating characteristic curve,** or an **OC curve.** An OC curve reports the percent defective along the horizontal axis and the probability of accepting that percent defective along the vertical axis. A smooth curve is usually drawn connecting all the possible levels of quality. The binomial distribution is used to develop the probabilities for an OC curve.

▶ **EXAMPLE**

Sims Software, as mentioned earlier, purchases DVDs from DVD International. The DVDs are packaged in lots of 1,000 each. Blair Sims, president of Sims Software, has agreed to accept lots with 10% or fewer defective DVDs. Blair has directed his inspection department to select a random sample of 20 DVDs and examine them carefully. Blair will accept the lot if it has two or fewer defectives in the sample. Develop an OC curve for this inspection plan. What is the probability of accepting a lot that is 10% defective?

SOLUTION

This type of sampling is called **attribute sampling** because the sampled item, a DVD in this case, is classified as acceptable or unacceptable. No "reading" or "measurement" is obtained on the DVD. Let π represent the actual proportion defective in the population.

The lot is good if $\pi \leq .10$.
The lot is bad if $\pi > .10$.

Let x be the number of defects in the sample. The decision rule is:

Accept the lot if $x \leq 2$.
Reject the lot if $x \geq 3$.

Here the acceptable lot is one with 10% or fewer defective DVDs. If the lot is acceptable when it has exactly 10% defectives, it would be even more acceptable if it contained fewer than 10% defectives. Hence, it is the usual practice to work with the upper limit of the percent of defectives.

The binomial distribution is used to compute the various values on the OC curve. Recall that for us to use the binomial, there are four requirements:

1. There are only two possible outcomes: The sampled DVD is either acceptable or unacceptable.
2. There are a fixed number of trials. The number of trials is the sample size of 20.
3. There is a constant probability of success. A success is finding a defective DVD. The probability of success is assumed to be .10.
4. The trials are independent. The probability of obtaining a defective DVD on the third one selected is not related to the likelihood of finding a defect on the fourth DVD selected.

Appendix B.1 gives various binomial probabilities. However, the tables in Appendix B.1 go up to only 15, that is, $n = 15$. For this problem, $n = 20$, so we will use Excel to compute the various binomial probabilities. The following Excel output shows the binomial probabilities for $n = 20$ when π is equal to .05, .10, .15, .20, .25, and .30.

We need to convert the terms used in Chapter 6 to acceptance sampling vocabulary. We let π refer to the probability of finding a defect, c the number of defects allowed, and n the number of items sampled. In this case, we will allow up to two defects, so $c = 2$. This means that we will allow 0, 1, or 2 of the 20 items sampled to be defective and still accept the incoming shipment of DVDs.

To begin, we determine the probability of accepting a lot that is 5% defective. This means that $\pi = .05$, $c = 2$, and $n = 20$. From the Excel output, the likelihood of selecting a sample of 20 items from a shipment that contained 5% defective and finding exactly 0 defects is .358. The likelihood of finding exactly 1 defect is .377, and finding 2 is .189. Hence, the likelihood of 2 or fewer defects is .924, found by .358 + .377 + .189. This result is usually written in shorthand notation as follows (recall that bar "|" means "given that").

$$P(x \leq 2 \mid \pi = .05 \text{ and } n = 20) = .358 + .377 + .189 = .924$$

Incoming Lot Fraction Defective

Number of Defects	Probability					
	0.05	0.10	0.15	0.20	0.25	0.30
0	0.358	0.122	0.039	0.012	0.003	0.001
1	0.377	0.270	0.137	0.058	0.021	0.007
2	0.189	0.285	0.229	0.137	0.067	0.028
3	0.060	0.190	0.243	0.205	0.134	0.072
4	0.013	0.090	0.182	0.218	0.190	0.130
5	0.002	0.032	0.103	0.175	0.202	0.179
6	0.000	0.009	0.045	0.109	0.169	0.192
7	0.000	0.002	0.016	0.055	0.112	0.164
8	0.000	0.000	0.005	0.022	0.061	0.114
9	0.000	0.000	0.001	0.007	0.027	0.065
10	0.000	0.000	0.000	0.002	0.010	0.031
11	0.000	0.000	0.000	0.000	0.003	0.012
12	0.000	0.000	0.000	0.000	0.001	0.004
13	0.000	0.000	0.000	0.000	0.000	0.001
14	0.000	0.000	0.000	0.000	0.000	0.000
*	*	*	*	*	*	*
20	0.000	0.000	0.000	0.000	0.000	0.000

Microsoft Excel

Continuing, the likelihood of accepting a lot that is actually 10% defective is .677. That is:

$$P(x \leq 2 \mid \pi = .10 \text{ and } n = 20) = .122 + .270 + .285 = .677$$

The complete OC curve in Chart 19–8 shows the smoothed curve for all values of π between 0 and about 30%. There is no need to show values larger than 30% because their probability is very close to 0. The likelihood of accepting lots of selected quality levels is shown in table form on the right-hand side of Chart 19–8. With the OC curve, the management of Sims Software will be able to quickly evaluate the probabilities of various quality levels.

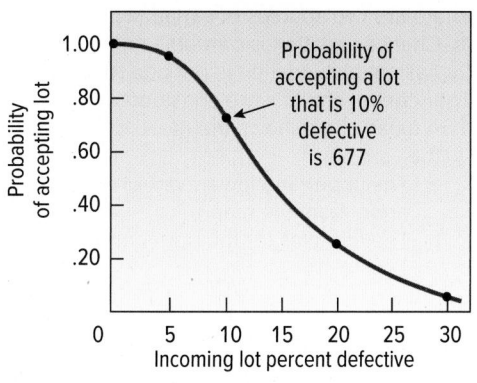

Lot percent defective	Probability of accepting lot
0	1.000
5	.924
10	.677
20	.207
30	.036

CHART 19–8 OC Curve for Sampling Plan ($n = 20$, $c = 2$)

SELF-REVIEW 19–4

Compute the probability of accepting a lot of DVDs that is actually 30% defective, using the sampling plan for Sims Software.

EXERCISES

15. Determine the probability of accepting lots that are 10%, 20%, 30%, and 40% defective using a sample of size 12 and an acceptance number of 2.

16. Determine the probability of accepting lots that are 10%, 20%, 30%, and 40% defective using a sample of size 14 and an acceptance number of 3.

17. Warren Electric manufactures fuses for many customers. To ensure the quality of the outgoing product, it tests 10 fuses each hour. If no more than one fuse is defective, it packages the fuses and prepares them for shipment. Develop an OC curve for this sampling plan. Compute the probabilities of accepting lots that are 10%, 20%, 30%, and 40% defective. Draw the OC curve for this sampling plan using the four quality levels.

18. Grills Video Products purchases LCDs from Mira Electronics. The company's sampling plan states that it will accept a shipment of LCDs if 3 or fewer are defective in a sample of 25. Develop an OC curve for these percents defective: 10%, 20%, 30%, and 40%. You will need a statistical software package.

CHAPTER SUMMARY

I. The objective of statistical quality control is to monitor the quality of the product or service as it is being developed.

II. A Pareto chart is a technique for tallying the number and type of defects that happen within a product or service.
   A. This chart was named after an Italian scientist, Vilfredo Pareto.
   B. The concept of the chart is that 80% of the activity is caused by 20% of the factors.

III. A fishbone diagram emphasizes the relationship between a possible problem cause that will produce the particular effect.
   A. It is also called a cause-and-effect diagram.
   B. The usual approach is to consider four problem areas: methods, materials, equipment, and personnel.

IV. The purpose of a control chart is to monitor graphically the quality of a product or service.
   A. There are two types of control charts.
      1. A variable control chart is the result of a measurement.
      2. An attribute chart shows whether the product or service is acceptable or not acceptable.

B. There are two sources of variation in the quality of a product or service.
  1. Chance variation is random in nature and cannot be controlled or eliminated.
  2. Assignable variation is not due to random causes and can be eliminated.
C. Four control charts were considered in this chapter.
  1. A mean chart shows the mean of a variable, and a range chart shows the range of the variable.
    a. The upper and lower control limits are set at plus and minus three standard errors from the mean.
    b. The formulas for the upper and lower control limits for the mean are:

$$UCL = \bar{\bar{x}} + A_2\bar{R} \qquad LCL = \bar{\bar{x}} - A_2\bar{R} \tag{19–4}$$

    c. The formulas for the upper and lower control limits for the range are:

$$UCL = D_4\bar{R} \qquad LCL = D_3\bar{R} \tag{19–5}$$

  2. A *p*-chart is an attribute chart that shows the proportion of the product or service that does not conform to the standard.
    a. The mean proportion defective is found by

$$p = \frac{\text{Total number defective}}{\text{Total number of items sampled}} \tag{19–6}$$

    b. The control limits for the proportion defective are determined from the equation

$$LCL, UCL = p \pm 3\sqrt{\frac{p(1-p)}{n}} \tag{19–8}$$

  3. A *c*-bar chart refers to the number of defects per unit.
    a. It is based on the Poisson distribution.
    b. The mean number of defects per unit is $\bar{c}$.
    c. The control limits are determined from the following equation.

$$LCL, UCL = \bar{c} \pm 3\sqrt{\bar{c}} \tag{19–9}$$

V. Acceptance sampling is a method to determine whether an incoming lot of a product meets specified standards.
  A. It is based on random sampling techniques.
  B. A random sample of *n* units is selected from a population of *N* units.
  C. *c* is the maximum number of defective units that may be found in the sample of *n* and the lot is still considered acceptable.
  D. An OC (operating characteristic) curve is developed using the binomial probability distribution to determine the probability of accepting lots of various quality levels.

PRONUNCIATION KEY

SYMBOL	MEANING	PRONUNCIATION
$\bar{\bar{x}}$	Mean of the sample means	x double bar
$s_{\bar{x}}$	Standard error of the mean	s sub x bar
A_2	Constant used to determine the upper and lower control limit for the mean	A sub 2
$\bar{R}$	Mean of the sample ranges	R bar
D_3	Constant used to determine the lower control limit for the range	D sub 3
D_4	Constant used to determine the upper control limit for the range	D sub 4
$\bar{c}$	Mean number of defects per unit	c bar

CHAPTER EXERCISES

19. The production supervisor at Westburg Electric Inc. noted an increase in the number of electric motors rejected at the time of final inspection. Of the last 200 motors rejected, 80 of the defects were due to poor wiring, 60 contained a short in the coil, 50 involved a defective plug, and 10 involved other defects. Develop a Pareto chart to show the major problem areas.

20. **FILE** The manufacturer of running shoes conducted a study on its newly developed jogging shoe. Listed are the type and frequency of the nonconformities and failures found. Develop a Pareto chart to show the major problem areas.

Type of Nonconformity	Frequency	Type of Nonconformity	Frequency
Sole separation	34	Lace breakage	14
Heel separation	98	Eyelet failure	10
Sole penetration	62	Other	16

21. At Rumsey's Old Fashion Roast Beef, cola drinks are filled by an automatic machine whose operation is based on the weight of the drink. When the process is in control, the machine fills each cup so that the grand mean is 10.0 ounces and the mean range is 0.25 for samples of 5.

a. Determine the upper and lower control limits for the process for both the mean and the range.

b. The manager of the I-280 store tested five soft drinks served last hour and found that the mean was 10.16 ounces and the range was 0.35 ounce. Is the process in control? Should other action be taken?

22. **FILE** A new machine has just been installed to produce printed circuit boards. One of the critical measurements is the thickness of the resistance layer. The quality control inspector randomly selects five boards each half-hour, measures the thickness, and records the results. The measurements (in millimeters) for the period 8:00 a.m. to 10:30 a.m. follow:

	Thickness (millimeters)				
Time	1	2	3	4	5
8:00	87.1	87.3	87.9	87.0	87.0
8:30	86.9	88.5	87.6	87.5	87.4
9:00	87.5	88.4	86.9	87.6	88.2
9:30	86.0	88.0	87.2	87.6	87.1
10:00	87.1	87.1	87.1	87.1	87.1
10:30	88.0	86.2	87.4	87.3	87.8

a. Determine the control limits for the mean and the range.

b. Plot the control limits for the mean outside diameter and the range.

c. Are there any points on the mean or the range chart that are out of control? Comment on the chart.

23. **FILE** Long Last Tire Company, as part of its inspection process, tests its tires for tread wear under simulated road conditions. Twenty samples of three tires each were selected from different shifts over the last month of operation. The tread wear is reported in hundredths of an inch.

Sample	Tread Wear			Sample	Tread Wear		
1	44	41	19	11	11	33	34
2	39	31	21	12	51	34	39
3	38	16	25	13	30	16	30
4	20	33	26	14	22	21	35
5	34	33	36	15	11	28	38
6	28	23	39	16	49	25	36
7	40	15	34	17	20	31	33
8	36	36	34	18	26	18	36
9	32	29	30	19	26	47	26
10	29	38	34	20	34	29	32

a. Determine the control limits for the mean and the range.

b. Plot the control limits for the mean tread wear and the range.

c. Are there any points on the mean or the range chart that are "out of control"? Comment on the chart.

24. **FILE** Charter National Bank has a staff of loan officers located in its branch offices throughout the Southwest. Robert Kerns, vice president of consumer lending, would like some information on the typical amount of loans and the range in the amount of the loans. A staff analyst of the vice president selected a sample of 10 loan officers and selected a sample of five loans each officer made last month. The data are reported here. Develop a control chart for the mean and the range. Do any of the officers appear to be "out of control"? Comment on your findings.

Officer	Loan Amount ($000)					Officer	Loan Amount ($000)				
	1	2	3	4	5		1	2	3	4	5
Weinraub	59	74	53	48	65	Bowyer	66	80	54	68	52
Visser	42	51	70	47	67	Kuhlman	74	43	45	65	49
Moore	52	42	53	87	85	Ludwig	75	53	68	50	31
Brunner	36	70	62	44	79	Longnecker	42	65	70	41	52
Wolf	34	59	39	78	61	Simonetti	43	38	10	19	47

25. **FILE** During the 2019 Masters Golf tournament Patrick Reed failed to repeat as champion. His scores relative to par in each round, on each hole are reported in the table. Develop and review appropriate control charts for his performance. Report your findings.

Hole	Round 1	Round 2	Round 3	Round 4
1	0	0	0	0
2	0	−1	0	0
3	0	−1	−1	1
4	1	1	0	0
5	0	0	1	0
6	0	1	0	0
7	1	0	0	0
8	0	0	−1	−1
9	0	0	0	0
10	−1	0	1	0
11	1	0	1	0
12	0	0	0	0
13	−2	−1	0	−1
14	1	0	0	0
15	−1	0	−1	−1
16	0	0	1	−1
17	0	−1	0	−1
18	1	0	1	1

26. **FILE** Early Morning Delivery Service guarantees delivery of small packages by 10:30 a.m. Of course, some of the packages are not delivered by 10:30 a.m. For a sample of 200 packages delivered each of the last 15 working days, the following numbers of packages were delivered after the deadline: 9, 14, 2, 13, 9, 5, 9, 3, 4, 3, 4, 3, 3, 8, and 4.

a. Determine the mean proportion of packages delivered after 10:30 a.m.

b. Determine the control limits for the proportion of packages delivered after 10:30 a.m. Were any of the sampled days out of control?

c. If 10 packages out of 200 in the sample were delivered after 10:30 a.m. today, is this sample within the control limits?

27. **FILE** An automatic machine produces 5.0-millimeter bolts at a high rate of speed. A quality control program has been initiated to control the number of defectives. The quality control inspector selects 50 bolts at random and determines how many are defective. The numbers of defectives in the first 10 samples are 3, 5, 0, 4, 1, 2, 6, 5, 7, and 7.

a. Design a *p*-chart. Insert the mean proportion defective, *UCL*, and *LCL*.

b. Plot the proportion defective for the first 10 samples on the chart.

c. Interpret the chart.

28. **FILE** Steele Breakfast Foods Inc. produces a popular brand of raisin bran cereal. The package indicates it contains 25.0 ounces of cereal. To ensure the product quality, the Steele inspection department makes hourly checks on the production process. As a part of the hourly check, four boxes are selected and their contents weighed. The results for 25 samples are as follows:

Sample	Weights				Sample	Weights			
1	26.1	24.4	25.6	25.2	14	23.1	23.3	24.4	24.7
2	25.2	25.9	25.1	24.8	15	24.6	25.1	24.0	25.3
3	25.6	24.5	25.7	25.1	16	24.4	24.4	22.8	23.4
4	25.5	26.8	25.1	25.0	17	25.1	24.1	23.9	26.2
5	25.2	25.2	26.3	25.7	18	24.5	24.5	26.0	26.2
6	26.6	24.1	25.5	24.0	19	25.3	27.5	24.3	25.5
7	27.6	26.0	24.9	25.3	20	24.6	25.3	25.5	24.3
8	24.5	23.1	23.9	24.7	21	24.9	24.4	25.4	24.8
9	24.1	25.0	23.5	24.9	22	25.7	24.6	26.8	26.9
10	25.8	25.7	24.3	27.3	23	24.8	24.3	25.0	27.2
11	22.5	23.0	23.7	24.0	24	25.4	25.9	26.6	24.8
12	24.5	24.8	23.2	24.2	25	26.2	23.5	23.7	25.0
13	24.4	24.5	25.9	25.5					

Develop an appropriate control chart. What are the limits? Is the process out of control at any time?

29. **FILE** An investor believes there is a 50–50 chance that a stock will increase on a particular day. To investigate this idea, for 30 consecutive trading days the investor selects a random sample of 50 stocks and counts the number that increase. The number of stocks in the sample that increased is reported here.

14	12	13	17	10	18	10	13	13	14
13	10	12	11	9	13	14	11	12	11
15	13	10	16	10	11	12	15	13	10

Develop a *p*-chart and write a brief report summarizing your findings. Based on these sample results, is it reasonable that the odds are 50–50 that a stock will increase? What percent of the stocks would need to increase in a day for the process to be "out of control"?

30. **FILE** Lahey Motors specializes in selling cars to buyers with a poor credit history. Listed is the number of cars that were repossessed from Lahey customers because they did not meet the payment obligations over each of the last 36 months.

6	5	8	20	11	10	9	3	9	9
15	12	4	11	9	9	6	18	6	8
9	7	13	7	11	8	11	13	6	14
13	5	5	8	10	11				

Develop a *c*-bar chart for the number repossessed. Were there any months when the number was out of control? Write a brief report summarizing your findings.

31. A process engineer is considering two sampling plans. In the first, a sample of 10 will be selected and the lot accepted if 3 or fewer are found defective. In the second, the sample size is 20 and the acceptance number is 5. Develop an OC curve for each. Compare the probability of acceptance for lots that are 5%, 10%, 20%, and 30% defective. Which of the plans would you recommend if you were the supplier?

32. **FILE** Christina Sanders is a member of the women's basketball team at Windy City College. Last season, she made 55% of her free throw attempts. In an effort to improve

this statistic, she attended a summer camp devoted to shooting techniques. The next 20 days she shot 100 free throws each day. She carefully recorded the number of free throws that she made each day. The results are as follows:

| 55 | 61 | 52 | 59 | 67 | 57 | 61 | 59 | 69 | 58 |
| 57 | 66 | 63 | 63 | 63 | 65 | 63 | 68 | 64 | 67 |

To interpret, the first day she made 55 out of 100, or 55%. The second day she made 61 shots, the third day 52 shots, the tenth day 58, the eleventh day 57 shots. The last day she made 67 of 100, or 67%.

a. Develop a control chart for the proportion of shots made. Over the 20 days of practice, what percent of attempts did she make? What are the upper and lower control limits for the proportion of shots made?

b. Is there any trend in her proportion made? Does she seem to be improving, staying the same, or getting worse?

c. Find the percent of attempts made for the last 5 days of practice. Use the hypothesis testing procedure, formula (10-4), to determine if there is an improvement from 55%.

33. **FILE** Eric's Cookie House sells chocolate chip cookies in shopping malls. Of concern is the number of chocolate chips in each cookie. Eric, the owner and president, would like to establish a control chart for the number of chocolate chips per cookie. He selects a sample of 15 cookies from today's production and counts the number of chocolate chips in each. The results are as follows: 6, 8, 20, 12, 20, 19, 11, 23, 12, 14, 15, 16, 12, 13, and 12.

a. Determine the centerline and the control limits.

b. Develop a control chart and plot the number of chocolate chips per cookie.

c. Interpret the chart. Does it appear that the number of chocolate chips is out of control in any of the cookies sampled?

34. **FILE** The numbers of "near misses" recorded for the last 20 months at Lima International Airport are 3, 2, 3, 2, 2, 3, 5, 1, 2, 2, 4, 4, 2, 6, 3, 5, 2, 5, 1, and 3. Develop an appropriate control chart. Determine the mean number of misses per month and the limits on the number of misses per month. Are there any months where the number of near misses is out of control?

35. **FILE** The following numbers of robberies were reported during the last 10 days to the robbery division of the Metro City Police: 10, 8, 8, 7, 8, 5, 8, 5, 4, and 7. Develop an appropriate control chart. Determine the mean number of robberies reported per day and determine the control limits. Are there any days when the number of robberies reported is out of control?

36. Swiss Watches Ltd. purchases watch stems for their watches in lots of 10,000. Their sampling plan calls for checking 20 stems, and if 3 or fewer stems are defective, the lot is accepted.

a. Based on the sampling plan, what is the probability that a lot of 40% defective will be accepted?

b. Design an OC curve for incoming lots that have zero, 10%, 20%, 30%, and 40% defective stems.

37. Automatic Screen Door Manufacturing Company purchases door latches from a number of vendors. The purchasing department is responsible for inspecting the incoming latches. Automatic purchases 10,000 door latches per month and inspects 20 latches selected at random. Develop an OC curve for the sampling plan if three latches can be defective and the incoming lot is still accepted.

38. At the beginning of each football season, Team Sports, the local sporting goods store, purchases 5,000 footballs. A sample of 25 balls is selected, and they are inflated, tested, and then deflated. If more than two balls are found defective, the lot of 5,000 is returned to the manufacturer. Develop an OC curve for this sampling plan.

a. What are the probabilities of accepting lots that are 10%, 20%, and 30% defective?

b. Estimate the probability of accepting a lot that is 15% defective.

c. John Brennen, owner of Team Sports, would like the probability of accepting a lot that is 5% defective to be more than 90%. Does this appear to be the case with this sampling plan?

Appendixes Introduction

A.1 Data Set 1—North Valley Real Estate Data

Variables
    Record = Property identification number
    Agent = Name of the real estate agent assigned to the property
    Price = Market price in dollars
    Size = Livable square feet of the property
    Bedrooms = Number of bedrooms
    Baths = Number of bathrooms
    Pool = Does the home have a pool? (1 = yes, 0 = no)
    Garage = Does the home have an attached garage (1 = yes, 0 = no)
    Days = Number of days of the property on the market
    Township = Area where the property is located
    Mortgage type = Fixed or adjustable. The fixed mortgage is a 30-year, fixed interest rate loan. The adjustable rate loan begins with an introductory interest rate of 3% for the first 5 years, then the interest rate is based on the current interest rates plus 1% (i.e., the interest rate AND the payment is likely to change each year after the fifth year.)
    Years = Number of years that the mortgage loan has been paid
    FICO = Credit score of the mortgage loan holder. The highest score is 850; an average score is 680, a low score is below 680. The score reflects a person's ability to pay debts.
    Default = Is the mortgage loan in default? (1 = yes, 0 = no)

Record	Agent	Price	Size	Bedrooms	Baths	Pool (Yes is 1)	Garage (Yes is 1)	Days	Township	Mortgage type	Years	FICO	Default (Yes is 1)
1	Marty	206424	1820	2	1.5	1	1	33	2	Fixed	2	824	0
2	Rose	346150	3010	3	2	0	0	36	4	Fixed	9	820	0
3	Carter	372360	3210	4	3	0	1	21	2	Fixed	18	819	0
4	Peterson	310622	3330	3	2.5	1	0	26	3	Fixed	17	817	0
5	Carter	496100	4510	6	4.5	0	1	13	4	Fixed	17	816	0
6	Peterson	294086	3440	4	3	1	1	31	4	Fixed	19	813	0
7	Carter	228810	2630	4	2.5	0	1	39	4	Adjustable	10	813	0
8	Isaacs	384420	4470	5	3.5	0	1	26	2	Fixed	6	812	0
9	Peterson	416120	4040	5	3.5	0	1	26	4	Fixed	3	810	0
10	Isaacs	487494	4380	6	4	1	1	32	3	Fixed	6	808	0
11	Rose	448800	5280	6	4	0	1	35	4	Fixed	8	806	1
12	Peterson	388960	4420	4	3	0	1	50	2	Adjustable	9	805	1
13	Marty	335610	2970	3	2.5	0	1	25	3	Adjustable	9	801	1
14	Rose	276000	2300	2	1.5	0	0	34	1	Fixed	20	798	0
15	Rose	346421	2970	4	3	1	1	17	3	Adjustable	10	795	0
16	Isaacs	453913	3660	6	4	1	1	12	3	Fixed	18	792	0
17	Carter	376146	3290	5	3.5	1	1	28	2	Adjustable	9	792	1
18	Peterson	694430	5900	5	3.5	1	1	36	3	Adjustable	10	788	0
19	Rose	251269	2050	3	2	1	1	38	3	Fixed	16	786	0
20	Rose	547596	4920	6	4.5	1	1	37	5	Fixed	2	785	0
21	Marty	214910	1950	2	1.5	1	0	20	4	Fixed	6	784	0
22	Rose	188799	1950	2	1.5	1	0	52	1	Fixed	10	782	0
23	Carter	459950	4680	4	3	1	1	31	4	Fixed	8	781	0
24	Isaacs	264160	2540	3	2.5	0	1	40	1	Fixed	18	780	0
25	Carter	393557	3180	4	3	1	1	54	1	Fixed	20	776	0
26	Isaacs	478675	4660	5	3.5	1	1	26	5	Adjustable	9	773	0
27	Carter	384020	4220	5	3.5	0	1	23	4	Adjustable	9	772	1
28	Marty	313200	3600	4	3	0	1	31	3	Fixed	19	772	0
29	Isaacs	274482	2990	3	2	1	0	37	3	Fixed	5	769	0
30	Marty	167962	1920	2	1.5	1	1	31	5	Fixed	6	769	0

(continued)

A.1 Data Set 1—North Valley Real Estate Data (*continued*)

Record	Agent	Price	Size	Bedrooms	Baths	Pool (Yes is 1)	Garage (Yes is 1)	Days	Township	Mortgage type	Years	FICO	Default (Yes is 1)
31	Isaacs	175823	1970	2	1.5	1	0	28	5	Adjustable	9	766	1
32	Isaacs	226498	2520	4	3	1	1	28	3	Fixed	8	763	1
33	Carter	316827	3150	4	3	1	1	22	4	Fixed	2	759	1
34	Carter	189984	1550	2	1.5	1	0	22	2	Fixed	17	758	0
35	Marty	366350	3090	3	2	1	1	23	3	Fixed	5	754	1
36	Isaacs	416160	4080	4	3	0	1	25	4	Fixed	12	753	0
37	Isaacs	308000	3500	4	3	0	1	37	2	Fixed	18	752	0
38	Rose	294357	2620	4	3	1	1	15	4	Fixed	10	751	0
39	Carter	337144	2790	4	3	1	1	19	3	Fixed	15	749	0
40	Peterson	299730	2910	3	2	0	0	31	2	Fixed	13	748	0
41	Rose	445740	4370	4	3	0	1	19	3	Fixed	5	746	0
42	Rose	410592	4200	4	3	1	1	27	1	Adjustable	9	741	1
43	Peterson	667732	5570	5	3.5	1	1	29	5	Fixed	4	740	0
44	Rose	523584	5050	6	4	1	1	19	5	Adjustable	10	739	0
45	Marty	336000	3360	3	2	0	0	32	3	Fixed	6	737	0
46	Marty	202598	2270	3	2	1	0	28	1	Fixed	10	737	0
47	Marty	326695	2830	3	2.5	1	0	30	4	Fixed	8	736	0
48	Rose	321320	2770	3	2	0	1	23	4	Fixed	6	736	0
49	Isaacs	246820	2870	4	3	0	1	27	5	Fixed	13	735	0
50	Isaacs	546084	5910	6	4	1	1	35	5	Adjustable	10	731	0
51	Isaacs	793084	6800	8	5.5	1	1	27	4	Fixed	6	729	0
52	Isaacs	174528	1600	2	1.5	1	0	39	2	Fixed	15	728	0
53	Peterson	392554	3970	4	3	1	1	30	4	Fixed	17	726	0
54	Peterson	263160	3060	3	2	0	1	26	3	Fixed	10	726	0
55	Rose	237120	1900	2	1.5	1	0	14	3	Fixed	18	723	0
56	Carter	225750	2150	2	1.5	1	1	27	2	Fixed	15	715	0
57	Isaacs	848420	7190	6	4	0	1	49	1	Fixed	5	710	0
58	Carter	371956	3110	5	3.5	1	1	29	5	Fixed	8	710	0
59	Carter	404538	3290	5	3.5	1	1	24	2	Fixed	14	707	0
60	Rose	250090	2810	4	3	0	1	18	5	Fixed	11	704	0
61	Peterson	369978	3830	4	2.5	1	1	27	4	Fixed	10	703	0
62	Peterson	209292	1630	2	1.5	1	0	18	3	Fixed	10	701	0
63	Isaacs	190032	1850	2	1.5	1	1	30	4	Adjustable	2	675	0
64	Isaacs	216720	2520	3	2.5	0	0	2	4	Adjustable	5	674	1
65	Marty	323417	3220	4	3	1	1	22	4	Adjustable	2	673	0
66	Isaacs	316210	3070	3	2	0	0	30	1	Adjustable	1	673	0
67	Peterson	226054	2090	2	1.5	1	1	28	1	Adjustable	6	670	0
68	Marty	183920	2090	3	2	0	0	30	2	Adjustable	8	669	1
69	Rose	248400	2300	3	2.5	1	1	50	2	Adjustable	4	667	0
70	Isaacs	466560	5760	5	3.5	0	1	42	4	Adjustable	3	665	0
71	Rose	667212	6110	6	4	1	1	21	3	Adjustable	8	662	1
72	Peterson	362710	4370	4	2.5	0	1	24	1	Adjustable	2	656	0
73	Rose	265440	3160	5	3.5	1	1	22	5	Adjustable	3	653	0
74	Rose	706596	6600	7	5	1	1	40	3	Adjustable	7	652	1
75	Marty	293700	3300	3	2	0	0	14	4	Adjustable	7	647	1
76	Marty	199448	2330	2	1.5	1	1	25	3	Adjustable	5	644	1
77	Carter	369533	4230	4	3	1	1	32	2	Adjustable	2	642	0
78	Marty	230121	2030	2	1.5	1	0	21	2	Adjustable	3	639	0
79	Marty	169000	1690	2	1.5	0	0	20	1	Adjustable	7	639	1
80	Peterson	190291	2040	2	1.5	1	1	31	4	Adjustable	6	631	1
81	Rose	393584	4660	4	3	1	1	34	3	Adjustable	7	630	1
82	Marty	363792	2860	3	2.5	1	1	48	5	Adjustable	3	626	0
83	Carter	360960	3840	6	4.5	0	1	32	2	Adjustable	5	626	1
84	Carter	310877	3180	3	2	1	1	40	1	Adjustable	6	624	1
85	Peterson	919480	7670	8	5.5	1	1	30	4	Adjustable	1	623	0
86	Carter	392904	3400	3	2	1	0	40	2	Adjustable	8	618	1
87	Carter	200928	1840	2	1.5	1	1	36	4	Adjustable	3	618	1

(continued)

Data Set 1—North Valley Real Estate Data (*concluded*)

Record	Agent	Price	Size	Bedrooms	Baths	Pool (Yes is 1)	Garage (Yes is 1)	Days	Township	Mortgage type	Years	FICO	Default (Yes is 1)
88	Carter	537900	4890	6	4	0	1	23	1	Adjustable	7	614	0
89	Rose	258120	2390	3	2.5	0	1	23	1	Adjustable	6	614	1
90	Carter	558342	6160	6	4	1	1	24	3	Adjustable	7	613	0
91	Marty	302720	3440	4	2.5	0	1	38	3	Adjustable	3	609	1
92	Isaacs	240115	2220	2	1.5	1	0	39	5	Adjustable	1	609	0
93	Carter	793656	6530	7	5	1	1	53	4	Adjustable	3	605	1
94	Peterson	218862	1930	2	1.5	1	0	58	4	Adjustable	1	604	0
95	Peterson	383081	3510	3	2	1	1	27	2	Adjustable	6	601	1
96	Marty	351520	3380	3	2	0	1	35	2	Adjustable	8	599	1
97	Peterson	841491	7030	6	4	1	1	50	4	Adjustable	8	596	1
98	Marty	336300	2850	3	2.5	0	0	28	1	Adjustable	6	595	1
99	Isaacs	312863	3750	6	4	1	1	12	4	Adjustable	2	595	0
100	Carter	275033	3060	3	2	1	1	27	3	Adjustable	3	593	0
101	Peterson	229990	2110	2	1.5	0	0	37	3	Adjustable	6	591	1
102	Isaacs	195257	2130	2	1.5	1	0	11	5	Adjustable	8	591	1
103	Marty	194238	1650	2	1.5	1	1	30	2	Adjustable	7	590	1
104	Peterson	348528	2740	4	3	1	1	27	5	Adjustable	3	584	1
105	Peterson	241920	2240	2	1.5	0	1	34	5	Adjustable	8	583	1

A.2 Data Set 2—Baseball Statistics, 2021 Season

Variables

Team = Team's name
League = American or National League
Year Opened = First year the team's stadium was used
Team Salary = Total team salary expressed in millions of dollars
Attendance = Total number of people attending regular season games expressed in millions
Wins = Number of regular season games won
ERA = Team earned run average
BA = Team batting average
HR = Team home runs
Net Worth = Net worth of a team expressed in billions of dollars
Average Salary = Average annual player salary in dollars
CPI = Consumer Price Index; base is 1982–1984.

Team	League	Year Opened	Team Salary ($Millions)	Attendance	Wins	ERA	BA	HR	Net worth ($billion)
Arizona Diamondbacks	National	1998	89.08	10,43,010	52	5.11	0.236	144	$1.320
Atlanta Braves	National	2017	134.46	23,00,247	88	3.88	0.244	239	$1.875
Baltimore Orioles	American	1992	45.70	7,93,229	52	5.84	0.239	195	$1.430
Boston Red Sox	American	1912	180.26	17,25,323	92	4.26	0.261	219	$3.465
Chicago Cubs	National	1914	149.67	19,78,934	71	4.87	0.237	210	$3.360
Chicago White Sox	American	1991	125.99	15,96,385	93	3.73	0.256	190	$1.685
Cincinnati Reds	National	2003	118.75	15,05,024	83	4.40	0.249	222	$1.085
Cleveland Indians	American	1994	46.83	11,14,368	80	4.34	0.238	203	$1.160
Colorado Rockies	National	1995	103.99	19,38,645	74	4.82	0.249	182	$1.300
Detroit Tigers	American	2000	80.40	11,02,623	77	4.32	0.242	179	$1.260
Houston Astros	American	2000	171.02	20,68,509	95	3.76	0.267	221	$1.870
Kansas City Royals	American	1973	87.78	11,59,613	74	4.65	0.249	163	$1.060
Los Angeles Angels	American	1966	177.35	15,12,033	77	4.69	0.245	190	$2.025
Los Angeles Dodgers	National	1962	235.41	28,04,693	106	3.01	0.244	237	$3.570
Miami Marlins	National	2012	49.43	6,42,617	67	3.96	0.233	158	$0.990
Milwaukee Brewers	National	2001	87.57	18,24,282	95	3.50	0.233	194	$1.220
Minnesota Twins	American	2010	121.00	13,10,199	73	4.83	0.241	228	$1.325
New York Mets	National	2009	167.42	14,84,665	77	3.90	0.238	176	$2.450
New York Yankees	American	2009	191.21	19,59,854	92	3.74	0.237	222	$5.250
Oakland Athletics	American	1966	74.62	7,01,430	86	4.02	0.238	199	$1.125
Philadelphia Phillies	National	2004	174.01	15,15,890	82	4.39	0.24	198	$2.050
Pittsburgh Pirates	National	2001	35.91	8,59,498	61	5.08	0.236	124	$1.285
San Diego Padres	National	2004	171.69	21,91,950	79	4.10	0.242	180	$1.500
San Francisco Giants	American	2000	127.89	16,79,484	107	3.24	0.249	241	$3.175
Seattle Mariners	National	1999	64.55	12,15,985	90	4.30	0.226	199	$1.630
St. Louis Cardinals	National	2006	135.05	21,02,530	90	3.98	0.244	198	$2.245
Tampa Bay Rays	American	1990	60.39	7,61,072	100	3.67	0.242	222	$1.055
Texas Rangers	American	1994	84.87	21,10,258	60	4.79	0.232	167	$1.785
Toronto Blue Jays	American	1989	137.13	8,09,557	91	3.91	0.266	262	$1.675
Washington Nationals	National	2008	161.91	14,65,543	65	4.80	0.258	182	$1.925

(continued)

A.2 Data Set 2—Baseball Statistics, 2021 Season (*concluded*)

Year	Annual Average Salary	CPI
2010	32,97,828	218.056
2011	33,05,393	224.939
2012	34,40,000	229.594
2013	36,50,000	232.957
2014	39,50,000	236.736
2015	42,50,000	237.017
2016	43,80,000	240.007
2017	40,97,122	245.12
2018	40,95,686	251.107
2019	40,50,000	255.657
2020	38,90,000	258.811
2021	41,70,000	270.97

* Note that the 2020 average salary was adjust upward to account for the effect of COVID-19 on salaries.

A.3 Data Set 3—Lincolnville School District Bus Data

Variables

ID = Bus identification number
Manufacturer = Source of the bus (Bluebird, Keiser, or Thompson)
Engine Type = If the engine is diesel then engine type = 0; if the engine is gasoline, then engine type = 1
Capacity = Number of seats on the bus
Maintenance Cost = Dollars spent to maintain a bus last year
Age = Number of years since the bus left the manufacturer
Odometer Miles = Total number of miles traveled by a bus
Miles = Number of miles traveled since last maintenance

ID	Manufacturer	Engine Type (0=diesel)	Capacity	Maintenance Cost	Age	Odometer Miles	Miles
10	Keiser	1	14	4646	5	54375	11973
396	Thompson	0	14	1072	2	21858	11969
122	Bluebird	1	55	9394	10	116580	11967
751	Keiser	0	14	1078	2	22444	11948
279	Bluebird	0	55	1008	2	22672	11925
500	Bluebird	1	55	5329	5	50765	11922
520	Bluebird	0	55	4794	10	119130	11896
759	Keiser	0	55	3952	8	87872	11883
714	Bluebird	0	42	3742	7	73703	11837
875	Bluebird	0	55	4376	9	97947	11814
600	Bluebird	0	55	4832	10	119860	11800
953	Bluebird	0	55	5160	10	117700	11798
101	Bluebird	0	55	1955	4	41096	11789
358	Bluebird	0	55	2775	6	70086	11782
29	Bluebird	1	55	5352	6	69438	11781
365	Keiser	0	55	3065	6	63384	11778
162	Keiser	1	55	3143	3	31266	11758
686	Bluebird	0	55	1569	3	34674	11757
370	Keiser	1	55	7766	8	86528	11707
887	Bluebird	0	55	3743	8	93672	11704
464	Bluebird	1	55	2540	3	34530	11698
948	Keiser	0	42	4342	9	97956	11691
678	Keiser	0	55	3361	7	75229	11668
481	Keiser	1	6	3097	3	34362	11662
43	Bluebird	1	55	8263	9	102969	11615
704	Bluebird	0	55	4218	8	83424	11610
814	Bluebird	0	55	2028	4	40824	11576
39	Bluebird	1	55	5821	6	69444	11533
699	Bluebird	1	55	9069	9	98307	11518
75	Bluebird	0	55	3011	6	71970	11462
693	Keiser	1	55	9193	9	101889	11461
989	Keiser	0	55	4795	9	106605	11418
982	Bluebird	0	55	505	1	10276	11359
321	Bluebird	0	42	2732	6	70122	11358
724	Keiser	0	42	3754	8	91968	11344
732	Keiser	0	42	4640	9	101196	11342
880	Keiser	1	55	8410	9	97065	11336
193	Thompson	0	14	5922	11	128711	11248
884	Bluebird	0	55	4364	9	92457	11231
57	Bluebird	0	55	3190	7	79240	11222
731	Bluebird	0	42	3213	6	68526	11168
61	Keiser	0	55	4139	9	103536	11148

(continued)

A.3 Data Set 3—Lincolnville School District Bus Data (*concluded*)

ID	Manufacturer	Engine Type (0=diesel)	Capacity	Maintenance Cost	Age	Odometer Miles	Miles
135	Bluebird	0	55	3560	7	76426	11127
833	Thompson	0	14	3920	8	90968	11112
671	Thompson	1	14	6733	8	89792	11100
692	Bluebird	0	55	3770	8	93248	11048
200	Bluebird	0	55	5168	10	103700	11018
754	Keiser	0	14	7380	14	146860	11003
540	Bluebird	1	55	3656	4	45284	10945
660	Bluebird	1	55	6213	6	64434	10911
353	Keiser	1	55	4279	4	45744	10902
482	Bluebird	1	55	10575	10	116534	10802
398	Thompson	0	6	4752	9	95922	10802
984	Bluebird	0	55	3809	8	87664	10760
977	Bluebird	0	55	3769	7	79422	10759
705	Keiser	0	42	2152	4	47596	10755
767	Keiser	0	55	2985	6	71538	10726
326	Bluebird	0	55	4563	9	107343	10724
120	Keiser	0	42	4723	10	110320	10674
554	Bluebird	0	42	1826	4	44604	10662
695	Bluebird	0	55	1061	2	23152	10633
9	Keiser	1	55	3527	4	46848	10591
861	Bluebird	1	55	9669	10	106040	10551
603	Keiser	0	14	2116	4	44384	10518
156	Thompson	0	14	6212	12	140460	10473
427	Keiser	1	55	6927	7	73423	10355
883	Bluebird	1	55	1881	2	20742	10344
168	Thompson	1	14	7004	7	83006	10315
954	Bluebird	0	42	5284	10	101000	10235
768	Bluebird	0	42	3173	7	71778	10227
490	Bluebird	1	55	10133	10	106240	10210
725	Bluebird	0	55	2356	5	57065	10209
45	Keiser	0	55	3124	6	60102	10167
38	Keiser	1	14	5976	6	61662	10140
314	Thompson	0	6	5408	11	128117	10128
507	Bluebird	0	55	3690	7	72849	10095
40	Bluebird	1	55	9573	10	118470	10081
918	Bluebird	0	55	2470	5	53620	10075
387	Bluebird	1	55	6863	8	89960	10055
418	Bluebird	0	55	4513	9	104715	10000

A.4   Data Set 4—Applewood Auto Group

Age = Age of the buyer at the time of the purchase
Profit = Amount earned by the dealership on the sale of each vehicle
Location = Dealership where the vehicle was purchased
Vehicle Type = SUV, sedan, compact, hybrid, or truck
Previous = Number of vehicles previously purchased at any of the four Applewood dealerships by the customer

Age	Profit	Location	Vehicle Type	Previous	Age	Profit	Location	Vehicle Type	Previous
21	$1,387	Tionesta	Sedan	0	40	1,509	Kane	SUV	2
23	1,754	Sheffield	SUV	1	40	1,638	Sheffield	Sedan	0
24	1,817	Sheffield	Hybrid	1	40	1,961	Sheffield	Sedan	1
25	1,040	Sheffield	Compact	0	40	2,127	Olean	Truck	0
26	1,273	Kane	Sedan	1	40	2,430	Tionesta	Sedan	1
27	1,529	Sheffield	Sedan	1	41	1,704	Sheffield	Sedan	1
27	3,082	Kane	Truck	0	41	1,876	Kane	Sedan	2
28	1,951	Kane	SUV	1	41	2,010	Tionesta	Sedan	1
28	2,692	Tionesta	Compact	0	41	2,165	Tionesta	SUV	0
29	1,206	Sheffield	Sedan	0	41	2,231	Tionesta	SUV	2
29	1,342	Kane	Sedan	2	41	2,389	Kane	Truck	1
30	443	Kane	Sedan	3	42	335	Olean	SUV	1
30	754	Olean	Sedan	2	42	963	Kane	Sedan	0
30	1,621	Sheffield	Truck	1	42	1,298	Tionesta	Sedan	1
31	870	Tionesta	Sedan	1	42	1,410	Kane	SUV	2
31	1,174	Kane	Truck	0	42	1,553	Tionesta	Compact	0
31	1,412	Sheffield	Sedan	1	42	1,648	Olean	SUV	0
31	1,809	Tionesta	Sedan	1	42	2,071	Kane	SUV	0
31	2,415	Kane	Sedan	0	42	2,116	Kane	Compact	2
32	1,546	Sheffield	Truck	3	43	1,500	Tionesta	Sedan	0
32	2,148	Tionesta	SUV	2	43	1,549	Kane	SUV	2
32	2,207	Sheffield	Compact	0	43	2,348	Tionesta	Sedan	0
32	2,252	Tionesta	SUV	0	43	2,498	Tionesta	SUV	1
33	1,428	Kane	SUV	2	44	294	Kane	SUV	1
33	1,889	Olean	SUV	1	44	1,115	Kane	Truck	0
34	1,166	Olean	Sedan	1	44	1,124	Tionesta	Compact	2
34	1,320	Tionesta	Sedan	1	44	1,532	Tionesta	SUV	3
34	2,265	Olean	Sedan	0	44	1,688	Kane	Sedan	4
35	1,323	Olean	Sedan	2	44	1,822	Kane	SUV	0
35	1,761	Kane	Sedan	1	44	1,897	Sheffield	Compact	0
35	1,919	Tionesta	SUV	1	44	2,445	Kane	SUV	0
36	2,357	Kane	SUV	2	44	2,886	Olean	SUV	1
36	2,866	Kane	Sedan	1	45	820	Kane	Compact	1
37	732	Olean	SUV	1	45	1,266	Olean	Sedan	0
37	1,464	Olean	Sedan	3	45	1,741	Olean	Compact	2
37	1,626	Tionesta	Compact	4	45	1,772	Olean	Compact	1
37	1,761	Olean	SUV	1	45	1,932	Tionesta	Sedan	1
37	1,915	Tionesta	SUV	2	45	2,350	Sheffield	Compact	0
37	2,119	Kane	Hybrid	1	45	2,422	Kane	Sedan	1
38	1,766	Sheffield	SUV	0	45	2,446	Olean	Compact	1
38	2,201	Sheffield	Truck	2	46	369	Olean	Sedan	1
39	996	Kane	Compact	2	46	978	Kane	Sedan	1
39	2,813	Tionesta	SUV	0	46	1,238	Sheffield	Compact	1
40	323	Kane	Sedan	0	46	1,818	Kane	SUV	0
40	352	Sheffield	Compact	0	46	1,824	Olean	Truck	0
40	482	Olean	Sedan	1	46	1,907	Olean	Sedan	0
40	1,144	Tionesta	Truck	0	46	1,938	Kane	Sedan	0
40	1,485	Sheffield	Compact	0	46	1,940	Kane	Truck	3

(continued)

Age	Profit	Location	Vehicle Type	Previous	Age	Profit	Location	Vehicle Type	Previous
46	2,197	Sheffield	Sedan	1	53	2,175	Olean	Sedan	1
46	2,646	Tionesta	Sedan	2	54	1,118	Sheffield	Compact	1
47	1,461	Kane	Sedan	0	54	2,584	Olean	Compact	2
47	1,731	Tionesta	Compact	0	54	2,666	Tionesta	Truck	0
47	2,230	Tionesta	Sedan	1	54	2,991	Tionesta	SUV	0
47	2,341	Sheffield	SUV	1	55	934	Sheffield	Truck	1
47	3,292	Olean	Sedan	2	55	2,063	Kane	SUV	1
48	1,108	Sheffield	Sedan	1	55	2,083	Sheffield	Sedan	1
48	1,295	Sheffield	SUV	1	55	2,856	Olean	Hybrid	1
48	1,344	Sheffield	SUV	0	55	2,989	Tionesta	Compact	1
48	1,906	Kane	Sedan	1	56	910	Sheffield	SUV	0
48	1,952	Tionesta	Compact	1	56	1,536	Kane	SUV	0
48	2,070	Kane	SUV	1	56	1,957	Sheffield	SUV	1
48	2,454	Kane	Sedan	1	56	2,240	Olean	Sedan	0
49	1,606	Olean	Compact	0	56	2,695	Kane	Sedan	2
49	1,680	Kane	SUV	3	57	1,325	Olean	Sedan	1
49	1,827	Tionesta	Truck	3	57	2,250	Sheffield	Sedan	2
49	1,915	Tionesta	SUV	1	57	2,279	Sheffield	Hybrid	1
49	2,084	Tionesta	Sedan	0	57	2,626	Sheffield	Sedan	2
49	2,639	Sheffield	SUV	0	58	1,501	Sheffield	Hybrid	1
50	842	Kane	SUV	0	58	1,752	Kane	Sedan	3
50	1,963	Sheffield	Sedan	1	58	2,058	Kane	SUV	1
50	2,059	Sheffield	Sedan	1	58	2,370	Tionesta	Compact	0
50	2,338	Tionesta	SUV	0	58	2,637	Sheffield	SUV	1
50	3,043	Kane	Sedan	0	59	1,426	Sheffield	Sedan	0
51	1,059	Kane	SUV	1	59	2,944	Olean	SUV	2
51	1,674	Sheffield	Sedan	1	60	2,147	Olean	Compact	2
51	1,807	Tionesta	Sedan	1	61	1,973	Kane	SUV	3
51	2,056	Sheffield	Hybrid	0	61	2,502	Olean	Sedan	0
51	2,236	Tionesta	SUV	2	62	783	Sheffield	Hybrid	1
51	2,928	Kane	SUV	0	62	1,538	Olean	Truck	1
52	1,269	Tionesta	Sedan	1	63	2,339	Olean	Compact	1
52	1,717	Sheffield	SUV	3	64	2,700	Kane	Truck	0
52	1,797	Kane	Sedan	1	65	2,222	Kane	Truck	1
52	1,955	Olean	Hybrid	2	65	2,597	Sheffield	Truck	0
52	2,199	Tionesta	SUV	0	65	2,742	Tionesta	SUV	2
52	2,482	Olean	Compact	0	68	1,837	Sheffield	Sedan	1
52	2,701	Sheffield	SUV	0	69	2,842	Kane	SUV	0
52	3,210	Olean	Truck	4	70	2,434	Olean	Sedan	4
53	377	Olean	SUV	1	72	1,640	Olean	Sedan	1
53	1,220	Olean	Sedan	0	72	1,821	Tionesta	SUV	1
53	1,401	Tionesta	SUV	2	73	2,487	Olean	Compact	4

A.5 Banking Data Set—Century National Bank Case

Balance = Account balance in $
ATM = Number of ATM transactions in the month
Services = Number of other bank services used
Debit = Account has a debit card (1 = yes, 0 = no)
Interest = Receives interest on the account (1 = yes, 0 = no)
City = City where banking is done

Balance	ATM	Services	Debit	Interest	City
1,756	13	4	0	1	2
748	9	2	1	0	1
1,501	10	1	0	0	1
1,831	10	4	0	1	3
1,622	14	6	0	1	4
1,886	17	3	0	1	1
740	6	3	0	0	3
1,593	10	8	1	0	1
1,169	6	4	0	0	4
2,125	18	6	0	0	2
1,554	12	6	1	0	3
1,474	12	7	1	0	1
1,913	6	5	0	0	1
1,218	10	3	1	0	1
1,006	12	4	0	0	1
2,215	20	3	1	0	4
137	7	2	0	0	3
167	5	4	0	0	4
343	7	2	0	0	1
2,557	20	7	1	0	4
2,276	15	4	1	0	3
1,494	11	2	0	1	1
2,144	17	3	0	0	3
1,995	10	7	0	0	2
1,053	8	4	1	0	3
1,526	8	4	0	1	2
1,120	8	6	1	0	3
1,838	7	5	1	1	3
1,746	11	2	0	0	2
1,616	10	4	1	1	2

Balance	ATM	Services	Debit	Interest	City
1,958	6	2	1	0	2
634	2	7	1	0	4
580	4	1	0	0	1
1,320	4	5	1	0	1
1,675	6	7	1	0	2
789	8	4	0	0	4
1,735	12	7	0	1	3
1,784	11	5	0	0	1
1,326	16	8	0	0	3
2,051	14	4	1	0	4
1,044	7	5	1	0	1
1,885	10	6	1	1	2
1,790	11	4	0	1	3
765	4	3	0	0	4
1,645	6	9	0	1	4
32	2	0	0	0	3
1,266	11	7	0	0	4
890	7	1	0	1	1
2,204	14	5	0	0	2
2,409	16	8	0	0	2
1,338	14	4	1	0	2
2,076	12	5	1	0	2
1,708	13	3	1	0	1
2,138	18	5	0	1	4
2,375	12	4	0	0	2
1,455	9	5	1	1	3
1,487	8	4	1	0	4
1,125	6	4	1	0	2
1,989	12	3	0	1	2
2,156	14	5	1	0	2

APPENDIX B: TABLES

B.1 Binomial Probability Distribution

n = 1
Probability

x	0.05	0.10	0.20	0.30	0.40	0.50	0.60	0.70	0.80	0.90	0.95
0	0.950	0.900	0.800	0.700	0.600	0.500	0.400	0.300	0.200	0.100	0.050
1	0.050	0.100	0.200	0.300	0.400	0.500	0.600	0.700	0.800	0.900	0.950

n = 2
Probability

x	0.05	0.10	0.20	0.30	0.40	0.50	0.60	0.70	0.80	0.90	0.95
0	0.903	0.810	0.640	0.490	0.360	0.250	0.160	0.090	0.040	0.010	0.003
1	0.095	0.180	0.320	0.420	0.480	0.500	0.480	0.420	0.320	0.180	0.095
2	0.003	0.010	0.040	0.090	0.160	0.250	0.360	0.490	0.640	0.810	0.903

n = 3
Probability

x	0.05	0.10	0.20	0.30	0.40	0.50	0.60	0.70	0.80	0.90	0.95
0	0.857	0.729	0.512	0.343	0.216	0.125	0.064	0.027	0.008	0.001	0.000
1	0.135	0.243	0.384	0.441	0.432	0.375	0.288	0.189	0.096	0.027	0.007
2	0.007	0.027	0.096	0.189	0.288	0.375	0.432	0.441	0.384	0.243	0.135
3	0.000	0.001	0.008	0.027	0.064	0.125	0.216	0.343	0.512	0.729	0.857

n = 4
Probability

x	0.05	0.10	0.20	0.30	0.40	0.50	0.60	0.70	0.80	0.90	0.95
0	0.815	0.656	0.410	0.240	0.130	0.063	0.026	0.008	0.002	0.000	0.000
1	0.171	0.292	0.410	0.412	0.346	0.250	0.154	0.076	0.026	0.004	0.000
2	0.014	0.049	0.154	0.265	0.346	0.375	0.346	0.265	0.154	0.049	0.014
3	0.000	0.004	0.026	0.076	0.154	0.250	0.346	0.412	0.410	0.292	0.171
4	0.000	0.000	0.002	0.008	0.026	0.063	0.130	0.240	0.410	0.656	0.815

n = 5
Probability

x	0.05	0.10	0.20	0.30	0.40	0.50	0.60	0.70	0.80	0.90	0.95
0	0.774	0.590	0.328	0.168	0.078	0.031	0.010	0.002	0.000	0.000	0.000
1	0.204	0.328	0.410	0.360	0.259	0.156	0.077	0.028	0.006	0.000	0.000
2	0.021	0.073	0.205	0.309	0.346	0.313	0.230	0.132	0.051	0.008	0.001
3	0.001	0.008	0.051	0.132	0.230	0.313	0.346	0.309	0.205	0.073	0.021
4	0.000	0.000	0.006	0.028	0.077	0.156	0.259	0.360	0.410	0.328	0.204
5	0.000	0.000	0.000	0.002	0.010	0.031	0.078	0.168	0.328	0.590	0.774

(continued)

B.1 Binomial Probability Distribution (*continued*)

n = 6
Probability

x	0.05	0.10	0.20	0.30	0.40	0.50	0.60	0.70	0.80	0.90	0.95
0	0.735	0.531	0.262	0.118	0.047	0.016	0.004	0.001	0.000	0.000	0.000
1	0.232	0.354	0.393	0.303	0.187	0.094	0.037	0.010	0.002	0.000	0.000
2	0.031	0.098	0.246	0.324	0.311	0.234	0.138	0.060	0.015	0.001	0.000
3	0.002	0.015	0.082	0.185	0.276	0.313	0.276	0.185	0.082	0.015	0.002
4	0.000	0.001	0.015	0.060	0.138	0.234	0.311	0.324	0.246	0.098	0.031
5	0.000	0.000	0.002	0.010	0.037	0.094	0.187	0.303	0.393	0.354	0.232
6	0.000	0.000	0.000	0.001	0.004	0.016	0.047	0.118	0.262	0.531	0.735

n = 7
Probability

x	0.05	0.10	0.20	0.30	0.40	0.50	0.60	0.70	0.80	0.90	0.95
0	0.698	0.478	0.210	0.082	0.028	0.008	0.002	0.000	0.000	0.000	0.000
1	0.257	0.372	0.367	0.247	0.131	0.055	0.017	0.004	0.000	0.000	0.000
2	0.041	0.124	0.275	0.318	0.261	0.164	0.077	0.025	0.004	0.000	0.000
3	0.004	0.023	0.115	0.227	0.290	0.273	0.194	0.097	0.029	0.003	0.000
4	0.000	0.003	0.029	0.097	0.194	0.273	0.290	0.227	0.115	0.023	0.004
5	0.000	0.000	0.004	0.025	0.077	0.164	0.261	0.318	0.275	0.124	0.041
6	0.000	0.000	0.000	0.004	0.017	0.055	0.131	0.247	0.367	0.372	0.257
7	0.000	0.000	0.000	0.000	0.002	0.008	0.028	0.082	0.210	0.478	0.698

n = 8
Probability

x	0.05	0.10	0.20	0.30	0.40	0.50	0.60	0.70	0.80	0.90	0.95
0	0.663	0.430	0.168	0.058	0.017	0.004	0.001	0.000	0.000	0.000	0.000
1	0.279	0.383	0.336	0.198	0.090	0.031	0.008	0.001	0.000	0.000	0.000
2	0.051	0.149	0.294	0.296	0.209	0.109	0.041	0.010	0.001	0.000	0.000
3	0.005	0.033	0.147	0.254	0.279	0.219	0.124	0.047	0.009	0.000	0.000
4	0.000	0.005	0.046	0.136	0.232	0.273	0.232	0.136	0.046	0.005	0.000
5	0.000	0.000	0.009	0.047	0.124	0.219	0.279	0.254	0.147	0.033	0.005
6	0.000	0.000	0.001	0.010	0.041	0.109	0.209	0.296	0.294	0.149	0.051
7	0.000	0.000	0.000	0.001	0.008	0.031	0.090	0.198	0.336	0.383	0.279
8	0.000	0.000	0.000	0.000	0.001	0.004	0.017	0.058	0.168	0.430	0.663

(*continued*)

B.1 Binomial Probability Distribution (*continued*)

n = 9
Probability

x	0.05	0.10	0.20	0.30	0.40	0.50	0.60	0.70	0.80	0.90	0.95
0	0.630	0.387	0.134	0.040	0.010	0.002	0.000	0.000	0.000	0.000	0.000
1	0.299	0.387	0.302	0.156	0.060	0.018	0.004	0.000	0.000	0.000	0.000
2	0.063	0.172	0.302	0.267	0.161	0.070	0.021	0.004	0.000	0.000	0.000
3	0.008	0.045	0.176	0.267	0.251	0.164	0.074	0.021	0.003	0.000	0.000
4	0.001	0.007	0.066	0.172	0.251	0.246	0.167	0.074	0.017	0.001	0.000
5	0.000	0.001	0.017	0.074	0.167	0.246	0.251	0.172	0.066	0.007	0.001
6	0.000	0.000	0.003	0.021	0.074	0.164	0.251	0.267	0.176	0.045	0.008
7	0.000	0.000	0.000	0.004	0.021	0.070	0.161	0.267	0.302	0.172	0.063
8	0.000	0.000	0.000	0.000	0.004	0.018	0.060	0.156	0.302	0.387	0.299
9	0.000	0.000	0.000	0.000	0.000	0.002	0.010	0.040	0.134	0.387	0.630

n = 10
Probability

x	0.05	0.10	0.20	0.30	0.40	0.50	0.60	0.70	0.80	0.90	0.95
0	0.599	0.349	0.107	0.028	0.006	0.001	0.000	0.000	0.000	0.000	0.000
1	0.315	0.387	0.268	0.121	0.040	0.010	0.002	0.000	0.000	0.000	0.000
2	0.075	0.194	0.302	0.233	0.121	0.044	0.011	0.001	0.000	0.000	0.000
3	0.010	0.057	0.201	0.267	0.215	0.117	0.042	0.009	0.001	0.000	0.000
4	0.001	0.011	0.088	0.200	0.251	0.205	0.111	0.037	0.006	0.000	0.000
5	0.000	0.001	0.026	0.103	0.201	0.246	0.201	0.103	0.026	0.001	0.000
6	0.000	0.000	0.006	0.037	0.111	0.205	0.251	0.200	0.088	0.011	0.001
7	0.000	0.000	0.001	0.009	0.042	0.117	0.215	0.267	0.201	0.057	0.010
8	0.000	0.000	0.000	0.001	0.011	0.044	0.121	0.233	0.302	0.194	0.075
9	0.000	0.000	0.000	0.000	0.002	0.010	0.040	0.121	0.268	0.387	0.315
10	0.000	0.000	0.000	0.000	0.000	0.001	0.006	0.028	0.107	0.349	0.599

n = 11
Probability

x	0.05	0.10	0.20	0.30	0.40	0.50	0.60	0.70	0.80	0.90	0.95
0	0.569	0.314	0.086	0.020	0.004	0.000	0.000	0.000	0.000	0.000	0.000
1	0.329	0.384	0.236	0.093	0.027	0.005	0.001	0.000	0.000	0.000	0.000
2	0.087	0.213	0.295	0.200	0.089	0.027	0.005	0.001	0.000	0.000	0.000
3	0.014	0.071	0.221	0.257	0.177	0.081	0.023	0.004	0.000	0.000	0.000
4	0.001	0.016	0.111	0.220	0.236	0.161	0.070	0.017	0.002	0.000	0.000
5	0.000	0.002	0.039	0.132	0.221	0.226	0.147	0.057	0.010	0.000	0.000
6	0.000	0.000	0.010	0.057	0.147	0.226	0.221	0.132	0.039	0.002	0.000
7	0.000	0.000	0.002	0.017	0.070	0.161	0.236	0.220	0.111	0.016	0.001
8	0.000	0.000	0.000	0.004	0.023	0.081	0.177	0.257	0.221	0.071	0.014
9	0.000	0.000	0.000	0.001	0.005	0.027	0.089	0.200	0.295	0.213	0.087
10	0.000	0.000	0.000	0.000	0.001	0.005	0.027	0.093	0.236	0.384	0.329
11	0.000	0.000	0.000	0.000	0.000	0.000	0.004	0.020	0.086	0.314	0.569

(continued)

B.1 Binomial Probability Distribution (*continued*)

n = 12
Probability

x	0.05	0.10	0.20	0.30	0.40	0.50	0.60	0.70	0.80	0.90	0.95
0	0.540	0.282	0.069	0.014	0.002	0.000	0.000	0.000	0.000	0.000	0.000
1	0.341	0.377	0.206	0.071	0.017	0.003	0.000	0.000	0.000	0.000	0.000
2	0.099	0.230	0.283	0.168	0.064	0.016	0.002	0.000	0.000	0.000	0.000
3	0.017	0.085	0.236	0.240	0.142	0.054	0.012	0.001	0.000	0.000	0.000
4	0.002	0.021	0.133	0.231	0.213	0.121	0.042	0.008	0.001	0.000	0.000
5	0.000	0.004	0.053	0.158	0.227	0.193	0.101	0.029	0.003	0.000	0.000
6	0.000	0.000	0.016	0.079	0.177	0.226	0.177	0.079	0.016	0.000	0.000
7	0.000	0.000	0.003	0.029	0.101	0.193	0.227	0.158	0.053	0.004	0.000
8	0.000	0.000	0.001	0.008	0.042	0.121	0.213	0.231	0.133	0.021	0.002
9	0.000	0.000	0.000	0.001	0.012	0.054	0.142	0.240	0.236	0.085	0.017
10	0.000	0.000	0.000	0.000	0.002	0.016	0.064	0.168	0.283	0.230	0.099
11	0.000	0.000	0.000	0.000	0.000	0.003	0.017	0.071	0.206	0.377	0.341
12	0.000	0.000	0.000	0.000	0.000	0.000	0.002	0.014	0.069	0.282	0.540

n = 13
Probability

x	0.05	0.10	0.20	0.30	0.40	0.50	0.60	0.70	0.80	0.90	0.95
0	0.513	0.254	0.055	0.010	0.001	0.000	0.000	0.000	0.000	0.000	0.000
1	0.351	0.367	0.179	0.054	0.011	0.002	0.000	0.000	0.000	0.000	0.000
2	0.111	0.245	0.268	0.139	0.045	0.010	0.001	0.000	0.000	0.000	0.000
3	0.021	0.100	0.246	0.218	0.111	0.035	0.006	0.001	0.000	0.000	0.000
4	0.003	0.028	0.154	0.234	0.184	0.087	0.024	0.003	0.000	0.000	0.000
5	0.000	0.006	0.069	0.180	0.221	0.157	0.066	0.014	0.001	0.000	0.000
6	0.000	0.001	0.023	0.103	0.197	0.209	0.131	0.044	0.006	0.000	0.000
7	0.000	0.000	0.006	0.044	0.131	0.209	0.197	0.103	0.023	0.001	0.000
8	0.000	0.000	0.001	0.014	0.066	0.157	0.221	0.180	0.069	0.006	0.000
9	0.000	0.000	0.000	0.003	0.024	0.087	0.184	0.234	0.154	0.028	0.003
10	0.000	0.000	0.000	0.001	0.006	0.035	0.111	0.218	0.246	0.100	0.021
11	0.000	0.000	0.000	0.000	0.001	0.010	0.045	0.139	0.268	0.245	0.111
12	0.000	0.000	0.000	0.000	0.000	0.002	0.011	0.054	0.179	0.367	0.351
13	0.000	0.000	0.000	0.000	0.000	0.000	0.001	0.010	0.055	0.254	0.513

(continued)

B.1 Binomial Probability Distribution (*concluded*)

$n = 14$

Probability

x	0.05	0.10	0.20	0.30	0.40	0.50	0.60	0.70	0.80	0.90	0.95
0	0.488	0.229	0.044	0.007	0.001	0.000	0.000	0.000	0.000	0.000	0.000
1	0.359	0.356	0.154	0.041	0.007	0.001	0.000	0.000	0.000	0.000	0.000
2	0.123	0.257	0.250	0.113	0.032	0.006	0.001	0.000	0.000	0.000	0.000
3	0.026	0.114	0.250	0.194	0.085	0.022	0.003	0.000	0.000	0.000	0.000
4	0.004	0.035	0.172	0.229	0.155	0.061	0.014	0.001	0.000	0.000	0.000
5	0.000	0.008	0.086	0.196	0.207	0.122	0.041	0.007	0.000	0.000	0.000
6	0.000	0.001	0.032	0.126	0.207	0.183	0.092	0.023	0.002	0.000	0.000
7	0.000	0.000	0.009	0.062	0.157	0.209	0.157	0.062	0.009	0.000	0.000
8	0.000	0.000	0.002	0.023	0.092	0.183	0.207	0.126	0.032	0.001	0.000
9	0.000	0.000	0.000	0.007	0.041	0.122	0.207	0.196	0.086	0.008	0.000
10	0.000	0.000	0.000	0.001	0.014	0.061	0.155	0.229	0.172	0.035	0.004
11	0.000	0.000	0.000	0.000	0.003	0.022	0.085	0.194	0.250	0.114	0.026
12	0.000	0.000	0.000	0.000	0.001	0.006	0.032	0.113	0.250	0.257	0.123
13	0.000	0.000	0.000	0.000	0.000	0.001	0.007	0.041	0.154	0.356	0.359
14	0.000	0.000	0.000	0.000	0.000	0.000	0.001	0.007	0.044	0.229	0.488

$n = 15$

Probability

x	0.05	0.10	0.20	0.30	0.40	0.50	0.60	0.70	0.80	0.90	0.95
0	0.463	0.206	0.035	0.005	0.000	0.000	0.000	0.000	0.000	0.000	0.000
1	0.366	0.343	0.132	0.031	0.005	0.000	0.000	0.000	0.000	0.000	0.000
2	0.135	0.267	0.231	0.092	0.022	0.003	0.000	0.000	0.000	0.000	0.000
3	0.031	0.129	0.250	0.170	0.063	0.014	0.002	0.000	0.000	0.000	0.000
4	0.005	0.043	0.188	0.219	0.127	0.042	0.007	0.001	0.000	0.000	0.000
5	0.001	0.010	0.103	0.206	0.186	0.092	0.024	0.003	0.000	0.000	0.000
6	0.000	0.002	0.043	0.147	0.207	0.153	0.061	0.012	0.001	0.000	0.000
7	0.000	0.000	0.014	0.081	0.177	0.196	0.118	0.035	0.003	0.000	0.000
8	0.000	0.000	0.003	0.035	0.118	0.196	0.177	0.081	0.014	0.000	0.000
9	0.000	0.000	0.001	0.012	0.061	0.153	0.207	0.147	0.043	0.002	0.000
10	0.000	0.000	0.000	0.003	0.024	0.092	0.186	0.206	0.103	0.010	0.001
11	0.000	0.000	0.000	0.001	0.007	0.042	0.127	0.219	0.188	0.043	0.005
12	0.000	0.000	0.000	0.000	0.002	0.014	0.063	0.170	0.250	0.129	0.031
13	0.000	0.000	0.000	0.000	0.000	0.003	0.022	0.092	0.231	0.267	0.135
14	0.000	0.000	0.000	0.000	0.000	0.000	0.005	0.031	0.132	0.343	0.366
15	0.000	0.000	0.000	0.000	0.000	0.000	0.000	0.005	0.035	0.206	0.463

B.2 Poisson Distribution

x	μ								
	0.1	0.2	0.3	0.4	0.5	0.6	0.7	0.8	0.9
0	0.9048	0.8187	0.7408	0.6703	0.6065	0.5488	0.4966	0.4493	0.4066
1	0.0905	0.1637	0.2222	0.2681	0.3033	0.3293	0.3476	0.3595	0.3659
2	0.0045	0.0164	0.0333	0.0536	0.0758	0.0988	0.1217	0.1438	0.1647
3	0.0002	0.0011	0.0033	0.0072	0.0126	0.0198	0.0284	0.0383	0.0494
4	0.0000	0.0001	0.0003	0.0007	0.0016	0.0030	0.0050	0.0077	0.0111
5	0.0000	0.0000	0.0000	0.0001	0.0002	0.0004	0.0007	0.0012	0.0020
6	0.0000	0.0000	0.0000	0.0000	0.0000	0.0000	0.0001	0.0002	0.0003
7	0.0000	0.0000	0.0000	0.0000	0.0000	0.0000	0.0000	0.0000	0.0000

x	μ								
	1.0	2.0	3.0	4.0	5.0	6.0	7.0	8.0	9.0
0	0.3679	0.1353	0.0498	0.0183	0.0067	0.0025	0.0009	0.0003	0.0001
1	0.3679	0.2707	0.1494	0.0733	0.0337	0.0149	0.0064	0.0027	0.0011
2	0.1839	0.2707	0.2240	0.1465	0.0842	0.0446	0.0223	0.0107	0.0050
3	0.0613	0.1804	0.2240	0.1954	0.1404	0.0892	0.0521	0.0286	0.0150
4	0.0153	0.0902	0.1680	0.1954	0.1755	0.1339	0.0912	0.0573	0.0337
5	0.0031	0.0361	0.1008	0.1563	0.1755	0.1606	0.1277	0.0916	0.0607
6	0.0005	0.0120	0.0504	0.1042	0.1462	0.1606	0.1490	0.1221	0.0911
7	0.0001	0.0034	0.0216	0.0595	0.1044	0.1377	0.1490	0.1396	0.1171
8	0.0000	0.0009	0.0081	0.0298	0.0653	0.1033	0.1304	0.1396	0.1318
9	0.0000	0.0002	0.0027	0.0132	0.0363	0.0688	0.1014	0.1241	0.1318
10	0.0000	0.0000	0.0008	0.0053	0.0181	0.0413	0.0710	0.0993	0.1186
11	0.0000	0.0000	0.0002	0.0019	0.0082	0.0225	0.0452	0.0722	0.0970
12	0.0000	0.0000	0.0001	0.0006	0.0034	0.0113	0.0263	0.0481	0.0728
13	0.0000	0.0000	0.0000	0.0002	0.0013	0.0052	0.0142	0.0296	0.0504
14	0.0000	0.0000	0.0000	0.0001	0.0005	0.0022	0.0071	0.0169	0.0324
15	0.0000	0.0000	0.0000	0.0000	0.0002	0.0009	0.0033	0.0090	0.0194
16	0.0000	0.0000	0.0000	0.0000	0.0000	0.0003	0.0014	0.0045	0.0109
17	0.0000	0.0000	0.0000	0.0000	0.0000	0.0001	0.0006	0.0021	0.0058
18	0.0000	0.0000	0.0000	0.0000	0.0000	0.0000	0.0002	0.0009	0.0029
19	0.0000	0.0000	0.0000	0.0000	0.0000	0.0000	0.0001	0.0004	0.0014
20	0.0000	0.0000	0.0000	0.0000	0.0000	0.0000	0.0000	0.0002	0.0006
21	0.0000	0.0000	0.0000	0.0000	0.0000	0.0000	0.0000	0.0001	0.0003
22	0.0000	0.0000	0.0000	0.0000	0.0000	0.0000	0.0000	0.0000	0.0001

B.3 Areas under the Normal Curve

Example:
If $z = 1.96$, then
$P(0 \text{ to } z) = 0.4750$.

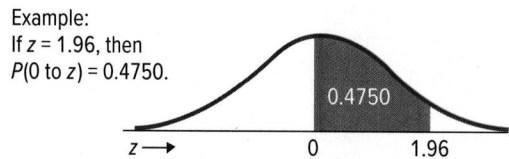

z	0.00	0.01	0.02	0.03	0.04	0.05	0.06	0.07	0.08	0.09
0.0	0.0000	0.0040	0.0080	0.0120	0.0160	0.0199	0.0239	0.0279	0.0319	0.0359
0.1	0.0398	0.0438	0.0478	0.0517	0.0557	0.0596	0.0636	0.0675	0.0714	0.0753
0.2	0.0793	0.0832	0.0871	0.0910	0.0948	0.0987	0.1026	0.1064	0.1103	0.1141
0.3	0.1179	0.1217	0.1255	0.1293	0.1331	0.1368	0.1406	0.1443	0.1480	0.1517
0.4	0.1554	0.1591	0.1628	0.1664	0.1700	0.1736	0.1772	0.1808	0.1844	0.1879
0.5	0.1915	0.1950	0.1985	0.2019	0.2054	0.2088	0.2123	0.2157	0.2190	0.2224
0.6	0.2257	0.2291	0.2324	0.2357	0.2389	0.2422	0.2454	0.2486	0.2517	0.2549
0.7	0.2580	0.2611	0.2642	0.2673	0.2704	0.2734	0.2764	0.2794	0.2823	0.2852
0.8	0.2881	0.2910	0.2939	0.2967	0.2995	0.3023	0.3051	0.3078	0.3106	0.3133
0.9	0.3159	0.3186	0.3212	0.3238	0.3264	0.3289	0.3315	0.3340	0.3365	0.3389
1.0	0.3413	0.3438	0.3461	0.3485	0.3508	0.3531	0.3554	0.3577	0.3599	0.3621
1.1	0.3643	0.3665	0.3686	0.3708	0.3729	0.3749	0.3770	0.3790	0.3810	0.3830
1.2	0.3849	0.3869	0.3888	0.3907	0.3925	0.3944	0.3962	0.3980	0.3997	0.4015
1.3	0.4032	0.4049	0.4066	0.4082	0.4099	0.4115	0.4131	0.4147	0.4162	0.4177
1.4	0.4192	0.4207	0.4222	0.4236	0.4251	0.4265	0.4279	0.4292	0.4306	0.4319
1.5	0.4332	0.4345	0.4357	0.4370	0.4382	0.4394	0.4406	0.4418	0.4429	0.4441
1.6	0.4452	0.4463	0.4474	0.4484	0.4495	0.4505	0.4515	0.4525	0.4535	0.4545
1.7	0.4554	0.4564	0.4573	0.4582	0.4591	0.4599	0.4608	0.4616	0.4625	0.4633
1.8	0.4641	0.4649	0.4656	0.4664	0.4671	0.4678	0.4686	0.4693	0.4699	0.4706
1.9	0.4713	0.4719	0.4726	0.4732	0.4738	0.4744	0.4750	0.4756	0.4761	0.4767
2.0	0.4772	0.4778	0.4783	0.4788	0.4793	0.4798	0.4803	0.4808	0.4812	0.4817
2.1	0.4821	0.4826	0.4830	0.4834	0.4838	0.4842	0.4846	0.4850	0.4854	0.4857
2.2	0.4861	0.4864	0.4868	0.4871	0.4875	0.4878	0.4881	0.4884	0.4887	0.4890
2.3	0.4893	0.4896	0.4898	0.4901	0.4904	0.4906	0.4909	0.4911	0.4913	0.4916
2.4	0.4918	0.4920	0.4922	0.4925	0.4927	0.4929	0.4931	0.4932	0.4934	0.4936
2.5	0.4938	0.4940	0.4941	0.4943	0.4945	0.4946	0.4948	0.4949	0.4951	0.4952
2.6	0.4953	0.4955	0.4956	0.4957	0.4959	0.4960	0.4961	0.4962	0.4963	0.4964
2.7	0.4965	0.4966	0.4967	0.4968	0.4969	0.4970	0.4971	0.4972	0.4973	0.4974
2.8	0.4974	0.4975	0.4976	0.4977	0.4977	0.4978	0.4979	0.4979	0.4980	0.4981
2.9	0.4981	0.4982	0.4982	0.4983	0.4984	0.4984	0.4985	0.4985	0.4986	0.4986
3.0	0.4987	0.4987	0.4987	0.4988	0.4988	0.4989	0.4989	0.4989	0.4990	0.4990

B.4 Table of Random Numbers

02711	08182	75997	79866	58095	83319	80295	79741	74599	84379
94873	90935	31684	63952	09865	14491	99518	93394	34691	14985
54921	78680	06635	98689	17306	25170	65928	87709	30533	89736
77640	97636	37397	93379	56454	59818	45827	74164	71666	46977
61545	00835	93251	87203	36759	49197	85967	01704	19634	21898
17147	19519	22497	16857	42426	84822	92598	49186	88247	39967
13748	04742	92460	85801	53444	65626	58710	55406	17173	69776
87455	14813	50373	28037	91182	32786	65261	11173	34376	36408
08999	57409	91185	10200	61411	23392	47797	56377	71635	08601
78804	81333	53809	32471	46034	36306	22498	19239	85428	55721
82173	26921	28472	98958	07960	66124	89731	95069	18625	92405
97594	25168	89178	68190	05043	17407	48201	83917	11413	72920
73881	67176	93504	42636	38233	16154	96451	57925	29667	30859
46071	22912	90326	42453	88108	72064	58601	32357	90610	32921
44492	19686	12495	93135	95185	77799	52441	88272	22024	80631
31864	72170	37722	55794	14636	05148	54505	50113	21119	25228
51574	90692	43339	65689	76539	27909	05467	21727	51141	72949
35350	76132	92925	92124	92634	35681	43690	89136	35599	84138
46943	36502	01172	46045	46991	33804	80006	35542	61056	75666
22665	87226	33304	57975	03985	21566	65796	72915	81466	89205
39437	97957	11838	10433	21564	51570	73558	27495	34533	57808
77082	47784	40098	97962	89845	28392	78187	06112	08169	11261
24544	25649	43370	28007	06779	72402	62632	53956	24709	06978
27503	15558	37738	24849	70722	71859	83736	06016	94397	12529
24590	24545	06435	52758	45685	90151	46516	49644	92686	84870
48155	86226	40359	28723	15364	69125	12609	57171	86857	31702
20226	53752	90648	24362	83314	00014	19207	69413	97016	86290
70178	73444	38790	53626	93780	18629	68766	24371	74639	30782
10169	41465	51935	05711	09799	79077	88159	33437	68519	03040
81084	03701	28598	70013	63794	53169	97054	60303	23259	96196
69202	20777	21727	81511	51887	16175	53746	46516	70339	62727
80561	95787	89426	93325	86412	57479	54194	52153	19197	81877
08199	26703	95128	48599	09333	12584	24374	31232	61782	44032
98883	28220	39358	53720	80161	83371	15181	11131	12219	55920
84568	69286	76054	21615	80883	36797	82845	39139	90900	18172
04269	35173	95745	53893	86022	77722	52498	84193	22448	22571
10538	13124	36099	13140	37706	44562	57179	44693	67877	01549
77843	24955	25900	63843	95029	93859	93634	20205	66294	41218
12034	94636	49455	76362	83532	31062	69903	91186	65768	55949
10524	72829	47641	93315	80875	28090	97728	52560	34937	79548
68935	76632	46984	61772	92786	22651	07086	89754	44143	97687
89450	65665	29190	43709	11172	34481	95977	47535	25658	73898
90696	20451	24211	97310	60446	73530	62865	96574	13829	72226
49006	32047	93086	00112	20470	17136	28255	86328	07293	38809
74591	87025	52368	59416	34417	70557	86746	55809	53628	12000
06315	17012	77103	00968	07235	10728	42189	33292	51487	64443
62386	09184	62092	46617	99419	64230	95034	85481	07857	42510
86848	82122	04028	36959	87827	12813	08627	80699	13345	51695
65643	69480	46598	04501	40403	91408	32343	48130	49303	90689
11084	46534	78957	77353	39578	77868	22970	84349	09184	70603

B.5 Student's *t*-Distribution

Confidence interval

Left-tailed test

Right-tailed test

Two-tailed test

	Confidence Intervals, c					
	80%	90%	95%	98%	99%	99.9%
	Level of Significance for One-Tailed Test, α					
df	0.10	0.05	0.025	0.01	0.005	0.0005
	Level of Significance for Two-Tailed Test, α					
	0.20	0.10	0.05	0.02	0.01	0.001
1	3.078	6.314	12.706	31.821	63.657	636.619
2	1.886	2.920	4.303	6.965	9.925	31.599
3	1.638	2.353	3.182	4.541	5.841	12.924
4	1.533	2.132	2.776	3.747	4.604	8.610
5	1.476	2.015	2.571	3.365	4.032	6.869
6	1.440	1.943	2.447	3.143	3.707	5.959
7	1.415	1.895	2.365	2.998	3.499	5.408
8	1.397	1.860	2.306	2.896	3.355	5.041
9	1.383	1.833	2.262	2.821	3.250	4.781
10	1.372	1.812	2.228	2.764	3.169	4.587
11	1.363	1.796	2.201	2.718	3.106	4.437
12	1.356	1.782	2.179	2.681	3.055	4.318
13	1.350	1.771	2.160	2.650	3.012	4.221
14	1.345	1.761	2.145	2.624	2.977	4.140
15	1.341	1.753	2.131	2.602	2.947	4.073
16	1.337	1.746	2.120	2.583	2.921	4.015
17	1.333	1.740	2.110	2.567	2.898	3.965
18	1.330	1.734	2.101	2.552	2.878	3.922
19	1.328	1.729	2.093	2.539	2.861	3.883
20	1.325	1.725	2.086	2.528	2.845	3.850
21	1.323	1.721	2.080	2.518	2.831	3.819
22	1.321	1.717	2.074	2.508	2.819	3.792
23	1.319	1.714	2.069	2.500	2.807	3.768
24	1.318	1.711	2.064	2.492	2.797	3.745
25	1.316	1.708	2.060	2.485	2.787	3.725
26	1.315	1.706	2.056	2.479	2.779	3.707
27	1.314	1.703	2.052	2.473	2.771	3.690
28	1.313	1.701	2.048	2.467	2.763	3.674
29	1.311	1.699	2.045	2.462	2.756	3.659
30	1.310	1.697	2.042	2.457	2.750	3.646
31	1.309	1.696	2.040	2.453	2.744	3.633
32	1.309	1.694	2.037	2.449	2.738	3.622
33	1.308	1.692	2.035	2.445	2.733	3.611
34	1.307	1.691	2.032	2.441	2.728	3.601
35	1.306	1.690	2.030	2.438	2.724	3.591

	Confidence Intervals, c					
	80%	90%	95%	98%	99%	99.9%
	Level of Significance for One-Tailed Test, α					
df	0.10	0.05	0.025	0.01	0.005	0.0005
	Level of Significance for Two-Tailed Test, α					
	0.20	0.10	0.05	0.02	0.01	0.001
36	1.306	1.688	2.028	2.434	2.719	3.582
37	1.305	1.687	2.026	2.431	2.715	3.574
38	1.304	1.686	2.024	2.429	2.712	3.566
39	1.304	1.685	2.023	2.426	2.708	3.558
40	1.303	1.684	2.021	2.423	2.704	3.551
41	1.303	1.683	2.020	2.421	2.701	3.544
42	1.302	1.682	2.018	2.418	2.698	3.538
43	1.302	1.681	2.017	2.416	2.695	3.532
44	1.301	1.680	2.015	2.414	2.692	3.526
45	1.301	1.679	2.014	2.412	2.690	3.520
46	1.300	1.679	2.013	2.410	2.687	3.515
47	1.300	1.678	2.012	2.408	2.685	3.510
48	1.299	1.677	2.011	2.407	2.682	3.505
49	1.299	1.677	2.010	2.405	2.680	3.500
50	1.299	1.676	2.009	2.403	2.678	3.496
51	1.298	1.675	2.008	2.402	2.676	3.492
52	1.298	1.675	2.007	2.400	2.674	3.488
53	1.298	1.674	2.006	2.399	2.672	3.484
54	1.297	1.674	2.005	2.397	2.670	3.480
55	1.297	1.673	2.004	2.396	2.668	3.476
56	1.297	1.673	2.003	2.395	2.667	3.473
57	1.297	1.672	2.002	2.394	2.665	3.470
58	1.296	1.672	2.002	2.392	2.663	3.466
59	1.296	1.671	2.001	2.391	2.662	3.463
60	1.296	1.671	2.000	2.390	2.660	3.460
61	1.296	1.670	2.000	2.389	2.659	3.457
62	1.295	1.670	1.999	2.388	2.657	3.454
63	1.295	1.669	1.998	2.387	2.656	3.452
64	1.295	1.669	1.998	2.386	2.655	3.449
65	1.295	1.669	1.997	2.385	2.654	3.447
66	1.295	1.668	1.997	2.384	2.652	3.444
67	1.294	1.668	1.996	2.383	2.651	3.442
68	1.294	1.668	1.995	2.382	2.650	3.439
69	1.294	1.667	1.995	2.382	2.649	3.437
70	1.294	1.667	1.994	2.381	2.648	3.435

(*continued*)

B.5 Student's *t*-Distribution (*concluded*)

	Confidence Intervals, *c*								Confidence Intervals, *c*					
	80%	**90%**	**95%**	**98%**	**99%**	**99.9%**		**80%**	**90%**	**95%**	**98%**	**99%**	**99.9%**
	Level of Significance for One-Tailed Test, α							Level of Significance for One-Tailed Test, α					
df	**0.10**	**0.05**	**0.025**	**0.01**	**0.005**	**0.0005**	*df*	**0.10**	**0.05**	**0.025**	**0.01**	**0.005**	**0.0005**
	Level of Significance for Two-Tailed Test, α							Level of Significance for Two-Tailed Test, α					
	0.20	**0.10**	**0.05**	**0.02**	**0.01**	**0.001**		**0.20**	**0.10**	**0.05**	**0.02**	**0.01**	**0.001**
71	1.294	1.667	1.994	2.380	2.647	3.433	89	1.291	1.662	1.987	2.369	2.632	3.403
72	1.293	1.666	1.993	2.379	2.646	3.431	90	1.291	1.662	1.987	2.368	2.632	3.402
73	1.293	1.666	1.993	2.379	2.645	3.429	91	1.291	1.662	1.986	2.368	2.631	3.401
74	1.293	1.666	1.993	2.378	2.644	3.427	92	1.291	1.662	1.986	2.368	2.630	3.399
75	1.293	1.665	1.992	2.377	2.643	3.425	93	1.291	1.661	1.986	2.367	2.630	3.398
76	1.293	1.665	1.992	2.376	2.642	3.423	94	1.291	1.661	1.986	2.367	2.629	3.397
77	1.293	1.665	1.991	2.376	2.641	3.421	95	1.291	1.661	1.985	2.366	2.629	3.396
78	1.292	1.665	1.991	2.375	2.640	3.420	96	1.290	1.661	1.985	2.366	2.628	3.395
79	1.292	1.664	1.990	2.374	2.640	3.418	97	1.290	1.661	1.985	2.365	2.627	3.394
80	1.292	1.664	1.990	2.374	2.639	3.416	98	1.290	1.661	1.984	2.365	2.627	3.393
81	1.292	1.664	1.990	2.373	2.638	3.415	99	1.290	1.660	1.984	2.365	2.626	3.392
82	1.292	1.664	1.989	2.373	2.637	3.413	100	1.290	1.660	1.984	2.364	2.626	3.390
83	1.292	1.663	1.989	2.372	2.636	3.412	120	1.289	1.658	1.980	2.358	2.617	3.373
84	1.292	1.663	1.989	2.372	2.636	3.410	140	1.288	1.656	1.977	2.353	2.611	3.361
85	1.292	1.663	1.988	2.371	2.635	3.409	160	1.287	1.654	1.975	2.350	2.607	3.352
86	1.291	1.663	1.988	2.370	2.634	3.407	180	1.286	1.653	1.973	2.347	2.603	3.345
87	1.291	1.663	1.988	2.370	2.634	3.406	200	1.286	1.653	1.972	2.345	2.601	3.340
88	1.291	1.662	1.987	2.369	2.633	3.405	∞	1.282	1.645	1.960	2.326	2.576	3.291

B.6A Critical Values of the *F*-Distribution ($\alpha = .05$)

							Degrees of Freedom for the Numerator										
	1	**2**	**3**	**4**	**5**	**6**	**7**	**8**	**9**	**10**	**11**	**12**	**15**	**20**	**25**	**30**	**40**
1	161.45	199.50	215.71	224.58	230.16	233.99	236.77	238.88	240.54	241.88	242.98	243.91	245.95	248.01	249.26	250.10	251.14
2	18.51	19.00	19.16	19.25	19.30	19.33	19.35	19.37	19.38	19.40	19.40	19.41	19.43	19.45	19.46	19.46	19.47
3	10.13	9.55	9.28	9.12	9.01	8.94	8.89	8.85	8.81	8.79	8.76	8.74	8.70	8.66	8.63	8.62	8.59
4	7.71	6.94	6.59	6.39	6.26	6.16	6.09	6.04	6.00	5.96	5.94	5.91	5.86	5.80	5.77	5.75	5.72
5	6.61	5.79	5.41	5.19	5.05	4.95	4.88	4.82	4.77	4.74	4.70	4.68	4.62	4.56	4.52	4.50	4.46
6	5.99	5.14	4.76	4.53	4.39	4.28	4.21	4.15	4.10	4.06	4.03	4.00	3.94	3.87	3.83	3.81	3.77
7	5.59	4.74	4.35	4.12	3.97	3.87	3.79	3.73	3.68	3.64	3.60	3.57	3.51	3.44	3.40	3.38	3.34
8	5.32	4.46	4.07	3.84	3.69	3.58	3.50	3.44	3.39	3.35	3.31	3.28	3.22	3.15	3.11	3.08	3.04
9	5.12	4.26	3.86	3.63	3.48	3.37	3.29	3.23	3.18	3.14	3.10	3.07	3.01	2.94	2.89	2.86	2.83
10	4.96	4.10	3.71	3.48	3.33	3.22	3.14	3.07	3.02	2.98	2.94	2.91	2.85	2.77	2.73	2.70	2.66
11	4.84	3.98	3.59	3.36	3.20	3.09	3.01	2.95	2.90	2.85	2.82	2.79	2.72	2.65	2.60	2.57	2.53
12	4.75	3.89	3.49	3.26	3.11	3.00	2.91	2.85	2.80	2.75	2.72	2.69	2.62	2.54	2.50	2.47	2.43
13	4.67	3.81	3.41	3.18	3.03	2.92	2.83	2.77	2.71	2.67	2.63	2.60	2.53	2.46	2.41	2.38	2.34
14	4.60	3.74	3.34	3.11	2.96	2.85	2.76	2.70	2.65	2.60	2.57	2.53	2.46	2.39	2.34	2.31	2.27
15	4.54	3.68	3.29	3.06	2.90	2.79	2.71	2.64	2.59	2.54	2.51	2.48	2.40	2.33	2.28	2.25	2.20
16	4.49	3.63	3.24	3.01	2.85	2.74	2.66	2.59	2.54	2.49	2.46	2.42	2.35	2.28	2.23	2.19	2.15
17	4.45	3.59	3.20	2.96	2.81	2.70	2.61	2.55	2.49	2.45	2.41	2.38	2.31	2.23	2.18	2.15	2.10
18	4.41	3.55	3.16	2.93	2.77	2.66	2.58	2.51	2.46	2.41	2.37	2.34	2.27	2.19	2.14	2.11	2.06
19	4.38	3.52	3.13	2.90	2.74	2.63	2.54	2.48	2.42	2.38	2.34	2.31	2.23	2.16	2.11	2.07	2.03
20	4.35	3.49	3.10	2.87	2.71	2.60	2.51	2.45	2.39	2.35	2.31	2.28	2.20	2.12	2.07	2.04	1.99
21	4.32	3.47	3.07	2.84	2.68	2.57	2.49	2.42	2.37	2.32	2.28	2.25	2.18	2.10	2.05	2.01	1.96
22	4.30	3.44	3.05	2.82	2.66	2.55	2.46	2.40	2.34	2.30	2.26	2.23	2.15	2.07	2.02	1.98	1.94
23	4.28	3.42	3.03	2.80	2.64	2.53	2.44	2.37	2.32	2.27	2.24	2.20	2.13	2.05	2.00	1.96	1.91
24	4.26	3.40	3.01	2.78	2.62	2.51	2.42	2.36	2.30	2.25	2.22	2.18	2.11	2.03	1.97	1.94	1.89
25	4.24	3.39	2.99	2.76	2.60	2.49	2.40	2.34	2.28	2.24	2.20	2.16	2.09	2.01	1.96	1.92	1.87
30	4.17	3.32	2.92	2.69	2.53	2.42	2.33	2.27	2.21	2.16	2.13	2.09	2.01	1.93	1.88	1.84	1.79
40	4.08	3.23	2.84	2.61	2.45	2.34	2.25	2.18	2.12	2.08	2.04	2.00	1.92	1.84	1.78	1.74	1.69
60	4.00	3.15	2.76	2.53	2.37	2.25	2.17	2.10	2.04	1.99	1.95	1.92	1.84	1.75	1.69	1.65	1.59
120	3.92	3.07	2.68	2.45	2.29	2.18	2.09	2.02	1.96	1.91	1.87	1.83	1.75	1.66	1.60	1.55	1.50
∞	3.84	3.00	2.60	2.37	2.21	2.10	2.01	1.94	1.88	1.83	1.79	1.75	1.67	1.57	1.51	1.46	1.39

Degrees of Freedom for the Denominator

B.6B Critical Values of the *F*-Distribution ($\alpha = .01$)

							Degrees of Freedom for the Numerator										
	1	**2**	**3**	**4**	**5**	**6**	**7**	**8**	**9**	**10**	**11**	**12**	**15**	**20**	**25**	**30**	**40**
1	4052.18	4999.50	5403.35	5624.58	5763.65	5858.99	5928.36	5981.07	6022.47	6055.85	6083.32	6106.32	6157.28	6208.73	6239.83	6260.65	6286.78
2	98.50	99.00	99.17	99.25	99.30	99.33	99.36	99.37	99.39	99.40	99.41	99.42	99.43	99.45	99.46	99.47	99.47
3	34.12	30.82	29.46	28.71	28.24	27.91	27.67	27.49	27.35	27.23	27.13	27.05	26.87	26.69	26.58	26.50	26.41
4	21.20	18.00	16.69	15.98	15.52	15.21	14.98	14.80	14.66	14.55	14.45	14.37	14.20	14.02	13.91	13.84	13.75
5	16.26	13.27	12.06	11.39	10.97	10.67	10.46	10.29	10.16	10.05	9.96	9.89	9.72	9.55	9.45	9.38	9.29
6	13.75	10.92	9.78	9.15	8.75	8.47	8.26	8.10	7.98	7.87	7.79	7.72	7.56	7.40	7.30	7.23	7.14
7	12.25	9.55	8.45	7.85	7.46	7.19	6.99	6.84	6.72	6.62	6.54	6.47	6.31	6.16	6.06	5.99	5.91
8	11.26	8.65	7.59	7.01	6.63	6.37	6.18	6.03	5.91	5.81	5.73	5.67	5.52	5.36	5.26	5.20	5.12
9	10.56	8.02	6.99	6.42	6.06	5.80	5.61	5.47	5.35	5.26	5.18	5.11	4.96	4.81	4.71	4.65	4.57
10	10.04	7.56	6.55	5.99	5.64	5.39	5.20	5.06	4.94	4.85	4.77	4.71	4.56	4.41	4.31	4.25	4.17
11	9.65	7.21	6.22	5.67	5.32	5.07	4.89	4.74	4.63	4.54	4.46	4.40	4.25	4.10	4.01	3.94	3.86
12	9.33	6.93	5.95	5.41	5.06	4.82	4.64	4.50	4.39	4.30	4.22	4.16	4.01	3.86	3.76	3.70	3.62
13	9.07	6.70	5.74	5.21	4.86	4.62	4.44	4.30	4.19	4.10	4.02	3.96	3.82	3.66	3.57	3.51	3.43
14	8.86	6.51	5.56	5.04	4.69	4.46	4.28	4.14	4.03	3.94	3.86	3.80	3.66	3.51	3.41	3.35	3.27
15	8.68	6.36	5.42	4.89	4.56	4.32	4.14	4.00	3.89	3.80	3.73	3.67	3.52	3.37	3.28	3.21	3.13
16	8.53	6.23	5.29	4.77	4.44	4.20	4.03	3.89	3.78	3.69	3.62	3.55	3.41	3.26	3.16	3.10	3.02
17	8.40	6.11	5.18	4.67	4.34	4.10	3.93	3.79	3.68	3.59	3.52	3.46	3.31	3.16	3.07	3.00	2.92
18	8.29	6.01	5.09	4.58	4.25	4.01	3.84	3.71	3.60	3.51	3.43	3.37	3.23	3.08	2.98	2.92	2.84
19	8.18	5.93	5.01	4.50	4.17	3.94	3.77	3.63	3.52	3.43	3.36	3.30	3.15	3.00	2.91	2.84	2.76
20	8.10	5.85	4.94	4.43	4.10	3.87	3.70	3.56	3.46	3.37	3.29	3.23	3.09	2.94	2.84	2.78	2.69
21	8.02	5.78	4.87	4.37	4.04	3.81	3.64	3.51	3.40	3.31	3.24	3.17	3.03	2.88	2.79	2.72	2.64
22	7.95	5.72	4.82	4.31	3.99	3.76	3.59	3.45	3.35	3.26	3.18	3.12	2.98	2.83	2.73	2.67	2.58
23	7.88	5.66	4.76	4.26	3.94	3.71	3.54	3.41	3.30	3.21	3.14	3.07	2.93	2.78	2.69	2.62	2.54
24	7.82	5.61	4.72	4.22	3.90	3.67	3.50	3.36	3.26	3.17	3.09	3.03	2.89	2.74	2.64	2.58	2.49
25	7.77	5.57	4.68	4.18	3.85	3.63	3.46	3.32	3.22	3.13	3.06	2.99	2.85	2.70	2.60	2.54	2.45
30	7.56	5.39	4.51	4.02	3.70	3.47	3.30	3.17	3.07	2.98	2.91	2.84	2.70	2.55	2.45	2.39	2.30
40	7.31	5.18	4.31	3.83	3.51	3.29	3.12	2.99	2.89	2.80	2.73	2.66	2.52	2.37	2.27	2.20	2.11
60	7.08	4.98	4.13	3.65	3.34	3.12	2.95	2.82	2.72	2.63	2.56	2.50	2.35	2.20	2.10	2.03	1.94
120	6.85	4.79	3.95	3.48	3.17	2.96	2.79	2.66	2.56	2.47	2.40	2.34	2.19	2.03	1.93	1.86	1.76
∞	6.63	4.61	3.78	3.32	3.02	2.80	2.64	2.51	2.41	2.32	2.25	2.18	2.04	1.88	1.77	1.70	1.59

Degrees of Freedom for the Denominator

B.7 Critical Values of Chi-Square

This table contains the values of χ^2 that correspond to a specific right-tail area and specific number of degrees of freedom.

Example: With 17 *df* and a 0.02 area in the upper tail, $\chi^2 = 30.995$

Degrees of Freedom, *df*	Right-Tail Area			
	0.10	0.05	0.02	0.01
1	2.706	3.841	5.412	6.635
2	4.605	5.991	7.824	9.210
3	6.251	7.815	9.837	11.345
4	7.779	9.488	11.668	13.277
5	9.236	11.070	13.388	15.086
6	10.645	12.592	15.033	16.812
7	12.017	14.067	16.622	18.475
8	13.362	15.507	18.168	20.090
9	14.684	16.919	19.679	21.666
10	15.987	18.307	21.161	23.209
11	17.275	19.675	22.618	24.725
12	18.549	21.026	24.054	26.217
13	19.812	22.362	25.472	27.688
14	21.064	23.685	26.873	29.141
15	22.307	24.996	28.259	30.578
16	23.542	26.296	29.633	32.000
17	24.769	27.587	30.995	33.409
18	25.989	28.869	32.346	34.805
19	27.204	30.144	33.687	36.191
20	28.412	31.410	35.020	37.566
21	29.615	32.671	36.343	38.932
22	30.813	33.924	37.659	40.289
23	32.007	35.172	38.968	41.638
24	33.196	36.415	40.270	42.980
25	34.382	37.652	41.566	44.314
26	35.563	38.885	42.856	45.642
27	36.741	40.113	44.140	46.963
28	37.916	41.337	45.419	48.278
29	39.087	42.557	46.693	49.588
30	40.256	43.773	47.962	50.892

B.8 Wilcoxon *T*-Values

	2α						
	.15	.10	.05	.04	.03	.02	.01
	α						
n	.075	.050	.025	.020	.015	.010	.005
4	0						
5	1	0					
6	2	2	0	0			
7	4	3	2	1	0	0	
8	7	5	3	3	2	1	0
9	9	8	5	5	4	3	1
10	12	10	8	7	6	5	3
11	16	13	10	9	8	7	5
12	19	17	13	12	11	9	7
13	24	21	17	16	14	12	9
14	28	25	21	19	18	15	12
15	33	30	25	23	21	19	15
16	39	35	29	28	26	23	19
17	45	41	34	33	30	27	23
18	51	47	40	38	35	32	27
19	58	53	46	43	41	37	32
20	65	60	52	50	47	43	37
21	73	67	58	56	53	49	42
22	81	75	65	63	59	55	48
23	89	83	73	70	66	62	54
24	98	91	81	78	74	69	61
25	108	100	89	86	82	76	68
26	118	110	98	94	90	84	75
27	128	119	107	103	99	92	83
28	138	130	116	112	108	101	91
29	150	140	126	122	117	110	100
30	161	151	137	132	127	120	109
31	173	163	147	143	137	130	118
32	186	175	159	154	148	140	128
33	199	187	170	165	159	151	138
34	212	200	182	177	171	162	148
35	226	213	195	189	182	173	159
40	302	286	264	257	249	238	220
50	487	466	434	425	413	397	373
60	718	690	648	636	620	600	567
70	995	960	907	891	872	846	805
80	1,318	1,276	1,211	1,192	1,168	1,136	1,086
90	1,688	1,638	1,560	1,537	1,509	1,471	1,410
100	2,105	2,045	1,955	1,928	1,894	1,850	1,779

B.9A Critical Values for the Durbin-Watson *d*-Statistic ($\alpha = .05$)

n	k = 1 $d_{L,.05}$	k = 1 $d_{U,.05}$	k = 2 $d_{L,.05}$	k = 2 $d_{U,.05}$	k = 3 $d_{L,.05}$	k = 3 $d_{U,.05}$	k = 4 $d_{L,.05}$	k = 4 $d_{U,.05}$	k = 5 $d_{L,.05}$	k = 5 $d_{U,.05}$
6	0.61	1.40	------	------	------	------	------	------	------	------
7	0.70	1.36	0.47	1.90	------	------	------	------	------	------
8	0.76	1.33	0.56	1.78	0.37	2.29	------	------	------	------
9	0.82	1.32	0.63	1.70	0.46	2.13	0.30	2.59	------	------
10	0.88	1.32	0.70	1.64	0.53	2.02	0.38	2.41	0.24	2.82
11	0.93	1.32	0.76	1.61	0.60	1.93	0.44	2.28	0.32	2.65
12	0.97	1.33	0.81	1.58	0.66	1.86	0.51	2.18	0.38	2.51
13	1.01	1.34	0.86	1.56	0.72	1.82	0.57	2.09	0.44	2.39
14	1.05	1.35	0.91	1.55	0.77	1.78	0.63	2.03	0.51	2.30
15	1.08	1.36	0.95	1.54	0.82	1.75	0.69	1.97	0.56	2.21
16	1.10	1.37	0.98	1.54	0.86	1.73	0.74	1.93	0.62	2.15
17	1.13	1.38	1.02	1.54	0.90	1.71	0.78	1.90	0.67	2.10
18	1.16	1.39	1.05	1.53	0.93	1.69	0.82	1.87	0.71	2.06
19	1.18	1.40	1.08	1.53	0.97	1.68	0.86	1.85	0.75	2.02
20	1.20	1.41	1.10	1.54	1.00	1.68	0.90	1.83	0.79	1.99
21	1.22	1.42	1.13	1.54	1.03	1.67	0.93	1.81	0.83	1.96
22	1.24	1.43	1.15	1.54	1.05	1.66	0.96	1.80	0.86	1.94
23	1.26	1.44	1.17	1.54	1.08	1.66	0.99	1.79	0.90	1.92
24	1.27	1.45	1.19	1.55	1.10	1.66	1.01	1.78	0.93	1.90
25	1.29	1.45	1.21	1.55	1.12	1.66	1.04	1.77	0.95	1.89
26	1.30	1.46	1.22	1.55	1.14	1.65	1.06	1.76	0.98	1.88
27	1.32	1.47	1.24	1.56	1.16	1.65	1.08	1.76	1.01	1.86
28	1.33	1.48	1.26	1.56	1.18	1.65	1.10	1.75	1.03	1.85
29	1.34	1.48	1.27	1.56	1.20	1.65	1.12	1.74	1.05	1.84
30	1.35	1.49	1.28	1.57	1.21	1.65	1.14	1.74	1.07	1.83
31	1.36	1.50	1.30	1.57	1.23	1.65	1.16	1.74	1.09	1.83
32	1.37	1.50	1.31	1.57	1.24	1.65	1.18	1.73	1.11	1.82
33	1.38	1.51	1.32	1.58	1.26	1.65	1.19	1.73	1.13	1.81
34	1.39	1.51	1.33	1.58	1.27	1.65	1.21	1.73	1.15	1.81
35	1.40	1.52	1.34	1.58	1.28	1.65	1.22	1.73	1.16	1.80
36	1.41	1.52	1.35	1.59	1.29	1.65	1.24	1.73	1.18	1.80
37	1.42	1.53	1.36	1.59	1.31	1.66	1.25	1.72	1.19	1.80
38	1.43	1.54	1.37	1.59	1.32	1.66	1.26	1.72	1.21	1.79
39	1.43	1.54	1.38	1.60	1.33	1.66	1.27	1.72	1.22	1.79
40	1.44	1.54	1.39	1.60	1.34	1.66	1.29	1.72	1.23	1.79
45	1.48	1.57	1.43	1.62	1.38	1.67	1.34	1.72	1.29	1.78
50	1.50	1.59	1.46	1.63	1.42	1.67	1.38	1.72	1.34	1.77
55	1.53	1.60	1.49	1.64	1.45	1.68	1.41	1.72	1.38	1.77
60	1.55	1.62	1.51	1.65	1.48	1.69	1.44	1.73	1.41	1.77
65	1.57	1.63	1.54	1.66	1.50	1.70	1.47	1.73	1.44	1.77
70	1.58	1.64	1.55	1.67	1.52	1.70	1.49	1.74	1.46	1.77
75	1.60	1.65	1.57	1.68	1.54	1.71	1.51	1.74	1.49	1.77
80	1.61	1.66	1.59	1.69	1.56	1.72	1.53	1.74	1.51	1.77
85	1.62	1.67	1.60	1.70	1.57	1.72	1.55	1.75	1.52	1.77
90	1.63	1.68	1.61	1.70	1.59	1.73	1.57	1.75	1.54	1.78
95	1.64	1.69	1.62	1.71	1.60	1.73	1.58	1.75	1.56	1.78
100	1.65	1.69	1.63	1.72	1.61	1.74	1.59	1.76	1.57	1.78

SOURCES: J. Durbin and G. S. Watson, "Testing for Serial Correlation in Least Squares Regression, II," *Biometrika* 30 (1951), pp. 159–178. Reproduced by permission of the Biometrika Trustees. N.E. Savin and K.J. White, "The Durbin-Watson Test for Serial Correlation with Extreme Sample Sizes or Many Regressors," *Econometrica* 45(8) (1977), pp. 1989–1996.

B.9B Critical Values for the Durbin-Watson *d*-Statistic ($\alpha = .025$)

n	k = 1		k = 2		k = 3		k = 4		k = 5	
	$d_{L,.025}$	$d_{U,.025}$	$d_{L,.025}$	$d_{U,.025}$	$d_{L,.025}$	$d_{U,.025}$	$d_{L,.025}$	$d_{U,.025}$	$d_{L,.025}$	$d_{U,.025}$
15	0.95	1.23	0.83	1.40	0.71	1.61	0.59	1.84	0.48	2.09
16	0.98	1.24	0.86	1.40	0.75	1.59	0.64	1.80	0.53	2.03
17	1.01	1.25	0.90	1.40	0.79	1.58	0.68	1.77	0.57	1.98
18	1.03	1.26	0.93	1.40	0.82	1.56	0.72	1.74	0.62	1.93
19	1.06	1.28	0.96	1.41	0.86	1.55	0.76	1.72	0.66	1.90
20	1.08	1.28	0.99	1.41	0.89	1.55	0.79	1.70	0.70	1.87
21	1.10	1.30	1.01	1.41	0.92	1.54	0.83	1.69	0.73	1.84
22	1.12	1.31	1.04	1.42	0.95	1.54	0.86	1.68	0.77	1.82
23	1.14	1.32	1.06	1.42	0.97	1.54	0.89	1.67	0.80	1.80
24	1.16	1.33	1.08	1.43	1.00	1.54	0.91	1.66	0.83	1.79
25	1.18	1.34	1.10	1.43	1.02	1.54	0.94	1.65	0.86	1.77
26	1.19	1.35	1.12	1.44	1.04	1.54	0.96	1.65	0.88	1.76
27	1.21	1.36	1.13	1.44	1.06	1.54	0.99	1.64	0.91	1.75
28	1.22	1.37	1.15	1.45	1.08	1.54	1.01	1.64	0.93	1.74
29	1.24	1.38	1.17	1.45	1.10	1.54	1.03	1.63	0.96	1.73
30	1.25	1.38	1.18	1.46	1.12	1.54	1.05	1.63	0.98	1.73
31	1.26	1.39	1.20	1.47	1.13	1.55	1.07	1.63	1.00	1.72
32	1.27	1.40	1.21	1.47	1.15	1.55	1.08	1.63	1.02	1.71
33	1.28	1.41	1.22	1.48	1.16	1.55	1.10	1.63	1.04	1.71
34	1.29	1.41	1.24	1.48	1.17	1.55	1.12	1.63	1.06	1.70
35	1.30	1.42	1.25	1.48	1.19	1.55	1.13	1.63	1.07	1.70
36	1.31	1.43	1.26	1.49	1.20	1.56	1.15	1.63	1.09	1.70
37	1.32	1.43	1.27	1.49	1.21	1.56	1.16	1.62	1.10	1.70
38	1.33	1.44	1.28	1.50	1.23	1.56	1.17	1.62	1.12	1.70
39	1.34	1.44	1.29	1.50	1.24	1.56	1.19	1.63	1.13	1.69
40	1.35	1.45	1.30	1.51	1.25	1.57	1.20	1.63	1.15	1.69
45	1.39	1.48	1.34	1.53	1.30	1.58	1.25	1.63	1.21	1.69
50	1.42	1.50	1.38	1.54	1.34	1.59	1.30	1.64	1.26	1.69
55	1.45	1.52	1.41	1.56	1.37	1.60	1.33	1.64	1.30	1.69
60	1.47	1.54	1.44	1.57	1.40	1.61	1.37	1.65	1.33	1.69
65	1.49	1.55	1.46	1.59	1.43	1.62	1.40	1.66	1.36	1.69
70	1.51	1.57	1.48	1.60	1.45	1.63	1.42	1.66	1.39	1.70
75	1.53	1.58	1.50	1.61	1.47	1.64	1.45	1.67	1.42	1.70
80	1.54	1.59	1.52	1.62	1.49	1.65	1.47	1.67	1.44	1.70
85	1.56	1.60	1.53	1.63	1.51	1.65	1.49	1.68	1.46	1.71
90	1.57	1.61	1.55	1.64	1.53	1.66	1.50	1.69	1.48	1.71
95	1.58	1.62	1.56	1.65	1.54	1.67	1.52	1.69	1.50	1.71
100	1.59	1.63	1.57	1.65	1.55	1.67	1.53	1.70	1.51	1.72

SOURCE: J. Durbin and G. S. Watson, "Testing for Serial Correlation in Least Squares Regression, II," *Biometrika* 30 (1951), pp. 159–178. Reproduced by permission of the Biometrika Trustees.

B.9C Critical Values for the Durbin-Watson d-Statistic ($\alpha = .01$)

n	k = 1		k = 2		k = 3		k = 4		k = 5	
	$d_{L,.01}$	$d_{U,.01}$	$d_{L,.01}$	$d_{U,.01}$	$d_{L,.01}$	$d_{U,.01}$	$d_{L,.01}$	$d_{U,.01}$	$d_{L,.01}$	$d_{U,.01}$
15	0.81	1.07	0.70	1.25	0.59	1.46	0.49	1.70	0.39	1.96
16	0.84	1.09	0.74	1.25	0.63	1.44	0.53	1.66	0.44	1.90
17	0.87	1.10	0.77	1.25	0.67	1.43	0.57	1.63	0.48	1.85
18	0.90	1.12	0.80	1.26	0.71	1.42	0.61	1.60	0.52	1.80
19	0.93	1.13	0.83	1.26	0.74	1.41	0.65	1.58	0.56	1.77
20	0.95	1.15	0.86	1.27	0.77	1.41	0.68	1.57	0.60	1.74
21	0.97	1.16	0.89	1.27	0.80	1.41	0.72	1.55	0.63	1.71
22	1.00	1.17	0.91	1.28	0.83	1.40	0.75	1.54	0.66	1.69
23	1.02	1.19	0.94	1.29	0.86	1.40	0.77	1.53	0.70	1.67
24	1.04	1.20	0.96	1.30	0.88	1.41	0.80	1.53	0.72	1.66
25	1.05	1.21	0.98	1.30	0.90	1.41	0.83	1.52	0.75	1.65
26	1.07	1.22	1.00	1.31	0.93	1.41	0.85	1.52	0.78	1.64
27	1.09	1.23	1.02	1.32	0.95	1.41	0.88	1.51	0.81	1.63
28	1.10	1.24	1.04	1.32	0.97	1.41	0.90	1.51	0.83	1.62
29	1.12	1.25	1.05	1.33	0.99	1.42	0.92	1.51	0.85	1.61
30	1.13	1.26	1.07	1.34	1.01	1.42	0.94	1.51	0.88	1.61
31	1.15	1.27	1.08	1.34	1.02	1.42	0.96	1.51	0.90	1.60
32	1.16	1.28	1.10	1.35	1.04	1.43	0.98	1.51	0.92	1.60
33	1.17	1.29	1.11	1.36	1.05	1.43	1.00	1.51	0.94	1.59
34	1.18	1.30	1.13	1.36	1.07	1.43	1.01	1.51	0.95	1.59
35	1.19	1.31	1.14	1.37	1.08	1.44	1.03	1.51	0.97	1.59
36	1.21	1.32	1.15	1.38	1.10	1.44	1.04	1.51	0.99	1.59
37	1.22	1.32	1.16	1.38	1.11	1.45	1.06	1.51	1.00	1.59
38	1.23	1.33	1.18	1.39	1.12	1.45	1.07	1.52	1.02	1.58
39	1.24	1.34	1.19	1.39	1.14	1.45	1.09	1.52	1.03	1.58
40	1.25	1.34	1.20	1.40	1.15	1.46	1.10	1.52	1.05	1.58
45	1.29	1.38	1.24	1.42	1.20	1.48	1.16	1.53	1.11	1.58
50	1.32	1.40	1.28	1.45	1.24	1.49	1.20	1.54	1.16	1.59
55	1.36	1.43	1.32	1.47	1.28	1.51	1.25	1.55	1.21	1.59
60	1.38	1.45	1.35	1.48	1.32	1.52	1.28	1.56	1.25	1.60
65	1.41	1.47	1.38	1.50	1.35	1.53	1.31	1.57	1.28	1.61
70	1.43	1.49	1.40	1.52	1.37	1.55	1.34	1.58	1.31	1.61
75	1.45	1.50	1.42	1.53	1.39	1.56	1.37	1.59	1.34	1.62
80	1.47	1.52	1.44	1.54	1.42	1.57	1.39	1.60	1.36	1.62
85	1,48	1.53	1.46	1.55	1.43	1.58	1.41	1.60	1.39	1.63
90	1.50	1.54	1.47	1.56	1.45	1.59	1.43	1.61	1.41	1.64
95	1.51	1.55	1.49	1.57	1.47	1.60	1.45	1.62	1.42	1.64
100	1.52	1.56	1.50	1.58	1.48	1.60	1.46	1.63	1.44	1.65

SOURCE: J. Durbin and G. S. Watson, "Testing for Serial Correlation in Least Squares Regression, II," *Biometrika* 30 (1951), pp. 159–178. Reproduced by permission of the Biometrika Trustees.

B.10 Factors for Control Charts

Number of Items in Sample, n	Chart for Averages	Chart for Ranges		
	Factors for Control Limits	Factors for Central Line	Factors for Control Limits	
	A_2	d_2	D_3	D_4
2	1.880	1.128	0	3.267
3	1.023	1.693	0	2.575
4	.729	2.059	0	2.282
5	.577	2.326	0	2.115
6	.483	2.534	0	2.004
7	.419	2.704	.076	1.924
8	.373	2.847	.136	1.864
9	.337	2.970	.184	1.816
10	.308	3.078	.223	1.777
11	.285	3.173	.256	1.744
12	.266	3.258	.284	1.716
13	.249	3.336	.308	1.692
14	.235	3.407	.329	1.671
15	.223	3.472	.348	1.652

SOURCE: Adapted from American Society for Testing and Materials, *Manual on Quality Control of Materials,* 1951, Table B2, p. 115. For a more detailed table and explanation, see J. Duncan Acheson, *Quality Control and Industrial Statistics,* 3rd ed. (Homewood, Ill.: Richard D. Irwin, 1974), Table M, p. 927.

Answers to Odd-Numbered Chapter Exercises

CHAPTER 1

1. **a.** Interval **d.** Nominal
   b. Ratio **e.** Ordinal
   c. Nominal **f.** Ratio
3. Answers will vary.
5. Qualitative data are not numerical, whereas quantitative data are numerical. Examples will vary by student.
7. A discrete variable may assume only certain values. A continuous variable may assume an infinite number of values within a given range. The number of traffic citations issued each day during February in Garden City Beach, South Carolina, is a discrete variable. The weight of commercial trucks passing the weigh station at milepost 195 on Interstate 95 in North Carolina is a continuous variable.
9. **a.** Ordinal
   b. Ratio
   c. The newer system provides information on the distance between exits.
11. **a.** The ranking of wearable technologies would most likely be based on a population. All possible brands and models could be listed.
    b. Since the ratings are self-reported, it is very likely that not all users submitted a rating. Therefore, the ratings are a sample or subset of the population.
13.

	Discrete Variable	Continuous Variable
Qualitative	b. Country d. Energy drink preference g. Student rank in class h. Rating of a finance professor	
Quantitative	c. Sales volume of treadmills f. SAT scores i. Number of home video devices	a. Salary e. Temperature

	Discrete	Continuous
Nominal	b. Country	
Ordinal	d. Energy drink preference g. Student rank in class h. Rating of a finance professor	
Interval	f. SAT scores	e. Temperature
Ratio	c. Sales volume of treadmills i. Number of video devices	a. Salary

15. According to the sample information, 120/300 or 40% would accept a job transfer.
17. **a.** From differences, it is clear that the sales of almost every brand decreased from 2019 to 2020. The primary causes are the effects of the COVID-19 pandemic on the economy and the manufacturing supply chain.

Brand	Difference
Tesla	97,777
Volvo	1,903
Mazda	526
Alfa Romeo	291
Porsche	−4,282
Genesis	−4,853
Fiat	−4,900
Lincoln	−6,702
Volkswagen	−7,638
Mini	−8,118
Jaguar	−9,219
Land Rover	−14,703
Chrysler	−16,687
Acura	−20,403
Lexus	−23,070
Cadillac	−26,755
Mercedes-Benz	−27,421
Kia	−28,608
Mitsubishi	−33,663
Audi	−37,486
Infiniti	−38,205
Buick	−44,177
BMW	−44,528
GMC	−49,637
Hyundai	−68,846
Ram	−78,386
Subaru	−88,179
Jeep	−127,986
Dodge	−155,562
Chevrolet	−212,006
Toyota	−247,308
Honda	−251,180
Ford	−355,230
Nissan	−390,211

b. This analysis shows that only Tesla, Volvo, and Alfa Romeo were able to sustain an increase in sales from 2019 to 2020. All other brands experienced decreases in sales ranging from 2.1% to 53.2%. Over time, decreases like these are very unusual. Again, the data reflect the effects of the pandemic.

Brand	Percent Change from 2019
Tesla	50.1%
Volvo	1.8%
Alfa Romeo	1.6%
Mazda	0.2%
Volkswagen	−2.1%
Kia	−4.7%
Lincoln	−6.0%
Porsche	−7.0%
Lexus	−7.7%
Mercedes-Benz	−7.8%

Brand	Percent Change from 2019
GMC	−8.8%
Hyundai	−10.0%
Chevrolet	−10.9%
Ram	−11.1%
Toyota	−11.9%
Subaru	−12.6%
Acura	−13.0%
Chrysler	−13.1%
BMW	−13.7%
Jeep	−13.9%
Land Rover	−15.5%
Ford	−15.6%
Audi	−16.7%
Cadillac	−17.1%
Honda	−17.3%
Buick	−21.3%
Mini	−22.4%
Genesis	−22.9%
Mitsubishi	−27.8%
Jaguar	−29.7%
Nissan	−31.8%
Infiniti	−32.5%
Dodge	−36.8%
Fiat	−53.2%

c. These graphs help to show the comparison in sales and percent change in sales for 2019 and 2020. In general, they show that each of the top 10 auto brands lost sales from 2019 to 2020. Further, the percent decreases ranged from about 30% for Nissan to 5% for Kia.

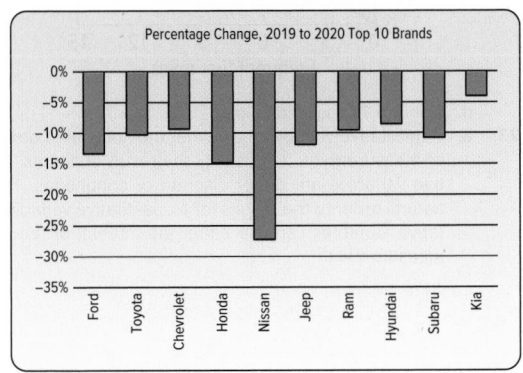

19. The graph shows that earnings increase about $15 billion per year over the period. However, 2008 sees a very large increase and 2009 sees a large decrease. Perhaps the earnings were affected by the Great Recession during the years 2008–2010. Perhaps the variability of earnings from 2013–2017 are related to supply and demand of oil. Supply may have increased with new production in North Dakota. Demand may be affected by other sources of energy, such as wind and solar energy generation. Also, the use of natural gas to generate energy may be substituting for oil. In 2020, the earnings were most likely affected by the global COVID-19 pandemic.

21. a. League is a qualitative variable; the others are quantitative.
    b. League is a nominal-level variable; the others are ratio-level variables.

CHAPTER 2

1. 25% market share.
3.

Season	Frequency	Relative Frequency
Winter	100	.10
Spring	300	.30
Summer	400	.40
Fall	200	.20
	1,000	1.00

5. a. A frequency table.

Color	Frequency	Relative Frequency
Bright White	130	0.10
Metallic Black	104	0.08
Magnetic Lime	325	0.25
Tangerine Orange	455	0.35
Fusion Red	286	0.22
Total	1,300	1.00

b.

c.

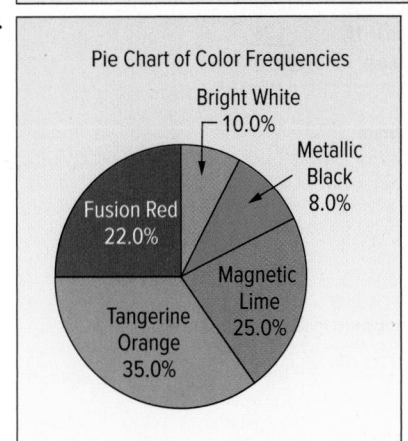

d. 350,000 orange, 250,000 lime, 220,000 red, 100,000 white, and 80,000 black, found by multiplying relative frequency by 1,000,000 production.

7. $2^5 = 32$, $2^6 = 64$, therefore, 6 classes.

9. $2^7 = 128$, $2^8 = 256$, suggests 8 classes.

$i \geq \dfrac{\$567 - \$235}{8} = 41$ Class intervals of 45 or 50 would be acceptable.

11. a. $2^4 = 16$ suggests 5 classes.

b. $i \geq \dfrac{31 - 25}{5} = 1.2$ Use interval of 1.5.

c. 24

d.

Units	f	Relative Frequency
24.0 up to 25.5	2	0.125
25.5 up to 27.0	4	0.250
27.0 up to 28.5	8	0.500
28.5 up to 30.0	0	0.000
30.0 up to 31.5	2	0.125
Total	16	1.000

e. The number of units produced in the past 16 days range between 24 and 31 units. The class with the highest frequency or relative frequency is the mode. The highest frequency is in the 27 up to 28.5 class. On 50% of the 16 days, the company produced between 27 and 28.5 units.

13. a.

Number of Visits	f
0 up to 3	9
3 up to 6	21
6 up to 9	13
9 up to 12	4
12 up to 15	3
15 up to 18	1
Total	51

b. The mode or largest group of shoppers (21) shop at BiLo 3, 4, or 5 times per month. Most shoppers make less than 9 visits. A small number of visitors make 9 or more visits.

c.

Number of Visits	Percent of Total
0 up to 3	17.65
3 up to 6	41.18
6 up to 9	25.49
9 up to 12	7.84
12 up to 15	5.88
15 up to 18	1.96
Total	100.00

15. a. Histogram
b. 100
c. 5
d. 28
e. 0.28
f. 12.5
g. 13

17. a. 50
b. 1.5 thousand miles, or 1,500 miles.

c.

d. $X = 1.5$, $Y = 5$

e.

f. For the 50 employees, about half traveled between 6,000 and 9,000 miles. Five employees traveled less than 3,000 miles, and 2 traveled more than 12,000 miles.

19. a. 40
b. 5
c. 11 or 12
d. About $18/hr
e. About $9/hr
f. About 75%

21. a. 5

b.

Miles	CF
Less than 3	5
Less than 6	17
Less than 9	40
Less than 12	48
Less than 15	50

c.

d. About 8.7 thousand miles

23. a. A qualitative variable uses either the nominal or ordinal scale of measurement. It is usually the result of counts. Quantitative variables are either discrete or continuous. There is a natural order to the results for a quantitative variable. Quantitative variables can use either the interval or ratio scale of measurement.

b. Both types of variables can be used for samples and populations.

25. a. Frequency table

b.

c.

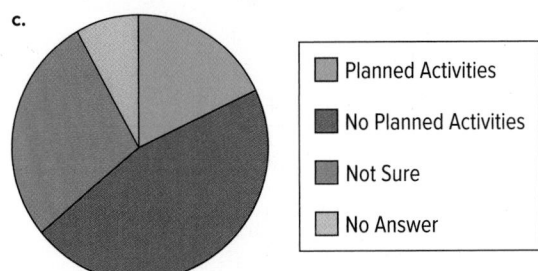

- Planned Activities
- No Planned Activities
- Not Sure
- No Answer

d. A pie chart would be better because it clearly shows that nearly half of the customers prefer no planned activities.

27. $2^6 = 64$ and $2^7 = 128$, suggest 7 classes

29. a. 5, because $2^4 = 16 < 25$ and $2^5 = 32 > 25$

b. $i \geq \dfrac{48 - 16}{5} = 6.4$ Use interval of 7.

c. 15

d.

Class		Frequency
15 up to 22	|||	3
22 up to 29	ⅧⅠ |||	8
29 up to 36	ⅧⅠ ||	7
36 up to 43	ⅧⅠ	5
43 up to 50	||	2
		25

e. Based on the frequency distribution the minutes to commute range between 15 and 50 minutes. The distribution shows that most common commute times are from 22 minutes up to 36 minutes. Commute times greater than 43 minutes are very infrequent.

31. a. $2^5 = 32$, $2^6 = 64$, 6 classes recommended.

b. $i = \dfrac{10 - 1}{6} = 1.5$ use an interval of 2.

c. 0

d.

Class	Frequency
0 up to 2	1
2 up to 4	5
4 up to 6	12
6 up to 8	17
8 up to 10	8
10 up to 12	2

e. The distribution is fairly symmetric or bell shaped with a mode in the middle of the two classes of 4 up to 8.

33. a. 4 because $2^3 = 12 < 15 < 16 = 2^4$. The interval width should be at least 11.75 as $i \geq (51 - 4)/4 = 11.75$. Round up and use 12 as the class interval.
Start the first interval at 4 because it is the minimum number of years.

Number of Calls	Frequency
4–15	5
16–27	3
28–39	6
40–51	1
Grand Total	**15**

b. The mode is the 28–39 class. There appears to be one outlier in the 40 up to 51 class.

35. a. 56

b. 10 (found by 60 − 50)

c. 55

d. 17

37. a. $2^5 = 32 < 33 < 64 = 2^6$. Thus 6 classes are recommended. The minimum class interval size would be $30.50 as $i \geq (265 - 82)/6$ thus an interval of 35 would work. Start the first class at 80, as 82 is the minimum value.

b.

Class	Frequency
$80 up to $115	6
115 up to 150	20
150 up to 185	10
185 up to 220	3
220 up to 255	4
255 up to 290	1
Total	44

c. Based on the frequency distribution the purchases ranged from a low of about $80 to a high of about $290. The highest frequency is in the $115 up to $150 class.

39. a.

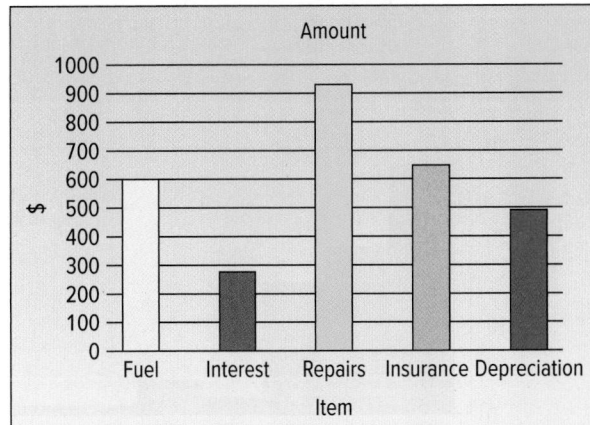

b. The data are qualitative and can be represented with either a bar chart or a pie chart. Bar charts are preferred when the goal is to compare the actual amount in each category.

c. Of the five classes, car owners spend the most on repairs, followed by insurance, fuel, depreciation, and loan interest.

41.

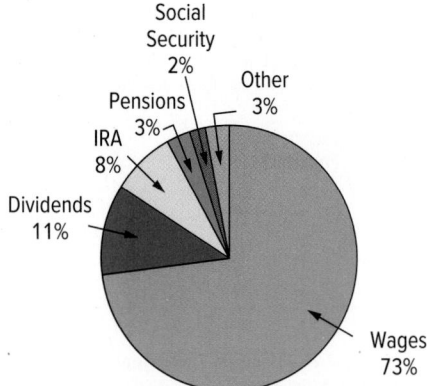

SC Income	Percent	Cumulative
Wages	73	73
Dividends	11	84
IRA	8	92
Pensions	3	95
Social Security	2	97
Other	3	100

By far the largest part of income in South Carolina is wages. Almost three-fourths of the adjusted gross income comes from wages. Dividends and IRAs each contribute roughly another 10%.

43. a. Since $2^6 = 64 < 70 < 128 = 2^7$, 7 classes are recommended. The interval should be at least $(1002.2 - 3.3)/7 = 142.7$; use 150 as a convenient value.

Class	Frequency
0 up to 150	28
150 up to 300	19
300 up to 450	15
450 up to 600	2
600 up to 750	4
750 up to 900	1
900 up to 1050	1
Grand Total	70

b.

c. Based on the histogram, the majority of people have less than $500,000 in their investment portfolio and may not have enough money for retirement. Merrill Lynch financial advisors need to promote the importance of investing for retirement in this age group.

45. a. Pie chart
b. 700, found by 0.7(1,000)
c. Yes, 0.70 + 0.20 = 0.90

47. a.

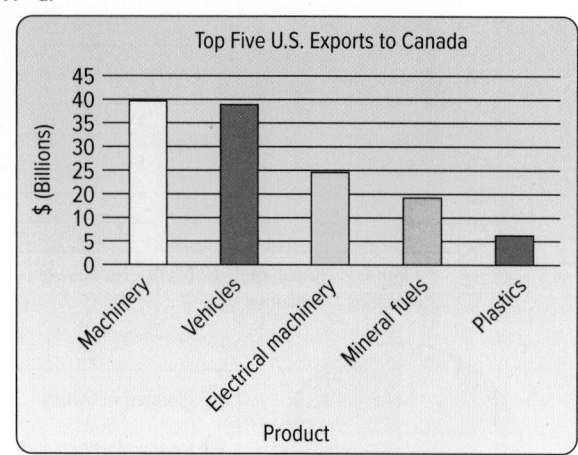

b.

Export	Percent of Total Exports
Machinery	15%
Vehicles	15%
Electrical machinery	9%
Mineral fuels	6%
Plastics	5%

c. Subtracting (15% + 15% + 9% + 6% + 5%) from 100%, all other exports account for 50% of the total exports to Canada.
d. For the total of $256.2 billion of exports, a pie chart shows the percentages for each class.

U.S. Product Exports to Canada

49.

M&Ms

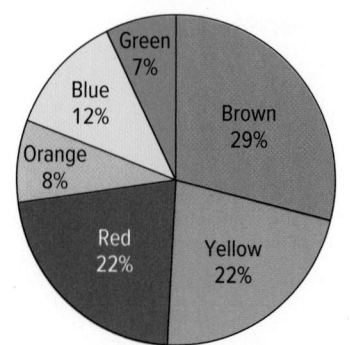

Brown, yellow, and red make up almost 75% of the candies. The other 25% is composed of blue, orange, and green.

51. There are many choices and possibilities here. For example you could choose to start the first class at 160,000 rather than 120,000. The choice is yours!
$i \geq (919,480 - 167,962)/7 = 107,360$. Use intervals of 120,000.

Selling Price (000)	Frequency	Cumulative Frequency
120 up to 240	26	26
240 up to 360	36	62
360 up to 480	27	89
480 up to 600	7	96
600 up to 720	4	100
720 up to 840	2	102
840 up to 960	1	105

a. Most homes (60%) sell between $240,000 and $480,000.

b. The typical price in the first class is $180,000 and in the last class it is $900,000

c.

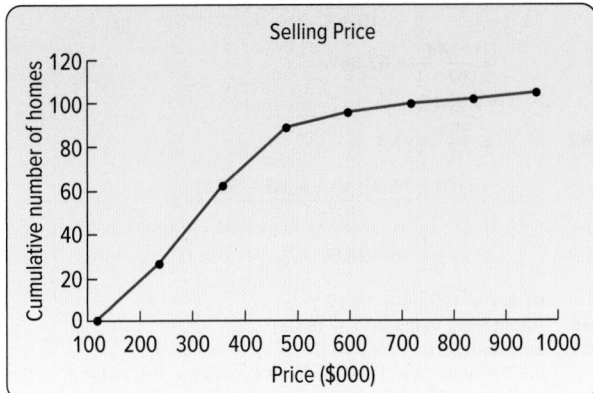

Fifty percent (about 52) of the homes sold for about $320,000 or less.
The top 10% (about 90) of homes sold for at least $520,000
About 41% (about 41) of the homes sold for less than $300,000.

d.

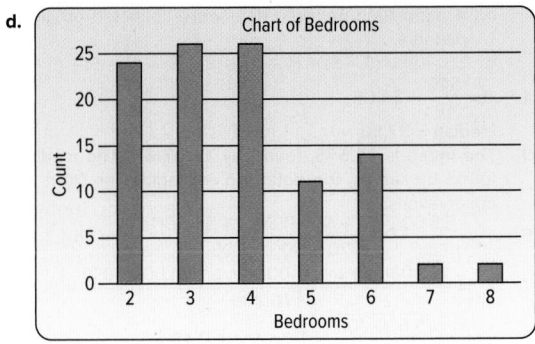

Two-, three-, and four-bedroom houses are most common with about 25 houses each. Seven- and eight-bedroom houses are rather rare.

53. Since $2^6 = 64 < 80 < 128 = 2^7$, use seven classes. The interval should be at least $(11,973 - 10,000)/7 = 281$ miles. Use 300. The resulting frequency distribution is:

Class	f
9,900 up to 10,200	8
10,200 up to 10,500	8
10,500 up to 10,800	11
10,800 up to 11,100	8
11,110 up to 11,400	13
11,400 up to 11,700	12
11,700 up to 12,000	20

a. The typical amount driven, or the middle of the distribution is about 11,100 miles. Based on the frequency distribution, the range is from 9,900 up to 12,000 miles.

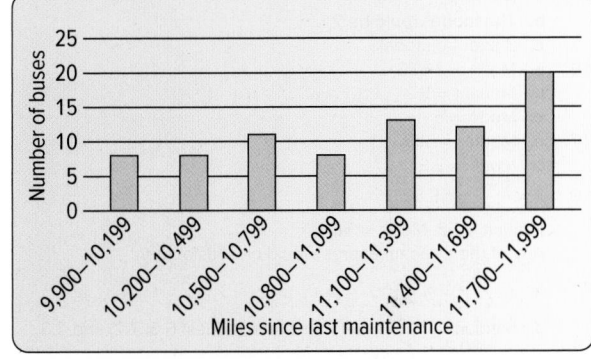

b. The distribution is somewhat "skewed" with a longer "tail" to the left and no outliers.

c.

Forty percent of the buses were driven fewer than about 10800 miles. About 30% of the 80 buses (about 24) were driven less than 10,500 miles.

d. The first diagram shows that Bluebird makes about 59% of the buses, Keiser about 31%, and Thompson only about 10%. The second chart shows that nearly 69% of the buses have 55 seats.

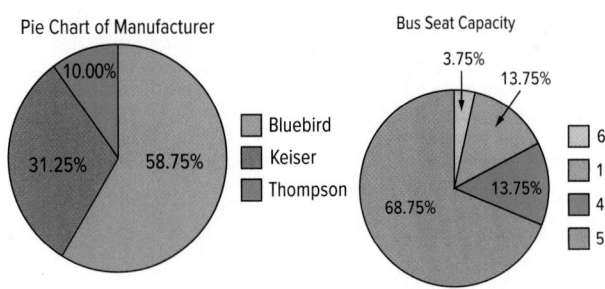

CHAPTER 3

1. $\mu = 5.4$, found by 27/5
3. **a.** $\bar{x} = 7.0$, found by 28/4
   b. $(5 - 7) + (9 - 7) + (4 - 7) + (10 - 7) = 0$
5. $\bar{x} = 14.58$, found by 43.74/3
7. **a.** 15.4, found by 154/10
   b. Population parameter, since it includes all the salespeople at Midtown Ford
9. **a.** $54.55, found by $1,091/20
   b. A sample statistic—assuming that the power company serves more than 20 customers
11. $\bar{x} = \dfrac{\Sigma x}{n}$ so
    $\Sigma x = \bar{x} \cdot n = (\$5{,}430)(30) = \$162{,}900$
13. **a.** No mode
    b. The mode would be 21.
    c. 3 and 4 bimodal
15. **a.** Mean = 3.583
    b. Median = 5
    c. Mode = 5
17. **a.** Median = 2.9
    b. Mode = 2.9
19. $\bar{x} = \dfrac{647}{11} = 58.82$
    Median = 58, Mode = 58
    Any of the three measures would be satisfactory.
21. **a.** $\bar{x} = \dfrac{85.9}{12} = 7.16$
    b. Median = 7.2. There are several modes: 6.6, 7.2, and 7.3.
    c. $\bar{x} = \dfrac{30.7}{4} = 7.675$,
       Median = 7.85
       About 0.5 percentage point higher in winter
23. 87.73, found by $\dfrac{300(\$65) + 400(\$90) + 400(\$80)}{300 + 400 + 400}$
25. $22.50, found by [50($12) + 50($20) + 100($29)]/200
27. 12.8%, found by $\sqrt[5]{(1.08)(1.12)(1.14)(1.26)(1.05)} = 1.128$
29. 12.28% increase, found by
    $\sqrt[5]{(1.094)(1.138)(1.117)(1.119)(1.147)} = 1.1228$
31. To achieve your investment goals, your investments would need to average an annual percent return of 16.59%.
    $GM = \sqrt[30]{\dfrac{1{,}000{,}000}{10{,}000}} - 1 = \sqrt[30]{100} - 1 = 1.1659 - 1 = 16.59\%$
33. 1.98% found by $\sqrt[10]{\dfrac{260.229}{213.967}} - 1$
35. **a.** 1.77% found by $\sqrt[10]{\dfrac{276.7}{232.2}} - 1$
    b. Using the 1.77% average annual increase,
    Number of 2021 users = (2020 users)(1 + 0.0177) = 276.7(1.0177) = 281.6
    Number of 2022 users = (2021 users)(1 + 0.0177) = 281.6(1.0177) = 289.6
37. **a.** 7, found by 10 − 3
    b. 6, found by 30/5
    c. 6.8, found by 34/5
    d. The difference between the highest number sold (10) and the smallest number sold (3) is 7. The typical squared deviation from 6 is 6.8.
39. **a.** 30, found by 54 − 24
    b. 38, found by 380/10
    c. 74.4, found by 744/10
    d. The difference between 54 and 24 is 30. The average of the squared deviations from 38 is 74.4.
41.

State	Mean	Median	Range
California	33.10	34.0	32
Iowa	24.50	25.0	19

The mean and median ratings were higher, but there was also more variation in California.
43. **a.** 5
    b. 4.4, found by
    $$\dfrac{(8 - 5)^2 + (3 - 5)^2 + (7 - 5)^2 + (3 - 5)^2 + (4 - 5)^2}{5}$$
45. **a.** $2.77
    b. 1.26, found by
    $$\dfrac{(2.68 - 2.77)^2 + (1.03 - 2.77)^2 + (2.26 - 2.77)^2}{5}$$
    $$\dfrac{+ (4.30 - 2.77)^2 + (3.58 - 277)^2}{5}$$
47. **a.** Range: 7.3, found by 11.6 − 4.3. Arithmetic mean: 6.94, found by 34.7/5. Variance: 6.5944, found by 32.972/5. Standard deviation: 2.568, found by $\sqrt{6.5944}$.
    b. Dennis has a higher mean return (11.76 > 6.94). However, Dennis has greater spread in its gross profits (16.89 > 6.59).
49. **a.** $\bar{x} = 4$
    $s^2 = \dfrac{(7 - 4)^2 + \cdots + (3 - 4)^2}{5 - 1} = \dfrac{22}{5 - 1} = 5.5$
    b. $s = 2.3452$
51. **a.** $\bar{x} = 38$
    $s^2 = \dfrac{(28 - 38)^2 + \cdots + (42 - 38)^2}{10 - 1}$
    $= \dfrac{744}{10 - 1} = 82.667$
    b. $s = 9.0921$
53. **a.** $\bar{x} = \dfrac{951}{10} = 95.1$
    $s^2 = \dfrac{(101 - 95.1)^2 + \cdots + (88 - 95.1)^2}{10 - 1}$
    $= \dfrac{1{,}112.9}{9} = 123.66$
    b. $s = \sqrt{123.66} = 11.12$
55. About 69%, found by $1 - 1/(1.8)^2$
57. **a.** About 95%
    b. The bell-shaped distribution is symmetric. $\bar{x} + 2s$ is half of the 95%, or 47.5%.
    The entire curve is 100%; the entire half above the mean is 50%. So, (50% − 47.5%) = 2.5% of the weights are more than $\bar{x} + 2s$.
59. **a.** Mean = 5, found by (6 + 4 + 3 + 7 + 5)/5.
    Median is 5, found by sorting the values (3, 4, 5, 6, 7) and selecting the middle value.
    b. A population because data were collected on all 5 senior partners.
    c. $\Sigma(x - \mu) = (6 - 5) + (4 - 5) + (3 - 5) + (7 - 5) + (5 - 5) = 0$
61. $\bar{x} = \dfrac{545}{16} = 34.06$
    Median = 37.50
63. The mean is 35.675, found by 1,427/40. The median is 36, found by sorting the data and averaging the 20th and 21st observations.
65. $\bar{x}_w = \dfrac{\$5.00(270) + \$6.50(300) + \$8.00(100)}{270 + 300 + 100} = \$6.12$
67. $\bar{x}_w = \dfrac{15{,}300(4.5) + 10{,}400(3.0) + 150{,}600(10.2)}{176{,}300} = 9.28$
69. $GM = \sqrt[54]{\dfrac{5{,}600{,}000}{42{,}000}} - 1$, so about 9.48%
71. **a.** 55, found by 72 − 17
    b. 17.6245, found by the square root of 2795.6/9
73. **a.** This is a population because it includes all the public universities in Ohio.
    b. The mean is 16,394.
    c. The median is 14,406 (University of Toledo).
    d. There is no mode for this data.

e. I would select the median because the mean is biased by a few schools (Ohio State, Cincinnati, Kent State, and Ohio University) that have extremely high enrollments compared to the other schools.
f. The range is $(46{,}984 - 3{,}304) = 43{,}680$.
g. The standard deviation is 11,039.45.

75. a. There were 13 flights, so all items are considered.
   b. $\mu = \dfrac{2{,}259}{13} = 173.77$
   c. Range $= 301 - 7 = 294$
   $$s = \sqrt{\dfrac{133{,}846}{13}} = 101.47$$

77. a. The mean is $717.20, found by $17,930/25. The median is $717.00 and there are two modes, $710 and $722.
   b. The range is $90, found by $771 − $681, and the standard deviation is $24.87, found by the square root of 14,850/24.
   c. From $667.46 up to $766.94, found by $717.20 ± 2($24.87)
   d. $\bar{x} = \dfrac{270}{30} = 9.0$

   $$s = \sqrt{\dfrac{366}{30 - 1}} = 3.552$$

   The mean and standard deviation from grouped data are estimates of the mean and standard deviations of the actual values.

79. a. 1. The mean team salary is $119.71 million, and the median is $123.50 million.
      Since the distribution is skewed, the median value of $123.50 million is more typical.
      2. The range is $199.5 million; found by $235.41 million −35.91 million. The standard deviation is $51.51 million. At least 95% of the team salaries are between $16.70 million and $222.72 million; found by $119.71 plus or minus 2($51.51).
   b. .435% per year, found by $\sqrt[21]{\dfrac{4{,}170{,}000}{1{,}990{,}000}} - 1 = 1.00435 = 0.435\%$

CHAPTER 4

1. In a histogram, observations are grouped so their individual identity is lost. With a dot plot, the identity of each observation is maintained.

3. a. Dot plot
   b. 15
   c. The minimum value is 1; the maximum value is 7. The range is $7 - 1 = 6$.
   d. The shape of the distribution is positively skewed with most of the data in the left of the distribution.
   e. A reasonable estimate is about 2 or 3.
   f. The mode of the distribution is 2. This value occurs most frequently at 5.
   g. The median is 3. There are 15 observations in the data set. Half of 15 is 7.5. So, in an ordered listing of the data, the median would be the 8th observation. Carefully counting from the left of the dot plot, the 8th value corresponds to a value of 3. 3 is the median because 50% of the values are less than 3; 50% of the values are more than 3.
   h. Starting at the left end of the distribution, and using the frequency for each value of employees, calculate the numerator as:
      a. $(2)(1) + (5)(2) + (4)(3) + (2)(4) + (1)(5) + (0)(6) + (1)(7)$
      b. The numerator is equal to 44.
      c. The denominator is equal to the sum of weights, or the frequency for each value. The sum is 15.

d. The mean is $44/15 = 2.93$.
i. The mode = 2; the median is 3; the mean is 2.93. The values are not equal. These results suggest that the distribution's shape is not symmetric.

5. Median = 53 found by (11 + 1)(1/2), therefore the 6th value in from lowest.
The median means that 50% of the 11 observed values are less than 53.
$Q_1 = 49$ found by (11 + 1)(1/4), therefore the 3rd value in from lowest.
The first quartile means that 25% of the 11 observed values are less than 49.
$Q_3 = 55$ found by (11 + 1)(3/4), therefore the 9th value in from lowest.
The third quartile means that 75% of the 11 observed values are less than 55.

7. a. $Q_1 = 33.25$ $Q_3 = 50.25$
      The first quartile means that 25% of the 30 observed values are less than 33.25.
      The third quartile means that 75% of the 30 observed values are less than 50.25.
   b. $D_2 = 27.8$ $D_8 = 52.6$
      The second decile means that 20% of the 30 observed values are less than 27.8.
      The eighth decile means that 80% of the 30 observed values are less than 52.6.
   c. $P_{67} = 47$. The 67th percentile means that 67% of the 30 observed values are less than 47.

9. a. 800
   b. $Q_1 = 500$, $Q_3 = 1{,}200$
   c. 700, found by $1{,}200 - 500$
   d. The upper outlier boundary is $1{,}200 + 1.5(700) = 1{,}200 + 1{,}050 = 2{,}250$.
   e. There are no outliers.
   f. The distribution is positively skewed.

11.

The distribution is somewhat positively skewed. Note that the dashed line above 35 is longer than below 18.

13. a. The mean is 30.8, found by 154/5. The median is 31.0, and the standard deviation is 3.96, found by

   $$s = \sqrt{\dfrac{62.8}{4}} = 3.96$$

   b. −0.15, found by $\dfrac{3(30.8 - 31.0)}{3.96}$

   c.

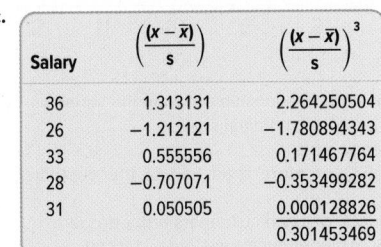

Salary	$\left(\dfrac{(x - \bar{x})}{s}\right)$	$\left(\dfrac{(x - \bar{x})}{s}\right)^3$
36	1.313131	2.264250504
26	−1.212121	−1.780894343
33	0.555556	0.171467764
28	−0.707071	−0.353499282
31	0.050505	0.000128826
		0.301453469

   0.125, found by $[5/(4 \times 3)] \times 0.301$

15. a. Note there are outliers in this data!
      The five-number summary is: minimum = 3.9; first quartile = 10.6; median = 15.8; third quartile = 22.3; maximum = 87.7.

The upper outlier boundary is $38.6 + 1.5(22.3 - 10.6) = 39.85$. The first value less than 39.85 in the data is 38.6.

b.

c. 0.868, found by $\dfrac{3(21.93 - 15.8)}{21.18}$

d. 2.444, found by $\left(\dfrac{15}{14 \cdot 13}\right)[29.658]$

e. Both measures of skewness indicate a positive skew. The boxplot also shows the positive skew with the longer upper whisker and the outliers.

17. The correlation coefficient is 0.86. Larger values of x are associated with larger values of y. The relationship is fairly strong.

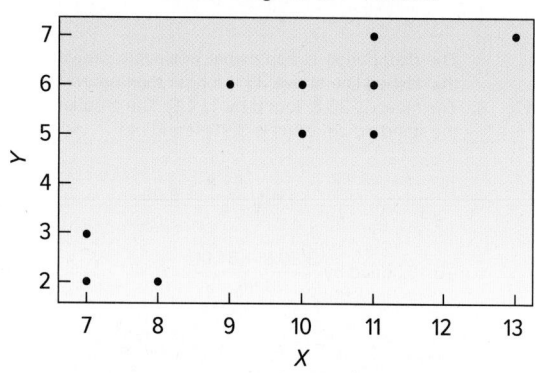

There is a positive relationship between the variables.
19. a. Both variables are nominal scale.
   b. Contingency table
   c. Yes, 58.5%, or more than half of the customer's order dessert.
      No, only 32% of lunch customers order dessert.
      Yes, 85% of dinner customers order dessert.
21. a. Dot plot
   b. 15
   c. 5

23. a. $L_{50} = (20 + 1)\dfrac{50}{100} = 10.50$

   $\text{Median} = \dfrac{83.7 + 85.6}{2} = 84.65$

   $L_{25} = (21)(.25) = 5.25$
   $Q_1 = 66.6 + .25(72.9 - 66.6) = 68.175$
   $L_{75} = 21(.75) = 15.75$
   $Q_3 = 87.1 + .75(90.2 - 87.1) = 89.425$

   b. $L_{26} = 21(.26) = 5.46$
   $P_{26} = 66.6 + .46(72.9 - 66.6) = 69.498$
   $L_{83} = 21(.83) = 17.43$
   $P_{83} = 93.3 + .43(98.6 - 93.3)$
   $\phantom{P_{83}} = 95.579$

   c.

25. a. $Q_1 = 26.25$, $Q_3 = 35.75$, Median = 31.50

   b. $Q_1 = 33.25$, $Q_3 = 38.75$, Median = 37.50

   c. The median time for public transportation is about 6 minutes less. There is more variation in public transportation. The difference between Q_1 and Q_3 is 9.5 minutes for public transportation and 5.5 minutes for private transportation.
27. The distribution is positively skewed. The first quartile is about $20 and the third quartile is about $90. There is one outlier located at $255. The median is about $50.
29. a.
   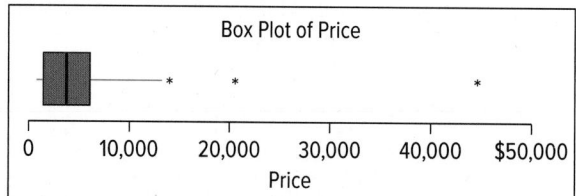

   Median is 3,733. First quartile is 1,478. Third quartile is 6,141. So prices over 13,135.5, found by $6{,}141 + 1.5 \times (6{,}141 - 1{,}478)$, are outliers. There are three (13,925; 20,413; and 44,312).
   b.
   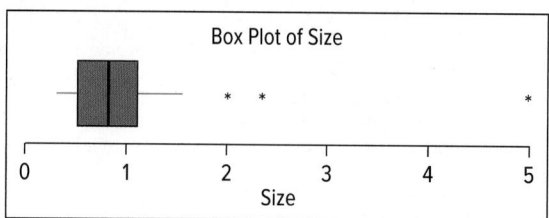

784

Median is 0.84. First quartile is 0.515. Third quartile is 1.12. So sizes over 2.0275, found by 1.12 + 1.5 (1.12 − 0.515), are outliers. There are three (2.03, 2.35, and 5.03).

c.

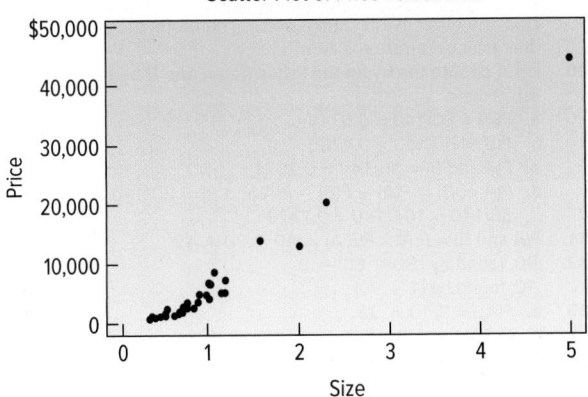

Scatter Plot of Price versus Size

There is a direct association between them. The first observation is larger on both scales.

d.

Shape/ Cut	Average	Good	Ideal	Premium	Ultra Ideal	All
Emerald	0	0	1	0	0	1
Marquise	0	2	0	1	0	3
Oval	0	0	0	1	0	1
Princess	1	0	2	2	0	5
Round	1	3	3	13	3	23
Total	2	5	6	17	3	33

The majority of the diamonds are round (23). Premium cut is most common (17). The Round Premium combination occurs most often (13).

31. $sk = 0.065$ or $sk = \dfrac{3(7.7143 − 8.0)}{3.9036} = −0.22$

33.

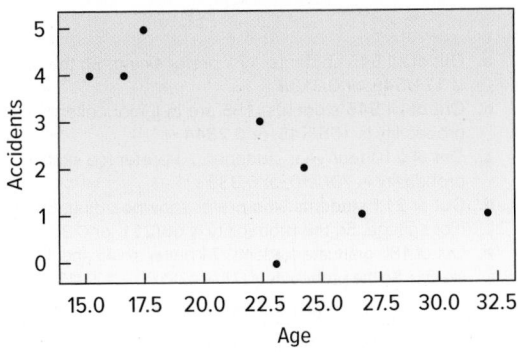

Scatter Plot of Accidents versus Age

As age increases, the number of accidents decreases.

35.
a. 139,340,000
b. 5.4% unemployed, found by (7,523/139,340)100
c. Men = 5.64%
   Women = 5.12%

37. a. Box-plot of age assuming the current year is 2021.

Distribution of stadium is highly positively skewed to the right. Any stadium older than 53.375 years (Q3 + 1.5(Q3 − Q1) = 31.25 + 1.5(31.25 − 16.5) is an outlier. There outliers are: Boston, Chicago Cubs, LA Dodgers, Oakland Athletics, and LA Angels.

b.

The first quartile is $78.95 million and the third is $168.32 million. Outliers are greater than Q3 + 1.5(Q3 − Q1) or 168.32 + 1.5*(168.32 − 78.95) = $302.38 million. The distribution is positively skewed. However, in 2021, there were no outliers.

c.

Wins versus. Salary

The correlation coefficient is 0.42. The relationship is generally positive, but the relationship is generally weak. Higher salaries are not strongly associated with more wins.

d.

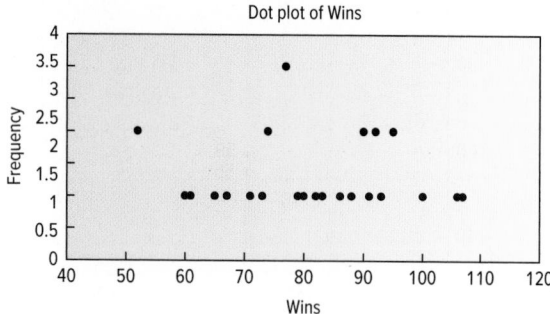

Dot plot of Wins

The dot plot shows a range of wins from the low 50s to the 100s. Most teams appear to win between 60 and 90 games in a season; 11 teams won 90 or more games; 2 teams won less than 60 games. That leaves 17 teams that won between 60 and 90 games.

CHAPTER 5

1. a. 78,960,960
   b. 840, found by (7)(6)(5)(4), that is 7!/3!
   c. 10, found by 5!/3!2!

3. a. 210 found by

$$_nC_r = \frac{n!}{r!(n-r)!} = \frac{10!}{4!(10-4)!} = (10)(9)(8)(7)/(4)(3)(2)$$

   b. 10 found by $_nC_r = \frac{n!}{r!(n-r)!} = \frac{10!}{1!(10-1)!} = \frac{10}{1} = 10.$

   Probability is 10/210 = 0.048

5. 120 found by 5!

7. (4)(8)(3) = 96 combinations.

9.

Outcome	Person 1	Person 2
1	A	A
2	A	F
3	F	A
4	F	F

The probability that both favor is ¼ = 0.25.
The probability that either favor is 2/4 = 0.50.

11. a. .176, found by $\frac{6}{34}$
   b. Empirical

13. a. Empirical
   b. Classical
   c. Classical
   d. Empirical, based on seismological data

15. a. The survey of 40 people about environmental issues
   b. 26 or more respond yes, for example.
   c. 10/40 = .25
   d. Empirical

17. a. Answers will vary. Here are some possibilities: 1236, 5124, 6125, 9999.
   b. $(1/10)^4$
   c. Classical

19. P(A or B) = P(A) + P(B) = .30 + .20 = .50
P(neither) = 1 − .50 = .50.

21. a. 102/200 = .51
   b. .49, found by 61/200 + 37/200 = .305 + .185. Special rule of addition.

23. P(above C) = .25 + .50 = .75

25. P(A or B) = P(A) + P(B) − P(A and B) = .20 + .30 − .15 = .35

27. When two events are mutually exclusive, it means that if one occurs, the other event cannot occur. Therefore, the probability of their joint occurrence is zero.

29. Let A denote the event the fish is green and B be the event the fish is male.
   a. P(A) = 80/140 = 0.5714
   b. P(B) = 60/140 = 0.4286
   c. P(A and B) = 36/140 = 0.2571
   d. P(A or B) = P(A) + P(B) − P(A and B) = 80/140 + 60/140 − 36/140 = 104/140 = 0.7429

31. P(A and B) = P(A) × P(B|A) = .40 × .30 = .12

33. .90, found by (.80 + .60) − .5
.10, found by (1 − .90)

35. a. $P(A_1) = 3/10 = .30$
   b. $P(B_1|A_2) = 1/3 = .33$
   c. $P(B_2 \text{ and } A_3) = 1/10 = .10$

37. a. A contingency table
   b. .27, found by 300/500 × 135/300
   c. The tree diagram would appear as:

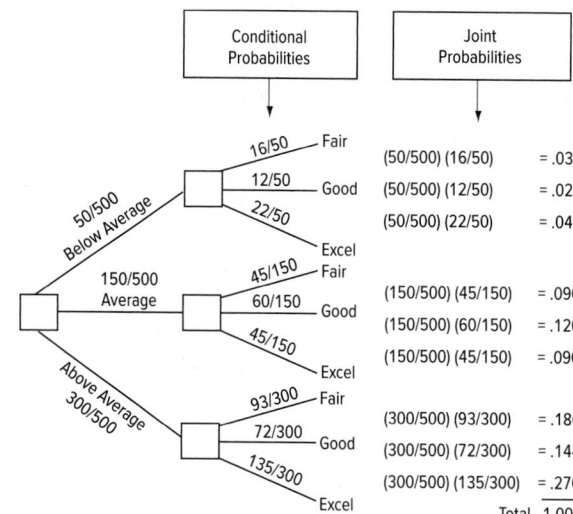

39. a. Out of all 545 students, 171 prefer skiing. So the probability is 171/545, or 0.3138.
   b. Out of all 545 students, 155 are in junior college. Thus, the probability is 155/545, or 0.2844.
   c. Out of 210 four-year students, 70 prefer ice skating. So the probability is 70/210, or 0.3333.
   d. Out of 211 students who prefer snowboarding, 68 are in junior college. So the probability is 68/211, or 0.3223.
   e. Out of 180 graduate students, 74 prefer skiing and 47 prefer ice skating. So the probability is (74 + 47)/180 = 121/180, or 0.6722.

41. $P(A_1|B_1) = \dfrac{P(A_1) \times P(B_1|A_1)}{P(A_1) \times P(B_1|A_1) + P(A_2) \times P(B_1|A_2)}$

$$= \frac{.60 \times .05}{(.60 \times .50) + (.40 \times .10)} = .4286$$

43. $P(\text{night}|\text{win}) = \dfrac{P(\text{night})P(\text{win}|\text{night})}{P(\text{night})P(\text{win}|\text{night}) + P(\text{day})P(\text{win}|\text{day})}$

$$= \frac{(.70)(.50)}{[(.70)(.50)] + [(.30)(.90)]} = .5645$$

45. $P(\text{cash} \mid > \$50)$

$$= \frac{P(\text{cash})\, P(> \$50 \mid \text{cash})}{[P(\text{cash})\, P(> \$50 \mid \text{cash})}$$
$$+ P(\text{credit})\, P(> \$50 \mid \text{credit})$$
$$+ P(\text{debit})\, P(> \$50 \mid \text{debit})]$$

$$= \frac{(.30)(.20)}{(0.30)(.20) + (.30)(.90) + (.40)(.60)} = .1053$$

47. a. Asking teenagers to compare their reactions to a newly developed soft drink.
   b. Answers will vary. One possibility is more than half of the respondents like it.
49. Subjective
51. a. 4/9, found by (2/3) · (2/3)
   b. 3/4, because (3/4) · (2/3) = 0.5
53. a. .8145, found by $(.95)^4$
   b. Special rule of multiplication
   c. $P(A \text{ and } B \text{ and } C \text{ and } D) = P(A) \times P(B) \times P(C) \times P(D)$
55. a. .08, found by .80 × .10
   b. No; 90% of females attended college, 78% of males
   c.

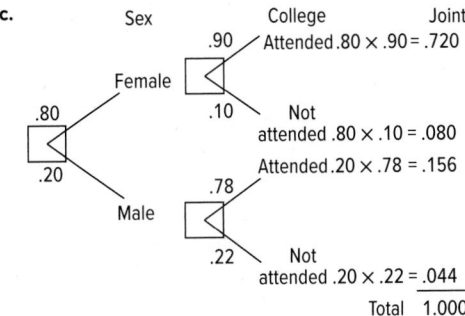

   d. Yes, because all the possible outcomes are shown on the tree diagram.
57. a. 0.57, found by 57/100
   b. 0.97, found by (57/100) + (40/100)
   c. Yes, because an employee cannot be both.
   d. 0.03, found by 1 − 0.97
59. a. 1/2, found by (2/3)(3/4)
   b. 1/12, found by (1/3)(1/4)
   c. 11/12, found by 1 − 1/12
61. a. 0.9039, found by $(0.98)^5$
   b. 0.0961, found by 1 − 0.9039
63. a. 0.0333, found by (4/10)(3/9)(2/8)
   b. 0.1667, found by (6/10)(5/9)(4/8)
   c. 0.8333, found by 1 − 0.1667
   d. Dependent
65. a. 0.3818, found by (9/12)(8/11)(7/10)
   b. 0.6182, found by 1 − 0.3818
67. a. $P(S) \cdot P(R \mid S) = .60(.85) = 0.51$
   b. $P(S) \cdot P(PR \mid S) = .60(1 - .85) = 0.09$
69. a. $P(\text{not perfect}) = P(\text{bad sector}) + P(\text{defective})$

$$= \frac{112}{1,000} + \frac{31}{1,000} = .143$$

   b. $P(\text{defective} \mid \text{not perfect}) = \dfrac{.031}{.143} = .217$

71. $P(\text{poor} \mid \text{profit}) = \dfrac{.10(.20)}{.10(.20) + .60(.80) + .30(.60)} = 0.294$

73. a. 0.1 + 0.02 = 0.12
   b. 1 − 0.12 = 0.88
   c. $(0.88)^3 = 0.6815$
   d. 1 − .6815 = 0.3185

75. Yes, 256 is found by 2^8
77. .9744, found by $1 - (.40)^4$
79. a. 0.193, found by .15 + .05 − .0075 = .193
   b. .0075, found by (.15)(.05)
81. a. $P(F \text{ and } > 60) = .25$, found by solving with the general rule of multiplication: $P(F) \cdot P(>60 \mid F) = (.5)(.5)$
   b. 0
   c. .3333, found by 1/3
83. $26^4 = 456,976$
85. 1/3, 628,800
87. a. $P(D) = .20(.03) + .30(.04) + .25(.07) + .25(.065) = .05175$
   b. $P(\text{Tyson} \mid \text{defective}) = \dfrac{.20(.30)}{[.20(.30) + .30(.04)} = .1159$
$$+ .25(.07) + .25(.065)]$$

Supplier	Joint	Revised
Tyson	.00600	.1159
Fuji	.01200	.2319
Kirkpatricks	.01750	.3382
Parts	.01625	.3140
	.05175	1.0000

89. 0.512, found by $(0.8)^3$
91. .525, found by $1 - (.78)^3$
93. a.

Wins	# Teams
50–59	2
60–69	4
70–79	8
80–89	5
90–99	8
100–109	3
Grand Total	**30**

   1. 11/30 = 0.37
   2. 10/11 = 0.91
   3. Winning 90 or more games in a season does not guarantee a place in the end-of-season playoffs.

   b.

	League		
Home runs	American	National	Grand Total
120–149	0	2	2
150–179	3	2	5
180–209	5	7	12
210–239	5	4	9
240–269	2	0	2
Grand Total	15	15	30

   1. In the American League, the probability that a team hits 180 or more homeruns is 0.80.
   2. In the National League, the probability that a team hits 180 or more homeruns is 0.73.
   3. There is clear difference in the distribution of homeruns between the American and National Leagues. There are many potential reasons for the difference. One of the reasons may be the use of a designated hitter.

CHAPTER 6

1. a. The values of the random variable are 0, 1, 2, and 3.
   b. Mean = 1.3

c. Standard deviation = 0.90 = $\sigma = \sqrt{\text{variance}} = \sqrt{.81}$
Variance = 0.81 found by:

$\mu = \Sigma XP(X) = 0(.20) + 1(.40) + 2(.30) + 3(.10) = 1.3$

$\sigma^2 = \Sigma(X - \mu)^2 P(X)$

$= (0 - 1.3)^2(0.2) + (1 - 1.3)^2(0.4) + (2 - 1.3)^2(0.3) + (3 - 1.3)^2(0.1)$

$= 0.81$

    d. $P(x > 1) = P(x = 2) + P(x = 3) = 0.3 + 0.1 = 0.4$

    e. $P(x \geq 0) = 1 - P(x = 0) = 1 - 0.2 = 0.8$

3. **a.** The values of the random variable are 5, 10, 15, and 20.

    b. $\mu = 14.5$, $5(.1) + 10(.3) + 15(.2) + 20(.4) = 14.5$

    c. Standard deviation = $5.2202 = \sigma = \sqrt{\text{variance}} = \sqrt{27.25}$

    $\sigma^2 = (5 - 14.5)^2(.1) + (10 - 14.5)^2(.3) + (15 - 14.5)^2(.2) +$
    $(20 - 14.5)^2(.4) = 27.25$

    d. $P(x \neq 5) = P(x = 10) + P(x = 15) + P(x = 20) = 0.3 + 0.2 + 0.4$
    $= 0.9$

    e. $P(x \leq 15) = P(x = 15) + P(x = 10) + P(x = 5) = 0.2 + 0.3 + 0.1$
    $= 0.6$

5. **a.**

Calls, x	Frequency	P(x)	xP(x)	$(x - \mu)^2 P(x)$
0	8	.16	0	.4624
1	10	.20	.20	.0980
2	22	.44	.88	.0396
3	9	.18	.54	.3042
4	1	.02	.08	.1058
	50		1.70	1.0100

    b. Discrete distribution, because only certain outcomes are possible.

    c. 0.20 found by $P(x = 3) + P(x = 4) = 0.18 + 0.02 = 0.20$

    d. $\mu = \Sigma x \cdot P(x) = 1.70$

    e. $\sigma = \sqrt{1.01} = 1.005$

7.

Amount	P(x)	xP(x)	$(x - \mu)^2 P(x)$
10	.50	5	60.50
25	.40	10	6.40
50	.08	4	67.28
100	.02	2	124.82
		21	259.00

    a. 0.10 found by $P(x = 50) + P(x = 100) = 0.08 + 0.02 = 0.10$

    b. $\mu = \Sigma xP(x) = 21$

    c. $\sigma^2 = \Sigma(x - \mu)^2 P(x) = 259$

    $\sigma = \sqrt{259} = 16.093$

9. Using the binomial table, Excel, or the binomial formula:

x	P(x)
0	0.4096
1	0.4096
2	0.1536
3	0.0256
4	0.0016

Using the binomial formula with $x = 2$ as an example:

$P(2) = \dfrac{4!}{2!(4 - 2)!}(.2)^2(.8)^{4-2} = 0.1536$

11. **a.**

x	P(x)
0	.064
1	.288
2	.432
3	.216

    b. $\mu = 1.8$

    $\Sigma^2 = 0.72$

    $\Sigma = \sqrt{0.72} = .8485$

13. **a.** .2668, found by $P(2) = \dfrac{9!}{(9 - 2)!2!}(.3)^2(.7)^7$

    b. .1715, found by $P(4) = \dfrac{9!}{(9 - 4)!4!}(.3)^4(.7)^5$

    c. .0404, found by $P(0) = \dfrac{9!}{(9 - 0)!0!}(.3)^0(.7)^9$

15. **a.** .2824, found by $P(0) = \dfrac{12!}{(12 - 0)!0!}(.1)^0(.9)^{12}$

    b. .3766, found by $P(1) = \dfrac{12!}{(12 - 1)!1!}(.1)^1(.9)^{11}$

    c. .2301, found by $P(2) = \dfrac{12!}{(12 - 2)!2!}(.1)^2(.9)^{10}$

    d. $\mu = 1.2$, found by 12(.1)

    $\sigma = 1.0392$, found by $\sqrt{1.08}$

17. **a.** The random variable is the count of the 15 accountants who have a CPA. The random variable follows a binomial probability distribution. The random variable meets all 4 criteria for a binomial distributor: (1) Fixed number of trials (15), (2) each trial results in a success or failure (the accountant has a CPA or not), (3) known probability of success (0.52), and (4) each trial is independent of any other selection.

    b. Using the binomial table, Excel, or the binomial formula, the probability distribution follows. $P(5$ of the 15 accountants with a CPA) = 0.0741.

x	P(x)	x	P(x)
0	0.0000	8	Q.2020
1	0.0003	9	0.1702
2	0.0020	10	0.1106
3	0.0096	11	0,0545
4	0.0311	12	0.0197
5	0.0741	13	0.0049
6	0.1338	14	0.0008
7	0.1864	15	0.0001

    c. 0.3884 found by $P(x = 7) + P(x = 8)$

    d. Mean $= n\pi = (15)(.52) = 7.8$ accountants

    e. Variance $= n\pi(1 - \pi) = (15)(.52)(.48) = 3.744$

19. **a.** 0.296, found by using Appendix B.1 with n of 8, π of 0.30, and x of 2

    b. $P(x \leq 2) = 0.058 + 0.198 + 0.296 = 0.552$

    c. 0.448, found by $P(x \geq 3) = 1 - P(x \leq 2) = 1 - 0.552$

21. **a.** 0.387, found from Appendix B.1 with n of 9, π of 0.90, and x of 9

    b. $P(x < 5) = 0.001$

    c. 0.992, found by $1 - 0.008$

    d. 0.947, found by $1 - 0.053$

23. **a.** $\mu = 10.5$, found by 15(0.7) and $\sigma = \sqrt{15(0.7)(0.3)} = 1.7748$

    b. 0.2061, found by $\dfrac{15!}{10!5!}(0.7)^{10}(0.3)^5$

    c. 0.4247, found by $0.2061 + 0.2186$

    d. 0.5154, found by $0.2186 + 0.1700 + 0.0916 + 0.0305 + 0.0047$

25. **a.** Given $N = 12$, 7 boys and 5 girls.

    $P(3 \text{ boys on a team of } 5) = \dfrac{(_7C_3)(_5C_2)}{(_{12}C_5)} = .4419$

    OR

    $P(2 \text{ girls on a team of } 5) = \dfrac{(_5C_2)(_7C_3)}{(_{12}C_5)} = .4419$

b. $P(5 \text{ boys on a team of } 5) = \dfrac{(_7C_5)(_5C_0)}{(_{12}C_5)} = 0.027$

c. Using the complement rule: $P(1 \text{ or more girls}) = 1 - P(0 \text{ girls}$ on a team of 5)

$$= 1 - \dfrac{(_5C_0)(_7C_5)}{(_{12}C_5)} = 1 - 0.027 = 0.973$$

27. N is 10, the number of loans in the population; S is 3, the number of underwater loans in the population; x is 0, the number of selected underwater loans in the sample; and n is 2, the size of the sample. Use formula (6–6) to find

$$P(0) = \dfrac{(_7C_2)(_3C_0)}{_{10}C_2} = \dfrac{21(1)}{45} = 0.4667$$

29. $P(2) = \dfrac{[_9C_3][_6C_2]}{[_{12}C_5]} = \dfrac{84(15)}{3003} = .4196$

31. a. .6703
b. .3297

33. a. .0613
b. .0803

35. $\mu = 6$
$P(x \geq 5) = 1 - (.0025 + .0149 + .0446 + .0892 + .1339) = .7149$

37. A random variable is an outcome that results from a chance experiment. A probability distribution also includes the likelihood of each possible outcome.

39. $\mu = \$1{,}000(.25) + \$2{,}000(.60) + \$5{,}000(.15) = \$2{,}200$
$\sigma^2 = (1{,}000 - 2{,}200)^2 .25 + (2{,}000 - 2{,}200)^2 .60 +$
$\qquad (5{,}000 - 2{,}200)^2 .15$
$\qquad = 1{,}560{,}000$

41. $\mu = 12(.25) + \cdots + 15(.1) = 13.2$
$\sigma^2 = (12 - 13.2)^2 .25 + \cdots + (15 - 13.2)^2 .10 = 0.86$
$\sigma = \sqrt{0.86} = .927$

43. a. $5 \cdot 10(.35) = 3.5$
b. $P(x = 4) = {}_{10}C_4(.35)^4(.65)^6 = 210(.0150)(.0754) = .2375$
c. $P(x \geq 4) = {}_{10}C_x(.35)^x(.65)^{10-x}$
$\qquad = 2375 + .1536 + \cdots + .0000 = .4862$

45. a. 6, found by 0.4×15
b. 0.0245, found by $\dfrac{15!}{10!5!}(0.4)^{10}(0.6)^5$
c. 0.0338, found by
$0.0245 + 0.0074 + 0.0016 + 0.0003 + 0.0000$
d. 0.0093, found by $0.0338 - 0.0245$

47. a. $\mu = 20(0.075) = 1.5$
$\sigma = \sqrt{20(0.075)(0.925)} = 1.1779$
b. 0.2103, found by $\dfrac{20!}{0!20!}(0.075)^0(0.925)^{20}$
c. 0.7897, found by $1 - 0.2103$

49. a. 0.2285, found by $\dfrac{16!}{3!13!}(0.15)^3(0.85)^{13}$
b. 2.4, found by $(0.15)(16)$
c. 0.79, found by $.0743 + .2097 + .2775 + .2285$

51. 0.2784, found by $0.1472 + 0.0811 + 0.0348 + 0.0116 + 0.0030 + 0.0006 + 0.0001 + 0.0000$

53. a.

0	0.0002	7	0.2075
1	0.0019	8	0.1405
2	0.0116	9	0.0676
3	0.0418	10	0.0220
4	0.1020	11	0.0043
5	0.1768	12	0.0004
6	0.2234		

b. $\mu = 12(0.52) = 6.24 \quad \sigma = \sqrt{12(0.52)(0.48)} = 1.7307$
c. 0.1768
d. 0.3343, found by
$0.0002 + 0.0019 + 0.0116 + 0.0418 + 0.1020 + 0.1768$

55. a. $P(1) = \dfrac{[_7C_2][_3C_1]}{[_{10}C_3]} = \dfrac{(21)(3)}{120} = .5250$
b. $P(0) = \dfrac{[_7C_3][_3C_0]}{[_{10}C_3]} = \dfrac{(35)(1)}{120} = .2917$
$P(x \geq 1) = 1 - P(0) = 1 - .2917 = .7083$

57. $P(x = 0) = \dfrac{[_8C_4][_4C_0]}{[_{12}C_4]} = \dfrac{70}{495} = .141$

59. a. .0498
b. .7746, found by $(1 - .0498)^5$

61. a. .0183
b. .1954
c. .6289
d. .5665

63. a. 0.1733, found by $\dfrac{(3.1)^4 e^{-3.1}}{4!}$
b. 0.0450, found by $\dfrac{(3.1)^0 e^{-3.1}}{0!}$
c. 0.9550, found by $1 - 0.0450$

65. $\mu = n\pi = 20(1/276) = 0.0725$
$P(0) = \dfrac{0.0725^0 e^{-0.0725}}{0!} = 0.930$
$P(1) = \dfrac{0.0725^1 e^{-0.0725}}{1!} = 0.067$
$P(x > 0) = 1 - P(x = 0) = 1 - 0.930 = 0.070$

67. Let $\mu = n\pi = 155(1/3{,}709) = 0.042$
$P(4) = \dfrac{0.042^4 e^{-0.042}}{4!} = 0.00000012 \qquad$ Very unlikely!

69. a. Using the entire binomial probability distribution, with a probability of success equal to 30% and number of trials equal to 40, there is an 80% chance of leasing 10 or more cars. Note that the expected value or number of cars sold with probability of success equal to 30% and trials equal to 40 is: $n\pi = (40)$ $(0.30) = 12$.
b. Of the 40 vehicles that Zook Motors sold only 10, or 25%, were leased. So Zook's probability of success (leasing a car) is 25%. Using .25 as the probability of success, Zook's probability of leasing 10 or more vehicles in 40 trials is only 56%. The data indicates that Zoot leases vehicles at a lower rate than the national average.

71. The mean number of home runs per game is 2.4461. The average season home runs per team is 198.133. Then $198.133/162 \times 2 = 2.4461$.
a. $P(x = 0) = \dfrac{\mu^0 e^{-2.4461}}{0!} = .0865$
b. $P(x = 2) = \dfrac{\mu^2 e^{-2.4461}}{2!} = .2591$
c. $P(X \geq 4) = 0.2313$, found by $1 - P(X < 4) = 1 - (.0865 + .2117 + .2591 + .2114) = 1 - .7687 = .2313$

CHAPTER 7

1. a. $b = 10, a = 6$ **b.** $\mu = \dfrac{6 + 10}{2} = 8$
c. $\sigma = \sqrt{\dfrac{(10 - 6)^2}{12}} = 1.1547$
d. Area $= \dfrac{1}{(10 - 6)} \cdot \dfrac{(10 - 6)}{1} = 1$

e. $P(x > 7) = \dfrac{1}{(10-6)} \cdot \dfrac{10-7}{1} = \dfrac{3}{4} = .75$

f. $P(7 \le x \le 9) = \dfrac{1}{(10-6)} \cdot \dfrac{(9-7)}{1} = \dfrac{2}{4} = .50$

g. P (x = 7.91) = 0.
For a continuous probability distribution, the area for a point value is zero.

3. a. 0.30, found by (30 − 27)/(30 − 20)
  b. 0.40, found by (24 − 20)/(30 − 20)

5. a. $a = 0.5, b = 3.00$
  b. $\mu = \dfrac{0.5 + 3.00}{2} = 1.75$

    $\sigma = \sqrt{\dfrac{(3.00 - .50)^2}{12}} = .72$

  c. $P(x < 1) = \dfrac{1}{(3.0 - 0.5)} \cdot \dfrac{1 - .5}{1} = \dfrac{.5}{2.5} = 0.2$

  d. 0, found by $\dfrac{1}{(3.0 - 0.5)} \dfrac{(1.0 - 1.0)}{1}$

  e. $P(x > 1.5) = \dfrac{1}{(3.0 - 0.5)} \cdot \dfrac{3.0 - 1.5}{1} = \dfrac{1.5}{2.5} = 0.6$

7. a. 1.25, found by $z = \dfrac{25 - 20}{4.0} = 1.25$
  b. 0.3944, found in Appendix B.3
  c. 0.3085, found by $z = \dfrac{18 - 20}{4.0} = -0.5$
    Find 0.1915 in Appendix B.3 for $z = -0.5$, then 0.5000 − 0.1915 = 0.3085.

9. a. .2123, found by $z = \dfrac{35.00 - 29.81}{9.31} = 0.56$
    Then find .2123 in Appendix B.3 for a $z = 0.56$.
  b. .2877, found by 0.5000 − .2123 = 0.2869
  c. 0.1469, found by $z = \dfrac{20.00 - 29.81}{9.31} = -1.05$
    For a $z = -1.05$, find 0.3531 in Appendix B.3, then 0.5000 − 0.3531 = 0.1469.

11. a. 0.8276: First find $z = -1.5$, found by (44 − 50)/4 and $z = 1.25 = (55 - 50)/4$. The area between −1.5 and 0 is 0.4332 and the area between 0 and 1.25 is 0.3944, both from Appendix B.3. Then adding the two areas we find that 0.4332 + 0.3944 = 0.8276.
  b. 0.1056, found by 0.5000 − .3944, where $z = 1.25$
  c. 0.2029: Recall that the area for $z = 1.25$ is 0.3944, and the area for $z = 0.5$, found by (52 − 50)/4, is 0.1915. Then subtract 0.3944 − 0.1915 and find 0.2029.

13. a. 0.1151: Begin by using formula (7−5) to find the z-value for $3,500, which is (3,500 − 3,401)/82.5, or 1.20. Then see Appendix B.3 to find the area between 0 and 1.20, which is 0.3849.
    Finally, since the area of interest is beyond 1.20, subtract that probability from 0.5000. The result is 0.5000 − 0.3849, or 0.1151.
  b. 0.0997: Use formula (7−5) to find the z-value for $3,579, which is (3,579 − 3,401)/82.5 or 2.16. Then see Appendix B.3 for the area under the standard normal curve. That probability is 0.4846. Since the two points (1.20 and 2.16) are on the same side of the mean, subtract the smaller probability from the larger. The result is 0.4846 − 0.3849 = 0.0997.
  c. 0.8058: Use formula (7−5) to find the z-value for $3,325, which is − 0.92, found by (3,325 − 3,401)/82.5. The corresponding area is 0.3212. Since − 0.92 and 2.16 are on different sides of the mean, add the corresponding probabilities. Thus, we find 0.3212 + 0. 4846 = 0.8058.

15. a. 0.0764, found by $z = (20 - 15)/3.5 = 1.43$, then 0.5000 − 0.4236 = 0.0764
  b. 0.9236, found by 0.5000 + 0.4236, where $z = 1.43$
  c. 0.1185, found by $z = (12 - 15)/3.5 = -0.86$.

The area under the curve is 0.3051, then $z = (10 - 15)/3.5 = -1.43$. The area is 0.4236. Finally, 0.4236 − 0.3051 = 0.1185.

17. $x = 56.60$, found by adding 0.5000 (the area left of the mean) and then finding a z-value that forces 45% of the data to fall inside the curve. Solving for x: 1.65 = (x − 50)/4, so x = 56.60.

19. $1,630, found by $2,100 − 1.88($250)

21. a. 214.8 hours: Find a z-value where 0.4900 of area is between 0 and z. That value is z = 2.33. Then solve for x: 2.33 = (x − 195)/8.5, so x = 214.8 hours.
  b. 270.2 hours: Find a z-value where 0.4900 of area is between 0 and (−z). That value is z = −2.33. Then solve for x: −2.33 = (x − 290)/8.5, so x = 270.2 hours.

23. 41.7%, found by 12 + 1.65(18)

25. The actual shape of a normal distribution depends on its mean and standard deviation. Thus, there is a normal distribution, and an accompanying normal curve, for a mean of 7 and a standard deviation of 2. There is another normal curve for a mean of $25,000 and a standard deviation of $1,742, and so on.

27. a. 490 and 510, found by 500 ± 1(10)
  b. 480 and 520, found by 500 ± 2(10)
  c. 470 and 530, found by 500 ± 3(10)

29. $z_{Rob} = \dfrac{\$70{,}000 - \$80{,}000}{\$5{,}000} = -2$

    $z_{Rachel} = \dfrac{\$70{,}000 - \$55{,}000}{\$8{,}000} = 1.875$

Adjusting for their industries, Rob is well below average and Rachel well above.

31. a. 0.3935, found by $1 - e^{[(-1/60)(30)]}$
  b. 0.1353, found by $e^{[(-1/60)(120)]}$
  c. 0.1859, found by $e^{[(-1/60)(45)]} - e^{[(-1/60)(75)]}$
  d. 41.59 seconds, found by $-60 \ln(0.5)$

33. a. 0.3836, found by $1 - e^{(-1/31)(15)}$ and 0.1243, found by $1 - e^{(-1/113)(15)}$
  b. 0.0208, found by $e^{(-1/31)(120)}$ and 0.3458, found by $e^{(-1/113)(120)}$
  c. 0.3252 found by $e^{(-1/31)(30)} - e^{(-1/113)(90)} = .3800 - .0548$ and 0.3159, found by $e^{(-1/113)(30)} - e^{(-1/113)(90)} = .7668 - .4509$
  d. 6.92 minutes, found by $-31 \ln(0.8)$ and 25.22 minutes, found by $-113 \ln(0.8)$

35. a. 0. For a continuous probability distribution, there is no area for a point value.
  b. 0. For a continuous probability distribution, there is no area for a point value.

37. a. $\mu = \dfrac{11.96 + 12.05}{2} = 12.005$
  b. $\sigma = \sqrt{\dfrac{(12.05 - 11.96)^2}{12}} = .0260$
  c. $P(x < 12) = \dfrac{1}{(12.05 - 11.96)} \dfrac{12.00 - 11.96}{1} = \dfrac{.04}{.09} = .44$
  d. $P(x > 11.98) = \dfrac{1}{(12.05 - 11.96)} \left(\dfrac{12.05 - 11.98}{1} \right)$
    $= \dfrac{.07}{.09} = .78$
  e. All cans have more than 11.00 ounces, so the probability is 100%.

39. a. $\mu = \dfrac{4 + 10}{2} = 7$
  b. $\sigma = \sqrt{\dfrac{(10 - 4)^2}{12}} = 1.732$
  c. $P(x < 6) = \dfrac{1}{(10 - 4)} \times \left(\dfrac{6 - 4}{1} \right) = \dfrac{2}{6} = .33$
  d. $P(x > 5) = \dfrac{1}{(10 - 4)} \times \left(\dfrac{10 - 5}{1} \right) = \dfrac{5}{6} = .83$

41. Based on the friend's information, the probability that the wait time is any value more than 30 minutes is zero. Given the data (wait time was 35 minutes), the friend's information should be rejected. It was false.

43. a. 0.4222, z for 900 is: $\dfrac{1200 - 1{,}370.10}{120} = -1.42$. Using the z-table, probability is .4222.

b. 0.0778, found by 0.5000 − 0.4222 [0.4222 found in part (a)]

c. 0.7821; z for 1200 is: $\dfrac{1200 - 1{,}370.1}{120} = -1.42$, z for 1,500 is: $\dfrac{1{,}500 - 1{,}370.1}{120} = 1.08$.

Adding the two corresponding probabilities 0.4222 + 0.3599 = .7821

d. 0.2032; z for 1200 is: $\dfrac{1200 - 1{,}370.1}{120} = -1.42$, z for 1300 is: $\dfrac{1{,}300 - 1{,}370.1}{120} = -0.58$.

Subtracting the two corresponding probabilities, 0.4222 − 0.2190 = .2032.

45. a. 0.3015, found by 0.5000 − 0.1985

b. 0.2579, found by 0.4564 − 0.1985

c. 0.0011, found by 0.5000 − 0.4989

d. 1,818, found by 1,280 + 1.28(420)

47. a. 0.0968, z for 300 is: $\dfrac{300 - 270}{23} = 1.30$. Using the z-table, probability is .4032. Subtracting from 0.5, 0.5000 − 0.4032 = 0.0968.

b. 0.9850, z for 220 is: $\dfrac{220 - 270}{23} = -2.17$. Using the z-table, probability is .4850. Adding 0.5, 0.5000 + 0.4850 = 0.9850.

c. 0.8882; Using the results from parts (a) and (b), the z for 220 is − 2.17 with a probability of .4850; the z for 300 is 1.30 with a probability of 0.4032. Adding the two probabilities, (0.4032 + 0.4850) = 0.8882.

d. 293.92 2x; The z-score for the upper 15% of the distribution is 1.04. So the time associated with the upper 15% is 1.04 standard deviations added to the mean, or 270 + 1.04 (23) = 293.92 minutes.

49. About 4,099 units, found by solving for x. 1.65 = $(x − 4{,}000)/60$

51. a. 15.39%, found by (8 − 10.3)/2.25 = −1.02, then 0.5000 − 0.3461 = 0.1539.

b. 17.31%, found by:

z = (12 − 10.3)/2.25 = 0.76. Area is 0.2764.

z = (14 − 10.3)/2.25 = 1.64. Area is 0.4495.

The area between 12 and 14 is 0.1731, found by 0.4495 − 0.2764.

c. The probability is virtually zero. Applying the Empirical Rule, for 99.73% of the days, returns are between 3.55 and 17.05, found by 10.3 ± 3(2.25). Thus, the chance of less than 3.55 returns is rather remote.

53. a. 21.19%, found by z = (9.00 − 9.20)/0.25 = −0.80, so 0.5000 − 0.2881 = 0.2119.

b. Increase the mean. z = (9.00 − 9.25)/0.25 = −1.00, P = 0.5000 − 0.3413 = 0.1587.

Reduce the standard deviation. σ = (9.00 − 9.20)/0.15 = −1.33; P = 0.5000 − 0.4082 = 0.0918.

Reducing the standard deviation is better because a smaller percent of the hams will be below the limit.

55. The z-score associated with $50,000 is 8.25: (50,000 − 33,500)/2000. That is, $50,000 is 8.25 standard deviations above the mean salary. Conclusion: The probability that someone in the same business has a salary of $50,000 is zero. This salary would be exceptionally unusual.

57. a. 0.4262, found by $1 - e^{[(-1/27)(15)]}$

b. 0.1084, found by $e^{[(-1/27)(60)]}$

c. 0.1403, found by $e^{[(-1/27)(30)]} - e^{[(-1/27)(45)]}$

d. 2.84 secs, found by −27 ln(0.9)

59. a. 0.2835, found by $1 - e^{[(-1/300{,}000)(100{,}000)]}$

b. 0.1889, found by $e^{[(-1/300{,}000)(500{,}000)]}$

c. 0.2020, found by $e^{[(-1/300{,}000)(200{,}000)]} - e^{[(-1/300{,}000)(350{,}000)]}$

d. Both the mean and standard deviation are 300,000 hours.

61. a.

Team Salary ($Millions)	
Mean	119.71
Median	123.50
Population standard deviation	51.51
Skewness	0.16
Range	199.51
Minimum	35.91
Maximum	235.41

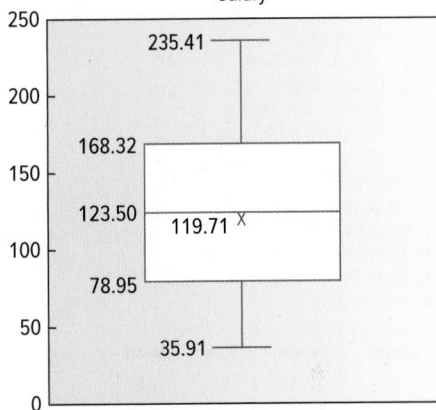

The distribution of salary is approximately normal. The mean and median are about the same, and skewness is about zero. These statistics indicate a normal symmetric distribution. The box-plot also supports a conclusion that the distribution of salary is normal.

b.

Age	
Mean	30.37
Median	21.50
Population standard deviation	25.12
Skewness	2.16
Range	105.00
Minimum	4.00
Maximum	109.00

Based on the descriptive statistics and the box-plot, stadium age is not normally distributed. The distribution is highly skewed toward the oldest stadiums. See the coefficient of skewness. Also see that the mean and median are very different. The difference is because the mean is affected by the two oldest stadium ages.

CHAPTER 8

1. **a.** 303 Louisiana, 5155 S. Main, 3501 Monroe, 2652 W. Central
   b. Answers will vary.
   c. 630 Dixie Hwy, 835 S. McCord Rd, 4624 Woodville Rd
   d. Answers will vary.
3. **a.** Bob Schmidt Chevrolet
   Great Lakes Ford Nissan
   Grogan Towne Chrysler
   Southside Lincoln Mercury
   Rouen Chrysler Jeep Eagle
   b. Answers will vary.
   c. York Automotive
   Thayer Chevrolet Toyota
   Franklin Park Lincoln Mercury
   Mathews Ford Oregon Inc.
   Valiton Chrysler
5. **a.**

Sample	Values	Sum	Mean
1	12, 12	24	12
2	12, 14	26	13
3	12, 16	28	14
4	12, 14	26	13
5	12, 16	28	14
6	14, 16	30	15

   b. $\mu_{\bar{x}} = (12 + 13 + 14 + 13 + 14 + 15)/6 = 13.5$
   $\mu = (12 + 12 + 14 + 16)/4 = 13.5$
   c. More dispersion with population data compared to the sample means. The sample means vary from 12 to 15, whereas the population varies from 12 to 16.
7. **a.**

Sample	Values	Sum	Mean
1	12, 12, 14	38	12.66
2	12, 12, 15	39	13.00
3	12, 12, 20	44	14.66
4	14, 15, 20	49	16.33
5	12, 14, 15	41	13.66
6	12, 14, 15	41	13.66
7	12, 15, 20	47	15.66
8	12, 15, 20	47	15.66
9	12, 14, 20	46	15.33
10	12, 14, 20	46	15.33

   b. $\mu_{\bar{x}} = \dfrac{(12.66 + \cdots + 15.33 + 15.33)}{10} = 14.6$
   $\mu = (12 + 12 + 14 + 15 + 20)/5 = 14.6$
   c. The dispersion of the population is greater than that of the sample means. The sample means vary from 12.66 to 16.33, whereas the population varies from 12 to 20.
9. **a.** 20, found by $_6C_3$
   b.

Sample	Cases	Sum	Mean
Ruud, Wu, Sass	3, 6, 3	12	4.00
Ruud, Sass, Flores	3, 3, 3	9	3.00
⋮	⋮	⋮	⋮
Sass, Flores, Schueller	3, 3, 1	7	2.33

c. $\mu_{\bar{x}} = 2.67$, found by $\dfrac{53.33}{20}$
$\mu = 2.67$, found by $(3 + 6 + 3 + 3 + 0 + 1)/6$.

They are equal.

d.

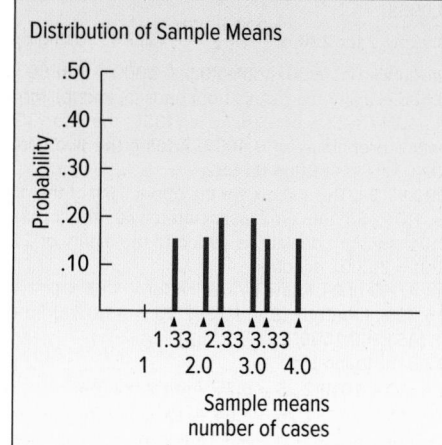

Sample Mean	Number of Means	Probability
1.33	3	.1500
2.00	3	.1500
2.33	4	.2000
3.00	4	.2000
3.33	3	.1500
4.00	3	.1500
	20	1.0000

The population has more dispersion than the sample means. The sample means vary from 1.33 to 4.0. The population varies from 0 to 6.

11. **a.**

$$\mu = \frac{0 + 1 + \cdots + 9}{10} = 4.5$$

b.

Sample	Sum	$\bar{x}$	Sample	Sum	$\bar{x}$
1	11	2.2	6	20	4.0
2	31	6.2	7	23	4.6
3	21	4.2	8	29	5.8
4	24	4.8	9	35	7.0
5	21	4.2	10	27	5.4

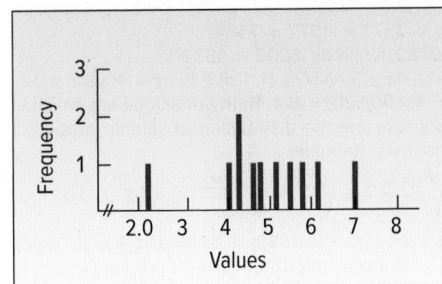

The mean of the 10 sample means is 4.84, which is close to the population mean of 4.5. The sample means range from 2.2 to 7.0, whereas the population values range from 0 to 9. From the above graph, the sample means tend to cluster between 4 and 5.

13. a.–c. Answers will vary depending on the coins in your possession.

f. Sampling error of more than 1 hour corresponds to times of less than 34 or more than 36 hours. $z = \frac{34 - 35}{5.5/\sqrt{25}} = -0.91$; $z = \frac{36 - 35}{5.5/\sqrt{25}} = 0.91$. Subtracting: $0.5 - .3186 = .1814$ in each tail. Multiplying by 2, the final probability is .3628.

15. a. $z = \frac{63 - 60}{12/\sqrt{9}} = 0.75$. So probability is 0.2266, found by $0.5000 - 0.2734$.

b. $z = \frac{56 - 60}{12/\sqrt{9}} = -1$ So the probability is 0.1587, found by $0.5000 - 0.3413$

c. 0.6147, found by $0.3413 + 0.2734$

17. $z = \frac{1,950 - 2,200}{250/\sqrt{50}} = -7.07$ $p = 1$, or virtually certain

19. a. $n\pi \geq 5$ AND $n\pi (1 - \pi) \geq 5$. $n\pi = 30(.7) = 21$ $n\pi (1 - \pi) = 30(.7)(.3) = 6.3$;
Both conditions are satisfied. We can approximate the distribution of sample proportions with a normal distribution.

b. .0837; $\sqrt{\frac{\pi(1 - \pi)}{n}} = \sqrt{\frac{.7(1 - .7)}{30}} = .0837$

c. .2743 found by $z = \frac{p - \pi}{\sqrt{\frac{\pi(1 - \pi)}{n}}} = \frac{.75 - .70}{\sqrt{\frac{.7(1 - .7)}{30}}} = \frac{.05}{.0837}$
$= .5974$ rounded to .60; probability is. $5000 - .2257 = .2743$

d. .0014 found by $z = \frac{p - \pi}{\sqrt{\frac{\pi(1 - \pi)}{n}}} = \frac{.45 - .70}{\sqrt{\frac{.7(1 - .7)}{30}}} = \frac{.25}{.0837}$
$= 2.9869$ rounded to 2.99; probability is $.5000 - .4986 = .0014$

e. .7243 found by using the results from parts (c) and (d). Add $.2257 + .4986 = .7243$

f. .0028 found by $z = \frac{p - \pi}{\sqrt{\frac{\pi(1 - \pi)}{n}}} = \frac{.50 - .70}{\sqrt{\frac{.7(1 - .7)}{30}}} = \frac{.20}{.0837}$
$= 2.3895$ rounded to 2.39; probability less than .5 is $.5000 - .4986 = .0014$

AND $z = \frac{p - \pi}{\sqrt{\frac{\pi(1 - \pi)}{n}}} = \frac{.90 - .70}{\sqrt{\frac{.7(1 - .7)}{30}}} = \frac{.20}{.0837} = 2.3995$
rounded to 2.39; probability is $.5000 - .4986 = .0014$

The probability that the sampling error of the sample proportion is .20 or more is $2(.0014) = .0028$.

21. a. $n\pi \geq 5$ AND $n\pi (1 - \pi) \geq 5$; $n\pi = 50(.8) = 40$ $n\pi (1 - \pi) = 50(.8)(.2) = 8$. Both conditions are satisfied. We can apply the central limit theorem and use the normal distribution.

b. The standard error is: $\sqrt{\frac{\pi(1 - \pi)}{n}} = \sqrt{\frac{.8(1 - .8)}{50}} = .0566$

$z = \frac{p - \pi}{\sqrt{\frac{\pi(1 - \pi)}{n}}} = \frac{.5 - .80}{\sqrt{\frac{.8(1 - 8)}{50}}} = \frac{-.30}{.0566} = -5.3004$ rounded to -5.30; probability is 1.000

The probability is approximately 1.000. The event that more than 50% of the sampled apartments sell within the range is virtually certain.

23. a. Kiehl's, Banana Republic, Cariloha, Nike, and Windsor.

b. Answers may vary.

c. Tilly's, Fabletics, Banana Republic, Madewell, Nike, Guess, Ragstock, Soma

25. a.

Samples	Mean	Deviation from Mean	Square of Deviation
1, 1	1.0	−1.0	1.0
1, 2	1.5	−0.5	0.25
1, 3	2.0	0.0	0.0
2, 1	1.5	−0.5	0.25
2, 2	2.0	0.0	0.0
2, 3	2.5	0.5	0.25
3, 1	2.0	0.0	0.0
3, 2	2.5	0.5	0.25
3, 3	3.0	1.0	1.0

b. Mean of sample means is $(1.0 + 1.5 + 2.0 + \ldots + 3.0)/9 = 18/9 = 2.0$. The population mean is $(1 + 2 + 3)/3 = 6/3 = 2$. They are the same value.

c. Variance of sample means is $(1.0 + 0.25 + 0.0 + \ldots + 3.0)/9 = 3/9 = 1/3$. Variance of the population values is $(1 + 0 + 1)/3 = 2/3$. The variance of the population is twice as large as that of the sample means.

d. Sample means follow a triangular shape peaking at 2. The population is uniform between 1 and 3.

27. Larger samples provide narrower estimates of a population mean. So the company with 200 sampled customers can provide more precise estimates. In addition, they selected consumers who are familiar with laptop computers and may be better able to evaluate the new computer.

29. a. We selected 60, 104, 75, 72, and 48. Answers will vary.

b. We selected the third observation. So the sample consists of 75, 72, 68, 82, 48. Answers will vary.

c. Number the first 20 motels from 00 to 19. Randomly select three numbers. Then number the last five numbers 20 to 24. Randomly select two numbers from that group.

31. a. $(79 + 64 + 84 + 82 + 92 + 77)/6 = 79.67\%$

b. 15 found by $_6C_2$

c.

Sample	Value	Sum	Mean
1	79, 64	143	71.5
2	79, 84	163	81.5
⋮	⋮	⋮	⋮
15	92, 77	169	84.5
			1,195.0

d. $\mu_{\bar{x}} = 79.67$, found by 1,195/15.
$\mu = 79.67$, found by 478/6.
They are equal.

e. Answers will vary. Not likely as the student is not graded on all available information. Based on these test scores however, this student has a 8/15 chance of receiving a higher grade with this method than the average and a 7/15 chance of receiving a lower grade.

33. a. 10, found by $_5C_2$

b.

Number of Shutdowns	Mean	Number of Shutdowns	Mean
4, 3	3.5	3, 3	3.0
4, 5	4.5	3, 2	2.5
4, 3	3.5	5, 3	4.0
4, 2	3.0	5, 2	3.5
3, 5	4.0	3, 2	2.5

Sample Mean	Frequency	Probability
2.5	2	.20
3.0	2	.20
3.5	3	.30
4.0	2	.20
4.5	1	.10
	10	1.00

c. $\mu_{\bar{x}} = (3.5 + 4.5 + \cdots + 2.5)/10 = 3.4$
$\mu = (4 + 3 + 5 + 3 + 2)/5 = 3.4$
The two means are equal.

d. The population values are relatively uniform in shape. The distribution of sample means tends toward normality.

35. a. The distribution will be normal.

b. $\sigma_{\bar{x}} = \dfrac{5.5}{\sqrt{25}} = 1.1$

c. $z = \dfrac{36 - 35}{5.5\sqrt{25}} = 0.91$
$p = 0.1814$, found by $0.5000 - 0.3186$

d. $z = \dfrac{34.5 - 35}{5.5/\sqrt{25}} = -0.45$
$p = 0.6736$, found by $0.5000 + 0.1736$

e. 0.4922, found by $0.3186 + 0.1736$

f. Sampling error of more than 1 hour corresponds to times of less than 34 or more than 36 hours. $z = \dfrac{34 - 35}{5.5/\sqrt{25}} = -0.91$;
$z = \dfrac{36 - 35}{5.5/\sqrt{2.5}} = 0.91$ Subtracting: $0.5 - .3186 = .1814$ in each tail. Multiplying by 2, the final probability is .3628.

37. $z = \dfrac{\$335 - \$350}{\$45/\sqrt{40}} = -2.11$
$p = 0.9826$, found by $0.5000 + 0.4826$

39. $z = \dfrac{29.3 - 29}{2.5/\sqrt{60}} = 0.93$
$p = 0.8238$, found by $0.5000 + 0.3238$

41. Between 5,954 and 6,046, found by $6,000 \pm 1.96(150/\sqrt{40})$

43. $z = \dfrac{900 - 947}{205/\sqrt{60}} = -1.78$
$p = 0.0375$, found by $0.5000 - 0.4625$

45. a. Alaska, Connecticut, Georgia, Kansas, Nebraska, South Carolina, Virginia, Utah

b. Arizona, Florida, Iowa, Massachusetts, Nebraska, North Carolina, Rhode Island, Vermont

47. a. $z = \dfrac{600 - 510}{14.28/\sqrt{10}} = 19.9$, $P = 0.00$, or virtually never

b. $z = \dfrac{500 - 510}{14.28/\sqrt{10}} = -2.21$
$p = 0.4864 + 0.5000 = 0.9864$

c. $z = \dfrac{500 - 510}{14.28/\sqrt{10}} = -2.21$
$p = 0.5000 - 0.4864 = 0.0136$

49. a. $\sigma_{\bar{x}} = \dfrac{2.1}{\sqrt{81}} = 0.23$

b. $z = \dfrac{7.0 - 6.5}{2.1/\sqrt{81}} = 2.14$, $z = \dfrac{6.0 - 6.4}{2.1/\sqrt{81}} = -2.14$,
$p = .4838 + .4838 = .9676$

c. $z = \dfrac{6.75 - 6.5}{2.1/\sqrt{81}} = 1.07$, $z = \dfrac{6.25 - 6.5}{2.1/\sqrt{81}} = -1.07$,
$p = .3577 + .3577 = .7154$

d. .0162, found by $.5000 - .4838$

51. a. yes; $n\pi \geq 5$ AND $n\pi (1 - \pi) \geq 5$. $n\pi = 40(.80) = 32$ $n\pi (1 - \pi) = 40(.80)(.20) = 6.4$. Both conditions are satisfied. We can approximate the distribution of sample proportions with a normal distribution.

b. $\sqrt{\dfrac{\pi(1 - \pi)}{n}} = \sqrt{\dfrac{.20(1 - .8)20)}{40}} = .0632$

c. $\pi \pm 2\sigma = .8 - 2(.0632) = .6736$ and $.8 + 2(.0632) = .9264$. So, approximately 95% of sample proportions are in the interval: $.6736 < p < .9264$.

53. a. $n\pi \geq 5$ AND $n\pi (1 - \pi) \geq 5$. $n\pi = 60(.90) = 45$ $n\pi (1 - \pi) = 60(.90)(.10) = 5.4$.
Both conditions are satisfied. We can approximate the distribution of sample proportions with a normal distribution.

b. .0387; $\sqrt{\dfrac{\pi(1 - \pi)}{n}} = \dfrac{\sqrt{.90(1 - .90)}}{60} = .0387$

c.
.0915 found by $z = \dfrac{p - \pi}{\sqrt{\dfrac{\pi(1 - \pi)}{n}}} = \dfrac{.95 - .90}{\sqrt{\dfrac{.90(1 - .90)}{60}}} = \dfrac{.05}{.0387} = 1.2920$
rounded to 1.29; probability is $.5000 - .4085 = .0915$

d. .0505 found by $z = \dfrac{p - \pi}{\sqrt{\dfrac{\pi(1 - \pi)}{n}}} = \dfrac{.75 - .90}{\sqrt{\dfrac{.90(1 - .90)}{60}}} = \dfrac{-.15}{.0915} = -$
1.6393 rounded to -1.64; probability is $.5000 - .4495 = .0505$

e. .8580 found by using the results from parts (c) and (d). $.4085 + .4495 = .8580$

f. .9902 found by $z = \dfrac{p - \pi}{\sqrt{\dfrac{\pi(1 - \pi)}{n}}} = \dfrac{1.00 - .90}{\sqrt{\dfrac{.90(1 - .90)}{60}}} = \dfrac{.10}{.0387} =$
2.5840 rounded to -2.58; probability is .4951
AND $z = \dfrac{p - \pi}{\sqrt{\dfrac{\pi(1 - \pi)}{n}}} = \dfrac{.80 - .90}{\sqrt{\dfrac{.90(1 - .90)}{60}}} = \dfrac{-.10}{.0387} = -2.5840$
rounded to -2.58; probability is .4951. Adding the two probabilities, the probability that the sampling error is .1 or less is $.2(.4951) = .9902$.

55. a. $n\pi \geq 5$ AND $n\pi (1 - \pi) \geq 5$; $n\pi = 100(.90) = 90$ $n\pi (1 - \pi) = 100(.90)(.10) = 9$. Both conditions are satisfied. We can apply the central limit theorem and use the normal distribution.

b. The standard error is: $\sqrt{\dfrac{\pi(1 - \pi)}{n}} = \sqrt{\dfrac{.9(1 - .9)}{100}} = .0009$.

5 students would be a proportion of 5/100 or .05. So, we want to find the probability of a sample proportion of $p < .05$.
$z = \dfrac{p - \pi}{\sqrt{\dfrac{\pi(1 - \pi)}{n}}} = \dfrac{.05 - .90}{\sqrt{\dfrac{.9(1 - .9)}{100}}} = \dfrac{-.85}{.0009} = -944.4444$ rounded to
-944.44; probability is 0.0000

57. Mean 2021 attendance was 1.509 million. Likelihood of a sample mean this small or smaller is .0000, found by $0.5000 - 0.4999$, where $z = \dfrac{1.509 - 2.45}{\dfrac{0.71}{\sqrt{30}}} = -7.26$

Based on normally distributed attendance with a mean of 2.45 million, the probability of a season mean of 1.509 million is zero. See that 2021 attendance was clearly affected by various COVID-19 pandemic policies.

CHAPTER 9

1. 51.314 and 58.686, found by $55 \pm 2.58(10/\sqrt{49})$

3. a. 1.581, found by $\sigma_{\bar{x}} = 25/\sqrt{250}$
   b. The population is normally distributed and the population variance is known. In addition, the central limit theorem says that the sampling distribution of sample means will be normally distributed.
   c. 16.901 and 23.099, found by 20 ± 3.099

5. a. $20. It is our best estimate of the population mean.
   b. $18.60 and $21.40, found by $20 \pm 1.96(\$5/\sqrt{49})$. About 95% of the intervals similarly constructed will include the population mean.

7. a. 8.60 gallons
   b. 7.83 and 9.37, found by $8.60 \pm 2.58(2.30/\sqrt{60})$
   c. If 100 such intervals were determined, the population mean would be included in about 99 intervals.

9. a. 2.201
   b. 1.729
   c. 3.499

11. Using the last row in the *t*-table with infinite degrees of freedom, find:
   a. 1.960
   b. 1.645
   c. 1.282

13. a. The population mean is unknown, but the best estimate is 20, the sample mean.
   b. Use the *t*-distribution since the standard deviation is unknown. However, assume the population is normally distributed.
   c. 2.093
   d. Margin of error = $2.093(2/\sqrt{20}) = 0.94$
   e. Between 19.06 and 20.94, found by $20 \pm 2.093(2/\sqrt{20})$
   f. Neither value is reasonable because they are not inside the interval.

15. Between 95.39 and 101.81, found by $98.6 \pm 1.833(5.54/\sqrt{10})$

17. a. 0.85 found by 85/100
   b. Between 0.78 and 0.92%, found by
   $$0.85 \pm 1.96\left(\sqrt{\dfrac{0.85(1-0.85)}{100}}\right)$$
   c. We are reasonably sure the population proportion is between 78 and 92%.

19. a. 0.625, found by 250/400
   b. Between 0.563 and 0.687, found by
   $$0.625 \pm 2.58\left(\sqrt{\dfrac{0.625(1-0.625)}{400}}\right)$$
   c. We are reasonably sure the population proportion is between 56 and 69%. Because the estimated population proportion is more than 50%, the results indicate that Fox TV should schedule the new comedy show.

21. 33.41 and 36.59, found by
   $$35 \pm 2.030\left(\dfrac{5}{\sqrt{36}}\right)\sqrt{\dfrac{300-36}{300-1}}$$

23. 1.683 and 2.037, found by
   $$1.86 \pm 2.680\left(\dfrac{0.5}{\sqrt{50}}\right)\sqrt{\dfrac{400-50}{400-1}}$$

25. 97, found by $n = \left(\dfrac{1.96 \times 10}{2}\right)^2 = 96.04$

27. 339, found by $n = 0.15(0.85)\left(\dfrac{2.576}{0.05}\right)^2 = 338.4245$

29. 237, found by $n = \left(\dfrac{1.282}{0.25}\right)^2 = 236.6675$

31. a. 577, found by $n = 0.60(0.40)\left(\dfrac{1.96}{0.04}\right)^2 = 576.24$
   b. 601, found by $n = 0.50(0.50)\left(\dfrac{1.96}{0.04}\right)^2 = 600.25$

33. 6.13 years to 6.87 years, found by $6.5 \pm 1.989(1.7/\sqrt{85})$

35. a. The sample mean, $1,147, is the point estimate of the population mean.
   b. The sample standard deviation, $50, is the point estimate of the population standard deviation.
   c. Margin of error = $2.426\left(\dfrac{50}{\sqrt{40}}\right) = 19.18$
   d. Between $1,127.82 and 1,166.18, found by $1,147 \pm 2.426\left(\dfrac{50}{\sqrt{40}}\right)$. $1,250 is not reasonable because it is outside of the confidence interval.

37. a. The population mean is unknown. The point estimate of the population mean is the sample mean, 8.32 years.
   b. Between 7.50 and 9.14, found by $8.32 \pm 1.685(3.07/\sqrt{40})$
   c. 10 is not reasonable because it is outside the confidence interval.

39. a. 65.49 up to 71.71 hours, found by $68.6 \pm 2.680(8.2\sqrt{50})$
   b. The value suggested by the NCAA is included in the confidence interval. Therefore, it is reasonable.
   c. Changing the confidence interval to 95 would reduce the width of the interval. The value of 2.680 would change to 2.010.

41. 61.47, rounded to 62. Found by solving for *n* in the equation:
   $$1.96(16/\sqrt{n}) = 4$$

43. a. Between 52,461.11 up to 57,640.77 found by
   $$55.051 \pm 1.711\left(\dfrac{7,568}{\sqrt{25}}\right)$$
   b. $55,000 is reasonable because it is inside of the confidence interval.

45. a. 82.58, found by 991/12.
   b. 3.94 is the sample standard deviation.
   c. Margin of error = $1.796\left(\dfrac{3.94}{\sqrt{12}}\right) = 2.04$
   d. Between 80.54 and $84.62, found by
   $$82.58 \pm 1.796\left(\dfrac{3.94}{\sqrt{12}}\right)$$
   e. 80 is not reasonable because it is outside of the confidence interval.

47. a. 89.467, found by 1342/15, is the point estimate of the population mean.
   b. Between 84.992 and 93.942, found by
   $$89.4667 \pm 2.145\left(\dfrac{8.08}{\sqrt{15}}\right)$$
   c. No, the stress level is higher because even the lower limit of the confidence interval is above 80.

49. a. 14/400 = .035, or 3.5%, is the point estimate of the population proportion.
   b. Margin of error = $2.576\left(\sqrt{\dfrac{(0.035)(1-0.035)}{400}}\right) = 0.24$
   c. The confidence interval is between 0.011 and 0.059;
   $$0.035 \pm 2.576\left(\sqrt{\dfrac{(0.035)(1-0.035)}{400}}\right)$$

d. It would be reasonable to conclude that 5% of the employees are failing the test because 0.05, or 5%, is inside the confidence interval.

51. a. Between 0.648 and 0.752, found by

$$.7 \pm 2.58\left(\sqrt{\frac{0.7(1-0.7)}{500}}\right)\left(\sqrt{\frac{20,000-500}{200,000-1}}\right)$$

b. Based on this sample we would confirm Ms. Miller will receive a majority of the votes as the lower limit of the confidence interval is above 0.500.

53. a. Margin of error $= 2.032\left(\dfrac{4.50}{\sqrt{35}}\right)\left(\sqrt{\dfrac{(500-35)}{500-1}}\right) = \$1.49$

b. $52.51 and $55.49, found by

$$\$54.00 \pm 2.032\frac{\$4.50}{\sqrt{35}}\sqrt{\frac{(500-35)}{500-1}}$$

55. 369, found by $n = 0.60(1-0.60)(1.96/0.05)^2$
57. 97, found by $[(1.96 \times 500)/100]^2$
59. a. Between 7,849 and 8,151, found by
$8,000 \pm 2.756(300/\sqrt{30})$

b. 554, found by $n = \left(\dfrac{(1.96)(300)}{25}\right)^2$

61. a. Between 75.44 and 80.56, found by $78 \pm 2.010(9/\sqrt{50})$

b. 220, found by $n = \left(\dfrac{(1.645)(9)}{1.0}\right)^2$

63. a. The point estimate of the population mean is the sample mean, $650.
b. The point estimate of the population standard deviation is the sample standard deviation, $24.
c. 4, found by $24/\sqrt{36}$
d. Between $641.88 and $658.12, found by

$$650 \pm 2.030\left(\frac{24}{\sqrt{36}}\right)$$

e. 23, found by $n = [(1.96 \times 24)/10]^2 = 22.13$
65. a. 708.13, rounded up to 709, found by
$0.21(1-0.21)(1.96/0.03)^2$
b. 1,068, found by $0.50(0.50)(1.96/0.03)^2$
67. a. Between 0.156 and 0.184, found by

$$0.17 \pm 1.96\sqrt{\frac{(0.17)(1-0.17)}{2700}}$$

b. Yes, because 18% are inside the confidence interval.
c. 21,682; found by $0.17(1-0.17)[1.96/0.005]^2$
69. Between 12.69 and 14.11, found by $13.4 \pm 1.96(6.8/\sqrt{352})$
71. a. Answers will vary.
b. Answers will vary.
c. Answers will vary.
d. Answers may vary.
e. Select a different sample of 20 homes and compute a confidence interval using the new sample. There is a 5% probability that a sample mean will be more than 1.96 standard errors from the mean. If this happens, the confidence interval will not include the population mean.
73. a. Between $4,033.1476 and $5,070.6274, found by 4,551.8875 ± 518.7399.
b. Between 71,040.0894 and 84,877.1106, found by 77,958.6000 ± 6,918.5106.
c. In general, the confidence intervals indicate that the average maintenance cost and the average odometer reading suggest an aging bus fleet.

CHAPTER 10

1. a. Two-tailed, because the alternate hypothesis does not indicate a direction.
b. Reject H_0 when z does not fall in the region from −1.96 and 1.96
c. −1.2, found by $z = \dfrac{49-50}{(5/\sqrt{36})}$. The test statistic is in the nonrejection zone.

d. Using the z-table, the p-value is 0.2302, found by 2(0.5000 − 0.3849). There is a 23.02% chance of finding a z-value this large by "sampling error" when H_0 is true.
e. Fail to reject H_0. The sample evidence is not sufficient to reject the null hypothesis.
3. a. One-tailed, because the alternate hypothesis indicates a greater than direction.
b. Reject H_0 when $z > 1.65$
c. 1.2, found by $z = \dfrac{21-20}{(5/\sqrt{36})}$. The test statistic does not exceed the critical value.
d. Using the z-table, p-value = 0.1151, found by 0.5000 − 0.3849. There is an 11.51% chance of finding a z-value this large or larger by "sampling error" when H_0 is true.
e. Fail to reject H_0. The sample evidence is strong enough to infer that $\mu > 20$.
5. a. H_0: $\mu = 60,000$ H_1: $\mu \neq 60,000$
b. Reject H_0 if $z < -1.96$ or $z > 1.96$
c. −0.69, found by $z = \dfrac{59,500-60,000}{(5000/\sqrt{48})}$. The test statistic is in the nonrejection zone.
d. Using the z-table, p-value = 0.4902, found by 2(0.5000 − 0.2549)
e. Do not reject H_0. Crosset's experience is not different from that claimed by the manufacturer.
7. a. H_0: $\mu \geq 6.8$ H_1: $\mu < 6.8$
b. Reject H_0 if $z < -1.65$
c. −2.0, found by $z = \dfrac{6.2-6.8}{1.8/\sqrt{36}}$. The test statistic is less than critical value.
d. Using the z-table, p-value = 0.0228.
e. H_0 is rejected. The mean number of DVDs watched is less than 6.8 per month.
9. a. Reject H_0 when $t < 1.833$
b. $t = \dfrac{12-10}{(3/\sqrt{10})} = 2.108$
c. Reject H_0. The mean is greater than 10.
11. H_0: $\mu \leq 40$ H_1: $\mu > 40$
Reject H_0 if $t > 1.703$.

$$t = \frac{42-40}{2.1\sqrt{28}} = 5.040$$

Reject H_0 and conclude that the mean number of calls is greater than 40 per week.
13. H_0: $\mu \leq 50,000$ H_1: $\mu > 50,000$
Reject H_0 if $t > 1.833$.

$$t = \frac{(60,000-50,000)}{(10,000/\sqrt{10})} = 3.16$$

Reject H_0 and conclude that the mean income in Wilmington is greater than $50,000.
15. a. Reject H_0 if $t < -3.747$.

b. $\bar{x} = 17$ and $s = \sqrt{\dfrac{50}{5-1}} = 3.536$

$$t = \frac{17-20}{(3.536/\sqrt{5})} = -1.90$$

c. Using a p-value calculator or statistical software, the p-value is .0653.
d. Do not reject H_0. We cannot conclude the population mean is less than 20.
17. H_0: $\mu \leq 1.4$ H_1: $\mu > 1.4$
Reject H_0 if $t > 2.821$.

$$t = \frac{1.6-1.4}{0.216/\sqrt{10}} = 2.93$$

Reject H_0 and conclude that the water consumption has increased. Using a p-value calculator or statistical software, the p-value is .0084. There is a slight probability that the sampling error, .2 liter, could occur by chance.

19. $H_0: \mu \le 67$ $H_1: \mu > 67$
Reject H_0 if $t > 1.796$

$$t = \frac{(82.5 - 67)}{(59.5/\sqrt{12})} = 0.902$$

Fail to reject H_0 and conclude that the mean number of text messages is not greater than 67. Using a *p*-value calculator or statistical software, the *p*-value is .1932. There is a good probability (about 19%) of selecting a sample of size 12 with a sample mean of 82.5.

21. 1.05, found by $z = (9{,}992 - 9{,}880)/(400/\sqrt{100})$. Then $0.5000 - 0.3531 = 0.1469$, which is the probability of a Type II error.

23. $H_0: \mu \ge 60$ $H_1: \mu < 60$
Reject H_0 if $z < -1.282$; the critical value is 59.29.

$$z = \frac{58 - 60}{(2.7/\sqrt{24})} = -3.629$$

Reject H_0. The mean assembly time is less than 60 minutes. Using the sample mean, 58, as μ_1, the *z*-score for 59.29 is 2.34. So the probability for values between 58 and 59.29 is .4904. The Type II error is the area to the right of 59.29 or $.5000 - .4904 = .0096$.

25. **a.** H_0 is rejected if $z > 1.645$

b. 1.09, found by $z = \dfrac{0.75 - 0.70}{\sqrt{\dfrac{0.70(0.30)}{100}}}$

c. H_0 is not rejected

27. **Step 1:** $H_0: \pi = 0.10$ $H_1: \pi \ne 0.10$
Step 2: The 0.01 significance level was chosen
Step 3: Use the *z*-statistic as the binomial distribution can be approximated by the normal distribution as $n\pi = 30 > 5$ and $n(1 - \pi) = 270 > 5$.
Step 4: Reject H_0 if $z > 2.326$
Step 5: $z = \dfrac{(63/300) - 0.10}{\sqrt{(0.10)(0.90)/300}} = 6.35$. Reject H_0.
Step 6: We conclude that the proportion of carpooling cars on the Turnpike is not 10%.

29. **Step 1:** $H_0: \pi \ge 0.9$ $H_1: \pi < 0.9$
Step 2: The 0.10 significance level was chosen.
Step 3: Use the *z*-statistic as the binomial distribution can be approximated by the normal distribution as $n\pi = 90 > 5$ and $n(1 - \pi) = 10 > 5$.
Step 4: Reject H_0 if $z < -1.282$
Step 5: $z = \{82/100 - 0.9/\sqrt{(0.9(0.1)/100)}\} = -2.67$. Reject H_0.
Step 6: Less than 90% of the customers receive their orders in less than 10 minutes.

31. $H_0: \mu = \$45{,}000$ $H_1: \mu \ne \$45{,}000$
Reject H_0 if $z < -1.65$ or $z > 1.65$.

$$z = \frac{\$45{,}500 - \$45{,}000}{\$3000/\sqrt{120}} = 1.83$$

Using the *z*-table, the *p*-value is 0.0672, found by $2(0.5000 - 0.4664)$.
Reject H_0. We can conclude that the mean salary is not $45,000.

33. $H_0: \mu \ge 10$ $H_1: \mu < 10$
Reject H_0 if $z < -1.65$.

$$z = \frac{9.0 - 10.0}{28/\sqrt{50}} = -2.53$$

Using the z-table, *p*-value $= 0.5000 - 0.4943 = 0.0057$.
Reject H_0. The mean weight loss is less than 10 pounds.

35. $H_0: \mu \ge 7.0$ $H_1: \mu < 7.0$
Assuming a 5% significance level, reject H_0 if $t < -1.677$.

$$t = \frac{6.8 - 7.0}{0.9/\sqrt{50}} = -1.57$$

Using a *p*-value calculator or statistical software, the *p*-value is 0.0614.
Do not reject H_0. West Virginia students are not sleeping less than 6 hours.

37. $H_0: \mu \ge 3.13$ $H_1: \mu < 3.13$
Reject H_0 if $t < -1.711$

$$t = \frac{2.86 - 3.13}{1.20/\sqrt{25}} = -1.13$$

We fail to reject H_0 and conclude that the mean number of residents is not necessarily less than 3.13.

39. $H_0: \mu \ge \$8{,}000$ $H_1: \mu < \$8{,}000$
Reject H_0 if $t < -1.796$

$$\bar{x} = \frac{85{,}936}{12} = 7{,}163.58 \quad s = \sqrt{\frac{9{,}768{,}674.92}{12 - 1}} = 942.37$$

$$t = \frac{7{,}163.58 - 8{,}000}{942.37/\sqrt{12}} = -3.07$$

Reject H_0. First, the test statistic (-3.07) is less than the critical value, 1.796. Second, using a *p*-value calculator or statistical software, the *p*-value is .0053 and less than the significance level, .05. We conclude that the mean interest paid is less than $8,000.

41. $H_0: \mu = 3.1$ $H_1: \mu \ne 3.1$ Assume a normal population.
Reject H_0 if $t < -2.201$ or $t > 2.201$.

$$\bar{x} = \frac{41.1}{12} = 3.425$$

$$s = \sqrt{\frac{4.0625}{12 - 1}} = .6077$$

$$t = \frac{3.425 - 3.1}{.6077/\sqrt{2}} = 1.853$$

Using a *p*-value calculator or statistical software, the *p*-value is .0910.
Do not reject H_0. Cannot show a difference between senior citizens and the national average.

43. $H_0: \mu \ge 6.5$ $H_1: \mu < 6.5$ Assume a normal population.
Reject H_0 if $t < -2.718$.
$\bar{x} = 5.1667$ $s = 3.1575$

$$t = \frac{5.1667 - 6.5}{3.1575/\sqrt{12}} = -1.463$$

Using a *p*-value calculator or statistical software, the *p*-value is .0861.
Do not reject H_0.

45. $H_0: \mu = 0$ $H_1: \mu \ne 0$
Reject H_0 if $t < -2.110$ or $t > 2.110$.
$\bar{x} = -0.2322$ $s = 0.3120$

$$t = \frac{-0.2322 - 0}{0.3120/\sqrt{8}} = -3.158$$

Using a *p*-value calculator or statistical software, the *p*-value is .0057.
Reject H_0. The mean gain or loss does not equal 0.

47. $H_0: \mu \le 100$ $H_1: \mu > 100$ Assume a normal population.
Reject H_0 if $t > 1.761$.

$$\bar{x} = \frac{1{,}641}{15} = 109.4$$

$$s = \sqrt{\frac{1{,}389.6}{15 - 1}} = 9.9628$$

$$t = \frac{109.4 - 100}{9.9628/\sqrt{15}} = 3.654$$

Using a *p*-value calculator or statistical software, the *p*-value is .0013.
Reject H_0. The mean number with the scanner is greater than 100.

49. $H_0: \mu = 1.5$ $H_1: \mu \ne 1.5$
Reject H_0 if $t > 3.250$ or $t < -3.250$

$$t = \frac{1.3 - 1.5}{0.9/\sqrt{10}} = -0.703$$

Using a *p*-value calculator or statistical software, the *p*-value is .4998.
Fail to reject H_0.

51. $H_0: \mu \geq 30$ $H_1: \mu < 30$
Reject H_0 if $t < -1.895$.

$$\bar{x} = \frac{238.3}{8} = 29.7875 \quad s = \sqrt{\frac{5.889}{8-1}} = 0.9172$$

$$t = \frac{29.7875 - 30}{0.9172/\sqrt{8}} = -0.655$$

Using a p-value calculator or statistical software, the p-value is .2667.
Do not reject H_0. The cost is not less than \$30,000.

53. a. $9.00 \pm 1.645(1/\sqrt{36}) = 9.00 \pm 0.274$.
So the limits are 8.726 and 9.274.

b. $z = \dfrac{8.726 - 8.6}{1/\sqrt{36}} = 0.756$.

$P(z < 0.756) = 0.5000 + 0.2764 = .7764$

c. $z = \dfrac{9.274 - 9.6}{1/\sqrt{36}} = -1.956$.

$P(z > -1.96) = 0.4750 + 0.5000 = .9750$

55. $50 + 2.33\dfrac{10}{\sqrt{n}} = 55 - .525\dfrac{10}{\sqrt{n}} \quad n = (5.71)^2 = 32.6$

Let $n = 33$

57. a. $H_0: \pi = 0.50$ $H_1: \pi \neq 0.50$
b. Yes. Both $n\pi$ and $n(1 - \pi)$ are equal to 25 and exceed 5.
c. Reject H_0 if z is not between -2.576 and 2.576.

d. $z = \dfrac{\dfrac{36}{53} - 0.5}{\sqrt{0.5(1 - 0.5)/53}} = 2.61$

We reject the null hypothesis.
e. Using a p-value calculator (rounding to three decimal places) or a z-table, the p-value is 0.009, found by 2(0.5000 − 0.4955). The data indicates that the National Football Conference is luckier than the American Conference in calling the flip of a coin.

59. $H_0: \pi \leq 0.60$ $H_1: \pi > 0.60$
H_0 is rejected if $z > 2.33$.

$$z = \frac{.07 - .60}{\sqrt{\dfrac{.60(.40)}{200}}} = 2.89$$

H_0 is rejected. Ms. Dennis is correct. More than 60% of the accounts are more than 3 months old.

61. $H_0: \pi \leq 0.44$ $H_1: \pi > 0.44$
H_0 is rejected if $z > 1.65$.

$$z = \frac{0.480 - 0.44}{\sqrt{(0.44 \times 0.56)/1.000}} = 2.55$$

H_0 is rejected. We conclude that there has been an increase in the proportion of people wanting to go to Europe.

63. $H_0: \pi \leq 0.20$ $H_1: \pi > 0.20$
H_0 is rejected if $z > 2.33$.

$$z = \frac{(56/200) - 0.20}{\sqrt{(0.20 \times 0.80)/200}} = 2.83$$

H_0 is rejected. More than 20% of the owners move during a particular year. p-value $= 0.5000 - 0.4977 = 0.0023$.

65. $H_0: \pi \geq 0.0008$ $H_1: \pi < 0.0008$
H_0 is rejected if $z < -1.645$.

$$z = \frac{0.0006 - 0.0008}{\sqrt{\dfrac{0.0008\,(0.9992)}{10,000}}} = -0.707 \quad H_0 \text{ is not rejected.}$$

These data do not prove there is a reduced fatality rate.

67. $H_0\ \mu = 130$ $H_1: \mu \neq 130$
Reject H_0 if t is not between -2.045 and 2.045.

$$t = \frac{119.71 - 130}{51.51/\sqrt{30}} = -1.904$$

Using a p-value calculator or statistical software, the p-value is .2829.

Fail to reject the null. Based on the sample data, we cannot infer that the mean salary is not equal to \$130 million.
b. $H_0: \mu \leq 2,000,000$ $H_1: \mu > 2,000,000$ Reject H_0 if t is > 1.699.

$$t = \frac{1,509 - 2}{.550/\sqrt{30}} = -4.990.$$

Using a p-value calculator or statistical software, p-value is .9999.
Fail to reject the null. Based on the sample data, we cannot infer that the mean attendace is more than 2,000,000. Note that the year of COVID-19 severely affected attendance.

CHAPTER 11

1. a. 9.01, from Appendix B.6
3. Reject H_0 if $F > 10.5$, where degrees of freedom in the numerator are 7 and 5 in the denominator. Computed $F = 2.04$, found by:

$$F = \frac{s_1^2}{s_2^2} = \frac{(10)^2}{(7)^2} = 2.04$$

Do not reject H_0. There is no difference in the variations of the two populations.
5. a. $H_0: \sigma_1^2 = \sigma_2^2$ $H_1: \sigma_1^2 \neq \sigma_2^2$
b. df in numerator are 11 and 9 in the denominator.
Reject H_0 where $F > 3.10$ (3.10 is about halfway between 3.14 and 3.07)

c. $F = 1.44$, found by $F = \dfrac{(12)^2}{(10)^2} = 1.44$

d. Using a p-value calculator or statistical software, the p-value is .2964.
e. Do not reject H_0.
f. It is reasonable to conclude variations of the two populations could be the same.
7. a. Two-tailed test
b. Reject H_0 if $z < -2.05$ or $z > 2.05$

c. $z = \dfrac{102 - 99}{\sqrt{\dfrac{5^2}{40} + \dfrac{6^2}{50}}} = 2.59$

d. Reject H_0.
e. Using the z-table, the p-value is $= .0096$, found by 2(.5000 −.4952).
9. **Step 1** $H_0: \mu_1 \geq \mu_2$ $H_1: \mu_1 < \mu_2$
Step 2 The .05 significance level was chosen.
Step 3 Reject H_0 if $z < -1.65$.
Step 4 -0.94, found by:

$$z = \frac{7.6 - 8.1}{\sqrt{\dfrac{(2.3)^2}{40} + \dfrac{(2.9)^2}{55}}} = -0.94$$

Step 5 Fail to reject H_0.
Step 6 Babies using the Gibbs brand did not gain less weight. Using the z-table, the p-value is $= .1736$, found by .5000 −.3264.
11. **Step 1** $H_0: \mu_{married} = \mu_{unmarried}$ $H_1: \mu_{married} \neq \mu_{unmarried}$
Step 2 The 0.05 significance level was chosen.
Step 3 Use a z-statistic as both population standard deviations are known.
Step 4 If $z < -1.960$ or $z > 1.960$, reject H_0.

Step 5 $z = \dfrac{4.0 - 4.4}{\sqrt{\dfrac{(1.2)^2}{45} + \dfrac{(1.1)^2}{39}}} = -1.59$

Fail to reject the null.
Step 6 It is reasonable to conclude that the time that married and unmarried women spend each week is not significantly different. Using the z-table, the p-value is .1142. The difference of 0.4 hour per week could be explained by sampling error.

13. H_0: variances are equal. From the F-table, the F critical value with 7 (numerator) and 9 (denominator) degrees of freedom is 3.29. Computed F-statistic $= 25/16 = 1.5625$. Fail to reject H_0. Cannot reject the hypothesis that the variances are equal. Proceed to pool the variances.

a. Reject H_0 if $t > 2.120$ or $t < -2.120$ df $= 10 + 8 - 2 = 16$

b. $s_p^2 = \dfrac{(10 - 1)(4)^2 + (8 - 1)(5)^2}{10 + 8 - 2} = 19.9375$

c. $t = \dfrac{23 - 26}{\sqrt{19.9375\left(\frac{1}{10} + \frac{1}{8}\right)}} = -1.416$

d. Using a p-value calculator or statistical software, the p-value is .1759. From the t-table we estimate the p-value is greater than 0.10 and less than 0.20.

e. Do not reject H_0.

15. H_0: variances are equal. From the F-table, F critical value with 14 (numerator) and 12 (denominator) degrees of freedom (computed) is 2.64. Computed F-statistic $= 65.862/44.936 = 1.466$. Fail to reject H_0. Cannot reject the hypothesis that the variances are equal. Proceed to pool the variances.

Step 1: H_0: $\mu_{\text{Pitchers}} = \mu_{\text{Position Players}}$ H_1: $\mu_{\text{Pitchers}} \neq \mu_{\text{Position Players}}$

Step 2: The 0.01 significance level was chosen.

Step 3: Use a t-statistic assuming a pooled variance with equal and unknown standard deviations.

Step 4: df $= 15 + 13 - 2 = 26$ Reject H_0 if t is not between -2.779 and 2.779.

$s_p^2 = \dfrac{(15 - 1)(8.116)^2 + (13 - 1)(6.703)^2}{15 + 13 - 2} = 56.205$

$t = \dfrac{5.822 - 5.519}{\sqrt{56.205 * \left(\frac{1}{15} + \frac{1}{13}\right)}} = .1067$

Using a p-value calculator or statistical software, the p-value is 0.9160.

Step 5: Do not reject H_0.

Step 6: There is no difference in the mean salaries of pitchers and position players.

17. a. H_0: variances are equal. From the F-table, F critical value with 6 (numerator) and 5 (denominator) degrees of freedom is 4.95. Computed F-statistic $= 249.238/149.9 = 1.6627$. Fail to reject H_0. Cannot reject the hypothesis that the variances are equal. Proceed to pool the variances.

b.

Step 1: H_0: $\mu_s \leq \mu_a$ H_1: $\mu_s > \mu_a$ From the F-table,

Step 2: The 0.10 significance level was chosen

Step 3: Use a t-statistic assuming a pooled variance with the standard deviation unknown.

Step 4: df $= 6 + 7 - 2 = 11$ Reject H_0 if $t > 1.363$

$s_p^2 = \dfrac{(6 - 1)(12.243)^2 + (7 - 1)(15.787)^2}{6 + 7 - 2} = 204.076$

Step 5: $t = \dfrac{142.5 - 130.3}{\sqrt{204.076\left(\frac{1}{6} + \frac{1}{7}\right)}} = 1.535$

Using a p-value calculator or statistical software, the p-value is 0.0763.

Reject H_0.

Step 6: The mean daily expenses are greater for the sales staff.

19. H_0: variances are equal. From the F-table, F critical value with 11 (numerator) and 14 (denominator) degrees of freedom is 2.57. Computed F-statistic $= 225/25 = 9.00$. Reject H_0. The population variances are not equal.

a. If $t < -2.179$ or $t > 2.179$, then reject H_0.

b. df $= 12$, found by:

$\dfrac{(5^2/15 + 15^2/12)^2}{\dfrac{(5^2/15)^2}{14} + \dfrac{(15^2/12)^2}{11}} = 12.96$

c. $t = \dfrac{50 - 46}{\sqrt{\dfrac{5^2}{15} + \dfrac{15^2}{12}}} = 0.885$

d. Using a p-value calculator, p-value $= .1968$

e. Fail to reject the null hypothesis.

21. H_0: variances are equal. From the F-table, F critical value with 17 (numerator) and 15 (denominator) degrees of freedom (computed) is 2.368. Computed F-statistic $= 2{,}387{,}025/697{,}225 = 3.424$. Reject H_0. The population variances are not equal.

a. H_0: $\mu_{\text{Private}} \leq \mu_{\text{Public}}$ H_1: $\mu_{\text{Private}} > \mu_{\text{Public}}$ If $t > 1.706$, then reject H_0.

b. df $= 26$, found by $\dfrac{(1{,}545^2/18 + 835^2/16)^2}{\dfrac{(1{,}545^2/18)^2}{17} + \dfrac{(835^2/16)^2}{15}} = 26.7$

c. $t = \dfrac{22{,}840 - 21{,}045}{\sqrt{\dfrac{1{,}545^2}{18} + \dfrac{835^2}{16}}} = 4.276$

d. The p-value is: .0001

e. Reject the null hypothesis and find evidence indicating the mean cost at a private agency is larger.

23. Reject H_0 if $t > 2.353$.

a. $\bar{d} = \dfrac{12}{4} = 3.00$

$s_d = \sqrt{\dfrac{(2 - 3)^2 + (3 - 3)^2 + (3 - 3)^2 + (4 - 3)^2}{4 - 1}} = 0.816$

$t = \dfrac{3}{0.816\sqrt{4}} = 7.353$

Using a p-value calculator or statistical software, the p-value is .0026.

b. Reject the H_0. The test statistic is greater than the critical value. The p-value is less than .05.

c. There are more defective parts produced on the day shift.

25. a. Step 1: H_0: $\mu_d \geq 0$ H_1: $\mu_d < 0$

Step 2: The 0.05 significance level was chosen.

Step 3: Use a t-statistic with the standard deviation unknown for a paired sample.

Step 4: Reject H_0 if $t < -1.796$.

b. Step 5:

$$\bar{d} = -25.917$$

$$s_d = 40.791 \quad t = \dfrac{-25.917}{40.791/\sqrt{2}} = -2.201$$

Using a p-value calculator or statistical software, the p-value is .0250.

c. Reject H_0. The test statistic is greater than the critical value. The p-value is less than .05.

d. Step 6: The incentive plan resulted in an increase in daily income.

27. a. H_0 is rejected if $z > 1.65$.

b. 0.64, found by $p_c = \dfrac{70 + 90}{100 + 150}$

c. 1.61, found by

$$z = \dfrac{0.70 - 0.60}{\sqrt{[(0.64 \times 0.36)/100] + [(0.64 \times 0.36)/150]}}$$

d. H_0 is not rejected.

29. a. H_0: $\pi_1 = \pi_2$ H_1: $\pi_1 \neq \pi_2$

b. H_0 is rejected if $z < -1.96$ or $z > 1.96$.

c. $p_c = \dfrac{24 + 40}{400 + 400} = 0.08$

d. -2.09, found by

$$z = \dfrac{0.06 - 0.10}{\sqrt{[(0.08 \times .092)/400] + [(0.08 \times 0.92)/400]}}$$

e. H_0 is rejected. The proportion infested is not the same in the two fields.

31. $H_0: \pi_d \leq \pi_r$ $H_1: \pi_d > \pi_r$
H_0 is rejected if $z > 2.05$.

$$p_c = \frac{168 + 200}{800 + 1,000} = 0.2044$$

$$z = \frac{0.21 - 0.20}{\sqrt{\frac{(0.2044)(0.7956)}{800} + \frac{(0.2044)(0.7956)}{1,000}}} = 0.52$$

H_0 is not rejected. We cannot conclude that a larger proportion of Democrats favor lowering the standards. p-value $= .3015$.

33. $H_0: \sigma_1^2 \leq \sigma_2^2; H_1: \sigma_1^2 > \sigma_2^2$ $df_1 = 21 - 1 = 20$; $df_2 = 18 - 1 = 17$. H_0 is rejected if $F > 3.16$.

$$F = \frac{(45,600)^2}{(21,330)^2} = 4.57$$

Reject H_0. There is more variation in the selling price of ocean-front homes.

35. a. $H_0: \mu_{Men} = \mu_{Women}$ $H_1: \mu_{Men} \neq \mu_{Women}$ Reject H_0 if $z < -2.576$ or $z > 2.576$

b. $z = \frac{24.51 - 22.69}{\sqrt{\frac{3.86^2}{40} + \frac{4.48^2}{35}}} = 1.82$

c. Using a p-value calculator or statistical software, the p-value is .0687.

d. Do not reject the null hypothesis. The test statistic is less than the critical value. The p-value is more than .01.

e. There is no difference in the means.

37. a. $H_0: \mu_{Gael} = \mu_{Leslie}; H_1: \mu_{Gael} \neq \mu_{Leslie}$ Reject H_0 if $z < -1.96$ or $z > 1.96$

b. $z = \frac{4.77 - 5.02}{\sqrt{\frac{(1.05)^2}{40} + \frac{(1.23)^2}{50}}} = -1.04$

c. Using a z-table or a p-value calculator or statistical software, the p-value is .2983.

d. H_0 is not rejected. The test statistic is less than the critical value. The p-value is more than .05.

e. The sample evidence is not sufficient to say that there is no difference in the mean number of calls.

39. a. H_0: variances are equal. From the F-table, F critical value with 30 (numerator) and 25 (denominator) degrees of freedom is 1.92. Computed F-statistic $= 9,200^2/6500^2 = 2.003$. Using a significance level of .10, reject H_0. The population variances are not equal.

b. $H_0: \mu_A \geq \mu_B$ $H_1: \mu_A < \mu_B$ Reject H_0 if $t < -1.674$.

$df = 53$ found by $\frac{\left(\frac{9200^2}{31} + \frac{6500^2}{26}\right)^2}{\frac{(9200^2/31)^2}{30} + \frac{(6500^2/26)^2}{25}} = 53.567$

c. $t = \frac{57000 - 61000}{\sqrt{\left(\frac{9200^2}{31} + \frac{6500^2}{26}\right)}} = -1.967$

d. Using a p-value calculator or statistical software, the p-value is .0272.

e. Reject H_0. The test statistic is less than the critical value. Reject H_0 if $t < -1.674$. The p-value is less than .05.

f. The mean income of those selecting Plan B is larger.

41. a. H_0: variances are equal. From the F-table, F critical value with 11 (numerator) and 11 (denominator) degrees of freedom is 2.82. Computed F-statistic $= .56^2/.30^2 = 3.484$. Reject H_0, the variances are not equal.

b. $H_0: \mu_{Apple} = \mu_{Spotify}$ $H_1: \mu_{Apple} \neq \mu_{Spotify}$; reject H_0 if $t < -2.120$ or $t > 2.120$

c. $df = 16$, found by $\frac{(0.56^2/12 + 0.3^2/12)^2}{\frac{(0.56^2/12)^2}{11} + \frac{(0.3^2/12)^2}{11}} = 16.8$

$t = \frac{1.65 - 2.2}{\sqrt{\frac{0.56^2}{12} + \frac{0.3^2}{12}}} = -2.999$

d. Using a p-value calculator or statistical software, the p-value is .0085.

e. Reject H_0. The test statistic is outside the interval. The p-value is less than .05.

f. The number of average monthly households using Apple Music and Spotify differ.

43. a. H_0: variances are equal. F critical value with 11 (numerator) and 9 (denominator) degrees of freedom is 3.10. Computed F-statistic $= 14.25^2/10.5^2 = 1.842$. Using a p-value calculator, p-value $= .36$. (Remember this is a two-tail test.) Using a significance level of .10, fail to reject H_0. The sample data are not sufficient to say the variances are not equal.

b. $H_0: \mu_n = \mu_s$ $H_1: \mu_n \neq \mu_s$; reject H_0 if $t < -2.086$ or $t > 2.086$
$df = 12 + 10 - 2 = 20$

$$s_p^2 = \frac{(12 - 1)(14.25)^2 + (10 - 1)(10.5)^2}{12 + 10 - 2} = 161.297$$

c. $t = \frac{83.55 - 78.8}{\sqrt{161.297\left(\frac{1}{12} + \frac{1}{10}\right)}} = .8735$

d. Using a p-value calculator or statistical software, the p-value is .3928.

e. Do not reject H_0. The test statistic is inside the interval. The p-value is greater than .05.

f. There is no difference in the mean number of hamburgers sold at the two locations.

45. a. H_0: variances are equal. From the F-table, F critical value with 12 (numerator) and 9 (denominator) degrees of freedom is 3.07. Computed F-statistic $= 2.45^2/2.33^2 = 1.10$. Fail to reject H_0. The sample data are not sufficient to say the variances are not equal.

b. $H_0: \mu_{Peach} = \mu_{Plum}$ $H_1: \mu_{Peach} \neq \mu_{Plum}$ Reject H_0 if $t < -2.831$ or $t > 2.831$

c. $df = 13 + 10 - 2 = 21$

$$s_p^2 = \frac{(13 - 1)(2.45)^2 + (10 - 1)(2.33)^2}{13 + 10 - 2} = 5.75$$

$$t = \frac{15.87 - 18.56}{\sqrt{5.75\left(\frac{1}{13} + \frac{1}{10}\right)}} = -2.67$$

d. Using a p-value calculator or statistical software, the p-value is .0143.

e. Do not reject H_0. The test statistic is inside the interval. The p-value is more than .01.

f. With a significance level of .01, there is no difference in the mean amount purchased.

47. a. H_0: variances are equal. From the F-table, F critical value with 10 (numerator) and 7 (denominator) degrees of freedom is 3.64. Computed F-statistic $= 2.46^2/2.26^2 = 1.18$. Fail to reject H_0. The sample data are not sufficient to say the variances are not equal.

b. $H_0: \mu_{Under\,25} \leq \mu_{Over\,65}$ $H_1: \mu_{Under\,25} > \mu_{Over\,65}$; reject H_0 if $t > 2.567$;
$df = 11 + 8 - 2 = 17$

c. $s_p^2 = \frac{(11 - 1)(2.46)^2 + (8 - 1)(2.26)^2}{11 + 8 - 2} = 5.67$

$t = \frac{10.375 - 5.636}{\sqrt{5.67\left(\frac{1}{11} + \frac{1}{8}\right)}} = 4.28$

d. Using a p-value calculator or statistical software, the p-value is .0002.

e. Reject H_0. The test statistic is greater than the critical value. The p-value is less than .01.

f. Customers who are under 25 years of age use ATMs more than customers who are over 60 years of age.

49. a. H_0: variances are equal. From the F-table, F critical value with 6 (numerator) and 7 (denominator) degrees of freedom is 3.87. Computed F-statistic $= 19.91^2/15.09^2 = 1.74$. Fail to reject H_0. The sample data are not sufficient to say the variances are not equal.

b. H_0: $\mu_{Reduced} \le \mu_{Regular}$ H_1: $\mu_{Reduced} > \mu_{Regular}$
$df = 8 + 7 - 2 = 13$: Reject H_0 if $t > 2.650$

c. $\overline{X}_1 = 125.125$ $s_1 = 15.094$ $\overline{X}_2 = 177.714$ $s_2 = 19.914$

$$s_p^2 = \frac{(8-1)(15.094)^2 + (7-1)(19.914)^2}{8+7-2} = 305.78$$

$$t = \frac{125.125 - 117.714}{\sqrt{305.708\left(\frac{1}{8} + \frac{1}{7}\right)}} = 0.819$$

d. Using a p-value calculator or statistical software, the p-value is .2138.

e. Do not reject H_0. The test statistic is inside the interval. The p-value is more than .01.

f. The sample data do not provide evidence that the reduced price increased sales.

51. a. H_0: $\mu_{Before} - \mu_{After} = \mu_d \le 0$ H_1: $\mu_d > 0$
Reject H_0 if $t > 1.895$.

b. $\overline{d} = 1.75$ $s_d = 2.9155$ $t = \dfrac{1.75}{2.9155/\sqrt{8}} = 1.698$

c. Using a p-value calculator or statistical software, the p-value is .0667.

d. Do not reject H_0. The test statistic is less than the critical value. The p-value is greater than .05.

e. We fail to find evidence the change reduced absences.

53. a. H_0: $\mu_1 = \mu_2$ H_1: $\mu_1 \ne \mu_2$
Reject H_0 if $t < -2.024$ or $t > 2.024$.

b. $s_p^2 = \dfrac{(15-1)(40,000)^2 + (25-1)(30,000)^2}{15+25-2} = 1,157,894,737$

$$t = \frac{150,000 - 180,000}{\sqrt{1.157,894,737\left(\frac{1}{15} + \frac{1}{25}\right)}} = -2.699$$

c. Using a p-value calculator or statistical software, the p-value is .0103.

d. Reject H_0. The test statistic is outside the interval. The p-value is less than .05.

e. The data indicate that the population means are different.

55. a. H_0: $\mu_{Before} - \mu_{After} = \mu_d \le 0$ H_1: $\mu_d > 0$
Reject H_0 if $t > 1.895$.

b. $\overline{d} = 3.113$ $s_d = 2.911$ $t = \dfrac{3.113}{2.911\sqrt{8}} = 3.025$

c. Using a p-value calculator or statistical software, the p-value is .0096.

d. Reject H_0. The test statistic is outside the interval. The p-value is less than .05.

e. We find evidence the average contamination is lower after the new soap is used.

57. a. H_0: $\mu_{Ocean\ Drive} = \mu_{Rio\ Rancho}$; H_1: $\mu_{Ocean\ Drive} \ne \mu_{Rio\ Rancho}$
Reject H_0 if $t < -2.008$ or $t > 2.008$.

b. $s_p^2 = \dfrac{(25-1)(23.43)\,2 + (28-1)(24.12)^2}{25+28-2} = 566$

$$t = \frac{86.2 - 92.0}{\sqrt{566\left(\frac{1}{25} + \frac{1}{28}\right)}} = -0.886$$

c. Using a p-value calculator or statistical software, the p-value is .3798.

d. Do not reject H_0. The test statistic is inside the interval. The p-value is more than .05.

e. It is reasonable to conclude there is no difference in the mean number of cars in the two lots.

59. a. H_0: $\mu_{US\ 17} - \mu_{SC\ 707} = \mu_d \le 0$ H_1: $\mu_d > 0$
Reject H_0 if $t > 1.711$.

b. $\overline{d} = 28$ $s_d = 6.589$ $t = \dfrac{2.8}{6.589/\sqrt{25}} = 2.125$

c. Using a p-value calculator or statistical software, the p-value is .0220.

d. Reject H_0. The test statistic is greater than the test statistic. The p-value is less than .05.

e. On average, there are more cars in the US 17 lot.

61. H_0: $\pi_1 \le \pi_2$ H_1: $\pi_1 > \pi_2$
If it $z > 2.33$, reject H_0.

$$p_c = \frac{990 + 970}{1,500 + 1,600} = 0.63$$

$$z = \frac{.6600 - .60625}{\sqrt{\frac{.63(.34)}{1,500} + \frac{.63(.37)}{1,600}}} = 3.10$$

Reject the null hypothesis. We can conclude the proportion of men who believe the division is fair is greater.

63. H_0: $\pi_1 \le \pi_2$ H_1: $\pi_1 > \pi_2$ H_0 is rejected if $z > 1.65$.

$$p_c = \frac{.091 + .0.85}{2} = .088$$

$$z = \frac{0.091 - 0.085}{\sqrt{\frac{(0.088)(0.912)}{5,000} + \frac{(0.088)(0.912)}{5,000}}} = 1.059$$

H_0 is not rejected. There has not been an increase in the proportion calling conditions "good" The p-value is. 1446, found by .5000 − .3554. The increase in the percentages will happen by chance in one out of every seven cases.

65. H_0: $\pi_1 = \pi_2$ H_1: $\pi_1 \ne \pi_2$
H_0 is rejected of z is not between −1.96 and 1.96.

$$p_c = \frac{100 + 36}{300 + 200} = .272$$

$$z = \frac{\frac{100}{300} - \frac{36}{200}}{\sqrt{\frac{(0.272)(0.728)}{300} + \frac{(0.272)(0.728)}{200}}} = 3.755$$

67. a. Using statistical software, the result is that we fail to reject the null hypothesis that the mean prices of homes with and without pools are equal. Assuming equal population variances, the p-value is 0.4908.

b. Using statistical software, the result is that we reject the null hypothesis that the mean prices of homes with and without garages are equal. There is a large difference in mean prices between homes with and without garages. Assuming equal population variances, the p-value is less than 0.0001.

c. Using statistical software, the result is that we fail to reject the null hypothesis that the mean prices of homes are equal with mortgages in default and not in default. Assuming equal population variances, the p-value is 0.6980.

69. Using statistical software, the result is that we reject the null hypothesis that the mean maintenance cost of buses powered by diesel and gasoline engines is the same. Assuming equal population variances, the p-value is less than 0.0001.

CHAPTER 12

1. a. H_0: $\mu_1 = \mu_2 = \mu_3$; H_1: Treatment means are not all the same.
b. Reject H_0 if $F > 4.26$.
c & d.

Source	SS	df	MS	F
Treatment	62.17	2	31.08	21.94
Error	12.75	9	1.42	
Total	74.92	11		

e. Reject H_0. The treatment means are not all the same.

3. a. H_0: $\mu_{Southwyck} = \mu_{Franklin} = \mu_{Old\ Orchard}$ H_1: Treatment means are not all the same.
b. Reject H_0 if $F > 4.26$.

c.

Source	SS	df	MS	F
Treatment	276.50	2	138.25	14.18
Error	87.75	9	9.75	

d. Using a p-value calculator or statistical software, the p-value is .0017.

e. Reject H_0. The test statistic is greater than the critical value. The p-value is less than .05.

f. The mean incomes are not all the same for the three tracks of land.

5. a. $H_0: \mu_1 = \mu_2 = \mu_3$ H_1: Treatment means are not all the same.

b. Reject H_0 if $F > 4.26$.

c. SST = 107.20   SSE = 9.47   SS total = 116.67

d. Using Excel,

ANOVA

Source of Variation	SS	df	MS	F	P-value	F crit
Treatment	107.2000	2	53.6000	50.9577	0.0000	4.2565
Error	9.4667	9	1.0519			
Total	116.6667	11				

e. Since $50.96 > 4.26$, H_0 is rejected. At least one of the means differ.

f. $(\overline{X}_1 - \overline{X}_2) \pm t\sqrt{MSE(1/n_1 + 1/n_2)}$

$(9.667 - 2.20) \pm 2.262\sqrt{1.052(1/3 + 1/5)}$

7.467 ± 1.69

[5.777, 9.157] Yes, we can conclude that treatments 1 and 2 have different means.

7. a. $H_0: \mu_1 = \mu_2 = \mu_3 = \mu_4$ H_1: Treatment means are not all equal. Reject H_0 if $F > 3.71$.

b. The F-test statistic is 2.36.

c. The p-value is .133.

d. H_0 is not rejected. The test statistic, 2.36 is less than the critical value, 3.71. The p-value is more than .05.

e. There is no difference in the mean number of weeks.

9. a. $H_0: \mu_1 = \mu_2$ H_1: Not all treatment means are equal.

b. Reject H_0 if $F > 18.5$.

c. $H_0: \mu_A = \mu_B = \mu_C$ H_1: Not all block means are equal. Reject H_0 if $F > 19.0$

d. SSTotal $= (46.0 - 36.5)^2 + \cdots (35.0 - 36.5)^2 = 289.5$

$SST = 3\left(\left(42.33 - {}^{219}/_6\right)^2\right) + 3\left(\left(30.67 - {}^{219}/_6\right)^2\right)$
$= 204.167$

$SSB = 2\left(\left(38.5 - {}^{219}/_6\right)^2\right) + 2\left(\left(31.5 - {}^{219}/_6\right)^2\right) +$
$2\left(\left(39.5 - {}^{219}/_6\right)^2\right) = 76.00$

SSE = SSTotal − SST − SSB = 289.5 − 204.1667 − 76
= 9.333

e.

Source	SS	df	MS	F	p-Value
Treatment	204.167	1	204.167	43.75	0.0221
Blocks	76.000	2	38.000	8.14	0.1094
Error	9.333	2	4.667		
Total	289.5000	5			

f. The F-statistic is significant: $43.75 > 18.5$; p-value is less than .05. so reject H_0. There is a difference in the treatment means: $8.14 < 19.0$. For the blocks, $8.14 < 19.0$; p-value is more than .05, so fail to reject H_0 for blocks. There is no difference between blocks.

11. a. For treatment
$H_0: \mu_{Day} = \mu_{Afternoon} = \mu_{Night}$
H_1: Not all means equal

b. Reject if $F > 4.46$.

c. For blocks: $H_0: \mu_S = \mu_L = \mu_C = \mu_T = \mu_M$ H_1: Not all means are equal. Reject if $F > 3.84$.

d. $SSTotal = (31 - 433/15)^2 + \cdots + (27 - 433/15)^2 = 139.73$

$SST = 5\left(\left(30 - {}^{433}/_{15}\right)^2\right) + 5\left(\left(26 - {}^{433}/_{15}\right)^2\right)$
$+ 5\left(\left(30.6 - {}^{433}/_{15}\right)^2\right) = 62.53$

$SSB = 3\left(\left(30.33 - {}^{433}/_{15}\right)^2\right) + 3\left(\left(30.67 - {}^{433}/_{15}\right)^2\right)$
$+ 3\left(\left(27.3 - {}^{433}/_{15}\right)^2\right) + 3\left(\left(29 - {}^{433}/_{15}\right)^2\right)$
$+ 3\left(\left(27 - {}^{433}/_{15}\right)^2\right) = 33.73$

SSE = (SSTotal − SST − SSB) = 139.73 − 62.53 − 33.73
= 43.47

e. Here is the ANOVA table:

Source	SS	df	MS	F	p-Value
Treatment	62.53	2	31.2667	5.75	.0283
Blocks	33.73	4	8.4333	1.55	.2767
Error	43.47	8	5.4333		
Total	139.73	14			

f. As $5.75 > 4.46$ the null for treatments is rejected, but the null for blocks is not rejected as $1.55 < 3.84$. There is a difference in means by shifts, but not by employee.

13.

Source	SS	df	MS	F	P
Size	156.333	2	78.1667	1.98	0.180
Weight	98.000	1	98.000	2.48	0.141
Interaction	36.333	2	18.1667	0.46	0.642
Error	473.333	12	39.444		
Total	764.000	17			

a. Since the p-value (0.18) is greater than 0.05, there is no difference in the Size means.

b. The p-value for Weight (0.141) is also greater than 0.05. Thus, there is no difference in those means.

c. There is no significant interaction because the p-value (0.642) is greater than 0.05.

15. a.

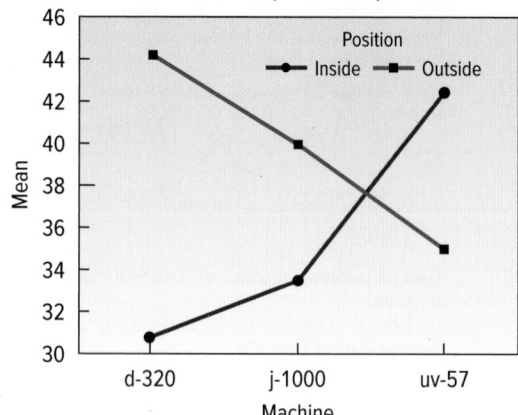

Interaction Plot (data means) for Sales

Yes, there appears to be an interaction effect. Sales are different based on machine position, either in the inside or outside position.

b.

Two-way ANOVA: Sales versus Position, Machine					
Source	df	SS	MS	F	P
Position	1	104.167	104.167	9.12	0.007
Machine	2	16.333	8.167	0.72	0.502
Interaction	2	457.333	228.667	20.03	0.000
Error	18	205.500	11.417		
Total	23	783.333			

The position and the interaction of position and machine effects are significant. The effect of machine on sales is not significant.

c.

One-way ANOVA: D-320 Sales versus Position					
Source	df	SS	MS	F	P
Position	1	364.50	364.50	40.88	0.001
Error	6	53.50	8.92		
Total	7	418.00			

One-way ANOVA: J-1000 Sales versus Position					
Source	df	SS	MS	F	P
Position	1	84.5	84.5	5.83	0.052
Error	6	87.0	14.5		
Total	7	171.5			

One-way ANOVA: UV-57 Sales versus Position					
Source	df	SS	MS	F	P
Position	1	112.5	112.5	10.38	0.018
Error	6	65.0	10.8		
Total	7	177.5			

Recommendations using the statistical results and mean sales plotted in part (a): Position the D-320 machine outside. Statistically, the position of the J-1000 does not matter. Position the UV-57 machine inside.

17. a. $H_0: \mu_1 = \mu_2 = \mu_3 = \mu_4$
H_1: Treatment means are not all equal.
b. $\alpha = .05$ Reject H_0 if $F > 3.10$.
c.

Source	SS	df	MS	F
Treatment	50	$4 - 1 = 3$	50/3	1.67
Error	200	$24 - 4 = 20$	10	
Total	250	$24 - 1 = 23$		

d. Do not reject H_0.
19. a. $H_0: \mu_{Discount} = \mu_{Variety} = \mu_{Department}$ H_1: Not all means are equal.
H_0 is rejected if $F > 3.89$.
b. From Excel, single-factor ANOVA,

ANOVA						
Source of Variation	SS	df	MS	F	P-value	F crit
Treatment	63.3333	2	31.6667	13.3803	0.0009	3.8853
Error	28.4000	12	2.3667			
Total	91.7333	14				

c. The F-test statistic is 13.3803.
d. p-Value = .0009.

e. H_0 is rejected. The F-statistic exceeds the critical value; the p-value is less than .05.
f. There is a difference in the treatment means.
21. a. $H_0: \mu_{Rec\ Center} = \mu_{Key\ Street} = \mu_{Monclova} = \mu_{Whitehouse}$ H_1: Not all means are equal. H_0 is rejected if $F > 3.10$.
b. From Excel, single-factor ANOVA,

ANOVA						
Source of Variation	SS	df	MS	F	P-value	F crit
Treatment	87.7917	3	29.2639	9.1212	0.0005	3.0984
Error	64.1667	20	3.2083			
Total	151.9583	23				

c. The F-test statistic is 9.1212.
d. p-value = .0005.
e. Since computed F of $9.1212 > 3.10$, and the p-value is less than .05, the null hypothesis of no difference is rejected
f. There is evidence the number of crimes differs by district.
23. a. $H_0: \mu_{Lecture} = \mu_{Distance}$ $H_1: \mu_{Lecture} \neq \mu_{Distance}$
Critical value of $F = 4.75$. Reject H_0 if the F-stat > 4.75.

ANOVA						
Source of Variation	SS	df	MS	F	P-value	F crit
Treatment	219.4286	1	219.4286	23.0977	0.0004	4.7472
Error	114.0000	12	9.5000			
Total	333.4286	13				

Reject H_0 in favor of the alternative.

b. $t = \dfrac{37 - 45}{\sqrt{9.5\left(\dfrac{1}{6} + \dfrac{1}{18}\right)}} - 4.806$

Since $t^2 = F$. That is $(-4.806)^2 = 23.098$. The p-value for this statistic is 0.0004 as well. Reject H_0 in favor of the alternative.

c. There is a difference in the mean scores between lecture and distance-based formats.
25. a. $H_0: \mu_{Compact} = \mu_{Midsize} = \mu_{Large}$ H_1: Not all means are equal.
H_0 is rejected if $F > 3.10$.
b. The F-test statistic is 8.258752.
c. p-value is .0019.
d. The null hypothesis of equal means is rejected because the F-statistic (8.258752) is greater than the critical value (3.10). The p-value (0.0019) is also less than the significance level (0.05).
e. The mean miles per gallon for the three car types are different.
27. $H_0: \mu_1 = \mu_2 = \mu_3 = \mu_4$. H_1: At least one mean is different. Reject H_0 if $F > 2.7395$. Since $13.74 > 2.74$, reject H_0. You can also see this from the p-value of $0.0001 < 0.05$. Priority mail express is faster than all three of the other classes, and priority mail is faster than either first-class or standard. However, first-class and standard mail may be the same.
29. a. $H_0: \mu_{Red} = \mu_{Blue} = \mu_{Orange} = \mu_{Green}$ H_1: At least one pair of means is significantly different.

$H_0: \mu_{Small} = \mu_{Medium} = \mu_{Large}$ H_1: At least one pair of means is significantly different.

b. From Excel, two-factor ANOVA without replication,

ANOVA

Source of Variation	SS	df	MS	F	P-value	F crit
Blocks	21.5000	2	10.7500	7.5882	0.0227	5.1433
Treatments	25.0000	3	8.3333	5.8824	0.0321	4.7571
Error	8.5000	6	1.4167			
Total	55	11				

For the blocks, $F = 7.5882$. For treatments, $F = 5.8824$.

c. For the blocks, p-value $= .0227$. For treatments, p-value $= .0321$.

d. For both treatments and blocks (color and size), H_0 is rejected.

e. At least one mean differs for color and at least one mean differs for size.

31. a. H_0: $\mu_{Zawodny} = \mu_{Norman} = \mu_{Cingle} = \mu_{Holiday}$ H_1: At least one pair of means is significantly different.

H_0: $\mu_A = \mu_B = \mu_{C} = \mu_D = \mu_E$ H_1: At least one pair of means is significantly different.

b. From Excel, two-factor ANOVA without replication,

ANOVA

Source of Variation	SS	df	MS	F	P-value	F crit
Block (home)	4278.7000	4	1069.6750	100.2037	0.0000	3.2592
Treatments (Assessor)	21.4000	3	7.1333	0.6682	0.5876	3.4903
Error	128.1000	12	10.6750			
Total	4428.2	19				

For the blocks, $F = 100.2037$. For treatments, $F = .6682$.

c. For the blocks, p-value $= .0000$. For treatments, p-value $= .5816$.

d. Reject H_0 for homes. Fail to reject H_0 for assessors.

e. The mean assessed values for the homes are statistically different. The mean assessed values for each assessor are not statistically different.

33. a.

For Gasoline

H_0: $\mu_R = \mu_M = \mu_S$
H_1: Mean mileage is not the same for gas
H_0 is rejected if $F > 3.89$

For Automobile

H_0: $\mu_1 = \mu_2 = \ldots \mu_7$
H_1: Mean mileage is not the same for cars
H_0 is rejected if $F > 3.00$

b. From Excel, two-factor ANOVA without replication,

ANOVA

Source of Variation	SS	df	MS	F	P-value	F crit
Blocks (Auto)	77.2381	6	12.8730	15.5962	0.0000	2.9961
Treatment (Brand)	44.0952	2	22.0476	26.7115	0.0000	3.8853
Error	9.9048	12	0.8254			
Total	131.2381	20				

For the blocks, $F = 15.5962$. For treatments, $F = 26.7115$.

c. For the blocks, p-value $= .0000$. For treatments, p-value $= .0000$.

d. Reject H_0 for Automobile. Reject H_0 for Brand.

e. The mean miles per gallon for automobiles are statistically different. The mean miles per gallon for each gasoline brand are statistically different.

35. a. H_0: $\mu_R = \mu_O = \mu_Y = \mu_B = \mu_T = \mu_G$ H_1: The treatment means are not equal. Reject H_0 if $F > 2.37$

b. From Excel, single-factor ANOVA,

ANOVA

Source of Variation	SS	df	MS	F	P-value	F crit
Treatment	0.0348	5	0.0070	3.8645	0.0043	2.3738
Error	0.1044	58	0.0018			
Total	0.1392	63				

For treatments, $F = 3.8645$.

c. For treatments, p-value $= .0043$.

d. Reject H_0 for color.

e. The mean weight of M&M's differ by color.

37. a.

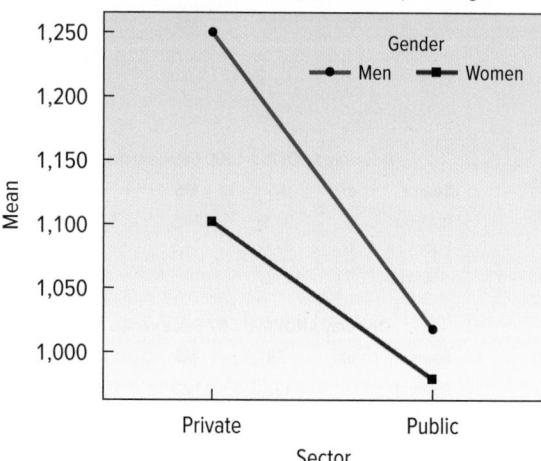

Interaction Plot (data means) for Wage

b. Two-way ANOVA: Wage versus Gender, Sector

```
Source        DF       SS       MS       F       P
Gender         1    44086    44086   11.44   0.004
Sector         1   156468   156468   40.61   0.000
Interaction    1    14851    14851    3.85   0.067
Error         16    61640     3853
Total         19   277046
```

There is no interaction effect of gender and sector on wages. However, there are significant differences in mean wages based on gender and significant differences in mean wages based on sector.

c. One-way ANOVA: Wage versus Sector

```
Source    DF        SS        MS        F        P
Sector     1    156468    156468    23.36    0.000
Error     18    120578      6699
Total     19    277046
```

$s = 81.85$ R-$Sq = 56.48\%$ R-$Sq(adj) = 54.06\%$

One-way ANOVA: Wage versus Gender

```
Source    DF        SS        MS       F        P
Gender     1     44086     44086    3.41    0.081
Error     18    232960     12942
Total     19    277046
```

$s = 113.8$ R-$Sq = 15.91\%$ R-$Sq(adj) = 11.24\%$

d. The statistical results show that only sector, private or public, has a significant effect on the wages of accountants.

39. a. $H_0: \sigma_p^2 = \sigma_{np}^2 \qquad H_1: \sigma_p^2 \neq \sigma_{np}^2$
Reject H_0. The p-value is less than 0.05. There is a difference in the variance of average selling prices between houses with pools and houses without pools.

b. $H_0: \sigma_g^2 = \sigma_{ng}^2 \quad H_1: \sigma_g^2 \neq \sigma_{ng}^2$
Reject H_0. There is a difference in the variance of average selling prices between house with garages and houses without garages. The p-value is < 0.0001.

c. $H_0: \mu_1 = \mu_2 = \mu_3 = \mu_4 = \mu_5; H_1$: Not all treatment means are equal.
Fail to reject H_0. The p-value is much larger than 0.05. There is no statistical evidence of differences in the mean selling price between the five townships.

d. $H_0: \mu_c = \mu_i = \mu_m = \mu_p = \mu_r, H_1$: Not all treatment means are equal. Fail to reject H_0. The p-value is much larger than 0.05. There is no statistical evidence of differences in the mean selling price between the five agents. Is fairness of assignment based on the overall mean price, or based on the comparison of the means of the prices assigned to the agents?
While the p-value is not less than 0.05, it may indicate that the pairwise differences should be reviewed. These indicate that Marty's comparisons to the other agents are significantly different.

e. The results show that the mortgage type is a significant effect on the mean years of occupancy ($p = 0.0227$). The interaction effect is also significant ($p = 0.0026$).

41. a. $H_0: \mu_B = \mu_K = \mu_T \qquad H_1$: Not all treatment (manufacturer) mean maintenance costs, are equal.
Do not reject H_0. ($p = 0.7664$). The mean maintenance costs by the bus manufacturer is not different.

b. $H_0: \mu_B = \mu_K = \mu_T \qquad H_1$: Not all treatments have equal mean miles since the last maintenance.
Do not reject H_0. The mean miles since the last maintenance by the bus manufacturer is not different. P-value = 0.4828.

CHAPTER 13

1. $\Sigma(x - \bar{x})(y - \bar{y}) = 10.6, s_x = 2.7, s_y = 1.3$

$$r = \frac{10.6}{(5.1)(2.709)(1.38)} = 0.75$$

3. a. Sales.
b.

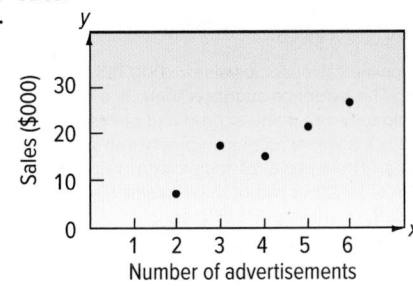

c. $\Sigma(x - \bar{x})(y - \bar{y}) = 36, n = 5, s_x = 1.5811, s_y = 6.1237$

$$r = \frac{36}{(5 - 1)(1.5811)(6.1237)} = 0.9295$$

d. There is a strong positive association between the variables.
5. a. Either variable could be independent. In the scatter plot, police is the independent variable.

b.

c. $n = 8, \Sigma(x - \bar{x})(y - \bar{y}) = -231.75$
$s_x = 5.8737, s_y = 6.4462$
$$r = \frac{-231.75}{(8 - 1)(5.8737)(6.4462)} = -0.8744$$

d. Strong inverse relationship. As the number of police increases, the crime decreases or, as crime increases the number of police decrease.

7. Reject H_0 if $t > 1.812$.

$$t = \frac{.32\sqrt{12 - 2}}{\sqrt{1 - (.32)^2}} = 1.068$$

Do not reject H_0.

9. $H_0: \rho \leq 0; H_1: \rho > 0$. Reject H_0 if $t > 2.552$. $df = 18$.

$$t = \frac{.78\sqrt{20 - 2}}{\sqrt{1 - (.78)^2}} = 5.288$$

Reject H_0. There is a positive correlation between gallons sold and the pump price.

11. $H_0: \rho \leq 0 \qquad H_1: \rho > 0$
Reject H_0 if $t > 2.650$ with $df = 13$.

$$t = \frac{0.667\sqrt{15 - 2}}{\sqrt{1 - 0.667^2}} = 3.228$$

Reject H_0. There is a positive correlation between the number of passengers and plane weight.

13. a. $\hat{y} = 3.7671 + 0.3630x$

$$b = 0.7522\left(\frac{1.3038}{2.7019}\right) = 0.3630$$

$$a = 5.8 - 0.3630(5.6) = 3.7671$$

b. 6.3081, found by $\hat{y} = 3.7671 + 0.3630(7)$
15. a. $\Sigma(x - \bar{x})(y - \bar{y}) = 44.6, s_x = 2.726, s_y = 2.011$

$$r = \frac{44.6}{(10 - 1)(2.726)(2.011)} = .904$$

$$b = .904\left(\frac{2.011}{2.726}\right) = 0.667$$

$$a = 7.4 - .677(9.1) = 1.333$$

b. $\hat{Y} = 1.333 + .667(6) = 5.335$
17. a.

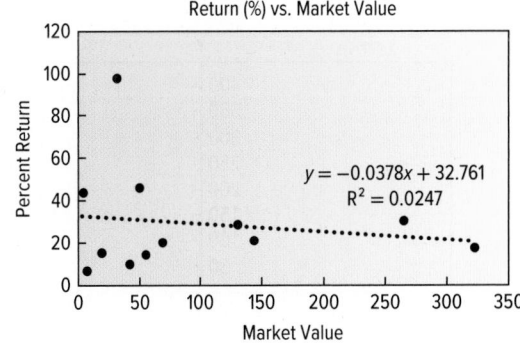

b. Computing correlation in Excel, $r = -.157206$

	Market Value ($ billions)	3-Year Annualized Return (%)
Mean	95.00833	29.16667
Standard Deviation	103.20771	24.83898
Count	12	12

c.

$$b = -.15720 \frac{24.8390}{103.2077} = -.0378;$$
$$a = 29.16667 - (-0.0378)(95.00833) = 32.7580$$

d. $\hat{Y} = 32.7580 + (-0.0378)(100.0) = 28.98\%$.

19. a. $b = -.8744\left(\frac{6.4462}{5.8737}\right) = -0.9596$

$$a = \frac{95}{8} - (-0.9596)\left(\frac{146}{8}\right) = 29.3877$$

b. 10.1957, found by $29.3877 - 0.9596(20)$
c. For each police officer added, crime goes down by almost one.

21. $H_0: \beta \geq 0$ $H_1: \beta < 0$ $df = n - 2 = 8 - 2 = 6$
Reject H_0 if $t < -1.943$.

$$t = -0.96/0.22 = -4.364$$

Reject H_0 and conclude the slope is less than zero.

23. $H_0: \beta = 0$ $H_1: \beta \neq 0$ $df = n - 2 = 12 - 2 = 10$
Reject H_0 if t not between -2.228 and 2.228.

$$t = -.03/.08 = -.375$$

Fail to reject. We cannot conclude the slope is different from zero.

25. The standard error of estimate is 3.378, found by $\sqrt{\frac{68.4814}{8-2}}$.
The coefficient of determination is 0.76, found by $(-0.874)^2$. Seventy-six percent of the variation in crimes can be explained by the variation in police.

27. The standard error of estimate is 0.913, found by $\sqrt{\frac{6.667}{10-2}}$. The coefficient of determination is 0.82, found by $29.733/36.4$. Eighty-two percent of the variation in kilowatt hours can be explained by the variation in the number of rooms.

29. a. $r^2 = \frac{1,000}{1,500} = .6667$

b. $r = \sqrt{.6667} = .8165$

c. $s_{y \cdot x} = \sqrt{\frac{500}{13}} = 6.2017$

31. a. $6.308 \pm (3.182)(.993)\sqrt{.2 + \frac{(7 - 5.6)^2}{29.2}}$

$$= 6.308 \pm 1.633$$
$$= [4.675, 7.941]$$

b. $6.308 \pm (3.182)(.993)\sqrt{1 + 1/5 + .0671}$
$$= [2.751, 9.865]$$

33. a. 4.2939, 6.3721
b. 2.9854, 7.6806

35. a

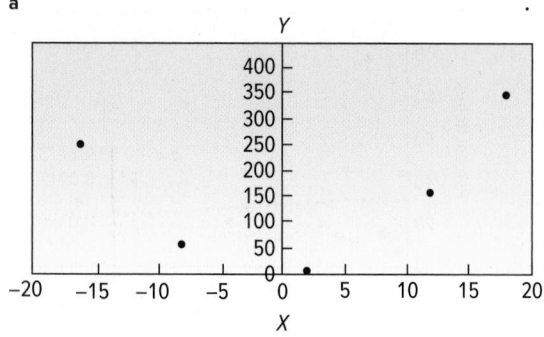

The correlation of X and Y is 0.2975. The scatter plot reveals the variables do not appear to be linearly related. In fact, the pattern is U shaped.
b. The correlation coefficient is .2975.
c. Perform the task.
d.

e. The correlation between Y and $X^2 = .9975$.
f. The relationship between Y and X is nonlinear. The relationship between Y and the transformed X^2 in nearly perfectly linear.
g. Linear regression analysis can be used to estimate the linear relationship: $Y = a + b(X)^2$.

37. $H_0: \rho \leq 0; H_1: \rho > 0$. Reject H_0 if $t > 1.714$.

$$t = \frac{.94\sqrt{25-2}}{\sqrt{1-(.94)^2}} = 13.213$$

Reject H_0. There is a positive correlation between passengers and weight of luggage.

39. $H_0: \rho \leq 0; H_1: \rho > 0$. Reject H_0 if $t > 2.764$.

$$t = \frac{.47\sqrt{12-2}}{\sqrt{1-(.47)^2}} = 1.684$$

Do not reject H_0. Using an online p-value calculator or statistical software, the p-value is 0.0615.

41. a. The correlation is -0.563. There is a moderate inverse linear relationship between points allowed and points scored. As the number of points scored increases, the number of points allowed decreases.
b. $H_0: \rho \geq 0$ $H_1: \rho < 0$ Reject H_0 if $t < -1.697$ $df = 30$

$$t = \frac{-0.563\sqrt{32-2}}{\sqrt{1-(-0.563)^2}} = -3.731.$$

Using an online calculator, p-value $= .000398$.
Reject H_0. The evidence suggests there is a significant inverse relationship between points scored and points allowed.

43. a. There is a positive relationship between wins and point differential. There were 14 teams with losing records (won 8 games or less) but two of these teams (Denver and Seattle) recorded a positive point differential.

Scatter Plot 2021 NFL Season Wins versus Point Differential

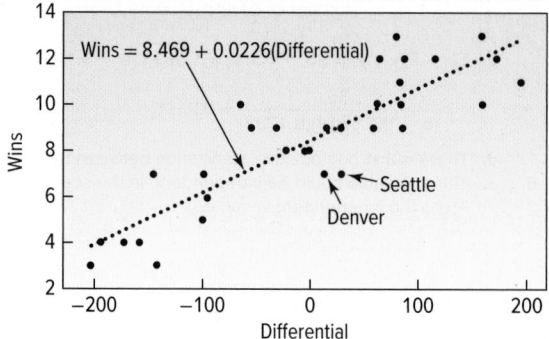

b. $r = .876$. There is a strong, positive relationship between wins and point differential.

c. The $R^2 = 76.65\%$. Point differential accounts for 76.65% of the variation in wins.

SUMMARY OUTPUT

Regression Statistics

Multiple R	0.8755
R Square	0.7665
Standard Error	1.4278
Observations	32

ANOVA

	df	SS	MS	F	p-value
Regression	1	200.8064	200.8064	98.4952	0.0000
Residual	30	61.1623	2.0387		
Total	31	261.9688			

	Coefficients	Standard Error	t Stat	P-value
Intercept	8.4688	0.2524	33.5516	0.0000
Diff	0.0226	0.0023	9.9245	0.0000

d. Wins = 8.469 + .0226 (point differential)

e. Setting differential equal to 100, then Wins = 8.469 + .0226(100) = 10.73. We estimate that a team with a point differential of 100 to win 11 games. Note that we rounded up to the next whole number.

f. The slope indicates that for every single point increase in point differential, wins increase .0226. An increase in the differential of 45 points would result in an additional win This is found by solving for point differential in the following equation:
1 = .0226(point differential). The result is 44.248 points or rounding up to 45 points.

45. a.

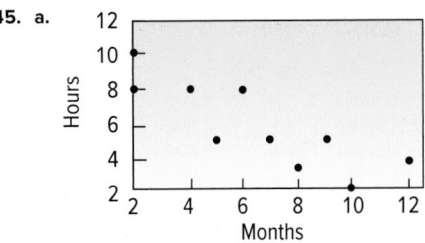

There is an inverse relationship between the variables. As the months owned increase, the number of hours exercised decreases.

b. $r = -0.827$ The correlation coefficient indicates a strong, inverse linear relationship between months owned and hours exercised.

c. $H_0: \rho \geq 0; H_1: \rho < 0$. Reject H_0 if $t < -2.896$.

$$t = \frac{-0.827\sqrt{10-2}}{\sqrt{1-(-0.827)^2}} = -4.16$$

Reject H_0. There is a negative association between months owned and hours exercised.

47. a. The appears to be a weak positive relationship between population and median age.

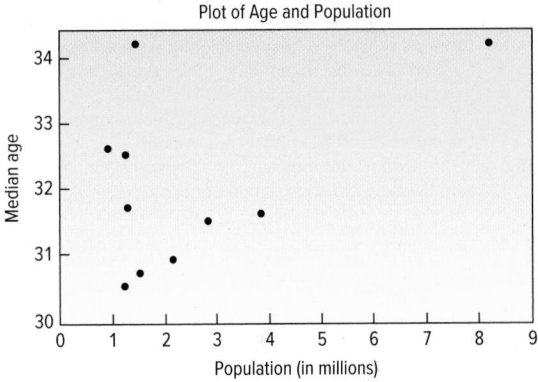

Plot of Age and Population

b. Compute by hand or use Excel to compute the correlation coefficient.

Population (millions) X	Median Age Y	$(X - \bar{X})$	$(X - \bar{X})^2$	$(Y - \bar{Y})$	$(Y - \bar{Y})^2$	$(X - \bar{X})(Y - \bar{Y})$
2.833	31.5	0.3612	0.130465	−0.54	0.2916	−0.19505
1.233	30.5	−1.2388	1.534625	−1.54	2.3716	1.907752
2.144	30.9	−0.3278	0.107453	−1.14	1.2996	0.373692
3.849	31.6	1.3772	1.89668	−0.44	0.1936	−0.60597
8.214	34.2	5.7422	32.97286	2.16	4.6656	12.40315
1.448	34.2	−1.0238	1.048166	2.16	4.6656	−2.21141
1.513	30.7	−0.9588	0.919297	−1.34	1.7956	1.284792
1.297	31.7	−1.1748	1.380155	−0.34	0.1156	0.399432
1.257	32.5	−1.2148	1.475739	0.46	0.2116	−0.55881
0.93	32.6	−1.5418	2.377147	0.56	0.3136	−0.86341
24.718	320.4		43.84259		15.924	11.93418

The correlation coefficient indicates a weak positive relationship between population and median age.

c. The slope of 0.272 indicates that for each increase of 1 million in the population that the median age increases on average by 0.272 year.

$$\bar{X} = \frac{24.718}{10} = 2.4718 \quad \bar{Y} = \frac{320.4}{10} = 32.04 \quad s_x = \sqrt{\frac{43.84259}{9}}$$
$$= 2.207$$

$$s_y = \sqrt{\frac{15.924}{9}} = 1.330$$

$$r = \frac{11.93418}{(10-1)(2.207)(1.330)} = 0.452$$

SUMMARY OUTPUT

Regression Statistics

Multiple R	0.4517
R Square	0.2040
Adjusted R Square	0.1045
Standard Error	1.2587
Observations	10

ANOVA

	df	SS	MS	F	p-Value
Regression	1	3.2485	3.2485	2.0503	0.1901
Residual	8	12.6755	1.5844		
Total	9	15.9240			

	Coefficients	Standard Error	t-Stat	p-Value	Lower 95%	Upper 95%	Lower 95.0%	Upper 95.0%
Intercept	31.3672	0.6158	50.9348	0.0000	29.9471	32.7873	29.9471	32.7873
Population	0.2722	0.1901	1.4319	0.1901	−0.1662	0.7106	−0.1662	0.7106

d. Median age = 31.3672 + .2722 (population). For a city with 2.5 million people, the predicted median age is 32.08 years, found by 31.4 + 0.272 (2.5).

e. The p-value (0.190) for the population variable is greater than, say 0.05. A test for significance of that coefficient would fail to be rejected. In other words, it is possible the population coefficient is zero.

f. The results indicate no significant linear relationship between a city's median age and its population.

49. a. The scatter plot indicates an inverse relationship between the winning bid and the number of bidders.

Bidders Line Fit Plot

b. Using the following Excel software output, the correlation coefficient is − .7064. It indicates a moderate inverse relationship between winning bid and number of bidders.

c.

SUMMARY OUTPUT

Regression Statistics

Multiple R	0.7064
R Square	0.4990
Adjusted R Square	0.4604
Standard Error	1.1138
Observations	15

ANOVA

	df	SS	MS	F	p-Value
Regression	1	16.0616	16.0616	12.9467	0.0032
Residual	13	16.1277	1.2406		
Total	14	32.1893			

	Coefficients	Standard Error	t-Stat	p-Value	Lower 95%	Upper 95%	Lower 95.0%	Upper 95.0%
Intercept	11.2360	0.9689	11.5961	0.0000	9.1427	13.3293	9.1427	13.3293
Bidders	−0.4667	0.1297	−3.5982	0.0032	−0.7470	−0.1865	−0.7470	−0.1865

The $R^2 = 49.90\%$; the "number of bidders" accounts for 49.90% of the variance of the "winning bid cost".

d. The regression equation is Winning bid = 11.236 − 0.4667 (number of bidders).

e. This indicates there is a negative relationship between the number of bids (X) and the winning bid (Y) and that for each additional bidder the winning bid decreases by 0.4667 million. The slope is significantly different from zero because its p-value, .0032, is less than .05.

f. "Winning bid cost" = 11.235986 − 0.466727(7.0) = $7.968897 million

g. $7.9689 \pm (2.160)(1.114)\sqrt{1 + \dfrac{1}{15} + \dfrac{(7 - 7.1333)^2}{837 - \dfrac{(107)^2}{15}}}$

7.9689 ± 2.4854

$[5.4835, 10.4543]$

51. a. There appears to be a relationship between the two variables. As the distance increases, so does the shipping time.

SUMMARY OUTPUT

Regression Statistics

Multiple R	0.6921
R Square	0.4790
Adjusted R Square	0.4501
Standard Error	2.0044
Observations	20

ANOVA

	df	SS	MS	F	p-Value
Regression	1	66.4864	66.4864	16.5495	0.0007
Residual	18	72.3136	4.0174		
Total	19	138.8000			

	Coefficients	Standard Error	t-Stat	p-Value	Lower 95%	Upper 95%	Lower 95.0%	Upper 95.0%
Intercept	−7.1264	3.8428	−1.8545	0.0801	−15.1999	0.9471	−15.1999	0.9471
Miles	0.0214	0.0053	4.0681	0.0007	0.0103	0.0324	0.0103	0.0324

b. From the regression output, $r = .6921$

$H_0: \rho \leq 0$ $H_0: \rho > 0$ Reject H_0 if $t > 1.734$.

$t = \dfrac{0.6921 \sqrt{20 - 2}}{1 - (0.6921)^2} = 4.0681$; the one-sided p-value

(.0007/2) is .0004. H_0 is rejected. There is a positive association between shipping distance and shipping time.

c. $R^2 = (0.6921)^2 = 0.4790$, nearly half of the variation in shipping time is explained by shipping distance.

d. The standard error of estimate is $2.0044 = \sqrt{72.3136/18}$.

e. Predicting days based on miles will not be very accurate. The standard error of the estimate indicates that the prediction of days may be off by nearly 2 days. The regression equation only accounts for about half of the variation in shipping time with distance.

53.

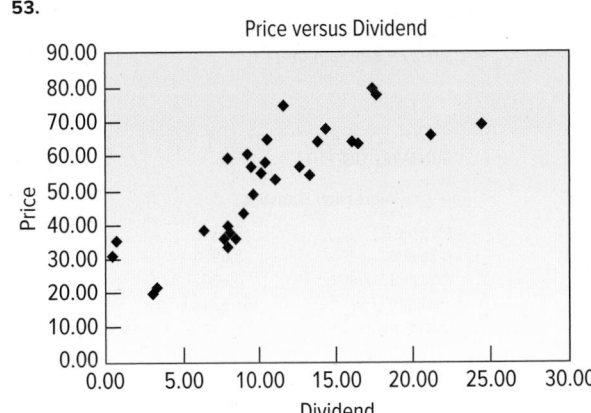

SUMMARY OUTPUT

Regression Statistics

Multiple R	0.8114
R Square	0.6583
Adjusted R Square	0.6461
Standard Error	9.6828
Observations	30

ANOVA

	df	SS	MS	F	p-Value
Regression	1	5057.5543	5057.5543	53.9438	0.0000
Residual	28	2625.1662	93.7559		
Total	29	7682.7205			

	Coefficients	Standard Error	t-Stat	p-Value	Lower 95%	Upper 95%	Lower 95.0%	Upper 95.0%
Intercept	26.8054	3.9220	6.8346	0.0000	18.7715	34.8393	18.7715	34.8393
Dividend	2.4082	0.3279	7.3446	0.0000	1.7365	3.0798	1.7365	3.0798

a. The regression equation is: Price = 26.8054 + 2.4082 dividend. For each additional dollar paid out in a dividend, the per share price increases by \$2.4082 on average.

b. $H_0: \beta = 0$ $H_1: \beta \neq 0$ At the 5% level, reject H_0 if t is not between -2.048 and 2.048. $t = 2.4082/0.3279 = 7.3446$ Reject H_0 and conclude slope is not zero.

c. $R^2 = \dfrac{\text{Reg SS}}{\text{Total SS}} = \dfrac{5057.5543}{7682.7205} = .6583$. 65.83% of the variation in price is explained by the dividend.

d. $r = \sqrt{.6583} = .8114$; 28 df; $H_0: \rho \leq 0\ H_1: \rho > 0$. At the 5% level, reject H_0 when $t > 1.701$.

$t = \dfrac{0.8114\sqrt{30-2}}{\sqrt{1-(0.8114)^2}} = 7.3457$; using a p-value calculator, p-value is less than .00001.

Thus H_0 is rejected. The population correlation is positive.

e. Price = 26.8054 + 2.4082 (\$10) = \$50.8874

f. $50.8874 \pm 2.048(9.6828)\sqrt{1 + \dfrac{1}{30} + \dfrac{(10 - 10.6777)^2}{872.1023}}$

The interval is (\$30.7241, \$71.0507).

55. a. 35

b. $s_{y \cdot x} = \sqrt{29{,}778{,}406} = 5{,}456.96$

c. $r^2 = \dfrac{13{,}548{,}662{,}082}{14{,}531{,}349{,}474} = 0.932$

d. $r = \sqrt{0.932} = 0.966$

e. $H_0: \rho \leq 0, H_1: \rho > 0$; reject H_0 if $t > 1.692$.

$t = \dfrac{.966\sqrt{35-2}}{\sqrt{1-(.966)^2}} = 21.46$

Reject H_0. There is a direct relationship between size of the house and its market value.

57.

SUMMARY OUTPUT

Regression Statistics

Multiple R	0.8346
R Square	0.6966
Adjusted R Square	0.6662
Standard Error	161.6244
Observations	12

ANOVA

	df	SS	MS	F	p-Value
Regression	1	599639.0413	599639.0413	22.9549	0.0007
Residual	10	261224.4587	26122.4459		
Total	11	860863.5000			

	Coefficients	Standard Error	t-Stat	p-Value	Lower 95%	Upper 95%	Lower 95.0%	Upper 95.0%
Intercept	−386.5455	246.8853	−1.5657	0.1485	−936.6403	163.5494	−936.6403	163.5494
Speed	703.9669	146.9313	4.7911	0.0007	376.5837	1031.3502	376.5837	1031.3502

a. The correlation of Speed and Price is 0.8346.

H_0: $\rho \le 0$ H_1: $\rho > 0$ Reject H_0 if $t > 1.8125$.

$t = \dfrac{0.8346 \sqrt{12 - 2}}{\sqrt{1 - (0.8346)^2}} = 4.7911$. Using a p-value calculator or statistical software, the p-value is 0.0004.

Reject H_0. It is reasonable to say the population correlation is positive.

b. The regression equation is Price $= -386.5455 + 703.9669$ Speed.

c. The standard error of the estimate is 161.6244. Any prediction with a residual more than the standard error would be unusual. The computers 2, 3, and 10 have errors in excess of $200.00.

59.

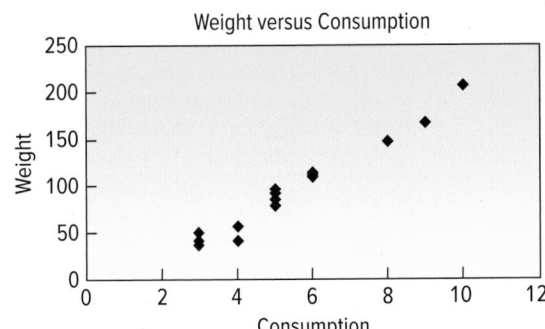
Weight versus Consumption

SUMMARY OUTPUT

Regression Statistics

Multiple R	0.9872
R Square	0.9746
Adjusted R Square	0.9730
Standard Error	7.7485
Observations	18

ANOVA

	df	SS	MS	F	p-Value
Regression	1	36815.6444	36815.6444	613.1895	0.0000
Residual	16	960.6333	60.0396		
Total	17	37776.2778			

	Coefficients	Standard Error	t-Stat	p-Value	Lower 95%	Upper 95%	Lower 95.0%	Upper 95.0%
Intercept	−29.7000	5.2662	−5.6398	0.0000	−40.8638	−18.5362	−40.8638	−18.5362
Consumption	22.9333	0.9261	24.7627	0.0000	20.9700	24.8966	20.9700	24.8966

a. The correlation of Weight and Consumption is 0.9872.

H_0: $\rho \le 0$ H_1: $\rho > 0$ Reject H_0 if $t > 1.746$.

$t = \dfrac{0.9872 \sqrt{18 - 2}}{1 - (0.9872)^2} = 24.7627$. Using a p-value calculator or statistical software, the p-value is less than .00001.

Reject H_0. It is quite reasonable to say the population correlation is positive!

b. The regression equation is Weight $= -29.7000 + 22.9333$(Consumption). Each additional cup increases the estimated weight by 22.9333 pounds.

c. The fourth dog has the largest residual weighing 21 pounds less than the regression equation would estimate. The 16th dog's residual of 10.03 also exceeds the standard error of the estimate; it weights 10.03 pounds more that the predicted weight.

61. a. The relationship is direct. Fares increase for longer flights.

Fare versus Distance

b. The correlation between Distance and Fare is 0.6556.

SUMMARY OUTPUT

Regression Statistics

Multiple R	0.6556
R Square	0.4298
Adjusted R Square	0.4094
Standard Error	46.3194
Observations	30

ANOVA

	df	SS	MS	F	p-Value
Regression	1	45279.0688	45279.0688	21.1043	0.0001
Residual	28	60073.5978	2145.4856		
Total	29	105352.6667			

	Coefficients	Standard Error	t-Stat	p-Value	Lower 95%	Upper 95%	Lower 95.0%	Upper 95.0%
Intercept	147.0812	15.8503	9.2794	0.0000	114.6133	179.5490	114.6133	179.5490
Distance	0.0527	0.0115	4.5939	0.0001	0.0292	0.0761	0.0292	0.0761

H_0: $\rho \le 0$; H_1: $\rho > 0$; Reject H_0 if $t > 1.701$. $df = 28$

$t = \dfrac{0.6556 \sqrt{30-2}}{\sqrt{1 - (0.6556)^2}} = 4.5939$. Using a p-value calculator or

statistical software, the p-value is .000042.
Reject H_0. There is a significant positive correlation between fares and distances.

c. 42.98 percent, found by $(0.6556)^2$, of the variation in fares is explained by the variation in distance.

d. The regression equation is Fare = 147.0812 + 0.0527(Distance). Each additional mile adds $0.0527 to the fare. A 1500-mile flight would cost $226.1312, found by $147.0812 + 0.0527(1500)$.

e. A flight of 4218 miles is outside the range of the sampled data. So the regression equation may not be useful.

63. a. There does seem to be a direct relationship between the variables.

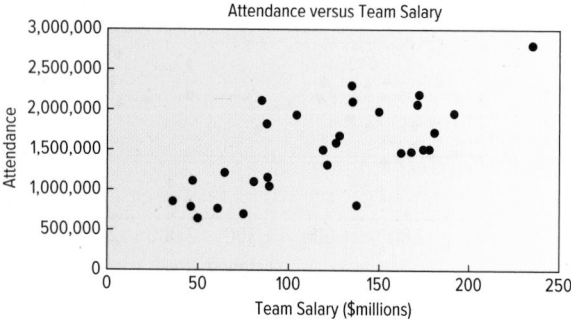

b. The regression analysis of attendance versus team salary follows:

SUMMARY OUTPUT

Regression Statistics

Multiple R	0.7051
R Square	0.4971
Adjusted R Square	0.4792
Standard Error	396718.4889
Observations	30

ANOVA

	df	SS	MS	F	Significance F
Regression	1	4.35657E+12	4.35657E+12	27.6809	0.0000
Residual	28	4.4068E+12	1.57386E+11		
Total	29	8.76337E+12			

	Coefficients	Standard Error	t Stat	P-value
Intercept	608411.7451	185910.4376	3.2726	0.0028
Team Salary ($Millions)	7525.1434	1430.2925	5.2613	0.0000

The regression equation is:
Attendance = 608,411.7451 + .7525.1434(Team Salary).
Expected Attendance with a salary of $100 million is 1,360,926 million, found by Attendance = 608,411.7451 + 7525.1434(100).

c. Increasing salary by 30 million will increase attendance by 225,754.30 on average, found by 7525.1434 (30).

d. H_0: $\beta \le 0$ H_1: $\beta > 0$ df $= n - 2 = 30 - 2 = 28$ Reject H_0 if $t > 1.701$ $t = 7525.1434/1430.2925 = 5.2613$
Using a p-value calculator or statistical software, the p-value is less than .00001.
Reject H_0 and conclude the slope is positive.

e. 0.4971 or 49.71% of the variation in attendance is explained by variation in salary.

f.

Correlation Matrix			
	Attendance	**ERA**	**BA**
Attendance	1		
ERA	−0.3667	1	
BA	0.1386	−0.1835	1

The correlation between attendance and batting average is 0.1386.

$H_0: \rho \le 0$ $H_1: \rho > 0$ At the 5% level, reject H_0 if $t > 1.701$.

$$t = \frac{0.1386\sqrt{30-2}}{\sqrt{1-(0.1386)^2}} = 0.7405$$

Using a p-value calculator or statistical software, the p-value is .2326. Fail to reject H_0.

The batting average and attendance are not positively correlated.

The correlation between attendance and ERA is −0.3667. The correlation between attendance and ERA is stronger than the correlation between attendance and batting average.

$H_0: \rho \le 0$ $H_1: \rho < 0$ At the 5% level, reject H_0 if $t < -1.701$.

$$t = \frac{-0.3667\sqrt{30-2}}{\sqrt{1-(-0.3667)^2}} = -2.086$$

Using a p-value calculator or statistical software, the p-value is .0231. Reject H_0.

ERA and attendance are negatively correlated. Attendance increases when ERA decreases.

CHAPTER 14

1. a. It is called multiple regression analysis because the analysis is based on more than one independent variable.

b. +9.6 is the coefficient of the independent variable, per capita income. It means that for a 1-unit increase in per capita income, sales will increase $9.60.

c. − 11,600 is the coefficient of the independent variable, regional unemployment rate. Note that this coefficient is negative. It means that for a 1-unit increase in regional unemployment rate, sales will decrease $11,600.

d. $374,748 found by = 64,100 + 0.394(796,000) + 9.6(6940) 11,600(6.0)

3. a. 497.736, found by

$$\hat{y} = 16.24 + 0.017(18) + 0.0028(26,500) + 42(3)$$
$$+ 0.0012(156,000) + 0.19(141) + 26.8(2.5)$$

b. Two more social activities. Income added only 28 to the index; social activities added 53.6.

5. a. $$s_{Y \cdot 12} = \sqrt{\frac{SSE}{n-(k+1)}} = \sqrt{\frac{583.693}{65-(2+1)}}$$
$$= \sqrt{9.414} = 3.068$$

Based on the empirical rule, about 95% of the residuals will be between ± 6.136, found by 2(3.068).

b. $$R^2 = \frac{SSR}{SS\ total} = \frac{77.907}{661.6} = .118$$

The independent variables explain 11.8% of the variation.

c. $$R^2_{adj} = 1 - \frac{\dfrac{SSE}{n-(k+1)}}{\dfrac{SS\ total}{n-1}} = 1 - \frac{\dfrac{583.693}{65-(2+1)}}{\dfrac{661.6}{65-1}}$$

$$= 1 - \frac{9.414}{10.3375} = 1 - .911 = .089$$

Using two independent variables in the regression equation explains only 8.9% of the variation in the dependent variable. The adjusted R^2 is less than the unadjusted R^2 because the adjusted R^2 recognizes that the number of variables in the regression equation will increase the unadjusted R^2 value. The adjusted R^2 removes this effect.

7. a. $\hat{y} = 84.998 + 2.391x_1 - 0.4086x_2$

b. 90.0674, found by $\hat{y} = 84.998 + 2.391(4) - 0.4086(11)$

c. $n = 65$ and $k = 2$

d. $H_0: \beta_1 = \beta_2 = 0$ H_1: Not all βs are 0
Reject H_0 if $F > 3.15$.
$F = 4.14$, reject H_0. Not all net regression coefficients equal zero.

e. For x_1 For x_2
$H_0: \beta_1 = 0$ $H_0: \beta_2 = 0$
$H_1: \beta_1 \ne 0$ $H_1: \beta_2 \ne 0$
$t = 1.99$ $t = -2.38$
Reject H_0 if $t > 2.0$ or $t < - 2.0$.
Delete variable 1 and keep 2.

f. Strictly speaking, both independent variables are significantly different from zero. Therefore, neither variable would be deleted from the regression equation.

9. a. The regression equation is: Performance = 29.3 + 5.22 Aptitude + 22.1 Union

Predictor	Coef	SE Coef	T	P
Constant	29.28	12.77	2.29	0.041
Aptitude	5.222	1.702	3.07	0.010
Union	22.135	8.852	2.50	0.028

$S = 16.9166\ R\text{-}Sq = 53.3\%\ R\text{-}Sq\ (adj) = 45.5\%$

Analysis of Variance

Source	DF	SS	MS	F	P
Regression	2	3919.3	1959.6	6.85	0.010
Residual Error	12	3434.0	286.2		
Total	14	7353.3			

b. These variables are both statistically significant in predicting performance. They explain 45.5% of the variation in performance. In particular union membership increases the typical performance by 22.1. A 1-unit increase in aptitude predicts a 5.222 increase in performance score.

c. $H_0: \beta_2 = 0$ $H_1: \beta_2 \ne 0$
Reject H_0 if $t < - 2.179$ or $t > 2.179$. Since 2.50 is greater than 2.179, we reject the null hypothesis and conclude that union membership is significant and should be included. The corresponding p-value is .028.

d. When you consider the interaction variable, the regression equation is Performance = 38.7 + 3.80 Aptitude − 0.1 Union + 3.61 x_1x_2.

Predictor	Coef	SE Coef	T	P
Constant	38.69	15.62	2.48	0.031
Aptitude	3.802	2.179	1.74	0.109
Union	−0.10	23.14	−0.00	0.997
X_1X_2	3.610	3.473	1.04	0.321

The t-value corresponding to the interaction term is 1.04. The p-value is .321 This is not significant. So we conclude there is no interaction between aptitude and union membership when predicting job performance.

11. a. The regression equation is
Price = 3,080 − 54.2 Bidders + 16.3 Age

Predictor	Coef	SE Coef	T	P
Constant	3080.1	343.9	8.96	0.000
Bidders	−54.19	12.28	−4.41	0.000
Age	16.289	3.784	4.30	0.000

The price decreases $54.2 as each additional bidder participates. Meanwhile the price increases $16.3 as the painting age increases by 1 year. While one would expect older paintings to be worth more, it is unexpected that the price goes down as more bidders participate!

b. The regression equation is
Price = 3,972 − 185 Bidders + 6.35 Age + 1.46 (Bidders) (Age)

```
Predictor        Coef    SE Coef      T      P
Constant       3971.7      850.2   4.67  0.000
Bidders        −185.0      114.9  −1.61  0.122
Age             6.353      9.455   0.67  0.509
(Bidders)(Age) 1.462       1.277   1.15  0.265
```

The t-value corresponding to the interaction term is 1.15. This is not significant. So we conclude there is no interaction.

c. The interaction term is insignificant. So, the result in part (a) should be reported.

13. a. Total df = 35 + 4 = 39, so $n = 40$

b. 4

c. R^2 = REG SS/Total SS = 750/1,250 = .60. Note total SS is the sum of regression SS and error SS.

d. $s_{y \cdot 1234} = \sqrt{500/35} = 3.7796$

e. $H_0: \beta_1 = \beta_2 = \beta_3 = \beta_4 = 0$
H_1: Not all the βs equal zero.
H_0 is rejected if $F > 2.65$.

$$F = \frac{750/4}{500/35} = 13.125$$

H_0 is rejected. At least one β_j does not equal zero.

15. a. $n = 26$

b. $R^2 = 100/140 = .7143$

c. 1.4142, found by $\sqrt{\text{Error SS/Error DF}} = \sqrt{40/20} = \sqrt{2}$

d. $H_0: \beta_1 = \beta_2 = \beta_3 = \beta_4 = \beta_5 = 0$
H_1: Not all the βs are 0.
H_0 is rejected if $F > 2.71$.
Computed $F = 10.0$. Reject H_0. At least one regression coefficient is not zero.

e. H_0 is rejected in each case if $t < -2.086$ or $t > 2.086$. x_1 and x_5 should be dropped.

17. a. $28,000

b. $R^2 = \dfrac{\text{SSR}}{\text{SS total}} = \dfrac{3,050}{5,250} = .5809$

c. 9.199 found by $\sqrt{\text{Error SS/Error DF}} = \sqrt{2,200/26} = \sqrt{84.62}$

d. H_0 is rejected if $F > 2.97$ (approximately)

Computed $F = \dfrac{1,016.67}{84.62} = 12.01$

H_0 is rejected. At least one regression coefficient is not zero.

e. If computed t is to the left of -2.056 or to the right of 2.056, the null hypothesis in each of these cases is rejected. Computed t for x_2 and x_3 exceed the critical value. Thus, "population" and "advertising expenses" should be retained and "number of competitors," x_1, dropped.

19. a. The strongest correlation is between High School GPA and Paralegal GPA. No problem with multicollinearity.

b. $R^2 = \dfrac{4.3595}{5.0631} = .8610$

86.10% of the variance in paralegal GPA is explained with the three independent variables.

c. H_0 is rejected if $F > 5.41$.

$$F = \frac{1,4532}{0.1407} = 10.328$$

At least one coefficient is not zero.

d. Any H_0 is rejected if $t < -2.571$ or $t > 2.571$. It appears that only High School GPA is significant. Verbal and math could be eliminated.

e. $R^2 = \dfrac{4.2061}{5.0631} = .8307$

R^2 has only been reduced .0303.

f. The residuals appear slightly skewed (positive) but acceptable.

g. There does not seem to be a problem with the plot.

21. a. The correlation of Screen and Price is 0.893. So there does appear to be a linear relationship between the two.

b. Price is the "dependent" variable.

c. The regression equation is Price = − 1242.1 + 50.671 (screen size). For each inch increase in screen size, the price increases $50.671 on average.

d. Using a "dummy" variable for Sony, the regression equation is Price = 11145.6 + 46.955 (Screen) + 187.10 (Sony). If we set "Sony" = 0, then the manufacturer is Samsung and the price is predicted only by screen size. If we set "Sony" = 1, then the manufacturer is Sony. Therefore, Sony TV's are, on average, $187.10 higher in price than Samsung TVs.

e. Here is some of the output.

Coefficients

Term	Coef	SE Coef	95% CI	t-Value	p-Value
Constant	−1145.6	220.7	(−1606.1, −685.2)	−5.19	<0.0001
Screen	46.955	5.149	(36.215, 57.695)	9.12	<0.0001
Sony					
1	187.10	71.84	(37.24, 336.96)	2.60	0.0170

Based on the p-values, screen size and manufacturer are both significant in predicting price.

f. A histogram of the residuals indicates they follow a normal distribution.

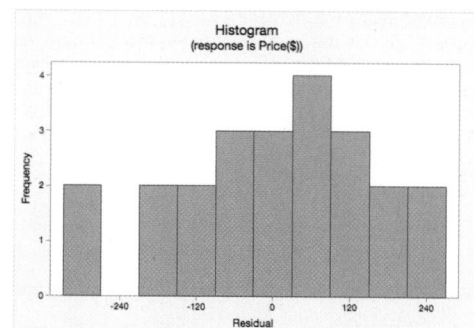

g. There is no apparent relationship in the residuals, but the residual variation may be increasing with larger fitted values.

23. a.

Scatter Diagram of Sales vs. Advertising, Accounts, Competitors, Potential

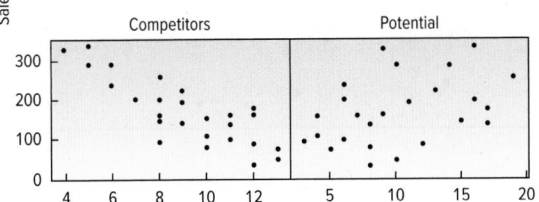

Sales seem to fall with increasing number of competitors and rise with increasing number of accounts and potential.

b. Pearson correlations

	Sales	Advertising	Accounts	Competitors
Advertising	0.159			
Accounts	0.783	0.173		
Competitors	−0.833	−0.038	−0.324	
Potential	0.407	−0.071	0.468	−0.202

The number of accounts and the market potential are moderately correlated.

c. The regression equation is:
Sales = 178 + 1.81 Advertising + 3.32 Accounts − 21.2 Competitors + 0.325 Potential

Predictor	Coef	SE Coef	T	P
Constant	178.32	12.96	13.76	0.000
Advertising	1.807	1.081	1.67	0.109
Accounts	3.3178	0.1629	20.37	0.000
Competitors	−21.1850	0.7879	−26.89	0.000
Potential	0.3245	0.4678	0.69	0.495

$S = 9.60441$ $R\text{-}Sq = 98.9\%$ $R\text{-}Sq(adj) = 98.7\%$

Analysis of Variance

Source	DF	SS	MS	F	P
Regression	4	176777	44194	479.10	0.000
Residual Error	21	1937	92		
Total	25	178714			

The computed F-value is quite large. So we can reject the null hypothesis that all of the regression coefficients are zero. We conclude that some of the independent variables are effective in explaining sales.

d. Market potential and advertising have large p-values (0.495 and 0.109, respectively). You would probably drop them.

e. If you omit potential, the regression equation is:
Sales = 180 + 1.68 Advertising + 3.37 Accounts − 21.2 Competitors

Predictor	Coef	SE Coef	T	P
Constant	179.84	12.62	14.25	0.000
Advertising	1.677	1.052	1.59	0.125
Accounts	3.3694	0.1432	23.52	0.000
Competitors	−21.2165	0.7773	−27.30	0.000

Now advertising is not significant. That would also lead you to cut out the advertising variable and report that the polished regression equation is: Sales = 187 + 3.41 Accounts − 21.2 Competitors

Predictor	Coef	SE Coef	T	P
Constant	186.69	12.26	15.23	0.000
Accounts	3.4081	0.1458	23.37	0.000
Competitors	−21.1930	0.8028	−26.40	0.000

f.

Histogram of the Residuals
(Response Is Sales)

The histogram looks to be normal. There are no problems shown in this plot.

g. The results of regressing number of accounts with number of competitors follow:

ANOVA

	df	SS	MS	F	p-Value
Regression	1	531.2157	531.2157	2.8205	0.1060
Residual	24	4520.1689	188.3404		
Total	25	5051.3846			

	Coefficients	Standard Error	t Stat	P-value
Intercept	68.1205	10.0572	6.7733	0.0000
Number of Competitors	−1.7854	1.0631	−1.6794	0.1060

Regressing number of accounts with number of competitors, the R^2 is 0.1052. The variance inflation factor is $(1/(1 − 0.1052))$ or 1.1176 which is less than 10. There is no indication of multicollinearity.

25. The computer output is:

Predictor	Coef	StDev	t-ratio	p
Constant	651.9	345.3	1.89	0.071
Service	13.422	5.125	2.62	0.015
Age	−6.710	6.349	−1.06	0.301
Sex	205.65	90.27	2.28	0.032
Job	−33.45	89.55	−0.37	0.712

Analysis of Variance

SOURCE	DF	SS	MS	F	p
Regression	4	1066830	266708	4.77	0.005
Error	25	1398651	55946		
Total	29	2465481			

a. $\hat{y} = 651.9 + 13.422x_1 − 6.710x_2 + 205.65x_3 − 33.45x_4$

b. $R^2 = .433$, which is somewhat low for this type of study.

c. $H_0: \beta_1 = \beta_2 = \beta_3 = \beta_4 = 0$; H_1: Not all βs equal zero.
Reject H_0 if $F > 2.76$.

$$F = \frac{1,066,830/4}{1,398,651/25} = 4.77$$

H_0 is rejected. Not all the β_is equal 0.

d. Using the .05 significance level, reject the hypothesis that the regression coefficient is 0 if $t < -2.060$ or $t > 2.060$. Service and sex should remain in the analyses; age and job should be dropped.

e. Following is the computer output using the independent variables service and sex.

```
Predictor      Coef   StDev  t-ratio       p
Constant      784.2   316.8     2.48   0.020
Service       9.021   3.106     2.90   0.007
Sex          224.41   87.35     2.57   0.016

Analysis of Variance
SOURCE     DF       SS      MS      F       p
Regression  2   998779  499389   9.19   0.001
Error      27  1466703   54322
Total      29  2465481
```

A male earns $224 more per month than a female. The difference between management and engineering positions is not significant.

27. a. The correlation between the independent variables, yield and EPS, is small, .16195. Multicollinearity should not be an issue.

Correlation Matrix			
	P/E	**EPS**	**Yield**
P/E	1		
EPS	−0.60229	1	
Yield	0.05363	0.16195	1

b. Here is part of the software output:

Predictor	Coef	SE Coef	t	p-Value
Constant	29.913	5.767	5.19	0.000
EPS	−5.324	1.634	−3.26	0.005
Yield	1.449	1.798	0.81	0.431

The regression equation is P/E = 29.913 − 5.324 EPS + 1.449 Yield.

c. EPS has a significant relationship with P/E (p-value = .005) but not with Yield (p-value = .431).

The regression equation is P/E = 33.5688 − 5.1107 EPS.

d. If EPS increases by one, P/E decreases by 5.1107

e. Yes, the residuals are evenly distributed above and below the horizontal line (residual = 0).

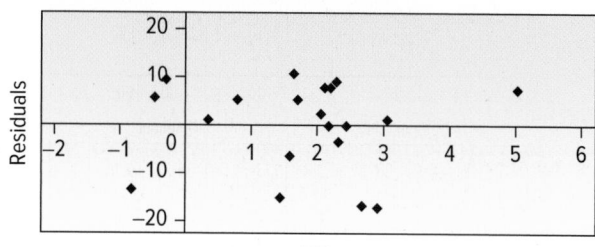

EPS Residual Plot

f. No. the adjusted R^2 indicates that the regression equation only accounts for 32.78% of the variation in P/E. The predictions will not be accurate.

29. a. The regression equation is
Sales (000) = 1.02 + 0.0829 Infomercials.

```
Predictor        Coef    SE Coef       T        P
Constant       1.0188     0.3105    3.28    0.006
Infomercials  0.08291    0.01680    4.94    0.000

Analysis of Variance
Source          DF       SS       MS       F       P
Regression       1   2.3214   2.3214   24.36   0.000
Residual Error  13   1.2386   0.0953
Total           14   3.5600
```

The global test demonstrates there is a relationship between sales and the number of infomercials.

SUMMARY OUTPUT

Regression Statistics

Multiple R	0.6023
R Square	0.3628
Adjusted R Square	0.3274
Standard Error	9.4562
Observations	20

ANOVA

	df	SS	MS	F	p-Value
Regression	1	916.2448	916.2448	10.2466	0.0050
Residual	18	1609.5483	89.4193		
Total	19	2525.7931			

	Coefficients	Standard Error	t-Stat	p-Value	Lower 95%	Upper 95%	Lower 95.0%	Upper 95.0%
Intercept	33.5688	3.5282	9.5145	0.0000	26.1564	40.9812	26.1564	40.9812
EPS	−5.1107	1.5966	−3.2010	0.0050	−8.4650	−1.7564	−8.4650	−1.7564

b.

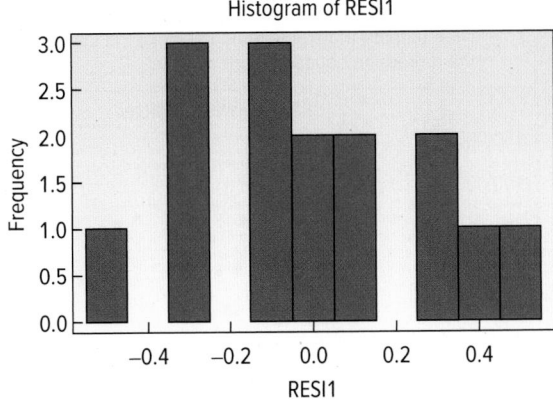

Histogram of RESI1

The residuals appear to follow the normal distribution.

31. a.

Regression Statistics

Multiple R	0.9391
R Square	0.8819
Adjusted R Square	0.8598
Standard Error	7066.4013
Observations	20

ANOVA

	df	SS	MS	F	p-Value
Regression	3	5966725060.72	1988908353.58	39.8307	0.0000
Residual	16	798944439.28	49934027.45		
Total	19	6765669500.00			

	Coefficients	Standard Error	t Stat	P-value
Intercept	− 118929.4614	19733.6074	− 6.0267	0.0000
Loan ($)	1.6268	0.1809	8.9926	0.0000
Payment ($)	2.0623	14.9484	0.1380	0.8920
Payments Male	50.3378	134.9139	0.3731	0.7140

The regression equation is Auction Price = − 11,892.46149 + 1.6268 Loan + 2.0623 Monthly Payment + 50.3378 Payments Made

To test the global hypothesis, the computed F is 39.8307. It is much larger than the critical value 3.24. The p-value is also quite small. Thus, the null hypothesis that all the regression coefficients are zero is rejected. At least one of the multiple regression coefficients is different from zero.

b. The null hypothesis is that the coefficient is zero in each individual test. It would be rejected if p-value is less than 0.05. In this analysis the p-values for monthly payment and number of payments made are much larger than 0.05. Thus, both variables are not significantly related to auction price and should be removed.

c.

Regression Statistics

Multiple R	0.9384
R Square	0.8807
Adjusted R Square	0.8740
Standard Error	6697.2345
Observations	20

ANOVA

	df	SS	MS	F	p-Value
Regression	1	5958316391.8476	5958316391.8476	132.8411	0.0000
Residual	18	807353108.1524	44852950.4529		
Total	19	6765669500.0000			

	Coefficients	Standard Error	t Stat	P-value
Intercept	− 119892.8731	14846.0435	− 8.0757	0.0000
Loan ($)	1.6666	0.1446	11.5257	0.0000

The revised regression equation is: Auction Price = − 119,893.8731 + 1.6666 Loan. For each dollar increase in the mortgage loan amount, the auction price increases $1.666. The R^2 is .8807. So, using only the mortgage loan amount, 88.07% of the variation in auction price is explained with the regression model.

33. a. The correlation matrix is as follows:

	Price	Bedrooms	Size (square feet)	Baths	Days on Market
Price	1.000				
Bedrooms	0.844	1.000			
Size (square feet)	0.952	0.877	1.000		
Baths	0.825	0.985	0.851	1.000	
Days on market	0.185	0.002	0.159	−0.002	1

The correlations for strong, positive relationships between "Price" and the independent variables "Bedrooms," "Size," and "Baths." There appears to be no relationship between "Price" and Days-on-the-Market. The correlations among the independent variables are very strong. So, there would be a high degree of multicollinearity in a multiple regression equation if all the variables were included. We will need to be careful in selecting the best independent variable to predict price.

b.

SUMMARY OUTPUT

Regression Statistics

Multiple R	0.952
R Square	0.905
Adjusted R Square	0.905
Standard Error	49655.822
Observations	105.000

ANOVA

	df	SS	MS	F	Significance F
Regression	1	2.432E+12	2.432E+12	9.862E+02	1.46136E-54
Residual	103	2.540E+11	2.466E+09		
Total	104	2.686E+12			

	Coefficients	Standard Error	t-Stat	p-Value
Intercept	−15775.955	12821.967	−1.230	0.221
Size (square feet)	108.364	3.451	31.405	0.000

The regression analysis shows a significant relationship between price and house size. The *p*-value of the *F*-statistic is 0.00, so the null hypothesis of "no relationship" is rejected. Also, the *p*-value associated with the regression coefficient of "size" is 0.000. Therefore, this coefficient is clearly different from zero.

The regression equation is: Price = − 15775.995 + 108.364 Size.

In terms of pricing, the regression equation suggests that houses are priced at about $108 per square foot.

c. The regression analyses of price and size with the qualitative variables pool and garage follow. The results show that the variable "pool" is statistically significant in the equation. The regression coefficient indicates that if a house has a pool, it adds about $28,575 to the price. The analysis of including "garage" to the analysis indicates that it does not affect the pricing of the house.

Adding pool to the regression equation increases the *R*-square by about 1%.

SUMMARY OUTPUT

Regression Statistics

Multiple R	0.955
R Square	0.913
Adjusted R Square	0.911
Standard Error	47914.856
Observations	105

ANOVA

	df	SS	MS	F	Significance F
Regression	2.00	2451577033207.43	1225788516603.72	533.92	0.00
Residual	102.00	234175013207.24	2295833462.82		
Total	104.00	2685752046414.68			

	Coefficients	Standard Error	t-Stat	p-Value
Intercept	−34640.573	13941.203	−2.485	0.015
Size (square feet)	108.547	3.330	32.595	0.000
Pool (yes is 1)	28575.145	9732.223	2.936	0.004

d. The following histogram was developed using the residuals from part (c). The normality assumption is reasonable.

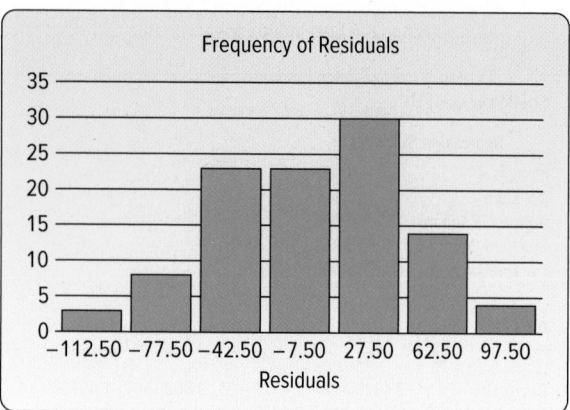

e. The following scatter diagram is based on the residuals in part (c) with the predicted dependent variable on the horizontal axis and residuals on the vertical axis. There does appear that the variance of the residuals increases with higher

values of the predicted price. You can experiment with transformations such as the Log of Price or the square root of price and observe the changes in the graphs of residuals. Note that the transformations will make the interpretation of the regression equation more difficult.

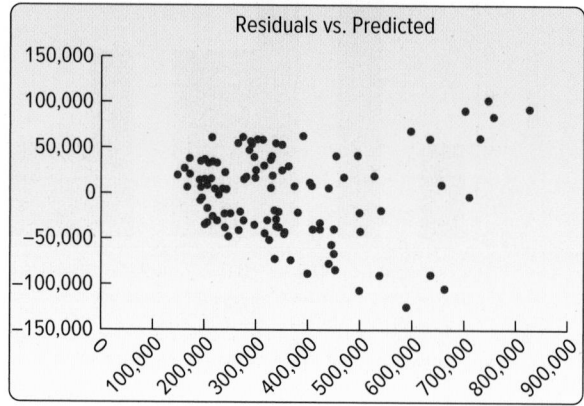

35. a.

	Maintenance Cost ($)	Age (years)	Odometer Miles	Miles since Last Maintenance
Maintenance cost ($)	1			
Age (years)	0.710194278	1		
Odometer miles	0.700439797	0.990675674	1	
Miles since last maint.	−0.160275988	−0.140196856	−0.118982823	1

The correlation analysis shows that age and odometer miles are positively correlated with cost and that "miles since last maintenance" shows that costs increase with fewer miles between maintenance. The analysis also shows a strong correlation between age and odometer miles. This indicates the strong possibility of multicollinearity if age and odometer miles are included in a regression equation.

b. There are a number of analyses to do. First, using Age or Odometer Miles as an independent variable. When you review these analyses, both result in significant relationships. However, Age has a slightly higher R^2. So I would select age as the first independent variable. The interpretation of the coefficient using age is bit more useful for practical use. That is, we can expect about an average of $600 increase in maintenance costs for each additional year a bus ages. The results are:

SUMMARY OUTPUT

Regression Statistics

Multiple R	0.708
R Square	0.501
Adjusted R Square	0.494
Standard Error	1658.097
Observations	80

ANOVA

	df	SS	MS	F	Significance F
Regression	1	215003471.845	215003471.845	78.203	0.000
Residual	78	214444212.142	2749284.771		
Total	79	429447683.988			

	Coefficients	Standard Error	t-Stat	p-Value
Intercept	337.297	511.372	0.660	0.511
Age (years)	603.161	68.206	8.843	0.000

We can also explore including the variable "miles since last maintenance" with Age. Your analysis will show that "miles since last maintenance" is not significantly related to costs. Last, it is possible that maintenance costs are different for diesel versus gasoline engines. So, adding this variable to the analysis shows:

SUMMARY OUTPUT

Regression Statistics

Multiple R	0.960
R Square	0.922
Adjusted R Square	0.920
Standard Error	658.369
Observations	80

ANOVA

	df	SS	MS	F	Significance F
Regression	2	396072093.763	198036046.881	456.884	0.000
Residual	77	33375590.225	433449.224		
Total	79	429447683.988			

	Coefficients	Standard Error	t-Stat	p-Value
Intercept	−1028.539	213.761	−4.812	0.000
Age (years)	644.528	27.157	23.733	0.000
Engine Type (0=diesel)	3190.481	156.100	20.439	0.000

The results show that the engine type is statistically significant and increases the R^2 to 92.2%. Now the practical interpretation of the analysis is that, on average, buses with gasoline engines cost about $3,190 more to maintain. Also, the maintenance costs increase with bus age at an average of $644 per year of bus age.

c. The normality conjecture appears realistic.

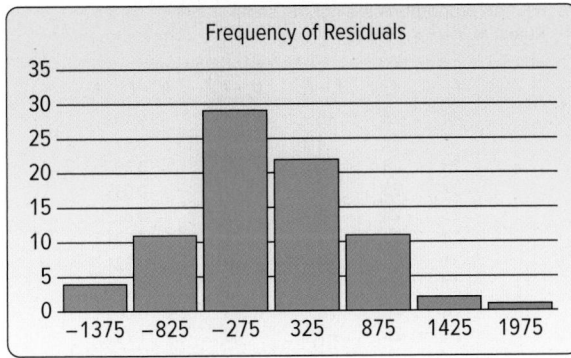
Frequency of Residuals

d. The plot of residuals versus predicted values shows the following. There are clearly patterns in the graph that indicate that the residuals do not follow the assumptions required for the tests of hypotheses.

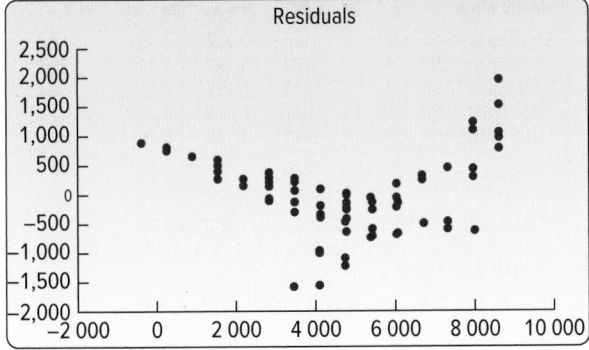
Residuals

Let's remember the scatter plot of costs versus age. The graph clearly shows the effect of engine type on costs. So there are essentially two regression equations depending on the type of engine.

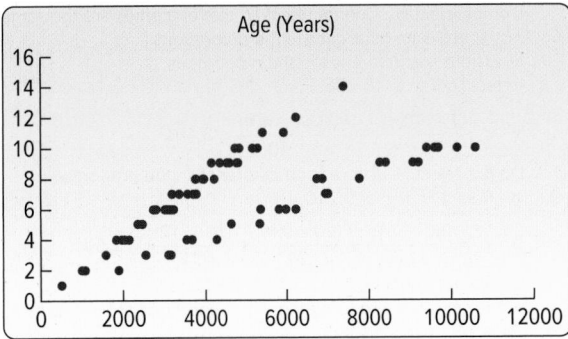
Age (Years)

So based on our knowledge of the data, let's create a residual plot of costs for each engine type.

Residuals for Diesel Engines

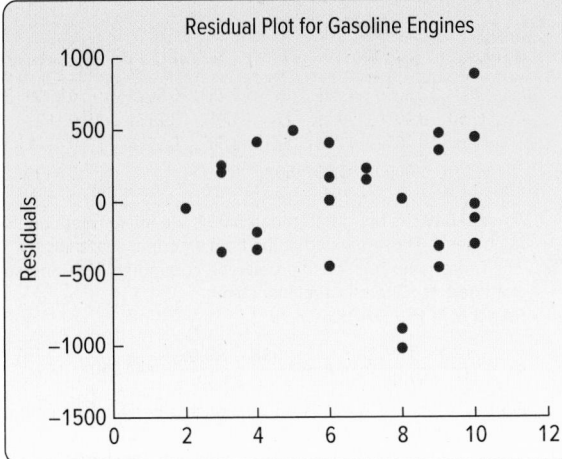
Residual Plot for Gasoline Engines

The graphs show a much better distribution of residuals.

CHAPTER 15

1. **a.** 3
   b. 7.815
3. **a.** Reject H_0 if $\chi^2 > 5.991$.

   b. $\chi^2 = \dfrac{(10 - 20)^2}{20} + \dfrac{(20 - 20)^2}{20} + \dfrac{(30 - 20)^2}{20} = 10.0$
   c. Reject H_0. The proportions are not equal.

5. H_0: The outcomes are the same; H_1: The outcomes are not the same. Reject H_0 if $\chi^2 > 9.236$.

$$\chi^2 = \frac{(3-5)^2}{5} + \cdots + \frac{(7-5)^2}{5} = 7.60$$

Do not reject H_0. Cannot reject H_0 that outcomes are the same.

7. H_0: There is no difference in the proportions.
H_1: There is a difference in the proportions.
Reject H_0 if $\chi^2 > 15.086$.

$$\chi^2 = \frac{(47-40)^2}{40} + \cdots + \frac{(34-40)^2}{40} = 3.400$$

Do not reject H_0. There is no difference in the proportions.

9. a. Reject H_0 if $\chi^2 > 9.210$.

b. $\chi^2 = \frac{(30-24)^2}{24} + \frac{(20-24)^2}{24} + \frac{(10-12)^2}{12} = 2.50$

c. Do not reject H_0.

11. H_0: Proportions are as stated; H_1: Proportions are not as stated.
Reject H_0 if $\chi^2 > 11.345$.

$$\chi^2 = \frac{(50-25)^2}{25} + \cdots + \frac{(160-275)^2}{275} = 115.22$$

Reject H_0. The proportions are not as stated.

13.

Number of Clients	z-Values	Area	Found by	f_e
Under 30	Under −1.58	0.0571	0.5000 − 0.4429	2.855
30 up to 40	−1.58 up to −0.51	0.2479	0.4429 − 0.1950	12.395
40 up to 50	−0.51 up to 0.55	0.4038	0.1950 + 0.2088	20.19
50 up to 60	0.55 up to 1.62	0.2386	0.4474 − 0.2088	11.93
60 or more	1.62 or more	0.0526	0.5000 − 0.4474	2.63

The first and last class both have expected frequencies smaller than 5. They are combined with adjacent classes.
H_0: The population of clients follows a normal distribution.
H_1: The population of clients does not follow a normal distribution.
Reject the null if $\chi^2 > 5.991$.

Number of Clients	Area	f_e	f_o	$f_e - f_o$	$(f_o - f_e)^2$	$[(f_o - f_e)^2]/f_e$
Under 40	0.3050	15.25	16	−0.75	0.5625	0.0369
40 up to 50	0.4038	20.19	22	−1.81	3.2761	0.1623
50 or more	0.2912	14.56	12	2.56	6.5536	0.4501
Total	1.0000	50.00	50	0		0.6493

Since 0.6493 is not greater than 5.991, we fail to reject the null hypothesis. These data could be from a normal distribution.

15. H_0: There is no relationship between community size and section read. H_1: There is a relationship.
Reject H_0 if $\chi^2 > 9.488$.

$$\chi^2 = \frac{(170 - 157.50)^2}{157.50} + \cdots + \frac{(88 - 83.62)^2}{83.62} = 7.340$$

Do not reject H_0. There is no relationship between community size and section read.

17. H_0: No relationship between error rates and item type.
H_1: There is a relationship between error rates and item type.
Reject H_0 if $\pi^2 > 9.21$.

$$\chi^2 = \frac{(20 - 14.1)^2}{14.1} + \cdots + \frac{(225 - 225.25)^2}{225.25} = 8.033$$

Do not reject H_0. There is not a relationship between error rates and item type.

19. H_0: $B_s = 0.50$, $B_r = B_s = 0.25$ H_1: Distribution is not as stated.
$df = 2$ Reject H_0 if $\chi^2 > 4.605$.

Turn	f_o	f_e	$f_o - f_e$	$(f_o - f_e)^2/f_e$
Straight	112	100	12	1.44
Right	48	50	−2	0.08
Left	40	50	−10	2.00
Total	200	200		3.52

H_0 is not rejected. The proportions are as given in the null hypothesis.

21. H_0: There is no preference with respect to TV stations.
H_1: There is a preference with respect to TV stations.
$df = 3 - 1 = 2$. H_0 is rejected if $\chi^2 > 5.991$.

TV Station	f_o	f_e	$f_o - f_e$	$(f_o - f_e)^2$	$(f_o - f_e)^2/f_e$
WNAE	53	50	3	9	0.18
WRRN	64	50	14	196	3.92
WSPD	33	50	−17	289	5.78
	150	150	0		9.88

H_0 is rejected. There is a preference for TV stations.

23. H_0: $\pi_n = 0.21$, $\pi_m = 0.24$, $\pi_s = 0.35$, $\pi_w = 0.20$
H_1: The distribution is not as given.
Reject H_0 if $\chi^2 > 11.345$.

Region	f_o	f_e	$f_o - f_e$	$(f_o - f_e)^2/f_e$
Northeast	68	84	−16	3.0476
Midwest	104	96	8	0.6667
South	155	140	15	1.6071
West	73	80	−7	0.6125
Total	400	400	0	5.9339

H_0 is not rejected. The distribution of order destinations reflects the population.

25. H_0: The proportions are the same.
H_1: The proportions are not the same.
Reject H_0 if $\chi^2 > 16.919$.

f_o	f_e	$f_o - f_e$	$(f_o - f_e)^2$	$(f_o - f_e)^2/f_e$
44	28	16	256	9.143
32	28	4	16	0.571
23	28	−5	25	0.893
27	28	−1	1	0.036
23	28	−5	25	0.893
24	28	−4	16	0.571
31	28	3	9	0.321
27	28	−1	1	0.036
28	28	0	0	0.000
21	28	−7	49	1.750
				14.214

Do not reject H_0. The digits are evenly distributed.

27.

Hourly Wage	f	M	fM	$M - x$	$(M - x)^2$	$f(M - x)^2$
$5.50 up to 6.50	20	6	120	−2.222	4.938	98.8
6.50 up to 7.50	24	7	168	−1.222	1.494	35.9
7.50 up to 8.50	130	8	1040	−0.222	0.049	6.4
8.50 up to 9.50	68	9	612	0.778	0.605	41.1
9.50 up to 10.50	28	10	280	1.778	3.161	88.5
Total	270		2220			270.7

The sample mean is 8.222, found by 2,220/270.
The sample standard deviation is 1.003, found as the square root of 270.7/269.

H_0: The population of wages follows a normal distribution.
H_1: The population of hourly wages does not follow a normal distribution.
Reject the null if $\chi^2 > 4.605$.

Wage	z-Values	Area	Found by	f_e	f_o	$f_e - f_o$	$(f_o - f_e)^2$	$[(f_o - f_e)^2]/f_e$
Under $6.50	Under −1.72	0.0427	0.5000 − 0.4573	11.529	20	−8.471	71.7578	6.2241
6.50 up to 7.50	−1.72 up to −0.72	0.1931	0.4573 − 0.2642	52.137	24	28.137	791.6908	15.1848
7.50 up to 8.50	−0.72 up to 0.28	0.3745	0.2642 + 0.1103	101.115	130	−28.885	834.3432	8.2514
8.50 up to 9.50	0.28 up to 1.27	0.2877	0.3980 − 0.1103	77.679	68	9.679	93.6830	1.2060
9.50 or more	1.27 or more	0.1020	0.5000 − 0.3980	27.54	28	−0.46	0.2116	0.0077
Total		1.0000			270	270	0	30.874

Since 30.874 is greater than 4.605, we reject the null hypothesis not from a normal distribution.

29.

	Men	Women
Dogs are better listeners	36	100
Dogs are not better listeners	164	200

H_0: Listening and sex are not related.
H_1: Listening and sex are related.
Reject H_0 if $\chi^2 > 3.841$

$$\chi^2 = \frac{(36 - 54.4)^2}{54.4} + \cdots + \frac{(200 - 218.4)^2}{218.4} = 14.182$$

Reject H_0. There is a relationship between opinion of listening and sex.

31. H_0: Sex and attitude toward the deficit are not related.
H_1: Sex and attitude toward the deficit are related.
Reject H_0 if $\chi^2 > 5.991$.

$$\chi^2 = \frac{(244 - 292.41)^2}{292.41} + \frac{(194 - 164.05)^2}{164.05}$$
$$+ \frac{(68 - 49.53)^2}{49.53} + \frac{(305 - 256.59)^2}{256.59}$$
$$+ \frac{(114 - 143.95)^2}{143.95} + \frac{(25 - 43.47)^2}{43.47} = 43.578$$

Since 43.578 > 5.991, you reject H_0. A person's position on the deficit is influenced by his or her sex.

33. H_0: Whether a claim is filed and age are not related.
H_1: Whether a claim is filed and age are related.
Reject H_0 if $\chi^2 > 7.815$.

$$\chi^2 = \frac{(170 - 203.33)^2}{203.33} + \cdots + \frac{(24 - 35.67)^2}{35.67} = 53.639$$

Reject H_0. Age is related to whether a claim is filed.

35. H_0: $\pi_{BL} = \pi_O = .23$, $\pi_Y = \pi_G = .15$, $\pi_{BR} = \pi_R = .12$.
H_1: The proportions are not as given. Reject H_0 if $\chi^2 > 15.086$.

Color	f_o	f_e	$(f_o - f_e)^2/f_e$
Blue	12	16.56	1.256
Brown	14	8.64	3.325
Yellow	13	10.80	0.448
Red	14	8.64	3.325
Orange	7	16.56	5.519
Green	12	10.80	0.133
Total	72		14.006

Do not reject H_0. The color distribution agrees with the manufacturer's information.

37. H_0: Salary and winning are not related.
H_1: Salary and winning are related.
Reject H_0 if $\chi^2 > 3.841$ with 1 degree of freedom.

	Salary		
Winning	Lower Half	Top Half	Total
No	10	6	16
Yes	5	9	14
Total	15	15	

$$\chi^2 = \frac{(10 - 8)^2}{8} + \frac{(5 - 7)^2}{7} + \frac{(6 - 8)^2}{8} + \frac{(9 - 7)^2}{7} = 2.1432$$

Fail to reject H_0. Cannot conclude that salary and winning are related.

CHAPTER 16

1. a. If the number of pluses (successes) in the sample is 9 or more, reject H_0.
b. Reject H_0 because the cumulative probability associated with nine or more successes (.073) does not exceed the significance level (.10).

3. a. H_0: $\pi \le .50$; H_1: $\pi > .50$; $n = 10$
b. H_0 is rejected if there are nine or more plus signs. A "+" represents a loss.
c. Reject H_0. It is an effective program because there were nine people who lost weight.

5. a. H_0: median $70,720 \qquad H_1$: median > $70,720
b. Reject H_0 if 12 or more earned than $70,720.
c. 13 of the 18 chiropractors earned more than $70,720 so reject H_0. The results indicate the starting salary for chiropractors is more than $70,720.

7.

Couple	Difference	Rank
1	550	7
2	190	5
3	250	6
4	−120	3
5	−70	1
6	130	4
7	90	2

Sums: − 4, +24. So $T = 4$ (the smaller of the two sums). From Appendix B.8, .05 level, one-tailed test, $n = 7$, the critical value is 3. Since the T of 4 > 3, do not reject H_0 (one-tailed test). There is no difference in square footage. Professional couples do not live in larger homes.

9. a. H_0: The production is the same for the two systems.
H_1: Production using the new procedure is greater.
b. H_0 is rejected if $T \le 21$, $n = 13$.
c. The calculations for the first three employees are:

Employee	Old	New	d	Rank	R^1	R^2
A	60	64	4	6	6	
B	40	52	12	12.5	12.5	
C	59	58	−1	2		2

The sum of the negative ranks is 6.5. Since 6.5 is less than 21, H_0 is rejected. Production using the new procedure is greater.

11. H_0: The distributions are the same. H_1: The distributions are not the same. Reject H_0 if $z, 21.96$ or $z > 1.96$.

A		B	
Score	Rank	Score	Rank
38	4	26	1
45	6	31	2
56	9	35	3
57	10.5	42	5
61	12	51	7
69	14	52	8
70	15	57	10.5
79	16	62	13
	86.5		49.5

$$z = \frac{86.5 - \frac{8(8 + 8 + 1)}{2}}{\sqrt{\frac{8(8)(8 + 8 + 1)}{12}}} = 1.943$$

H_0 is not rejected. There is no difference in the two populations.

13. H_0: The distributions are the same. H_1: The distribution of Campus is to the right. Reject H_0 if $z > 1.65$.

Campus		Online	
Age	Rank	Age	Rank
26	6	28	8
42	16.5	16	1
65	22	42	16.5
38	13	29	9.5
29	9.5	31	11
32	12	22	3
59	21	50	20
42	16.5	42	16.5
27	7	23	4
41	14	25	5
46	19		94.5
18	2		
	158.5		

$$z = \frac{158.5 - \frac{12(12 + 10 + 1)}{2}}{\sqrt{\frac{12(10)(12 + 10 + 1)}{12}}} = 1.35$$

H_0 is not rejected. There is no difference in the distributions.

15. ANOVA requires that we have two or more populations, the data are interval- or ratio-level, the populations are normally distributed, and the population standard deviations are equal. Kruskal-Wallis requires only ordinal-level data, and no assumptions are made regarding the shape of the populations.

17. **a.** H_0: The three population distributions are equal.
H_1: Not all of the distributions are the same.
b. Reject H_0 if $H > 5.991$.
c.

Sample 1 Rank	Sample 2 Rank	Sample 3 Rank
8	5	1
11	6.5	2
14.5	6.5	3
14.5	10	4
16	12	9
64	13	19
	53	

$$H = \frac{12}{16(16 + 1)}\left[\frac{(64)^2}{5} + \frac{(53)^2}{6} + \frac{(19)^2}{5}\right] - 3(16 + 1)$$
$$= 59.98 - 51 = 8.98$$

d. Reject H_0 because $8.98 > 5.991$. The three distributions are not equal.

19. H_0: The distributions of the lengths of life are the same.
H_1: The distributions of the lengths of life are not the same.
H_0 is rejected if $H > 9.210$.

Salt		Fresh		Others	
Hours	Rank	Hours	Rank	Hours	Rank
167.3	3	160.6	1	182.7	13
189.6	15	177.6	11	165.4	2
177.2	10	185.3	14	172.9	7
169.4	6	168.6	4	169.2	5
180.3	12	176.6	9	174.7	8
	46		39		35

$$H = \frac{12}{15(16)}\left[\frac{(46)^2}{5} + \frac{(39)^2}{5} + \frac{(35)^2}{5}\right] - 3(16) = 0.62$$

H_0 is not rejected. There is no difference in the three distributions.

21. **a.** The data from the two raters are the ordinal scale.
b. No outliers. Appears to be a weak association

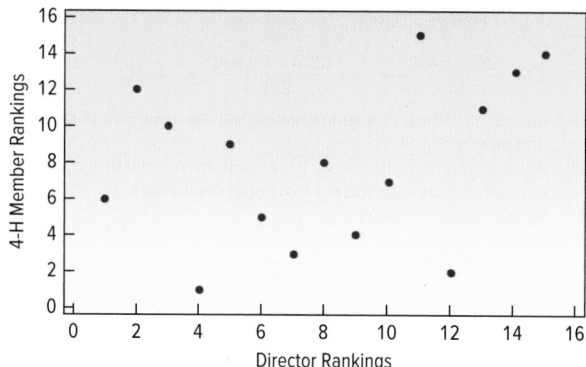

Scatterplot of 4-H Member vs Director

c. $r_s = 1 - \frac{6\Sigma d^2}{n(n^2 - 1)} = 1 - \frac{6(372)}{15(15^2 - 1)} = 0.336$

d. H_0: No correlation between the raters
H_1: A positive correlation between the raters
Reject H_0 if $t > 1.771$

$$t = .336\sqrt{\frac{15 - 2}{1 - .336^2}} = 1.663$$

H_0 is not rejected. We conclude the correlation in population among the ranks is not positive. We cannot conclude that the two raters agree.

23.

Representative	Sales	Rank	Training Rank	d	d^2
1	319	8	8	0	0
2	150	1	2	1	1
3	175	2	5	3	9
4	460	10	10	0	0
5	348	9	7	−2	4
6	300	6.5	1	5.5	30.25
7	280	5	6	1	1
8	200	4	9	5	25
9	190	3	4	1	1
10	300	6.5	3	−3.5	12.25
					83.50

a. $r_s = 1 - \dfrac{6(83.5)}{10(10^2 - 1)} = 0.494$

A moderate positive correlation

b. H_0: No correlation among the ranks. H_1: A positive correlation among the ranks. Reject H_0 if $t > 1.860$.

$$t = 0.494 \sqrt{\dfrac{10 - 2}{1 - (0.494)^2}} = 1.607$$

H_0 is not rejected. The correlation in population among the ranks could be 0.

25. H_0: $\pi = .50$. H_1: $\pi = .50$. Use a software package to develop the binomial probability distribution for $n = 19$ and $\pi = .50$. H_0 is rejected if there are either 5 or fewer "+" signs, or 14 or more. The total of 12 "+" signs falls in the acceptance region. H_0 is not rejected. There is no preference between the two shows.

27. H_0: $\pi = .50$ H_1: $\pi = .50$
H_0 is rejected if there are 12 or more or 3 or fewer plus signs. Because there are only 8 plus signs, H_0 is not rejected. There is no preference with respect to the two brands of components.

29. a. H_0: $= 0.50$ H_1: 0.50 $n = 22$; 2 were indifferent, so $n = 20$. 5 preferred pulp; 15 preferred no pulp.
b. As a two-tailed test, reject if 5 or less preferred pulp, or 14 or more preferred pulp.
c. Reject H_0. There is a difference in the preference for the two types of orange juice.

31. H_0: Rates are the same; H_1: The rates are not the same.
H_0 is rejected if $H > 5.991$. $H = .082$. Do not reject H_0.

33. H_0: The populations are the same. H_1: The populations differ. Reject H_0 if $H > 7.815$. $H = 14.30$. Reject H_0.

35. $r_s = 1 - \dfrac{6(78)}{12(12^2 - 1)} = 0.727$

H_0: There is no correlation between the rankings of the coaches and of the sportswriters.
H_1: There is a positive correlation between the rankings of the coaches and of the sportswriters. Reject H_0 if $t > 1.812$.

$$t = 0.727 \sqrt{\dfrac{12 - 2}{1 - (.727)^2}} = 3.348$$

H_0 is rejected. There is a positive correlation between the sportswriters and the coaches.

37. a. H_0: There is no difference in the distributions of the selling prices in the five townships.
H_1: There is a difference in the distributions of the selling prices of the five townships.
H_0 is rejected if H is greater than 9.488. The computed value of H is 2.70, so the null hypothesis is not rejected. The sample data does not suggest a difference in the distributions of selling prices.
b. H_0: There is no difference in the distributions of the selling prices depending on the number of bedrooms.
H_1: There is a difference in the distributions of the selling prices depending on the number of bedrooms.
H_0 is rejected if H is greater than 9.488. The computed value of H is 75.71, so the null hypothesis is rejected. The sample data indicates there is a difference in the distributions of selling prices based on the number of bedrooms.
c. H_0: There is no difference in the distributions of FICO scores depending on the type of mortgage the occupant has on the home.
H_1: There is a difference in the distributions of FICO scores depending on the type of mortgage the occupant has on the home.
H_0 is rejected if H is greater than 3.841. The computed value of H is 41.04, so the null hypothesis is rejected. The sample data suggests a difference in the distributions of the FICO scores. The data show that home occupants with lower FICO scores tended to use adjustable rate mortgages.

39. a. H_0: The distributions of the maintenance costs are the same for all capacities.
H_1: The distributions of the costs are not the same.
H_0 is rejected if $H > 7.815$, from χ^2 with 3 degrees of freedom.

$$H = \dfrac{12}{80(81)} \left[\dfrac{(132)^2}{3} + \dfrac{(501)^2}{11} + \dfrac{(349)^2}{11} + \dfrac{(2258)^2}{55} \right] - 3(81) = 2.186$$

Fail to reject H_0. There is no difference in the maintenance cost for the four bus capacities.
b. H_0: The distributions of maintenance costs by fuel type are the same.
H_1: The distributions are different.
Reject H_0 if $z < -1.96$ or $z > 1.96$.

$$z = \dfrac{1693 - \dfrac{53(53 + 27 + 1)}{2}}{\sqrt{\dfrac{(53)(27)(53 + 27 + 1)}{12}}} = -4.614$$

We reject reject H_0 and conclude that maintenance costs are different for diesel and gasoline fueled buses.
c. H_0: The distributions of the maintenance costs are the same for the three bus manufacturers.
H_1: The distributions of the costs are not the same.
H_0 is rejected if $H > 5.991$, from χ^2 with 2 degrees of freedom.

$$H = \dfrac{12}{80(81)} \left[\dfrac{(414)^2}{8} + \dfrac{(1005)^2}{25} + \dfrac{(1821)^2}{47} \right] - 3(81) = 2.147$$

H_0 is not rejected. There may be no difference in the maintenance cost for the three different manufacturers. The distributions could be the same.

CHAPTER 17

1.

Year	Loans ($ millions)	Index (base = 2010)
2010	55,177	100.0
2011	65,694	119.1
2012	83,040	150.5
2013	88,378	160.2
2014	97,420	176.6
2015	98,608	178.7
2016	101,364	183.7
2017	110,527	200.3
2018	116,364	210.9

3. The mean sales for the earliest 3 years is $(486.6 + 522.2)/3 or $505.2.
2017: 90.4, found by (456.6/505.2) (100)
2018: 85.8, found by (433.3/505.2) (100)
Net sales decreased by 9.6% and 14.2% from the 2009–2010 period to 2017 and 2018, respectively.

5. a. $P_t = \dfrac{3.35}{2.49}(100) = 134.54$ $P_s = \dfrac{4.49}{3.29}(100) = 136.47$

$P_c = \dfrac{4.19}{1.59}(100) = 263.52$ $P_a = \dfrac{2.49}{1.79}(100) = 139.11$

b. $P = \dfrac{14.52}{9.16}(100) = 158.52$

c. $P = \dfrac{\$3.35(6) + 4.49(4) + 4.19(2) + 2.49(3)}{\$2.49(6) + 3.29(4) + 1.59(2) + 1.79(3)}(100) = 147.1$

d. $P = \dfrac{\$3.35(6) + 4.49(5) + 4.19(3) + 2.49(4)}{\$2.49(6) + 3.29(5) + 1.59(3) + 1.79(4)}(100) = 150.2$

e. $I = \sqrt{(147.1)(150.2)} = 148.64$

7. a. $P_W = \dfrac{0.10}{0.07}(100) = 142.9$ $P_C = \dfrac{0.03}{0.04}(100) = 75.0$

$P_S = \dfrac{0.15}{0.15}(100) = 100$ $P_H = \dfrac{0.10}{0.08}(100) = 125.0$

b. $P = \dfrac{0.38}{0.34}(100) = 111.8$

c.

$P = \dfrac{0.10(17,000) + 0.03(125,000) + 0.15(40,000) + 0.10(62,000)}{0.07(17,000) + 0.04(125,000) + 0.15(40,000) + 0.08(62,000)} \times$
$(100) = 102.92$

d.

$P = \dfrac{0.10(20,000) + 0.03(130,000) + 0.15(42,000) + 0.10(65,000)}{0.07(20,000) + 0.04(130,000) + 0.15(42,000) + 0.08(65,000)} \times$
$(100) = 103.32$

e. $I = \sqrt{102.92(103.32)} = 103.12$

9.

	2015			2020		
	Price	Quantity		Price	Quantity	
Grain	Bushels	(1000 MT)	Price * Quantity	Bushels	(1000 MT)	Price * Quantity
Oats	3.21	1298	4166.58	2.82	949	2676.18
Wheat	5.99	56117	336140.83	4.58	49691	227584.78
Corn	3.7	345506	1278372.2	3.56	360252	1282497.12
Barley	5.3	4750	25175	4.69	3600	16884
		Sum=	1,643,854.61			1,529,642.08
		Value Index	93.052			

11. a. $I = \dfrac{6.8}{5.3}(0.20) + \dfrac{362.26}{265.88}(0.40) + \dfrac{125.0}{109.6}(0.25)$

$+ \dfrac{622,864}{529,917}(0.15) = 1.263.$

Index is 126.3.

b. Business activity increased 26.3% from 2010 to 2022.

13. The real income is $X = (\$106,100)/2.7097 = \$39,156$
"Real" salary increased $\$39,156 - \$19,800 = \$19,356$

15.

Year	Tinora	Tinora Index	National Index
2010	$28,650	100.0	100
2015	$33,972	118.6	122.5
2022	$37,382	130.5	136.9

The Tinora teachers received smaller increases than the national average.

The Tinora teachers received smaller increases than the national average.

17.

Year	Domestic Sales (Base = 2016)
2016	100.00
2017	105.43
2018	110.77
2019	105.69
2020	114.08

Compared to 2016, Sales are 14.08% higher.

19.

Year	International Sales (Base = 2016)
2016	100.00
2017	107.36
2018	116.49
2019	123.53
2020	115.76

Compared to 2016, Sales are 15.76% higher.

21.

Year	Employees (Base = 2016)
2016	100
2017	106.01
2018	106.88
2019	104.59
2020	107.20

Compared to 2016, number of employees is 7.20% higher.

23.

Year	Revenue ($ Billion)	Index Base = 2015
2015	94.49	100.00
2016	103.3	109.32
2017	99.28	105.07
2018	97.01	102.67
2019	95.21	100.76
2020	79.62	84.26

Compared to 2015, Revenue decreased 15.74%.

25.

Year	Employees (thousands)	Index Base = 2015
2015	333	100.00
2016	295	88.59
2017	313	93.99
2018	283	84.98
2019	205	61.56
2020	174	52.25

Compared to 2015, the number of employee decreased 47.75%.

27. $P_{ma} = \dfrac{2.00}{0.81}(100) = 246.91$ $P_{sh} = \dfrac{1.88}{0.84}(100) = 223.81$

$P_{mi} = \dfrac{2.89}{1.44}(100) = 200.69$ $P_{po} = \dfrac{3.99}{2.91}(100) = 137.11$

29. $P = \dfrac{\$2.00(18) + 1.88(5) + 2.89(70) + 3.99(27)}{\$0.81(18) + 0.84(5) + 1.44(70) + 2.91(27)}(100) = 179.37$

31. $I = \sqrt{179.37(178.23)} = 178.80$

33. $P_R = \dfrac{0.60}{0.50}(100) = 120$ $P_S = \dfrac{0.90}{1.20}(100) = 75.0$

$P_W = \dfrac{1.00}{0.85}(100) = 117.65$

35. $P = \dfrac{0.60(320) + 0.90(110) + 1.00(230)}{0.50(320) + 1.20(110) + 0.85(230)}(100) = 106.87$

37. $P = \sqrt{(106.87)(106.04)} = 106.45$

39. $P_C = \dfrac{0.05}{0.06}(100) = 83.33$ $P_C = \dfrac{0.12}{0.10}(100) = 120$

$P_P = \dfrac{0.18}{0.20}(100) = 90$ $P_E = \dfrac{.015}{0.15}(100) = 100$

41. $P = \dfrac{0.05(2,000) + 0.12(200) + 0.18(400) + 0.15(100)}{0.06(2,000) + 0.10(200) + 0.20(400) + 0.15(100)}(100)$
$= 89.79$

43. $I = \sqrt{(89.79)(91.25)} = 90.52$

45. $P_A = \dfrac{.86}{.82}(100) = 104.9$ $P_N = \dfrac{2.99}{4.37}(100) = 68.4$

$P_{PET} = \dfrac{58.15}{71.21}(100) = 81.7$ $P_{PL} = \dfrac{1292.53}{1743.6}(100) = 74.1$

47. $P_{Laspeyres} =$

$$\dfrac{.86(1000) + 2.99(5000) + 58.15(60000) + 1292.53(500)}{.82(1000) + 4.37(5000) + 71.21(60000) + 1743.60(500)}(100)$$

$= 80.34$

49. $I = \sqrt{(80.34)(80.14)} = 80.24$

51. $I = \Big[100\dfrac{1971.0}{1159.0}(0.20) + \dfrac{91}{87}(0.10) + \dfrac{114.7}{110.6}(0.40)$

$\quad + \dfrac{1501000}{1214000}(0.30)\Big] = 123.05$

The economy is up 23.05 percent from 1996 to 2016.

53. February : $I = 100\Big[\dfrac{6.8}{8.0}(0.40) + \dfrac{23}{20}(0.35) + \dfrac{303}{300}(0.25)\Big]$

$\qquad\qquad = 99.50$

$\qquad$ March : $I = 100\Big[\dfrac{6.4}{8.0}(0.40) + \dfrac{21}{20}(0.35) + \dfrac{297}{300}(0.25)\Big]$

$\qquad\qquad = 93.50$

55. For 2015: $1,293,801, found by $2,400,000/1.855
For 2020: $1,816,295, found by $3,500,000/1.927

CHAPTER 18

1. Any graphs similar to the following:

Stationary Trend

Positive Trend

Negative Trend

3. The irregular component is the randomness in a time series that cannot be described by any trend, seasonal, or cyclical pattern. The irregular component is used to estimate forecast error.

5. **a.** The graph shows a stationary pattern.

b. & c.

Period	Demand	3 Month SMA	Absolute Error	Absolute Percent Error
1	104			
2	132			
3	143			
4	137	126.33	10.67	7.8%
5	146	137.33	8.67	5.9%
6	150	142	8	5.3%
7	101	144.33	43.33	42.9%
8	126	132.33	6.33	5.0%
9	116	125.67	9.67	8.3%
10	115	114.33	0.67	0.6%
11		119	MAD = 12.48	MAPE = 10.84%

d. The forecast demand for period 11 is 119.
e. The MAD of 12.48 and MAPE of 10.84% are the reported measure of errors. So, the forecast is 119 $\pm$ 12.48. And the average percent error is 10.84%.

7. **a.** The graph shows a stationary pattern.

b. c. and d.

Period	Demand	4 Month SMA	6 Month SMA	4 Month Absolute Error	6 Month Absolute Error	4 Month Absolute Percent Error	6 Month Absolute Percent Error
1	126						
2	112						
3	135						
4	145						
5	106	129.5		23.5		22.17%	
6	101	124.5		23.5		23.27%	
7	132	121.75	120.8	10.25	11.2	7.77%	8.48%
8	141	121	121.8	20	19.2	14.18%	13.62%
9	110	120	126.7	10	16.7	9.09%	15.18%
10	131	121	122.5	10	8.5	7.63%	6.49%
11		128.5	120.2	MAD = 16.21	MAD = 13.9	MAPE = 14.02%	MAPE = 10.94%

e. The 6-month moving average MAD of 13.90 and MAPE of 10.94% are less than the 4-month MAD of 16.21 and MAPE of 14.02%. This is one reason to prefer using the 6-month rather than the 4-month moving average.

9. a. The graph shows a stationary pattern.

Demand

b. and c.

		alpha =	0.3			ABS
Period	Demand	Exp Smooth	Error	ABS Error	Percent error	
1	104					
2	132	104	28	28.00	21.21%	
3	143	112.4	30.6	30.60	21.40%	
4	137	121.6	15.4	15.40	11.24%	
5	146	126.2	19.8	19.80	13.56%	
6	150	132.1	17.9	17.90	11.93%	
7	101	137.5	−36.5	36.50	36.14%	
8	126	126.6	−0.6	0.60	0.48%	
9	116	126.4	−10.4	10.40	8.97%	
10	115	123.3	−8.3	8.30	7.22%	
11		120.8		MAD = 18.61	MAPE = 14.68%	

d. Period 11 forecast = 120.80

e. The MAD of 18.61, is the reported measure of error. So, the forecast is 120.8 ± 18.61. The MAPE is 14.68%. So, the average relative error in the forecasts is 14.68%.

11. a. The graph shows a stationary pattern.

Demand

b. and c.

Period	Demand	alpha = 0.35 Exp Smooth	Error	ABS Error	ABS Percent Error
1	126				
2	112	126	−14	14	12.50%
3	135	121.1	13.9	13.9	10.30%
4	145	126	19	19	13.10%
5	106	132.7	−26.7	26.7	25.19%
6	101	123.4	−22.4	22.4	22.18%
7	132	115.6	16.4	16.4	12.42%
8	141	121.3	19.7	19.7	13.97%
9	110	128.2	−18.2	18.2	16.55%
10	131	121.8	9.2	9.2	7.02%
11		125		MAD = 17.72	MAPE = 14.8%

Period	Demand	alpha = 0.85 Exp Smooth	Error	ABS Error	ABS Percent Error
1	126				
2	112	126	−14	14	12.50%
3	135	114.1	20.9	20.9	15.48%
4	145	131.9	13.1	13.1	9.03%
5	106	143	−37	37	34.91%
6	101	111.6	−10.6	10.6	10.50%
7	132	102.6	29.4	29.4	22.27%
8	141	127.6	13.4	13.4	9.50%
9	110	139	−29	29	26.36%
10	131	114.4	16.6	16.6	12.67%
11		128.5		MAD = 20.44	MAPE = 17.03%

d. For an alpha of .35, the MAD = 17.72, the MAPE is 14.8%.
For an alpha of .85, the MAD = 20.45, the MAPE is 17.03%.

e. Because it has the lower measure of error (MAD and MAPE), choose exponential smoothing with alpha = .35.

13. a.

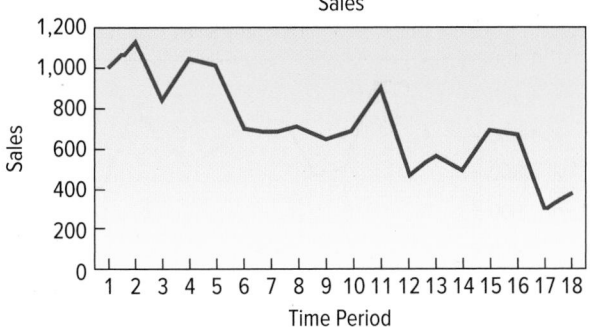

Sales

b. The graph shows a negative time series trend in sales.

c. A trend model is appropriate because we want to estimate the decreasing change in sales per time period.

d. Based on the regression analysis; the trend equation is: Sales = 1062.86 − 36.24 (time period); sales are declining at a historical rate of 36.24 for each increment of 1 time period. Based on the MAD, the average forecast error for this model is 111.15.

SUMMARY OUTPUT

Regression Statistics

Multiple R	0.83
R Square	0.69
Adjusted R Square	0.67
Standard Error	134.97
Observations	18

ANOVA

	df	SS	MS	F	p-Value
Regression	1	636183.06	636183.06	34.92	0.00
Residual	16	291455.22	18215.95		
Total	17	927638.28			

	Coefficients	Standard Error	t Stat	P-value
Intercept	1062.86	66.37	16.01	0.00
Period	−36.24	6.13	−5.91	0.00

Period	Sales	Predicted	Abs err	Abs % err
1	1001	1026.62	25.61988	2.56%
2	1129	990.3836	138.6164	12.28%
3	841	954.1472	113.1472	13.45%
4	1044	917.9109	126.0891	12.08%
5	1012	881.6746	130.3254	12.88%
6	703	845.4383	142.4383	20.26%
7	682	809.2019	127.2019	18.65%
8	712	772.9656	60.9656	8.56%
9	646	736.7293	90.72927	14.04%
10	686	700.4929	14.49295	2.11%
11	909	664.2566	244.7434	26.92%
12	469	628.0203	159.0203	33.91%
13	566	591.784	25.78397	4.56%

Period	Sales	Predicted	Abs err	Abs % err
14	488	555.5476	67.54764	13.84%
15	688	519.3113	168.6887	24.52%
16	675	483.075	191.925	28.43%
17	303	446.8387	143.8387	47.47%
18	381	410.6023	29.60234	7.77%
19		374.366	MAD	MAPE
20		338.1297	111.1542	16.91%
21		301.8934		

e. Sales are declining at a historical rate of 36.24 for each increment of 1 time period.

f. Sales (19) = 1062.86 − 36.24 (19) = 374.37
Sales (20) = 1062.86 − 36.24 (20) = 338.13
Sales (21) = 1062.86 − 36.24 (21) = 301.89
The MAD or error associated with each forecast is 111.15. The MAPE is 16.91%.

15. a.

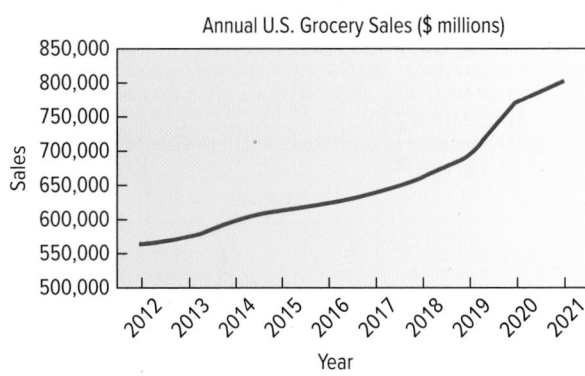

Annual U.S. Grocery Sales ($ millions)

b. The graph shows a positive time series trend in grocery sales.

c. A trend model is appropriate because we want to estimate the increasing change in sales per time year.

d. Predicted annual U.S. grocery sales = − 50,726,733.9151 + 25,307.4303 (year). The forecast error computed with the MAD is 20,869.92. The MAPE is a low 3.1%.

SUMMARY OUTPUT

Regression Statistics

Multiple R	0.9522
R Square	0.9067
Adjusted R Square	0.8950
Standard Error	26073.3727
Observations	10

ANOVA

	df	SS	MS	F	p-Value
Regression	1	52838447354.7758	52838447354.7758	77.7241	0.0000
Residual	8	5438566120.8242	679820765.1030		
Total	9	58277013475.6000			

	Coefficients	Standard Error	t Stat	P-value
Intercept	−50377734.0061	5788538.2261	−8.7030	0.0000
Year	25307.4303	2870.5839	8.8161	0.0000

Observation	Predicted Sales	Residuals	ABS error	ABS Percent Error
2012	540815.7636	22829.23636	22829.23636	4.22%
2013	566123.1939	8423.806061	8423.806061	1.49%
2014	591430.6242	8172.375758	8172.375758	1.38%
2015	616738.0545	−3579.054545	3579.054545	0.58%
2016	642045.4848	−16750.48485	16750.48485	2.61%
2017	667352.9152	−28191.91515	28191.91515	4.22%
2018	692660.3455	−30875.34545	30875.34545	4.46%
2019	717967.7758	−24952.77576	24952.77576	3.48%
2020	743275.2061	30465.79394	30465.79394	4.10%
2021	768582.6364	34458.36364	34458.36364	4.48%
			MAD = 20869.92	MAPE = 3.1%

e. Sales are increasing at a historical rate of $25,307.4303 million per year.

f. Annual U.S. grocery sales (2022) = − 50,726,733.9151+ 25,307.4303 (2022). = $793,890.07 (millions).

Annual U.S. grocery sales (2023) = − 50,726,733.9151+ 25,307.4303 (2023). = $819,197.50 (millions).

Annual U.S. grocery sales (2024) = − 50,726,733.9151+ 25,307.4303 (2024). = $844,504.93 (millions).

The MAD associated with each forecast is 20,869.92. The MAPE is 3.1%.

17. a. The graph of residuals does not show evidence of a pattern or autocorrelation.

Residuals

b.

Period	Sales	Forecast	Residuals	Lagged Residuals	Squared Difference	Squared Residuals
1	1001	1026.620	−25.620			656.38
2	1129	990.384	138.616	−25.620	26973.57	19214.52
3	841	954.147	−113.147	138.616	63384.95	12802.30
4	1044	917.911	126.089	−113.147	57234.02	15898.46
5	1012	881.675	130.325	126.089	17.95	16984.72
6	703	845.438	−142.438	130.325	74400.02	20288.66
7	682	809.202	−127.202	−142.438	232.15	16180.33
8	712	772.966	−60.966	−127.202	4387.25	3716.80
9	646	736.729	−90.729	−60.966	885.88	8231.80
10	686	700.493	−14.493	−90.729	5811.98	210.05
11	909	664.257	244.743	−14.493	67203.47	59899.32
12	469	628.020	−159.020	244.743	163025.10	25287.45
13	566	591.784	−25.784	−159.020	17751.92	664.81
14	488	555.548	−67.548	−25.784	1744.20	4562.68
15	688	519.311	168.689	−67.548	55807.60	28455.87
16	675	483.075	191.925	168.689	539.93	36835.21
17	303	446.839	−143.839	191.925	112737.24	20689.56
18	381	410.602	−29.602	−143.839	13049.94	876.30
				Column sums:	665187.17	291455.22

d = 2.282

No autocorrelation d table values: 1.16,1.39

c. The d-test statistic is 2.282. It is larger than the upper d-critical value of 1.39. Therefore, fail to reject the null hypothesis of "no autocorrelation" and conclude that there is no autocorrelation in the data. We can use the results of the hypothesis tests associated with the regression analysis.

19. a.

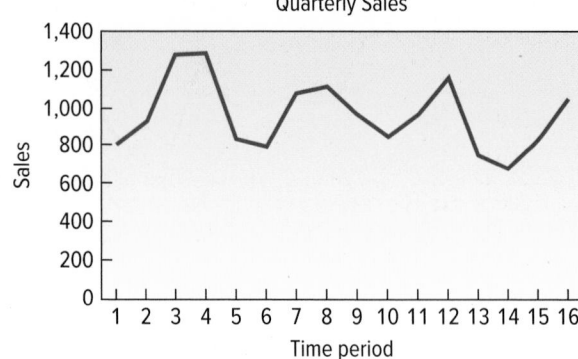

Quarterly Sales

b. The quarterly time series shows two patterns, negative trend, and seasonality. The seasonality is indicated with quarters 3 and 4 always with high sales, and quarters 1 and 2 always with low sales.

c. A trend model is appropriate because we want to estimate the decreasing change in sales per quarter. A model with seasonal indexes is appropriate because we want to quantify the seasonal effects for each quarter.

d. e.

SUMMARY OUTPUT

Regression Statistics

Multiple R	0.262
R Square	0.069
Adjusted R Square	0.002
Standard Error	182.671
Observations	16

ANOVA

	df	SS	MS	F	p-Value
Regression	1	34552.224	34552.224	1.035	0.326
Residual	14	467162.213	33368.730		
Total	15	501714.438			

	Coefficients	Standard Error	t-Stat	p-Value
Intercept	1041.875	95.794	10.876	0.000
period	−10.081	9.907	−1.018	0.326

period	qtr	Sales	trend	index	Forecast	ABS Error	ABS Percent Error
1	1	812	1031.794	0.787	893.851	81.851	10.08%
2	2	920	1021.713	0.900	856.087	63.913	6.95%
3	3	1268	1011.632	1.253	1092.042	175.958	13.88%
4	4	1280	1001.551	1.278	1218.004	61.996	4.84%
5	1	832	991.471	0.839	858.918	26.918	3.24%
6	2	791	981.390	0.806	822.300	31.300	3.96%
7	3	1071	971.309	1.103	1048.514	22.486	2.10%
8	4	1109	961.228	1.154	1168.966	59.966	5.41%
9	1	965	951.147	1.015	823.986	141.014	14.61%
10	2	844	941.066	0.897	788.513	55.487	6.57%
11	3	961	930.985	1.032	1004.985	43.985	4.58%
12	4	1160	920.904	1.260	1119.928	40.072	3.45%
13	1	751	910.824	0.825	789.053	38.053	5.07%
14	2	674	900.743	0.748	754.727	80.727	11.98%
15	3	828	890.662	0.930	961.456	133.456	16.12%
16	4	1033	880.581	1.173	1070.890	37.890	3.67%
						MAD = 68.44	MAPE = 7.28%

Quarter	Index
1	0.866
2	0.838
3	1.079
4	1.216

f. Sales = [1041.875 − 10.081 (time period)] [quarterly index for the time period]

Period 17 Sales = [1041.875 − 10.081 (17)] [.866] = [870.498] [.866] = 753.851

Period 18 Sales = [1041.875 − 10.081 (18)] [.838] = [860.417] [.838] = 721.029

Period 19 Sales = [1041.875 − 10.081 (19)] [1.079] = [850.336] [1.079] = 917.513

Period 20 Sales = [1041.875 − 10.081 (20)] [1.216] = [840.255] [1.216] = 1021.750

21. a.

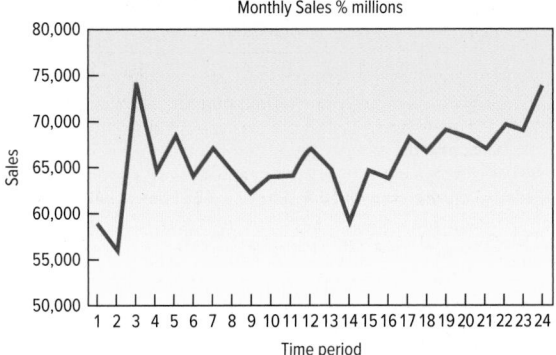

Monthly Sales % millions

b. The monthly time series shows two patterns, positive trend and seasonality. The seasonality is indicated with month 2 (February) the lowest of the months 1 through 12 and month 12 (December) the highest sales among the 12 months.

c. A trend model is appropriate because we want to estimate the increasing change in sales per month. A model with seasonal indexes is appropriate because we want to quantify the seasonal effects for each month.

d. and e. The MAD is 1439.97. The MAPE is 2.15%.

SUMMARY OUTPUT

Regression Statistics

Multiple R	0.4837
R Square	0.2340
Adjusted R Square	0.1991
Standard Error	3782.7887
Observations	24

ANOVA

	df	SS	MS	F	p-Value
Regression	1	96145121.9617	96145121.9617	6.7190	0.0166
Residual	22	314808790.5383	14309490.4790		
Total	23	410953912.5000			

	Coefficients	Standard Error	t Stat	P-value
Intercept	62084.9457	1593.8799	38.9521	0.0000
period	289.1443	111.5484	2.5921	0.0166

period	Mth Yr	Month	Sales $Millions	Trend	Index	Forecast	ABS error	% Abs error
1	1/1/20	1	58,722	62374.090	0.941	60046.532	1324.532	2.26%
2	2/1/20	2	55,870	62663.234	0.892	55895.781	25.781	0.05%
3	3/1/20	3	73,901	62952.379	1.174	67626.725	6274.275	8.49%
4	4/1/20	4	64,383	63241.523	1.018	62408.169	1974.831	3.07%
5	5/1/20	5	68,436	63530.667	1.077	66464.362	1971.638	2.88%
6	6/1/20	6	63,973	63819.812	1.002	63536.691	436.309	0.68%
7	7/1/20	7	66,892	64108.956	1.043	66138.123	753.877	1.13%
8	8/1/20	8	64,500	64398.100	1.002	64634.635	134.635	0.21%
9	9/1/20	9	62,100	64687.245	0.960	62815.636	715.636	1.15%
10	10/1/20	10	64,017	64976.389	0.985	65007.839	990.839	1.55%
11	11/1/20	11	63,920	65265.533	0.979	64693.765	773.765	1.21%
12	12/1/20	12	67,027	65554.678	1.022	68471.703	1444.703	2.16%
13	1/1/21	1	64,785	65843.822	0.984	63386.787	1398.213	2.16%
14	2/1/21	2	59,018	66132.967	0.892	58990.792	27.208	0.05%
15	3/1/21	3	64,734	66422.111	0.975	71354.092	6620.092	10.23%
16	4/1/21	4	63,749	66711.255	0.956	65832.180	2083.180	3.27%
17	5/1/21	5	68,015	67000.400	1.015	70094.319	2079.319	3.06%
18	6/1/21	6	66,531	67289.544	0.989	66991.030	460.030	0.69%
19	7/1/21	7	68,923	67578.688	1.020	69717.679	794.679	1.15%
20	8/1/21	8	68,259	67867.833	1.006	68117.111	141.889	0.21%
21	9/1/21	9	66,939	68156.977	0.982	66184.978	754.022	1.13%
22	10/1/21	10	69,523	68446.121	1.016	68479.250	1043.750	1.50%
23	11/1/21	11	68,948	68735.266	1.003	68133.100	814.900	1.18%
24	12/1/21	12	73,617	69024.410	1.067	72095.830	1521.170	2.07%

MAD = 1439.97   MAPE = 2.15%

Month	Index	Month	Index
1	0.9627	7	1.0317
2	0.8920	8	1.0037
3	1.0743	9	0.9711
4	0.9868	10	1.0005
5	1.0462	11	0.9912
6	0.9956	12	1.0445

f. Sales = [62,084.9457 + 289.1443 (time period)] [monthly index for the time period]

Period 25 Sales = [62,084.9457 + 289.1443 (25)] [0.9627]
= [69,313.55] [0.9627] = 66,727.04 Million$

Period 26 Sales = [62,084.9457 + 289.1443 (26)] [0.8920]
= [69,602.70] [0.8920] = 62,085.80 Million$

Period 27 Sales = [62,084.9457 + 289.1443 (27)] [1.0743]
= [69,891.84] [1.0743] = 75,081.46 Million$

Period 28 Sales = [62,084.9457 + 289.1443 (28)] [0.9868]
= [70,180.99] [0.9868] = 69,256.19 Million$

23. Both techniques are used when a time series has no trend or seasonality. The pattern only shows random variation. Simple moving average selects a fixed number of data points from the past and uses the average as a forecast. All past data is equally weighted. Simple exponential smoothing uses all past available data and adjusts the weights of the past information based on the forecaster's choice of a smoothing constant.

25. The time series has no seasonality.

27. a. The graph does not show any trend or seasonality. The graph shows a stationary pattern. Simple moving average models would be a good choice to compute forecasts.

Demand

b. and c.

Period	Demand	3 month SMA	ABS Error	ABS Percent Error
1	104			
2	132			
3	117			
4	120			
5	104			
6	141	115.4	25.6	18.6%
7	120	122.8	2.8	2.33%
8	136	120.4	15.6	11.47%
9	109	124.2	15.2	13.94%
10	143	122	21.0	14.69%
11	142	129.8	12.2	8.59%
12	109	130	21.0	19.27%
13	113	127.8	14.8	13.10%
14	124	123.2	0.8	0.65%
15	113	126.2	13.2	11.68%
16	104	120.2	16.2	15.58%
17		112.6	MAD = 14.4	MAPE = 11.77%

d. The forecast demand for period 17 is 112.6 units.

e. The forecasting error is estimated with the MAD, which is 14.4. The MAPE is 11.77%. Applying the MAD, the forecast demand is most likely between 98.2, or 112.6 − 14.4, and 127.0, or 112.6 + 14.4. Based on the MAPE, we expect the period 17 forecast error to be about 11.77% in error.

29. a. The graph does not show any trend or seasonality. The graph shows a stationary pattern. Simple exponential smoothing models would be a good choice to compute forecasts.

Demand

b., c., and d.

Period	Demand	Exp with 0.4	Error	ABS Error	ABS Percent Error
1	138				
2	131	138.00	−7.00	7.00	5.34%
3	149	135.20	13.80	13.80	9.26%
4	110	140.72	−30.72	30.72	27.93%
5	175	128.43	46.57	46.57	26.61%
6	194	147.06	46.94	46.94	24.20%
7	166	165.84	0.16	0.16	0.10%
8	103	165.90	−62.90	62.90	61.07%
9	142	140.74	1.26	1.26	0.89%
10	122	141.24	−19.24	19.24	15.77%
11	121	133.55	−12.55	12.55	10.37%
12	130	128.53	1.47	1.47	1.13%
13	126	129.12	−3.12	3.12	2.47%
14	140	127.87	12.13	12.13	8.66%
15		132.72		MAD = 19.84	MAPE = 14.91%

Period	Demand	Exp with 0.9	Error	ABS Error	ABS Percent Error
1	138				
2	131	138.00	−7.00	7.00	5.34%
3	149	131.70	17.30	17.30	11.61%
4	110	147.27	−37.27	37.27	33.88%
5	175	113.73	61.27	61.27	35.01%
6	194	168.87	25.13	25.13	12.95%
7	166	191.49	−25.49	25.49	15.35%
8	103	168.55	−65.55	65.55	63.64%
9	142	109.55	32.45	32.45	22.85%
10	122	138.76	−16.76	16.76	13.73%
11	121	123.68	−2.68	2.68	2.21%
12	130	121.27	8.73	8.73	6.72%
13	126	129.13	−3.13	3.13	2.48%
14	140	126.31	13.69	13.69	9.78%
15		138.63		MAD = 24.34	MAPE = 18.12%

e. Comparing the MAD's and MAPE's the simple exponential smoothing model with α = 0.4 forecasts had less error.

31. a.

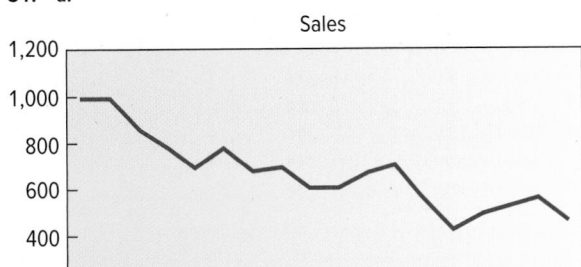

Sales

b. The graph shows a downward, negative trend in sales.

c. Forecasting with a trend model will reveal the average, per period, change in sales.

d. The Trend forecast model is Sales = 930.954 − 27.457 (time period). Based on the MAD, the forecasting error is ± 58.53. The relative percent error, MAPE, is 9.20%

SUMMARY OUTPUT

Regression Statistics

Multiple R	0.900
R Square	0.811
Adjusted R Square	0.799
Standard Error	72.991
Observations	18

ANOVA

	df	SS	MS	F	p-Value
Regression	1	365262.764	365262.764	68.559	0.000
Residual	16	85243.014	5327.688		
Total	17	450505.778			

	Coefficient	Standard Error	t-Stat	p-Value
Intercept	930.954	35.894	25.936	0.000
Time period	− 27.457	3.316	− 8.280	0.000

Period	Sales	Predicted Sales	ABS Error	ABS Percent Error
1	988	903.497	84.503	8.55%
2	990	876.040	113.960	11.51%
3	859	848.583	10.417	1.21%
4	781	821.126	40.126	5.14%
5	691	793.668	102.668	14.86%
6	776	766.211	9.789	1.26%
7	677	738.754	61.754	9.12%
8	690	711.297	21.297	3.09%
9	605	683.840	78.840	13.03%
10	604	656.383	52.383	8.67%
11	670	628.925	41.075	6.13%
12	703	601.468	101.532	14.44%
13	550	574.011	24.011	4.37%
14	427	546.554	119.554	28.00%
15	493	519.097	26.097	5.29%
16	524	491.639	32.361	6.18%
17	563	464.182	98.818	17.55%
18	471	436.725	34.275	7.28%
19		409.268	MAD=58.53	MAPE= 9.2%
20		381.811		
21		354.354		

e. Based on the slope from the regression analysis, sales are decreasing at a rate of 27.457 units per period.

f. Forecasts for periods 19, 20, and 21 are:
Sales = 930.954 − 27.457 (19) = 409.271
Sales = 930.954 − 27.457 (20) = 379.814
Sales = 930.954 − 27.457 (21) = 352.357

33. a.

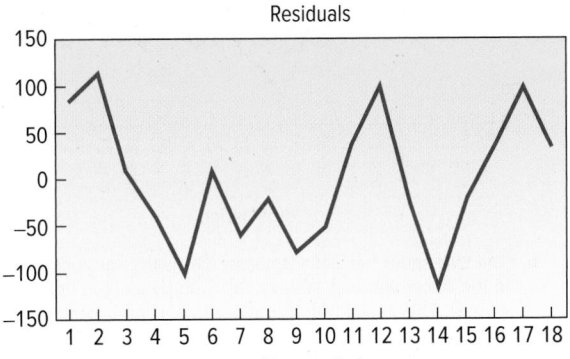

Residuals

b.

Period	Sales	Predicted	Residuals	Lagged Residual	Squared Differences	Squared Residuals
1	988	903.4971	84.5029			7140.7442
2	990	876.0399	113.9601	84.5029	867.7250	12986.9036
3	859	848.5827	10.4173	113.9601	10721.1172	108.5195
4	781	821.1256	−40.1256	10.4173	2554.5774	1610.0605
5	691	793.6684	−102.6684	−40.1256	3911.6053	10540.7976
6	776	766.2112	9.7888	−102.6684	12646.6156	95.8203
7	677	738.7540	−61.7540	9.7888	5118.3762	3813.5617
8	690	711.2969	−21.2969	−61.7540	1636.7828	453.5567
9	605	683.8397	−78.8397	−21.2969	3311.1770	6215.6979
10	604	656.3825	−52.3825	−78.8397	699.9820	2743.9289
11	670	628.9254	41.0746	−52.3825	8734.2431	1687.1267
12	703	601.4682	101.5318	41.0746	3655.0697	10308.7104
13	550	574.0110	−24.0110	101.5318	15761.0016	576.5285
14	427	546.5538	−119.5538	−24.0110	9128.4319	14293.1196
15	493	519.0967	−26.0967	−119.5538	8734.2431	681.0358
16	524	491.6395	32.3605	−26.0967	3417.2410	1047.2026
17	563	464.1823	98.8177	32.3605	4416.5558	9764.9342
18	471	436.7251	34.2749	98.8177	4165.7766	1174.7656

Sums: 99480.5211   85243.0141

d = 1.1670

c. Based on d = 1.1670, the result of the hypothesis test is inconclusive. We cannot make any determination regarding the presence of autocorrelation in the data.

35. a.

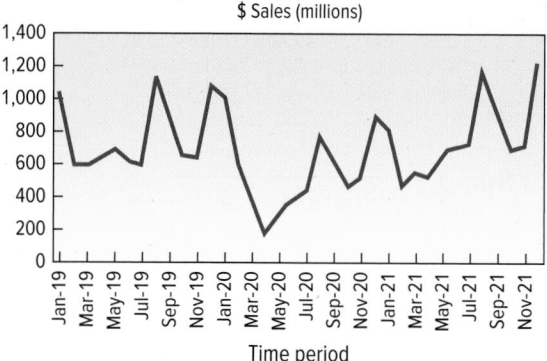

$ Sales (millions)

Time period

b. The time series has definite seasonality with peaks occurring in the December and January, followed by a regular peak in August. There may be a slight positive trend over the time span.

c. The choice of this forecasting model is appropriate because of the seasonality and the hint of a small positive trend.

d. d, e, and f.   The MAD is 115.0112. The MAPE is 22.68%.

SUMMARY OUTPUT

Regression Statistics	
Multiple *R*	0.0811
R Square	0.0066
Adjusted *R* Square	− 0.0226
Standard Error	247.2114
Observations	36

ANOVA

	dd	SS	MS	F	p-Value
Regression	1	13760.1113	13760.1113	0.2252	0.6382
Residual	34	2077858.6387	61113.4894		
Total	35	2091618.7500			

	Coefficients	*Standard Error*	*t Stat*	*P-value*
Intercept	650.1000	84.1511	7.7254	0.0000
period	1.8820	3.9662	0.4745	0.6382

Year	Month	Month Number	$ Sales (millions)	Period	Trend	Index	Forecast	ABS(Error)	ABS (Percent Error)
2019	January	1	1,029	1	651.9820	1.5783	917.5763	111.4237	10.83%
2019	February	2	585	2	653.8640	0.8947	529.1814	55.8186	9.54%
2019	March	3	603	3	655.7459	0.9196	502.4112	100.5888	16.68%
2019	April	4	650	4	657.6279	0.9884	431.4517	218.5483	33.62%
2019	May	5	696	5	659.5099	1.0553	517.7952	178.2048	25.60%
2019	June	6	613	6	661.3919	0.9268	548.7496	64.2504	10.48%
2019	July	7	591	7	663.2739	0.8910	560.0720	30.9280	5.23%
2019	August	8	1,124	8	665.1559	1.6898	983.1117	140.8883	12.53%
2019	September	9	871	9	667.0378	1.3058	765.8990	105.1010	12.07%
2019	October	10	650	10	668.9198	0.9717	581.0178	68.9822	10.61%
2019	November	11	640	11	670.8018	0.9541	594.3934	45.6066	7.13%
2019	December	12	1,074	12	672.6838	1.5966	1024.0242	49.9758	4.65%
2020	January	1	990	13	674.5658	1.4676	949.3599	40.6401	4.11%
2020	February	2	593	14	676.4477	0.8766	547.4588	45.5412	7.68%
2020	March	3	406	15	678.3297	0.5985	519.7142	113.7142	28.01%
2020	April	4	169	16	680.2117	0.2485	446.2683	277.2683	164.06%
2020	May	5	275	17	682.0937	0.4032	535.5262	260.5262	94.74%
2020	June	6	388	18	683.9757	0.5673	567.4871	179.4871	46.26%
2020	July	7	437	19	685.8577	0.6372	579.1419	142.1419	32.53%
2020	August	8	770	20	687.7396	1.1196	1016.4910	246.4910	32.01%
2020	September	9	620	21	689.6216	0.8990	791.8299	171.8299	27.71%
2020	October	10	455	22	691.5036	0.6580	600.6339	145.6339	32.01%
2020	November	11	496	23	693.3856	0.7153	614.4048	118.4048	23.87%
2020	December	12	900	24	695.2676	1.2945	1058.4035	158.4035	17.60%
2021	January	1	820	25	697.1495	1.1762	981.1435	161.1435	19.65%
2021	February	2	459	26	699.0315	0.6566	565.7361	106.7361	23.25%
2021	March	3	547	27	700.9135	0.7804	537.0172	9.9828	1.83%
2021	April	4	514	28	702.7955	0.7314	461.0849	52.9151	10.29%
2021	May	5	632	29	704.6775	0.8969	553.2573	78.7427	12.46%
2021	June	6	703	30	706.5595	0.9950	586.2246	116.7754	16.61%
2021	July	7	712	31	708.4414	1.0050	598.2118	113.7882	15.98%
2021	August	8	1,154	32	710.3234	1.6246	1049.8702	104.1298	9.02%

Year	Month	Month Number	$ Sales (millions)	Period	Trend	Index	Forecast	ABS(Error)	ABS (Percent Error)
2021	September	9	883	33	712.2054	1.2398	817.7608	65.2392	7.39%
2021	October	10	697	34	714.0874	0.9761	620.2500	76.7500	11.01%
2021	November	11	708	35	715.9694	0.9889	634.4161	73.5839	10.39%
2021	December	12	1,203	36	717.8514	1.6758	1092.7827	110.2173	9.16%
2022	January	1		37	719.7333		1012.9271	MAD= 115.01	MAPE= 22.68%
2022	February	2		38	721.6153		584.0135		
2022	March	3		39	723.4973		554.3201		
2022	April	4		40	725.3793		475.9015		
2022	May	5		41	727.2613		570.9883		
2022	June	6		42	729.1432		604.9622		
2022	July	7		43	731.0252		617.2816		
2022	August	8		44	732.9072		1083.2494		
2022	September	9		45	734.7892		843.6917		

Month	Index	Month	Index
1	1.4074	7	0.8444
2	0.8093	8	1.4780
3	0.7662	9	1.1482
4	0.6561	10	0.8686
5	0.7851	11	0.8861
6	0.8297	12	1.5223

e. The regression analysis shows a small increase of 1.8820 million dollars per month.

f. Book sales are highest in December (52.23% higher than average) and August (47.80% higher than average). Book sales are lowest from February through July.

g.

Year	Month	Forecast Sales
2022	January	1,012.93
2022	February	584.01
2022	March	554.32
2022	April	475.90
2022	May	570.99
2022	June	604.96
2022	July	617.28
2022	August	1,083.25
2022	September	843.69

h. Given the MAD's estimate of error in the forecasting model, the forecasts could be off by $\pm$ 115.0112 million dollars. Based on the MAPE, the average absolute percent error is 22.68%. Because a time series approach to forecasting replicates historical patterns in sales, note that, starting in March 2020, the time series was affected by the COVID-19 pandemic. In fact, you may try using only the data starting in March 2020. You will see a much better time series model. The MAD is 47.7 and the MAPE is 8.4%.

37. The linear trend line for net sales is $\hat{Y} = 12{,}457 + 3{,}648 \cdot t$. The logarithmic trend line is $\hat{Y} = 4.2680 + 0.0325 \cdot t$. The base year (1993) is 0. The linear equation appears better because R^2 is larger at 0.8996 compared to 0.7869. The years 2021 and 2022 would be coded $t = 29$ and 30, respectively.

The 20121 forecast is $\hat{Y} = 12{,}457 + 3{,}648 (29)$ or \$118,249 million. The 2022 forecast is $\hat{Y} = 12{,}457 + 3{,}648 (30)$ or \$121,897 million.

39. Here is the output from regression software.

SUMMARY OUTPUT

Regression Statistics

Multiple R	0.9976
R Square	0.9952
Adjusted R Square	0.9948
Standard Error	2277.4710
Observations	28

ANOVA

	df	SS	MS	F	p-Value
Regression	2	26901495466.60	13450747733.30	2593.23	0.0000
Residual	27	129671851.82	5186874.07		
Total	27	27031167318.43			

	Coefficients	Standard Error	t Stat	P-value
Intercept	−74030.7635	5842.2927	−12.6715	0.0000
Associates	132.9193	11.8415	11.2248	0.0000
Average Ticket Sale	1883.8798	167.9100	11.2196	0.0000

The regression equation is:
Sales = − 74,030.76 + 1,883.88 (Average Ticket Sale) + 132.92 Associates

The null hypothesis is no autocorrelation, and the alternate is there is positive autocorrelation. There are 2 independent variables (k) and the sample size (n) is 28. For a significance level of 0.05 the lower value is 1.26 and the upper value is 1.56 from Appendix B.9. To compute the test statistic (d), you need the residuals, the difference between successive residuals, the squares of both and their totals.

Observation	Predicted	Residuals	Lagged Residuals	Residual Squared	Squared Diff
1	6411.16927	2827.83073		7996626.638	
2	12700.10178	−223.101777	2827.83073	49774.40292	9308189.163
3	15417.61328	52.38671621	−223.101777	2744.368035	75893.90991
4	18301.11972	1233.880276	52.38671621	1522460.536	1395927.032
5	24698.07193	−542.0719262	1233.880276	293841.9732	3154006.225
6	31666.47429	−1447.474286	−542.0719262	2095181.809	819753.4332
7	42920.50756	−4466.507558	−1447.474286	19949689.76	9114561.896
8	47832.54339	−2094.543392	−4466.507558	4387112.022	5626214.003
9	51668.36398	1884.636024	−2094.543392	3551852.942	15833868.82
10	56426.44353	1820.556467	1884.636024	3314425.85	4106.189592
11	62045.97207	2770.027928	1820.556467	7673054.72	901496.0544
12	72321.62127	772.378731	2770.027928	596568.904	3990602.313
13	81027.15844	483.8415595	772.378731	234102.6547	83253.69932
14	85365.54593	−6343.545927	483.8415595	40240574.93	46613219.89
15	78250.93235	−901.932349	−6343.545927	813481.9622	29611158.33
16	73531.80351	−2243.803511	−901.932349	5034654.197	1800618.216
17	65614.26981	561.7301857	−2243.803511	315540.8015	7871019.324
18	66466.20654	1530.793463	561.7301857	2343328.625	939083.6346
19	70338.63717	56.36283462	1530.793463	3176.769127	2173945.677
20	74567.95725	186.0427462	56.36283462	34611.90343	16816.87948
21	81413.79472	−2601.794716	186.0427462	6769335.745	7772037.717
22	84302.41703	−1126.417035	−2601.794716	1268815.336	2176739.303
23	87858.77891	660.2210938	−1126.417035	435891.8927	3192075.802
24	93626.61407	968.3859311	660.2210938	937771.3116	94965.56698
25	99662.36337	1241.636635	968.3859311	1541661.532	74665.94697
26	104711.1612	3491.838756	1241.636635	12192937.89	5063409.585
27	107915.8523	2309.147681	3491.838756	5332163.011	1398758.179
28	132970.5053	−860.505279	2309.147681	740469.3352	10046699.89
			Sums:	129,671,851.82	169,153,086.68
			$d=$	1.304470356	

The Durbin-Watson d is 169,153,087/129,671,851 = 1.30. Since the computed value is between the lower and upper limits, we neither accept or reject the hypothesis of no autocorrelation.

CHAPTER 19

1.

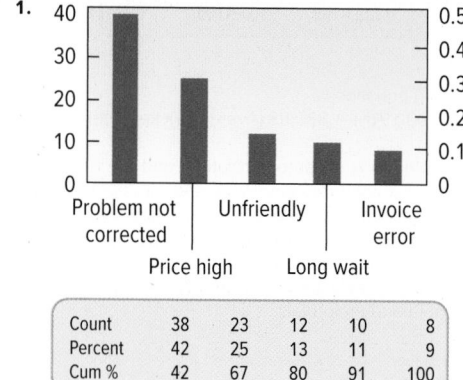

Count	38	23	12	10	8
Percent	42	25	13	11	9
Cum %	42	67	80	91	100

About 67% of the complaints concern the problem not being corrected and the price being too high.

3. Chance variation is random in nature; because the cause is a variety of factors, it cannot be entirely eliminated. Assignable variation is not random; it is usually due to a specific cause and can be eliminated.

5. a. The A_2 factor is 0.729.
   b. The value for D_3 is 0, and for D_4 it is 2.282.

7. a.

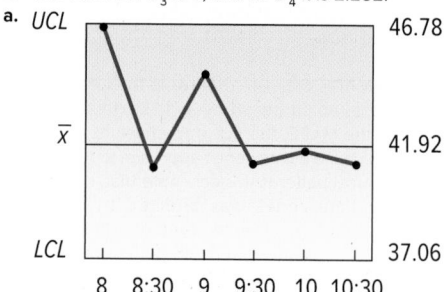

Time	$\bar{x}$, Arithmetic Means	R, Range
8:00 a.m.	46	16
8:30 a.m.	40.5	6
9:00 a.m.	44	6
9:30 a.m.	40	2
10:00 a.m.	41.5	9
10:30 a.m.	39.5	1
	251.5	40

$$\overline{\overline{x}} = \frac{2515}{6} = 41.92 \quad \overline{R} = \frac{40}{6} = 6.67$$

$$UCL = 41.92 + 0.729(6.67) = 46.78$$
$$LCL = 41.92 - 0.729(6.67) = 37.06$$

  b. Interpreting, the mean reading was 341.92 degrees Fahrenheit. If the oven continues operating as evidenced by the first six hourly readings, about 99.7% of the mean readings will lie between 337.06 degrees and 346.78 degrees.

9. **a.** The fraction defective is 0.0507. The upper control limit is 0.0801 and the lower control limit is 0.0213.

  b. Yes, the seventh and ninth samples indicate the process is out of control.

  c. The process appears to stay the same.

11. $\overline{c} = \dfrac{37}{14} = 2.64$

$$2.64 \pm 3\sqrt{2.64}$$

The control limits are 0 and 7.5. The process is out of control on the seventh day.

13. $\overline{c} = \dfrac{6}{11} = 0.545$

$$0.545 \pm 2\sqrt{0.545} = 0.545 \pm 2.215$$

The control limits are from 0 to 2.760, so there are no receipts out of control.

15.

Percent Defective	Probability of Accepting Lot
10	.889
20	.558
30	.253
40	.083

17. $P(x \le 1 \mid n = 10, \pi = .10) = .736$
$P(x \le 1 \mid n = 10, \pi = .20) = .375$
$P(x \le 1 \mid n = 10, \pi = .30) = .149$
$P(x \le 1 \mid n = 10, \pi = .40) = .046$

19.

Reason	Poor wiring	Short coil	Defective plug	Other
Count	80	60	50	10
Percent	40.0	30.0	25.0	5.0
Cum %	40.0	70.0	95.0	100.0

21. **a.** Mean: $UCL = 10.0 + 0.577(0.25) = 10.0 + 0.14425$
$\qquad\qquad\qquad = 10.14425$
$\qquad\quad LCL = 10.0 - 0.577(0.25) = 10.0 - 0.14425$
$\qquad\qquad\qquad = 9.85575$
  Range: $UCL = 2.115(0.25) = 0.52875$
$\qquad\quad LCL = 0(0.25) = 0$

  b. The mean is 10.16, which is above the upper control limit and is out of control. There is too much cola in the soft drinks. The process is in control for variation; an adjustment is needed.

23. **a.** $\overline{\overline{x}} = \dfrac{611.3333}{20} = 30.57$

$$\overline{R} = \frac{312}{20} = 15.6$$

  Mean: $UCL = 30.5665 + (1.023)(15.6) = 46.53$
$\qquad\quad LCL = 30.5665 - (1.023)(15.6) = 14.61$
  Range: $UCL = 2.575(15.6) = 40.17$

  b.

  c. The points all seem to be within the control limits. No adjustments are necessary.

25. $\overline{\overline{x}} = \dfrac{-0.5}{18} = -0.0278 \quad \overline{R} = \dfrac{27}{18} = 1.5$

$$UCL = -.0278 + (0.729)(1.5) = 1.065$$
$$LCL = -.0278 - (0.729)(1.5) = -1.121$$
$$UCL = 2.282(1.5) = 3.423$$

The X-bar chart indicates that the "process" was in control. However, the R-bar chart indicates that the performance on hole 12 was outside the limits.

27. **a.** $p = \dfrac{40}{10(50)} = 0.08 \quad 3\sqrt{\dfrac{0.08(0.92)}{50}} = 0.115$

$$UCL = 0.08 + 0.115 = 0.195$$
$$LCL = 0.08 - 0.115 = 0$$

  b.

  c. There are no points that exceed the limits.

29.

P Chart for C1

These sample results indicate that the odds are much less than 50-50 for an increase. The percent of stocks that increase is "in control" around 0.25, or 25%. The control limits are 0.06629 and 0.4337.

31. $P(x \leq 3 \mid n = 10, \pi = 0.05) = 0.999$
$P(x \leq 3 \mid n = 10, \pi = 0.10) = 0.987$
$P(x \leq 3 \mid n = 10, \pi = 0.20) = 0.878$
$P(x \leq 3 \mid n = 10, \pi = 0.30) = 0.649$
$P(x \leq 5 \mid n = 20, \pi = 0.05) = 0.999$
$P(x \leq 5 \mid n = 20, \pi = 0.10) = 0.989$
$P(x \leq 5 \mid n = 20, \pi = 0.20) = 0.805$
$P(x \leq 5 \mid n = 20, \pi = 0.30) = 0.417$

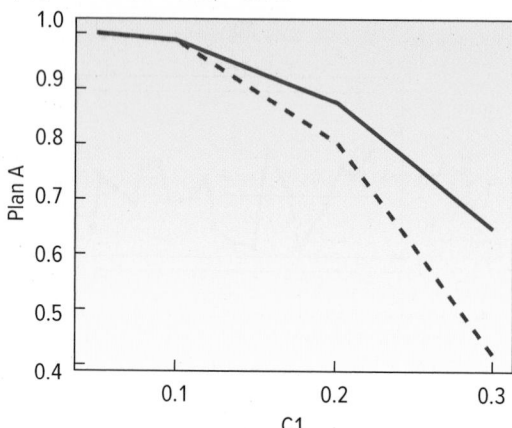

The solid line is the operating characteristic curve for the first plan, and the dashed line, the second. The supplier would prefer the first because the probability of acceptance is higher (above). However, if he is really sure of his quality, the second plan seems higher at the very low range of defect percentages and might be preferred.

33. **a.** $\bar{c} = \dfrac{213}{15} = 14.2 \; ; \; 3\sqrt{14.2} = 11.30$

$UCL = 14.2 + 11.3 = 25.5$
$LCL = 14.2 - 11.3 = 2.9$

b.

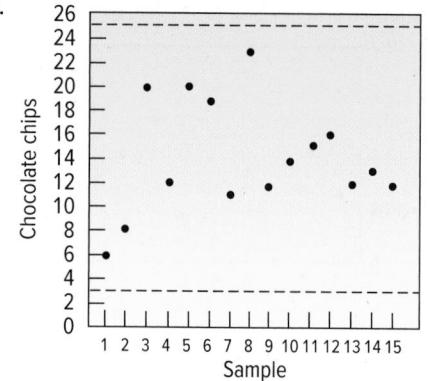

c. All the points are in control.

35. $\bar{c} = \dfrac{70}{10} = 7.0$

$UCL = 7.0 + 3\sqrt{7} = 14.9$
$LCL = 7.0 - 3\sqrt{7} = 0$

37. $P(x \leq 3 \mid n = 20, \pi = .10) = .867$
$P(x \leq 3 \mid n = 20, \pi = .20) = .412$
$P(x \leq 3 \mid n = 20, \pi = .30) = .108$

836

APPENDIX C: ANSWERS

Answers to Odd-Numbered Review Exercises

REVIEW OF CHAPTERS 1–4
PROBLEMS

1. a. Mean is 147.9. Median is 148.5. Standard deviation is 69.24.
 b. The first quartile is 106. The third quartile is 186.25.
 c.

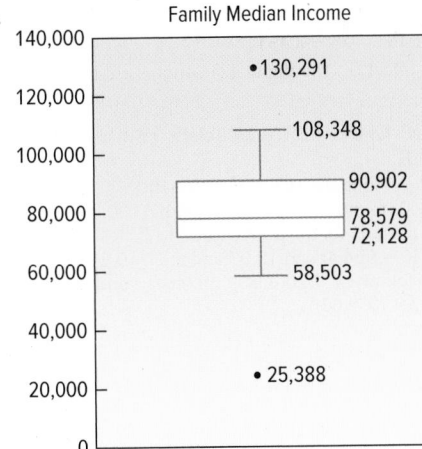

There are no outliers. The distribution is symmetric. The whiskers and the boxes are about equal on the two sides.

 d. $2^6 = 64$, use six classes; $i = \dfrac{299 - 14}{6} = 47.5$, use $i = 50$.

Amount	Frequency
$\$\ \ 0$ up to $\$\ 50$	3
50 up to 100	8
100 up to 150	15
150 up to 200	13
200 up to 250	7
250 up to 300	7
Total	50

 e. Answers will vary but include all of the above information.
3. a. Minimum = 25,388; lower outlier boundary = 58,503; first quartile = 72,128; median = 78,579; third quartile = 90,902; upper outlier boundary = 108,348; maximum = 130,291.
 b. The interquartile range is (90,902 − 72,128) = 18,774; 50% of the 52 observations have median family incomes in this range.
 c.

Family Median Income

```
140,000
                    •130,291
120,000

100,000          ── 108,348

                           ── 90,902
 80,000     ┌────────┐── 78,579
            │        │── 72,128
 60,000     └── 58,503

 40,000

                • 25,388
 20,000

      0
```

The distribution appears symmetric. However, there are two observations that are outliers. The District of Columbia with an extremely high median family income of $130,291 and Puerto Rico with an extremely low family median income of $25,388.

 d.

Median Income	Number of States (including Washington, D.C. and Puerto Rico)
$25000–41999	1
42000–58999	1
59000–75999	19
76000–92999	20
93000–109999	10
127000–143999	1
Grand Total	**52**

 e. The distribution of state median annual income shows 39 states between $59,000 and $93,000. Ten states exceed $93,000; one state (Mississippi) is lower with $58,503; the territory of Puerto Rico is the smallest with $25,388.
5. a. Box plot.
 b. Median is 48, the first quartile is 24, and the third quartile is 84.
 c. Positively skewed with the long tail to the right.
 d. You cannot determine the number of observations.

REVIEW OF CHAPTERS 5–7
PROBLEMS

1. a. .035
 b. .018
 c. .648
3. a. .0401
 b. .6147
 c. 7,440
5. a. $\mu = 1.10$
   $\sigma = 1.18$
 b. About 550
 c. $\mu = 1.833$

REVIEW OF CHAPTERS 8 AND 9
PROBLEMS

1. $z = \dfrac{8.8 - 8.6}{2.0/\sqrt{35}} = 0.59, .5000 - .2224 = .2776$

3. $160 \pm 2.426 \dfrac{20}{\sqrt{40}}$, 152.33 up to 167.67

5. $985.5 \pm 2.571 \dfrac{115.5}{\sqrt{6}}$, 864.27 up to 1,106.73

7. $240 \pm 2.131 \dfrac{35}{\sqrt{16}}$, 221.35 up to 258.65

 Because 250 is in the interval, the evidence does *not* indicate an increase in production.

9. $n = \left[\dfrac{1.96(25)}{4} \right]^2 = 150$

11. $n = .30(.70) \left(\dfrac{2.33}{0.02} \right)^2 = 2851$

13. $n = .4(.6) \left(\dfrac{2.33}{0.03} \right)^2 = 1,448$

REVIEW OF CHAPTERS 10–12
PROBLEMS

1. $H_0: \mu \geq 36$; $H_1: \mu < 36$. Reject H_0 if $t < -1.683$.

$$t = \frac{35.5 - 36.0}{0.9/\sqrt{42}} = -3.60$$

Reject H_0. The mean height is less than 36 inches.

3. We test the assumption or hypothesis that the population variances are equal.

$$H_0 : \sigma_e^2 = \sigma_h^2$$
$$H_1 : \sigma_e^2 \neq \sigma_h^2$$

This a two-tail test. To use the F-table in the text, we select a significance level, α, of .10 and divide by 2 to use the F-table with a right tail area of .05. With 9 degrees of freedom in the numerator and 11 degrees of freedom in the denominator, the F critical value is 2.90.

Using the sample standard deviations, we calculate the F-statistic:

$$F = \frac{s_w^2}{s_a^2} = \frac{8^2}{5^2} = 2.56$$

The calculated F-statistic is less than 5.19. We fail to reject the null hypothesis. The sample data are not sufficient to conclude that the population variances are different. We will use the pooled sample variances as the best estimate of the population variance.

$H_0: \mu_1 = \mu_2$ $H_1: \mu_1 \neq \mu_2$

Reject H_0 if $t < -2.845$ or $t > 2.845$.

$$s_p^2 = \frac{(12 - 1)(5)^2 + (10 - 1)(8)^2}{12 + 10 + 2} = 42.55$$

$$t = \frac{250 - 252}{\sqrt{42.55\left(\frac{1}{12} + \frac{1}{10}\right)}} = -0.716$$

H_0 is not rejected. There is no difference in the mean strength of the two glues.

5. $H_0: \mu_1 = \mu_2 = \mu_3 = \mu_4$ H_1: The means are not all the same.

H_0 rejected if $F > 3.29$.

Source	SS	df	MS	F
Treatments	20.736	3	6.91	1.04
Error	100.00	15	6.67	
Total	120.736	18		

H_0 is not rejected. There is no difference in the mean sales.

7. **a.** From the graph, marketing salaries may be acting differently.

b. $H_0: \mu_1 = \mu_2 = \mu_3 = \mu_4$

H_1: At least one mean is different (for four majors).

$H_0: \mu_1 = \mu_2 = \mu_3$

H_1: At least one mean is different (for 3 years).

H_0: There is no interaction.

H_1: There is interaction.

c. The p-value (.482) is high. Do not reject the hypothesis of no interaction.

d. The p-value for majors is small (.034 < .05), so there is a difference among mean salaries by major. There is no difference from one year to the next in mean salaries (.894 > .05).

REVIEW OF CHAPTERS 13 AND 14
PROBLEMS

1. **a.** Profit

b. $\hat{y} = a + b_1x_1 + b_2x_2 + b_3x_3 + b_4x_4$

c. $163,200

d. About 86% of the variation in net profit is explained by the four variables.

e. About 68% of the net profits would be within $3,000 of the estimates; about 95% would be within 2($3,000), or $6,000, of the estimates; and virtually all would be within 3($3,000), or $9,000, of the estimates.

3. **a.** 0.9261

b. 2.0469, found by $\sqrt{83.8/20}$

c. $H_0: \beta_1 = \beta_2 = \beta_3 = \beta_4 = 0$

H_1: Not all coefficients are zero.

Reject if $F > 2.87$; computed $F = 62.697$, found by 162.70/4.19.

d. Could delete x_2 because t-ratio (1.29) is less than the critical t-value of 2.086. Otherwise, reject H_0 for x_1, x_3, and x_4 because all of those t-ratios are greater than 2.086.

REVIEW OF CHAPTERS 15 AND 16
PROBLEMS

1. H_0: Median ≤ 60

H_1: Median > 60

$\mu = 20(.5) = 10$

$\sigma = \sqrt{20(.5)(.5)} = 2.2361$

H_0 is rejected if $z > 1.65$. There are 16 observations greater than 60.

$$z = \frac{15.5 - 10.0}{2.2361} = 2.46$$

Reject H_0. The median sales per day are greater than 60.

3. H_0: The population lengths are the same.

H_1: The population lengths are not the same.

H_0 is rejected if H is > 5.991.

$$H = \frac{12}{24(24 + 1)}\left[\frac{(104.5)^2}{7} + \frac{(125.5)^2}{9} + \frac{(70)^2}{8}\right] - 3(24 + 1)$$

$$= 78.451 - 75 = 3.451$$

Do not reject H_0. The population lengths are the same.

REVIEW OF CHAPTERS 17 AND 18
PROBLEMS

1. **a.** 156.6, found by (16,915/10,799)100

b. 153.0, found by (16,615/11,056.7)100. Note: 11,056.7 is the average for the period 2008 to 2010.

c. $9,535 + 854.4t$ and 18,079, found by $9,535 + 854.4 (10)$

3. 55.44, found by 1.20[3.5 + (0.7)(61)], and 44.73, found by 0.90[3.5 + (0.7)(66)]

Solutions to Practice Tests

PRACTICE TEST (AFTER CHAPTER 4)
PART 1
1. statistics
2. descriptive statistics
3. population
4. quantitative and qualitative
5. discrete
6. nominal
7. nominal
8. zero
9. seven
10. 50
11. variance
12. never
13. median

PART 2
1. $\sqrt[3]{(1.18)(1.04)(1.02)} = 1.0777$, *or* 7.77%
2. a. $30,000
   b. 105
   c. 52
   d. 0.19, found by 20/105
   e. 165
   f. 120 and 330
3. a. 70
   b. 71.5
   c. 67.8
   d. 28
   e. 9.34
4. $44.20, found by [(200)$36 + (300)$40 + (500)$50]/1,000
5. a. pie chart
   b. 11.1
   c. three times
   d. 65%

PRACTICE TEST (AFTER CHAPTER 7)
PART 1
1. never
2. experiment
3. event
4. joint
5. a. permutation
   b. combination
6. one
7. three or more outcomes
8. infinite
9. one
10. 0.2764
11. 0.0475
12. independent
13. mutually exclusive
14. only two outcomes
15. bell-shaped

PART 2
1. a. 0.0526, found by (5/20)(4/19)
   b. 0.4474, found by 1 − (15/20)(14/19)
2. a. 0.2097, found by $16(.15)(.85)^{15}$
   b. 0.9257, found by $1 − (.85)^{16}$

3. 720, found by $6 \times 5 \times 4 \times 3 \times 2$
4. a. 2.2, found by .2(1) + .5(2) + .2(3) + .1(4)
   b. 0.76, found by .2(1.44) + .5(0.04) + .2(0.64) + .1(3.24)
5. a. 0.1808. The *z*-value for $2,000 is 0.47, found by (2,000 − 1,600)/850.
   b. 0.4747, found by 0.2939 + 0.1808
   c. 0.0301, found by 0.5000 − 0.4699
6. a. contingency table
   b. 0.625, found by 50/80
   c. 0.75, found by 60/80
   d. 0.40, found by 20/50
   e. 0.125, found by 10/80
7. a. 0.0498, found by $\dfrac{3^0 e^{-3}}{0!}$
   b. 0.2240, found by $\dfrac{3^3 e^{-3}}{3!}$
   c. 0.1847, found by 1 − [0.0498 + 0.1494 + 0.2240 + 0.2240 + 0.1680]
   d. .0025

PRACTICE TEST (AFTER CHAPTER 9)
PART 1
1. random sample
2. sampling error
3. standard error
4. become smaller
5. point estimate
6. confidence interval
7. population size
8. proportion
9. positively skewed
10. 0.5

PART 2
1. 0.0351, found by 0.5000 − 0.4649. The corresponding
$$z = \frac{11 - 12.2}{2.3/\sqrt{12}} = -1.81$$
2. a. The population mean is unknown.
   b. 9.3 years, which is the sample mean
   c. 0.3922, found by $2/\sqrt{26}$
   d. The confidence interval is from 8.63 up to 9.97, found by
$$9.3 \pm 1.708\left(\frac{2}{\sqrt{26}}\right)$$
3. 2,675, found by $.27(1 - .27)\left(\dfrac{2.33}{.02}\right)^2$
4. The confidence interval is from 0.5459 up to 0.7341, found by
$$.64 \pm 1.96\sqrt{\frac{.64(1 - .64)}{100}}$$

PRACTICE TEST (AFTER CHAPTER 12)
PART 1
1. null hypothesis
2. significance level
3. *p*-value
4. standard deviation
5. normality
6. test statistic
7. split evenly between the two tails
8. range from negative infinity to positive infinity

9. independent

10. three and 20

PART 2

1. $H_0: \mu \le 90$ $H_1: \mu > 90$ If $t > 2.567$, reject H_0.

$$t = \frac{96 - 90}{12/\sqrt{18}} = 2.12$$

Do not reject the null. The mean time in the park could be 90 minutes.

2. We test the assumption or hypothesis that the population variances are equal.

$$H_0: \sigma_y^2 = \sigma_h^2$$
$$H_1: \sigma_y^2 \ne \sigma_h^2$$

This a two-tail test. To use the F-table in the text, we select a significance level, α, of .10 and divide by 2 to use the F-table with a right tail area of .05. With 11 degrees of freedom in the numerator and 13 degrees of freedom in the denominator, the F critical value is 2.63.

Using the sample standard deviations, we calculate the F-statistic:

$$F = \frac{s_y^2}{s_h^2} = \frac{40^2}{30^2} = 1.778$$

The calculated F-statistic is less than 2.63. We fail to reject the null hypothesis. The sample data are not sufficient to conclude that the population variances are different. We will use the pooled sample variances as the best estimate of the population variance.

$H_0: \mu_1 = \mu_2$ $H_1: \mu_1 \ne \mu_2$
$df = 14 + 12 - 2 = 24$
If $t < -2.064$ or $t > 2.064$, then reject H_0.

$$s_p^2 = \frac{(14 - 1)(30)^2 + (12 - 1)(40)^2}{14 + 12 - 2} = 1,220.83$$

$$t = \frac{837 - 797}{\sqrt{1,220.83\left(\frac{1}{14} + \frac{1}{12}\right)}} = \frac{40.0}{13.7455} = 2.910$$

Reject the null hypothesis. There is a difference in the mean miles traveled.

3.
  a. three, because there are 2 df between groups.
  b. 21, found by the total degrees of freedom plus 1.
  c. If the significance level is .05, the critical value is 3.55.
  d. $H_0: \mu_1 = \mu_2 = \mu_3$ H_1: Treatment means are not all the same.
  e. At a 5% significance level, the null hypothesis is rejected.
  f. At a 5% significance level, we can conclude the treatment means differ.

PRACTICE TEST (AFTER CHAPTER 14)
PART 1

1. vertical
2. interval
3. zero
4. -0.77
5. never
6. 7
7. decrease of .5
8. -0.9
9. zero
10. unlimited
11. linear
12. residual
13. two

14. correlation matrix
15. normal distribution

PART 2

1.
  a. 30
  b. The regression equation is $\hat{y} = 90.619X - 0.9401$. If X is zero, the line crosses the vertical axis at -0.9401. As the independent variable increases by one unit, the dependent variable increases by 90.619 units.
  c. 905.2499
  d. 0.3412, found by 129.7275/380.1667. Thirty-four percent of the variation in the dependent variable is explained by the independent variable.
  e. 0.5842, found by $\sqrt{0.3412}$ $H_0: p \ge 0$ $H_1: p < 0$
     Using a significance level of .01, reject H_0 if $t > 2.467$.

$$t = \frac{0.5842\sqrt{30 - 2}}{\sqrt{1 - (0.5842)^2}} = 3.81$$

     Reject H_0. There is a negative correlation between the variables.

2.
  a. 30
  b. 4
  c. 0.5974, found by 227.0928/380.1667
  d. $H_0: \beta_1 = \beta_2 = \beta_3 = \beta_4 = 0$ H_1: Not all βs are 0. Reject H_0 if $F > 4.18$ (using a 1% level of significance). Since the computed value of F is 9.27, reject H_0. Not all of the regression coefficients are zero.
  e. Reject H_0 if $t > 2.787$ or $t < -2.787$ (using a 1% level of significance). Drop variable 2 initially and then rerun. Perhaps you will delete variable(s) 1 and/or 4 also.

PRACTICE TEST (AFTER CHAPTER 16)
PART 1

1. nominal
2. at least 30 observations
3. two
4. 6
5. number of categories
6. dependent
7. binomial
8. comparing two or more independent samples
9. never
10. normal populations, equal standard deviations

PART 2

1. H_0: The proportions are as stated.
     H_1: The proportions are not as stated.
     Using a significance level of .05, reject H_0 if $\chi^2 > 7.815$.

$$x^2 = \frac{(120 - 130)^2}{130} + \frac{(40 - 40)^2}{40}$$
$$+ \frac{(30 - 20)^2}{20} + \frac{(10 - 10)^2}{10} = 5.769$$

     Do not reject H_0. Proportions could be as declared.

2. H_0: No relationship between sex and book type.
     H_1: There is a relationship between sex and book type.
     Using a significance level of .01, reject H_0 if $\chi^2 > 9.21$.

$$x^2 = \frac{(250 - 197.3)^2}{197.3} + \cdots + \frac{(200 - 187.5)^2}{187.5} = 54.84$$

     Reject H_0. There is a relationship between sex and book type.

3. H_0: The distributions are the same.
     H_1: The distributions are not the same.
     H_0 is rejected if $H > 5.99$.

8:00 a.m. Ranks		10:00 a.m. Ranks		1:30 p.m. Ranks	
68	6	59	1.5	67	5
84	20	59	1.5	69	7
75	10.5	63	4	75	10.5
78	15.5	62	3	76	12.5
70	8	78	15.5	79	17
77	14	76	12.5	83	19
88	24	80	18	86	21.5
71	9			86	21.5
				87	23
Sums	107		56		137
Count	8		7		9

$$H = \frac{12}{24(25)}\left[\frac{107^2}{8} + \frac{56^2}{7} + \frac{137^2}{9}\right] - 3(25) = 4.29$$

H_0 is not rejected. There is no difference in the three distributions.

4. $H_0: \pi \leq 1/3$ $H_1: \pi > 1/3$

At the .01 significance level, the decision rule is to reject H_0 if $z > 2.326$.

$$z = \frac{\left[\frac{210}{500} - \frac{1}{3}\right]}{\sqrt{\frac{\left(\frac{1}{3}\right)\left(1 - \frac{1}{3}\right)}{500}}} = \frac{0.08667}{0.02108} = 4.11$$

Reject the null hypothesis.

The actual proportion of Louisiana children who were obese or overweight is more than one out of three.

PRACTICE TEST (AFTER CHAPTER 18)

PART 1

1. denominator
2. index
3. quantity
4. base period
5. 1982–1984
6. trend
7. moving average
8. autocorrelation
9. residual
10. same

PART 2

1. **a.** 111.54, found by (145,000/130,000) × 100 for 2013 92.31, found by
    (120,000/130,000) × 100 for 2014 130.77, found by
    (170,000/130,000) × 100 for 2015 146.15, found by
    (190,000/130,000) × 100 for 2016
   b. 87.27, found by (120,000/137,500) × 100 for 2014 126.64, found by
    (170,000/137,500) × 100 for 2015 138.18, found by
    (190,000/137,500) × 100 for 2016
2. **a.** 108.91, found by (1,100/1,010) × 100
   b. 111.18, found by (4,525/4,070) × 100
   c. 110.20, found by (5,400/4,900) × 100
   d. 110.69, found by the square root of (111.18) × (110.20)
3. For January of the fifth year, the seasonally adjusted forecast is 70.0875, found by 1.05 × [5.50 + 1.25(49)].
   For February of the fifth year, the seasonally adjusted forecast is 66.844, found by 0.983 × [5.50 + 1.25(50)].

CHAPTER 1

1.1 **a.** Inferential statistics, because a sample was used to draw a conclusion about how all consumers in the population would react if the chicken dinner were marketed.

b. On the basis of the sample of 1,960 consumers, we estimate that, if it is marketed, 60% of all consumers will purchase the chicken dinner: $(1,176/1,960) \times 100 = 60\%$.

1.2 **a.** Age is a ratio-scale variable. A 40-year-old is twice as old as someone 20 years old.

b. The two variables are: (1) if a person owns a luxury car, and (2) the state of residence. Both are measured on a nominal scale.

CHAPTER 2

2.1 **a.** Qualitative data, because the customers' response to the taste test is the name of a beverage.

b. Frequency table. It shows the number of people who prefer each beverage.

c.

d.

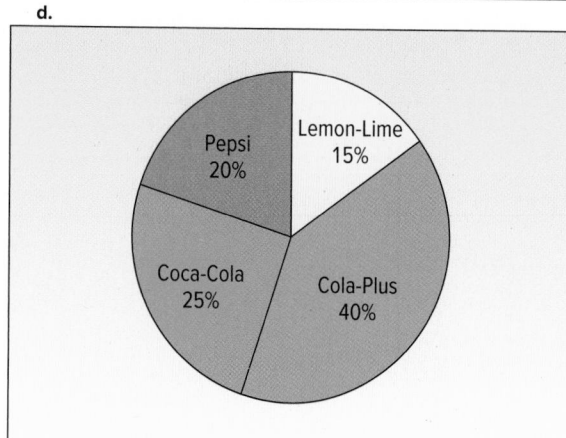

2.2 **a.** Raw or ungrouped data.

b.

Commission	Number of Sales people
$1,400 up to $1,500	2
1,500 up to 1,600	5
1,600 up to 1,700	3
1,700 up to 1,800	1
Total	11

c. Class frequencies.

d. The largest concentration of commissions is $1,500 up to $1,600. The smallest commission is about $1,400 and the largest is about $1,800. The typical amount earned is $1,550.

2.3 **a.** $2^6 = 64 < 73 < 128 = 2^7$, so seven classes are recommended.

b. The interval width should be at least $(488 - 320)/7 = 24$. Class intervals of either 25 or 30 are reasonable.

c. Assuming a class interval of 25 and beginning with a lower limit of 300, eight classes are required. If we use an interval of 30 and begin with a lower limit of 300, only 7 classes are required. Seven classes is the better alternative.

Distance Classes	Frequency	Percent
300 up to 330	2	2.7%
330 up to 360	2	2.7
360 up to 390	17	23.3
390 up to 420	27	37.0
420 up to 450	22	30.1
450 up to 480	1	1.4
480 up to 510	2	2.7
Grand Total	73	100.00

d. 17

e. 23.3%, found by 17/73

f. 71.2%, found by $(27 + 22 + 1 + 2)/73$

2.4 **a.**

b.

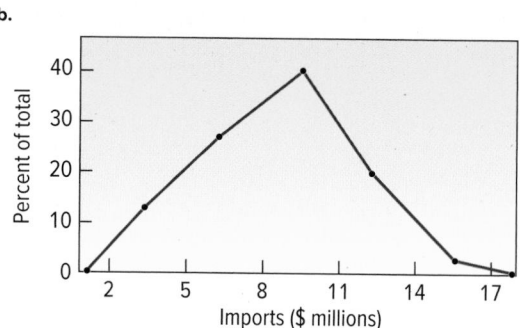

The plots are: (3.5, 12), (6.5, 26), (9.5, 40), (12.5, 20), and (15.5, 2).

c. The smallest annual volume of imports by a supplier is about $2 million, the largest about $17 million. The highest frequency is between $8 million and $11 million.

2.5 **a.** A frequency distribution.

b.

Hourly Wages	Cumulative Number
Less than $8	0
Less than $10	3
Less than $12	10
Less than $14	14
Less than $16	15

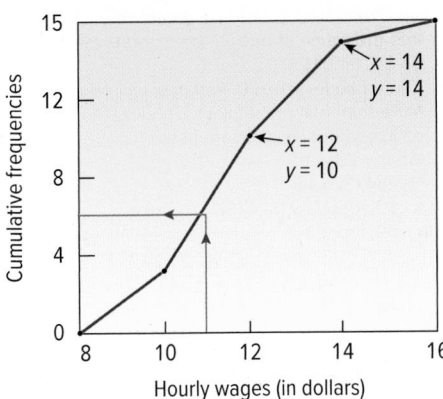

c. About seven employees earn $11.00 or less.

CHAPTER 3

3–1 1. a. $\bar{x} = \dfrac{\Sigma x}{n}$ Add the four values and divide by the number of values.

b. $\bar{x} = \dfrac{\$62,900 + \$69,100 + \$58,300 + \$76,800}{4}$
$= \$66,775$

c. Statistic, because the data are a sample from a population.

d. $66,775. The sample mean is our best estimate of the population mean.

2. a. $\mu = \dfrac{\Sigma x}{N}$ Add the six values and divide by the number of values.

b. $\mu = \dfrac{92 + 96 + 61 + 86 + 79 + 84}{6} = 83$

c. Parameter, because it was computed using all the population values.

3–2 1. a. $878

b. 3, 3

2. There are an even number of observations, so the middle two values are averaged to find the median.

a. 17, found by (15 + 19)/2 = 17

b. 5, 5

c. There are 3 values that occur twice: 11, 15, and 19. There are three modes.

3–3 a.

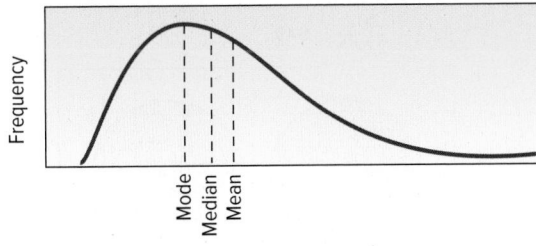

Weekly sales

b. Positively skewed, because the mean is the largest average and the mode is the smallest.

3–4 a. $237, found by:

$$\dfrac{(95 \times \$400) + (126 \times \$200) + (79 \times \$100)}{95 + 126 + 79} = \$237.00$$

b. The profit per suit is $12, found by $237 − $200 cost − $25 commission. The total profit for the 300 suits is $3,600, found by 300 × $12.

3–5 1. a. About 9.9%, found by $\sqrt[6]{1458602236}$ then 1.099 − 1.00 = .099

b. About 10.095%

c. Greater than, because 10.095 > 9.9

2. 8.63%, found by $\sqrt[20]{\dfrac{120,520}{23,000}} - 1 = 1.0863 - 1$

3–6 a. 22 thousands of pounds, found by 112 − 90

b. $\bar{x} = \dfrac{824}{8} = 103$ thousands of pounds

c. Variance $= \dfrac{373}{8} = 46.625$

$$\sigma^2 = \dfrac{(95 - 103)^2 + (103 - 103)^2 \cdots + (112 - 103)^2 + (90 - 103)^2}{8}$$

3–7 a. $\mu = \dfrac{\$16,900}{5} = \$3,380$

b. $\sigma^2 = \dfrac{(3,536 - 3,380)^2 + \cdots + (3,622 - 3,380)^2}{5}$

$= \dfrac{(156)^2 + (-207)^2 + (68)^2 + (-259)^2 + (242)^2}{5}$

$= \dfrac{197,454}{5} = 39,490.8$

c. $\sigma = \sqrt{39,490.8} = 198.72$

d. There is more variation in the Pittsburgh office because the standard deviation is larger. The mean is also larger in the Pittsburgh office.

3–8 2.33, found by:

$$\bar{x} = \dfrac{\Sigma x}{n} = \dfrac{28}{7} = 4$$

$$s^2 = \dfrac{\Sigma(x - \bar{x})^2}{n - 1}$$

$$= \dfrac{14}{7 - 1}$$

$$= 2.33$$

$$s = \sqrt{2.33} = 1.53$$

3–9 $k = \dfrac{14.15 - 14.00}{.10} = 1.5$

a. $k = \dfrac{13.85 - 14.0}{.10} = -1.5$

$1 - \dfrac{1}{(1.5)^2} = 1 - .44 = .56$

b. 13.8 and 14.2

CHAPTER 4

4–1 1. (a) The minimum value is 79 employees; the maximum value is 105 employees. The range is 105 − 79 = 26.

(b) The shape of the distribution is symmetric with most of the data in the middle of the range with few data points at the ends of the range.

(c) A reasonable estimate is about 92 employees.

(d) The mode of the distribution is 91. This value occurs most frequently at 15 stores.

(e) The median is 92 employees. There are 142 observations in the data set. Half of 142 is 71. So, in an ordered listing of the data, the median would be the average of the 71st and 72nd observations. Carefully counting from the dot plot, the 71st and 72nd values correspond to value of 92. The average is 92; 92 is the median because 50% of the values are less than 92, and 50% of the values are more than 92.

(f) Starting at the left end of the distribution, and using the frequency for each value of employees, calculate the numerator as:

   a. $(1)(79) + (0)(80) + (0)(81) + (2)(8) + (1)(83) + (2)(84) + (7)(85) + (3)(86) + \ldots + (1)(101) + (3)(102) + (1)(104) + (1)(105)$

   b. The numerator is equal to 13,055.

   c. The denominator is equal to the sum of weights, or the frequency of stores for each value. The sum is 142.

   d. The mean number of employees in a store is $13{,}055/142 = 91.94$.

(g) The mode $= 91$; the median is 92; the mean is 91.94 or about 92. The values are nearly equal and indicate the distribution's location is about 91 or 92. Because the values are nearly equal, these results also suggest that the distribution's shape is symmetric.

4–2 **a.** 7.9
   b. $Q_1 = 7.76, Q_3 = 8.015$

4–3 **a.** 10 and 85
   b. 40
   c. 25 and 60
   d. Fifty percent of the observations are between 25 and 60, 25% are less than 25, and 25% are more than 60.
   e. No. The right whisker is longer than the left whisker. Also, the box is not centered on the median.
   f. Upper outlier boundary = Q3 + 1.5(interquartile range) = $60 + 1.5(35) = 112.5$. There are no large outliers because the maximum value is 85 and less than 112.5.

4–4 **a.** $\bar{x} = \dfrac{407}{5} = 81.4$

   $s = \sqrt{\dfrac{923.2}{5 - 1}} = 15.19$, Median $= 84$

   b. $sk = \dfrac{3(81.4 - 84.0)}{15.19} = -0.51$

   c. $sk = \dfrac{5}{(4)(3)}[-1.3154] = -0.5481$

   d. The distribution is somewhat negatively skewed.

4–5 **a.**

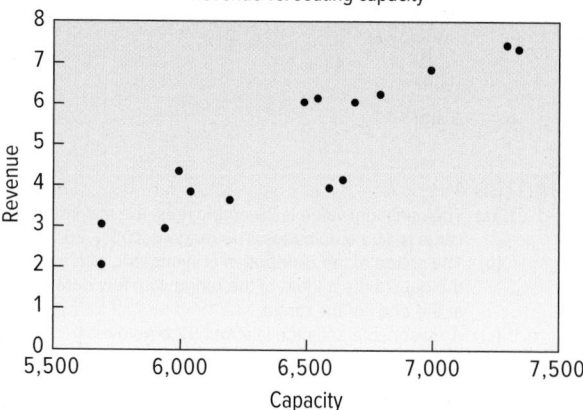

Revenue vs. seating capacity

b. The correlation coefficient is 0.90.
c. $7,500
d. Strong and positive. Revenue is positively related to seating capacity.

CHAPTER 5

5–1 **a.** Count the number who think the new game is playable.
   b. Seventy-three players found the game playable. Many other answers are possible.
   c. No. Probability cannot be greater than 1. The probability that the game, if put on the market, will be successful is 65/80, or .8125.
   d. Cannot be less than 0. Perhaps a mistake in arithmetic.
   e. More than half of the players testing the game liked it. (Of course, other answers are possible.)

5–2 **1.** $(5)(4) = 20$
   2. $(3)(2)(4)(3) = 72$

5–3 **1.** **a.** 60, found by $(5)(4)(3)$.
   b. 60, found by:

   $$\frac{5!}{(5 - 3)!} = \frac{5 \cdot 4 \cdot 3 \cdot \cancel{2} \cdot \cancel{1}}{\cancel{2} \cdot \cancel{1}}$$

   2. 5,040, found by:

   $$\frac{10!}{(10 - 4)!} = \frac{10 \cdot 9 \cdot 8 \cdot 7 \cdot \cancel{6} \cdot \cancel{5} \cdot \cancel{4} \cdot \cancel{3} \cdot \cancel{2} \cdot \cancel{1}}{\cancel{6} \cdot \cancel{5} \cdot \cancel{4} \cdot \cancel{3} \cdot \cancel{2} \cdot \cancel{1}}$$

   3. **a.** 35 is correct, found by:

   $$_7C_3 = \frac{n!}{r!(n - r)!} = \frac{7!}{3!(7 - 3)!} = 35$$

   b. Yes. There are 21 combinations, found by:

   $$_7C_5 = \frac{n!}{r!(n - r)!} = \frac{7!}{5!(7 - 5)!} = 21$$

   c.

   $$_nC_r = \frac{n!}{r!(n - r)!} = \frac{7!}{1!(7 - 1)!} = \frac{7 \cdot 6 \cdot 5 \cdot 4 \cdot 3 \cdot 2 \cdot 1}{1(6 \cdot 5 \cdot 4 \cdot 3 \cdot 2 \cdot 1)} = \frac{7}{1} = 7$$

   Using part (b), the probability of weekend team membership $= 7/21 = 0.3333$

   4. **a.** $_{50}P_3 = \dfrac{50!}{(50 - 3)!} = 117{,}600$

   b. $_{50}C_3 = \dfrac{50!}{3!(50 - 3)!} = 19{,}600$

5–4 **1.** $\dfrac{4 \text{ queens in deck}}{52 \text{ cards total}} = \dfrac{4}{52} = .0769$

   Classical.

   2. $\dfrac{182}{539} = .338$ Empirical.

   3. The probability of the outcome is estimated by applying the subjective approach to estimating a probability. If you think that it is likely that you will save $1 million, then your probability should be between .5 and 1.0.

5–5 **a.** **i.** $\dfrac{(50 + 68)}{2{,}000} = .059$

   ii. $1 - \dfrac{302}{2{,}000} = .849$

   b.

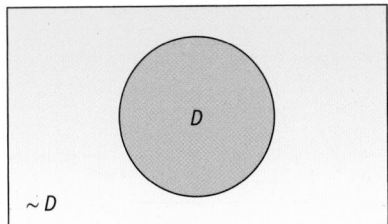

c. They are not complementary, but are mutually exclusive.

5–6 **a.** Need for corrective shoes is event *A*. Need for major dental work is event *B*.

$$P(A \text{ or } B) = P(A) + P(B) - P(A \text{ and } B)$$
$$= .08 + .15 - .03$$
$$= .20$$

b. One possibility is:

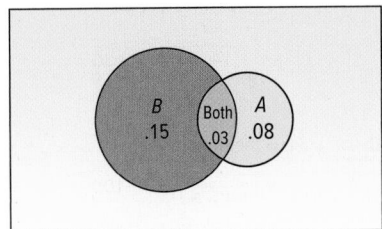

5–7 $(.95)(.95)(.95)(.95) = .8145$

5–8 **a.** .002, found by:

$$\left(\frac{4}{12}\right)\left(\frac{3}{11}\right)\left(\frac{2}{10}\right)\left(\frac{1}{9}\right) = \frac{24}{11,880} = .002$$

b. .14, found by:

$$\left(\frac{8}{12}\right)\left(\frac{7}{11}\right)\left(\frac{6}{10}\right)\left(\frac{5}{9}\right) = \frac{1,680}{11,880} = .1414$$

c. No, because there are other possibilities, such as three women and one man.

5–9 **a.** $P(B_2) = \frac{225}{500} = .45$

b. The two events are mutually exclusive, so apply the special rule of addition.

$$P(B_1 \text{ or } B_2) = P(B_1) + P(B_2) = \frac{100}{500} + \frac{225}{500} = .65$$

c. The two events are not mutually exclusive, so apply the general rule of addition.

$$P(B_1 \text{ or } A_1) = P(B_1) + P(A_1) - P(B_1 \text{ and } A_1)$$
$$= \frac{100}{500} + \frac{75}{500} - \frac{15}{500} = .32$$

d. As shown in the example/solution, movies attended per month and age are not independent, so apply the general rule of multiplication.

$$P(B_1 \text{ and } A_1) = P(B_1)P(A_1|B_1)$$
$$= \left(\frac{100}{500}\right)\left(\frac{15}{100}\right) = .03$$

5–10 **a.** $P(\text{visited often}) = \frac{80}{195} = .41$

b. $P(\text{visited a store in an enclosed mall}) = \frac{90}{195} = .46$

c. The two events are not mutually exclusive, so apply the general rule of addition.
$P(\text{visited often or visited a Sears in an enclosed mall})$
$= P(\text{often}) + P(\text{enclosed mall}) - P(\text{often and enclosed mall})$
$$= \frac{80}{195} + \frac{90}{195} - \frac{60}{195} = .56$$

d. $P(\text{visited often} \mid \text{went to a Sears in an enclosed mall})$
$$= \frac{60}{90} = .67$$

e. Independence requires that $P(A \mid B) = P(A)$. One possibility is: $P(\text{visit often} \mid \text{visited an enclosed mall}) = P(\text{visit often})$. Does 60/90 = 80/195? No, the two variables are not independent. Therefore, any joint probability in the table must be computed by using the general rule of multiplication.

f. As shown in part (e), visits often and enclosed mall are not independent, so apply the general rule of multiplication.

$$P(\text{often and enclosed mall}) = P(\text{often})P(\text{enclosed}|\text{often})$$
$$= \left(\frac{80}{195}\right)\left(\frac{60}{80}\right) = .31$$

g.

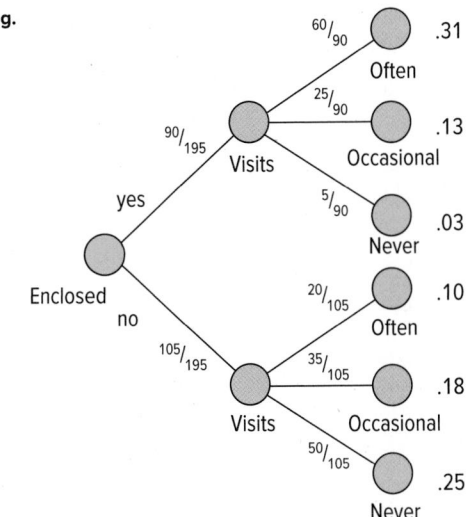

5–11 **a.** $P(A_3|B_2) = \dfrac{P(A_3)P(B_2|A_3)}{P(A_1)P(B_2|A_1) + P(A_2)P(B_2|A_2) + P(A_3)P(B_2|A_3)}$

b. $= \dfrac{(.50)(.96)}{(.30)(.97) + (.20)(.95) + (.50)(.96)}$
$$= \frac{.480}{.961} = .499$$

CHAPTER 6

6–1 **a.**

Number of Spots	Probability
1	$\frac{1}{6}$
2	$\frac{1}{6}$
3	$\frac{1}{6}$
4	$\frac{1}{6}$
5	$\frac{1}{6}$
6	$\frac{1}{6}$
Total	$\frac{6}{6} = 1.00$

b.

c. $\frac{6}{6}$ or 1.

6–2 **a.** It is discrete because the values \$1.99, \$2.49, and \$2.89 are clearly separated from each other. Also the sum of the probabilities is 1.00, and the outcomes are mutually exclusive.

b.

x	P(x)	xP(x)
1.99	.30	0.597
2.49	.50	1.245
2.89	.20	0.578
		Sum is 2.42

Mean is 2.42

c.

x	P(x)	$(x - \mu)$	$(x - \mu)^2 P(x)$
1.99	.30	−0.43	0.05547
2.49	.50	0.07	0.00245
2.89	.20	0.47	0.04418
			0.10210

The variance is 0.10208, and the standard deviation is 31.95 cents.

d. 0.30

e. 0.70

6–3 **a.** It is reasonable because each employee either uses direct deposit or does not; employees are independent; the probability of using direct deposit is 0.95 for all; and we count the number using the service out of 7.

b. $P(7) = {}_7C_7 (.95)^7 (.05)^0 = .6983$

c. $P(4) = {}_7C_4 (.95)^4 (.05)^3 = .0036$

d. Answers are in agreement.

6–4 **a.** $n = 8, \pi = .40$

b. $P(x = 3) = .2787$

c. $P(x > 0) = 1 - P(x = 0) = 1 - .0168 = .9832$

6–5 $P(3) = \dfrac{{}_8C_3 \, {}_4C_2}{{}_{12}C_5} = \dfrac{\left(\dfrac{8!}{3!5!}\right)\left(\dfrac{4!}{2!2!}\right)}{\dfrac{12!}{5!7!}}$

$\qquad = \dfrac{(56)(6)}{792} = .424$

6–6 $\mu = 4{,}000(.0002) = 0.8$

$P(1) = \dfrac{0.8^1 e^{-0.8}}{1!} = .3595$

CHAPTER 7

7–1 **a.** $P(x)$

b. $P(x) = \text{(height)(base)}$

$\qquad = \left(\dfrac{1}{14 - 8}\right)(14 - 8)$

$\qquad = \left(\dfrac{1}{6}\right)(6) = 1.00$

c. $\mu = \dfrac{a + b}{2} = \dfrac{14 + 8}{2} = \dfrac{22}{2} = 11$

$\sigma = \sqrt{\dfrac{(b - a)^2}{12}} = \sqrt{\dfrac{(14 - 8)^2}{12}} = \sqrt{\dfrac{36}{12}} = \sqrt{3}$

$\qquad = 1.73$

d. $P(10 < x < 14) = \text{(height)(base)}$

$\qquad = \left(\dfrac{1}{14 - 8}\right)(14 - 10)$

$\qquad = \dfrac{1}{6}(4)$

$\qquad = .667$

e. $P(x < 9) = \text{(height)(base)}$

$\qquad = \left(\dfrac{1}{14 - 8}\right)(9 - 8)$

$\qquad = 0.167$

7–2 **a.** $z = (64 - 48)/12.8 = 1.25$. This person's difference of 16 ounces more than average is 1.25 standard deviations above the average.

b. $z = (32 - 48)/12.8 = -1.25$. This person's difference of 16 ounces less than average is 1.25 standard deviations below the average.

7–3 **a.** Computing z:

$$z = \frac{154 - 150}{5} = 0.80$$

Referring to Appendix B.3, the area is .2881. So $P(150 < \text{temp} < 154) = .2881$.

b. Computing z:

$$z = \frac{164 - 150}{5} = 2.80$$

Referring to Appendix B.3, the area is .4974. So $P(164 > \text{temp}) = .5000 - .4974 = .0026$

7–4 **a.** Computing the z-values:

$$z = \frac{146 - 150}{5} = -0.80 \quad \text{and} \quad z = \frac{156 - 150}{5} = 1.20$$

$P(146 < \text{temp} < 156) = P(-0.80 < z < 1.20)$
$\qquad\qquad\qquad\qquad\quad = .2881 + .3849 = .6730$

b. Computing the z-values:

$$z = \frac{162 - 150}{5} = 2.40 \quad \text{and} \quad z = \frac{156 - 150}{5} = 1.20$$

$P(156 < \text{temp} < 162) = P(1.20 < z < 2.40)$
$\qquad\qquad\qquad\qquad\quad = .4918 - .3849 = .1069$

7–5 85.24 (instructor would no doubt make it 85). The closest area to .4000 is .3997; z is 1.28. Then:

$$1.28 = \frac{x - 75}{8}$$
$$10.24 = x - 75$$
$$x = 85.24$$

7–6 **a.** $46,400 and $48,000, found by $47,200 ± 1($800).
  b. $45,600 and $48,800, found by $47,200 ± 2($800).
  c. $44,800 and $49,600, found by $47,200 ± 3($800).
  d. $47,200. The mean, median, and mode are equal for a normal distribution.
  e. Yes, a normal distribution is symmetrical.

7–7 **a.** .7769, found by:

$$P(\text{Arrival} < 15) = 1 - e^{-\frac{1}{10}(15)}$$
$$= 1 - .2231 = .7769$$

  b. .0821, found by:

$$P(\text{Arrival} > 25) = e^{-\frac{1}{10}(25)} = .0821$$

  c. .1410, found by

$$P(15 < x < 25) = P(\text{Arrival} < 25) - P(\text{Arrival} < 15)$$
$$= .9179 - .7769 = .1410$$

  d. 16.09 minutes, found by:

$$.80 = 1 - e^{-\frac{1}{10}(x)}$$
$$-\ln 0.20 = \frac{1}{10}x$$
$$x = -(-1.609)(10) = 1.609(10) = 16.09$$

CHAPTER 8

8–1 **a.** Students selected are Lehman, Edinger, Nickens, Chontos, St. John, and Kemp.
  b. Answers will vary.
  c. Skip it and move to the next random number.

8–2 The students selected are Berry, Francis, Kopp, Poteau, and Swetye.

8–3 **a.** 10, found by:

$$_5C_2 = \frac{5!}{2!(5-2)!}$$

  b.

	Service	Sample Mean
Snow, Tolson	20, 22	21
Snow, Kraft	20, 26	23
Snow, Irwin	20, 24	22
Snow, Jones	20, 28	24
Tolson, Kraft	22, 26	24
Tolson, Irwin	22, 24	23
Tolson, Jones	22, 28	25
Kraft, Irwin	26, 24	25
Kraft, Jones	26, 28	27
Irwin, Jones	24, 28	26

  c.

Mean	Number	Probability
21	1	.10
22	1	.10
23	2	.20
24	2	.20
25	2	.20
26	1	.10
27	1	.10
	10	1.00

  d. Identical: population mean, μ, is 24, and mean of sample means, is also 24.
  e. Sample means range from 21 to 27. Population values go from 20 to 28.
  f. No, the population is uniformly distributed.
  g. Yes.

8–4 The answers will vary. Here is one solution.

	Sample Number									
	1	**2**	**3**	**4**	**5**	**6**	**7**	**8**	**9**	**10**
	8	2	2	19	3	4	0	4	1	2
	19	1	14	9	2	5	8	2	14	4
	8	3	4	2	4	4	1	14	4	1
	0	3	2	3	1	2	16	1	2	3
	2	1	7	2	19	18	18	16	3	7
Total	37	10	29	35	29	33	43	37	24	17
$\bar{x}$	7.4	2	5.8	7.0	5.8	6.6	8.6	7.4	4.8	3.4

Mean of the 10 sample means is 5.88.

8–5 $z = \dfrac{31.08 - 31.20}{0.4/\sqrt{16}} = -1.20$

The probability that z is greater than -1.20 is $.5000 + .3849 = .8849$. There is more than an 88% chance the filling operation will produce bottles with at least 31.08 ounces.

8–6 **a.** $np = 12.5$, $np(1 - p) = 6.25$. Both are greater than 5 so we can apply the central limit theorem.

$$z = \frac{p - \pi}{\sqrt{\dfrac{\pi(1-\pi)}{n}}} = \frac{.2 - .5}{\sqrt{\dfrac{.5(1-.5)}{25}}} = -3.00$$

Using the standard normal table, the probability associated with -3.00 is .4987. Therefore, the probability of proportions less than .20 is $.5000 - .4987 = .0013$. The probability that the proportion of 25 bottles with less than 20 ounces of water is .20 or less (i.e., 5 or less bottles) is .0013.

CHAPTER 9

9–1 **a.** Unknown. This is the value we wish to estimate.
  b. The sample mean of $20,000 is the point estimate of the population mean daily franchise sales.
  c. $20,000 \pm 1.960\dfrac{\$3,000}{\sqrt{40}} = \$20,000 \pm \$930$
  d. The estimate of the population mean daily sales for the Bun-and-Run franchises is between $19,070 and $20,930. About 95% all possible samples of 40 Bun-and-Run franchises would include the population mean.

9–2 **a.** $\bar{x} = \dfrac{18}{10} = 1.8$ $s = \sqrt{\dfrac{11.6}{10-1}} = 1.1353$
  b. The population mean is not known. The best estimate is the sample mean, 1.8 days.
  c. $1.80 \pm 2.262\dfrac{1.1353}{\sqrt{10}} = 1.80 \pm 0.81$
  The endpoints are 0.99 and 2.61.
  d. t is used because the population standard deviation is unknown.

e. The value of 0 is not in the interval. It is unreasonable to conclude that the mean number of days of work missed is 0 per employee.

9-3 a. $p = \dfrac{420}{1,400} = .30$

b. $.30 \pm 2.576\,(.0122) = .30 \pm .03$

c. The interval is between .27 and .33. About 99% of the similarly constructed intervals would include the population mean.

9-4 $.375 \pm 1.96\sqrt{\dfrac{.375(1 - .375)}{40}}\sqrt{\dfrac{250 - 40}{250 - 1}} =$

$.375 \pm 1.96(.0765)(.9184) = .375 \pm .138$

9-5 $n = \left(\dfrac{2.576(.279)}{.05}\right)^2 = 206.6$. The sample should be rounded to 207.

CHAPTER 10

10-1 a. $H_0: \mu = 16.0;\ H_1: \mu \neq 16.0$

b. .05

c. $z = \dfrac{\bar{x} - \mu}{\sigma/\sqrt{n}}$

d. Reject H_0 if $z < -1.96$ or $z > 1.96$.

e. $z = \dfrac{16.017 - 16.0}{0.15/\sqrt{50}} = \dfrac{0.0170}{0.0212} = 0.80$

f. Do not reject H_0.

g. We cannot conclude the mean amount dispensed is different from 16.0 ounces.

10-2 a. $H_0: \mu \leq 16.0;\ H_1: \mu > 16.0$

b. Reject H_0 if $z > 1.645$.

c. The sampling error is $16.04 - 16.00 = 0.04$ ounce.

d. $z = \dfrac{16.040 - 16.0}{0.15/\sqrt{50}} = \dfrac{.0400}{.0212} = 1.89$

e. Reject H_0.

f. The mean amount dispensed is more than 16.0 ounces.

g. p-Value $= .5000 - .4706 = .0294$. The p-value is less than α (.05), so H_0 is rejected. It is the same conclusion as in part (d).

10-3 a. $H_0: \mu \leq 305;\ H_1: \mu > 305$

b. $df = n - 1 = 20 - 1 = 19$
The decision rule is to reject H_0 if $t > 1.729$.

c. $t = \dfrac{\bar{X} - \mu}{s/\sqrt{n}} = \dfrac{311 - 305}{12/\sqrt{20}} = 2.236$
Reject H_0 because $2.236 > 1.729$. The modification increased the mean battery life to more than 305 days.

10-4 a. $H_0: \mu \geq 9.0;\ H_1: \mu < 9.0$

b. 7, found by $n - 1 = 8 - 1 = 7$

c. Reject H_0 if $t < -2.998$.

d. $t = -2.494$, found by:

$$s = \sqrt{\dfrac{0.36}{8 - 1}} = 0.2268$$

$$\bar{x} = \dfrac{70.4}{8} = 8.8$$

Then

$$t = \dfrac{8.8 - 9.0}{0.2268/\sqrt{8}} = -2.494$$

Since -2.494 lies to the right of -2.998, H_0 is not rejected. We have not shown that the mean is less than 9.0.

e. The p-value is between .025 and .010.

f. The p-value is greater than 0.01. Fail to reject the null hypothesis.

10-5 .0054, found by determining the area under the curve between 10,078 and 10,180.

$$z = \dfrac{\bar{x}_c - \mu_1}{\sigma/\sqrt{n}}$$

$$= \dfrac{10,078 - 10,180}{400/\sqrt{100}} = -2.55$$

The area under the curve for a z of -2.55 is .4946 (Appendix B.3), and $.5000 - .4946 = .0054$.

10-6 a. Yes, because both $n\pi$ and $n(1 - \pi)$ exceed 5: $n\pi = 200(.40) = 80$, and $n(1 - \pi) = 200(.60) = 120$.

b. $H_0: \pi \geq .40$
$H_1: \pi < .40$

c. Reject H_0 if $z < -2.326$.

d. The p-value is .1922, found by $.5000 - .3078$.

e. $z = -0.87$, found by:

$$z = \dfrac{.37 - .40}{\sqrt{\dfrac{.40(1 - .40)}{200}}} = \dfrac{-.03}{\sqrt{.0012}} = -0.87$$

Do not reject H_0.

CHAPTER 11

11-1 Let Mark's assemblies be population 1, then $H_0: \sigma_1^2 \leq \sigma_2^2$; $H_1: \sigma_1^2 > \sigma_2^2$ $df_1 = 10 - 1 = 9$; and df_2 also equals 9. H_0 is rejected if $F > 3.18$.

$$F = \dfrac{(2.0)^2}{(1.5)^2} = 1.78$$

H_0 is not rejected. The variation is the same for both employees.

11-2 a. $H_0: \mu_W \leq \mu_M$ $\quad H_1: \mu_W > \mu_M$
The subscript W refers to the women and M to the men.

b. Reject H_0 if $z > 1.645$.

c. $z = \dfrac{\$1,500 - \$1,400}{\sqrt{\dfrac{(\$250)^2}{50} + \dfrac{(\$200)^2}{40}}} = 2.11$

d. Reject the null hypothesis.

e. p-Value $= .5000 - .4826 = .0174$

f. The mean amount sold per day is larger for women.

11-3 Reject H_0 that the two population variances are equal if $F >$ 4.88, where degrees of freedom in the numerator are 7 and 5 in the denominator. Computed $F = 2.57$, found by:

$$F = \frac{s_a^2}{s_d^2} = \frac{5.1429}{2.000} = 2.57$$

The test statistic does not exceed the critical value and the p-value is .1579. Fail to reject H_0. There is no difference in the two population variances.

a. $H_0: \mu_d = \mu_a$ $H_1: \mu_d \neq \mu_a$

b. $df = 6 + 8 - 2 = 12$

Reject H_0 if $t < -2.179$ or $t > 2.179$.

c. $\bar{x}_1 = \frac{42}{6} = 7.00$ $s_1 = \sqrt{\frac{10}{6-1}} = 1.4142$

$\bar{x}_2 = \frac{80}{8} = 10.00$ $s_2 = \sqrt{\frac{36}{8-1}} = 2.2678$

$s_p^2 = \frac{(6-1)(1.4142)^2 + (8-1)(2.2678)^2}{6+8-2}$

$= 3.8333$

$t = \frac{7.00 - 10.00}{\sqrt{3.8333\left(\frac{1}{6}+\frac{1}{8}\right)}} = -2.837$

d. Reject H_0 because -2.837 is less than the critical value.

e. The p-value is less than .02.

f. The mean number of defects is not the same on the two shifts.

g. Independent populations, populations follow the normal distribution, populations have equal standard deviations.

11-4 Reject H_0 that the two population variances are equal if $F >$ 3.68, where degrees of freedom in the numerator are 9 and 7 in the denominator. Computed $F = 5.795$, found by:

$$F = \frac{s_c^2}{s_a^2} = \frac{734,449}{126,736} = 5.795$$

The test statistic exceeds the critical value, and the p-value is .0152. Reject H_0. The two population variances are different.

a. $H_0: \mu_c \geq \mu_a$ $H_1: \mu_c < \mu_a$

b. $df = \frac{[(356^2/10) + (857^2/8)]^2}{\frac{(356^2/10)^2}{10-1} + \frac{(857^2/8)^2}{8-1}} = 8.93$

so $df = 8$

c. Reject H_0 if $t < -1.860$.

d. $t = \frac{\$1{,}568 - \$1{,}967}{\sqrt{\frac{356^2}{10} + \frac{857^2}{8}}} = \frac{-399.00}{323.23} = -1.234$

e. Do not reject H_0.

f. There is no difference in the mean account balance of those who applied for their card or were contacted by a telemarketer.

11-5 a. $H_0: \mu_d \geq 0, H_1: \mu_d > 0$

b. Reject H_0 if $t > 2.998$.

c.

Name	Before	After	d	$(d - \bar{d})$	$(d - \bar{d})^2$
Hunter	155	154	1	−7.875	62.0156
Cashman	228	207	21	12.125	147.0156
Mervine	141	147	−6	−14.875	221.2656
Massa	162	157	5	−3.875	15.0156
Creola	211	196	15	6.125	37.5156
Peterson	164	150	14	5.125	26.2656
Redding	184	170	14	5.125	26.2656
Poust	172	165	7	−1.875	3.5156
			71		538.8750

$$\bar{d} = \frac{71}{8} = 8.875$$

$$s_d = \sqrt{\frac{538.875}{8-1}} = 8.774$$

$$t = \frac{8.875}{8.774/\sqrt{8}} = 2.861$$

d. p-Value = .0122

e. Do not reject H_0. We cannot conclude that the students lost weight.

f. The distribution of the differences must be approximately normal.

11-6 a. $H_0: \pi_a = \pi_{ch}$

$H_1: \pi_a \neq \pi_{ch}$

b. .10

c. Two-tailed

d. Reject H_0 if $z < -1.645$ or $z > 1.645$.

e. $p_c = \frac{87 + 123}{150 + 200} = \frac{210}{350} = .60$

$p_a = \frac{87}{150} = .58$ $p_{ch} = \frac{123}{200} = .615$

$z = \frac{.58 - .615}{\sqrt{\frac{.60(.40)}{150} + \frac{.60(.40)}{200}}} = -0.66$

CHAPTER 12

12-1 a. $H_0: \mu_1 = \mu_2 = \mu_3$

H_1: At least one treatment mean is different.

b. Reject H_0 if $F > 4.26$.

c. $\bar{x} = \frac{240}{12} = 20$

SS total $= (18 - 20)^2 + \cdots + (32 - 20)^2$

$= 578$

SSE $= (18 - 17)^2 + (14 - 17)^2 + \cdots + (32 - 29)^2$

$= 74$

SST $= 578 - 74 = 504$

d.

Source	Sum of Squares	Degrees of Freedom	Mean Square	F
Treatment	504	2	252	30.65
Error	74	9	8.22	
Total	578	11		

The F-test statistic, 30.65.

e. H_0 is rejected. There is a difference in the mean number of bottles sold at the various locations.

12-2 a. $H_0: \mu_1 = \mu_2 = \mu_3$

H_1: Not all means are equal.

b. H_0 is rejected if $F > 3.98$.

c.

ANOVA: Single Factor

Groups	Count	Sum	Average	Variance
Northeast	5	205	41	1
Southeast	4	155	38.75	0.916667
West	5	184	36.8	0.7

ANOVA

Source of Variation	SS	df	MS	F	p-Value
Between Groups	44.16429	2	22.08214	25.43493	7.49E-05
Within Groups	9.55	11	0.868182		
Total	53.71429	13			

d. H_0 is rejected. The treatment means differ.

e. $(41 - 36.8) \pm 2.201 \sqrt{0.8682\left(\frac{1}{5} + \frac{1}{5}\right)} = 4.2 \pm 1.3 = 2.9$

and 5.50. The means are significantly different. Zero is not in the interval.

These treatment means differ because both endpoints of the confidence interval are of the same sign.

12–3 **a.** For types:
$H_0: \mu_1 = \mu_2 = \mu_3$
$H_1:$ The treatment means are not equal.
Reject H_0 if $F > 4.46$.
For months:
$H_0: \mu_1 = \mu_2 = \mu_3 = \mu_4 = \mu_5$
$H_1:$ The block means are not equal.

b. Reject H_0 if $F > 3.84$.

c. The analysis of variance table is as follows:

Source	df	SS	MS	F	p-Value
Types	2	3.60	1.80	0.39	0.2397
Months	4	31.73	7.93	1.71	0.6902
Error	8	37.07	4.63		
Total	14	72.40			

d. Fail to reject both hypotheses. The p-values are more than .05.

e. There is no difference in the mean sales among types or months.

12–4 **a.** There are four levels of Factor A. The p-value is less than .05, so Factor A means differ.

b. There are three levels of Factor B. The p-value is less than .05, so the Factor B means differ.

c. There are three observations in each cell. There is an interaction between Factor A and Factor B means because the p-value is less than .05.

CHAPTER 13

13–1 **a.** Advertising expense is the independent variable, and sales revenue is the dependent variable.

b.

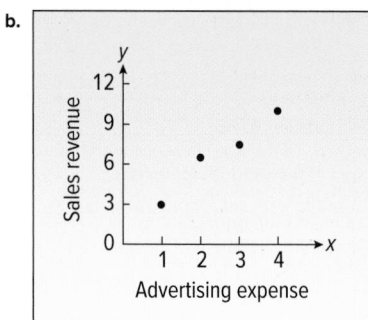

c.

x	y	$(x - \bar{x})$	$(x - \bar{x})^2$	$(y - \bar{y})$	$(y - \bar{y})^2$	$(x - \bar{x})(y - \bar{y})$
2	7	−0.5	.25	0	0	0
1	3	−1.5	2.25	−4	16	6
3	8	0.5	.25	1	1	0.5
4	10	1.5	2.25	3	9	4.5
10	28		5.00		26	11.0

$\bar{x} = \frac{10}{4} = 2.5 \quad \bar{y} = \frac{28}{4} = 7$

$s_x = \sqrt{\frac{5}{3}} = 1.2910$

$s_y = \sqrt{\frac{26}{3}} = 2.9439$

$r = \frac{\Sigma(X - \bar{X})(y - \bar{y})}{(n - 1)s_x s_y} = \frac{11}{(4 - 1)(1.2910)(2.9439)}$

$\quad = 0.9648$

d. There is a strong correlation between the advertising expense and sales.

13–2 $H_0: \rho \le 0, H_1: \rho > 0$. H_0 is rejected if $t > 1.714$.

$t = \frac{.43\sqrt{25 - 2}}{\sqrt{1 - (.43)^2}} = 2.284$

H_0 is rejected. There is a positive correlation between the percent of the vote received and the amount spent on the campaign.

13–3 **a.** See the calculations in Self-Review 13–1, part (c).

$b = \frac{rs_y}{s_x} = \frac{(0.9648)(2.9439)}{1.2910} = 2.2$

$a = \frac{28}{4} - 2.2\left(\frac{10}{4}\right) = 7 - 5.5 = 1.5$

b. The slope is 2.2. This indicates that an increase of $1 million in advertising will result in an increase of $2.2 million in sales. The intercept is 1.5. If there was no expenditure for advertising, sales would be $1.5 million.

c. $\hat{Y} = 1.5 + 2.2(3) = 8.1$

13–4 $H_0: \beta_1 \le 0; H_1: \beta > 0$. Reject H_0 if $t > 3.182$.

$t = \frac{2.2 - 0}{0.4243} = 5.1850$

Reject H_0. The slope of the line is greater than 0.

13–5 **a.**

y	$\hat{y}$	$(y - \hat{y})$	$(y - \hat{y})^2$
7	5.9	1.1	1.21
3	3.7	−0.7	.49
8	8.1	−0.1	.01
10	10.3	−0.3	.09
			1.80

$s_{y \cdot x} = \sqrt{\frac{\Sigma(y - \hat{y})^2}{n - 2}}$

$\quad = \sqrt{\frac{1.80}{4 - 2}} = .9487$

b. $r^2 = (.9648)^2 = .9308$

c. Ninety-three percent of the variation in sales is accounted for by advertising expense.

13–6 6.58 and 9.62, since for an x of 3 is 8.1, found by $\hat{y} = 1.5 + 2.3(3) = 8.1$, then $\bar{x} = 2.5$ and $\Sigma(x - \bar{x})^2 = 5$. t from Appendix B.5 for $4 - 2 = 2$ degrees of freedom at the .10 level is 2.920.

$\hat{y} \pm t(s_{y \cdot x})\sqrt{\frac{1}{n} + \frac{(x - \bar{x})^2}{\Sigma(x - \bar{x})^2}}$

$= 8.1 \pm 2.920(0.9487)\sqrt{\frac{1}{4} + \frac{(3 - 2.5)^2}{5}}$

$= 8.1 \pm 2.920(0.9487)(0.5477)$

$= 6.58$ and 9.62 (in $ millions)

CHAPTER 14

14–1 **a.** $389,500 or 389.5 (in $000); found by $2.5 + 3(40) + 4(72) - 3(10) + .2(20) + 1(5) = 3,895$

b. The b_2 of 4 shows profit will go up $4,000 for each extra hour the restaurant is open (if none of the other variables change). The b_3 of -3 implies profit will fall \$3,000 for each added mile away from the central area (if none of the other variables change).

14–2 **a.** The total degrees of freedom $(n - 1)$ is 25. So the sample size is 26.
    b. There are 5 independent variables.
    c. There is only 1 dependent variable (profit).
    d. $S_{Y.12345} = 1.414$, found by $\sqrt{2}$. Ninety-five percent of the residuals will be between -2.828 and 2.828, found by $\pm 2(1.414)$.
    e. $R^2 = .714$, found by $100/140$. 71.4% of the deviation in profit is accounted for by these five variables.
    f. $R_{adj}^2 = .643$, found by

$$1 - \left[\frac{40}{(26 - (5 + 1))}\right] \Big/ \left[\frac{140}{(26 - 1)}\right]$$

14–3 **a.** $H_0: \beta_1 = \beta_2 = \beta_3 = \beta_4 = \beta_5 = 0$
      H_1: Not all of the βs are 0.
    The decision rule is to reject H_0 if $F > 2.71$. The computed value of F is 10, found by $20/2$. So, you reject H_0, which indicates at least one of the regression coefficients is different from zero.
    Based on p-values, the decision rule is to reject the null hypothesis if the p-value is less than .05. The computed value of F is 10, found by $20/2$, and has a p-value of .000. Thus, we reject the null hypothesis, which indicates that at least one of the regression coefficients is different from zero.
    b. For variable 1: $H_0: \beta_1 = 0$ and $H_1: \beta_1 \neq 0$
    The decision rule is to reject H_0 if $t < -2.086$ or $t > 2.086$. Since 2.000 does not go beyond either of those limits, we fail to reject the null hypothesis. This regression coefficient could be zero. We can consider dropping this variable. By parallel logic, the null hypothesis is rejected for variables 3 and 4.
    For variable 1, the decision rule is to reject $H_0: \beta_1 = 0$ if the p-value is less than .05. Because the p-value is .056, we cannot reject the null hypothesis. This regression coefficient could be zero. Therefore, we can consider dropping this variable. By parallel logic, we reject the null hypothesis for variables 3 and 4.
    c. We should consider dropping variables 1, 2, and 5. Variable 5 has the smallest absolute value of t or largest p-value. So delete it first and compute the regression equation again.
      $\hat{y} = 15.7625 + 0.4415x_1 + 3.8598x_2$

14–4 **a.** $\hat{y} = 15.7625 + 0.4415(30) + 3.8598(1)$
      $= 32.87$
    b. Female agents make \$3,860 more than male agents.
    c. $H_0: \beta_3 = 0$
      $H_1: \beta_3 \neq 0$
      $df = 17$; reject H_0 if $t < -2.110$ or $t > 2.110$

$$t = \frac{3.8598 - 0}{1.4724} = 2.621$$

    The t-statistic exceeds the critical value of 2.110. Also, the p-value $= .0179$ and is less than .05. Reject H_0. Sex should be included in the regression equation.

CHAPTER 15

15–1 **a.** Observed frequencies
    b. Six (six days of the week)
    c. 10. Total observed frequencies $\div 6 = 60/6 = 10$.
    d. 5; $k - 1 = 6 - 1 = 5$

e. 15.086 (from the chi-square table in Appendix B.7).
f. $\chi^2 = \Sigma \left[\frac{(f_o - f_e)^2}{f_e}\right] = \frac{(12 - 10)^2}{10} + \cdots + \frac{(9 - 10)^2}{10} = 0.8$
g. Do not reject H_0.
h. Evidence fails to show a difference in the proportion of absences by day of the week.

15–2 $H_0: P_C = .60$, $P_L = .30$, and $P_U = .10$.
    H_1: Distribution is not as above.
    Reject H_0 if $\chi^2 > 5.991$.

Category	f_o	f_e	$\frac{(f_o - f_e)^2}{f_e}$
Current	320	300	1.33
Late	120	150	6.00
Uncollectible	60	50	2.00
	500	500	9.33

Reject H_0. The accounts receivable data do not reflect the national average.

15–3 **a.** Contingency table
    b. H_0: There is no relationship between income and whether the person played the lottery. H_1: There is a relationship between income and whether the person played the lottery.
    c. Reject H_0 if $\chi^2 > 5.991$.
    d. $\chi^2 = \frac{(46 - 40.71)^2}{40.71} + \frac{(28 - 27.14)^2}{27.14} + \frac{(21 - 27.14)^2}{27.14}$

$$+ \frac{(14 - 19.29)^2}{19.29} + \frac{(12 - 12.86)^2}{12.86} + \frac{(19 - 12.86)^2}{12.86}$$

$$= 6.544$$

    e. Reject H_0. There is a relationship between income level and playing the lottery.

CHAPTER 16

16–1 **a.** Two-tailed because H_1 does not state a direction.
    b.

Adding down, $.000 + .003 + .016 = .019$. This is the largest cumulative probability up to but not exceeding .050, which is half the level of significance. The decision rule is to reject H_0 if the number of plus signs is 2 or less or 10 or more.
    c. Reject H_0; accept H_1. There is a preference.

16–2 H_0: median = \$84,352, H_1: median ≠ \$84,352
Binomial distribution with $n = 20$, and $\pi = 0.5$

x	P(x)	Cumulative probabilities in the tails
0	0.000	
1	0.000	0.000
2	0.000	0.000
3	0.001	0.001
4	0.005	0.006
5	0.015	0.019
6	0.037	0.052
7	0.074	
8	0.120	
9	0.160	
10	0.176	
11	0.160	
12	0.120	
13	0.074	
14	0.037	0.052
15	0.015	0.019
16	0.005	0.006
17	0.001	0.001
18	0.000	0.000
19	0.000	0.000
20	0.000	

Reject H_0: median = \$84,352 if number of successes is 5 or less, or the number of success is 15 or more. In this example, the number of successes is 13. Therefore, fail to reject H_0.

16–3 **a.** $n = 10$ (because there was no change for A. A.)

b.

Before	After	Difference	Absolute Difference	Rank	R^-	R^+
17	18	−1	1	1.5	1.5	
21	23	−2	2	3.0	3.0	
25	22	3	3	5.0		5.0
15	25	−10	10	8.0	8.0	
10	28	−18	18	10.0	10.0	
16	16	—	—	—	—	—
10	22	−12	12	9.0	9.0	
20	19	1	1	1.5		1.5
17	20	−3	3	5.0	5.0	
24	30	−6	6	7.0	7.0	
23	26	−3	3	5.0	5.0	
					48.5	6.5

H_0: Production is the same.
H_1: Production has increased.
The sum of the positive signed ranks is 6.5; the negative sum is 48.5. From Appendix B.8, one-tailed test, $n = 10$, the critical value is 10. Since 6.5 is less than 10, reject the null hypothesis and accept the alternate. New procedures did increase production.

c. No assumption regarding the shape of the distribution is necessary.

16–4 H_0: There is no difference in the distances traveled by the XL-5000 and by the D2.
H_1: There is a difference in the distances traveled by the XL-5000 and by the D2.

Do not reject H_0 if the computed z is between 1.96 and −1.96 (from Appendix B.3); otherwise, reject H_0 and accept H_1. $n_1 = 8$, the number of observations in the first sample.

XL-5000		D2	
Distance	Rank	Distance	Rank
252	4	262	9
263	10	242	2
279	15	256	5
273	14	260	8
271	13	258	7
265	11.5	243	3
257	6	239	1
280	16	265	11.5
Total	89.5		46.5

$W = 89.5$

$$z = \frac{89.5 - \dfrac{8(8 + 8 + 1)}{2}}{\sqrt{\dfrac{(8)(8)(8 + 8 + 1)}{12}}}$$

$$= \frac{21.5}{9.52} = 2.26$$

Reject H_0; accept H_1. There is evidence of a difference in the distances traveled by the two golf balls.

16–5

Ranks			
Englewood	West Side	Great Northern	Sylvania
17	5	19	7
20	1	9.5	11
16	3	21	15
13	5	22	9.5
5	2	14	8
18			12

$\Sigma R_1 = 89 \quad \Sigma R_2 = 16 \quad \Sigma R_3 = 85.5 \quad \Sigma R_4 = 62.5$
$n_1 = 6 \quad n_2 = 5 \quad n_3 = 6 \quad n_4 = 6$

H_0: The population distributions are identical.
H_1: The population distributions are not identical.

$$H = \frac{12}{22(22 + 1)}\left[\frac{(89)^2}{6} + \frac{(16)^2}{5} + \frac{(85.5)^2}{5} + \frac{(62.5)^2}{6}\right] - 3(22 + 1)$$
$$= 13.635$$

The critical value of chi-square for $k - 1 = 4 - 1 = 3$ degrees of freedom is 11.345. Since the computed value of 13.635 is greater than 11.345, the null hypothesis is rejected. We conclude that the number of transactions is not the same.

16–6 a.

		Rank			
x	y	x	y	d	d^2
805	23	5.5	1	4.5	20.25
777	62	3.0	9	−6.0	36.00
820	60	8.5	8	0.5	0.25
682	40	1.0	4	−3.0	9.00
777	70	3.0	10	−7.0	49.00
810	28	7.0	2	5.0	25.00
805	30	5.5	3	2.5	6.25
840	42	10.0	5	5.0	25.00
777	55	3.0	7	−4.0	16.00
820	51	8.5	6	2.5	6.25
				0	193.00

$$r_s = 1 - \frac{6(193)}{10(99)} = -.170$$

b. $H_0: \rho = 0; H_1: \rho \neq 0$. Reject H_0 if $t < -2.306$ or $t > 2.306$.

$$t = -.170\sqrt{\frac{10 - 2}{1 - (-0.170)^2}} = -0.488$$

H_0 is not rejected. We have not shown a relationship between the two tests.

CHAPTER 17

17–1 1.

Country	Amount	Index (Based = US)
China	1,032	1200.0
India	119	138.4
Japan	96	111.6
United States	86	100.0
Russia	76	88.4

China produced 1200% more steel than the U.S.

2. a.

Year	Median Annual Wage	Index (Base = 2016)
2016	$30,533.31	100.00
2017	31,561.49	103.37
2018	32,828.45	107.52
2019	34,248.45	112.17
2020	34,621.04	113.36

The 2020 median wage increase 13.36% compared to 2016.

b.

Year	Median Annual Wage	Index (Base = 2016–17)
2016	$30,533.31	98.34
2017	31,561.49	101.66
2018	32,828.05	105.74
2019	34,248.45	110.31
2020	34,612.04	111.48

The 2020 median wage increase 11.48% compared to the average of 2010 and 2012.

17–2 1. a. $P_1 = (\$85/\$75)(100) = 113.3$
$P_2 = (\$45/\$40)(100) = 112.5$
$P = (113.3 + 112.5)/2 = 112.9$

b. $P = (\$130/\$115)(100) = 113.0$

c. $P = \dfrac{\$85(500)+\$45(1,200)}{\$75(500)+\$40(1,200)}(100)$

$= \dfrac{\$96,500}{85,500}(100) = 112.9$

d. $P = \dfrac{\$85(520)+\$45(1,300)}{\$75(520)+\$40(1,300)}(100)$

$= \dfrac{\$102,700}{\$91,000}(100) = 112.9$

e. $P = \sqrt{(112.9)(112.9)} = 112.9$

17–3 a. $P = \dfrac{\$4(9,000)+\$5(200)+\$8(5,000)}{\$3(10,000)+\$1(600)+\$10(3,000)}(100)$

$= \dfrac{\$77,000}{60,600}(100) = 127.1$

b. The value of sales went up 27.1% from 2015 to 2022.

17–4 a.

For 2020	
Item	Weight
Cotton	($0.25/$0.20)(100)(.10) = 12.50
Autos	(1,200/1,000)(100)(.30) = 36.00
Money turnover	(90/80)(100)(.60) = 67.50
Total	116.00

For 2021	
Item	Weight
Cotton	($0.50/$0.20)(100)(.10) = 25.00
Autos	(900/1,000)(100)(.30) = 27.00
Money turnover	(75/80)(100)(.60) = 56.25
Total	108.25

b. Business activity decreased 7.75% from 2020 to 2021.

17–5 In terms of the base period, Jodie's salary was $14,518 in 2000 and $22,143 in 2021. This indicates that take-home pay increased at a faster rate than the rate of prices paid for food, transportation, etc.

17–6 $0.36, round by ($1.00/274.138)(100). The purchasing power has declined by $0.64.

17–7

	Florida		New York		Illinois		California	
Year	Florida	Index	New York	Index	Illinois	Index	California	Index
2016	3,176	100.0	1,041	100.0	1,078	100.0	3,837	100.0
2017	3,116	98.1	1,006	96.6	1,090	101.1	3,884	101.2
2018	3,135	98.7	964	92.6	1,035	96.0	3,798	99.0
2019	3,183	100.2	913	87.7	1,009	93.6	3,606	94.0
2020	2,915	91.8	943	90.6	1,031	95.6	3,568	93.0

a. See above.
b. There was a 1.2% increase.
c. There was a decrease of 12.3%.
d. There was an 8.4% decrease.
e. All indexes for 2020 are less than 100.0. So, the number of fatalities decreased in the selected states over the period.

CHAPTER 18

18–1 a.

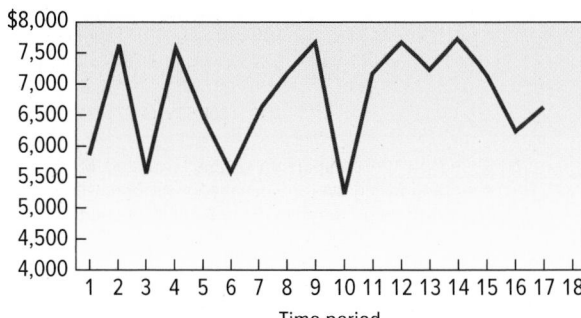

b. Over the 18 months, the graph of the time series does not show any trend or seasonal patterns.
c. Because the graph does not show any trend or seasonal patterns, the pattern is random and stationary. Therefore, the best time series forecasting method is an averaging method, such as a simple moving average.
d. and e. The MAD is 751.79 and the MAPE is 11.56%. The four period forecast is 6,938.

Period	Revenue	Four-Period Average	Absolute Error	Absolute Percent Error
March	5,874			
April	7,651			
May	5,546			
June	7,594			
July	6,450	6,666	216.25	3.35%
August	5,580	6,810	1230.25	22.05%
September	6,560	6,293	267.50	4.08%
October	7,209	6,546	663.00	9.20%
November	7,679	6,450	1229.251	6.01%
December	5,192	6,757	1565.00	30.14%
January	7,177	6,660	517.00	7.20%
February	7,693	6,814	878.75	11.42%
March	7,232	6,935	296.75	4.10%
April	7,742	6,824	918.50	11.86%
May	7,142	7,461	319.00	4.47%
June	6,227	7,452	1225.25	19.68%
July	6,639	7,086	446.75	6.73%
August		6,938		
			MAD = 751.79	MAPE = 11.56%

f. The MAD is 808.53 and the MAPE is 12.14%. The four-period forecast is 6,881.

Period	Revenue	Four-Period Average	Absolute Error	Absolute Percent Error
March	5,874			
April	7,651			
May	5,546			
June	7,594			
July	6,450			
August	5,580			
September	6,560			
October	7,209			
November	7,679	6,558	1121.00	14.60%
December	5,192	6,784	1591.63	30.66%
January	7,177	6,476	700.75	9.76%
February	7,693	6,680	1012.88	13.17%
March	7,232	6,693	539.50	7.46%
April	7,742	6,790	951.75	12.29%
May	7,142	7,061	81.50	1.14%
June	6,227	7,133	906.25	14.55%
July	6,639	7,011	371.50	5.60%
August		6,881		
			MAD = 808.53	MAPE = 12.14%

g. Based on the comparison of the MAD and MAPE the 4-month moving average has the lower forecasting error and would be preferred over the 8-month average.

18–2   a.

b. Over the 18 months, the graph of the time series does not show any trend or seasonal patterns.

c. Because the graph does not show any trend or seasonal patterns, the pattern is random and stationary. Therefore, the best time series forecasting method is an averaging method. Simple exponential smoothing is a good choice.

d. and e. The forecast for August is $6,849.7643. The error of the forecast is the MAD, 823.3141. The MAPE is 12.16%.

Period	Revenue	Forecast (0.2)	ABS (error)	ABS (percent error)
March	$5,874			
April	7,651	$5874.0000	1777.0000	23.23%
May	5,546	6229.4000	683.4000	12.32%
June	7,594	6092.7200	1501.2800	19.77%
July	6,450	6392.9760	57.0240	0.88%
August	5,580	6404.3808	824.3808	14.77%
September	6,560	6239.5046	320.4954	4.89%
October	7,209	6303.6037	905.3963	12.56%
November	7,679	6484.6830	1194.3170	15.55%
December	5,192	6723.5464	1531.5464	29.50%
January	7,177	6417.2371	759.7629	10.59%
February	7,693	6569.1897	1123.8103	14.61%
March	7,232	6793.9517	438.0483	6.06%
April	7,742	6881.5614	860.4386	11.11%
May	7,142	7053.6491	88.3509	1.24%
June	6,227	7071.3193	844.3193	13.56%
July	6,639	6902.4554	263.4554	3.97
August		6,849.7643	MAD 823.3141	MAPE 12.16%

f. Using an $\alpha = 0.7$, the forecast for August is $6,610.2779. The error of the forecast is the MAD, 977.1302. The MAPE is 15.01%.

Period	Revenue	Forecast (0.7)	ABS (error)	ABS (percent
March	$5,874			
April	7,651	$5874.0000	1777.0000	23.23%
May	5,546	7117.9000	1571.9000	28.34%
June	7,594	6017.5700	1576.4300	20.76%
July	6,450	7121.0710	671.0710	10.40%
August	5,580	6651.3213	1071.3213	19.20%
September	6,560	5901.3964	658.6036	10.04%
October	7,209	6362.4189	846.5811	11.74%
November	7,679	6955.0257	723.9743	9.43%
December	5,192	7461.8077	2269.8077	43.72%
January	7,177	5872.9423	1304.0577	18.17%
February	7,693	6785.7827	907.2173	11.79%
March	7,232	7420.8348	188.8348	2.61%
April	7,742	7288.6504	453.3496	5.86%
May	7,142	7605.9951	463.9951	6.50%
June	6,227	7281.1985	1054.1985	16.93%
July	6,639	6543.2596	95.7404	1.44%
August		6,610.2779	MAD 977.1302	MAPE 15.01%

g. Based on the comparison of the MAD and MAPE the exponential smoothing model with α of 0.2 is preferred because it as has a lower MAD and MAPE than the exponential smoothing model with α of 0.7.

18–3 a.

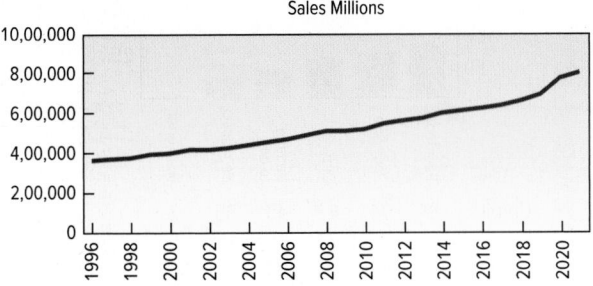

Sales Millions

b. The time series graph shows a gradual increase in U.S. total grocery store annual sales between 1996 and 2021.

c. A trend model is appropriate because we would like to estimate the average annual increase shown by the trend pattern in the time series graph.

d. Sales = 314,671.2215 + 15,657.7785 (time period). The MAD is 20,446.64. The MAPE is 3.81%. Notice that the error as a percent of the forecast is very small.

e. The predicted annual change in total U.S. grocery sales dollars is $15,657.7785 million.

SUMMARY OUTPUT

Regression Statistics

Multiple R	0.9750
R Square	0.9507
Adjusted R Square	0.9486
Standard Error	27837.4373
Observations	26

ANOVA

	df	SS	MS	F	p-Value
Regression	1	3.59E+11	3.59E+11	4.63E+02	3.41E-17
Residual	24	1.86E+10	7.75E+08		
Total	25	3.77E+11			

	Coefficients	Standard Error	t Stat	P-value
Intercept	314671.2215	11241.5321	27.9918	0.0000
Period	15657.7785	727.9161	21.5104	0.0000

Year	Period	Sales	Predicted	|Error|	|Percent Error|
1996	1	365547	330329.00	35218.00	9.63%
1997	2	372570	345986.78	26583.22	7.14%
1998	3	378188	361644.56	16543.44	4.37%
1999	4	394250	377302.34	16947.66	4.30%
2000	5	402515	392960.11	9554.89	2.37%
2001	6	418127	408617.89	9509.11	2.27%
2002	7	419813	424275.67	4462.67	1.06%
2003	8	427987	439933.45	11946.45	2.79%
2004	9	441136	455591.23	14455.23	3.28%
2005	10	457667	471249.01	13582.01	2.97%
2006	11	471699	486906.78	15207.78	3.22%
2007	12	491360	502564.56	11204.56	2.28%
2008	13	511222	518222.34	7000.34	1.37%
2009	14	510033	533880.12	23847.12	4.68%
2010	15	520750	549537.90	28787.90	5.53%
2011	16	547476	565195.68	17719.68	3.24%
2012	17	563645	580853.46	17208.46	3.05%
2013	18	574547	596511.23	21964.23	3.82%
2014	19	599603	612169.0	112566.01	2.10%
2015	20	613159	627826.79	14667.79	2.39%
2016	21	625295	643484.57	18189.57	2.91%
2017	22	639161	659142.35	19981.35	3.13%
2018	23	661785	674800.13	13015.13	1.97%
2019	24	693015	690457.90	2557.10	0.37%
2020	25	773741	706115.68	67625.32	8.74%
2021	26	803041	721773.46	81267.54	10.12%
2022	27		737431.24		
2023	28		753089.02		
2024	29		768746.80		
		MAD =	20446.64		MAPE = 3.81%

f. Sales = 314,671.2215 + 15,657.7785 (time period). The next 3 years-2022, 2023, and 2024-are periods 27, 28, and 29.
2022 sales = 314,671.2215 + 15,657.7785 (27) = 737,431.24
2023 sales = 314,671.2215 + 15,657.7785 (28) = 753,089.02
2024 sales = 314,671.2215 + 15,657.7785 (29) = 768,746.80

18–4 a.

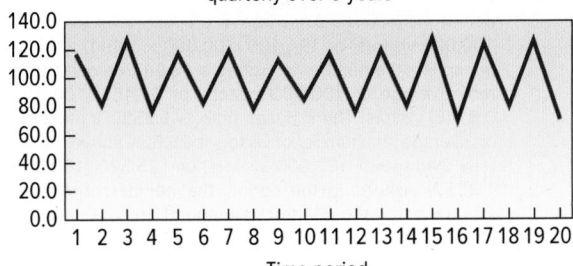

Visitors (1,000s) quarterly over 5 years

Time period

b. The pattern in the time series is clearly seasonality. During a 4-quarter time span, winter and summer are always the highest number of visitors; spring and fall are always the lowest number of visitors.

c. In this time series, there is virtually no trend. So using the overall average as the base of the seasonal indexes would be a logical choice.

d. Computing the indexes by dividing each period's visitors by 100 shows the following results.

Season	Time Period	Visitors	Indexes (Base = 100)
Winter	1	117.0	1.17
Spring	2	80.7	0.807
Summer	3	129.6	1.296
Fall	4	76.1	0.761
Winter	5	118.6	1.186
Spring	6	82.5	0.825
Summer	7	121.4	1.214
Fall	8	77.0	0.77
Winter	9	114.0	1.14
Spring	10	84.3	0.843
Summer	11	119.1	1.191
Fall	12	75.0	0.75
Winter	13	120.7	1.207
Spring	14	79.6	0.796
Summer	15	129.9	1.299
Fall	16	69.5	0.695
Winter	17	125.2	1.252
Spring	18	80.2	0.802
Summer	19	127.6	1.276
Fall	20	72.0	0.72

Quarter	Seasonal Index
Winter	1.191
Spri ng	0.8146
Summer	1.2552
Fall	0.7392

e. The winter index is 1.191. It means that on average, the number of visitors is 19.1% above the quarterly average of 100,000 visitors, or 191,100 (100,000 × 1.191) visitors. In the spring, the number of visitors is 18.54% below the quarterly average of 100,000 visitors, or 81,460 (100,000 × 0.8146) visitors. The summer index is 1.2552. It means that on average, the number of visitors is 25.52% above the quarterly average of 100,000 visitors, or 125,520 (100,000 × 1.2552) visitors. In the spring, the number of visitors is 26.08% below the quarterly average of 100,000 visitors, or 73,920 (100,000 × 0.7392) visitors.

CHAPTER 19

19–1

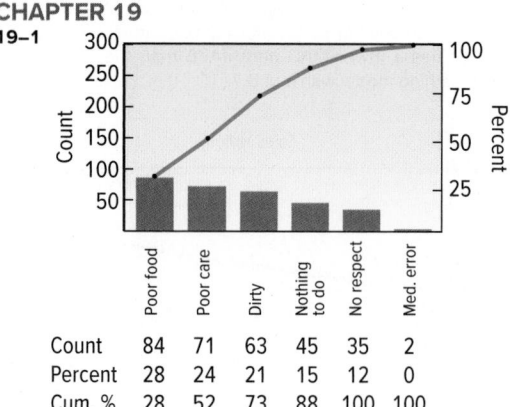

	Poor food	Poor care	Dirty	Nothing to do	No respect	Med. error
Count	84	71	63	45	35	2
Percent	28	24	21	15	12	0
Cum. %	28	52	73	88	100	100

Seventy-three percent of the complaints involve poor food, poor care, or dirty conditions. These are the factors the administrator should address.

19–2 a.

Sample Times						
1	2	3	4	Total	Average	Range
1	4	5	2	12	3	4
2	3	2	1	8	2	2
1	7	3	5	16	$\frac{4}{9}$	$\frac{6}{12}$

$$\bar{\bar{x}} = \frac{9}{3} = 3 \quad \bar{R} = \frac{12}{3} = 4$$

$$UCL \text{ and } LCL = \bar{\bar{x}} \pm A_2\bar{R}$$

$$= 3 \pm 0.729(4)$$

$$UCL = 5.916 \quad LCL = 0.084$$

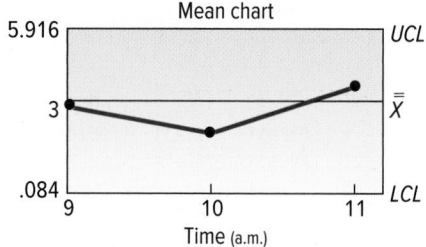

$$LCL = D_3\bar{R} = 0(4) = 0$$

$$UCL = D_4\bar{R} = 2.282(4) = 9.128$$

b. Yes. Both the mean chart and the range chart indicate that the process is in control.

19–3 $\bar{c} = \dfrac{25}{12} = 2.083$

$UCL = 2.083 + 3\sqrt{2.083} = 6.143$

$LCL = 2.083 - 3\sqrt{2.083} = -2.247$

Because LCL is a negative value, we set $LCL = 0$. The shift with seven defects is out of control.

19–4 $P(x \le 2 \mid \pi = .30 \text{ and } n = 20) = .036$

CHAPTER 20

20–1

Event	Payoff	Probability of Event	Expected Value
Market rise	$2,200	.60	$1,320
Market decline	1,100	.40	440
			$1,760

20–2 **a.** Suppose the investor purchased Rim Homes stock, and the value of the stock in a bear market dropped to $1,100 as anticipated (Table 20–1). Instead, had the investor purchased Texas Electronics and the market declined, the value of the Texas Electronics stock would be $1,150. The difference of $50, found by $1,150 − $1,100, represents the investor's regret for buying Rim Homes stock.

b. Suppose the investor purchased Texas Electronics stock, and then a bull market developed. The stock rose to $1,900, as anticipated (Table 20–1). However, had the investor bought Kayser Chemicals stock and the market value increased to $2,400 as anticipated, the difference of $500 represents the extra profit the investor could have made by purchasing Kayser Chemicals stock.

20–3

Event	Payoff	Probability of Event	Expected Opportunity Value
Market rise	$500	.60	$300
Market decline	0	.40	0
			$300

20–4 **a.**

Event	Payoff	Probability of Event	Expected Value
Market rise	$1,900	.40	$ 760
Market decline	1,150	.60	690
			$1,450

b.

Event	Payoff	Probability of Event	Expected Value
Market rise	$2,400	.50	$1,200
Market decline	1,000	.50	500
			$1,700

20–5 For probabilities of a market rise (or decline) down to .333, Kayser Chemicals stock would provide the largest expected profit. For probabilities .333 to .143, Rim Homes would be the best buy. For .143 and below, Texas Electronics would give the largest expected profit. Algebraic solutions:

Kayser: $2,400p + (1 - p)1,000$

Rim: $\quad\dfrac{2,200p + (1 - p)1,100}{1,400p + 1,000 = 1,100p + 1,100}$

$p = .333$

Rim: $\quad 2,200p + (1 - p)1,100$

Texas: $\dfrac{1,900p + (1 - p)1,150}{1,100p + 1,100 = 750p + 1,150}$

$p = .143$

Glossary

α   The probability of making a Type I error, represented by the Greek letter alpha.

Alternate hypothesis   A statement that is accepted if the sample data provide sufficient evidence that the null hypothesis is false.

Analysis of variance (ANOVA)   A technique used to test simultaneously whether the means of several populations are equal. It uses the *F*-distribution as the distribution of the test statistic.

Assignable variation   Variation that is not random. It can be eliminated or reduced by investigating the problem and finding the cause.

Attribute control chart   An attribute control chart plots a count of a nominal variable over time.

Autocorrelation   Successive residuals in a time series are correlated.

β   The probability of making a Type II error, represented by the Greek letter beta.

Bar chart   A graph that shows qualitative classes on the horizontal axis and the class frequencies on the vertical axis. The class frequencies are proportional to the heights of the bars.

Bayes' theorem   Developed by Reverend Bayes in the 1700s, it is designed to find the probability of one event, *A*, occurring, given that another event, *B*, has already occurred.

Binomial probability distribution   A probability distribution based on a discrete random variable. Its major characteristics are: 1. Each outcome can be classified into one of two mutually exclusive categories. 2. The distribution is the result of counting the number of successes. 3. Each trial is independent, meaning that the answer to trial 1 (correct or wrong) in no way affects the answer to trial 2. 4. The probability of a success stays the same from trial to trial.

Blocking variable   A second treatment variable that when included in the ANOVA analysis will have the effect of reducing the SSE term.

Box plot   A graphic display that shows the general shape of a variable's distribution. It is based on five descriptive statistics: the maximum and minimum values, the first and third quartiles, and the median.

Cause-and-effect diagram   A diagram used to illustrate the relationship between a problem and a set of the problem's possible causes.

Central limit theorem   If all samples of a particular size are selected from any population, the sampling distribution of the sample mean is approximately a normal distribution. This approximation improves with larger samples.

Chance variation   Variation that is random in nature. This type of variation cannot be completely eliminated unless there is a major change in the techniques, technologies, methods, equipment, or materials used in the process.

Chebyshev's theorem   For any set of observations (sample or population), the proportion of the values that lie within *k* standard deviations of the mean is at least $1 - 1/k^2$, where *k* is any value greater than 1.

Classical probability   Probability based on the assumption we know the number of possible outcomes and that each of the outcomes is equally likely.

Cluster sampling   A population is divided into clusters using naturally occurring geographic or other boundaries. Then, clusters are randomly selected and a sample is collected by randomly selecting from each cluster.

Collectively exhaustive   At least one of the events must occur when an experiment is conducted.

Combination formula   A formula to count the number of possible arrangements when the order of the outcomes is not important. For example, the outcome {a, b, c} is considered the same as {c, b, a}.

Conditional probability   The probability of a particular event occurring, given that another event has occurred.

Confidence interval   A range of values constructed from sample data so that the population parameter is likely to occur within that range at a specified probability. The specified probability is called the *level of confidence*.

Consumer Price Index   An index reported monthly by the U.S. Department of Labor. It describes the change in a market basket of goods and services from the base period of 1982–1984 to the present.

Consumer's risk   The error of accepting a lot, when the lot should be rejected.

Contingency table   A table used to classify sample observations according to two identifiable characteristics.

Continuity correction factor   Used to improve the accuracy of estimating or approximating a discrete distribution with a continuous distribution.

Continuous random variable   A random variable that may assume an infinite number of values within a given range.

Correlation analysis   A group of techniques to measure the relationship between two variables.

Correlation coefficient   A measure of the strength of association between two variables.

Critical value   The dividing point between the region where the null hypothesis is rejected and the region where it is not rejected.

Cyclical pattern   A pattern of highs and lows occurring over periods of many years.

Deciles   Values of an ordered (minimum to maximum) data set that divide the data into 10 equal parts.

Dependent variable   The variable that is being predicted or estimated.

Descriptive statistics   The techniques used to describe the important characteristics of a set of data. This includes organizing the data values into a frequency distribution, computing measures of location, and computing measures of dispersion and skewness.

Discrete random variable   A random variable that can assume only certain clearly separated values.

Dot plot   A dot plot summarizes the distribution of one variable by stacking dots at points on a number line that shows the values of the variable. A dot plot shows all values.

Dummy variable   A variable in which there are only two possible outcomes. For analysis, one of the outcomes is coded a 1 and the other a 0.

Empirical probability   The probability of an event based on a collection of observations or data.

Empirical Rule   For a symmetrical, bell-shaped frequency distribution, approximately 68% of the observations lie within ± 1 standard deviation of the mean; about 95% of the observations lie within ± 2 standard deviations of the mean; and practically all (99.7%) lie within ± 3 standard deviations of the mean.

Event   A collection of one or more outcomes of an experiment.

Experiment   A process that leads to the occurrence of one and only one of several possible results.

Finite-population correction factor (FPC)   When sampling without replacement from a finite population, a correction term is used to reduce the standard error of the mean according to the relative size of the sample to the size of the population. The correction factor is used when the sample is more than 5% of a finite population.

Fishbone diagram   A diagram used to illustrate the relationship between a problem and a set of the problem's possible causes.

Frequency distribution   A grouping of quantitative data into mutually exclusive and collectively exhaustive classes showing the number of observations in each class.

Frequency table   A grouping of qualitative data into mutually exclusive classes showing the number of observations in each class.

Global test   A test used to determine if any of the set of independent variables has regression coefficients different from zero.

Histogram   A graph in which the classes are marked on the horizontal axis and the class frequencies on the vertical axis. The class frequencies are represented by the heights of the bars, and the bars are drawn adjacent to each other.

Homoscedasticity   The variation around the regression equation is the same for all of the values of the independent variables.

Hypergeometric distribution   A probability distribution based on a discrete random variable. Its major characteristics are a fixed number of trials, only two possible outcomes, and the probability of success is not the same on each trial.

Independent events   The occurrence of one event has no effect on the probability of another event.

Independent variable   A variable that provides the basis for estimation.

Index number   A number that expresses the relative change in price, quantity, or value compared to a base period.

Inferential statistics   The methods used to estimate a property of a population on the basis of a sample.

Interaction effect   The effect of one factor on a response variable differs depending on the value of another factor.

Interquartile range   The absolute numerical difference between the first and third quartiles. Fifty percent of a distribution's values occur in this range.

Interval level of measurement   For data recorded at the interval level of measurement, the interval or the distance between values is meaningful. The interval level of measurement is based on a scale with a known unit of measurement.

Irregular component   The random variation in a time series.

Joint probability   A probability that measures the likelihood two or more events will happen concurrently.

Kruskal-Wallis one-way analysis of variance by ranks   A test used when the assumptions for parametric analysis of variance (ANOVA) cannot be met. Its purpose is to test whether several populations are the same. The data must be at least ordinal scale.

Law of large numbers   Over a large number of trials, the empirical probability of an event will approach its true probability.

Least Squares Principle   A mathematical procedure that uses the data to position a line with the objective of minimizing the sum of the squares of the vertical distances between the actual y-values and the predicted values of y.

Measure of dispersion   A value that shows the spread of a data set. The range, variance, and standard deviation are measures of dispersion.

Measure of location   A single value that is typical of the data. It pinpoints the center of a distribution. The arithmetic mean, weighted mean, median, mode, and geometric mean are measures of location.

Median   The value of the middle observation after all the observations have been arranged from low to high. For example, if observations 6, 9, 4 are rearranged to read 4, 6, 9, the median is 6, the middle value.

Mode The value that appears most frequently in a set of data. For grouped data, it is the midpoint of the class containing the largest number of values.

Multiplication formula If there are m ways of doing one thing and n ways of doing another thing, there are $m \times n$ ways of doing both.

Mutually exclusive The occurrence of one event means that none of the other events can occur at the same time.

Nominal level of measurement Data recorded at the nominal level of measurement is represented as labels or names. They have no order. They can only be classified and counted.

Null hypothesis A statement about the value of a population parameter developed for the purpose of testing numerical evidence.

Ordinal level of measurement Data recorded at the ordinal level of measurement is based on a relative ranking or rating of items based on a defined attribute or qualitative variable. Variables based on this level of measurement are only ranked or counted.

Outcome A particular result of an experiment.

Outlier A data point that is unusually far from the others. An accepted rule is to classify an observation as an outlier if it is 1.5 times the interquartile range above the third quartile or below the first quartile.

p-value The probability of observing a sample value as extreme as, or more extreme than, the value observed, given that the null hypothesis is true.

Parameter A characteristic of a population.

Percentiles Values of an ordered (minimum to maximum) data set that divide the data into 100 intervals.

Permutation Any arrangement of r objects selected from a single group of n possible objects.

Permutation formula A formula to count the number of possible arrangements when the order of the outcomes is important. For example, the outcome {a, b, c} is considered different from {c, b, a}.

Pie chart A chart that shows the proportion or percentage that each class represents of the total number of frequencies.

Point estimate A single value computed from a sample and used to estimate a population parameter. Example: If the sample mean is 1,020, it is the best estimate of the population mean.

Point estimates The statistic, computed from sample information, that estimates a population parameter.

Poisson probability distribution A discrete probability distribution often used to approximate binomial probabilities when n is large and π is small.

Population The entire set of individuals or objects of interest or the measurements obtained from all individuals or objects of interest.

Posterior probability A revised probability based on additional information.

Prior probability The initial probability based on the present level of information.

Probability A value between 0 and 1, inclusive, that reports the likelihood that a specific event will occur.

Probability distribution A listing of all possible outcomes of an experiment and the probability associated with each outcome.

Producer Price Index An index that measures change over time in the selling prices received by domestic producers for their output.

Producer's risk The error of rejecting a lot, when the lot is acceptable.

Qualitative variables A nominal-scale variable coded to assume only one nonnumeric outcome or category. For example, a person is considered either employed or unemployed.

Quartiles Values of an ordered (minimum to maximum) data set that divide the data into four intervals.

Random variable A variable measured or observed as the result of an experiment. By chance, the variable can have different values.

Random variation The sum of the squared differences between each observation and its treatment mean.

Range A measure of dispersion found by subtracting the minimum value from the maximum value.

Ratio level of measurement Data recorded at the ratio level of measurement are based on a scale with a known unit of measurement and a meaningful interpretation of zero on the scale.

Regression equation An equation that expresses the linear relationship between two variables.

Residual The difference between the actual value of the dependent variable and the estimated value of the dependent variable.

Sample A portion, or part, of the population of interest.

Sampling distribution of the sample mean A probability distribution of all possible sample means of a given sample size.

Sampling error The difference between a sample statistic and its corresponding population parameter.

Scatter diagram Graphical technique used to show the relationship between two variables measured with interval or ratio scales.

Seasonality Patterns of highs and lows in a time series within a calendar year. These patterns tend to repeat each year.

Sign test A test used for dependent samples. The sign test is used to find whether there is a brand preference for two products or to determine whether performance after an experiment is greater than before the experiment. Also, the sign test is used to test a hypothesis about the median.

Simple random sample A sample selected so that each item or person in the population has the same chance of being included.

Special rule of addition A rule used to find the probabilities of events made up of A or B when the events are mutually exclusive.

Special rule of multiplication A rule used to find the probability of the joint occurrence of independent events.

Standard error of estimate A measure of the dispersion, or scatter, of the observed values around the line of regression for a given value of x.

Statistic A characteristic of a sample.

Statistics The science of collecting, organizing, analyzing, and interpreting data for the purpose of making more effective decisions.

Stem-and-leaf display A method to display a variable's distribution using every value. Values are classified by the data's leading digit. For example, if a data set contains values between 13 and 84, eight classes based on the 10s digit would be used for the stems. The 1s digits would be the leaves.

Stepwise regression A step-by-step method to determine a regression equation that begins with a single independent variable and adds or deletes independent variables one by one. Only independent variables with nonzero regression coefficients are included in the regression equation.

Stratified random sample A population is divided into subgroups, called strata, and a sample is randomly selected from each stratum.

Subjective concept of probability The probability or likelihood of an event that is assigned by an individual based on their experience and knowledge.

Systematic random sampling A random starting point is selected, and then every kth member of the population is selected.

Test statistic A value, computed from sample information, used to decide whether to reject or fail to reject the null hypothesis.

Total variation The sum of the squared differences between each observation and the overall mean.

Treatment variation The sum of the squared differences between each treatment mean and the grand or overall mean. Each squared difference is multiplied by the number of observations in the treatment.

Trend The change of a variable over time.

Type I error Rejecting the null hypothesis, H_0, when it is true.

Type II error Not rejecting the null hypothesis, H_0, when it is false.

Value of perfect information The difference between the maximum payoff under conditions of certainty and the maximum payoff under uncertainty.

Variable control chart A variable control chart plots the mean of an interval or ratio measurement over time.

Variance A measure of dispersion based on the average squared differences from the arithmetic mean.

Variance inflation factor A test used to detect correlation among independent variables.

Weighted index The prices in the base period and the given period are multiplied by quantities (weights).

Wilcoxon rank-sum test A nonparametric test requiring independent samples. The data must be at least ordinal level. That is, the data must be capable of being ranked. The test is used when the assumptions for the parametric Student's t-test cannot be met. The objective of the test is to find whether two independent samples can be considered as coming from the same population. It is used if the assumptions required for the paired t-test cannot be met.

***z*-Value** It is the distance between a selected value and the mean measured in units of the standard deviation.

Index

KEY FORMULAS Lind, Marchal, and Wathen · *Statistical Techniques in Business & Economics, 19th edition*

CHAPTER 3

- Population mean

$$\mu = \frac{\Sigma x}{N} \qquad (3\text{–}1)$$

- Sample mean, raw data

$$\bar{x} = \frac{\Sigma x}{n} \qquad (3\text{–}2)$$

- Weighted mean

$$\bar{x}_w = \frac{w_1 x_1 + w_2 x_2 + \cdots + w_n x_n}{w_1 + w_2 + \cdots + w_n} \qquad (3\text{–}3)$$

- Geometric mean

$$GM = \sqrt[n]{(x_1)(x_2)(x_3)\ldots(x_n)} \qquad (3\text{–}4)$$

- Geometric mean rate of increase

$$GM = \sqrt[n]{\frac{\text{Value at end of period}}{\text{Value at start of period}}} - 1.0 \qquad (3\text{–}5)$$

- Range

$$\text{Range} = \text{Maximum value} - \text{Minimum value} \qquad (3\text{–}6)$$

- Population variance

$$\sigma^2 = \frac{\Sigma(x - \mu)^2}{N} \qquad (3\text{–}7)$$

- Population standard deviation

$$\sigma = \sqrt{\frac{\Sigma(x - \mu)^2}{N}} \qquad (3\text{–}8)$$

- Sample variance

$$s^2 = \frac{\Sigma(x - \bar{x})^2}{n - 1} \qquad (3\text{–}9)$$

- Sample standard deviation

$$s = \sqrt{\frac{\Sigma(x - \bar{x})^2}{n - 1}} \qquad (3\text{–}10)$$

CHAPTER 4

- Location of a percentile

$$L_p = (n + 1)\frac{P}{100} \qquad (4\text{–}1)$$

- Pearson's coefficient of skewness

$$sk = \frac{3(\bar{x} - \text{Median})}{s} \qquad (4\text{–}2)$$

- Software coefficient of skewness

$$sk = \frac{n}{(n - 1)(n - 2)}\left[\Sigma \left(\frac{x - \bar{x}}{s} \right)^3 \right] \qquad (4\text{–}3)$$

- Correlation coefficient

$$r = \frac{\Sigma(x - \bar{x})(y - \bar{y})}{(n - 1)\, s_x s_y} \qquad (4\text{–}4)$$

CHAPTER 5

- Multiplication formula

$$\text{Total arrangements} = (m)(n) \qquad (5\text{–}2)$$

- Number of permutations

$$_nP_r = \frac{n!}{(n - r)!} \qquad (5\text{–}3)$$

- Number of combinations

$$_nC_r = \frac{n!}{r!(n - r)!} \qquad (5\text{–}4)$$

- Special rule of addition

$$P(A \text{ or } B) = P(A) + P(B) \qquad (5\text{–}5)$$

- Complement rule

$$P(A) = 1 - P(\sim A) \qquad (5\text{–}6)$$

- General rule of addition

$$P(A \text{ or } B) = P(A) + P(B) - P(A \text{ and } B) \qquad (5\text{–}7)$$

- Special rule of multiplication

$$P(A \text{ and } B) = P(A)P(B) \qquad (5\text{–}8)$$

- General rule of multiplication

$$P(A \text{ and } B) = P(A)P(B|A) \qquad (5\text{–}9)$$

- Bayes' theorem

$$P(A_1|B) = \frac{P(A_1)P(B|A_1)}{P(A_1)P(B|A_1) + P(A_2)P(B|A_2)} \qquad (5\text{–}10)$$

CHAPTER 6

- Mean of a probability distribution

$$\mu = \Sigma[xP(x)] \qquad (6\text{–}1)$$

- Variance of a probability distribution

$$\sigma^2 = \Sigma[(x - \mu)^2 P(x)] \qquad (6\text{–}2)$$

- Binomial probability distribution

$$P(x) = {}_nC_x \pi^x (1 - \pi)^{n - x} \qquad (6\text{–}3)$$

- Mean of a binomial distribution

$$\mu = n\pi \qquad (6\text{–}4)$$

- Variance of a binomial distribution

$$\sigma^2 = n\pi(1 - \pi) \qquad (6\text{–}5)$$

- Hypergeometric probability distribution

$$P(x) = \frac{({}_SC_x)({}_{N-S}C_{n-x})}{{}_NC_n} \qquad (6\text{–}6)$$

- Poisson probability distribution

$$P(x) = \frac{\mu^x e^{-\mu}}{x!} \qquad (6\text{–}7)$$

- Mean of a Poisson distribution

$$\mu = n\pi \qquad (6\text{–}8)$$

- Variance of a Poisson distribution

$$\sigma^2 = n\pi \qquad (6\text{–}9)$$

CHAPTER 7

- Uniform probability distribution

$$P(x) = \frac{1}{b-a} \tag{7-1}$$

if $a \leq x \leq b$ and 0 elsewhere

- Mean of a uniform distribution

$$\mu = \frac{a+b}{2} \tag{7-2}$$

- Standard deviation of a uniform distribution

$$\sigma = \sqrt{\frac{(b-a)^2}{12}} \tag{7-3}$$

- Normal probability distribution

$$P(x) = \frac{1}{\sigma\sqrt{2\pi}} e^{-\left[\frac{(x-\mu)^2}{2\sigma^2}\right]} \tag{7-4}$$

- Standard normal value

$$z = \frac{x-\mu}{\sigma} \tag{7-5}$$

- Exponential distribution

$$P(x) = \lambda e^{-\lambda x} \tag{7-6}$$

- Finding a probability using the exponential distribution

$$P(\text{Arrival time} < x) = 1 - e^{-\lambda x} \tag{7-7}$$

CHAPTER 8

- Standard error of mean

$$\sigma_{\bar{x}} = \frac{\sigma}{\sqrt{n}} \tag{8-1}$$

- z-value, μ and σ known

$$z = \frac{\bar{x}-\mu}{\sigma/\sqrt{n}} \tag{8-2}$$

- Sample proportion

$$p = \frac{x}{n} \tag{8-3}$$

- Standard error of the proportion

$$\sigma_p = \sqrt{\frac{\pi(1-\pi)}{n}} \tag{8-4}$$

- z-Value for a sample proportion

$$z = \frac{p-\pi}{\sqrt{\frac{\pi(1-\pi)}{n}}} \tag{8-5}$$

CHAPTER 9

- Confidence interval for μ, with σ known

$$\bar{x} \pm z\frac{\sigma}{\sqrt{n}} \tag{9-1}$$

- Confidence interval for μ, σ unknown

$$\bar{x} \pm t\frac{s}{\sqrt{n}} \tag{9-2}$$

- Sample proportion

$$p = \frac{x}{n} \tag{9-3}$$

- Confidence interval for proportion

$$p \pm z\sqrt{\frac{p(1-p)}{n}} \tag{9-4}$$

- Sample size for estimating mean

$$n = \left(\frac{z\sigma}{E}\right)^2 \tag{9-5}$$

- Sample size for a proportion

$$n = \pi(1-\pi)\left(\frac{z}{E}\right)^2 \tag{9-6}$$

CHAPTER 10

- Testing a mean, σ known

$$z = \frac{\bar{x}-\mu}{\sigma/\sqrt{n}} \tag{10-1}$$

- Testing a mean, σ unknown

$$t = \frac{\bar{x}-\mu}{s/\sqrt{n}} \tag{10-2}$$

- Type II error

$$z = \frac{\bar{x}_c - \mu_1}{\sigma/\sqrt{n}} \tag{10-3}$$

- Test of hypothesis, one proportion

$$z = \frac{p-\pi}{\sqrt{\frac{\pi(1-\pi)}{n}}} \tag{10-4}$$

CHAPTER 11

- Test for comparing two variances

$$F = \frac{s_1^2}{s_2^2} \tag{11-1}$$

- Variance of the distribution of difference in means

$$\sigma_{\bar{x}_1-\bar{x}_2}^2 = \frac{\sigma_1^2}{n_1} + \frac{\sigma_2^2}{n_2} \tag{11-2}$$

- Two-sample test of means, known σ

$$z = \frac{\bar{x}_1 - \bar{x}_2}{\sqrt{\frac{\sigma_1^2}{n_1} + \frac{\sigma_2^2}{n_2}}} \tag{11-3}$$

- Pooled variance

$$s_p^2 = \frac{(n_1-1)s_1^2 + (n_2-1)s_2^2}{n_1+n_2-2} \tag{11-4}$$

- Two-sample test of means, unknown but equal σ^2s

$$t = \frac{\bar{x}_1 - \bar{x}_2}{\sqrt{s_p^2\left(\frac{1}{n_1} + \frac{1}{n_2}\right)}} \tag{11-5}$$

- Two-sample tests of means, unknown and unequal σ^2s

$$t = \frac{\bar{x}_1 - \bar{x}_2}{\sqrt{\frac{s_1^2}{n_1} + \frac{s_2^2}{n_2}}} \tag{11-6}$$

- Degrees of freedom for unequal variance test

$$df = \frac{[(s_1^2/n_1) + (s_2^2/n_2)]^2}{\frac{(s_1^2/n_1)^2}{n_1-1} + \frac{(s_2^2/n_2)^2}{n_2-1}} \tag{11-7}$$

- Paired t test

$$t = \frac{\bar{d}}{s_d/\sqrt{n}} \tag{11-8}$$

- Two-sample test of proportions

$$z = \frac{p_1 - p_2}{\sqrt{\dfrac{p_c(1 - p_c)}{n_1} + \dfrac{p_c(1 - p_c)}{n_2}}} \quad \text{(11–9)}$$

- Pooled proportion

$$p_c = \frac{x_1 + x_2}{n_1 + n_2} \quad \text{(11–10)}$$

CHAPTER 12

- Sum of squares, total

$$\text{SS total} = \Sigma(x - \bar{x}_G)^2 \quad \text{(12–1)}$$

- Sum of squares, error

$$\text{SSE} = \Sigma(x - \bar{x}_c)^2 \quad \text{(12–2)}$$

- Sum of squares, treatments

$$\text{SST} = \text{SS total} - \text{SSE} \quad \text{(12–3)}$$

- Confidence interval for differences in treatment means

$$(\bar{x}_1 - \bar{x}_2) \pm t \sqrt{\text{MSE}\left(\frac{1}{n_1} + \frac{1}{n_2}\right)} \quad \text{(12–4)}$$

- Sum of squares, blocks

$$\text{SSB} = k\Sigma(\bar{x}_b - \bar{x}_G)^2 \quad \text{(12–5)}$$

- Sum of squares error, two-way ANOVA

$$\text{SSE} = \text{SS total} - \text{SST} - \text{SSB} \quad \text{(12–6)}$$

CHAPTER 13

- Correlation coefficient

$$r = \frac{\Sigma(x - \bar{x})(y - \bar{y})}{(n - 1) s_x s_y} \quad \text{(13–1)}$$

- Test for significant correlation

$$t = \frac{r\sqrt{n - 2}}{\sqrt{1 - r^2}} \quad \text{(13–2)}$$

- Linear regression equation

$$\hat{y} = a + bx \quad \text{(13–3)}$$

- Slope of the regression line

$$b = r\frac{s_y}{s_x} \quad \text{(13–4)}$$

- Intercept of the regression line

$$a = \bar{y} - b\bar{x} \quad \text{(13–5)}$$

- Test for a zero slope

$$t = \frac{b - 0}{s_b} \quad \text{(13–6)}$$

- Standard error of estimate

$$s_{y \cdot x} = \sqrt{\frac{\Sigma(y - \hat{y})^2}{n - 2}} \quad \text{(13–7)}$$

- Coefficient of determination

$$r^2 = \frac{\text{SSR}}{\text{SS Total}} = 1 - \frac{\text{SSE}}{\text{SS Total}} \quad \text{(13–8)}$$

- Standard error of estimate

$$s_{y \cdot x} = \sqrt{\frac{\text{SSE}}{n - 2}} \quad \text{(13–9)}$$

- Standard error of the estimate

$$s_{y \cdot x} = \sqrt{\text{Residual mean square}} \quad \text{(13–10)}$$

- Confidence interval

$$\hat{y} \pm ts_{y \cdot x} \sqrt{\frac{1}{n} + \frac{(x - \bar{x})^2}{\Sigma(x - \bar{x})^2}} \quad \text{(13–11)}$$

- Prediction interval

$$\hat{y} \pm ts_{y \cdot x} \sqrt{1 + \frac{1}{n} + \frac{(x - \bar{x})^2}{\Sigma(x - \bar{x})^2}} \quad \text{(13–12)}$$

CHAPTER 14

- Multiple regression equation

$$\hat{y} = a + b_1 x_1 + b_2 x_2 + \cdots + b_k x_k \quad \text{(14–1)}$$

- Multiple standard error of estimate

$$s_{y \cdot 123 \ldots k} = \sqrt{\frac{\Sigma(y - \hat{y})^2}{n - (k + 1)}} = \sqrt{\frac{\text{SSE}}{n - (k + 1)}} \quad \text{(14–2)}$$

- Coefficient of multiple determination

$$R^2 = \frac{\text{SSE}}{\text{SS total}} \quad \text{(14–3)}$$

- Adjusted coefficient of determination

$$R^2_{adj} = 1 - \frac{\dfrac{\text{SSE}}{n - (k + 1)}}{\dfrac{\text{SS total}}{n - 1}} \quad \text{(14–4)}$$

- Global test of hypothesis

$$F = \frac{\text{SSR}/k}{\text{SSE}/[n - (k + 1)]} \quad \text{(14–5)}$$

- Testing for a particular regression coefficient

$$t = \frac{b_i - 0}{s_{b_i}} \quad \text{(14–6)}$$

- Variance inflation factor

$$VIF = \frac{1}{1 - R_j^2} \quad \text{(14–7)}$$

CHAPTER 15

- Chi-square test statistic

$$\chi^2 = \Sigma\left[\frac{(f_o - f_e)^2}{f_e}\right] \quad \text{(15–1)}$$

- Expected frequency

$$f_e = \frac{(\text{Row total})(\text{Column total})}{\text{Grand total}} \quad \text{(15–2)}$$

CHAPTER 16

- Wilcoxon rank-sum test

$$z = \frac{W - \dfrac{n_1(n_1 + n_2 + 1)}{2}}{\sqrt{\dfrac{n_1 n_2(n_1 + n_2 + 1)}{12}}} \quad \text{(16–1)}$$

- Kruskal-Wallis test

$$H = \frac{12}{n(n+1)}\left[\frac{(\Sigma R_1)^2}{n_1} + \frac{(\Sigma R_2)^2}{n_2} + \cdots + \frac{(\Sigma R_k)^2}{n_k}\right] - 3(n+1) \qquad \text{(16–2)}$$

- Spearman coefficient of rank correlation

$$r_s = 1 - \frac{6\Sigma d^2}{n(n^2-1)} \qquad \text{(16–3)}$$

- Hypothesis test, rank correlation

$$t = r_s\sqrt{\frac{n-2}{1-r_s^2}} \qquad \text{(16–4)}$$

CHAPTER 17
- Simple index

$$P = \frac{p_t}{p_0}(100) \qquad \text{(17–1)}$$

- Simple average of price relatives

$$P = \frac{\Sigma P_i}{n} \qquad \text{(17–2)}$$

- Simple aggregate index

$$P = \frac{\Sigma p_t}{\Sigma p_0}(100) \qquad \text{(17–3)}$$

- Laspeyres' price index

$$P = \frac{\Sigma p_t q_0}{\Sigma p_0 q_0}(100) \qquad \text{(17–4)}$$

- Paasche' price index

$$P = \frac{\Sigma p_t q_t}{\Sigma p_0 q_t}(100) \qquad \text{(17–5)}$$

- Fisher's ideal index

$$\sqrt{(\text{Laspeyres' price index})(\text{Paasche's price index})} \qquad \text{(17–6)}$$

- Value index

$$V = \frac{\Sigma p_t q_t}{\Sigma p_0 q_0}(100) \qquad \text{(17–7)}$$

- Real income

$$\text{Real income} = \frac{\text{Money income}}{\text{CPI}}(100) \qquad \text{(17–8)}$$

- Using an index as a deflator

$$\text{Deflated sales} = \frac{\text{Actual sales}}{\text{Index}}(100) \qquad \text{(17–9)}$$

- Purchasing power

$$\text{Purchasing power} = \frac{\$1}{\text{CPI}}(100) \qquad \text{(17–10)}$$

CHAPTER 18
- Forecast error

$$\text{Forecast Error} = \text{Actual} - \text{Forecast} \qquad \text{(18–1)}$$

- Mean absolute deviation

$$\text{MAD} = \frac{\Sigma|\text{Error}|}{n} \qquad \text{(18–2)}$$

- Mean absolute percent error

$$\text{MAPE} = \frac{\Sigma|\text{Percent Error}|}{n} \qquad \text{(18–3)}$$

- Exponential smoothing

$$\text{Forecast}_{t+1} = \alpha(\text{Observed Value})_t + (1-\alpha)(\text{Forecast})_t \qquad \text{(18–4)}$$

- Exponential smoothing revised

$$\text{Forecast}_{t+1} = \text{Forecast}_t + \alpha(\text{Error})_t \qquad \text{(18–5)}$$

- Linear trend regression equation

$$\text{Time Series Variable} = \text{Intercept} + \text{slope (time period)} \qquad \text{(18–6)}$$

- Durbin-Watson statistic

$$d = \frac{\sum_{t=2}^{n}(e_t - e_{t-1})^2}{\sum_{t=1}^{n}e_t^2} \qquad \text{(18–7)}$$

CHAPTER 19
- Grand mean

$$\bar{\bar{x}} = \frac{\Sigma\bar{x}}{k} \qquad \text{(19–1)}$$

- Control limits for the mean

$$UCL = \bar{\bar{x}} + 3\frac{s}{\sqrt{n}} \quad \text{and} \quad LCL = \bar{\bar{x}} - 3\frac{s}{\sqrt{n}} \qquad \text{(19–3)}$$

- Control limits, mean

$$UCL = \bar{\bar{x}} + A_2\bar{R} \qquad LCL = \bar{\bar{x}} - A_2\bar{R} \qquad \text{(19–4)}$$

- Control limits, range

$$UCL = D_4\bar{R} \qquad LCL = D_3\bar{R} \qquad \text{(19–5)}$$

- Mean proportion defective

$$p = \frac{\text{Total number defective}}{\text{Total number of items sampled}} \qquad \text{(19–6)}$$

- Control limits, proportion

$$UCL \text{ and } LCL = p \pm 3\sqrt{\frac{p(1-p)}{n}} \qquad \text{(19–8)}$$

- Control limits, c-bar chart

$$UCL \text{ and } LCL = \bar{c} \pm 3\sqrt{\bar{c}} \qquad \text{(19–9)}$$

CHAPTER 20
- Expected monetary value

$$\text{EMV}(A_i) = \Sigma[P(S_j) \cdot V(A_i, S_j)] \qquad \text{(20–1)}$$

- Expected opportunity loss

$$\text{EOL}(A_i) = \Sigma[P(S_j) \cdot R(A_i, S_j)] \qquad \text{(20–2)}$$

- Expected value of perfect information

$$\text{EVPI} = \text{Expected value under conditions of certainty} - \text{Expected value of optimal decision under conditions of uncertainty} \qquad \text{(20–3)}$$

Student's *t*-Distribution

Confidence interval

Left-tailed test

Right-tailed test

Two-tailed test

(continued)

	Confidence Intervals, *c*					
	80%	**90%**	**95%**	**98%**	**99%**	**99.9%**
	Level of Significance for One-Tailed Test, α					
df	**0.10**	**0.05**	**0.025**	**0.01**	**0.005**	**0.0005**
	Level of Significance for Two-Tailed Test, α					
	0.20	**0.10**	**0.05**	**0.02**	**0.01**	**0.001**
1	3.078	6.314	12.706	31.821	63.657	636.619
2	1.886	2.920	4.303	6.965	9.925	31.599
3	1.638	2.353	3.182	4.541	5.841	12.924
4	1.533	2.132	2.776	3.747	4.604	8.610
5	1.476	2.015	2.571	3.365	4.032	6.869
6	1.440	1.943	2.447	3.143	3.707	5.959
7	1.415	1.895	2.365	2.998	3.499	5.408
8	1.397	1.860	2.306	2.896	3.355	5.041
9	1.383	1.833	2.262	2.821	3.250	4.781
10	1.372	1.812	2.228	2.764	3.169	4.587
11	1.363	1.796	2.201	2.718	3.106	4.437
12	1.356	1.782	2.179	2.681	3.055	4.318
13	1.350	1.771	2.160	2.650	3.012	4.221
14	1.345	1.761	2.145	2.624	2.977	4.140
15	1.341	1.753	2.131	2.602	2.947	4.073
16	1.337	1.746	2.120	2.583	2.921	4.015
17	1.333	1.740	2.110	2.567	2.898	3.965
18	1.330	1.734	2.101	2.552	2.878	3.922
19	1.328	1.729	2.093	2.539	2.861	3.883
20	1.325	1.725	2.086	2.528	2.845	3.850
21	1.323	1.721	2.080	2.518	2.831	3.819
22	1.321	1.717	2.074	2.508	2.819	3.792
23	1.319	1.714	2.069	2.500	2.807	3.768
24	1.318	1.711	2.064	2.492	2.797	3.745
25	1.316	1.708	2.060	2.485	2.787	3.725
26	1.315	1.706	2.056	2.479	2.779	3.707
27	1.314	1.703	2.052	2.473	2.771	3.690
28	1.313	1.701	2.048	2.467	2.763	3.674
29	1.311	1.699	2.045	2.462	2.756	3.659
30	1.310	1.697	2.042	2.457	2.750	3.646
31	1.309	1.696	2.040	2.453	2.744	3.633
32	1.309	1.694	2.037	2.449	2.738	3.622
33	1.308	1.692	2.035	2.445	2.733	3.611
34	1.307	1.691	2.032	2.441	2.728	3.601
35	1.306	1.690	2.030	2.438	2.724	3.591

(continued-top right)

	Confidence Intervals, *c*					
	80%	**90%**	**95%**	**98%**	**99%**	**99.9%**
	Level of Significance for One-Tailed Test, α					
df	**0.10**	**0.05**	**0.025**	**0.01**	**0.005**	**0.0005**
	Level of Significance for Two-Tailed Test, α					
	0.20	**0.10**	**0.05**	**0.02**	**0.01**	**0.001**
36	1.306	1.688	2.028	2.434	2.719	3.582
37	1.305	1.687	2.026	2.431	2.715	3.574
38	1.304	1.686	2.024	2.429	2.712	3.566
39	1.304	1.685	2.023	2.426	2.708	3.558
40	1.303	1.684	2.021	2.423	2.704	3.551
41	1.303	1.683	2.020	2.421	2.701	3.544
42	1.302	1.682	2.018	2.418	2.698	3.538
43	1.302	1.681	2.017	2.416	2.695	3.532
44	1.301	1.680	2.015	2.414	2.692	3.526
45	1.301	1.679	2.014	2.412	2.690	3.520
46	1.300	1.679	2.013	2.410	2.687	3.515
47	1.300	1.678	2.012	2.408	2.685	3.510
48	1.299	1.677	2.011	2.407	2.682	3.505
49	1.299	1.677	2.010	2.405	2.680	3.500
50	1.299	1.676	2.009	2.403	2.678	3.496
51	1.298	1.675	2.008	2.402	2.676	3.492
52	1.298	1.675	2.007	2.400	2.674	3.488
53	1.298	1.674	2.006	2.399	2.672	3.484
54	1.297	1.674	2.005	2.397	2.670	3.480
55	1.297	1.673	2.004	2.396	2.668	3.476
56	1.297	1.673	2.003	2.395	2.667	3.473
57	1.297	1.672	2.002	2.394	2.665	3.470
58	1.296	1.672	2.002	2.392	2.663	3.466
59	1.296	1.671	2.001	2.391	2.662	3.463
60	1.296	1.671	2.000	2.390	2.660	3.460
61	1.296	1.670	2.000	2.389	2.659	3.457
62	1.295	1.670	1.999	2.388	2.657	3.454
63	1.295	1.669	1.998	2.387	2.656	3.452
64	1.295	1.669	1.998	2.386	2.655	3.449
65	1.295	1.669	1.997	2.385	2.654	3.447
66	1.295	1.668	1.997	2.384	2.652	3.444
67	1.294	1.668	1.996	2.383	2.651	3.442
68	1.294	1.668	1.995	2.382	2.650	3.439
69	1.294	1.667	1.995	2.382	2.649	3.437
70	1.294	1.667	1.994	2.381	2.648	3.435

(continued)

Student's *t*-Distribution (*concluded*)

df	Confidence Intervals, c					
	80%	90%	95%	98%	99%	99.9%
	Level of Significance for One-Tailed Test, α					
	0.10	0.05	0.025	0.01	0.005	0.0005
	Level of Significance for Two-Tailed Test, α					
	0.20	0.10	0.05	0.02	0.01	0.001
71	1.294	1.667	1.994	2.380	2.647	3.433
72	1.293	1.666	1.993	2.379	2.646	3.431
73	1.293	1.666	1.993	2.379	2.645	3.429
74	1.293	1.666	1.993	2.378	2.644	3.427
75	1.293	1.665	1.992	2.377	2.643	3.425
76	1.293	1.665	1.992	2.376	2.642	3.423
77	1.293	1.665	1.991	2.376	2.641	3.421
78	1.292	1.665	1.991	2.375	2.640	3.420
79	1.292	1.664	1.990	2.374	2.640	3.418
80	1.292	1.664	1.990	2.374	2.639	3.416
81	1.292	1.664	1.990	2.373	2.638	3.415
82	1.292	1.664	1.989	2.373	2.637	3.413
83	1.292	1.663	1.989	2.372	2.636	3.412
84	1.292	1.663	1.989	2.372	2.636	3.410
85	1.292	1.663	1.988	2.371	2.635	3.409
86	1.291	1.663	1.988	2.370	2.634	3.407
87	1.291	1.663	1.988	2.370	2.634	3.406
88	1.291	1.662	1.987	2.369	2.633	3.405
89	1.291	1.662	1.987	2.369	2.632	3.403
90	1.291	1.662	1.987	2.368	2.632	3.402
91	1.291	1.662	1.986	2.368	2.631	3.401
92	1.291	1.662	1.986	2.368	2.630	3.399
93	1.291	1.661	1.986	2.367	2.630	3.398
94	1.291	1.661	1.986	2.367	2.629	3.397
95	1.291	1.661	1.985	2.366	2.629	3.396
96	1.290	1.661	1.985	2.366	2.628	3.395
97	1.290	1.661	1.985	2.365	2.627	3.394
98	1.290	1.661	1.984	2.365	2.627	3.393
99	1.290	1.660	1.984	2.365	2.626	3.392
100	1.290	1.660	1.984	2.364	2.626	3.390
120	1.289	1.658	1.980	2.358	2.617	3.373
140	1.288	1.656	1.977	2.353	2.611	3.361
160	1.287	1.654	1.975	2.350	2.607	3.352
180	1.286	1.653	1.973	2.347	2.603	3.345
200	1.286	1.653	1.972	2.345	2.601	3.340
∞	1.282	1.645	1.960	2.326	2.576	3.291

Areas under the Normal Curve

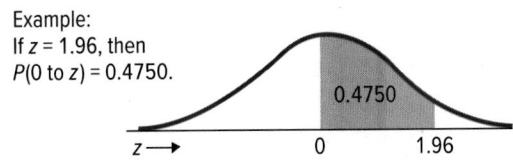

z	0.00	0.01	0.02	0.03	0.04	0.05	0.06	0.07	0.08	0.09
0.0	0.0000	0.0040	0.0080	0.0120	0.0160	0.0199	0.0239	0.0279	0.0319	0.0359
0.1	0.0398	0.0438	0.0478	0.0517	0.0557	0.0596	0.0636	0.0675	0.0714	0.0753
0.2	0.0793	0.0832	0.0871	0.0910	0.0948	0.0987	0.1026	0.1064	0.1103	0.1141
0.3	0.1179	0.1217	0.1255	0.1293	0.1331	0.1368	0.1406	0.1443	0.1480	0.1517
0.4	0.1554	0.1591	0.1628	0.1664	0.1700	0.1736	0.1772	0.1808	0.1844	0.1879
0.5	0.1915	0.1950	0.1985	0.2019	0.2054	0.2088	0.2123	0.2157	0.2190	0.2224
0.6	0.2257	0.2291	0.2324	0.2357	0.2389	0.2422	0.2454	0.2486	0.2517	0.2549
0.7	0.2580	0.2611	0.2642	0.2673	0.2704	0.2734	0.2764	0.2794	0.2823	0.2852
0.8	0.2881	0.2910	0.2939	0.2967	0.2995	0.3023	0.3051	0.3078	0.3106	0.3133
0.9	0.3159	0.3186	0.3212	0.3238	0.3264	0.3289	0.3315	0.3340	0.3365	0.3389
1.0	0.3413	0.3438	0.3461	0.3485	0.3508	0.3531	0.3554	0.3577	0.3599	0.3621
1.1	0.3643	0.3665	0.3686	0.3708	0.3729	0.3749	0.3770	0.3790	0.3810	0.3830
1.2	0.3849	0.3869	0.3888	0.3907	0.3925	0.3944	0.3962	0.3980	0.3997	0.4015
1.3	0.4032	0.4049	0.4066	0.4082	0.4099	0.4115	0.4131	0.4147	0.4162	0.4177
1.4	0.4192	0.4207	0.4222	0.4236	0.4251	0.4265	0.4279	0.4292	0.4306	0.4319
1.5	0.4332	0.4345	0.4357	0.4370	0.4382	0.4394	0.4406	0.4418	0.4429	0.4441
1.6	0.4452	0.4463	0.4474	0.4484	0.4495	0.4505	0.4515	0.4525	0.4535	0.4545
1.7	0.4554	0.4564	0.4573	0.4582	0.4591	0.4599	0.4608	0.4616	0.4625	0.4633
1.8	0.4641	0.4649	0.4656	0.4664	0.4671	0.4678	0.4686	0.4693	0.4699	0.4706
1.9	0.4713	0.4719	0.4726	0.4732	0.4738	0.4744	0.4750	0.4756	0.4761	0.4767
2.0	0.4772	0.4778	0.4783	0.4788	0.4793	0.4798	0.4803	0.4808	0.4812	0.4817
2.1	0.4821	0.4826	0.4830	0.4834	0.4838	0.4842	0.4846	0.4850	0.4854	0.4857
2.2	0.4861	0.4864	0.4868	0.4871	0.4875	0.4878	0.4881	0.4884	0.4887	0.4890
2.3	0.4893	0.4896	0.4898	0.4901	0.4904	0.4906	0.4909	0.4911	0.4913	0.4916
2.4	0.4918	0.4920	0.4922	0.4925	0.4927	0.4929	0.4931	0.4932	0.4934	0.4936
2.5	0.4938	0.4940	0.4941	0.4943	0.4945	0.4946	0.4948	0.4949	0.4951	0.4952
2.6	0.4953	0.4955	0.4956	0.4957	0.4959	0.4960	0.4961	0.4962	0.4963	0.4964
2.7	0.4965	0.4966	0.4967	0.4968	0.4969	0.4970	0.4971	0.4972	0.4973	0.4974
2.8	0.4974	0.4975	0.4976	0.4977	0.4977	0.4978	0.4979	0.4979	0.4980	0.4981
2.9	0.4981	0.4982	0.4982	0.4983	0.4984	0.4984	0.4985	0.4985	0.4986	0.4986
3.0	0.4987	0.4987	0.4987	0.4988	0.4988	0.4989	0.4989	0.4989	0.4990	0.4990